Sp73f

Opin 9-11-15

THE

WILLARD J. GRAHAM SERIES

IN ACCOUNTING

BOOKS IN
THE WILLARD J. GRAHAM SERIES IN ACCOUNTING

CONSULTING EDITOR ROBERT N. ANTHONY *Harvard University*

Intermediate
Accounting

Intermediate
Accounting

GLENN A. WELSCH, Ph.D., C.P.A.
Professor of Accounting

CHARLES T. ZLATKOVICH, Ph.D., C.P.A.
Professor of Accounting

JOHN ARCH WHITE, Ph.D.
Professor of Accounting, Emeritus

All of the Graduate School of Business
University of Texas at Austin

1972

Third Edition
RICHARD D. IRWIN, INC.
HOMEWOOD, ILLINOIS 60430
IRWIN–DORSEY LIMITED, GEORGETOWN, ONTARIO

© RICHARD D. IRWIN, INC., 1963, 1968, and 1972

All rights reserved. No part of this publication may be
reproduced, stored in a retrieval system, or transmitted,
in any form or by any means, electronic, mechanical,
photocopying, recording, or otherwise, without the prior
written permission of the publisher.

Third Edition

First Printing, January, 1972

Second Printing, July, 1972

Library of Congress Catalog Card No. 71–153164

Printed in the United States of America

LEARNING SYSTEMS COMPANY—
a division of Richard D. Irwin, Inc.—has developed a
PROGRAMMED LEARNING AID
to accompany texts in this subject area.
Copies can be purchased through your bookstore
or by writing PLAIDS.
1818 Ridge Road, Homewood, Illinois   60430.

Preface

This textbook is designed for students who have completed the study of two semesters or quarters of accounting principles. It is structured for a two-semester sequence, but with judicious selection and emphasis of material the text is readily adaptable to shorter courses or to the needs of schools using the quarter plan. It is designed to integrate with a principles text coauthored by one of the same authors,[1] but may be used following the completion by the student of any reasonably complete first-year text in accounting.

Accounting theory is emphasized throughout. Students are given reasons for the various treatments presented; they will learn the more important "why" along with the "how" of accounting procedures. This edition continues the comprehensive features which gained wide recognition for the prior editions. Upon completion, the student should be well prepared for the theory and practice sections of the Uniform CPA Examination and advanced courses in accounting. A salient feature of this book is that, rather than avoiding troublesome complexities, it deals with them directly, and alternative viewpoints are presented. Inspection of the chapters will reveal that all aspects of each topic are considered, consistent with the objectives of the book, despite the fact that this imposes on the text a high level of sophistication.

Significantly, this edition introduces the concepts of present value early and utilizes them throughout. This feature reflects the very recent, and significant, trend in the accounting profession to ap-

[1]William W. Pyle and John Arch White, *Fundamental Accounting Principles* (6th ed.; Homewood, Ill.: Richard D. Irwin, Inc., 1972).

propriately reflect present values for certain debt and receivable transactions, in the amortization of discounts and premiums, and in certain other types of transactions. The critical areas of leases, fund accumulations, and installment debt require, more than ever before, widespread utilization of future- and present-value determinations. Experience of the authors has confirmed that these concepts are not particularly troublesome to accounting students if introduced early in intermediate accounting and used subsequently throughout the course. Rather than moving to a less sophisticated (and inadequate) instructional content, the authors have moved forward to reflect the increasing sophistication in accounting being reflected in recent (and expected) Opinions of the Accounting Principles Board, on the CPA examinations, and in professional and private practice.

The latest terminology is used, and references to pronouncements of the American Institute of Certified Public Accountants, the American Accounting Association, and the Securities and Exchange Commission pervade the 29 chapters. Recognizing that students learn much of their accounting at this stage of development by solution of assigned materials, the authors have provided a wealth of question, exercise, and problem material. In addition, decision cases designed for discussion in class and/or homework solution on an essay, rather than on a "columnar," basis accompany almost all chapters. An appropriate selection of materials from Uniform CPA Examinations is to be found in the assignment material. The instructor is given a wide range of problem material of varying difficulty so he can select that best suited to his class. The teacher's manual and examination booklet provides helpful suggestions and step-by-step computations to maximize user convenience.

Chapters are arranged in a teachable and logical sequence. They are grouped to facilitate any desired rearrangement of materials to suit individual preferences. The first chapter sets the stage for all that follows by presenting an integrating overview of the foundations of accounting theory. It is followed by three chapters which review the accounting cycle and which at the same time carry the student somewhat beyond equivalent coverage in the traditional elementary accounting course.

Chapter 5 presents the concepts of present-value and actuarial mathematics in their practical applications to accounting problems. This chapter has been moved to this location since the concepts are fundamental to practically all of the subsequent chapters. It makes possible effective instruction in this increasingly important area as a unit as opposed to oblique references to it. This location significantly simplifies explanations, illustrations, and understandings in numerous instances throughout the course of intermediate instruction (and advanced courses as well). The authors also took note of the recent trend to include some instruction in present-value concepts in elementary accounting textbooks; the instruction should be continued on a higher level of sophistication at the intermediate level.

Chapters 6 through 15 represent a comprehensive treatment of assets incorporating new materials on intercorporate investments (including the purchase and pooling-of-interest concepts). Chapters 16 and 17 are devoted to liabilities. Chapter 18 is unique in that it presents an intermediate-level discussion of pensions and leases. Chapters 19 through 22 incorporate an unusually complete treatment of corporations. Chapter 23 discusses special income-determination problems including income tax allocation and price-level effects. Chapter 24 is essentially new in that it treats comprehensively the evolving problem of accounting changes, the subject of a recent APB Opinion. The last five chapters are devoted to funds flow (including the all-resources concept), ratio analyses, variation analysis, consignments, and installment sales in that order. Each of these chapters (as well as certain others) may be omitted without affecting the continuity of the course.

We are indebted to numerous colleagues from universities throughout the nation whose comments and suggestions led to many improvements in this third edition. We appreciate the permission granted by the American Accounting Association and the American Institute of CPAs to quote from their various pronouncements.

The latter organization also permitted us to make liberal use of materials adapted from their Uniform CPA Examinations. We are very appreciative of the many valuable suggestions provided by our colleagues and friends Kermit D. Larson, Lewis L. Davidson, Jim G. Ashburne, Charles H. Griffin, Gary L. Holstrum, Don Vickrey, William L. Talbert, and Jerry L. Morgan. We also express our thanks to numerous users of the prior edition for valuable suggestions in respect to content and arrangement.

Austin, Texas   GLENN A. WELSCH
December, 1971   CHARLES T. ZLATKOVICH
                                       JOHN A. WHITE

Contents

Acquisition of Fixed Assets: *Nature of Fixed Assets. Capital and Revenue Expenditures. Valuation Principles Underlying Fixed Asset Accounting. Assets Acquired for Cash. Assets Acquired on Deferred Payment Plan. Assets Acquired in Exchange for Securities. Assets Acquired through Exchanges. Departures from Cost in Accounting for Tangible Fixed Assets. Donated Assets and Discovery Value. Write-Down of Tangible Fixed Assets Based on Decreased Use Value. Outlays Subsequent to Acquisition but Prior to Use. Acquisitions of Groups of Fixed Assets. Fixed Assets Constructed for Own Use. Interest during Construction Period.* Cost Outlays Subsequent to Acquisition: *Repairs and Maintenance. Replacements and Renewals. Betterment and Improvements. Additions. Rearrangements of Assets. Acquisition Costs of Specific Property.* Retirement of Tangible Fixed Assets: *General. Control of Tangible Fixed Assets.*

Depreciation: *Nature of Depreciation. Causes of Depreciation. Factors in Determining the Depreciation Charge. Recording Depreciation. Methods of Depreciation. Compound Interest Methods. Special Depreciation Systems. Depreciation Policy. Depreciation for Income Tax Purposes. Changes and Correction of Depreciation. Depreciation and a Changing Price Level. The Investment Credit.* Depletion: *Nature of Depletion.* Revaluation of Fixed Assets: *Write-Up of Tangible Fixed Assets Based on Appraisals.*

Part A—Intangible Assets: *Nature and Classification of Intangible Assets. Accounting Valuation of Intangibles at Acquisition. Classification of the Cost of Intangibles. Amortization of Intangible Costs. Limitation on the Write-Off of Intangibles. Patents. Experimental, Research, and Development Costs. Goodwill. Amortization of Goodwill. Estimating Goodwill. Present Value Estimation of Goodwill. Organization Costs. Leaseholds. Other Intangible Assets.* Part B—Deferred Charges: *Prepaid Expenses and Deferred Charges Distinguished.* Part C—

chapter 1 | # The Foundations of Accounting Theory

INTRODUCTION

The broad objectives of accounting are three-fold: (a) To provide relevant and understandable data concerning the financial affairs of an enterprise to external parties (such as investors and creditors); (b) To provide relevant data for decision making by the managers of the enterprise; and (c) To facilitate the broad socio-economic operations of organized society (such as taxation, labor-management relations, regulation of commerce, environmental planning and control, and social programs). This textbook focuses primarily on the first object.

While a comprehensive treatment of all of these broad aspects of accounting would be desirable, sound exposition and space limitations necessitate some selectivity of subject matter. In accordance with these objectives, we present in the first chapter a systematic formulation of the *foundations of accounting theory*. This approach aims to provide a basic foundation for what follows, since theory is the thread that necessarily should run all the way through financial accounting. By including highlights of introductory accounting in Chapters 2 through 4, these chapters not only provide a broad review but also augment the foundation for the study of what is to follow. Beginning with Chapter 5, each succeeding chapter examines particular major accounting problems and applications in greater depth.

Your authors made the decision to present this discussion of the foundations of accounting theory as the first chapter for very specific reasons. Primary was concern with the fact that when these foundations are discussed fragmentarily in the intensive coverage of varied topics, as they necessarily are, it follows that they seldom come out clearly and structurally related as far as the student is concerned. The other basic reason is that throughout the study of accounting as presented in this and similar books, the student continuously needs to "hang his hat" on a solid foundation of theoretical structure. Consistent with these reasons, we urge that the student repeatedly return to this chapter to find the rationale for the accounting determinations and practices discussed and illustrated in the chapters to follow. As we state below, most of accounting as it is practiced today can find its rationale in the outline of the broad structure of accounting theory discussed in this chapter. One final suggestion to the student: as the chapters to follow are mastered you will find that this structure will become more meaningful and, more importantly, helpful in determining what is sound accounting without memorization of a specific set of rules or a sequential series of accounting entries. When you have finished the book, come back and study this chapter constructively and critically.

In the broad sense, accounting data are not only essential to the effective functioning of business enterprise but more and more are being utilized in national planning and in making distributions of the total product among the several beneficiaries. Government relies on certain accounting data in shaping tax programs and in legislating relative to commerce and industry. Labor organizations frequently base claims for wage adjustments on reported profits and productivity measurements. Dividend expectations by stockholders are determined in large part by reported profits. The consumer is appropriately concerned with the relationship of reported profits, investment, and prices. Effective management of the individual business unit is directly related to enlightened use of appropriate accounting data. Socioeconomic accounting and environmental accounting reflect recent extensions that focus on some of the evolving problems that confront society generally. Thus considerable significance should be attached to the central purposes of accounting, that is, to accumulate, classify, and report on the financial activities of enterprises—both business and nonbusiness.

Since accounting data are of such significance to investors, managements, employees, consumers, creditors, government administrators, and others, it is imperative that the accounting process be based on a sound theoretical foundation. Confidence in, and reliance on, accounting data are directly related to the usefulness, objectivity, feasibility, and accuracy of these data. To have confidence in financial statements,

readers must have an unequivocal basis for assuming that such statements have been prepared in accordance with generally accepted
standards and procedures consistent with the broad objectives of
accounting. These standards and procedures should be well defined,
capable of near-universal application, communicated to the *users*, and
followed explicitly by the accounting profession. Thus the accounting
profession has the dual responsibility of developing and disseminating
a foundation of "accounting theory and practice."

Over the years the accounting profession has devoted much time
and attention to the problem of "generally accepted accounting principles." Today accountants generally have a common understanding of
accounting principles, concepts, standards, and procedures, although
there is no single authoritative statement of them that has wide agreement.

During the period 1938 through 1958 the Committee on Accounting
Procedure of the American Institute of Certified Public Accountants
issued a series of pronouncements dealing with accounting principles,
procedures, and terminology. Primary among these were the *Accounting Research* and *Accounting Terminology Bulletins* (with revisions).
This series of statements was combined and published in 1961 by the
institute as the *Final Edition*.[1] Rather than attempting to develop a
comprehensive statement of principles, the series dealt with specific
problem areas. The terminology bulletins recognized a very serious
problem of semantics: various terms were being used by the profession rather loosely much to the confusion of the financial community
and the interested public generally.

The Accounting Principles Board (APB) was organized by the Institute in 1959 to replace the Committee on Accounting Procedure. In
October 1965, in an "opinion," the APB adopted until further notice
the opinions of the predecessor committee. In the last few years the
APB has issued a number of opinions and revisions of prior opinions.
As a foundation for new and revised opinions the Institute has sponsored and published a number of *Accounting Research Studies*.[2] A
particularly significant milestone in the development of accounting
practice occurred in October 1964 when the Council of the Institute
adopted recommendations requiring that for fiscal periods that began
after December 31, 1965, *departures from accounting principles*

---

[1] AICPA, *Accounting Research and Terminology Bulletins, Final Edition* (New York,
1961). This was a compilation of the 43 *Accounting Research Bulletins* and the 4 *Accounting Terminology Bulletins*. For brevity, AICPA will be used in the text to identify
the American Institute of Certified Public Accountants. The American Accounting
Association will be identified as the AAA.

[2] For example in "Inventory of Generally Accepted Accounting Principles for Business Enterprises, 1965," *Accounting Research Study No. 7*, the AICPA brought together (*a*) the basic concepts to which accounting principles are oriented; (*b*) a list of the
accounting principles (or practices); and (*c*) the pronouncements of its committees.

accepted in APB opinions and the preceding Accounting Research Bulletins *be disclosed in footnotes to financial statements or in independent auditors' reports when the effect of any such departure on the financial statements was material.*

Since 1936 the American Accounting Association through its committees has issued a series of statements relating to accounting theory. Starting in June 1936 with "A Tentative Statement of Accounting Principles Underlying Corporate Financial Statements," the Association carried on an active program of research related to accounting theory. These statements were issued as pamphlets and as articles in the *Accounting Review*. The 1936 statement was revised and supplemented three times; the latest revision was called "Accounting and Reporting Standards for Corporate Financial Statements, 1957 Revision." This statement, along with the preceding statements and nine supplements, was published in a single pamphlet by the association in 1957. The latest statement, prepared by a special AAA committee, was published in 1966 and was entitled *A Statement of Basic Accounting Theory*. Like prior AAA statements, it dealt primarily with fundamental accounting theory, as opposed to accounting practice and procedures. The committee was more concerned with "what should be, as opposed to what was, or what is."[3] The statements relating to accounting principles issued by the Association tended to be more general, theoretical, and oriented toward future practice, whereas those issued by the AICPA primarily dealt with problems arising in current practice. The major statements published by the AAA also tended to deal more with the broad theoretical structure of accounting and less with detailed aspects thereof. Both organizations are continuing active research in accounting theory. Numerous references to these statements will be made throughout the discussions in this book.

THE NATURE OF ACCOUNTING PRINCIPLES

In dealing with the foundations of accounting theory, one is confronted with a serious problem of terminology—both from point of view of current usage and that of preferable usage. Throughout the literature of accounting there are numerous references to the basic foundation of accounting theory in the following terms: principles, concepts, conventions, doctrines, standards, rules, underlying assumptions, procedures, and postulates. Although each of these terms is subject to precise definition, general usage by the profession has served to give them loose and overlapping meanings. Precise definitions taken from standard dictionaries do not satisfy the need for acceptable and descriptive nomenclature for the broad concept of the "founda-

---

[3] AAA, *A Statement of Basic Accounting Theory* (Evanston, Ill., 1966).

tions of accounting theory." For example, various authorities use such diverse terms as "the money *convention,*" the "*doctrine* of conservatism," the "cost *principle,*" the "entity *theory,*" and the "realization *postulate.*" This wide diversity in terminology to express the basic frame of reference can only serve to confuse the learner, to say the least. In addition, the foundations of accounting theory should be formulated within some logical and articulate structure. A series of unrelated concepts, ideas, rules, and standards can hardly qualify as a body of theory—there must be an underlying stucture that is logical, consistent, and systematic. The special committee of the AAA stated: "We define 'theory' as a cohesive set of hypothetical, conceptual, and pragmatic principles forming a general frame of reference for a field of study."[4] Despite this significant effort, by and large, accounting theory as currently expressed continues to be plagued by a lack of (*a*) uniform terminology and (*b*) a systematic underlying structure.[5]

In studying accounting at the level of this book it is imperative that some structure to accounting theory be provided. In view of the present state of the art (as indicated above), a completely adequate structure cannot be presented. Nevertheless, your authors have attempted to present a broad structure that is tentative but which should aid the student of accounting in gaining a better understanding of the foundations of accounting theory. Accordingly, in order to establish a basis for study and consistent treatment throughout this book, your authors have selected the frame of reference (structure) and terminology outlined below and discussed in detail subsequently. As the student studies the various chapters, it may be observed that most of accounting can be explained in terms of this structure. It appears that this frame of reference is easily understood, is closely related to current thinking, and should serve to provide a consistent structure that is articulate and at the same time suitable for the readership of this book. It would be indeed fortunate for accountancy if in the near future there would emerge a more general agreement, a more logical underlying structure, and more consistency in the terminology area.

The APB recently issued their *Statement No. 4,* "Basic Concepts and Accounting Principles Underlying Financial Statements of Business Enterprises." Although the statement does not present an integrated theoretical structure, it does effectively discuss the nature of financial accounting, its objectives, and the principles, procedures, and practices widely used at the present time. There are good reasons to hope that it will serve to advance the "written expression of finan-

---

[4] Ibid., p. 1.

[5] For those who desire to pursue in depth the subject of financial accounting theory the authors recommend the following: Eldon S. Hendriksen, *Accounting Theory,* (rev. ed.; Homewood, Ill.: Richard D. Irwin, Inc., 1970).

cial accounting principles."[6] This statement is briefly reviewed at the end of this chapter.

The broad structure of accounting theory developed by the authors is outlined below and is explained in detail in the pages that follow. Each of the four basic categories are defined followed by an exposition of each of the related subconcepts.

THE BROAD STRUCTURE OF ACCOUNTING THEORY OUTLINED

1. Fundamental underlying assumptions:
   a) The separate-entity assumption
   b) The continuity assumption
   c) The unit-of-measure assumption
   d) The time-period assumption
2. Fundamental theoretical concepts:
   a) The entity theory
   b) The proprietary theory
   c) The funds theory
3. Generally accepted accounting principles:
   a) The cost principle
   b) The revenue principle
   c) The matching principle
   d) The objectivity principle
   e) The consistency principle
   f) The full-disclosure principle
   g) The exception principle
      (1) Materiality
      (2) Conservatism
      (3) Industry peculiarities
4. Accounting procedures:
   a) Those related to income determination
   b) Those related to presentation of data
   c) Those not affecting either income determination or the presentation of data

Fundamental Underlying Assumptions

The fundamental underlying assumptions are broad yet specific aspects of the total *environment* in which accounting normally operates, and they are of direct significance in relationship to the broad spectrum of the objectives of accounting. The underlying assumptions do not include all aspects of the environment but only those significant ones that directly affect and in large part determine the underlying theoretical concepts and foundations of generally accepted principles.

---

[6] "Basic Concepts and Accounting Principles Underlying Financial Statements of Business Enterprises," *Statement No. 4* (New York: Accounting Research Division, AICPA, 1971).

The underlying assumptions—*separate entity, continuity, unit of measure,* and *time period*—suggest pervasive and accepted characteristics of the business environment that are broader even than accounting. The essence of the fundamental underlying assumptions is that aside from accounting, in the absence of evidence to the contrary, the business community (*a*) views the individual business unit as a *separate entity* distinct and apart from the owners; (*b*) generally accepts the idea that *continuity* of operations in the individual business unit will prevail in the forseeable future; (*c*) negotiates and consummates business transactions in an acceptable monetary unit (dollars), whatever their value; and (*d*) relates business activities to specific, short-run *time periods.*

These four fundamental underlying assumptions directly affecting accounting theory, principles, and practices are discussed below.

The Separate-Entity Assumption.   Accounting is concerned with specific and separate enterprise units or entities. Thus each enterprise is considered as an *accounting unit* separate and apart from the owner or owners and from other firms having separate legal and accounting frames of reference. For accounting purposes, partnerships and sole proprietorships are treated as entirely separate and apart from the owners thereof despite the fact that this distinction is not made in the legal sense. Thus this assumption identifies the business unit as an entity separate and distinct from the owners.

Under the separate-entity concept the business entity is considered to own all resources committed to its purpose, subject to the rights and interests of creditors. The separate-entity assumption gives recognition to the fact that transactions of the business and those of the owners should be accounted for and reported separately. In carrying out the accounting function, the assets, equities, and operations also are segregated for each separate entity. All records and reports are developed from the viewpoint of the particular entity. This viewpoint affects the analysis of transactions, accumulation and classification of data, and the resultant financial reporting. Thus the separate-entity concept has significantly influenced the development of present-day accounting. It provides a basis for clear-cut distinction in analyzing transactions between the enterprise and the owners. As an example, the personal residence of an individual owning an unincorporated business is not considered to be an appropriate item to report for the business, although there is a common owner. In this example the accounting entity makes a distinction that is not made in the legal sense; creditors may look to both the personal residence and the business assets for satisfaction of claims against the common owner.

The separate-entity concept is important in determining the results of operations (net income or loss) of a business unit, since personal transactions should not be included in such determination. The accountant would be in an untenable situation from time to time if he did not have this basic concept to rely on in making distinctions between personal and business transactions. Pressures to overlook this distinction are encountered by accountants occasionally.

Accounting fundamentally expresses the economic substance of the entity through an economic model: Assets = Liabilities + Proprietary Equity. Exchange transactions in which the entity is involved are analyzed, recorded, and reported in terms of this model.

The Continuity Assumption. The continuity assumption is frequently referred to as the "going-concern concept." The continuity assumption implies indefinite continuance of the enterprise or accounting entity, that is, that the business is not expected to liquidate in the foreseeable future. The assumption does not imply that accountancy assumes permanent continuance; rather there is a presumption of stability and continuity for a period of time sufficient to carry out contemplated operations, contracts, and commitments. This concept establishes the rationale of accounting on a *nonliquidation basis*, and thus provides the theoretical foundation for many of the valuations and allocations common in accounting. For example, depreciation and amortization procedures rest upon this concept.

This assumption generally underlies the decisions of investors to commit capital to the enterprise. Therefore, accounting for these commitments and the resulting incomes and losses must be based upon the assumption that the enterprise will continue to function in the contemplated manner, performing the business activities consistent with prior objectives including the earning of a return for the entrepreneur. In other words, this concept, as applied to accounting, holds that continuity of business activity is the reasonable expectation for the business unit for which the accounting function is being performed. If the particular entity should be faced with serious loss and probable liquidation, conventional accounting based on the continuity assumption would not be appropriate for determining and reporting the true conditions. In such cases *liquidation* accounting is appropriate wherein all valuations are accounted for at immediate realizable amounts.

Accountants are fully cognizant of the fact that no business entity will continue forever. To satisfy the continuity assumption, it is essential only that on the basis of present facts it appears that the business will continue so that its present resources are utilized according to plan without serious loss of capital investment. Only on the basis of this assumption can the accounting process remain stable and achieve the objective of accurately recording and reporting on the capital commitments, the efficiency of management, and the financial status of the enterprise as a going concern. Under this assumption neither higher current market values nor liquidation values are of particular importance in accounting; rather the assumption provides a basis for the utilization of *cost* in accounting for assets, liabilities, and capital.

The Unit-of-Measure Assumption. Some unit of exchange is essential to raise the level of commerce above that of barter. Similarly, some unit of measurement is necessary in accounting; with so many diverse assets and equities that must be recorded, analyzed, and reported, there is the necessity of expressing them in terms of a common denominator. Obviously, to be of maximum usefulness, accounting ideally should employ the same unit of measure as employed by the business community, that is, the dollar. Accounting may deal with some data in nonmonetary units; however the monetary unit certainly predominates. Thus money becomes the common denominator—the yardstick—in the accounting process.

At this point we encounter a particularly critical problem in accounting: unlike the yardstick which is always 36 inches long, the monetary unit (dollar) changes in value or purchasing power. As a consequence, when there is inflation or deflation, dollars of different size (value) are entered in the accounts over a period of time and dollars of cost are intermingled in the accounts as if they were of equal purchasing power. Because of this practice it is said that accounting either "assumes a perfectly stable monetary unit" or that "changes in the value of money are not significant."

In the United States the rate of price change was not viewed as particularly significant prior to World War II, although there was a significant deflationary period in the early 1930s. In view of the comparatively rapid inflation during and since World War II, accountants have become quite concerned with the stable-money assumption. The accounting profession has devoted considerable attention to the problem, and numerous suggestions have been made to account for the effects of changes in the purchasing power of the dollar. A substantive amount of literature has been written on this problem, and the leading professional organizations are constantly studying it. To date, the profession (and the businessman) has taken few definite steps toward discarding the unit-of-measure assumption.

The unit-of-measure assumption has exerted a particularly significant impact on the development of accounting. The basic theoretical concepts discussed in the next section of this chapter in part rest upon this assumption. Adherence to the cost principle (discussed below) and cost apportionments are related to this assumption. It is the basis for accounting in terms of *original* dollars of inflow and outflow.

The unit-of-measure assumption also has been explained without the assumption that the unit of measure is a "value" measurement in the following manner. This explanation, called the money convention, holds that accounting should record "money invested" and "money borrowed," trace the various recommitments of this "money capital" as it is invested and reinvested in the business process, and finally measure out of gross "money revenue" resulting from business activity the return or recapture of "money capital" with any remainder being designated as "money income." Thus the balance sheet reports, in effect, the number of dollars received from every source, whether from creditors, owners, or retained income. Against this listing of dollar capital by sources, the asset side of the balance sheet reveals where these dollar funds have been invested such as current assets, fixed assets, etc. This view of the balance sheet is strictly one of accountability for that which was received—dollars. Under this concept the view is that it is not the function of accounting to account for *value*. It clearly recognizes that the value of a dollar is often in a state of change, perhaps substantially, from one period to another. However, the explanation says that accounting should not be influenced by these changes, since the primary objective is to "account for dollars." Since the objective is to account for that which has been received (dollars), "counting dollars" must continue despite continuous and often material changes in the purchasing power of those dollars. Pragmatically, the "dollar count" can be done with a high degree of accuracy and objectivity, while the determination of value is both subjective and dependent upon the course of future events. Under this concept, the accountant must recognize, however, that supplementary analyses of such data to report the effects of price-level changes are quite useful and should be utilized, particularly during periods of significant inflation or deflation.

Still another view of the unit-of-measure assumption is that changes in the purchasing power of the monetary unit are not important. It is on the basis of this assumption that dollars of cost are intermingled in the accounts as though they were of equal purchasing power at the time incurred, although, as a matter of fact, it is well recognized that they are not. Dollars of revenue are treated as the equivalent of dollars of cost allocated to the same period regardless of any material changes in the purchasing power of the dollar between the time the costs were incurred and the time they are matched against revenues.[7]

Despite the arguments for adhering to "historical cost" in accounting, there are many cogent arguments for some form of "price-level" and "current value" accounting. Various academicians have spoken eloquently in their favor. Similarly, numerous committees of the American Accounting Association have tended in this direction. In a similar vein the Accounting Principles Board in June 1969 issued its *Statement No. 3*, "Financial Statements Restated for General Price-Level Changes." This statement explains the effects on financial

---

[7] Robert L. Kane, Jr. (ed.), *CPA Handbook* (New York: American Institute of Accountants, 1953), vol. II, chap. xvii, p. 13. Also see *Changing Concepts of Business Income* (New York: The Macmillan Co., 1952), p. 20. (Copyright by the AICPA.)

statements of changes in the general purchasing power of the monetary unit and gives some general guidance on how to prepare and present price-level adjusted financial statements. In this statement the APB recommended that, although price-level adjusted statements are not required, they may be quite useful if presented in conjunction with historical-dollar financial statements. Notwithstanding these activities generally accepted accounting principles continue to adhere to the historical-dollar cost concept in accounting for assets, liabilities, and capital.[8]

The unit-of-measure assumption is considered at greater length in Chapter 23.

The Time-Period Assumption.   Although the results of operations of a specific business enterprise cannot be known precisely until it has completed its life span (final liquidation), *interim* financial reports are necessary. Thus the environment—the business community and government—has imposed upon accounting a calendar constraint, that is, the necessity for assigning changes in wealth of a firm to a series of short time periods. These time periods vary; however, the year is the most common interval as a result of established business practice, tradition, and governmental requirements. Some firms adhere to the calendar year; however, more and more firms are changing to the "natural" business year, the end of which is marked by the lowest point of business activity in each 12-month period. Practically all entities extend the segmentation of operations into monthly periods for internal purposes.

The continuity in business operations tends to obscure the results of these interim "test readings" which the accountant is required to render in the form of periodic financial statements. There are many difficulties involved in the allocation of costs and revenue to a series of relatively short periods. Despite these difficulties, short-term reports are of such significance to management, owners, and creditors that the accounting process must be designed to meet and resolve them. The time-period assumption recognizes this need despite the fact that precision in segmentation on a short-term basis frequently is difficult to attain. This assumption is an established foundation of accounting theory. Many continuous and interrelated streams of data are arbitrarily severed in the preparation of short-term reports. However, it is fully recognized that the difficulties and shortcomings of the

---

[8] AICPA, "Financial Statements Restated for General Price-Level Changes," *Statement No. 3* (New York, June 1969). The reader should observe that to date the APB has issued or authored the publication of three different series of publications: (*a*) Opinions, which have the force of "generally accepted accounting"; (*b*) Statements, which are recommendations only, designed to "lead" in the development of desirable accounting practices and principles; and (*c*) Research Studies, which report the results of research and directions which support both the Opinions and Statements and provide a basis for future changes in accounting.

periodic financial statements are far overbalanced by their usefulness.

The time-period assumption underlies the whole area of *accruals* and *deferrals* affecting significantly the income statement, the balance sheet, and the statement of retained earnings. As noted above it has its roots in the environment that is, in the business practices of the economy and the continuously increasing demands for more information about operations.

Fundamental Theoretical Concepts

The fundamental theoretical concepts are broad notions relating to the underlying financial structure of a business enterprise. They are concerned with the theoretical nature of the accounting entities that operate in a free economy characterized by private ownership of property. Thus these concepts—the *entity theory*, the *proprietary theory*, and the *funds theory*—are concerned with a theoretical explanation of the *equities* currently recognized in the business environment, and the manner in which the accounting therefor should be carried out fundamentally. They are not concerned with techniques but with the basic problem of defining accounting entities, thereby providing a philosophical basis for the general principles of accounting.

In contrast with the underlying assumptions (as discussed above), all of which are independently applicable, in a sense, the three theoretical concepts are competing explanations of the nature of the individual business entity. The theorist would insist on a choice of one from among the three to provide a theoretical explanation of equities of the business unit. The question is: Which one of the three theories best defines and delineates the real theoretical nature of the accounting entity and thus serves best to identify the primary objectives of accounting so that there is established a sound point of departure for the application of generally accepted accounting principles and procedures within the separate business unit?

Only the entity and proprietary theories have gained any general acceptance as being expressive of the fundamental nature of the accounting entity. These two theories in particular have had a significant impact on accounting thought, and each underlies a number of different accounting rules and procedures. It appears that at least in recent years, the entity theory has had the greater impact on the evolving "body of accounting theory." The three theories of accounting entities are discussed briefly in the following paragraphs.

The Entity Theory.   The entity theory is said to be "income centered." In the entity theory, the focal point of accounting is the business unit (the entity) not the proprietor. Assets belong to the entity, and liabilities and capital represent sources of the assets. Revenue and expense are viewed from the point of view of the enterprise rather than from that of the owners. Primary importance is attached to income determination, and the income statement is given primary consideration.

This theory arose from the legal view of the corporation as a separate entity (or person) in its own right. The entity stands in relationship to stockholders, creditors, employees, and the general public as a trustee of ownership. This position of accountability is discharged primarily in terms of *operating results* and productivity of the *total* capital employed. The entity "accounts for" resources entrusted to it in terms of measurement of accomplishment or productivity (called revenue) and business effort (costs and expenses). The difference, *net income*, is the fundamental index of the effectiveness of the management in employing the resources entrusted to the entity and in discharging the responsibilities to equity holders. Accounting thus is income centered under the entity theory instead of being "asset centered" as under the proprietary theory.

An illustration of the application of the entity theory relates to inventory valuation. The entity theory would tend to support the conclusion that *Lifo* inventory valuation theoretically may be preferable to *Fifo* if better income determination is achieved thereby. Lifo tends to match current revenue and current cost more effectively than Fifo; inventory valuation on the balance sheet is considered to be of less significance.

The Proprietary Theory. The proprietary theory is said to be "asset centered." This theory emphasizes the economic aspects of the enterprise as revolving around proprietary (owner) equity. The focus is on ownership, since the central concept evolved during the original development of accounting long before the corporate form became so dominant. The proprietary theory generally is viewed as having greater relevance for closely held enterprises such as a proprietorship or partnership than for widely held corporations.

The proprietary theory conceives of the primary and overriding objective of accounting as being the proper determination of owner equity. Emphasis is on the accounting equation expressed as Assets — Liabilities = Owner Equity. The proprietary theory is said to be asset centered, since attention is directed primarily to the determination of asset values and liability amounts (considered as negative assets) so that their difference accurately reflects the proprietorship element. The major accounting effort is viewed in terms of reporting assets (and their valuation), and the most important single financial statement is the balance sheet. Revenue and income are defined as increases in proprietorship not resulting from proprietary investments, and expenses and losses are viewed as decreases in proprietorship not resulting from withdrawals of capital by the proprietor. The principal objective of business is viewed as that of increasing proprietorship through augmentation of assets. It follows that the balance sheet properly prepared would report the all-important assets and proprietorship; thus all questions of accounting measurement should be resolved in favor of the balance sheet.

To continue the prior example under the proprietary theory, stronger theoretical support is provided for Fifo than Lifo in inventory valuation. Since the proprietary theory is asset centered, inventory valuation for balance sheet purposes is of more significance than for income determination. Fifo would tend to result in a more realistic asset valuation (inventory), although current costs may not be matched effectively with current revenue.

The Funds Theory. Under this theory the assets are viewed as a "fund" and the employment of those assets in terms of activities or purposes is fundamental. The right side of the balance sheet reports a series of *restrictions* against those assets — legal and economic. Here the center of accounting focus is defined in terms of a group of assets and the uses to which those assets are committed. The funds theory therefore is asset centered. The administration and appropriate use of those assets is the principal motivation in managerial employment of the funds. Liabilities are restrictions against the funds in that they must be paid from the fund of assets. Under the funds theory, activities employing the fund assets are not necessarily related to profit making. Augmentation of assets is not a primary aspect of the employment of fund assets, whereas velocity of funds flow is. As a consequence of these concepts, income determination is viewed as a secondary objective of financial reporting.

The funds theory is more applicable to fiduciary, governmental, and institutional accounting than to industrial accounting. However, some aspects of industrial accounting have relevance in the funds theory. Certainly, the concept has application in accounting for sinking funds and other segregations of assets. In overall perspective the funds theory seemingly had relatively little impact on accounting thought.[9]

Generally Accepted Accounting Principles

The term *generally accepted accounting principles* is used widely in discussions of accounting theory and with considerable variation as to meaning. Your authors have chosen to use the term very broadly and in a pragmatic sense rather than in a narrow theoretical sense. Accordingly, generally accepted accounting principles are defined for our considerations to include those *broad rules* of accounting action developed and accepted by the accounting profession in con-

---

[9] For an excellent discussion, see Morton Backer (ed.), *Modern Accounting Theory* (Englewood Cliffs, N.J.: Prentice-Hall, Inc., 1966), chap. xii.

formity with the objectives of accounting, the fundamental underlying assumptions, and the basic theoretical concepts. They do not include the accounting procedures and mechanics. For example, one principle is known as the cost principle. Applied to inventories it holds that they should be valued at historical *cost;* in applying this principle one becomes involved in an accounting procedure, that is, whether to apply Fifo, Lifo, average, or some other procedure, each of which applies the cost principle but in a different way mechanically.

Generally accepted accounting principles are not immutable principles of nature like those found in physics and chemistry, but they are developed by man, as a result of specific needs; hence they are subject to change when the basic needs or the related environment are altered. These principles cannot be rigid; they must be changeable since accountants develop them to be of greatest usefulness to users of the resulting data consistent with the concepts of truth and fairness. Generally accepted accounting principles also must have the *substantial authoritative support* of the profession. One broad view of generally accepted accounting principles is described in the *CPA Handbook* as follows:

principles of accounting might be considered as being in the nature of rules of human behavior adopted by man with a view to their usefulness for the particular needs of society at the time and place. From such a viewpoint, principles of accounting would be subject to evolution and change. They would be similar to principles of law such as the principles of evidence, trust, and corporate responsibility; or to principles of education such as teaching methods, classroom management and school supervision; or to principles of social etiquette such as form of introduction, table manners and marriage practices.[10]

The seven generally accepted accounting principles listed on page 6 are discussed in the following paragraphs.

The Cost Principle.   This is one of the more basic principles underlying the accounting process. It may be more appropriately designated as the "historical cost principle" as opposed to the current cost and reproduction cost theories. The cost principle holds that *cost* is the appropriate basis for initial accounting recognition (at date of acquisition) of all asset acquisitions, service acquisitions, expenses, costs, creditor equities, and owner equities. It also holds that subsequent to acquisition cost values are retained throughout the accounting process. The cost principle recognizes the basic subject matter of accounting as completed transactions which are to be translated into their financial effect on the entity in terms of the exchange price

---

[10]*CPA Handbook*, vol. II, chap. xvii, p. 1.

established at the date of the completed transaction. The cost principle was defined authoritatively as follows:

Factors of production and other resources of an enterprise are measured at the date of acquisition by costs incurred or amounts invested, on a cash or cash-equivalent basis, and at later dates by the balances of costs incurred or amounts invested after taking into account the effects of operation and other subsequent events. Similarly the rights of creditors and stockholders are measured initially by amounts contributed, on a cash or cash-equivalent basis, and subsequently reflect the cumulative results of operations, distributions, and other corporate activities.[11]

In applying the cost principle, the accountant frequently is confronted with a serious problem of *determining* cost, that is, where noncash considerations are involved. In determining cost the "cash bargained price" is utilized. Where considerations other than cash are involved, the cost measure is the cash equivalent of the consideration given up in the transaction or the cash equivalent of the asset or service acquired, whichever is the more clearly evident. Thus, where capital stock is issued to pay for land acquired, the asset is recorded at the fair market value of the stock if determinable; otherwise the fair market value of the land must be determined as objectively as is possible.

It should be emphasized that the cost principle is applicable to the measurement of equities (creditor and owner) as well as to assets, expenses, and services. Liabilities should be measured at their cash equivalent, and capital transactions likewise should be recorded and reported in accordance with the cost principle. Detailed discussions of these applications, as well as certain exceptions to the cost principle, appear in subsequent chapters.

The Revenue Principle.   The revenue principle (*a*) defines revenue, (*b*) specifies how revenue should be measured, and (*c*) pinpoints the timing of revenue recognition. Each of the three facets of the revenue principle presents difficult conceptual and operational problems and clarity of thought requires that each be defined independently. On this basis revenue can be appropriately defined as "the creation of goods or services by an enterprise during a specific interval of time." Note that this definition does not dictate either the measurement (amount) or timing (date of recognition) of the revenue, but is neutral in respect to them."[12] Another useful definition, from a different viewpoint, is: "Revenue . . . is the monetary expression of the aggregate of products or services transferred by an enterprise to its customers

---

[11] AAA, "Accounting Principles Underlying Corporate Financial Statements," *Accounting Review*, June 1941, p. 3.

[12] Adapted from Eldon S. Hendriksen, *Accounting Theory* (rev. ed.; Homewood, Ill.: Richard D. Irwin, Inc., 1970), p. 161.

during a period of time."[13] Thus, the revenue principle holds that revenue should include all changes in the net assets of the firm other than those arising from capital transactions. That is, revenue is the measure of new assets received for (a) the sale of goods and services; (b) interest, rents, royalties, etc.; (c) net gain on the sale of assets other than stock-in-trade; and (d) gain from advantageous settlement of liabilities. In applying the broad principle we will see in later chapters that adequate reporting (under the full-disclosure principle) requires that revenue be reported in segments such as operating revenue and extraordinary gains and losses.

In respect to measurement of revenue, the principle holds that revenue is best measured by the cash exchange value of the product, service, or asset exchanged (provided). This concept requires that discounts be viewed as adjustments that are made to reach the true cash exchange value (i.e., sales discounts should be deducted from sales revenues) and that in noncash transactions the fair market value of the consideration given or received, whichever is the more clearly determinable, should be used as the cash exchange value of the revenue.

In respect to timing of revenue recognition, accountants generally rely on a subprinciple known as the *realization concept*. It is a pragmatic test for the timing of revenue recognition since it is characterized by operational rather than by strict theoretical content. Specifically it holds that revenue should be recognized when an exchange or severance has occurred. Thus, the primary test of revenue recognition is the point of sale (or point at which services are rendered). The point of sale generally is viewed as the time when legal title to the goods passes. For example, in the case of goods shipped f.o.b. shipping point, title legally passes at the time they are turned over to the shipper, hence revenue would be recognized at this point; whereas goods shipped f.o.b. destination give rise to revenue only upon delivery at destination. In the case where services rather than goods are involved, revenue is realized under the sales basis when the services are rendered. As a practical matter, the realization of revenue frequently is recognized when the service is completed and billed.

The *sales basis* should be used where the following conditions exist: (a) the ultimate realization of the sales price is reasonably certain and (b) the costs and expenses related to the particular transaction appear to be determinable with reasonable accuracy in the period of sale.

The *cash basis* also is used to a limited extent as a determination of when to recognize revenue. Under this basis revenue is recognized only upon receipt of the sales price in cash. This basis should be used

---

[13] AAA, Committee on Accounting Concepts and Standards, *Accounting and Reporting Standards for Corporate Financial Statements and Preceding Statements and Supplements* (Columbus, Ohio, 1957), p. 5.

only where the sales basis is not appropriate due to the absence of reasonable assurance that ultimate collection will be made, or where the related and significant expenses and costs cannot yet be determined with any degree of accuracy. The "installment method" of recognizing revenue on installment sales discussed in a subsequent chapter is an example of the use of the cash basis in revenue recognition. Another basis is the *production basis;* that is, revenue is recognized as production progresses rather than at final date of transfer. A variation of this method is known as the percentage-completion method on long-term contracts. To illustrate, assume a building contractor has only one contract in process, that is, to construct a large building which will require approximately three years. According to the terms of the contract he is to receive monthly payments based on "percent of the contract completed." In this case, he may adopt an accounting procedure to recognize some revenue each period rather than to defer all revenue until the end of the three-year period. Another example of the production basis relates to cost-plus-fixed-fee contracts.

A fourth and rarely used basis for recognition of revenue is the *cost-recovery* or *sunk cost basis.* On this basis *all* related costs are recovered before any revenue is recognized. The sunk cost basis is applicable only in highly speculative transactions where the ultimate outcome is completely unpredictable. For example, an investor may have purchased bonds where the interest was in default for a number of years. The purchase price was at a fraction of the maturity value of the bonds because of the improbability of final collection. The transaction was highly speculative. Under the sunk cost basis, receipts of interest would not be taken up as revenue until the original investment was recovered; collections subsequent to this point would be recognized as revenue.

Clearly the problem of determining when revenue should be recognized is a critical one. Due to diverse transactions involving revenue, no single theoretical rule can apply to all situations; therefore, accountants necessarily have developed the realistic guidelines explained above to determine when revenue should be recognized in point of time.

The Matching Principle. The matching principle holds that for any period for which net income is to be reported, the revenues to be recognized should be determined and then the incurred costs related to that revenue should be determined and reported for that period. If revenue is carried over from a prior period or deferred to a future period in accordance with the revenue principle, all elements of cost and expense related to that revenue likewise should be carried over from a prior period or deferred, as the case may be. This matching of costs with revenue frequently is a difficult problem; however, careful matching is an essential function of accounting if there is to be a proper determination of periodic net income.

Application of the matching principle often requires the accountant to deal with estimates. For example, assume a home appliance is being sold with a 12-month guarantee. Costs of making good on the guarantee should be matched against the revenue from those sales despite the fact that the guaranty costs actually will be incurred in the year following sale. In this case matching of cost with revenue is possible only through an estimate of the future costs as is done (and for the same reason) with respect to the allowance for doubtful accounts.

The Objectivity Principle. The objectivity principle holds that to the fullest extent possible, accounting should be based on objective data and determinations. In recording and reporting the results of transactions, accounting should look to completed transactions resulting from bargaining between parties having adverse interests. Thus, the legal concept of an "arm's-length" transaction is especially important in accounting. To the fullest extent possible, accounting data must be supported by formal and verifiable business documents originating outside the entity. Under this principle, opinions, estimates, and judgmental decisions should be kept to a minimum consistent with the necessities of the situation.

Accountants fully realize that many aspects of accounting are not completely factual and that some amounts reported on the financial statements are not entirely factual but necessarily involve estimates of values and are founded on certain expectations about the future. Depreciation charges, amortizations, accruals, and deferrals of both revenue and costs involve estimates from time to time. Many estimates necessarily must enter the accounting process. However, the objectivity principle exerts a very significant and beneficial impact on accounting principles, assumptions, and procedures. The objectivity principle also is fundamental to the professional "independence" of the practicing CPA in that certain amounts reported on the financial statements are wholly or partially verified by objective means independently from the client's own records.

The Consistency Principle. The consistency principle holds that in an accounting entity accounting must be the result of consistent application of accounting theory, practice, and methods from one period to the next. Consistent accounting for the entity should be followed so that the resulting financial data of successive periods are comparable. Comparability is essential so that trends and differences may be identified, evaluated, and appraised. In addition, inconsistency in the application of certain accounting methods (such as changing the method of depreciation) may materially affect the reported net income and balance sheet. Inconsistency, if allowed, would open the door to manipulation of both reported assets and net income.

The consistency principle does not preclude changes in the accounting to improve the measurements and reporting. When changes in accounting are desirable for sound reasons, a description of the change and the dollar effect should be reported in conformance with the full-disclosure principle on the financial statements in the year of change and in later years for which comparative data are presented.

The opinion by the independent auditor recognizes consistency as an especially important aspect in audited financial statements. The AICPA *Statements on Auditing Procedure No. 33,* issued in 1963, suggested the following wording where an unqualified opinion by the auditor is expressed:

In our opinion, the accompanying balance sheet and statement(s) of income and retained earnings present fairly the financial position of X Company at June 30, 19 – , and the results of its operations for the year then ended, in conformity with generally accepted accounting principles applied on a basis consistent with that of the preceding year.[14]

In harmony with this principle, in the absence of clear statements to the contrary, those using financial statements can assume that generally accepted accounting principles and procedures have been followed in a consistent manner. The reader has assurance that the financial statements reflect consistent treatment from period to period of such items as inventories, depreciation, amortizations, accruals, and deferrals. Only by being able to rely upon adherence to the consistency principle can confidence in financial reports be maintained.

In *Statements on Auditing Procedure No. 33* the objective of the consistency standard is stated as follows:

(1) To give assurance that the comparability of financial statements as between periods has not been materially affected by changes in the accounting principles employed or in the method of their application; or
(2) If comparability has been materially affected by such changes, to require a statement of the nature of the changes and their effects on the financial statements.[15]

The Full-Disclosure Principle. The full-disclosure principle holds that there should be complete and understandable reporting on the financial statements of all significant information relating to the economic affairs of the accounting entity. The degree of disclosure should be such that the financial statements will not be misleading. The principle is especially applicable to unusual events and major changes in expectations. Full disclosure may involve additional

---

[14]Committee on Auditing Procedure AICPA, *Statements on Auditing Procedure No. 33* (New York, 1963), p. 57.

[15]Ibid., p. 42.

information within the body of the affected report, by footnote, or by extended explanations appended to the statements. Practically all footnotes observed in the published financial reports reflect the impact of the full-disclosure principle.

The disclosure of certain poststatement findings that may significantly affect the financial condition of the entity is required by this principle. The full-disclosure principle places a heavy responsibility on the accountant to exercise sound judgment as to the additional information that should be reported by separate footnote or comment.

The Exception Principle. In a preceding paragraph the point was made that accounting principles are not principles of nature but are man-made. Further, accounting principles are subject to change when there is a change in the environment in which they operate, or in the related needs of the users of financial statements. Accounting principles are very pragmatic and must be applied to a very diverse set of facts and conditions. In view of these considerations some exceptions are to be expected. The exception principle encompasses three fairly specific concepts which have been widely recognized and accepted in accounting as essential to accomplishment of the broad objectives of accounting. These three concepts comprise the exception principle and are discussed below:

Materiality. This concept holds that items of small significance need not be accorded strict theoretical treatment. Accounting deals with the practical affairs of business; accuracy and compliance with accounting theory are important. Yet from the practical point of view the accountant must weigh the worth of strict accuracy and compliance with theory against the *cost* thereof. Accordingly, under the materiality concept, strict adherence to principle is not required where the accuracy of the financial report is not significantly influenced.

With respect to determination of materiality, the *CPA Handbook* states:

An item in relation to a financial statement would be considered material only if it would have a significant effect upon an important judgment based on that statement. Whether a particular item is material or significant cannot be determined by consideration only of the item itself. Its relationship to other items and to the surrounding circumstances have to be known before that judgment can be made.[16]

To illustrate, most concerns have a minimum cost of capital additions below which such items are expensed directly, although there may be a continuing benefit for several periods. A pencil sharpener costing $1.89 may last for three years; theoretically the cost should be allocated (depreciated) over the three years. However, the cost of the

---

[16] *CPA Handbook*, vol. II, chap. xvii, p. 24.

detailed accounting required might well exceed the cost of the asset. Since the cost of the item obviously is immaterial when related to overall operations, it may be expensed when acquired. It is highly desirable that the accounting entity establish uniform policies to govern these exceptions to accounting theory and that these policies be followed consistently.

Conservatism. The concept of conservatism as applied in accounting holds that where alternatives for an accounting determination are available, each having some reasonable support, that alternative having the *least favorable immediate influence* on the proprietary equity should be selected. In recognizing assets where two alternative valuations have some merit, the lower should be selected, and the higher of two alternative liability amounts should be recorded; in determining the amount of costs, expenses, and revenues where there is reasonable doubt as to the appropriateness of alternative amounts, the one having the least favorable effect on net income should be chosen. Thus, where there is a choice among alternative valuations, accounting seeks to avoid favorable exaggeration by relying on rational conservatism. Conservatism in accounting frequently results in an exception from theoretical treatment. For example, "lower of cost or market" as used in costing inventories is a departure from the cost principle.

Although the accounting profession has generally accepted the concept that profits should not be anticipated and that probable losses should be recognized as soon as the amounts thereof are reasonably determinable, overconservatism usually results in misrepresentation. The accountant should be fully aware of the pitfalls of ultraconservatism. Reliance on conservatism should never be used as an escape from the more laborious procedures to attain reasonable accuracy. It is recognized that many errors in accounting have been committed as a result of overconservatism. A modified view of conservatism currently exerts an impact on accounting thought and practices.

Industry Peculiarities. In view of the focus of accounting on usefulness, feasibility, and appropriateness, the peculiarities of an industry (not an individual company) warrant certain exceptions to accounting principles and practices. The exception principle provides for a special accounting for specific items where there is a clear precedent in the industry based on real need, rationale, and feasibility. It is appropriate also to note that some aspects of accounting are in response to legal requirements; this is especially true with respect to corporate capital.

Accounting Procedures

Although accounting procedures were listed on page 6 as a category of the "foundations of accounting theory," they are not basically theoretical considerations but rather are related to the "how" of accounting; they result from the application of accounting theory and principles. Accounting procedures may be defined as those methods, practices, and approaches generally used to implement the accounting function in conformance with the underlying assumptions, theoretical concepts, and generally accepted accounting principles. Thus accounting procedures are concerned with the mechanics of accounting, details of applying accounting theory, and data processing in specific accounting entities. There is a pervasive and unfortunate confusion in much of the literature (and related discussions) between accounting theory and accounting procedures. This confusion has been one of the primary roadblocks to the development of an integrated theoretical structure which should underlie accounting procedures. Accounting procedures vary widely from firm to firm and from industry to industry. Unfortunately the application of different accounting procedures may have a significant effect on the values reported on financial statements. As a consequence the accounting profession must be very attentive to accounting procedures in order to assure (a) that they do not violate accounting theory and principles and (b) that a selected procedure is appropriate for the particular situation to which it is being applied. To illustrate, a fixed asset having a limited life, such as a machine, is recorded at its cost in harmony with the cost principle; subsequent to acquisition its cost is amortized over its useful life (depreciation) as an offset to revenue in conformance with the matching principle. There are numerous depreciation procedures that can be used, such as straight line, output, and declining balance, each of which is in conformance with the cost and matching principles. On the other hand, for a particular asset in a particular environment there is only one depreciation method that is appropriate; it is the one that best relates the depreciation charge each period to the "decrease in economic usefulness of the asset to the enterprise for the purpose for which acquired." As another example, for inventory purposes, Fifo, Lifo, and weighted average satisfy the cost and matching principles. In apply these accounting procedures one is faced, in each situation, with selecting the one that best applies the matching principle taking into account the situation and the broad objectives of financial reporting.

Some examples of accounting procedures are:

a) Those related to income determination:
   1) Method of estimating depreciation (straight line, declining charge, etc.).
   2) Method of costing inventories (Fifo, Lifo, etc.).
   3) Method of retail inventory.
   4) Use and application of overhead rates.

b) Those related to presentation of data:
    5) Method of reporting nonrecurring gains and losses.
    6) Arrangement of data and headings on financial statements.
    7) Selection of terminology in accounting reports.
c) Those not affecting either income determination or the presentation of data:
    8) Use of controlling accounts and related subsidiaries.
    9) Method of processing data (manual, machine, computer).
    10) Arrangement and organization of journals and ledgers.
    11) Preparation of adjusting, closing, and reversing entries.

The above list of examples of accounting procedures is suggestive of their nature; numerous additional examples could be provided. Throughout this book much of the discussion will concern accounting procedures.

Basic Concepts and Accounting Principles

In October 1970 the APB issued *Statement No. 4* entitled "Basic Concepts and Accounting Principles Underlying Financial Statements of Business Enterprises." The Statement represents a major step toward the development of an articulated statement of accounting theory and principles. It purposes were stated to be: (1) To advance the written expression of financial principles, (2) To discuss the nature of financial accounting, (3) To set forth the objectives of financial accounting, and (4) to present a description of *present* generally accepted accounting principles. To quote from the Statement:

The Statement is a step toward development of a more consistent and comprehensive structure of financial accounting and of more useful financial information. It is intended to provide a framework within which the problems of financial accounting may be solved, although it does not propose solutions to those problems and does not attempt to indicate what generally accepted accounting principles should be. Evaluation of present accounting principles and determination of changes that are desirable are left to future pronouncements of the Board. . . . Publication of this Statement does not constitute approval by the Board of accounting principles that are not covered in its Opinions.

Space constraints precludes detailed explanation of this lengthy Statement; however, an outline of its basic components follows. The outline indicates that the Statement presents *three* major categories of items with numerous subitems under each. For convenience in reference, the Statement provided special designations for the "principles"; these are indicated below in the second column of Table 1–1.

Table 1–1
Outline of APB *Statement 4*

Categories	*Designation (if any)*

I. Basic *features* of financial accounting

   1. Accounting entity
   2. Going concern
   3. Measurement of economic resources and obligations
   4. Time periods
   5. Measurement in terms of money
   6. Accrual
   7. Exchange price
   8. Approximation
   9. Judgment
  10. General-purpose financial information
  11. Fundamentally related financial statements
  12. Substance over form
  13. Materiality

II. Basic *elements* of financial accounting

   Financial position

   1. Assets
   2. Liabilities
   3. Owners' equity

   Results of operations

   4. Revenue
   5. Expenses
   6. Net income

III. Generally accepted *accounting principles*

   1. Pervasive principles

    a) Pervasive measurement principles

     Initial recording of assets and liabilities P-1
     Realization P-2
     Associating cause and effect P-3
     Systematic and rational allocation P-4
     Immediate recognition...P-5
     Unit of measure P-6

    b) Modifying conventions

     1. Conservatism
     2. Emphasis on income
     3. Application of judgment

   2. Broad operating principles

    a) Principles of selection (S) and measurement (M)

     Exchanges recorded S-1
     Exchange prices...M-1
     Owners' investments and withdrawals recorded........................S-2
     Owners' investments and withdrawals measured.......................M-2
     Nonreciprocal transfers recorded S-3
     Nonreciprocal transfers measured M-3
     Favorable external events other than transfers generally
       not recorded..S-4
     Retention of recorded amounts M-4
     Unfavorable external events other than transfers recorded..........S-5
     Measuring unfavorable events M-5

Table 1–1 (continued)

Categories	Designation (if any)

Production recorded..S-6
Production measurement M-6
Casualties S-7
Measuring casualties M-7

b) Principles that determine effects on assets, liabilities,
    owners' equity, revenues, and expenses.

Dual effects...E-1
Increases in assets...E-2
Decreases in assets E-3
Increases in liabilities E-4
Decreases in liabilities E-5
Increases in owners' equity..E-6
Decreases in owners' equity...E-7
Revenue E-8
Expenses E-9
Effects of accounting for assets and liabilities that are not
    resources or obligations E-10

c) Principles of financial statement presentation

Basic financial statements R-1
Complete balance sheet..R-2
Complete income statement...R-3
Accounting period..R-4
Consolidated financial statements R-5
Equity basis R-6
Translation of foreign balances R-7
Classification and segregation..R-8
Other disclosures R-9
Form of financial statement presentation R-10
Earnings per share R-11

d) Detailed principles

The large body of practices and procedures that prescribe
definitively how transactions and other events should be
recorded, classified, summarized, and presented are the
means of implementing the broad and pervasive principles.
They are not identified in the Statement.

The above outline merely serves to indicate the broad approach to be found in the Statement. Clearly, the approach varies somewhat from that presented in the prior paragraphs of this chapter. At this point in time it is impossible to assess the reactions to the Statement; however, in the opinion of these authors it is a major step that warrants serious study and constructive evaluation. The APB has clearly stated that the Statement represents accounting as it "now is" and that it is viewed as an essential step in moving forward in the continuing evolution of accounting to meeting the increasingly sophisticated needs of a complex society. Serious students of accounting would be well advised to acquire a copy of this Statement for study and evaluation.

CONCLUSION

The discussions of the "foundations of accounting theory" in this chapter are intended to provide the student with a frame of reference for study of subsequent chapters. Rather than presenting these concepts piecemeal throughout the text, the authors have chosen to present them briefly in an earlier chapter. In considering the subject matter in subsequent chapters, these concepts will be reconsidered and related to the problem or practice at hand.

After having studied the contents of this book it might be advisable for the student to return to this chapter for a critical study of it. Out of such an approach a firm foundation of theory might be attained on the part of the student. Your authors cannot overemphasize the importance of an understanding and appreciation of the foundations of accounting theory as opposed to a mere memorization of procedures and techniques. The accountant, whether in public practice or in industry, is faced continually with accounting problems that do not fit precisely what may have been encountered or considered previously; somehow many of them do not fit neatly into specific accounting practice and procedures. As a consequence, many very practical judgments and decisions must be made by the accountant, and they should be resolved on the basis of sound theoretical analysis. For this approach to resolving problems there must exist a logical and articulate structure of accounting theory. An accountant must have a deep understanding of the meaning and relevance of accounting theory to be successful as a professional man. In this connection, we might repeat the hope, expressed earlier in this chapter, that there will emerge in the relatively near future an improved formulation of the foundations of accounting theory as contrasted with the implementing principles, procedures, and practices.

QUESTIONS FOR CLASS DISCUSSION

1. List and briefly explain the four basic categories of the "foundations of accounting theory."
2. Give the four underlying assumptions presented in the chapter and briefly explain each.
3. Give the three fundamental theoretical concepts presented and briefly explain each.
4. Give the seven generally accepted accounting principles listed in the chapter and briefly explain each.
5. What is the "going-concern" concept?
6. When is "liquidation" accounting appropriate?
7. What primary problem is created in depreciation accounting if the unit-of-measure assumption is not valid?
8. Relate the cost principle and the matching principle.
9. How is cost measured in noncash transactions?

10. On what basis should there be "revenue recognition" under the revenue principle?

11. Relate the consistency, exception, and full-disclosure principles to an audit report by an independent accountant.

12. What are some of the hazards of overconservatism in accounting?

DECISION CASE 1-1

In making an audit of a corporation you find certain liabilities, such as taxes, which appear to be overstated. Also some semiobsolete inventory items seem to be undervalued, and the tendency is to expense rather than to capitalize as many items as possible.

In talking with the management about the policies, you are told that "the company has always taken a very conservative view of the business and its future prospects." Management suggests that they do not wish to weaken the company by reporting any more earnings or paying any more dividends than are absolutely necessary, since they do not expect business to continue to be good. They point out that the undervaluation of assets, etc., does not lose anything for the company and creates reserves for "hard times."

Required:

You are to discuss fully the policies followed by the company and comment on each of the arguments presented by management.

(AICPA adapted)

DECISION CASE 1-2

The general manager of the Cumberland Manufacturing Company received an income statement from his controller. The statement covered the calendar year. "Joe," he said to the controller, "this statement indicates that a net income of only $100,000 was earned last year. You know the value of the company is much more than it was this time last year."

"You're probably right," replied the controller. "You see, there are factors in accounting which sometimes keep reported operating results from reflecting the change in the fair market value of the company."

Required:

Present a detailed explanation of the accounting theories, principles, and practices to which the controller referred. Include justification, to the extent possible, for the generally used accounting principles and methods.

(AICPA adapted)

EXERCISES

Exercise 1-1

State the generally accepted accounting principles applicable to the valuation in the balance sheet of each of the following assets:

a) Accounts receivable.

b) Fixed assets.

c) Inventories.

d) Marketable securities.

e) Prepaid expenses.

Exercise 1-2

In applying the revenue principle, the problem of when revenue should be recognized is critical. For each of the proposals below, indicate the theoretical aspects of revenue recognition:

a) When cash is collected for sales or services.

b) Upon delivery of the goods or completion of the service.

c) In proportion to percentage completion of production.

d) Upon segregation of goods for the purchaser or completion of all plans to render the service.

Exercise 1-3

When a business is purchased as an entity, the price paid often differs from the equity shown by the records of the vendor.

Required:

Explain fully why the sale value of a going business may differ from the book value even where acceptable accounting practices have been followed in keeping the accounts of the business.   (AICPA adapted)

Exercise 1-4

What is your understanding of the meaning of *consistency* in the application of accounting principles — for example, as used in the standard form of an independent public accountant's report?   (AICPA adapted)

Exercise 1-5

Accountants frequently refer to a concept of "conservatism." Explain what is meant by conservatism in accounting. Discuss the question of the extent to which it is possible to follow accounting procedures which will result in consistently conservative financial statements over a considerable number of years. Give an example of an application of conservatism in accounting.   (AICPA adapted)

PROBLEMS

Problem 1-1

Appraise each of the following statements in terms of accounting theory:

a) Anticipate no profits and recognize all possible losses.

b) Lower of cost or market should be used in valuing all inventories.

c) Reported net income is affected more by judgment than by fact.

d) When in doubt be conservative.

e) Full disclosure presumes an informed reader.

f) The cost principle primarily affects only the income statement.

Problem 1-2

Present accounting theory is based on the assumption that the "value of money" is relatively stable. If there is a significant change in the price level, or in the purchasing power of the dollar, problems arise in interpreting income data as determined under conventional accounting procedures.

Required:

State and explain briefly the nature of such problems as related to inventories and fixed assets. You need not attempt to offer specific solutions to these problems.   (AICPA adapted)

Problem 1–3

Inventories are often valued at the "lower of cost or market." This traditional method of valuation is frequently defended as "conservative," and like any other valuation method adopted, it should be followed consistently.

Required:

In your opinion, is a company which regularly follows the practice of valuing its inventory at the lower of cost or market being "consistent and conservative"? Discuss critically, including a discussion of the meaning of the terms *consistent* and *conservative*.   (AICPA adapted)

Problem 1–4

You are engaged in the audit of the Willis Corporation which opened its first branch office in 19A. During the audit the Willis president raises the question of the accounting treatment of the operating loss of the branch office for its first year, which is material in amount.

The president proposes to capitalize the operating loss as a "starting-up" expense to be amortized over a five-year period. He states that branch offices of other firms engaged in the same field generally suffer a first-year operating loss which is often capitalized; and you are aware of this practice. He argues, therefore, that the loss should be capitalized so that the accounting will be conservative; further, he argues that the accounting must be consistent with established industry practice.

Required:

1. Discuss the president's use of the words *conservative* and *consistent* from the standpoint of accounting terminology. Discuss the accounting treatment you would recommend.

2. What disclosure, if any, would be required in the financial statements?
                                                          (AICPA adapted)

Problem 1–5

The general ledger of Enter-tane, Inc., a corporation engaged in the development and production of television programs for commercial sponsorship, contains the following accounts before amortization at the end of the current year:

Account	Balance (debit)
Sealing Wax and Kings	$51,000
The Messenger	36,000
The Desperado	17,500
Shin Bone	8,000
Studio Rearrangement	5,000

An examination of contracts and records revealed the following information:

a) The first two accounts listed above represent the total cost of completed programs that were televised during the accounting period just ended. Under the terms of an existing contract, Sealing Wax and Kings will be rerun during the next accounting period at a fee equal to 50% of the fee for the first televising of the program. The contract for the first run produced $300,000 of revenue. The contract with the sponsor of The Messenger provides that he may, at his option, rerun the program during the next season at a fee of 75% of the fee on the first televising of the program.

b) The balance in The Desperado account is the cost of a new program which has just been completed and is being considered by several companies for commercial sponsorship.

c) The balance in the Shin Bone account represents the cost of a partially completed program for a projected series that has been abandoned.

d) The balance of the Studio Rearrangement account consists of payments made to a firm of engineers which prepared a report relative to the more efficient utilization of existing studio space and equipment.

Required:

1. State the general principle (or principles) of accounting that are applicable to the first *four* accounts.

2. How would you report each of the first *four* accounts in the financial statements of Enter-tane, Inc.? Explain.

3. In what way, if at all, does the Studio Rearrangement account differ from the first four? Explain.   (AICPA adapted)

chapter **2** | # The Accounting Process

The first step in the accounting process is the recording of transactions affecting the entity for which accounting is being done. A preliminary to this step is the *recognition* of transactions which ought to be recorded. Transaction recognition is treated briefly in this chapter. The emphasis of this chapter is on the recording of transactions during the accounting period and on end-of-the-period procedures leading to preparation of financial statements.

Traditionally, transactions are first recorded in books of original entry. Such books commonly are called *journals*, and recording transactions in them is called *journalizing*. While a few accounting entities do not carry the recording process beyond journalizing, the traditional process includes subsequent transfer of the recorded information to the *ledger*. A ledger is a group of summarizing devices known as *accounts*. *Posting* is the designation given to the transferring of journalized transaction data from the journal to the ledger. Journalizing and posting comprise the major steps in the recording process.

The design of journals and ledgers is quite important and is part of an area of accounting work known as *systems*. The efficiency with which recording is done depends largely on the effectiveness of the systems accountant in designing journals and ledgers to fit the organization and informational needs of the accounting entity. Some of the more spectacular developments in the whole field of accounting since World War II have been in the systems field. Many new methods and techniques have been developed to keep pace with the increasing size of accounting entities and increased informational needs of business management. It is possible only to scratch the surface of some of these systems matters in a single chapter.

Necessity to Summarize Data

The whole accounting process is largely one of summarization. Notice the importance of summarizing activities in the following well-known definition of accounting in that two of the three key participles are *classifying* and *summarizing:* "Accounting is the art of recording, classifying, and summarizing in a significant manner and in terms of money, transactions and events which are, in part at least, of a financial character, and interpreting the results thereof."[1]

A primary problem facing an accountant when he is designing a system for an accounting entity is to ascertain significant information needs. Once he has determined what information is needed to manage the unit effectively and to enable it to meet the requirements of outsiders such as stockholders, lenders, taxing and regulatory authorities, he can proceed to design the ledger and journal structure. For even the smallest business it is impossible to portray its financial position and operating results without summarization. For all accounting entities it is necessary to select and summarize significant common elements from among the dozens to millions of transactions per period in order to reduce them to understandable proportions. A very small business unit is likely to have many transactions within a single period which are alike in one or more respects. While it may have many receipts, nearly all of them are likely to be for cash sales of goods or services or collections of receivables previously created. Its relatively large number of sales may include only one or a limited number of classes of goods or services and are likely to be either for cash or credit transactions.

Summarization of these transactions into their common elements such as increases in cash, increases or decreases in receivables, sales of A, and sales of B, etc., can be accomplished in the journal or in the ledger. The point is that by the time ledger posting has been done, a great deal of summarization has occurred.

Transaction Analysis

Discussion of the recording process is a logical juncture at which to deal generally with the subject of transaction recognition and analysis. Much of the material from this point to the end of the book is devoted

---

[1]This definition was first formulated by the Committee on Terminology of the AICPA in 1941 and was reaffirmed in 1953 by the same committee in *Accounting Terminology Bulletin No. 1*, "Review and Résumé."

to transaction *recognition* and *analysis,* but the bulk of that discussion is in a specific context such as cash, receivables, depreciation, and so on. Generally speaking, transactions are of two types: (1) external transactions executed with outsiders, such as sales, purchases, payments and receipts of cash; and (2) internal transactions which are reapportionments of costs within the business, such as depreciation of fixed assets, and the consumption of supplies and raw materials in the productive activities of the concern. Most external transactions are easy to recognize in that an asset leaves or enters the entity, or as in the case of a sale, assets both leave and enter. Sometimes a claim arises or is extinguished as a result of a transaction. These claims may be receivables, amounts owed to the entity by outsiders, or payables, or amounts owed by the entity to outsiders. Some internal transactions are obvious and easy to recognize; others are subtle and easily overlooked. The transfer of raw materials to work in process involving a noticeable physical event supported by business papers is less likely to go unrecognized than internal transactions which occur gradually and receive only periodic recognition, such as depreciation, amortization, and certain cost expirations.

Accounting is performed in a double-entry model. The analysis of transactions results in a breakdown of each into an equality of debits and credits. Proof of this equality is undertaken from time to time, as when a journal is crossfooted to determine the equality of debits and credits recorded therein or when a trial balance of a ledger is taken.

Accounts are sometimes classified as *nominal, real,* or *mixed.* Nominal accounts are those whose balances are normally transferred (closed) to other accounts when the books are closed. Real accounts are those which remain open and which normally do reflect a balance after the books have been closed. Mixed accounts are those with balances reflecting nominal and real elements prior to completion of the adjusting entries. The following schematic based on the "normal" status in each account serves to illustrate these concepts:

			Debits	Credits
Real accounts	Assets		+	−
	Equities	Liabilities	−	+
		Capital	−	+
Nominal accounts	Revenue or Income		−	+
	Expense or Cost		+	−
Mixed accounts	Balance may reflect a mixture of asset and expense.			
	Balance may reflect a mixture of liability and revenue.			

Examples of mixed accounts include Insurance prior to separation of expense from the prepaid premium portion in adjusting, or Rent Income where the balance represents both some rent earned and some rent applicable to future accounting periods.

After the books are closed, real account balances are reflected principally on the balance sheet, and nominal accounts on the income statement. Mixed accounts are separated into real and nominal elements in the adjusting process. The statement of retained earnings (earned surplus) commonly reflects a mixture of real and nominal balances (e.g., real: Retained Earnings, Reserve for Sinking Fund; nominal: Net Income).

A subclassification of accounts is variously known as *auxiliary, offset, negative,* or *contra* accounts. Such accounts are used to show reductions from related accounts reflecting positive balances. Accumulated Depreciation is an offset to accounts reflecting original cost of fixed assets. Purchase Returns and Allowances is an offset to Purchases and enables both gross and net purchases to be portrayed. Treasury Stock is commonly subtracted from Capital Stock to show both issued and outstanding stock.

Transactions ordinarily are journalized only after having been evidenced on a business form received from outsiders or originated within the recording entity. Some forms never leave the entity originating them; examples include time reports, readings of cash register totals, and journal vouchers. Other forms are sent to outsiders who also use them as a basis for recording transactions. For example, if a business sold merchandise on account to customers, it would send the original copy of an invoice to each customer who will use it as the basis of recording a purchase; the retained carbon copy would be used as a basis of recording the sale.

Journal and Ledger Structure

The *general journal* is an all-purpose book of original entry that can be used to record all transactions of an accounting entity in chronological order. In view of the number of transactions of specific types, it is seldom feasible to use only a general journal. Whenever a comparatively large number of transactions have some common characteristic (such as an increase in cash), a special column or special book (such as the cash receipts journal) should be used. Later portions of this chapter illustrate several special journals including the sales journal, sales returns and allowances journal, cash receipts journal, cash payments journal, and voucher register. Regardless of the variety and nature of the special journals, certain entries cannot be made in them; consequently they are recorded in the general journal.

A ledger is a group of accounts. If only one ledger is maintained, it is called the *general ledger.* If several ledgers are maintained, the principal ledger will be known as the general ledger and others will be known as *subsidiary ledgers.* The separate subsidiary ledgers provide additional detail supporting the balances of specific control accounts in the general ledger. For example, a single Accounts Payable account may be carried in the general ledger, in which case individual accounts with each creditor will be found in a subsidiary accounts payable ledger. The Accounts Payable account in this case is known as a *controlling account,* and its balance should equal the sum of balances of individual creditor accounts in the accounts payable subsidiary ledger. Separate subsidiary ledgers are commonly maintained for accounts receivable and accounts payable; different classes of expenses such as selling, general, and manufacturing; assets of like kind owned in quantity; stockholder accounts; etc.

Electronic Data Processing

During the period since the mid-1950s there have been tremendous changes in methods of recording for virtually all larger entities and for many smaller ones as well. The central device which made this accounting revolution possible was the electronic computer; its development spawned the creation of new peripheral devices such as tape units, high-speed printers, and remote station satellite devices which enable individual offices and branches to communicate directly with the central computer. This method of accounting has come to be known as electronic data processing; in some forms it is also known as integrated data processing.

Any effort to describe a computer system concisely can be only partially successful. While the accounting data are undergoing transformation in a computer system, they bear little mechanical or physical resemblance to their counterparts in a conventional, less sophisticated system. Men have learned how to translate the numerical and alphabetical symbols used in traditional accounting systems into various forms which computers and their related hardware can read and manipulate, then emit in a format which we are accustomed to using. The chief advantages of doing so are that the computer can perform the desired data processing at very high speeds and with a degree of accuracy seldom attainable by humans. Further, it can summarize and recombine data in many different forms at lower cost and provide greater accessibility to it than conventional recording methods have been able to achieve.

Each procedure which is to be processed by a computer must first be analyzed carefully, and then written as a series of detailed steps or instructions in a form which the computer can read and store in a portion of its memory. These instructions are known as a *program.* The program then causes the transaction data to be read into the computer memory, after which they are mathematically processed and summarized in whatever fashion the systems analyst and programmer desire. The program also causes the processed information to be emitted whenever it is wanted in a form we can understand and use. Input data are usually put on punch cards or tapes (from conventional forms or as a by-product of preparing the forms), then read into the computer. Computer output is also often in the form of cards or tapes which are read by printers that turn out forms and reports similar to those produced by less sophisticated machines or by manual methods. Obviously the traditional forms of journals and ledgers have undergone a very substantial transformation in a computer system, yet their counterparts are to be found in it, and the computer can be programmed to produce reports bearing considerable resemblance to traditional journals or ledgers. Study of computer programming and the analysis which must precede it is usually undertaken in the Accounting Systems course. Further consideration of the topic is beyond the scope of this textbook, and we now return to a coverage of conventional recording methods which are still used by most smaller business units and by a substantial number of larger ones as well.

The Accounting Cycle

The steps in the accounting cycle performed in traditional systems (and with some variations in computer systems as well) are as follows:

1. Documents (or forms) are received or created to provide the first record of transactions.
2. Transactions are journalized on the basis of advice conveyed by the forms which commonly are referenced to provide an *audit trail* and support for the journal entries.
3. Journal entries are posted to the ledger.
4. The balance of the general ledger is proved by taking a trial balance while subsidiary ledgers are checked for agreement with their controlling accounts.
5. A work sheet is prepared. This commonly starts with the general ledger trial balance and incorporates adjustment columns to reflect changes in cost or expense accounts, revenues, assets, and liabilities.
6. Adjusting entries are entered in the journal and posted to the ledger.
7. Statements are prepared from the adjusted account balances.
8. The ledger is closed; i.e., all nominal account balances are transferred to appropriate real accounts. The net income or loss for the period is summarized and transferred to the appropriate proprietorship account.
9. Reversing entries are made if desirable.
10. As a proof of the mechanical accuracy of steps 5, 6, 8, and 9, a post-closing trial balance is taken.

Journals Illustrated

Special journals of various kinds are illustrated in the next few pages. In examining these specimens the reader should bear in mind that—

a) These illustrations typify what is encountered in practice but that many variations and adaptions to the needs of individual businesses are to be expected.

b) Larger entities use accounting machines extensively, and as a consequence they often combine journalization and posting with an attendant need to modify forms. The journals illustrated are intended primarily for handwritten systems.

c) Any special journal is justified by volume of data and other considerations previously cited. Any transaction recorded in a special journal can be recorded instead in the general journal or on journal vouchers or both.

Sales Journal. Entries for the sales of merchandise or service are recorded in this journal. Debits to individual customer accounts are posted daily or at short intervals while the totals are posted at the end of the month (or other period) as a debit to Accounts Receivable and a credit to Sales (see Illustration 2–1).

Illustration 2–1
Sales Journal

Date	Inv. No.	Account Debited	Address	Terms	L.F.	Amount
19–						
Dec. 29	819	Acme Wholesale Co.	New Orleans, La.	2/10, n/30		350.25
30	820	M. R. Brush	Dallas, Texas	n/60		402.00
		Accounts	Receivable, Dr. –	Sales, Cr.		10,809.80

Of course for entities having numerous relatively small sales (such as department stores), a different journalizing procedure may be desirable. In such an enterprise, posting to customer accounts could be made directly from sales tickets with daily totals entered in a sales journal or analysis sheet for summarization before posting to the general ledger. Such a journal might appear as in Illustration 2–2.

The daily sales amount of each department is secured by totaling sales tickets accumulated (or subsequently sorted) by departments. The sales tickets are then alphabetized to facilitate posting to the alphabetically arranged customers' accounts in the accounts receivable ledger. It is essential to maintain control of the recording process by ascertaining that there is agreement between (*a*) total sales tickets for each day, (*b*) journalized subtotals, and (*c*) changes in the balances of subsidiary accounts receivable.

Illustration 2–2
Sales Journal

Date	Dept. 1	Dept. 2	Dept. 3	Dept. 4	Dept. 5	Dept. 6	Dept. 7	Dept. 8	Dept. 9	Dept. 10	Dept. 11	Total
1–												
Dec. 1	1220 40	816 20	405 10	1005 30	218 20	259 70	102 60	918 50	114 05	704 00	192 10	5,956.45
2	865 90	509 10	500 05	715 00	302 80	119 10	209 00	1010 60	95 15	398 60	184 80	4910 10
4	1009 00	780 40	316 90	985 40	258 65	404 25	96 80	856 20	118 00	682 40	108 90	5616 90
31	1340 20	941 70	398 25	1102 40	365 80	284 60	111 30	761 65	109 90	521 20	90 10	5927 10
	26601 30	17910 90	9982 20	24009 60	7118 40	7205 00	2919 80	23748 70	2445 10	15108 20	2928 40	140177 60

Sales Returns and Allowances Journal. Entries for the credits to customers for all sales returns and allowances are made in this journal. The credits to the customers' accounts are posted daily, and the total is posted at the end of the month to the general ledger as a debit to Sales Returns and Allowances and as a credit to Accounts Receivable (see Illustration 2–3).

Cash Receipts Journal. All cash receipts are entered in this journal. Credits for collections from customers are entered in the Accounts Receivable column with any discount allowed on the account placed in

Illustration 2–3
Sales Returns and Allowances Journal

Date	Account Credited	Explanation	Credit Memo No.	L.F.	Amount
19–					
Dec. 2	A. C. Burton	Mdse. returned	218		42.00
26	M. R. Allen	Damaged in transit	239		10.60
	Sales Returns	and Allowances, Dr. —	— Accts. Rec.	Cr.	712.40

the Sales Discount column and the net cash received in the Cash debit column. All other credits are entered in the General credit column.

Daily postings are made of all amounts in the Accounts Receivable column. The amounts in the General ledger column are posted to the individual accounts indicated; the total of the General column is not posted, but the totals of the other columns are posted as indicated in the headings (see Illustration 2–4).

Illustration 2–4
Cash Receipts Journal

Date	Account Credited	Explanation	L.F.	General Credit	Accts. Rec. Credit	Sales Disc. Debit	Cash Debit
19 – Dec. 1	M. R. Allen	Paid Inv. 724			762.20	15.24	746.96
1	Notes payable	Loan – 1st Nat'l.		3,000.00			3,000.00
5	Sales	Cash sales		900.00			900.00
30	Burns & Co.	On account			210.00		210.00
31	Office postage	Sold stamps		10.00			10.00
				4,034.10	8,692.60	108.30	12,618.40

Cash Payments Journal. All payments of cash are entered in this journal. Since the design of the journal assumes that a voucher register is used, the full amount of each liability being paid is entered in the Vouchers Payable[2] debit column. Any discounts allowed are entered in the Purchases Discounts column with the amount of the check entered in the Cash credit column. The checks are numbered consecutively; in Illustration 2–5, checks issued during December were

Illustration 2–5
Cash Payments Journal

Date	Name of Payee	Check No.	Voucher No.	Vouchers Payable Debit	Purchases Discounts Credit	Cash Credit
Dec. 1	Morris Davis Co.	592	716	205.00		205.00
20	Baker Milling Co.	641	741	800.00	16.00	784.00
30	State of Texas	642	757	1,124.60		1,124.60
				11,981.50	215.20	11,766.30

numbered from 592 to 642 inclusive. The numbers of the vouchers being paid correspond to the numbers assigned to these vouchers in the voucher register. The only daily notation that might be made from the cash payment book is to the voucher register in which the vouchers which have been paid are marked paid in the "payment"

---

[2] Alternatively, this could be captioned Accounts Payable.

Illustration 2-6
Voucher Register

Date	Vo. No.	Payee	Terms	Payment Date	Check No.	Vouchers Payable, Cr.	Purchases Dr.	Freight-in, Dr.	Factory Expenses, Dr.	Selling Expenses, Dr.	General Expenses, Dr.	Sundry Debits Amount	F	Account
19– Dec. 1	716	Morris Davis Co.	Cash	Dec. 1	592	205.00						205.00		Machinery
1	717	Brown, Brown, and Stacey	30 days			420.00					420.00			
1	718	Baker Milling Co.	2/10, n/30	CM	Dec. 18	(50.00) 719.50	(50.00) 719.50							
29	753	Central Freight Lines	Cash	Dec. 29	620	116.30		116.30						
30	754	First National Bank		Dec. 30	637	1,530.00						30.00 1,500.00		Interest expense Notes payable
30	755	Petty cash		Dec. 30	638	96.00		2.00		45.00	49.00			
30	756	Payroll	Cash	Dec. 30	639	2,820.60			1,540.50	910.10	370.00			
30	757	State of Texas		Dec. 30	642	1,124.60					1,124.60			
						(50.00) 16,764.40	(50.00) 6,230.70	418.00	3,921.20	1,870.40	2,316.10	2,008.00		

column. At the end of the month, the totals of the three columns are posted to the general ledger as indicated in the headings of the columns.

Voucher Register. The voucher register is a special journal used for the purpose of recording the analysis of all purchases of merchandise, services, commodities, and other expense items. As soon as a liability is incurred, a voucher is issued in the name of the particular creditor and this paper form supports the journal entry in the voucher register. The entry in the voucher register debits the account to which the expenditure should be charged and credits Vouchers Payable. This is true whether the expenditure is on credit or whether it is a cash transaction. An entry must be made in the voucher register first.

The only individual postings made from the voucher register are the sundry debit items, those items for which special columns were not provided. At the end of the month, the totals of the various columns, except the total of the Sundry column, are posted to the general ledger as indicated in the headings of the columns. The voucher register is shown in Illustration 2–6.

General Journal. Transactions which cannot be recorded in special journals are entered in the general journal. In addition to entries for current transactions for which no special journals have been provided, correcting, adjusting, closing, and reversing entries are made in the general journal.

The general journal may be a two-column, simple journal, or it may be a multicolumned journal, the special columns being used to summarize entries for posting purposes. When basic vouchers are prepared to supply all the details and explanations for journal entries, the form of the general journal is modified to eliminate from the journal record everything except amounts, filing references, and account codes for the detail posting. The account codes are used in lieu of the account names. An example of such a journal is shown in Illustration 2–7.

Illustration 2–7
General Journal

Date	Journal Voucher No.	General Ledger			Factory Expense		Selling Expense		General Expense	
		Debit Amount	Code	Credit Amount	Code	Amount	Code	Amount	Code	Amount
19— June 7	473	265.30	2R 2	265.30						

The larger accounting entity finds it advantageous to prepare journal entries in as highly summarized form as possible. The summarized entries are supported by files of underlying vouchers and other business documents. By referencing the identifying number of supporting documents in the journal and by filing these forms sequentially, any necessary reference to the underlying documents is facilitated.

Form and content of journal vouchers, as noted earlier, should vary according to the particular requirements of the accounting entity. The form shown in Illustration 2–8 is one of many possible designs. Pre-

Illustration 2–8
Journal Voucher

DATE June 7, 19—			VOUCHER NO. 473	
Accounts	Detailed Amount	Code	Debit	Credit
Allowance for Doubtful Accounts		2R	2 6 5 30	
Accounts Receivable		2		2 6 5 30
Willard Byver	1 0 5 10	✓		
Marshall & Co.	1 6 0 20	✓		

EXPLANATORY MEMORANDUM
To write off as uncollectible receivables of customers certified insolvent by credit dept.

PREPARED BY	AUDITED BY	APPROVED
W. A. Thomas	D. G. R.	Ted Thome

printing of account titles and codes (numbers) will reduce the likelihood that an essential element of a recurring entry such as an adjustment or closing entry will be overlooked. If an account should not be involved for some reason during the period for which such a journal voucher is prepared, the amount space opposite such an account can be filled with xxx's or a zero.

Ledgers—General and Subsidiary

Each account in the general ledger having a balance is reflected in the principal trial balance. The general ledger provides information for the basic financial and operating statements. In addition to the general ledger, subsidiary ledgers may be used to supply details in classes of accounts not included in the general ledger because they are too numerous or otherwise inappropriate. Postings to subsidiary ledgers are fairly commonly made directly from business forms or vouchers, e.g., posting to customer's ledger from invoices or sales tickets.

Balancing of subsidiary ledger totals to control account balances at frequent intervals is essential from a control standpoint. How often a trial balance of a subsidiary ledger should be taken depends on several factors including (a) volume of recording activity, (b) size of the subsidiary ledger and attendant difficulty of finding errors if they occur, and (c) importance of the content of the subsidiary ledger. When mechanized accounting is employed, the machines commonly provide means of proving posting accuracy as a by-product of recording, and complete trial balances of subsidiary ledgers are therefore seldom necessary.

In situations where the entries in a ledger are largely of one type (e.g., debits to expense accounts), it is not uncommon to find that each account consists simply of a single money column and that a rather large subsidiary ledger can be accommodated on a single sheet of multicolumn paper. When an occasional opposite type entry is required (e.g., credits to expense accounts), use of a parenthesis, an asterisk, or the like will suffice. Subsidiary expense ledgers of the one-column variety are "closed" simply by removing them from the current ledger binder, filing them, and starting the next period by insertion of a new set of blank columnar forms.

The Trial Balance. In order to prove the mechanical accuracy of the journalizing and posting processes, a trial balance is prepared from the general ledger. This is a listing of all accounts in the ledger and their balances, showing the total of accounts with debit balances and the total of accounts with credit balances.

Use of Work Sheet

The processes of accounting all lead toward the preparation of reports which are useful to business management and others needing financial data with respect to the operations of the business enterprise. After the results of business transactions have been analyzed and summarized in ledger form, the preliminary work in the reporting process is undertaken. The preliminary work includes the securing of adjustment data and the preparation of the entries for adjusting the ledger balances. As a means of facilitating this preliminary work and the preparation of statements with the least possible delay, a work sheet may be prepared. These several related processes will be described in detail. The work sheet techniques and their use are illustrated in a subsequent section of this chapter.

Securing the Adjustment Data

After the analysis of transactions has been posted to the ledger, a review of the records may reveal that certain unrecorded changes in the amounts of assets, liabilities, expenses, and incomes have occurred through the passage of time, through the consumption of assets in operations, and from various causes other than the completion of formal transactions. The purpose of the resulting adjusting entries is to change the ledger record so that it will reflect these changes and cause them to be reflected on the financial statements.

The procedure for securing adjustment data consists of systematic arrangement of subsidiary records so that they will supply information, and analyzing the ledger accounts to determine whether their balances represent the true condition on the particular statement date. Expired insurance may be obtained from the insurance register or other records; depreciation, from the subsidiary records of fixed assets; inventories of merchandise and supplies, by actual count or from perpetual (book) inventory records; the data for a cash adjustment, from the count and reconciliation of cash; accrued payrolls, from payroll records: accrued income, from records of interest-bearing assets. Other adjustment data may be obtained at the end of an accounting period by the application of foresight and systematic arrangement.

Usually data are needed for the following kinds of adjustment:

1. Merchandise inventories
2. Prepaid expenses
3. Accrued expenses
4. Prepaid income
5. Accrued income
6. Depreciation expense
7. Credit losses — bad debt expense

Each of the types of adjustments will now be discussed in the order listed.

Inventories

The kind and number of adjustments affecting inventories will depend on the nature of the inventories and the company's accounting procedures. Should the accounting entity maintain a running or perpetual inventory record of supplies, materials, and goods ready for sale, the only adjustments normally called for would be to bring book inventory figures into agreement with the findings of a physical inventory, since entries are made currently to the inventory accounts as the materials and goods move into and out of the stock room, factory, and warehouse.

For those concerns which do not maintain perpetual inventories, it is necessary to determine the inventory of unsold merchandise and to adjust the ledger accounts to reflect this new inventory. To illustrate, assume that a mercantile concern closing its books on the calendar year basis ascertains that the inventory is $25,000 on December 31.

The ledger record before adjustment reveals that the inventory on January 1 of that year was $30,000. The entries necessary to record this inventory change are:

```
Income Summary (sometimes called Profit and Loss)..............30,000
    Merchandise Inventory .............................................        30,000
    To close the beginning inventory of merchandise.

Merchandise Inventory .......................................................25,000
    Income Summary ......................................................        25,000
    To record the final inventory of merchandise.
```

After the net costs of purchases are transferred to Income Summary, that account will reflect the cost of goods sold (prior to other closing entries).

Inventory adjustments for a manufacturing concern must take into account the three types of inventories, viz, raw material, work in process, and finished goods. The beginning inventory is closed to the appropriate summary account, then the new inventory is set up with an offsetting credit to the appropriate summary account. Therefore, the inventory adjustments for the manufacturing concern would appear as follows:

```
Manufacturing (sometimes called Cost of Goods
Manufactured)........................................................................20,000
    Raw Material Inventory...............................................        20,000
    To transfer cost of opening inventory to Manufacturing sum-
    mary account.

Raw Materials Inventory ....................................................23,000
    Manufacturing........................................................        23,000
    To record final inventory.

Manufacturing..................................................................... 7,600
    Work in Process Inventory...........................................        7,600
    To transfer opening inventory of work in process to Manu-
    facturing summary account.

Work in Process Inventory................................................. 7,000
    Manufacturing........................................................        7,000
    To record final inventory.

Income Summary .............................................................30,000
    Finished Goods Inventory............................................        30,000
    To transfer cost of opening inventory to Income Summary.

Finished Goods Inventory....................................................25,000
    Income Summary .....................................................        25,000
    To record final inventory.
```

The periodic (physical) inventory method of accounting requires the addition of the cost of the opening inventory to the cost of goods acquired to obtain the total cost of goods available; from this total is deducted the final inventory to secure cost of goods sold (or cost of raw materials used, or other cost figure according to the purpose of the computation).

Prepaid Expenses

The adjustment to be made for prepaid or deferred expenses like-wise depends on the entry originally made giving effect to the acquisition of the material or services. Theoretically at least, at the date of purchase of a service which is not immediately consumed, the cost of such service is an asset. As the service is consumed through operations, the asset value lessens and a transfer to cost ensues. While this is the nature of what actually happens from day to day, the bookkeeping for such daily changes seems hardly practicable. Consequently, the purchase price of services not immediately consumed may be recorded either as an asset or as an expense. If initially recorded as an asset, i.e., prepaid expense, it becomes necessary periodically to relieve that asset account of the expense or cost portion, as for example:

```
Insurance Expense...................................................................300
      Prepaid Insurance................................................................      300
      To record the amount of insurance expired for the year and to re-
      lieve the Prepaid Insurance account in accordance with analysis of
      the insurance register.
```

Perhaps the more usual entry affecting prepayments of costs at date of purchase is to debit an expense account as shown below:

December 1

```
Cash .....................................................................................49,500
Interest Expense ....................................................................   500
      Note Payable ....................................................................      50,000
      To record discounting of a 60-day, 6% note at the First Na-
      tional Bank.
```

It is necessary under such circumstances to correct these expense accounts at statement dates by deferring such amounts as are applicable to future periods by an entry as follows:

December 31

```
Prepaid Interest Expense........................................................250
      Interest Expense................................................................      250
      To record the amount of bank discount on note to First National Bank
      applicable to the subsequent period.
```

Accrued Expenses

Some expense items may have been incurred for the period but may not have been paid or recorded — an accrued expense. It is necessary to adjust the accounts so that this expense is added to expenses and the liability therefor is recorded. For example, if wages are paid on every Saturday and the accounting period ends on some other day, the entry to adjust for the unpaid and unrecorded wages would be:

Wages..1,200
    Accrued Wages (or Wages Payable)....................................   1,200
    To record accrued wages at end of period.

Prepaid Income

Income may be collected before it is earned. That portion of income collected and recorded in the income account but unearned when the books are to be closed is "prepaid income."[3] If on November 1, a concern rents one of its unused warehouses and collects six months' rental in advance totaling $3,000, four sixths of that income is unearned at the end of the accounting period at December 31. If this income was credited at the time of collection to the Rental Income account, it is necessary to adjust that account by removing the unearned portion. The adjusting entry would be:

Rental Income...2,000
    Prepaid Rental Income..   2,000
    To adjust the Rental Income account for four months' rental on
    warehouse collected in advance.

If the collection of income had been credited originally to Prepaid Rental Income at the time of its first recording, the adjusting entry would transfer the earned portion to the Rental Income account. The adjusting entry would be:

Prepaid Rental Income...1,000
    Rental Income..   1,000
    To adjust Prepaid Rental Income to reflect rent earned.

Accrued Income

When the books are to be adjusted and closed, it may be found that some income has been earned, but since it is not due and has not been collected, no record of this earning has been made. For example, bond investments may be held which bear a stipulated rate of interest. If that interest is collectible at some date after the close of the fiscal year, an entry should be made to record the earned income. The adjusting entry would take the form:

Accrued Interest Income[4] (or Interest Receivable)..........................200
    Interest Income   200
    To record interest earned but not collected on bond investments.

Depreciation, Depletion, and Amortization

The proper determination of periodic income must take into account the cost of fixed assets worn out or used up in the operating process. An adjusting entry must be made to record depreciation, that proportion of the cost of the asset which should be charged to the operation

---

[3] Alternative terms include *deferred income* and *unearned income*.

[4] An alternative title is "accrued interest receivable."

of the period as representative of the expired use value of that asset. The adjusting entry to record depreciation would be:

Depreciation of Equipment...2,000
    Accumulated Depreciation of Equipment   2,000
    To record the estimated depreciation expense due to deprecia-
    tion of equipment.

Similar adjusting entries should be made to record the depreciation of other fixed assets subject to wear and tear or loss of serviceability because of the passage of time, or use in operations, or obsolescence.

Depletion is that proportion of the cost of a wasting asset (natural resource) which should be charged against operations as a measure of the cost of the asset assignable to the production of this accounting period. The entry to record the estimated depletion would be:

Depletion Costs...3,000
    Accumulated Depletion   3,000
    To record estimated depletion of minerals @$1 per ton for 3,000
    tons extracted.

Other long-term prepayments representing asset values must be spread over the period of the prepayment's useful life. The process of apportioning this cost between accounting periods is called "amortization." For example, a patent may be purchased at a substantial cost. This patent represents the right to sell the registered device for a definite period of time. (The full legal life of a patent is 17 years.) Since the patent cost is an expense payment for benefit to be realized over a period longer than the accounting period, the patent cost should be allocated among the periods receiving benefits therefrom. It is necessary to make an adjusting entry each period to set up the charge for patent expense estimated as a proper charge against current revenue. Assuming a patent which cost $9,000 has a useful life of five years, the entry to record this adjustment is:

Amortization of Patent Cost...1,800
    Patents (or Accumulated Amortization)...............................   1,800
    To write off one fifth of the cost of patents, as the estimated use-
    ful life of the asset is five years.

It should be noted that depreciation, depletion, and amortization charges are all similar in nature. Each item represents a proportion of a cost outlay which it is felt should be charged as an expense to the operating period under review.

Credit Losses

Modern business finds it necessary to operate to a large extent upon credit. Credit is extended to customers usually with definite terms of payment. Credit risks are selected with a considerable degree of care in modern business; however, the granting of credit regardless of the degree of precaution taken nearly always results in losses due to inability to collect all of the accounts receivable. These losses are part of the expense of doing a credit business and, as such, are properly assignable to the period in which the credit sales are made. Under the *allowance method* of handling bad debts, an estimate of the bad debt expense for the period is made (or an estimate of the total estimated uncollected accounts is obtained) and the ledger accounts adjusted accordingly. The purpose of this adjusting entry is to set up the expense of bad debt losses and to create an allowance which when deducted from the receivables leaves the amount expected to be collected ultimately. The adjusting entry for bad debt losses is:

Loss from Bad Debts..2,300
    Allowance for Doubtful Accounts   2,300
    To set up the estimated bad debt loss computed at $1/2\%$ of net
    sales.

Another method of handling bad debts is the so-called charge-off method. This method makes no attempt to predict losses but merely takes up as an expense the bad debts as they are discovered. Because of the lack of a distribution of credit risk (e.g., where only a small number of ledger accounts constitute the accounts receivable), under certain circumstances this method must be used. When it is used, no adjusting entry is made at the end of the accounting period for bad debts.

Closing the Ledger

After the ledger accounts have been adjusted, the next step in the bookkeeping cycle is to prepare the financial and operating statements. These statements are the goal of the recording and reporting processes, for it is the statements which are the end of the bookkeeping process; it is the use of the statements which enables business to chart its future on the basis of past records and accomplishments. Since a more complete discussion of statements is necessary than can be attempted in this chapter, the development of that step in the bookkeeping cycle is deferred to a later chapter.

After the statements have been prepared, the ledger is closed. This means that the balances of all adjusted incomes and expenses are transferred to the Income Summary account. This latter account is a summary account in the ledger used to clear the details of operations from the original accounts, to summarize these, and to compute arithmetically the net results of operations. The books are closed in order to divide the accomplishments into periods, which are comparable in length, so that progress or lack of progress can be determined readily from the development of trends and by the comparison of the results of one period with those of another.

"Closing" is accomplished through the medium of closing entries in the general journal, which are posted to the general ledger. For the trading concern, these closing entries basically are three in number:

1. An entry to close all cost and expense balances to Income Summary — Income Summary is debited, and the cost and expense accounts are credited.
2. An entry to close all revenue to Income Summary — each revenue account is debited with its balance, and Income Summary is credited with their total.
3. The balance of Income Summary is determined after the posting of the above entries, and an entry is made to transfer this balance to the proprietory accounts — Income Summary is debited with the net income, and a capital account is credited. The closing entries for the manufacturing concern are illustrated on pages 58 and 59.

Readjusting the Ledger

Once the ledger has been closed, it may be desirable to close out all temporary summary accounts used in the adjusting process, such as accrued expenses, accrued incomes, prepaid expenses, and prepaid incomes. The process of transferring the balances in such temporary accounts to the appropriate income and expense accounts is usually referred to as "readjusting the ledger" by means of "reversing entries." Usually all balances of accrued expenses are closed out by transferring them to the appropriate expense accounts. This transfer does away with the necessity of analyzing expense payments made in the new period to determine what portion of each payment belonged to the past period and what part should be charged to the present period. For example, the adjusting entry made for accrued interest cost may be reversed by debiting the Accrued Interest Expense account and crediting the Interest Expense account. Then when interest payments are made, the entire amount of these payments may be charged to Interest Expense. The credit balance in the Interest Expense account resulting from the reversing entry will reduce the subsequent interest charges so that the remainder is the expense chargeable to the later period. Similarly, accrued incomes may be reversed and for the same reason. Any balances created in any prepaid income and prepaid expense accounts by the adjusting entries may be reversed. The concept of reversing entries considers all balances in accrued and prepaid accounts set up by the adjusting entries as being temporarily classified and, therefore, that all such balances should be returned to the accounts of their original classification. Consequently, all prepaid expense balances set up by adjusting entries in the prepaid expense accounts preferably should be reversed; all prepaid income balances created by adjusting entries similarly should be reversed. *The student should clearly understand that reversing entries are made to facilitate subsequent accounting; they are not mandatory but offer the advantage of simplifying subsequent accounting.*

The Accounting Work Sheet

The accounting work sheet, usually referred to simply as the work sheet, provides the accountant a technique for organizing in one place all accounting data necessary to adjust and close the books and to prepare operating statements and the balance sheet. By placing all adjusting and closing data on this accounting "scratch pad," the accountant can be reasonably sure of the accuracy of the amounts prior to actually placing the adjusting and closing entries on the books. It also permits the preparation of financial statements throughout the year without having to go through the lengthy and tedious work of formally adjusting and closing the books.

Work sheet preparation begins with the placing of the unadjusted trial balance figures in the first two columns of the work sheet. Then follows a recording of the adjusting entries in the debit and credit Adjustment columns. The final two columns are generally reserved for the balance sheet figures, with the space between the Adjustment and Balance Sheet columns required for the profit and loss elements.[5] The nature of the business and the amount of detailed profit and loss information required will determine the number of columns needed to reflect operating facts.

For the small mercantile concern, a work sheet with headings as follows will be adequate:

	Trial Balance		Adjustments		Income Summary		Balance Sheet	
	Dr.	Cr.	Dr.	Cr.	Dr.	Cr.	Dr.	Cr.
Accounts......								

The following example presents the typical column headings and adjustments of a manufacturing work sheet for the fourth quarter of a calendar year for a small manufacturing concern:

THE SMITHSON TOOL COMPANY
Adjustment Data for the Fourth Quarter, 19–

A. Merchandise inventories.
    1. Inventory of raw materials, $68,000.
    2. Inventory of unfinished work in process, $23,000.
    3. Inventory of finished goods, $35,000.

---

[5] Income Summary is the title chosen by the authors for the account used to summarize all revenue and expense or expired cost balances. Profit and Loss (Summary) is an alternative title which was once used almost universally; it is still encountered, but its usage today is somewhat less widespread.

B. Prepaid expenses.
    4. Other inventories and prepayments: factory supplies, $150; postage and office supplies, $260; coal, $480; shipping supplies, $170.
    5. Insurance expired: factory, $420; sales department, $280; general office $170.
C. Depreciation and amortization.
    6. Building, annual depreciation rate, 4%.
    7. Machinery and equipment, annual depreciation rate, 12%.
    8. Furniture and fixtures, sales department and general office, annual depreciation rate, 12%.
    9. Factory tools have been inventoried and found to have an estimated cost value of $3,900.
    10. Patents are being written off at the rate of $1,200 per year.
D. Credit losses.
    11. Accounts receivable totaling $780 should be written off as uncollectible.
    12. Estimated bad debts for the quarter are $\frac{1}{2}$% of sales.
E. Accrued expenses.
    13. Accrued payroll—factory, direct labor, $200, and indirect labor, $60; sales department, $120.
    14. Interest accrued on notes payable and mortgage payable, $1,050.
    15. Property taxes, $150.
F. Accrued income.
    16. Interest accrued on notes receivable, $780.
G. The following adjusted expense balances should be prorated to the factory, sales department, and general office. The percentages apply in the order given to factory, sales department, and general office.
    a) Heat, light, and power, 90%, 5%, 5%.
    b) Postage and stationery, 30%, 50%, 20%.
    c) Taxes, 60%, 30%, 10%.
    d) Depreciation of building, 70%, 20%, 10%.

Explanation of Adjusting Entries on the Smithson Tool Company Work Sheet. The adjusting entries on the work sheet of Illustration 2–9 are numbered to correspond with the numbers assigned the adjustment data given above. To facilitate the tracing of those entries and to make certain that each is understood, these explanations of the entries are given:

A. Merchandise inventories.
    1. The inventory adjustments were not made in the Adjusting Entry column in this illustration. Instead, the beginning in-

Illustration 2–9

THE SMITHSON TOOL COMPANY
Work Sheet for the Fourth Quarter, 19—

	Trial Balance		Adjusting Entries		Manufacturing		Income Summary		Balance Sheet	
	Dr.	Cr.	Dr.	Cr.	Dr.	Cr.	Dr.	Cr.	Dr.	Cr.
Cash	48,500								48,500	
Notes receivable	7,000								7,000	
Accounts receivable	76,000			(11) 780					75,220	
Allowance for doubtful accounts		980	(11) 780	(12) 1,300						1,500
Raw material inventory	72,000				72,000	68,000			68,000	
Work in process inventory	25,000				25,000	23,000			23,000	
Finished goods inventory	33,000						33,000	35,000	35,000	
Prepaid insurance	1,300			(5) 870					430	
Land	7,000								7,000	
Buildings	75,000								75,000	
Accumulated depreciation—building		15,000		(6) 750						15,750
Machinery and equipment	42,000								42,000	
Accumulated depreciation—machinery and equip		18,000		(7) 1,260 (9) 700						19,260
Factory tools	4,600								3,900	
Furniture and fixtures—sales department	16,400								16,400	
Accumulated depreciation—furn. and fixt., sales dept.		1,900		(8) 492						2,392
Furniture and equipment—general office	5,600								5,600	
Accumulated depreciation—furniture and equipment		1,020		(8) 168 (10) 300						1,188
Patents	3,600								3,300	
Accounts payable		38,800								38,800
Notes payable		30,000								30,000
Mortgage payable		65,000								65,000
Capital stock		100,000								100,000
Retained earnings		11,700								11,700
Sales		260,000						260,000		
Raw material purchases	62,000				62,000					
Freight-In	1,400				1,400					
Direct labor	30,900		(13) 200		31,100					
Indirect factory labor	4,600		(13) 60		4,660					
Heat, light, and power	7,500			(4) 480	6,318		702			
Factory repairs	860				860					
Factory supplies	750			(4) 150	600					
Sundry factory expense	470				470					
Sales department salaries	8,900		(13) 120				9,020			
Advertising	1,860						1,860			
Shipping expense	920			(4) 170			750			
Sales office expense	1,130						1,130			
General office salaries	1,980						1,980			
Postage and stationery	940			(4) 260	204		476			
Property taxes	450		(15) 150		360		240			
Sundry office expense	380						380			
Interest expense	160		(14) 1,050				1,210			
Interest income		90		(16) 780				870		
Sales discount	620						620			
Purchase discount		330						330		
	542,820	542,820								
Prepaid expenses (supplies, postage, coal, etc.)			(4) 1,060						1,060	
Insurance expired—										
Factory			(5) 420		420					
Sales dept			(5) 280				280			
Office			(5) 170				170			
Depreciation—										
Building			(6) 750		525		225			
Machinery			(7) 1,260		1,260					
Factory tools			(9) 700		700					
Furn. and equip.										
Sales dept			(8) 492				492			
General office			(8) 168				168			
Amortization—patents			(10) 300		300					
Bad debt expense			(12) 1,300				1,300			
Wages payable				(13) 380						380
Interest receivable			(16) 780						780	
Accrued interest payable				(14) 1,050						1,050
Taxes payable				(15) 150						150
			10,040	10,040	208,177	91,000				
Cost of goods manufactured						117,177	117,177			
					208,177	208,177	171,180	296,200	412,190	287,170
Income before federal income taxes							125,020			
Liability for federal income taxes										47,500
Net Income										77,520
							296,200	296,200	412,190	412,190

ventory is extended to the debit side of Manufacturing. The beginning inventory is an addition to cost and as such is extended to the debit side of Manufacturing. The final inventory then is entered in the Balance Sheet column as an asset and also entered on the credit side of Manufacturing, as a deduction from manufacturing cost. This method of handling the inventories shortens the work sheet. The entry closing the beginning inventory and setting up the final inventory is made when closing entries are taken from the work sheet. This procedure is illustrated subsequently.

2. In the same manner, the beginning inventory of work in process is extended to the debit side of Manufacturing, and the final inventory is set up as an asset in the Balance Sheet and shown as a credit to Manufacturing.

3. A similar technique is used in making the finished goods inventory adjustment. The beginning inventory of finished goods is extended to the debit side of Income Summary, and the final inventory of finished goods is set up on the debit side of the balance sheet as an asset and on the credit side of Income Summary as a deduction from cost of goods sold.

B. Prepaid expenses.

4. Adjusting entry No. 4 is entered in the Adjusting Entry column as a debit to Prepaid Expenses and a credit to Heat, Light, and Power (for unused coal), Factory Supplies (for unused supplies), Shipping Expenses (for unused shipping supplies), and to Postage and Stationery (for unused postage and office supplies). This adjustment transfers from the respective expense accounts to an asset account the cost of supplies purchased and charged to those expenses but not used during the accounting period just ended. If desired, separate prepaid expense accounts could be used for the several kinds of supplies remaining in the inventory.

5. Entry No. 5 transfers from the Prepaid Insurance account the insurance expired during the period, charging the appropriate expense accounts for insurance expense.

C. Depreciation and amortization.

6. Entry No. 6 records the estimated depreciation for the fourth quarter, debiting the depreciation expense account and crediting accumulated depreciation.

7. This entry records the estimated depreciation on machinery and equipment for the fourth quarter.

8. This entry records the estimated Depreciation — Furniture and Fixtures, Sales Department, and Furniture and Equipment, General Office.

9. This entry adjusts the Factory Tools account for the estimated

decreases in the cost value of the asset debiting Depreciation — Factory Tools and crediting the Factory Tools account directly. This method of inventorying factory tools is frequently used in lieu of estimation of depreciation based upon the costs of the asset. Since tools are small items and are frequently lost, it is more difficult to determine either separate service life of each tool or the composite life of the group. Therefore, the tools are inventoried at an estimated value based upon original cost.

   10. Entry No. 10 debits Amortization — Patents and credits the Patent account for the estimated proportion of the total cost assignable to the fourth quarter.

D. Credit losses.

   11. Entry No. 11 debits Allowance for Doubtful Accounts and credits Accounts Receivable for those accounts considered uncollectible.

   12. This entry records the estimated bad debt expense for the quarter.

E. Accrued expenses.

   13. This entry debits the wage expense accounts and credits Wages Payable for the unpaid total of the fourth quarter.

   14. Entry No. 14 debits Interest Expense and credits Accrued Interest Payable for unrecorded and unpaid interest on notes payable and mortgages payable.

   15. This entry records the unpaid taxes expense at the end of the fourth quarter.

F. Accrued income.

   16. Entry No. 16 debits the asset, Interest Receivable, and credits Interest Income for interest earned on notes receivable but not yet collected.

G. The several expenses which are to be divided between the factory, sales department, and general office are merely extended to the Manufacturing and Income Summary columns with the factory share of the expense being placed in the first of these summary columns and the sales department and general office shares are placed in the Income Summary account. No journal entries are necessary to effect this proration of expense.

Adjusting Journal Entries for the Smithson Tool Company. The adjusting entries may be taken directly from the work sheet. The adjusting entries are copied from the Adjusting Entry column, and they appear as follows:

(1), (2), and (3). These entries for the merchandise inventories in the illustration are not made with the adjusting entries on the work sheet, and as a consequence, they may be more easily taken off the work sheet along with the closing entries.

(4) Prepaid Expenses 1,060
         Heat, Light, and Power...   480
         Factory Supplies..   150
         Shipping Expense...   170
         Postage and Stationery..   260
         To adjust expense accounts for inventories and prepayments.

(5) Insurance Expired — Factory.............................   420
     Insurance Expired — Sales Department   280
     Insurance Expired — Office   170
         Prepaid Insurance...   870
         To record expired insurance.

(6) Depreciation — Building.................................   750
         Accumulated Depreciation — Building..........................   750
         To record estimated depreciation for the fourth quarter.

(7) Depreciation — Machinery 1,260
         Accumulated Depreciation — Machinery.......................   1,260
         To record estimated depreciation for the fourth quarter.

(8) Depreciation — Furniture and Equipment, Sales Department..   492
     Depreciation — Furniture and Fixtures, General Office...........   168
         Accumulated Depreciation — Furn. and Equip., Sales Dept..   492
         Accumulated Depreciation — Furn. and Fixt., Gen. Office..   168
         To record estimated depreciation for the fourth quarter.

(9) Depreciation — Factory Tools...........................   700
         Factory Tools   700
         To adjust the Factory Tools account for estimated costs chargeable to the period as an expense.

(10) Amortization — Patents   300
         Patents..   300
         To record estimated amortization of patent costs for fourth quarter.

(11) Allowance for Bad Debts   780
         Accounts Receivable   780
         To write off uncollectible accounts receivable.

(12) Bad Debt Expense 1,300
         Allowance for Doubtful Accounts..............................   1,300
         To record estimated bad debts at one half of 1% of the sales.

(13) Direct Labor...   200
     Indirect Labor   60
     Sales Department Salaries...............................   120
         Wages Payable..   380
         To record accrued and unpaid payrolls.

(14) Interest Expense..1,050
      Accrued Interest Payable 1,050
    To record interest accrued on notes payable and mortgages payable.

(15) Property Taxes... 150
      Taxes Payable.. 150
    To record unpaid taxes.

(16) Interest Receivable 780
      Interest Income 780
    To record interest accrued on notes receivable.

Closing Journal Entries for the Smithson Tool Company. The closing entries may be taken directly from the work sheet. Account balances to be closed are already conveniently grouped and totaled on the work sheet. All account balances appearing in the Manufacturing column should be closed to that summary account; all account balances appearing in the Income Summary column should be closed to that summary account. The closing entries would appear as follows:

Manufacturing 208,177
    Raw Material inventory... 72,000
    Work in Process inventory... 25,000
    Raw material purchases 62,000
    Freight-In 1,400
    Direct Labor.. 31,100
    Indirect Factory Labor.. 4,660
    Heat, Light, and Power.. 6,318
    Factory Repairs... 860
    Factory Supplies 600
    Sundry Factory Expense 470
    Postage and Stationery.. 204
    Property Taxes.. 360
    Insurance Expired — Factory 420
    Depreciation — Building 525
    Depreciation — Machinery 1,260
    Depreciation — Factory tools 700
    Amortization — Patents.. 300
    To close beginning factory inventories and all factory costs and expenses to the Manufacturing Summary account.

Raw Material inventory.................................... 68,000
Work in Process inventory................................ 23,000
    Manufacturing 91,000
    To set up final factory inventories.

Income Summary 171,180
    Finished Goods inventory.. 33,000
    Heat, Light, and Power.. 702
    Sales Department Salaries... 9,020
    Advertising... 1,860
    Shipping Expenses... 750
    Sales Office Expense 1,130
    General Office Expense 1,980
    Postage and Stationery.. 476
    Property Taxes.. 240

Income Summary (*Continued*)

Sundry Office Expense		380
Interest Expense...		1,210
Sales Discount...		620
Insurance Expired – Sales Department		280
Insurance Expired – Office		170
Depreciation – Building		225
Depreciation –		
Furniture and Fixtures, Sales Department		492
Furniture and Fixtures, General Office		168
Bad Debt Expense		1,300
Manufacturing		117,177

To close cost of goods manufactured, beginning inventory of finished goods, and operating expenses to income summary.

Finished Goods inventory...	35,000	
Sales..	260,000	
Interest Income	870	
Purchase Discount	330	
Income Summary..		296,200

To set up final inventory of finished goods, and to close income accounts to Income Summary.

Income Summary..	47,500	
Liability for Federal Income Taxes		47,500

To set up liability for income tax based on reported pretax income of $125,020. (Note: a separate Income Tax Expense account could be used.)

Income Summary..	77,520	
Retained Earnings...		77,520

To close net income to Retained Earnings.

The Interim Work Sheet

The interim work sheet may be used to record both the *transactions* and *adjustments* for a period and to modify the starting balance sheet or trial balance. This form of work sheet frequently is used to develop estimated statements when inadequate records have been maintained. In this latter situation a beginning balance sheet is prepared from an inventory of assets and liabilities (or from last year's income tax return). Then transactions are journalized (in summary form) by first making entries for all known transactions. It may be that total cash received can be obtained from memoranda records, bank statements, and the like, and at least a partial analysis of cash disbursements from the canceled checks (or check stubs). After entries are made for all the known transactions, the most plausible entries are then inserted to complete the picture. For example, if it is found that the beginning balance of Accounts Receivable was $5,000, and it is known that uncollectible accounts totaling $600 were written off and that $6,800 was collected from customers and that the final balance due from customers amounted to $5,300, with respect to this account the data might be completed as follows:

Balance at start of period...$5,000
Current debits (for credit sales).. ?
Current credits total ($600 + $6,800).................................... 7,400
Balance at end of period 5,300

Thus the debits in the account including the beginning balance must exceed the credits by $5,300, the final debit balance. Therefore, the debits total $12,700, and the amount of the debit for credit sales is $7,700.

In this form of work sheet the accounts with debit balances are listed first or above those with credit balances. The debit-over-credit form of work sheet is used to reduce the number of columns and thus provide a more compact form of work sheet. Where the approximate number of accounts is unknown when the work sheet is started, this form is highly adaptable, for by skipping space for adding accounts to both debits and credits a more ordered listing results than if both debit and credit accounts were listed together as they are needed. In the example of an interim work sheet shown in Illustration 2–10, the figures listed in boldface type represent known account balances; the beginning balances were provided by last year's balance sheet; and the final balances by inventories and partial records. It is desirable to show in as much detail as possible the journal entries to record the current transactions for the year and the adjustments to secure a correct income statement and balance sheet (see numbered explanations for transactions).

Illustrative Problem. Illustration 2–10 was prepared from the following information.

An annual recapitulation of the cashbook, which was in columnar form, disclosed the following column totals:

Receipt Side		Payment Side	
General.....................................$1,800°		General.....................................$3,500	
Accounts receivable................... 6,200°		Accounts payable 3,900	
Sales discount.......................... 108		Purchase discount .... 75°	
Cash 7,892		Cash .... 7,325°	

° Credits.

The General credits consisted of $400 from the sale of office furniture (cost, $1,000; depreciated value, $250), $100 for interest earned, and $1,300 from collection of notes receivable.

The General debits consisted of purchases of furniture and equipment, $800; expenses, $2,500; and withdrawals by Mr. Frank, $200.

Accounts receivable written off during the year as uncollectible totaled $100.

Illustration 2–10
Analytical Interim Work Sheet

	Balances 1/1/— Debit	Transactions Debit		Transactions Credit		Income Summary Debit	Balances° 12/31/— Debit
Cash	$ 1,220	(1)	$ 7,892	(2)	$ 7,325		$ 1,787
Notes receivable		(6)	1,800	(3)	1,300		500
Accounts receivable	2,100	(7)	7,700	(1)	6,200		3,500
				(5)	100		
Accrued interest income	40	(9)	10	(8)	40		10
Inventory	5,000	(11)	5,600	(10)	5,000		5,600
Furniture	4,800	(4)	800	(3)	1,000		4,600
Prepaid expense	200	(13)	300	(12)	200		300
General debits		(2)	3,500	(4)	3,500		
Depreciation		(18)	460			$ 460	
Sales discount		(1)	108			108	
Expenses		(4)	2,500	(13)	300	2,330	
		(12)	200	(15)	120		
		(16)	50				
R. D. Frank, personal		(4)	200	(19)	2,067		
		(20)	1,867				
Purchases		(10)	5,000	(11)	5,600	4,700	
		(14)	5,300				
Bad debt expense		(17)	130			130	
Net income		(19)	2,067			2,067	
	$13,360					$9,795	$16,297
	Credit					Credit	Credit
Accounts payable	$ 1,400	(2)	3,900	(14)	5,300		$ 2,800
Accrued expenses	120	(15)	120	(16)	50		50
Allowance for doubtful accounts	40	(5)	100	(17)	130		70
Accumulated depreciation	800	(3)	750	(18)	460		510
R. D. Frank, capital	11,000			(20)	1,867		12,867
Sales				(6)	1,800	$9,500	
				(7)	7,700		
General credits		(3)	1,800	(1)	1,800		
Purchase discount				(2)	75	75	
Gain on sale, fixed assets				(3)	150	150	
Interest income		(8)	40	(3)	100	70	
				(9)	10		
	$13,360		$52,194		$52,194	$9,795	$16,297

° Amounts not in bold face were derived; they were not given initially.

Explanations:†

(1) Entry to summarize the receipt side of cashbook. The total of the General (credit) column is credited to a temporary account, "General Credits," pending analysis.

(2) Entry to summarize payment side of cashbook. As in entry 1 the total of the General column is recorded in a temporary account.

(3) Closes out temporary account, "General Credits," and credits every account shown by analysis to have been entered in that column.

(4) Closes out "General Debits" and debits all accounts with balances in that column as shown by analysis.

Illustration 2–10 (continued)

(5) To record write off of bad accounts.

(6) Since all transactions given have been journalized, it is necessary to start back at the top of the work sheet and supply most plausible missing entries in accounts so as to arrive at known or computed final balances. This entry (No. 6) records receipt of enough notes so that with the given credit a final balance (given) of $500 remains. The most plausible source of these notes is from customers either on account or for sales.

(7) Records sufficient debit for credit sales so as to leave required balance in accounts receivables.

(8) Reverses beginning balance of accrued interest.

(9) Adjusting entry for accrued interest at end of period.

(10) Closes out beginning inventory to Purchases.

(11) Sets up final inventory as shown in final balance sheet.

(12) Reverses beginning balance of prepaid expenses.

(13) Adjusting entry for final prepaid expenses.

(14) Credits accounts payable with sufficient credit purchases to leave final balance given for the liability.

(15) Reverses beginning balance of accrued expenses.

(16) Adjusting entry for accrued expenses at end of period.

(17) Adjusts allowance for doubtful accounts to final balance given in ending balance sheet.

(18) Adjusts accumulated depreciation to final balance given.

(19) At this point all incomes and expenses are extended to the Income Summary column and the net income determined. An entry is then made to transfer the income to the proprietor's personal account.

(20) Entry to close the balance of the proprietor's personal account to his capital account.

---

† Explanations of journal entries are numbered to correspond with entries as numbered on the work sheet.

QUESTIONS FOR CLASS DISCUSSION

1. At the left below are six numbered phrases related to the early part of Chapter 2. At the right are some terms which can be identified with the phrases. Match the letter with the phrases.

(1) Must be done before recording proceeds. 　　　　*a)* Systems work.

(2) Books of original entry. 　　　　*b)* Ledger.

(3) A group of related accounts. 　　　　*c)* Accounting.

(4) Process of transferring entries from books of original entry to accounts. 　　　　*d)* Journals.
　　　　e) Transaction recognition.
　　　　f) Posting.

(5) That phase of accounting having to do with design of the forms and records.

(6) Art of recording, classifying, and summarizing financial transactions and interpreting the results thereof.

2. Comment on the accuracy of the statement that "summarization may be accomplished in the journal, the ledger, or both." Briefly support whatever position you take.

3. Transactions may be classed as external or internal. (*a*) Distinguish between the two and give three examples of each type. (*b*) Which are more subtle, hence less likely to be recognized and recorded?

4. Accounts may be classified as *nominal, real,* or *mixed.* Describe the meaning of each of these terms.

5. Classify the following accounts as nominal, real, or mixed:

   a) Accounts receivable.
   b) Interest income.
   c) Sales salaries.
   d) Prepaid taxes (prior to adjustment).
   e) Prepaid taxes (after adjustment).

   f) Delivery equipment.
   g) Accrued office salaries.
   h) Retained earnings.
   i) Sales.
   j) Notes payable.

6. *a*) What are auxiliary or offset accounts?
   b) Are they nominal or real?
   c) Give examples of auxiliary accounts.

7. What is a controlling account? In what type of ledger is a controlling account likely to be found? Give two examples of controlling accounts.

8. Distinguish controlling accounts from auxiliary accounts. Give two examples of the latter.

9. If the following statement is false, tell why and give an example in support of your answer: "All auxiliary accounts are nominal."

10. The following questions relate to *electronic data processing:*
    a) What is a program?
    b) To what mechanical form are input data to a computer usually reduced before being introduced into its memory?
    c) Are *printers* more associated with computer input or output?

11. What is meant by the term *accounting cycle?*

12. In a sense, the taking of a trial balance marks the approximate midpoint of the accounting cycle. Name at least two steps which precede the trial balance phase of the cycle and two which follow it.

13. In another sense it is erroneous to say the trial balance is near the midpoint of the accounting cycle. How is this so?

14. Entries belong in some particular special journal according to one or more common characteristics. What common characteristics do entries in the following special journals possess?
    a) Sales journal.
    b) Cash receipts journal.
    c) Cash payments journal (assuming voucher system is in use).

15. If entries fail to possess some of the common characteristics which cause them to belong in one of the special journals cited in the previous question or in some other special journal, where should they be initially recorded?

16. What information appears on a journal voucher that likely would not appear if the same entry were recorded in the general journal?

17. What factors determine the frequency with which a trial balance is taken of a subsidiary ledger? What goal or goals attend the taking of such a trial balance?

18. In a general sense, why are adjusting entries necessary?

19. Which of the following account titles is used by the authors of this book?

    a) Income and Expense.
    b) Income Summary.
    c) Profit and Loss.
    d) Revenue and Expense.
    e) None of the foregoing.

20. Write a suitable explanation for each of the following journal entries:

a) Wages...xx
       Accrued Wages.. xx
b) Retained Earnings xx
       Dividends... xx
c) Interest Earned xx
       Accrued Interest income... xx
d) Bond Interest Expense xx
       Discount on Bonds.. xx
e) Insurance Expense..xx
       Unexpired Insurance.. xx
    (Not an adjustment or correcting entry.)

21. Complete the following tabulation by substituting an amount in each blank space:

	Capital at Start of Period	Additional Investment by Owner	Withdrawals by Owner	Capital at End of Period	Net Income or (Loss)
a)	$10,000	$2,000	$1,000	$16,400	$____
b)	18,000	3,000	____	22,000	4,700
c)	____	1,200	800	30,000	(2,200)
d)	15,500	600	____	12,950	(2,000)
e)	18,000	____	2,700	22,000	4,700

22. Briefly describe the work sheets of the following types of businesses:
    a) Retail store with a single department.
    b) Manufacturing concern.
    c) Manufacturing concern with two sales departments, the gross margin to be determined for each department.
    d) Radio and TV station desiring to determine net income from each operation.

23. Complete the following tabulation by substituting an amount in each blank space:

	Sales	Finished Goods Initial Inventory	Cost of Goods Manufactured	Finished Goods Ending Inventory	Cost of Goods Sold	Gross Margin	Expenses	Net Income
a)	$____	$15,000	$60,000	$____	$67,000	$23,000	$____	$1 000
b)	80,000	____	48,000	2,000	____	23,000	18,000	____
c)	____	20,000	____	36,000	59,000	18,000	____	8,000

24. Name two different types of adjusting entries, the effects of which would be nullified (as to asset values) if they were reversed.

DECISION CASE 2–1

Elvin Furniture Manufacturing Corporation has grown from a small upholstering proprietorship founded 30 years ago by Mr. John Elvin, president, to an enterprise now employing over 200 persons and enjoying annual sales exceeding $3 million. At first Mr. Elvin kept the books, supervised the two employees, and was in direct contact with all customers and every aspect of the operations. As the business expanded and his four sons successively joined the organization he necessarily lost this intimate contact, but for some time was still quite aware of the day-to-day fortunes of the enterprise. Growth of the past decade had made it impossible for any one person to keep up with details of more than a limited phase of the activities, although almost anyone in the organization would be reluctant to make such an admission.

Twenty years ago when volume warranted it, Mr. Joe Flynn was hired as bookkeeper. He did all record keeping and prepared annual financial statements and tax returns. The accounting staff had grown to seven employees with Mr. Flynn in charge. He is now 63 years old and will retire in two years. Financial statements are still being turned out on an annual basis and usually are not ready until mid-March, some 10 weeks after close of the fiscal year.

Peter Elvin, youngest of four sons to join the business and a recent university accounting graduate, had recently begun work in the accounting department and may succeed Mr. Flynn upon his retirement. On learning of some of the accounting practices and that statements are being turned out only annually and so slowly, young Elvin was appalled. When he discussed the tardy and infrequent statements with Mr. Flynn, the latter pointed out "how much the cost of record keeping has risen over the years" and that to do what Peter suggested, namely "prepare monthly statements by the 10th of the next month, would be both impossible and prohibitive in cost."

Some of Mr. Flynn's specific arguments were:

  a) "It costs over $3,000 just to take inventory, and it is impossible to prepare statements without knowing the quantities and values of goods and supplies."

  b) "Monthly statements for January are simple enough because the books are closed as of December 31, but what about February, March, and later months when the figures are cumulative?" (Peter's plans do not envisage monthly closing of the books.)

  c) "The business is somewhat seasonal, and no one can estimate how good a year is likely to be until August at the earliest. Therefore, how is any income tax accrual going to be possible? By year-end the corporation might show a loss (though it has not done so for 25 years), find itself in the 22% tax bracket, or find it is in the 48% bracket (which is usually the case)."

  d) "The idea of preparing statements within 10 days of the end of the month is preposterous, and I do not want to discuss the possibility." Flynn says: "Other objections are enough to puncture young Mr. Elvin's dream, so this matter does not warrant discussion."

Peter Elvin sees great peril to the company in the present situation and has decided that waiting until Mr. Flynn's retirement to start his plan could be disastrous.

Required:

  1. What is the basic problem here as you see it?
  2. Does the company really have some alternatives? If so, what are they?

3. If you were Peter Elvin what would you say in response to Mr. Flynn's first three arguments?

DECISION CASE 2–2

A summary description of Rasco Store's procedures in respect to credit sales appears below.

Each sales clerk is provided with a book of sales tickets with triplicate forms; the original and duplicate copies are removable, while the final copy remains permanently bound in the book. When merchandise is sold on account, a sales ticket is prepared in triplicate, and the original and duplicate are removed by the sales clerk. The original goes to the customer with the merchandise. The duplicate is first filed in an unpaid invoice file which serves as the store's accounts receivable ledger. The sales books containing the permanently bound copies serve as a "sales journal."

When customers pay for or return goods their sales tickets are pulled from the unpaid invoice file. In the case of payments, they are attached to a tape accompanying the remittances, then filed permanently in a paid invoice file. In the case of returns, after verification and the proper approval, the tickets are filed permanently in a sales returns file.

Required:

The foregoing is but a summarized description; however, it should suffice to provide a basis for answering the following questions.

1. What recording economies are inherent in the procedure described?

2. What procedures can be installed to establish control over the receivables ledger?

3. What are some of the deficiencies of the system as described?

4. Under what circumstances, if any, would such a system be likely to work reasonably well?

EXERCISES

Exercise 2–1

Charles Philip Company uses a sales journal similar to the one shown in Illustration 2–1, a sales returns journal like the one in Illustration 2–3, and a cash receipts journal like the one in Illustration 2–4. Its sales terms are 2/10, 1/20, net/30. During May the following relevant transactions occurred:

May 2   Sold $575 of merchandise to Harris and Sons of Wichita, Kansas; Invoice No. 352.

5   Collected the amount due from Ed Sellers arising from a $830.20 sales invoice dated April 16.

8   Harris and Sons returned goods for $100 credit; issued Credit Memo No. 126.

10   Granted an allowance to Paul Starnes amounting to 10% of his April 22 purchase of $500; issued Credit Memo No. 127.

12   Collected the balances due from Paul Starnes and Harris and Sons.

13   Turner and Dee remitted $168.30 to apply on their $400 purchase dated April 24.

17   Sold $380 of merchandise to Grady Green, Tulsa, Oklahoma; Invoice No. 353.

24 Collected the balance due from Turner and Dee on their April 24 invoice.
29 Sold marketable securities for $400 which had cost $340 when purchased April 2.
30 Sold $210.40 of merchandise to Harris and Sons; Invoice No. 354.

Required:

1. Record the May transactions in the appropriate journals.
2. Indicate as to accounts to which column totals are posted whether they are real, nominal, or mixed.

Exercise 2–2

During March of this year Clara's Shoppe engaged in the transactions described below. Respectively, its sales, sales returns, and cash receipts journals are similar to those shown in Illustrations 2–1, 2–3, and 2–4. Sales terms are 1/10, net /30.

Mar. 1 Collected the amount due from C. D. Evans arising from our $400 Invoice No. 137 dated February 20.
3 Sold $350 merchandise to D. E. Fine of Albany, New York, on account; Invoice No. 191.
5 Sold $375 merchandise (net price) to Acme Corporation for cash.
6 D. E. Fine returned goods purchased March 3 for $50 credit. Issued Credit Memo No. 38.
7 Sold $600 merchandise to Davis Corporation of Hartford, Connecticut, on account; Invoice No. 192.
12 Collected the amount due from D. E. Fine on Invoice No. 191.
16 Collected $200 from Arthur and Company arising from a sale made February 14.
18 Brannons, Inc., were granted $40 credit on their purchase of February 28 because the merchandise was not wholly satisfactory; issued Credit Memo No. 39.
19 As an accommodation sold $20 worth of office supplies at cost to Marks and Due for cash.
26 Received $350 check from Davis Corporation to apply on their purchase of March 7.
30 Sold $256 merchandise to D. E. Fine on account; Invoice No. 193.

Required:

Record the foregoing transactions in the appropriate journals.

Exercise 2–3

Shelton Specialties uses a cash payments journal and a voucher register similar to those shown in Illustrations 2–5 and 2–6 plus, of course, a general journal which is in simple two-column form. Some of its transactions related to usage of these journals during July were as follows:

July 1 Paid Voucher No. 317, using Check No. 760 in the amount of $990. The voucher resulted from a purchase on June 21 involving terms of 1/10, net/30 from Jones Corporation.
3 Prepared Voucher No. 330 covering purchase of $400 from ABC Company under terms of 2/10, net/30.
5 Paid Voucher No. 310 in the amount of $750, using Check No. 761. The voucher resulted from buying three typewriters for use as fixed assets on June 26 under terms of 1/10, net/30 from Miller Office Supply.

9 Prepared Voucher No. 331 as a result of buying a new delivery truck from Muller Motors for $3,271.20; terms, cash. Check No. 762 was drawn to pay the voucher.

13 Check No. 763 was drawn in payment of Voucher No. 330.

15 Prepared Voucher No. 332 covering the semimonthly payroll which is summarized as follows:

Factory wages	3,900.00	
Sales salaries	3,050.00	
Office salaries	1,890.30	
Withholding taxes payable		1,420.10
Due to Blue Cross		288.10
Vouchers payable		7,132.10

Hint: Record the payroll in the general journal; place a check mark therein alongside each debit since these should be posted from the voucher register. In the voucher register indicate that the payee is Security Bank Payroll Account; enter the nonvoucher part of the liability in the sundry portion in red or in parentheses. Draw Check No. 764 to transfer funds to the payroll account.

19 Prepare Voucher No. 333 in favor of "Blue Cross, Texas District" to effect settlement of amounts withheld on the July 15 payroll. Pay this voucher with Check No. 765.

23 After extended negotiations we receive notification from Able, Inc., that they have granted us a $100 reduction on the price of goods purchased from them on June 26 under 30-day terms. The original Voucher No. 322 was for $880; as reduced it is now paid by Check No. 766. Hint: Since the voucher register entries of June were posted shortly after June 30, a new voucher (No. 334) should be drawn. In the general journal make the following entry:

Vouchers payable	880	
Purchase returns		100
Vouchers payable		780

27 Prepare Voucher No. 335 in favor of Mitchell & Breen for $1,630.70 for merchandise and an invoice received from them on this date. Terms: 2/10, net/30.

27 Draw Voucher No. 336 and pay it with Check No. 767 in the amount of $77.40. This is for freight connected with the purchase from Mitchell & Breen; the carrier is Atchison, Topeka, and Sante Fe Railroad.

29 Because some of the items bought July 27 were not wholly satisfactory, an allowance of $50 was granted by Mitchell & Breen.

Required:

1. Record the foregoing transactions in the appropriate journals.
2. Post your entries to T accounts.
3. Prove the equality of the debits and credits.

Exercise 2–4

Cox Department Store uses the following voucher register and cash payments journal forms for recording portions of its transactions:

Cash Payments Journal

Date	Name of Payee	Check No.	Voucher No.	Vouchers Payable Dr.	Purchases Discounts Cr.	Cash Cr.

Voucher Register

Date	Voucher No.	Payee	Terms	Payment		Vouchers Payable Cr.	Purchases Dept. A Dr.	Purchases Dept. B Dr.
				Date	Check No.			

Voucher Register (continued)

Purchases Dept. C Dr.	Selling Expenses Dr.	General Expenses Dr.	Sundry Debits		
			Amount	F	Accounts

Transactions during October were as follows:

Oct. 1   Drew Voucher No. 401 in favor of Earlham Insurance Agency to cover one-year fire insurance policy in the amount of $400 and paid this voucher immediately with Check No. 357. Charge asset account.

    2   Drew Check No. 358 to pay ABC Company's invoice dated September 22 covered on Voucher No. 396. This invoice covered purchase of $230.50 for merchandise bought for Department A and $273.50 for Department B; terms, 2/10, n/30.

    4   Prepared Voucher No. 402 covering purchases from Wilson Supply Company; Department A, $178; Department B, $720; Department C, $172; terms, 1/10, n/30.

    6   Drew Voucher No. 403 to Jackson Equipment, Limited, for purchase of new typewriter costing $350; terms, net 10 days.

    9   Received invoice from Display, Inc., covering September advertising. Drew Voucher No. 404 in the amount of $183.70.

  13   Paid Voucher No. 403 with Check No. 359.

  15   Bought merchandise from Adams & Baker for Department B, $520; terms, net 30 days. Drew Voucher No. 405.

  20   Returned $35 of goods bought from Adams & Baker for credit. Record in voucher register as adjustment of Voucher No. 405.

Oct. 21 A note payable for $1,500 to Owen Smith Corporation matured. The note has run 60 days and bears interest at 6%. Draw Voucher No. 406 and pay with Check No. 360.

23 Paid Voucher No. 397 covering purchase of stationery costing $80. Drew Check No. 361 to Brock Company.

25 Paid Voucher No. 404 with Check No. 362.

28 Received invoice from Willis Carpet Company for maintenance work on office floors; drew Voucher No. 407 for $32.

Required:

Record the October transactions in the forms shown above.

Exercise 2–5

Prepare a journal voucher for the issuance by the Bonham Pump Company, Houston, Texas, of capital stock par $100 per share as follows:

50 shares, Certificate No. 432, to R. O. Bedford in full payment for land valued at $5,200.

30 shares to R. C. Axe for legal services performed in organization of the corporation, billed at $3,000; Certificate No. 433.

5 shares to Miss Mary Day, Certificate No. 434, for services as secretary during period of organization of the corporation, issued at request of Miss Day in lieu of salary payable in cash, $510.

Exercise 2–6

For several years, Albers Company has sold wallpaper and paint both for cash and on open account. Initially, the volume of transactions was sufficiently small to warrant use of only a two-column general journal as the only book of original entry. Increasing volume has rendered this arrangement more and more unsatisfactory. Among other things, an indication of gross margin by the two principal product lines is needed.

Required:

1. Draft forms suitable for use as a complete set of books of original entry under the changed situation. Pay particular attention to providing special columns where appropriate.

2. Indicate which columns in your journals should be posted as single totals; if any columns are not to be posted at all this fact should also be indicated.

Exercise 2–7

Give the adjusting entries required on the books of Prince Company at October 31, 1972, for the fiscal year ended on that date. Indicate which entries call for reversal.

PART I

a) On July 1, 1972, $5,070 was credited to "Subscription Income." The amount received represented one year's prepayment by customers.

b) The company borrowed $100,000 on June 30, 1969, by issuance of 10-year bonds at par which pay 6% per annum each June 30 and December 31.

c) The Equipment account balances on October 31, 1971, and 1972 were $85,000 and $95,000, respectively. The regular rate of depreciation is 10% per annum. Acquisitions and retirements during a year are depreciated at half this rate, and there were no retirements between the two dates.

d) Insurance premiums are charged to Prepaid Insurance when paid. The following policies are in force:

Policy	Date Taken Out	Total Term	Cost
A......................	July 1, 1970	3 Years	$270
B......................	April 1, 1971	2 years	432
C......................	May 1, 1972	1 year	108

e) Supplies inventories at October 31, 1971, and 1972 were $3,540 and $2,260 respectively. Supplies purchased during the 1971–72 fiscal year cost $11,370 and were debited to Supplies Expense.

f) On September 1, 1972, the company borrowed from a bank by issuance of a 90-day, 6% note, making the following entry:

Cash	14,775	
Interest Expense	225	
Notes Payable		15,000

g) An officer borrowed $6,000 from the company on August 1, 1972, giving his 5% note which matures in one year, at which time both principal and interest are payable.

h) Accrued salaries at October 31, 1972, amount to $400 and are subject to F.I.C.A. taxes of $17. Accrue both amounts.

PART II

Refer to items (b), (d), and (e) in Part I.

b) If the bonds had been sold at a price other than par and at the time of each interest payment the following entry had been made:

Bond Interest Expense	2,850	
Premium on Bonds Payable	150	
Cash...		3,000

Give the October 31, 1972, adjustment.

d) Prepare the October 31 adjusting entry if the company had consistently debited premium payments to Insurance Expense.

e) Suppose the company had charged Supplies Inventory each time it bought supplies. Give the October 31, 1972, adjustment.

Exercise 2–8

Balances in certain accounts in the ledger of Myron Corporation were changed as a result of adjusting entries made at the end of its fiscal year.

Required:

For each case indicate the probable entry or entries causing the changes:

Balances

Case	Account or Accounts Affected	Before		After	
a)	Office salaries	Dr.	$11,000		$11,670
b)	Prepaid insurance	Dr.	670		120
c)	Allowance for doubtful accounts	Dr.	30	Cr.	450
d)	Rent income	Cr.	1,400		1,200
e)	Office supplies used		0	Dr.	240
f)	Interest income	Cr.	120		140
	Accrued interest income		0	Dr.	30
g)	Bond interest expense	Dr.	2,040		3.060
	Accrued bond interest expense		0	Cr.	1,000
h)	Accumulated depreciation	Cr.	250		800

Exercise 2–9

1. Record the following transactions occurring in 1972 in such a way that reversing entries will not be required when books are adjusted at December 31, 1972:

a) On November 10 collected $900 rent covering the period November 1, 1972, through April 30, 1973.
b) Purchased $200 worth of office supplies for cash on December 1.
c) Paid $120 premiums on insurance policy on September 1 running two years from that date.

2. At December 31, 1972, office supplies on hand are valued at $140. Give adjusting entries required on that date if books are being adjusted and closed (a) monthly and (b) annually.

Exercise 2–10

From the following prepare an interim work sheet showing entries summarizing the transactions and adjustments for the year and the adjusted income and expense account balances. Make entries first for the following summaries of given transactions; then make entries which seem most plausible to complete the changes between the opening and closing balance sheet accounts.

Summarized transactions given: credit sales, $100,000; credit purchases, $50,000. Fixed asset costing, $1,000; depreciated value, $600; sold for, $400. Bad debt written off, $600. The undisclosed expenses are 70% selling expense and 30% administrative expense.

Balance Sheets (opening and closing)

	Jan. 1	Dec. 31
Cash	$ 1,000	$ 1,500
Accounts receivable	5,000	4,000
Inventory	15,000	16,000
Fixed assets	35,000	34,000
Bond discount	100	80
	$56,100	$55,580

	Jan. 1	Dec. 31
Accounts payable	$ 2,000	$ 500
Bonds, 8%, due January 1, 19—	30,000	30,000
Allowance for bad debts	500	1,000
Accumulated depreciation	3,000	2,900
Capital stock	20,000	20,000
Retained earnings	600	1,180
	$56,100	$55,580

Exercise 2–11

Prepare a cost of goods manufactured statement and an income statement for Milholland Manufacturing Company based on the following data:

a) Cost of goods manufactured and cost of goods sold were respectively $148,500 and $120,000.

b) Gross margin based on selling prices was 40%. There were no purchase returns, but sales returns amounted to $5,000.

c) Inventory variations were as follows: raw materials, one third as much on hand at end of period as at start; no initial inventory of work in process, but at end of period $11,500 was on hand; finished goods inventory was four times as large at end of period as at the start.

d) Net income after taxes amounted to $21,000; income tax rate is 30%.

e) Purchases of raw materials amounted to twice as much as net income before taxes.

f) Breakdown of costs incurred in manufacturing was as follows:

          Raw materials consumed..........................50%
          Direct labor..30
          Overhead...20

g) Selling expenses amounted to one and one-half times as much as general expenses.

PROBLEMS

Problem 2–1

Kaneohe Bay Company was organized in January. At the end of January the different journals showed the following results:

General journal: General (Dr.), $40,720; Accounts Payable (Dr.), $1,500; General (Cr.), $39,750; Accounts Receivable (Cr.), $2,470. Analysis of "General" items revealed: *Debits:* Cash (opening entry), $5,000; Merchandise Inventory—Department 1, $2,500; Merchandise Inventory—Department 2, $3,000; Furniture and Fixtures, $2,000; Delivery Equipment, $1,000; Notes Receivable, $2,000; Accounts Receivable, $5,000; Subscriptions Receivable—Capital Stock, $10,000; Unissued Capital Stock, $10,000; Freight-In—Department 1, $100; Freight-In—Department 2, $120; *Credits:* Accounts Payable, $2,000; Notes Payable, $600; Allowance for Bad Debts, $500; Accumulated Depreciation—Delivery Equipment, $250; Accumulated Depreciation—Furniture and Fixtures, $400; Capital Stock Subscribed, $10,000; Authorized Capital Stock, $25,000; Premium on Capital Stock, $1,000.

Cash receipts journal: General, $14,900; Accounts Receivable, $6,200; Sales Discounts, $100; and Net Cash, $21,000. The "General" column contained: Cash Balance (opening entry), $5,000; Cash Sales, $4,000; Notes Payable, $350; Subscriptions Receivable, $5,000; and Interest Income, $50; Notes Receivable, $500.

Cash disbursements journal: General, $1,200; Office Expense, $100; Accounts Payable, $4,000; Purchase Discount, $200; and Net Cash, $5,100. Analysis of the "General" column showed: Advertising, $200; Unexpired Insurance, $240; Rent, $300; Notes Payable, $400; Interest Expense, $60.

Sales journal: Credit Sales, $12,000; Cash Sales, $4,000; Department 1, $8,700; and Department 2, $7,300.

Purchase journal: Total, $7,800; Department 1, $4,100; Department 2, $3,700.

Purchase returns and allowance journal: Total, $1,300; Department 1, $800; Department 2, $500.

Sales returns and allowance journal: Total, $1,020; Department 1, $600; Department 2, $420.

Required:

1. Set up ledger accounts and post the above journals.
2. Take a trial balance.

Problem 2–2

The following transactions occurred in the sequence they are listed below:

a) Miller National Bank informed us the note of Thomas Kay has been dishonored. This $1,500 note had borne interest at 6% and was held by us for 24 of its 60 days before being discounted at the bank at 5%. We paid the sum due plus a $5 protest fee.
b) A $70 account receivable owed by Lyndon King is written off as uncollectible. Assume such bad debts had been anticipated.
c) Purchased merchandise costing $2,400 giving our 60-day, 8% note.
d) Paid the note issued in (c) at maturity.
e) Borrowed from Zenith Bank by discounting our own $3,600, 120-day, 9% note (face amount).
f) Paid the note issued in (e) at maturity.

Required:

1. Record the transactions in general journal form; assume, however, that disbursement vouchers are used to control cash.
2. For each transaction indicate the book or books of original entry which would be used where a complete array of special journals and the voucher system are in use.

Problem 2–3

As of September 26, 1972, the general ledger trial balance and subsidiary ledgers of Theo's Stationers were as follows:

Cash	$ 3,000	
Accounts receivable	1,600	
Allowance for doubtful accounts		$ 200
Inventory – Department A	20,000	
Inventory – Department B	18,000	
Unexpired insurance	200	
Delivery equipment	6,300	
Accumulated depreciation – delivery equipment		500
Notes payable		500
Accounts payable		2,900
Capital stock		25,000
Retained earnings		1,595
Sales – Department A		45,000
Sales – Department B		60,000
Sales returns and allowances – Department A ..	250	
Sales returns and allowances – Department B ..	300	
Purchases – Department A	28,000	
Purchases – Department B	35,000	
Purchase returns and allowances – Department A		150
Purchase returns and allowances – Department B		200
Freight-in – Department A	400	
Freight-in – Department B	475	
Selling expenses (control)	18,300	
General expenses (control)	4,200	
Interest expense	20	
	$136,045	$136,045

Subsidiary ledgers:

Accounts Receivable

James Blair	$ 500
Gerald Dean	300
Jim Smithson	400
Will Jaynes	400
	$1,600

Selling Expenses

Store rent	$ 1,000
Advertising	1,600
Salaries – Department A	5,000
Salaries – Department B	7,500
Delivery expense	3,200
	$18,300

Accounts Payable

W Company	$1,500
X Company	100
Y Company	600
Z Company	700
	$2,900

General Expenses

Office salaries	$2,000
Office supplies used	800
Property taxes	1,000
Utilities	400
	$4,200

Enter the foregoing accounts and amounts in ledgers as of September 26, using the one money column form for expense ledgers.

Cash sales are journalized both in cash receipts and sales journals; however, the columns headed "Cash Sales" are not posted from either journal.

Prepare journals according to the following format:

General Journal

Date	Accounts and Explanation	F	General Dr.	Accounts Payable Dr.	General Cr.	Accounts Receivable Cr.

Sales Journal

Date	Customer	Invoice Number	F	Accounts Receivable Dr.	Cash Sales	Sales Dept. A Cr.	Sales Dept. B Cr.

Purchases Journal

Date	Creditor	Number	F	Accounts Payable Cr.	Purchases Dept. A Dr.	Purchases Dept. B Dr.

Cash Receipts Journal

Date	Account	F	General Cr.	Cash Sales	Accounts Receivable Cr.	Cash Dr.

Cash Payments Journal

Date	Account	F	General Dr.	Selling Expense Dr.	General Expense Dr.	Accounts Payable Dr.	Cash Cr.

Transactions for the three days following the date of the trial balance are set out below:

September 27

Sales invoices: James Blair, No. 750, $200 on credit; cash sale, No. 751, $450, both Department A.

Disbursed $25 for office supplies.

Paid $1,000 on balance owed W Company.

Collected $250 from Will Jaynes.

Sales invoices: Will Jaynes, No. 752, $300 on credit; cash sale, No. 753, $500, both Department B.

Purchases on credit: Z Company, No. 450, $350, Department A, and $600, Department B.

Disbursed $100 for October rent.

Disbursed $200 for advertising.

Paid X Company $50 on account.

September 29

Sales invoices: Jim Smithson, No. 754, $500, Department A, and $200, Department B; Gerald Dean, No. 755, $600, Department A, and $400, Department B, all on credit.

Paid $1,000 for additional delivery equipment.

Paid $180 insurance premium.

Purchases on credit: Y Company, No. 451, $600, Department B.

Cash sales invoice: No. 756, $360, Department A, and $240, Department B.

Collections on account: $100 from Will Jaynes; and $400 from James Blair.

September 30

Disbursed $50 for utilities, $60 for delivery expense, and $50 for freight-in, Department A.

Cash sales Invoice No. 757: $500, Department A, and $400, Department B.

Cash purchase Invoice No. 452, $50, Department A, and $25, Department B.

Purchase Return Memo No. 46: returned $10 applicable to purchase Invoice No. 451.

Purchases on credit: Z Company, No. 453, $60, Department A, and $140, Department B.

Required:

1. Journalize the foregoing transactions; post.
2. Take a trial balance of the general ledger.
3. Prepare abstracts of the subsidiary ledgers as of September 30.

Schedule of accounts rec.

Problem 2–4

Because so many of its customers take the 2% cash discount offered for prompt payment, Miller Company has changed its accounting so that all sales on account are initially recorded "net." Thus, a sale which would ordinarily be recorded at $100 is recorded at $98. In the event the customer fails to pay within the discount period, the company would, upon collection of the $100, credit Accounts Receivable, $98, and credit Revenue from Lost Customer Discounts, $2.

All sales of merchandise described in the transactions are "gross," i.e., before deduction of discount. Credit terms are 2/10, n/30. The company uses single-column sales and sales returns journals and a cash receipts journal with the following columnar structure:

Date	Account Credited	Explanation	L.F.	General Cr.	Accounts Receivable Cr.	Revenue from Lost Discounts Cr.	Cash Dr.

December transactions were as follows:

Dec. 2 Sold goods to XYZ Company on Invoice No. 318 which totaled $800.
      4 Ten percent of the goods are returned by XYZ Company for credit; issued Credit Memo No. 60.
      5 Sold goods for $120 cash on Invoice No. 319.
      7 Sold goods to Parrish Company on Invoice No. 320 which totaled $165.50.
      7 Received proceeds of matured $2,000, 6% note receivable dated September 23.
     12 Collected balance due on Invoice No. 318.
     15 Collected $125 from Dean Brothers on Invoice No. 299 dated November 17.
     16 Granted allowances of $25 (gross figure) on Invoice No. 320; issued Credit Memo No. 61.
     17 Collected balance due on Invoice No. 320.
     18 Sold goods to Wilder and Wooley on Invoice No. 321 which totaled $671.10.
     23 Collected semiannual interest on AB Utility Corporation, $1,000, 8% bond which was purchased at par as permanent investment two years ago.
     28 Collected balance due on Invoice No. 321.
     29 Collected $426 from Ace Company on Invoice No. 317 dated November 27.

Required:

Record the foregoing transactions in the three journals.

Problem 2–5

The adjustment data set out below are to be handled twice as set out in the requirements. Date of adjustments is December 31 in each case.

a) Rent income of $1,200 covering the year beginning September 1 was collected on that date. A nominal account was credited.

b) On October 1 a $180 premium was paid on a three-year insurance policy running from that date. A real account was debited.

c) On February 1 the company borrowed $40,000 by issuing a three-year mortgage note bearing interest at 9% per annum. The interest is paid at quarterly intervals from February 1.

d) Bonds were purchased at par for $5,000 on April 1. These bonds are held as a permanent investment and bear interest at 8% per annum; interest is paid each April 1 and October 1.

e) The building occupied by the company cost $60,000 and has a 40-year estimated life with no expected salvage value.

f) The company pays property taxes for the preceding year each January 15. In the preceding year the total tax bill was $3,000. This year it is expected to be 10% higher.

g) On July 1, $100 was paid to the city for an annual license to do business and a nominal account was debited. The license must be renewed each July 1.

Required:

Head up the first pair of columns of a sheet of four-column paper "Case 1"; the second pair of columns should be headed "Case 2." Prepare adjusting entries in general journal form based on the data given above. For Case 1 assume ledger accounts have been adjusted and closed monthly and reversing entries have been made. For Case 2 assume accounts are adjusted and closed only at year-end and that no reversing entries have been made.

Problem 2–6

Data relating to the balances of various accounts affected by adjusting entires appear below; however the entries which caused the changes in the balances are not given. The books are adjusted and closed each December 31.

a) Allowance for doubtful accounts: Balance on January 1, $400; accounts written off during year as uncollectible, $4,200; balance after adjustment on December 31, $1,000.

b) Accumulated depreciation: Balance at January 1, $2,000. During the year a fixed asset which cost $8,000 was sold for $7,000 resulting in a loss of $400. Balance reported on December 31 balance sheet, $2,500.

c) For several years on each May 31 and November 30 the bond interest payments of $2,400 have been made. On the income statement for the year the bond interest expense is properly reported at $4,500.

d) Prepaid interest income at January 1, $60; interest collected during year, $800; interest income reported on income statement, $825.

e) Accounts payable at January 1, $6,000; at December 31, $5,000. Payments on account during year, $23,000; purchase discounts taken during year $400. (This simply reflects a missing entry, not an adjustment.)

f) Wage expense for the year, $7,125, accrued wages at January 1, $400; wage payments during year, $7,300.

g) Prepaid rent expense at January 1, $250; charges to prepaid rent during year, $1,750; prepaid rent reported on December 31 balance sheet, $500.

Required:

Supply the missing entries which would logically account for the changes and other data indicated; if in any instance you find it appropriate to make an assumption to justify your entry, briefly state the assumption.

Problem 2–7

Solution of this problem calls for use of a 10-column work sheet form. As a preliminary step, copy the unadjusted trial balance into the first pair of columns and the adjusted trial balance into the middle pair of columns, leaving a pair of blank columns between them.

	Unadjusted Trial Balance		Adjusted Trial Balance	
Accounts payable		$ 12,700		$ 12,700
Accounts receivable	$ 15,800		$ 15,800	
Accrued bond interest expense				600
Accumulated depreciation – delivery equipment		400		600
Accumulated depreciation – office equipment		90		140
Advertising expense	1,800		1,600	
Allowance for doubtful accounts		500		720
Bond interest expense			550	
Bonds payable		20,000		20,000
Capital stock		20,000		20,000
Cash	4,400		4,400	
Cost of goods sold			67,270	
Delivery equipment	1,600		1,600	
Delivery supplies inventory	180		30	
Delivery supplies used			150	
Depreciation of delivery equipment			200	
Depreciation of office equipment			50	
Freight-in	950			
Insurance expired – delivery equipment			60	
Insurance expired – merchandise			20	
Insurance expired – office equipment			10	
Interest expense	100		90	
Interest income		60		70
Interest payable				15
Interest receivable			30	
Land	25,000		25,000	
Loss from doubtful accounts			220	
Merchandise inventory	17,500		18,000	
Notes payable		1,800		1,800
Notes receivable	600		600	
Office equipment	430		430	
Office salaries	2,700		2,900	
Office supplies inventory	100		25	
Office supplies used			75	
Premiums on bonds payable		200		150
Prepaid advertising			200	
Prepaid insurance	290		200	
Prepaid interest expense			25	
Prepaid interest income				20
Prepaid rent expense			200	
Purchases	67,000			
Purchase returns		180		
Rent expense	2,600		2,400	
Retained earnings		3,070		3,070
Salaries of salesmen	6,550		6,700	
Salaries payable				350
Sales		89,100		89,100
Sales returns	500		500	
	$148,100	$148,100	$149,335	$149,335

Required:

Complete the work sheet by heading the pair of blank columns between the two sets of trial balance columns "Adjustments." Enter the apparent adjustment on each line where a balance has changed. Head the last two pairs of columns "Income Summary" and "Balance Sheet" respectively. Extend the adjusted trial balance amounts into these final columns and complete the work sheet.

Problem 2–8

At December 31, 1972, the unadjusted trial balance of Bainbridge Corporation was as set out below. Inventories appearing therein are as of January 1, 1972. Respectively, the ending inventories of Raw Materials, Work in Process, and Finished Goods at December 31 were $8,000, $10,100 and $5,000.

	Debit	Credit
Cash	$ 12,830	
Accounts receivable	23,000	
Raw materials	9,220	
Work in process	9,000	
Finished goods	11,000	
Fixed assets	30,000	
Accumulated depreciation		$ 2,000
Accounts payable		5,000
Capital stock		60,000
Retained earnings		15,455
Sales		70,000
Purchases of raw materials	20,000	
Direct labor	20,000	
Sales salaries	5,000	
Administrative expenses	4,900	
Insurance expense	500	
Factory supply expense	850	
Advertising	345	
Property taxes	800	
Indirect labor	3,010	
Freight-out	2,000	
	$152,455	$152,455

Adjustment data as of December 31, 1972 are as follows:

a) Accrued payroll totals $500; of this amount, $400 relates to direct labor and the remainder to sales salaries.

b) Prepaid insurance amounts to $250; half of the insurance expense relates to manufacturing operations, the other half to selling and administrative activities.

c) Factory supplies on hand are valued at $300.

d) Depreciation for the year amounts to $1,800; two thirds of this amount pertains to manufacturing operations, the remainder to selling and administrative activities.

e) Analysis of accounts receivable at December 31 indicates a probable loss from uncollectible accounts of $100.

f) Property tax expense for the year is fully reflected in the trial balance. The expense is to be apportioned in the same ratio as insurance.

Required:

Prepare a manufacturing work sheet similar to Illustration 2–9.

Problem 2–9

Set up a work sheet with the following columnar headings: Balance Sheet, January 1; Transactions (Dr. and Cr.); Income Summary (Dr. and Cr.); Balance Sheet, December 31. Enter the amounts given in the first and last columns, skipping two lines after "Cash" and another after "Accounts receivable."

	January 1	December 31
Cash	$ 10,000	$ 18,000
Accounts receivable	30,000	42,000
Inventory	30,000	24,800
Prepaid expenses	2,000	1,600
Fixed assets	40,000	35,000
Discount on bonds payable	1,000	900
	$113,000	$122,300
Accrued payroll	$ 200	$ 300
Accounts payable	15,000	18,000
Bonds payable – 4%	20,000	20,000
Allowance for bad debts	1,300	1,500
Accumulated depreciation	8,000	9,000
Capital stock	60,000	60,000
Retained earnings	8,500	13,500
	$113,000	$122,300

A limited amount of additional data is given, but for other amounts and transactions you will have to apply logical accounting processes.

Added data:

a) Sales: for cash, $10,000; on account, $120,000.

b) Cash payments: on accounts payable, $75,000; dividends, $3,000; payroll, $20,500; miscellaneous expenses, $10,900; other payments not given.

c) Accounts written off as uncollectible, $1,000.

d) Fixed assets which had cost $5,000 were sold for $1,200 cash at a time when their book value was $1,000.

Required:

Using the same letters as under added data, give effect to these data in the Transactions columns. Then using letters *e* and beyond, complete the Transactions column on the basis of what can logically be inferred. Complete the remainder of the work sheet.

Problem 2–10

Balance sheets as of January 1 and December 31 are given below. Certain transaction data are also given; both the balance sheet and transaction data are to be entered in an interim work sheet form (see the instructions for Problem 2–9 above which also are relevant to this problem).

	January 1	December 31
Cash	$10,000	$ 17,500
Accounts receivable	15,000	23,800
Inventory	18,000	12,000
Fixed assets	55,000	60,000
	$98,000	$113,300

	January 1	December 31
Premium on bonds payable	$ 400	$ 350
Accounts payable	13,500	10,500
Bonds payable–5%	30,000	30,000
Allowance for bad debts	1,000	800
Accumulated depreciation	12,000	15,000
Capital stock	25,000	35,000
Premium on capital stock	5,000	6,000
Retained earnings	11,100	15,650
	$98,000	$113,300

Added data:

a) Cash collections: cash sales, $30,000; fixed assets sold for $4,000 which had a book value of $3,000 and which had originally cost $10,000. The remainder of cash collected was from sale of capital stock and collection of receivables.

b) Total sales on account during the year amounted to $150,000.

c) The adjustment for bad debt expense recorded on December 31 amounted to $1,000.

d) Cash payments: payroll, $40,000; miscellaneous expenses, $20,000; dividends, four percent based on par value of stock outstanding at January 1; bond interest, regular amount based on par value of bonds outstanding; fixed assets purchased new, amount undisclosed; to merchandise creditors, $100,000; total payments, $177,500.

Beyond the foregoing data it will be necessary to apply logical accounting processes to account for the changes between beginning and ending balance sheet amounts.

Required:

Using the same letters as under added data give effect to these data in the transactions column of your interim work sheet. Then using letters e and beyond, complete the transactions column and the remainder of the interim work sheet.

Problem 2–11

You were given the following trial balances of the Baker Company. The trial balance as of December 31, 1972, was taken on a gross basis; that is, the totals of the debits and of the credits in each of the ledger accounts, including any balance from the after-closing trial balance at June 30, 1972, rather than the final balance, have been included. You are advised that the company records all disbursements for expense items through liability accounts prior to making payment.

Trial Balances

Account	June 30, 1972		December 31, 1972	
Cash in bank	$ 21,849		$ 285,016	$ 256,972
Investments	30,500		50,712	15,000
Accounts receivable	47,420		301,425	248,979
Merchandise inventory	55,542		208,856	153,495
Office furniture and fixtures	8,663		11,164	365
Accumulated depreciation		$ 4,967	176	5,940
Bank loans		30,000	10,000	30,000
Accounts payable		15,879	211,658	233,986
Accrued income tax		7,350	5,658	10,350
Capital stock		50,000		50,000
Retained earnings		55,778	10,000	55,778
Sales			481	254,005
Cost of goods sold			151,914	
Executive salaries			15,500	
Other administrative expense			21,567	
Selling expense			25,348	
Bad debt losses			665	
Write-down of obsolete merchandise			1,025	
Profit on sale of investment				168
Loss on sale of fixtures			23	
Interest expense			850	
Income tax expense			3,000	
	$163,974	$163,974	$1,315,038	$1,315,038

Required:

Reconstruct the ledger accounts as they probably appear. Record the transactions for the period in journal form and in skeleton ledger accounts keyed to the journal entries. You need not prepare financial statements.

(AICPA adapted)

Problem 2–12

Mrs. A and Mrs. B operate a skating rink as a partnership, sharing profits equally. They manage the business themselves, employing high school students for ticket takers and skate boys. Income is from admissions, skate rentals, and sales of soft drinks and candy, some of which is sold on credit.

The business records consist of a single-entry cashbook in which the details of all cash receipts and disbursements are entered. The business fiscal year ends on March 31.

The balance sheet of the partnership at March 31, 1972, was as follows:

ASSETS

Cash on hand and in bank	$1,295
Accounts receivable	86
Inventory (soft drinks and candy)	119
Prepaid insurance	270
Land	500
Building and building improvements	6,628
Equipment	2,522
Accumulated depreciation	(5,476)
	$5,944

LIABILITIES AND PARTNERS' CAPITAL

Accounts payable	$ 882
Taxes payable (including $38 withheld from employees)	208
Capital — Mrs. A	2,427
Capital — Mrs. B	2,427
	$5,944

The summary of the cashbook for the year ended March 31, 1973, is as follows:

	Debit	Credit
Admissions		$4,817
City admissions tax collected		231
Skate rentals		1,899
Sales — soft drinks and candy		3,112
State sales tax collected		56
Wages paid	$ 696	
Purchases — soft drinks and candy	2,434	
Insurance expense	750	
Heat, fuel, and telephone	579	
Supplies	309	
Payroll taxes paid	142	
City admissions tax paid	239	
State sales and excise taxes paid	179	
Property taxes paid	74	
Equipment repairs	260	
Building repairs and improvements	2,914	
Miscellaneous expense	199	
Drawings — Mrs. A	1,434	
Drawings — Mrs. B	840	

The following balances at March 31, 1973, were furnished by the client and are assumed to be correct:

Cash on hand	$ 55
Inventory	108
Accounts receivable	15
Amounts withheld from employees	16

The details of accounts payable and taxes payable were as follows:

	March 31 1972	March 31 1973
Accounts payable —		
Merchandise	$160	$ 71
Heat, fuel, and telephone	63	43
Supplies	32	14
Building repairs and improvements	540	
Equipment repairs	56	16
Miscellaneous	31	5
	$882	$149

March 31

	1972	1973
Taxes payable—		
Payroll taxes (including amounts withheld from employees)	$ 72	$ 23
City admissions tax	39	31
State sales and excise taxes	23	16
Property taxes	74	147
	$208	$217

A review of cash transactions revealed the following:

a) In accordance with established policy of purchasing insurance covering one-year periods, the following purchases were made during the year ended March 31, 1973:

Fire insurance, policy expires August 1, 1973		$144
Liability insurance, policy expires October 15, 1973		360
Fire and liability insurance on partners' homes and automobiles, policies expire June 30, 1973:		
Mrs. A	$110	
Mrs. B	136	246
		$750

b) Depreciation is computed on a straight line basis over a 20-year period for building, five years for building improvements, and various rates for the equipment. One-half year's depreciation is taken in year of acquisition. Based on the asset balances at the beginning of the year, depreciation expense for the year would be $817. No fixed assets were disposed of during the year.

c) Building repairs and improvements include $1,898 in full payment of a city assessment for paving streets and alleys in the area, $560 for painting exterior of the building, and the balance for normal building maintenance.

d) During the year $62 was withheld from employees' wages for social security and withholding taxes.

Required:

1. A work sheet showing:
   a) Adjustments to the beginning balance sheet and to the income and expense accounts,
   b) The financial position of the partnership at March 31, 1973, and
   c) The results of its operations for the year then ended on the accrual basis.

2. The entries in journal form to adjust the accounts, including entries necessary to place the books on an accrual basis. Give brief explanations for each adjustment, and key the journal form adjustments to the adjustments in the work sheet.

(AICPA adapted)

chapter 3 | The Reporting Process — The Balance Sheet

Management, stockholders, creditors, and other properly interested parties need information concerning the business unit in respect to (*a*) the results of operations for definite periods (months and years) and (*b*) the financial position of the enterprise at the end of such time periods. More extended consideration of these parties' needs and their usage of financial reports is to be found throughout this book. Suffice it to say for the present that the balance sheet (discussed in this chapter) and the income statement and statement of retained earnings (discussed in the next chapter) are the principal means by which the financial change and standing of an entity are ascertained and evaluated by shareholders and other nonmanagerial groups.

The accounting profession has developed, over the years, fairly standardized formats to meet these needs in part. Variations abound, but at the same time it is accurate to say that the principal financial exhibits of all profit-oriented enterprises follow the basic patterns of balance sheets discussed here and those of income statements and statements of retained earnings as presented in Chapter 4. Special statements such as the statement of changes in financial position, formerly known as the source and application of funds, manufacturing, and costs, depending on the nature of the entity and special features of its method of operating and financing, frequently are prepared to supplement the basic statements. The statement of changes in financial position was once optional but is now required; it is discussed in Chapter 25. If the entity is affected seriously by inflation or other changes in the value of money (as would be the case when a high proportion of the assets have a low turnover or if a foreign currency has been unstable and operations in that foreign country are significant), supplemental price-level adjusted statements should be prepared. The latter are discussed in Chapter 23.

The balance sheet is the *position statement;* that is, it presents the cumulative financial position of a firm at a specific date. Since all financial aspects are in effect *stopped* for the moment of the balance sheet, it has been appropriately described as a "snapshot or still picture" of the financial position of a business entity. In contrast, the income statement has been described as a "motion picture" of the financial activities of an entity, since it reports on the operations for a given period of time as opposed to a specific point in time.

The balance sheet reports financial position in terms of the basic economic model of the enterprise:

$$\text{Assets} = \text{Creditors' Equity} + \text{Owners' Equity}$$

While the term *balance sheet* is widely used, alternate (and preferable) terms such as *statement of financial position* are being used with more frequency. Essentially the balance sheet is a historical report in that most of the data thereon represent the result of past and completed transactions; it does not report projected or budgeted data but does reflect some estimates of future values such as the net amount of receivables to be collected (accounts receivable less estimated losses on doubtful accounts).

In *Statement 4,* the Accounting Principles Board (APB) of the AICPA stated that:

The *financial position* of an enterprise at a particular time comprises its assets, liabilities, and owners' equity and the relationship among them, plus contingencies, commitments, and other financial matters that pertain to the enterprise at that time. The financial position of an enterprise is presented in the *balance sheet* and in notes to the financial statements.[1]

The APB listed the "elements" of the financial position as assets, liabilities, and owners' equity and then defined them as follows:

Assets — economic resources of an enterprise that are recognized and measured in conformity with generally accepted accounting principles. Assets also include certain deferred charges that are not resources but that are recognized and measured in conformity with generally accepted accounting principles.[2]

---

[1] AICPA, "Basic Concepts and Accounting Principles Underlying Financial Statements," *Statement of the Accounting Principles Board 4,* (New York, 1970), pp. 49–50.

[2] Deferred charges that are not resources include items such as "charges from income tax allocation," and deferred credits that are not resources include items such as "credits from income tax allocation." See Chapter 23.

Liabilities—economic obligations of an enterprise that are recognized and measured in conformity with generally accepted accounting principles. Liabilities also include certain deferred credits that are not obligations but that are recognized and measured in conformity with generally accepted accounting principles.[3]

Owners' equity—the interest of owners in an enterprise, which is the excess of an enterprise's assets over its liabilities.

A significant aspect of these definitions are that they define each element in terms of *generally accepted accounting principles* rather than on a conceptual basis; an approach that is subject to considerable criticism.

Corporations generally caption the capital section of the balance sheet as stockholders' equity or shareholders' equity. The term *capital* is used less as a balance sheet caption than in the past; it still is widely used by unincorporated entities.[4]

Balance Sheet Classifications

To facilitate the analysis, interpretation, and use of the mass of financial data frequently found on a balance sheet, items usually are grouped according to some common characteristic. Broadly, assets and liabilities are classified as current or short-term items and non-current or long-term items. The classifications used in a balance sheet and the array of items to be found under each classification depend somewhat on the size and nature of the business and its method of operation. For example, two similar businesses, one of which owns its property and the other of which leases the major portion of such property, will show quite different detail on the balance sheets. So also will the balance sheet of a logging and timber enterprise differ from that of a retail grocery chain because of the difference in operations conducted. Insofar as it is feasible to generalize concerning major balance sheet captions, in view of the great varieties of captions encountered in practice, the following classifications are representative of sound accounting practice.

Assets: 1. Current assets (including prepaid expenses).
2. Investments and funds.
3. Fixed assets—tangible.
4. Fixed assets—intangible.
5. Other assets.
6. Deferred charges.

Liabilities: 1. Current liabilities.
2. Long-term liabilities.

---

[3] See footnote 2.

[4] Based upon data reported in the 1970 edition of *Accounting Trends and Techniques*, an annual publication of the AICPA which sets out in considerable detail the reporting practices of 600 industrial and commerical corporations as reflected in their annual reports to stockholders. Since practices of the same companies in earlier years are also tabulated, it is easy to recognize trends in reporting practices.

Stockholders' equity: 1. Contributed capital.

    a) Capital stock.

    b) Contributions in excess of par or stated value.

    2. Retained earnings.

    a) Appropriated.

    b) Unappropriated.

It should be noted that the foregoing classification structure provides for only three major headings: viz, assets, liabilities, and stockholders' equity. Accounting practice increasingly has tended to add a somewhat anomalous fourth category of items usually captioned "deferred incomes" or "deferred credits." Where found, this fourth category is placed between liabilities and capital. Typical items presented under the caption include premium on bonds payable, expected profit on transactions which has yet to be earned or realized, and in the case of consolidated statements, excess of book value of parent company's equity over the price paid for that equity.[5] More extended coverage of deferred credits is to be found in Chapter 16. In theory, it is difficult to justify such a fundamental deviation as "deferred credits" from the basic model: Assets = Liabilities + Capital.

Current Assets

Current assets are cash and other assets or resources reasonably expected to be realized in cash or sold or consumed within one year, or during the *normal operating cycle* of the business, whichever is longer. Current assets generally are listed on the balance sheet in order of their liquidity. Assets classified as current frequently command more attention than do any others. Solvency and the financial strength to carry out expansion, dividends, and investment policies are largely dependent on the working capital position. *Working capital* is defined as the excess of current assets over current liabilities.

In addition to cash, current assets include the following major categories of items: receivables, inventories, marketable securities representing the investment of temporary cash excess balances, prepaid expenses, and supplies.

The *operating cycle* is the period of time between the acquisition of inventory (for sale) or items which will be processed to become salable inventory and the final cash realization from their sale. Briefly stated, the cycle is cash to inventory, to sale, to receivables, to cash. For most businesses this cycle is shorter than one year. For example, if a business enjoys an inventory turnover of six times per year and

---

[5] A summarized treatment of consolidated statements will be found in Chapter 11. For a complete treatment see Griffin, Williams, and Larson, *Advanced Accounting*, (rev. ed.; Homewood, Ill.: Richard D. Irwin, Inc., 1971).

sells on 30-day credit terms (so that its accounts receivable turnover should be about 12 times per year), its operating cycle would be approximately three months. There are however certain businesses whose operating cycle extends beyond 12 months. Industry examples include sugar plantations, distilleries, logging, and shipbuilding, all of whose production cycles are extended. Similarly, due to the extended collection period, dealers who sell on installment terms and who carry their receivables often have an operating cycle exceeding one year. The length of the operating cycle is important because it determines whether assets and liabilities should be classed as current or noncurrent.

The AICPA's Committee on Accounting Procedure stated:

For accounting purposes, the term *current assets* is used to designate cash and other assets or resources commonly identified as those which are reasonably expected to be realized in cash or sold or consumed during the normal operating cycle of the business. Thus the term comprehends in general such resources as (a) cash available for current operations and items which are the equivalent of cash; (b) inventories of merchandise, raw materials, goods in process, finished goods, operating supplies, and ordinary maintenance material and parts; (c) trade accounts, notes, and acceptances receivable; (d) receivables from officers, employees, affiliates, and others, if collectible in the ordinary course of business within a year; (e) instalment or deferred accounts and notes receivable if they conform generally to normal trade practices and terms within the business; (f) marketable securities representing the investment of cash available for current operations; and (g) short-term prepaid expenses such as insurance, interest, rents, taxes, unused royalties, current paid advertising service not yet received, and operating supplies. Prepaid expenses are not current assets in the sense that they will be converted into cash but in the sense that, if not paid in advance, they would require the use of current assets during the operating cycle.

This concept of the nature of current assets contemplates the exclusion from that classification of such resources as: (a) cash and claims to cash which are restricted as to withdrawal or use for other than current operations, are designated for expenditure in the acquisition or construction of noncurrent assets, or are segregated for the liquidation of long-term debts; (b) investments in securities (whether marketable or not) or advances which have been made for the purposes of control, affiliation, or other continuing business advantage; (c) receivables arising from unusual transactions (such as the sale of capital assets, or loans or advances to affiliates, officers, or employees) which are not expected to be collected within 12 months; (d) cash surrender value of life insurance policies; (e) land and other natural resources; (f) depreciable assets; and (g) deferred charges, that is, long-term prepayments which are chargeable to the operations of several years, such as bonus payments under a long-term lease, costs of rearrangement of factory layout or removal to a new location, and certain types of research and development costs.[6]

---

[6]*Accounting Research and Terminology Bulletins, Final Edition*, pp. 20–21.

Bearing in mind the implications of the operating cycle and the one-year limitation, the following accounts typify what is reported as *positive* elements under the current asset classification: Cash (unless restricted), Receivables, Certificates of Deposit, Inventories including Finished Goods, Work in Process, Raw Materials, and Supplies, Marketable Securities, Advances of Cash, and Prepaid Expenses, *Negative* elements under the current asset classification typically include Allowance for Doubtful Receivables, Notes Receivable Discounted, and Allowance to Reduce to Market (used in connection with inventories and marketable securities). The basis of valuation of marketable securities and of inventories should be disclosed in the balance Sheet.

Investments and Funds

Permanent investments are assets (generally securities but may include such items as land) acquired to be held for a considerable period of time for the income or the financial advantages accruing therefrom. The following accounts are typical of those to be found under this classification: Investments in Securities, Long-Term Advances to Affiliated Companies, Time Deposits (for nonworking capital purposes), Funds (of various types such as Sinking Funds, Plant Expansion Funds, and Preferred Stock Retirement Funds), and Cash Surrender Value of Life Insurance.

Certain tangible assets held for resale (other than inventory) may be reported under this caption. This treatment would appear to be proper, as for example, where land was purchased speculatively in the expectation of a rise in its value. Assets formerly or prospectively to be used as tangible fixed assets may be reported under this caption pending final disposition. Machinery retired from use and held for sale and land purchased for use as a future plant site are examples. Neither item should be classed under "fixed assets" when not actually in use; alternatively either item also could be shown as "other assets," depending upon the future expectations with respect to their use or disposition.

Fixed Assets — Tangible

Tangible fixed assets are defined as those having usefulness because of their physical characteristics and are used or consumed in the operation of the business. If the fixed assets are to be used, they are, with the exception of land, depreciable; if they are to be consumed, they are wasting assets (i.e., natural resources). The following accounts are typical of those to be found as *positive* elements under the "fixed assets — tangible" classification: Land, Building, Machinery, Equipment, Furniture and Fixtures, Natural Resources (such as timberland, mineral-bearing property), Tools, and Returnable Containers. *Negative* elements under this classification include the various specific accumulated depreciation and accumulated depletion accounts. As will be seen in Chapter 13, appraisals should not be reflected in the accounts except in rather rare circumstances; however, where they have already been recorded, it is preferable to set out four special accounts for each appraised depreciable asset. For example, Buildings—Cost, Buildings—Unrealized Appraisal Increment, and as negative or contra accounts, Accumulated Depreciation of Buildings—Cost and Accumulated Depreciation of Buildings—Unrealized Appraisal Increment.

Fixed Assets—Intangible

Fixed assets having no physical existence (though they may be evidenced by various tangible documents) whose values are dependent on the rights their possession confers on the owner are defined as intangible fixed assets. Account titles commonly found under this classification include Patents, Copyrights, Goodwill, Trademarks and Brand Names, Leaseholds, Leasehold Improvements, Formulas and Processes, Research and Development Costs, Licenses and Franchises, Organization Costs, and Rights (such as water and mineral). There is not complete agreement among accounting authorities as to the classification of leaseholds and leasehold improvements. While these two items sometimes are reported as intangibles, the Securities and Exchange Commission (SEC) classifies leasehold improvements as tangible fixed assets. Similarly, a substantial number of the companies included in the survey reported in *Accounting Trends and Techniques* followed this practice. Intangible assets are commonly reported at their "book" values (cost less amortization to date) without a separate contra or offset account; this treatment contrasts with that usually accorded depreciable tangible assets. Presumably as evidence of extreme conservatism, a few companies report their intangibles (at least on the balance sheet) at $1 or some other relatively nominal value. This practice is unsound; it is sometimes followed in connection with goodwill, patents, and trademarks, and is rare insofar as the other assets are concerned.

Other Assets

"Other assets" are those which cannot be reasonably categorized under the asset classifications discussed specifically. Examples include cash in closed banks, subscriptions receivable (when demand for payment will not be made in the near future), and fixed assets held for resale. Items should be analyzed carefully before being reported as other assets because often there is a logical basis for classifying them elsewhere. Items such as strike losses and flood losses intended to be written off in time occasionally are sometimes reported as other assets. This treatment is unsupportable inasmuch as there is no element of future benefit associated with such losses, hence there is no asset value.

Deferred Charges

Deferred charges represent debit balances derived from expenditures not recognized as costs of operations of current or prior periods but involving a future benefit hence are carried forward to be matched with future revenues. The everyday meaning of deferred is *delayed*, and charge is synonymous with *debit;* hence these "delayed debits" have been held for matching against future revenues. Deferred charges are distinguished from prepaid expenses on the basis of the *time* over which they will be amortized, that is, they involve a longer period of time than do prepaid expenses. The following accounts typify those to be found under the "deferred charges" caption: Machinery Rearrangement Costs, Research and Development Costs, Taxes (especially in connection with tax deferments such as discussed in Chapter 23), Organization Costs (alternatively shown under "intangibles"), Pension Costs Paid in Advance and Insurance Prepayments (long-term prepayments not classed as current), and Unamortized Bond Discount. The last-mentioned item, especially if it relates essentially to discount and not to expenses of debt incurrence, is preferably shown contra (offset) to long-term debt. Although some companies continue to present short-term prepaid expenses under deferred charges, the practice is waning apparently in response to a pronouncement of the AICPA's Committee on Accounting Procedure which expressed a preference for classing prepaid expenses as current assets.

Current Liabilities

Current liabilities were described by the AICPA's Committee on Accounting Procedure as those obligations —

whose liquidation is reasonably expected to require the use of existing resources properly classifiable as current assets, or the creation of other current liabilities. As a balance-sheet category, the classification is intended to include obligations for items which have entered into the operating cycle, such as payables incurred in the acquisition of materials and supplies to be used in the production of goods or in providing services to be offered for sale; collections received in advance of the delivery of goods or performance of services; and debts which arise from operations directly related to the operating cycle, such as accruals for wages, salaries, commissions, rentals, royalties, and income and other taxes. Other liabilities whose regular and ordinary liquidation is expected to occur within a relatively short period of time, usually 12 months, are also intended for inclusion, such as short-term debts arising from the acquisition of capital assets, serial maturities of long-term obligations, amounts required to be expended within one year under sinking fund provisions, and agency obligations arising from the collection or acceptance of cash or other assets for the account of third persons.[7]

Current liabilities should not include long-term bonds or notes whose maturity dates have become imminent where such debts are expected to be refunded, but there should be disclosure that they have been omitted from current liabilities and the reason therefor given. Similarly, debts to be liquidated by use of noncurrent assets should be excluded from current liabilities. Obviously, reclassification after 9 years of a 10-year bond issue and its related sinking fund would seriously distort the current ratio for the 10th year and render comparisons with that ratio for several preceding periods somewhat meaningless.

Typical accounts to be found under current liabilities include Accounts and Notes Payable, Accrued Expenses, Taxes Payable, Unearned Income, Advances from Customers, and Cash Dividends Payable.

Offsetting of current assets and liabilities is improper because this practice avoids full disclosure and would permit a business to show a more favorable current ratio than actually exists. For example, a business whose current assets consist of cash of $20,000 and receivables of $25,000 and currently owing notes payable of $10,000 and accounts payable of $5,000 has a current ratio of 3 to 1. If the intent to use $10,000 of the cash to pay the notes is reflected in the balance sheet by offsetting, the current ratio would rise to 7 to 1. Offsetting is permissible only where a legal right of offset exists; thus, it would be proper to offset a $5,000 overdraft in one account with a bank against another account reflecting $8,000 on deposit in that same bank. Offsetting the two amounts where two different banks are involved is unacceptable.

Long-Term Liabilities

Debts not classed as current liabilities are reported under this caption. The most common items include Bonds Payable, Long-term Notes Payable, and Deferred Tax Liabilities. Two contra or offset items sometimes reported in this classification include Unamortized Discount on Bonds Payable, and Treasury Bonds held alive and uncancelled.

Justification for this treatment of unamortized discount on bonds payable rests on these arguments: (1) Bond discount ultimately is chargeable to interest expense but is not interest paid in advance; rather, it is unpaid interest and hence cannot be shown as an asset (deferred charge). (2) The investor who purchased the bonds regards

---

[7] Ibid.

the asset value as the price paid; therefore, the issuer should reflect as debt the amount received. As the maturity date approaches, both parties will have amortized the bond values toward par or the redemption amount. Unamortized premium on bonds payable theoretically should be reported as an addition to the related bonds under the long-term debt caption rather than separately under deferred credits.

Use of "funded debt" as a caption for this subdivision of liabilities is not recommended because this term implies specific funding arrangements have been made; some elements of long-term debt may be unfunded. It is customary and desirable to include relevant descriptive information concerning long-term debts. Indications as to whether the debts are secured, interest rates, maturity dates, provision for funding, and conditions, such as debt convertibility or subordination,[8] typify the types of disclosures that should be included on the balance sheet or in accompanying notes.

Deferred Credits

Deferred credits can be said to be the counterparts of deferred charges; i.e., they represent credit balances carried forward to be adjusted and closed into Income Summary in the matching process in future periods. However it was noted earlier in the chapter that they do not really fit the basic accounting equation because a deferred credit is neither a liability nor a part of owners' equity. Although it is theoretically possible to condemn and exorcise deferred credits, the world of accounting practice finds it increasingly difficult to get along without them. More detailed discussion of deferred credits appears in Chapter 16.

Deferred Profit on Sales, Income Payments Received in Advance, Deferred Income Taxes, and Unamortized Premium on Bonds Payable typify items reported under Deferred Credits on balance sheets of major companies. When the caption Deferred Credits is used it is ordinarily found between Liabilities and Stockholders' Equity.

Capital Stock

Details of each class of capital shares should be set out separately in the balance sheet, including titles of the issues; number of shares authorized, issued, and subscribed; conversion features and basis of conversion; callability; and preferences upon liquidation (if other than par). Obligations to issue additional shares stemming from subscriptions, stock options granted, or stock dividends declared simi-

---

[8]Convertible debt securities are those which, at the option of their holders and subject to specified limitations, may be exchanged under certain conditions for stocks or other securities of the issuer. Convertible securities increased greatly in use in the last half of the 1960s. Subordinated debts are those to be paid after those owing to general creditors. Such arrangements may be agreed to when creditors of a debtor in financial straits have faith in the debtor's ultimate ability to pay.

larly call for disclosure. Par or other nominal values also should be indicated. Account titles reflecting positive (credit) balances in this category include (with appropriate description) Capital Stock, Subscribed Stock, and Stock Dividends Payable. Account titles reflecting contra (debit) elements include Unissued Stock and Treasury Stock.

Capital Contributed in Excess of Nominal Values

Where shares are other than true no-par stock, premiums, discounts, and other amount variations from the par or stated values should be reported separately. These amounts may be reported with the related stock amounts indicated in the foregoing caption or under a separate caption such as Contributions in Excess of Par (or Stated) Value, Capital in Excess of Par (or Stated) Value, other Paid-in Capital, or Paid-in Surplus.[9]

Retained Earnings

Corporate retained earnings may consist of unappropriated retained earnings and appropriated retained earnings. Restrictions on retained earnings whether or not reflected in accounts as appropriations formally should be disclosed. A detailed discussion of appropriations of retained earnings is to be found in Chapter 22. The primary reasons for appropriation or restriction of retained earnings may be summarized as follows:

1. To fulfill a legal requirement as in the case of a restriction on retained earnings equivalent to the cost of treasury stock held.
2. To fulfill a contractual agreement as in the case of a bond issue where the bond indenture carries a stipulation providing for a restriction on retained earnings.
3. To record formally an action by the board of directors to restrict a portion of retained earnings as a matter of financial planning. (Example: reserve for plant expansion.)
4. To record formally an action by the board of directors to restrict a portion of retained earnings in anticipation of possible future losses. (Example: reserve for self-insured losses.)

A negative or debit balance in retained earnings is commonly called a *deficit*.

Contingencies

Full disclosure requires that accounting take cognizance of contingencies. In the general sense, a contingency is a possible or not un-

---

[9] Despite efforts to eliminate usage of the term *surplus* (coupled with such modifiers as "earned" or "paid-in"), the term refused to disappear. Well over a quarter of the 600 companies included in the 1970 edition of *Accounting Trends and Techniques* used the term *surplus* in their balance sheet captions.

likely future event or condition. However, accounting must observe a more specific definition, since all aspects of the future involve contingencies of varying degrees. Thus, from the accounting point of view a contingency arises from acts, events, or circumstances occurring before the date of the balance sheet or from conditions existing as of that date, but for which any asset inflow or indebtedness is contingent upon some future event or circumstance.

Various past events, transactions, or contracts may give rise to *contingent assets* or to *contingent liabilities* as of the balance-sheet date. Skilled judgment is required in deciding which contingencies to disclose and which ones should not be reported. The difficulty is twofold: (*a*) there is uncertainty as to whether any given contingency will eventuate; (*b*) the impact of contingencies which materialize is often difficult to assess in advance. Excessive zeal in disclosing contingencies could result in cluttering statements with insignificant items. On the other hand, failure to disclose contingencies which culminate later with material impact is clearly undesirable and fails to satisfy the full-disclosure principle. It seems reasonable to generalize that there should be greater readiness to disclose the existence of contingent liabilities than of contingent assets; however, disclosure of either is often warranted. Contingent liabilities can arise from guarantees of loans and accommodation endorsements, endorsement of notes receivable discounted, actual or prospective litigation in which the company is defendant, possible added tax assessments, and purchase or repurchase commitments. Contingent assets can arise from claims for tax refunds, carryforward of tax losses of former years, suits for recovery of damages where the company is plaintiff, and from contingent donations. The most common method of disclosure of contingencies is by means of footnotes or notes to the statements, although it is not unusual to observe contingencies reported in the body of the financial statements as contra accounts. Discounted notes receivable commonly are reflected by either (*a*) subtracting the balance of notes receivable discounted from the balance of notes receivable; (*b*) showing notes receivable at a net figure and setting out notes receivable discounted under liabilities with the amount extended "short," i.e., not included in the liability total; or (*c*) showing the notes receivable net and reporting the discounted notes in a footnote. The authors prefer the first method.

Post-Balance Sheet Disclosures

Closely related to contingencies are those events occurring or becoming known subsequent to the date in the heading of the balance sheet but prior to its issuance. These events may have a significant effect on future financial standing of the firm and, therefore, require disclosure to prevent the statement from becoming misleading.

The AICPA's Committee on Auditing Procedure has said:

An independent auditor's report is ordinarily rendered in connection with financial statements which purport to present financial position at a stated date and results of operations for a period ended on that date. Such financial statements are essentially historical in character. Financial statements for a given period represent one installment in the financial history of a business enterprise. They are so considered by the auditor in making his examination and in expressing his opinion with regard to the statements. However, events or transactions sometimes occur subsequent to the balance-sheet date which may have a material effect on the financial statements or which may be important in connection with consideration of the statements and, therefore, require adjustment or annotation of the statements.[10]

A recent edition of *Accounting Trends and Techniques* indicated that 258 of the 600 companies included in the survey referred to post-balance sheet events in their published annual reports. These disclosures ordinarily were presented in notes to the financial statements or the accompanying president's letter. Typical post-balance sheet disclosures relate to extra stock distributions proposed or approved, adoption or modification of employee benefit plans, mergers (pending, proposed, or effected), contracts negotiated or canceled, and litigation.

Special Problems Related to Consolidated Balance Sheets

A brief discussion of consolidated statements is presented in Chapter 11. At this point brief cognizance will be taken of two important matters peculiar to such statements. A consolidated balance sheet is one in which the assets and liabilities of the subsidiary companies (subsidiaries) are combined with those of the controlling corporation (parent) in such a way as to disclose the financial position of the related companies as though they were a single entity. Such statements call for a special heading which indicates they apply to more than one enterprise.

Where subsidiaries are not wholly owned, that portion of capital not owned by the parent corporation is commonly referred to as the *minority interest*. The minority interests, appropriately described, are commonly reported immediately above capital. Minority interests are sometimes also shown within the stockholders' equity section.

Footnotes to the Balance Sheet

When reporting within the balance sheet does not meet the requirements of *full disclosure*, the use of appropriate footnotes is required. Several common situations are discussed below. Where needed, balance sheets should include either within the body or in accompanying explanatory notes such data as assets subject to lien (mortgaged); and the secured obligations must be identified. If there have been de-

---

[10] AICPA, *Statement on Auditing Procedure No. 33* (New York, 1963), p. 75.

faults as to principal, interest, sinking fund or redemption provisions, or any breach of covenant of a related indenture, such facts must be part of the balance sheet or set out in accompanying notes.

A brief description of the essential provisions of any employee pension or retirement plan should be given, together with an identification or description of the employee groups covered. The company's accounting and funding policies should be described. The excess, if any, of the actuarially computed value of vested benefits over the total of the pension fund and any balance sheet pension accruals less any pension prepayments or deferred charges should be disclosed in the balance sheet itself or in accompanying notes. Pension plan accounting is covered in more detail in Chapter 18.

Provision for the purchase of a corporation's stock by officers and other employees is a common practice. Where such stock option plans exist, the number of shares under option, option prices, and the number of shares as to which options are exercisable should be disclosed in the balance sheet or accompanying notes. The subject of accounting for stock options is covered in greater detail in Chapter 22.

Compliance with authoritative pronouncements may require that more important details as to true leases (as distinguished from asset-purchase contracts which are sometimes called leases) be set out in accompanying notes to the financial statements.[11] Coverage of this topic will be found in Chapter 18.

In addition to the matters noted in the foregoing paragraphs, there may well be other events, contracts, or transactions which have important effects on the entity being reported upon but which are not manifest in the typical summarization to be found in the usual financial statements. Where knowledge of such items is essential to obtain a fair evaluation of an entity on the part of readers of its financial statements, it is important that the statements themselves or notes accompanying them inform the reader fully of the essential features of the events, contracts, or transactions.

Rounding of Amounts

Amounts in published financial statements commonly are rounded to the nearest dollar, or in the case of larger entities, to the nearest hundreds or thousands of dollars. Statements filed with the Securities and Exchange Commission[12] (SEC) may be rounded to the nearest

---

[11] AICPA, *Opinion of the Accounting Principles Board No. 7* (New York, 1966); and AAA, *A Statement of Basic Accounting Theory* (Evanston, Ill., 1966), pp. 32–33.

[12] The SEC is a federal agency which, since its inception in 1934, has had the power to prevent unfair practices in the securities market. Its chief means of accomplishing this is through *disclosure*. Generally speaking, securities offerings in excess of $300,000 must be preceded by the filing of detailed financial statements and other data with the commission; these data are available to interested investors and to the public generally. Companies whose securities are listed on exchanges must keep such data up to date to maintain their listings.

dollar or thousands of dollars provided that in the latter case notation to that effect is inserted immediately beneath the statement heading or at the top of each money column. The SEC also allows the practice of rounding to the nearest dollar or thousand if it is stated in a note that the failure of items to add to the totals shown is due to the dropping of amounts less than $1 or $1,000, as appropriate.

This practice of rounding on statements is not to be confused with so-called centsless accounting in which many transactions are accounted for in journals and ledgers to the nearest dollar with pennies dropped. While a majority of companies do not drop pennies or larger amounts in their basic recording, many do round off amounts on statements to the nearest dollar or some larger amount.

Balance Sheet Forms

Balance sheets commonly are presented in annual reports in one of two general forms, with variations of each format. The most widely used form, commonly referred to as the account form, follows the basic model: Assets = Liabilities + Capital. This format customarily reflects the assets on the left and the liabilities and capital on the right. The other format, commonly referred to as the financial position or vertical form, reflects the assets with a subtraction of liabilities, with the resultant owners' equity. One widely used variation of this format reports current assets less current liabilities, giving net working capital. To this subtotal other assets are added and other liabilities deducted giving the resultant final total of owners' equity.

The 1970 edition of *Accounting Trends and Techniques*[13] revealed the following practices as to terminology and form in respect to presentation of balance sheets by 600 large companies.

```
Titles used:
Balance sheet............................................................................................512
Statement of financial position ............................................................. 61
Statement of financial condition ........................................................... 27
     Total................................................................................................600

Forms used:
Assets = Liabilities + Capital..................................................................567
Working Capital + Other Assets − Other Liabilities = Capital .................. 27
Other forms ...............................................................................................6
     Total................................................................................................600
```

Illustrative Balance Sheet

To enrich your study of financial statements in a practical vein the balance sheet of Trans World Airlines, Inc., on a *consolidated comparative* basis at December 31, 1969 and 1968, is presented in Illustration 3–1. The notes to these statements, which are an integral part

---

[13]*Accounting Trends and Techniques*, 1970 ed., p. 43.

of them, and the accompanying independent accountants' opinion are also shown here. Chapter 4 discusses the income statement and statement of retained earnings; these statements for the same company appear in Illustration 4–10. Several references to this company's statements will be found in subsequent chapters when such matters as leases, pensions, and convertible debt are specifically discussed.

Illustration 3–1
TRANS WORLD AIRLINES, INC. AND SUBSIDIARIES
CONSOLIDATED BALANCE SHEET
December 31, 1969 and 1968

ASSETS

	1969	1968
Current Assets:		
Cash...$	20,862,000	$ 30,139,000
Marketable securities and other short-term investments,		
at cost or less, plus accrued interest (approximates market)...................	124,581,000	37,548,000
Receivables, less reserve (1969 – $3,321,000; 1968 – $3,978,000).................	148,508,000	109,214,000
Refundable deposits on equipment to be leased (Note 3)	33,683,000	–
Refund of federal income taxes (Note 2)	6,278,000	21,886,000
Spare parts, materials, and supplies, at average cost less		
obsolescence reserve (1969 – $12,725,000; 1968 – $10,145,000)	40,789,000	41,979,000
Other current assets	12,285,000	5,658,000
Total Current Assets...$	386,986,000	$ 246,424,000
Special Funds and Investments:		
Flight equipment deposits (Note 3)...$	141,166,000	$ 156,414,000
Equity in Hilton International Co. (Note 1)	33,045,000	27,615,000
Other...	31,361,000	1,539,000
Total Special Funds and Investments..................................$	205,572,000	$ 185,568,000
Property and Equipment:		
Flight equipment, at cost (Note 3) $1,169,449,000		$1,017,821,000
Less accumulated depreciation (Note 4)	471,926,000	397,386,000
Flight equipment – net ....$	697,523,000	$ 620,435,000
Other property and equipment, at cost ....$	162,886,000	$ 132,951,000
Less accumulated depreciation (Note 4)	53,289,000	46,141,000
Other property and equipment – net...$	109,597,000	$ 86,810,000
Property and Equipment – Net ....$	807,120,000	$ 707,245,000
Deferred Charges:		
Aircraft development and integration costs (Note 3).............................$	7,550,000	$ 9,985,000
Unamortized debt expense..	6,462,000	5,242,000
Long-term prepayments and other deferred charges...............................	8,206,000	5,465,000
Total Deferred Charges ....$	22,218,000	$ 20,692,000
Total $1,421,896,000		$1,159,929,000

LIABILITIES

	1969	1968
Current Liabilities:		
Current maturities of long-term debt...$	23,214,000	$ 21,969,000
Accounts payable and accrued liabilities	152,748,000	116,599,000
Accrued income taxes..	1,131,000	1,124,000
Customer deposits	5,706,000	5,538,000
Advance ticket sales..	32,883,000	24,742,000
Total Current Liabilities...$	215,682,000	$ 169,972,000

Illustration 3–1 (continued)

Long-Term Debt, less current maturities (Note 8).......................................$	757,179,000	$ 570,123,000

Deferred Credits:

Deferred federal income taxes (Note 2) ....$	85,182,000	$ 76,946,000
Other...	2,024,000	1,635,000
Total Deferred Credits ....$	87,206,000	$ 78,581,000

	Number of Shares			
	1969	1968		
Shareholders' Equity:				
Preferred Stock, without par value, stated value $2.50, liquidating preference $50 per share (aggregate $49,970,000):				
Authorized...............	7,000,000	3,500,000		
Issued and outstanding	999,392	973,719	2,498,000	2,434,000
Reserved (Note 5)..	70,269	98,220		
Common stock, par value $5 per share:				
Authorized...............	40,000,000	20,000,000		
Issued and outstanding	10,200,250	10,032,612	51,001,000	50,163,000
Reserved (Note 5)..	7,411,243	4,692,980		
Capital surplus			114,644,000	107,848,000
Retained earnings (Note 8)..			193,686,000	180,808,000
Total Shareholders' Equity ....$			361,829,000	$ 341,253,000
Total ....$			1,421,896,000	$1,159,929,000

Notes To Financial Statements

1. Principles of Consolidation

The accompanying financial statements show TWA's equity in the net assets and in the results of operations of Hilton International Co. and subsidiaries. All other subsidiaries are consolidated in the accompanying financial statements. All subsidiaries are wholly owned.

2. Income Taxes

Provision (credit) for income taxes is as follows:

	(Amounts in Thousands) Year Ended December 31	
	1969	1968
Current Federal Income Taxes Refundable:		
Gross tax ....$	(7,178)	$(28,065)
Less investment tax credit..	1,763	7,016
Net current...$	(5,415)	$(21,049)
Deferred Federal Income Taxes:		
Gross tax ....$	12,633	$ 33,528
Less investment tax credit..	(10,169)	(18,652)
Net deferred ....$	2,464	$ 14,876
State and foreign income taxes...	—	59
Total..$	(2,951)	$ (6,114)

The net tax credit for 1969 is comprised of amounts applicable to the current year only and to an examination by the Internal Revenue Service of the company's tax returns for the years 1963 through 1968 as follows:

Illustration 3–1 (continued)

(Amounts in Thousands)

	Current Year	Prior Years	Net 1969
Current:			
Gross tax	$(16,246)	$ 9,068	$ (7,178)
Less investment tax credit	4,061	(2,298)	1,763
Net current	$(12,185)	$ 6,770	$ (5,415)
Deferred:			
Gross tax	$ 22,577	$(9,944)	$12,633
Less investment tax credit	(12,708)	2,539	(10,169)
Net deferred	$ 9,869	$(7,405)	$ 2,464
Total	$ (2,316)	$ (635)	$ (2,951)

Certain issues raised in the examination for prior years have not been settled, but the company believes that adequate provision has been made for income taxes.

Accelerated methods and rates of depreciation are used for income tax purposes; thus depreciation deductions in tax returns exceed those in the income statements in earlier years of the life of aircraft and such differences reverse in later years. Similar timing differences between tax returns and income statements also exist with respect to other items of lesser amounts. The provision (credit) for current taxes is based on estimated amounts to be shown in tax returns or refund claims (arising from tax loss carrybacks) to be filed, while the provision for deferred tax is based on timing differences in depreciation and other items.

At December 31, 1969, accumulated investment tax credits of approximately $52,000,000 (including $400,000 expiring in 1970) are available for use on future tax returns, subject to a number of restrictive provisions in the Internal Revenue Code, of which $10,300,000 is available in computing future current and deferred tax provisions for accounting purposes.

3. Leases, Equipment Acquisitions and Related Guarantees

Forty-three aircraft were operated under long-term leases at December 31, 1969, at an aggregate annual rental of approximately $26,000,000. Thirty-eight of these aircraft are leased for a period of 15 years from delivery in 1968 and 1969, with options to purchase at market value upon termination of the lease. The lessor's purchase cost was financed in part by loans from others, evidenced by notes payable in installments over the term of the leases from rental proceeds under the leases. TWA has guaranteed the payment of these notes, even though rental payments will be sufficient to amortize the notes and pay interest thereon. The five remaining aircraft involve long-term leases of the airframes only, with options to purchase.

TWA has assigned purchase agreements with respect to eight Boeing 727 and two Boeing 747 aircraft, scheduled for delivery in 1970, to Bankers Trust Company (Owner Trustee) under an arrangement providing for purchase of such aircraft by the Owner Trustee on behalf of First National City Bank (the Lessor). If the aggregate purchase price of the 10 aircraft exceeds $96,730,000, TWA will pay the excess. These aircraft will be leased by TWA for a period of 15 years from delivery with options to purchase at market value upon termination of the leases. The Owner Trustee has sold to the public $70,000,000 of Guaranteed Loan Certificates for payment of 70% of the Lessor's cost of the aircraft and certain expenses of the lease transaction and public offering. The Loan Certificates are guaranteed by TWA and are secured by, among other things, a mortgage on the aircraft and an assignment of the lease, even though rental payments will exceed the Trustee's principal and interest payments. Aggregate annual rentals under the lease will approximate $10,586,000. TWA's purchase deposits with Boeing under the assigned purchase agreements approximate $33,683,000 at December 31, 1969, refundable to TWA as to each aircraft upon purchase by the Owner Trustee.

Additional agreements at December 31, 1969, provide for purchase of 11 Boeing 747, 2 Boeing 707, 3 Boeing 727 and 44 Lockheed 1011 aircraft. Eleven of the Lock-

Illustration 3–1 (continued)

heed 1011 aircraft are subject to TWA's right to cancel the purchase of such aircraft prior to June 30, 1971. Upon such cancellation TWA would forfeit $40,000 of the advance deposit for each aircraft not purchased. Deposits and advances for all aircraft under these agreements were $136,041,000 at December 31, 1969, and additional scheduled deposits, together with payments due on delivery, approximate $757,000,000.

Early in 1970 an agreement was entered into between TWA and Eastern Air Lines for purchase by TWA of four additional Boeing 747 aircraft at an estimated cost of $78,000,000, for delivery in 1972 after prior use by Eastern.

Advance deposits of $2,960,000 were made in connection with preliminary orders for 18 proposed supersonic aircraft, both U.S. and foreign made, the cost of which is not presently determinable. TWA is also a participant in a plan for financing the development of U.S. supersonic (SST) aircraft by Boeing. Under terms of this plan, $11,500,000 was paid for TWA's 12 reserved delivery positions. Such funds were restricted solely for use in development of SST aircraft and are at total risk; therefore, the $11,500,000 is being amortized to expense over a five-year period beginning in 1968. In consideration of its participation, TWA is entitled to "royalties," if any, up to $1,500,000 for each $1,000,000 paid with respect to its first 10 delivery positions and up to $750,000 for each $750,000 paid for each of its additional 2 delivery positions.

Leases for terminals, overhaul base, hangars, office and other space are for varying terms. The aggregate annual rental for facilities in service under such leases is approximately $22,000,000 at December 31, 1969. In addition, the aggregate annual rental of a computerized reservation system is approximately $4,200,000. Other ground equipment, including other computer systems, is leased principally for relatively short periods or under cancellable leases.

4. *Depreciation*

Provision for depreciation in the financial statements is based on estimated service lives of the respective classes of property and is computed on the straightline depreciation method.

5. *Capital Stock*

Capital stock reserved for various purposes at December 31, 1969 and 1968, is as follows:

	Number of Shares	
	1969	1968
Preferred Stock:		
Hilton Hotels Corporation warrants (a)	50,853	74,870
Hilton International Co. stock options (b)	19,416	23,350
Total	70,269	98,220
Common Stock:		
TWA warrants (c)	2,094,820	2,094,978
Hilton Hotels Corporation warrants (a)	27,970	41,131
4% Subordinated Debentures (d)	1,110,618	1,000,000
5% Subordinated Debentures (e)	2,777,777	–
Series A Preferred Stock (f)	534,831	535,970
TWA stock options (g)	444,141	467,296
Hilton International Co. stock options (b)	10,670	12,830
Stock purchase plans for employees (h)	160,416	290,775
Employee incentive compensation plan (i)	250,000	250,000
Total	7,411,243	4,692,980

(a) Hilton Hotels Corporation warrants outstanding at the date of acquisition of Hilton International Co. by TWA permit the holder to purchase as a unit, at any time on or before October 15, 1971, one share of common stock of Hilton Hotels Corporation and .144375 of a share of TWA Common Stock and .2625 of a share of TWA Series A Preferred Stock. Of the total exercise price of $50 for such a unit TWA would receive $23.80.

Illustration 3–1 (continued)

(b) Hilton International Co. stock options outstanding at the date of acquisition by TWA, exercisable at prices from $18.57 to $24.50 a share of Hilton International stock, became convertible into .5 of a share of TWA Series A Preferred Stock and .275 of a share of TWA Common Stock for each share of Hilton International stock under option. See Note 5(g).

(c) Warrants issued with the 6½% Subordinated Income Debentures are exercisable at a price of $22 for a share of Common Stock until December 1, 1973, payable either in cash or in such Debentures at par.

(d) 4% Subordinated Debentures are convertible into Common Stock on or prior to September 1, 1981. As of January 30, 1969, coincident with the sale of 5% Subordinated Debentures, the conversion price of the 4% Subordinated Debentures was adjusted from $100 to $90.04 per share and common shares reserved for conversion were increased to 1,110, 618 in accordance with the terms of such Debentures.

(e) 5% Subordinated Debentures are convertible into Common Stock on or prior to July 1, 1983, at a price of $54 per share.

(f) Series A Preferred Stock is convertible into .5 of a share of Common Stock or each share of Series A Preferred Stock.

(g) Transactions for 1969 under stock options plans are summarized below:

	Shares	Option Price per Share
TWA Stock Options:		
Outstanding, January 1, 1969	339,708	$ 8.20 to $86.60
Granted	145,700	22.00 to 45.85
Exercised	(23,155)	8.20 to 38.35
Cancelled	(35,575)	8.20 to 86.60
Outstanding, December 31, 1969		
(currently exercisable 203,515 shares)	426,678	8.20 to 86.60
Reserved for future grants	17,463	
Total	444,141	

	Shares		Option Price per Unit
	Common	Preferred	
Hilton International Co. Stock Options:			
Outstanding, January 1, 1969	12,830	23,350	See
Exercised	(1,002)	(1,824)	Note
Cancelled	(1,158)	(2,110)	5 (b)
Outstanding, December 31, 1969	10,670	19,416	

(h) Comprised of Employee Stock Purchase Plan and the Thrift Plan for Non-Contract Employees; under both plans the Trustees purchase unissued stock from TWA at market value or, with TWA's consent, purchase stock in the open market.

(i) Any incentive compensation awards payable in unissued capital stock are to be charged to the Incentive Compensation Reserve at the average of closing market prices on the last trading day of each month of the calendar year preceding the year in which the award is made.

6. Earnings per Share

Computation of "Earnings Per Common Share" is as follows:

	(Amounts in Thousands) Year Ended December 31	
	1969	1968
Adjustment of Net Income:		
Net income	$19,894	$21,537
Preferred dividends	(1,977)	(1,923)
Reduction in interest expense, net of income tax, for the assumed tender of 6½% Debentures if TWA warrants were exercised	2,000	1,917
Adjusted Net Earnings—Common and Common Equivalent Shares	$19,917	$21,531
Adjustment of Shares Outstanding:		
Average shares of common stock outstanding	10,120	9,960
Assumed exercise of warrants and options:		
TWA warrants	2,095	2,095
TWA and Hilton stock options	37	62
Total Average Common and Common Equivalent Shares	12,252	12,117

Illustration 3–1 (continued)

See Note 5 for a description of rights and privileges of outstanding convertible securities, warrants and options entering into the computation of earnings per share. The Company believes that the present likelihood of full conversion and exercise of such securities is remote.

Earnings per common and common equivalent share were computed by dividing adjusted earnings available for such shares by the weighted average number of shares assumed to be outstanding. Warrants and options are considered to be common stock equivalents from issuance except they are excluded from the computation in any period in which they would increase the earnings per share. As to TWA warrants, net earnings were adjusted for a portion of the interest, net of tax effect, for the assumed surrender of the $6\frac{1}{2}\%$ Subordinated Debentures in an amount sufficient to exercise all warrants. As to TWA and Hilton stock options, the increase in the number of common shares was reduced by the number of shares assumed to have been purchased, at the average market price of TWA common stock during the year, with the assumed proceeds from exercise of such options. Conversion of all other convertible securities would not have had a dilutive effect on earnings per share.

7. *Retirement Plans*

Retirement plans cover substantially all employees. These are generally voluntary contributory plans except that the Company pays the full cost of plans for certain employee groups pursuant to collective bargaining agreements and for certain employees in foreign countries. TWA's policy is to fund pension costs. The total pension expense for the year was $9,878,000, which includes provision for funding of prior service costs over a 30-year period. Additionally, trust fund contributions by the Company for certain employee groups, pursuant to collective bargaining agreements, were $8,715,000 for the year.

8. *Long-Term Debt*

Long-term debt consisted of:

	(Amounts in Thousands) December 31	
	1969	1968
Senior Notes:		
Series A, $6\frac{1}{2}\%$ due 1970–1972	$ 34,800	$ 46,400
Series B, 6 % due 1970–1977	76,000	86,000
Series D, $5\frac{1}{4}\%$ due 1973–1986	100,000	100,000
Series E, $5\frac{3}{8}\%$ due 1973–1986	100,000	100,000
Series F, $6\frac{1}{2}\%$ due 1975–1994	94,050	–
4% Subordinated Debentures due March 1, 1992 (Note 5)	100,000	100,000
5% Subordinated Debentures due January 1, 1994 (Note 5)	150,000	–
$6\frac{1}{2}\%$ Subordinated Income Debentures due June 1, 1978 (Note 5)	96,438	96,439
Revolving Credit Notes	25,000	62,000(a)
Revolving Credit Notes Overseas	720	–
Installment purchase contracts, final payment due 1976	3,385	1,253
Total	$780,393	$592,092
Less amounts due within one year	23,214	21,969
	$757,179	$570,123

(a) A revolving credit arrangement with a group of banks and Irving Trust Company, as Agent, permits TWA to borrow and reborrow amounts of as much as $250,000,000 until December 31, 1972, and lesser amounts thereafter until June 30, 1976. A commitment fee of $\frac{1}{4}$ of 1% per annum is paid on the unused portion of the revolving credit. Interest on amounts borrowed is (i) during the period until July 1, 1972, at a rate each day equal to Irving Trust Company's prime rate for such day, and (ii) beginning July 1, 1972, at a rate each day of $\frac{1}{4}$ of 1% above Irving Trust Company's prime rate for such day.

Illustration 3-1 (continued)

Agreements relating to long-term debt contain certain limitations on the payment of cash dividends. Under the most restrictive of these limitations, retained earnings available for payment of cash dividends approximated $65,000,000 at December 31, 1969.

9. *Contingencies etc.*

In June 1961, TWA brought suit in the U.S. District Court for the Southern District of New York against Howard R. Hughes, Hughes Tool Company and Raymond M. Holliday based on violations of the antitrust laws and other actions. TWA requested damages of $145,000,000. The Honorable Herbert Brownell, acting as Special Master, submitted a report to the District Court in September 1968 with proposed findings that the defendants shall pay TWA damages of $137,611,436. Objections to the report were filed with the District Court by both TWA and the defendants. On December 23, 1969, the District Court confirmed the Special Master's report. When entered, the judgment of the District Court will be subject to appeal. It is the position of the defendants that their objections, if sustained, would preclude any recovery by TWA. No effect has been given in the accompanying financial statements to any recovery which may be received by the Company as a result of this litigation.

TWA has also brought an action in the Chancery Court in Delaware against Hughes Tool Company and Howard R. Hughes based on breach of fiduciary duty, and Hughes Tool Company has filed counterclaims similar to those asserted and dismissed in the Federal Court action. Discovery proceedings in this action have been stayed pending further action of the Chancery Court.

Certain contingent liabilities exist but the possibility of material payments resulting therefrom is remote. TWA and its legal counsel know of no litigation pending or threatened which in their opinion would result in liability which, over and above any insurance coverage in respect thereof, would materially affect TWA's financial condition or interfere with its operations.

Depending upon the results of negotiations with insurance carriers with respect to damage to an aircraft on August 29, 1969, insurance premium expense, net of related income taxes, will be decreased by approximately $1,150,000 or increased by approximately $450,000.

Accountants' Opinion

Haskins & Sells
Certified Public Accountants

To the Shareholders and Board of Directors of Trans World Airlines, Inc.:

We have examined the consolidated balance sheet of Trans World Airlines, Inc., and its subsidiaries, except as stated below, as of December 31, 1969, the related statements of consolidated income, retained earnings and capital surplus for the year then ended, and the supplemental schedule of source and disposition of funds. Our examination was made in accordance with generally accepted auditing standards, and accordingly included such tests of the accounting records and such other auditing procedures as we considered necessary in the circumstances. As to certain subsidiaries of Hilton International Co., we were furnished the reports of other accountants on their examination of the financial statements of those companies for the year.

In our opinion, based on our examination and the reports of other accountants referred to above, and subject to the possible recovery of damages which may be received by the Company but is not presently recorded as an asset (see Note 9 to the financial statements), the accompanying financial statements present fairly the financial position of the companies at December 31, 1969, and the results of their operations for the year then ended, in conformity with generally accepted accounting principles applied on a basis consistent with that of the preceding year, and the accompanying supplemental schedule of source and disposition of funds, when considered in relation to the basic financial statements, presents fairly in all material respects the information shown therein.

Kansas City, Missouri   February 20, 1970

The statements of Trans World Airlines, Inc., were selected for study since they represent better than average standards of reporting and they are comprehensive in that numerous types of transactions are reflected. Your authors now comment specifically on several items in the statements because they relate particularly to the subject matter of this chapter.

1. The independent accountants' *opinion* is technically correct and includes a "subject to" comment in the second paragraph. You should reflect carefully on this opinion as it is by far the primary single element of the financial report. Specifically, it tells the reader the extent to which the overall financial report is useful and the extent to which generally accepted accounting principles have not been followed by the enterprise.

2. The major balance sheet captions largely accord to the authors' preferences as reflected in the chapter. The only major exception is "deferred credits."

3. Items reported under each major caption appear to be representative of current practice. Preferably "unamortized debt expense" should be deducted from long-term debt. Observe the deduction of "reserve" from receivables which involves obsolete terminology. Unfortunately the term *surplus* appears once in the shareholders' equity section; however, we must recognize that use of this term in this respect is not uncommon.

4. The amount of detail in respect to assets and liabilities is generally better than that usually observed.

5. Similarly, the amount of disclosure in respect to leases, equipment acquisitions, and related guarantees appears to be generally better than usual.

6. Note 9 discloses a material contingency (also noted in the opinion).

7. On balance, the quality of disclosure, classification, and terminology employed (including the notes) is somewhat better than the usual case. Unfortunately it is superior to the reporting practices today of a number of enterprises who should do better.

Reserves

The Committee on Terminology of the AICPA noted that in accounting practice the term *reserves* has been used in at least four senses, namely:

(1) To describe a deduction which is made (a) from the face amount of an asset in order to arrive at the amount expected to be realized, as in the case of a reserve for uncollectible accounts, or (b) from the cost or other basic value of an asset, representing the portion of the cost which has been amortized or allocated to income, in order to arrive at the amount properly chargeable to future operations, as in the case of a reserve for deprecia-

tion. In this sense the term has been said to refer to valuation reserves, reflected in the asset section of the balance sheet.

(2) To indicate an estimate of (a) an admitted liability of uncertain amount, as in the case of a reserve for damages, (b) the probable amount of a disputed claim, as in the case of a reserve for additional taxes, or (c) a liability or loss which is not certain to occur but is so likely do so as to require recognition, as in the case of a reserve for self-insurance. These reserves have been included in the *liability* section of the balance sheet, or in a section immediately below the ordinary liabilities, or in the *proprietary* section. In the insurance field the term is used in this sense as referring to the portion of the total assets derived from premiums which is expected to be required to meet future payments under policies.

(3) To indicate that an undivided or unidentified portion of the net assets, in a stated amount, is being held or retained for a special purpose, as in the case of a reserve (a) for betterments or plant extensions, or (b) for excess cost of replacement of property, or (c) for possible future inventory losses, or (d) for general contingencies. In this sense a reserve is frequently referred to as an appropriation of retained income.

(4) In the income statement, to indicate a variety of charges, including losses estimated as likely to be sustained because of uncollectible accounts, depreciation, depletion, amortization, and general or specific contingencies. It is to be noted here that the term refers to the charge by means of which a reserve (in any of the three preceding senses) is created.[14]

As early as 1948 the committee recommended that in accounting practice use of the term *reserve* be *limited to the third of the four senses*. Soundness of this recommendation is increasingly recognized in practice. The committee noted that the first two accounting usages of reserve seem both contrary to the everyday meaning and lacking in technical justification.

The Committee on Concepts and Standards of the American Accounting Association has gone farther and concluded the term *reserve* should not be employed in financial statements at all. This group expressed the opinion that appropriations of retained earnings encountered in current practice vary so widely in purpose and scope and carry such uninformative captions that statement readers unable to secure added information concerning them are confused or misled. Disclosure of restrictions on retained earnings can most be effectively accomplished through statement footnotes in the opinion of the AAA committee.[15]

QUESTIONS FOR CLASS DISCUSSION

1. What are the two principal financial statements? What statements are generally prepared to supplement them?

[14]*Accounting Research and Terminology Bulletins, Final Edition*, pp. 26–27.

[15]"Reserves and Retained Income" in the AAA publication *Accounting and Reporting Standards for Corporate Financial Statements and Preceding Statements and Supplements* (Columbus, Ohio, 1957), p. 21.

2. The balance sheet is an expression of a model or equation. Explain.

3. A balance sheet essentially reflects history. Indicate some ways in which it may reflect future values.

4. For a corporation, the excess of assets over liabilities commonly is represented by several items. What are they? What is the caption placed over them.

5. What are the major subdivisions of *assets* and of *liabilities* to be found in a classified balance sheet?

6. What is *working capital?* Is working capital related to the items usually found under the balance sheet caption *deferred credits?* Explain.

7. What is the meaning of the term *operating cycle?* Does it have any bearing on the classification of balance sheet items as current or noncurrent? If so, explain.

8. Explain the reasoning underlying the classification of such items as office supplies and unexpired insurance as current assets.

9. Name some balance sheet accounts which would have balances but whose amounts would be incorrect if the adjusting entries were omitted or made in the wrong amounts.

10. Where would the following items appear on the classified balance sheet of a department store?
    a) Income taxes withheld from employees' salaries.
    b) Notes receivable discounted.
    c) Mortgage notes payable due in 3, 9, 15, 21, and 27 months.
    d) Merchandise held for customers who have made 5% layaway deposits.
    e) Deposits from customers to cover layaway purchases.
    f) Accrued interest on bonds held as permanent investment.
    g) Cash in change and petty cash funds.
    h) Wrapping and packaging supplies.

11. a) What types of receivables should appear under the current asset caption?
    b) What types of liabilities should appear under the current liability caption?

12. Under what circumstances would cash on hand or on deposit not be classed as current asset?

13. You are engaged as independent accountant to prepare audited financial statements for a jewelry store which has had an average inventory turnover of 6 times in the most recent 10 years. What portions of the inventory would you classify as current assets? Explain.

14. Name some of the principal assets to be found under the intangibles asset classification.

15. Under what caption on a classified balance sheet should the following items appear? (a) Retired equipment held for sale, (b) Subscription receivable (for which no call is expected to be made).

16. What is the meaning of the term *deferred charges?* Distinguish these from prepaid expenses. What types of items appear under the deferred charges caption of a classified balance sheet?

17. Under what circumstances might payable balances due within a few months properly be excluded from the current liabilities classification?

18. (a) Broadly, total retained earnings may consist of two major categories of items or amounts. Explain. (b) What term is used to describe existence of a debit balance in Retained Earnings?

19. (a) Under some circumstances it is proper for a balance sheet to report certain matters which arose after the date of the statement. Explain. (b) Give examples of typical items which should be reported as postbalance disclosures.

20. Name some items (which are not postbalance sheet items) which commonly give rise to notes accompanying the balance sheet.

21. Describe the principal forms employed for balance sheet preparation. Besides the term *balance sheet*, what titles are used to caption the statement?

22. Briefly explain the various past usages of the term *reserve* in accounting practice. Which usage, in the opinion of an AICPA committee, reflects good practice today? What is the position of the AAA committee?

DECISION CASE 3–1

Angus McDougald and Sons is a family corporation operating a chain of seven retail men's clothing stores in the Southwest. The total capital of approximately $5 million is owned by Angus McDougald, president and founder, and eight men and women in the McDougald family. Except for accounts payable, modest amounts of four-month bank credit, and the usual accrued short-term liabilities, the entire resources of the enterprise have come from contributed capital and retained earnings. The general business reputation of the organization is excellent, and there have never been complaints about slowness of paying its liabilities. The family now sees an opportunity to undertake a profitable expansion to 10 or 11 stores and estimates that upwards of $1,500,000 would be required for the purpose. It will be necessary to borrow this sum, and the issuance of five- to eight-year mortgage notes is contemplated.

Because the business is closely held and has never before borrowed to an extent that made issuance of financial statements to outsiders necessary, the only persons who have seen the corporation's statements are members of the family, a few top employees, and some governmental officials, chiefly tax agents. When Angus McDougald was told by a prospective lender he would have to provide detailed financial statements for the past five years and audited statements for the most recent year as a basis for considering the loan, Angus' initial reaction was to "hit the ceiling." After consideration, however, he switched his position to a willingness to have the audit made and to releasing balance sheets as of the end of each of the most recent five years. He was, as yet, unwilling to release income statements and retained earnings statements, and a majority of the other owners agreed with his stand.

Required:

1. If these five balance sheets are quite detailed, what can prospective lenders ascertain from them?

2. In your opinion would the five balance sheets give enough information to warrant granting a $1,500,000 secured intermediate-term loan?

3. If you were the lending officer of the prospective creditor and sought a compromise in the form of getting some added financial facts without receiving summarized income and retained earnings statements, what added data would be most useful to you?

4. Why does the intermediate-term creditor need information that the short-term creditors may not require?

EXERCISES

Exercise 3–1

Indicate the best answer in each of the following:

1. Working capital means –
   - *a*) Excess of current assets over current liabilities.
   - *b*) Current assets.
   - *c*) Capital contributed by stockholders.
   - *d*) Capital contributed by stockholders plus retained earnings.
2. The distinction between current and noncurrent assets and liabilities is now based primarily on –
   - *a*) One year; no exceptions.
   - *b*) One year or operating cycle, whichever is shorter.
   - *c*) One year or operating cycle, whichever is longer.
   - *d*) Operating cycle; no exceptions.
3. Under current accounting theory unexpired insurance is a –
   - *a*) Current asset.
   - *b*) Deferred charge.
   - *c*) Sundry asset.
   - *d*) Temporary investment.
4. Which of the following is not a current asset?
   - *a*) Office supplies.
   - *b*) Temporary investment.
   - *c*) Petty cash.
   - *d*) Cash surrender value of life insurance.
5. Which of the following is not a current liability?
   - *a*) Accrued interest on notes payable.
   - *b*) Accrued interest on bonds payable.
   - *c*) Rent collected in advance.
   - *d*) Premium on bonds payable.
6. A deficit is synonymous with –
   - *a*) A net loss
   - *b*) A cash overdraft.
   - *c*) Negative working capital.
   - *d*) A debit balance in retained earnings.
7. A balance sheet is an expression of the model –
   - *a*) Assets = Equities.
   - *b*) Assets = Liabilities − Capital.
   - *c*) Assets + Liabilities = Capital.
   - *d*) Working Capital − Other Assets − Long-Term Liabilities = Capital.

8. Contingencies are —
    a) Synonymous with postbalance sheet events.
    b) Related to liabilities but not to assets.
    c) Often disclosed by means of footnotes.
    d) Usually caused by deferred credits.

9. A modern acceptable usage of the term *reserve* is reflected by —
    a) Deduction made from the initial value of an asset to reflect a reduced value.
    b) Terminology applied to a liability of indeterminate amount.
    c) Appropriation of retained earnings.
    d) An income statement charge (e.g., depletion).

10. Which terminology essentially is not synonymous with "balance sheet"?
    a) Operating statement.
    b) Statement of financial condition.
    c) Statement of financial position.
    d) Statement of assets and equities.

11. The "operating cycle concept" —
    a) Causes the distinction between current and noncurrent items to depend on whether they will affect *cash* within one year.
    b) Permits some assets to be classed as current even though they are more than one year removed from becoming cash.
    c) Is rapidly becoming somewhat obsolete.
    d) Affects the income statement but not the balance sheet.

Exercise 3–2

The following quotation appeared in the 1950s in what was then a basic document dealing with accounting principles: "With the increasing importance of the income statement there has been a tendency to regard the balance sheet as the connecting link between successive income statements; however this concept should not obscure the fact that the balance sheet has significant uses of its own." This statement has since been reaffirmed by the AICPA's Accounting Principles Board within the past decade, and since that body keeps its pronouncements under more-or-less continuous surveillance, it can be assumed to be a current statement.

Required:

In the order of their importance, as you see them, list the "significant uses of its own" of the corporate balance sheet.

Exercise 3–3

This is a library assignment which can be fulfilled by consulting the annual compilation *Accounting Trends and Techniques* published by the American Institute of CPAs. Be sure you cite which edition and page numbers were used in obtaining the data.

Required:

Prepare a report in good form showing terminology used in the title of published balance sheets over the four most recent years for which you can obtain data.

Exercise 3–4

The following trial balance was prepared by Ace Company as of December 31, 1971:

Cash	$ 7,200	
Accounts receivable	14,000	
Inventories	13,000	
Equipment	28,000	
Land	6,000	
Building	8,000	
Deferred charges	1,100	
Accounts payable		$ 5,500
Note payable—6%		8,000
Capital stock (par $10)		40,000
Earned surplus		23,800
	$77,300	$77,300

You ascertain that certain errors of omission and commission are reflected in the above, including the following:

1. There are two different bank accounts in separate banks; one has a positive balance of $9,000; the other is overdrawn.

2. The $14,000 balance in accounts receivable represents the entire amount owing to the company; of this sum, $12,500 is from trade customers, and 5% of that amount is estimated to be uncollectible. The remaining sum owed to the company represents a long-term advance to its president.

3. Inventories include $2,000 of goods erroneously billed to the company at double the agreed price; the bill is unpaid and no correction has been recorded as yet. Office supplies of $400 are also included in the balance of inventories.

4. When equipment and building were purchased new on January 1, 1967, they had respectively estimated lives of 10 and 25 years. They have been depreciated by the straight line method on the assumption of zero salvage values, and depreciation has been credited directly to these assets.

5. The balance of the land account includes a $1,000 payment made as a deposit of earnest money on the purchase of an adjoining tract. The option to buy it has not yet been exercised.

6. The note matures March 31, 1972, having been drawn July 1, 1971. Interest on it has been ignored.

7. On November 15, 1971, 5% annual dividends were declared on the capital stock payable January 15, 1972, to stockholders of record of December 15, 1971. Accounts payable was credited.

Required:

Prepare a correct classified balance sheet using preferred terminology. Use whichever form is specified by your instructor.

Exercise 3–5

1. Match the numbered items with the lettered ones appearing below.

a) Note receivable discounted. 5   (1) Long-term liabilities.
b) Statement of financial position. 1   (2) Valuation item.

c) Prepaid rent income. 3
d) Equities. 6
e) Leasehold improvements. 8
f) Allowance for doubtful accounts. 2
g) Machinery rearrangement costs. 4
h) Cash in closed bank. 9

(3) Deferred credit.
(4) Deferred charge.
(5) Contingent liability.
(6) Liabilities and capital.
(7) Balance sheet.
(8) Intangible.
(9) Other asset.

2. Describe concisely the circumstances, if any, under which a period of more than 12 months would be used as a determinant of whether to class certain balance sheet assets and liabilities as current or noncurrent.

3. The term *reserve* is now supposed to be used in respect to only one category of balance sheet items. Indicate what this correct usage is (as a class, not just by a single example).

Exercise 3–6

A balance sheet has the following captions:

A. Current assets.
B. Investments and funds.
C. Fixed assets – tangible.
D. Fixed assets – intangibles.
E. Other assets.
F. Deferred charges.

G. Current liabilities.
H. Long-term liabilities.
I. Capital stock.
J. Contributions in excess of par or stated value.
K. Retained earnings.

Required:

Indicate by letter (use capitals and print) how each of the following would be classified: (Where an item is negative in a caption, place a minus sign before it.)

1. Accounts payable.
2. Bond sinking fund.
3. Equipment.
4. Machinery rearrangement costs.
5. Notes receivable discounted.
6. Accumulated depreciation.
7. Petty cash fund.
8. Prepaid insurance.
9. Treasury stock.

10. Office supplies.
11. Dividends payable (in stock).
12. Land held for resale (not part of inventory).
13. Allowance for doubtful accounts.
14. Reserve for sinking fund.
15. Franchise (not perpetual).
16. Prepaid interest on notes receivable.

Exercise 3–7

This is a library assignment which can be fulfilled by consulting the annual compilation *Accounting Trends and Techniques* published by the American Institute of CPAs.

Required:

Prepare a report which includes a table showing the types of postbalance sheet disclosures made in published reports for the most recent year for which you can obtain data. Be sure you specify the edition and page numbers used in obtaining your data.

Exercise 3-8

On a balance sheet with the following captions:

A. Current assets.
B. Investment and funds.
C. Tangible fixed assets.
D. Intangible fixed assets.
E. Other assets.
F. Deferred charges.

G. Current liabilities.
H. Long-term liabilities.
I. Capital stock.
J. Contributions in excess of par or stated value.
K. Retained earnings.

Required:

Indicate by letter how each of the following would be classified:

1. Cash dividend payable.
2. Payroll fund.
3. Leasehold improvements.
4. Bonds payable (due in six months; adequate sinking fund exists).
5. Fully depreciated fixtures held for sale.
6. Accrued interest on bonds payable.
7. Marketable securities held in bond sinking fund.
8. Merchandise inventory.
9. Prepaid interest on notes payable.
10. Premium on bonds payable.
11. Organization expense (being amortized over five-year period).
12. Debentures payable.
13. Patents.
14. Advances to salesmen.
15. Reserve for plant expansion.
16. Accrued salaries.
17. Capital stock subscribed.
18. Retired equipment held for sale.
19. Machinery rearrangement costs.
20. Premium on capital stock.

Exercise 3-9

The following balance sheet has come to your attention:

BLAUVELT CORPORATION
Balance Sheet
For Year Ended December 31, 1971

ASSETS

Current Assets:			
Cash		$ 36,000	
Receivables	$ 29,000		
Less: Reserve for bad debts	700	28,300	
Inventories		42,000	
			$106,300
Investments and Funds:			
Petty cash fund		$ 200	
Sinking fund		65,000	
			65,200
Fixed Assets:			
Land and buildings	$140,000		
Less: Reserve for depreciation	9,000	$131,000	
Equipment	$ 84,000		
Less: Reserve for depreciation	29,000	55,000	
			186,000

Other Assets:
Prepaid expenses.. $ 2,700
Accrued sinking fund income.........................   600

         3,300

      Total Assets..................................... $360,800

LIABILITIES

Current Liabilities:
Accrued interest on mortgage.......................... $ 700
Accounts payable...   36,500
Estimated income taxes payable......................$ 13,000
    Less: U.S. government bonds....................... 8,000   5,000

         $ 42,200

Long-Term Liabilities:
Mortgage payable°.. $ 70,000
Notes receivable discounted   4,000

         74,000

CAPITAL

Capital stock $100,000
Earned surplus unappropriated†......................   52,400
Reserve for contingencies   68,000

     $220,400
    Less: Treasury stock ....,.....   24,200

         244,600
         $360,800

°The mortgage payable matures April 18, 1972, and is largely funded by the sinking fund.

†On December 20, 1971, the directors declared a 6% dividend payable in cash on February 1, 1972, to stockholders of record on January 20, 1972.

Required:

List your criticisms of the balance sheet and its accompanying notes.

Exercise 3–10

The ledger of Simple Manufacturing Company reflects obsolete terminology but you find its books have been, on the whole, accurately kept. After the most recent closing of the books at December 31, 1971, the following accounts are submitted to you for the preparation of a balance sheet.

Accounts payable ....$	2,700	Raw materials.....................$	9,600
Accounts receivable.............	9,800	Reserve for bad debts..........	500
Accrued expenses................	800	Reserve for depreciation	9,000
Bonds payable — 7%.............	25,000	Rent paid in advance...........	4,000
Capital stock ($100 par)........	100,000	Sinking fund.......................	8,000
Cash.................................	18,200	Treasury stock (at cost)	15,000
Earned surplus	xx,xxx	Tools	6,600
Factory equipment..............	31,200	Work in process	18,300
Finished goods	11,100		
Investments.......................	13,700		
Office equipment	9,500		

You ascertain that two thirds of the depreciation relates to factory and one third to office equipment and that $4,000 of the balance in the Investments account can be properly classified as a current asset while the remainder represents a long-term commitment. Tools are not depreciated directly but are inventoried periodically for this purpose. The treasury stock consists of 100 shares. Prepaid rent covers the factory and office space and represents payment for the forthcoming year and the final year of a lease which has six more years to run.

Required:
Prepare a classified balance sheet using preferred terminology.

Exercise 3–11
You have been asked to assist the chief accountant of the Chenault Corporation in the preparation of a balance sheet. The outline presented below represents the various classifications suggested by the chief accountant for the balance sheet; classification "O" has been added for items to be excluded from the balance sheet.

Assets	*Liabilities and Capital*
A. Current.	G. Current.
B. Investments.	H. Long term.
C. Plant and equipment.	I. Other liabilities.
D. Intangibles.	J. Preferred stock.
E. Deferred charges.	K. Common stock.
F. Other assets.	L. Contributions in excess of par or stated value.
	M. Retained earnings.
	N. Other capital.
	O. Items excluded from the balance sheet.

Required:
Using the *letters* above, classify the following accounts according to the *preferred* balance sheet presentation. If the account is an offsetting or valuation account, mark an "X" before the letter. For example, "Allowance for Doubtful Accounts" would be "X-A."

1. Dividend payable (on Chenault's preferred stock).
2. Plant construction in progress.
3. Factory building (retired from use and held for sale).
4. Reserve for higher plant replacement costs.
5. Land (held for possible future building site).
6. Stock dividend payable (in common stock to common stockholders and to be issued at par).
7. Office supplies inventory.
8. Sinking fund cash (First National Bank, Trustee).
9. Reserve for retirement of preferred stock.
10. Installment sales accounts receivable (average collection period 18 months).
11. Reserve for possible decline in inventory value.
12. Advances to officers (indefinite repayment date).

13. Unredeemed merchandise coupons.
14. Reserve for self-insurance.
15. Inventory of small tools.
16. Unissued common stock.
17. Reserve to reduce inventory to market.
18. Common stock subscribed (Chenault Corporation's stock).
19. Reserve for sinking fund.
20. Securities held as collateral.
21. Bank overdraft.   (AICPA adapted)

Exercise 3-12

You are given a trial balance of Trugood Sales Company, embodying the following accounts, and are requested to prepare a balance sheet. Prepare such statement (account form) without use of amounts, setting out only the accounts properly classified.

Capital stock, traveling expense, sinking fund, prepaid rent, accumulated depreciation, taxes (state and city), accounts receivable (customers'), sales, insurance (all expired), purchases, depreciation, accrued bond interest income, notes receivable (customers'), U.S. income taxes paid, furniture and fixtures, retained earnings, U.S. treasury bonds, long-term advance to officers, allowance for doubtful accounts, trade acceptances receivable, bond interest expense, cash, auto trucks, general expense, collections on bad debts previously charged off, dividends declared but not paid, notes receivable discounted, merchandise inventory (at beginning of period—the inventory at the date of the trial balance is also given you), returns and allowances on sales, interest received on U.S. bonds, discounts received on purchases, dividends paid, trade acceptances payable, discounts allowed on sales, notes payable (officers), treasury stock, and bonds payable.

PROBLEMS

Problem 3-1

The president of Bright Manufacturing Company is a personal friend of yours. He tells you the company has never had an audit and is contemplating having one principally because he suspects the financial statements are not well prepared. As an example he hands you the following balance sheet for review:

BRIGHT MANUFACTURING COMPANY
Balance Sheet
For the Year Ended December 31, 1972

ASSETS

Current Assets:

Cash in banks and on hand	$12,000
Receivables from various sources net of reserve for bad debts	5,000
Inventories	6,000
Cash for restricted uses	500
Total Current Assets	$23,500

Other Assets:

Treasury stock	$ 5,000
Fixed assets (net)	$26,000
Total Assets	$54,500

LIABILITIES AND NET WORTH

Current Liabilities:

Trade accounts payable		$ 3,000
Accrued salaries payable		1,000
Total Current Liabilities		$ 4,000

Long-term Liability:

Mortgage note payable		$ 7,000

Stockholders' Equity:

Capital stock	$30,000	
Earned surplus	13,500	
Total Stockholders' Equity		43,500
Total Liabilities and Stockholders' Equity		$54,500

Required:

1. List your criticisms of the balance sheet.
2. Assuming the balance sheet is symptomatic of the general efficiency with which the books are kept, what would be your advice as to the desirability of going ahead with the audit which is contemplated?

Problem 3–2

As of December 31, 1972, the real account balances on the books of Martin Corporation were as follows:

Accounts payable	$10,100
Accounts receivable	11,800
Accrued interest income	70
Advertising — prepaid	100
Allowance for doubtful accounts	270
Bonds payable	25,000
Building	57,000
Capital stock, par $100	50,000
Cash in bank	7,200
Depreciation accrued to date — building	6,000
Depreciation accrued to date — equipment	3,150
Discount on bonds payable	600
Equipment	16,100
Equipment held for resale	200
Goodwill	5,000
Imprest petty cash fund	100
Land	2,800
Merchandise inventory	18,630
Notes payable	2,100
Notes receivable	11,000
Notes receivable discounted	1,000
Prepaid insurance	385
Reserve for sinking fund	5,000
Retained earnings	?
Sinking fund	5,000
Stock subscribed	8,000
Subscriptions receivable (current)	3,000
Taxes payable	6,325

Required:

Prepare a classified balance sheet.

Problem 3–3

After the books of Parkinson Corporation were closed at October 31, the ledger reflected the balances which appear below. Par value of the corporation's stock is $50 per share.

Furniture and fixtures	$ 62,100
Organization costs	2,000
Cash	31,213
Accumulated depreciation—building	5,400
Dividends payable	4,200
Inventory	14,000
Accrued expenses	1,329
Unexpired insurance	400
Capital contributed in excess of par	2,100
Notes receivable discounted	500
Bonds payable	45,000
Authorized capital stock	100,000
Sinking fund	6,000
Accounts payable	12,647
Building	50,000
Supplies	800
Accumulated depreciation—furniture and fixtures	9,200
Unissued capital stock	15,000
Land	9,200
Notes receivable	4,250
Reserve for sinking fund	6,000
Accounts receivable	22,030
Retained earnings	?
Fees collected in advance	3,500

Required:

Prepare a statement of financial position using appropriate major classifications. Set out fixed assets on a single line with supporting details shown in a separate schedule.

Problem 3–4

Pasco Corporation's adjusted ledger as of December 31, 1972, included the following balances:

Accounts payable	$18,210
Accounts receivable	11,365
Accrued interest income	35
Advertising—prepaid	120
Allowance for doubtful accounts	210
Building	52,300
Capital stock, par $100	55,000
Cash in bank	3,418
Depreciation accrued to date—building	3,185
Depreciation accrued to date—equipment	2,700
Equipment	23,200
Equipment held for resale	550
Goodwill	2,000
Imprest petty cash fund	50
Land	3,000
Merchandise inventory	11,460
Mortgage payable	15,000

Notes payable	1,600
Notes receivable	9,000
Notes receivable discounted	1,200
Patents	3,000
Prepaid insurance	365
Reserve for plant expansion	6,000
Retained earnings	?
Stock subscribed	10,000
Subscriptions receivable (current)	4,000
Taxes payable	2,740
U.S. treasury bonds	14,500

Required:

Prepare a classified balance sheet.

Problem 3-5

The adjusted real accounts for Davis Enterprises, Inc., as of December 31, 1972, are listed below. The net income or loss for 1972 has not yet been closed to retained earnings.

Goods in process	$ 25,000	Patents	$ 16,500
Accrued interest on notes payable	1,000	Reserve for sinking fund	2,500
Accrued interest on notes receivable	750	Accumulated depreciation—office equipment	1,550
Accrued income on temporary investments	1,250	Accumulated depreciation—buildings	4,800
Common stock subscribed	40,000	Unissued common stock	50,000
Cash on hand	500	Trademarks	1,000
Inventory out on consignment	2,500	Chattel mortgage payable	5,000
Allowance to reduce marketable securities to market value	5,000	Real estate held for resale	25,000
Dividends payable on common stock	7,000	Supplies on hand	4,500
		Stock investments in subsidiary company	68,000
Accumulated depreciation—delivery equipment	4,000	Precollected rent income	500
Authorized preferred stock	300,000	Small tools	3,000
Goodwill	25,000	Sinking fund investments	2,500
Finished goods	48,000	Taxes accrued	2,500
Bonds payable (due in 6 years)	50,000	Raw materials	15,000
Accounts payable	55,000	Notes receivable	35,000
Advances to salesmen	1,500	Retained earnings	87,500
Accounts receivable	90,000	Wages accrued	1,250
Accumulated depreciation—machinery and plant equipment	5,000	Notes receivable discounted	10,000
Land, railway siding, driveway	100,000	Subscribers to common stock (current)	20,000
Buildings	100,000	Office equipment	15,500
Machinery and plant equipment	50,000	Authorized common stock	200,000
Prepaid interest expense	500	Allowance for doubtful accounts	4,250
Cash in bank	32,000	Treasury common stock (at par)	10,000
Organization expenses	4,000	Notes payable	20,000
Premium on bonds payable	600	Temporary investments	60,000
Raw material scrap	150	Discount on preferred stock	30,000
Delivery equipment	19,000	Dividends payable on preferred stock	2,250
Interest accrued on chattel mortgage	250	Prepaid advertising	3,000
Estimated federal taxes payable	20,000	Deferred machinery rearrangement costs	11,500
Prepaid insurance	1,250	Deposits by customers on sales orders	2,000

Required:

Determine the net income for 1972 (the balancing figure for the foregoing) and prepare a classified balance sheet using the following captions:

a) Current assets.
b) Investments and funds.
c) Property, plant, and equipment.
d) Intangibles.
e) Deferred charges.
f) Current liabilties.
g) Deferred credits.
h) Long-term liabilities.
i) Capital.

Par value of all shares of the corporation's stock is $100 per share.

Problem 3–6

The CPA for whom you work received the following letter:

Miles Products Company

Dear Sir:

Our bank has asked us for a statement for credit purposes. Will you please prepare one for us?

Our plants stand at their cost price, which is $60,400. We have taken depreciation of $10,200 on them. There is a $20,000 mortgage on the plant which bears interest at 6% and is paid up to three months ago. We hold $10,000 of notes receivable and have discounted $25,000 of notes receivable with our bank. Our accounts receivable, which we consider good, amount to $18,000, including $3,000 due from one of our employees on personal account. Our trade accounts receivable are subject to 5% discount if paid at due date, and only $1,000 is now past due. In addition to the foregoing accounts we have customers' accounts in suspense amounting to $4,000. These accounts are all over 60 days past due. I believe that these are 50% good. We have ordered a new machine to cost $6,000, but it has not yet been delivered. We have endorsed a note for $6,000 for our friends, the A B Company, but I am confident they will take care of it when it is due. Our accounts payable amount to $4,200. Our insurance amounts to $400 a year and has six months to run. We have a note at the bank for $5,000, interest paid to date. We own 50 shares of stock in the company from which we buy our material. They cost us $2,800 and are surely worth it, though we might have some difficulty selling them in a hurry. Our inventory is taken at a low selling price, which is 10% more than it cost us. The amount is $17,600. Our cash in bank is $4,800, and cash in hand, $200.

Our company was organized five years ago when capital stock of a par value of $50,000 was sold at a premium of 10%. No changes in capital have occurred since that time other than the retention of profits in the business.

I have told you all the facts I think you need. Perhaps some are not required, but I want to give the bankers all the information they ought to have in the way they expect to get it.

I do not, of course, expect you to accept any responsibility for the figures in the statement, but simply to prepare the statement in the best form you can from this letter. If you have any suggestions as to how I can better meet the bank's requirements, let me have them.

(Signed) *H. A. Miles*
PRESIDENT

Required:

Draft the requested statement for review by your employer.

Problem 3–7

The most recent balance sheet of Carter Corporation appears below.

CARTER CORPORATION
Balance Sheet
For the Year Ended December 31, 1971

ASSETS

Current Assets:

Cash	$ 5,000	
Marketable securities	10,000	
Accounts receivable	30,000	
Merchandise inventory	25,000	
Supplies inventory	5,000	
Stock of subsidiary company	17,000	$ 92,000

Investments:

Cash surrender value of life insurance	$20,000	
Treasury stock	25,000	45,000

Tangible Fixed Assets:

Buildings and land	$56,000		
Less: reserve for depreciation	10,000	$46,000	
Equipment	$15,000		
Less: Reserve for depreciation	10,000	5,000	51,000
Total Assets			$188,000

LIABILITIES AND CAPITAL

Current Liabilities:

Accounts payable	$16,900	
Reserve for income taxes	17,000	
Customers' accounts with credit balance	100	$ 34,000

Long-term Liabilities:

Bonds payable	$45,000	45,000
Total Liabilities		$ 79,000

Capital Stock:

Capital stock, par $10	$75,000	
Retained earnings	25,000	
Cash dividends declared	9,000	109,000
Total Liabilities and Capital		$188,000

Required:

List your criticisms, taking note of misclassifications and poor terminology. Where a deficiency is cited, state briefly the proper treatment. Do not concern yourself with arithmetic.

Problem 3–8

When Mattern Corporation was organized January 1, 1972, the authorized stock of 500 shares (par $100) was sold immediately for cash at $110 per share. Six months later the company suffered a severe fire. Only portions of the records were saved.

The company leased its quarters, paying $2,400 rent covering the first year on January 1. All other fixed assets were acquired for cash on this date. Annual depreciation on fixtures amounts to $1,200 and on delivery equipment to $800. Estimated scrap values and estimated lives are, respectively: fixtures, $1,000, and eight years; delivery equipment, $500, and five years.

Purchases through June 30 amounted to $150,000; all but 10% were paid for. Sales amounted to $210,000 and represented an average markup of 50% on cost. Half of the sales were for cash; of those on open account, many were collected within the discount period as evidenced by a $1,200 balance in the Sales Discount account. The credit terms were 2/10, net /30. No receivables have been written off as uncollectible, but an allowance for bad debts of $200 amounting to 2% of uncollected accounts is thought to be adequate.

Aside from other expenses stated or implied, the company has paid $30,000 selling expenses and $20,000 general expenses. Accrued expenses of both types amounted to an additional 10%. The company borrowed $20,000 on May 1 by discounting its own 6%, 90-day note. A 3% dividend was declared May 1 and paid June 1. Insurance expense amounts to $250; all policies were taken out January 1, at which time annual premiums were paid in advance.

Solution Hint: It is suggested you use T-accounts rather than a work sheet. Your Cash account should be submitted as part of your solution; the ending balance should be $69,000.

Required:

Prepare a classified balance sheet as of June 30, 1972, and an income statement covering the six-month period ended that date.

Problem 3–9

The balance sheet shown below, which was submitted to you for review, has been prepared for inclusion in the published annual report of the XYZ Company for the year ended December 31, 1972.

XYZ COMPANY
Balance Sheet
December 31, 1972

ASSETS

Current Assets:

Cash..		$ 1,900,000
Accounts receivable customers $3,900,000		
Less: Reserve for bad debts	50,000	3,850,000
Inventories – at the lower of cost (determined by the first-in, first-out method) or market...		3,500,000
Total Current Assets		$ 9,250,000

Fixed Assets:

Land—at cost		$ 200,000	
Buildings, machinery and equipment, furniture and fixtures—at cost	$4,200,000		
Less: Reserves for depreciation	1,490,000	2,710,000	$ 2,910,000

Deferred Charges and Other Assets:

Cash surrender value of life insurance	$ 15,000	
Unamortized discount on first-mortgage note	42,000	
Prepaid expenses	40,000	97,000
Total Assets		$12,257,000

LIABILITIES

Current Liabilities:

Notes payable to bank—unsecured	$ 750,000
Current maturities of first-mortgage note	600,000
Accounts payable—trade	1,900,000
Reserve for income taxes for the year ended December 31, 1968	700,000
Accrued expenses	550,000
	$ 4,500,000

Funded Debt:

4% first-mortgage note payable in quarterly installments of $150,000	$4,200,000	
Less: Current maturities	600,000	3,600,000

Reserves:

Reserve for damages	$ 50,000	
Reserve for possible future inventory losses	300,000	
Reserve for contingencies	500,000	
Reserve for additional federal income taxes	100,000	950,000

Capital:

Capital stock—authorized, issued and outstanding 100,000 shares of $10 par value	$1,000,000	
Capital surplus	300,000	
Earned surplus	1,907,000	3,207,000
Total Liabilities		$12,257,000

Additional data:

1. Reserve for damages was set up by a charge against current fiscal year's income to cover damages possibly payable by the company as a defendant in a law suit in progress at the balance sheet date. Suit was subsequently compromised for $50,000 prior to issuance of the statement.

2. Reserve for possible future inventory losses was set up in prior years, by action of board of directors, by charges against Earned Surplus. No change occurred in the account during the current fiscal year.

3. Reserve for contingencies was set up by charges against Earned Surplus over a period of several years by the board of directors to provide for a possible future recession in general business conditions.

4. Reserve for federal income taxes was set up in a prior year and relates to additional taxes which the Internal Revenue Service contends the com-

pany owes. The company believes that settlement will be effected for the $100,000 amount set up on the balance sheet.

5. Capital surplus consists of the difference between the par value of $10 per share of capital stock and the price at which the stock was actually issued.

Required:

State what changes in classification or terminology you would advocate in the presentation of this balance sheet to make it conform with generally accepted accounting principles and with present-day terminology. State your reasons for your suggested changes.

The client has requested that the "customary" form of balance sheet be presented so that no consideration should be given to changing the form to such variations of the balance sheet as a statement of financial position, financial condition, etc.   (AICPA adapted)

Problem 3–10

A common means of analyzing a company from a financial viewpoint is to make use of comparative financial statements, i.e., to study its statements for two or more recent successive fiscal periods. Although this topic is not covered in depth until Chapter 26 of this textbook, your prior study of elementary accounting has probably given you some exposure to the subject. Even without such specific exposure it is likely that by now you have developed some feel for certain accounting relationships and trends as would be manifested in successive balance sheets.

Required:

1. Briefly discuss wherein comparative balance sheets are likely to be superior to a single (most recent) balance sheet as a financial indicator.

2. "Even comparative balance sheets have limitations or may be misleading." Indicate wherein this statement may be true.

3. Some of the figures on a balance sheet, as of the time it is dated, can be said to reflect "current dollars or values" whereas others distinctly do not. Which items are likely to be current?   (AICPA adapted)

	The Reporting Process—
	The Income and
chapter **4**	Retained Earnings
	Statements

Purpose of the Income Statement

Income is measured by matching costs consumed or expired against revenues realized. The purpose of the income statement is to report the results of the accounting process of matching the revenue of a specified period with the costs reasonably assignable to that revenue thus deriving the net results (net income) of the business activities for the period. Income has been defined by the Supreme Court as "the gain derived from capital, from labor, or from both combined, provided it be understood to include profit gained through a sale or conversion of capital assets. . . ."[1] Income is evidenced by an increment in the assets of the business (or other accountable unit) not resulting from external contributions or investment. If income is to be correctly recognized, the measurement of the increment must be in accordance with accounting principles and procedures developed and accepted by the accounting profession. These principles and procedures were discussed in general terms in Chapter 1 and are discussed in detail throughout this text.

---

[1] *Eisner v. Macomber*, 252 U.S. 189.

Varying titles for the income statement are used. Such titles as statement of "operations," "profit and loss," "income and expense," and "earnings" are in use. However, in line with the recommendation of the Committee on Terminology of the AICPA,[2] most published statements of operations by profit-making units now use the key word *income* in describing this important financial report.

Form of the Income Statement

Numerous variations of the income statement may be observed in practice. The principal formats are referred to as the multiple-step form and the single-step form. These are illustrated respectively in Illustrations 4–1 and 4–3. It is not uncommon for the main portion of each form to be followed by a separate last section presenting various nonrecurring items.

The income statement frequently is combined with a presentation detailing changes in retained earnings for the same period. This latter practice has increased in popularity, at least among larger corporations. There does not appear to be any particular pattern relating use of the single-step form to combining the income statement with the retained earnings statement. In other words some users of the single-step form combine the income and retained earnings statements while others issue separate statements. The same can be said for users of the multiple-step form.[3] A combined comparative operations and retained earnings statement for Caterpillar Tractor Co. is shown in Illustration 4–4.

The format and detail should be determined primarily by the purpose for which the statement is prepared. Ths users of financial and operating statements may be divided into three principal classes: (1) those directly concerned with the management of the business; (2) outsiders such as stockholders, creditors, and the general public; and (3) government agencies such as public-utility commissions, the Securities and Exchange Commission, and the Internal Revenue Service. Statements prepared for the management necessarily contain or are supported by considerable detail. Statements prepared

---

[2] Committee on Terminology, AICPA, "Review and Resumé," Accounting Terminology Bulletin No. I, (New York, 1961), p. 14. The 1969 edition of *Accounting Trends and Techniques* revealed that 383 of the 600 companies reported upon used the key word *income;* 183 used *earnings;* 18 used *operations* and 6 used other terminology.

[3] A definite preference for the single-step form is revealed in *Accounting Trends and Techniques:*

	1969	1968	1967	1965	1955
Single-step form	400	410	396	366	268
Multiple-step form	200	190	204	234	330
No income statement	—	—	—	—	2
Total	600	600	600	600	600

for outsiders are usually somewhat more condensed, emphasizing somewhat broader aspects of operations and the results thereof. Statements prepared for governmental units vary with the requirements of such agencies.

The income statement of a manufacturing concern varies from that of a trading concern only in the manner in which cost of goods sold is reported. In a trading concern the goods are purchased ready for sale, but in the manufacturing concern the goods for sale are manufactured. In the latter case "purchases" is replaced by the "cost of goods manufactured," and a statement of cost of goods manufactured is prepared as a supporting schedule to the income statement. If the Melon Company manufactured the goods sold, the cost of goods sold section of the income statement in Illustration 4–1 would appear as follows:

Cost of Goods Sold for Manufacturing Firm
Finished goods inventory, January 1, 1972 .... $152,000
Cost of goods manufactured (see Schedule –) 365,500
    Total Cost of Goods Available for Sale $517,500
  Less: Finished goods inventory, December 31, 1972 159,500
    Cost of Goods Sold $358,000

The schedule of the cost of goods manufactured reports the detail of the costs of production. Such a schedule might appear as shown in Illustration 4–2.

Variations in Classification

On the *multiple-step* income statement (as shown for the Melon Company in Illustration 4–1), costs and expenses often are classified according to the major *functions* of the business. For most items no special problems of classifications arise, but some items such as bad debt expense require special consideration. Some of the special items commonly encountered are discussed below.

Freight-Out. Freight on sales paid by the vendor and not charged to the customer is properly classified as a selling expense on the same basis that delivery expenses are so classified. If, however, the regular selling price is increased by the amount of the freight on particular sales, then the freight charges to be paid to the carrier (and charged to freight-out) should be reported as a deduction from sales on the income statement, otherwise the net sales figure would be overstated.

Bad Debts. Little uniformity is found on income statements with respect to classification of bad debt expense. This item is variously listed as a selling, administrative, or financial expense. The circumstances in a given situation may indicate that any one of these classifications is correct. The determining factor in the classification of this item is the organizational position of the department or office having

Illustration 4-1
Multiple-Step Income Statement
THE MELON COMPANY
Income Statement
For Year Ended December 31, 1972

Revenue:			
Gross sales			$600,000
Less: Sales returns and allowances		$ 11,100	
Sales discounts		7,500	18,600
Net sales			$581,400
Costs and expenses:			
Cost of goods sold:			
Merchandise inventory, January 1, 1972		$152,000	
Add: Merchandise purchases	$376,500		
Freight-in	1,200		
Cost of purchases	$377,700		
Less: Purchases returns and allowances	$8,200		
Purchase discounts	4,000	12,200	365,500
Total Goods Available for Sale		$517,500	
Deduct: Merchandise inventory December 31, 1972		159,500	
Cost of goods sold			358,000
Gross margin on sales			$223,400
Operating expenses:			
Selling expenses:			
Advertising	$ 32,000		
Salaries	35,000		
Commissions	31,000		
Freight-out	3,000		
Insurance on inventory	1,000		
Other selling expenses	8.000	$110,000	
General and administrative expenses:			
Office expenses	$ 4,800		
Office payroll	32,100		
Depreciation of office equipment	1,100		
Rent	2,000		
Bad debt expense	3,000	43,000	153,000
Income from operations			$ 70,400
Deduct:			
Other expenses:			
Bond interest expense	$ 4,200		
Interest on notes payable	720	$ 4,920	
Other incomes:			
Interest income	$ 860		
Dividend income	450	1.310	3,610
Net income before income taxes			$ 66,790
Less: Provision for income taxes			25,916
Net Income for the Year			$ 40,874

supervision over the granting of credit and the collection of accounts. If the credit and collection function is under the sales department, bad debt expense should be classified as a selling expense. Since credit and collection is frequently a responsibility of general administration, bad debt expense is generally reported under the general administrative expense caption.

Illustration 4–2
Manufacturing Schedule
THE MELON COMPANY
Cost of Goods Manufactured
For Year Ended December 31, 1972

Raw material:			
Inventory, January 1, 1972		$ 28,000	
Purchases	$196,400		
Less: Returned purchases	800	195,600	
Freight-in		900	
Material available for issue		$224,500	
Inventory, December 31, 1972		31,000	
Cost of material consumed			$193,500
Direct labor			106,200
Manufacturing expenses:			
Depreciation—buildings		$ 2,200	
Depreciation—machinery		15,100	
Fuel		20,900	
Insurance—buildings and machinery		480	
Indirect labor		16,100	
Repairs—buildings		1,920	
Repairs—machinery		2,800	
Taxes—plant and equipment		1,600	
			61,100
Goods in process:			
Inventory, January 1, 1972		$ 26,800	
Inventory, December 31, 1972		22,100	
Decrease			4,700
Cost of Goods Manufactured			$365,500

Packaging Supplies. Cartons, packages, cans, boxes, and other nonreturnable containers are considered manufacturing costs if the merchandise is packed in the factory and delivered to the warehouse and to the customer in the original package. When, however, goods are normally delivered from the factory in bulk to be sold in varying weights and quantities, the cost of packing and wrapping should be reported as a selling expense.

Depreciation. Operating statements prepared for internal use should identify depreciation with the particular division of the organization making use of the property depreciated. *Opinion No. 12,* issued in December 1967 by the AICPA's Accounting Principles Board, indicates that published statements or their accompanying notes should disclose separately the depreciation expense for the period.

Taxes. Taxes on property should be prorated to the functions of the business utilizing the assets on the basis of the cost of the property. Social security taxes should be allocated to the respective departments or functions where the related salaries or wages were incurred. Excise or revenue taxes imposed on the manufacture of goods is a manufacturing cost. Likewise, severance tax on natural resources should be shown as a cost of the extracted commodity. Revenue and excise taxes based on quantity or amount of sales, when paid by the vendor are selling expenses. Until recent years income taxes were not considered as a proper expense charge on the income statement. This view is no longer held. Income taxes should be shown in full on the income statement as an expense, although the difficulty of classification does not permit its assignment to one or more of the operating cost and expense classifications shown on the statement. Income taxes on operating income may be reported either as "other expenses and deductions" or as a separate item before "net income." Frequently the terminology "net income before income taxes" is used so as to emphasize the significance of tax expense.

In addition to the problem of reporting of controversial items, the accountant must also face the problem of apportionment or allocation of certain expenses, Although items such as depreciation, insurance, and taxes usually can be logically allocated to the functions of manufacturing, selling, and administrative, in actual practice the accountant is frequently confronted with items recorded in accounts descriptive of the expense but not identified as to function to which they pertain. It becomes the task of the accountant in such instances to determine a logical basis for reporting. If, as is sometimes the case, no logical basis for allocation is apparent, then the only alternative is to classify the item under the grouping to which the major portion of the expense ordinarily would apply.

Purchase Discounts. Several variations in reporting cash discount on purchases may be observed in actual practice. Some statements report purchase discounts on the income statement as an "other income"; others show this item as a deduction from purchases. Theoretically, purchase discounts should be reported as a direct deduction from the cost of the items purchased. No income can be earned by simply purchasing goods and paying for them, yet the other income method gives this effect.

The true nature of purchase discounts as a deduction from invoice price to secure cost is recognized by many companies at the time purchases are entered on the books. These companies debit Purchases and credit Accounts Payable with invoice price less *allowable* cash discounts. The item "purchase discounts" never shows on the books and statements. If the invoice is not paid in time to obtain the discount, the entry for payment is a credit to Cash with debits to Accounts Payable and Purchase Discounts Lost.[4] The latter ac-

---

[4] Theoretically correct accounting also would require an adjusting entry for "Estimated Liability for Purchase Discounts Lost" on unpaid accounts still within the discount period when the financial statements are prepared. The adjusting entry would

count records the cost of penalty for late payments. Purchase discounts lost should be classified as "other expense," since it is similar to interest expense.

In the maintenance of perpetual inventories it is often inexpedient to adjust the unit prices on the purchase invoice for the amount of the anticipated cash discount. In these cases no serious objection is raised to showing the item as an "other income" purely for practical reasons. However, the inventory reported at the end of the period should be reduced by the amount of discount contained therein if that amount is material. An extended discussion of purchase discounts may be found in Chapter 8.

Appropriation Section

Sometimes an appropriation section is added to the income statement, thus permitting a clear picture of what disposition was made of the net income. The following form is indicative of the procedure:

```
Net income for period .............................................    $......
Appropriations:
    Annual sinking fund provision................................$......
    Dividends on preferred stock ..................................  ......    ......
Net income added to retained earnings .......................
```

Single-Step versus Multiple-Step Income Statement

The single-step income statement is a simplified form of statement devoid of all classification except that of separating revenue and income on the one hand from costs, expenses, and other deductions on the other. The multiple-step statement (Illustration 4–1) provides a classification which will at least show sales revenue, cost of goods sold, resulting gross margin, operating expenses, other income and expenses, and final net income. The preceding illustration (4–1) of the report form statement is also an example of the multiple-step statement. Illustration 4–3 is a single-step form of income statement commonly found in annual reports to stockholders.

One principal reason for use of the single-step income statement is that it treats all costs and expenses alike as deductions from revenue. It does not first deduct cost of goods sold from revenue, then operating expenses, and last, other expenses as does the multiple-step income statement. It does not recognize any "profit" at intermediate stages, such as "gross margin" or "net income before taxes," both of which are commonly set forth in the multiple-step statement. And all revenue including miscellaneous incomes, such as interest, rents, divi-

---

involve a debit to Purchase Discounts Lost and a credit to "Estimated Liability for Purchase Discounts Lost"; the entry should be reversed at the beginning of the next period.

Illustration 4–3
Single-Step Income Statement
THE STANDARD CORPORATION
Statement of Income
For Year Ended December 31, 1972

Revenue:

Sales less allowance and discounts $312,440		$6,540,000
Dividends, interest, and other incomes		106,300
Total Revenue		$6,646,300
Costs and Expenses:		
Cost of goods sold	$3,900,000	
Selling expenses	1,010,700	
General and administrative expenses	407,600	
Depreciation	133,500	
Interest on bonds payable	64,000	
Federal taxes on income	587,200	
Total Costs and Expenses		6,103,000
Net Income		$ 543,300

Earnings per share $1.62 based on average number of shares outstanding for the year of 335,400.

dends, and royalties, are grouped in the operating picture on the single-step statement so as to appear to bear a part of the expense burden. On the multiple-step statement these incomes appear to be somewhat fortuitous, earned at no expense to the company.

Another apparent reason for the growth in use of the single-step

Illustration 4–4
CATERPILLAR TRACTOR COMPANY
Consolidated Results of Operations (in millions of dollars)

	1969	1968
Sales	$2,001.6	$1,707.1
Costs:		
Inventories brought forward from previous year	$ 488.8	$ 462.0
Materials, supplies, services purchased, etc.	1,068.2	845.6
Wages, salaries, and contributions for employee benefits	652.9	571.6
Depreciation (portion of original cost of buildings, machinery, and equipment allocated to operations)	95.9	82.2
Interest on borrowed funds	26.6	23.0
U.S. and foreign income taxes	126.7	90.5
	$2,459.1	$2,074.9
Deduct: inventories carried forward to following year	599.0	488.8
Costs allocated to year°	$1,860.1	$1,586.1
	$ 141.5	$ 121.0
Profit of subsidiary credit companies	1.0	.6
Profit for year—consolidated (per share:† 1969—$2.51; 1968—$2.14)	$ 142.5	$ 121.6
Profit employed in the business at beginning of year	689.2	635.7
	$ 831.7	$ 757.3
Dividends paid in cash during year—$1.20 per share	68.3	68.1
Profit employed in the business at end of year	$ 763.4	$ 689.2

° Includes cost of goods sold: 1969—$1,531.0; 1968—$1,330.3
† Computed on weighted average number of shares outstanding.

form is that it tends to be compact and relatively uncluttered. It has become fairly common practice, especially on single-step form statements, to set out costs and expenses largely on an *object* (nature) classification rather than on a *function* (purpose) classification basis. As an example, note in Illustration 4–4, the comparative (consolidated) operations statements of Caterpillar Tractor Company for 1968 and 1969, all costs are set out on an object basis. In other words, the nature of each cost rather than whether it accomplished production, selling, delivery, administration, or some other function is indicated. At the bottom of the statement labor, materials, depreciation, and other overhead elements which combined to comprise "cost of goods sold" are recombined and set out as single totals (hence functionally). Certain notes accompanied the statement in the 1969 annual report of Caterpillar but they are not germane to this discussion and are not reproduced here.

Concepts of Reporting Income

For a number of years two somewhat different concepts of income reporting have been prominent in both accounting practice and literature. Usually they are referred to as the *current operating performance concept* and the *all-inclusive concept.*[5] They differed in that certain items which would appear on the retained earnings statement rather than on the income statement under the current operating performance concept would be reported on the income statement under all-inclusive concept. These items were principally material extraordinary or nonrecurring gains and losses and corrections of the net income of prior periods. It is generally correct to say that historically recommendations of AICPA committees favored use of current operating performance concept while those of the AAA's committees leaned to the all-inclusive concept.

With the issuance of *Opinion No. 9* in December 1966, the Accounting Principles Board reversed the AICPA's long-held stand against the all-inclusive concept. The opinion made an exception in the case of *prior period adjustments* (which were carefully defined); aside from these, all items of gain or loss recognized during a period should be reported on the income statement. The opinion states that *extraordinary items* should be segregated on the income statement unless their effects are immaterial. The one topic on which the board was less than perfectly clear in its opinion was the matter of how to deal with certain accounting changes. *APB Opinion 20* on accounting changes has just been issued (see Chapter 24).

Some significant excerpts from the board's opinion follow.

---

[5] Some synonyms for *current operating performance* include "earning power" and for *all-inclusive* include "clean surplus" and "historical."

1. The fundamental viewpoint:

Net income should reflect all items of profit and loss recognized during the period with the sole exception of the prior period adjustments described below. *Extraordinary items* should, however, be segregated from the results of ordinary operations and shown separately in the income statement, with disclosure of the nature and amounts thereof. The criteria for determination of extraordinary items are described . . . below.[6]

2. Financial statement form:

Under this approach, the income statement should disclose the following elements:

Income before extraordinary items
Extraordinary items
   (less applicable income tax)
Net income

3. Extraordinary items related to current period defined:

Such events and transactions are identified primarily by the nature of the underlying occurrence. They will be of a character significantly different from the typical or customary business activities of the entity. Accordingly, they will be events and transactions of material effect which would not be expected to recur frequently and which would not be considered as recurring factors in any evaluation of the ordinary operating processes of the business.

4. Criteria for prior period adjustments:

Adjustments related to prior periods—and thus excluded in the determination of net income for the current period—are limited to those material adjustments which (a) can be specifically identified with and directly related to the business activities of particular prior periods, and (b) are not attributed to economic events occurring subsequent to the date of the financial statements for prior period, and (c) depend primarily on determinations by persons other than management and (d) were not susceptible of reasonable estimation prior to such determination. Such adjustments are rare in modern financial accounting.

Some elaboration on the fundamental position expressed above is in order. Examples of items to be reported on the income statement as extraordinary items include material (i.e., relatively consequential in terms of amount) gains or losses from (a) sale or abandonment of a plant or major segment of the business, (b) sale of an investment not acquired for resale, (c) write-off of goodwill or other intangibles due to unusual events or developments within the period, (d) property condemnation or expropriation, and (e) major devaluation of a foreign

---

[6] This quotation and those immediately following are rearranged to facilitate presentation, but are taken from AICPA, *Opinion of the Accounting Principles Board No. 9* (New York, 1966).

currency. Examples of gains or losses (or provisions therefor) which, regardless of size, constitute neither extraordinary items nor prior period adjustments (therefore are operating items in the income statement) include (*a*) write-downs of receivables, inventories, and research and development costs; (*b*) adjustments of accrued contract prices; and (*c*) gains or losses from ordinary foreign exchange fluctuations.

Examples of prior period adjustments (to be reported on the statement of retained earnings), which it is repeated are rare, include material, nonrecurring adjustments or settlements of income taxes, of renegotiation proceedings, or of public-utility revenue under rate regulation. Settlements of significant amounts resulting from litigation or similar claims may also constitute prior period adjustments. On the other hand, treatment as prior period adjustments should *not* be applied to normal, recurring corrections and adjustments which are the natural result of the use of commonplace accounting estimates. Thus, changes in the estimated remaining lives of fixed assets affect the computed amounts of depreciation, but such changes should be viewed as prospective in nature rather than as prior period adjustments. Similarly, immaterial adjustments of provisions for liabilities (such as for taxes) made in prior periods should be considered recurring items to be reflected in current period operations. Other uncertainties which would *not* qualify for prior period adjustment treatment include those relating to collectibility of receivables, ultimate recovery of deferred costs, or realizability of inventories or other assets. Such items fail to qualify as prior period adjustments because *current* economic events (i.e., subsequent to the period in which they were initially recognized) enter into a determination of their most recent status or values.

Accounting Changes

Accounting changes are discussed in detail in Chapter 24; however, it is necessary at this point to take some cognizance of them. Accounting changes involve four distinctly different types of situations; and each requires a different approach to resolution. The four types of accounting changes are:

1. Accounting errors. The use of inappropriate accounting principles (including procedures) and unsupportable estimates, outright mathematical mistakes, oversights, and failure to properly reflect the economic essence of a transaction all constitute accounting errors.

2. Changes in estimates. The use of estimates (such as in determining depreciation or bad debt expense) is a natural consequence of the accounting process. From time to time, experience and additional information make it possible for estimates to be improved. For example, a fixed asset, after having been used (and depreciated) for 6

years, may realistically be changed from the original 10-year estimated life to a 15-year estimated life. Changes of this type are referred
to as "changes in estimates" and are to be distinguished from an error
or change in accounting principle.

3. Changes in accounting principle. Because of a change in circumstances, or the development of a new accounting principle, a change
in the record-keeping and financial reporting approach to one or more
types of transactions may be desirable or necessary. For example, a
change in circumstances may make it desirable, from the accounting
point of view, to change from expensing research and development
costs to capitalizing them. This would be a change in accounting principle, that is, a change from one acceptable principle to another acceptable principle.

4. Change in the accounting entity.

Now let's review briefly the accounting and reporting approach
that is appropriate for each of these accounting changes. You should
observe in this brief discussion that each type of accounting change
calls for a different approach to accommodate it appropriately.

Treatment of Accounting Errors. Clearly, when an error in the
accounting process is identified it should be corrected immediately
in such a way as to reflect what the results would have been had the
error not been committed. Thus, when an error is found that was
committed in the *current year,* the accounts (and related schedules)
should be corrected prior to preparation of the current financial
reports. This normally can be best effected by reversing the incorrect
entry and reentering the transaction correctly. Not infrequently an
error is located during the current period that was committed during
some *prior* period. In this situation a *correcting entry* usually is
required which places in the *real* (balance sheet) accounts the correct
balance and provides for entering for the current period the correct
amount in the nominal accounts affected. Frequently correcting
entries of this type require recognition of a *prior period adjustment*
to retained earnings. To illustrate, assume a machine that cost $10,000
(10-year estimated life and no residual value) when purchased on
January 1, 19A was incorrectly debited to an expense account. The
error was discovered near the end of 19D; the correcting entry would
be:

Asset—Machinery	10,000	
Depreciation Expense (for 19D)	1,000	
Accumulated Depreciation (four years)		4,000
Correction—Prior Period Adjustment		7,000

Any financial statements for the four-year period presented after
discovery of the error must be corrected. The approach described for
the correction of previously reported amounts is frequently referred
to as *retroactive adjustment.*

Treatment of Changes in Estimates. Changes of this type are made on a *prospective basis;* that is, the effect of *prior* accountings are not disturbed.[7] The change is made so that the new estimate is reflected only in the *current and future* financial statements and entries. To illustrate, assume a building that cost $162,000 (no residual value) has been depreciated for 6 years on the basis of a 10-year life (straight line); in the 7th year, on a realistic basis, the estimated life is revised to 15 years (i.e., 9 years of remaining life). Since this is a change in estimate no correcting entry is required; instead the depreciation for the seventh (and each remaining year of life) would be recorded as follows:

Depreciation Expense−Building° 7,200
    Accumulated Depreciation−Building   7,200

° Computations:
  Original cost..$162,000
  Depreciation to date ($162,000 × 6/10).............................   97,200
  To be depreciated over remaining life...$ 64,800

Annual depreciation under new estimate: $64,800 ÷ 9 years = $7,200

Treatment of Changes in Accounting Principles. This type of change is somewhat more complex than the others. Briefly stated, when a change in accounting *principle* is made, the accounts for the current period must be restated on the basis of what they would have been had the newly adopted principle been in effect from the beginning. This usually necessitates a correcting entry which will include a "catch-up" adjustment recorded and reported as an *extraordinary item* on the income statement for the current period. To illustrate, assume research and development costs have been expensed in the past and it is decided, starting with 19X to capitalize them followed by amortizing them over 10 years. Assume that at the end of 19X, prior to amortization, an analysis shows that prior and current costs of $60,000 should have been capitalized. The related entries would be:

To correct accounts for change in accounting principle:

Deferred Research and Development Costs...........................60,000
    Extraordinary Item−Change in Accounting Principle........   60,000

To record amortization for current year, 19X:

Research and Development Costs Amortized.......................... 6,000
    Deferred Research and Development Costs........................   6,000

The extraordinary item would be reported on the income statement for 19X and an appropriate footnote would be required in respect to

---

[7] AICPA, Accounting Principles Board, *Opinions 9 and 20.* (New York, 1966 and 1971).

the change in accounting principle in order to meet the requirements of full disclosure.[8]

Intraperiod (or Interstatement) Income Tax Allocation

Because of their amount, income taxes paid by corporations have come to be viewed as an expense of doing business (as opposed to a distribution of profits) by the accounting profession and by industry. Proper reporting of net income and certain other amounts on the financial statements, as well as full-disclosure requirements, have given rise to comprehensive tax allocation procedures of two types:

1. Interperiod. The allocation of income tax expense between *periods* due to the fact that some items of revenue, or expense, appear on the periodic financial statement either before or after they are permitted on the income tax return. This phase of income tax allocation is discussed in Chapter 23.

2. Intraperiod or interstatement. The allocation of income tax expense between *statements;* discussed below and elaborated on in Chapter 23.

Intraperiod (or interstatement) income tax allocation is the process of assigning total income tax expense for the period to the income statement, the statement of retained earnings, and the balance sheet to the extent that items thereon gave rise to tax consequences. *APB Opinion 11* states:[9]

The need for tax allocation within a period arises because items included in the determination of taxable income may be presented for accounting purposes as (*a*) extraordinary items, (*b*) adjustments of prior periods (or of the opening balance of retained earnings) or (*c*) as direct entries to other stockholders' accounts.

The underlying concept of interstatement tax allocation is that the tax consequences should follow the item that gave rise to it on the financial statements. Thus, total income tax expense for the period must be allocated to (1) income before extraordinary items, (2) extraordinary items, (3) prior period adjustments (retained earnings), and (4) direct entries to other stockholders' accounts to the extent that there are items in each category that affected total income tax expense for the period. Clearly, in most cases income tax expense for the period will be directly related to the first two categories — income before extraordinary items and extraordinary items. Seldom do the last two categories (prior period adjustments and other owners' equity accounts) affect income taxes.

---

[8] AICPA, "Accounting Changes," *APB Opinion 20* (New York, July, 1971) see Chapter 24 for a detailed discussion of accounting changes.

[9] AICPA, "Accounting for Income Taxes," *Accounting Principles Board Opinion 11,* (New York, 1967).

Intraperiod allocation of income tax expense is complicated by the fact that there are differential income tax rates. In the recent past, and for 1971 at least, corporation tax rates are 22% on the first $25,000 of net income before taxes and 48% on all income above $25,000. In addition, long-term capital gains generally are taxed at the 25% rate. There are numerous other special provisions that affect the amount of income taxes payable in a particular year; however, these are sufficient for purposes of this discussion. For purposes of simplicity in illustrations and assignment material throughout this book we will frequently utilize a flat rate such as 40%.

The latest pronouncement of the AICPA on income tax allocation was *APB Opinion 11* (December 1967). In respect to *intraperiod* tax allocation that Opinion specifies the approach as follows:

The income tax expense attributable to income before extraordinary items is computed by determining the income tax expense related to revenue and expense transactions entering into the determination of such income, without giving effect to the tax consequences of the items excluded from the determination of income before extraordinary items. The income tax expense attributable to other items is determined by the tax consequences of transactions involving these items. If an operating loss exists before extraordinary items, the tax consequences of such loss should be associated with the loss.

Interstatement income tax allocation is not complex or controversial. Illustrations 4–5, 4–6, and 4–7 are presented to reflect the appli-

Illustration 4–5
Intraperiod Tax Allocation – with Extraordinary Gain

Situation
A Corporation accounts for the period reflected the following:
1) Income before income taxes and before extraordinary items, $100,000
2) Gain on sale of plant, $40,000
3) Income tax expense, $51,500°

A CORPORATION
Partial Income Statement

Income before income taxes and extraordinary items		$100,000
Less: Applicable income taxes		41,500
Income before extraordinary items		58,500
Extraordinary items:		
Gain on sale of plant	$40,000	
Less: Applicable income tax	10,000	
Extraordinary gain, net of applicable income tax		30,000
Net income		$ 88,500

° Computation of tax allocation

Tax on ordinary income		
$25,000 × 22% = $ 5,500		
$75,000 × 48% = 36,000	$41,500	
Tax on extraordinary item		
$40,000 × 25% =	10,000	
Total income tax allocated	$51,500	

Illustration 4–6
Intraperiod Tax Allocation — with Extraordinary Loss

Situation

B Corporation accounts for the period reflected the following:
  1) Income before income taxes and before extraordinary items, $100,000
  2) Loss on sale of plant, $40,000
  3) Income tax expense, $22,300°

B CORPORATION
Partial Income Statement

Income before income taxes and extraordinary items	$100,000
Less: Applicable income taxes..	41,500
Income before extraordinary items..	$ 58,500
Extraordinary items:	
Loss on sale of plant...$40,000	
Less: Applicable tax reduction............................. 19,200	
Extraordinary loss, net of applicable income tax	(20,800)
Net income	$37,700

° Computation of tax allocation

Tax on ordinary income		
$25,000 × 22% = $ 5,500		
$75,000 × 48% = 36,000	$41,500	
Tax Saving on extraordinary loss		
$40,000 × 48% =	(19,200)	
Total income tax allocated	$22,300	

cation of interstatement allocation. Note on each illustration that the total income tax for the period is simply allocated to each of the four categories (listed above) so that the tax consequence follows the item that gives rise to the tax effect. You should particularly be aware in each illustration of the several amounts that would be incorrectly reported without intraperiod allocation of income tax expense. For example, in Illustration 4–7, if one were to report total tax expense ($118,300) as a direct reduction from pretax income ($100,000) at least four amounts would be misstated: income before extraordinary items, net extraordinary loss, net income, and restated balance of retained earnings.

Another method of computing the interstatement tax allocation that has been widely used is based on an "average" tax rate for the period. Essentially this method involves computation of the average tax rate for the period then allocating income taxes to each classification on a proportional basis by utilizing this average. Since the issuance of *APB Opionion 11* in 1967 the averaging method has been utilized much less.

The other, and more complex, aspect of tax allocation, known as *interperiod* tax allocation, involves the allocation of income taxes between the current and future *periods*. It arises when there is a *timing difference* (lag) between the reporting of certain revenues and

Illustration 4–7
Intraperiod Tax Allocation—Retained Earnings Affected

Situation

C Corporation records for the period reflected the following:
1) Income before income taxes and before extraordinary items, $100,000
2) Loss of sale of plant, $40,000
3) Income tax expense, $118,300°
4) Claim for damages settled and collected (lawsuit), $200,000
5) Balance retained earnings, beginning of period, $140,000
6) Dividends paid during year, $20,000

C CORPORATION
Partial Income Statement

Income before income taxes and extraordinary items..................		$100,000
Less: Applicable income tax reduction.................................		41,500
Income before extraordinary items		$ 58,500
Extraordinary items:		
Loss on sale of plant..	$ 40,000	
Less: Applicable income tax reduction.............................	19,200	
Extraordinary loss, net of applicable income tax....................		(20,800)
Net income...		$ 37,700

C CORPORATION
Statement of Retained Earnings

Retained earnings at beginning of period:		
As previously reported..		$140,000
Add: Damages collected (lawsuit settled)............................	$200,000	
Less: Applicable income tax	96,000	104,000
Beginning balance restated...		244,000
Add: Net income for period...		37,700
		281,700
Deduct: Dividends paid during period		20,000
Retained earnings, end of period..		$261,700

° Computation of tax allocation

Tax on ordinary loss		
$25,000 × 22% = $ 5,500		
$75,000 × 48% = 36,000	$41,500	
Tax saving on extraordinary item		
$40,000 × 48% =	(19,200)	
Tax on retained earnings item		
$200,000 × 48% =	96,000	
Total taxes allocated	$118,300	

expenses on the periodic financial statement before or after they are reported on the income tax return. Accrual accounting suggests that the tax effect of these timing differences should be recorded in the accounts and reported on the financial statements. To illustrate, assume a $5,000 gross profit on an installment sale, made in 19A, was recorded in the books and reported on the financial statement in year 19A; however, tax regulations permit recognition of such profit only in the year collected, say in 19B. Therefore, at the end of 19A, assuming a 40% rate, the following tax allocation entry must be made to recognize the deferred income taxes:

Income Tax Expense – 19A ($5,000 × 40%)..............................2,000
    Deferred Income Taxes (liability)..   2,000

Clearly, at the end of 19B the following related entry would be made to reflect payment of the deferred tax liability:

Deferred Income Taxes (liability)..2,000
    Cash (payment of taxes)...   2,000

The purpose of *interperiod* tax allocation is to reflect on the period financial statement the amount of income tax expense related, on an accrual basis, to the items appearing on the statement rather than the specific amount of income taxes payable for that period as reflected on the income tax return. Clearly, it is a quite different concept than interstatement tax allocation discussed above.[10]

The Retained Earnings Statement

The retained earnings statement reports separately each major category of changes in retained earnings during a fiscal period. If a portion of retained earnings has been appropriated (i.e., made unavailable for dividends), the retained earnings statement may well consist of two major segments — one reporting changes in unappropriated or "free" retained earnings, the other showing changes in the one or more appropriated portions of retained earnings. For example if $10,000 is added during the year to a Reserve for Plant Expansion, in the unappropriated section of the statement the $10,000 is reported as a decrease in unappropriated retained earnings, while in the appropriated section it would be shown as a $10,000 addition to Reserve for Plant Expansion (also known as Retained Earnings Appropriated for Plant Expansion). Sometimes the retained earnings statement is referred to as a reconciliation; it begins with the start-of-the-period balance of retained earnings and ends with the end-of-the-period balance. Basically the statement explains the change from the initial balance to the ending one and thus reconciles the two or accounts for the changes in them.

Under the concept of reporting advocated by the Accounting Principles Board and described and illustrated on pages 136 and 145, the principal increases in unappropriated retained earnings would result from net income, from transfers back to unappropriated retained earnings of amounts previously appropriated, and from prior period adjustments which resulted in an increase in net assets or a decrease

---

[10] Interstatement allocation procedures involve both timing and permanent tax differences, whereas interperiod tax allocation is limited strictly to timing tax differences; see Chapter 23.

in liabilities without a corresponding change in other assets or liabilities. The principal decreases in unappropriated retained earnings would result from net losses, from dividend declarations, from prior period adjustments opposite to those described above, from transfers to appropriated retained earnings accounts, and from certain types of capital transactions described in Chapters 12 and 20.[11] The latest edition of *Accounting Trends and Techniques* reveals that 80% of the corporations included in that study which paid cash dividends reported the amount of dividends per share in their retained earnings statements and that 60% of the companies paying preferred dividends disclosed the per share amounts.

There has been a trend, among larger companies at least, toward preparing combined income and retained earnings statements, but separate retained earnings statements are still quite common in published annual reports. An example of a typical retained earnings statement is shown in Illustration 4–8.

Illustration 4–8
THE MASSEY CORPORATION
Statement of Retained Earnings
For Year Ended, December 31, 1971

Retained Earnings Appropriated:		
Balance reserve for bond sinking fund, January 1, 1971	$ 50,000	
Appropriation for current year.....................................	25,000	
Total Appropriated Balance, December 31, 1971...		$ 75,000
Retained Earnings Unappropriated:		
Balance, January 1, 1971	$162,800	
Add: Net income for year per income statement.........	80,000	
	$242,800	
Less: Appropriation to bond sinking fund reserve $25,000		
Dividends declared $1.60 per share......................... 32,000	57,000	
Total Unappropriated Balance, December 31, 1971		185,800
Total Appropriated and Unappropriated Balance Retained Earnings, December 31, 1971......		$260,800

Combined Income and Retained Earnings Statement

When the income and retained earnings statements are combined (as has been done on an increasing scale in practice), some economies of space required for the presentation are achieved. With only a slight modification of the title of the income statement, its heading will serve for both since obviously the name of the entity and the period or periods involved are common to both the income statement and retained earnings data. Another space-saving technique is to use the last figure on the income statement—net income—as the first

---

[11] These would include purchase of treasury stock at a higher price per share than realized when it was originally issued, quasi-reorganizations, and a few other types of transactions which generally occur rather rarely.

element of the retained earnings portion of the combined statement. To the net income is added the beginning balance of retained earnings and any other additions. From the total of these elements, dividends and any other reductions during the period are subtracted; the statement concludes with the retained earnings balance at the end of the period. This approach is demonstrated in Illustration 4–4.

Computation and Reporting of Earnings per Share

Reporting of earnings per share on outstanding *common stock* has long been a commonplace practice, not only on financial statements but in many other types of releases directed to the financial community. The practice has grown and, for accountants, has undergone a rapid recent evolution which has now proceeded to the point that reporting earnings per share on the face of the income statement, on which the accountant is expressing his professional opinion, is mandatory.

Historically, reporting earnings per share on statements appearing in annual reports was optional prior to the issuance of *APB Opinion 9* in December 1966. In that Opinion the Accounting Principles Board stated "that earnings per share data are most useful when furnished in conjunction with a statement of income. Accordingly, the Board *strongly recommends* that earnings per share be disclosed in the statement of income. It is the Board's opinion that the reporting of per share data should disclose amounts for (*a*) income before extraordinary items, (*b*) extraordinary items, if any (less applicable income tax), and (*c*) net income—the total of (*a*) and (*b*)."[12] *APB Opinion 15* issued in May 1969 changed the recommendation to a *requirement*. The new Opinion calls for two presentations of earnings per share on the income statement—(*a*) primary earnings per share and (*b*) fully diluted earnings per share. These terms are explained and discussed later in this section.

APB Opinion 15 is a lengthy, complex document. Only its highlights will be presented here; it is not feasible to attempt a discussion of all of the details covered in its more than 60 pages of text and exhibits. Further, approximately a year after its publication *Opinion 15* was supplemented by an interpretive booklet of well over 100 pages of explanatory material.

The simplest possible calculation of earnings per share in compliance with *Opinion 15* would involve a company with but a single class of shares authorized, all of which had remained outstanding throughout its fiscal year. If such a company had only ordinary in-

---

[12] "Reporting the Results of Operations," *APB Opinion 9*, p. 119 (emphasis supplied). *Opinion 15* requires EPS for (*a*) income before extraordinary items and (*b*) net income. EPS on extraordinary items is recommended but not mandatory.

come, i.e., no extraordinary items, calculation of its earnings per share for the year would merely involve dividing the net income by the number of shares. See Case A of Illustration 4–9.

Illustration 4–9
Calculation of Earnings per Share under Increasingly Complex Cases

Assumptions	*Calculation and Reporting EPS*

Case A

Assumptions: 30,000 shares outstanding throughout the year; net income for the year $48,000.	Net income...$48,000	
	Earnings per common share.....................	$1.60

Case B

Assumptions: 30,000 shares outstanding throughout the year; income before extraordinary items, $27,000; gain on sale of property less applicable taxes, $21,000; net income for year $48,000.	Income before extraordinary item.............$27,000	
	Extraordinary item – gain on sale of property less applicable tax 21,000	
	Net income.................................$48,000	
	Earnings per common share:	
	Income before extraordinary item..........$	$0.90
	Extraordinary item..............................	0.70
	Net income.................................$	$1.60

Case C–1

Assumptions: 30,000 shares outstanding from January 1 through April 1, on which date an additional 10,000 shares were sold°; other data as in Case B.	Income before extraordinary item.............$27,000	
	Extraordinary item – gain on sale of property less applicable tax 21,000	
	Net income.................................$48,000	
	Earnings per common share:	
	Income before extraordinary item..........$	$0.72
	Extraordinary item..............................	0.56
	Net income.................................$	$1.28

Case C–2

Assumptions: 30,000 shares outstanding from January 1 through April 1, on which date an additional 10,000 shares were issued as a stock dividend†; other data as in Case B	Income before extraordinary item.............$27,000	
	Extraordinary item – gain on sale of property less applicable tax 21,000	
	Net income.................................$48,000	
	Earnings per common share:	
	Income before extraordinary item..........$	$0.675
	Extraordinary item..............................	0.525
	Net income.................................$	$1.20

Case D‡

Assumptions: 10,000 shares of preferred stock are outstanding on which the annual cumulative dividend requirement is $3 per share; 30,000 shares of common stock are outstanding throughout the year§; net income for the year $48,000	Net income...$48,000	
	Earnings per common share.....................	$0.60

Illustration 4–9 (continued)

Assumptions	*Calculation and Reporting EPS*

Case E‡

Assumptions: The capital structure consists of:

Shares	Class	Annual Dividends
5,000	A Pfd.	$3
5,000	B Pfd.	4
20,000	Common	Open

The Class A is cumulative, nonconvertible; the Class B is noncumulative, each share is convertible to 7 shares of common. Net income for the year $48,000.

Net income $48,000

Earnings per common share‖ $0.65

Earnings per common share assuming full dilution¶ 0.60

° Calculation of weighted average of shares:

Inclusive dates	Months	Shares	Product
Jan. 1–Apr. 1	3	30,000	90,000
Apr. 1–Dec. 31	9	40,000	360,000
	12		450,000

Average: 450,000 ÷ 12 = 37,500

†As provided in *APB Opinion 9* when the change in the number of shares is due to a stock dividend, the proper divisor is the year-end number of outstanding shares; in this instance, 40,000.

‡In neither Case D or Case E is any preferred stock a "common stock equilivant" nor is stock convertible unless it is so designated.

§Per share data on common stock is after recognition of the dividend requirements ($30,000) on the preferred stock.

‖Holders of shares of Class B preferred stock can exchange them for 3.5 shares of common stock at their option. Earning per common share were calculated by dividing net income for the year by the number of common shares outstanding after allowing for full dividends on both classes of preferred stock; $15,000 on Class A and $20,000 on Class B: $48,000 − ($15,000 + $20,000) ÷ 20,000 shares = $0.65.

¶Earnings per share assuming full dilution were calculated on the assumption that all Class B holders exercised their options to become common stockholders as of the start of the year: ($48,000 − $15,000) ÷ (35,000 + 20,000) = $0.60.

A slight advance in complexity would have the company experience an extraordinary gain or loss in arriving at its net income. In this case, earnings per share figures would be reported for income before extraordinary items and for net income. See Case B of Illustration 4–9. *Opinion 15* states "It may also be desirable to present earnings per share amounts for extraordinary items."

The next advance in complexity would involve a company with a single class of authorized securities to have an increase in the number of shares outstanding during the period. A material increase due to the sale of additional shares would call for the calculation of the weighted average of the number of shares outstanding. See Case C–1 of Illustration 4–9. A material increase due to a stock dividend or stock split would call for simply dividing by the number of shares outstanding at year-end.[13] See Case C–2 of Illustration 4–9.

---

[13] If the common shares change as a result of a stock dividend or split (or reverse split), the computations should give retroactive recognition to an appropriate equivalent

Another step up the ladder of complexity would be for a corporation to have nonconvertible senior securities outstanding. Senior securities are those for which interest or dividend requirements take precedence over common stock dividends. Generally, senior securities include bonds and preferred stocks, especially cumulative preferred shares. Interest or dividends on such securities take precedence over common stock dividends. Claims of senior securities on earnings of a period should be deducted from net income (and from income before extraordinary items) before computing earnings per share on common stock. Dividends on cumulative preferred stock should be deducted from net income whether earned or not. In case there is a net loss, the amount of the loss should be increased by any cumulative dividends for the period to arrive at a loss per share figure on the common stock. See Case D of Illustration 4–9.

The next illustration (Case E) of earnings per share calculations involves some aspects of the "common stock equivalent." *APB Opinion 15* defines a common stock equivalent as "a security which is not. in form, a common stock but which usually contains provisions to enable its holder to become a common stockholder and which, because of its terms and the circumstances under which it was issued, is in substance equivalent to a common stock. The holders of these securities can expect to participate in the appreciation of the value of the common stock resulting principally from the earnings and earnings potential of the issuing corporation." Companies with complex capital structures which include convertible debt and other convertible securities and options or warrants that upon exercise or conversion will dilute earnings per common share must present two per share amounts on the face of the income statement for all periods set forth. The first is "primary earnings per share," and the second, "fully diluted earnings per share." Further, if there is more than a single income figure (net income) as would be the case when extraordinary items are reported, both primary and fully diluted per share figures must be presented for income before extraordinary items as well as for net income.

Primary earnings per share should be based on the number of common shares outstanding *plus* common stock equivalents. A convertible security is a common stock equivalent if at the time of its issuance its cash yield, based on its market price, is less than two thirds of the then current bank prime rate of interest. This determination is made when convertible securities are issued and is not altered

change in capital structure for all periods presented in the case of comparative statements. Where such changes occur after the close of a fiscal period but before statements are issued, per share computations should be based on the new number of shares since readers' primary interests are presumably related to current capitalization. Disclosure should reflect the number of shares in the calculation.

by later events. Stock options and warrants are always regarded as common stock equivalents, but the board's rules for determination of their dilutive effects, if any, are much too complex and lengthy for consideration here.

Fully diluted earnings per share are computed on the assumption that all convertible securities, options, or warrants, if dilutive, have been converted or exercised. Since the purpose is to show *maximum* potential dilution of current earnings per share on a *prospective* basis, the computation should exclude those securities whose conversion or issuance would have the effect of increasing earnings per share or of decreasing loss per share. However, in case any earnings per share amount calculated in accordance with provisions of the Opinion is diluted by less than 3%, such diluted amount need not be presented. In applying this provision, only security issues which individually reduce earnings per share should be considered. The 3% test is then applied in the aggregate.

Choice of a Fiscal Period

Many, probably most, businesses close their books and prepare annual statements each December 31. It is fairly easy to understand how this practice arose; at the same time there are good reasons why many such entities should have chosen some date other than December 31 as the last date of their fiscal year. For years, the accounting profession, SEC, and others have been advocating the use of the "natural business year." The natural business year is the period of 12 consecutive months which ends when business's activities have reached the lowest ebb in its annual cycle. End of the natural business year for any particular business would be marked by lows or near-lows for the year of inventories, sales, production, and probably also receivables and current liabilities, and by annual highs of cash. In *Accounting Series Release No. 17*, the SEC's chief accountant said:

The advantages to be obtained from the adoption of a fiscal-year-end date which coincides with the lowest point in the annual cycle of operations are clear and to my mind have never been shown to be outweighted by related disadvantages. Among the more important advantages there may be mentioned the probability of obtaining more complete and reliable financial statements since at the close of the natural business year incomplete transactions, and such items as inventories, would ordinarily be at a minimum. Mention may also be made of the fact that the general adoption of the natural business year would facilitate the work of public accountants by permitting them to spread much of their work throughout the calendar year, and thus aid them in rendering the most effective service to their clients.[14]

---

[14] Securities Exchange Commission, *Accounting Series Release No. 17* (Washington, D.C., March 18, 1940).

In addition to the stated and implied advantages cited in the SEC release, some other advantages of adoption of the natural business year include:

1. Future planning is simplified. There is a natural break for changes in cost standards, establishment of sales, and other budget quotas, and planning of future operations.

2. The cost of inventory taking and valuation is reduced because all inventories are at a low. Further, the taking of a physical inventory would probably cause least interference with sales and production activities and personnel to assist with the inventory would be available.

3. Work load of the accounting department is smoothed because there would be less conflict with preparation of annual government payroll, tax, and other information returns filed on a calendar year basis (unless, of course, the natural business year and calendar year coincided).

4. Assessment of annual operating results and of financial position can probably be done somewhat more efficiently when statements are prepared at the close of a natural cycle of operations rather than somewhere in the middle of the cycle.

Despite years of promotional effort urging initial adoption of the natural business year or conversion to it, a majority of business entities end their fiscal years on December 31.[15] It is unlikely that for most of them this date marks the close of their natural business years.

Examples of Published Income Statements

Balance sheets and accompanying notes for Trans World Airlines, Inc., as of December 31, 1969 and 1968 were presented in Chapter 3. The related income statements and retained earnings statements are shown in Illustration 4–10.

The income and retained earnings statements of Tenneco, Inc., and relevant accompanying notes are shown in Illustration 4–11. The income statements of both TWA and Tenneco are noteworthy in that operating revenues reflect a breakdown into major sources – a commendable practice which all too few companies have seen fit to adopt in their annual reports. The income statements of Tenneco are interesting because, in one year at least, material amounts of extraordinary income are reported and the earnings per share situation is complex, yet clearly presented.

---

[15] Recent editions of *Accounting Trends and Techniques* indicates slow progress is being made toward adoption of the natural business year. Among the 600 companies in the survey there has been a steady decline in the number with December fiscal closings as shown in this tabulation.

	1968 & 1969	1967	1960	1955
Non-December closings	215	206	194	179
December closings	385	394	406	421

Illustration 4–10
TRANS WORLD AIRLINES, INC., AND SUBSIDIARIES
Statement of Consolidated Income
For the Years Ended December 31, 1969 and 1968

	1969	1968
Operating Revenues:		
Passenger	$ 925,709,000	$788,910,000
Cargo	114,669,000	97,963,000
Other	58,062,000	61,371,000
Total operating revenues	$1,098,440,000	$948,244,000
Operating Expenses:		
Flying, in-flight, and ground servicing	$ 574,230,000	$482,870,000
Maintenance	149,096,000	134,393,000
Depreciation and amortization (Note 4)	96,361,000	83,259,000
Selling and advertising	151,618,000	132,464,000
General and administrative	46,850,000	44,069,000
Employees' welfare	46,548,000	40,967,000
Contribution to other airlines – mutual aid agreement	8,651,000	–
Total operating expenses	$1,073,354,000	$918,022,000
Operating Profit	$ 25,086,000	$ 30,222,000
Income Charges (Credits):		
Interest – net, less amount capitalized	$ 20,871,000	$ 22,261,000
Loss (gain) on disposition of aircraft – net	(3,787,000)	286,000
Other – net	(1,011,000)	(1,546,000)
Total income charges – net	$ 16,073,000	$ 21,001,000
Income before Provision for Income Taxes	$ 9,013,000	$ 9,221,000
Provision (Credit) for Income Taxes (Note 2)	(2,951,000)	(6,114,000)
Income from Airline Operations	$ 11,964,000	$ 15,335,000
Income from Hotel Operations	7,930,000	6,202,000
Net Income for the Year	$ 19,894,000	$ 21,537,000
Earnings per Common Share (Note 6):		
On outstanding and equivalent shares	$ 1.63	$ 1.78
Assuming full dilution	$ 1.63	$ 1.78

Statement of Consolidated Retained Earnings

Balance at beginning of year	$ 180,808,000	$171,154,000
Net income	19,894,000	21,537,000
Cash dividends:		
Common stock – per share, $0.50 in 1969 and $1.00 in 1968	(5,039,000)	(9,960,000)
Preferred stock – per share, $2.00	(1,977,000)	(1,923,000)
Balance at end of year	$ 193,686,000	$180,808,000

Illustration 4–10 (continued)
Statement of Consolidated Capital Surplus

Balance at beginning of year ....$	107,848,000	$101,164,000
Amounts received in excess of par value of capital stock issued under employee stock option and purchase plans and upon exercise of warrants......................................	6,796,000	6,684,000
Balance at end of year ....$	114,644,000	$107,848,000

See notes to Financial statements in Illustration 3–1.

Illustration 4–11
TENNECO, INC., AND SUBSIDIARY COMPANIES
Consolidated Income

	Year Ended December 31	
	1969	1968 (Note 1)
Revenues:		
Operating revenues —		
Machinery, equipment, and shipbuilding..........$	861,829,533	$ 579,467,347
Gas sales and transportation	563,357,774	533,552,582
Refined products..	258,726,709	241,007,144
Crude oil and condensate...............................	140,341,235	138,232,904
Chemicals..	248,963,910	241,808,436
Packaging..	257,226,252	238,785,430
Land use and other	120,151,650	105,036,382
	$2,450,597,063	$2,077,890,225
Nonoperating income and expense (net).............	42,509,702	38,467,378
	$2,493,106,765	$2,116,357,603
Costs and Expenses (Notes 2 and 3):		
Cost of sales and operating expenses ....$	2,030,688,095	$1,683,618,299
Depreciation, depletion, and amortization	167,231,508	155,395,128
Interest expense..	116,492,792	98,727,717
Interest charged to construction	(16,421,129)°	(14,263,157)
Federal income taxes—Current	25,230,148	29,689,329
Federal income taxes—Deferred	2,257,788	324,402
	$2,325,479,202	$1,953,491,718
Income before equity in undistributed earnings of 50% owned companies, outside stockholders' interest, and extraordinary items..........$	167,627,563	$ 162,865,885
Equity in undistributed earnings of 50% owned companies..	3,098,088	3,342,718
Income before outside stockholders' interest and extraordinary items ....$	170,725,651	$ 166,208,603
Outside Stockholders' Interest in Subsidiaries' Net Income:		
Preferred stock ....$	4,749,850	$ 4,895,205
Common stock...	710,330	3,698,777
	$ 5,460,180	$ 8,593,982
Income before extraordinary items.......................$	165,265,471	$ 157,614,621
Extraordinary items, net of tax effect (Note 4)	225,073	9,587,041
Net Income...$	165,490,544	$ 167,201,662
Preferred and preference stock dividends..............	38,324,700	39,765,500
Net Income to Common Stock............................$	127,165,844	$ 127,436,162

Illustration 4–11 (continued)

Year Ended December 31

	1969	1968 (Note 1)
Earnings per Share of Common Stock (Note 9):		
Average shares outstanding—		
Income before extraordinary items........................$	2.31	$ 2.21
Extraordinary items, net of tax............................	—	.18
Net income ....$	2.31	$ 2.39
Fully diluted—		
Income before extraordinary items........................$	2.06	$ 1.98
Extraordinary items, net of tax............................	—	.12
Net income ....$	2.06	$ 2.10

Consolidated Retained Earnings

	1969	1968
Balance, beginning of year:		
As previously reported ....$	419,465,664	$ 365.036,282
Retained earnings of companies pooled in 1969	1,360,284	945,465
Adjustment resulting from acquisitions in 1969 accounted for as poolings of interests..............	(1,683,240)	(1,683,240)
	$ 419,142,708	$ 364,298,507
Add:		
Net income	165,490,544	167,201,662
	$ 584,633,252	$ 531,500,169
Deduct:		
Cash dividends—		
Cumulative preferred stock..............................$	8,527,204	$ 8,248,422
Cumulative convertible second preferred stock...	6,096,079	7,671,773
Cumulative convertible preference stock............	23,701,417	23,845,305
Common stock..	70,903,168	67,194,824
Plant, property, and equipment adjustments resulting from Federal Power Commission original cost determination applicable to the years 1953–1967	—	3,623,773
Cash dividends of subsidiaries, prior to pooling.....	—	36,887
Other (net)..	487,282	1,736,477
	$ 109,715,150	$ 112,357,461
Balance, end of year (Note 6) ....$	474,918,102	$ 419,142,708

Notes to Financial Statements

1. *Principles of Consolidation*

The consolidated financial statements of Tenneco Inc. include all majority-owned subsidiaries other than inactive and finance subsidiaries.

On September 4, 1968, the plan of merger between Tenneco Corporation, a subsidiary, and Newport News Shipbuilding and Dry Dock Company was consummated. Pursuant to the terms of the merger, Tenneco Corporation acquired all of the outstanding common stock of Newport News in exchange for 852,810 shares of Tenneco Inc., common stock which it held and $102,338,000 principal amount of its 7% Debentures. This transaction was accounted for as a purchase and, accordingly, the results of operations of Newport News have been included in the financial statements since the date of acquisition. Operating revenues of Newport News amounted to $97,521,696 from date of acquisition to December 31, 1968, and $313,-877,195 for the year 1969.

In 1969, Tenneco Corporation, a subsidiary, acquired the assets and liabilities of California Almonds, Inc., and Qualitron Aero, Inc., in exchange for 114,357 shares of Tenneco Inc. common stock. The financial statements for 1968 have been restated to reflect such transactions in accordance with the pooling-of-interests principle of accounting. For the year 1968, total operating revenues and earnings of the pooled companies amounted to $14,411,705 and $269,914, respectively. Also during the last quarter of 1969, Tenneco Inc., through a subsidiary, increased its interest in J. I. Case Company from 56% to 91%; the shares of Case so acquired and 423,172 shares of Tenneco Inc. preference stock owned by such subsidiary are pledged to secure $78,244,185 of short-term notes payable.

Unconsolidated majority-owned subsidiaries and 50% owned companies are carried at cost plus undistributed earnings since date of acquisition. Such undistributed earnings amounted to $44,717,192 and $37,819,106 at December 31, 1969 and 1968, respectively.

In 1967, Tenneco Inc. acquired the business and assets of Kern County Land Company in exchange for 4,332,093 shares of $5.50 Cumulative Convertible Preference Stock. Several legal actions against Tenneco Inc. were instituted in connection with such acquisition, two of which are still pending. One action asserts a claim for at least $20,000,000, and another action asserts claims aggregating at least $160,-000,000; however, in the opinion of counsel for Tenneco Inc. such claims are without merit and will be successfully defended.

2. *Plant Property and Equipment*

The plant, property and equipment balances at December 31, 1969, are set forth in the following tabulation:

	Gross Plant, Property and Equipment	Less Reserves for Depreciation, Depletion, and Amortization	Net Plant, Property, and Equipment
Gas transmission	$1,913,133,197	$ 608,783,482	$1,304,349,715
Producing and undeveloped oil and gas	894,613,964	144,064,251	750,549,713
Producing leasehold interest, subject to redetermination	159,463,500	60,785,875	98,677,625
Refining and marketing	211,539,771	75,315,045	136,224,726
Machinery, equipment and shipbuilding	386,507,472	158,691,509	227,815,963
Packaging	272,264,727	126,033,257	146,231,470
Chemicals	252,528,205	88,520,074	164,008,131
Land use and other	98,581,800	26,762,678	71,819,122
	$4,188,632,636	$1,288,956,171	$2,899,676,465

Tenneco Inc. and its subsidiaries capitalize all productive and nonproductive well drilling costs applicable to the exploration for and development of oil and gas reserves. Depreciation, depletion, and amortization of producing and undeveloped oil and gas properties is provided on a composite basis using the unit-of-production method. With respect to properties supplying its regulated gas pipeline system, a rate is determined for each production area by dividing the total unrecovered book cost of all producing and undeveloped oil and gas properties by the total quantity of remaining reserves. As to other domestic and the Canadian properties, a rate is determined by dividing the total unrecovered book cost of all such properties by the total quantity of remaining reserves; similarly, rates are determined for overseas properties. Nonproducing leases are charged to the composite reserve when abandoned.

Depreciation of the other properties is provided on a straight-line basis in amounts which, in the opinion of management, are adequate to allocate the cost of properties over their estimated useful lives.

3. *Federal Income Taxes*

Substantial amounts of the costs incurred in exploration for and development of oil and gas reserves, which are capitalized for financial purposes, are deducted as incurred for tax purposes.

The investment tax credit has been recorded on the flow-through method of accounting whereby the benefit of such credit is currently reflected in the income statement. The total consolidated investment tax credit so utilized and reflected for the years 1969 and 1968 was $15,000,000 and $15,800,000, respectively. Based on the average shares of common stock outstanding for the applicable periods, such amounts per share were 27¢ and 30¢, respectively. At December 31, 1969, the companies' unused investment tax credit aggregated approximately $25,000,000. Under the Tax Reform Act of 1969, the investment tax credit has been repealed for all property acquisitions or construction after April 18, 1969, subject to certain exceptions, and utilization of the unused investment tax credit carry-over as of December 31, 1969, is limited to 20% annually.

The Tax Reform Act also covers many other areas which, in the aggregate, Tenneco Inc. presently believes will not have a significant effect on future operations.

The pipeline companies regulated by the Federal Power Commission follow the flow-through method of accounting for the current tax reduction resulting from the use of liberalized depreciation for federal income tax purposes, pursuant to orders by the Commission. Prior to adopting such accounting method the amount of taxes currently deferred was charged to income and credited to a reserve for deferred federal income taxes, which is now being amortized over a period of 13 years from January 1, 1967 (annual amortization of $3,370,000). The subsidiary companies not regulated by the Federal Power Commission continue to follow deferred tax accounting for the current income tax reduction resulting from the use of liberalized depreciation for tax purposes, and such reserves will be charged with the increase in income taxes payable in future years as a result of using these tax deductions currently.

4. *Extraordinary Items*

A tabulation of the extraordinary items for the years 1969 and 1968 is set forth below:

1969 – Gain on sale of Fibreboard Corporation warrants ($11,157,873), less write-down of Moonie Field, Australia properties to estimated salvage value ($5,655,564) and abandonment of domestic plant facilities applicable to discontinued operations ($5,604,436), net of tax effect ($327,200)... $ 225,073

1968 – Gain on sale of investment in Watkins-Johnson Company ($53,871,147), less loss on certain foreign investments ($32,731,506), primarily Nigeria, net of tax effect ($11,552,600) $9,587,041

6. *Restrictions on Payment of Dividends*

At December 31, 1969, after giving effect to certain restrictions, approximately $319,000,000 of consolidated retained earnings was not restricted for payment of dividends on common stock.

9. *Common Stock and Stock Option Plans*

Earnings per share of common stock are based on the average number of shares of common stock outstanding during each period adjusted to reflect shares issued in connection with the poolings of interests referred to in Note 1. Such adjusted average shares outstanding were 55,011,314 and 53,270,535 shares for the years 1969 and 1968, respectively. Earnings per share computations assuming full dilution additionally include the average common shares issuable for convertible or exchangeable securities, stock options, warrants, and other contingently issuable shares during each period and the elimination of the related dividend and interest requirements, less applicable federal income taxes. Such average shares assuming full dilution were 81,557,467 and 79,455,709 shares for the years 1969 and 1968, respectively.

At December 31, 1969, the shares of Tenneco Inc. common stock reserved for issuance were as follows:

Conversion of second preferred stock	3,561,820
Conversion of preference stock (including 1,667,419 shares of common stock issuable to a subsidiary)	15,615,706
Exercise of common stock warrants (at $32 per share through April 1, 1979)	2,500,000
Exchange of Tenneco Corporation second preferred stock, stated value $27.75 (share for share basis to May 1, 1983)	1,970,365
Exchange of Tenneco Corporation debentures (at $30 per share through September 30, 1992)	3,333,267
Stock option plans	450,161
Contingently issuable depending on future earnings of certain acquired companies	353,600
	27,784,919

The number of shares issuable, as set forth above, is subject to adjustment under certain conditions to protect against dilution.

Tenneco Inc. has reserved and granted options for the purchase of an aggregate of 1,218,594 shares of common stock under a Restricted Stock Option Plan which provided for the granting of options at 95% of the fair market value at the date of grant. At December 31, 1969, options for the purchase of 1,126,856 shares had been exercised. In addition, Tenneco Inc. has reserved an aggregate of 500,000 shares of common stock under a Qualified Stock Option Plan which provides for the granting of options at 100% of the fair market value at date of grant. At December 31, 1969, options had been granted for 455,617 shares under such plan; options for the purchase of 175,327 shares had been exercised. Tenneco Inc. has also reserved 33,750 shares of its common stock for conversion of preference stock options which were granted in substitution for Kern County Land Company common stock options outstanding at date of acquisition.

During 1969, 1,287,809 shares were issued upon conversion or exchange of securities and 58,135 shares were issued in connection with stock options.

Cash dividends on common stock have been paid at a quarterly rate of 32¢ per share through September 31, 1969. In December 1969, a fourth quarter cash dividend of 33¢ was paid.

°( ) Denotes deduction.

QUESTIONS FOR CLASS DISCUSSION

1. What titles are used in lieu of "income statement?"

2. Distinguish the "multiple-step" from the "single-step" form of income statement.

3. Since the cost of goods manufactured is a part of the cost of goods sold, why not compute the cost of goods manufactured in the cost of goods sold section of the income statement?

4. Assuming a manufacturing corporation employs the single-step form of income statement supported by a separate statement of cost of goods manufactured and that the income statement has sections which set forth (1) income before extraordinary items, (2) extraordinary items (less applicable income tax), and (3) net income (or loss), using the numbers,

(1), (2), and (3) as above, plus (4) for the manufacturing statement, where would the following appear?

a) Discount on sales.
b) Duty on imported materials.
c) Excise taxes (on units of product made).
d) Income taxes.
e) Loss from bad debts.
f) Superintendence.
g) Freight-out.
h) Taxes on plant and equipment.
i) Cash discount on raw material purchases.
j) Taxes on finished goods inventory.
k) Indirect labor.
l) Officers' salaries.
m) Freight on returned sales.
n) Interest expense.
o) Net loss for period.
p) Gain on sale of machinery.
q) Tax on gain in (p).

5. Refer to Question 4 above. If the income statement is in multiple-step form and there are separate captions for (1) selling, (2) general, and (3) other expenses, how would the following be reported?: (e), (g), (j), (l), (m), (n).

6. Would a listing of all expenses under the categories set out below reflect classification on the basis of *object* or *function?*

a) Salaries
b) Depreciation
c) Taxes
d) Insurance
e) Utilities
f) Supplies used

However you answer, explain what the other basis of classification means.

7. Very briefly, explain the differences between the *current operating performance* and *all-inclusive* concepts of income reporting. Give a synonym for each.

8. As between the current operating performance and all-inclusive concepts, which is preferred by the AICPA's Accounting Principles Board? What basic format of income statement does the board recommend?

9. All elements of this question relate to *prior period adjustments.* (a) In general terms, what are they? (b) By what criteria can they be determined? (c) How, according to the Accounting Principles Board, should they be reported in financial statements? (d) Give a specific example of one.

10. Do any of the following qualify as prior period adjustments? If so, which ones?

a) R Company sold in 1971 at a large gain bonds bought in 1966 when interest on them was in default.
b) S Corporation found it has been underdepreciating some piers and other harbor facilities it owns because action of the sea and some of its creatures has seriously weakened them. Correction of the earlier underdepreciation is now being reflected.
c) T Publishing Company wins an appeal to the Supreme Court of a libel suit decision which was lost in lower courts and for which $500,000

was set up as a liability two years ago. As a result of the Supreme Court decision, damages are now scaled down to $75,000.

d) U Corporation made a substantial increase in its balance of Allowance for Doubtful Accounts at year-end 1971 when it learned the billing department fell down on the job and failed to bill many of the customers currently or to send follow-up notices to those who had not paid after being billed once. An intensive follow-up collection campaign in 1972 has been so fruitful it is now obvious the allowance account is grossly excessive, so a correcting entry is being made in 1972.

11. Office equipment with a five-year life and no salvage value was bought early in 1969 but the $900 charge was erroneously made to Office Expense. The error went undetected until statements were being prepared at year-end 1971. The corporation involved is quite small. Briefly describe proper presentation if:

   a) Only statements for 1971 are being prepared.

   b) Comparative statements are being prepared for 1969 through 1971.

12. Briefly explain the meaning of tax allocation.

13. Either of two basic procedures can be followed in connection with tax allocation; one of them involves "averaging." Explain what is meant.

14. Under the concept of reporting advocated by the Accounting Principles Board what are the major items of increase and decrease of unappropriated retained earnings to be reported on the retained earnings statement?

15. Is it now forbidden, optional, or mandatory to present earnings per share data on corporate income statements? In this connection, what has been the historical development?

16. XY Corporation has but a single class of shares; during the most recent fiscal year the number of outstanding shares increased materially. Under what circumstances would the average number of shares outstanding be used in earnings per share calculations? In what circumstances would the year-end number of shares be used?

17. Where a corporation has a complex capital structure and experiences nonoperating gains as well as ordinary income, in preparing comparative income statements for the current and preceding years, how many earnings per share figures will likely be required? Explain your answer.

18. The close of the *natural business year* for any given entity is usually marked by low ebbs of certain items. Name some of them and, in your own words, define natural business year.

DECISION CASE 4–1

The president of Taylor School Supply Company, a wholesaler, presents you with a comparison of distribution costs for two salesmen and wants to know if you think the salesmen's compensation plan is working to the detriment of the company. He supplies you with the following data:

	Salesmen	
	McKinney	Sim
Gross sales	$247,000	$142,000
Sales returns	17,000	2,000
Cost of goods sold	180,000	85,000
Reimbursed expenses (e.g., entertainment)	5,500	2,100
Other direct charges (e.g., samples distributed)	4,000	450
Commission rate on gross sales dollars	5%	5%

Required:

1. A salesman's compensation plan encourages him to work to increase the measure of performance to which his compensation is related. List the questionable sales practices by a salesman that might be encouraged by basing commissions on gross sales.

2. *a)* What evidence that the compensation plan may be working to the detriment of the company can be found in the data?

   b) What other information should the president obtain before reaching definite conclusions about this particular situation? Why?

(AICPA adapted)

DECISION CASE 4–2

J. B. Jacobson opened a small retail cash-and-carry grocery business with an investment of $1,000 cash, $5,000 of merchandise, and a lot and building valued at $18,000. Fixtures were obtained by signing a note repayable in equal installments over a 36-month period. He pays cash for all his merchandise purchases and keeps no formal accounting records. When asked how he knew how well he was doing and where he stood, Jacobson made the following statement: "As long as I do not buy or sell anything except merchandise and that remains fairly constant, I can judge my profit or loss by the increase or decrease in my bank balance."

Required:

Evaluate his statement in the light of the facts known.

EXERCISES

Exercise 4–1

The December 31, 1972, trial balance of King Corporation which appears below reflects year-end adjustments except for the fact the inventory figure is as of January 1. The December 31 inventory is $35,370.

Advertising	$ 5,100
Bond interest expense	4,000
Bonuses to salesmen	10,350
Depreciation – building	1,200
Depreciation – office equipment	850
Depreciation – sales fixtures	1,600
Dividends paid	2,200
Freight-in	730
Gain on sale of equipment	4,400
Income tax expense	?

Inventory	$ 14,050
Office salaries	21,360
Payroll taxes	2,110
Repairs and maintenances	770
Purchases	260,400
Sales (including sales taxes)	401,200
Sales salaries and commissions	45,020
Sales taxes	7,700
Taxes and licenses	2,030

The gain on sale of equipment is taxable at the capital gains rate of 30% except when allocable tax on regular basis would be lower. The company is subject to income tax rates of 22% on the first $25,000 of net income before taxes and 48% on all above that amount.

Required:

Following the Accounting Principles Board's recommendations, prepare an income statement for 1972 in single-step form, combining it with a retained earnings statement. (The January 1, 1972, balance of retained earnings unappropriated was $31,400, while a Reserve for Plant Expansion account balance on the same date was $10,000; during 1972 an added $5,000 was transferred to the reserve.) Common stock outstanding throughout the year was 2,200 shares; show dividends and earnings per share figures.

Exercise 4–2

The following accounts are found on the books of the Vickrey Products Company on December 31. All adjustments except for final inventories and federal income taxes (40%) have been made.

Sales	$280,000
Materials purchases	50,000
Inventories, January 1:	
Raw materials	10,000
Work in process	6,000
Finished goods	15,000
Direct labor	50,000
Indirect labor	10,000
Superintendence	9,000
Light, heat, and power	15,000
Rent of factory building	4,000
Repairs on machinery	2,000
Sundry factory expense	6,000
Sales salaries	22,000
Advertising	8,000
Freight-out	3,000
Office salaries	7,000
Rent of office	2,000
Depreciation—office equipment	200
Depreciation—store equipment	1,000
Depreciation—plant equipment	3,000
Sales returns and allowances	2,800
Interest income	200
Miscellaneous general expense	600

The final inventories were: raw material, $14,000; work in process, $8,700; and finished goods, $10,000.

Required:

Prepare a multiple-step income statement for the year supported by a separate manufacturing statement. Show earnings per share; the company had 5,700 shares of stock outstanding from January 1 through June 30; on July 1 an additional 600 shares were sold on the open market.

Exercise 4–3

The following balances appear in the adjusted ledger of Myer Company at year-end 1972:

Advertising ....$	5,900
Bond interest expense	4,400
Contributions to charities...	1,000
Depreciation – building	2,000
Depreciation – office equipment	600
Depreciation – sales fixtures	1,150
Destruction loss – warehouse...	7,200
Freight-in	780
Freight-out...	1,120
Income tax expense..	?
Inventory, January 1...	24,390
Office salaries..	24,700
Payroll taxes..	2,900
Repairs and maintenance...	800
Purchases..	169,330
Sales	288,660
Sales returns and allowances..	4,100
Sales salaries and commissions...	30,470
Taxes..	2,200

The company is subject to income tax rates of 22% on the first $25,000 of net income before taxes and 48% on all above that amount. The inventory at December 31, 1972, amounts to $21,160. Depreciation – building, repairs, and taxes should be split evenly between selling and general expenses (except that payroll taxes should be split in proportion to salaries). Use the averaging method of allocating tax to the warehouse loss.

Required:

Prepare an income statement using the following broad format:

Sales   Income before taxes and extraor-
Cost of goods sold   dinary items
Gross margin   Income tax
Selling expenses   Income before extraordinary items
General expenses   Extraordinary items
Financial items   Net income

Calculate earnings per share. The company had an average of 6,000 shares of stock outstanding during 1972.

Exercise 4–4

The following data are to be used in preparing statements for Carlos Manufacturing Company for its fiscal year ended September 30, 1972:

Sales $1,200,000
Cost of goods sold (four fifths of production) (exclusive of
　　depreciation) 700,000
Gain on sale of fixed assets 25,000
Depreciation (60% factory, 25% selling, 15% general) 80,000
Selling expenses (exclusive of depreciation) 200,000
Balance of retained earnings, January 1 402,000
General expenses (exclusive of depreciation) 80,000
Additional assessment of 1969 income tax (by IRS) 20,000
Loss on retirement of River Plant 12,000
Gain on purchase and sale of treasury stock 5,000
Dividends paid on capital stock ($2 per share) 50,000

It is also discovered that minor selling expense accruals of $500 were not set up at the end of the preceding year. No attempt has been made to correct this error.

As to income taxes, regular income is taxed at 22% on the first $25,000 of pretax income; amounts above that are taxed at 48%. The gain on sale of fixed assets is subject to tax at only 30% provided there is any advantage to that alternative. Loss on Retirement of River Plant has the same tax effect as an expense of the same amount. Items pertaining to prior years are not to affect determination of income tax of the current year. Do not use averaging in allocating tax to the River Plant loss.

Required:

Prepare a combined income and retained earnings statement complying with recommendations of the AICPA's Accounting Principles Board and following the single-step form. Show per share amounts where appropriate.

Exercise 4-5

Nominal accounts in the ledger of QST, Inc., after year-end adjusting entries at December 31, 1971, were as follows:

Abandonment loss — Richfield properties .... $ 6,000
Bad debt expense 800
Bonus to executives 9,300
Building rental expense 11,400
Depreciation — office equipment 800
Depreciation — sales fixtures 1,800
Dividends paid ($1 per share) 12,000
Franchise amortization 750
Gain on sale of securities 9,200
Insurance expense 640
Inventory, January 1 10,800
Office and administrative salaries 21,100
Payroll taxes 2,020
Repairs and maintenance 760
Purchases 302,200
Sales 455,700
Sales salaries and commissions 45,300
Supplies used 700
Taxes and licenses 2,600

The abandonment loss has the same tax effect as an expense of the same amount. The gain on sale of securities is taxable at the capital gains rate of 30% except when allocable tax on regular basis would be lower. The company is subject to income tax rates of 22% on the first $25,000 of net income before taxes and 48% on all above that amount. The ending inventory is valued at $8,880.

Required:

Prepare an income statement for 1971 in the single-step form and in accordance with the recommendations of the AICPA's Accounting Principles Board. The corporation's outstanding stock remained constant during the year. In applying tax allocation to the abandonment loss do not use the averaging procedure.

Exercise 4–6

Progresso Corporation is a newly formed audit client of yours. Its president learns that the company will be required to report earnings per share data in the first year's annual report and has requested that you furnish certain information to him about this reporting.

Required:

a) Define the term *earnings per share* as it applies to a corporation with a capitalization structure composed of only one class of common stock and explain how earnings per share should be computed and how the information should be disclosed in the corporation's financial statements.

b) Discuss the treatment, if any, which should be given to each of the following items in computing earnings per share of common stock for financial statement reporting:

1. The declaration of current dividends on cumulative preferred stock.
2. A two-for-one split of common stock during the current fiscal year.
3. A provision created out of retained earnings for a contingent liability from a possible lawsuit.
4. The replacement of a machine immediately prior to the close of the current fiscal year at a cost of 20% above the original cost of the replaced machine. The new machine will perform the same function as the old machine which was sold for its book value.

(AICPA adapted)

Exercise 4–7

The following financial statements have come to you for review:

BROWN PRODUCTION COMPANY
Income Statement
December 31, 1972

Revenue:		
Gross sales	$256,800	
Less: Sales discount	5,120	
Net sales		$251,680

Costs and expenses:
Cost of goods sold:

Inventory, January 1		$ 98,500	
Purchases	$132,600		
Less: Purchases discount	2,780	129,820	
		$228,320	
Inventory, December 31		102,300	
Cost of goods sold			126,020
Gross profit			$125,660
Operating expenses:			
Selling expenses		$ 38,000	
General and administrative expenses:			
General expenses	$ 20,000		
Depreciation	8,800		
Bad debt expense	1,080	29,880	
Total Operating Expenses			67,880
Income from operations			$ 57,780
Other income:			
Interest income			970
Net income before federal income taxes			$ 58,750
Less: Federal income taxes			28,720
Net Income			$ 30,030

BROWN PRODUCTION COMPANY
Statement of Retained Earnings
December 31, 1972

Retained earnings appropriated:			
Balance reserve for plant expansion, January 1, 1972		$ 60,000	
Appropriation for current year		20,000	
Total appropriated balance, December 31, 1972			$ 80,000
Retained earnings unappropriated:			
Balance, January 1		$187,600	
Corrections applicable to past periods:			
Additions:			
Depreciation overstated		3,400	
Adjusted balance		$191,000	
Additions during current year:			
Net income	$30,030		
Gain on sale of land	8,200	38,230	
		$229,230	
Deductions during current year:			
Dividends	$30,000		
Loss on sale of machinery	9,650		
Appropriation for plant expansion	20,000	59,650	
Total unappropriated balance, December 31, 1972			169,580
Total Appropriated and Unappropriated Balance Retained Earnings, December 31, 1972			$249,580

Required:

1. State whether the statements were apparently prepared under the old "current operating performance" or "all-inclusive" concept. Briefly cite two specifics in support of your answer.

2. In the light of more modern recommendations as to such statements, what changes should be made in them?

Exercise 4–8

The following data related to 1972 operations of Lido Sales Company are made available to you:

a) The January 1 inventory is $20,000 larger than the December 31 inventory; the latter amounts to 20% of purchases for the year.
b) Two thirds of the operating expenses relate to sales activities; the remainder of operating expenses are broadly classed as "general expenses." Total operating expenses amount to 75% of gross margin.
c) Cost of goods sold amounts to $120,000.
d) The income tax rate is 40%.
e) Gross margin is 40% of net sales.
f) Sales returns amount to $3,000.
g) Losses from bad debts comprise 10% of the general expenses; the remainder of that category of expenses is equally divided between office salaries and administrative salaries.

Required:

On the basis of the foregoing data prepare an income statement for 1972 in multiple-step form. Assume the company has 5,000 shares outstanding and that these are subject to dilution or expansion to 6,000 shares.

Exercise 4–9

A condensed adjusted trial balance for Rion Corporation as of December 31, 1972, appears below:

Assets (net)	$ 489,280	
Capital stock (par $50)		$ 300,000
Cost of goods sold	640,400	
Depreciation	18,425	
Dividends paid	15,000	
Gain on sale of investments		30,000
Insurance expense	6,760	
Liabilities		86,330
Loss from fire damage	38,400	
Other expenses of operation	81,510	
Reserve for plant expansion		20,000
Retained earnings		57,445
Sales		960,815
Salaries	164,815	
	$1,454,590	$1,454,590

Assume that the company's operating income is subject to a 40% income tax rate, that the fire loss had the same effect on income as operating expense of the same amount, and that its gain on sale of investments is taxable at the 30% rate for capital gains. By action of the board of directors, reserve for plant expansion was doubled during 1972.

Required:

Prepare a combined income and retained earnings statement in accordance with recommendations of the Accounting Principles Board. The period is the year 1972; follow the single-step form. The number of shares outstanding is subject to dilution or expansion by an additional 10%.

Exercise 4–10

For a considerable number of years, *Forbes* magazine has published each January an "Annual Report on American Industry." This is a library assignment which calls for you to consult that report for the most recent year for which you can obtain a copy.

Required:

Prepare a report showing:

a) The five corporations which showed the greatest five-year annual earnings per share growth in the survey. Indicate also how these same companies performed as to sales growth during the period. For each company report the percent of earnings per share and sales growth.

b) Which companies which were still profitable did relatively worst in terms of earnings per share performance? Name at least five companies. Name three companies which had been profitable in the past which in the year of the survey you examined had slipped to a loss or deficit status.

c) In terms of *sales* growth for the period covered by your survey, name five corporations with outstanding performance records.

d) The survey is broken down into coverage in greater detail of specific industries. Which specific industry groups were accorded this kind of attention in the year you reported upon?

Exercise 4–11

Many business enterprises have a natural business year. The natural business year varies according to the type and nature of the enterprise and frequently does not coincide with the calendar year.

Required:

1. Define "natural business year."
2. Discuss briefly the reasons for changing the accounting period of a company to a "natural business year."

(AICPA adapted)

PROBLEMS

Problem 4–1

The ledger of Marden Corporation after adjustment at December 31, 1972, reflected (among others) the following balances: sales, $2,003,520; purchases, $1,170,550; freight-in, $4,700; freight-out, $8,960; sales salaries, $203,680; office salaries, $56,220; executive salaries, $52,890; depreciation of delivery equipment, $14,200; depreciation of office equipment, $6,000; building rent, $63,000; taxes (other than on income) $42,600; inventory, $173,800.

You ascertain that the inventory balance is the January 1, 1972, figure and that the inventory at December 31, 1972, is $110,580. For allocation purposes expenses such as rent, executive salaries, etc., are considered two thirds selling and one third general or administrative. The income tax rate is 22% on the first $25,000 and 48% on all income in excess of that amount. The average number of common shares outstanding during 1972 was 50,000; there were no senior securities but the common shares are subject to a potential dilution of 22% if various options are exercised.

Required:

Prepare a condensed single-step income statement for 1972 on *a*) an *object* basis and *b*) a *function* basis.

Problem 4–2

This is a library assignment which calls for you to consult an investments guide such as *Moody's Manual – Industrials* or *Standard and Poors*. Look up financial data on three leading corporations engaged in the manufacturing of cans and other food containers. Some representative companies include: American Can Company; Continental Can Co., Inc.; Crown Cork and Seal Co., Inc.; Hunt Foods and Industries, Inc.; Owens-Illinois, Inc.; and U.S. Hoffman Machinery Corporation.

Required:

For each of the three corporations selected:

a) Set out the income statement highlights for the most recent year for which you can obtain data, together with the same kind of information pertaining to the preceding year plus counterpart information (to the extent it is given) for the earliest year for which data are available in the particular volume used.

b) Indicate the number of subsidiary companies owned by the company reported on (for the most recent year only).

c) How many kinds of capital stock did the company have outstanding (for the most recent year only)? Briefly describe it.

d) Who is listed as their auditors? (In closing, be sure to cite date and title of the publication used, together with page numbers on which data were found.)

Problem 4–3

Information related to Electrax Corporation's operations during the years ended December 31, 1973 and 1974 is presented below.

	1973	1974
Sales	$550,000	$602,000
Sales returns and allowances	1,500	2,000
Cost of goods sold	330,000°	397,210°
Selling expenses	40,000	42,500
Depreciation	12,000	13,750
General expenses	75,000	95,000
Gain on sale of plant	—	15,000
Interest income	12,000	12,500
Preferred dividends (1,000 shares)†	5,000	6,000

Common stock outstanding, January 1 (in shares)	10,000	12,000
Common stock sold (in shares):		
April 1	1,000	
October 1	1,000	
June 1		1,000

°Electrax's 1973 ending inventory was overstated by $20,000; the results of this error are reflected in the company's cost of goods sold figures.

†Each share of the company's preferred stock is convertible into five shares of its common.

Required:

Prepare comparative single-step statements of income for Electrax Corporation following the recommendations of the AICPA's Accounting Principles Board and the recommendations made in this text, assuming that the gain on sale of plant is taxed at 30% and that all other items affecting income are taxed at 50%.

Problem 4-4

IRON PRODUCTS COMPANY
Balances of Operating Accounts, December 31, 1972

Advertising	$54,600	Light, fuel, and power (factory)	$ 8,350
Freight on purchases	120	Purchases — raw material	381,500
Freight on sales	1,000	Royalty on production	30,000
Depreciation —		Repairs to equipment	7,600
Factory furniture	320	Rent of factory building	4,300
Office furniture	580	Salesmen's salaries and expenses	21,000
Machinery and factory build-		Superintendent and factory clerks	9,050
ings	19,120	Salaries of officers	24,000
Discount on sales	10,150	Factory supplies	19,000
Discount on purchases	12,500	Taxes on real estate (factory)	1,700
Factory expenses	5,100	Plating expenditures	20,500
Office expenses	20,200	Bad debt expense	1,000
Interest paid	70	Sales	660,000
Insurance — machinery and factory			
buildings	3,880	Inventories, December 31:	
Inventories, January 1:		Raw materials	140,000
Raw materials	90,000	Goods in process	22,000
Goods in process	10,000	Finished goods	75,000
Finished goods	60,000	Gain from sale of securities	50,000
Dividends paid	40,000	Direct labor	37,900

The books of the Iron Products Company disclose the following data for the fiscal year:

Twenty-five percent of the office expenses and salaries are considered as entering into the cost of production; 65% of these amounts are deemed to be selling expenses, and 10% are considered general. Bad debt expense and depreciation on office furniture are not allocated.

Required:

Prepare (1) a statement of cost of goods manufactured; (2) a multiple-step income statement assuming a federal income tax rate of 45%; and (3) a statement of retained earnings; balance January 1, $84,700. Follow the recommendations of the Accounting Principles Board as to form. The tax rate applicable to the extraordinary gain is 30%. Common shares outstanding averaged 9,000 for the year.

Problem 4–5

As of December 31, 1971, Beene Manufacturing Company, with outstanding stock consisting of 3,000 shares of stock, $10 par value per share, had the following assets and liabilities:

Cash	$ 5,000
Accounts receivable	10,000
Raw material inventory	4,000
Work in process inventory	2,000
Finished goods inventory	6,000
Prepaid expenses	500
Fixed assets (net)	30,000
Current liabilities	17,500

During the year 1972, the retained earnings increased 50% as a result of the year's business. No dividends were paid during the year. Balances of accounts receivable, prepaid expenses, current liabilities, and capital stock were exactly the same on December 31, 1972, as they had been one year earlier. Inventories were reduced by exactly 50% except for the finished goods inventory which was reduced by one third. Fixed assets (net) were reduced by depreciation of $4,000, charged three fourths to manufacturing expenses and one fourth to general expense. Sales were made at 50% above their cost of $40,000. Direct labor cost was $9,000, and manufacturing expense was applied at a rate of 100% of direct labor cost, leaving $2,000 unapplied which was included in the cost of goods sold. Total general expense and selling expense amounted to 15% and 10% respectively of the gross sales.

Required:

Prepare an income statement for 1972 separately supported by a cost of goods manufactured statement and a balance sheet. The income statement should be in multiple-step form, and the balance sheet should be classified. It is suggested that as a preliminary step you prepare an interim work sheet similar to the one illustrated in Chapter 2.

(AICPA adapted)

Problem 4–6

The following year-end financial statements were prepared by the Colesar Corporation's bookkeeper. The Colesar Corporation operates a chain of retail stores.

COLESAR CORPORATION
Balance Sheet
June 30, 1972

ASSETS

Current Assets:

Cash	$	90,000
Notes receivable		100,000
Accounts receivable, less reserve for doubtful accounts		75,000
Inventories		395,500
Investment securities, at cost		100,000
Total Current Assets	$	760,500

Property, Plant, and Equipment:

Land, at cost (Note 1)...	$175,000	
Buildings, at cost less accumulated depreciation of $350,000..	500,000	
Equipment, at cost less accumulated depreciation of $180,000..	400,000	1,075,000
Intangibles		450,000

Other Assets:

Prepaid expenses		6,405
Total Assets		$2,291,905

LIABILITIES AND OWNERS' EQUITY

Current Liabilities:

Accounts payable..		$ 25,500
Estimated income taxes payable		160,000
Contingent liability on discounted notes receivable..		75,000
Total Current Liabilities		$ 260,500

Long-Term Liabilities:

5% serial bonds, $50,000 due annually on December 31 Maturity value.............................	$850,000	
Less: Unamortized discount	35,000	815,000
Total Liabilities.......................................		$1,075,500

Owners' Equity:

Common stock, stated value $10 (authorized and issued, 75,000 shares)		$750,000	
Retained earnings:			
Appropriated (Note 2) $110,000			
Free.. 356,405		466,405	1,216,405
Total Liabilities and Owners' Equity...........			$2,291,905

COLESAR CORPORATION
Income Statement
As at June 30, 1972

Sales..			$2,500,000
Interest income..			6,000
Total revenue			$2,506,000
Cost of goods sold			1,780,000
Gross margin			$ 726,000
Operating expenses:			
Selling expenses:			
Salaries	$ 95,000		
Advertising..	85,000		
Sales returns and allowances	50,000	$230,000	
General and administrative expenses:			
Salaries	$ 84,000		
Property taxes	38,000		
Depreciation and amortization	86,000		
Rent (Note 3)	75,000		
Interest on serial bonds....................................	48,000	331,000	561,000
Net income before taxes.......................................			$ 165,000
Provision for federal income taxes...........................			160,000
Net Income			$ 5,000

Notes to Financial Statements

1. Includes a future store site acquired during the year at a cost of $75,000.
2. Retained earnings in the amount of $110,000 have been set aside to finance expansion.
3. During the year the company acquired certain equipment under a long-term lease.

Required:

Identify and discuss the defects in the above financial statements with respect to terminology, disclosure, and classification. Your discussion should explain why you consider them to be defects. Do not prepare revised statements. (You should assume that the arithmetic is correct.)

(AICPA adapted)

Problem 4–7

Presented below are the comparative statements of consolidated income and retained earnings of the Sureal Corporation for the years ended December 31, 1972 and 1973, as prepared by the corporation's president.

SUREAL CORPORATION
Statements of Consolidated Income and Retained Earnings
Years Ended December 31

	1973	1972
Revenues:		
Sales	$275,000	$233,000
Other income	10,000	7,500
Gain on sale of fixed assets		10,000
Refund of income taxes from 1968	13,750	
Total Revenues	$298,750	$250,500
Expenses:		
Cost of goods sold	$115,000	$102,000
Depreciation	17,000	15,000
Selling expenses	45,000	49,000
General and administrative expenses	57,000	54,000
Loss on destruction of plant	12,000	
Correction of 1972 ending inventory	8,000	
Federal income tax expense	15,500	13,250
Total Expenses	$269,500	$233,250
Net Income	$ 29,250	$ 17,250
Retained earnings, January 1	$ 14,225	$ 4,975
Add net income	29,250	17,250
Total	$ 43,475	$ 22,225
Deduct preferred dividends	12,000	8,000
Retained earnings, December 31	$ 31,475	$ 14,225

Required:

Recast these statements in single-step form in conformity with the recommendations of the Accounting Principles Board and the recommendations made in this text, assuming the gain on sale of fixed assets is taxed at 30% and all other items affecting income are taxed at 50%. Also, assume that the schedule below reflects changes in Sureal's outstanding common stocks during 1972 and 1973.

	Shares
Common stock outstanding, January 1, 1972	10,000
Common stock sold:	
April 1, 1972	3,000
October 1, 1972	2,000
January 1, 1973	1,000
July 1, 1973	2,000
Common stock outstanding December 31, 1973	18,000

Mathematical Principles
chapter **5** | and Applications

The accountant's knowledge necessarily must include an understanding of the concepts of compound interest and their adaptation in the determination of the accounting values and entries in respect to certain contracts, monetary transactions, and internal allocations. For example, how much will $10,000 placed in a sinking fund today amount to in 10 years including compound interest at 6%? Or, what is the amount to be paid today (present value) in settlement of a contractual debt due five years hence assuming interest at 8%? The company sets aside $1,000 per year as an asset replacement fund for 10 years at 6% compound interest; what will be the balance of the fund and the interest earned at the end of each period? A five-year lease with annual rentals of $1,000 is to be paid in one lump sum in advance; what will that advance payment be, assuming a compound interest rate of 6%? How should the rent prepayment be amortized? Answers to questions such as these frequently have a direct bearing on the proper recording of the results of certain transactions for accounting purposes and for subsequent reporting. Further, the increasing involvement of accountants in management science and the related mathematical techniques, such as discounted cash-flow analyses of proposed capital expenditures, suggests the essentiality of at least a minimum competence in this important area.

The basic concepts of compound interest and the use of prepared tables are developed in Part A of this chapter. Part B provides an

176

expanded discussion of the concepts and their interrelationships by means of a series of applications to special problems. Part B may be omitted if only a general knowledge of the concepts is desired. Part C emphasizes some selected applications of compound interest concepts to accounting problems.[1]

PART A—BASIC CONCEPTS AND USE OF PREPARED TABLES

Compound Interest

Interest is identified as *compound* when after a stated period of time, accrued interest is added to the original amount, and thereafter for each period interest is computed on both the original amount and the accrued interest. For example, $1 invested at 5% interest becomes $1.05 at the end of the first specified period. For the second period interest is computed (compounded) on $1.05, and at the end of the second period the amount becomes $1.1025; at the end of a third period, $1.157625, etc. A total that accumulates as a result of leaving a given sum invested at compounded interest is known as the *amount* of the given sum. In the example above, the *amount* of $1 left at 5% compound interest for three interest periods is $1.157625.

Four basic amounts or values are used in discussion of compound interest, viz:

1. *Amount of 1*—the future value of $1 at the end of n periods at i compound interest rate.

$$[a = (1 + i)^n; \text{ see Table 5–1.}]$$

2. *Present value of 1*—the present value (worth) of $1 due n periods hence, discounted at i compound interest rate:

$$\left[p = \frac{1}{(1 + i)^n}; \text{ see Table 5–2.} \right]$$

3. *Amount of annuity of 1*—the future value of n periodic contributions (rents) of $1 each plus accumulated compound interest at i rate.[2]

$$\left[A \text{ (or } s_{\overline{n}|i}) = \frac{(1 + i)^n - 1}{i}; \text{ see Table 5–3.} \right]$$

4. *Present value of annuity of 1*—the present value (worth) of $1 to be received (or paid) each period (rents) for n periods, discounted at i compounded interest rate. Stated another way: The amount that

---

[1] The exercises and problems to be found at the end of this chapter are grouped to correspond to the three parts of the chapter: A, B, and C.

[2] These are ordinary annuities, not annuities due.

must be invested today at i compounded interest rate in order to receive n periodic receipts in the future of $1 each.[3]

$$\left[P \text{ (or } a_{\overline{n}|i}) = \frac{1 - \dfrac{1}{(1 + i)^n}}{i} \text{ ; see Table 5-4.} \right]$$

Interest Periods

Contracts between debtors and creditors which call for compound interest usually specify the interest rate on an *annual* basis. The interest periods—those intervals at which interest is accrued and added to the principal—may or may not be as much as one year apart. For example, a contract may call for "interest at 6% compounded annually," or for "interest at 6% compounded semiannually." In the first instance the rate is 6% for one interest period of a year; in the second instance the rate is 3% for each interest period of six months. If interest of 6% is compounded quarterly, the rate per period (quarter) is $1\frac{1}{2}\%$, and there would be four interest periods per year. If an annual rate is stated and there is no mention of the frequency of compounding, interest is assumed to be compounded annually.

Compound Amount (Amount of 1)

Calculation of Amount of 1. The amount of 1 is the future value of $1 at a specific rate of interest compounded for a given number of periods in the future. It is convenient and customary to use a base figure of 1 in compound interest calculations. In the United States it would be natural to think of 1 as $1. The figure 1 could just as readily stand for one peso or one of some other unit of currency.

We can determine how much an investment of $1 would be worth after being left for a specified number of periods at a specified compounding rate per period by any one of several methods. To illustrate, assume $1 is invested for six years at 5% compounded annually. The total of principal and compound interest at the end of the six years may be determined by any one of the following methods:

1. *By successive interest computations*—multiply the principal ($1) by the interest rate (.05) and add the $.05 interest thus obtained for the first period and the sum ($1.05) is the amount ($a$) at the end of the first period. This amount becomes the interest-bearing principal for the second period. This sum is principal plus interest $(1 + i)$, which may then be used as the multiplier in each succeeding period to secure the compound amount. Illustration 5-1 uses this multiplier to secure the amount (a) at the end of each of the six periods.

2. *By formula*—substitute in a formula which states that for n interest periods at i rate of interest the amount of 1 is, $a = (1 + i)^n$.

---

[3]These are ordinary annuities, not annuities due.

Illustration 5–1

Period	Balance at Start of Period	Multiplier (1 + i)	Amount at End of Period
1 .... $1	1.05	$1.05
2 .... 1.05	1.05	1.1025
3 .... 1.1025	1.05	1.157625
4 .... 1.157625	1.05	1.21550625
5 .... 1.21550625	1.05	1.27628156 (rounded)
6 .... 1.27628156	1.05	1.34009564 (rounded)

Substituting, we would say $1 invested at 5% annual compound interest for six years = $(\$1 + .05)^6$, or $1.34+. (Verifiable in Table 5–1). Sixth power multiplication is a laborious process and would be especially so where the exponent is large. A less time-consuming computation would employ logarithms as follows:

$$\log 1.05 = .021189$$
$$\log (1.05)^6 = 6 \times .021189 = .127134$$
$$\text{antilog } .127134 = 1.34009, \text{ the compound}$$
$$\text{amount } (a) \text{ for six periods}$$

3. *By table* — use a compound interest (amount of 1) table. Reference to Table 5–1, down the 5% column and across on the six-period line, reveals the compound amount of 1 is 1.34009564 (i.e., $1.34+).

Compound Amount of Specified Principal. Suppose we want to know the amount to which $10 will accumulate at 5% compounded annually for six years. Multiply $10 by 1.34009564 (amount of 1 at 5% for six periods from Table 5–1) to get $13.40. If instead the principal is $180, multiply this amount by 1.34009564. The answer, $241.22, can be computed with sufficient precision by use of the comparatively short value, 1.34009. If, however, the principal is a large sum such as $200,000, it becomes necessary to use the more precise value, 1.34009564, to get a more accurate answer, $268.019.13. Use of 1.34009 gives a close but less accurate result of $268,018.00. Even use of an eight-decimal value of 1 will often yield a result that is slightly incorrect as to the periodic values.

As another example, suppose we wish to calculate the compound amount of $3,000 left at 7% per annum compounded semiannually for four years. Since the interest periods are one-half year, there are eight interest periods and the compound interest rate becomes $3\frac{1}{2}\%$ (one half of 7% per annum). Reference to the $3\frac{1}{2}\%$ column for eight periods on Table 5–1 reveals the amount of 1 to be 1.31680904. Multiplying this value times the given initial amount of $3,000 gives an answer of $3,950.43. In other words, $3,000 left on deposit at 7% interest compounded semiannually for four years would accumulate to $3,950.43.

Determination of Other Values Related to Amount of 1

In each example above, *three* values were given; to restate one example: (*a*) principal, $200,000; (*b*) interest rate, 5%; and (*c*) periods, 6. A fourth value, the future amount $268,019.13, was computed. Obviously, if *any* three of these four values are known, the other one can be derived. Thus, there are three types of problems that may be encountered; viz:

1. To determine the future value (discussed above — compound amount of specified principal).
2. To determine the required interest rate (discussed below — determination of compound interest rate).
3. To determine the required number of interest periods (discussed below — determination of number of periods).

Determination of the Compound Interest Rate

If the amount to which a given principal sum will accumulate (or is desired to accumulate) is known, and the number of periods is known, the required rate of compound interest can be calculated from tables or, in case tables are not available, by use of logarithms.

As an example, if it is desired to invest $1,315.10 at interest compounded annually for 10 years so as to accumulate $2,142.16, what rate of interest is required or implied? To find the rate the following steps may be taken:

1. $2,142.16 ÷ $1,315.10 = $1.628895 (rounded) the amount to which $1 would accumulate at the unknown interest rate by the end of the 10-year period.
2. Referring to an amount of 1 table (Table 5–1) and reading across the 10-period line we find the amount of 1.62889463 under the 5% column; thus, this is the implied interest rate.

This illustration was designed so as to give an approximate rate of 5% as shown in the table. Often it is necessary to interpolate to derive the required rate. Suppose once again $1,315.10 is to be invested for 10 years. In this case it is desired to accumulate $1,642.83. Here the rate of increase is the same as if $1 had grown to $1.249205 ($1,642.83 ÷ $1,315.10). Referring to the 10-period line, we find the value under 2% is 1.21899442; under the next higher rate, $2\frac{1}{2}$%, it is 1.28008454. Therefore, the rate is between 2 and $2\frac{1}{2}$% — somewhat closer to the former — not quite one half of the way between them. We can conclude that the interest earned was about $2\frac{1}{4}$% [2% + $\frac{1}{2}$ ($2\frac{1}{2}$ − 2)]. Or more precisely with insignificant rounding applied:[4]

$$\left[2\% + \frac{1.249205 - 1.218994}{1.280085 - 1.218994} \, (2\tfrac{1}{2} - 2)\right] = 2.248 + \%$$

---

[4] *Linear* interpolation was illustrated; calculus or methods of finite differences could have been used.

Determination of Number of Periods

If the amount to which a given sum will accumulate is known, and the interest rate is known, the required number of periods can be calculated. To use the above example again, assume the following is known: (*a*) investment to be made $1,315.10; (*b*) accumulation desired $2,142.16; and (*c*) the desired interest rate to be 5%. To compute the required number of interest periods —

(1) $2,142.16 ÷ $1,315.10 = $1.628895 (rounded), the amount $1 would accumulate at 5% for the unknown number of interest periods.

(2) Referring to an amount of 1 table (Table 5–1) and reading down the 5% column we find 1.628895 (rounded) on the 10-year line, thus the required (implied) number of interest periods is 10.

Present Value (Worth)

Present Value (Worth) at Compound Interest (Compound Discount). Present value (worth) is the equivalent value *now* of future dollars discounted back from a specified future due date to the present date at a given rate of compound interest (discount). For example, $1 due two years in the future, when discounted back at 5% compound interest for two years, has a present value of $.907. We have seen that $1 invested at i interest rate per period has a future value of $(1 + i)^n$ dollars due in n periods. It would follow that $(1 + i)^n$ dollars due in n periods would have a present value of $1. Therefore, a reciprocal relationship exists between amount of 1 and present value of 1; i.e., the present value of

$$\$1 = \frac{1}{(1 + i)^n}$$

The very name "present value" is an implication that we tend to think in terms of *now*, and to *discount* a sum of money (to be received or paid in the future) is to find its present value. To illustrate the distinction, $1 deposited now will amount to $1.16 (more accurately, $1.157625) at the end of three periods assuming compound interest at 5%; conversely, $1 due at the end of three periods in the future, discounted at 5%, now is worth $.86 ($.8638376).

"Present Value of 1" Tables. The uses of "amount of 1" tables have already been demonstrated. It is obvious that such a table could be used to compute a table for "present value of 1" simply by dividing each value therein into 1. A *present value table* for the same interest rates and number of periods as the counterpart "amount of 1" in Table 5–1 appears in Table 5–2. The reciprocal relationship of the value in each table

$$\left(\frac{1}{1.020000} =_{,}.98039216 \right)$$

exists for every counterpart set of values throughout both tables.

Table 5-1
Amount of 1, $a = (1 + i)^n$

Periods	1½%	2%	2½%	3%	3½%	4%
0	1.	1.	1.	1.	1.	1.
1	1.015 25	1.02	1.025 25	1.03	1.035 25	1.04
2	1.0302 25	1.0404	1.0506 25	1.0609	1.0712 25	1.0816
3	1.0456 7838	1.0612 08	1.0768 9063	1.0927 27	1.1087 1788	1.1248 64
4	1.0613 6355	1.0824 3216	1.1038 1289	1.1255 0881	1.1475 2300	1.1698 5856
5	1.0772 8400	1.1040 8080	1.1314 0821	1.1592 7407	1.1876 8631	1.2166 5290
6	1.0934 4326	1.1261 6242	1.1596 9342	1.1940 5230	1.2292 5533	1.2653 1902
7	1.1098 4491	1.1486 8567	1.1886 8575	1.2298 7387	1.2722 7926	1.3159 3178
8	1.1264 9259	1.1716 5938	1.2184 0290	1.2667 7008	1.3168 0904	1.3685 6905
9	1.1433 8998	1.1950 9257	1.2488 6297	1.3047 7318	1.3628 9735	1.4233 1181
10	1.1605 4083	1.2189 9442	1.2800 8454	1.3439 1638	1.4105 9876	1.4802 4428
11	1.1779 4894	1.2433 7431	1.3120 8666	1.3842 3387	1.4599 6972	1.5394 5406
12	1.1956 1817	1.2682 4179	1.3448 8882	1.4257 6089	1.5110 6866	1.6010 3222
13	1.2135 5244	1.2936 0663	1.3785 1104	1.4685 3371	1.5639 5606	1.6650 7351
14	1.2317 5573	1.3194 7876	1.4129 7382	1.5125 8972	1.6186 9452	1.7316 7645
15	1.2502 3207	1.3458 6834	1.4482 9817	1.5579 6742	1.6753 4883	1.8009 4351
16	1.2689 8555	1.3727 8571	1.4845 0562	1.6047 0644	1.7339 8604	1.8729 8125
17	1.2880 2033	1.4002 4142	1.5216 1826	1.6528 4763	1.7946 7555	1.9479 0050
18	1.3073 4064	1.4282 4625	1.5596 5872	1.7024 3306	1.8574 8920	2.0258 1652
19	1.3269 5075	1.4568 1117	1.5986 5019	1.7535 0605	1.9225 0132	2.1068 4918
20	1.3468 5501	1.4859 4740	1.6386 1644	1.8061 1123	1.9897 8886	2.1911 2314
21	1.3670 5783	1.5156 6634	1.6795 8185	1.8602 9457	2.0594 3147	2.2787 6807
22	1.3875 6370	1.5459 7967	1.7215 7140	1.9161 0341	2.1315 1158	2.3699 1879
23	1.4083 7715	1.5768 9926	1.7646 1068	1.9735 8651	2.2061 1448	2.4647 1554
24	1.4295 0281	1.6084 3725	1.8087 2595	2.0327 9411	2.2833 2849	2.5633 0416
25	1.4509 4535	1.6406 0599	1.8539 4410	2.0937 7793	2.3632 4498	2.6658 3633

5%	6%	6½%	7%	7½%	8%	8½%
1.	1.	1.	1.	1.	1.	1.
1.05	1.06	1.065	1.07	1.075	1.08	1.055
1.1025 25	1.1236	1.1342 25	1.1449	1.1556 25	1.1664	1.1772 25
1.1576 25	1.1910 16	1.2079 4963	1.2250 43	1.2422 9688	1.2597 12	1.2772 8913
1.2155 0625	1.2624 7696	1.2864 6635	1.3107 9601	1.3354 6914	1.3604 8896	1.3858 5870
1.2762 8156	1.3382 2558	1.3700 8666	1.4025 5173	1.4356 2933	1.4693 2808	1.5036 5669
1.3400 9564	1.4185 1911	1.4591 4230	1.5007 3035	1.5433 0153	1.5868 7432	1.6314 6751
1.4071 0042	1.5036 3026	1.5539 8655	1.6057 8148	1.6590 4914	1.7138 2427	1.7701 4225
1.4774 5544	1.5938 4807	1.6549 9567	1.7181 8618	1.7834 7783	1.8509 3021	1.9206 0434
1.5513 2822	1.6894 7896	1.7625 7039	1.8384 5921	1.9172 3866	1.9990 0463	2.0838 5571
1.6288 9463	1.7908 4770	1.8771 3747	1.9671 5136	2.0610 3156	2.1589 2500	2.2609 8344
1.7103 3936	1.8982 9856	1.9991 5140	2.1048 5195	2.2156 0893	2.3316 3900	2.4531 6703
1.7958 5633	2.0121 9647	2.1290 9624	2.2521 9159	2.3817 7960	2.5181 7012	2.6616 8623
1.8856 4914	2.1329 2826	2.2674 8750	2.4098 4500	2.5604 1307	2.7196 2373	2.8879 2956
1.9799 3160	2.2609 0396	2.4148 7418	2.5785 3415	2.7524 4405	2.9371 9362	3.1334 0357
2.0789 2818	2.3965 5819	2.5718 4101	2.7590 3154	2.9588 7735	3.1721 6911	3.3997 4288
2.1828 7459	2.5403 5168	2.7390 1067	2.9521 6375	3.1807 9315	3.4259 4264	3.6887 2102
2.2920 1832	2.6927 7279	2.9170 4637	3.1588 1521	3.4193 5264	3.7000 1805	4.0022 6231
2.4066 1923	2.8543 3915	3.1066 5438	3.3799 3228	3.6758 0409	3.9960 1950	4.3424 5461
2.5269 5020	3.0255 9950	3.3085 8691	3.6165 2754	3.9514 8940	4.3157 0106	4.7115 6325
2.6532 9771	3.2071 3547	3.5236 4506	3.8696 8446	4.2478 5110	4.6609 5714	5.1120 4612
2.7859 6259	3.3995 6360	3.7526 8199	4.1405 6237	4.5664 3993	5.0338 3372	5.5465 7005
2.9252 6072	3.6035 3742	3.9966 0632	4.4304 0174	4.9089 2293	5.4365 4041	6.0180 2850
3.0715 2376	3.8197 4966	4.2563 8573	4.7405 2986	5.2770 9215	5.8714 6365	6.5295 6092
3.2250 9994	4.0489 3464	4.5330 5081	5.0723 6695	5.6728 7406	6.3411 8074	7.0845 7360
3.3863 5494	4.2918 7072	4.8276 9911	5.4274 3264	6.0983 3961	6.8484 7520	7.6867 6236

Table 5-2
Present Value of 1, $p = \dfrac{1}{(1+i)^n}$

Periods	1½%	2%	2½%	3%	3½%	4%
1	0.9852 2167	0.9803 9216	0.9756 0976	0.9708 7379	0.9661 8357	0.9615 3846
2	0.9706 6175	0.9611 6878	0.9518 1440	0.9425 9591	0.9335 1070	0.9245 5621
3	0.9563 1699	0.9423 2233	0.9285 9941	0.9151 4166	0.9019 4271	0.8889 9636
4	0.9421 8423	0.9238 4543	0.9059 5064	0.8884 8705	0.8714 4222	0.8548 0419
5	0.9282 6033	0.9057 3081	0.8838 5429	0.8626 0878	0.8419 7317	0.8219 2711
6	0.9145 4219	0.8879 7138	0.8622 9687	0.8374 8426	0.8135 0064	0.7903 1453
7	0.9010 2679	0.8705 6018	0.8412 6524	0.8130 9151	0.7859 9096	0.7599 1781
8	0.8877 1112	0.8534 9037	0.8207 4657	0.7894 0923	0.7594 1156	0.7306 9021
9	0.8745 9224	0.8367 5527	0.8007 2836	0.7664 1673	0.7337 3097	0.7025 8674
10	0.8616 6723	0.8203 4830	0.7819 8402	0.7440 9391	0.7089 1881	0.6755 6417
11	0.8489 3323	0.8042 6304	0.7621 4478	0.7224 2128	0.6849 4571	0.6495 8093
12	0.8363 8742	0.7884 9318	0.7435 5589	0.7013 7988	0.6617 8330	0.6245 9705
13	0.8240 2702	0.7730 3253	0.7254 2038	0.6809 5134	0.6394 0415	0.6005 7409
14	0.8118 4928	0.7578 7502	0.7077 2720	0.6611 1781	0.6177 8179	0.5774 7508
15	0.7998 5150	0.7430 1473	0.6904 6556	0.6418 6195	0.5968 9062	0.5552 6450
16	0.7880 3104	0.7284 4581	0.6736 2493	0.6231 6694	0.5767 0591	0.5339 0818
17	0.7763 8526	0.7141 6256	0.6571 9506	0.6050 1645	0.5572 0378	0.5133 7325
18	0.7649 1159	0.7001 5937	0.6411 6591	0.5873 9461	0.5383 6114	0.4936 2812
19	0.7536 0747	0.6864 3076	0.6255 2772	0.5702 8603	0.5201 5569	0.4746 4242
20	0.7424 7042	0.6729 7133	0.6102 0943	0.5536 7575	0.5025 6588	0.4563 8695
21	0.7314 9795	0.6597 7582	0.5953 8629	0.5375 4928	0.4855 7090	0.4388 3360
22	0.7206 8763	0.6468 3904	0.5808 6467	0.5218 9250	0.4691 5063	0.4219 5539
23	0.7100 3708	0.6341 5592	0.5666 9724	0.5066 9175	0.4532 8563	0.4057 2633
24	0.6995 4392	0.6217 2149	0.5528 7535	0.4919 3374	0.4379 5713	0.3901 2147
25	0.6892 0583	0.6095 3087	0.5393 9059	0.4776 0557	0.4231 4699	0.3751 1680

5%	6%	6½%	7%	7½%	8%	8½%
0.9523 8095	0.9433 9623	0.9389 6714	0.9345 7944	0.9302 3256	0.9259 2593	0.9216 5899
0.9070 2948	0.8899 9644	0.8816 5928	0.8734 3873	0.8653 3261	0.8573 3882	0.8494 5529
0.8638 3760	0.8396 1928	0.8278 4909	0.8162 9788	0.8049 6057	0.7938 3224	0.7829 0810
0.8227 0247	0.7920 9366	0.7773 2309	0.7628 9521	0.7488 0053	0.7350 2985	0.7215 7428
0.7835 2617	0.7472 5817	0.7298 8084	0.7129 8618	0.6965 5863	0.6805 8320	0.6650 4542
0.7462 1540	0.7049 6054	0.6853 3412	0.6663 4222	0.6479 6152	0.6301 6963	0.6129 4509
0.7106 8133	0.6650 5711	0.6435 0621	0.6227 4974	0.6027 5490	0.5834 9040	0.5649 2635
0.6768 3936	0.6274 1237	0.6042 3119	0.5820 0910	0.5607 0223	0.5402 6888	0.5206 6945
0.6446 0892	0.5918 9846	0.5673 5323	0.5439 3374	0.5215 8347	0.5002 4897	0.4798 7968
0.6139 1325	0.5583 9478	0.5327 2604	0.5083 4929	0.4851 9393	0.4631 9349	0.4422 8542
0.5846 7929	0.5267 8753	0.5002 1224	0.4750 9280	0.4513 4319	0.4288 8286	0.4076 3633
0.5568 3742	0.4969 6936	0.4696 8285	0.4440 1196	0.4198 5413	0.3971 1376	0.3757 0168
0.5303 2135	0.4688 3902	0.4410 1676	0.4149 6445	0.3905 6198	0.3670 9792	0.3462 6883
0.5050 6795	0.4423 0096	0.4141 0025	0.3878 1724	0.3633 1347	0.3404 6104	0.3191 4178
0.4810 1710	0.4172 6506	0.3888 2652	0.3624 4602	0.3379 6602	0.3152 4170	0.2941 3989
0.4581 1152	0.3936 4628	0.3650 9533	0.3387 3460	0.3143 8699	0.2918 9047	0.2710 9667
0.4362 9669	0.3713 6442	0.3428 1251	0.3165 7439	0.2924 5302	0.2702 6895	0.2498 5869
0.4155 2065	0.3503 4379	0.3218 8969	0.2958 6392	0.2720 4932	0.2502 4903	0.2302 8450
0.3957 3396	0.3305 1301	0.3022 4384	0.2765 0832	0.2530 6913	0.2317 1206	0.2122 4378
0.3768 8948	0.3118 0473	0.2837 9703	0.2584 1900	0.2354 1315	0.2145 4821	0.1956 1639
0.3589 4236	0.2941 5540	0.2664 7608	0.2415 1309	0.2189 8897	0.1986 5575	0.1802 9160
0.3418 4987	0.2775 0510	0.2502 1228	0.2257 1317	0.2037 1067	0.1839 4051	0.1661 6738
0.3255 7131	0.2617 9726	0.2349 4111	0.2109 4688	0.1894 9830	0.1703 1528	0.1531 4965
0.3100 6791	0.2469 7855	0.2206 0198	0.1971 4662	0.1762 7749	0.1576 9934	0.1411 5176
0.2953 0277	0.2329 9863	0.2071 3801	0.1842 4918	0.1639 7906	0.1460 1790	0.1300 9378

To illustrate use of the present value of 1 (Table 5–2), suppose we wish to calculate the amount that must be deposited *now* in a fund (present value) to meet an obligation of $50,000 due 15 years in the future, assuming the fund will earn 6%. Reference to the 6% column in Table 5–2 for 15 periods reveals that present value of 1 to be .41726506. Multiplying this value times the stipulated *future* amount of $50,000 gives an answer of $20,863.25. In other words, $20,863.25 left on deposit at 6% compound interest would accumulate to $50,000 at the end of 15 years (periods). Determination of other values related to the present value of 1 may be made in a manner similar to that illustrated previously for the amount of 1.

Annuities

Nature of Annuities. The term *annuity* implies a series of periodic payments (or receipts) called *rents*. The periods involved are of equal length and the rents of a constant amount. For example, the monthly loan payments made on the purchase of an auto, or home, constitute an annuity; there are equal periodic rents comprised in part of principal and in part of interest. From the point of view of the creditor the annuity represents periodic receipts of cash, whereas from the point of view of the debtor the annuity represents periodic (and equal) payments of cash. Thus, a series of equal rents, paid or received at regular time intervals (periods) characterize an *annuity*. While the term *annuity* may imply *annual* rents to some people, we should note that equal rents spread over any series of equal time intervals (monthly, quarterly, semiannually, or annually) constitute an annuity. Accounting frequently encounters transactions involving annuities; common examples include interest payments on bonds (owed or held as an investment), contributions to sinking funds, amortization of long-term prepayments, and leaseholds.

Amount of an Annuity. The *amount of an annuity* is the *future* value (sum) of all its rents plus the compound interest on each of them. Consider a simple example. Suppose a person deposits $100 per year for four years (periods) in a fund which earns compound interest at 6% per annum. At the date of the last deposit, the first rent will have earned compound interest for three years, the second for two years, the third for one year. Applying principles we learned in the section on amount of 1, the accumulation at the date of the last deposit will be seen to consist of—

Date of
Deposit

Year 1	$100 × (1.06)³ = $119.10
Year 2	$100 × (1.06)² = 112.36
Year 3	$100 × (1.06)¹ = 106.00
Year 4	$100 = 100.00
Amount of Annuity (Ordinary)	$437.46

Note should be taken of the fact that in the above illustration, no interest was included after the last rent; hence, interest was involved for only three periods, although there were four rents. One less interest period than rents is a characteristic of the amount of *ordinary annuities* since they "end" on the *date of the last rent*. In contrast, the *amount of an annuity due* ends one period *after* the last rent; as a consequence the latter would involve the *same* number of interest periods (4 in the example) as rents. Annuities *due* are discussed in a subsequent section of this chapter.

Two different symbols are variously used to refer to the amount of annuity of 1, A and $S_{\overline{n}|i}$. With respect to the latter notation, "n" refers to the number of periodic rents and "i" to the interest rate per period. For example $S_{\overline{10}|.05}$ refers to the amount of an annuity of 1 for 10 periodic rents at 5% interest. The amount of an annuity is derived by the formula

$$A = \frac{(1 + i)^n - 1}{i}$$

It will be noted in the heading of Table 5–3 that this is the indicated formula for the table values.

Use of Table of Amount of Annuity of 1. A limited table showing the amount of an ordinary annuity of 1 over a limited range of periodic rents and interest rates is shown in Table 5–3.

Tables of amounts of annuities are commonly used to calculate the future amount (worth) of an annuity where the rents, interest rate, and number of rents are known.

To illustrate use of Table 5–3, assume a company desires to know the future amount that will accumulate in a sinking fund when regular payments (rents) of $6,000 are made each 6 months for 10 years and invested at 6% per annum, compounded semiannually. The problem may be expressed, $A = S_{\overline{20}|.03}$, since there are 20 semiannual rents and a *period* interest rate of .03. Reference to the 3% column in Table 5–3 (amount of annuity of 1) for 20 rents shows a value of 26.8703745. Multiplication of this table value times the periodic rent of $6,000 gives $161,222 (rounded) the accumulation in the sinking fund at the end of 10 years.

Determination of Other Values Related to Amount of Annuity. In the immediately preceding example, *three* values were given as follows: (1) periodic rents, $6,000; (2) number of rents, 20; and (3) the periodic interest rate, 3%. A fourth value, the future accumulation in a sinking fund $161,222 was computed. Obviously, if *any* three of these four values are known, the other one can be derived. Thus, as was illustrated with respect to the amount of 1 (Table 5–1), there are four types of potential problems that may be encountered; viz:

1. To determine the future accumulation (value); discussed immediately above.

Table 5-3
Amount of Annuity of 1 (Ordinary), $A = S_{\overline{n}|i} = \dfrac{(1+i)^n - 1}{i}$

Periodic rents	1½%	2%	2¼%	2½%	3%	3½%	4%
1	1.	1.	1.	1.	1.	1.	1.
2	2.015 2250	2.020	2.0225 0625	2.025 6250	2.030 9000	2.035 25	2.040 6000
3	3.045	3.060	3.0680 0625	3.075 6250	3.090 9000	3.1062 25	3.121 6000
4	4.090 9034	4.121 6800	4.1370 3639	4.152 5156	4.183 6270	4.2149 4288	4.246 4640
5	5.152 2669	5.204 0402	5.2301 1971	5.256 3285	5.309 1358	5.3624 6588	5.416 3226
6	6.229 5509	6.308 1210	6.3477 9740	6.387 7367	6.468 4099	6.5501 5218	6.632 9755
7	7.322 9942	7.434 2833	7.4906 2284	7.547 4301	7.662 4622	7.7794 0751	7.898 2945
8	8.432 8391	8.582 9610	8.6591 6186	8.736 1159	8.892 3361	9.0516 8677	9.214 2263
9	9.559 3317	9.754 6284	9.8539 9300	9.954 5188	10.159 1061	10.3684 9581	10.582 7953
10	10.702 7217	10.949 7210	11.0757 0784	11.203 3818	11.463 8793	11.7313 9316	12.006 1071
11	11.863 2625	12.168 7154	12.3249 1127	12.483 4663	12.807 7957	13.1419 9192	13.486 3514
12	13.041 2114	13.412 0897	13.6022 2177	13.795 5530	14.192 0296	14.6019 6164	15.025 8055
13	14.236 8296	14.680 3315	14.9082 7176	15.140 4418	15.617 7905	16.1130 3030	16.626 8377
14	15.450 3820	15.973 3982	16.2437 0788	16.518 9528	17.086 3242	17.6769 8636	18.291 9112
15	16.682 1378	17.293 4169	17.6091 9130	17.931 9267	18.598 9139	19.2956 8088	20.023 5876
16	17.932 3698	18.639 2853	19.0053 9811	19.380 2248	20.156 8813	20.9710 2971	21.824 5311
17	19.201 3554	20.012 0710	20.4330 1957	20.864 7304	21.761 5877	22.7050 1575	23.697 5124
18	20.489 3757	21.412 3124	21.8927 6251	22.386 3487	23.414 4354	24.4996 9130	25.645 4129
19	21.796 7164	22.840 5586	23.3853 4966	23.946 0074	25.116 8684	26.3571 8050	27.671 2294
20	23.123 6671	24.297 3698	24.9115 2003	25.544 6576	26.870 3745	28.2796 8181	29.778 0786
21	24.470 5221	25.783 3172	26.4720 2923	27.183 2741	28.676 4857	30.2694 7068	31.969 2017
22	25.837 5799	27.298 9835	28.0676 4989	28.862 8559	30.536 7803	32.3289 0215	34.247 9698
23	27.225 1436	28.844 9632	29.6991 7201	30.584 4273	32.452 8837	34.4604 1373	36.617 8886
24	28.633 5208	30.421 8625	31.3674 0338	32.349 0380	34.426 4702	36.6665 2821	39.082 6041
25	30.063 1236	32.030 2997	33.0731 6996	34.157 7639	36.459 2643	38.9498 5669	41.645 9083

4½%	5%	6%	6½%	7%	7½%	8%	8½%
1.	1.	1.	1.	1.	1.	1.	1.
2.045	2.050	2.060 0000	2.065	2.07	2.075	2.08	2.085
3.1370 25	3.152 5000	3.183 6000	3.1992 25	3.2149	3.2306 25	3.2464	3.2622 25
4.2781 9113	4.310 1250	4.374 6160	4.4071 746	4.4399 430	4.4729 219	4.5061 12	4.5395 141
5.4707 0973	5.525 6313	5.637 0930	5.6936 410	5.7507 390	5.8083 910	5.8666 01	5.9253 728
6.7168 9166	6.801 9128	6.975 3185	7.0637 276	7.1532 907	7.2440 203	7.3359 290	7.4290 295
8.0191 5179	8.142 0085	8.393 8377	8.5228 694	8.6540 211	8.7873 219	8.9228 034	9.0604 970
9.3800 1362	9.549 1089	9.897 4679	10.0768 565	10.2598 026	10.4463 710	10.6366 276	10.8306 393
10.8021 1423	11.026 5643	11.491 3160	11.7318 522	11.9779 888	12.2298 488	12.4875 578	12.7512 436
12.2882 0937	12.577 8925	13.180 7949	13.4944 225	13.8164 480	14.1470 075	14.4865 625	14.8350 993
13.8411 7879	14.206 7872	14.971 6426	15.3715 600	15.7835 993	16.2081 191	16.6454 875	17.0960 828
15.4640 3184	15.917 1265	16.869 9412	17.3707 114	17.8884 513	18.4237 280	18.9771 265	19.5492 498
17.1599 1327	17.712 9829	18.882 1377	19.4998 077	20.1406 429	20.8055 076	21.4952 966	22.2109 360
18.9321 0937	19.598 6320	21.015 0659	21.7672 952	22.5504 879	23.3659 207	24.2149 203	25.0988 656
20.7840 5429	21.578 5636	23.275 9699	24.1821 693	25.1290 220	26.1183 647	27.1521 139	28.2322 692
22.7193 3673	23.657 4918	25.672 5281	26.7540 103	27.8880 536	29.0772 421	30.3242 830	31.6320 120
24.7417 0689	25.840 3664	28.212 8798	29.4930 210	30.8402 173	32.2580 352	33.7502 257	35.3207 331
26.8550 8370	28.132 3847	30.905 6526	32.4100 674	33.9990 325	35.6773 879	37.4502 437	39.3229 934
29.0635 6246	30.539 0039	33.759 9917	35.5167 218	37.3789 648	39.3531 919	41.4462 632	43.6654 500
31.3714 2277	33.065 9541	36.785 5912	38.8253 087	40.9954 923	43.3046 813	45.7619 643	48.3770 132
33.7831 3680	35.719 2518	39.992 7267	42.3489 537	44.8651 763	47.5525 324	50.4229 214	53.4890 594
36.3033 7795	38.505 2144	43.392 2903	46.1016 357	49.0057 392	52.1189 724	55.4567 552	59.0356 294
38.9370 2996	41.430 4751	46.995 8277	50.0982 421	53.4361 409	57.0278 953	60.8932 956	65.0536 579
41.6891 9631	44.501 9989	50.815 5774	54.3546 278	58.1766 708	62.3049 874	66.7647 592	71.5832 188
44.5652 1015	47.727 0988	54.864 5120	58.8876 786	63.2490 377	67.9778 615	73.1059 400	78.6677 924

2. To determine an unknown interest rate.

   Example (based on above data):

   Given: *a*) Periodic rents, $6,000.

           b) Rents, 20.

           c) Future accumulation desired, $161,222.

   To derive the implied interest rate:

       a) $161,222 ÷ $6,000 = 26.87037 (table value for 20 rents at unknown interest rate).

       b) Reference to Table 5–3, *line* for 20 rents indicates the interest rate to be 3% (rounded).

3. To determine an unknown number of periodic rents.

   Example (based on above data):

   Given: *a*) Periodic rents, $6,000.

           b) Future accumulation desired, $161,222.

           c) Interest rate, 3% per period.

   To derive the implied number of rents.

       a) $161,222 ÷ $6,000 = 26.87037 (table value for $1 at 3% for unknown number of rents).

       b) Reference to Table 5–3, *column* for 3% interest indicates the number of rents to be 20.

4. To determine the unknown amount of each rent.

   Example (based on above data):

   Given: *a*) Rents, 20.

           b) Interest rate per period, 3%.

           c) Future accumulation desired, $161,222.

   To derive the unknown amount of each rent:

       a) Reference to Table 5–3, column for 3% and line for 20 rents gives the value 26.87037.

       b) $161,222 ÷ 26.87037 = $6,000 – the period rent required (rounded).

Present Value of Annuities.   The present value (worth) of an *annuity* is the equivalent value *now* of a series of future dollars (periodic rents) discounted back from a series of specified future dates (periods) to the present date at a given rate of compound interest (discount). For example, $1 (the periodic rent) due at the *end* of *each* of three periods in the future (total sum due $3), when discounted back at 5% compound interest, has a present value of $2.72+. Alternatively, $2.72 deposited today at 5% compound interest per period would pay back $1 at the end of each of the three future periods. Significantly, it should be noted that the rents on the present value of an ordinary annuity are assumed to be at the *end* of each period; hence, in contrast to the amount of an annuity of 1, there are the same number of interest periods as rents.[5]

---

[5] In both instances an *ordinary* annuity is assumed; *annuity due* is discussed in the next section.

As another example, suppose an expert estimate indicates that a certain mine should produce a net income of $15,000 annually for the next 10 years. Assuming a 5% interest rate; what should be the maximum paid for the mine (i.e., what is the present value of the mine)? This situation may be compared to the lump-sum purchase of an ordinary annuity of 10 periodic rents of $15,000, or alternatively, the calculation of the present value of such an annuity.

From a table of *present value of an annuity of 1* such as appears in Table 5–4, the present value of the 10 rents of $15,000 each can be calculated by multiplying the rent by the present value of an annuity of $1:

$$\$15,000 \times 7.7217349 = \$115,826.02$$

Two different symbols are variously used for the present value of an annuity, P and $A_{\overline{n}|i}$. In the latter, n indicates number of periodic rents and i the periodic interest rate. The detailed formula for Table 5–4 is:

$$\frac{1 - \dfrac{1}{(1 + i)^n}}{i}$$

Determination of Other Values Related to Present Value of Annuity

Tables of present values of annuities are commonly used to calculate the present value of an annuity where the rents, interest rate, and number of periodic rents are known as illustrated in the preceding paragraph. They may also be used to calculate the rents if, instead, the present value as well as other factors are known. In the immediately preceding example, *three* values were given as follows: (1) periodic rents of $15,000 each; (2) number of periodic rents, 10; and (3) interest rate, 5%. A fourth value, the present value of the future rents was computed. Obviously, if *any* three of these four values are known, the other one can be derived. Thus, as was illustrated previously with respect to the amount of an annuity of 1 (Table 5–3), there are four types of potential problems that may be encountered; viz:

1. To determine the present value of a series of future rents (discussed and illustrated immediately above).
2. To determine an unknown interest rate.
   Example (based on above data):
   Given: *a*) Periodic rents, $15,000.
         b) Number of periodic rents, 10.
         c) Present value of the future rents, $115,826.02.
   To derive the implied interest rate:
      a) $115,826.02 ÷ $15,000 = $7.7217347 (approximate table value for 10 periods at unknown interest rate).

Table 5-4

Present Value of Annuity of 1 (Ordinary), $P = a_{\overline{n}|i} = \dfrac{1 - \dfrac{1}{(1+i)^n}}{i}$

Periodic Rents	1½%	2%	2½%	3%	3½%	4%
1	0.985 2217	0.980 3922	0.975 6098	0.970 8738	0.9661 8357	0.961 5385
2	1.955 8834	1.941 5609	1.927 4242	1.913 4697	1.8996 9428	1.886 0947
3	2.912 2004	2.883 8833	2.856 0236	2.828 6114	2.8016 3698	2.775 0910
4	3.854 3847	3.807 7287	3.761 9742	3.717 0984	3.6730 7921	3.629 8952
5	4.782 6450	4.713 4595	4.645 8285	4.579 7072	4.5150 5238	4.451 8223
6	5.697 1872	5.601 4309	5.508 1254	5.417 1914	5.3285 5302	5.242 1369
7	6.598 2140	6.471 9911	6.349 3906	6.230 2830	6.1145 4398	6.002 0547
8	7.485 9251	7.325 4814	7.170 1372	7.019 6922	6.8739 5554	6.732 7449
9	8.360 5173	8.162 2367	7.970 8655	7.786 1089	7.6076 8651	7.435 3316
10	9.222 1846	8.982 5850	8.752 0639	8.530 2028	8.3166 0532	8.110 8958
11	10.071 1178	9.786 8481	9.514 2087	9.252 6241	9.0015 5104	8.760 4767
12	10.907 5052	10.575 3412	10.257 7646	9.954 0040	9.6633 3433	9.385 0738
13	11.731 5322	11.348 3738	10.983 1850	10.634 9553	10.3027 3849	9.985 6479
14	12.543 3815	12.106 2488	11.690 9122	11.296 0731	10.9205 2028	10.563 1229
15	13.343 2330	12.849 2635	12.381 3777	11.937 9351	11.5174 1090	11.118 3874
16	14.131 2641	13.577 7093	13.055 0027	12.561 1020	12.0941 1681	11.652 2956
17	14.907 6493	14.291 8719	13.712 1977	13.166 1185	12.6513 2059	12.165 6689
18	15.672 5609	14.992 0313	14.353 3636	13.753 5131	13.1896 8173	12.659 2970
19	16.426 1684	15.678 4620	14.978 8913	14.323 7991	13.7098 3742	13.133 9394
20	17.168 6388	16.351 4333	15.589 1623	14.877 4749	14.2124 0330	13.590 3263
21	17.900 1367	17.011 2092	16.184 5486	15.415 0241	14.6979 7420	14.029 1600
22	18.620 8244	17.658 0482	16.765 4132	15.936 9166	15.1671 2484	14.451 1153
23	19.330 8615	18.292 2041	17.332 1105	16.443 6084	15.6204 1047	14.856 8417
24	20.030 4054	18.913 9256	17.884 9858	16.935 5421	16.0583 6760	15.246 9631
25	20.719 6112	19.523 4565	18.424 3764	17.413 1477	16.4815 1459	15.622 0799

5%	6%	6½%	7%	7½%	8%	8½%
0.952 3810	0.943 3962	0.9389 671	0.9345 794	0.9302 326	0.9259 259	0.9216 590
1.859 4104	1.833 3927	1.8206 264	1.8080 182	1.7955 652	1.7832 648	1.7711 143
2.723 2480	2.673 0120	2.6484 755	2.6243 160	2.6005 257	2.5770 970	2.5540 224
3.545 9505	3.465 1056	3.4257 986	3.3872 113	3.3493 263	3.3121 268	3.2755 967
4.329 4767	4.212 3638	4.1556 794	4.1001 974	4.0458 849	3.9927 100	3.9406 421
5.075 6921	4.917 3243	4.8410 136	4.7665 397	4.6938 464	4.6228 797	4.5535 872
5.786 3734	5.582 3814	5.4845 198	5.3892 894	5.2966 013	5.2063 701	5.1185 135
6.463 2128	6.209 7938	6.0887 510	5.9712 985	5.8573 036	5.7466 389	5.6391 830
7.107 8217	6.801 6923	6.6561 042	6.5152 323	6.3788 870	6.2468 879	6.1190 626
7.721 7349	7.360 0871	7.1888 302	7.0235 815	6.8640 810	6.7100 814	6.5613 481
8.306 4142	7.886 8746	7.6890 425	7.4986 743	7.3154 242	7.1389 643	6.9689 844
8.863 2516	8.383 8439	8.1587 253	7.9426 863	7.7352 783	7.5360 780	7.3446 861
9.393 5730	8.852 6830	8.5997 421	8.3576 507	8.1258 403	7.9037 759	7.6909 549
9.898 6409	9.294 9839	9.0138 423	8.7454 680	8.4891 537	8.2442 370	8.0100 967
10.379 6580	9.712 2490	9.4026 689	9.1079 140	8.8271 197	8.5594 787	8.3042 366
10.837 7696	10.105 8953	9.7677 642	9.4466 480	9.1415 067	8.8513 692	8.5753 333
11.274 0663	10.477 2597	10.1105 767	9.7632 230	9.4339 598	9.1216 381	8.8251 919
11.689 5869	10.827 6035	10.4324 664	10.0590 864	9.7060 091	9.3718 871	9.0554 764
12.085 3209	11.158 1165	10.7347 102	10.3355 952	9.9590 782	9.6035 992	9.2677 202
12.462 2103	11.469 9212	11.0185 073	10.5940 143	10.1944 914	9.8181 474	9.4633 366
12.821 1527	11.764 0766	11.2849 833	10.8355 273	10.4134 803	10.0168 032	9.6436 282
13.163 0026	12.041 5817	11.5351 956	11.0612 405	10.6171 910	10.2007 437	9.8097 956
13.488 5739	12.303 3790	11.7701 367	11.2721 874	10.8066 893	10.3710 590	9.9629 452
13.798 6418	12.550 3575	11.9907 387	11.4693 340	10.9829 668	10.5287 583	10.1040 970
14.093 9446	12.783 3562	12.1978 767	11.6535 832	11.1469 459	10.6747 762	10.2341 908

   b) Reference to Table 5–4, line for 10 rents, indicates the interest rate to be 5%.
3. To determine an unknown number of periodic rents.
   Example (based on above data):
   Given: *a)* Periodic rents, $15,000.
          b) Interest rate, 5%.
          c) Present value of the future rents, $115,826.02.
   To derive the unknown number of periodic rents:
   a) $115,826.02 ÷ $15,000 = 7.7217347 (approximate table value at 5% at unknown number of rents).
   b) Reference to Table 5–4, column for 5%, indicates 10 periodic rents.
4. To determine the unknown amount of each rent.
   Example (based on above data):
   Given: *a)* Number of periodic rents, 10.
          b) Interest rate per period, 5%.
          c) Present value of the future rents, $115,826.02.
   To derive the amount of each rent:
   a) Table 5–4 value at 5%, 10 rents = 7.7217349.
   b) $115,826.03 ÷ 7.7217349 = $15,000 (the periodic rent).

Frequently, it is desirable to develop a *tabulation* of annuity results for accounting purposes. For illustration, another example is presented that is identical with 4 immediately above, except for changed data. Assume a debtor owes $6,600 bearing 5% interest payable annually. The debt and interest is to be paid in four equal installments commencing one year hence. What are the annual payments (rents)?

Analysis: Data provided: (*a*) present value of annuity, $6,600; (*b*) interest rate, 5%; and (*c*) rents, 4. To compute the *annual rent:*

$6,600 ÷ 3.545905 (Table 5–4 value) = $1,861.28 (annual rent)

Having computed the annual rent, payment of the principal and interest may be tabulated as shown in Illustration 5–2.

Illustration 5–2

Payment (Rent)	Total Paid	Interest Expense	Payment on Principal	Unpaid Principal
				$6,600.00°
First......................$1,861.28		$330.00	$1,531.28	5,068.72
Second................... 1,861.28		253.44	1,607.84	3,460.88
Third 1,861.28		173.04	1,688.24	1,772.64
Fourth................... 1,861.27		88.63	1,772.64	0

° Successive computations:
   $6,600 × 5% = $330.00.
   $1,861.28 − $330.00 = $1,531.28.
   $6,600 − $1,531.28 = $5,068.72.

We may note that each line indicates an accounting entry, for example to record the first payment:

Notes Payable	1,531.28	
Interest Expense	330.00	
Cash		1,861.28

Annuities Due

Discussion of annuities to this point has been confined to *ordinary annuities* since they represent the more or less "normal" situation encountered. It will be recalled that with respect to ordinary annuities, very specific assumptions were noted in the preceding discussions relative to the *timing* of the rents and the interest periods. *Annuities due* involve very different assumptions with respect to the time and interest period viewpoints. In order to clearly understand the distinction between *ordinary* annuities and annuities *due*, the *amount* of an annuity (Table 5–3) must be considered separately from the *present value* of an annuity (Table 5–4).

Amount of Annuity Due. In the case of the amount of an ordinary annuity the *amount* is the future value on the date of the *last* rent; hence, there is one less interest period than rents. In contrast, in an *annuity due* the *amount* is the future value one period *after* the date of the last rent; hence, there are the same number of interest periods as rents. The distinction may be graphically shown in Illustration 5–3.

Clearly, the difference is one of time viewpoint. The *amount of an annuity due* is the value of the annuity one period *after* the date of the final rent or payment. The *amount of an ordinary annuity* is the value of the annuity *on* the date of the final rent or payment. In solving annuity problems care must be exercised to determine which situation is involved. Table 5–3 given above was for *ordinary* annuities; annuity due tables are generally available. However, when annuity due tables are not available, the necessary value can be derived from the table for ordinary annuities; the annuity due value simply requires that the reading from the ordinary table be one greater than the number of rents, then subtraction of the numeral 1 from it.[6] To illustrate—

Ordinary Annuity Example. If seven payments of $3,000 are deposited each January 1, beginning January 1, 1967, and continuing through January 1, 1973 (date of last rent), determination of the sum on deposit January 1, 1973, calls for calculation of the amount of an *ordinary* annuity for seven rents. Assuming an interest rate of 5% for the seven rents, from Table 5–3 we get 8.1420085, then—

$$\$3,000 \times 8.1420085 = \$24,426.03$$

---

[6] Frequently expressed as $(n + 1 \text{ rents}) - \$1$.

Illustration 5–3
Amount of Ordinary Annuity and Annuity Due Compared

AMOUNT OF ORDINARY ANNUITY OF 1

No Interest after Last Rent—Four Rents and Three Interest Periods

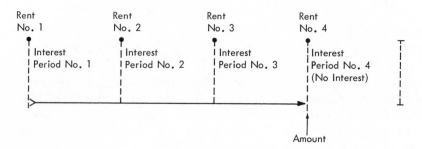

AMOUNT OF ANNUITY DUE OF 1

Interest after Last Rent—Four Rents and Four Interest Periods

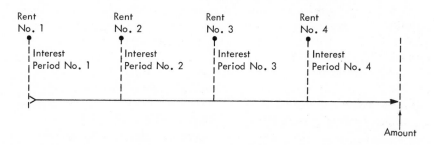

Annuity Due Example. If, on the other hand, the same seven $3,000 deposits are made on the same seven dates and a 5% rate is earned, and we wish to determine the amount on deposit January 1, 1974 (one year later, hence one more interest period), calculation of the amount of an annuity *due* for *seven* periods is necessary. We would take our reading for *eight* rents from Table 5–3 (amount of an ordinary annuity) and subtract *1* because there is no eighth rent on July 1, 1974:

$$\$3,000 \times (9.5491089 - 1) = \$25,647.33$$

The difference is that in the latter case each payment has earned compound interest for one additional period whereas the rents remained the same. An alternative way to arrive at the same result is to take the ordinary annuity accumulation of $24,426.03 and to compound interest on it at 5% for an additional year, viz:

$$\$24,426.03 \times 1.05 = \$25,647.33$$

Present Value of Annuity Due.   In the case of the present value of an *ordinary* annuity, the value *now* is discounted back one period from the first rent; therefore, the number of rents and the number of discount periods are the same. In contrast, with respect to the present value of an *annuity due,* since there is no discount back from the first rent, there is *one less* discount period than rents. The distinction may be graphically shown as in Illustration 5–4.

Illustration 5–4
Present Value of Ordinary Annuity and Annuity Due Compared
PRESENT VALUE OF ORDINARY ANNUITY OF 1
Four Rents and Four Discount Periods

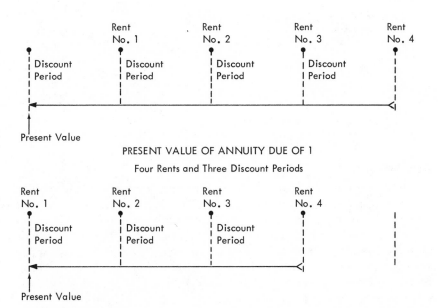

PRESENT VALUE OF ANNUITY DUE OF 1
Four Rents and Three Discount Periods

Clearly, the difference, again is one of time viewpoint. In solving problems care must be exercised to determine which situation is involved. If a table for present value for annuity *due* of 1 is not available, the ordinary annuity table may be used. To determine the present value of an annuity due of n rents of $1, find the present value of an ordinary annuity of $n - 1$ rents, then add $1, that is, $[(n - 1$ rents$) + \$1]$.

To illustrate, suppose a tenant paying annual rentals of $500 in advance desires to prepay the rent for the remainder of his lease which has four years to run. The payment immediately due on, say, January 1, 1971, covers the year 1971. If the lessor is willing to accept a lump sum on this date, discounted at 8%, settlement could be effected by payment of $1,788.55 (an annuity due); calculated as follows:

To calculate present value of an annuity due for: (a) 4 rents, (b) at 8% interest per period, and (c) rents, $500.

1. Table value for annuity due from a table of ordinary annuities (Table 5–4): $(n - 1$ rents$) + \$1 = (4 - 1$ rents$) + \$1$

   3 rents at 8%   = 2.577097
   2.577097 + 1.00   = 3.577097
2. $500 × 3.577097   = $1,788.55

Proof of Calculation

Jan. 1, 1971	Total present value	$1,788.55
	Rent due January 1, 1971 (no interest on first rent)	500.00
	Remainder	$1,288.55
Jan. 1, 1972	Interest at 8% of $1,288.55	103.08
	Total	$1,391.63
	Rent due, January 1, 1972	500.00
	Remainder	$ 891.63
Jan. 1, 1973	Interest at 8% of $891.63	71.33
	Total	$ 962.96
	Rent due, January 1, 1973	500.00
	Remainder	$ 462.96
Jan. 1, 1974	Interest at 8% of $462.96	37.04
	Rent Due, January 1, 1974	$ 500.00

Deferred Annuities

An annuity in which more than one period is to expire before rents are begun is known as a deferred annuity. The *amount* of a deferred annuity is the same as the amount of an ordinary annuity of like payments, interest, and number of rents. The *present value* of a deferred annuity is not the same, however, as the present value of an ordinary annuity, at least not until only one period before the first rent is to be paid. At this time, of course, it would no longer be a deferred annuity, but would instead have become an ordinary annuity.

For example, on January 1, 1968, an annuity contract was executed calling for five equal annual payments of $200 each with the first payment to be made at the *end* of the eighth year (1975) and a 5% interest rate. This deferred annuity may be diagrammed as follows:

Rents $200 $200 $200 $200 $200
                                                     ↓   ↓   ↓   ↓   ↓
Years | 1968 | 1969 | 1970 | 1971 | 1972 | 1973 | 1974 | 1975 | 1976 | 1977 | 1978 | 1979 |

This is essentially an ordinary annuity of five rents, deferred seven years. We can compute both its future amount and its present value. The *future amount* of this annuity on the date of the last rent (end of 1979) would be:

$$\text{Rent} \times S_{\overline{5}|.05} = \$200 \times 5.5256313 = \$1{,}105.13$$

Its present value (on January 1, 1968) may be computed as follows: (1) Determine the present value of an ordinary annuity of 1 at the given interest rate for the specified number of rents. (2) Multiply the value in (1) by the amount of the rent. At this stage we have computed the present value of an ordinary annuity as of one year before the date of the first rent. (3) Multiply the result in (2) by the present value of 1 for the number of deferred periods, viz:

1. Present value of ordinary annuity of 1 at 5% for five years is 4.329477 (present value of 1 at beginning of 1975).
2. Annual rents of $200 × 4.329477 = $865.90 (amount at beginning of 1975).
3. The present value of 1 for seven periods at 5% = .710681. $865.90 × .710681 = $615.38, present value of annuity of five rents of $200, deferred seven periods (present value at beginning of 1968).

Formulas and table-value derivation and interrelationships are presented in an appendix to this chapter.

PART B – APPLICATION OF FUNDAMENTAL PROCESSES AND FORMULAS

This part of the chapter is designed to recapitulate and summarize by way of a common example the fundamental processes (and the four tables presented). The illustrations are presented in the same sequence as the topics were discussed in Part A. To the fullest extent possible a common set of figures are utilized, viz: interest rate, 5%, compounded annually; number of periods (or rents), 10; deposit, rent, or ending amount (as the case may be), $1,000.

Each solution utilizes formulas and table values and restates the "given" values in order to facilitate study.

Amount of 1:

1. How much will $1,000 deposited at 5% for 10 years accumulate? Date of deposit, January 1, 1967; end date, January 1, 1977.

$$\$1{,}000 \times a = \$1{,}000 \times (1+i)^n$$
$$\$1{,}000 \times (1+.05)^{10} = \$1{,}000 \times 1.62889463 \text{ (Table 5–1)}$$
$$= \$1{,}628.89$$

Present Value of 1:

2. How much must be deposited in a lump sum at 5% if $1,000 is desired in 10 years? Date of deposit, January 1, 1967; end date, January 1, 1977.

$$\$1,000 \times p = \$1,000 \times \frac{1}{(1 + i)^n}$$

$$\$1,000 \times \frac{1}{(1 + .05)^{10}} = \$1,000 \times .61391325 \text{ (Table 5-2)}$$

$$= \$613.91$$

Amount of Ordinary Annuity:

3. If $1,000 is deposited annually at 5% for 10 years, how much will accumulate on the date of the last deposit? Date of first deposit, January 1, 1967; end date, January 1, 1976.

$$\$1,000 \times A = \$1,000 \times \frac{(1 + i)^n - 1}{i}$$

$$\$1,000 \times \frac{(1 + .05)^{10} - 1}{.05} = \$1,000 \times 12.5778925 \text{ (Table 5-3)}$$

$$= \$12,577.89$$

4. How much must be deposited each year for 10 years at 5% to produce a fund of $1,000 on the date of the last deposit? Date of first deposit, January 1, 1967; end date, January 1, 1976.

$$\$1,000 \div A = \$1,000 \div \frac{(1 + i)^n - 1}{i}$$

$$\$1,000 \div \frac{(1 + .05)^{10} - 1}{.05} = \$1,000 \div 12.5778925 \text{ (Table 5-3)}$$

$$= \$79.50$$

Present Value of Ordinary Annuity:

5. How much must be invested at 5% to provide for 10 annual rents of $1,000, the first to be made one year after the investment? Date of investment, January 1, 1967; date of first rent, January 1, 1968.

$$\$1,000 \times P = \$1,000 \times \frac{1 - \dfrac{1}{(1 + i)^n}}{i}$$

$$\$1,000 \times \frac{1 - \dfrac{1}{(1 + .05)^{10}}}{.05} = \$1,000 \times 7.7217349$$

$$= \$7,721.73 \qquad \text{(Table 5-4)}$$

6. *a)* If $1,000 is deposited at 5% to produce 10 equal annual rents, the first of which is payable after one year, how large is each

rent? Date of deposit, January 1, 1967; date of first rent, January 1, 1968.

$$\$1,000 \div P = \$1,000 \div \frac{1 - \dfrac{1}{(1 + i)^n}}{i}$$

$$\$1,000 \div \frac{1 - \dfrac{1}{(1 + .05)^{10}}}{.05} = \$1,000 \div 7.72173493$$

$$= \$129.50$$

b) It would follow that a debt of $1,000, bearing interest at 5% and payable in 10 equal annual installments, would require payments of $129.50 starting one year hence.

Amount of Annuity Due:

7. If $1,000 is deposited annually at 5% for 10 years, how much will accumulate in 10 years after the first deposit (i.e., one year after the last deposit)? Date of first deposit, January 1, 1967; end date, January 1, 1977.

$$\$1,000 \times (A - 1) = \$1,000 \times \left[\frac{(1 + i)^n - 1}{i} - 1 \right]$$

$$\$1,000 \times \left[\frac{(1 + .05)^{11} - 1}{.05} - 1 \right] = \$1,000 \times (14.2067872 - 1)$$

(Table 5–3)

$$= \$13,206.79$$

(Note: Since this is an annuity due, use a value of A for 11 years and subtract 1.)

8. How much must be deposited each year for 10 years to produce a fund of $1,000 one year after the date of the last deposit? Date of first deposit, January 1, 1967; end date, January 1, 1977.

$$\$1,000 \div (A - 1) = \$1,000 \div \left[\frac{(1 + i)^n - 1}{i} - 1 \right]$$

$$\$1,000 \div \left[\frac{(1 + .05)^{11} - 1}{.05} - 1 \right] = \$1,000 \div (14.20678716 - 1)$$

(Table 5–3)

$$= \$1,000 \div 13.20678716$$
$$= \$75.72$$

(Note: Since this is an annuity due, use a value of A for 11 years and subtract 1.)

Present Value of Annuity Due:

9. How much must be invested at 5% to provide 10 annual rents of $1,000, the first to be made immediately? Date of first deposit and rent, January 1, 1967; date of last rent, January 1, 1976. We have an annuity due of 10 rents. This is the same as an annuity of nine rents, plus one immediate rent. Accordingly, we can use the present value of nine future rents from Table 5–4 and add 1.

$$\$1,000 \times (P + 1) = \$1,000 \times \left[\frac{1 - \frac{1}{(1 + i)^n}}{i} + 1 \right]$$

$$\$1,000 \times \left[\frac{1 - \frac{1}{(1 + .05)^9}}{.05} + 1 \right] = \$1,000 \times (7.1078217 + 1)$$

$$= \$8,107.82$$

10. If $1,000 is deposited at 5% to produce 10 equal rents, the first of which is payable immediately, how large is each rent? Date of deposit and first rent, January 1, 1967; date of last rent, January 1, 1976.

Since each rent is payable at the beginning of a period, we have an annuity due of 10 rents. This is the same as an annuity of nine rents, plus one immediate rent. Accordingly, we can use the present value of nine future rents from Table 5–4 and add 1.

$$\$1,000 \div (P + 1) = \$1,000 \div \left[\frac{1 - \frac{1}{(1 + i)^n}}{i} + 1 \right]$$

$$\$1,000 \div \left[\frac{1 - \frac{1}{(1 + .05)^9}}{.05} + 1 \right] = \$1,000 \div (7.1078217 + 1)$$

$$= \$123.34$$

Deferred Annuities:

11. How much must be invested at 5% to provide for 10 annual rents of $1,000, the first to be made 5 years after the investment? Date of investment, January 1, 1967; date of first rent, January 1, 1972.

This is an ordinary annuity of 10 rents deferred 4 periods. We can solve the problem by first calculating how much must be invested to produce 10 rents of $1,000 each (as in example no. 5). Taking the value in 5 = $7,721.73, we must then discount it for four periods at 5%.

$$\$7,721.73 \times p = \$7,721.73 \times \frac{1}{(1+i)^n}$$

$$\$7,721.73 \times \frac{1}{(1+.05)^4} = \$7,721.73 \times .82270247 \quad \text{(Table 5–2)}$$

$$= \$6,352.69$$

12. If \$1,000 is deposited at 5% to produce 10 equal annual rents, the first of which is payable after 5 years, how large is each rent? Date of deposit, January 1, 1967; date of first rent, January 1, 1972. Again, this is an ordinary annuity of 10 rents, deferred four periods. We can solve the problem by first looking up the present value of an ordinary annuity of 10 rents at 5%, then discounting this figure as above in 11, and dividing the result into \$1,000.

a) Present value of annuity of 1 for 10 rents at 5% = 7.721735
b) Divide \$1,000 by present value of 1 at 5% for four periods
  (÷ .8227025.)
c) $\dfrac{(\$1,000 \div .8227025)}{7.721735} = \$157.41.$

Special Problems.   Careful analysis of problems involving compound interest is necessary to determine what tables to use and the procedures to apply. Not uncommonly, problems are encountered that represent a combination of elements. It is first necessary to separate and identify each element before deciding what procedure to follow in developing a solution. Some examples of problems calling for special analysis follow.

Example 1.   On January 1, 1957, \$4,000 was deposited to earn 4%, compounded annually. In consideration of an additional deposit of \$3,000 on January 1, 1967, the interest rate is raised to 5% and compounding is to occur semiannually. What will be on deposit at January 1, 1977?

Element No. 1	Amount of 1 at 4% for 10 periods	1.48024428
	Multiply by \$4,000 original deposit	×\$4,000
	Amount of original deposit by January 1, 1967	\$ 5,920.98
	Additional deposit on January 1, 1967	3,000.00
	Amount on deposit at January 1, 1967	\$ 8,920.98
Element No. 2	Multiply by amount of 1 at 2½% for 20 periods	×1.63861644
	Amount on Deposit at January 1, 1977	\$14,618.06

Example 2.   Beginning July 1, 1957, \$1,000 is deposited annually in a fund. Beginning July 1, 1962, the annual deposits are increased to \$2,000. (*a*) What amount will be on deposit at July 1, 1971, if interest is compounded annually at 4%? (*b*) Assuming no additional

deposits are made after July 1, 1971, what will be the amount of the fund on July 1, 1977, if interest is continued at 4%, compounded annually?

Probably the easiest approach to this problem is solve it as two separate annuities: $1,000 for 15 years, and the increase starting July 1, 1962, as a $1,000 annuity for 10 years; then add the two amounts to get the total as of July 1, 1971.

> a) Amount of ordinary annuity of 15 rents of 1 at 4% 20.0235876
> Multiply by $1,000 .... ×$1,000
> $20,023.59
> Amount of ordinary annuity of 10 rents of 1 at 4% 12.0061071
> Multiply by $1,000 .... ×$1,000
> $12,006.11
> Total Amount at July 1, 1971 .... $32.029.70

Part (b) seeks to find the compound amount of the total available as of July 1, 1971, if it remains on deposit at compound interest until July 1, 1977.

> b) Amount at July 1, 1971 as determined above $32,029.70
> Multiply by amount of 1 for six periods at 4% 1.26531902
> Amount at July 1, 1977 .... $40,527.79

Example 3. A serial bond issue of $400,000 is to remain outstanding for seven years, at the end of which time $100,000 is to be repaid. Like amounts will be retired the three successive years thereafter. A sinking fund is created to provide for these payments. Assuming the fund is scheduled to earn 5% per annum, what annual equal contributions will be required?

If the $400,000 were needed in a lump sum at the end of the 10th year, we would divide $400,000 by 12.5778925 (amount of an annuity of 10 rents of 1 at 5%) to get $31,801.83 as the annual rent. Most of the money is needed earlier, however. So while $400,000 needs to

		Lost Interest	
Date Paid	*Yrs.*	*Amount* × *(Amount of 1)* − 1	
End 7th year	3	100,000 × (1.157625 − 1)	= $ 15,762.50
End 8th year	2	100,000 × (1.102500 − 1)	= 10,250.00
End 9th year	1	100,000 × (1.050000 − 1)	= 5,000.00

Total amount of lost interest ....$ 31,012.50
Add principal to be retired 400,000.00
Amount to divide by amount of annuity of 10 rents $431,012.50

$431,012.50 ÷ 12.5778925 = $34,267.47 annual rent.

be accumulated, the rents (contributions) must be more than \$31,-801.83. The rents must be increased to cover the lost compound interest on three \$100,000 installments paid out before the 10th year; that is, for 3 years on the 7th payment, 2 years on the 8th payment, and 1 year on the 9th payment as shown above.

This problem can also be solved by assuming the \$100,000 withdrawals are an annuity earning the same 5% rate as the fund. It would be an ordinary four-period annuity, the amount of which is 4.310125. Multiplying by the rent of \$100,000, we get \$431,012.50 as before.

PART C—SOME SELECTED ACCOUNTING APPLICATIONS

Having considered the concepts of compound interest related to future amounts and present values we can now introduce and illustrate some relevant applications in accounting. There are numerous situations, in the context of business operations and the analysis of their economic effects, where compound interest applications are essential. Throughout this book and other more advanced accounting treatments, the student can expect to encounter these concepts. Finally, accounting is rapidly becoming more basic as an important element in interfacing with the complexities of modern civilization; this calls for precise and sophisticated expressions of "values" as opposed to oversimplifications. Thus, the accounting profession is applying the concepts of present and future values more than ever before, and it is safe to project that this trend will continue.

Some of the more commonly encountered accounting applications are:

1. Valuation of noninterest-bearing notes for recording purposes.
2. Analysis and recording of assets acquired for debt (as opposed to cash).
3. Analysis and recording of installment contracts.
4. Accounting for sinking fund transactions.
5. Amortization of premium and discount on debt (and receivables).
6. Analysis and recording of long-term leases.
7. Accounting for depreciation on fixed assets.
8. Analysis and accounting for future commitments to furnish assets or services.
9. Analysis and accounting for future commitments involving debt.
10. Evaluation of capital additions projects.

In this section we will introduce and illustrate the first four applications. Subsequent chapters will elaborate on them and consider others.

Noninterest-Bearing Notes Receivable

A noninterest-bearing note is so designated because the interest is included in the face (maturity value). Obviously, all notes involve interest whether specified or not. Conceptually a note should be recorded at its present value. An interest-bearing note, assuming the specified interest is the going rate, has identical present and maturity values. In contrast the difference between the present value and the maturity value of a noninterest-bearing note is the implied (imputed) interest. To illustrate accounting for such a note assume that M Corporation sold goods and received therefor a two-year non-interest-bearing note, face amount $5,000. Assuming a 7% rate of interest the present value of the note receivable at date of the sale would be:

$$\$5,000 \times .87343873 \text{ (Table 5-2)} = \$4,367.19$$

The accounting entries in respect to the notes receivable should be as below.

To record the sale:[7]

Notes Receivable — Trade	4,367.19	
Sales		4,367.19

To record interest income at end of first year:

Notes Receivable — Trade	305.70	
Interest Income ($4,367.19 × 7%)		305.70

To record interest income at end of second year:

Notes Receivable — Trade	327.11	
Interest Income ($4,367.19 + $305.70)7%		327.11

To record collection of the note:

Cash	5,000.00	
Notes Receivable Trade		5,000.00

Purchase Asset for Noninterest-Bearing Debt

Assets purchased should be recorded at their "true cost" exclusive of any interest charges. Frequently, the implied interest is overlooked which is conceptually incorrect. To illustrate, assume Company M purchased a new machine having an invoice price of $10,000. However, the vendor agreed to sell the machine at that price to be "paid at the end of 24 months with no interest charge." Assuming a going rate of 8% the asset should be valued at acquisition as follows:

$$\$10,000 \times .85733882 \text{ (Table 5-2)} = \$8,573.39$$

The accounting entries in respect to the open account payable should be as below.

---

[7] Alternatively, the sale could be recorded as follows with same results:

Notes receivable — trade	5,000.00	
Deferred Interest Income		632.81
Sales		4,367.19

To record the purchase of the machine:[8]

Asset—Machine	8,573.39	
Deferred Interest Expense	1,426.61	
Account Payable (Machinery)		10,000.00

To record interest expense at end of first year:

Interest Expense	685.87	
Deferred Interest Expense ($8,573.39 × 8%)		685.87

To record interest expense at end of second year:

Interest Expense	740.74	
Deferred Interest Expense ($8,573.39 + $685.57)8%		740.74

To record payment of the liability:

Account Payable (Machinery)	10,000.00	
Cash		10,000.00

Installment Contracts

Contracts calling for regular and equal payments over a period of time invariably involve an interest element. The interest (amount or rate) may not be clearly spelled out but it is there, nonetheless. It is illogical that a purchase calling for installment payments would re-

Illustration 5–5

		Allocation of Payment to—		
Month	Cash (Cr.)	Interest Expense (Dr.)	Liability (Dr.)	Liability Balance (Unpaid)
Initial balance				$3,600.00
First	$309.84[a]	$18.00[b]	$291.84[c]	3,308.16[d]
Second	309.84	16.54	293.30	3,014.86
Third	309.84	15.07	294.77	2,720.09
Fourth	309.84	13.60	296.24	2,423.85
Fifth	309.84	12.12	297.72	2,126.13
Sixth	309.84	10.63	299.21	1,826.92
Seventh	309.84	9.13	300.71	1,526.21
Eighth	309.84	7.63	302.21	1,224.00
Ninth	309.84	6.12	303.72	920.28
Tenth	309.84	4.60	305.24	615.04
Eleventh	309.84	3.08	306.76	308.28
Twelfth	309.82	1.54	308.28	—
	$3,718.08	$118.08	$3,600.00	

Sequential computations:
[a] Constant from formula—$309.84.
[b] $3,600 × .005 = $18.00.
[c] $309.84 − $18.00 = $291.84.
[d] $3,600.00 − $291.84 = $3,308.16.

[8] Alternatively, the purchase could be recorded as follows with the same results:

Asset—Machine	8,573.39	
Accounts Payable (Machinery)		8,573.39

quire a lump-sum payment equal to the sum of the installment payments either in advance or at the time the last payment is due. The total payment at the contract date (purchase) would undoubtedly be less; alternatively a lump-sum payment at the end of the contract period would be greater than the sum of the installments.

The periodic payments can be thought of as annuity rents. Their amount can be determined by dividing the current debt (sale price) by the present value of an annuity for the number of rents (payments) at an appropriate rate. For example if a $3,600 loan on an automobile is to be liquidated over a term of 12 months at an interest rate of $\frac{1}{2}\%$ per month, we can divide $3,600 by 11.6189321 (present value of an annuity of 1 for 12 periods at $\frac{1}{2}\%$) to derive the installment payment ($309.84). We can then prepare an *amortization* table such as Illustration 5–5 which shows for each payment (1) the amount of interest and (2) the reduction of principal, as well as the unpaid balance. In addition, the related accounting entries are indicated. (Note that the $3,600 is the current debt [a present value] excluding interest; if the $3,600 were a future debt value, including interest, the computation would be $3,600 divided by the appropriate Table 5–3 value.)

A particularly common sinking fund contract calls for the accumulation of a sum of money over a specified future term by means of equal periodic payments to the fund balance. The periodic increases to include: (1) the contribution (payments) to the fund, plus (2) interest earned on the fund balance. The increases in the fund balance are greater each year since the periodic contribution is constant while the interest earned is increasing in amount each period.

To illustrate, assume $100,000 is to be accumulated through a contribution each year for 10 years, with compound interest at 4% per year on the fund balance, the periodic contributions to be equal in

Illustration 5–6. Sinking Fund Accumulation Table* (Ordinary annuity basis)

Rent	Cash (Cr.)°°	Interest Income°°° (Cr.)	Sinking Fund (Dr.)	Sinking Fund Balance°°
Start				
1	$ 8,329.09		$ 8,329.09	$ 8,329.09
2	8,329.09	$ 333.16	8,662.25	16,991.34
3	8,329.09	679.65	9,008.74	26,000.08
4	8,329.09	1,040.00	9,369.09	35,369.17
5	8,329.09	1,414.77	9,743.86	45,113.03
6	8,329.09	1,804.52	10,133.61	55,246.64
7	8,329.09	2,209.87	10,538.96	65,785.60
8	8,329.09	2,631.42	10,960.51	76,746.11
9	8,329.09	3,069.85	11,398.94	88,145.05
10	8,329.09	3,525.86	11,854.95	100,000.00
	$83,290.90	$16,709.10	$100,000.00	

° Adjusting entries not indicated.
°° Values at start of period.
°°° Values at end of period.

amount each year. Clearly, the periodic contribution will be less than $10,000 per year. We have seen that the contribution (rent) is $100,000 ÷ $S_{\overline{10}|.04}$, or $100,000 ÷ 12.0061071 (Table 5–3) = $8,329.09. Convenience, from the accounting point of view, would suggest that a fund accumulation table be developed as shown in Illustration 5–6 assuming an ordinary annuity situation.

APPENDIX – COMPOUND INTEREST RELATIONSHIPS

This is a technical expansion of the derivation of formulas and the compound interest tables. It elaborates on the interrelationships between them and is useful for a higher level of sophistication than ordinarily required. It is not essential for most applications and discussions of compound interest concepts.

Four basic compound interest values have been discussed, and an abbreviated table for each has been given.

	Symbol	Formula
1. Amount of 1:	a	$(1 + i)^n$
2. Present value of 1:	p	$\dfrac{1}{(1 + i)^n}$
3. Amount of annuity of 1:	A (also $S_{\overline{n}|i}$)	$\dfrac{(1 + i)^n - 1}{i}$
4. Present value of annuity of 1:	P (also $A_{\overline{n}|i}$)	$\dfrac{1 - \dfrac{1}{(1 + i)^n}}{i}$

The four values and their symbols are so interrelated that if the table for any one is available, it can be used to calculate values for any of the other three. Certain interrelationships between the four table values are very apparent when the mathematical formulas are compared. Note that the formula for the amount of 1, $(1 + i)^n$, appears as the dominant part of each of the three other formulas.

Up to this point there has been an effort to minimize emphasis on formulas. For certain purposes, much time can be saved if the formula approach is taken. The following symbols, in addition to those given above, have become fairly standard in actuarial mathematics:

$$i = \text{interest rate per period}$$
$$n = \text{number of periods or rents}$$
$$I = \text{compound interest } (a - 1)$$
$$D = \text{compound discount } (1 - p)$$

With the above symbols and formulas we may analyze briefly the relationships between the four basic compound interest values (tables).

We have noted the reciprocal relationship between the amount of 1

(a in Table 5–1) and the present value of 1 (b in Table 5–2); these relationships may be expressed as follows:

$$a = (1 + i)^n \qquad \text{or} \qquad a = \frac{1}{p}$$

and

$$p = \frac{1}{(1 + i)^n} \qquad \text{or} \qquad p = \frac{1}{a}$$

Examples:

Given $a = 1.1025$ (5%, 2 periods from Table 5–1), find p.

$$p = \frac{1}{a} = \frac{1}{1.1025} = .90702948 \text{ (verifiable in Table 5–2).}$$

Alternatively: Given $p = .90702948$ (from Table 5–2), find a.

$$a = \frac{1}{p} = \frac{1}{.90702948} = 1.1025 \text{ (verifiable in Table 5–1).}$$

Thus, one can readily derive either table value if the other one is known.

Next, let's examine the relationship between the amount of 1 (a in Table 5–1) and the amount of an annuity of 1 (A in Table 5–3). We noted above that I = compound interest; it is the difference between $1 and its future value; that is $I = a - 1$. For example, the amount of $1 at 5% for 2 periods is $1.1025; and $I = \$.1025$ ($I = a - 1 = \$1.1025 - \$1.00$). The amount of an annuity of 1 then is:

$$A = \frac{I}{i}$$

Substituting: $\qquad A = \dfrac{a - 1}{i}$

Substituting: $\qquad A = \dfrac{(1 + i)^n - 1}{i}$ (the formula for Table 5–3).

Examples:

Given $a = 1.1025$ (5%, 2 periods from Table 5–1), find A.

$$A = \frac{a - 1}{i} = \frac{1.1025 - 1}{.05} = 2.050 \text{ (verifiable in Table 5–3).}$$

Alternatively: Given $A = 2.050$ (from Table 5–3), find a.

$$A = \frac{a - 1}{i}.$$

Transforming: $a = (A \times i) + 1$

$\quad\quad\quad\quad\quad a = (2.050 \times .05) + 1 = 1.1025$ (verifiable in Table 5–1).

To examine the relationship between the present value of 1 (p in Table 5–2) and the present value of an annuity of 1 (P in Table 5–4) we must refer to D (compound discount). Compound discount is the difference between \$1 and its present value, that is, $D = 1 - p$. For example, the present value of \$1 discounted at 5% for 2 periods is \$.90702948, and $D = \$1.00 - \$.90702948 = \$.09297052$. The present value of an annuity of 1 then is:

$$P = \frac{D}{i}$$

Substituting: $\quad\quad P = \frac{1-p}{i}$

Substituting: $\quad\quad P = \dfrac{1 - \dfrac{1}{(1+i)^n}}{i}$ (the formula for Table 5–4).

Examples:

Given $p = .90702948$ (5%, 2 periods, from Table 5–2), find P.

$$P = \frac{1-p}{i} = \frac{1 - .90702948}{.05} = 1.8594104 \text{ (verifiable in Table 5–4).}$$

Alternatively: Given $P = 1.8594104$ (from Table 5–4), find p.

$$P = \frac{1-p}{i}$$

Transforming: $p = 1 - (P \times i)$

$\quad\quad\quad\quad\quad = 1 - (1.8594104 \times .05)$

$\quad\quad\quad\quad\quad = .90702948$ (verifiable in Table 5–2).

The following example summarizes these relationships by deriving the three other table values from a given *amount of 1* at 5% for three periods.

Given a: Amount of $1 = (1 + i)^n = (1 + .05)^3 = 1.157625$ (from Table 5–1 or computed directly):

1. To find p: Present value of $1 = \left[\dfrac{1}{(1+i)^n}\right] = \dfrac{1}{(1+.05)^3} = \dfrac{1}{1.157625} =$ .86383760 (verifiable in Table 5–2).

2. To find A: Amount of ordinary annuity of $1 = \left[\dfrac{(1+i)^n - 1}{i}\right] =$

$\dfrac{(1+.05)^3 - 1}{.05} = \dfrac{1.157625 - 1}{.05} = \dfrac{.157625}{.05} = 3.1525$ (verifiable in Table 5–3).

3. To find P: Present value of ordinary annuity of $1 = \left[\dfrac{1 - \dfrac{1}{(1+i)^n}}{i}\right] =$

$$\dfrac{1 - \dfrac{1}{(1+.05)^3}}{.05} = \dfrac{1 - .86383760}{.05} = \dfrac{.13616240}{.05} = 2.723248 \text{ (verifiable}$$

in Table 5–4).

QUESTIONS FOR CLASS DISCUSSION

1. Explain briefly why accountants should have an understanding of the concepts of compound interest.

2. Briefly explain each of the following:
   a) Amount of 1.
   b) Present value of 1.
   c) Amount of annuity of 1.
   d) Present value of annuity of 1.

3. Give the numerical values of n and of i in determining the compound amount of a sum for 10 years for each of the following:
   a) 5% compounded annually.
   b) 5% compounded semiannually.
   c) 8% compounded quarterly.
   d) 6% compounded monthly.

4. Explain the meaning of the amount of 1 formula and relate it to an amount of 1 table.

5. Indicate three different ways by which the amount of 1 may be obtained.

6. To what rate columns and what number of periods would you refer in looking up the following in an amount of 1 table?

Annual Rate	Number of Years Invested or Deposited	Frequency of Compounding
a) 6%	10	Quarterly
b) 4%	5	Semiannually
c) 3%	6	Annually

7. Explain what is meant by the present value of 1. Relate it to the amount of 1.

8. If the table value for amount of 1 is known, how may it be converted to the table value for present value of 1?

9. Define an annuity in general terms. Explain rents and relate them to time periods and interest rates.

10. Explain what is meant by amount of an annuity. Explain the symbol $S_{\overline{n}|i}$.

11. The table for amount of an annuity provides the value 3.09 (rounded) at 3% for three periods; explain the meaning of the table value.

12. Explain what is meant by present value of annuities. Explain the symbol $A_{\overline{n}|i}$.

13. Explain the fundamental difference between (a) amount of an ordinary annuity and (b) amount of an annuity due.

14. Explain the fundamental difference between (*a*) present value of an ordinary annuity and (*b*) present value of an annuity due.

15. What is a deferred annuity?

16. Complete the following table:

	Symbol	Formula
a) Amount of 1	_____	_____
b) Present value of 1	_____	_____
c) Amount of annuity of 1	_____	_____
d) Present value of annuity of 1	_____	_____

17. The amount of an annuity of 1 may be expressed as: $A = I/i$; show how this expression may be reformulated as a detailed formula for the amount of an annuity of 1.

18. The present value of an annuity of 1 may be expressed as $P = D/i$; show how this expression may be reformulated as a detailed formula for the present value of an annuity of 1.

19. What are the primary accounting applications of future amounts and present values?

20. Relate sinking fund accounting to the concepts of compound interest.

DECISION CASE 5–1

You are a CPA, grateful that tax season has ended, enjoying a comparatively peaceful morning in your office when the calm is shattered by the unexpected appearance of a middle-aged widow excitedly clutching an ad she has just clipped from the *Wall Street Journal*. Her husband was a client who recently passed away and you have assisted in several matters related to the estate including preparation of tax returns, advice about the sale of certain properties, etc.

"Look at this!" she almost shouts as she thrusts the ad at you. After a time you manage to comprehend the essential contents of the ad between her interruptions and you ascertain that what has so aroused her interest is the fact that she could take $15,000 of cash from the assets of the estate of her late husband, deposit the money for five years with the First National Bank of Denham Springs, Louisiana, receive immediately either $3,750 cash or a fully equipped 1970 Ford Galaxie 500, Pontiac Catalina, or Chevrolet Impala with airconditioning, power steering and brakes, and all taxes and licenses paid. After five years her $15,000 will be returned; meanwhile the entire amount will have been insured by the FDIC. Although she has 90 days in which to take advantage of the offer, you sense that in her present frame of mind she will probably beat the deadline by at least 87 days.

Required:

1. Aside from whether she needs a new car worth approximately $3,750 or whether she should reduce her cash position by $11,250, determine for her what approximate rate of return she would be receiving on an annual compounding basis. Support your findings.

2. After the client leaves with your promise to call her with your findings, you take a more detailed look at the copy of the ad. You also note that the

bank also is offering the following alternatives for "depositing for five years." Immediate delivery of:

a) $1,050 cash or a 14' boat with trolling motor and a galvanized trailer for a deposit of $4,200, or

b) $625 cash or a 1971 RCA 23" color console TV for a deposit of $2,500, or

c) $6,250 cash or a 1970 Cadillac Coupe deVille with many extras for a deposit of $25,000.

In each case the bank will return the amount deposited in full after five years. Savings are insured up to $20,000 by the FDIC. Are the returns on these alternative offers comparable to the one which so intrigued your client? Support your findings.

DECISION CASE 5-2

Drexo Corporation has been quite successful and somewhat dominant in the market in which it operates. As a consequence it has accumulated relatively large cash balances. Managers of the company draw comparatively high salaries, own about 55% of the stock, and are, for the most part, comparatively well-to-do.

With the approval of the entire management team, several senior officers have been permitted to borrow amounts ranging up to $25,000 each from the company by signing noninterest-bearing notes which mature two years from the dates they were drawn.

Acting on the instruction of the controller (who has not been one of the borrowers), the Drexo accounting staff prepared financial statements which report the notes at face value on the balance sheet and reflect no interest income on the income statement. These facts literally accord with the terms of the notes.

Required:

1. If the statements are not modified, would you, as an independent CPA of Drexo Corporation, be able to express an unqualified opinion as to the fairness of presentation of the statements? Why or why not?

2. From a theoretical standpoint, how should the note transactions have been treated? Supply specific figures with respect to a $20,000 note received and dated October 1, 1971, to illustrate your points; assume financial statements are being prepared as of December 31, 1971. Provide entries for the life of the note. Indicate how you arrived at your figures and where you might turn for specific data.

EXERCISES

Part A (1 through 14)

Exercise 5-1

Determine how much $2,000 will accumulate to in five years under each separate case. (Use table values to five decimal places and show detailed computations.)

Case A – 8% annual interest.

Case B – 5% annual interest.

Case C – 12% annual interest compounded semiannually.

Case D – 16% annual interest compounded quarterly.

Exercise 5–2

If $35,000 is invested today, how much would accumulate at the end of six years if the interest is:

a) 6% compounded annually?
b) 6% compounded semiannually?
c) 6% compounded quarterly?
d) 4% compounded semiannually?

Show computations in detail.

Exercise 5–3

An investor planned to deposit $50,000 in a savings account for 10 years at 6% interest. He had determined that the resultant accumulation would be $89,542.39.

Required:

(*Show computations in detail.*)

1. Show how he computed the accumulation.

2. Assuming the interest rate was not known but that the other three values were known, show how the unknown interest rate could be derived.

3. Assuming the number of interest periods was not known but that the other three values were known, show how the unknown number of periods could be derived.

Exercise 5–4

1. An investor has $10,000 to invest for a period of 12 years and he desires an accumulation of $20,000 at the end of the period. Approximately what rate of compound interest must his money earn? (Do not interpolate; show computations.)

2. Another investor has $30,000 to invest at 5% compound interest and he desires an accumulation of $60,000 at the end of a certain number of years. Approximately how many years will be required? (Do not interpolate; show computations.)

Exercise 5–5

An investor has $10,000 to invest at compound interest for a period of 10 years at which time he expects an accumulation (fund) of $20,000. Determine the exact rate of interest required. Interpolate; to simplify carry table values to only three decimal places (rounded).

Exercise 5–6

An investor wishes to have $30,000 at the end of five years. How much would he have to invest as a lump sum today if the interest is:

a) 7% compounded annually?
b) 8% compounded semiannually?
c) 6% compounded quarterly?
d) 6% compounded semiannually?

Set up a tabulation to show the detailed computations. Use table values to four decimal places (rounded).

Exercise 5–7

Calculate the accumulation at the end of 10 years of periodic rents of $300 where each rent is paid every interest compounding date assuming:

a) Annual compound interest at 5%.
b) Semiannual compound interest at 6% per annum.
c) Semiannual compound interest at 4½% per annum.
d) Annual compound interest at 3½%.

Set up a table to show the detailed computations; use table values rounded to four decimal places and assume ordinary annuity.

Exercise 5–8

An investor planned to deposit $10,000 per year in a savings account for 10 years at 7% compound interest. He determined that the resultant accumulation at the end on the 10th year (on date of the last deposit) would be $138,164.48.

Required:

(*Show details of computations.*)
1. Show how he computed the accumulation.
2. Assuming the interest rate was unknown but that the other three values were known, show how the unknown interest rate could be computed.
3. Assuming the number of deposits (rents) was unknown but that the other three values were known, show how the unknown number of rents could be computed.
4. Assuming the amount of each rent was unknown but that the other three values were known, show how the unknown amount of each rent could be computed.

Exercise 5–9

A debtor desires to accumulate a fund to retire a debt of $40,000 due eight years hence. How much will he have to pay into the fund each of the eight years assuming the last payment is on the due date of the loan and that—
Case A—interest is 6% per annum.
Case B—interest is 8% per annum.
Round table values to four decimal places. Do not interpolate.

Exercise 5–10

Marley Scrooge is to receive $1,000 per year for five years, starting one year hence. Assuming an interest rate of 6% he has calculated that this stream of equal periodic incomes (rents) has a present value (now) of $4,212.36.

Required:

(Show detailed computations.)

1. Show how he computed the present value.

2. Assuming the interest rate was not known but that the other three values were known, show how the unknown interest rate could be computed.

3. Assuming the number of periods (rents) was not known but that the other three values were known, show how the unknown number of periods could be derived.

4. Assuming the amount of each rent was not known but that the other three values were known, show how the unknown amount of each rent could be derived.

Exercise 5–11

Calculate the present value of an ordinary annuity covering six years with periodic rents of $4,000 each assuming:

Case A — annual rents at 6% per annum.

Case B — semiannual rents at 6% per annum.

Case C — quarterly rents at 6% per annum.

Set up a table to show the detailed computations; round table values to four decimal places.

Exercise 5–12

X Company's management is contemplating depositing $20,000 per period (rents) for five years and expects a compound interest rate of 6%. The deposits are to create an "asset replacement fund."

Required:

(Show details of computations; round table values to four places.)

1. Compute the accumulation in the fund assuming an ordinary annuity.

2. Compute the accumulation in the fund assuming an annuity due.

3. Write an explanation to the investor of the reason for the different results as between 1 and 2.

Exercise 5–13

The management of Dee Company is contemplating paying rent five years in advance; the annual rent is $6,000. Assuming compound interest of 6%, what single sum would have to be paid now for the advance rent assuming:

a) An ordinary annuity situation.

b) An annuity due situation.

Write an explanation of the reason for the different results as between *(a)* and *(b)*.

Exercise 5–14

Find the present value as of January 1, 1971, of an annuity contract calling for four annual rents of $500 each, the first to be paid on January 1, 1974. Interest rate is 6%. Prove your calculations with a tabular statement similar to the one shown in the chapter.

Part B (15 through 18)

Exercise 5–15

1. Using an amount of annuity of 1 table indicate the values of the following:

a) Annuity of seven payments of $6,000; interest rate, 5%.
b) Annuity due of five payments of $7,800; interest rate, 3½%.

2. Calculate the present value of—

a) Annuity of seven payments of $6,000; interest rate, 5%.
b) Annuity due of five payments of $7,800; interest rate, 3½%.
c) Annuity of seven payments of $6,000 deferred for five periods; interest rate, 5%.

Exercise 5–16

1. What will be the amount of each rent if an annuity of 25 rents is purchased for $25,000 and the interest rate is a) 6%? b) 8%?
2. What will be the lump-sum purchase price of an annuity of 25 annual rents of $1,000 each if the interest rate is a) 6%? b) 8%?

Exercise 5–17

A $10,000 bond has coupons attached to it calling for payment of $225 (each), due at the end of every six months for the next five years.

Required:

1. What is the present value of the coupons if they can be invested as they mature at 4% compounded semiannually?
2. What is the compound amount of the coupons at the end of five years?

Exercise 5–18

A $1,000 bond maturing in 10 years has 20 coupons attached calling for payment of $17.50 each at six-month intervals over the term.

Required:

What is the bond worth—
a) If money is now earning 8% compounded semiannually?
b) If money is earning 6% compounded semiannually?

Part C (19 through 24)

Exercise 5–19

Company K owes a $10,000 liability which is to be paid in 10 equal semi-annual installments (payable at the end of each period) at 8% annual interest. Compute the amount of the semiannual installments and prepare a debt reduction schedule that reflects the journal entries and the liability balance.

Exercise 5–20

On April 1, 1971, $24,000 was deposited in trust to pay a series of 15 annual payments on a loan, the first of which was payable immediately. How large was each payment assuming an interest rate (a) of 4%? (b) of 5%?

Exercise 5–21

An outboard cruiser can be purchased for six semiannual payments of $500 each. What should be the cash price if money is (a) worth 5% per annum? (b) worth 6%? Prove your answer to (b) by means of a table of entries.

Exercise 5–22

1. What annual deposits are required each year on June 30 to produce a fund of $5,000 by June 30, 1972 (date of last deposit), if the first deposit is made June 30, 1968, and interest is compounded annually at 6%?

2. Assume same facts as in (1) except it is desired to accumulate the $5,000 by June 30, 1973. How large must each of the five deposits be?

3. Assume facts as in (1) except the $5,000 is desired by June 30, 1977. How large must each of the five deposits be?

4. Tabulate the entries for (1).

Exercise 5–23

On June 30, 19A, Marks Service Company completed a service job and billed the customer for $4,000. The customer suffered a severe fire loss and asked for a 12-month extension which was granted "with no interest charge." Marks closes its books on December 31; the going rate of interest was $8\frac{1}{2}\%$ per annum. Give all entries indicated through collection on July 1, 19B.

Exercise 5–24

On June 30, 19B, Johnson Grocery purchased a large stock of groceries on a special deal. In view of a tight cash position, Johnson was granted 12 months to pay; the payment to be made on July 1, 19C, was $55,000. Johnson closes his books on December 31; he has been paying $7\frac{1}{2}\%$ interest on short-term loans. Give all entries indicated through July 1, 19C.

PROBLEMS

Part A (1 through 6)

Problem 5–1

Compute the balance at the end of 1973 of a savings account on which interest is compounded semiannually if $3,500 is left on January 1, 1965, to earn interest as indicated below:

Years	Annual Rate
1965–67	5%
1968–69	4%
1970–73	5%

Problem 5–2

If $38,000 is paid for an annuity of five payments on March 1, 1967, the first payment to be made on March 1, 1968, how much will each payment be providing the interest rate is a) 5%? b) 7%?

Prepare a table to prove your answer to (a).

Problem 5–3

Annual deposits of $2,000 were placed in a building fund beginning October 1, 1967, and are to continue through October 1, 1973. On October 1, 1974, the annual deposits will be raised to $2,500.

Required:

1. What balance will be in the fund on October 1, 1977, if interest is compounded annually at 5%?

2. If no further deposits are made after October, 1977, and the balance is left to earn interest at the same rate, what will be accumulated by October 1, 1987?

3. Solve for 1 and 2 using another method.

Problem 5–4

What lump sum must be invested at 6% compounded semiannually to permit withdrawal of $5,000 at the end of every second year over a six-year span?

Problem 5–5

1. A CPA contemplating retirement on his 65th birthday desires an income of $8,000 per year for eight years. How much must he invest in a lump sum on his 55th birthday if 5% interest can be expected? First payment is to occur on his 65th birthday.

2. Assume same facts as in 1 except that starting on his 55th birthday the CPA wishes to make a series of annual payments through his 64th birthday which will provide the desired income. How large must each payment be?

Problem 5–6

A. Weller Able promised his son and daughter-in-law he would deposit $100 each year for each grandchild for 17 years in a trust fund to provide for their education. By agreement these deposits were to be begun on January 1 following the year of birth of each grandchild. Dates of birth of the grandchildren follow:

> November 15,1963............................A. Weller Able III
> August 25, 1966...............................Martha Able
> September 26, 1970...........................Hardy Lee Able

Required:

1. The grandfather made good on his promise, and the deposits earned 4% compounded *semiannually*. How much was on deposit July 1, 1972?

2. The accumulation for A. Weller Able III was withdrawn on January 2, 1980. Assuming the fund earned 4% compounded *annually*, how much could properly be withdrawn? How much remained for Martha and Hardy Lee?

Part B (7 through 11)

Problem 5–7

On January 1, 1964, $6,000 was deposited to earn 5% compounded semiannually. When the bank announced that effective after January 1, 1968, the interest rate was to be dropped to 4% compounded semiannually, half of the balance was withdrawn. What balance will be on deposit January 1, 1974?

Problem 5-8

An investor plans to deposit $700 each year beginning July 1, 1970, and continuing thereafter each July 1 through 1973.

Required:

1. How much will be accumulated on July 1, 1973, if interest is a) 6% compounded annually? b) 6% compounded semiannually?

2. How much will accumulate by July 1, 1975, assuming no additional deposits are made and the interest is continued at a) 6% compounded annually? b) 6% compounded semiannually?

3. Prove answers in 1(a) and 2(a) by preparing an accumulation table.

Problem 5-9

On July 1, 1970, an investor purchased for $25,000 an annuity of 10 rents. Interest was 6% per annum. Calculate the amount of each rent assuming the first is payable at:

a) July 1, 1971.
b) July 1, 1972.
c) July 1, 1973.

Problem 5-10

1. A single deposit of $1,000 is placed in a savings account. Interest is compounded semiannually. The following annual rates prevail:

> First four years............................5%
> Next six years 6
> Last five years.............................5

How much will be accumulated at the end of 15 years?

2. How much must be deposited in a fund which will earn 5% compounded annually to permit three withdrawals of $4,000 at the end of every third year?

Problem 5-11

1. Compute the amount accumulated at the end of 10 years in a savings account to which annual contributions of $1,000 are made if for the first three years 3% annual interest is earned; for the next three years, $3\frac{1}{2}\%$; and for the next four years, 4%. Deposits made at year-end.

2. A debt of $5,000 on which 6% interest is compounded annually is being paid off in 10 equal annual payments. After making seven payments, the debtor becomes able to pay off the balance in a lump sum. What amount is owed just after the seventh payment?

Part C (12 through 16)

Problem 5-12

1. Determine the price which should be paid for a building which can be

leased out for $10,000 annual rental (free of all costs) for 15 years after which it can be sold for $20,000. Assume money is worth 8% and rents are payable at the end of the year.

2. Determine the maximum price to pay for an asset with a four-year life and a residual value at the end of four years of $10,000. Assume an interest rate of 8% and anticipated annual earnings (at year-end) as follows:

Year	Annual Earnings
1	$25,000
2	20,000
3	15,000
4	10,000

Problem 5–13

A sinking fund to retire a $500,000, 18-year bond issue is to be accumulated by means of equal annual payments to a trustee. The expected interest rates during this time are as follows:

First five years	$4\frac{1}{2}\%$
Next five years	4
Remaining years	$3\frac{1}{2}$

Required:

1. Compute the amount of the annual payment into the fund assuming the $500,000 balance is to be accumulated as of the date of the last rent.

2. Compute the amount of the annual payment into the fund assuming the $500,000 balance is to be accumulated at the end of the period of the last rent.

3. Give journal entries for the first two payments in (1), include interest.

Problem 5–14

On July 1, 1967, an issue of $6\frac{3}{4}\%$ serial bonds was sold to mature as follows:

Redemption Date	Face Amount
July 1, 1975	$200,000
July 1, 1977	200,000
July 1, 1979	200,000

Beginning July 1, 1968, it is desired to start making equal annual contributions to a sinking fund with which to retire the bond issue. Assuming the fund can earn 6%, what amount of annual contribution will achieve what is wanted? Give entries for first two periods, including interest.

Problem 5–15

How much must be set aside each year to provide a debt retirement fund according to the following plan? A borrowed $20,000 on March 1, 1966. This amount plus accrued interest at 8% compounded semiannually is to be repaid March 1, 1976. Until March 1, 1971, nothing is to be contributed to the retirement fund. On that date, however, and for the next four years equal amounts are to be set aside. It is believed the fund will earn 6% per annum. Also give entries, including interest, for the first two payments into the fund.

Problem 5–16

The Port Authority of the City of A contracted with a bridge construction firm whereby the latter would build a bridge across a river for $15 million and accept in payment the 20-year 3% bonds of the Authority. Interest is payable annually. Semiannual payments are to be made by the authority to a sinking fund for retirement of the bonds. Assume the sinking fund will earn $3\frac{1}{2}$% compounded annually. Annual maintenance and operating costs on the bridge are expected to average $75,000.

It is anticipated that revenue from bridge tolls will be sufficient to service the debt and cover maintenance costs. Pedestrians are to be charged 5 cents; vehicles, which are expected to be 10 times as numerous, are to be charged 50 cents. How many tolls will be necessary each year to avoid the necessity of the Port Authority's dipping into its resources to meet annual costs on the bridge?   (AICPA adapted)

Cash and Temporary Investments

chapter **6**

Temporary investments are substitutes for cash; they are made to avoid losses of revenue attendant upon idle cash balances. Their interchangeability and other similarities warrant discussion of both cash and temporary investments in a single chapter. Accounting for cash and temporary investments is relatively simple from valuation and classification standpoints; on the other hand, achieving accounting control over these assets frequently poses a major challenge.[1]

CASH

Composition of Cash

Two principal characteristics of cash are (1) its availability as a medium of exchange and (2) principally that it is the measure used in accounting for all other items. Although its purchasing power may change, accountants make no effort to revalue cash. Some special measures which can be taken in conjunction with the effects of price-level changes on certain other financial statement items are discussed in Chapter 23. Cash includes coins, currency, and certain types of formal negotiable paper which are acceptable by banks for deposit,

---

[1] See Chapter 25 for an extended discussion of cash flow.

but excludes certain items commonly intermingled with cash. Examples of *exclusions* include postage stamps, and cash-due memos. When stamps are received in payment for merchandise, such as inexpensive articles sold by mail, they should be accounted for on the basis of their intrinsic characteristics, not as the money for which substituted. Similarly, cash-due memos or I.O.U.'s from officers, owners, or cashiers should be classiffied as special receivables, not as cash. Formal *negotiable* paper which is due at sight may be treated as cash. Thus, bank drafts, cashier's checks, money orders, certified checks, and ordinary checks constitute cash for accounting purposes. Balances on deposit in commercial banks should be considered as cash if subject to immediate withdrawal. Balances in savings accounts should be classed as temporary investments because the bank usually has a legal right to demand some advance notice of withdrawal; as a practical matter this right is rarely exercised, and as a consequence the classification of cash in savings accounts as ordinary cash is unobjectionable. Demand certificates of deposit are properly classed as cash; time certificates of deposit, depending on maturity dates and managerial intent, may be current assets but should not be captioned as "cash."

Deposits in foreign banks give rise to two special problems, viz: (1) foreign currency units such as pounds or pesos first must be converted to dollars and (2) it is not uncommon for the foreign deposits to be subject to restricted withdrawal and conversion. Treatment of conversion of deposits in foreign banks is beyond the scope of this book. Even when spendable immediately or in the near future, cash in foreign banks should be set out separately on the balance sheet.

The nature of current assets was discussed in Chapter 3. The AICPA Committee on Accounting Procedure, in *Accounting Research Bulletin No. 43*, stated that such resources as "cash and claims to cash which are restricted as to withdrawal or use for other than current operations, are designated for expenditure in the acquisition or construction of noncurrent assets, or are segregated for the liquidation of long-term debts" should be excluded from current assets. The committee then added:

Even though not actually set aside in special accounts, funds that are clearly to be used in the near future for the liquidation of long-term debts, payments to sinking funds, or for similar purposes should also, under this concept, be excluded from current assets. However, where such funds are considered to offset maturing debt which has properly been set up as a current liability, they may be included within the current asset classification.[2]

---

[2]Committee on Accounting Procedure, AICPA, "Restatement and Revision of Accounting Research Bulletins," *Accounting Research Bulletin No. 43* (New York, 1961), p. 21.

Petty cash funds and cash in the hands of branches or divisions properly are includable under cash because these ordinarily are used to meet current operating expenses or to liquidate current liabilities.

Checks which have been drawn against a bank balance but which have not been mailed or otherwise delivered to the payees should not be deducted from the cash balance. If such checks, properly drawn but still under the firm's control, have been entered in the cash payment records, the accountant should add them back to cash and to accounts payable before preparing the financial statements. An overdraft in a bank account ordinarily should be shown as a current liability. However, where a depositor has overdrawn one account with Bank A but has positive balances in other accounts in that bank, it is appropriate to offset and show the net asset or liability on the balance sheet. It is improper to offset an overdraft in Bank A against a balance on deposit in Bank B.

Sources of Cash Receipts

Cash flows into the business from various sources, the main stream being from sales and services transactions, with smaller streams coming from conversions of noncurrent assets and through increase of company liabilities. Although a complete list of all such sources would be beyond the scope of this work, the following list is representative:

1. The sale of merchandise for cash.
2. The collection of accounts and notes receivable from customers.
3. The collection of charges for services rendered to customers.
4. The renting of property or the lending of money.
5. Notes payable discounted by banks, new bonds and capital stock issued.
6. The sale of scrap, waste, by-products, and nonmerchandise items.
7. The sale of special and miscellaneous assets.
8. The return of cash where erroneous or excess payments have been made on purchases.
9. The receipt of deposits as guarantees, subject to withdrawal.

Control over Cash Receipts

The first step in developing control over cash receipts is to determine whether the entity is so organized as to permit continuous, uninterrupted flow of cash from the instant of initial receipt to deposit in an authorized bank account. During this handling period no one person should have physical control of cash without there being at least one other individual cognizant of that person's accountability.

Separation of the responsibility for *cash handling* from *cash recording* is, therefore, essential. The next step is to determine whether proper precaution and supervision are being exercised directly toward continuation of effective control. A concern may have the finest accounting system installed, but unless it is being used properly it can be of little value in the safeguarding of cash receipts.

The separation of cash handling responsibilities from cash recording responsibilities is accomplished most effectively by assigning the cash handling responsibilities to the treasurer.

Each entity has a need for some internal auditing, and this function should not be performed by those persons responsible for the recording function. In larger organizations this can be accomplished by placing responsibility on the controller for all recording and auditing. The controller, being unable personally to handle all the details, should have under him a chief accountant responsible for the recording function and an auditor responsible for the internal control function. The records maintained under the supervision of the chief accountant serve as a check on the work of the treasurer and are available to the internal auditor in the verification process.

Analysis of Cash Disbursements

The primary transactions which occasion the disbursement of company funds are as follows:

1. Purchase of finished goods, raw materials, supplies, and fixed assets.
2. Payments for employment costs.
3. Payments for other items constituting the bulk of the operating expenses.
4. Purchase of securities and other income-producing property.
5. Retirement of bank loans, bonds issued, and capital stock.
6. Miscellaneous payments such as those resulting from lawsuits, dividend declarations, patent infringement, and the refunding of customer deposits.

Control of Cash Payments and Petty Cash

The cash disbursement transactions listed above are significant in an industrial concern. In recognition of the need for internal control, such payments are practically always made by check coupled with a carefully designed voucher and approval system.

Even in those companies where most payments are made by check, it is necessary to make many small payments in currency and coin. These small payments may be controlled more effectively if one or more petty cash funds are established from which to make the payments. One cashier should be made responsible for each petty cash fund—its initial balance, the documents taken from those to whom payments are made, and the accountability for its periodic replenishment. Petty cash funds should be replenished only by check; this should be done when balances are appropriately low or at the end of each fiscal period. To support replenishment, each petty cashier should turn in receipts (documents) evidencing all payments made since the last reimbursement. These receipts should be attached to a disbursements voucher and subjected to the usual procedures which attend the approval and payment of vouchers. Upon such approval, a check payable to "cash" is drawn which enables the petty cashier to begin the cycle anew. Opportunities for misappropriation from petty cash may be relatively small. Sometimes, however, these funds are sizeable and even where they are not the fact that the same type of fraud can be perpetrated repeatedly should prompt management to initiate sound and stringent control measures over petty cash.

The initial entry to record creation of a petty cash fund involves a debit to Petty Cash and a credit to Cash. Recording thereafter may vary somewhat depending on the system design and arrangement and on whether the petty cash fund is operated under (a) a fluctuating system, or (b) a nonfluctuating (imprest) system.

A typical arrangement under a fluctuating fund system requires the responsible cashier to maintain a "petty cash book." Payments are classified and summarized in this record which is then used as a basic record when the fund is replenished. Various accounts are debited for the individual payments and Petty Cash is credited. The entry for replenishment of the fund gives rise to a debit to Petty Cash and a credit to Cash. Reimbursement is ordinarily in terms of a round, even amount, while the expenditures usually total to some odd figure. Clearly, under this approach the balance in the Petty Cash account fluctuates.

Under the nonfluctuating (imprest) system, petty cash payments are also recorded and summarized in a petty cash book, and when the fund is low, the petty cash book is "ruled" and presented together with the supporting vouchers; a check is drawn in favor of petty cash for the *exact* amount of these expenses, giving rise to a journal entry involving debits to various expense accounts and credit to Cash. The fluctuating fund system is less desirable than the nonfluctuating system because it is somewhat more difficult to audit.

Overage and Shortage

Cash is susceptible to being lost or stolen, and errors in making change are almost inevitable; therefore, cash should be counted at relatively short intervals. When an error is detected, a correcting entry must be made to a Cash Over and Short account. The use of this special account facilitates comparison and analyses. A small balance should be recognized as a financial expense (or income). A large balance caused by defalcation should be charged against the person responsible for the embezzlement or the bonding company (as a receivable), or as a loss depending on whether or not there is a possibility that the loss will be made up.

Reconciliation of Cash Balance

At the end of each month the actual cash on hand and on deposit in the bank (as shown on the monthly bank statement) should be reconciled with the balance of cash as shown in the accounts. This reconciliation of actual cash and bank balances with the balance of the cash account involves an analysis of the *monthly bank statement* and the cash records developed in the company. Generally there will be a difference between the two cash records. The usual causes of differences between the cash balance per the bank statement and the cash balance per the books of the company may be classified as follows:

A. Items already recorded as cash receipts in the books of the company but not yet added to the bank balance per the bank statement.

   Examples:

   1. Deposits made up and charged to the bank by the company but not received and reported by the bank until the next bank statement.
   2. Deposits actually made late in the period but reported in the next period by the bank because of the timing of the bank statement.
   3. Undeposited cash on hand.

B. Items already added to the bank balance but not the balance on the company books.

   Examples:

   1. Interest allowed the depositor by the bank but not yet recorded on the company books.
   2. Collections (and deposits) of notes and drafts by the bank for the depositor but not yet recorded on the company books.

C. Items already recorded as cash disbursements on the company books but not deducted by the bank from the bank balance.

   Example:

   1. Outstanding checks—checks written and properly recorded in the company books but not yet cleared through the bank.

D. Items already deducted from the bank balance but not from the book balance.

Examples:

1. Customers' checks returned to the company by the bank (because of NSF—not sufficient funds) but not yet recorded on the books of the company.
2. Interest charged by the bank on an overdraft not yet recorded on the books of the company.
3. Service charges made by the bank but not yet recorded on the books of the company.

The cash balance per company books (designated by CB) and the bank balance per bank statement (designated by BB) can be reconciled best in three ways (A, B, C, and D used as defined above) as follows:

1. Work from both cash balance per company books and bank balance to *correct* (true) cash balance (designated by TB), formulas:

$$TB = BB + A - C$$
$$TB = CB + B - D$$

2. Work from book balance to bank balance, formula:

$$CB - A + B + C - D = BB$$

3. Work from bank balance to book balance, formula:

$$BB + A - B - C + D = CB$$

The first approach definitely is preferable for the following reasons:

1. The reconciliation naturally falls into two parts (Books and Bank), and all the reconciling entries to be made in the books are grouped in the section devoted to the *book balance.*

2. It is less confusing. After the correctness of each item has been verified, the reconciliation merely involves placing such items under the appropriate part as an addition or deduction.

3. The reconciliation can be used as a schedule supporting the Cash balance as reported on the balance sheet; the last line on the reconciliation is reported on the balance sheet.

Illustrative Problem. The first method of reconciling the cash balances is illustrated below based on the following data:

From the bank statement at end of the period:

Interest collected on note for the company by the bank..........$ 20
Bank charges   4
Ending balance...$1,404

From the cash records of the company at the end of the period:

Unrecorded deposit		$ 450
Cash on hand		100
Outstanding checks:		
No. 401	$150	
No. 410	200	
No. 412	53	403
Ending balance		$1,535

Solution — Bank and Book Balances to Correct Balance:

BANK BALANCE

Balance per bank		$1,404
Additions:		
Unrecorded deposit	$450	
Cash on hand	100	550
		$1,954
Deductions:		
Outstanding checks:		
No. 401	$150	
No. 410	200	
No. 412	53	403
Correct Cash Balance		$1,551

BOOK BALANCE

Balance per books	$1,535
Additions:	
Interest collected by bank	20
	$1,555
Deductions:	
Bank charges	4
Correct Cash Balance	$1,551

Entries to record items on the bank reconciliation which have not been recognized on the books previously may be taken directly from the bank reconciliation. If the method of reconciliation illustrated above is used, those items listed under the caption "book balance" constitute the amounts to be recognized. The entries necessary to reflect the correct cash balance in the books ($1,551 in the illustration) are as follows:

Cash	20	
Interest Income		20
Expense — Bank Charges	4	
Cash		4

The company would report a cash balance of $1,551 on the balance sheet. The second method is illustrated in the footnote; the third method, obviously, would simply be the inverse of the second method.[3] Note that the *correct* balance does not appear.

Comprehensive Reconciliation

Comprehensive reconciliation or reconciliation of receipts and disbursements for a month (or an entire fiscal period) is sometimes undertaken by accountants and auditors.[4]

Comprehensive reconciliation is akin to true balance reconciliation; it differs in that it also reconciles receipts and payments for the period under consideration and begins with a true balance type reconciliation (made as of the end of the prior period). The procedure is explained by way of illustration.

Illustrative Problem. Refer to the true balance reconciliation on page 231 and assume it was made March 31 and that necessary entries to correct Cash were reflected in the company's account as of that date. April transactions reflected on the bank statement and the company's Cash account are as below:

Data on Cash

April Bank Statement°

March 31	Balance forward	$ 1,404
April 1	Deposit..	550
	The $450 unrecorded deposit + $100	
	undeposited cash as of March 31.	
2–29	Deposits..	10,800
	Other April receipts deposited.	
30	Note collected..................................	515
	$500 note + $15 interest collected	
	by bank in behalf of company.	
	Total Receipts...........................	$11,865
	Initial balance + receipts................	$13,269

---

[3] *Solution — Book Balance to Bank Balance:*

Balance per books....................................			$1,535
Less ("A" items):			
Unrecorded deposit.............................	$450		
Cash on hand	100	550	
			$ 985
Add:			
("B" items):			
Interest allowed by bank		$ 20	
("C" items):			
Outstanding checks:			
No. 401..	$150		
No. 410..	200		
No. 412..	53	403	423
			$1,408
Less ("D" items):			
Bank charges..			4
Balance per Bank....................................			$1,404

[4] Coverage of this topic should be regarded as optional at the discretion of the instructor.

Charges for Checks°

April	1	Numbers 401 and 410 ....$	350
		March checks cleared in April.	
	2–29	Numbers 413–430.............................	10,700
		April checks cleared in April.	
	30	April service charge............................	10
		Total April charges....................	$11,060
	30	Balance	$ 2,209

April Cash Account†

March 31		Cash balance .... $	1,551
		Reflects entries called for by	
		March 31 reconciliation.	
April	2–29	Receipts.....................................	10,800
		Receipts which were also deposited	
		during April.	
	30	Receipts.....................................	400
		Deposit in transit at April 30.	
	30	Receipts.....................................	200
		Cash on hand at April 30.	
		Total receipts...........................	$11,400
		Initial balance + receipts....................	$12,951

April Checks†

April	2–29	Numbers 413–430..............................	$10,700
		April checks cleared in April.	
	30	Number 431....................................	100
		April check outstanding April 30.	
			$10,800
	30	Balance	2,151

° Explanation in italics not part of the bank statement.

† Explanation in italics not part of the cash record.

Comprehensive Reconciliation

	Balance March 31	April Receipts	April Payments	Balance April 30
Balances per bank.......................$1,404		$11,865	$11,060	$2,209
Unrecorded deposits:				
March 31.................................	450	450°		
April 30		400		400
Undeposited cash:				
March 31.................................	100	100°		
April 30		200		200
Outstanding checks:				
March 31 #401	150°		150°	
#410	200°		200°	
#412	53°			53°
April 30 #431			100	100°
Correct balances $1,551		$11,915	$10,810	$2,656
Balances per company's books........$1,551		$11,400	$10,800	$2,151
April service charge			10	10°
Note and interest collected		515		515
Correct balances $1,551		$11,915	$10,810	$2,656

° Deduction.

Observe that check #412 for $53 which was outstanding at March 31 is still outstanding at April 30 and that payment on it has not been stopped. The comprehensive reconciliation for April would appear as shown on page 233.

Entries needed to record the correct cash balance as of April 30 are as follows:

```
Cash.................................................................................515
    Note Receivable ................................................................        500
    Interest Income.................................................................         15
Expense—Bank Charges.............................................................  10
    Cash..........................................................................         10
```

The company should report a cash balance of $2,656 on its April 30 balance sheet.

Management of Cash

Effective management of cash is of crucial importance because cash is the lifeblood of business. It is the principal means of acquiring goods and services and is generally the most readily misappropriated of all assets. Thus far, we have stressed cash content and internal control over cash. The remainder of this segment of the chapter deals with planning cash receipts and disbursements with a view to determining borrowing needs or other financing requirements or, conversely, of determining investment opportunities that may arise if excess funds are to be generated by operations or other activities.

Planning Cash Position and Requirements

There are two principal approaches to the planning of cash receipts and disbursements. One, the receipts and disbursements method, entails an analysis of certain estimates (plans) in order to derive probable cash receipts and payments during a specified future period. The other method is generally referred to as cash flow analysis and is discussed in Chapter 25. Both, of course, start from present cash position and add to it projected cash inflows and outflows according to the factors perceived and the analytical method used.

The receipts and disbursements method analyzes probable future receipts and payments in terms of the factors arrayed on pages 226 and 227. The illustrative problem which follows typifies this kind of analysis.

Illustrative Problem. The Astromotion Wholesale Corporation's fiscal year ends on December 31. The information below related to

Astromotion's operations is available for use in preparing a cash forecast for the first quarter of the company's 19B fiscal year.

1. Projected sales for the first six months of 19B.

January	$ 300,000
February	400,000
March	550,000
April	500,000
May	480,000
June	525,000
Total	$2,755,000

2. Actual sales for the fourth quarter of 19A:

October	$ 480,000
November	470,000
December	500,000
	$1,450,000

3. Selected account balances as of December 31, 19A, are:

   a) Cash – $75,000.
   b) Accounts receivable trade – $105,000.
   c) Accounts payable merchandise – $240,000.
   d) Merchandise inventory – $420,000.

4. All of Astromotion's sales are on credit. The schedule below indicates the period of time over which a typical month's sales are collected.

   During month of sale – 70%.
   During first subsequent month – 20%.
   During second subsequent month – 9%.
   Uncollectible – 1%.

5. The company's cost of goods sold averages 60% of sales. Each month's merchandise purchases are paid for during the following month. The company policy is to have a two months' supply of inventory on hand at the beginning of each month.
6. Monthly cash disbursements for operating expenses usually amount to 5% of sales plus $15,000.
7. Cash disbursements for fixed assets and installments on notes total about $22,500 per month.
8. Federal income taxes of $50,000 will be paid on March 15, 19B.
9. Cash dividends of $30,000 are paid the second month of each quarter.

Solution:

THE ASTROMOTION WHOLESALE CORPORATION
Cash Forecast
First Quarter, 19B

	January	February	March
Beginning cash balance	$ 75,000	$134,800	$102,300
Cash receipts (Schedule 1)	352,300	385,000	492,000
Total	$427,300	$519,800	$594,300
Cash disbursements:			
Merchandise purchases (Schedule 2 and 3)	$240,000	$330,000	$300,000
Operating expenses (Schedule 4)	30,000	35,000	42,500
Fixed asset purchases and installments on notes	22,500	22,500	22,500
Federal income taxes			50,000
Dividends		30,000	
	$292,500	$417,500	$415,000
Ending Cash Balance	$134,800	$102,300	$179,300

Schedule 1
Cash Receipts from Sales

	Cash Receipts — Sales		
	January 19B	February 19B	March 19B
From sales in:			
November 19A ($470,000 × 9%)	$ 42,300		
December 19A	100,000	$ 45,000	
January 19B	210,000	60,000	$ 27,000
February 19B		280,000	80,000
March 19B			385,000
Total Receipts	$352,300	$385,000	$492,000

Schedule 2
Merchandise Purchases

	January 19B	February 19B
Desired ending inventory	$570,000*	$630,000†
Add projected cost of sales	180,000	240,000
Total	$750,000	$870,000
Less actual or projected beginning inventory	420,000	570,000
Purchases required	$330,000	$300,000

*($400,000 + $550,000) × .60 = $570,000.
†($550,000 + 500,000) × .60 = $630,000.

Schedule 3
Cash Disbursements — Merchandise Purchases

Cash Disbursements — Merchandise

	January 19B	February 19B	March 19B
For merchandise purchased in:			
December 19A	$240,000		
January 19B		$330,000	
February 19B			$300,000

Schedule 4
Cash Disbursements — Operating Expenses

Cash Disbursements — Operating Expenses

	January 19B	February 19B	March 19B
Variable:			
5% × $300,000.....................................	$ 15,000		
5% × $400,000.....................................		$ 20,000	27,500
5% × $550,000.....................................			
Fixed...	15,000	15,000	15,000
	$ 30,000	$ 35,000	$ 42,500

TEMPORARY INVESTMENTS

Types of Investments

Prior to a discussion of accounting for temporary investments, it is appropriate to describe briefly the nature and types of investments. Investments generally are classified for balance sheet purposes as either *temporary* or *permanent*. This distinction is entirely one of accounting and not of law and arises out of the nature of the security and the purpose of the investment. Investment purposes may be outlined as follows:

A. Temporary investments (short-term investments in marketable securities).
  1. Funds set aside for emergency use on a current basis and invested in marketable securities.
  2. Investment of working capital funds made idle by seasonal business.
  3. Speculative holdings (short duration).
B. Permanent investments[5] (long-term investments).
  1. Stocks and bonds of outside companies held for purposes of business profit and control. Control may be exercised through full ownership of all securities issued by the subsidiary company or through only a controlling interest.

---

[5] Discussed in Chapters 11, 15, and 17.

2. Advances to affiliates or subsidiaries.
3. Funds earmarked for a designated purpose such as retirement of a funded debt, replacement of plant and equipment, or payment of pensions.
4. Cash value of life insurance on company executives.
5. Major expenditures for certain types of memberships in associations and exchanges, such as a broker's "seat" on a stock exchange.
6. Fixed assets, land in particular, not used in regular business operations; held for sale or speculation.
7. Funds invested in long-term assets not directly related to the primary operations of the company. For example, the National Laundry Machinery Company purchased a patent on a special pressing device, developed it for use in a field not in competition with its own operations, and secured regular royalties from its licensing. The cost of this patent should be accounted for as an investment rather than as an intangible fixed asset.

Temporary Investments – Defined

Temporary investments are reported on the balance sheet under the current asset caption. To be classified as a current asset a temporary investment must meet the following twofold test:

1. The security must be readily marketable. It must be a security which is regularly traded on a security exchange or for which there is an established market.
2. It must be the intention of the company's management to convert the securities into cash in the short run and hence back into the normal operations for which working capital is used. This criterion has proven somewhat troublesome to auditors in practice. "Intentions" are elusive and prone to change from one period to the next.

Valuation of Temporary Investments

Temporary investments are recorded initially at cost in conformance with the cost principle. Subsequent to acquisition they may be accounted for at—

1. Cost.
2. Cost or market, whichever is lower.
3. Market. (See especially the discussion of this valuation basis in Chapter 11.)

Cost includes brokerage costs, taxes, and all other costs incurred in acquisition, as well as the agreed upon purchase price. It does not, in the case of bonds, include accrued interest purchased. Cost as a basis for valuation subsequent to acquisition is appropriate provided market fluctuations are minor or insignificant. To illustrate, assume Company R purchased, as a temporary investment, $100,000 par value U.S. government 5⅜ bonds at 101⅝ (no accrued interest), or a cost of $101,625. If at the date of the balance sheet this security is quoted at 101⅛, or $101,125, since market is below cost, the temporary investment should be reported at cost with the market price indicated parenthetically as follows:

Current Assets:
U.S. treasury bonds at cost (market, $101,125)................................$101,625

If after investigation it is found that there has been a substantial shrinkage in market value of the securities held, valuation at cost generally is considered inappropriate; in its place the lower of cost or market valuation should be used.

Valuation of temporary investments at the lower of cost or market is justified on the basis of conservatism, that is, when there has been a significant decrease in value the loss should be recognized currently rather than at the date of sale of the temporary investment. In applying the lower of cost or market approach the investment portfolio is considered as one unit as opposed to individual items. For example, assume the following temporary securities were shown on the books of Company S:

Name and Description	Cost	Market
American Amalgamated Glass, 5½% bonds...............	$ 66,360	$ 46,800
Southwest Forge, 7% bonds	67,723	52,308
U.S. Treasury, 6¼% bonds......................................	98,932	103,256
Majik Appliances, Inc., 7% bonds	48,280	33,902
Reliable Motors common stock	84,425	57,714
Perfect Metals, Inc., 6% preferred stock..................	18,880	14,220
Total..	$384,600	$308,200

In this example the investments should be reported on the balance sheet at $308,200. This figure is the total market value of all the investments in the portfolio. It should be noted that the application of the principle of "the lower of cost or market" to temporary investments involves the use of the lower of *total* cost or *total* market, without the alternatives permitted in inventory accounting of applying the rule to individual items, classes of items, or to totals. (See Chapter 8.) The difference between total cost and total market, $76,400, should be reflected as a holding loss in the year in which the market decline occurred, and the balance sheet would reflect the investment status as follows:

Current Assets:
Marketable securities valued at lower of cost or market
   (cost, $384,600)..$308,200

Market Value. At this writing temporary investments, under generally accepted accounting principles, should be accounted for at cost or lower of cost or market as explained above. However, many investment institutions (such as insurance companies) currently are reporting (and accounting for) marketable securities at their fair market value at each balance sheet date. There is currently a very strong movement among accountants to move to "fair value" accounting for all marketable securities, particularly those classified as current assets. This trend reflects the positions that (*a*) the needs of the user of the statements are better served and (*b*) the market is the only true measure of the availability of funds and hence of the true value of temporary investments in judging financial position. Currently, according to published information, the APB is drafting an Opinion that would require fair value accounting for marketable equity securities (stock). Accounting on this basis would require that, at each statement date, the temporary investments be restated to market value. If no market value is readily available it should be approximated. In the absence of any basis for restatement the temporary investments should be accounted for at cost. In applying the fair value basis the net effects of the market changes, both unrealized and realized, should be reported on the income statement as a separate item, but not as an extraordinary gain or loss.[6] To illustrate, the following events are utilized.

To record purchase of 5,000 shares of common stock in X Corporation at $20 per share as a temporary investment:

Marketable Securities (5,000 shares common stock, X Corporation) 100,000
    Cash..   100,000

To record subsequent sale of 2,000 shares at $30 per share:

Cash... 60,000
    Gain on Sale of Marketable Securities...........................   20,000
    Marketable Securities (2,000 shares common stock, X Corporation)   40,000

To record market value of securities on hand at end of accounting period:

Marketable Securities (X Corporation common stock)........... 30,000
    Gain on Market Value of Marketable Securities (3,000 shares × $10)   30,000

Reporting on financial statements:

Income statement:
Gain on sale of marketable securities...$50,000

Balance sheet:
Temporary investments at market (cost $60,000) $90,000

---

[6] See Chapters 11 and 22 for discussions of long-term investments in marketable securities.

The arguments advanced against the use of market value for temporary investments are: (*a*) market value is rather tenuous; it changes constantly and even erratically, (*b*) an unrealized profit should not be recognized, and (*c*) it encourages management to utilize temporary investments to "manipulate" periodic income. Despite these arguments, many accountants feel that the arguments for market value far outweigh them. The authors prefer market value and believe that in the very near future generally accepted accounting principles will require its use for temporary investments. Many accountants argue for identifying the *market* gain or loss as "unrealized" and not to include it as an element of net income, but rather as a direct credit to owners' equity.

Accounting for Lower of Cost or Market

The requirements of income determination under the lower of cost of market method for temporary investments require that *cost* be recorded initially and remain on the books until sold. Valuation adjustments should be recorded in special accounts in the books so as not to disturb basic cost amounts. This recording may be accomplished by the use of a valuation account, Allowance to Reduce Temporary Investments to LCM. This account is adjusted at the end of the fiscal year with month-to-month fluctuations generally ignored. When the market value of securities is lower than their cost, the allowance (no previous balance assumed) is credited with the excess of aggregate cost over aggregate market with the offsetting debit to Loss Due to Reduction of Temporary Investments from Cost to LCM. The loss is closed to the Income Summary account for the period; the allowance account remains on the books until subsequent analysis and comparison of security costs and market prices indicate a need for its adjustment. A credit balance in the allowance account, when deducted from the cost of the securities as shown in the temporary investment account, reduces the value of the investment from cost to market.

To illustrate, assume the Crown Rubber Company had temporary investments in stocks on the books acquired at a cost of $30,000. The market value of these securities on December 31, 19A, was $27,000. The following adjustment is indicated:

December 31, 19A

Loss Due to Reduction of Temporary Investments from Cost to
  LCM 3,000
    Allowance to Reduce Temporary Investments to LCM..........   3,000
  To record the difference between cost and market of temporary
  investments (the allowance account had no previous balance).

The temporary investments then should be reported on the balance sheet as follows:

Current Assets:
   Marketable securities at lower of cost or market (cost $30,000) $27,000

If one third of these securities were sold on September 1, 19B, for $8,000, the entry to record the sale would be:

```
Cash..............................................................................8,000
Loss on Sale of Temporary Investments....................................2,000
     Marketable Securities (one third of $30,000)......................          10,000
     To record sale of temporary investments, original cost, $10,000.
```

The allowance account is not debited in this entry for a proportionate part (in this case one third) since to do so would offset a holding (market) loss against the loss between actual cost and sales price. (See footnote 7.)

At the end of the second year, the aggregate cost of all temporary investment securities again is compared with their aggregate market value. Many purchases and sales may have been made since the allowance was established (or last adjusted), but the Allowance to Reduce Temporary Investments to LCM is a composite allowance, applying to all temporary investments held. If the Crown Rubber Company made no other purchases and sales of securities during the year, the adjusting entry required at the end of the second year would be as follows, assuming that the market value of the investments retained is $19,500:

December 31, 19B

```
Allowance to Reduce Temporary Investments to LCM...............2,500
     Recovery in Market Value of Temporary Investments.............          2,500
     To adjust allowance balance so that it will equal present excess of
     cost over market value of securities.°
```

   °Calculation: Cost of securities on hand, $20,000 − Market value of securities, $19,500 = Excess of cost over market, $500. Unadjusted balance of allowance, $3,000 − Required balance, $500 = Recovery in market value, $2,500.

Recovery in Market Value of Temporary Investments is closed to the Income Summary account.[7]

---

[7] An alternative treatment would be as follows:

```
Cash .............................................................................8,000
Allowance to Reduce Temporary Investments to LCM..............1,000
Loss on Sale of Temporary Investments..................................1,000
     Temporary Investments ...............................................          10,000
     To record sale of one third of the temporary investments.
```

```
Allowance to Reduce Temporary Investments to LCM ..............1,500
     Recovery in Market Value of Temporary Investments .........          1,500
     To adjust allowance account on December 31, 19B.
```

Clearly, the first treatment is the preferable one because the latter, in reflecting a $1,000 loss is actually netting a $2,000 realized loss on the sale against the $1,000 "unrealized" market loss previously recognized.

Identification of Units

When temporary investments are sold, or otherwise disposed of, a question frequently is posed in respect to identification of unit cost (or other value). For example, assume three purchases of stock in XY Corporation as follows: purchase No. 1, 200 shares@ $80; purchase No. 2, 300 shares@ $100; and purchase No. 3, 100 shares@ $110. Now assume 100 shares are sold at $120; what is cost? Specific identification of the particular shares sold is preferable; however, in cases where such identification is not feasible, a Fifo or average cost flow may be assumed; the former appears to be more generally used. The Internal Revenue Service, however, does not permit the use of average cost, but it requires that if shares of stock are sold from lots purchased at different dates or at different prices and the identity of the lots cannot be determined, the stock sold is from the earliest purchases of such stock. For accounting purposes the first-in, first-out rule (or average) applies only where there is identification neither by certificate nor by designation of the taxpayer. The question of sufficiency of identification shades off into very close decisions, which are outside the scope of this text. It should be noted that the use of the valuation account to reduce the cost value of temporary investments to a lower market value does not affect the determination of gain or loss on their sale as being the difference between sales price and original cost. Both loss due to reduction of security values to market and gain from recovery in the market value of securities are closed to the Income Summary account as separate loss and gain items, the loss as an unrealized loss and the recovery gain as an adjustment of losses previously taken up and never actually realized.

Illustrative Entries for Temporary Investments

The illustrative problem which follows was designed to present preferable accounting for the numerous aspects of temporary investments. On November 1, 19A, the XYZ Corporation purchased as temporary investments: six, $1,000, 5% bonds (interest payable on March 1 and September 1 of each year) of Baxter Company at 104 plus accrued interest; and 40 shares of stock of Watson and Wiley, Inc., at 26, plus brokerage fees of $20. Related entries are listed in Illustration 6–1. The following points should be kept in mind with respect to it. Bonds customarily are issued in $1,000 denominations and pay interest semiannually though the rate is stated on annual basis. Shares of stock listed on exchanges frequently pay dividends quarterly. Interest accrues legally on bonds but dividends do not accrue on stocks. Since the planned holding period of temporary investments is short, bond premium or discount obviously should not be amortized in this instance.

Illustration 6–1

Transaction	Entry
Nov. 1, 19A: Purchase of temporary investments. Baxter bonds: Six bonds ($6,000 × 104) ....$6,240 Accrued interest ($6,000 × .05 × 2/12)......................... 50 Cash Paid.........................$6,290 Watson and Wiley stock: Forty shares @ $26...................$1,040 Brokerage fees....................... 20 Cash Paid...........................$1,060	Temporary Investments— Baxter Bonds ....6,240 Interest Income .... 50 Cash .... 6,290 Temporary Investments— Watson and Wiley, Inc., Stock ....1,060 Cash 1,060
Dec. 31, 19A: Accrual of four months. (Sept. 1 to Dec. 31) interest on Baxter bonds. $6,000 × .05 × 4/12 = $100 To close interest income: Credit $100 − Debit $50 = $50	Interest Receivable .... 100 Interest Income .... 100 Interest Income .... 50 Income Summary 50
Jan. 1, 19B: To reverse adjusting entry for accrued interest on Baxter bonds.	Interest Income .... 100 Interest Receivable 100
Mar. 1, 19B: Collected semiannual interest on the Baxter bonds. $6,000 × .05 × 6/12 = $150	Cash .... 150 Interest Income 150
Mar. 20, 19B: Received dividend of 50 cents per share on Watson and Wiley stock. (40 × $.50 = $20)	Cash .... 20 Dividend Income......... 20
Apr. 30, 19B: Sold the six Baxter bonds at 103 and ¾ plus accrued interest. Cost.......................................$6,240 Sales price ($1,000 @ 103¾ = $1,037.50 × 6) .... 6,225 Loss on Sale ....$ 15 Accrued interest—$6,000 × .05 × 2/12 = $50	Cash ($6,225 + $50)............6,275 Loss on Sale of Bonds......... 15 Interest Income .... 50 Temporary investments —Baxter Bonds 6,240
June 20, 19B: Received dividend of 50 cents per share on Watson and Wiley stock. (40 × $.50 = $20)	Cash .... 20 Dividend Income......... 20

Illustration 6–1 (continued)

Transaction	Entry
July 1, 19B: Sold 30 shares of the Watson and Wiley stock at 29 and $\frac{1}{2}$. Sales proceeds (30 × $29.50)...................... $ 885 885 Cost of 40 shares.......$1,060 Less 10 shares retained ($\frac{1}{4}$ × $1,060)................... 265 Cost of 30 shares sold 795 Gain on Sale............. $ 90	Cash .... 885 Temporary Investments —Watson and Wiley, Inc., Stock.............. 795 Gain on Sale of Stock ... 90
Sept. 20, 19B: Received dividend of 50 cents per share on Watson and Wiley stock. (10 × $.50 = $5)	Cash .... 5 Dividend Income........ 5
Oct. 1, 19B: Purchased nine $1,000 bonds of Markwell Corporation at 98 plus brokerage fees of $40 and accrued interest. These 4% bonds pay interest each May 1 and November 1. Cash – $1,000 @ 98 × 9 = $8,820 + $40 = $8,860 Accrued interest – $9,000 × .04 × 5/12 = $150	Temporary Investments— Bonds of Markwell Corp...8,860 Interest Income .... 150 Cash 9,010
Oct. 10, 19B: Sold remaining 10 shares of Watson and Wiley stock at 30.	Cash .... 300 Temporary Investments —Watson and Wiley, Inc., Stock............... 265 Gain on Sale of Stock..... 35
Nov. 1, 19B: Collected semiannual interest on Markwell bonds. $9,000 × .04 = 6/12 = $180	Cash .... 180 Interest Income 180
Dec. 31, 19B: Adjust books for accrued interest. $9,000 × .04 × 2/12 = $60	Interest receivable .... 60 Interest Income 60
Dec. 31, 19B: Adjust books; the Markwell bonds are now quoted at 97 and $\frac{1}{2}$ plus accrued interest. Cost....................................$8,860 Market ($9,000 × 97$\frac{1}{2}$) .... 8,775 Adjustment Required...............$ 85	Decline in Value of Temporary Investments°............ 85 Allowance to Reduce Temporary Investments to LCM 85
Dec. 31, 19B: Close books; this entry reflects a reversing entry which was made on January 1 concerning accrued interest on Baxter bonds.	Gain on Sale of Stock........... 125 Interest Income .... 190 Dividend Income............... 45 Loss on Sale of Bonds... 15 Decline in Value of Temporary Investments°... 85 Income Summary......... 260

° Alternatively, this could be called "Loss due to reduction of temporary investments from cost to LCM." This entry assumes lower of cost or market valuation.

Market prices of both bonds and stocks are quoted at so much per bond or per share. The smallest fraction used is $\frac{1}{8}$. Thus, a $1,000 face value bond quoted at 103 and $\frac{1}{8}$ would sell for $1,031.25 and a $100 bond for $103.125; a share of stock quoted at 47 and $\frac{1}{4}$ would sell for $47.25 regardless of the par or stated value of each share.

QUESTIONS FOR CLASS DISCUSSION

1. Define cash in the accounting sense.

2. An accounting executive said, "In one respect cash is the easiest of all items to account for; in another respect it is perhaps the most difficult." What thoughts probably underlie this remark?

3. Wherein might deposits in foreign banks give rise to special problems?

4. Under what circumstances, if any, is it permissible to offset a bank overdraft against a positive balance in another bank account?

5. If you were called upon to establish a petty cash system that would be particularly effective from the standpoint of internal control, what important features would you incorporate in it?

6. Explain the usage of a Cash Over and Short account.

7. Basically what are the differences between a fluctuating and a nonfluctuating system of petty cash?

8. Where (if at all) do items (a) through (g) belong in the following reconciliation?

```
Balance per bank statement, June 30 ............................................$x,xxx.xx
    Plus ..............................................................................._____
    Minus ............................................................................._____
    June 30 true balance...................................................$9,600.00

Balance per our ledger, June 30 ...............................................$x,xxx.xx
    Plus ..............................................................................._____
    Minus ............................................................................._____
    June 30 true balance...................................................$9,600.00
```

a) Note collected by bank for depositor on June 29; notification was received July 2 when the June 30 bank statement was delivered by the postman.

b) Checks drawn in June which had not cleared bank by June 30.

c) Check of a depositor with a similar name which was returned with checks accompanying June 30 bank statement and which was charged to our account.

d) Bank service charge for which notification was received upon receipt of bank statement.

e) Deposit mailed June 30 which reached bank July 1.

f) Notification of charge for imprinting our name on blank checks was received with the June 30 bank statement.

g) Upon refooting cash receipts book we discovered that one receipt was omitted in arriving at the total which was posted to the Cash account in the ledger.

9. Indicate the various methods of effecting reconciliation of cash in bank with cash per books. If one of the methods has advantages over the others, indicate these advantages. Do not discuss "comprehensive reconciliation."

10. Briefly describe "comprehensive" bank reconciliation. Tell how this system may resemble any other reconciliation technique.

11. What are the two principal approaches to forecasting of cash position and requirements?

12. Define temporary investments.

13. How should temporary investments be valued for accounting purposes?

14. What is included in the cost of temporary investments?

15. Is the "cost or market" method applied to temporary investments in the same way as to inventories? If not, indicate the difference.

16. Why is interest on bonds purchased accrued but not dividends on purchased stocks?

17. An investor purchased 100 shares of XY Company stock in January for $6,700 and another 100 in February for $7,000. In August he sold 150 shares at 77. What is the amount of his gain or loss? Discuss briefly.

18. Under what circumstances would credit entries properly be made to Allowance to Reduce Security Values to LCM? Under what circumstances would this account be debited?

19. How is the accounting for premium or discount on bonds purchased as a temporary investment accomplished?

DECISION CASE 6–1

The president of a small factory came to you for advice. His bookkeeper had told him that the business "has been just about breaking even." He also said that the inventories, receivables, and payables have not varied much since the corporation was organized 10 years ago but that cash had constantly increased; therefore, he "thinks that the business has been making money and that there is an error." The president stated that there had been no sale of assets, refinancing of indebtedness, or change in corporate structure, such as sale of stock.

Required:

1. Present briefly an *explanation* that you might give the president for the continued increase in cash under the circumstances as stated.

2. Give examples of transactions that would illustrate your explanation.

3. What financial statements would you suggest to better inform the president on the present predicament?

(AICPA adapted)

EXERCISES

Exercise 6–1

Indicate the amount (and how derived) which could be properly set out as cash under current assets for each of the following independent cases:

a) Balance in Bank P., $3,100; overdraft in Bank Q, $600; check in drawer from company president for $300 received six weeks ago in settlement of advance to him.

b) Balance in Bank P, $20,000; refundable deposit with state treasurer to guarantee performance of highway contract in progress, $10,000; balance in Banco de Sud America, $2,000 (restricted).

c) Cash on hand, $500; cash in Bank C, $9,000; cash in hands of salesmen as advances on expense accounts, $800; postage stamps in cash drawer received from mail-order customers, $50.

d) Deposit balance in checking account, $10,000; demand certificates of deposits, $5,000, both in Bank C. Deposit with bond sinking fund trustee, $15,000; cash on hand, $1,000.

e) Checks in cash drawer on December 31:

From	Date of Check	Other Data	
Customer W	Dec. 29	On past-due account	$500
Customer X	Dec. 30	In payment of $1,000 invoice of Dec. 23, 2/10, n/30	700
Customer Y	Dec. 24	Previously deposited and returned "NSF."	300
Customer Z	Jan. 2	In full payment of account	400

Exercise 6–2

As a part of their newly designed internal control system, the Mark Corporation established a petty cash fund. Operations for the first month were:

a) Placed in the fund $600 on August 1.

b) Summary of the petty cash record:

	Aug. 1–15	Aug. 16–31
Postage	$ 48	$ 46
Supplies	330	320
Delivery costs	90	150
Miscellaneous expenses	20	30
Total	$488	$546

c) Fund replenished on August 16.

d) Fund replenished on August 31 and increased by $200.

Required:

Give all entries indicated assuming:

a) Fluctuating system.

b) Nonfluctuating (imprest) system.

Exercise 6–3

On beginning an audit of the books and records of the Denny Company for the fiscal year ended December 31, 19A, the following items were found in the petty cash drawer on January 1, 19B, by the auditor:

a) Currency and coin .... $ 9.50
b) Check drawn by the Denny Company to petty cash 55.00
c) Four tickets to a football game purchased by the petty cashier for
   A. B. Carr, a director of the company, reimbursement to be received
   on delivery of the tickets 30.00
d) Postage stamps on hand (purchased on voucher in [g]) 90
e) Employee's check marked "NSF." 10.00
f) Employee's check dated January 15, 19B 10.00
g) Petty cash vouchers for:
   Stamps ....$ 5.00
   Carfare 3.00
   Typewriter repairs 7.00
   Electric utility bill for Mr. Denny's home 19.50   34.50
                                                       $149.90

The Petty Cash account in the general ledger showed a balance of $150.

Required:

1. What entries should be made before statements are prepared?
2. What is the correct amount of petty cash for the balance sheet as of December 31, 19B?

Exercise 6–4

Myles, Ltd., as a matter of policy deposits all receipts and makes all payments by check. The following data were taken from the cash records:

Reconciliation at May 31

Balance per bank $7,000
   Add: Outstanding deposits 1,200
                                       $8,200
   Deduct: Outstanding checks 1,500
Balance per Books $6,700

June Results

	Per Bank	Per Books
Balance, June 30	$ 4,090	$ 5,100
June deposits	10,600	12,300
June checks	14,500	13,900
June note collected	1,000	—
June bank charges	10	—

Required:

1. Compute the unrecorded deposits and outstanding checks.
2. Reconcile the bank account.
3. Give any correcting entries indicated.

Exercise 6–5

Reconciliation of Cox Company's bank account at May 31 was as follows:

Balance per bank statement $14,000
Deposits outstanding.. 800
Checks outstanding.. 150°
$14,650

Balance per books.. 14,664
Unrecorded service charge... 14°
$14,650

°Denotes deduction.

June data are as follows:

	Bank	Books
Checks recorded..	$11,500	$11,800
Deposits recorded..	10,100	11,000
Service charges recorded.................................	12	14
Collection by bank ($800 note plus interest).......	820	–
NSF check returned with June 30 statement (will be redeposited; assumed to be good)....	50	–
Balances June 30..	13,694	14,186

Required:

1. Compute unrecorded deposits and outstanding checks at June 30.
2. Prepare a reconciliation for June.
3. Prepare entries needed at June 30.

Exercise 6-6

At April 30 the cash balances per bank statement and per company records of Crown Company were respectively $750 and $625. They failed to agree because at the time outstanding checks and deposits were respectively $400 and $270 and the bank had recorded a $5 service charge in late April which Crown did not record until May 5.

During May total receipts recorded by the bank and by Crown were $4,000 and $3,900 while payments recorded were $3,750 and $3,625, respectively. The latter figure included the company's recording of the $5 service charge.

As of May 31 you ascertain that Crown has not recorded collection of a $200 noninterest-bearing note receivable on its behalf by the bank which took place late in May and that bank payments include a $12 service charge not reflected on Crown's books. Further, late in May the bank returned to Crown a $38 check which Crown had received from a customer and deposited. While Crown expects it will ultimately realize this $38 it believes it would be futile to redeposit the check immediately and it has made no entry since receiving the check back from the bank. The check was returned because the drawer had insufficient funds on deposit.

Crown makes all payments by check and deposits all receipts daily. At May 31 the balances per bank statement and per Crown books (cash account) were $1,000 and $900, respectively.

Required:

1. Determine apparent outstanding checks and deposits as of May 31.

2. Prepare a comprehensive reconciliation for May.

3. Give entries needed to correct Crown's accounts as of May 31.

Exercise 6–7

From the following data relative to the operation of the Happy Home Project during 1972 you are requested to prepare a schedule showing cash collections of rents for the year.

Gross potential rents	$211,688
Vacancies	42,609
Space occupied by corporation for own use	4,925
Prepaid rent:	
Beginning of period	302
End of period	984
Delinquent rent:	
Beginning of period	377
End of period	79
Deposits (tenants') forfeited	100
Refunds to tenants	20
Uncollectible rents	80

(AICPA adapted)

Exercise 6–8

Information related to the operations of Astromotion Incorporated is presented below.

Actual or projected sales December 1971 through April 1972:

	Cash	Credit	Total
December 1971 (actual)	$20,100	$402,000	$422,100
January 1972 (projected)	20,000	400,000	420,000
February 1972 (projected)	22,500	410,000	432,500
March 1972 (projected)	20,250	405,000	425,250
April 1972 (projected)	20,350	407,000	427,350

Other information:

1. Merchandise inventory is marked up 30% on sales price.

2. Astromotion's cash balance as of December 31, 1971, is $15,000.

3. Typically, 60% of each month's credit sales are collected in the month sold; about 40% of each month's credit sales are collected in the following month.

4. The company follows the practice of purchasing merchandise for cash the month prior to the month in which it will be sold.

5. Cash disbursements for items other than merchandise, including installments on notes payable, salaries, equipment purchases, etc., amount to about $115,000 per month.

Required:

Prepare cash budgets for January, February, and March of 1972.

Exercise 6–9

1. Give journal entries to record the purchase on March 1 of $20,000 par

value bonds of K Corporation for a total consideration (including any accrued interest) of $21,100. The 6% per annum interest on these bonds is payable each June 1 and December 1. The bonds are to be held as a temporary investment.

2. Record the collection of interest at June 1.

3. If the investor adjusts and closes books on June 30 and the market value of the bonds is $20,600 excluding interest, make all necessary entries (assume LCM).

4. Make any entries necessary on July 1.

5. Record the sale of the bonds on July 30 for a total consideration (including any accrued interest) of $20,900.

Exercise 6–10

a) Purchased bonds $40,000 par value on January 1, 19A, at 100 as a temporary investment. (Disregard interest so as to concentrate on other aspects of the accounting.)

b) Market value was 96 at December 31, 19A.

c) January 2, 19B: Sold ¼ of the bonds at 95.

d) Market value was 94 at December 31, 19B.

Required:

Give all entries, assuming the "allowance" account for lower of cost or market is adjusted: (*a*) only at year-end and (*b*) at date of sale and at year-end. Compare the results.

Exercise 6–11

Prepare journal entries to record the following transactions relating to 4% bonds of Dial Corporation purchased as a temporary investment. These bonds pay interest each May 1 and November 1.

Aug. 1   Cash of $39,800 is disbursed for $40,000 par value bonds including interest.

Nov. 1   Collected interest.

Dec. 31   Adjust and close the books for the year. The market value of the bonds is 98 excluding interest (assume LCM).

Jan. 1   Make any necessary reversing entries.

Feb. 1   Sold half of the bonds, receiving a check for $19,600, including accrued interest.

May 1   Collected interest.

Exercise 6–12

A commission consisting of three members, A, B, C, was sent on a special mission; on their return an expense account was turned in by the chairman, A, as follows:

```
Expenses:
    Three airline tickets, at $45.50 .........................$136.50
    One cash fare.................................  46.00
    Ground transportation ....................   9.00
    Hotel, etc...................................  47.50
    To B for incidentals .....................  25.00
    To C for incidentals .....................  22.00
    To A for incidentals .....................  19.50  $305.50
```

Refunds:

One ticket returned for redemption	$ 45.50	
Cash returned by B	15.30	
Cash returned by C	9.90	
Cash returned to balance	23.80	94.50
		$400.00
Cash Advanced		$400.00

Required:

An expense account clerk under your supervision came to you with the statement, "Something is wrong here but I am not sure just what." To help him, the two of you revised the report. Show the revision and explain any errors found.

PROBLEMS

Problem 6–1

The following transactions pertained to petty cash:

a) Jan. 1 19A: Established imprest cash fund $500

b) Jan. 10: Summary of expenditures from the fund from reimbursement voucher:

Expenses (specific)	120
Supplies	90
Advances to employees	240
Miscellaneous items of expense	30

c) Jan. 15: Increased fund by $200.

d) Jan. 31: Summary of expenditures from reimbursement voucher:

Expenses (specific)	160
Supplies	100
Advances to employees	380
Miscellaneous items of expense	40

e) Jan. 31: Count of items in petty cash box:

Currency and coins	692
Stamps (purchased from petty cash)	3

Required:

1. Reconcile the petty cash fund and indicate amount to be reported on the balance sheet.

2. Give all entries indicated.

Problem 6–2

A surprise count of the Y Company's imprest petty cash fund, carried on the books at $5,000 was made on November 10, 1972.

The company acts as agent for an express company in the issuance and sale of money orders. Blank money orders are held by the cashier for issuance upon payments of the designated amounts by employees. Settlement with the express company is made weekly with its representative who calls at the Y Company office. At that time he collects for orders issued, accounts for unissued orders, and leaves additional blank money orders serially numbered.

The count of the items presented by the cashier as composing the fund was as follows:

Currency (bills and coin)...$2,200
Cashed checks 500
Vouchers (made out in pencil and signed by recipient)................ 740
NSF checks (dated June 10 and 15, 1972) 260
Copy of petty cash receipt vouchers:
    Return of expense advance $200
    Sale of money orders (#C1015–1021)............................ 100   300
Blank money orders – claimed to have been purchased
    for $100 each from the express company (#C1022
    to 1027).. 600

At the time of the count there was also on hand the following:

Unissued money orders #C1028–1037.
Unclaimed wage envelopes (sealed and amounts not shown).

The following day the custodian of the fund produced vouchers aggregating $400 and explained that these vouchers had been temporarily misplaced the previous day. They were for wage advances to employees.

Required:

Show the proper composition of the fund at November 10, 1972.

(AICPA adapted)

Problem 6–3

The cash records for the Champ Company provided the following data for the month of March:

	March 1	March 31
Balances per bank statement	$15,600.09	$14,459.91
Balances per company books	14,375.00	13,409.00

Relevant items:

a) Outstanding checks March 31 (verified as correct)....................................$1,400
b) Deposits in transit March 31 (verified as correct)..................................... 800
c) Interest earned on bank balance (reported on bank statement)................... 18
d) NSF check (customer check returned with bank statement)....................... 50
e) Service charge by bank (reported on bank statement) 7
f) Error in deposit for cash sales (deposit slip showed overage, corrected
    by bank).. 10
g) Error by bank (check for $10.89 cleared at $10.98) ....
h) Note collected by bank for us (including $30 interest) 1,030
i) Deduction for church (per signed pledge form)... 20
j) Cash on hand.. 500

Required:

1. Prepare a bank reconciliation in good form showing correct balance for the balance sheet.
2. Prepare necessary entries at March 31.

Problem 6–4

The records pertaining to cash for the Willis Company provided the following data for May:

Bank Statement:
- a) Balance, May 31 ....$34,500
- b) Service charges for May... 5
- c) NSF check returned with May statement; customer gave this check, will redeposit next week, assumed to be good...................................... 50
- d) Note receivable ($5,000) collected for Willis by the bank and added to balance... 5,200
- e) Error from previous month in interest collected on another note receivable; bank credited Willis account in May for the amount............. 100

Books:
- f) Balance, May 31 30,700
- g) Cash on hand 400
- h) Unrecorded deposit... 3,700
- i) Outstanding checks... 2,665

Required:

1. Prepare a bank reconciliation in good form. Assume all amounts provided above are correct.

2. Give required entries for May 31.

Problem 6–5

X Company regularly deposits all its cash receipts and makes all its cash disbursements through its account with the Third State Bank by check. A summary of its Cash account and of the bank's account with X Company for January and February appear below. Use these data to prepare an overall reconciliation for February. The following information relates to lettered items in the accounts:

a) Inquiry at the bank concerning a $20 check drawn early in January revealed that as of February 27, the check had still not cleared. The bank had been contacted by telephone; it will accept only written stop payment orders and order was not drawn until February 28, hence had not become effective at the bank during February.

b) The $200 represents proceeds of a customer of X's note. X had turned the note over to the bank for collection (which occurred late in February). Advice of the collection was not conveyed to X until early in March.

c) Check from a customer of X deposited late in February proved to be NSF.

X COMPANY

Cash in Bank

1/1 balance	$1,000	Jan. checks	$3,100
Jan. receipts	3,740	1/31 balance	1,640
	$4,740		$4,740
2/1 balance	$1,640	Service charge	$ 5
Feb. receipts	3,900	Feb. checks	4,030
(a)	20	2/28 balance	1,525
	$5,560		$5,560
3/1 balance	$1,525		

THIRD STATE BANK

X Co. Checking Account

Checks cleared	$3,020	1/1 balance	$1,000
Service charge	5	Receipts	3,500
1/31 balance	1,475		
	$4,500		$4,500
Checks cleared	$4,040	2/1 balance	$1,475
NSF check (c)	35	Regular receipts	3,800
2/28 balance	1,400	(b)	200
	$5,475		$5,475
		3/1 balance	$1,400

Required:

Prepare an overall reconciliation for February.

Problem 6-6

The following information was obtained in an audit of the cash account of Tuck Company as of December 31, 1971. Assume that the CPA has satisfied himself as to the validity of the cash book, the bank statements, and the returned checks, except as noted.

1. The bookkeeper's bank reconciliation at November 30, 1971.

Balance per bank statement		$ 19,400
Add deposit in transit		1,100
Total		$ 20,500
Less outstanding checks		
#2540	$140	
1501	750	
1503	480	
1504	800	
1505	30	2,300
Balance per books		$ 18,200

2. A summary of the bank statement for December 1971.

Balance brought forward	$ 19,400
Deposits	148,700
	$168,100
Charges	132,500
Balance, December 31, 1971	$ 35,600

3. A summary of the cash book for December 1971 before adjustments.

Balance brought forward	$ 18,200
Receipts	149,690
	$167,890
Disbursements	124,885
Balance, December 31, 1971	$ 43,005

4. Included with the canceled checks returned with the December bank statement were the following:

Number	Date of Check	Amount of Check	
#1501	Nov. 28, 1971	$75	This check was in payment of an invoice for $750 and was recorded in the cash book as $750.
#1503	Nov. 28, 1971	$580	This check was in payment of an invoice for $580 and was recorded in the cash book as $580.
#1523	Dec. 5, 1971	$150	Examination of this check revealed that it was unsigned. A discussion with the client disclosed that it had been mailed inadvertently before it was signed. The check was endorsed and deposited by the payee and processed by the bank even though it was a legal nullity. The check was recorded in the cash disbursements.
#1528	Dec. 12, 1971	$800	This check replaced #1504 that was returned by the payee because it was mutilated. Check #1504 was not canceled on the books.
–	Dec. 19, 1971	$200	This was a counter check drawn at the bank by the president of the company as a cash advance for travel expense. The president overlooked informing the bookkeeper about the check.
–	Dec. 20, 1971	$300	The drawer of this check was the Tucker Company.
#1535	Dec. 20, 1971	$350	This check had been labeled NSF and returned to the payee because the bank had erroneously believed that the check was drawn by the Luck Company. Subsequently the payee was advised to redeposit the check.
#1575	Jan. 5, 1972	$10,000	This check was given to the payee on December 30, 1971, as a postdated check with the understanding that it would not be deposited until January 5. The check was not recorded on the books in December.

5. The Tuck Company discounted its own 60-day note for $9,000 with the bank on December 1, 1971. The discount rate was 6%. The bookkeeper recorded the proceeds as a cash receipt at the face value of the note.

6. The bookkeeper records customers' dishonored checks as a reduction of cash receipts. When the dishonored checks are redeposited they are recorded as a regular cash receipt. Two NSF checks for $180 and $220 were returned by the bank during December. The $180 check was redeposited but the $220 check was still on hand at December 31.

Cancellations of Tuck Company checks are recorded by a reduction of cash disbursements.

7. December bank charges were $20. In addition a $10 service charge was made in December for the collection of a foreign draft in November. These charges were not recorded on the books.

8. Check #2540 listed in the November outstanding checks was drawn in 1971. Since the payee cannot be located, the president of Tuck Company agreed to the CPA's suggestion that the check be written back into the accounts by a journal entry.

9. Outstanding checks at December 31, 1971, totaled $4,000 excluding checks #2540 and #1504.

10. The cut-off bank statement disclosed that the bank had recorded a deposit of $2,400 on January 2, 1972. The bookkeeper had recorded this deposit on the books on December 31, 1971, and then mailed the deposit to the bank.

Required:

Prepare a four-column reconciliation (sometimes called a "proof of cash") of the cash receipts and cash disbursements recorded on the bank statement and on the company's books for the month of December 1971. The reconciliation should agree with the cash figure that will appear in the company's financial statements. (AICPA adapted)

Problem 6–7

Selected data related to the operations of Nod Incorporated are presented below.

Excerpted account balances as of December 31, 1971:

Cash	$ 11,100
Accounts receivable (trade)	115,000
Merchandise inventory	151,800
Accounts payable (merchandise)	25,000
Wages and commissions payable	7,250
Notes payable	10,000

Actual or forecast sales — October 1971 to June 1972:

	Cash	Credit	Total
October 1971 (actual)	$10,000	$100,000	$110,000
November 1971 (actual)	11,000	110,000	121,000
December 1971 (actual)	10,500	105,000	115,500
January 1972 (projected)	11,000	110,000	121,000
February 1972 (projected)	12,000	120,000	132,000
March 1972 (projected)	11,500	115,000	126,500
April 1972 (projected)	12,100	121,000	133,100
May 1972 (projected)	11,700	117,000	128,700
June 1972 (projected)	11,800	118,000	129,800

Other pertinent information:

1. In general, 50% of a month's credit sales are collected in the month sold, 40% in the following month, and 8% in the second following month. About 2% of each month's credit sales is never collected.

2. Inventory is marked up 40% on sales price, and a two month's supply of inventory should be on hand at the end of each month. Merchandise is purchased on credit with terms of 2/10, n/30 throughout each month; merchandise purchases are recorded net. All discounts are taken.

3. The monthly installments on the notes payable amount to $1,000.

4. The company plans to purchase a new machine in January 1972 for cash. The cost of the machine is expected to be $20,000.

5. A $10,000 cash balance is required at the beginning of each month. Money may be borrowed in multiples of $1,000 for 30-day, 60-day, 90-day, and 120-day periods at 6%. Interest is payable when the loans are repaid.

6. Wages and sales commissions are paid semimonthly one-half month after they are earned. Wages amount to $4,000 per month, and sales commissions equal 10% of sales.

7. Other operating expenses total $13,000 each month; this figure includes $2,500 of depreciation and $500 amortization of intangibles.

Required:

Prepare cash budgets for January, February, and March of 1972. Your budgets should indicate the amount of cash borrowings and repayments which should occur each month.

Problem 6–8

You are called upon to develop a monthly cash budget for Thrifty Department Store and in the course of your investigation ascertain the following facts.

Thrifty has been a somewhat seasonal business. Over the past several years the following pattern has evolved and is expected to continue into the period being budgeted:

| | | Percent of Month's Sales | |
Month	Percent of Year's Sales	For Cash	On Credit
January	6	30	70
February	6	40	60
March	9	40	60
April	10	50	50
May	11	40	60
June	11	40	60
July	10	40	60
August	8	35	65
Etc.	—	=	=
	100		

The budgeted profit plan for the year is as follows:

Sales		$4,000,000
Cost of sales:		
Inventory, January 1	$ 200,000	
Purchases	2,350,000	
	$2,550,000	
Inventory, December 31	150,000	2,400,000
Gross margin		$1,600,000
Expenses:		
Selling expenses	$ 980,000	
General expenses	220,000	1,200,000
		$ 400,000

Miscellaneous items:

Purchase discounts..$	26,000	
Loss on bad debts	38,000	12,000
Net Income before Taxes		$ 388,000

Sales are made at a uniform rate of markup throughout the year. Purchases are planned to increase the inventory 10% over the end of each previous month's balance through March; inventory is then to be held constant through June, and then to drop a uniform amount per month to attain the budgeted year-end level.

Purchases are regularly paid for within the discount period: 40% in the same month as purchased, 60% in the following month. Discounts average 1%. Receivables collections amount to 70% the month following sale, 29% in the next month, the remainder prove worthless. Selling expenses are paid as incurred (and the variable portion varies in direct proportion to sales at 20%); $180,000 of the selling expenses are fixed, of which one third is depreciation. General expenses are similarly paid as incurred, are all fixed, and include $40,000 of depreciation.

Required:

Prepare a cash flow budget for March, April, and May. Cash on hand March 1 has been forecast to be $120,000.

Solution suggestions: Prepare the following schedules:

No. 1—Analysis of Sales, Inventory, Purchases, and Variable Sales Expense.

Side captions: Jan., Feb., Mar., Apr., and May.

Top captions: Total Sales, Cash, On Account, Cost of Sales, Planned Inventory Increase, Purchases Required, and Variable Sales Expense.

No. 2—Collection Schedule (Accounts Receivable).

Side captions: Jan. Sales, Feb. Sales, March Sales, April Sales.

Top captions: Jan., Feb., Mar., Apr., May, June, Losses, Total.

No. 3—Accounts Payable (Purchases) Schedule.

Side captions: Jan. Purchases, Feb. Purchases, March Purchases, April Purchases, May Purchases, Total before Discount, Payment Required.

Top captions: Jan., Feb., Mar., Apr., May, June, and Total.

No. 4—Cash Flow Budget.

Side captions:

Balance start of month

Receipts:

Cash sales

Collections

Total receipts

Payments:

Fixed selling expenses

Fixed general expenses

Variable selling expenses

Accounts payable (purchases)
Total payments
Excess receipts over payments
Balance, end of month
Top captions: March, April, and May.
Solution Hint: May 31, cash balance, $191,574.

Problem 6–9

The Standard Mercantile Corporation is a wholesaler and ends its fiscal year on December 31. As the company's CPA you have been requested in early January 19B to assist in the preparation of a cash forecast. The following information is available regarding the company's operations:

1. Management believes the 19A sales pattern is a reasonable estimate of 19B sales. Sales in 19A were as follows:

January	$ 360,000
February	420,000
March	600,000
April	540,000
May	480,000
June	400,000
July	350,000
August	550,000
September	500,000
October	400,000
November	600,000
December	800,000
Total	$6,000,000

2. The accounts receivable at December 31 total $380,000. Sales collections are generally made as follows:

During month of sale	60%
In first subsequent month	30
In second subsequent month	9
Uncollectible	1

3. The purchase cost of goods averages 60% of selling price. The cost of the inventory on hand at December 31 is $840,000 of which $30,000 is obsolete. Arrangements have been made to sell the obsolete inventory in January at half of the normal selling price on a c.o.d. basis.

The company wishes to maintain the inventory as of the first of each month at a level of three months sales as determined by the sales forecast for the next three months. All purchases are paid for on the 10th of the following month. Accounts payable for purchases at December 31 total $370,000.

4. Recurring fixed expenses amount to $120,000 per month including depreciation of $20,000. For accounting purposes the company apportions the recurring fixed expenses to the various months in the same proportion as that month's estimated sales bears to the estimated total annual sales. Variable expenses amount to 10% of sales. Payments for expenses are made as follows:

	During Month Incurred	Following Month
Fixed expenses 55%		45%
Variable expenses.........................70		30

5. Annual property taxes amount to $50,000 and are paid in equal installments on December 31 and March 31. The property taxes are in addition to the expenses in item "4" above.

6. It is anticipated that cash dividends of $20,000 will be paid each quarter on the 15th day of the third month of the quarter.

7. During the winter unusual advertising costs will be incurred which will require cash payments of $10,000 in February and $15,000 in March. The advertising costs are in addition to the expenses in item "4" above.

8. Equipment replacements are made at the rate of $3,000 per month. The equipment has an average estimated life of six years.

9. On March 15, 19B, the company expects to pay $60,000 on its income tax liability.

10. At December 31, 19A, the company owed $280,000 on an unpaid bank loan. This loan requires a principal payment of $20,000 on the last day of each month plus interest at one half of 1% per month on the unpaid balance at the first of the month. The remaining balance is due on March 31, 19B.

11. The cash balance at December 31, 19A, is $100,000.

Required:

Prepare a cash forecast by months for the first three months of 19B for the Standard Mercantile Corporation. The statement should show the amount of cash on hand (or deficiency of cash) at the end of each month. All computations and supporting schedules should be presented in good form.

(AICPA adapted)

Problem 6–10

The balance sheet at the start of the year 19B showed:

Marketable securities at cost $865,000
Dividends receivable ($2 per share on 1,500, Security B) 3,000

Using the following data, show how the marketable securities would affect the balance sheet as of December 31, 19B, and the income for the year, if the first-in, first-out method of determining the cost of securities sold is used. (Use an allowance account to record any market decline in the price of securities on hand at the end.)

Marketable Securities on Hand, December 31, 19A

Shares	Security	Cost	Shares	Security	Cost
1,000...........................A		$ 90,000	1,000...........................F		$130,000
1,500...........................B		120,000	800...........................G		85,000
600...........................C		60,000	1,000...........................H		70,000
1,500...........................D		95,000	2,000...........................I		130,000
1,200...........................E		85,000			
			Total.....................		$865,000

Cash Purchases — 19B

Date	Security	Shares	Cost	Date	Security	Shares	Cost
Mar. 20 ....A		200	$20,000	July 15 ....K		300	$40,000
Apr. 15 ....B		500	50,000	July 25 ....G		200	20,000
Apr. 25 ....J		200	15,000	Aug. 15 ....G		200	25,000
May 10 ....J		300	25,000	Sept. 15 ....K		1,000	90,000

Cash Sales — 19B

Date	Security	Shares	Price	Date	Security	Shares	Price
Jan. 15 ....A		200	$ 19,000	July 20............A		500	$ 50,000
Mar. 10 ....F		200	30,000	Aug. 20............H		1,000	30,000
Apr. 10 ....E		1,200	110,000	Sept. 15............B		1,000	125,000
June 15 ....F		300	50,000				

Additional data:

a) Cash dividends received — 19B: A, $5,000; B, $12,000; D, $4,000; F, $6,000; G, $5,000; I, $9,000; J, $1,000.

b) Stock dividend received June 15, 19B: H, 100%.

c) Purchased December 31, 19B, for delivery and payment January 2, 19C: 200 shares G, $25,000.

d) Dividends declared in 19B payable in cash in 19C: H, $1 per share to stockholders of record December 31, 19B; D, $1 per share to stockholders of record January 2, 19C.

e) Market value of all securities owned: December 31, 19A, $850,000; December 31, 19B, $800,000.

Solution suggestion: Set up a work sheet with side captions for each security, providing five lines for each so as to account for purchases and sales. Top captions: No. Shares, Cost per Share, Amount, Sales Price, Gain or Loss, and Balance on Hand (at Cost).

Problem 6–11

At January 1 the ledger of Shelton Company, insofar as temporary investments are concerned, reflected the following accounts and balances after posting January 1 reversing entries:

8% Bonds of AB Company		Interest Income	
1/1 (par $6,000) 6,050		1/1	$40

5% Pref. Stock of MN Corporation		Allowance to Reduce Temporary Investments to Market	
1/1 (par $4,000) 5,720		1/1	200

The balance in the Allowance to Reduce Temporary Investments to Market arose as a result of the following situation as of December 31:

Security	Cost	Market
8% bonds of AB Company (excluding interest)	$ 6,050	$ 6,070
5% Pref. stock of MN Corporation	5,720	5,500
Total Values	$11,770	$11,570

Transactions in respect to these and other temporary investments throughout the following year were as follows:

Jan. 15 Collected quarterly dividend on MN stock.
Feb. 1 Purchased 9% bonds of CD Incorporated for a total consideration of $8,040. Par value of these bonds which pay interest each May 1 and November 1 is $8,000.
Apr. 15 Collected quarterly dividend on MN stock.
May 1 Collected semiannual interest on CD bonds.
June 1 Collected semiannual interest on AB bonds.
July 1 Sold MN stock for $5,600.
Aug. 1 Sold half of AB bonds at par plus accrued interest.
Nov. 1 Collected semiannual interest on CD bonds.
Dec. 1 Collected semiannual interest on AB bonds.
Dec. 18 Bought 40 shares of PQ Corporation common stock at 38½ plus brokerage fees totaling $40.
Dec. 31 Adjust and close books at year-end, taking into consideration the following quotations which for bonds do not include accrued interest: AB, 102½; CD, 97; PQ, 39.

Required:

Journalize the foregoing transactions assuming LCM; adjust and close the books at December 31.

Hint: Do not overlook reversal of accrued interest on AB bonds on January 1.

Problem 6–12

The following transactions relate to temporary investments. The fiscal year ends December 31.

19A:

a) Mar. 1 Purchased 10 $1,000 6% bonds (interest payable on April 1 and October 1 each year) of Abel Company at the quoted market of 95 (exclusive of accrued interest).
b) Apr. 1 Collected interest on Abel bonds.
c) May 1 Purchased 50 shares of Byrd Corporation $100 par value, common stock at 59½ plus brokerage fees of $25.
d) Sept. 10 Dividends declared and received on Byrd Stock $275.
e) Oct. 1 Collected interest on Abel bonds.
f) Adjusted and closed books. Market values on Dec. 31, 19A: Abel bonds, 91½ (ex-interest); Byrd stock, 62.

19B:

g) Apr. 1 Collected interest on Abel bonds.
h) June 1 Sold four of the Abel bonds $4,000 including accrued interest.
i) Aug. 1 Sold 30 shares of Byrd stock for $1,700.
j) Sept. 15 Dividends declared and received on Byrd stock (8% on par).

k) Oct. 1 Collected interest on Abel bonds.
l) Adjusted and closed books. Market values on December 31, 19B: Abel bonds, $5,640 (ex-interest); Byrd stock, $1,060.

Required:

1. Give all entries indicated.
2. Show how the temporary investments should be reported on the balance sheet December 31, 19B.

Problem 6-13

Walsh Manufacturing Company's temporary investment portfolio included the following at December 31, 19A:

	Cost
AB Company, nine 5% bonds (face, $9,000)	$9,300
BC Corporation common, 50 shares, no par	1,800
CD Corporation, 4% preferred, 150 shares (par, $40)	8,000

Transactions relating to the securities during 19B were as follows:

Jan. 25 Received semiannual dividend check on CD shares.
Mar. 1 Collected semiannual interest on AB bonds.
Apr. 15 Sold 30 shares of BC Corporation stock for $1,020.
May 1 Sold six of the AB bonds for a total consideration (including accrued interest) of $6,350.
June 20 Purchased 50 shares of EF Corporation, common at 47 plus $30 brokerage fees.
July 25 Received semiannual dividend check on CD shares.
Sept. 1 Collected semiannual interest on AB bonds.
Oct. 1 Purchased a $1,000 6% bond of DE, Inc., for total consideration of $1,100. Interest payment dates on this bond are February 1 and August 1.
Nov. 17 Sold remaining BC Corporation shares for $700.
Dec. 2 Received $60 dividend check from EF Corporation.
31 Preparatory to adjusting and closing the books for the year the following data as to current market values of securities held were obtained:

Security	*Market*
AB bonds (ex-interest)	103
CD preferred	54
DE, Inc., bond (ex-interest)	106
EF common	45

Required:

Journalize the foregoing transactions; adjust and close the books at December 31, 19B: Value the total portfolio of securities at market by means of an Allowance to Reduce Temporary Investments to Market account.

Hint: Do not overlook reversal of accrued interest adjustment on AB bonds on January 1, 19B.

chapter 7 | Receivables

This chapter focuses on the classification, valuation, and accounting for receivables. Broadly speaking, the term *receivables* encompasses claims of the entity for money, goods, or services from other entities or persons. In most companies receivables largely consist of amounts due from customers and clients arising from the normal operations of the firm; however, a variety of other types of receivables are encountered from time to time. This chapter discusses the following aspects of receivables:

1. Trade receivables
   a) Accounts receivable
   b) Notes receivable
2. Special receivables
   a) Deposits
   b) Claims against various parties
   c) Advances to employees
3. Collection expectations
   a) Current
   b) Noncurrent
4. Receivables used for borrowing
   a) Accounts receivable assignment and factoring
   b) Notes receivable discounting

TRADE RECEIVABLES

Trade receivables mark the first point in the sequence of merchandising transactions which include a potential profit. Prior to this point, transfers (from cash to materials, to work in process, to finished goods) have been at cost. The amounts billed as accounts receivable usually include a gross margin. The initial value placed on receivables, ordinarily, is the maximum that can be realized in cash. From this value an allowance for estimated bad debt losses is subsequently subtracted. The two principal classes of trade receivables are accounts receivable and notes receivable; they are discussed in that order.

Accounts Receivable

The term *accounts receivable* is commonly used to designate trade debtors' accounts. Other receivables are separately designated in special accounts as explained in the next section of this chapter. We may note that considerable objection may be raised against the unqualified title "accounts receivable." Strictly speaking, any claim for which no written statement of the obligation (such as a note) signed by the obligor has been received by the creditor is an account receivable to the creditor. The careless use of a title so broadly inclusive is not sufficiently descriptive to convey the true nature of the various assets included. It is preferable to employ more descriptive titles for the various classes of accounts receivable, such as, "accounts receivable—trade debtors" for accounts due for regular sales to customers. Such usage facilitates the classification (and interpretation) of these assets on the balance sheet. Ordinarily accounts receivable are classified under the current asset caption on the balance sheet, yet there are many special accounts receivable which should not be classified as current.

Valuation of Accounts Receivable. Valuation of accounts receivable poses a problem of estimating the amount which will be realized from the accounts through collection.[1] In estimating the value of trade accounts receivable, deductions must be made for estimated losses from bad debts. In addition, in special situations it may be necessary to estimate freight costs which must be paid on goods returned by customers, allowances to be made next period on present receivables, and cash discounts which will be taken on present receivables. The most important allowance, and the one which is almost invariably needed, is the Allowance for Doubtful Accounts (or alternatively, Allowance for Bad Debts).

There are two common approaches to estimating the Allowance for Doubtful Accounts for trade receivables (including trade notes receivable); each approach has two variations as follows:

---

[1] Receivables arising from sales and services should be recorded at net of any trade discounts; see Chapter 8 for a complete discussion of accounting for cash discounts on receivables.

1. Estimation of the expense of extending credit:
   a) On the basis of past experience a percentage relationship between losses from bad debts and net credit sales is ascertained. This percentage is then applied to the net credit sales of the period to determine the current addition to the allowance for doubtful accounts.
   b) Use the same procedure as in (a) except that the percentage of bad debts to total sales is used. This method is deficient because it relates the losses from bad debts to cash as well as credit sales.
2. Estimation of the value of present receivables:
   a) Determine from past experience the ratio of bad debts to outstanding accounts receivable and then apply this ratio to the present balance in the Accounts Receivable account. The balance in the allowance account is then increased so that its balance equals the total of the estimated uncollectible accounts. For a rough estimate of bad debts this method may be used. It is, however, not to be recommended since it gives no weight to varying ages of accounts; it is applied to all outstanding account balances rather than to only current additions.
   b) Age the accounts receivable, and from the resulting analysis and other available information estimate the total uncollectible accounts. The balance in the allowance account is then increased so that its balance equals the total of the estimated uncollectible accounts. In aging accounts receivable, the customers' accounts are listed and the items therein classified according to whether they are not yet due, just due, a little past due, or considerably past due. Each of these classes is examined for items that should be separately valued, and the remainder are evaluated by average percentages which increase with the age of the items. The older the account after becoming past due, the less likelihood of its being collected, since it must either be in dispute or due from a poor credit risk.

The use of any of these approaches to estimating bad debts must take cognizance of changes in credit policy, of changes in economic conditions, and of any other external factors which might have a bearing upon the ability of customers to pay their debts. After a method is selected it should be subjected to a more or less continuous review on the part of the accountant and the officers of the company so that rates may be revised or the approach changed to secure reliable results.

Allowance for Doubtful Accounts. The title of the account used to reflect the estimate of losses from failure to collect the full amount of trade receivables initially recorded is variously titled in practice. Combinations of such terms as *allowance, reserve,* or *provision* with the terms *doubtful accounts, bad debts,* or *estimated losses* are to be found in practice. Use of the term *reserve* in this connection has been rejected by authoritative committees and is disappearing gradually. Allowance for Doubtful Accounts is the terminology most commonly used; accordingly it is used throughout this book.

Under either of the two approaches outlined above the related adjusting entry for estimated bad debts involves a debit to an expense account with an offsetting credit to the account Allowance for Doubtful Accounts. An illustrative problem is presented below to demonstrate the basic accounting for doubtful accounts.

Illustrative Problem. Starting balances: Accounts Receivable, $100,000; Allowance for Doubtful Accounts, $2,000 (credit).

Transactions: sales on credit, $500,000; collections, $420,000; accounts written off as uncollectible, $2,500. Make appropriate adjusting entry.

Solution:

The write-off of uncollectible accounts ordinarily would occur throughout the period and would precede the end-of-period adjusting entry; in some cases the write-off may create a temporary debit balance in the allowance account. After posting the following entry, Allowance for Doubtful Accounts has a *debit* balance of $500.

Allowance for Doubtful Accounts 2,500
    Accounts Receivable 2,500
    To write off accounts considered worthless.

The two different approaches to the adjusting entry are now shown:

1. Adjustment of the allowance by estimating the expense of extending credit. Assuming past experience has indicated that 1% of credit sales normally is not collected and that this pattern is likely to continue, the following entry should be made:

Bad Debt Expense (.01 × $500,000) 5,000
    Allowance for Doubtful Accounts 5,000

Upon posting this entry the allowance account has a $4,500 credit balance which should be deducted from trade accounts receivable on the balance sheet.

2. Adjustment of the allowance by estimating the value of the present receivables. Assume it is decided that 2.4% of the balance of trade receivables ($177,500) will not be collected. In this instance the following entry would be made:

Bad Debt Expense...4,760
    Allowance for Doubtful Accounts 4,760
    To adjust to the desired credit balance as follows:
      Desired balance (2.4% of $177,500) $4,260
      Debit balance in allowance before adjustment............ 500
      Amount of Credit Needed......................................$4,760

The debit balance in the allowance account before adjustment at the end of the period may mean that inadequate provisions have been made in the past. On the other hand, it may indicate merely that the expected current period's charge-offs have been made against Allowance for Doubtful Accounts prior to the period's adjustment of that account. If it is determined that the provision for bad debts is inappropriate (either too high or too low) the loss percentage (rate) should be changed prospectively (see page 269).

Bad Debts Collected. When an amount is collected from a customer whose account was previously written off as uncollectible, the customer's account should be recharged with that amount (or with the entire balance written off if it now appears collectible) and the allowance account should be credited for the same amount. This entry will cause the debtor's account to reflect the complete record of the credit and related collections in detail. Such information may be useful in future dealings with the customer.

Estimating the Valuation of Uncollectible Receivables. As noted and illustrated above, adjustment of the Allowance for Doubtful Accounts may be based upon (1) net sales, (2) credit sales, (3) a percentage of present receivables, or (4) an aging analysis of present receivables. The net sales (cash plus credit sales) basis emphasizes the matching of sales revenue with the bad debt expense (cost of extending credit). It is based upon the theoretical premise that all sales, not just credit sales, are influenced by the credit policies of the company. It is especially appropriate for short-term interim statements (monthly or quarterly) and for highly seasonal situations. Basing estimated bad debt losses on net sales is simple, widely practiced, and theoretically defensible.

The credit sales basis also emphasizes matching sales revenue and the cost of extending credit. It is based upon a more theoretically feasible premise that only credit sales give rise to bad debt losses. It also recognizes a fairly common pattern, that is, that bad debt losses in most situations tend to correlate to a higher degree with credit sales than with any other index. If in a given situation bad debt losses do correlate with credit sales to a higher degree than with net sales, a shift in the relationship of cash sales to credit sales would distort the effect of a ratio based on net sales but would not distort a ratio based on credit sales. The credit sales basis is simple, theoretically sound, and it is used perhaps more widely than any other basis.

Both of the bases discussed above theoretically are preferable from the standpoint of the income statement since they directly match bad debt expense with current sales. The "credit-sales" basis theoretically is preferable. In contrast, the two bases to be discussed next emphasize the reliable value of all trade receivables uncollected at balance sheet date. Therefore, these bases tend to emphasize the viewpoint of the balance sheet.

The percentage of present-receivables basis may yield a fairly accurate estimate of the amount to be collected provided the credit manager or other person making the estimate has thorough knowledge of general characteristics of the receivables, is experienced, and is alert to current economic conditions which would affect collectibility of accounts generally. The chief advantage of this method is its simplicity. It may work rather satisfactorily if the bad debt adjustment is made annually. If it is applied at short intervals such as monthly or quarterly, it is likely to result in recurring charges for balances extant at the end of earlier periods which remain uncollected at the close of successive periods. The method suffers from the possibility that the bad debt expense reported on the current income statement may not be particularly related to current sales, thus violating the matching principle.

Aging of accounts receivable involves the analysis of each individual account balance with a view to determining amounts not yet due, amounts moderately past due, and amounts considerably past due. The example in Illustration 7–1 shows a typical aging procedure.

Illustration 7–1
Aging Accounts Receivable

Customer	Receivable Balance Dec. 31, 19–	Not Past Due	Past Due		
			1–30 Days	31–60 Days	Over 60 Days
Davis	$ 500	$ 400	$ 100		
Evans	900	900			
Field	1,650		1,350	$ 300	
Harris	90			30	$ 60
King	800	700	60	40	
Zilch	250	250			
Total	$32,500	$26,000	$4,200	$2,000	$300

Ideally, each account would be reviewed by credit department personnel with a view to determining its whole or partial collectibility. Such a procedure could become prohibitively time consuming if a large number of customer accounts were involved. Somewhat more feasible in such cases would be the development of estimated loss percentages for each category based on previous loss experience and application of these percentages to the totals as shown in Illustration 7-2.

Illustration 7-2
Estimating Allowance for Doubtful Accounts

Status	Total Balances	Loss Experience Percentage	Estimated Amount to Be Lost
Not due..................................	$26,000	1%	$ 260
1–30 days past due	4,200	8	336
30–60 days past due	2,000	25	500
Over 60 days past due	300	50	150
	$32,500		$1,246

Anticipating Customer Discounts and Returns. If customers are granted cash discounts for prompt payment, then, theoretically, estimates reflecting the expected experience should be recorded. Similarly, if they are granted allowances or can return goods for credit, a case can be made for anticipatory recording of these items. In practice, few companies attempt to reflect such future events in their accounts. To illustrate, if anticipatory recording of customer discounts were undertaken by a concern which grants 2% discounts and which has $20,000 of receivables on which the discount period has not expired as of the end of a period, assuming three fourths of the credit sales to customers normally is paid within the discount period, the following entry could be made:

Sales Discounts (2% of three fourths of $20,000) 300
    Allowance for Cash Discounts   300

This entry would be reversed at the start of the next period so that normal recording could be followed as to all discounts taken during the first few days of the period. In other words, any discount taken subsequently would result in a debit to Sales Discounts, and it would not be necessary to analyze collections to determine whether an anticipated discount was being taken. Similar procedures could be followed for anticipated sales returns and allowances. The balance in the allowance account would be presented on the balance sheet as a deduction from receivables.

Allowance for Freight and Containers. When merchandise is sold f.o.b. destination with an arrangement that any freight paid by the customer will result in a reduction of his remittance settling the charge for goods, accounting in anticipation of such reductions may be desirable if the amounts involved are material. This may be accomplished in several ways; two appropriate approaches are illustrated.

Assume a sale for $1,000 with the agreement that the purchaser will pay the freight upon delivery but that he will deduct it from his payment; the freight paid was $100. The indicated entries by the vendor are:

At date of sale:		*Allowance Approach*		*Net Due Approach*
Accounts Receivable 1,000			900	
Sales...		1,000		900
Freight-out (estimated)	100			
Allowance for Freight-out		100		
At date of payment:				
Cash...	900		900	
Allowance for Freight-out	100			
Accounts Receivable		1,000		900

A balance in the allowance account would be reported as a deduction from Accounts Receivable; Freight-out should be deducted from gross sales. In the above example the estimated freight and the actual freight turned out to be the same amount which may not be the case in some situations; in such instances, since the amount normally is small in amount, the simplest approach is to close it to Freight-out at the end of the period for such known differences.

Products may be delivered to customers in containers for which a refundable charge is made; accounting procedures for this situation are discussed in Chapter 16.

Customers' Credit Balances. When individual customers' accounts have credit balances, the amount may be deducted from the debit balances of the customers' accounts if immaterial in amount. If they are material in amount, separate disclosure under liabilities is called for; "credit balance of customers' accounts" is a suitable title.

Average Due Date of an Account. Frequently, it is desirable to determine the average *due date* of an account receivable (or payable) where several amounts comprise the balance. For example, assume an account receivable having two charges, one on February 15 for $100 and another on March 15 for $100. Assume further that the amounts are due 30 days after date of charge and if not paid by regular due date, interest at 5% is chargeable. Obviously, the average due date in this illustration would be April 1: settlement of the $200 as one payment on that date could avoid the interest charge. In the above illustration the average due date was obvious since (a) there were only two amounts and dates involved, and (b) the respective amounts were equal. Where several different dates and amounts are involved the computation must give weight to both the differing dates and amounts. Therefore, in computing the average due date of an account receivable (or payable), *each entry* (debit and credit) must be considered as to amount and date. The dates involved in averaging are the dates on which the elements affecting the balance are worth their *face value;* more appropriately the date may be designated as the *date of face value.* Time periods should be counted so as to avoid advantage to either debtor or creditor; thus the *date of face value* for the several items of debits and credits to be found in an account receivable are:

Items	Date of Face Value
Cash sales	Date of sale
Credit sales	Date when payment should be made in full
Return or allowance	Same due date as that used for the invoice to which the return or allowance applies
Interest-bearing note	Date of note
Noninterest-bearing note	Due date of note
Partial payment on account	Date of payment

A *focal date* must be chosen when the average due date computation is undertaken. The focal date is an arbitrary base point from which the computation proceeds. While any date may be selected as the focal date, it is recommended that the date chosen be the date preceding the earliest *date of face values* determined according to the tabulation above. Since the due date must be a later date, such a choice has the advantages of avoiding plus and minus items in either segment of the calculation and of reducing the "dollar days" amounts.

As a simple illustration, suppose credit terms are 1/10, n/30 and a customer's account reflects the following:

Customer Receivable

March 5 (invoice)	1,000
March 23 (invoice)	200

Assume that by April 6 this customer had made no payment. Obviously, the $1,000 is past due, while the $200 is not yet due. The creditor has already sustained a possible loss of interest on the $1,000 (through potential reinvestment), while payment by the debtor of the $200 on April 6 would cost the latter a theoretical loss of interest. Computation of the average due date is shown below. Following the recommendation made earlier, since the first "date of face value" is April 4, April 3 is chosen as the focal date:

(a)	(b)	(c)	(d) Days from Date of Face Value to Focal	(e)
Date	Amount	Date of Face Value	Date of April 3	Dollar Days (b) × (d)
Mar. 5...............$1,000		Apr. 4	1	$1,000
Mar. 23................... 200		Apr. 22	19	3,800
	$1,200			$4,800

$\Sigma(e) \div \Sigma(b) =$ Number of days after focal date to yield average due date; $\$4,800 \div \$1,200 = 4$. Four days after April 3 makes April 7 the average due date. Hence, full payment should be on April 7 to avoid interest gain or loss to either party.

Illustrative Problem. A more extended illustration involving an account receivable containing both debits and credits follows:

Customer Receivable

May 16	2/10, n/30	425	May 26	Payment	225
May 31	2/10, n/60	325	June 11	Payment	150
June 5	c.o.d.	250			

Compute the average date of the foregoing account using as a focal date May 25, the day preceding the earliest date of face value:

		(a)	(b)	(c)	(d) Days from Date of Face Value to Focal Date of May 25	(e) Dollar Days (b) × (d)
		Date	Amount	Date of Face Value		
		5/16	$ 425	6/15	21	$ 8,925
		5/31	325	7/30	66	21,450
Debits		6/5	250	6/5	11	2,750
			$1,000			$33,125
		5/26	$ 225	5/26	1	$ 225
Credits		6/11	150	6/11	17	2,550
			$ 375			$ 2,775
Balance			$ 625			$30,350

$\$30,350 \div \$625 = 48.56$ days.
48.56 or 49 days forward from May 25 yields July 13 as the average date of the account.

If the account had only debits, the average date would be 33 days forward from May 25 ($\$33,125 \div \$1,000$), or June 27.

The average due date, frequently referred to as the average date, is used in several situations, among which are the following:

1. Payment of an account where interest is chargeable after due date but payment on the average due date avoids interest.
2. Dating of a note receivable in full settlement of an account; the note should be dated as of the average due date of the account.
3. Computation of interest charges on past-due receivables.
4. Factoring of accounts receivable (discussed below).
5. Settlement of notes receivable, accounts payable, and notes payable in situations similar to 1, 2, and 3 immediately above.

Notes Receivable

Notes receivable may consist of trade notes receivable, which arise from regular operations, and special notes receivable. Trade notes receivable are by far the most common in the usual company. When material amounts are involved, trade notes and special notes should be accounted for and reported separately.

Notes receivable are unconditional written promises to pay the payee or holder of the note (holder in due course) a specified sum. The payee ordinarily would be in possession unless he had endorsed the notes to a subsequent holder in due course. Not all notes are negotiable (transferable by endorsement); hence one classification of notes would be whether they are negotiable or nonnegotiable. Requisites for negotiability are a matter of law.

Notes may be designated as interest bearing or noninterest bearing; although strictly speaking practically all notes are interest bearing. Interest-bearing notes require payment of the *face value* of the note plus interest at maturity. In contrast, a noninterest-bearing note includes the interest in the face value. Thus the present value of an interest-bearing note is the same as its maturity value (i.e., its face value). Again in contrast, the present value of a noninterest-bearing note is less than its maturity (face) value. For example, the present value of one-year $1,080, 8% interest-bearing note is $1,080; on the other hand, the present value of an $1,080 noninterest-bearing note is $1,000 one year prior to maturity assuming the implied interest rate is 8% per year (i.e., $1,080 ÷ 1.08 = $1,000).

Whether a note is interest bearing or not frequently affects the recording of the transaction. To illustrate, assume a $2,000 sale and receipt of a one-year 8% note receivable in payment. The indicated entries under two different conditions follows:

	Interest-Bearing Note		Noninterest-Bearing Note	
At date note received:				
Notes Receivable	2,000		2,160	
Unearned Discount on Notes Receivable				160
Sales		2,000		2,000
At end of six months (end of fiscal period):				
Interest Receivable	80			
Unearned Discount on Notes Receivable			80	
Interest Income		80		80
At date of payment:				
Cash	2,160		2,160	
Unearned Discount on Notes Receivable			80	
Interest Receivable		80		
Interest Income		80		80
Notes Receivable		2,000		2,160

On interim balance sheets the balance in Unearned Discount on Notes Receivable should be deducted from Notes Receivable.

Though not all of the documents reported under the caption "notes receivable" technically are notes, the distinctions between them are seldom deemed vital enough to warrant the use of separate accounts for each type. For example, bills of exchange and trade acceptances usually are included in the category notes receivable. A draft, trade acceptance, and other bills of exchange are written orders drawn by one party on a second party to pay a third party an amount of money under specified conditions.

The Notes Receivable account should include only commercial paper with trade debtors which is related to the operating cycle and not past due. All other notes including those between the entity and its officers, employees, or stockholders should be reported separately. Notes of affiliated companies also should be shown separately.

Balance sheet classification of notes receivable must be consistent with the definition of current assets; therefore, they may be either current or noncurrent depending upon collection expectations.

Provision for Losses on Notes. Provision for bad notes from trade customers normally should be included in the provision credited to Allowance for Doubtful Accounts.

Interest and Maturity Date Calculation Reviewed. Interest normally is calculated on the basis of a 360-day year. Thus, interest on an $1,800 note maturing in 60 days and bearing interest at 6% would be calculated:

$$\$1,800 \times .06 \times \frac{60}{360} = \$18$$

Discounting of Notes Receivable Reviewed. If a negotiable note receivable is endorsed to another payee before maturity, the original payee receives money (through the discounting) before maturity but may become *contingently liable* for payment of the note. The contingent liability depends on whether or not the note was endorsed in a regular manner (with recourse) or "without recourse." Since the bank or other endorsee normally is unwilling to accept the note with the latter type of endorsement, most notes give rise to a contingent liability upon their being discounted.

The interest cost of discounting is calculated as follows:

Discount = Maturity Value of Note × Rate × Time to be Held by Endorsee

Thus, a 60-day, 6% note for $1,800 would have a maturity value of $1,818. However, if discounted at 5% after being held 36 days from its issue date, the proceeds would be $1,811.94, as shown in this calculation:

$$\text{Maturity Value} = \$1,800 \times .06 \times \frac{60}{360} = \$18 + \$1,800 = \$1,818$$

$$\text{Discount} = \$1,818 \times .05 \times \frac{24}{360} = \$6.06$$

$$\text{Proceeds} = \$1,818 - \$6.06 = \$1,811.94$$

Upon discounting the endorser should make either of the following entries:

	Interest Expense and Income Recognized Separately		Interest Expense and Income Offset	
Cash..	1,811.94		1,811.94	
Interest Expense	6.06		0	
Notes Receivable Discounted.....		1,800.00		1,800.00
Interest Income°		18.00		11.94

° Theoretically, if material in amount, this should be recognized over the remaining life of the note.

The first entry is preferable theoretically; however, for practical reasons the second entry generally is made. If the note had been endorsed "without recourse," the $1,800 credit would be made to Notes Receivable instead of to Notes Receivable Discounted. When a discounted note is paid by the maker, the original payee must debit Notes Receivable Discounted and credit Notes Receivable.

Notes Receivable Discounted on Balance Sheet. The contingent liability represented by notes receivable discounted may be shown on the balance sheet in one of several different ways. One method which is not used as extensively now as in former years is to show the contingent liability as a deduction from Notes Receivable, with the latter account containing both notes on hand and notes discounted.

Current Assets:
Notes Receivable $10,000
Less: Notes Receivable Discounted.................................. 4,000 $6,000

Published statements of the more prominent corporations at the present time more frequently show the contingent liability for discounted notes receivable in a footnote either immediately following the listing of notes receivable or at the end of the balance sheet, thus:

Current Assets:
Notes receivable (contingent liability for notes
    discounted, $4,000)...$6,000

or, thus:

Current Assets:

Notes receivable...$6,000°

      ° The contingent liability on June 30, 19A, for customers' notes discounted was $4,000

Still another method which is sometimes used is to enter the amount of the contingent liability short (i.e., entered in the items column and not added in with total liabilities) on the liability side of the balance sheet, thus:

Current Assets:

Notes receivable $6,000

Current Liabilities:

Notes receivable discounted..$4,000

Dishonored Notes Receivable. When a note receivable is not paid or renewed at maturity it is said to be dishonored. The accounting procedure for a dishonored note depends on whether or not the note has been discounted. If a dishonored note has been discounted, ordinarily it will be necessary for the original payee to pay it (unless he endorsed it "without recourse"). If the note discounted in the illustration on page 277–78 is dishonored, upon payment by the original payee, his entries would be as follows:

Notes Receivable Discounted...1,800
    Notes Receivable...   1,800
Accounts Receivable (name)..1,818
    Cash..   1,818

In case protest fees were paid by the payee, the amount involved would be added to the second entry.

On the other hand, if this same note had not been discounted, upon dishonor the required entry would have been:

Accounts Receivable (name)..1,818
    Notes Receivable...   1,800
    Interest Income ($1,800 × .06 × 60/360)   18
    To charge dishonored note to account of maker together with accrued interest to maturity date.

Some accountants feel that an additional entry preferably should be made transferring the balance to a Dishonored Notes Receivable account as shown below:

Dishonored Notes Receivable 1,818
    Accounts Receivable (name)..   1,818

After dishonor, interest accrues on the maturity value of the note plus any protest fees at the *legal* rate of interest. However, if the note is bad the claim for interest is similarly worthless and should perhaps be ignored.

Balance sheet presentation of dishonored notes receivable favored by the authors is to show them as past-due notes receivable together with subtraction of an appropriate allowance for the estimated uncollectible portion. They should be classified as current or noncurrent depending on collection expectations.

SPECIAL RECEIVABLES

Receivables other than trade receivables generally are classified as special receivables. They may be represented by open accounts or notes and may be current or noncurrent. Some of the usual types of special receivables are:

1. Deposits made to other parties to cover potential damages, and deposits as a guarantee of performance of a contract or payment of an expense.
2. Prepayments to others on contingent purchases and expense contracts.
3. Claims against creditors for damaged or lost or returned goods.
4. Claims against common carriers for lost or damaged goods.
5. Claims against the government for rebates and the like.
6. Claims against officers and employees.
7. Claims against customers for return of containers (no deposit).
8. Advances to subsidiaries.
9. Advances to officers and employees.
10. Dividends receivable (declared).
11. Unexpended balances of working funds in the hands of agents.
12. Claims against insurance companies for losses sustained.
13. Claims in litigation.
14. Unpaid calls on stock subscriptions (subscriptions receivable).

Special receivables that are related to the operating cycle or are collectible within one year should be appropriately designated and reported in the current asset section of the balance sheet. Other special receivables normally are reported on the balance sheet under a caption such as "other assets." Thus, receivables from officers, employees, or affiliates, whether arising from cash advances or from sales, would be classed as noncurrent if not collectible within one year. Examples of other exclusions from current assets include receivables arising from sale of capital assets not due within one year and cash surrender value of life insurance policies.

Special receivables should be evaluated independently, and a special allowance for doubtful accounts for this class of receivables should be established when warranted by the prevailing circumstances.

USE OF RECEIVABLES TO SECURE IMMEDIATE CASH

Companies frequently utilize receivables to secure immediate cash prior to the regular collection date. The more common methods of obtaining immediate cash on receivables are: (1) discounting of notes receivable (discussed above), (2) assignment of accounts receivable, (3) factoring of accounts receivable, (4) outright sale of accounts receivable, and (5) pledging accounts receivable. While detailed contractual arrangements may vary, the following brief description generally typifies these transactions and the accounting for them.[2]

Assignment

Accounts receivable financing frequently involves the assignment to a financing institution of receivables arising on open-account sales. Frequently, these assignments are made on a "with recourse, nonnotification" basis. "With recourse" means that accounts becoming excessively delinquent or uncollectible must be repurchased by the seller or replaced with other accounts receivable of equivalent value. "Nonnotification" means debtors are not informed of the assignment, and hence remit to the seller in the usual way. As the seller collects invoices which have been assigned, the cash is transmitted to the finance company.

The cash advanced may range from 70 to 95% of the gross value of the accounts. Interest rates charged vary somewhat, but one fortieth of 1% per day is a representative figure. Thus, if 90% of the gross value of the invoices has been advanced, an annual effective rate of just over 10% results. Annual rates charged may range as high as 18 to 20% where risks are greater and the low dollar volume per account causes high costs.

Assignment of receivables with recourse is akin to the discounting of notes receivable, and the accounting procedure is somewhat parallel. An illustrative problem is presented to demonstrate the essential accounting procedure involved in the assignment of accounts receivable.

Illustrative Problem. W Company assigned $40,000 of its receivables to Z Finance Company under a contract, including a promissory note, whereby the latter agreed to advance 85% of their gross value.

---

[2] Some of the following added details may be of interest. Accounts financed are commonly owed by other businesses rather than consumers. The volume and popularity of this kind of financing have increased markedly, especially since World War II. Contrary to popular belief, many very solvent businesses with excellent credit ratings use accounts receivable financing.

W's debtors remit directly to it since the assignment was "with recourse, and nonnotification." The series of transactions and related entries are shown in Illustration 7–3.

Illustration 7–3
Assignment of Accounts Receivable

Transaction	Entries on W's Books
Jan. 2: Assigned $40,000 accounts receivable: advance received 85%; gave note payable.	Accounts Receivable Assigned ....40,000 Accounts Receivable 40,000
	Cash ($40,000 × 85%) ....34,000 Notes Payable (Z Finance Co.).......... 34,000
Jan: Collected $30,000 of assigned accounts less cash discounts $300 and sales returns $500.	Cash ....29,700 Sales Discounts...................................... 300 Sales Returns .... 500 Accounts Receivable Assigned.......... 30,500
Jan. 31: Remitted collections to finance company plus $250 interest.	Financing Expense............................... 250 Notes Payable (Z Finance Co.)................29,700 Cash 29,950
Feb: Collected balance of assigned accounts except $200 written off as uncollectible.	Cash .... 9,300 Allowance for Doubtful Accounts............ 200 Accounts Receivable Assigned.......... 9,500
Feb. 28: Remitted balance due to finance company plus $80 interest.	Financing Expense............................... 80 Notes Payable (Z Finance Co.)................ 4,300 Cash 4,380

On January 31 the balance sheet would reflect the following:

Current Assets:
Accounts receivable... $150,000
Accounts receivable assigned $9,500
Less: Note payable on assigned accounts...................... 4,300
Equity in accounts receivable assigned.........................   5,200
    Total Accounts Receivable $155,200

Obviously, the details of a contract, such as the one illustrated above, will determine the details of the accounting entries.

Factoring

Accounts receivable may be sold on a *without recourse* basis to factors.[3] Customers whose accounts are sold are notified to pay directly to the factor who assumes the functions of billing, collecting, etc.

---

[3] Factors are financing organizations which buy trade receivables. Factoring is encountered in many lines of industry but is especially widespread in the textile industry.

Under a factoring contract, the factor passes on the granting of credit for the client. As the latter sells to customers, copies of the sales invoices and supporting documents are sent to the factor. The client usually obtains cash immediately upon transferring the invoices. Gross amounts of the invoices less any discounts and allowances and less the factor's commission and a margin or reserve (factor's margin or reserve) to cover expected returns and claims is the measure of cash available. Interest (above the factor's commission) is charged only on cash drawn *prior* to the average due date of the factored invoices. Available money not drawn plus the amount reserved becomes available without interest cost on the average due date. (Refer to the previous section on computation of the average due date of an account.)

In addition to interest, factors charge commissions to compensate for their credit and collection services and the credit losses they must bear. Since cash needs are often seasonal, proportions of available cash drawn probably will vary throughout the term of the factoring arrangement. Commissions range from less than 1% to over 2% of the value of receivables factored, while interest charges usually are around 8% on an annual basis. An illustrative problem is presented to demonstrate the essential accounting procedures related to factoring arrangements.

Illustrative Problem. The following invoices arising from sales on 1/10, n/30 terms are sold to a factor on May 15, the related computation of the average due date, for interest purposes, is included:

Invoice Date	Discount Period Due Date + 10 Days°	Invoice Amount		Days from Focal Date (May 26)	Dollar Days
		Gross	Net		
May 7 ....5/27		$ 800	$ 792	1	$ 792
8 ....5/28		1,100	1,089	2	2,178
9 ....5/29		3,300	3,267	3	9,801
11 ....5/31		2,500	2,475	5	12,375
13 .... 6/2		4,600	4,554	7	31,878
		$12,300	$12,177		$57,024

° This is the earliest date on which invoices are payable plus the cash discount period per the agreement and plus an agreed upon 10-day period for collection delays, clearing of checks, etc. Thus, as shown in the illustrative problem, an invoice dated May 7 with 1/10, n/30 terms would have a discount period due date of May 17, plus 10 days, making a face value date of May 27. Otherwise, computations are as shown earlier in this chapter.

Division of total of dollar days ($57,024) by the total of net invoice amount ($12,177) yields a quotient of 4.68 days. Thus, the average date is May 31, i.e., May 26 plus five days (after rounding). Money drawn prior to May 31 would give rise to interest charges based on the amount drawn. If the commission is 1 and ½% of the net amount of the

Illustration 7–4
Factoring Receivables

Entries on Borrower's Books

Transaction			
May 15: Sale of $12,300 accounts receivable to factor per contract.	Factor's Commission (1 and ½% of $12,177)............	182.66	
	Sales Discount ($12,300 × 1%)............	123.00	
	Factor's Margin°	1,199.43	
	Receivable from Factor (residual amount)............	10,794.91	
	Accounts Receivable............		12,300.00
	° .10[$12,300 − ($182.66 + $123.00)].		
May 19: Draw of $5,000 cash against the factor; 12 days prior to average due date of May 31 and at agreed interest rate of 6% per annum.	Cash............	5,000	
	Interest Expense............	10	
	Receivable from Factor............		5,010
May 31: Draw of balance due from factor ($10,794.91 − $5,010.00 = $5,784.91)	Cash............	5,784.91	
	Receivable from Factor............		5,784.91
June 2: Received report from factor that accounts receivable of $500 were being returned in view of disagreement with the customer in respect to the merchandise. A check for the balance of the factor's margin was included ($1,199.43 − $500.00 = $699.43).	Cash............	699.43	
	Accounts Receivable............	500.00	
	Factors Margin............		1,199.43

invoices and the safety factor (factor's margin) is 10% of the net receivables discounted, the factoring would be recorded as in Illustration 7–4.

The balance in Factor's Margin plus Receivable from Factor would be reported as a current asset. No contingent liability exists relative to the receivables factored.

Outright Sale of Accounts Receivable

Occasionally accounts receivable are sold outright to a third party, usually without recourse. Outright sale involves a prohibitively high discount rate, varying from 15 to 50%, depending upon the circumstances. Outright sale occurs most frequently when a business is in serious financial difficulty. No unique accounting problems are involved; discounting losses preferably should be reported as an extraordinary item on the income statement.

Pledging

Loans are sometimes obtained from banks and other lenders by pledging accounts receivable as security. The borrower continues to • collect his receivables and usually is required to apply collections to reduction of the loan. This method of lending on receivables is sometimes used because commerical banks may lack express or implied power to purchase accounts receivable. Disclosure of the fact that portions of the accounts receivable balance have been pledged should be accomplished by balance sheet footnotes or appropriate parenthetical notations. The accounting by the borrower is essentially the same as that illustrated above for assignment.

QUESTIONS FOR CLASS DISCUSSION

1. Define receivables and indicate the types of receivables encountered generally.
2. What is meant by trade receivables?
3. How should trade accounts receivable and trade notes receivable be valued? Explain.
4. How should special receivables be valued?
5. Outline the basic approaches in estimating the allowance for doubtful accounts for trade receivables. Evaluate each approach.
6. What entry or entries should be made when an account previously written off as bad is collected? Explain.
7. How should customers' credit balances be reported?
8. What is meant by "average due date"? Indicate the primary situations where it may be useful.
9. A $1,000, 5%, 90-day, interest-bearing note receivable is discounted at 6% at the end of 30 days. Compute the cash received upon discounting.
10. With respect to the note in 9 above give the following entries: (a) at re-

ceipt of the note, (b) at date of discounting; (c) at date of payment by the maker, and (d) assuming the maker defaulted and payment is made by the endorser including a $15 protest fee.

11. Indicate several ways of reporting notes receivable discounted on the balance sheet.

12. Indicate the proper accounting and reporting for special receivables.

13. What are the primary methods of securing immediate cash from receivables?

14. Explain the essential differences between assignment and factoring of accounts receivable.

DECISION CASE 7–1

Stardust Store has accounted for bad debt losses by a direct charge-off to expense with no allowance for doubtful accounts. (When an account is deemed bad, expense is debited and receivables credited at that time.) All sales are on 30-day net credit terms, and cycle billing is used.[4] Monthly financial statements are prepared for the management. The 20 stockholders receive quarterly statements in addition to annual reports dated each December 31. An analysis of sales and receivables together with the amounts charged off as uncollectible over the 15-month period ended December 31, 1971, appears below.

Date	Sales	Uncollected from Two Months Back or More	Uncollected from One to Two Months Back	Uncollected Current Month's Receivables	Written Off during Month
1970:					
Oct	$ 50,000	$ 3,000	$ 20,000	$ 40,700	$ 800
Nov	80,000	4,300	32,100	60,300	500
Dec	106,000	5,500	40,000	90,500	900
1971:					
Jan	65,000	7,200	24,000	51,300	200
Feb	37,000	8,000	30,300	31,100	800
Mar	42,000	7,000	20,000	38,800	1,000
Apr	58,000	7,700	21,000	51,000	1,400
May	50,000	8,200	30,500	46,000	450
June	44,000	10,100	31,100	42,900	1,300
July	45,000	9,700	28,800	41,600	850
Aug	42,000	8,700	31,400	39,700	1,800
Sept	49,000	10,300	34,000	43,400	300
Oct	57,000	8,000	29,000	55,000	2,200
Nov	91,000	10,500	40,300	86,600	700
Dec	126,000	12,800	62,000	111,000	1,800
Total	$942,000	$121,000	$474,500	$829,900	$15,000

[4]Cycle billing is a procedure whereby customers are billed at regular staggered intervals throughout a month. Thus, customers whose last name begins with letters A through D might be billed on the fifth of the month, those in the E through H group billed on the ninth, etc.

Required:

1. Evaluate the suitability of the company's bad debt loss procedure from the standpoint of financial statements prepared for management. Analyze to the fullest extent possible based on the above data.

2. Would you recommend continuance of the present bad debt procedure used or would something different be preferable? Support your position.

DECISION CASE 7–2

Part A

During the audit of accounts receivable your client asks why the current year's expense for bad debts is charged merely because some accounts may become uncollectible next year. He then said that he had read that financial statements should be based upon verifiable, objective evidence, and that it seemed to him to be much more objective to wait until individual accounts receivable were actually determined to be uncollectible before charging them to expense.

Required:

1. Discuss the theoretical justification of the allowance method as contrasted with the direct write-off method of accounting for bad debts.

2. Describe the following two methods of estimating bad debts. Include a discussion of how well each accomplishes the objectives of the allowance method of accounting for bad debts.

a) The percentage of sales method.
b) The aging method.

3. Of what merit is your client's contention that the allowance method lacks the objectivity of the direct write-off method? Discuss in terms of accounting's measurement function.

Part B

Due to calamitous earthquake losses the Morgan Company, one of your client's oldest and largest customers, suddenly and unexpectedly became bankrupt. Approximately 30% of your client's total sales have been made to the Morgan Company during each of the past several years.

The amount due from Morgan Company—none of which is collectible—equals 25% of total accounts receivable, an amount which is considerably in excess of what was determined to be an adequate provision for doubtful accounts at the close of the preceding year.

Required:

How should your client record the write-off of the Morgan Company receivable if it is using the allowance method of accounting for bad debts? Justify your suggested treatment.   (AICPA adapted)

EXERCISES

Exercise 7–1

A corporation selling appliances on 20-month installment terms has the following items included in a single account entitled "Receivables."

a) Past-due balance owed by customer.
b) Advance to affiliate company—due in 10 months.
c) Loan to vice president—due in 16 months.
d) Meter deposits for utilities.
e) Investment in joint venture (all assets of which are current).
f) Income tax refund claim (not yet approved by government).
g) Balances due from customers.
h) Damage claim against railroad (approved for payment).
i) Subscriptions receivable—common stock.

Required:

Indicate (*a*) the preferable account title and (*b*) the preferable balance sheet classification for each item. Assume each is material in amount.

Exercise 7–2

In an audit of the Beta Company you find that the receivables and payables are kept in one controlling account (called Receivables) which shows a debit balance of $29,900. An analysis of the details reveals the following:

	Debits	Credits
Accounts receivable—customers	$60,000	
Accounts receivable—officers	5,000	
Debit balances—creditors	3,000	
Fire insurance premiums paid day prior to audit	1,200	
Capital stock subscriptions not fully paid	10,000	
Accounts payable—creditors		$40,000
Unpaid officers' salaries		7,500
Credit balances—customers		1,000
Payments received in advance for shipments not yet made		800

Required:

1. What disposition would you make of these items? Give entry to reflect correct treatment and to clear this account.
2. How should they be reported on the balance sheet?

Exercise 7–3

An analysis of the receivables account (balance, $40,800) of the Conger Company revealed the following on December 31:

a) Accounts from regular sales (current) ... $30,000
b) Accounts known to be uncollectible ... 1,000
c) Dishonored notes charged back to customers' accounts ... 4,000
d) Credit balances in customers' accounts ... 200
e) Accounts of customers past due ... 3,000
f) Due from employees ... 3,000

The Allowance for Doubtful Accounts is adjusted annually on December 31. Its balance before adjustment on December 31 was a $800 debit. It was estimated that losses on receivables of December 31 would average as follows: 1% on item (*a*); 20% on item (*c*); 5% on item (*e*).

Required:

1. Give entries to close the old account and to reflect properly the above items.

2. Indicate proper reporting on the balance sheet. Assume all amounts to be material.

Exercise 7–4

The following data are available for the month of January:

Cash sales	$200,000
Credit sales	100,000
Accounts receivable, beginning balance	82,000
Accounts receivable, ending balance	80,000
Allowance for doubtful accounts, beginning balance	1,000 (credit)
Uncollectible accounts to be written off	2,000

Required:

Give entry for bad debt expense for the month of January assuming:

a) Basis is net sales (cash plus credit sales) and that the estimate is 2%.

b) Basis is credit sales and that the estimate is 5%.

c) Basis of a flat percent of uncollected receivables and that the estimate is 7½%.

d) Basis is an analysis of uncollected receivables (aging) and that the estimate is: on ⅘ of the receivables, 2½%; on ⅕ of the receivables, 25%.

Show all computations and indicate ending balance in the allowance account.

Exercise 7–5

Excerpts from the trial balance of Koker Company as of December 31 include:

Accounts receivable	$29,000
Notes receivable	4,000
Allowance for doubtful accounts	400 (debit balance)
Sales	95,500
Sales returns and allowances	3,500

The accountant estimated that 3% of all the outstanding receivables would not be collected. The credit manager estimated that 1% of net sales should be "reserved" for bad debts.

Required:

1. Indicate the amounts to be charged to Bad Debt Expense for the current year under the two approaches and give the entry to reflect each opinion.

2. Indicate the ending balance in the allowance account under each method.

3. Conceptually what are the basic differences between the two approaches?

Exercise 7–6

Compute the average due date of the following account under each independent assumption given below:

Account Receivable – J. A. Rye

Sept. 3	Sale	70	Oct. 5	Cash	50
Sept. 21	Sale	60	Oct. 6	Return°	10
Oct. 10	Sale	45			

° Applies to sale of September 21.

a) Assume that all balances are due the first of the month following the date of charges.

b) Assume that all sales are made on terms of 1/10, n/30.

Exercise 7–7

Mr. A. B. Coe, a customer, has indicated that he would like to "settle his accounts and handle the interest fairly." Accordingly, the company has decided to compute the average date of his account which follows. Since details concerning the note are not provided you are to make the computation under each of two assumptions.

Account Receivable – A. B. Coe

Apr. 12	2/10, n/30	500	May 22	Cash	500
May 4	2/10, n/30	325	June 27	Note°	200
June 18	n/30	105			

a) Assume the note marked ° is dated June 26, is noninterest bearing, and matures in 30 days.

b) Assume instead the note marked ° is dated June 24, bears interest at 6%, and matures in 60 days.

Exercise 7–8

The Brown Company accepted a trade note from a customer. In respect to the note give the indicated journal entry for each of the following events; show computations:

a) Received a trade note receivable, face $2,000, 6% interest bearing, dated August 18, maturing in 120 days.

b) Discounted the above note at the end of 60 days at 8% interest. Give two methods of recording.

c) The maker paid the note at maturity.

d) The maker defaulted and the original payee had to pay the note at maturity together with a protest fee of $10.

Exercise 7–9

Lamar Finance Company loaned Smith Brothers 80% on accounts receivable assigned with recourse and nonnotification basis on August 1. A flat 2% commission on the assigned accounts was charged at the date of the loan. A promissory note to the finance company was signed for $80,000.

On August 31 Smith's records reflected the following in respect to the assigned accounts:

Cash collected		$25,000
Sales discount allowed		480
Notes receivable		2,000
Accounts determined to be bad:		
A. B. Cox	$200	
P. E. Spers	150	350

Cash was remitted to the finance company in accordance with the contract which specified that each month Smith would remit cash equal to 80% of all cash collected on the accounts plus interest amounting to .005 per month on all uncollected accounts at month-end plus an amount equal to all items settled on a noncash basis. Smith made the remittance accordingly.

On September 30 Smith's records reflected that all of the remaining assigned accounts had been collected, less sales discounts of $1,000. Accordingly, Smith made a final remittance to the finance company.

Required:

1. Make entries for each of the three intervals indicated: August 1, August, and September. Show computations.

2. Show how the relevant amounts would be reflected on the balance sheet at the end of August.

Exercise 7–10

On December 1, 19A, the Cage Company received two notes from two customers for goods sold to them. Each note was in settlement for a sale of goods for $10,000. Customer A gave a 6%, 60-day, interest-bearing note. Customer B gave a 60-day noninterest-bearing note with an implied interest rate of 6% (i.e., 6% interest was included in the face of the note).

Required:

1. Give all entries in respect to the two notes from date of receipt through date of payment assuming the end of the fiscal accounting period is December 31, 19A.

2. Show how the notes should be reflected on the December 31, 19A, balance sheet.

PROBLEMS

Problem 7–1

Recently the management of the Baker Trading Company became concerned about certain estimates and procedures used in the accounting function. One concern relates to the approach to accounting for doubtful accounts. The records of the company provided the following relevant information:

Cash sales for the month $800,000
Credit sales for the month 500,000
Balance in accounts receivable (trade) on first of month.................. 100,000
Balance in accounts receivable (trade) at end of month.................... 120,000
Balance in allowance for doubtful accounts on first of month............   2,000 (credit)
Bad debts written off during month   3,000

The company has been estimating bad debt expense on an informal basis; the management is reviewing the procedure with the distinct possibility of a change in approach.

Required:

Four different approaches are being considered. You are to list these different approaches and briefly explain each. After each explanation you are to give the indicated entry for the month for bad debt expense (show computations) and immediately following each entry indicate the advantages of the approach. For solution purposes use the following simplified estimates:

a) Bad debt expense approximates $\frac{1}{4}$ of 1% of net sales (cash plus credit sales).
b) Bad debt expense approximates $\frac{3}{5}$ of 1% of credit sales.
c) As a rough estimate 5% of the uncollected accounts receivable will be bad at any one time.
d) Aging of the accounts at the end of the month indicated that three fourths of them will incur a 3% loss and one fourth of them will incur an 8% loss.

Problem 7–2

Provide journal entries, supported by detailed computations, for each of the following independent situations:

a) The relative effects of four different approaches in determining the bad debt expense are under consideration. You are to provide the appropriate entry for each approach based on the following data (December):

Cash sales..$90,000
Credit sales.. 70,000
Beginning balance in accounts receivable 17,000
Ending balance in accounts receivable.. 22,000
Beginning balance in allowance for doubtful accounts (credit)............   3,000
Pertinent estimates of bad debt expense:
  As a percent of cash plus credit sales – 3%
  As a percent of credit sales – 7%
  As a percent of uncollected receivables – 20%
  As a percent of due dates (aging analysis) of receivables:
    On one fourth of uncollected receivables – 40%
    On three fourths of uncollected receivables – 15%
  Uncollectible accounts to be written off during month...................   5,000

b) An allowance for doubtful accounts is used. The $5,000 written off in December was comprised of a $2,000 and a $3,000 receivable. During the following fiscal year the first account was collected in full and $1,000 on the second account was collected. You are to provide all entries indicated.

Problem 7–3

The Installment Jewelry Company has been in business for five years but has never had an audit made of its financial statements. Engaged to make an audit for 1971, you find that the company's balance sheet carries no allowance for doubtful accounts, uncollectible accounts having been expensed as written off and recoveries credited to income as collected. The company's policy is to write off at December 31 of each year those accounts on which no collections have been received for three months. The installment contracts generally provide for uniform monthly collections over a time span of two years from date of sale.

Upon your recommendation the company agrees to revise its accounts for 1971 in order to account for bad debts on the allowance basis. The allowance is to be based on a percentage of sales which is derived from the experience of prior years.

Statistics for the past five years are as follows:

Year	Charge Sales	Accounts Written Off and Year of Sale			Recoveries and Year of Sale
1967	$100,000	(1967) 550			
1968	250,000	(1967) 1,500	(1968) $1,000		(1967) $100
1969	300,000	(1967) 500	(1968) 4,000	(1969) $1,300	(1968) 400
1970	325,000	(1968) 1,200	(1969) 4,500	(1970) 1,500	(1969) 500
1971	275,000	(1969) 2,700	(1970) 5,000	(1971) 1,400	(1970) 600

Accounts receivable at December 31, 1971, were as follows:

1970 sales	$ 15,000
1971 sales	135,000
	$150,000

Required:

Prepare the adjusting journal entry or entries with appropriate explanations to set up the Allowance for Doubtful Accounts. (Support each item with organized computations; income tax implications should be ignored. The books have been adjusted but not closed at December 31, 1971.)

(AICPA adapted)

Problem 7–4

The Downs Store estimates the allowance for doubtful accounts by aging the accounts at the end of each period. It is May 31 and the accounts are to be aged. The following data were provided by the company records:

a) Balance in the Allowance for Doubtful Accounts, $200.31 (credit).

b) Bad account to be written off immediately, $300.

c) Excerpts from the journals for the period; credit terms are net, 30 days:

Sales Journal

Date	Customer	Invoice No.	Amount
Feb. 10	Gerrah Bros.	3671	$ 215.10
12	Ferris and Ferris	3679	1,100.00
21	Ingalls, Inc.	3810	307.40
Mar. 4	Kermit and Son	4103	111.85
6	Gerrah Bros.	4182	280.00
9	Martinson Mart	4222	608.20
Apr. 13	Lewis and Quine	4714	503.50
20	Ferris and Ferris	4917	381.30
26	Hendrix Stores	5300	344.60
29	Gerrah Bros.	5614	301.90
May 3	Ingalls, Inc.	5839	218.00
11	Ferris and Ferris	5902	124.80
13	Hendrix Stores	5966	606.75
14	Lewis and Quine	6034	39.80
18	Jackson and Gill	6110	131.10
28	Lewis and Quine	6299	103.35
31	Ingalls, Inc.	6416	493.30

Cash Receipts Book

Date	Customer or Account	Reference	Cr. Accounts Receivable	Cr. General Ledger
Mar. 13	Ferris and Ferris	3679	$950.00	
14	Gerrah Bros.	3671	215.10	
20	Ingalls, Inc.	3810	260.00	
Apr. 16	Martinson Mart	4222	200.00	
May 6	Notes receivable	NR No. 3		$280.00
6	Interest income	NR No. 3		1.40

General Journal

Feb. 26   Sales Returns and Allowances 150.00
         Accounts Receivable – Ferris and Ferris 150.00
         To record return of merchandise bought 2/12.

Apr. 6   Notes Receivable (No. 3) 280.00
         Accounts Receivable – Gerrah Bros. 280.00
         To record receipt of 30-day, 6% note on account balance.

Apr. 8   Sales Returns and Allowances 47.40
         Accounts Receivable – Ingalls, Inc. 47.40
         Allowance granted for damage to goods shipped 2/21.

d) Loss percentages expected; based on past experience.

<table>
<tr><td></td><td>% Loss</td></tr>
</table>

	% Loss
Not due	1
1–30 days past due	10
Over 30 days past due	25

Required:

1. Age the accounts as of May 31 (in 30-day steps).
2. Give adjusting entry as of May 31.

Problem 7–5

The Miller Company (a sole proprietorship) has experienced a cash flow problem largely occasioned by collection problems. As a consequence it has become involved in numerous transactions involving notes receivable. The following note transactions occurred during a three-month period ending June 30:

Apr. 5 Received a $5,000, 90-day, 6% interest-bearing note dated April 5 from E. M. Smith, a customer.

10 Discounted a personal, 90-day interest-bearing note, face $3,000, at the bank at 6%.

21 Received a $4,000, 60-day 5% interest-bearing note dated April 20 from Mike Johnson, a customer.

30 Discounted the Johnson note at the bank at 8%.

May 1 Discounted the Smith note at the bank at 6%.

20 Received a $2,500, 90-day, 6% interest-bearing note dated May 19 from S. O. Brock, a customer.

25 Received from A. R. Allen, a customer, a $2,000, 60-day, 6% note dated May 15, payable to Allen and signed by the Cable Company. Upon endorsement, gave the customer credit for the maturity value of the note less discount at 7%.

31 Received a one-year, noninterest-bearing note, dated May 31 from Don Karnes, a customer, in settlement of a $4,000 account receivable. The implied interest rate was 8%.

June 20 Received a bank notice that the Johnson note was not paid at maturity. The bank charged Miller's account for $2,003 including a protest fee.

25 Received payment from Johnson on his dishonored note, including interest at 6% on the face value of the note from the maturity date.

Required:

1. Give journal entries for the above transactions.
2. Give the adjusting entries required at June 30, end of the fiscal period.

Problem 7–6

F. W. King and Sons secured a loan (promissory note) from the Commercial Finance Company by pledging $100,000 of accounts receivable as security. The loan provisions were as follows:

a) The finance company agreed to advance 80% of the face value of the receivables less an advance commission of 5% of pledged accounts.

b) King and Sons agreed to make collections of the pledged accounts and to make remittances to the finance company each month for the accounts settled so as to maintain a 20% margin (i.e., 20% of the uncollected accounts) with that company. Interest of one half of 1% per month on the unsettled accounts at the end of the month would also be paid the finance company.

The following is a summary of the transactions affecting the pledged accounts:

	First Month	Second Month	Third Month
Cash collected	$26,000	$42,000	$10,800
Sales discounts allowed	480	60	–
Notes taken on account	–	–	1,200

King and Sons rendered a report and made payment of all amounts due the finance company at the end of each month.

Required:

Prepare all entries on the books of King and Sons to record the transactions related to the financing transactions and the related receivables.

Problem 7–7

The Doe Company finances some of its current operations by assigning accounts receivable to a finance company. On July 1, 19A, it assigned, under guarantee, accounts amounting to $40,000, the finance company advancing to them 80% of the accounts assigned (20% of the total to be withheld until the finance company has made full recovery), less a commission charge of one half of 1% the total accounts assigned.

On July 31, the Doe Company received a statement that the finance company had collected $21,000 of these accounts, and had made an additional charge of one half of 1% of the total accounts outstanding as of July 31 – this charge to be deducted at the time of the first remittance due Doe Company from the finance company. On August 31, the Doe Company received a second statement from the finance company, together with a check for the amount due. The statement indicated that the finance company had collected an additional $16,000 and had made a further charge of one half of 1% of the balance outstanding as of August 31.

Required (on books of Doe Company):

1. Give the entry to record the assignment of the accounts on a notification basis (July 1). *Hint:* Set up an account entitled "Equity in Accounts Assigned."

2. Give entry to record the data from the first report from the finance company (July 31).

3. Reconstruct the report submitted by the finance company on August 31; show details to explain cash remitted and the uncollected accounts still held by the finance company.

4. Give the entry to record the data in the report of August 31.

5. Explain how the items should be reported on the financial statements of Doe Company at July 31 and August 31.

(AICPA adapted)

Problem 7-8

An agreement dated January 2, 19A, between Down Sales Company and May Factors concerning sale of Down trade receivables to May included the following provisions:

a) The agreement applied only to receivables created after January 15, 19A, and to specific invoices on which May gives prior credit approval.

b) A 20% holdback applied to the face of each invoice net of discount and commission.

c) A commission of 1¼% applied to the net amount of each invoice after deducting any sales returns.

d) Interest shall be computed at 6% per annum on amounts drawn by Down before the average due date. Withdrawals on and after the average due date are interest free.

e) Sales returns and allowances up to 25% of the invoice total shall not affect commissions once computed.

f) Discounts shall not affect commissions regardless of whether taken or not.

On February 3, 19A, Down first availed itself of the factoring arrangement by selling the following receivables to May:

Invoice Date	Customer	Invoice Amount
1/27	A. B. Beene & Co.	$ 1,100
1/28	John Shelton	3,220
1/31	Penn-Collins, Inc.	830
2/1	Walton Da Vega Co.	3,750
2/3	Meyers and Barr	460
2/3	John Shelton	1,040
		$10,400

All credit terms are 1/10, n/30. On February 8 Down drew $6,000 from May. On February 10 Meyers and Barr returned goods for credit, $100.

Required:

1. Give entry on February 3 to record on Down's books the six invoices, amounting to $10,400, factored.

2. Give entry to record the cash draw on February 8.

3. Give entry to record the returned goods on February 10.

4. Compute the average due date assuming the "date of face value" is the last day on which the customer may take advantage of the cash discount plus 10 days for "processing paper work, etc., as specified in the contract."

5. Give entry for final settlement with the factor including withdrawal of all cash available under the factoring. Settlement was on February 20 and all invoices were paid within the discount period.

Problem 7-9

From the following postclosing trial balance, prepared by the Alexander Company from its records at September 30, 1971, and the supplementary information outlined below, prepare a columnar work sheet, setting forth the necessary adjustments and corrections to the accounts.

Accounts	Debit	Credit
Accounts payable and other current liabilities....................		$ 1,830,000
Accounts receivable ....$	3,800,000	
Bonds payable – 4% – 1975..		2,000,000
Capital stock...		4,000,000
Cash...	1,983,333	
Deferred income on discounts receivable		375,000
Discounts receivable	3,216,667	
Fixed assets...	4,000,000	
Goodwill...	80,000	
Notes payable...		1,000,000
Accumulated depreciation...		1,000,000
Allowance for doubtful accounts		625,000
Retained earnings:		
Balance – October 1, 1970		1,915,000
Income for the year ended September 30, 1971...............		435,000
Treasury stock	100,000	
	$13,180,000	$13,180,000

It has been determined that the following transactions or circumstances have not been adequately considered by the company in the preparation of the above trial balance:

a) Discounts receivable represent the uncollected balances of a considerable number of notes receivable, acquired on a discount basis, in the aggregate original amount of $3,750,000. The discount rate was 10%, and the deferred income of $375,000 was the full amount of the discount at the dates of acquisition as follows:

Date	(Maturity Value) Aggregate Amount
June 15, 1971..$	2,000,000
July 21, 1971	1,000,000
Sept. 10, 1971	750,000

By their terms, the notes are collectible in equal monthly installments over a period of 15 months. The management is of the opinion that the aggregate discount on the notes acquired should be regarded as earned over the life of the notes and has requested that the "sum of months' digits" method of transferring discount to income be used. It has been agreed that this method is acceptable, but it has been agreed further that no discount will be transferred to income in the month of acquisition.

b) The company executed a lease agreement (for a building it needed) in July 1971, for a five-year period beginning September 1, 1971, which stipulated an annual rental of $10,000. Under the provisions of the lease, the annual rental is due on the first day of each lease year, but no rent had been paid or accrued at September 30, 1971.

c) A 2% dividend was declared on September 30, 1971, to stockholders of record on October 15, 1971. The dividend is payable on November 1, 1971.

d) Under a contract with an advertising agency, payments of $110,000 were made during the year in connection with a direct mail campaign. The payments represented a deposit ($25,000) and services and expenses through August 31 ($85,000). In addition, a bill for services and expenses for the month of September has been received in the amount of $60,000. All payments have been charged to expense; no accruals have been reflected in the records.

e) Cash for the payment of the semiannual bond interest, due October 15, 1971, was deposited in advance with the trustee in September. The transfer of cash was treated as a charge against income.

(AICPA adapted)

| chapter 8 | Inventories — General Problems |

Introduction

The basic purpose in accounting for inventories is the proper determination of net income through the matching of appropriate inventory cost against revenue; a secondary purpose is to provide an inventory valuation for the balance sheet. Inventories present problems of considerable magnitude for both the accountant and management. Both must seriously consider such inventory problems as valuation, control, safeguarding, and cost allocation. All of these problems are especially critical in view of the materiality of inventories in the typical firm and the fact that inventories directly affect both the income statement and the balance sheet. These factors have caused the accounting profession to give particular attention to the problems related to inventories. This and the two following chapters present the principal problems and accounting procedures relating to inventories of all types.

The Nature of Inventories

As an accounting category, *inventories* is an asset represented by goods owned by the firm at a particular point in time and held for the purpose of future sale or for utilization in the manufacture of goods for sale. No other asset includes so great a variety of properties under a single heading, for practically all kinds of tangible goods and properties are found in the inventories of one business or another. The

300

machinery and equipment are fixed assets of the business using them, but constituted at one time a part of the inventory of the manufacturer of such equipment. Even a building until finished and turned over to a buyer is an inventory item, a "contract in process," among the assets of the builder.

In many firms inventories represent a significant portion of current assets or even total assets. Inventories generally represent a very active asset in that there is constant usage and replacement. Although many inventory items are of small size they frequently have considerable value; therefore, the problem of safeguarding ranks next to that for cash. The advisability of adequate stocking of items for sale, coupled with the risk of loss and cost of overstocking, creates critical management planning and control problems. Failure to control inventories adequately and to account for inventory quantities and costs might well lead to business failure.

At date of acquisition inventory items are recorded at cost in harmony with the cost principle; subsequently when sold or utilized the cost is matched with revenue in accordance with the matching principle. Inventory items remaining on hand at the end of an accounting period are valued on the basis of the cost principle except when their "value" has been eroded through damage, obsolescence, erosion of replacement cost, and similar factors, in which case they are "valued" in accordance with the concept of conservatism (for example, by the lower of cost or market procedure). The discussions to follow in this and the next two chapters consider special inventory problems and procedures within the context to these broad theoretical requirements.

Classification of Inventories

Inventories commonly are classified as follows:

1. Merchandise inventory — the goods on hand purchased by a trading concern for resale. The physical form of the goods is not altered prior to resale.
2. Manufacturing inventory — the combined inventories of a manufacturing concern consisting of:
   a) Raw materials inventory — the tangible goods purchased or obtained from natural sources and on hand principally for direct use in the manufacture of goods for resale. Parts or subassemblies manufactured prior to use are sometimes classified as raw materials; however, a preferable treatment would report them as *parts inventory*.
   b) Goods in process inventory — the goods partly processed and requiring further processing before sale. Goods (work) in process inventory normally is valued at the sum of *direct ma-*

terial, direct labor, and *allocated manufacturing overhead* costs incurred to date of the inventory.

  c) Finished goods inventory—the manufactured articles completed and being held for sale. Finished goods inventory normally is valued at the sum of *direct material, direct labor,* and *allocated manufacturing overhead* costs related to their manufacture.

  d) Manufacturing supplies inventory—the items on hand such as lube oils for the machinery, cleaning materials, and supply items which comprise an insignificant part of the finished product as, for example, the thread and glue used in binding this book.

3. Miscellaneous inventories such as office supplies, janitorial supplies, and shipping supplies. Inventories of this type normally are used in the near future and usually are charged to selling and general expense; consequently, these asset values are generally reported as prepaid expenses.

The Dual Phase of the Inventory Problem

The basic cause of many inventory problems faced by the accountant is the fact that goods sold during a fiscal period seldom correspond exactly to those produced or bought during that period. Consequently, the typical situation is one where physical inventory is being increased or decreased. This increase or decrease in physical inventory necessitates a corresponding *allocation* of the cost of goods *available* for sale or use between (*a*) those goods that were sold or used and (*b*) those that were not sold or used. This situation creates two distinct problems in inventory determination, viz:

1. Determination of the *physical goods* (items and quantities) to be included in inventory.
2. Determination of the *accounting values* to be assigned to the physical goods included in inventory.

Goods (Items) to Be Included in Inventory

In determining physical goods to be included in inventory, accountants apply the general rule that all goods should be included to which the concern has *legal title* at inventory date irrespective of location. Accordingly, the seller should include in his inventory goods under contract for sale but not yet segregated and applied to the contract. Further, mere segregation does not create a "passage of title"; the terms of the contract itself must be determining. Since at the close of an accounting period, a business may (*a*) hold goods which it does not own or (*b*) own goods which it does not hold, care must be exercised in determination of the goods properly includable in inventory.

Goods purchased though not received should be included in the inventory of the purchaser provided title to such goods has passed. Application of the "passage of title" rule requires the following: if the goods are shipped f.o.b. *destination*, title does not pass until the purchaser receives the goods from the common carrier; if the goods are shipped f.o.b. *shipping point*, title passes when the seller delivers them to the common carrier.

All goods owned by the concern, regardless of location, should be included in the inventory. Goods *out* on consignment, those held by agents, and those located at branches should be included in inventory. On the other hand, goods *held* (but owned by someone else) for sale on commission or consignment and those received from vendors but rejected and awaiting return for credit should be excluded from the inventory.

In determining goods to be admitted to inventory, in cases where there is some question as to whether title has passed, the accountant must exercise judgment in the light of the particular situation. Obviously the legal position should be followed; however, the accountant will face many situations where a strict legal determination is impractical. In such cases the intent of the sales agreement, policies of the parties involved, industry practices, and other available evidences of intent must be considered.

Determination of Physical Quantities in Inventory

The physical quantities in inventory may be determined by means of (a) a *periodic (physical) inventory* or (b) a *perpetual inventory*. When a periodic or physical inventory system is used, an actual count of the goods on hand is taken at the end of each period for which financial statements are to be prepared. The goods are counted, weighed, or otherwise measured, then *unit prices* are applied to items in order to derive the inventory valuation. When a periodic inventory system is used, end-of-the-period entries are required for (a) adjusting or closing the beginning inventory and (b) recording the ending inventory. On the income statement the cost of goods sold becomes a *residual* amount (determined by subtraction) when a periodic inventory system is used.

When a *perpetual* or continuous inventory system is used, detailed subsidiary records are maintained for each item of inventory. The Inventory Control account is maintained on a current basis; consequently, the detailed inventory records for each different item will provide for recording (a) receipts, (b) issues, and (c) balances on hand, usually in both quantities and dollar amounts. Thus, the physical amount and valuation of goods on hand at any time are readily available from the accounting records; consequently, a physical inventory count is unnecessary except to check on the accuracy of the inventory records from time to time. Such checks (physical counts) are usually made at least annually or on a continuous rotation basis when large inventories are involved. When a discrepancy is found, the perpetual inventory records must be adjusted to the physical count. In such cases the Inventory account is debited or credited as necessary for correction and an inventory adjustment account such as "Inventory Overages or Shortages" is used for the contra amount. The Inventory Adjustment account is closed to the Income Summary account at the end of the period.

A perpetual inventory system is particularly useful (*a*) in the control and safeguarding of inventory and (*b*) when monthly statements are prepared. A perpetual inventory is generally considered to be one of the essential characteristics of a good cost accounting system.

A typical subsidiary record for Raw Material X (perpetual inventory record) is shown in Illustration 8–1. Data indicated by the inventory record for Raw Material X are as follows:

a) Beginning inventory......................1,000 units @ $.40......................$400
b) January 10 purchase (entry):
    Raw Material..200
    Cash...   200
c) January 18 issue (entry):
    Material in Process (manufacturing)..............................240
    Raw Material..   240
d) Ending inventory.......................... 900 units @ $.40......................$360
e) Raw material on order: 700 units of Raw Material X.

Effect of Incorrect Inventory

Failure to include or exclude physical units correctly for inventory purposes will result in errors in the financial statements. The following errors are not uncommon:[1]

Inclusion of items that should not be admitted to final inventory:

1. *Incorrect inclusion of items in inventory, and the purchase incorrectly recorded.* These two errors result in an overstatement of inventory, purchases, and accounts payable. In this case net income will be correctly stated, since the errors in inventory and purchases will offset; however, the assets and liabilities on the balance sheet each will be overstated by the same amount.
2. *Incorrect inclusion of items in inventory, but purchase not recorded.* This error results in an overstatement of the final inventory, hence both net income and assets are overstated by the same amounts.

Exclusion of items that should be admitted to final inventory:

3. *Incorrect exclusion of items from inventory, but the purchase correctly recorded.* This error results in an understatement of the

---

[1] Some of the effects of these errors will differ depending on the inventory flow method used, that is, Fifo, Lifo, etc.

Illustration 8–1
Perpetual Inventory Record

SUBSIDIARY LEDGER

PERPETUAL INVENTORY RECORD

Article _Raw Material X_

Location _L-15_

Unit _lbs._

Bin No. _32_

Maximum _1,600_

Minimum _800_

Verification Dates

Date	Ordered		Received or Completed					Issued or Sold				Balance on Hand		
	Order No.	Units	Order No.	Ref.	Units	Unit Cost	Total Cost	Ref.	Units	Unit Cost	Total Cost	Units	Unit Cost	Total Cost
Jan. 1												1,000	$.40	$400
10			17		500	$.40	$200					1,500	.40	600
18									600	$.40	$240	900	.40	360
19	18	700												

final inventory, hence an understatement of both net income and assets by the same amounts.

4. *Incorrect exclusion of items from inventory, and the purchase not recorded.* These two errors result in an understatement of inventory, purchases, and accounts payable. In this case net income will be correctly stated, since the errors in inventory and purchases will offset; however, the assets and liabilities on the balance sheet each will be understated by the same amount.

The effects of each situation are demonstrated in Illustration 8–2.

Errors similar to those discussed above, which related to purchases, may also arise in connection with goods when sold.

Determination of the Accounting Value of Inventory

The *accounting value* of inventories represents an *acceptable* allocation of the total cost of goods or materials *available* between that portion used or sold (cost of goods sold) and that portion held as an asset for subsequent use or sale (inventory). There are a number of procedures for determining the accounting value of inventories that satisfy the theoretical requirements. The acceptability of a number of procedures, as opposed to a single one, suggests the wide variation in inventory characteristics and conditions as related to particular situations and purposes. Basically the accounting values for inventories serve two somewhat opposing purposes. The accomplishment of one purpose implies procedures that may not appear to be entirely appropriate for the accomplishment of the other purpose. One of these purposes is to develop a monetary value for the inventory listed on the *balance sheet.* There it is desirable to show this resource at cost or at its future utility to the business, whichever is lower. The other purpose, directed toward the *income statement,* is to measure the inventory value so that a proper determination of income as between accounting periods results. Conservatism with respect to inventory values in terms of one objective may not be conservative in terms of the other objective. In recent years the income measurement objective has predominated as indicated by the following quotation from *Accounting Research Bulletin No. 43:*

In accounting for the goods in the inventory at any point of time, the major objective is the matching of appropriate costs against revenues in order that there may be a proper determination of the realized income. Thus, the inventory at any given date is the balance of costs applicable to goods on hand remaining after the matching of absorbed costs with concurrent revenues. This balance is appropriately carried to future periods provided it does not exceed an amount properly chargeable against the revenues expected to be obtained from ultimate disposition of the goods carried forward. In practice,

Illustration 8–2
Effects of Inventory Errors

	Correct Amounts	(1) Inventory Error Incorrectly Included $1,000 in Final Inventory Purchases in Error (Was Recorded)	(2) Inventory Error Incorrectly Included $1,000 in Final Inventory Purchases Are Correct (Was Not Recorded)	(3) Inventory Error Incorrectly Excluded $1,000 from Final Inventory Purchases Are Correct (Was Recorded)	(4) Inventory Error Incorrectly Excluded $1,000 from Final Inventory Purchases in Error (Was Not Recorded)
Income Statement:					
Sales	$10,000	$10,000	$10,000	$10,000	$10,000
Initial inventory	$ 3,000	$ 3,000	$ 3,000	$ 3,000	$ 3,000
Purchases	12,000	13,000†	12,000	12,000	11,000°
Total	$15,000	$16,000	$15,000	$15,000	$14,000
Final inventory	8,000	9,000†	9,000†	7,000°	7,000°
Cost of goods sold	$ 7,000	$ 7,000	$ 6,000	$ 8,000	$ 7,000
Gross margin	$ 3,000	$ 3,000	$ 4,000	$ 2,000	$ 3,000
Expenses	1,000	1,000	1,000	1,000	1,000
Net Profit	$ 2,000	$ 2,000	$ 3,000†	$ 1,000°	$ 2,000
Balance Sheet:					
Assets (inventory)	$ 8,000	$ 9,000†	$ 9,000†	$ 7,000°	$ 7,000°
Liabilities (payables)	12,000	13,000†	12,000	12,000	11,000°
Retained earnings	20,000	20,000	21,000†	19,000°	20,000

°Under
†Over.

this balance is determined by the process of pricing the articles comprised in the inventory.[2]

Determination of an acceptable accounting value for inventory involves two distinct problems, viz:

1. Inventory Valuation—selection of an appropriate *unit price* for valuation of the items in inventory. The principal bases or *inventory valuation methods* are:
    a) Cost basis:
       (1) Cost.
    b) Departure from cost basis:
       (2) Lower of cost or market.
       (3) Selling price.
       (4) Cash realizable value.
       (5) Direct cost.
2. Inventory Flow—selection of an appropriate inventory flow method, that is, selection of an appropriate *assumed flow* of inventory costs. The principal *inventory flow methods* (discussed in Chapter 9) are:
    a) Specific cost.
    b) Average cost.
    c) First-in, first-out.
    d) Last-in, first-out.
    e) Base stock.

Cost for Inventory Valuation

The selection of an appropriate inventory *valuation* (unit price) method is determined largely by the condition of the specific items included in the inventory and the trend of cost of the goods involved. The cost-principle provides the theoretical foundation for inventory valuation.

The primary basis of accounting for inventories is cost, which has been defined generally as the price paid or consideration given to acquire an asset. As applied to inventories, cost means in principle the sum of the applicable expenditures and charges directly or indirectly incurred in bringing an article to its existing condition and location.[3]

Thus inventory costs are measured by the total outlay made to acquire the goods in question and get them ready for the market. These costs include not only the purchase price but also those incidental costs such as excise and sales taxes, duties, freight, storage,

---

[2]Committee on Accounting Procedure, AICPA, "Restatement and Revision of Accounting Research Bulletins," *Accounting Research Bulletin No. 43* (New York, 1961), p. 28.

[3]Ibid., p. 28.

insurance on the merchandise while in transit or in storage, and all other costs incurred on the goods up to the time they are ready for use or for sale to the customer. Some incidental costs, such as freight-in, frequently can be identified directly with specific goods, while other incidental costs may require an allocation to specific goods on some reasonable basis. As a practical matter many incidental costs, although theoretically a cost of goods purchased, frequently are not included in inventory valuation but reported as a separate expense; the cost of allocating may not be warranted by the slight increase in accuracy. In such cases consistency in application is particularly important.

Freight-In and Purchase Returns. Freight, drayage, and other incidental costs paid in connection with purchase of materials for use or merchandise for resale are proper additions to the cost of such materials. Where such charges can be identified with specific goods, they should be charged to such goods. However, in many cases such identification is impractical if not impossible. Consequently, it is frequently advisable to record transportation costs in a special account such as Freight-in and to report it as an addition to cost of sales in the case of a trading concern and to cost of materials used in a manufacturing concern. However, in this case failure to add freight costs to the purchase price directly causes cost of goods sold to be overstated and inventory to be understated. Theoretically, freight-in should be apportioned to cost of goods sold and final inventory in proportion to the quantity of goods involved in each. Purchase returns should be deducted from the related purchases.

Treatment of Purchase Discounts. Theoretically, all cash discounts permitted, whether taken or not, upon payment of invoices for materials or goods purchased, should be treated as reductions in the cost of the items to which they relate. Discounts permitted but not taken (lost) theoretically constitute a financing expense. Since cash discounts are reductions in the cost of specific goods, they reduce both cost of purchases and inventory valuation. Practical considerations frequently have resulted in the use of methods that are not strictly sound from a theoretical point of view.

Although numerous treatments have been accorded purchase discounts, three methods are found in general use. In order to explain and illustrate each method assume a purchase of merchandise listed at $1,000, terms, 2/10, n/30, and that three fourths of the goods are paid for within the discount period.

Method 1. Record purchases and accounts payable at gross.

To record the purchase at gross:

```
Purchases...................................................................1,000
    Accounts Payable.........................................................     1,000
```

To record payment of three fourths of the liability within the discount period:

Accounts Payable	750	
Cash		735
Discount on Purchases		15

To record payment for one fourth of the liability after the discount period:

Accounts Payable	250	
Cash		250

Under this method the Discount on Purchases credit balance is variously reported as (a) financial income or (b) a deduction from purchases in the cost of goods sold section of the income statement. Under this method both the inventory and cost of purchases would be valued on a unit cost basis at cost *prior* to deduction of the cash discount. Therefore, when purchase discount is recorded as above and reported as a *financial income*, there is a consequent overstatement of purchases, inventory, and accounts payable. In addition, there is no theoretical justification for reporting a financial income, since an income cannot accrue as a result of merely purchasing and paying for goods whether sold or not. This approach has no justification except that it is "simple." When purchase discount is reported as a deduction from purchases, the result has some theoretical basis. However, there still remains some misstatement of amounts; inventory is overstated and purchases correspondingly understated, since there is no deduction for discount from the cost of goods remaining in inventory. In view of the fact that the misstatement usually is insignificant in amount, this approach has received wide acceptance despite the theoretical objections.

Method 2. Record purchases at net of discount and accounts payable at gross.

To record the purchase:

Purchases (net of discount)	980	
Allowance for Purchase Discounts	20	
Accounts Payable (at gross)		1,000

If financial statements were developed at this point, the physical inventory would be valued on a unit cost basis net of discount (whether taken or not). The $20 debit balance in Allowance for Purchase Discounts would be deducted from accounts payable on the balance sheet.

To record payment of three fourths of the liability within the discount period:

Accounts Payable	750	
Allowance for Purchase Discounts		15
Cash		735

To record payment of one fourth of the liability after the discount period:

```
Accounts Payable ......................................................................250
Purchase Discounts Lost ............................................... 5
     Cash ...........................................................................          250
     Allowance for Purchase Discounts.........................          5
```

Under this method purchases are correctly reported—in the illustration at $980. Theoretically, this is the true cost whether or not the discount is taken since failure to take the discount gives rise to *interest expense*—the seller is temporarily providing funds to finance the purchase. For this reason the Purchase Discounts Lost balance (debit) is reported as a financial expense on the income statement. The Allowance for Purchase Discounts balance (debit) is reported as a deduction from Accounts Payable on the assumption that the discount normally will be taken. If this is not the normal case, Allowance for Purchase Discounts might be reported as a prepaid expense on the basis that when recognized as *lost* it will be reported as an expense. Method 2 is theoretically sound in that purchase discount (whether taken or not) is deducted in part from cost of goods purchased and in part from inventory, and in that purchase discounts *not taken* are recognized as a cost of financing (i.e., an interest cost). Despite its theoretical soundness it is not widely used which is unfortunate.

Method 3. Record both purchases and accounts payable at net. To record the purchase at net:

```
Purchases (net of discount) ........................................................980
     Accounts Payable................................................................          980
```

To record payment of three fourths of the liability within the discount period:

```
Accounts Payable........................................................................735
     Cash................................................................................          735
```

To record payment of one fourth of the liability after the discount period:

```
Accounts Payable........................................................................245
Purchase Discounts Lost................................................. 5
     Cash................................................................................          250
```

Under this method purchases theoretically would be reported correctly at $980. The $5 discounts lost would be shown on the income statement as a financial expense. Since all purchases are recorded at net this method results in the discount being properly deducted in part from cost of goods sold and in part from inventory. It also presumes that the physical inventory will be valued on a unit cost basis net of discount. If the payment after the discount period is anticipated in a later accounting period, correct accounting would require the following *adjusting entry* at the end of the accounting period in which the purchase was made:

Purchase Discounts Lost (estimated)..5
    Estimated Liability for Purchase Discounts Lost.............................   5

The Discounts Lost (estimated) represents an estimate of the discounts that will not be taken on outstanding payables (as of the end of the current period) and would be shown on the current income statement as a financial expense. The Estimated Liability for Purchase Discounts Lost would be shown on the current balance sheet as a current liability (generally as an addition to accounts payable). It would be preferable to reverse the adjusting entry at the beginning of the new accounting period. Although theoretically correct, this method (No. 3) has not been widely used because of the complication introduced by the need for the adjusting and reversing entries. Thus, practical reasons illogically have tended to outweigh theoretical considerations.

Lower of Cost or Market

Under certain circumstances a departure from cost for inventory valuation purposes is acceptable. One circumstance is when the current replacement or reproductive cost of items in inventory is *less* than the original cost of those items. In this situation accountants generally agree that current replacement cost (market) should be used. This position has been accepted by the accounting profession on the basis of (*a*) the matching principle; that is, the utility of the goods on hand is less than original cost, hence there has been a loss which should be recognized for the period in which the decline in utility took place, and revenue should be matched with the replacement cost of goods sold; and (*b*) from the point of view of balance sheet conservatism the asset inventory should be reported at the lower figure. It is particularly important to realize also that there is an implicit assumption in the lower of cost or market rule that selling prices decrease in direct proportion to decreases in replacement cost. The position of the Committee on Accounting Procedure of the AICPA as expressed in *Accounting Research Bulletin No. 43* is as follows:

A departure from the cost basis of pricing the inventory is required when the utility of the goods is no longer as great as its cost. Where there is evidence that the utility of goods, in their disposal in the ordinary course of business, will be less than cost, whether due to physical deterioration, obsolescence, changes in price levels, or other causes, the difference should be recognized as a loss of the current period. This is generally accomplished by stating such goods at a lower level commonly designated as *market*.[4]

---

[4] Ibid., p. 30.

Cost, as used in these discussions, refers to "actual" cost determined through the application of an acceptable inventory flow method such as Fifo, Lifo, or average (see Chapter 9).

Market Defined. The definition of *market* used by accountants generally and by the Treasury Department for income tax purposes is the same, viz: "Under ordinary circumstances 'market' means the current bid price prevailing at the date of the inventory for the particular merchandise in the volume in which usually purchased by the taxpayer." In applying this definition the type of firm and the nature and condition of the items in the inventory must be taken into account as follows:

1. For stock-in-trade, raw materials, and purchased parts use purchase or replacement basis — *market* for the stock-in-trade of a trading concern is the current bid prices from the normal suppliers related to the volume normally purchased, adjusted for regular transportation costs and other necessary expenses to secure the goods from the usual outlets.

2. For goods in process and finished goods use reproduction basis — *market* for the goods in process and finished goods inventories for the manufacturer is based on the cost of manufacturing the items at the prevailing market prices for raw materials, labor, and other factory costs.

3. For damaged and deteriorated items use realization basis — *market* frequently must be interpreted in terms of the *condition* of the items in inventory. Damaged, obsolete, depreciated, used, and otherwise deteriorated items in inventory seldom will have a determinable replacement value in their current condition; therefore, accountants generally agree that such items should be valued for inventory purposes at their *realizable value.* The Committee on Concepts and Standards of the American Accounting Association appeared to take the position that realization basis should be *net realizable value,* that is "the estimated amount of sales proceeds less direct expense of completion and disposal."[5] Some accountants prefer realizable value less an *allowance* for normal profit. For example, the inventory under each of these concepts would be calculated as follows:

Final inventory, 1,000 units at estimated sales price	$1,000
Less: Estimated distribution cost at $.40 per unit	400
Inventory at *net realizable value*	$ 600
Less: Allowance for normal profit (10% on sales)	100
Inventory at *Net Realizable Value* Less Normal Profit	$ 500

[5] Committee on Accounting Concepts and Standards, AAA, "Inventory Pricing and Changes in Price Levels," *Accounting and Reporting Standards for Corporate Financial Statements and Preceding Statements and Supplements* (Columbus, Ohio, 1957), p. 36.

Exceptions to Market. In applying the lower of cost or market procedure, certain *exceptions* were recognized by the Committee on Accounting Procedure of the AICPA. "Judgment must always be exercised and no loss should be recognized unless the evidence indicates clearly that a loss has been sustained. There are, therefore, exceptions to such a standard." These exceptions were then listed as "Statement 6," viz:

As used in the phrase *lower of cost or market* the term *market* means current replacement cost (by purchase or by reproduction, as the case may be) except that:

(1) Market should not exceed the net realizable value (i.e., estimated selling price in the ordinary course of business less reasonably predictable costs of completion and disposal); and

(2) Market should not be less than net realizable value reduced by an allowance for an approximately normal profit margin.[6]

These exceptions in effect establish a "ceiling" and a "floor" for *market* in the comparison with original *cost* in applying the procedure. Illustration 8–3 gives several completely independent situations under which the lower of cost or market rule might be applied. The cost and other values are those of a single unit. Observe in the

Illustration 8–3
Computation of Lower of Cost or Market

	Case I	II	III	IV
a) Cost (per unit)	$1.00	$1.00	$1.00	$.45
b) Current replacement cost (per unit)	.55	.65	.45	.40
c) Ceiling (net realizable value-estimated sales price less predictable cost of completion and disposal)°	.60	.60	.60	.60
d) Floor (net realizable value less a normal profit margin)°	.50	.50	.50	.50
e) Market (selected from b, c, and d values)	.55	.60	.50	.50
f) Inventory valuation under lower of cost or market rule (selected from a and e)	.55	.60	.50	.45

° Additional data to verify ceiling and floor:

	I	II	III	IV
Estimated selling price	$.85	$.90	$.80	$.75
Less: Estimated cost to complete and sell	.25	.30	.20	.15
Net realizable value (ceiling)	$.60	$.60	$.60	$.60
Less: Estimated normal profit	.10	.10	.10	.10
Net realizable value less profit (floor)	$.50	$.50	$.50	$.50

[6]*Accounting Research Bulletin No. 43*, p. 31.

illustration that "market" is the result of a choice among current replacement cost, the ceiling (net realizable value), and the floor (net realizable value less normal profit). The market thus derived is compared with "cost" in order to determine the appropriate inventory valuation.

The limits (ceiling and floor) are considered necessary in order properly to measure the economic utility of the items in inventory. For example, in Case II in Illustration 8–3, current replacement cost is $.65 and the net realizable value (ceiling) is $.60. To carry the $.65 forward in inventory which is more than the net realizable value would result in a charge against future sales greater than the economic utility of the goods, and a charge against current income for an amount less than the anticipated loss; hence the reported profit and inventory value of each period would be incorrect. In Case III (Illustration 8–3), the net realizable value less normal profit (floor) is greater than current replacement cost, hence the floor value ($.50) should be carried forward in inventory. To carry forward a market value of $.45 would result in an understatement of the inventory since at $.50 a normal profit margin will be earned when the item is sold. Therefore, if current replacement cost as the market value ($.45) were carried forward in this case, future profits on the inventory items would be overstated, and current period profits understated.

In applying the exceptions *Bulletin No. 43* states: "Because of the many variations of circumstances encountered in inventory pricing, Statement 6 (see above quotation) is intended as a guide rather than a literal rule. It should be applied realistically in the light of the objectives expressed in this chapter and with due regard to the form, content, and composition of the inventory."

Accounting Problems in Applying Lower of Cost or Market

In applying the lower of cost or market procedure two primary problems of an accounting nature arise, viz:

1. How shall the procedure be applied in determination of the overall inventory valuation?

2. How shall the resulting inventory valuation be recorded in the accounts?

In applying the cost or market procedure in determining the overall inventory valuation, three approaches have been suggested: (1) by comparison of cost and market separately for each item of inventory, (2) by comparison of cost and market separately for each *classification* of inventory, and (3) by comparison of *total* cost with *total* market for the inventory. Illustration 8–4 shows the application of each approach.

The most common practice in the application of the lower of cost or market procedure is by *individual items*. However, under certain

Illustration 8–4
Applying Lower of Cost or Market

| | | | Lower of Cost or Market Applied by — | | |
| | | | Individual | | |
Commodity	Cost	Market	Items	Classification	Total
Classification A:					
Item 1..................$10,000		$ 9,500	$ 9,500		
Item 2.................. 8,000		9,000	8,000		
$18,000		$18,500		$18,000	
Classification B:					
Item 3..................$21,000		$22,000	21,000		
Item 4.................. 32,000		29,000	29,000		
$53,000		$51,000		51,000	
Total..............$71,000		$69,500			$69,500
Inventory Valuation ...			$67,500	$69,000	$69,500

circumstances, application of the procedure to classifications or totals may have the greatest significance for accounting purposes. For example, in applying the procedure to the raw materials inventory of a manufacturer producing only one major product and using several raw materials having common characteristics, the utility of the total stock of raw material may have more significance than the individual market prices of each raw material. Consistency in application is essential.

A particular problem arises when there are several unit costs with respect to a particular commodity to be compared with a single unit *market* price. This situation frequently arises when first-in, first-out (discussed in next chapter) and similar inventory flow procedures are used. In such cases the aggregate cost for the commodity should be compared with the aggregate market (see Illustration 8–5).

With respect to departures from cost in inventory valuation, once an item in inventory has been reduced to a value lower than cost,

Illustration 8–5
Lower of Cost or Market and Fifo

| | | Unit Prices | | | | Inventory Valuation | |
| | Units on | Actual | Current | Aggregate | Aggregate | | |
Commodity	Hand	Cost	Market	Cost	Market	Unit	Total
A	10,000	$4.00⎫	$3.90	$ 78,500	$ 78,000	$3.90	$78,000
	10,000	3.85⎭					
B	10,000	7.70⎫	7.90	157,000	158,000	⎰7.70	77,000
	10,000	8.00⎭				⎱8.00	80,000

subsequent accounting would consider the reduced value as "cost" for that particular item. Items once reduced for inventory valuation purposes should not be subsequently recorded at their original cost.

Recording Lower of Cost or Market in the Accounts. It will be recalled that purchases are initially recorded at cost; therefore, if inventories subsequently are to be recorded at *less than cost* (i.e., market when lower), two distinctly different *items* must be recognized: (*a*) the actual *cost* of goods used or sold and (*b*) the *loss* due to decline in utility of the inventory, that is, the difference between cost and market (frequently referred to as a holding loss). Good accounting would require that these two distinctly different items — cost and loss — be accounted for and reported separately. Three methods of recording the results of the lower of the cost or market rule in the accounts are found in practice:

1. Direct inventory reduction method wherein the actual cost of goods sold or used and the loss in inventory utility are *not* separately accounted for and reported.
2. Direct inventory reduction method wherein the cost and loss are separately accounted for and reported for the *ending inventory only.*
3. Inventory allowance method wherein the cost and loss are separately accounted for and reported for *both* the beginning and ending inventories.

Recording in the accounts is further complicated by the fact that some firms employ a *periodic* or physical inventory system, whereas other firms employ a *perpetual* inventory system.

In order to illustrate and compare the three methods outlined above, assume the following inventories for the years 19A and 19B:

Inventory Date	At Original Cost	At Lower of Cost or Market	Difference (Loss)
January 1, 19A $75,000		$75,000	$ –0–
December 31, 19A........... 80,000		70,000	(10,000)
December 31, 19B........... 60,000		56,000	(4,000)

The three methods are illustrated below for both perpetual and periodic inventory assumptions. The related income statements are shown in Illustration 8–6 on a comparative basis so that the effect of each method on the statement may be compared and evaluated readily.

1. *Direct Inventory Reduction Method — Loss Not Recognized Separately.* Assuming the company utilizes a *periodic* or physical inventory system, the entries relating to inventories for 19A and 19B would be as follows:

For 19A:

a) Income Summary...75,000
      Inventory.. 75,000
    To close beginning inventory.

b) Inventory...70,000
      Income Summary... 70,000
    To record ending inventory at lower of cost or market.

For 19B:

c) Income Summary...70,000
      Inventory.. 70,000
    To close beginning inventory.

d) Inventory...56,000
      Income Summary... 56,000
    To record ending inventory at lower of cost or market.

Assuming the company utilizes a *perpetual* inventory system, the entries would be as shown below and *unit costs* on the subsidiary inventory records would be reduced to a comparable basis:

For 19A:

a) Cost of Goods Sold..10,000
      Inventory.. 10,000
    To reduce the ending inventory from cost basis of $80,000
    to lower of cost or market basis of $70,000.

For 19B:

b) Cost of Goods Sold.. 4,000
      Inventory.. 4,000
    To reduce the ending inventory to lower of cost or market
    ($60,000 − $56,000).

2. *Direct Inventory Reduction—Loss in Ending Inventory Recognized Separately.* Assuming the company utilizes a *periodic* inventory system, the entries would be:

For 19A:

a) Income Summary...75,000
      Inventory.. 75,000
    To close the beginning inventory.

b) Loss on Inventory Reduction to Market..............................10,000
      Inventory.. 10,000
    To record the inventory holding loss.

c) Inventory...80,000
      Income Summary... 80,000
    To record ending inventory.

Entries (*b*) and (*c*) could well be combined.

d) Income Summary...10,000
      Loss on Inventory Reduction to Market...................... 10,000
    To close the holding loss account.

For 19B:

e) Income Summary...70,000
       Inventory...   70,000
       To close the beginning inventory.

f) Loss on Inventory Reduction to Market............................ 4,000
       Inventory...   4,000
       To record the inventory holding loss.

g) Inventory...60,000
       Income Summary..   60,000
       To record ending inventory.

Entries (*f*) and (*g*) could well be combined.

h) Income Summary... 4,000
       Loss on Inventory Reduction to Market......................   4,000
       To close the holding loss account.

Assuming the company utilizes a *perpetual* inventory system, the entries would be as shown below and the subsidiary inventory records would be adjusted to a comparable basis:
    For 19A:

a) Loss on Inventory Reduction to Market............................10,000
       Inventory...   10,000
       To reduce the ending inventory to lower of cost or market
       ($80,00 − $70,000).

For 19B:

b) Loss on Inventory Reduction to Market..............................4,000
       Inventory...   4,000
       To reduce the ending inventory to lower of cost or market
       ($60,000 − $56,000).

The Loss on Inventory Reduction to Market, if small in amount may be closed to cost of sales. On the other hand, "when substantial and unusual losses result from the application of this rule it will frequently be desirable to disclose the amount of the loss in the income statement as a charge separately identified from the consumed inventory costs described as *cost of goods sold.*"[7] There is an inherent inconsistency in this method between the initial and final inventory (see Illustration 8–6).

    3. *Inventory Allowance Method—Loss Recognized Separately for Both Beginning and Ending Inventory.* Assuming the company utilizes a *periodic* inventory system, the entries would be:
    For 19A

a) Income Summary...75,000
       Inventory...   75,000
       To close the beginning inventory.

---

[7] Ibid., p. 33.

b) Inventory..80,000
    Loss on Inventory Reduction to Market............................10,000
        Income Summary...   80,000
        Allowance for Inventory Reduction to Market.............   10,000
      To record ending inventory at cost and to record the loss
      separately. This could be effected in two entries.

For 19B:

c) Income Summary...80,000
    Inventory..   80,000
      To close the beginning inventory.

d) Inventory...60,000
    Allowance for Inventory Reduction to Market................... 6,000
        Income Summary...   60,000
        Gain on Inventory Adjustment to Market.....................   6,000
      To record ending inventory at cost and to record loss (gain)
      separately. This could be effected in two entries.

Assuming the company utilizes a *perpetual* inventory system the entries would be as shown below:

For 19A:

a) Loss on Inventory Reduction to Market............................10,000
      Allowance for Inventory Reduction to Market.............   10,000
      To reduce the ending inventory to lower of cost or market.

For 19B:

b) Allowance for Inventory Reduction to Market.................... 6,000
      Gain on Inventory Adjustment to Market.....................   6,000
      To adjust the allowance account to lower of cost or market.

The credit balance in the Allowance for Inventory Reduction to Market account should be shown on the balance sheet as a deduction from the related inventory, thus stating the inventory at "market." This method of accounting for the lower of cost or market is sometimes referred to as the "reserve" method; the allowance account frequently is inappropriately designated as a "reserve" account.

In evaluating the three methods illustrated to record the results of the lower of cost or market procedure, it may be observed on the income statements (Illustration 8–6) that each produces the same reported net income. On the other hand, there are significant internal differences on the income statements which should be evaluated.

The direct inventory reduction method where the market loss is not recognized separately (No. 1) has the practical advantage of simplicity. The primary disadvantages of this method that have been advanced are: (*a*) there is no distinction on the income statement between actual cost and market (holding) loss with a consequent overstatement of cost of sales and understatement of gross margin based on cost; (*b*) subsidiary perpetual inventory records must be adjusted to the reduced value; and (*c*) there is an implication that the inventory will be reported on the balance sheet as one figure at the reduced value. With respect to balance sheet presentation when lower of cost or market is used, it is desirable that original cost be shown parenthetically or in some similar manner. Because of practical considerations, the parenthetical method is frequently used.

The direct inventory reduction method, where the market loss is recognized separately for the ending inventory (No. 2), is widely used since it also has the practical advantage of simplicity and offers a satisfactory approach since theoretically there is a logical matching of cost and revenue. The primary disadvantages that have been offered are: (*a*) the inventories may be shown at somewhat inconsistent values on the income statement as in this case since the beginning inventory is shown at lower of cost or market and the ending inventory at cost; (*b*) cost of goods sold is not reported at actual cost; and (*c*) subsidiary perpetual inventory records must be adjusted to the reduced value.

The allowance method (No. 3) is theoretically preferable in that there is a complete distinction between actual cost and market loss on the income statement and balance sheet. Provision is made for reporting the inventory on the balance sheet at cost and subtracting therefrom the balance in the Allowance for Inventory Reduction to Market account. It is maintained that the effect of market fluctuations are correctly reported even though there may be a *gain* to be recognized. For example, in Illustration 8–6 the $6,000 *gain* for 19B is comprised of the $10,000 *loss* relating to the beginning inventory (taken up as a loss in the prior period), offset by the $4,000 *loss* relating to the 19B ending inventory. These two amounts offset to a *gain*, since the beginning inventory is *added* as a cost and the ending inventory is *subtracted* as a cost in view of the computation of cost of sales in terms of original cost. In view of the current market value of $4,000 below cost, the position is taken that in terms of original cost and in recognition of the $10,000 loss previously recorded, there is a $6,000 gain that should be recognized in the current period.

The nature of the *gain* that frequently is reported may be seen more clearly by assuming that market is below cost at the end of one period and that there is no ending inventory at the end of the next period. The write-down in the prior period shifts cost (or rather a loss) from one period to the other. For example, assume the ending inventories are: Period 1 – cost, $20,000, and market, $19,000; Period 2 – no ending inventory (see Illustration 8–7).

The $1,000 market loss in Period 1 appears reasonable. The $1,000 market gain in Period 2 is in effect an adjustment of the initial inventory figure to $19,000. On the basis of actual cost the $1,000 must be added as income in the second period, since this same $1,000 was reported as a *loss* in the prior period.

Illustration 8–6
Reporting Inventory Holding Losses
Income Statement for the Year Ended December 31, 19A

	Direct Inventory Reduction Method—Loss Not Recognized Separately	Direct Inventory Reduction Method—Loss in Ending Inventory Recognized Separately	Inventory Allowance Method—Loss Recognized for Both Beginning and Ending Inventory
Sales	$200,000	$200,000	$200,000
Cost of goods sold:			
Beginning inventory	(Cost) $ 75,000	(Cost) $ 75,000	(Cost) $ 75,000
Purchases	115,000	115,000	115,000
Goods available for sale	$190,000	$190,000	$190,000
Less: Ending inventory	(LCM) 70,000 / 120,000	(Cost) 80,000° / 110,000	(Cost) 80,000 / 110,000
Gross margin	$ 80,000	$ 90,000	$ 90,000
Less: Expenses	60,000	60,000	60,000
	$ 20,000	$ 30,000	$ 30,000
Less: Loss on inventory reduction to market		10,000	10,000
Add: Gain on inventory adjustment to market			
Net Income	$ 20,000	$ 20,000	$ 20,000

Income Statement for the Year Ended December 31, 19B

Sales	$220,000	$220,000	$220,000
Cost of goods sold:			
Beginning inventory	(LCM) $ 70,000	(LCM) $ 70,000°	(Cost) $ 80,000
Purchases	118,000	118,000	118,000
Goods available for sale	$188,000	$188,000	$198,000
Less: Ending inventory	(LCM) 56,000 / 132,000	(Cost) 60,000 / 128,000	(Cost) 60,000 / 138,000
Gross margin	$ 88,000	$ 92,000	$ 82,000
Less: Expenses	66,000	66,000	66,000
	$ 22,000	$ 26,000	$ 16,000
Less: Loss on inventory reduction to market		4,000	6,000
Add: Gain on inventory adjustment to market			
Net Income	$ 22,000	$ 22,000	$ 22,000

° Note this inherent inconsistency in this method.

Illustration 8–7
Effect of Inventory Holding Losses on Net Income

	Period 1 — Final Inventory at Market Is $1,000 below Cost		Period 2 — No Final Inventory	
	At Actual Cost	At Lower Cost or Market (Allowance Method)	At Actual Cost	At Lower Cost or Market (Allowance Method)
Sales	$100,000	$100,000	$200,000	$200,000
Beginning inventory	$ 10,000	$ 10,000	$ 20,000	$ 20,000
Purchases	70,000	70,000	100,000	100,000
Total	$ 80,000	$ 80,000	$120,000	$120,000
Ending inventory	20,000	20,000	–	–
Cost of sales..................	$ 60,000	$ 60,000	$120,000	$120,000
Gross margin.................	$ 40,000	$ 40,000	$ 80,000	$ 80,000
Market loss (gain)..........		1,000		(1,000)
Net	$ 40,000	$ 39,000	$ 80,000	$ 81,000

Another advantage frequently cited for the allowance method is that when a company maintains a perpetual inventory system, the subsidiary inventory records need not be adjusted to a reduced value since the inventory control accounts remain at original cost. The position appears sound for a trading concern; however, there is a serious question as to whether it is equally sound for a manufacturing company, since failure to adjust the raw material inventory values to the reduced value might result in questionable costs for goods in process and finished goods inventories when the materials are issued. The primary disadvantages of the allowance method that have been suggested are (a) complexity and (b) reporting a gain such as discussed above is impractical. However, it must be realized that this effect is implicit in the other methods although not explicitly reported.

Inventories Valued above Cost at Selling Price or Realizable Value

Another departure from the cost principle in selecting an accounting value of inventories is acceptable where selling price may be used under highly unusual circumstances as follows:

It is generally recognized that income accrues only at the time of sale, and that gains may not be anticipated by reflecting assets at their current sales prices. For certain articles, however, exceptions are permissible. Inventories of gold and silver, when there is an effective government-controlled market at a fixed monetary value, are ordinarily reflected at selling prices. A similar treatment is not uncommon for inventories representing agricultural, mineral, and other products, units of which are interchangeable and have an immediate marketability at quoted prices and for which appropriate costs may be difficult to obtain. Where such inventories are stated at sales prices, they should of course be reduced by expenditures to be incurred in disposal, and the use of such basis should be fully disclosed in the financial statements.[8]

The preceding quotation states that, in conformance with the revenue principle, income should be recognized only at time of sale. In this connection it may be noted that unrealized profits should not be included in the inventory valuation except as noted in the above quotation. For example, some firms follow the practice of transferring items of inventory from one major subdivision of the company to another subdivision (interdivisional transfers) at a figure above cost. This procedure is used to facilitate management control by placing each subdivision on a separate profit-making basis. Although interdivisional transfers made in this manner may be highly desirable for internal purposes, when the overall financial statements are prepared the interdivisional profits in inventories must be removed, otherwise those items of inventory that have been transferred at a value above cost, and consequently the reported income, will include unrealized profits.

In special circumstances a variation in the use of selling price for inventory valuation is acceptable in some situations where realizable value must be used because actual costs are indeterminate. For example, assume in a meat-packing plant that 1,000 pounds of a certain by-product is on hand. In view of the nature of the processing it is impossible to derive a "cost" for the by-product, yet it has a sales value of $.21 per pound. The inventory value of the by-product may be determined as follows:

Sales value (1.000 × $.21)	$210
Less: Estimated disposal costs (1,000 × $.05)	50
Net realizable value	$160
Less: Normal profit (10%)	21
Net Realizable Value Less Normal Profit	$139

In this situation sales value clearly is unacceptable; therefore, the inventory could be valued at $160 on the theory that no profit is earned on the by-product. Preferably, the inventory may be valued at $139 in anticipation of a normal profit on the by-product at time of sale. Since cost is indeterminable in this situation, the problem is one of cost apportionment on the basis of sales value, since this value provides some indication of utility in the inventory.

---

[8] Ibid., p. 34.

Damaged, Obsolete, and Depreciated Inventory

In the discussion of the lower of cost or market procedure (page 313), it was stated that deteriorated and damaged items in inventory should be valued on a net realization basis. Goods on hand that have deteriorated in value due to obsolescence, use, casualty damage, and technological changes, as well as repossessed merchandise, frequently should be accorded special treatment in the accounts consistent with the net realization basis valuation. The loss in value due to the more or less normal consequences of business such as style changes, shop wear, change in local demand, and similar operational conditions should be accounted for in the manner described previously for the lower of cost or market rule. Losses resulting from storm, fire, flood, and other extraordinary events should be set out separately as extraneous losses. Damaged, obsolete, and depreciated items on hand should be carried in a special inventory account.

Inventories Valued at Direct Cost

Within recent years a "system" of cost accounting, commonly referred to as *variable* or *direct costing*, has been utilized by a growing number of companies. In comparison with traditional "full-cost" procedures, the essential features of the direct costing are: (*a*) fixed and variable costs are separately recorded in the accounts; (*b*) inventories are valued at the sum of the variable manufacturing costs — direct material, direct labor, and variable factory overhead; (*c*) fixed factory overhead is treated as a *period* cost as opposed to a product cost; and (*d*) the financial statements clearly present the distinctions indicated in (*a*), (*b*), and (*c*). Illustration 8–8 shows the basic distinction between full or absorption costing and direct costing.

Illustration 8–8
Full Costing and Direct Costing Compared

	Full or Absorption Costing	*Direct Costing*
100 units manufactured:		
Direct material — variable	$1,500	$1,500
Direct labor — variable	500	500
Factory overhead — variable	2,000	2,000
Factory overhead — fixed	1,000	–0–
Cost of manufacturing — Total	$5,000	$4,000
— Per Unit	$50	$40
60 units sold:		
Cost of sales	$3,000	$2,400
40 units in inventory:		
Inventory valuation	2,000	1,600
Period charge on income statement:		
Fixed factory overhead	–0–	1,000

The principal argument for direct costing relates to its particular application to internal management problems such as planning, controlling, differential cost analysis, and alternative choices. The significant aspect is that fixed and variable costs are identified, classified, and reported separately.

The direct costing advocates take the position that the fixed manufacturing costs are "costs of getting ready to produce, hence are period costs and not related to production" and the variable manufacturing costs are "activity costs, hence are inventoriable costs."[9] Under direct costing, gross margin and net income fluctuate with changes in sales since variable costs on a *unit cost basis* are constant irrespective of volume changes. Therefore, it is claimed that *only direct costing* provides a theoretically correct inventory valuation.

To date, the direct cost method of inventory valuation has not been accorded general acceptance by the accounting profession nor by the Internal Revenue Service. *Accounting Research Bulletin No. 43* (Chapter 4, Statement 3) expresses a position that is cited as limiting the acceptability of direct costing for external reporting, viz: "As applied to inventories, cost means in principle the sum of the applicable expenditures and charges directly or *indirectly* incurred in bringing an article to its existing condition and location." (Italics supplied.)

Relative Sales Value Method

When two or more items having different characteristics are purchased for a lump price and a separate cost for each item is required for accounting purposes, some method of apportioning the *joint cost* must be used. The apportionment of the lump cost logically should be related to the economic utility of each item and the quantities involved. Since *sales value* of a particular item may be a reasonable indication of its relative utility, apportionment of the joint cost of "basket purchases" is usually made on the basis of the *relative sales value* of the several items or commodities. Also, when joint costs are incurred subsequent to purchase, such costs frequently are allocated on the basis of relative sales value. To illustrate, assume a packing plant purchases 1,000 bushels of orchard-run apples (ungraded) for $1,000, and that after purchase the apples are sorted into three grades at a cost of $35 with the following results: Grade A, 200 bushels; Grade B, 300 bushels; and Grade C, 500 bushels. Assume further that sorted apples are selling at the following prices: Grade A, $2; Grade B, $1.50; and Grade C, $.60. The cost apportionment may be made as shown in Illustration 8–9.

Assuming a perpetual inventory system, the purchase would be recorded as follows:

---

[9] Period costs are charged to the period in which the costs are incurred, whereas inventoriable costs are charged to the period in which the goods are sold.

Raw material — Apples Grade A (200 @ $1.80) 360
Raw material — Apples Grade B (300 @ $1.35) 405
Raw material — Apples Grade C (500 @ $.54)...............................270
   Cash   1,035

Illustration 8–9
Relative Sales Value Method

Grade	Quantity (Bushels)	Unit Sales Price	Total Sales Value	Multi-plier°	Apportioned Cost Total†	Per Bushel‡
A.......................	200	$2.00	$ 400	.90	$ 360	$1.80
B.......................	300	1.50	450	.90	405	1.35
C.......................	500	.60	300	.90	270	.54
	1,000		$1,150		$1,035	

°Total cost divided by total sales value, i.e., $1,035 ÷ $1,150 = .90.
†Total sales value times multiplier.
‡Unit sales price times multiplier.

In cost allocations such as illustrated above, quantities lost due to shrinkage or spoilage should be ignored thereby resulting in a greater unit cost for the remaining units. In the case of real estate developments, improvements such as streets and parks may be allocated in this manner to the cost of the salable areas. While the relative sales value method is frequently used, other bases such as Btu's in petroleum products are sometimes used.

In summary, the accounting for inventories rests upon the theoretical foundation of the cost and matching principles. In application certain exceptions have been accorded limited acceptability in recognition of special circumstances; the exceptions discussed in this chapter were: (a) lower of cost or market; (b) selling price; (c) cash realizable value; and (d) direct costing.

QUESTIONS FOR CLASS DISCUSSION

1. In general why should (a) accountants and (b) management be concerned with inventories?

2. What broad theoretical requirements underlie accounting for inventories?

3. List and briefly explain the usual classifications of inventories.

4. Distinguish between raw materials inventory and factory supplies inventory.

5. Why are inventories such as office supplies, janitorial supplies, and shipping supplies frequently shown as prepaid expenses rather than as inventory?

6. What general rule is applied by accountants in determining what goods should be admitted to inventory?

7. Assume you are in the process of adjusting and closing the books at the end of the fiscal year, what treatment for inventory purposes would you

accord the following goods in transit? (*a*) invoice received for $5,000, shipped f.o.b. shipping point; (*b*) invoice received for $10,000, shipped f.o.b. destination; and (*c*) invoice received for $1,000, shipped f.o.b. shipping point and delivery refused on the last day of the period due to damaged condition.

8. Complete the following:

	Include in Inventory		Valuation
	Yes	*No*	
a) Goods out on consignment.	___	___	___
b) Goods held on consignment.	___	___	___
c) Merchandise at branch for sale.	___	___	___
d) Merchandise at conventions for display purposes.	___	___	___
e) Goods held by our agents.	___	___	___
f) Goods held for sale on commission.	___	___	___
g) Goods held but awaiting return to vendor due to damaged condition.	___	___	___
h) Goods returned to us from buyer, reason unknown to date.	___	___	___

9. Compare a periodic inventory system with a perpetual inventory system. What are the advantages and disadvantages of each?

10. Explain the effect of each of the following errors in the final inventory of a trading concern:
   a) Incorrectly included 100 units of Commodity A, valued at $1 per unit, in the final inventory; the purchase was recorded.
   b) Incorrectly included 200 units of Commodity B, valued at $2 per unit, in the final inventory; the purchase was not recorded.
   c) Incorrectly excluded 300 units of Commodity C, valued at $3 per unit, from the final inventory; the purchase was recorded.
   d) Incorrectly excluded 400 units of Commodity D, valued at $4 per unit, from the final inventory; the purchase was not recorded.

11. What is meant by the "accounting value" of inventories? What objective predominates in determining this value for inventories?

12. Cost is the primary basis for inventory valuation. List the four exceptions to cost discussed in the chapter. What exceptions are "generally acceptable" under specified conditions?

13. In determining *cost* for inventory purposes, how should the following items be treated?
   a) Freight on goods or materials purchased.
   b) Purchase returns.
   c) Purchase discounts.
   d) Storage costs.

14. Do you think purchase discounts should be (*a*) deducted in total in the income statement for the period in which the discounts arose or (*b*) deducted in part in the income statement and in part from inventory on the balance sheet? Explain.

15. Explain why the concept of "lower of cost or market" is applied to inventory valuation.

16. What is meant by "realization basis"?

17. What is the nature and purpose of the Allowance for Inventory Reduction to Market account?

18. In what specific situations may inventories be valued above cost at selling price?

19. How should damaged, obsolete, and depreciated merchandise on hand at the end of the period be valued for inventory purposes?

20. What are the essential features of *direct costing?* Has the inventory valuation implicit in direct costing been accorded general acceptance by the accounting profession?

21. What are the basis assumptions underlying the relative sales value method when used in allocating costs for inventory purposes?

DECISION CASE 8-1

The Ward Manufacturing Company has been in operation since 1952 and has experienced a reasonably satisfactory growth since that time. Mr. Ward, the organizer, was an experienced and skilled machinist having operated a small custom machine shop for years. In 1952, with the financial assistance of a friend, he organized the company to manufacture specially designed trailers for the transportation of horses. Most of the trailers manufactured were designed to haul one horse; consequently, they were built to meet the particular desires of each customer. These trailers varied from a fairly standard type to some super deluxe models in keeping with the "horse-show tradition."

In 1960 the company started making trailers for boats. Two standard models were developed for sale to sporting goods stores, and in addition trailers were made to meet the specifications of individual buyers. The company recently experienced an unexpected demand for boat trailers which was attributed to their quality, competitive price, and design. Mr. Ward is having considerable difficulty keeping up with this demand. He hesitates to add capacity, workers, and materials needed on the basis of expectations rather than on the basis of firm orders. As a consequence the firm has lost some business. Customarily a 50% deposit is required on all custom-made trailers.

Mr. Ward has been particularly interested in the manufacturing side of the business, although the financial and management aspects appear to be a problem. He is not inclined to be the "executive type." As a result of some income tax difficulties Mr. Ward engaged an outside certified public accountant to "set up some records and help with the financial management of the company." One of the employees spends part time on the present record keeping which involves minimum records relative to cash, salaries, receivables, and wages.

The company regularly stocks 23 different items of "raw materials" and numerous small supplies such as bolts, screws, welding materials, and paint. The company loses about two thirds of the available cash discounts on purchases through oversight. Customarily the company pays freight on the purchases. Finished goods "on the lot" generally consist of 8 to 15 horse trailers, 20 to 35 boat trailers, plus small quantities of eight other small items generally manufactured. Frequently, customers leave trailers "on the lot" a week or more before picking them up. Several items of raw materials currently on hand are of such a nature that the replacement cost is less than the original cost. The company has always had difficulty with raw materials and supplies; frequently shortages hold up work on jobs for days. Frequently, substitutions of higher cost materials are necessary due to items being out of stock. The raw materials are stored both outside and inside, and individual workmen select the material as they need it on a help-yourself basis. Mr. Ward feels that the company cannot afford an "inventory clerk." Items are reordered from a notebook kept on Mr. Ward's desk where individual workmen are instructed to "write down any items that are low or out of stock." When raw materials are received they are moved to the storage area and placed "wherever space is available." Space is a problem. No inventory records are maintained. No payments are made for raw materials unless the invoice is signed by the employee that checked in the goods. Theft is no problem for the company.

The certified public accountant has decided to install a job-order cost system so that costs will be accumulated by job for direct material, direct labor, and manufacturing overhead. He recognizes that in view of the smallness of the company, the overall system must be simple and easy to operate.

The accountant is concerned about the raw material and finished goods inventory situations in particular and asks you as one of his staff to make recommendations relative to the inventory problem. He has decided to employ Fifo and lower of cost or market. Specifically, he wants your suggestions for the company relative to (1) determination of quantities in inventory, (2) treatment of freight-in and purchases discount, (3) the accounting treatment of the results of application of the lower of cost or market, and (4) recommendations for better control of inventory. He expects sound reasons for your suggestions.

Narrate your recommendations to the company giving particular attention to the raw materials and finished goods inventories. Give supporting reasons.

EXERCISES

Exercise 8–1

For each of the items listed below for the Slavin Sales Company indicate whether or not they should be included in the regular inventory or excluded from the regular inventory. The company transfers damaged goods to a special inventory. State reasons for your assumptions in each case that might be doubtful. The company policy is "satisfied customers." Also indicate the inventory valuation for each item and in total.

	Cost
a) Items included in warehouse count, specifically segregated for shipment next period per sales contract	300
b) Items in receiving department, returned by customer, no notification received	50
c) Items ordered and in the receiving department, invoice not received	400

d) Invoice received for goods ordered, goods shipped but not received (we pay freight) 500
e) Items shipped today, f.o.b. destination, invoice mailed to customer............ 300
f) Items counted in warehouse 20,000
g) Items currently being used for window displays 900
h) Items on counters for sale... 7,000
i) Items in shipping department, invoice not mailed to customer 150
j) Items in receiving department, refused by us because of damage 100
k) Items shipped today, f.o.b. shipping point, invoice mailed to customer........ 100
l) Items included in warehouse count, damaged, not returnable.................... 60

Exercise 8–2

The public accountant for the Petrie Company found the errors indicated below in the records of the company. Set up a table to reflect the uncorrected balances, changes occasioned by the errors, and the corrected balances for (1) purchases, (2) net income, (3) accounts payable, and (4) inventory. The records (uncorrected) showed the following amounts: (*a*) net purchases, $166,000; (*b*) net income, $14,500; (*c*) accounts payable, $19,500; and (*d*) inventory at the end of the period, $39,000.

a) Incorrect exclusion of an invoice for $1,000 from the inventory count at the end of the period. The goods were in transit (f.o.b. shipping point); the invoice had been received, and the purchase recorded.
b) Inclusion of items on the receiving dock that were being held for return to the vendor because of damage. In counting the goods in the receiving department these items were incorrectly included. With respect to these goods a purchase of $3,000 had been recorded.
c) Incorrect exclusion from the final inventory of items costing $1,000 for which the purchase was not recorded.
d) Inclusion in the final inventory of goods costing $5,000, although the purchase was not recorded. The goods in question were being held on consignment from the Baker Company.

Exercise 8–3

The Larson Company utilizes a perpetual inventory system. The items on hand are inventoried on a rotation basis throughout the year in such manner that all items are checked twice each year. During the month of March the following data relating to goods on hand are available:

	Per Perpetual Inventory		Per Physical Count
Product	Units	Unit Cost	Units
A......................	100	$ 1.20	90
B......................	1,400	2.50	1,410
C......................	2,100	3.44	2,110
D	7,000	.90	7,000
E......................	13,340	2.00	13,310
F......................	532	21.00	530
G	9,427	4.50	9,428
H	11,110	1.70	11,100
I.......................	3,783	20.00	3,773
J.......................	4,576	9.60	4,567

Required:

Determine the amount of the inventory overage or shortage and give the indicated entry. Indicate the final disposition of any discrepancy that is recorded.

Exercise 8-4

The Myron Company purchased 7,000 pounds of Commodity X at $4 per pound. In addition the company paid $230 freight on the purchase. The company also purchased 10,000 pounds of Commodity Y at $3 per pound and 3,000 gallons of Commodity Z at $10 per gallon. In connection with these two purchases, which were delivered simultaneously by the trucking line, a freight charge (not detailed by product) was paid amounting to $400. The company utilizes a perpetual inventory system.

Required:

1. Give combined entry to record the purchases from a theoretical point of view.

2. From a more practical point of view how would you suggest that the purchases be recorded?

3. If you suggested a different entry from the practical point of view, indicate the basis for your suggestion.

Exercise 8-5

The Congress Trading Company purchased merchandise listed at $18,000; terms, 2/15, n/30. Payment of $12,000 of this amount was made during the discount period; the balance was paid after the discount period.

Required:

Give entries to record the purchase and payments of the invoices assuming:

a) Purchases and accounts payable are recorded at gross.
b) Purchases recorded at net and accounts payable recorded at gross.
c) Purchases and accounts payable recorded at net.

Exercise 8-6

The Local Trading Company purchased merchandise listed at $40,000; terms, 2/10, n/30. Payment was made within the discount period. At the end of the fiscal period one fourth of this merchandise was unsold. Determine (1) the cost of sales that would be reported on the income statement and (2) the final inventory valuation as regards this particular lot of merchandise assuming:

a) Purchases and accounts payable are recorded at gross and discounts are shown on the income statement as other income.
b) Purchases and accounts payable are recorded at gross and discounts are deducted in total from purchases on the income statement.
c) Purchases are recorded at net and accounts payable recorded at gross.
d) Purchases and accounts payable both are recorded at net.

Exercise 8-7

The recapitulation of inventory taken on December 31 was as follows for the Roberts Company:

a) Merchandise in the store at 10% above cost.............................$106,800
b) Merchandise out on consignment billed at sales price (including markup, 20% on selling price)... 2,400
c) Goods held on consignment from the Fairfax Electrical Company at sales price (sales commission, 20% of sales price included) 2,000
d) Goods purchased in transit (shipped f.o.b. shipping point; estimated freight, $600), invoice price 4,800
e) Goods out on approval (sales price, $1,500) costing.................... 1,000

    Total Inventory..$117,000

Required:

Compute the correct final inventory.

Exercise 8-8

The HiFi Company, a large dealer in radio and television sets, buys large quantities of a television model which costs $400. The contract reads that if 100 or more are purchased during the year, a bonus or rebate of $15 per set will be made. On December 15, the records showed that 150 sets had been purchased and that 10 remained on hand in inventory. A claim for the rebate was made to the jobber, and a check was received on January 20 after the books were closed.

Required:

1. At what valuation should the inventory be shown on December 31?
2. What entry should be made relative to the rebate on December 31?
3. What entry would be made on January 20?

Exercise 8-9

The Walker Company has 1,000 units of Product A in inventory at the end of the fiscal period. The unit cost was $60; estimated distribution costs are $3 per unit; and the "normal" profit is $4 per unit. Compute the unit valuation of the inventory under each separate case listed below. Apply the lower of cost or market procedure in accordance with the "exceptions" specified by the Committee on Accounting Procedure of the AICPA.

Case	Anticipated Sales Price	Current Replacement Cost	Case	Anticipated Sales Price	Current Replacement Cost
a).........$65		$61	f).........$68		$61
b).......... 70		62	g).......... 50		44
c).......... 60		58	h).......... 59		57
d).......... 58		50	i).......... 61		53
e).......... 66		57	j).......... 73		59

Exercise 8-10

In the process of auditing the records of the K Company, your client takes the position that under the cost or market procedure the two items listed below should be reported in the final inventory at $88,000 (total). Do you agree? If not indicate the correct inventory valuation by item. Show computations.

"Handyman" hedge clippers: 1,000 on hand; cost, $22 each; reproduction cost, $16; estimated sales price, $30; estimated distribution cost, $9 each; and normal profit, 10% on the sales price.

"Handyman" edgers: 2,000 on hand; cost, $40 each; reproduction cost, $36 each; estimated sales price, $90; estimated distribution cost, $28; and normal profit, 20% of sales.

Exercise 8–11

The inventory records of the TW Company showed the following data:

		Unit Basis	
Product	Units	Cost	Market
A.....................300		$1.50	$1.55
B.....................200		1.40	1.30
C.....................500		3.00	3.20
D.....................400		2.00	2.10

Required:

Determine the value of the inventory assuming the lower of cost or market procedure is applied:

a) To individual items.
b) To groups assuming A and B are in one group and C and D are in another group.
c) To totals.

Exercise 8–12

The inventories for the years 19A and 19B are shown below for Diamonds, Incorporated:

Inventory Date	Original Cost	Lower of Cost or Market	Difference
Jan. 1, 19A.....................$10,000		$10,000	$ –0–
Dec. 31, 19A................. 12,000		11,000	1,000
Dec. 31, 19B................. 14,000		12,000	2,000

Required:

Give the journal entries to apply the lower of cost or market procedure to the inventories for 19A and 19B, assuming the company utilizes the direct inventory reduction method where the loss is not separately recognized under (a) periodic inventory procedures and (b) perpetual inventory procedures.

Exercise 8–13

Utilizing the data given in Exercise 8–12, give the journal entries to apply the lower of cost or market procedure to the inventories for 19A and 19B, assuming the company utilizes the direct inventory reduction method where the loss in the ending inventory is recognized separately under (a) periodic inventory procedures and (b) perpetual inventory procedures.

Exercise 8–14

Utilizing the data given in Exercise 8–12, give the journal entries to apply the lower of cost or market procedure to the inventories for 19A and 19B, assuming the company utilizes the inventory allowance method where the losses in the beginning and ending inventories are separately recognized under (a) periodic inventory procedures and (b) perpetual inventory procedures.

Exercise 8–15

The Green Canning Company purchased 1,500 bushels of ungraded peaches at $2.42 per bushel. The peaches were sorted as follows: Grade One, 500 bushels; Grade Two, 300 bushels; Grade Three, 650 bushels. Handling and sorting costs amounted to $205. The current market prices for graded peaches were: Grade One, $4 per bushel; Grade Two, $2 per bushel; and Grade Three, $1 per bushel. The company utilizes a perpetual inventory system. What entry would be made to record the purchase? Show computations of total and unit costs for each grade assuming the relative sales value method of cost allocation is used.

Exercise 8–16

The Ace Development Corporation purchased a tract of land for development purposes. The tract was subdivided as follows: 50 lots to sell at $300 per lot, and 150 lots to sell at $400 per lot. The tract cost $22,500, and an additional $8,250 was spent in general developmental costs. Assuming cost allocation is based on the relative sales value method, give entries for (a) purchase of the tract, (b) payment of the developmental costs, (c) sale of one $300 lot, and (d) sale of one $400 lot.

Exercise 8–17

The Royal Realty Company purchased and subdivided a tract of land at a cost of $385,000. The subdivision was on the following basis:

20% used for streets, alleys, and parks.
30% divided into 300 lots to sell for $800 each.
40% divided into 400 lots to sell for $700 each.
10% divided into 100 lots to sell for $300 each.

Required:

Assuming the relative sales value method is used, compute the valuation of the inventory of lots at the end of the first year assuming 100, $800 lots; 200, $700 lots; and 20, $300 lots are on hand. (Ignore paving costs and other deferrable items.)

Exercise 8–18

The Sweet Candy Company purchased 1,000 bags of orchard-run pecans at a cost of $3,460. In addition the company incurred $50 for transportation and grading. The pecans graded out as follows:

Grade	Quantity	Current Market Price per Bag
A	300	$7.00
B	500	6.00
C	150	5.00
Waste	50	

Required:

Assuming the relative sales value method is used to allocate joint costs, give (a) the entry for purchase assuming a perpetual inventory (show computations) and (b) valuation of final inventory assuming the following quantities are on hand: Grade A, 100 bags; Grade B, 80 bags; and Grade C, 20 bags.

PROBLEMS

Problem 8–1

In an audit for the year ended December 31, 19A, you find the following transactions near the closing date:

a) Merchandise costing $1,822 was received on January 3, 19B, and the related purchase invoice recorded January 5. The invoice showed the shipment was made on December 29, 19A, f.o.b. *destination.*

b) Merchandise costing $625 was received on December 28, 19A, and the invoice was not recorded. You located it in the hands of the purchasing agent; it was marked *on consignment in.*

c) A packing case containing a product costing $816 was standing in the shipping room when the physical inventory was taken. It was not included in the inventory because it was marked *"Hold for shipping instructions."* Your investigation revealed that the customer's order was dated December 18, 19A, but that the case was shipped and the customer billed on January 10, 19B. The product was a stock item of your client.

d) Merchandise received on January 6, 19B, costing $720 was entered in the purchase register on January 7, 19B. The invoice showed shipment was made f.o.b. supplier's warehouse on December 31, 19A. Since it was not on hand at December 31, it was not included in the inventory.

e) A special machine, fabricated to order for a customer, was finished and in the shipping room on December 31, 19A. The customer was billed on that date, and the machine was excluded from inventory, although it was shipped on January 4, 19B.

Assume that each amount is material.

Required:

1. State whether the merchandise should be included in the client's inventory.

2. Give your reason for your decision on each item in (1) above.

(AICPA adapted)

Problem 8–2

Assume you are the independent accountant for the Powell Manufacturing Corporation and that the company is in the process of determining the final inventories for the year ended December 31, 19A. The following matters related to the final inventory have arisen, and the company accountant requests your advice on them. Compute the valuation of the final inventory of raw materials and finished goods indicating specifically what items you would include and exclude. Give assumptions and reasons you would present to the company relative to any doubtful items.

	Material A @$2	Material B @$3
Raw material inventory data on December 31, 19A (in units):		
a) Items counted in bins	10,000	1,600
b) Invoice received, items not received (f.o.b. shipping point)		300
c) Items counted in bins, set aside for shipment next period per contract of sale to subsidiary	300	
d) Items counted in bins that had been issued to factory and returned by them in damaged condition, not returnable to vendor		60
e) Items counted in bins, from a shipment partly damaged, returnable for replacement		40
f) Items on receiving dock, refused because of damage	50	
g) Items on receiving dock, invoice not received	300	400
h) Items counted in bins, to be returned; rejected for incorrect specs	200	
i) Invoice received, items not received (f.o.b. destination)	20	100

	Product X @$10	Product Y @$20
Finished goods inventory data on December 31, 19A (in units):		
j) Items counted in warehouse	9,000	18,000
k) Items shipped on December 31, 19A, invoice mailed (f.o.b. shipping point)	200	600
l) Items completed by factory, counted in the work in process inventory; not transported to warehouse	700	700
m) Items on receiving dock, returned by customer because of damage; notification from customer received		50
n) Items on trucking company dock, invoice mailed to customer, buyer pays freight	500	2,000
o) Items held by wholly owned subsidiary — Cox Corporation	2,000	4,000
p) Items counted in warehouse, damaged condition	40	30
q) Items in shipping department, invoice not mailed to customer	100	300
r) Items shipped yesterday, invoice mailed (f.o.b. destination)	100	
s) Items on consignment to Brady Distributing Company	500	800
t) Items counted in warehouse, specifically segregated and crated for shipment to branch	400	200
u) Items used for display purposes	100	300
v) Items counted in warehouse, specifically segregated and crated for shipment early next period per sales contract	1,000	
w) Items on receiving dock, returned by customer, no notification received (not damaged)	20	

Problem 8–3

The Wells Company fiscal period ends on December 31, 19A. Shortly thereafter an audit for the year was completed by a certified public accountant. During the process of auditing, numerous errors in the records were found. The more significant errors related to determination of the final inventory. The company utilized physical inventory procedures. The certified public accountant was employed after the end of the year and, therefore, could not observe the taking of the physical inventory. As a result a particularly critical examination was made of the inventory records, purchases, and sales. The following data were found in the course of this examination:

a) Merchandise in transit costing $9,000 was excluded from inventory, and the purchase was not recorded. The goods had been shipped by the vendor f.o.b. shipping point.

b) Merchandise costing $6,000 was included in the final inventory. The goods had been rejected because of incorrect specifications and were being held for return to the vendor. The merchandise had been recorded as a purchase.

c) Merchandise costing $20,000 was excluded from the inventory; the sale at $22,000 was recorded. The goods had been segregated in the warehouse for shipment; there was no contract for sale, merely a purchase order from the customer; therefore the auditor assumed no sale at inventory date.

d) Merchandise costing $6,000 was out on consignment to the Campbell Distributing Company and was included in the final inventory. The merchandise had not been recorded as a sale.

e) Merchandise costing $10,000 and sold for $14,000 was included in the final inventory. The sale was recorded, since the goods were in transit; the inventory clerk failed to note that the goods were shipped f.o.b. shipping point.

f) Merchandise costing $5,000 was excluded from the final inventory, and the sale at $6,000 was not recorded. The goods had been specifically segregated, however, according to the terms of the contract of sale title did not pass until actual delivery.

g) Merchandise costing $13,000 was included in the final inventory, and the related purchase was not recorded. The goods had been shipped by the vendor f.o.b. destination, and the invoice, but not the goods, had been received.

h) Merchandise in transit costing $15,000 was excluded from inventory, although the shipment was f.o.b. shipping point. The purchase had been recorded.

The financial statements (uncorrected) showed the following: final inventory, $40,000; accounts receivable, $32,000; accounts payable, $17,000; net sales $320,000; net purchases, $140,000; and net income, $14,000.

Required:

Prepare a schedule with one column for each account (starting with the uncorrected balances) showing the corrections to each balance given above and the correct balances.

Problem 8–4

The Boise Company purchased merchandise during its first year of operations at an invoice price of $475,000 plus $25,000 freight. The freight was paid upon delivery and was identified or allocated to each purchase. At the end of the fiscal year, one fifth of the goods remains on hand. The company was eligible for a 2% discount on the merchandise; however, due to a shortage of cash some discounts have been lost. Cash payments on purchases during the year were $372,700, of which $161,700 was paid on accounts within the discount period. It is estimated that one fifth of the discounts on unpaid accounts payable will be lost.

Required:

Give entries for the purchases and payments during the year and compute the valuation of the inventory and cost of sales under each of the four methods of accounting for purchase discount listed below:

a) Purchases and accounts payable are recorded at gross, and the discounts shown on the income statement as other income.
b) Purchases and accounts payable are recorded at gross, and the discounts are deducted in total from purchases on the income statement.
c) Purchases are recorded at net, and accounts payable at gross.
d) Purchases and accounts payable both are recorded at net.

Problem 8–5

The Phoenix Stores are in the process of determining the final inventory for the fiscal period. The inventory sheets for Department A carried the following data:

Items	Units per Physical Inventory	Unit Cost	Current Replacement Cost
A-1	3,100	$1.00	$1.10
A-2	1,000	.95	.90
A-3	2,500	.60	.60
A-4	1,400 1,200	3.00 3.30	3.10
A-5	2,100 1,800	4.00 5.00	4.60
A-6	3,000 1,000	1.20 1.40	1.20
A-7	4,000 6,000	1.60 1.80	1.70
A-8	2,000 2,300 2,500	3.40 3.00 3.20	3.30
A-9	4,000 4,400 4,000	5.10 5.20 5.40	5.30
A-10	9,000	9.70	9.60

Required:

You are requested to compute the valuation of the final inventory for the department assuming (*a*) cost and (*b*) lower of cost or market, applied item by item.

Problem 8–6

The information shown below relating to the final inventory was taken from the records of the Banner Publishing Company:

		Per Unit	
Inventory Classification	Quantity	Cost	Market
Newsprint:			
Grade A	200	$300	$330
B	60	250	230
C	40	240	240
Special stock (white):			
Stock H	20	70	65
I	10	60	62
J	5	80	80
K	3	120	110
L	4	90	85
M	3	140	150
N	6	60	60
Special stock (colored):			
Stock S	8	75	70
T	4	90	80
U	7	100	110
V	3	70	70
W	5	80	70

Required:

Determine the valuation of the above inventory at lower of cost or market and cost assuming application by (*a*) item by item, (*b*) by classifications, and (*c*) total inventory.

Problem 8–7

The Harris Company records provide the following data relating to inventories for the years 19A and 19B:

Inventory Date	Original Cost	At Lower of Cost or Market
January 1, 19A	$30,000	$30,000
December 31, 19A	40,000	36,000
December 31, 19B	30,000	27,000

Other data available are:

	19A	19B
Sales	$200,000	$230,000
Purchases	125,000	140,000
Administrative and selling expenses	51,000	61,000

The company values inventories on the basis of lower of cost or market.

Required:

1. Give journal entries for 19A and 19B relating to inventories to apply lower of cost or market through the direct inventory reduction method where the inventory holding loss is not reported separately assuming the company utilizes (*a*) periodic inventory procedures and (*b*) perpetual inventory procedures.

2. Give journal entries for 19A and 19B to apply lower of cost or market through the direct inventory reduction method where the inventory holding loss in the ending inventory is reported separately assuming the company utilizes (*a*) periodic inventory procedures and (*b*) perpetual inventory procedures.

3. Give journal entries for 19A and 19B to apply the lower of cost or market rule through the inventory allowance method where inventory holding losses in the beginning and ending inventories are reported separately assuming (*a*) periodic inventory procedures and (*b*) perpetual inventory procedures.

4. Prepare income statements for each year comparing the results of the three procedures. Utilize a six-column form similar to that illustrated in the text.

Problem 8–8

The summarized income statements for the Walton Company are shown below as developed by the company. The inventories are valued at cost.

	19A	19B
Sales	$104,000	$97,000
Cost of sales:		
Beginning inventory	$ 25,000	$20,000
Purchases	75,000	73,000
Total	$100,000	$93,000
Ending inventory	20,000	15,000
Cost of sales	$ 80,000	$78,000
Gross margin	$ 24,000	$19,000
Less: Operating expenses	14,000	12,000
Net Income	$ 10,000	$ 7,000

The inventories valued at lower of cost or market would have been at the beginning of 19A, $25,000; end of 19A, $17,000; and end of 19B, $14,000.

Required:

Restate the 19A and 19B income statements applying the lower of cost or market rule for each of the following procedures (use six-column work sheet similar to that illustrated in the text):

a) Direct inventory reduction method where the inventory holding loss is not reported separately.
b) Direct inventory reduction method where the inventory holding loss in the final inventory is reported separately.
c) Allowance method where the inventory holding losses in both beginning and ending inventories are reported separately.

Problem 8–9

On June 1, Able and Baker invested $20,000 cash each for the purpose of purchasing and subdividing a tract of land for residential building purposes.

On June 1, they purchased 30 acres comprising the subdivision, at $2,000 per acre, paying $10,000 in cash and giving a 6% interest-bearing note (with mortgage) for the balance.

The property was subdivided into 300 lots of equal size, 100 of which were to sell at $800 each and the balance at $600 each. Lots are released from the mortgage by payments on the note of cash equal to 125% of the cost of the lots (computed by the relative sales value method) and the accrued interest on the portion of the note paid.

Costs of subdividing incurred and paid in cash amounted to $12,000.

During June, the following sales were made for one-half cash and the balance on 5% interest-bearing notes.

	Lots
Group A (sold at $600 each)	30
Group B (sold at $800 each)	20

The lots sold were released from the mortgage by payments on the notes as per agreement, payments and releases being made on the last day of each month.

Operating expenses amounted to $8,500 by the end of June.

Required:

1. Journal entries for all of the above transactions.
2. Statement of income for the month of June.
3. Complete final inventory of unsold lots on June 30.

Problem 8–10

The Palace Fruit Company purchased a large quantity of mixed grapefruit for $21,000, which it sorted at a cost of $700 as indicated below. Sales (at the sales prices indicated) and losses (frozen, theft, rotten, etc.) are also listed.

Grade	Baskets Bought	Sales Price per Basket	Baskets Sold	Baskets Lost
A	3,000	$3.00	2,000	50
B	4,000	2.00	3,000	60
C	10,000	1.00	8,000	80
D	6,000	.60	4,000	
Culls	1,000	.40	900	
Loss	55			

Required:

1. Give entry for purchase assuming a perpetual inventory system. Show computations.
2. Give entries to record the sales and cost of goods sold.

3. Give entry relative to the losses assuming the losses are recorded separately from cost of sales.

4. Determine the valuation of the final inventory.

5. Compute the direct contribution for each grade of grapefruit. (Disregard operating, administrative, and selling expenses.)

Chapter **9** | Inventories — Flow
and Matching Procedures

In Chapter 8 we noted that one of the important inventory problems relates to the selection of an appropriate *inventory flow method*, that is, the selection of an appropriate *assumed flow* of inventory *costs* such as Fifo, Lifo, etc. During a period of time such as a month or year, items frequently are manufactured or purchased at different unit costs. Upon issue or sale of the items where more than one unit cost is involved, the accountant is faced with the problem of selecting an appropriate unit cost for accounting purposes. Alternatively, the problem can be viewed as one of costing the units remaining on hand in inventory. Selection of an appropriate unit cost for issues and for inventory purposes on a consistent basis necessitates the establishment of a definite inventory flow policy by the management of the firm. As a matter of actual practice the management usually relies upon the accountant to recommend a policy appropriate for the situation. Acceptance of a specific inventory flow method concurrently determines the costing of issues or sales as the case may be. This chapter considers the theory, procedures, and results of the principal *inventory flow methods*.

When goods are manufactured or purchased there is an inflow of cost; when the goods are issued or sold there is an outflow of cost; the net difference between inflow and outflow of such costs is represented by the costs remaining in inventory. In selecting an inventory flow method a policy is established as to the *assumed flow of costs* that is to be used in costing both inventory and issues or sales. Although some inventory flow methods may be consistent with the *physical flow of goods* in a specific case, inventory flow methods are concerned primarily with the flow of costs rather than with the flow of physical goods. The Accounting Procedure Committee of the AICPA took the position that acceptability of a particular inventory flow method does not rest upon the physical flow of goods but upon its appropriateness in reflecting periodic income. On this point *Bulletin 43* of the AICPA Committee stated: "Cost for inventory purposes may be determined under any one of several assumptions as to the flow of cost factors (such as first-in first-out, average, and last-in first-out); the major objective in selecting a method should be to choose the one which, under the circumstances, most clearly reflects periodic income."[1]

We should specifically observe that application of each of the inventory flow methods conforms with the *cost principle;* they do not involve departures from cost. As a consequence, the selection of an inventory flow method reflects an application of the *matching principle;* the method selected should be the one that best matches cost with revenue (i.e., "most clearly reflects periodic income.") in the particular situation.

The inventory flow methods discussed in this chapter are:

1. Specific cost.
2. Average cost (simple average, weighted average, and moving average).
3. First-in, first-out.
4. Last-in, first-out (priced currently and at end of the period).
5. Base stock.
6. Miscellaneous methods.

For purposes of illustrating the various methods, the simplified data in Table 9–1 are used.

Table 9–1

| | | Received | | | Units on |
	Transactions	Units	Unit Cost	Units Issued	Hand
Jan. 1	Inventory (@ $1).......				200
9	Purchase..................300		$1.10		500
10	Sale..........................			400	100
15	Purchase..................400		1.16		500
18	Sale..........................			300	200
24	Purchase..................100		1.26		300

[1] Committee on Accounting Procedure, AICPA, "Restatement and Revision of Accounting Research Bulletins," *Accounting Research Bulletin No. 43* (New York, 1961), p. 29.

The above data indicate a final inventory of 300 units for January which must be given a value (costed) for accounting purposes. Including the unit cost in the beginning inventory, four different unit costs are involved.

The application of the several inventory flow methods will usually vary somewhat depending on whether *periodic* (physical) inventory procedures or *perpetual* inventory procedures are utilized. The discussions to follow will distinguish between each of these procedures as they affect the application of the inventory flow method. It will be recalled that under periodic (physical) inventory procedures, the ending inventory is determined by a physical unit count; the units are then priced utilizing one of the methods discussed in this chapter. The cost of goods sold (or used) is determined by subtracting the final inventory cost from the *goods available* amount. Under perpetual inventory procedures, all receipts and issues of inventory items are directly recorded so that an up-to-date or running inventory balance is maintained perpetually in the records.

Specific Cost

In case the goods involved are relatively large in size or high in cost and small quantities are handled, it may be feasible to tag or number each item when purchased or manufactured, as the case may be, so that the actual unit cost is indicated on each item. This procedure makes it possible readily to identify the unit *cost* for each issue or sale and also for each item on hand to be included in inventory. The specific cost method identifies the *cost flow* with the specific flow of physical goods and may be applied with either periodic or perpetual inventory procedures. The specific cost method requires careful identification of each item; consequently, it is seldom used because of the practical limitation created by the detailed record keeping involved and because specific items remaining (as opposed to specific items issued) frequently are there more or less by accident. There is also the possibility of profit manipulation by arbitrary selection of items.

Average Costs

The average cost methods of inventory flow are based on some form of average unit cost. A simple average, weighted average, or moving average unit cost may be employed.

Simple Average. A simple or straight average of the individual unit purchase prices (including the initial inventory price) could be used to cost final inventory and issues. The simple average for the illustrative data would be computed as follows:

$$\frac{\$1.00 + \$1.10 + \$1.16 + \$1.26}{4} = \$1.13 \text{ cost per unit}$$

If *periodic* inventory procedures were employed, the 300 units in the ending inventory (obtained by physical count) would be valued at $339 (300 × $1.13). The cost of sales (or issues) then could be determined as follows:

Initial inventory		$ 200
Purchases:		
Jan. 9................300 @ $1.10.................$330		
15................400 @ $1.16................. 464		
24................100 @ $1.26................. 126		920
Total available...................................		$1,120
Less: Final inventory 300 @ $1.13		339
Cost of Goods Sold (issues)°		$ 781

° Note: The issues (700 units) are not priced at $1.13 under this procedure due to the fact that the simple average is not representative of the unit cost when different quantities are involved.

If *perpetual* inventory procedures were employed, the *issues* (sales) and *balances on hand* must be recorded in *units* only throughout the period since the average unit cost cannot be computed until the last purchase for the period is recorded. At the end of the period when the simple average unit cost is computed, the issues and balance on hand could then be expressed in dollars by extending the units times the unit price. This procedure would require an adjustment on the inventory card to bring the sum of the issues and the final inventory into agreement with the total goods available for sale or issue (see note below the preceding illustration). This practical difficulty and the necessity of deferring the pricing of issues to the end of the period generally precludes the use of a simple average when perpetual inventory procedures are employed.

More significantly, the simple average is seldom acceptable since a serious theoretical weakness is involved in that each unit purchase price is given equal weight irrespective of the variation in units from purchase to purchase. For example, in the illustration the $1.26 unit cost is given the same weight as the $1.16 unit cost, although four times as many units were purchased at the latter price. Since it would be theoretically acceptable only when purchased quantities are equal, the only favorable argument is that it is easy to compute. It has been included herein to emphasize its inappropriateness.

Weighted Average. The weighted average is based upon both the unit purchase price and the number of units involved in each purchase; therefore, to compute the weighted average unit cost, the cost of all goods available for sale or issue is divided by the total number of units available for sale or issue. Applied to the illustrative data the weighted average unit cost computation and costing of the inventory and issues would be as shown in Illustration 9–1.

When *periodic* inventory procedures are used, the computation of the weighted average unit cost is based upon data from the beginning

Illustration 9-1

Inventory—Weighted Average Illustrated

	Units	Unit Price	Total Cost
Goods available:			
Jan. 1 Inventory.......................... 200		$1.00	$ 200
9 Purchase.......................... 300		1.10	330
15 Purchase.......................... 400		1.16	464
24 Purchase.......................... 100		1.26	126
Total 1,000		1.12°	$1,120
Issues at weighted average cost:			
Jan. 10 400		1.12	$ 448
18 300		1.12	336
700			$ 784
Final inventory at weighted average cost:			
Jan. 31 300		1.12	$ 336

° Weighted average unit cost ($1,120 ÷ 1,000 = $1.12).

inventory and purchases records. The units in the final inventory, obtained by physical count, are priced at the computed average price as shown above.

Where *perpetual* inventory procedures are used, the pricing of issues must be held up until the end of the period for the obvious reason that the average cost per unit cannot be computed until the last purchase for the period is recorded. Significantly, the weighted average method does not require the troublesome adjustment as does the simple average method—the reason being that a weighted average is a *representative* average. The weighted average method is used frequently, since it is theoretically and mathematically sound and is relatively easy to apply particularly when periodic inventory procedures are employed. Average costs minimize the effect of extreme variations in purchase prices; on a rising market, weighted average cost will be lower than current cost, and on a declining market, it will be higher than current cost.

Moving Average. When perpetual inventory procedures are employed, a moving average rather than the weighted average is generally used in order to facilitate the costing of issues or sales currently rather than at the end of the period. For obvious reasons it is rarely used with periodic inventory procedures. The moving average procedure involves the calculation of a new unit cost after each purchase. The method is shown in Illustration 9-2 and based on the data given in Table 9-1.

Note that the moving average unit cost is computed directly on the inventory card *after each purchase*, thus facilitating the current costing of issues during the period. On January 9 the $1.06 moving average cost was derived by dividing the total cost $530 by the total units 500; on January 15 the $1.14 moving average was derived by dividing

Illustration 9–2
Perpetual Inventory Record
(moving average illustrated)

Date	Received			Issued			Balance		
	Units	Unit Cost	Total Cost	Units	Unit Cost	Total Cost	Units	Unit Cost	Total Cost
Jan. 1							200	$1.00	$200
9	300	$1.10	$330				500	1.06°	530
10				400	$1.06	$424	100	1.06	106
15	400	1.16	464				500	1.14°	570
18				300	1.14	342	200	1.14	228
24	100	1.26	126				300	1.18°	354

° New average computed.

$570 by 500 units; and on January 24, $354 divided by 300 units gave the $1.18 moving average. The moving average does not involve the theoretical weakness noted with respect to the simple average. It is a representative average that is more "current" than the weighted average. In the above example the unit costs are even; obviously, in actual situations this will seldom be the case. Many firms avoid this problem by pricing the first issue after each purchase so that an even unit cost remains in the Balance column. The moving average method is conceptually sound and is especially suitable when computers are used to maintain inventory records.

First-In, First-Out

The first-in, first-out method (*Fifo*) rests upon the flow-of-cost assumption that the cost of goods purchased or manufactured should be transferred out as sales or issues take place in the same order that the costs flowed in (were incurred); as a consequence, issues are costed at the *oldest* unit costs and the remaining inventory is costed at the *most recent* unit costs. Using the illustrative data the *Fifo* method would be applied as follows assuming *physical* inventory procedures:

Beginning inventory (200 units @ $1)...................... $ 200
Add purchases during the period (computed above) ... 920
Goods available $1,120
Inventory Computation
Deduct final inventory (300 units per physical inventory count):
    100 units @ $1.26 (most recent purchase) $126
    200 units @ $1.16 (next most recent purchase) 232
        Total inventory 358
Cost of Goods Sold (or Issues) .... $ 762

The *Fifo* method is adaptable for *perpetual* inventory procedures as shown in Illustration 9–3 utilizing the same data. Note in particular the maintenance of "inventory layers" for each different unit cost in the Balance column.

Illustration 9–3
Perpetual Inventory Record
(Fifo illustrated)

Date	Received			Issued			Balance		
	Units	Unit Cost	Total Cost	Units	Unit Cost	Total Cost	Units	Unit Cost	Total Cost
Jan. 1							200	$1.00	$200
9	300	$1.10	$330				200 300	1.00 1.10	200 330
10				200 200	$1.00 1.10	$200 220	100	1.10	110
15	400	1.16	464				100 400	1.10 1.16	110 464
18				100 200	1.10 1.16	110 232	200	1.16	232
24	100	1.26	126				200 100	1.16 1.26	232⎱ 126⎰ $358

The final inventory of 300 units is valued at $358, the same as derived under the *Fifo* physical inventory procedure. Thus the final inventory derived under perpetual inventory procedures may be quickly verified as follows:

Most recent purchase (Jan. 24).....................................100 @ $1.26 $126
Next most recent purchase (Jan. 15)..............................200 @ 1.16   232
    Total Inventory (Jan. 31)....................................300 $358

For perpetual inventory purposes *Fifo* applied on a *current* basis or on an *end-of-the-period* basis gives the same dollar results for issues and final inventory. That is, the issues may be costed on the inventory card as they occur in time, or at the end of the period with identical resultant values. This is not the case with *Lifo*, as is illustrated in the next section.

Fifo is widely used for inventory costing purposes since (*a*) it is adaptable to either periodic or perpetual inventory procedures, (*b*) it produces an inventory valuation which approximates current replacement cost, and (c) it does not suffer from the theoretical weakness of being a nonrepresentative cost as does the simple average method. It cannot be said that the resulting cost flow is precisely consistent with the physical flow of goods in all or even most situations where it is used.

Last-In, First-Out

The last-in, first-out (*Lifo*) method of inventory flow is based upon the flow of cost assumption that current acquisition costs are largely incurred, if not wholly incurred, for the purpose of meeting current sales or manufacturing requirements; and as a consequence, the latest costs should be charged against current sales or manufacturing costs as the case may be. Under this method the cost of the units remaining in inventory represents the *oldest* costs available; conversely, the issues are costed at the *newest* costs available.

Lifo may be applied under either periodic or perpetual inventory procedures. Using the illustrative data given in Table 9–1, *Lifo* would be applied as follows assuming *periodic* inventory procedures:

	Goods available (per above)	$1,120
	Deduct final inventory (300 units per physical inventory count):	
	200 units @ $1.00 (oldest costs available; from	
Inventory	Jan. 1 inventory) $200	
Computation	100 units @ $1.10 (next oldest costs available;	
	from Jan. 9 purchase) 110	
Goods Sold	Total inventory	310
	Cost of Goods Sold (or Issues)	$ 810

When *Lifo* is applied with *perpetual* inventory procedures, the *issues* may be costed on the inventory card (a) currently throughout the period or (b) at the end of the period. With respect to *Lifo* the timing of the costing of issues becomes important, since costing currently may result in a different inventory valuation (and valuation of issues) than costing at the end of a period on the inventory card. Costing at the end of the period will give the same results as periodic inventory procedures. The applications of *Lifo* under perpetual inventory procedures are shown in Illustrations 9–4 and 9–5. Illustration 9–4 shows the application of *Lifo* when issues are costed currently throughout the period. Illustration 9–5 shows the issues costed at the end of the period. Note the maintenance of "inventory layers" for each different unit cost in the Balance column.

The items shown in *italics* in Illustration 9–5 were entered at the end of the period. Note that Illustration 9–5 (costed at end of period) provides the same inventory valuation ($310) as the periodic inventory computation. On the other hand, Illustration 9–4 (costed currently) provides an inventory valuation of $342. The $32 difference is due to the fact that the issues on January 10 and 18 were out of different "inventory layers" as a result of the difference in the timing in costing issues. The difference between the *cost of issues* on the two records is also $32. From this illustration it is apparent that the *Lifo* inventory valuation costed at the end of the period (but not when costed currently) may be verified readily by pricing the number of units in inventory out of the oldest unit costs. *Lifo* is usually applied on a current basis when perpetual inventory procedures are employed and on an end-of-the-period basis when periodic inventory procedures are employed.

Illustration 9–4
Perpetual Inventory Record
(Lifo illustrated — costed currently)

Date	Received			Issued or Sold			Balance		
	Units	Unit Cost	Total Cost	Units	Unit Cost	Total Cost	Units	Unit Cost	Total Cost
Jan. 1							200	$1.00	$200
9	300	$1.10	$330				200 300	1.00 1.10	200 330
10				300 100	$1.10 1.00	$330 100	100	1.00	100
15	400	1.16	464				100 400	1.00 1.16	100 464
18				300	1.16	348	100 100	1.00 1.16	100 116
24	100	1.26	126				100 100 100	1.00 1.16 1.26	100 ⎫ 116 ⎬ 126 ⎭ $342

Proponents of *Lifo*, relying on the matching principle, maintain that it assigns cost to inventory and to cost of sales (or issues) in the order in which the two cost commitments are conceived to be made in normal merchandising or manufacturing activity. First, a requisite inventory of goods is created or acquired; then as goods are sold or used, sufficient goods must be produced or acquired to meet those requirements. It is the cost of this latter effort which should be matched with the sales revenue or reflected as cost of manufacturing for the period. There is no claim that the flow of costs parallels the

Illustration 9–5
Perpetual Inventory Record
(Lifo illustrated – costed at end of period)

	Received			Issued or Sold			Balance		
Date	Units	Unit Cost	Total Cost	Units	Unit Cost	Total Cost	Units	Unit Cost	Total Cost
Jan. 1							200	$1.00	$200
9	300	$1.10	$330				500		
10				400° Detail: 100 300	$1.26 1.16	$126 348	100		
15	400	1.16	464				500		
18				300 Detail: 100 200	1.16 1.10	116 220	200		
24	100	1.26	126				300 Detail: 200 100	1.00 1.10	200⎫ 110⎭ $310

° Since pricing of issues is delayed until the end of the period, the first issue (400 units) is priced out of the last purchase (100 units at $1.26), and so on.

flow of physical goods. The thing that is important is the association of the cost of effort or purchasing (acquisition, either production or buying) with the revenue occasioning that effort. The argument continues that it is the volume of sales that determines the amount of purchases or effort needed in production, and if economic reasonableness be the test of association, it is reasonable to match the current effort born of current demand against the revenue from that demand.

Special Problems in Applying Last-In, First-Out. The application of *Lifo* frequently presents problems requiring special attention. Five special problems frequently encountered are discussed below.

1. *Variation in Costing Incremental Layers.* When periodic inventory procedures or perpetual inventory procedures (costed at the end of the period) are employed with *Lifo* there is some variation in practice with respect to pricing the new or incremental inventory layers. For example, in Illustration 9–5 the final inventory could be costed either of two ways. The two variant practices observed in handling the incremental layers are illustrated below based on the data in Illustration 9–5:

a) Base inventory layer maintained; incremental inventory layers costed at oldest applicable unit costs (as shown in Illustration 9–5):

Base layer...200 units @ $1.00..............$200
Incremental layer (oldest unit costs).................100 units @ $1.10.............._110
                                                     300

    Inventory valuation..$310

b) Base layer maintained; one incremental layer at average unit cost of purchases:

Base layer...200 @ $1.00......................$200
Incremental layer (average unit cost)...............100 @ $1.15°.................... 115
                                                     300

    Inventory valuation..$315

        ° 300 units @ $1.10 = $330
        400 units @ 1.16 = 464
        100 units @ 1.26 = 126
        800 units @ 1.15 = $920

The first alternative is preferable from the theoretical and accounting viewpoints; however, either alternative is acceptable for federal income tax purposes. Tax regulations further stipulate that *Lifo* can be used for tax purposes only when the method is also employed for financial accounting purposes.

2. *Inventory Liquidation.* A problem not infrequently encountered under *Lifo* procedures relates to the failure of a company to maintain the "normal" inventory position. To illustrate, assume the following:

	Units	Unit Cost	Total Cost
Beginning inventory (assumed to be the "normal" inventory position)......................	10,000	$1.00	$10,000
Purchases...	40,000	1.50	60,000
Total Available for Sale	50,000		$70,000
Sales (44,000 units, issues on Lifo basis)	{ 40,000	1.50	$60,000
	{ 4,000	1.00	4,000
	44,000		$64,000
Final Inventory	6,000	1.00	$ 6,000

In the above example the company failed to maintain the "normal" inventory position by 4,000 units. This failure may have been due to—

a) Voluntary inventory liquidation. Management may have decided to reduce "normal" inventory quantity for some reason such as shortage of liquid funds, anticipation of a decline in prices, or anticipation of an improvement in the product.[2]

---

[2] A major criticism of Lifo is that it lends itself to profit manipulation, e.g., year-end purchasing policy can be used (1) to reduce reported profits by heavy buying, if prices have increased; and (2) to overstate profits by permitting inventories to decline and "old" low prices to be charged to cost of sales.

b) Involuntary inventory liquidation. Uncontrollable causes such as shortages, strikes, delayed delivery dates, or unexpected demands may have forced the inventory reduction.

As a result of the liquidation of a part of the "normal" inventory, cost of sales includes 4,000 units costed at an old cost ($1 per unit) which is matched against current revenue thereby "distorting the reported net income." Assuming the inventory liquidation is temporary, should the 4,000 units be costed out at $1 per unit or at some other cost? The problem is further complicated if the 4,000 units are replaced in the next period, say at $1.60 per unit. Should the restoration of the "normal inventory position" be at $1 per unit or at $1.60 per unit? A common practice when the inventory liquidation is temporary involves charging cost of sales (issues) with the replacement cost, crediting inventory with *Lifo* cost, and crediting the difference to a special account as follows (assuming perpetual inventory procedures):

Cost of Goods Sold (40,000 @ $1.50) + (4,000 @ $1.60) 66,400
    Inventory (per above)... 64,000
    Excess of Replacement Cost of Lifo Inventory Temporarily
        Liquidated (4,000 @ $.60)[3].. 2,400

When the liquidated inventory is replaced (normal position restored) the following entry is made:

Inventory (4,000 @ $1.00)... 4,000
Excess of Replacement Cost of Lifo Inventory Temporarily
    Liquidated (4,000 @ $.60)... 2,400
    Accounts Payable (4,000 @ $1.60) 6,400

In practice, a balance (credit) in the Excess of Replacement Cost of *Lifo* Inventory Temporarily Liquidated is variously reported (*a*) under a special caption between liabilities and owners' equity and (*b*) as a special current liability. The latter treatment is correct because it represents an amount which will have to be spent or incurred as a current liability without a corresponding increase in inventories. There is disagreement in respect to the theoretical correctness of this procedure. Some feel that it is necessary to protect the integrity of the *Lifo* concept. Others feel that, although at one time it was approved for tax purposes, it results in "income manipulation" and is not in accord with sound accounting theory.

3. *Lifo Application in Cost Systems.* The full impact possible from *Lifo* frequently cannot be secured unless the inventory and issues are costed at the end of the complete fiscal period which is usually one year; consequently, a severe limitation is imposed from the point of view of the cost accountant. Cost systems generally are designed so that *issues* are costed out currently, even daily. Although issues are costed currently in the accounts, some firms deem it de-

---

[3] This account sometimes is incorrectly labeled as an "Inventory Reserve."

sirable to cost the inventory at the end of the year for tax and external reporting purposes. To illustrate a probable procedure, assuming the *Lifo* example shown in Illustrations 9–4 and 9–5 relates to a *year* rather than to just January, the following results are indicated:

	Inventory		Issues	
	Units	Amount	Units	Amount
Costed currently (Illustration 9–4) 300		$342	700	$778
Costed end of period (Illustration 9–5)..................300		310	700	810
Difference...		$ 32		$ 32

Assuming the company has costed issues *currently* in the accounts, the following entry may be made to recognize the effect of costing at the end of the period:

```
Cost of Goods Sold° .........................................................................32
    Allowance to Reduce Lifo Priced Currently to Lifo Priced at End of
        Period† ...............................................................................        32
```

° If the inventory were raw materials, instead of finished goods as assumed, the $32 (if material in amount) should be apportioned to work in process inventory, cost of sales, and finished goods inventory in proportion to the relative costs therein.

† This account frequently is incorrectly labeled as an "inventory reserve."

The allowance (credit) would be shown on the balance sheet as a reduction of inventory. In the succeeding periods the allowance would be adjusted to the amount required to account for the difference in results for the period between the two applications. A theoretical complication would arise in the case of falling prices, since the allowance account may show a debit balance (rather than a credit balance) which would require an addition to inventory on the balance sheet.

4. *Adoption of Lifo.* When a company decides to change the method of costing inventory, the full-disclosure principle requires that the change be explained and that the net effect of such change be fully reported in the financial statements for the year in which the change was instituted.[4] In order to compute the net effect of such a change the beginning inventory must be valued in terms of both the old and new method. For example, using the illustrative data given in Table 9–1, assume the company had been employing *Fifo* and has decided to change to *Lifo;* the final inventory for the preceding period would be recomputed as follows since it will be the beginning inventory for the current period:

```
Final inventory—300 units:
  Fifo basis (former basis):
    100 units @ $1.26 .........................................................................$126
    200 units @   1.16 ......................................................................... 232
        Total...................................................................................        $358
```

[4] Such changes require approval of the Internal Revenue Service for tax purposes.

Lifo basis (periodic) (new basis):
200 units @ $1.00 ....$200
100 units @ 1.10 110

    Total... <u>310</u>
Difference—net effect (decrease) on inventory valuation and income
    (before income taxes)... <u>$ 48</u>

The financial statements or accompanying footnotes should indicate that there has been a change from *Fifo* to *Lifo* and that the inventory valuation and net income (before income taxes) each are $48 less as a result of the change. In case the beginning inventory contained several layers, the average unit cost of the beginning inventory would be used in establishing the base *Lifo* layer.

If a significant drop in the price level occurs subsequent to the adoption of *Lifo*, the replacement cost of the items in inventory might be below the cost carried forward in the *Lifo* inventory. In such a case, should the *Lifo* cost be carried forward in the inventory or should the lower of cost or market rule be applied? Strict application of the *Lifo* rule would preclude the use of lower of cost or market. However, it is doubtful whether the accountant should insist on such a strict application of *Lifo* in this situation. In this connection it may be noted that for income tax purposes lower of cost or market cannot be applied when *Lifo* is used.

5. *Dollar-Value Lifo.* In the preceding illustrations relating to *Lifo* the inventory layers were determined by reference to quantities and unit costs of *each item* in an inventory. This procedure imposes a formidable record-keeping task for the firm handling hundreds or thousands of individual items. A procedure has been developed (and accepted for tax purposes), known as *dollar-value Lifo*, to avoid the necessity for extensive clerical detail. Under *dollar-value Lifo*, aggregate dollars, rather than quantities of specific items, are used as the basis for determining *Lifo* inventory layers. Thus, a wholesale grocer carrying a stock of 2,000 items might group the items by broad product categories and apply the dollar-value method, rather than the specific quantities, to determine the *Lifo* layers. The dollar-value *Lifo* application involves numerous complexities; the presentation here is intended only to pose its basic characteristic.[5]

The method involves a comparison of the beginning inventory in dollars of cost (at the beginning-of-the-year prices) with the ending inventory in dollars of cost (at end-of-the-year prices); hence, an adjustment for changes in purchase price is necessary to determine the *Lifo* layers. The method may be applied in several ways; however, one illustration is sufficient to indicate the concept involved.

---

[5] For a more complete treatment see Raymond A. Hoffman, *Lifo: A Review of Its Application in Valuing Inventories* (Chicago: Price Waterhouse and Co., 1953).

Assume the following data are available:

Inventory at end of 19A (*Lifo* basis)....................................$100,000
Inventory at end of 19B (at 19B cost) 121,000
Inventory increase due to both quantity and cost...............$ 21,000

Average increase in cost during 19B (estimated)................. 10%

Problem:

Restate the 19B inventory in terms of *Lifo* layers.

Solution:

19B inventory at 19A cost ($121,000 ÷ 110%) $110,000
   Less: 19A inventory... 100,000   (Due to
19B increment at 19A cost...$ 10,000   quantity change
19B increment at 19B cost ($10,000 × 110%)..............$ 11,000   only)

19B *Lifo* inventory layers:
   19A inventory layer at 19A cost............................. $100,000
   19B increment at 19B cost......................................   11,000
      Total (19B inventory at *Lifo*).......................... $111,000

Evaluation of Last-In, First-Out. The effects of *Lifo* may be emphasized by comparing it with *Fifo*. As long as unit cost prices remain constant, the two methods give the same results; when unit cost prices change materially, the two methods provide significantly different effects on assets (inventories) and net income (costs). In comparing *Lifo* with *Fifo* it is important to note that the comparative effect will depend upon the direction of the change in unit cost prices. With *rising* prices *Fifo* matches the low costs (oldest costs) with the increased sales revenue (inflated dollars) and provides an inventory valuation approximating the higher current replacement cost, whereas *Lifo* matches the high costs (newest costs) with the increased sales revenue and provides an inventory valuation on a low-cost (oldest cost) basis. Conversely, with *declining* prices *Fifo* matches the high costs (oldest costs) with the decreased sales revenue and provides an inventory valuation approximating the lower current replacement cost, whereas *Lifo* matches the low costs (newest costs) with the decreased sales revenue and provides an inventory valuation on a high-cost (oldest cost) basis.

The question is largely one of *periodic* distribution of income and periodic inventory valuations. Over a period of time covering a complete cycle of price changes, the two methods would produce the same overall results. On the other hand, the question is vital from the standpoint of preparing realistic financial statements (and tax returns) on a periodic basis.

The proponents of *Lifo* maintain that a more appropriate *matching* of costs and revenues results than when *Fifo* is employed in that *Lifo* matches current costs with current revenues. On the other hand, the opponents of *Lifo* maintain that for balance sheet purposes *Lifo* provides an unrealistic inventory valuation thereby distorting the current ratio and other amounts related to current assets. They also maintain that *Lifo* does not provide a correct cost in that it does not recognize the actual flow of physical goods that normally occurs.

Lifo has been widely adopted in recent years primarily because of the tax advantage to be gained in a period of rising prices and the apparent conviction by some individuals that the resulting income figures are more realistic and that the income statement should take precedence over the balance sheet. The only sound argument for *Lifo* must be based on the resulting matching of current costs and current revenues. On the other hand, in addition to questioning the costflow assumption and inventory valuation, many accountants feel that profits occasionally are "arbitrarily equalized" or manipulated under *Lifo* through excessive or deficient purchases (when compared with the "normal" inventory position) at the end of the period (see page 354).

The statement of the Accounting Procedures Committee of the AICPA quoted on page 345 appears to indicate acceptance of *Lifo* when the assumption as to the flow of cost factors with regard to the particular situation most clearly reflects periodic income. In determination of the acceptance of a particular method the committee clearly preferred the criteria of income measurement rather than the flow of physical goods and balance sheet considerations.

The Committee on Accounting Concepts and Standards of the American Accounting Association, on the other hand, appeared to take the position that *specific* identification of cost with physical goods is preferable, and where this is impractical, the assumed flow of costs should "reflect the dominant characteristics of the actual flow of goods." When *Lifo* cost flow does not approximate the actual flow of goods, "grave doubts exist as to whether the accuracy of such artificial matching is sufficient to justify the resultant departure from realism." The statement of the American Accounting Association is quoted below in part.

1) Ideally, the measurement of accounting profit involves the matching precisely of the identified costs of specific units of product with the sales revenues derived therefrom.

2) Where conditions are such that precise matching of identified costs with revenues is impracticable, identified cost matching may be simulated by the adoption of an assumed flow of costs.

3) A flow assumption can be *realistic*, in that it reflects the dominant characteristics of the actual flow of goods; thus it may reflect an actual dominance of first-in, first-out (Fifo), average, or last-in, first-out (Lifo) movement. A flow assumption can be *artificial*, on the other hand, in that it premises a flow of costs that is clearly in contrast with actual physical movement.

4) The Lifo flow assumption now has wide usage although in very few, if any, instances of its application can the assumption be justified on the ground that it corresponds even approximately with the actual flow of goods. *Artificial* Lifo has appeal to some during periods of markedly changing price levels as a means of approaching a matching of current costs (dollar costs adjusted to reflect changes in the general purchasing power of the monetary unit) with current revenues; however, grave doubt exists as to whether the accuracy of such artificial matching is sufficient to justify the resultant departure from realism. Present use of the method should be considered a transitory step which may ultimately be supplanted by better methods of accomplishing the intended result.[6]

Base Stock

The base stock (or normal stock) method is based upon the assumption that there is a minimum or base stock of goods that must be kept on hand at all times for continued operations. It is generally viewed as the predecessor of the *Lifo* method. The base stock method assumes that a minimum or base stock represents a more or less permanent commitment of resources as in the case of a fixed asset and as with *Lifo;* current acquirement costs should be matched against the current demands (revenue). Since the base stock is viewed as a long-term business requirement somewhat like fixed assets, it should be valued at a normal or a long-run price and should be maintained at this constant figure. Extra stock (and issues) should be priced on a current *Lifo* basis. At the end of the period the number of units on hand is determined and the base quantity is priced at the base cost. The extra units in inventory should be costed on a *Lifo* basis; however, application of an average or even a *Fifo* basis occasionally is observed notwithstanding the theoretical inconsistency involved. The *Lifo* alternative clearly is more consistent with the base stock concept. For example, if the base stock for a particular concern has been set at 10,000 units at the long-run or normal price of $1 per unit, current issues and the ending inventory should be costed as follows:

Base Stock. Perpetual Inventory. Current issues costed currently on *Lifo* basis:

---

[6]Committee on Accounting Concepts and Standards, AAA, "Inventory Pricing and Changes in the Price Levels," *Accounting and Reporting Standards for Corporate Financial Statements and Supplements* (Columbus, Ohio, 1957), pp. 36–37.

	Units	Unit Cost	Amount
Base stock	10,000	$1.00	$10,000
Extra stock	2,000	1.20	2,400
Total beginning inventory	12,000		$12,400
First purchase	2,000	1.30	2,600
Total	14,000		$15,000
First sale (4,000 units)	2,000	1.30	2,600
	2,000	1.20	2,400
Total	10,000		$10,000
Second purchase	6,000	1.40	8,400
Total	16,000		$18,400
Second sale (5,000 units)	5,000	1.40	7,000
Ending inventory (11,000 units):			
Base stock	10,000	1.00	$10,000
Extra stock (oldest unit cost)	1,000	1.40	1,400
Total	11,000		$11,400

Base Stock. Periodic Inventory. Current issues costed at end of period on *Lifo* basis:

	Units	Unit Cost	Amount
Base stock	10,000	$1.00	$10,000
Extra stock	2,000	1.20	2,400
Total beginning inventory	12,000		$12,400
Purchases:			
First	2,000	1.30	2,600
Second	6,000	1.40	8,400
Total Available	20,000		$23,400
Ending inventory (11,000 units per count):			
Base stock	10,000	1.00	$10,000
Extra stock	1,000	1.20	1,200
Total	11,000		$11,200
Cost of Goods Sold	9,000		$12,200

You should note that the difference in results shown above (final inventory of $11,400 versus $11,200) is due to perpetual versus periodic procedures rather than as a peculiarity of the base stock method; we observed this same effect in respect to *Lifo*.

As with *Lifo*, erosion of the base stock presents a particular problem. To illustrate, if sales were 12,000 units with a resulting final inventory of 8,000, a deficiency in the base stock would exist and special treatment would be required. Such a deficiency should not be allowed to occur except under the most unusual circumstances; in such cases it generally means that the base is too low. However, in such cases the value of the final inventory is determined by deducting the cost of replacement of the deficient stock from the normal value of the base stock in the following manner in order to maintain the "costing" integrity of the system:

Final inventory:

Base stock	10,000	$1.00	$10,000
Deficient stock	2,000	1.40	2,800
Inventory Value	8,000		$ 7,200

The deduction of deficient stock at replacement cost is based upon the theory that the stock was borrowed from the base stock to meet unexpectedly large sales requirements and that the best measure of the cost of its replacement is the current price of such merchandise and that the correct charge against the sales revenue of such merchandise is the estimated cost of its replacement. It follows that the succeeding period's purchase or production volume should be sufficient to restore at least the base stock and cover the sales requirements for that period.

The purpose of the base stock method is similar to that of last-in, first-out, that is, the matching of current costs with current revenues. The permanency assumed with respect to the base stock provides another avenue for attempted justification. The method is not acceptable for federal income tax purposes and is not in general use. The reasons for nonacceptance are the arbitrary nature of both the quantity and unit values of the assumed base stock and the fact that essentially similar results may be obtained under *Lifo.*

Miscellaneous Methods

Numerous methods in addition to those discussed herein have been proposed from various quarters. None of them has attained the status of acceptability. Examples are the *Nifo* and cost-of-last-purchase methods.

Nifo refers to next-in, first-out. Under this method the cost of sales or issues is costed at the unit of cost anticipated for the next purchase of a like volume. The idea is to match precisely the cost of sales with the actual cost of replacing the goods sold. It is maintained that *Lifo* fails to precisely match replacement cost with current revenues in that the method employs the cost of the latest purchase *prior* to the actual sale.

Cost-of-the-last-purchase method also has been proposed as a method of overcoming the inherent *lag* in ordinary *Lifo* procedures. Under this method *all issues* are priced at the last actual purchase price irrespective of the number of units involved. Under certain conditions relating to price change and quantities, this method conceivably could produce a negative inventory value. For this and other obvious reasons these methods have received little attention.

Selection of a Flow Method

It is interesting to note that a recent issue of *Accounting Trends and Techniques*[7] indicates that approximately 36% of the reporting companies utilize Fifo; 20% utilize Lifo; 27% utilize average; 4% utilize standard cost; 3% utilize the retail method; and the remaining utilize several miscellaneous methods. The same report also indicates that approximately 72% of the approximately 600 companies whose reports were analyzed utilize lower of cost or market.

The selection of an appropriate inventory flow method is a serious problem confronting many firms. Obviously, income measurement and income tax considerations will be paramount in the thinking of the practical businessman. The accountant should advocate the maintenance of sound accounting practices. Consistency from period to period is especially important. It has been noted that an AICPA Committee preferred income measurement, whereas an American Accounting Association Committee preferred the dominant characteristics of the actual flow of goods, as the primary criterion of acceptability of a given method. Methods encompassing both flow of goods and flow of cost assumptions have been approved for income tax purposes (specific identification, average, Fifo, and Lifo).

Recent trends toward emphasis on the income statement rather than on the balance sheet suggest that the primary consideration is tending toward the accuracy with which a given method matches cost and revenue. The point of argument hinges around the concept of "cost." Do we mean current cost, specific cost, oldest cost, or some other cost? It would appear that the following factors, in addition to those previously noted, should be considered in reaching a decision in a specific situation as to the inventory flow method to be adopted:

1. Responsiveness of the selling price of the goods to changes in their cost.
2. Nature of the goods involved.
3. Industry characteristics and practices.
4. Income tax considerations.
5. Trend of the general price level.

Standard Costs for Inventory

In manufacturing concerns using a standard cost system, the inventories are valued, recorded, and reported on the basis of a standard unit cost. The standard cost approximates an ideal or expected cost, and its use prevents the inflation of inventory values by excluding losses and expenses due to inefficiency, waste, or abnormal conditions. Under this method the *differences* between actual cost and standard

---

[7] AICPA, *Accounting Trends and Techniques* (24th ed.; New York, 1970), p. 56.

cost are set up in separate variance accounts which are written off in the current period as a loss or period cost rather than being capitalized in inventory. Standard costs may be applied to raw materials, work in process, and finished goods inventories. To illustrate the utilization of standard costs for raw materials in a simple manner, assume a particular company has just adopted standard cost procedures and that the initial inventory is zero. During the current period the company makes two purchases and one issue and records them as follows:

1. To record the purchase of 10,000 units of raw material at $1.10 actual cost; standard cost has been established at $1:

Raw Materials (10,000 units @ $1)......................................10,000
Raw Materials Purchase Price Variation
   (10,000 units @ $.10) 1,000
      Accounts Payable (10,000 units @ $1.10)........................   11,000

2. To record issuance of 8,000 units of raw material to factory for processing:

Material in Process 8,000
   Raw Materials (8,000 units @ $1).....................................   8,000

3. To record the purchase of 2,000 units of raw material at $.95:

Raw Materials (2,000 units @ $1)..2,000
Raw Materials Purchase Price Variation
   (2,000 units @ $.05)   100
   Accounts Payable (2,000 units @ $.95)   1,900

Results for the period:

Purchases at actual cost:
   10,000 units @ $1.10 ....$11,000
    2,000 units @   .95 1,900
      Total.. $12,900
Issues at standard cost:
    8,000 units @ $1...$ 8,000
Final inventory at standard cost:
    4,000 units @ $1 4,000   12,000
Raw Materials Purchase Price Variation (debit – charged
   against current income as a *loss*)................................ $ 900

Under the procedures illustrated above for raw material there would be no need for consideration of inventory flow methods such as *Lifo, Fifo,* and average, since only one cost—the standard cost—appears in the records. In addition, perpetual inventory records could be maintained in *units only*, since all issues and inventory valuations are at the constant standard price. Clearly standard cost represents a departure from the cost principle as currently interpreted. We have included this brief discussion of it at this point in view of the fact that for external reporting the standard cost values usually are "converted" to an actual cost basis. For example a simple conversion approach frequently used is:

	At Standard		At Actual
Final inventory	$ 4,000	$\frac{1}{3} \times \$12,900 =$	$ 4,300
Cost of issues	8,000	$\frac{2}{3} \times \$12,900 =$	8,600
	$12,000		$12,900

A detailed discussion of standard cost procedures is beyond the scope of this text and can be found in any complete cost accounting textbook.

QUESTIONS FOR CLASS DISCUSSION

1. Explain the importance of inventory flow methods in accounting for inventories and issues of the related goods.

2. Explain the specific cost method and indicate the objections to it.

3. List the three types of averages used for inventory costing. Indicate arguments for and against each.

4. Explain the basic differences between periodic inventory procedures and perpetual inventory procedures.

5. What are the primary advantages of perpetual inventory procedures over periodic inventory procedures?

6. Does the adoption of perpetual inventory procedures eliminate the need for physical count or measurement of inventories? Explain.

7. Explain the essential features of first-in, first-out. What are the primary advantages and disadvantages of Fifo? Explain the difference in the application of Fifo under (a) periodic inventory procedures and (b) perpetual inventory procedures.

8. Explain the essential features of last-in, first-out. What are the primary advantages and disadvantages of Lifo? Explain the difference in application of Lifo under (a) periodic inventory procedures and (b) perpetual inventory procedures.

9. Explain why Lifo costed currently and Lifo costed at the end of the month may give different results.

10. What is meant by "inventory layers"? Why are they significant with respect to the Fifo, Lifo, and base stock methods?

11. Compare the effects of Fifo versus Lifo (a) when prices are rising and (b) when prices are declining.

12. Explain the essential features of the base stock method of inventory costing.

13. You have just completed an audit of the XY Corporation. At the beginning of the year under audit, the company changed from Fifo to Lifo. Explain the implications and your recommendations relative to the financial statements being prepared for publication.

14. Discuss the important considerations in selecting an inventory flow method.

DECISION CASE 9–1

As a member of the controller's department of XYZ Corporation you have been involved in an initial discussion with some other company executives concerning the merits of Lifo versus Fifo inventory procedures for the company. The following items were listed during the initial discussion:

	Characteristic of		
	Fifo	*Lifo*	
1. Matches actual physical flow of goods..................	Yes	No	Explanation
2. Levels income			
3. Tends to cause income to vary with prices			
4. Matches old cost with new prices........................			
5. Costs inventory at approximate replacement cost ..			
6. Matches new cost with new prices			
7. Emphasizes balance sheet.................................			
8. Emphasizes income statement			
9. Opens door for "profit manipulation"			
10. Gives higher profits when prices rise...................			
11. Gives lower profits when prices fall			
12. Procession of costs same order as incurred			
13. Matches current costs with current revenue			
14. Acceptable for income tax purposes....................			
15. Income figure more accurately reflects profits that are available to owners			

Required:

1. Complete the tabulation.
2. Be prepared to discuss each item in detail.
3. Explain and illustrate item 15.

EXERCISES

Exercise 9–1

The raw material records of the Craig Manufacturing Corporation for the month of September showed the following data relative to item P-9:

			Units	*Unit Cost*
Sept.	1	Inventory...........................	300	$2.00
	3	Purchase............................	700	2.10
	11	Issue.................................	600	
	17	Purchase............................	300	2.14
	18	Issue.................................	500	
	29	Purchase............................	800	2.20

Compute the cost of issues for the period and the final inventory assuming (*a*) the simple average method is used, (*b*) the weighted average method is used, and (*c*) the moving average method is used. Under what circumstances would each be preferable?

Exercise 9–2

Utilizing the data given in Exercise 9–1 compute the cost of issues for the period and the final inventory assuming (a) Fifo, (b) Lifo costed out currently, and (c) Lifo costed out at the end of the period. What would be two important factors in selecting between costing currently or at end of the period under Lifo?

Exercise 9–3

The inventory records of the Miller Company provided the following data for one item of finished goods:

	Units	Unit Cost	Amount
Goods available for sale:			
Beginning inventory	400	$1.00	$ 400
Purchases: May 5	700	.90	630
May 12	600	.85	510
May 28	300	.80	240
Total	2,000		$1,780
Sales: May 10	800		
May 15	500		
May 29	200		
	1,500		
Final Inventory	500		

Required:

Use shortcut methods to complete the following:

	Valuation	
	Final Inventory	Cost of Sales
a) Fifo	$_____	$_____
b) Lifo (costed out at end of period)	$_____	$_____
c) Simple average	$_____	$_____
d) Weighted average	$_____	$_____
e) Base stock (base 300 units @ $1)	$_____	$_____

Exercise 9–4

The Nixon Corporation manufactures three different products which are "stocked" for regular sale. The principal product is referred to as "Benders." The records of the company for the month of November provided the following data relative to "Benders." The company maintains perpetual inventory records for finished goods.

Nov.	1	In stock	30 units @ $6.00
	10	Received from factory	10 " @ 6.40
	14	Shipments	20 "
	18	Received from factory	40 " @ 6.25
	21	Shipments	50 "
	28	Received from factory	20 " @ 6.05
	30	Shipments	12 "

Required:

Reconstruct the perpetual inventory record for Benders under each of the following assumptions:

a) Moving average method.
b) Weighted average method.

Exercise 9–5

Utilizing the data given in Exercise 9–4 reconstruct the perpetual inventory record under each of the following assumptions:

a) First-in, first-out.
b) Last-in, first-out, costed out currently.

Exercise 9–6

The Garza Company utilized Lifo flow and perpetual inventory procedures and considered 5,000 units of the primary raw material to be their "normal inventory position." For Period A, the following data were available relative to the primary raw material:

	Units	Unit Cost
Beginning inventory (normal)	5,000	$2.00
Beginning inventory (excess)	1,000	2.10
Purchases	19,000	2.20
Issues	22,000	

The first purchase in Period B was 10,000 units at $2.30 per unit.

Required:

1. Compute the final inventory and issues (units, unit cost, and total cost) for Period A.
2. Give journal entries for purchase and issues, recognizing the inventory liquidation in Period A.
3. Give journal entry for the purchase in Period B.
4. How should the inventory and any related accounts be reported on the balance sheet at the end of Period A?

Exercise 9–7

The records of the Coker Corporation showed a beginning inventory of 2,000 units of Item KB-20 at a unit cost of $5. Purchases during the period were: No. 1–3,000 units @ $5.20; No. 2–7,000 units @ $5.30; and No. 3–8,000 units @ $5.10. The company utilizes periodic inventory procedures; the final inventory count showed 6,000 units on hand. Compute the final inventory valuation and the cost of issues assuming Lifo under each of the following assumptions:

a) Incremental inventory layers priced at the oldest prices.
b) Incremental inventory layers priced at the average cost for the period.
c) Which approach is preferable? Why?

Exercise 9–8

Utilizing the data given in Exercise 9–7 for the Coker Corporation, compute the effect on (1) the inventory valuation and (2) income before taxes assuming the company has been using Fifo procedures and at the end of the current period changed to Lifo with incremental layers priced at the oldest prices. Indicate the proper treatment on the financial statements of the effect of the change in methods.

Exercise 9–9

The Blasdel Company uses the base stock method of inventory and for costing raw material into production. At the beginning of the period the inventory of raw material MN consisted of base stock, 1,000 units at $1; and extra stock, 500 units at $1.60. During the period the following purchases were made: No. 1–5,000 units @ $1.70; No. 2–3,000 units @ $1.50; and No. 3–2,000 units @ $1.80. The inventory on hand at the end of the period amounted to 2,100 units. Compute the cost of the raw material issued to production and the valuation of the final inventory assuming a periodic inventory procedure. Assume Lifo flow above the base stock.

Exercise 9–10

The Savoy Corporation utilizes *Lifo* flow and perpetual inventory procedures. For a particular period the inventory record for one item of finished goods showed the following:

Perpetual Inventory Card
(Lifo, costed out currently)

	Receipts			Issues			Balance		
	Units	Unit Cost	Total	Units	Unit Cost	Total	Units	Unit Cost	Total
a) Inventory....................							600	$1.00	$600
b) Purchase....................800		$1.10	880				600	1.00	600
							800	1.10	880
c) Issue...........................				700	$1.10	$770	600	1.00	600
							100	1.10	110
d) Purchase....................500		1.25	625				600	1.00	600
							100	1.10	110
							500	1.25	625
e) Issue...........................				400	1.25	500	600	1.00	600
							100	1.10	110
							100	1.25	125

The corporation follows the practice of adjusting the accounts to Lifo costed at the end of the period in order to "realize the full impact of Lifo."

Required:

1. Compute the difference between the two Lifo approaches as they effect inventory and issues.

2. Give entry to recognize the difference.
3. Show how the final inventory should be reported on the balance sheet.

Exercise 9-11

The Featherweight Company produced 70,000 units during the year. Sales were 60,000 units, and the final inventory totaled 40,000 units. The unit cost of production for the year was $10, and the initial inventory was carried at $270,000. Complete the following:

	Final Inventory		
Computations		Amount	Net Income
a) First-in, first-out		$_____	$ 90,000
b) Last-in, first-out		$_____	$_____
c) Weighted average		$_____	$_____
d) Base stock (25,000 units at $8.50)		$_____	$_____

Exercise 9-12

The Wilson Wholesale Grocery Company utilizes the dollar-value Lifo method for inventory purposes. The inventory for 19A (Lifo basis) amounted to $260,000. The physical inventory taken at the end of 19B, at 19B costs, amounted to $336,000. The management estimates that they paid 12% more for goods purchased during 19B than the costs in the 19A inventory. Determine the 19B final inventory.

Exercise 9-13

The Standard Products Company utilizes standard costs in the accounts. The raw material inventory records are maintained at standard. When raw materials are purchased, the difference between the standard cost and the actual cost is recorded in a separate account and treated as a *loss or gain* for the period in which the goods were purchased. The records relating to one item of raw material showed the following: standard cost per unit, $4; beginning inventory, 500 units; purchases during the period were No. 1—1,000 units at $4.30, No. 2—500 units at $3.80, and No. 3—800 units at $4; and issues 2,000 units.

Required:

1. Give journal entries for the purchases and issues.
2. Summarize the results for the period relative to the raw material item.

PROBLEMS

Problem 9-1

The Rogers Company records showed the following data relative to Raw Material W:

			Units	Unit Cost
July	1	Inventory	300	$5.00
	10	Purchase	400	4.90
	12	Issue	500	
	15	Purchase	700	4.80
	21	Issue	600	
	27	Purchase	100	4.70

Required:

Using shortcut approaches compute the cost of the issues and final inventory in each of the following completely independent situations (round unit costs to even cents):

	Final Inventory	Issues
a) Simple average	$	$
b) Weighted average	$	$
c) Moving average	$	$
d) Fifo	$	$
e) Lifo costed currently	$	$
f) Lifo costed at end of period	$	$
g) Base stock (base stock is 100 units)	$	$
h) Standard cost (standard cost is $4.75)	$	$

Problem 9-2

The records of the Fast Trading Company showed the following data relating to the major item sold:

			Units	Unit Cost
Aug.	1	Inventory	4,000	$6.00
	5	Purchase	3,000	6.20
	8	Sales	5,000	
	9	Purchase	9,000	6.30
	10	Sales	7,000	
	20	Purchase	6,000	6.40
	25	Sales	8,000	
	27	Purchase	4,000	6.50

Required:

Compute the valuation of the final inventory and the cost of sales under each of the following separate assumptions:

a) Fifo, periodic inventory procedures.
b) Lifo, periodic inventory procedures.
c) Weighted average, periodic inventory procedures. (Carry unit cost to three places.)
d) Moving average, perpetual inventory procedures (prepare the perpetual inventory record; carry unit cost to two places and throw rounding error to inventory).

Problem 9–3

The following purchases and issues of a raw material were made by the Massey Manufacturing Company during June (inventory on June 1 was 800 units valued at $600):

| | Purchases | | Units |
Date	Units	Unit Cost	Issued
3	500	$.80	800
5	1,600	.75	600
9	–	–	200
15	–	–	400
17	900	.82	–
19	600	.80	300
24	–	–	900
26	–	–	500
29	300	.77	–

Required:

Calculate the value of the issues and the inventory using the following methods (assume purchases before issues were on the same date):

a) First-in, first-out.
b) Weighted average cost (round units cost to three places).
c) Last-in, first-out, costed out currently.
d) Last-in, first-out, costed out at end of period.
e) Base stock, assuming a normal unit cost of $.75, a normal quantity of 780 units, and a Lifo flow above the base stock.

Problem 9–4

The records of the Samson Company showed the following relative to one of the major items being sold. Assume the transactions occurred in the order given.

	Units	Unit Cost
Beginning inventory	5,000	$1.00
Purchase No. 1	5,000	1.20
Sale No. 1	2,000	
Purchase No. 2	10,000	1.31
Sale No. 2	11,000	

Required:

Compute the cost of the issues and the valuation of the final inventory under each of the following assumptions (set up perpetual inventory record when needed; round unit costs to nearest cent).

a) Weighted average cost with periodic inventory procedures.
b) Moving average cost with perpetual inventory procedures.
c) Fifo with periodic inventory procedures.
d) Lifo with periodic inventory procedures, priced at end of period.
e) Base stock with periodic inventory procedures; assume base stock is 5,000 units @ $1 and Lifo flow above the base stock.

f) Standard cost assuming the standard unit cost is $1. What is the amount of the standard cost variations?

Problem 9–5

The records of the Ralph Company showed the following data with respect to one raw material utilized in the manufacturing process. Assume the transactions occurred in the order given.

	Units	Unit Cost
Inventory	6,000	$1.50
Purchase No. 1	3,000	1.60
Issue No. 1	4,000	
Purchase No. 2	5,000	1.70
Issue No. 2	7,000	
Purchase No. 3	4,000	1.75

Required:

Compute the cost of issues and the valuation of the final inventory under each of the following separate assumptions. Assume periodic inventories.

a) First-in, first-out.

b) Last-in, first-out, incremental layers costed at oldest prices (normal inventory position 6,000 units).

c) Last-in, first-out, incremental layers costed at average price (normal inventory position 6,000 units).

d) Base stock, extra stock costed on Lifo basis (base stock 5,000 @ $1.50).

e) Base stock, extra stock costed on average basis.

Problem 9–6

The Jackson Manufacturing Company manufactures one main product. Two raw materials are used in the manufacture of this product. The company utilizes standard costs in the accounts and carries the inventories at standard. The records of the company showed the following:

	Material A	Material B
Beginning inventory (units)	8,000	5,000
Standard cost per unit	$ 4.00	$ 8.00
Purchases during the period:		
No. 1	10,000 @ $4.00	7,000 @ $8.00
No. 2	20,000 @ 3.80	8,000 @ 8.10
Issues during the period (units)	28,000	16,000
Final inventory per physical count	10,000	3,900

Required:

1. Give all entries indicated relative to raw materials.

2. Determine the value of the final inventory and cost issues for each raw material.

3. Determine the amount of the variations from standard for each raw material and indicate the disposition of such amounts.

Problem 9-7

The Perez Company executives decided at the beginning of the current period to change from Fifo to Lifo. The records of the company showed the following data for the current period relative to one major item in inventory:

	Units	Unit Cost
Beginning inventory (Fifo layers averaged)	10,000	$3.00
Purchases and issues (in the order given):		
1 Purchase	8,000	2.80
2 Issue..	9,000	
3 Issue..	5,000	
4 Purchase	7,000	3.10
5 Purchase	6,000	3.40
6 Issue..	8,000	
7 Purchase	3,000	3.20

Required:

1. Compute the Lifo value of the inventory and the cost of issues assuming periodic inventory procedures.

2. Assuming periodic inventory procedures prepare comments suitable for the financial statements in view of the change from Fifo to Lifo.

Problem 9-8

The Carson Company utilizes periodic inventory procedures and has changed from Fifo to Lifo for the current and future periods. The records of the company pertaining to the main product provided the following information:

	Units	Unit Cost
Beginning inventory	5,000	$6.00
Purchases:		
No. 41...		
42...		
43...	4,000	6.20
44...	2,000	6.10
45...	6,000	5.90
46...		
47...		
48...	5,000	6.00
49...	8,000	5.80
50...		
Final inventory	10,000	

Required:

1. Compute the final inventory valuation and the cost of issues for the product assuming Lifo and that incremental inventory layers are costed at the oldest prices.

2. Prepare comments suitable for the financial statements in view of the change from Fifo to Lifo.

3. Explain why net income changes in the direction that it does in this instance.

Problem 9–9

The Holstrom Corporation maintains perpetual inventory records on a Fifo basis for the three main products distributed by the company. A physical inventory is taken at the end of each six months in order to check the perpetual inventory records. The following information relating to one of the products for the year was taken from the records of the company:

		Product A
Beginning inventory	9,000 units	@ $7.00
Purchases and sales (in the order given):		
Purchase No. 11	5,000 units	@ 7.50
Sale No. 1	10,000 units	
Purchase No. 12	16,000 units	@ 7.30
Sale No. 2	11,000 units	
Purchase No. 13	4,000 units	@ 7.20
Purchase No. 14	7,000 units	@ 7.10
Sale No. 3	14,000 units	
Purchase No. 15	5,000 units	@ 6.70
Ending inventory (per count)	10,000	
Replacement cost (per unit)	$6.50	

Required:

1. Reconstruct the perpetual inventory record for Product A.
2. Give all entries indicated by the above data assuming selling price is $12 per unit and that the company employs the direct inventory reduction method in recognizing lower of cost or market.

Problem 9–10

The Bagley Trading Company sells three main products. In the past periodic inventory procedures have been employed on a Fifo basis. The records of the company showed the following information relating to one of the products:

Beginning inventory	3,000 units	@ $2.00
Purchases and sales (in the order given):		
Purchase No. 1	3,000 units	@ 2.20
Purchase No. 2	5,000 units	@ 2.00
Sale No. 1	6,000 units	
Purchase No. 3	7,000 units	@ 2.30
Sale No. 2	8,000 units	
Sale No. 3	2,000 units	
Purchase No. 4	7,000 units	@ 2.10

In considering a change in inventory policy the following summary was prepared:

	Illustration			
	(1)	(2)	(3)	(4)
Sales	$50,000	$50,000	$50,000	$50,000
Cost of sales	34,100	34,176	34,700	34,800
Gross margin	$15,900	$15,824	$15,300	$15,200

Required:

Identify the inventory flow method used for each illustration assuming the ending inventory only was affected. (Hint: As the first step compute total goods available for sale.)

Problem 9–11

The Griffin Company uses the Fifo method in costing their raw material inventory. Over the first three years of operation, the inventory at the end of each year computed by different methods for comparative purposes was as follows:

	Final Inventory		
	19A	*19B*	*19C*
Fifo	$380,000	$460,000	$400,000
Lifo	300,000	375,000	430,000
Average cost (weighted)	350,000	440,000	420,000

Required:

Compute net income resulting under each method. Actual results under Fifo method are given. (Hint: Beginning and ending inventories have opposite effects on net income.)

	Net Income		
	19A	*19B*	*19C*
Fifo	$100,000	$150,000	$200,000
Lifo	$	$	$
Average cost	$	$	$

chapter 10 | Inventories – Estimating Procedures

There are numerous situations where the accountant must be concerned with estimates relating to inventories. As a result of these situations certain inventory estimating procedures have gained wide acceptance. The principal estimating procedures are discussed in this chapter under the captions (*a*) the gross margin (profit) method, (*b*) the retail inventory method, and (*c*) inventory allowances. These topics are followed by a discussion of several miscellaneous inventory problems not treated in Chapters 8 and 9.

Gross Margin Method

The gross margin[1] method represents an approach frequently used in approximating the valuation of the inventory independently of a physical count of the goods and as a check on the detailed inventory records in the case of perpetual inventory procedures. The method is based on the assumption that the short-run *rate of gross margin* (gross margin divided by sales) is approximately the same from one period to the next. The method involves computation of total goods *available* for sale in the normal manner based on data provided by the regular accounts. Next the estimated cost of goods sold is determined by applying the estimated gross margin rate to net sales and deducting this

---

[1]The method traditionally has been referred to as the gross profit method, nevertheless the more modern terminology *gross margin* is used throughout these discussions. (Ref. AICPA *Terminology Bulletin No. 2*.)

amount from sales to derive estimated cost of goods sold. Deduction of the estimated cost of goods sold from the cost of goods available for sale gives the ending inventory at estimated cost. For example, if the rate of gross margin for a concern has been uniformly 40% of sales, the final inventory may be approximated as follows:

	Known Data	Computations	Order of Computations
Net sales	$10,000°		
Cost of goods sold:			
Initial inventory ....$ 5,000†			
Add: Purchases .... 8,000°			
Goods available			
for sale $13,000			
Less: Final inven-			
tory........................ ?		($13,000 − $6,000) = $7,000	3
Cost of goods sold	?	($10,000 − $4,000) = $6,000	2
Gross margin.................... 40%‡	?	($10,000 × 40%) = $4,000	1

° From company records.
† Final inventory from prior period.
‡ Based on recent past performance.

A more comprehensive example where the data are rearranged to facilitate computation follows.

Cost of goods available for sale:		
Beginning inventory...		$ 50,000°
Purchases during period ....$160,400°		
Freight-in... 9,800°		
Total purchases...$170,200		
Less: Purchase returns and allowances................... 200°		
Net purchases...	170,000	
Cost of goods available for sale............................	$220,000	
Deduct estimated cost of goods sold:		
Sales...$201,000°		
Less: Sales returns and allowances .... 1,000°		
Net sales..$200,000		
Less: Estimated gross margin ($200,000 × .20†)........ 40,000		
Estimated cost of goods sold	160,000	
Estimated Cost of Ending Inventory	$ 60,000	

° Data available from the records.
† Based on recent past performance.

In some problems relating to the gross margin method, a *cost* percentage or cost rate (cost of sales divided by sales) is given rather than the gross margin percentage or rate (gross margin divided by sales). If either percentage is known the other percentage may be readily determined, since the two percentages must sum to 100%. In the above example, since the rate of gross margin is 20%, the cost percentage is 80% (100% − 20%).

In other cases the gross margin rate may be given as a percent of *cost* of sales rather than as a percent of sales. In the above example the gross margin rate, or markup, was given as a percent of sales (20% markup on sales); however, it could have been stated as 25% of the *cost of goods sold* (markup on cost). In the latter case a conversion of the rate on cost to a rate on sales would be desirable. Conversion of a rate on cost to a rate on sales or vice versa may be accomplished algebraically as follows:

Symbols: *MS* — Markup on sales
     MC — Markup on cost

1. The markup on cost is 25%; determine the markup (gross margin rate) on sales.

$$MS = \frac{MC}{1 + MC} = \frac{.25}{1 + .25} = .20, \text{ or } 20\%$$

2. The markup on sales is 20%; determine the markup on cost.

$$MC = \frac{MS}{1 - MS} = \frac{.20}{1 - .20} = .25, \text{ or } 25\%$$

A more direct approach involves the use of fractions as illustrated below. Note that in all cases the numerator is the same; whereas when converting to a markup on sales, the denominator is the sum of the numerator and denominator of the cost fraction, and when converting to a markup on cost, the denominator is the difference between the numerator and the denominator of the sales fraction. Obviously the fraction or rate on sales must be smaller than the comparable fraction or rate on cost. Observe the relationship between the fractions on each line in the following example:

	Markup	
	On Cost	*On Sales*
a) Markup is 25% on cost; determine the markup on sales.....................	$\frac{1}{4}(25\%)$	$\frac{1}{5}(20\%)$
b) Markup is 33⅓% on sales; determine the markup on cost..............	$\frac{1}{2}(50\%)$	$\frac{1}{3}(33\frac{1}{3}\%)$
c) Markup is 66⅔% on cost; determine the markup on sales.....................	$\frac{2}{3}(66\frac{2}{3}\%)$	$\frac{2}{5}(40\%)$

The above techniques for converting from a markup on one base to markup on another base has numerous business applications and often appears on CPA examinations where the required rate frequently is not given directly. With respect to the gross margin method, it is generally preferable when a rate on cost is given to convert to the comparable rate on sales and then to solve in the manner illustrated on the immediately preceding page.[2]

The gross margin method frequently is employed in four different situations as follows:

1. By the auditor or others to test the reasonableness of an inventory valuation provided by some other person or determined by some other means, such as physical inventory, or perpetual inventory. To illustrate, assume the bookkeeper for the company referred to on page 378 submitted to the auditor an inventory valuation of $85,000. The gross margin method provides an approximation of $60,000, which would alert the auditor to investigate the inventory situation thoroughly. The "gross margin test" generally is considered to be a part of the normal audit program.

2. To estimate the final inventory for interim financial statements (monthly statements for example) prepared during the year where the taking of interim physical inventories is impractical. The method finds fairly wide application in this respect.

3. To estimate an inventory destroyed by some casualty such as fire or storm. Obviously, this application would be limited to those situations where the books of accounts are not destroyed since certain basic data from the accounts are essential. Valuation of inventory lost through casualty is necessary in order to (a) estimate the amount of loss and (b) as a basis for settlement of insurance claims related to the inventory loss.

4. To develop budget estimates of cost of sales, gross margin, and inventory after the sales budget is developed.

In applying the gross margin method the accountant must bear in mind that a possibility of error exists in view of (a) the assumption that the gross margin rate assumed is realistic and reasonably accurate and (b) the effect of using an *average* rate. In the usual situation a firm will carry a number of different lines of merchandise each having a different mark up or gross margin. Obviously, a change in markup on one or more lines, or a shift in the relative quantities of each line sold, will change the average gross margin rate (markup) thereby distorting the validity of the results derived by the method.

When the gross margin method is applied where significantly different rates of markup are involved, computations should be developed for each separate class of merchandise if practicable.

---

[2] An alternative computation (where markup is known on cost) giving the same results without a conversion to markup on sales could be made as follows:

Cost of goods available for sale (per above) $220,000
Deduct estimated cost of goods sold:
Sales reduced to estimated cost ($200,000 ÷ 1.25)..................... 160,000
Estimated Cost of Ending Inventory...$ 60,000

Retail Inventory Method

The retail method of inventory valuation is widely employed by retail stores, particularly department stores, which sell a great diversity of items. In such situations perpetual inventory procedures generally are impractical and the taking of complete physical inventories more often than annually is uncommon. Several features of department store operation make possible the utilization of the retail inventory method. Particular features are (a) the departments are frequently homogeneous with respect to the markup on items sold within the departments and (b) articles purchased are immediately priced for resale and displayed. The effect of this latter feature may be observed in the tendency by retailing establishments to relate markups, analyses, budgets, estimates, markdowns, etc., to *sales price* rather than to cost price. Whereas those in nonretailing endeavors tend to think of markup as being on cost, the retailer traditionally thinks of markup on selling price.

The use of the retail method makes possible interim operating statements by departments which would be impracticable if physical inventories had to be taken. The retail method has been actively sponsored by the National Retail Dry Goods Association and officially accepted by the Internal Revenue Service; consequently, it has become an important method of inventory determination. The accounting profession has accepted the method on its own merits as fundamentally sound where properly administered. It must be realized that the retail inventory method represents an approach in *estimating* the inventory position at a given date. The method as usually applied secures a valuation which approximates "cost or market, whichever is lower."

Application of the retail method requires that records be kept which show the following data:

1. Beginning inventory valued at both cost and retail.
2. Purchases during the period valued at both cost and retail.
3. Adjustments to the original marked retail price such as additional markups, markup cancellations, markdowns, employee discounts, and markdown cancellations.
4. Data relating to other adjustments such as interdepartmental transfers, returns, breakage, and damaged goods.
5. Sales.

This method is similar to the gross margin method in that the inventory valuation is based on the ratio of cost to selling price. Under the retail method records are maintained so that the ratio may be developed for the current period rather than being estimated from prior periods. The retail method involves computation of the goods available for sale at both *cost* and *retail*. Cost is divided by retail to obtain the *cost ratio*. Sales are then deducted from goods available for sale (at retail), the result being the inventory at retail. Multiplication of the inventory at retail by the cost ratio provides the estimated inventory valuation at cost. Determination of the final inventory valuation employing the retail method is illustrated below with simplified data:

	At Cost	At Retail
Goods available for sale:		
Beginning inventory (January 1)............................	$ 15,000°	$ 25,000°
Purchases during January	195,000°	275,000°
Cost of goods available for sale	$210,000	$300,000
Cost ratio: $210,000 ÷ $300,000 = 70%.		
Deduct January sales at retail..................................		260,000°
Ending inventory (January 31):		
At retail...		$ 40,000
At cost ($40,000 × 70%).......................................	$ 28,000	

° Data available from the records.

Since the retail inventory method provides merely an estimate of the final inventory, a physical inventory should be taken at least annually as a check on the accuracy of the estimates. Significant differences between the physical inventory and the retail inventory estimate should be carefully analyzed. Investigation may indicate (*a*) inventory shortages due to breakage, loss, or theft; (*b*) incorrect application of the retail method; (*c*) failure of departmental managers to report correctly markdowns, additional markups, or cancellations; (*d*) errors in the records; (*e*) errors in the physical inventory; or (*f*) inventory manipulation.

Since the retail inventory method is used widely with respect to internal statements and analyses, numerous applications have been developed. The primary uses of the retail method are as follows:

1. To provide estimated inventory valuations for interim periods (usually monthly) when physical inventories are impracticable. The method provides inventory valuations needed for monthly statements, analyses, control, and purchasing policy considerations.

2. To provide a means of converting a physical inventory, priced at retail, to a cost basis. In order to eliminate the necessity of marking the cost (in code) on the merchandise, or referring to invoices, many retail establishments, after physically counting the stock on hand, extend the inventory sheets at retail. The retail value is then converted to cost by applying the retail inventory method without reference to individual cost prices.

3. To provide a basis for interim control of inventory, purchases, theft, markdowns, and additional markups. Many department stores utilize the results of the retail inventory calculation by department for such interim control requirements.

Markups and Markdowns

The preceding illustration assumed that there were no changes in the *original* marked selling price. The original selling price is frequently raised or lowered, particularly at the end of the selling season or when replacement costs are changing. The retail method requires that a careful record be kept of all adjustments to the *original* marked selling price since these adjustments must be taken into account in the computation. In order to apply this rule it is important to distinguish between the following terms:

Terminology	*Definition*	*Example*
1. Cost.	Invoice cost of the merchandise plus incidental costs such as freight.	$ 8.00
2. Initial markup (markon).	The original or initial amount that the merchandise is marked up. The difference between cost and the original sales price marked on the merchandise. Sometimes referred to as markon.	+ 2.00
3. Original sales price.	Cost plus the initial markup. The regular selling price. *Note that this price represents the base for the terms defined below.*	$ 10.00

Revisions of Original Sales Price:

4. Additional markup.	A $1.50 upward revision of the original sales price of $10.	+ 1.50

Revised sales price (including initial markup and an additional markup) ....$ 11.50

5. Markup cancellation.	A $1.00 reduction in the *additional* markup. Does not reduce the selling price below the original sales price	− 1.00

Revised sales price (at this point there has been an initial markup of $2.00, an additional markup of $1.50, and a markup cancellation of $1.00) ....$ 10.50

6. Net additional markup.	The additional markups minus the markup cancellations. At this point in the example the net additional markup is $.50.	
7. Markdown.	A reduction in selling price below the *original* sales price. Assume the item is marked down to $7. Markdown $3.00 and markup cancellation $.50.	− 3.50

Revised sales price...$ 7.00

8. Markdown cancellation.	Cancellation of a markdown. Does not increase the sales price above the *original* sales price. Now assume a markdown cancellation of $2.50. (If the change here were $3.50 there would be a markdown cancellation of $3 and an additional markup of $.50)	+ 2.50

Revised sales price...$ 9.50

9. Net markdown.	The mark downs minus the markdown cancellations. In the example, at this point, the net markdown is $.50.	

If all of the changes indicated above had been made on 100 units of a particular item of merchandise, the following would have been reported to the accounting department for retail inventory purposes:

	Units	Per Unit	Amount
4. Additional markups	100	$1.50	$ 150
5. Markup cancellations	100	1.00	(100)
6. Markup cancellations	100	.50	(50)
7. Markdowns	100	3.00	(300)
8. Markdown cancellations	100	2.50	250
Total Effect ($10.00 − $9.50 × 100 units)			$(50)

The difference between cost and the final selling price ($9.50 − $8.00 = $1.50) is frequently referred to as the *maintained* markup. We may note that cancellations of markups or markdowns seldom equal the markup or markdown because after the markup or markdown some items are sold so even a complete cancellation will not result in a complete offset. For example, assume a department has on hand 100 items that were originally marked to sell at $20 each. It is decided to raise the selling price to $22. At this time the department manager marking up the goods must submit a report to the accounting department showing additional markups of $200 (100 items @ $2). Subsequently it is found that the items are not moving; therefore, it is decided to mark the remaining 20 to sell for $17 each. At this time the department manager must submit a report showing (a) markup cancellations of $40 (20 items @ $2) and (b) markdowns of $60 (20 items @ $3). Failure to report correctly these adjustments to the original sales price will give rise to an error in the retail inventory calculation.

The way in which markups and markdowns are included in the computation depends upon whether the inventory is to be valued at approximate *lower of cost or market* (Case A below); or at approximate cost (Case B below).

Illustrations Utilizing Retail Method of Inventory

To illustrate estimation of the final inventory utilizing the retail method for each of these two cases, the following data are assumed to have been taken from the accounting records:

	At Cost	At Retail
Inventory at beginning of period	$ 550	$ 900
Purchases during period	6,290	8,900
Additional markups during period		225
Markup cancellations during period		25
Markdowns during period		600
Markdown cancellations during period		100
Sales for the period		8,500

CASE A—Inventory valued at approximate lower of cost or market—include *only* net markups in the computation of the cost ratio; the markdowns are included in the determinations *after* the cost ratio computation.

	At Cost	At Retail
Goods available for sale:		
Beginning inventory	$ 550	$ 900
Purchases during period	6,290	8,900
Additional markups	$225	
Less: Markup cancellations	25	
Net additional markups		200
Goods available for sale	$6,840	$10,000
Cost ratio: $6,840 ÷ $10,000 = 68.4%		
Deduct:		
Sales		8,500
Remainder		$ 1,500
Markdowns	$600	
Less: Markdown cancellations	100	
Net markdowns		500
Ending inventory:		
At retail		$ 1,000
At lower of cost or market ($1,000 × 68.4%)	$ 684	

CASE B—Inventory valued at approximate cost—include both net markups and net markdowns in the computation of the cost ratio.

	At Cost	At Retail
Goods available for sale:		
Beginning inventory	$ 550	$ 900
Purchases during period	6,290	8,900
Additional markups during period	$225	
Less: Markup cancellations	25	
Net additional markups		200
Deduct:		
Markdowns during period	$600	
Less: Markdown cancellations	100	
Net markdowns		(500)
Goods available for sale	$6,840	$ 9,500
Cost ratio: $6,840 ÷ $9,500 = 72%		
Deduct:		
Sales		8,500
Ending inventory:		
At retail		$ 1,000
At Cost ($1,000 × 72%)	$ 720	

The inclusion of net additional markups and the exclusion of net markdowns in computing the cost ratio gives a conservative inventory valuation approximating the lower of cost or market as is indicated in Case A above. The lower of cost or market approach (Case A) appears to be used more frequently than the approximate cost approach (Case B). Therefore, throughout this book the lower of cost or market approach is assumed unless otherwise stated.

In the retail inventory computations, cash discounts should be excluded if they are considered to be financial items. If they are considered to be deductions from gross purchases or gross sales (theoretically preferable), as the case may be, then they must be accorded special treatment. In this case, purchase discounts should be treated as a reduction of purchase cost. Since sales discounts do not affect "retail" or cost they should be omitted from the computation unless they have been deducted from the sales amount, in which case they should be added back to sales. Special discounts to employees and preferred customers, and known or estimated normal losses from spoilage or breakage, should be included in the computations in a manner similar to markdowns. Return purchases are deducted from purchases at both cost and retail; return sales are deducted from gross sales. These items are included in the illustration below:

	At Cost	At Retail
Goods available for sale:		
Initial inventory	$ 5,000	$ 7,500
Purchases	23,000	32,800
Freight-in	1,000	
Purchase returns	(600)	(840)
Purchase discount (if considered a deduction from purchases)	(400)	
Net additional markups		540
Total goods available for sale	$28,000	$40,000
Cost ratio: $28,000 ÷ $40,000 = 70%		
Deduct:		
Sales (net of sales returns)	$30,000	
Net markdowns	3,000	
Employee discounts	2,000	35,000
Final inventory:		
At retail		$ 5,000
At lower of cost or market ($5,000 × 70%)	$ 3,500	

Approximating Lifo with the Retail Method (Lifo Retail Method)

The retail method may be adapted to approximate Lifo results by maintaining a distinction in the computations between the base (normal) inventory and subsequent inventory layers. The subsequent layers are determined through the use of a price index somewhat similar to that previously illustrated for dollar-value Lifo (page 357).

Adaptation of the retail method to provide Lifo results (Lifo retail method) poses two distinct problems, viz:

1. Procedures that should be used for changing from the method being used (such as the retail method, lower of cost or market) to the Lifo retail method.

2. Procedures to be used after the change. These procedures must maintain a separation of costs for the base inventory level and subsequent inventory levels on an approximate Lifo basis.

Procedures for Changing to Lifo Retail. To accommodate the change to Lifo retail the *beginning inventory* for the period in which the change is to be instituted must be restated and an adjusting entry recorded. The cost figure for the beginning inventory should be either the average cost or the cost of the purchases in the prior period; the latter usually is used as illustrated below. Since the prior inventory method normally is the traditional retail method, which approximates the lower of cost or market, the adjustment serves to restate the inventory to a cost basis. In developing the restatement to a cost basis the *cost ratio* is computed (*a*) by excluding the beginning inventory for the prior year and (*b*) by including markdowns and markups. The restated inventory is then recorded by means of an adjusting entry. To illustrate, assume a small department store had been utilizing the traditional retail method (lower of cost or market basis) and has decided to change to the Lifo retail method starting in 1971. The conventional retail method computations developed at the end of December, 1970 were as follows:

	At Cost	At Retail
Inventory, January 1, 1970	$ 5,700	$ 10,000
Purchases	78,300	138,000
Net additional markups		2,000
Total	$84,000	$150,000
Cost ratio: $84,000 ÷ $150,000 = 56%		
Net markdowns		5,000
Remainder		$145,000
Sales		115,000
Ending inventory, December 31, 1970:		
At retail		$ 30,000
At lower of cost or market ($30,000 × 56%)	$16,800	

The computations to restate the ending inventory for 1970 (beginning for 1971) were as follows. You should note the exclusion of the base inventory level and inclusion of both markups and markdowns in determination of the cost ratio.

	At Cost	At Retail
Purchases	$78,300	$138,000
Net additional markups		2,000
Net markdowns		(5,000)
Total	$78,300	$135,000
Cost ratio — cost basis: $78,300 ÷ $135,000 = 58%		
1970 ending inventory — cost basis ($30,000 × 58%)	$17,400	

The entry to restate the beginning inventory for 1971 would be as follows:

Beginning Inventory ($17,400 − $16,800)......................................600
　　Inventory Adjustment Due to Adoption of Lifo Retail...............   600

The inventory adjustment account would be closed to Income Summary at the end of 1971.

Procedures to Implement Lifo Retail after Change.　Lifo retail procedures may be outlined as follows:

1. In computing the cost ratio, markdowns as well as markups are included. Markdowns are included so that the valuation will approximate a cost basis rather than a lower of cost or market valuation.
2. The beginning inventory is disregarded in computing the cost ratio because under Lifo it is carried forward as a base layer at the original valuation and the cost ratio is used to estimate the new layer which should be valued at current cost.
3. A distinction is maintained between the base inventory layer and subsequent inventory layers. In identifying the new or incremental layer(s), the computed final inventory at retail must be restated by means of a *retail price index* applicable to the goods involved in the inventory.
4. If an inventory decrease follows one or more increases, the incremental layers are eaten away in Lifo order.

The small department store illustration is continued. Lifo retail inventory computations for the years 1971, 1972, and 1973 shown below are in Illustrations 10–1, 10–2 and 10–3, based upon the following data taken from the records of the company:

	1971 At Cost	1971 At Retail	1972 At Cost	1972 At Retail	1973 At Cost	1973 At Retail
Beginning inventory (per above).....	$17,400	$ 30,000				
Purchases.............	90,480	147,000	$101,500	$172,000	$109,800	$177,000
Net additional markups.........		8,800		9,000		7,000
Net markdowns.....		5,000		6,000		4,000
Sales....................		140,000		162,800		197,800
Applicable price index (1970 = 100)°		102		106		110

° A reliable index should be used which is representative of the conditions of the particular industry and region.

The computations for 1971 may be briefly elaborated on:

a) The ending inventory at retail ($40,800) is computed in the traditional retail manner except that the *cost ratio* (60%) is determined by (1) excluding the beginning inventory and (2) including both markups and markdowns.

b) Restatement on *cost* basis requires utilization of the price index in order to identify the new Lifo layer as follows:

1) The ending inventory as computed ($40,800) is deflated by utilizing the price index, that is $40,800 ÷ 1.02 = $40,000. This tells us what the final inventory would have been at retail had there been no price increase during 1971.

2) Subtraction of the beginning inventory layer ($30,000) from the final inventory as deflated ($40,000) derives the new layer added in 1971 (at deflated retail) amounting to $10,000.

3) The 1971 layer added must be returned to 1971 prices ($10,000 × 1.02 = $10,200). Finally it must be stated at cost ($10,200 × 60%) which is $6,120.

Illustration 10–1
Lifo Retail Computations for 1971

	At Cost	At Retail	Cost Ratio
Inventory, January 1, 1971	$ 17,400	$ 30,000	
Purchases	$ 90,480	$147,000	
Net additional markups		8,800	
Net markdowns		(5,000)	
Total (excluding beginning inventory)	$ 90,480	$150,800	60%
Total (including beginning inventory)	$107,880	$180,800	
Sales		140,000	
1971 ending inventory at retail		$ 40,800	
Restatement on cost basis:			
1971 ending inventory at 1970 prices ($40,800 ÷ 1.02)	$40,000		
Base layer (1970 per above)	30,000	$ 17,400°	
1971 layer:			
At 1970 prices	$10,000		
At 1971 prices ($10,000 × 1.02)	$10,200		
At 1971 cost ($10,200 × 60%)		6,120†	
1971 ending inventory at Lifo cost		$ 23,520	

° 1970 layer at cost from line 1.
† 1971 layer at cost.

The results of the computation of the new layer added in 1971, along with the data already at hand in respect to the beginning inventory, may be summarized as follows:

	At Cost	At 1970 Retail		At 1971 Retail
1971 ending inventory summarized:				
Base layer (1970 layer)	$17,400	$30,000	(× 1.02)	$30,600
1971 additional layer	6,120	10,000	(× 1.02)	10,200
Total Inventory	$23,520	$40,000	(× 1.02)	$40,800

The computations and summaries for 1972 and 1973 follow (Illustrations 10–2 and 10–3) without comment since the procedures are identical to those shown above.

Illustration 10–2
Lifo Retail Computations for 1972

	At Cost	At Retail	Cost Ratio
Inventory, January 1, 1972 (per above)	$ 23,520	$ 40,800	
Purchases	$101,500	$172,000	
Net additional markups		9,000	
Net markdowns		(6,000)	
Total (excluding beginning inventory)	$101,500	$175,000	58%
Total (including beginning inventory)	$125,020	$215,800	
Sales		162,800	
1972 ending inventory at retail		$ 53,000	

Restatement on cost basis:
1972 ending inventory at 1970 prices

($53,000 ÷ 1.06)	$50,000	
Base layer (1970 per above)	30,000	$ 17,400
Excess over base layer	$20,000	
1971 Lifo layer (per above)	10,000	6,120
1972 layer:		
At 1970 prices	$10,000	
At 1972 prices (10,000 × 1.06)	$10,600	
At 1972 cost ($10,600 × 58%)		6,148
1972 ending inventory at cost		$ 29,668

	At Cost	At 1970 Retail		At 1972 Retail
1972 ending inventory summarized:				
Base layer (1970 layer)	$17,400	$30,000	(× 1.06)	$31,800
1971 layer	6,120	10,000	(× 1.06)	10,600
1972 additional layer	6,148	10,000	(× 1.06)	10,600
Total Inventory at Lifo Cost	$29,668	$50,000	(× 1.06)	$53,000

The acceptability of Lifo retail method for federal income tax purposes has created widespread interest in the method. Many retail establishments in recent years have changed from the traditional retail method to the Lifo retail method. The tax regulations provide that in case of a change of method the change in the beginning inventory must be reported along the lines illustrated on page 356. Unfortunately, the regulations further require that the method must be used for "book purposes" to be acceptable for income tax purposes.

Inventories under Long-Term Construction Contracts

A special inventory problem arises in connection with long-term construction contracts extending beyond the end of the fiscal period. In cases where financial statements are prepared prior to the completion of the contract, the accountant must consider (a) inventory

Illustration 10–3
Lifo Retail Computations for 1973

	At Cost	At Retail	Cost Ratio
Inventory, January 1, 1973 (per above)	$ 29,668	$ 53,000	
Purchases	$109,800	$177,000	
Net additional markups		7,000	
Net markdowns		(4,000)	
Total (excluding beginning inventory)	$109,800	$180,000	61%
Total (including beginning inventory)	$139,468	$233,000	
Sales		197,800	
1973 ending inventory at retail		$ 35,200	

Restatement on cost basis:
1973 ending inventory at 1970 prices
($35,200 ÷ 1.10) $32,000
Base layer (1970 per above) .... 30,000 $ 17,400

Excess over base layer (from
1971 layer) ....$ 2,000

1971 layer:
At 1970 prices ....$ 2,000

At 1971 prices (using 1971 index)
($2,000 × 1.02) ....$ 2,040

At 1971 cost (using 1971 cost ratio)
($2,040 × 60%)   1,224
1973 ending inventory at Lifo cost .... $ 18,624

	At Cost	At 1970 Retail		At 1973 Retail
1973 ending inventory summarized:				
Base layer (1970)	$17,400	$30,000	(× 1.10)	$33,000
1971 layer	1,224	2,000	(× 1.10)	2,200
Total Inventory	$18,624	$32,000	(× 1.10)	$35,200

valuation and (*b*) income (or loss) earned to date with respect to such contracts. Should all of the costs incurred to date in connection with the construction contract be shown on financial statements as work in process inventory and no income or loss recognized prior to final completion? The accounting profession has recognized two methods in accounting for long-term construction contracts:[3]

1. The completed-contract method.
2. The percentage-of-completion method.

Under the *completed-contract method* all costs incurred in connection with the long-term construction contract are accumulated in a Construction in Process account, interim billings by the contractor as the construction proceeds are debited to Accounts Receivable and

---

[3]Committee on Accounting Procedure, AICPA, "Long-Term Construction-Type Contracts," *Accounting Research Bulletin No. 45* (New York, 1955).

credited to Revenue Billed on Construction Contracts, and no income is recognized prior to completion of the contract. The net balance between the Construction in Process (debit) and Revenue Billed on Construction Contracts (credit) accounts is shown on the balance sheet as a current asset if a debit and as a current liability if a credit.

To illustrate the completed-contract method the following data are assumed:

1. A contract is received to construct a building for a flat fee of $1,500,000 starting February 1, 1971; estimated time to complete $2\frac{1}{2}$ years.
2. Progress billings to be paid at the end of each month. Billings to be based on estimates of completion developed by the architects as of the 15th of each month.
3. Data covering the construction period:

	Cumulative		
	1971	1972	1973
Costs incurred to date	350,000	$900,000	$1,365,000
Estimated costs to complete	1,000,000	460,000	–
Progress billings to date	300,000	875,000	1,500,000
Progress collections to date	270,000	825,000	1,500,000

The accounting for the duration of the contract would be as follows:

Entries:

1. To record costs of construction:

	1971		1972		1973	
Construction in Process	350,000		550,000		465,000	
Cash, Payables, etc........		350,000		550,000		465,000

2. To record progress billings:

Accounts Receivable– Construction Contract Billings...........................	300,000		575,000		625,000	
Revenue Billed on Construction Contracts..........		300,000		575,000		625,000

3. To record collections:

Cash................................	270,000		555,000		675,000	
Accounts Receivable– Construction Contract Billings..............		270,000		555,000		675,000

4. To record income and close accounts:

Revenue Billed on Construction Contracts					1,500,000	
Construction in Process						1,365,000
Income on Construction Contracts						135,000

Financial Statement Presentation:

	1971	1972	1973
Balance Sheet:			
Current assets:			
Accounts receivable — construction contract billings	$30,000	$50,000	–0–
Construction in process.........$350,000		$900,000	
Less: Billings on contracts..................... 300,000		875,000	
Cost on incompleted contracts in excess of billings	50,000	25,000	–0–
Income Statement:			
Net income (loss)	–0–	–0–	$135,000

The completed-contract method conforms with the concept that income should not be recognized prior to point of sale. The method does not require an estimate of profits earned prior to completion of the contract for financial statement purposes; in this respect it is conservative. The primary disadvantage of the method is that, in the view of some, it may lead to distortion of revenue and earnings of the period. Net income may be low or even nonexistent for several years followed by extremely high profits during the year of completion, although operations may have been fairly uniform during the extended period. In the above example, is it reasonable to report that the $135,000 income was earned only in 1973? Many accountants feel strongly that such reporting is misleading. If a loss appears imminent with respect to a long-term contract, provision for it should be made irrespective of the method of accounting employed with respect to income and inventory. A possible loss should be recognized (*a*) as a loss in the accounts, (*b*) as a reservation of retained earnings, or (*c*) by footnotes depending upon the probabilities involved.

Under the *percentage-of-completion method* all costs incurred in connection with the long-term construction contract are accumulated in a Construction in Process account; interim billings as the construction proceeds are debited to Accounts Receivable and credited to Revenue Billed on Construction Contracts, and income (or loss) is recognized on the basis of percentage of completion. The income to be recognized on financial statements prior to completion of the contract is recorded by debiting Construction in Process and crediting Income on Construction in Process; the latter account then is closed to Income Summary at the end of each accounting period. The net balance between the Construction in Process (debit) and Revenue Billed on Construction (credit) accounts is shown on the balance sheet as a current asset if a debit and as a current liability if a credit.

Utilizing the data given above, the estimated income to be recognized under the percentage-of-completion method is computed below. The income to be recognized is determined by relating the costs incurred to date to the total estimated costs of the construction as follows:

	1971		1972		1973
Contract price		$1,500,000		$1,500,000		$1,500,000
Less cost:						
Incurred to date ......$ 350,000		$900,000		$1,365,000	
Estimated to						
complete 1,000,000	1,350,000	460,000	1,360,000	–0–	1,365,000
Income (estimated).....	$ 150,000		$ 140,000		$ 135,000
Income to be recog-					
nized	$ 38,889		$ 92,647		$ 135,000
Less income recog-					
nized to date....,....			38,889		92,647
Net..........................			$ 53,758		$ 42,353

Calculation: 1971 $350,000/$1,350,000 × $150,000 = $38,889; 1972, $900,000/$1,360,000 × $140,000 = $92,647.

The accounting for the duration of the contract would be as follows for the percentage-of-completion method:

Entries:

1. To record cost of construction:

	1971	1972	1973
Construction in			
Process..............350,000		550,000	465,000
Cash, Pay-			
ables, etc.....	350,000	550,000	465,000

2. To record progress billings:

Accounts Receiv-			
able – Construc-			
tion Contract			
Billings 300,000		575,000	625,000
Revenue Billed			
on Construc-			
tion Con-			
tracts...........	300,000	575,000	625,000

3. To record collections:

Cash 270,000		555,000	675,000
Accounts Re-			
ceivable –			
Construc-			
tion Con-			
tract Bill-			
ings	270,000	555,000	675,000

4. To recognize revenue (per computations above):

	1971	1972	1973
Construction in Process..............	38,889	53,758	
Income on Construction Contracts (estimated).........		38,889	53,758
Revenue Billed on Construction Contracts................			1,500,000
Construction in Process....			1,457,647
Income on Construction Contracts...........			42,353

Financial Statement Presentation:

	1971	1972	1973
a) Current assets:			
Accounts receivable — construction contract billings.....................	$30,000	$ 50,000	–0–
Construction in process.................$388,889		$992,647	
Less: Billings on contracts.......... 300,000		875,000	
Cost of incompleted contracts in excess of billings....................	88,889	117,647	–0–
b) Net income (loss)....................	38,889	53,758	$42,353

Accounts receivable — construction contract billings should be reported as a current asset.

The construction contract may provide for retention by the party for whom the contract is being performed of a stated percentage of each progress billing prior to final completion. For example, assume the contract provides for the retention of 5% of each progress billing. In this instance entry No. 2 for 1971 would be:

Accounts Receivable — Construction Contract Billings 285,000
Accounts Receivable — Retained Billings on Contracts (5%)... 15,000
    Billed Revenue on Construction Contracts.................... 300,000

The percentage of completion may be based on estimates of completion developed by construction engineers or architects rather than on the cost incurred basis as illustrated above.

The percentage-of-completion method has gained wide acceptance by the accounting profession, although the procedure must be viewed as applicable only in special circumstances. The principal disadvantage is that it is based on future estimates of costs which are subject to the considerable uncertainty inherent in long-term construction. The *Research Bulletin* of the AICPA includes the following statements relative to accounting for long-term contracts:

It is, however, a generally accepted accounting procedure to accrue revenues under certain types of contracts and thereby recognize profits, on the basis of partial performance, where the circumstances are such that total profit can be estimated with reasonable accuracy and ultimate realization is reasonably assured.[4]

The committee believes that in general when estimates of costs to complete and extent of progress toward completion of long-term contracts are reasonably dependable, the percentage-of-completion method is preferable. When lack of dependable estimates or inherent hazards cause forecasts to be doubtful, the completed-contract method is preferable.[5]

Federal income tax regulations permit the taxpayer to select either method for tax purposes but require consistency in application.

Inventory Reserves

Although recent trends in accounting definitely have been away from the term *reserve* as related to assets, one can still observe a fair number of published statements showing inventory "reserves" of one type or another. In Chapter 8 the "allowance for inventory reduction to market" was introduced in connection with the lower of cost or market procedures. The point was made that use of the term *reserve* in that situation is inappropriate. It will be recalled that this allowance relates to a decrease in market that has *already* taken place. Some companies follow the practice of establishing a "reserve for possible future inventory price decline" in anticipation of an expected *future* drop in market related to goods in inventory.[6] This provision is established by debiting Retained Earnings and crediting the reserve account; hence the provision represents an appropriation of retained earnings and is properly labeled a reserve and should be reported on the balance sheet under owners' equity. This reserve is not charged with losses and is returned to Retained Earnings when the purposes have been served.

Numerous other "reserves" related to inventories can be observed on published financial statements. For example, a recent edition of *Trends and Techniques* illustrated the following "inventory reserves."

1. *Reserve for Future Inventory Price Declines* (discussed above).

---

[4] Committee on Accounting Procedure, AICPA, "Restatement and Revision of Accounting Research Bulletins," *Accounting Research Bulletin No. 43* (New York, 1961), p. 95.

[5] *Accounting Research Bulletin No. 45*, p. 7.

[6] A preferred title would be "appropriation of retained earnings for possible future inventory price decline." Also see Chapter 21. This application is rare in practice.

2. *Reserve for Obsolescence of Inventory.* This account was created through the following entry:

```
Loss on Obsolescence of Inventory.................................................xxx
    Reserve for Obsolescence of Inventory.....................................    xxx
```

The entry properly recorded a current loss, however, the account credited should have been labeled an "allowance" rather than a "reserve." The allowance account would be deducted from the inventory valuation and removed upon disposal of the goods.

3. *Reserve for Reduction of Inventory to Lifo Basis.* This account was used to record the effect of a change in inventory basis. To illustrate, the company employing Fifo changed to Lifo with the following effect:

```
            Inventory on Fifo basis.................................$150,000
            Inventory on Lifo basis.................................  100,000
            Difference — reduction ...............................$ 50,000
```

The following entry was effected:

```
Nonrecurring Loss Due to Change from Fifo to Lifo ...............50,000
    Reserve to Reduce Inventory to Lifo Basis......................    50,000
```

The allowance should be deducted from the related inventory and is removed at the time of disposal of the goods. This procedure represents sound accounting; however, the word *reserve* should not be used in respect to it.

This same situation was illustrated in Chapter 9 (pages 356–57) without utilization of the allowance account; either procedure would accomplish the same results adequately.

4. *Reserve for Replacement of Basic Lifo Inventories.* This reserve was established because of the liquidation of the "normal" Lifo inventory position as illustrated in Chapter 9, inventory liquidation (pages 354 and 355). The procedure utilized was correct except for usage of the term *reserve;* a preferred title for the account would have been Excess of Replacement Cost of Lifo Inventory Temporarily Liquidated.

5. *Reserve for Adjustment of Inventory from Lifo to Fifo Basis.* In this particular case the inventory change gave rise to the following effect:

```
            Inventory — Fifo basis ...................................$250,000
            Inventory — Lifo basis ...................................  150,000
            Difference — increase ...........................$100,000
```

The following entry was made in this particular case:

```
Amount to Increase Inventory from Lifo to Fifo Basis..............100,000
    Reserve for Adjustment of Inventory from Lifo to
        Fifo Basis .................................................................    100,000
```

The debit account was reported as a current asset and the credit account as a reserve under capital. Obviously, the procedure directly violates sound accounting theory and practice. Assuming the change in inventory was justified and the amounts realistic, the entry should have been treated as a correction of prior years' earnings and appropriate terminology should have been employed.

The five illustrations above serve (1) to call attention to the continued misuse of the term *reserve* as an offset or contra to an asset account and (2) to indicate some of the special problems related to inventory adjustments. The inappropriate designation of inventory contra accounts, as reflected above, has not adequately served the principle of full disclosure.

Used, Damaged, and Repossessed Goods

Damaged, deteriorated, and shopworn goods should be carried in inventory at the lower of cost or net realizable value in their present condition. Used merchandise and merchandise received as a result of repossessions or trade-ins should be recorded at their estimated net realizable value. The net realizable value represents the estimated price at which the goods may be disposed of less costs of reconditioning and selling. For example, assume a refrigerator is received as a trade-in and it is estimated that after repairing it can be sold for $85, the inventory valuation might be derived as follows:

Estimated sales price		$85
Less:		
Estimated cost of repairing	$10	
Estimated selling costs	5	15
Inventory Valuation		$70

Many accountants prefer to reduce the valuation further for an estimated "normal profit."

Losses on Firm Purchase Commitments

Contracts frequently are made by a company to purchase a given quantity of specific goods at a fixed price in the future. If the commitment cannot be canceled, in the event of a decline in prices the apparent loss should be recognized in the current period. *Research Bulletin No. 43* of the AICPA states: "Accrued net losses on firm purchase commitments for goods for inventory, measured in the same way as are inventory losses, should, if material, be recognized in the accounts and the amounts thereof separately disclosed in the income statement."[7] In all instances this and similar events should be fully disclosed in the statements (or in footnotes in conformance with the full-disclosure principle.)

---

[7] *Accounting Research Bulletin No. 43*, p. 34.

Reporting Inventories on the Balance Sheet

In conformance with the operating-cycle concept used in defining current assets, inventories are reported on the balance sheet as current assets generally in order of their liquidity, although in some instances considerable time may pass before some of the inventory is realized in cash. Supplies on hand that are charged to selling and general expenses generally are reported as prepaid expenses rather than as inventory. Advances of cash made for future purchase commitments should not be shown as inventory but as a special receivable.

The principle of full disclosure frequently necessitates the inclusion of parenthetical notes concerning inventory. The inventory valuation method used (cost, lower of cost of market, cash realizable value, retail method, etc.) and the inventory flow method (specific cost, average cost, Fifo, Lifo, etc.) should be clearly indicated. If the accounting treatment accorded inventories has been changed, the effect of the change on net income and inventory valuation must be reported. It is advisable to identify the method utilized for tax purposes. If the inventory is pledged as security for a loan, this fact should be disclosed. In addition any unusual items concerning the inventory or any part of it should be explained clearly.

Some companies follow the practice of transferring items from one division of the company to another at a price in excess of actual cost — frequently at a price comparable to what would have to be paid to outside suppliers. This practice generally is the result of accounting for each subdivision of the company as a separate "profit center." Profit-center accounting is an important tool of management control; however, for external reporting purposes, all interdepartmental or interdivisional profits related to transferred goods still held by the entity must be removed.

Merchandise is frequently placed in wholesale or retail outlets "on consignment." A consignment contract reserves the title of the goods for the consignor; the consignee is responsible for their care and remits to the consignor only upon "sale" by the latter. Accordingly, goods out on consignment should be included in the inventory of the consignor and excluded from the inventory of the consignee. Normal transportation costs on consigned goods are a proper addition to inventory cost.

QUESTIONS FOR CLASS DISCUSSION

1. What is the basic assumption implicit in the gross margin method?

2. Approximate the valuation of the ending inventory assuming the following data are available:

Cost of goods available for sale	$100,000
Net sales	150,000
Gross margin rate (on sales)	40%

3. Distinguish between (a) gross margin rate on sales, (b) gross margin rate on cost of goods sold, (c) cost percentage, (d) markup on cost, and (e) markup on sales.

4. List the four principal uses of the gross margin method.

5. Why is it frequently desirable to apply the gross margin method by classes of merchandise?

6. Explain the basic approach in the retail method of estimating inventories. What data must be accumulated in order to apply the retail method?

7. The final inventory estimated by the retail inventory method was $40,000. A physical inventory of the merchandise on hand extended at retail showed $35,000. Suggest possible reasons for the discrepancy.

8. What are the primary uses of the retail method of estimating inventories?

9. Why are markdowns and markdown cancellations excluded in computing the cost ratio in the retail inventory method?

10. Why are return sales and cash discounts on sales treated differently in the retail inventory computations?

11. What adaptations are required to the conventional retail method to approximate *Lifo* results?

12. Explain the essential differences between (a) the completed-contract method and (b) the percentage-of-completion method of accounting for long-term construction contracts.

13. Distinguish between the (a) Allowance for Inventory Reduction to Market and (b) the Reserve for Possible Future Inventory Decline accounts.

14. The Cox Company repossessed a washing machine. It was estimated that after certain reconditioning the machine could be sold for $60. The reconditioning costs were estimated at $12 and selling costs at $6. At what value should the machine be shown while on hand?

DECISION CASE 10-1

Your client, the Brown Agency, sells new and used cars and has a service department. At audit date, April 30, 19A, the used car inventory consisted of four cars.

	Used Car Number			
	1	*2*	*3*	*4*
Allowed on trade-in	$1,700	$2,400	$1,000	$1,400
Overallowance (a)	300	300	200	200
Service department charges for work on car (b)	60	–	40	160
National Auto Dealers Association estimate of market value (at retail):				
At time of trade-in	1,600	2,200	875	1,200
At audit date	1,550	2,200	850	1,150
Probable sale price if sold during May, 19A (c)	1,600	2,150	825	1,300

a) During the year, new cars were being sold at less than list where no trade-in was involved. The amounts in this line represent the discount that would have been allowed on the new car sold had that new car been sold for cash with no trade-in.

b) The service department makes necessary repairs on used cars taken in trades and bills the used car department at cost plus a 33⅓% markup. The amounts in this line are the bills from the service department.

c) With the exception of cars 2 and 4, which are still on hand, the used cars were sold for cash during the first week of May 19A at the amounts shown on this line.

Discuss the various factors which should be considered in assigning a value to the inventory of used cars. Indicate the computations needed to arrive at an acceptable inventory value for each car as of April 30, 19A.

(AICPA adapted)

EXERCISES

Exercise 10–1

The books of Craig Company provided the following information:

Inventory, January 1 ....$ 9,000
Purchases to June 15... 70,000
Net sales to June 15... 93,000

On June 16, the assets of the company were totally destroyed by fire. The insurance company adjuster found that the average rate of gross margin for the past few years had been 33⅓%.

Required:

What was the approximate value of the inventory destroyed assuming the gross margin percentage given was based on (a) sales and (b) cost of goods sold?

Exercise 10–2

You are engaged in the audit of the records of Victor Company. A physical inventory has been taken by the company under your observation, although the extensions have not been completed to determine the valuation of the inventory. The records of the company provide the following data: sales, $400,000; return sales, $6,000; purchases (gross), $229,000; beginning inventory, $60,000; discount on purchases, $2,000; freight-in, $6,000; and purchase returns and allowances, $3,000. The gross margin last period was 32% of net sales; you anticipate that it will be 1% higher (i.e., 33%) for the year under audit. Determine the approximate value of the ending inventory.

Exercise 10–3

Income statement data for Tulsa Company follows:

Beginning inventory..$ 60,000
Purchases... 500,000
Sales 800,000

Required:

Estimate the ending inventory for each of the following independent assumptions:

a) Estimated gross margin on sales, 30%.
b) Estimated gross margin on cost, 100%.

Exercise 10–4

Assume the following data are known for the Mike Company for a particular period:

Sales		$100,000
Initial inventory	$ 10,000	
Purchases	70,000	
Goods Available	$ 80,000	

For each of the separate situations below estimate the final inventory:

a) Markup is 40% on sales.
b) Markup is one fourth on cost.
c) Markup is 60% on sales.
d) Markup is 50% on cost.
e) Markup is 57% on cost.

Exercise 10–5

The Blue Company utilizes the retail method of inventory. At the end of February the records of the company reflected the following:

Purchases for February: At cost, $236,000; at retail, $353,800.
Sales during February, $350,000.
Inventory February 1: At cost, $28,000; at retail, $46,200.

Estimate the ending inventory for February.

Exercise 10–6

The records of the Columbus Department Store showed the following data for Department 20 for January: beginning inventory at cost, $12,000, and $20,000 at selling price; purchases at cost, $152,000, and $286,000 at selling price; sales, $287,000; return sales, $7,000; purchase returns at cost, $4,000, and $6,000 at selling price; and freight-in of $5,000. Determine the approximate valuation of the final inventory utilizing the retail inventory method.

Exercise 10–7

Using the retail inventory method, determine the ending inventory for Rye Retailers at lower of cost or market from the following data:

	Cost	Retail
Inventory (initial)	$ 86,500	$120,000
Purchases	319,500	534,000
Purchases returned	9,000	12,000
Freight-in	6,000	
Additional markups	—	15,000
Markup cancellations	—	7,000
Markdowns	—	8,000
Markdown cancellations	—	3,000
Sales	—	556,000
Sales returned	—	11,000

Exercise 10–8

Assume the following events and transactions with respect to a particular item sold by the Economy Retailers:

Date		Per Unit
(1)	Cost of 10 units purchased	$ 20.00
	Initial markup on cost (50%)	+10.00
	Original sales price	$ 30.00
(2)	Sold 4 units	
(3)	Additional markup	+ 3.00
	Revised sales price	$ 33.00
(4)	Sold one unit	
(5)	Markup cancellation	− 1.00
	Revised sales price	$ 32.00
(6)	Sold one unit	
(7)	Reduction in sales price	− 5.00
	Revised sales price	$ 27.00
(8)	Sold 3 units	
(9)	Markdown cancellation	+ 1.00
	Revised sales price	$ 28.00
(10)	Sold remaining unit(s)	

Required:

Complete the following form to indicate what should be reported to the accounting department for retail inventory purposes.

Date	Description		Units	Per Unit	Retail Amount
(1)	Received	(10 units; cost $20 ea.; markup 50%)	10	$30	$300
(2)	Sales		(4)	30	120
.					
.					
.					
etc.					

Exercise 10–9

Penn Retail Store has just completed the annual physical inventory, which involved counting the goods on hand then pricing them at retail. The inventory valuation derived in this manner amounted to $76,000. The records of the company provide the following data: beginning inventory, $90,000 at retail and $51,000 at cost; purchases (including freight-in and returns), $800,000 at retail and $462,000 at cost; additional markups, $30,000; markup cancellations, $20,000; sales, $823,000; return sales $12,000; and markdowns, $7,000.

Required:

1. Estimate the cost of the ending inventory so as to approximate lower of cost or market.

2. Note any suggested discrepancies and indicate the possible reasons therefor.

Exercise 10–10

The following data were available from the records of the Popular Retail Store with respect to a particular item sold:

	At Cost	At Retail
Purchases	$2,500	$4,050
Additional markups		625
Markup cancellations		25
Sales		4,000
Markdowns		700
Markdown cancellations		200
Initial inventory	200	350

Required:

Estimate the final inventory valuations assuming (*a*) it is to be valued at approximate lower of cost or market and (*b*) it is to be valued at approximate cost.

Exercise 10–11

Ketchum and Cheatum were partners in a construction business, sharing profits 60% and 40%, respectively. They contracted to construct a school building for a flat price of $300,000. When the building was only partially completed, Ketchum died. The work to date had cost $110,400, and it was estimated that an additional $129,600 would be expended in completing the building. Calculate the share of profits earned to date which Ketchum's estate might claim.

Exercise 10–12

The Superior Construction Company entered into a contract to construct a building for a flat fee of $200,000. Construction commenced in 1970 and was completed in 1972. The transactions relating to the contract are summarized below:

	1970	1971	1972
Cost incurred during year	$ 35,200	$36,520	$ 89,280
Estimated costs to complete	124,800	91,280	–0–
Billings and collections during year	34,000	40,000	126,000

Required:

Compute the amount of income to be recognized each year by the Superior Construction Company assuming the percentage-of-completion method is employed.

PROBLEMS

Problem 10–1

The Farmer's Feed Store burned on March 19, 19D. The following information (up to the date of the fire) was taken from the records of the company which were stored in a safe: inventory, January 1, $25,000; sales, $120,000; purchases, $82,000; return sales, $4,000; purchase returns and allowances, $3,000; and freight-in, $6,000. The cost of goods sold and gross margins for the past three years were:

	Cost of Goods Sold	Gross Margin = 22%
19A	$425,000	$105,000
19B	394,550	125,450
19C	428,450	121,550

Required:

Estimate the value of the inventory destroyed by the fire.   19,520

Problem 10–2

The records of Eban Company revealed the following information on September 17, 19A:

Inventory, January 1 19A	$ 42,000
Purchases, January 1 to September 16	295,180
Sales, January 1 to September 16	337,200
Purchase returns and allowances	3,180
Sales returns	1,200
Freight-in	6,000

A disastrous fire completely destroyed the inventory on September 16, 19A, except for goods marked to sell at $5,200 which had an estimated salvage value of $4,000, and for goods in transit to which Eban Company had title, the purchase had been recorded. Invoices recorded on the latter show: merchandise cost, $1,750; and freight-in, $50.

The average rate of gross margin in recent years has been 25%. Compute the approximate fire loss if the gross margin percentage is based on (*a*) selling price and (*b*) cost.

Problem 10–3

The Freedom Company in the past carried inventories at cost. At the end of the current period the inventory was valued at 45% of selling price as a matter of convenience. The current financial statements have been prepared and the inventory sheets destroyed; consequently, you find it impossible to reconstruct the final inventory at actual cost. The following data are available:

Sales	$400,000
Final inventory (at 45% of selling price)............................	18,000
Cost of goods sold..	240,000
Net income	40,000
Beginning inventory (at cost)..	10,000

Required:

Utilizing the data available reconstruct the income statement making any adjustments to the data given that appears appropriate.

Problem 10–4

The Giles Retail Company is in the process of developing a profit plan. The following data were developed for a three-month future period.

a) January 1 planned inventory, $70,000.
b) Average rate of gross margin on sales planned, 22%.

Complete the following profit plan:

	Profit Plan Estimates			
	January	*February*	*March*	*Total*
Sales planned..............................$150,000		$170,000	$180,000	$500,000
Cost of sales:				
Beginning inventory.....................	?	?	?	?
Purchases budget........................$110,000		$130,000	$160,000	$400,000
Total goods available..............	?	?	?	?
Less: Final inventory	?	?	?	?
Cost of sales	?	?	?	?
Gross margin planned.....................	?	?	?	?

Problem 10–5

The records of Oxford Department Store provided the following data for the month of June:

Sales..................................	$685,000	Purchase returns:	
Return sales........................	8,000	At retail	$ 5,000
Additional markups	16,500	At cost	3,900
Markup cancellations...........	6,500	Freight on purchases.............	10,000
Markdowns.........................	6,000	Beginning inventory:	
Purchases:		At cost	51,300
At retail...........................	715,000	At retail	80,000
At cost	414,600	Employee discounts	1,000
		Markdown cancellations	4,000

Required:

Estimate the lower of cost or market valuation of the final inventory by utilizing the retail inventory method.

Problem 10–6

The records of Miami Retailers provided the following data for the year:

	At Retail	At Cost
Inventory January 1	$ 180,000	$105,000
Net purchases	1,312,000	714,000
Freight-in		21,000
Additional markups	14,000	
Markup cancellations	6,000	
Markdowns	10,000	
Sales	1,190,000	
Inventory December 31 (per physical count valued at retail)	265,000	

Required:

1. Calculate the estimated cost (LCM) of the final inventory.

2. Note any discrepancies that are indicated and suggest the possible reasons therefor.

3. What accounting treatment should be accorded the discrepancy (if any)?

Problem 10–7

Craig's Department Store uses the retail inventory method. Data for the year ended January 31, 1972, for one department appear below:

Inventory, January 31, 1971:	
Cost	$ 21,000
Sales price	36,000
Purchases for year ended January 31, 1972 (gross):	
Cost	128,800
Sales price	214,600
Sales for year (gross)	225,000
Freight on merchandise purchased	4,000
Returns:	
Purchases:	
Cost	1,300
Sales price	2,300
Sales	5,000
Additional markups	3,200
Markup cancellations	1,500
Markdowns	4,100
Markdown cancellations	1,200
Discounts (cash):	
Purchases	1,000
Sales	3,000
Employee discounts	1,100

Required:

Estimate the January 31, 1972, inventory valuation utilizing the retail inventory method assuming:

a) Cash discounts are treated as financial items. 15,860 + 26,000

b) Cash discounts are treated as reductions in gross purchases and sales.
15,756 + 26,000

Problem 10–8

The following monthly data relating to Department 5 were taken from the records of Dottie's, a ladies' ready-to-wear store: inventory March 1 at retail, $70,000, at cost, $46,500; sales, $768,900; return sales, $5,000; purchases at retail, $790,000, at cost, $515,600; freight on purchases, $12,000; purchase discounts, $2,500; special discounts on goods purchased by employees, $1,000; purchase returns at retail, $6,000, at cost, $4,000; additional markups, $14,000; markup cancellations, $8,000; markdowns, $7,000, markdown cancellations, $3,000; and loss of merchandise through spoilage and breakage, $1,100 (at retail). Estimate the cost of the final inventory for the department utilizing conventional retail inventory procedures. Assume cash discounts are treated as reductions of sales and purchases.

Problem 10–9

The Goode Department Store had been employing the conventional retail inventory method for some years. The management decided to continue the retail inventory method but with an adaptation to last-in, first-out. After some investigation the decision was made to change as of January 1, 1970. Using the data given below you are to compute the final inventories for the years 1970, 1971, and 1972, and to provide any adjusting entries required by the change in method.

a) The 1969 retail records showed the following:

	Cost	Retail
Beginning inventory	$ 32,000	$ 54,000
Purchases (net)	493,400	680,000
Net additional markups		6,000
Sales (net)		670,000
Net markdowns		10,000

b) Data for 1970–72:

	1970		1971		1972	
	Cost	Retail	Cost	Retail	Cost	Retail
Purchases (net)	$501,120	$689,000	$497,000	$711,000	$529,250	$722,000
Net additional markups		16,000		10,000		10,000
Net markdowns		9,000		11,000		7,000
Sales (net)		683,900		703,350		732,470
Applicable price index (1969 = 100)		103		105		108

Problem 10–10

Wonder Builders, Incorporated, entered into a contract to construct an office building for the Stecht Company for a flat fee of $100,000. Construction commenced on March 15, 1971, and was completed on December 7, 1972. Wonder Builders' fiscal year ends on December 31. Transactions by Wonder Builders relating to the contract are summarized below:

	Cumulative	
	Dec. 31, 1971	Dec. 31, 1972
Costs incurred to date	$32,000	$ 82,000
Estimated costs to complete	48,000	–0–
Progress billings to date	30,000	100,000
Progress collections to date	27,000	100,000

Required:

1. Give entries on the contractor's books assuming the completed-contract method is employed.

2. Give entries on the contractor's books assuming the percentage-of-completion method is employed (based on costs).

3. For each method indicate amounts to be shown on the balance sheet and income statement for each year.

Problem 10–11

Barkley and Cable Construction Company entered into a contract to build a dam for the city of Smithville for a flat fee of $900,000. The contract specified that the construction company be paid as the work progressed. The contract further specified that the engineers representing each party would develop estimates of percentage completion on the 15th of each month for the billing due at the end of the month. Barkley and Cable close their books each December 31. Work commenced under the contract on September 15, 1970, and was completed on March 30, 1972. Construction activities are summarized below by year:

1970 – Construction costs incurred during the year, $172,800; estimated costs to complete, $547,200; and collection from the city during the year, $170,000.

1971 – Construction costs incurred during the year, $385,450; estimated costs to complete, $166,750; and collections from the city during the year, $390,000.

1972 – Construction costs incurred during the year, $171,750. Since the contract was completed the remaining balance was collected per contract.

Since there was immediate collection on billings to the city the company did not record a receivable for "billings on contract."

Required:

1. Give entries for each year on the books of Barkley and Cable assuming income is recognized only upon completion of the contract. Indicate the amounts that would be reported on the balance sheet and income statement each year.

2. Give entries for each year on the books of Barkley and Cable assuming income is recognized each year in relationship of costs incurred to total estimated cost of the contract. Indicate the amounts that would be reported on the balance sheet and income statement each period.

Problem 10–12

The Richards Engineering Company entered into a contract to construct a bridge for a contract price of $660,000. Payments were to be received on the basis of approved engineering estimates of percentage of completion. The contract specified that 10% of each progress billing would be retained until final completion of the contract. Payment of a billing (less the 10%) is to be within five days after submission. The contract further specified that Richards would be advanced $50,000 prior to the start of construction for preparatory work; this amount to be deducted equally during the first two years.

Transactions relating to the contract are summarized below:

1970 — Advance received, $50,000; construction costs incurred during the year, $120,000; estimated costs to complete, $480,000; retention per contract, $9,500.

1971 — Construction costs incurred during the year, $246,000; estimated costs to complete, $244,000; retention per contract, $22,000; and collections during the year, $173,000.

1972 — Construction costs incurred during the year, $239,000. The remaining billings were submitted by October 1 and final collections completed on November 30.

Required:

1. Give entries for each year that would be made on the books of the contractor assuming the completed contract method is employed. Show amounts that would be reported on the financial statements for each year.

2. Give entries for each year that would be made on the books of the contractor assuming the percentage-of-completion method is employed. Show amounts that would be reported on the financial statements for each year.

chapter 11 | # Long-Term Investments in Stocks

Accounting for long-term (permanent) investments in stocks is discussed in this chapter. Long-term investments in bonds are covered in Chapter 17; investment funds are discussed in Chapter 15.

It was noted in Chapter 6 (cash and temporary investments) that investments are classed as current assets only where (a) they are readily marketable and (b) there is a clear intention of management to use them for working capital purposes. Investments not meeting these two requisites are classified as long term or permanent. Long-term investments are reported under a separate balance sheet caption entitled "Investments and Funds" which should appear between current and fixed assets. In conformity with the *cost principle*, cost is the basis of valuation for recording a permanent investment at date of acquisition; original cost may be modified as a result of amortization, receipt of stock rights, assessments, liquidating dividends, etc. Subsequent to initial recording, long-term investments in the stock of another entity may be accounted for under one of several methods. The appropriate method to be utilized subsequent to acquisition depends upon (a) the type of stock, (b) the number of shares owned (percent of ownership), and (c) the characteristics of the entities involved.

Cost of Long-Term Investments at Acquisition

Shares of stock may be acquired on various security markets. When purchased outright the full cost includes the basic cost of the security plus brokerage fees, excise taxes, and any other transfer costs incurred by the purchaser. Stocks may be purchased for cash, "on margin," or on a subscription basis. When stock is acquired on margin, only part of the purchase price is paid initially, the balance being borrowed. The stock should be recorded at its full cost and the liability to the lender should be recognized. A stock subscription or agreement to buy the stock of a corporation gives rise to an asset represented by the stock and a liability for the amount to be paid. Any interest paid on a subscription contract should be treated as interest expense and not capitalized as part of the cost of the investment.

When noncash considerations (property or services) are given for long-term investments the value assigned to the securities should be (1) the fair market value of the consideration given or (2) the fair market value of the investment whichever is more definitely determinable. Determination of either value in the case of unlisted or closely held securities being exchanged for property for which no established market value exists may force resort to appraisals or estimates.

Securities frequently may be purchased between regular interest or dividend dates. The general accounting rule is that interest is accrued but dividends are rarely accrued. In the case of a purchase of stock on which the issuing corporation has been regularly paying dividends and when the stock is cumulative, the correct treatment is debatable. The authors would not accrue dividends (even in this case) and thereby ignore the so-called accrued dividends because dividends legally do not accrue. Ordinarily the price paid when stock is purchased does not include any specific item of accrued dividends, except perhaps where preferred stock is issued initially between dividend dates. In this unusual instance an exception may be justified and the accrued dividend recognized. Theoretically dividends should be recognized when stock is purchased between the declaration date and record date (ex-dividend date).[1]

Special Cost Problems

A purchase of two or more classes of securities for a single lump sum calls for allocation of the cost according to relative sales values

---

[1] The price of a listed stock (especially preferred) tends to rise as the regular dividend date approaches and to decline by approximately the amount of the dividend as soon as the stock goes "ex dividends." Prices of such stocks are, however, subject to many variables which may somewhat obscure these pre- and post-dividend movements.

of the several classes. For example, if a block of Security A purchased alone would cost $1,000 and a block of Security B purchased separately would cost $2,000, one third of the total cost of a combination purchase of the two would be allocated to A and two thirds to B whether the combined price was $3,000 or some other amount. In case one class of securities has a known market value and the other does not, the known market value is used for that class and the remainder of the lump-sum price is allocated to the others. If neither has a known market value it is better to defer any apportionment until evidence of at least one value becomes sufficiently clear.

Securities sometimes are acquired in exchange for other securities. The new securities should be recorded at their fair market value or at the fair market value of those given up at the time of the exchange, whichever is more clearly determinable. To illustrate an exchange of securities, assume that each holder of a share of $100 par value preferred stock in AB Corporation becomes entitled to receive in exchange five shares of no-par common stock of the company. An investor who had paid $6,000 for 50 shares of preferred stock makes the exchange. At the time of the exchange the no-par common shares were selling at $27. The exchange would be recorded as follows:[2]

Investment in No-Par Common Stock of AB Corporation ($27 × 250 shares)..6,750		
Investment in Preferred Stock of AB Corporation—	6,000	
Extraordinary Gain—Conversion of Stock Investment...........	750	

Correct accounting requires that each lot or block of securities purchased must be identified separately as to number of shares (or other securities) and cost per share. In effect, this requires the maintenance of inventory records with respect to securities in order that they may be "costed out" upon disposition. For example, if 10 shares of X Corporation stock are purchased at $150 per share and later an additional 30 shares are purchased at $200 per share, the subsequent sale of 5 shares at $180 per share would pose a cost identification problem. If the five shares can be identified as a part of the first purchase, a gain of $30 per share should be recognized. Alternatively, if they came from the second purchase, a loss of $20 per share should be recognized. If an averaging procedure were applied, the result would be a loss per share computed as follows:

---

[2] A more extended discussion of the exchange of securities is presented in Chapter 17: an alternate treatment whereby no gain or loss is recognized also is presented. The authors are of the opinion that the treatment illustrated here is preferable, assuming materiality.

First purchase ....10 shares @ $150 = $1,500
Second purchase.....30 shares @ $200 =   6,000
          Total   40 $7,500

Average cost per share $7,500 ÷ 40 shares = $187.50
Sales price of 5 shares (per share)   =   180.00
          Loss per Share...............................$ 7.50

Identification of shares sold ordinarily is not difficult. However, where blocks of shares have been transferred through an estate, where the issuing corporation has exchanged substitute securities for those originally purchased, or the like, an identification problem can arise. Federal tax laws require use of "first-in, first-out" where specific identification is not made. Use of either Fifo or an *average cost* procedure is acceptable from the standpoint of accounting theory.

Accounting Subsequent to Acquisition

In accounting for stock investments subsequent to acquisition a careful distinction must be made between voting common stock and other types of stock. Fundamentally, long-term investments in the *voting common stock* of another corporation reflect one of two possible situations:

1. Noncontrolling interest. This is the situation where the investing company does not own enough of the voting shares of the other corporation to exercise a controlling influence over it. Ownership of less than 50% of the outstanding shares, in the absence of other compelling factors, would represent a noncontrolling interest.

2. Controlling interest. In this situation the investing company owns enough of the voting shares of the other corporation to effectively control it. Obviously, ownership of over 50% of the outstanding shares would assure control. On the other hand, circumstances frequently exist where ownership of something less than 50% may be a controlling interest. Factors such as number of shares outstanding, dispersion of the shares, and stockholder participation bear on the point at which a "controlling interest" is attained. The accounting profession has found it very difficult to develop an operational definition of control below 50% of the stock.

The issuance of *APB Opinion No. 18* (March, 1971) had a significant impact on the accounting for long-term investments. In view of *Opinion No. 18* (and certain other pronouncements) the accounting for long-term investments in *stocks* may be outlined as follows:

	Method of
Situation	*Accounting*

Noncontrolling ownership interest:
  A. Investments in stocks other than voting common stock ....Cost
  B. *Noncontrolling* interest in voting common stock if below   Cost or
     20% ownership interest in the outstanding stock ....Market Value
  C. *Noncontrolling* interest in voting common stock if 50%
     or less down to and including 20% ownership interest
     in the outstanding stock (investor-investee relationship) ....Equity

Controlling ownership interest:
  D. *Controlling* interest in voting common stock, but for
     special reasons not appropriate for consolidation
     (unconsolidated subsidiary)[3] ....Equity
  E. *Controlling* interest in voting common stock (parent-
     subsidiary relationship); usually over 50% ownership   Consolidated
     interest in the outstanding voting common stock..........................Basis

Accounting for Noncontrolling Ownership Interests

When a stock investment represents a noncontrolling interest, one of three accounting approaches must be utilized subsequent to acquisition: (1) cost, (2) equity, or (3) market. We will consider each of these approaches and indicate when they are appropriate.

Cost Method. Under this approach a long-term investment is initially recorded and reported at cost; subsequently it is carried and reported at cost. Unlike temporary investments, long-term investments are not subject to lower of cost or market. Minor declines in market values are disregarded; however, significant and permanent declines are recorded as an extraordinary loss. Dividends are recorded as investment income. Dividend procedures ordinarily call for recognition of three dates: (1) date of declaration, (2) date of record, and (3) date of payment. No two of them coincide except in the case of smaller corporations. The following is typical of the language used to announce dividends: "At their meeting of February 17, 1971, the directors declared a regular quarterly dividend on outstanding common stock of $1 per share payable on April 15, 1971, to stockholders of record at the close of business on March 31, 1971." A stockholder owning 400 common shares of this company should make the following entry in February:

Dividends Receivable 400	
Dividend Income...	400

To record right to receive a quarterly dividend of $1 per share on X common payable April 15, 1971.

---

[3] An unconsolidated subsidiary is one in which the parent has a controlling interest (usually over 50%) but which does not qualify for consolidation because it is not economically related and, therefore, not capable of meaningful assimilation in a consolidated statement. For example, banks, insurance companies, and finance companies, even though controlled, are not generally consolidated with the accounts of a manufacturing entity.

The receipt of the cash on date of payment (April 15) would be recorded as follows:

Cash 400
    Dividends Receivable   400
    To record receipt of cash dividend on X common stock.

Because the lag between declaration and payment dates ordinarily is short, and because the dividend is not taxable as income until received, many investors do not record dividends until the cash is received. In this instance Cash would be debited and Dividend Income credited. The authors already have indicated disapproval of the accruing of *undeclared* dividends no matter how regular past dividends have been and no matter what cumulative features the stock may have. Once a *cash* or *property* dividend is declared, however, a definite receivable is created insofar as the stockholders of record are concerned.

Dividends occasionally are paid with some medium (asset) other than cash, in which case they are referred to as *property dividends.* (See next section for discussion of stock dividends.) When property dividends are paid, the fair market value of the property received becomes the basis for recording the dividend by the recipient. Because they represent divisible units of uniform value, securities of other corporations (held as an investment) may be used as the payment medium of property dividends. In such cases, in order to effect equitable settlement among holders of small blocks of shares and among holders of other than the share-multiple required to be owned to receive a dividend share, fractional (part) payments usually are made in cash (also see Chapter 20).

Occasionally an investor receives a dividend that is entirely, or in part, a *liquidating dividend* (see Chapter 20). In such instances the investor should reduce the investment account for the amount of the liquidating portion of the dividend and credit investment income for the balance. Liquidating dividends received in the form of noncash assets generally should be recorded at the fair market value of the assets received.

Dividend and interest income from investments should be reported as *nonoperating income* (except in the case of a financial institution, holding company, or the like). Gains or losses from the disposition of investments should be set out separately on the income statement as *extraordinary items.*

In reflecting significant and relatively permanent declines in market values of long-term investments, the credit to record the decreased valuation may be made to an account entitled Allowance to Reduce Investments to Market Value rather than directly to the investment account, so as to preserve cost in the latter account. For example, if securities which cost $200,000 have declined to a market value of $175,000, reflection of these events in the accounts would be recorded as follows:

1. To record purchase of the stock:

Investment in Common Stock of K Company 200,000
    Cash   200,000

2. To record subsequent decline in market value:

Loss in Market Value of Investments.................................. 25,000
    Allowance to Reduce Investments to Market Value........   25,000

Such an *unrealized loss* cannot be claimed as an income tax deduction. The loss should be reported as an extraordinary item on the income statement and the allowance account should be subtracted from the investment account on the balance sheet. When investments are sold, realized gains and losses resulting from differences between the amount received for investments and their carrying values should be recognized in the accounts. To illustrate, assume the $200,000 investment for which the $25,000 market adjustment was made (above) is sold for $170,000. The recognized loss for accounting purposes would be $5,000. The sale would be recorded as follows:

Cash 170,000
Allowance to Reduce Investment to Market Value 25,000
Loss on Sale of Investment 5,000
    Investment in Common Stock of K Company   200,000

Note: In Chapter 6, with respect to temporary investments, a preference for an alternate treatment was expressed. The treatment illustrated above is preferred for *long-term investments* because typically the allowance relates to a single security and seldom arises.

If the market value rises in a subsequent period, consistency and theory would suggest that the allowance account be reduced and a gain reported. Generally subsequent gains in the market value are not recognized because of conservatism and the concept of lower of cost or market. There is increasing support for applying the concept of "fair value" accounting to all investments—current and long-term— on the basis that the decision-making needs of the user are better served.

In the light of *APB Opinion No. 18* (and certain other pronouncements), the cost method would be applied to all investments other than those that have been singled out for special treatment; these were indicated on page 415. The cost and equity methods are compared on p. 422 utilizing a common set of assumed data.

Market Value Method. This method requires, after acquisition, that the balance in the investment account be adjusted from cost to "fair value" which then becomes the carrying value for subsequent accounting. In the case of marketable securities, fair value is best determined by reference to the quoted market of the securities;

generally this is a readily obtainable, objective measurement from outside the entity. Dividends are recorded as investment income in the same manner as under the cost method. The change in the carrying value of the investment at the end of each period is reflected as (*a*) a gain or loss for the period or (*b*) an unrealized item in owners' equity. To illustrate, assume Company A purchased 3,000 shares (10%) of common stock of Company B for $50 per share and that the indicated events transpired over a three-year period:

a) Year 1—Purchased 3,000 shares of common stock in Company B, $50 per share:

```
Investment in Common Stock of Company B ......................150,000
    Cash ...................................................................................            150,000
```

b) Year 1—Company B reported profits of $20,000:

No entry required.

c) End of Year 1—Market value of the 3,000 shares, $55 per share:

```
Investment in Common Stock of Company B ...................... 15,000
    Gain/Loss on Marketable Securities (market
        appreciation)° .....................................................            15,000
```
° No distinction is assumed between realized and unrealized gains and losses.

d) End of Year 2—Company B reported profits of $22,000:

No entry required.

e) Year 2—Cash dividends paid by Company B, $10,000:

```
Cash ($10,000 × 10%)..................................................... 1,000
    Investment Income (dividends) ..................................            1,000
```

f) Year 3—Sold 1,000 of the shares at $54 per share:

```
Cash............................................................................ 54,000
Gain/Loss on Marketable Securities.................................. 1,000
    Investment in Common Stock of Company B
        (1,000 × $55)........................................................            55,000
```

Numerous arguments have been advanced in favor of and against the valuation of marketable securities at fair value. The principal arguments against it are: (*a*) it violates the cost principle and places on the balance sheet questionable and transitory values that tend to mislead the user, (*b*) it introduces another variance between book and tax values, (*c*) it violates the realization principle since revenue is recognized on market changes rather than on sale, and (*d*) it introduces a possible "Yo-Yo" effect on net income. In contrast, the proponents disagree with the first two points and further argue that (*a*) market values are much more relevant information for decision making by the user, (*b*) it avoids "managed" earnings, (*c*) stock yield including both dividends and appreciation should be reported on the income statement each period since that best reflects what is happening to the investment, and (d) investors make decisions on the basis of present and future values as opposed to historical costs.

The market method poses several serious problems; among them are the following:

1. Determination of fair value. In the case of a thin market, a large block of stock may be overvalued if the price per share prevailing at a given time is simply multiplied by the number of shares held. Additionally, many seriously question the realism of utilizing a price per share on a given day (last day of the period). Strong arguments have been made for utilization of some form of average price per share.

2. Reporting the market gain or loss. Many take the position that the market gain or loss should be viewed as "unrealized" and reported as an unrealized increment in owners' equity. The gain or loss would later be reported through the income statement as "realized" upon disposal of the investment. In contrast, realism, logic, and perhaps theory suggest that market gains and losses should be reported on the income statement in the period in which they occurred. In the illustration immediately above, this position was assumed. In contrast, if the market changes were accounted for as unrealized, the above entries would be changed as follows:

Entry (c):

```
Investment in Stock of Company B.......................................15,000
    Unrealized Market Gain on Investments (owners'
        equity) ...................................................................        15,000
```

Entry (f):

```
Cash ...............................................................................54,000
Unrealized Market Gain on Investments............................. 5,000
    Investment in Common Stock of Company B....................        55,000
    Gain on Sale of Investments (realized)...........................         4,000
```

For several years a large majority of the financial institutions have utilized the market value method in accounting for certain marketable securities. However, they have tended to account for the market gain or loss as unrealized. The APB currently is considering an Opinion which, it is anticipated, will require that marketable equity securities be accounted for under the market value method and that both realized and unrealized gains and losses be reported on the income statement in the period in which they transpire.[4]

Equity Method. Under this method a particular economic relationship between the two parties — the investor in voting common stock and the investee — is recognized. At date of acquisition the investment is recorded at cost; subsequently the investment account

---

[4] This position by the authors is based upon information disseminated by the APB.

is adjusted each period for the investor's share of the accumulated earnings (less dividends) of the investee. *APB Opinion No. 18* (The Equity Method of Accounting for Investments in Common Stock) stated that investors should use the equity method in accounting for "investments in common stock of all unconsolidated subsidiaries (foreign as well as domestic)" and also for all investments in common stock where the "investment in voting stock gives it the ability to exercise significant influence over operating and financial policies of an investee even though the investor holds 50% or less of the voting stock." The Opinion also states that "an investment (direct or indirect) of 20% or more of the voting stock of an investee should lead to a presumption that in absence of evidence to the contrary an investor has the ability to exercise significant influence over an investee."[5] *Opinion No. 18* sets forth procedures for applying the equity method; among them are the following:

a. Intercompany profits and losses should be eliminated until realized by the investor or investee as if a subsidiary, corporate joint venture or investee company were consolidated.
b. A difference between the cost of an investment and the amount of underlying equity in net assets of an investee should be accounted for as if the investee were a consolidated subsidiary.
c. The investment(s) in common stock should be shown in the balance sheet of an investor as a single amount, and the investor's share of earnings or losses of an investee(s) should ordinarily be shown in the income statement as a single amount except for the extraordinary items as specified in (d) below.
d. The investor's share of extraordinary items and its share of prior-period adjustments reported in the financial statements of the investee in accordance with *APB Opinion No. 9* should be classified in a similar manner unless they are immaterial in the income statement of the investor.
e. A transaction of an investee of a capital nature that affects the investor's share of stockholders' equity of the investee should be accounted for as if the investee were a consolidated subsidiary.
f. Sales of stock of an investee by an investor should be accounted for as gains or losses equal to the difference at the time of sale between selling price and carrying amount of the stock sold.

Thus, under the equity method the accounting procedure may be outlined as follows:

1. At acquisition of the investment, the investor records the stock purchase at cost.

---

[5] The equity method gives the same overall results on the financial statements as would consolidation procedures discussed in the next section; as a consequence it is frequently referred to as "one-line consolidation." Recognition and amortization of goodwill as well as intercompany transactions must be accounted for.

2. Subsequent to acquisition, each period the investor —
  a. Records his proportionate share of the investee's profits by debiting the investment account and crediting investment income. For a loss the investment account would be credited and investment loss debited.
  b. Records his proportionate share of any dividends declared by the investee by debiting dividends receivable and crediting the investment account.
  c. Records amortization of any *purchased goodwill* that was implicit in the purchase transaction. The debit should be to investment income and the credit to the investment account.
  d. Records depreciation on any increase in depreciable assets implicit in the purchase transaction. The debit should be to investment income and the credit to the investment account.
3. Upon sale, gain or loss is the difference between sales price and carrying value at date of sale.

To illustrate, assume that on January 1, 19A, Company R purchased 2,000 shares (20%) of the outstanding voting common stock of Company S for $300,000. At that date the balance sheet for Company S reflected the following book values:

Assets not subject to depreciation	$ 550,000
Assets subject to depreciation (net)	500,000
Total Assets	$1,050,000
Liabilities	50,000
Common stock (10,000 shares)	900,000
Retained earnings	100,000
Total Equities	$1,050,000

It was estimated that the assets subject to depreciation had a fair market value at date of acquisition of the stock of $700,000; consequently the *purchased* goodwill amounted to $60,000, viz:

Purchase price (for 20% ownership interest)	$300,000
Purchased book value ($1,000,000 × .20)	200,000
Difference	$100,000
Composition of the difference:	
Increase to market value of assets subject to depreciation ($700,000 − $500,000).20	$ 40,000
Goodwill purchased $300,000 − ($1,200,000 × .20)	60,000
	$100,000

The remaining life of the assets is assumed to be 10 years and goodwill is to be amortized over 40 years. At the end of 19A, Company S reported a net income of $110,000, including a $30,000 extraordinary gain. At year-end Company S declared a $50,000 dividend. The following presents the journal entries for acquisition and transactions during 19A under both the cost method and the equity method for Company R:[6]

a) To record purchase of 2,000 shares of Company S stock as a long-term investment:

Cost Method:

> Investment in Stock of Company S...................................300,000
>   Cash.. 300,000

Equity Method:

> Investment in Stock of Company S...................................300,000
>   Cash.. 300,000

b) To record profits of Company S (investee):

Cost Method:

> No entry

Equity Method:

> Investment in Stock of Company S° 22,000
>   Investment Income (ordinary)...................................... 16,000
>   Investment Income (extraordinary).............................. 6,000
>
> ° Computations: Ordinary: .20($80,000) = $16,000
>   Extraordinary: .20($30,000) = 6,000

c) To record dividends declared by Company S (investee):

Cost Method:

> Dividends Receivable° 10,000
>   Dividend Income.. 10,000
>
> ° Computation: .20($50,000) = $10,000

Equity Method:

> Dividends Receivable.. 10,000
>   Investment in Stock of Company S.............................. 10,000

d) To record amortization of implied goodwill (40 years):

Cost Method:

> Not recognized

Equity Method:

> Investment Income (ordinary)° 1,500
>   Investment in Stock of Company S.............................. 1,500
>
> ° Computation: $60,000 ÷ 40 years = $1,500

---

[6] This illustration assumes that the $700,000 is a valid estimate; the book value did not represent fair value. See Chapter 14 for a discussion of the amortization of intangibles.

e) To record depreciation on implicit asset increment (10 years):

Cost Method:

Not recognized

Equity Method:

Investment Income (ordinary)° 4,000
    Investment in Stock of Company S.............................   4,000

  ° Computation: (.20 × $200,000) ÷ 10 = $4,000.

	Cost Method	Equity Method
Recapitulation:		
Ending balance in investment account.................$300,000		$306,500
Net income effect on Company R:		
Ordinary income 10,000		10,500
Extraordinary items .... −0−		6,000

Consolidated Statements

When a *controlling interest* is acquired by one company in a different corporation, a special relationship is thereby created between the investor (parent company) and the controlled corporation (subsidiary). Accountants have long recognized that this economic relationship calls for special accounting and reporting. Typically in such cases, the parent carries the investment account at *either* the cost or equity method as discussed above. Significantly, however, the financial statements (income statement, balance sheet, statement of changes in financial position, etc.) are prepared on a *consolidated basis*. It is important to observe that whether the cost or equity method is utilized in the accounts of the parent company the *resultant consolidated financial statement is the same.* A work sheet approach is utilized for "converting" the amounts from the two sets of records (parent and subsidiary) to a single set of data to be reflected in the consolidated financial statement. "These statements are essentially summations of the assets, liabilities, revenues, and expenses of the individual affiliates, calculated on the basis of transactions with *nonaffiliates;* the statement formats and the account classifications parallel those of a single corporation."[7] Consolidated statements reflect all of the entities as a single economic unit. "There is a presumption that consolidated statements . . . are usually necessary for a fair presentation when one of the companies in the group directly or indirectly has a controlling financial interest in the other companies."[8] The criteria for including a subsidiary in the consolidated statements are:[9]

---

[7] Charles H. Griffin, Thomas H. Williams, and Kermit D. Larson, *Advanced Accounting* (rev. ed.; Homewood, Ill.: Richard D. Irwin, Inc., 1971).

[8] AICPA *Accounting Research Bulletin No. 51*, August 1959.

[9] Adapted from Griffin, Williams, and Larson, op. cit., p. 211.

1. The parent corporation must have the ability to govern, or effectively regulate, the subsidiary corporation's managerial decisions.
2. The parent must be so related to the subsidiary that the economic results of the subsidiary will accrue to the parent (allowing for allocations to the minority shareholders of the subsidiary).
3. Expectation of continuity of control.
4. The degree of existing restrictions upon the availability of earnings of the subsidiary to the parent (frequently a problem with foreign subsidiaries).
5. The general coincidence of accounting periods.
6. Degree of heterogeneity in the operations of the parent and the subsidiary.

Although each affiliate (parent and subsidiaries) keeps separate books and prepares separate financial statements, these individualized statements do not present a comprehensive report of the *economic unit* as a whole. Since the entire economic unit is under one management (and one group of stockholders), a financial report for that unit is essential to meet the needs of owners, creditors, and management. When a subsidiary is less than 100% owned, there is a group of minority shareholders (minority interest) to be recognized in the consolidated financial statements.

The essential steps in developing consolidated financial statements can be summarized as follows:[10]

a) The assets and liabilities of the subsidiary are substituted for the investment account as reflected on the books of the parent. This is accomplished by "eliminating" the owner equity accounts of the subsidiary against the investment account of the parent.
b) Elimination of intercompany receivables and payables.
c) Elimination of intercompany revenues, expenses, gains, and losses.
d) Elimination of other intercompany items.
e) Adjustments on the work sheet are made to reflect certain acquisition effects that differ from the book values.
f) The remaining revenues and expenses of the parent and subsidiary are combined to derive a consolidated income statement.
g) The assets and liabilities of the parent and subsidiary are combined to derive a consolidated balance sheet.
h) Utilize similar procedures to develop other desired financial statements on a consolidated basis.

---

[10] It is important to realize that these steps refer to work sheet entries and to the resultant financial statements and not to the books of accounts of the respective entities which are continued as the records of separate legal entities.

Consolidated financial statements are commonly prepared (*a*) at the date of acquisition of a controlling interest (balance sheet only) and (*b*) for each accounting period subsequent to acquisition (income statement, balance sheet, etc.).

Consolidated Statements at Date of Acquisition

Preparation of consolidated statements is facilitated by use of a *consolidation work sheet*. The work sheet provides for the data on each entity being consolidated and for the necessary eliminations and adjustments.[11] The preparation of consolidated statements under a variety of assumptions will be illustrated by utilizing the following series of cases:[12]

Consolidation at date of acquisition:

Case A: Parent company acquisition of 100% of subsidiary shares at a cost equal to subsidiary book value.

Case B: Parent company acquisition of 80% of subsidiary shares at a cost above book value (no goodwill).

Case C: Parent company acquisition of 80% of subsidiary shares at a cost above book value (goodwill).

Case D: Parent company acquisition of 80% of subsidiary shares at a cost below book value.

Consolidation subsequent to date of acquisition:

Case E: Parent company acquisition of 100% of subsidiary shares at book value (continuation of Case A).

Case F: Parent company acquisition of 80% of subsidiary shares at a cost above book value (continuation of Case C).

Case A.   Parent acquisition of 100% of subsidiary at book value. Assume Company A purchased, on the market, all of the outstanding shares of Company B on January 1, 19A, for $70,000 when the balance sheet of each company reflected the following (summarized):

	Company A (parent)	Company B (subsidiary)
Current assets	$200,000	$ 30,000
Fixed assets (net)	400,000	70,000
Total	$600,000	$100,000
Liabilities	$ 50,000	$ 30,000
Common stock	400,000	60,000
Retained earnings	150,000	10,000
	$600,000	$100,000

---

[11] All illustrations except one (Illustration 11–5) will be limited to the work sheet since the resultant statements can be taken directly therefrom and are cast in the standard format.

[12] Each case will assume that the acquisition is a "purchase"; the alternative situation known as a "pooling of interests" will be discussed in the next section.

Illustration 11-1

Case A — Work Sheet to Develop Consolidated Balance Sheet at Acquisition
Company A and Its Subsidiary, Company B (100% owned), at January 1, 19A

	At Book Value		Eliminations		
	Company A°	Company B	Debit	Credit	Consolidated
Current assets............	$130,000	$ 30,000			$160,000
Investment in					
Company B (100%)	70,000			(a) 70,000	
Fixed assets (net)........	400,000	70,000			470,000
Total..............	$600,000	$100,000			$630,000
Liabilities..................	$ 50,000	$ 30,000			$ 80,000
Common stock					
Company A	400,000				400,000
Company B		60,000	(a) 60,000		
Retained earnings					
Company A	150,000				150,000
Company B		10,000	(a) 10,000		
Total................	$600,000	$100,000			$630,000

° After recording the purchase entry.

Note: Since the subsidiary is 100% owned, there is no minority interest to be reflected.

At date of purchase, Company A (parent) would make this entry:

Investment in Common Stock of Company B 70,000
    Cash...   70,000

Immediately after the purchase a consolidated balance sheet is to be developed; a work sheet to combine the amounts and to resolve the eliminations could be prepared as shown in Illustration 11-1. In view of this simple situation there is only one entry on the work sheet, that is, to eliminate the investment account as reflected on the parent's books against the owners' equity reflected on the subsidiary books.

Case B. Parent acquisition of 80% of subsidiary above book value. Cases B, C, and D will utilize the same set of basic data. Assume Company P (parent) acquired 80% of the outstanding stock of Company S (subsidiary) on January 1, 19A, when the balance sheet of each company reflected the following:

	Company P (parent)	Company S (subsidiary)
Current assets..	$300,000	$ 60,000
Fixed assets	500,000	80,000
Total	$800,000	$140,000
Liabilities	$ 90,000	$ 30,000
Common stock..	600,000	100,000
Retained earnings	110,000	10,000
	$800,000	$140,000

Assume further that the purchase price was $96,000 for 80% of the outstanding shares; therefore, Company P would make this entry:

Investment in Common Stock of Company S 96,000
   Cash   96,000

The purchase may be analyzed as follows:

Purchase price $96,000
Book value purchased ($110,000 × .80) 88,000
   Differential (between purchase price and book value) ....$ 8,000

In the case of a "purchase," as in this instance, the *differential* must be accounted for as (*a*) an upward adjustment of the subsidiary assets to fair value and/or (*b*) purchased goodwill (preferably "cost of investment in excess of fair value of identifiable assets"). In this case we will assume the differential represents an upward adjustment of fixed assets to fair value.

The consolidation work sheet is shown in Illustration 11–2 (Case B). The entries on the work sheet are:

(a) To eliminate the parent's investment account balance against the owners' equity of the subsidiary on a proportionate ownership basis. Observe that since the purchase was not at book value that the *differential* must be recognized, viz:

Common Stock ($100,000 × 80%)...80,000
Retained Earnings ($10,000 × 80%)...................................... 8,000
Differential... 8,000
   Investment in Common Stock of Company S   96,000

(b) The differential is "apportioned" on the basis of data given: in this case to increase the fixed assets to fair value, viz:

Fixed Assets...8,000
   Differential   8,000

Obviously, in subsequent periods depreciation on this increase, if it relates to depreciable assets, must be entered on the consolidation work sheet.

You should observe that for consolidation purposes the fixed assets of the subsidiary are escalated to their fair value *related to the proportionate ownership interest*. That is, the $8,000 represents, in this case, 80% of the fair value. Thus, the fair value relating to the minority interest (20%) is not recognized on the basis that it was not "purchased." Although this procedure represents current practice, many accountants feel that the theoretical arguments for recognition of 100% of the increase in fair value are persuasive.[13]

Observe in particular that the *minority interest* in the subsidiary is identified. The $22,000 minority interest would be reflected on the consolidated balance sheet between liabilities and owners' equity (See Illustration 11–5).

---

[13] Further consideration of this important issue, as well as several others, is beyond the scope of this book. For an in-depth discussion of these issues, see Griffin, Williams, and Larson, op. cit.

Illustration 11–2
Work Sheet to Develop Consolidated Balance Sheet at Acquisition—Cases B, C, and D

	At Book Value		Adjustments and Eliminations		
	Parent Company	Subsidiary	Debit	Credit	Consolidated
Case B—Acquisition of 80% interest at book value:					
Current assets..................................	$204,000	$ 60,000			$264,000
Investment in Company S (80%)	96,000			(a) 96,000	
Fixed assets...................................	500,000	80,000	(b) 8,000		588,000
	$800,000	$140,000			$852,000
Differential.....................................			(a) 8,000	(b) 8,000	
Liabilities	$ 90,000	$ 30,000			$120,000
Common stock—Parent..................	600,000				600,000
, —Subsidiary.............		100,000	(a) 80,000		20,000M
Retained earnings—Parent..............	110,000				110,000
—Subsidiary		10,000	(a) 8,000		2,000M
	$800,000	$140,000			$852,000
Case C—Acquisition of 80% interest above the book value of the net assets of subsidiary:					
Current assets..................................	$188,000	$ 60,000			$248,000
Investment in Company S (80%)	112,000			(a) 112,000	
Fixed assets...................................	500,000	80,000	(b) 8,000		588,000
Goodwill..			(b) 16,000		16,000
	$800,000	$140,000			$852,000
Differential.....................................			(a) 24,000	(b) 24,000	
Liabilities	$ 90,000	$ 30,000			$120,000
Common stock—Parent..................	600,000				600,000
—Subsidiary.............		100,000	(a) 80,000		20,000M
Retained earnings—Parent..............	110,000				110,000
—Subsidiary		10,000	(a) 8,000		2,000M
	$800,000	$140,000			$852,000
Case D—Acquisition of 80% interest below the book value of the net assets of subsidiary:					
Current assets..................................	$217,000	$ 60,000			$277,000
Investment in Company S (80%)	83,000			(a) 83,000	
Fixed assets...................................	500,000	80,000		(b) 5,000	575,000
	$800,000	$140,000			$852,000
Differential.....................................			(b) 5,000	(a) 5,000	
Liabilities	$ 90,000	$ 30,000			$120,000
Common stock—Parent..................	600,000				600,000
—Subsidiary.............		100,000	(a) 80,000		20,000M
Retained earnings—Parent..............	110,000				110,000
—Subsidiary		10,000	(a) 8,000		2,000M
	$800,000	$140,000			$852,000

M—Minority interest.

Case C. The facts are identical to those in Case B except that:

1. The purchase price was $112,000 for an 80% interest.
2. The differential was allocated to fixed assets ($8,000) and the remainder to purchased goodwill.

Therefore, the purchase may be analyzed as follows:

Purchase price (for 80% interest)	$112,000
Book value purchased ($110,000 × 80%)	88,000
Differential	24,000
Allocation:	
To increase fixed assets to fair value	8,000
Balance to goodwill	$ 16,000

The consolidated work sheet is shown in Illustration 11–2 (Case C). The entries on the work sheet are:

(a) To eliminate investment account against subsidiary net worth:

Common Stock ($100,000 × 80%)	80,000	
Retained Earnings ($10,000 × 80%)	8,000	
Differential	24,000	
Investment in Company S		112,000

(b) To apportion the differential in accordance with data given:

Fixed Assets	8,000°	
Goodwill	16,000°	
Differential		24,000

° Observe that this represents 80% of the fair value of each item.

It is assumed that this "apportionment" of the differential is based upon a realistic and dependable determination of the fair value of the fixed assets, thus the remainder represents the "cost of the investment in excess of the fair value of the identifiable assets" (for convenience the term *goodwill* generally is used; we will use the term for the same reason). Again, as in the preceding case, we may observe that the differential (as allocated) represents only the proportionate share owned by the parent. Thus the $8,000 upward adjustment of the fixed assets of the subsidiary and the $16,000 goodwill (recognized for consolidation purposes only) represents, in this case, 80% of the values implicit in the acquisition. The minority share of these values is not recognized. Obviously, in subsequent periods, for consolidation purposes, depreciation on the increase in fixed assets and amortization of the goodwill must be included in the determinations (illustrated subsequently). Another theoretical point, beyond the scope of this text to discuss, is readily apparent in Illustration 11–2; that is, is it appropriate to reflect the minority interest at $22,000 in all three cases despite the fact that there are three significantly different market values?

Case D. Parent acquisition of 80% ownership at less than book value. Assume the same facts as Case B except that the acquisition price was $83,000 for an 80% interest. The purchase may be analyzed:

Purchase price (for 80% interest)... $83,000
Book value purchased ($110,000 × 80%) 88,000
  Differential (negative)..($ 5,000)

The purchase price indicates that the identifiable net assets are overvalued (at book value); we will assume that it relates to the fixed assets. The consolidation work sheet is shown in Illustration 11–2 (Case D). The entries thereon are:

(a) To eliminate the investment account against owner's equity of the subsidiary:

Common Stock ($100,000 × 80%)..80,000
Retained Earnings ($10,000 × 80%).. 8,000
  Investment in Common Stock of Company P.................... 83,000
  Differential.. 5,000

(b) To apportion the differential in accordance with assumed data:

Differential.. 5,000
  Fixed Assets 5,000

If these assets are subject to depreciation, the write-down will affect depreciation expense on future consolidation work sheets.

Consolidated Statements Subsequent to Acquisition

For periods subsequent to acquisition a combination consolidation work sheet is needed to develop appropriate values for each statement (income statement, balance sheet, etc.) Eliminations and adjustments must be entered on the work sheet similar to those illustrated above. Two separate cases will be presented.

Case E. Consolidation subsequent to acquisition, 100% ownership. Assume that at the end of 19A the income statement and balance sheet for Company P and its subsidiary, Company S (continuation of Case A, Illustration 11–1), reflected the following (summarized):

	End of Year – 19A	
	Company P (parent)	*Company S (subsidiary)*
Income Statement:		
Sales	$299,000	$100,000
Interest income	1,000	
Total	$300,000	$100,000
Cost of goods sold.................................	$230,000	$ 56,000
Depreciation	20,000	7,000
Other expenses.....................................	30,000	27,000
Total	$280,000	$ 90,000
Net Income...	$ 20,000	$ 10,000

Balance Sheet:	Company P (parent)	Company S (subsidiary)
Current assets	$180,000	$ 42,000
Investment in Company S (at cost)	70,000	
Fixed assets	380,000	63,000
Total	$630,000	$105,000
Liabilities	$ 60,000	$ 25,000
Common stock	400,000	60,000
Retained earnings	170,000	20,000
Total	$630,000	$105,000

The consolidation work sheet is shown in Illustration 11–3. You should observe carefully: (a) the subsections for the income statement and the balance sheet, (b) the manner in which the eliminations and

Illustration 11–3

Case E—Work Sheet to Develop Consolidated Income Statement and Balance Sheet
Company P and Its Subsidiary (100% owned), Company S, at December 31, 19A

	Reported Amounts 12/31/19A		Eliminations and Adjustments		Consoli-dated
	Company P	Company S	Debit	Credit	
Income Statement:					
Sales	$299,000	$100,000	(b) 6,000		$393,000
Interest income	1,000		(c) 1,000		
Total	$300,000	$100,000			$393,000
Cost of goods sold	$230,000	$ 56,000		(b) 6,000	$280,000
Depreciation	20,000	7,000			27,000
Other expenses	30,000	27,000		(c) 1,000	56,000
Total	$280,000	$ 90,000			$363,000
Income (down)	$ 20,000	$ 10,000			$ 30,000
Balance Sheet:					
Current assets	$180,000	$ 42,000		(d) 8,000	$214,000
Investment in Company S	70,000			(a) 70,000	
Fixed assets	380,000	63,000			443,000
Total	$630,000	$105,000			$657,000
Liabilities	$ 60,000	$ 25,000	(d) 8,000		$ 77,000
Stock—Company P	400,000				400,000
—Company S		60,000	(a) 60,000		
Retained earnings (at acquisition)					
—Company P	150,000				150,000
—Company S		10,000	(a) 10,000		
Add income (from above)	20,000	10,000			30,000
Total	$630,000	$105,000			$657,000

Assumption: Investment account is carried at cost.

Intercompany items (keyed to the work sheet eliminations and adjustments):
   (a) Parent investment and owners' equity of subsidiary.
   (b) Company P sold goods at cost to Company S amounting to $6,000.
   (c) Company P collected $1,000 interest income from Company S.
   (d) Company S owed Company P $8,000 at year-end (current item).

adjustments are entered, and (c) the procedure for "bringing down" the net income amounts in each column.[14]

Case F. Consolidation subsequent to acquisition, 80% owned. To illustrate, we will continue Case C (Illustration 11–2). Assume that at the end of year 19A the income statement and balance sheet for Company P (parent) and Company S (subsidiary) reflected the following:

	At December 31, 19A	
	Company P	*Company S*
Income Statement:		
Sales	$520,000	$105,000
Cost of goods sold	$300,000	$ 53,000
Depreciation	20,000	4,000
Other expenses	140,000	36,000
Total	$460,000	$ 93,000
Net Income	$ 60,000	$ 12,000
Balance Sheet:		
Current assets	$275,000	$ 86,000
Investment in Company (80%; at cost)	112,000	
Fixed assets	480,000	76,000
Total	$867,000	$162,000
Liabilities	$ 97,000	$ 40,000
Common stock	600,000	100,000
Retained earnings	170,000	22,000
Total	$867,000	$162,000

The consolidation work sheet is shown in Illustration 11–4 and the resultant financial statements are shown in Illustration 11–5. You should note in particular the procedures for identifying the *minority interest.*

In cases where there are several changes in retained earnings it may be desirable to add a middle subsection captioned Retained Earnings.

---

[14] The elimination of intercompany sales of $6,000 assumed the goods were transferred at cost. If (a) the transfer price included an element of profit for the selling entity and (b) the goods were still held by the purchasing entity, the profit residue (unrealized intercompany inventory profit) would be eliminated by debiting sales for the sales price, crediting cost of goods sold for the cost price, and crediting ending inventory for the markup on the work sheet.

Illustration 11-4

Case F—Work Sheet to Develop Consolidated Income Statement and Balance Sheet
Company P and Its Subsidiary, Company S (80% owned), at December 31, 19A

	Reported Amounts		Eliminations and Adjustments		Consolidated
	Company P	Company S	Debit	Credit	
Income Statement:					
Sales.................................	$520,000	$105,000	(d) 7,000		$618,000
Cost of goods sold...............	$300,000	53,000		(d) 7,000	$346,000
Depreciation........................	20,000	4,000	(c) 800		24,800
Other expenses...................	140,000	36,000			176,000
Amortization goodwill..........			(c) 400		400
Total..........................	$460,000	$ 93,000			$547,200
Income (down)...................	$ 60,000	$ 12,000			$ 70,800
Minority interest (20% × $12,000)....................					2,400
					$ 68,400
Parent interest................			(a) 24,000	(b) 24,000	
Differential........................					
Balance Sheet:					
Current assets.....................	$275,000	$ 86,000		(e) 3,000	$358,000
Investment in Company S.....	112,000			(a) 112,000	
Fixed assets (net)...............	480,000	76,000	(b) 8,000	(c) 800	563,200
Goodwill............................			(b) 16,000	(c) 400	15,600
Total..........................	$867,000	$162,000			$936,800
Liabilities...........................	$ 97,000	$ 40,000	(e) 3,000		$134,000
Common stock—					
Company P.....................	600,000				600,000
Company S.....................		100,000	(a) 80,000		20,000M
Retained earnings (at acquisition):					
Company P.....................	110,000				110,000
Company S.....................		10,000	(a) 8,000		2,000M
Income (from above)...........	60,000	12,000			2,400M
					68,400
Totals	$867,000	$162,000			$936,800

M—Minority interest.

Intercompany items (keyed to work sheet eliminations and adjustments):
  (a) Parent investment and owners' equity of subsidiary.
  (b) Apportionment of residual (see Case C, Illustration 11-2).
  (c) Depreciation on asset increase (10-year assumed remaining life) and amortization of goodwill (40 years).
  (d) Intercompany sales, $7,000 (at cost).
  (e) Intercompany debt, $3,000 (current).

Illustration 11-5
Company P and Subsidiary Company S
Consolidated Income Statement (unclassified)
for the Year Ended December 31, 19A

Sales		$618,000
Expenses:		
Cost of goods sold	$346,000	
Depreciation	24,800	
Other expenses	176,000	
Amortization of intangible (goodwill)	400	547,200
Combined net income		$ 70,800
Minority interest in net income (20%)		2,400
Consolidated net income		$ 68,400

Consolidated Balance Sheet (unclassified), December 31, 19A

ASSETS

Current assets		$358,000
Fixed assets (net)		563,200
Cost of investment in subsidiary in excess of fair value of identifiable assets		15,600
Total Assets		$936,800

EQUITIES

Liabilities		$134,000
Minority interest in Company S:		
Common stock	$ 20,000	
Retained earnings	4,400	24,400
Owners' equity:		
Common stock	$600,000	
Retained earnings	178,400	778,400
Total Equities		$936,800

Business Combinations—Purchase versus Pooling

In recent years there has been an increasing trend toward business combinations whereby two or more companies (usually corporations) are brought together for operating purposes. For example, Company P may desire to combine with Company S in order to improve their market position, to effect certain economies of scale, or for other reasons. In order to effect the combination Company P may *purchase* Company S outright or the two might *pool* their resources whereby Company S stock would be turned in (exchanged) for Company P stock.[15] Due to the many variations of arrangements possible, some of

---

[15] All of the discussions and illustrations up to this point in the chapter have assumed a "purchase."

which are rather complex, the accounting profession over the years has issued a number of pronouncements in respect to appropriate accounting procedures. The latest pronouncements were *APB Opinions No. 16* and *No. 17* dated August 1970. The discussions to follow are consistent with these two Opinions. Two accounting approaches are available for business combinations; they are not alternatives for the same situation but are required approaches depending upon the characteristics of the combination transaction. The two methods may be summarized as follows:

1. *Purchase Method.* This method must be followed when the combination transaction is in the nature of a purchase. Typically, this occurs when P, the acquiring company, pays cash, gives other assets, or issues debt to pay for the resources and operations of Company S (the acquired company). Under the purchase method the acquiring company reports the assets of the acquired company at their *fair value* at the date of the exchange transaction as would be done in respect to the purchase of any other asset. The preceding discussions on consolidated statements assumed a purchase situation in each case.

2. *Pooling of Interests Method.* This method must be followed when the combination transaction is in the nature of a continuation of the former ownership interests in combination. Pooling transactions are typified by agreements between shareholders of the companies to exchange stock in one company for stock of the other company so that there is a continuity of common ownership. Under this method the assets of the two companies are brought together at their prior *book values* in recognition of the fact that there has been no purchase but merely a rearrangement of shares.

One of the central problems faced by the accountant has been the difficulty of classifying some combinations within the above described frame of reference. Complex exchange transactions have evolved that make this difficult. For example, Company P may acquire Company S, paying one half in cash and one half in its own stock. This problem, along with the obvious attempts of some parties to utilize accounting alternatives as a means of misrepresenting economic realities (such as devising merger arrangements to inflate reported earnings and earnings per share amounts and then applying inappropriate accounting methods) led to extensive discussions during 1969 and 1970 by the APB, SEC, and industry. These discussions culminated in the issuance of *Opinion No. 16* which stated: "The purchase method and the pooling of interests method are both acceptable in accounting for business combinations, although not as alternative accounting procedures for the same business combination. A business combination which meets specified conditions requires accounting by the pooling of interests method and all other combinations must utilize the purchase method."

General Characteristics of Purchase Method. Although there are numerous complexities in the application of this method, the general characteristics may be outlined as follows:

1. The assets and liabilities of the acquired firm are reported by the acquiring firm at cost at date of acquisition in conformity with the cost principle. Cost is the price paid for the acquired company (cash equivalent cost) and is the *fair market value* at that date.
2. Individual assets acquired are reported at their individual fair values at date of acquisition. This includes all identifiable tangible and intangible assets (land, equipment, patents, etc.). Liabilities are reported at their present "debt" value.
3. The difference between the total purchase cost and the fair value of the identifiable assets acquired (less the liabilities acquired) is reported as "goodwill from acquisition."[16] Goodwill from acquisition is subsequently amortized as an income statement charge.
4. At date of combination, the retained earnings balance of the combined entity is defined as the retained earnings balance of the acquiring company; that is, the retained earnings balance of the acquired company is eliminated (not carried forward).
5. After the combination, financial statements which pertain to pre-combination periods must depict the historical data of the acquiring company only.

General Characteristics of Pooling of Interests Method. The general characteristics of this method may be indicated by summarizing the accounting distinctions and then listing the criteria. The accounting distinctions are:

1. The assets and liabilities of the combining companies are reported at the previously established *book values* of each. Although adjustments may be made to reflect consistent applications of accounting principles, the current fair values at the time of the combination are not used as a substitute for the book values at that date.
2. No goodwill results from the combination.
3. The retained earnings balances of the combining companies are added to determine the retained earnings balance of the combined companies at date of acquisition.

---

[16] If total purchase cost is less than the summed fair market values of individual assets and liabilities, the difference is applied to reduce the valuations of the identifiable tangible and intangible assets.

4. After combination, financial statements which pertain to precombination periods must be restated to reflect the data that would have been reported had the firms been combined throughout the precombination periods being reflected.

The APB specified in *Opinion No. 16* that the following conditions must be met in order to apply the pooling of interests method:

1. Each of the combining companies is autonomous and has not been a subsidiary or division of another corporation within two years before the plan of combination is initiated.
2. Each of the combining companies is independent of the other combining companies.
3. The combination is effected in a single transaction or is completed in accordance with a specific plan within one year after the plan is initiated.
4. A corporation offers and issues only common stock with rights identical to the majority of its outstanding voting common stock in exchange for substantially all of the voting common stock interest of another company at the date the plan of combination is consummated.
5. Each of the combining companies maintains substantially the same voting common stock interest.
6. Each of the combining companies reacquires shares of voting common stock only for purposes other than business combinations.
7. The ratio of the interest of an individual common stockholder to those of the other common stockholders in a combining company remains the same.
8. The combination is resolved at the date the plan is consummated and no provisions of the plan relating to the issue of securities or other consideration are pending.
9. There shall be no planned transactions after combination which are inconsistent with the combining of the entire existing interests of common stockholders.
10. Dissolution of a combining company is not a condition for applying the pooling of interests method.

These distinctions between *purchase* accounting and *pooling of interests* accounting are independent of the legal form of the surviving entity or entities. For example, the bringing together of two entities, say Company P and Company S, could have taken any one of the following legal forms:

a) Corporation X is formed and Companies P and S go out of existence.
b) Corporation P continues and S goes out of existence (or vice versa).
c) Corporation P and S continue in a parent-subsidiary relationship.

Informal surveys in the last few years have indicated that less than 2% of business combinations take the form of (*a*); whereas the remainder are approximately equally divided between the legal forms indicated in (*b*) and (*c*). In respect to the accounting format, in (*a*) the books of both P and S are discontinued, and in (*b*) the books of the nonsurvivor are discontinued. In contrast, in situation (*c*) the books of both P and S continue independently. Either *purchase* or *pooling of interests* accounting may be applied in each of the three legal forms. In the case of situations (*a*) and (*b*) the accounting method utilized for the combination would be reflected *both* in the books and on the financial statements of the continuing entity, whereas in situation (*c*) the accounting method utilized would be reflected *only* on the *consolidated* financial statements of the parent company. In situation (*c*) the investment of the parent company would be reflected on their *books* in an asset account entitled "Investment Stock of Corporation S." This account would be debited for an amount conditioned by the method of accounting applied (purchase or pooling) and subsequently would be carried on either a cost or equity basis as discussed in the preceding sections of this chapter.

Purchase and Pooling of Interests Methods Illustrated

The scope of this text limits our discussion of this important subject; therefore, we will present one simplified example designed to contrast the essential features of the purchase and pooling methods of accounting for a business combination. Assume that Company P and Company S are to be brought together as a combination when their records reflected the following:

	Company P Book Value	Company S Book Value	Company S Fair Value (Appraised)
Cash	$610,000	$ 20,000	$ 20,000
Inventories	20,000	30,000	25,000
Accounts receivable (net)	10,000	40,000	40,000
Plant and equipment (net)	200,000	110,000	151,000
Patents (net)	20,000	10,000	14,000
	$860,000	$210,000	$250,000
Current liabilities	$ 10,000	$ 20,000	
Long-term liabilities	50,000	40,000	
Common stock (par $100)	600,000	100,000	
Retained earnings	200,000	50,000	
	$860,000	$210,000	

Case A—Purchase Method. Assume Company P acquires Company S through purchase in the open market of all of the outstanding stock of the latter for $240,000 cash. Company S will continue as a legal entity as a subsidiary of Company P. At date of acquisition Company S owed Company P $5,000 accounts payable. Since the books of S will not be merged with P the following purchase entry should be made in the accounts of Company P:

```
Investment in Company S Stock (100%, at cost) .................240,000
    Cash .................................................................    240,000
```

Now, assume that Company P prepares a *consolidated* balance sheet immediately after the acquisition. Since the acquisition transaction clearly does not meet all of the criteria listed above for the pooling of interests method, it must utilize the purchase method and report the assets of Company S at their purchase price (fair value) at date of acquisition. The consolidation work sheet is shown in Illustration 11–6.

Illustration 11–6
Consolidation Work Sheet – Purchase Method (at date of acquisition)
Company P and Its Subsidiary, Company S (100% owned)

	Balances per Books of		Eliminations and Adjustments		Consolidated
	Company P	Company S	Debit	Credit	
Cash...............................	$370,000	$ 20,000			$390,000
Inventories.........................	20,000	30,000		(b) 5,000	45,000
Accounts receivable.............	10,000	40,000		(c) 5,000	45,000
Investment in Company S.....	240,000			(a) 240,000	
Plant and equipment (net) ...	200,000	110,000	(b) 41,000		351,000
Patents.............................	20,000	10,000	(b) 4,000		34,000
Goodwill...........................			(b) 50,000		50,000
	$860,000	$210,000			$915,000
Differential.......................			(a) 90,000	(b) 90,000	
Current liabilities...............	$ 10,000	$ 20,000	(c) 5,000		$ 25,000
Long-term liabilities............	50,000	40,000			90,000
Common stock –					
Company P......................	600,000				600,000
Company S......................		100,000	(a) 100,000		
Retained earnings –					
Company P......................	200,000				200,000
Company S......................		50,000	(a) 50,000		
	$860,000	$210,000			$915,000

Intercompany items (keyed to work sheet eliminations and adjustments):

(a) To eliminate investment account against subsidiary net worth (100% owned) and to recognize the differential.

(b) To apportion the differential on the basis of fair values at date of acquisition. Computation of goodwill:

```
Purchase price (100% interest)..........................................................$240,000
Book value (100% interest)...............................................  150,000
    Differential ...........................................................................$ 90,000
Allocation:
    Plant and equipment ($151,000 – $110,000).......................  $41,000
    Patents ($14,000 – $10,000) ...........................................    4,000
    Inventories ($25,000 – $30,000).......................................( 5,000)    40,000
    Balance to goodwill ...............................................................$ 50,000
```

(c) To eliminate intercompany debt of $5,000.

On the work sheet you can observe the following features of the purchase method:

1. Both tangible and identifiable intangible assets are reported at cost (fair value) at date of acquisition as opposed to prior book value.
2. Any excess of purchase price above the fair value of the assets (less liabilities assumed) is reflected as goodwill.
3. Depreciation, amortization of identifiable intangibles, and amortization of goodwill based on the new values must be reflected on future income statements.
4. Retained earnings of Company S is eliminated.

It is important to note that in Illustration 11–6, had the ownership interest been, say, 80%, only that proportion of the fair value changes would have been recognized.

Case B—Pooling of Interests Method. Assume instead that Company P exchanged 1,000 shares of its common stock for the 1,000 shares of Company S common stock outstanding. Thus, there is a continuity of ownership and we will assume that all of the other criteria (listed above) are met so that the pooling of interests method *must be applied.* Assume as above that Company S continues as a legal entity (subsidiary of P) and that there is a $5,000 intercompany debt. Under these circumstances Company P would record the pooling transaction as follows:

```
Investment in Company S (100% ownership).......................150,000
    Common Stock (1,000 shares at par)............................        100,000
    Contributed Capital......................................................        50,000
```

The preparation of a consolidated balance sheet, following the pooling of interests method using a consolidation work sheet, is shown in Illustration 11–7. In contrast with the purchase method, observe that the assets of both companies are combined at their book values (as opposed to fair value at date of acquisition), that no goodwill was reported, that retained earnings of both entities were combined, and that depreciation and amortization on future income statements will be based upon *prior book values.*

Amortization of Purchased Goodwill. The purchase method of accounting for business combinations frequently results in recognition of "goodwill from acquisition." *APB Opinion No. 17,* "Intangible Assets," states that "The portion of the cost of an acquired company not allocated to tangible assets, identifiable intangible assets, and liabilities should be assigned as the cost of goodwill." The *Opinion* then states that goodwill should be amortized, by systematic charges to income over the periods estimated to be benefited; however, the period should not exceed 40 years. In Illustration 11–6, the $50,000 goodwill recognized under the purchase method would be amortized over a "reasonable" life, say 10 years.

Illustration 11–7
Consolidation Work Sheet—Pooling of Interests Method (at date of acquisition)
Company P and Its Subsidiary Company S (100% owned)

| | Balance per Books of | | Eliminations | | |
	Company P	Company S	Debit	Credit	Consolidated
Cash................................	$ 610,000	$ 20,000			$630,000
Inventories........................	20,000	30,000			50,000
Accounts receivable...........	10,000	40,000		(b) 5,000	45,000
Investment in Company S...	150,000			(a) 150,000	
Plant and equipment.........	200,000	110,000			310,000
Patents............................	20,000	10,000			30,000
	$1,010,000	$210,000			$1,065,000
Current liabilities..............$	10,000	$ 20,000	(b) 5,000		$ 25,000
Long-term liabilities..........	50,000	40,000			90,000
Common stock (par $100)...	700,000	100,000	(a) 100,000		700,000
Retained earnings	200,000	50,000			250,000
Contributed capital	50,000		(a) 50,000		
	$1,010,000	$210,000			$1,065,000

Intercompany items (keyed to work sheet eliminations):
(a) To eliminate investment account against subsidiary net worth (100% owned).
(b) To eliminate intercompany debt of $5,000.

In the example relating to Company P and Company S the differences on the consolidated balance sheets were illustrated as between the purchase and pooling of interests methods. In respect to subsequent income statements prepared on a consolidated basis, the primary differences would be due to amortization of goodwill, depreciation of fixed assets, and amortization of intangibles other than goodwill. To illustrate, assume that depreciation and amortization of the patent and goodwill by Company P are based on a remaining life of 10 years. The comparative effect on the annual income statement, aside from the inventory adjustment, under each of the two methods would be (refer to Illustrations 11–6 and 11–7):

	Purchase Method	Pooling of Interests Method	Difference
Depreciation $35,100		$31,000	$4,100
Amortization of patent............................. 3,400		3,000	400
Amortization of goodwill.......................... 5,000		–0–	5,000
Total difference (in pretax profit)......			$9,500

This simple illustration clearly reveals a primary reason why the pooling of interests method was widely abused prior to the issuance of the strict accounting criteria in *APB Opinions No. 16* and *No. 17*.

Simply, the pooling method generally shows a higher reported net income amount and a lower reported investment base. It also obscures the long-range impact of a major expenditure such as was common in the history of many of the conglomerates of the 1960s. The pooling of interests method also made possible the reporting of "instant earnings." Some companies acquired another company (usually much smaller) under various cash, stock, and debt arrangements, then accounted for them on a pooling basis. A portion of the assets reported by the acquiring company at the depreciated book value of the acquired company frequently was immediately sold at the much higher market value giving rise to a "bookkeeping" gain which was included in the reported net income amount for the immediate period.

Significantly, in 1966, the Committee to Prepare a Statement of Accounting Theory of the AAA took a firm stand on the purchasing and pooling controversy as follows:[17]

Purchase and pooling. Although market transactions resulting in combinations or reorganizations of business entities are recorded, there is considerable freedom in recording such transactions as either a pooling of interests (where the market transaction is treated as if it created no *new* exchange values for the assets involved) or as a purchase (where new exchange values resulting from the market transaction are recognized). This is perhaps the classic case of quantifiability and verifiability warring with relevance. It is true that carrying forward the existing book values of the two combining entities is eminently quantifiable since the figures exist on the books. It is more than questionable that such a treatment, which essentially ignores the new exchange values created by a significant market transaction such as the combination of two companies, can be said to be relevant for investment decisions. When a single machine is purchased, the book value of that machine on the seller's books is considered irrelevant for the purchaser's records. The same is true when a company is merged or purchased. The committee feels that in most instances in such a transaction enough evidence exists to provide verifiability and freedom from bias, and that relevant exchange values resulting from such transactions should be recognized, and thus recommends that the pooling of interest technique be disallowed.

Recent constructive efforts of the APB as reflected in *Opinions No. 16* and *No. 17*, and the rulings of the SEC have served to minimize these unfortunate abuses although in the judgment of many they have not gone far enough in this direction.[18]

Pro Forma Entries and Statements

In contemplating major decisions the management of an enterprise generally insists upon a presentation of their potential effects

---

[17] AAA, *A Statement of Basic Accounting Theory* (Evanston, Ill., 1966), p. 33.

[18] A comprehensive treatment of all aspects of business combinations is presented in Griffin, Williams, and Larson, op. cit.

on the financial statements. How the decision will be reflected on the financial statements frequently is a particularly critical issue in the decision-making process. To illustrate, when two or more enterprises are planning to combine, the management of each entity may request "as if" financial statements for each of several alternative ways of combining. In such situations the management generally will request numerous "as if" financial statements, viz:

a) Assuming a purchase combination is decided upon.

b) Assuming a pooling combination is decided upon.

"As if" financial statements commonly are referred to as *pro forma* statements. Frequently, it is desirable to prepare pro forma journal entries, pro forma cash flow analyses, and pro forma projections—all of them being based on definitely specified assumptions. Pro forma entries, statements, and work sheets should be clearly defined as such and their assumptions should be specifically stated so that they could never be confused with "actual" data. Not infrequently, selected pro forma data are included in "actual" financial statements; for example, the "fully diluted" earnings per share amount frequently reported is a pro forma statistic (see Chapter 26).

Special Problems

Several problems relating to the acquisition, holding, and sale of stock investments are discussed in the remaining paragraphs.

Stock Dividends on Investment Shares. In order to conserve cash and yet make a distribution to shareholders, a corporation may declare and issue a dividend utilizing its own shares of stock as payment. Such a dividend commonly is referred to as a stock dividend. When a stock dividend is issued, the distributing corporation debits Retained Earnings and credits Stock Dividends Issuable (a capital account); when the stock is issued, Stock Dividends Issuable is debited and the appropriate capital stock account is credited. The effect of a stock dividend as far as the issuing corporation is concerned is to "capitalize" a part of retained earnings; significantly, a stock dividend does not decrease the assets of the issuing corporation.

From the investor's point of view, the nature of a stock dividend is suggested by the effect on the issuing corporation. In effect, the investor does not receive "assets" or "income" from the corporation; neither does he own more of the issuing corporation. He does have more shares to represent his same prior proportional ownership. Thus, the receipt of a stock dividend in the same class of shares as already owned results, from the standpoint of the investor's records, in more shares but no increase in the cost (carrying value) of his holdings. Since such a dividend involves no distribution of corporate assets and does not affect the proportional interest of the stockholder in the assets of the corporation whose stock he holds, the investor should make no entry for income nor change in his investment account other than a memorandum entry for the number of shares received. In case of a sale of any of these shares, a new cost per share is computed by adding the new shares to the old and dividing this sum into the carrying value. To illustrate, assume X purchased 100 shares of stock at $90 and subsequently received a 50% dividend payable in identical stock, and later sold 20 shares at $85. A schedule showing the gain or loss on the sale and the balance remaining in the investment account (cost method) follows:[19]

	Shares	Cost per Share	Total Cost Price	Sales Price	Gain, Loss°
Purchased 100		$90	$9,000		
Stock dividend........ 50			0		
Total............150		60	$9,000		
Sold...................... 20		60	1,200	$1,700	$500
Ending Balance 130		60	$7,800		

If the stock dividend is of a different class of stock than that on which the dividend is declared, such as preferred stock received as a dividend on common stock, three methods of accounting for the dividend have been suggested:

1. Record the new stock in terms of shares only, and when it is sold recognize the total sales price as a gain.
2. Record the new stock at an amount determined by apportioning the carrying value of the old stock between the new stock and the old stock on the basis of the fair market value of the different classes of stock *after* issuance of the dividend.
3. Do not change the carrying value of the old stock but record the new stock on the books at its market value upon receipt with an offsetting credit to dividend income. This method is predicated on the assumption that stock of a different class received as a dividend is no different from a property dividend.

Of these three methods the first is the most conservative, the second is theoretically sound and more in keeping with generally accepted accounting principles, while the third is the least logical. To illustrate the second method, assume an investor purchased 50 shares of X Company common stock for $7,500. When the market value of the common stock was $10,000 he received a stock dividend of 20 shares of X preferred having a fair market value of $2,500. Using the relative sales value method the cost may be apportioned as follows:

---

[19] Under the Internal Revenue Code stock dividends are exempt from taxation except (a) where the shareholder can elect to take cash rather than stock for the dividend and (b) when stock dividends satisfy dividend preference requirements.

$$\text{Apportioned cost} - \text{common} = \$7,500 \times \frac{\$10,000}{\$12,500} = \$6,000$$

$$\text{Apportioned cost} - \text{preferred} = \$7,500 \times \frac{\$2,500}{\$12,500} = \underline{1,500}$$

$$\underline{\underline{\$7,500}}$$

Indicated entry:

Investment in Preferred Stock of X Company 1,500
    Investment in Common Stock of X Company   1,500

Stock Split of Investment Shares. A stock split is effected when a corporation issues new or additional shares without "capitalizing" (debiting) retained earnings or otherwise adding to the amount of dollar *legal capital.* In a stock split the number of shares outstanding is increased, accompanied by a proportionate decrease in the par or stated value per share of stock (refer to Chapters 20 and 22). Thus, a stock split is essentially different from a stock dividend from the point of view of the issuer but very similar from the point of view of the holder. To the latter a stock dividend is not income. A two-for-one stock split means, for example, that the holder of shares at the date of the split will receive two shares in place of each old share held. To the investor this merely means that he has twice as many shares after the split to represent the same total cost as he had before. The accounting for investment shares where there is a stock split simply involves a memorandum entry for the number of shares received; the resulting "cost per share" is reduced proportionately.

Convertible Securities. In recent years there has been a significant increase in the use of convertible securities. An enterprise may invest in preferred stock or bonds that are convertible into common stock under specified conditions. An accounting measurement problem arises at the time of conversion since the cost of the convertible securities generally is different from the market value of the common stock received at the time of conversion. Two alternative views are held on this point:

1. At date of conversion record the cost of the convertible security given up as the cost of the new security received, thus no gain or loss upon conversion would be recognized. This position is supported by the arguments that (*a*) the original transaction is continuing to materialize; prearranged conversion does not constitute a distinct exchange transaction, (*b*) conversion usually is at the option of the investor, and (*c*) most conversions do not give rise to a taxable gain or loss.

2. At date of conversion record the new security received at its fair market value and recognize a gain or loss on conversion. This position is supported by the arguments that (*a*) a distinct and separate exchange transaction has occurred, (*b*) market value is objective evi-

dence of the "value received," and (c) this is similar to the exchange of any other asset and should be accounted for accordingly.

The former view tends to prevail in practice although the latter appears to be theoretically preferable. Also see Chapter 17.

Stock Rights on Investment Shares. The privilege accorded stockholders (investors) of purchasing additional shares of stock from the issuing corporation at a specific price and by a specified future date commonly is known as a *stock right*. The term *stock right* is usually interpreted to mean the right related to *each share of old stock*. Therefore, a holder of 10 shares of stock who receives the rights to subscribe for 5 new shares is said to own 10 stock rights rather than 5; that is, there is one right per old share irrespective of the "new" share arrangement. Rights have value when the holder can buy added shares through the *exercise* of his rights at a lower price per share than can persons buying similar shares on the market without rights. As the spread between the privileged subscription price and the market price of shares bought without rights changes subsequent to issuance of the rights, the value of the rights will change.

The accounting problems surrounding stock rights are important since some stockholders prefer to sell their rights rather than to exercise them, in which event any gain on rights sold must be determined and entries made to reflect the proper allocation of the cost of the old shares between the rights and the stock. After rights are received the investor has shares of stock and stock warrants (stock rights), both arising out of the single original cost commitment. To determine the gain or loss on the sale of either stock or rights, it is necessary to apportion the total cost of the investment between the stock and the rights. This is done by the use of the relative sales value method; i.e., the total cost of the old shares is divided between the old stock and the rights in proportion to their respective market values at the time that the rights are issued. For example, if the market value of a share of stock after the issuance of stock rights is $120 (ex rights) and the market value of the right is $20, the original cost of $100 for the old share would be divided between the share and right as follows:

Market value of share of stock on date right issued (ex rights)	$120
Market value of right on date issued	20
Total Market Value of Share and Right	$140

Allocation of the $100 cost of the investment:

$$\text{To share of stock: } \frac{120}{140} \times \$100 = \$\ 85.71$$

$$\text{To stock right: } \frac{20}{140} \times \$100 = \underline{\ \ 14.29}$$

Total Cost of Investment...$100.00

Indicated entry:

Investment in Stock Rights—X Company...................................14.29
    Investment in Stock—X Company..   14.29

When the intention to issue stock rights is declared, obviously the stock will start selling in the market "rights on"; i.e., purchasers have time to "register" newly bought shares in their names so as to secure the rights when issued. Therefore, the market price of the share sold "rights on" is the price of a share and a right. After the rights are issued the share will sell in the market "ex rights." After issuance, rights usually will have as ready a market as the related stock and thus will be quoted at a specific market price.

It is sometimes not possible to secure the market price of a right for the purpose of allocating the cost of the investment. In this case the *parity value* of the right may be used in lieu of the unobtainable market value. The parity value of a stock right is the theoretical sales value of the right; i.e., it is the approximate price which the right should bring in the market in view of the relationship between the privileged subscription price (the special price offered to the old stockholder) of a share and the market price of a share of stock. The parity value of a right is determined by dividing the difference between the market value of the old stock (rights on) and the privileged subscription price by the number of rights required to secure one new share *plus one*.[20] Or, if the market quotation on the stock is "ex rights," the market value of the old stock (ex right) minus the privileged subscription price should be divided by the number of rights required to secure one new share.

To illustrate, assume that a corporation whose old stock has a market value of $150 a share when quoted "rights on" issued warrants to subscribe for one share of stock at par of $100 for each four old shares. In this situation the formula and computation of parity value is:

$$V = \frac{M_a - S}{n + 1} \quad (\text{"rights on" formula})$$

$$= \frac{\$150 - \$100}{4 + 1} = \$10 \quad (\text{parity value per right})$$

when V is the parity value of the right; M_a is the market value of an old share "rights on"; S, the subscription price per share of new stock; and n, the number of old shares needed to secure the privilege of

---

[20] One must be added to adjust for the "rights on" aspect of the market value; referring to the illustration:

      Conversion price = $100} 4 rights
      Ex rights price   =   140}
      Rights on price =   150} 1
                            ——————
                          5 rights

subscribing for one new share. If the old stock is selling "ex rights" at $140, then the formula ($M_b$ represents the market value of an old share, ex rights) and solution would be:

$$V = \frac{M_b - S}{n} \text{ ("ex rights" formula)}$$

$$= \frac{\$140 - \$100}{4} = \$10 \text{ (parity value per right)}$$

The relative sales value method has long been used in this context for both financial accounting and federal income tax purposes. It requires an apportionment of the cost of the investment between the stock and the rights on the basis of the respective selling prices of each at the time the rights are issued. Once the relative market values of the old shares and the new stock rights are determined, the cost of the two investments may be determined. To continue the above illustration, assume that the old stock cost $75 per share; the allocation for one share would be as follows:

> Market value of share of stock (ex rights).............................$140
> Parity value of right... 10
>   Total Value of Share and Right....................................$150

Allocation of the $75 cost of investment:

$$\text{To share of stock: } \frac{140}{150} \times \$75 = \$70$$

$$\text{To stock right: } \frac{10}{150} \times \$75 = \underline{\quad 5}$$

> Total Cost of
>   Investment............... $75

Indicated entry:

> Investment in Stock Rights of Y Company..5
>   Investment in Stock of Y Company...   5

Continuing the illustration, assume that subsequently one right was sold for $11; the entry to record the sale would be:

> Cash...11
>   Investment in Stock Rights Y Company...   5
>   Gain on Sale of Stock Right   6

On the other hand, if the rights had been exercised instead of being sold, the cost of the rights plus the cash subscription price would be the cost of the new share (or shares) acquired. To illustrate, assume that the privileged subscription price (the special price offered to the old stockholder) authorized the stockholder to buy one new share at a special price of $100 along with the surrender (tender) of four stock rights. The old stockholder would surrender four rights, pay the $100, and receive therefor a new share of stock. The cost of the new share would be computed as follows:

Cost of rights (4 rights @ $5)...$ 20
Cash payment (special subscription price)........................ 100
    Cost of New Share..$120

Indicated entry:

Investment in Stock of Y Company..120
    Investment in Stock Rights of Y Company...................................   20
    Cash   100

If rights are not sold or exercised they will lapse, in which case, a loss equivalent to the cost allocated to the rights should be recognized.

Illustrative Problem.   A comprehensive illustration is now presented to indicate the entries which would be made in the case of stock rights. Assume an investor purchased 500 shares of stock in the XY Corporation at $93 per share, and later by reason of the ownership of such stock received 500 stock rights entitling him to subscribe to 100 additional shares at $100 per share. Upon the issuance of the rights each share of stock on which the rights were issued had a fair market value of $120 (ex rights), and the rights had a fair market value of $4 each when issued.

Case A: Assume that instead of subscribing for the additional shares, the investor later sold the rights at $4.50 each.

Case B: Assume the investor exercised his rights to subscribe to the additional shares and later sold one of the new shares for $140.

Solution:

Case A   Investor's Entries

a) Investment—Stock of XY Corporation...............................46,500
    Cash   46,500
        For purchase of 500 shares at $93 = $46,500.

b) Investment—Stock Rights XY Corporation°......................... 1,500
    Investment—Stock of XY Corporation...........................   1,500

°Calculation:
To allocate cost to 500 rights as follows:
    Shares: 500 × $120   = $60,000
    Rights: 500 = $4   =   2,000
        Total Market Value......$62,000

Allocation:
    Shares: $\frac{\$60,000}{\$62,000}$ × $46,500 = $45,000

    Rights: $\frac{\$2,000}{\$62,000}$ × $46,500 =   1,500
        Total Cost................$46,500

For the purpose of determining the gain or loss from the subsequent sale of the old stock on which the rights were issued, the adjusted cost of each share is $45,000 ÷ 500, or $90 per share.

c) Cash.. 2,250
        Investment—Stock Rights XY Corporation............   2,000
        Gain on sale of Stock Rights   250
    For sale of the 500 stock rights at $4.50 each.

Case B   Investor's Entries

a) Investment Stock of XY Corporation—First Purchase ...46,500
    Cash...   46,500
    To record purchase of 500 shares at $93 = $46,500.

b) Investment—Stock Rights XY Corporation................. 1,500
    Investment Stock of XY Corporation—First
        Purchase..   1,500
    To allocate cost of 500 rights as computed in Case A.

c) Investment Stock of XY Corporation—Second Purchase...11,500
        Investment—Stock Rights XY Corporation...........   1,500
        Cash...   10,000
    To record exercise of rights and receipt of 100 new shares of stock.

d) Cash.. 140
    Investment Stock of XY Corporation—Second Purchase...   115
    Gain on Sale of Stock Investment......................   25
    To record sale of one new share; cost, $11,500 ÷ 100 = $115.

QUESTIONS FOR CLASS DISCUSSION

1. Distinguish between long-term (permanent) and short-term (temporary) investments.
2. Define cost as applied to long-term investments at date of acquisition.
3. Why do accountants generally hold that dividends on stocks should not be accrued by the investor?
4. Why should each block or lot of shares acquired be accounted for separately?
5. Distinguish between a cash dividend and a property dividend. What particular accounting problems are posed for the investor with respect to each?
6. Indicate the importance of three dates relative to dividends.
7. Distinguish between a noncontrolling interest and a controlling interest.
8. Indicate when each of the following methods of accounting for a long-term investment should be used: (a) cost method, (b) market value method, (c) equity method, and (d) consolidation.
9. Explain the essential features of the cost method.

10. Explain the essential features of the market value method.

11. In applying the market value method a controversy continues in respect to reporting the gains and losses. Explain.

12. Explain the essential features of the equity method.

13. Why do market value and goodwill have an impact on the equity method?

14. Explain the essential features of consolidation at acquisition.

15. Why do market value and goodwill have an impact on consolidation procedures?

16. Distinguish between purchase and pooling of interests accounting in business combinations. When is each appropriate?

17. Contrast the effect on the balance sheet and the income statement of purchase versus pooling of interests accounting for business combinations.

18. How does a stock split differ from a stock dividend? Explain the effects on the accounting procedures by the investor.

19. What are stock rights? Basically, how are they accounted for by the investor?

DECISION CASE 11-1

Able Corporation, an old-line company that went public five years ago, was a family business prior to incorporation. It had a sound marketing base but had not grown with the times. At the time that it became a publicly held corporation a new management was brought in from the outside. In the last two years it had become acquisition-minded and, as a consequence, acquired two smaller enterprises; one in a purchase arrangement and the other in a pooling of interests agreement.

Currently negotiations are under way that may lead to a combination with Baker Corporation, a successful enterprise that would complement the operations of Able. An important facet in the negotiations has been the potential financial effects of the merger. Accordingly, the Able management has requested that pro forma financial statements be prepared under several assumptions.

Comparison of the financial statements for the two corporations for the year just ended (prior to combination) is shown in the accompanying table.

| | | Baker Corporation | |
	Able Corporation	Book Value	Appraised Value
Balance Sheet:			
Cash	$ 470,000	$ 12,000	
Receivables (net)	40,000	58,000	$ 50,000
Inventories	80,000	70,000	55,000
Investments	100,000		
Plant	650,000	100,000	250,000
Patents	10,000	30,000	50,000
	$1,350,000	$ 270,000	

	Able Corporation	Baker Corporation Book Value	Baker Corporation Appraised Value
Current liabilities	$ 50,000	$ 10,000	
Long-term liabilities	180,000	20,000	
Common stock (par $100)	1,000,000	200,000	
Retained earnings	120,000	40,000	
	$1,350,000	$ 270,000	
Income Statement:			
Sales	$6,000,000	$1,000,000	
Costs and expenses (excluding depreciation and amortization)	5,754,000	967,000	
Depreciation	65,000	10,000	
Amortization of patents	1,000	3,000	
Income	180,000	20,000	

At year-end Baker Corporation owed a $10,000 current liability to Able Corporation. For case purposes assume that all depreciable assets and intangible assets have a remaining useful life of 10 years from date of combination.

Required:

1. Assume that Able will purchase all of the outstanding stock of Baker for a cash consideration of $450,000.

a) Give the pro forma acquisition entry.
b) Prepare a pro forma balance sheet on the appropriate consolidation basis (or if you prefer, present a pro forma consolidation worksheet).

2. Assume instead that Able obtained all of the outstanding shares of Baker by exchanging stock on a share for share basis.

a) Give the pro forma acquisition entry.
b) Prepare a pro forma balance sheet (or work sheet) on the appropriate consolidation basis.

3. Identify the amount of the differences on the balance sheets between (1) and (2) above and explain the reasons for each. Identify and explain the values that will be different on the income statements for the next period as between (1) and (2).

EXERCISES

Exercise 11-1

Henna Company purchased shares in two corporations, as indicated below, with the intention of holding them as long-term investments; purchases were in the following order:

a) Purchased 50 shares of common stock of M corporation at $31 per share plus a 5% brokerage fee and transfer cost of $72.50.
b) Purchased 100 shares of preferred stock of N Corporation at $78 per share plus a 3% brokerage fee and transfer costs of $66.

c) Purchased 20 shares of common stock of M Corporation at $35 per share plus a 5% brokerage fee and transfer costs of $5.

d) Sold 10 shares of common stock of M Corporation at $41 per share.

Required:

(Assume the cost method is appropriate.)

1. Give all indicated entries for transactions (*a*), (*b*), and (*c*) on Henna's books.

2. Give entry for transaction (*d*) under each of the following assumptions: (*a*) The stock sold was specifically identified as coming from the second purchase; (*b*) the stock sold was accounted for on a Fifo basis; and (*c*) the stock sold was accounted for on an average basis.

3. What is the "book value" of the stock investment account after giving effect to the above transactions?

Exercise 11–2

Blue Company purchased common stock (par value $50) of the Doe Corporation as a permanent investment. Transactions related to this investment were as follows and in the order given.

a) Purchased 1,000 shares of the common stock at $90 per share (designated as lot No. 1).

b) Purchased 4,000 shares of the common stock at $95 per share (designated as lot No. 2). The 5,000 shares in total represented 15% of the outstanding shares of the Doe Corporation; it did not represent a controlling interest.

c) At the end of the first year Doe Corporation reported a net income of $12,000.

d) The Doe Corporation declared a dividend on the common stock of $2 per share.

e) The dividend was paid in cash.

f) After reporting a net income of $9,000 for the second year the Doe Corporation declared a stock dividend whereby each shareholder received one additional share for each two shares owned. At the time of the stock dividend (prior to declaration) the stock was selling at $85.

g) The Doe Corporation revised its charter to provide for two classes of stock, preferred and no-par common. The "old" common was canceled. Accordingly, holders of the old shares were directed to turn them in to the corporation and receive in exchange two shares of the new preferred (par $30 per share) for each old share owned.

Required:

(Assume cost method and no controlling interest.)

Give entries for each transaction as they should be made on the books of the investor, the Blue Company. Provide explanations and computations.

Exercise 11–3

On January 1, 19A, Company R purchased 5% of the 50,000 ($10 par value) shares of the outstanding common stock of Company S at $11 per share. During the years 19A, 19B, and 19C the following additional data were available:

	Company R	Company S
End of 19A:		
Reported profits	$200,000°	$30,000
Cash dividends declared	40,000	20,000
Market value per share	75	15
End of 19B:		
Reported profits	180,000°	20,000
Cash dividends declared	40,000	15,000
Market value per share	80	14

January 10, 19C:
Company R sold 500 shares of Company S stock at $17 per share.

°Prior to considering the investment in Company S.

Required:

(You may use abbreviated account titles; assume market value method.)
1. Give all entries indicated for Company R in parallel columns assuming:

a) market changes are considered "realized."
b) market changes are considered "unrealized."

2. In parallel columns for each assumption show the (a) balance of the investment account (shares, per share, and amount) and (b) net income after considering the investment in Company S, for each of the three periods.
3. Compute the balance in the "unrealized" account at the end of each period.

Exercise 11–4

On January 10, 19A, Company X purchased as a permanent investment 12% of the 10,000 shares of outstanding common stock of Company Y (par value $40 per share) at $50 per share. During 19A, 19B, and 19C the following additional data were available:

	19A	19B
Reported profits by Company Y at year-end	$30,000	$35,000
Cash dividends declared by Company Y at year-end	10,000	15,000
Quoted market price per share of Company Y stock at year-end	57	55
Reported profits by Company X at year-end (prior to considering the investment in Company Y)	70,000	80,000

On January 2, 19C, Company X sold 300 of the Company Y shares at $56 per share.

Required:

(Assume market value method is appropriate.)
1. Give all entries indicated in the accounts of Company X assuming market changes are considered as "realized."
2. Prepare a tabulation to show the net income of X Company and the balance in the investment account for the years 19A, 19B, and 19C.
3. Restate any entries that would be affected if market changes are considered "unrealized."

Exercise 11-5

On January 1, 19A, Company P purchased (for cash) 60% of the 10,000 outstanding voting common stock of Company S at $15 per share. At that date the following additional data in respect to Company S were available:

	At Book Value	Market Value per Appraisal
Assets not subject to depreciation	$ 80,000	$ 85,000
Assets subject to depreciation (10-year remaining life)	60,000	67,000
Total	$140,000	$152,000
Liabilities	$ 10,000	$ 10,000
Common stock ($10 par value)	100,000	
Retained earnings	30,000	
Total	$140,000	

At the end of 19A, Company S reported net income for the year of $20,000 (including a $5,000 extraordinary gain) and cash dividends declared of $8,000.

Required:

1. Compute (a) the implied goodwill, (b) the annual amortization of goodwill assuming a 20-year amortization period, and (c) the increase in annual depreciation for investment accounting purposes.

2. Assuming a purchase, give all entries indicated on the books of Company P for 19A assuming the equity method.

3. Prepare a table reflecting (a) the 19A ending balance in the investment account and (b) the effect on the 19A income statement of Company P.

4. How much income from Company S would Company P recognize in 19A under the cost method?

5. Give the entry required assuming Company P sold 600 shares of the stock of Company S on January 3, 19C, for $10,000 assuming (a) the equity method and (b) the cost method.

Exercise 11-6

During January 19A Company A purchased 40% of the 5,000 shares of outstanding common stock of Company B at $20 per share. At that date the following data were available:

	Company B	
	At Book Value	Market Value per Appraisal
Assets not subject to depreciation	$ 60,000	$63,000
Assets subject to depreciation (10-year remaining life)	40,000	45,000
	$100,000	
Liabilities	$ 20,000	20,000
Common stock (par value $10)	50,000	
Retained earnings	30,000	
	$100,000	

At the end of 19A Company B reported a net income of $15,000 and dividends declared of $5,000. At the end of 19A Company B common stock was quoted on the market at $22 per share.

At the end of 19A Company A reported a net income of $200,000 prior to considering the investment in Company B. In January 19C Company A sold 100 of the shares of Company B at $23 per share.

Required:

1. In parallel columns prepare entries for the accounts of Company A from the date of purchase of the long-term investment through date of sale of the 100 shares assuming: (a) the cost method is utilized, (b) the market value method is used (market changes are treated as "realized"), and (c) the equity method is utilized. Assume any goodwill amortization to be over a 20-year period.

2. Prepare a table for each assumption in requirement 1 to reflect (a) balances in the investment account and (b) net income (adjusted) for Company A at the end of 19A and after the 100 shares were sold.

Exercise 11-7

On January 1, 19A, Company P acquired a controlling interest in Company S when the balance sheets reflected the following (summarized):

	Company P	Company S
Assets not subject to depreciation	$180,000	$40,000
Assets subject to depreciation (10-year remaining life)	120,000	25,000
	$300,000	$65,000
Liabilities	$ 20,000	$ 5,000
Common stock	200,000	40,000°
Retained earnings	80,000	20,000
	$300,000	$65,000

° 4,000 shares, par value $10 per share.

Required:

(Assume Company P paid $60,000 for all of the outstanding stock of Company S.)

1. Give entry in the accounts of Company P for acquisition of the stock for cash assuming a long-term investment.

2. Prepare a consolidation work sheet at date of acquisition. Assume the assets of Company S at book value are realistically valued.

3. Prepare a consolidation work sheet assuming instead that Company P paid $48,000 for 80% of the outstanding common stock of Company S.

Exercise 11-8

Refer to the balance sheets for Company P and Company S as given in Exercise 11-7.

Required:

1. Assume that the assets of Company S were appraised at acquisition with the following results (these values have already been reduced for the proportionate ownership):

a) Assets not subject to depreciation to be increased in consolidation to $41,000.

b) Assets subject to depreciation to be increased in consolidation to $30,000.

Assume further that Company P purchased 90% of the outstanding common stock of Company S for $70,000. Prepare a consolidation work sheet at acquisition.

2. Assume instead that the appraisal reflects the following results:

a) Assets not subject to depreciation to be reduced in consolidation to $39,000.

b) Assets subject to depreciation to be reduced in consolidation to $23,000.

Assume further that Company P purchased 90% of the outstanding common stock of Company S for $51,000. Prepare a consolidation work sheet at date of acquisition.

Exercise 11–9

On January 1, 19A, Par Company purchased a 100% interest in Sub Company at book value. At the end of 19A the financial statements reflected the following (summarized):

	Reported at End of Year 19A	
	Par Company	Sub Company
Income Statement:		
Sales	$360,000	$ 80,000
Interest income		400
	$360,000	$ 80,400
Cost of goods sold	$150,000	$ 42,000
Other operating expenses	109,600	26,300
Interest expense	400	100
	$260,000	$ 68,400
Net Income	$100,000	$ 12,000
Balance Sheet:		
Current assets	$172,000	$ 80,000
Investment in Sub Company	128,000	
Fixed assets	400,000	90,000
	$700,000	$170,000
Current liabilities	$ 50,000	$ 30,000
Common stock	500,000	100,000
Retained earnings	150,000	40,000
	$700,000	$170,000

Intercompany items at year-end were:

1. Par Company sold Sub Company goods (at cost) during the year amounting to $5,000.
2. Par Company paid Sub Company $400 interest during the year.
3. Par Company owed Sub Company $3,000 at the end of the year.

Required:

Prepare a work sheet to develop a consolidated income statement and balance sheet at the end of 19A.

Exercise 11–10

Utilizing the income statements, balance sheets, and intercompany transactions given in Exercise 11–9 present a work sheet to develop a consolidated income statement and balance sheet assuming that Par Company acquired a 90% ownership interest at book value in Sub Company at a cost of $115,200. This assumption changes the balance sheet of Par Company as follows:

Current assets	$184,800
Investment in Sub Company	115,200

Exercise 11–11

On January 1, 19A, X Company purchased 80% of the outstanding common stock of Y Company at a cost of $137,200. At date of acquisition, on the basis of an appraisal of the assets of Y Company, the decision was made for consolidation purposes to (*a*) increase the current assets by $1,000 and (*b*) increase the fixed assets by $5,000. These were considered to be "fair" values for the assets.

After one year of operations each company prepared a balance sheet and income statement as follows (summarized):

	Reported at End of Year 19A	
	X Company	*Y Company*
Income Statement:		
Sales	$340,000	$ 90,000
Cost of goods sold	$190,000	$ 46,000
Depreciation	32,000	15,000
Other operating expenses	72,000	17,000
Interest expense	2,000	1,000
Total	$296,000	$ 79,000
Net Income	$ 44,000	$ 11,000
Balance Sheet:		
Current assets	$170,800	$ 40,000
Investment in Y Company	137,200	
Fixed assets	330,000	160,000
Total	$638,000	$200,000
Liabilities	$138,000	$ 30,000
Common stock	400,000	150,000
Retained earnings	100,000	20,000
Total	$638,000	$200,000

Intercompany items at year-end were determined to be:

1. Sales of X Company to Y Company during the year were $15,000 (at cost).

2. Depreciation on fixed assets; assume a 10-year remaining life.

3. Amortization of any goodwill; assume a 20-year amortization period.

Required:

Prepare a work sheet to develop a consolidated income statement and balance sheet at the end of 19A.

Exercise 11-12

Company P and Company S balance sheets reflected the following on a given date:

	Company P	Company S
Assets subject to depreciation (net)	$200,000	$ 80,000
Other assets (including cash)	340,000	120,000
Total Assets	$540,000	$200,000
Liabilities	$ 60,000	$ 20,000
Common stock (par $10)	400,000	150,000
Retained earnings	80,000	30,000
Total Liabilities	$540,000	$200,000

The fair market values of Company S assets, determined by appraisal on the balance sheet date, were: assets subject to depreciation, $120,000; other assets, $140,000.

> Case A—Company P purchases all of the outstanding stock of Company S for $270,000 cash; Company S will continue as a subsidiary of Company P.
>
> Case B—Company P exchanges its own stock for all of the outstanding stock of Company S on a share for share basis; Company S will continue as a subsidiary of Company P.

Required:

In parallel columns present the following for each case:

1. Entry on Company P books to record the combining transaction.

2. Values on the consolidated balance sheet prepared immediately after the combination.

3. Income statement amounts subsequently (annual basis), on a consolidated basis, for depreciation and any amortization of intangibles. Assume a 10-year remaining useful life in respect to depreciation and amortization.

Exercise 11-13

Grayson Company purchased for a lump sum of $103,000 the three different stocks listed below:

Company and Stock	Number of Shares
X Corporation, common stock, par $10	200
Y Corporation, preferred stock, par $100	400
Z Corporation, common stock, no par	500

In addition Grayson paid transfer fees and other costs related to the acquisition amounting to $790. At the time of purchase the stocks were quoted on the local market at the following prices per share: X common, $70; Y preferred, $120; and Z common, $90.

Required:

(Assume cost method.)

Give entry to record the purchase and payment of the transfer fees. Show computations. Record each stock in a separate account.

Exercise 11–14

Each of the following situations are completely independent; however, both of them relate to the receipt of a stock dividend by an investor.

Case A. Corporation K had 20,000 shares of $50 par value stock outstanding and a balance of $350,000 in retained earnings at which time the board of directors voted to issue a 25% stock dividend by capitalizing $250,000 of the retained earnings.

Required:

Give all entries on the books of a stockholder (investor) who had previously purchased 160 shares of Corporation K stock at $65 per share and who, after receiving the stock dividend, sold 20 shares of stock at the book value of the stock as shown on the books of Corporation K (after the stock dividend). Assume the cost method.

Case B. During the course of an audit you find accounts as follows:

Investments – Stock in A Company ($100 par per share)

Debits

Jan. 1	Cost of 100 shares	$17,500
Feb. 1	50 shares received as a stock dividend	5,000

Credits

July 1	25 shares of dividend stock sold at 125	$ 3,125

Income Summary

Credits

Feb. 1	Stock dividend on A Company stock (50%)	$ 5,000
July 1	Cash dividend on A Company stock	3,000

Required:

Assuming the cost method, what adjustments to these accounts would you make? Give reasons.

Exercise 11–15

Box Corporation issued rights to subscribe to new stock at par ($100) in the ratio of one new share for six old shares held. The stock "rights on" was quoted at $149. John Doe owned 300 shares of stock; cost, $22,350.

Required:

(Assume the cost method.)

1. How many "rights" did Doe receive?

2. Using the parity method, determine the cost of his stock rights.

3. Assuming that Doe exercised his rights, determine the cost of the new stock and give entries for receipt and exercise of the rights.

4. Assuming that Doe sold his rights at $7.40, make entry for the sale.

Exercise 11–16

Give entries under the cost method for the following transactions which occurred over a period of time and in the chronological order shown:

a) XY Corporation purchased 100 shares of Bell Corporation common stock at $99 per share as a permanent investment.

b) Bell Corporation issued a 10% dividend in additional shares of the same class of stock.

c) Bell Corporation issued rights to present common stockholders entitling each holder of five old shares to buy one additional share of new common stock at 95. At the time the rights sold for $4 each and the shares outstanding sold for $116 each (ex rights). Make an allocation to the rights.

d) XY Corporation exercised its rights and bought new shares.

e) XY Corporation sold 120 shares of Bell stock for $12,000 failing to identify the specific shares disposed of. (Use Fifo procedure.)

Exercise 11–17

An investor purchased 100 shares of X Corporation's common stock paying $90 per share. Shortly thereafter he received stock rights entitling him to purchase one additional share of stock for $65 for each 10 rights tendered. At the time the rights were issued the common stock was selling at $120, "rights on," per share.

Required:

1. Give entry to record the purchase of the investment assuming the cost method.

2. Give the entry to record the receipt of the rights by the investor.

3. Give entry assuming the investor sold 20 rights at $4 each.

4. Give entry assuming the investor exercised the remaining rights.

5. Compute the parity value of a right assuming that the stock was selling at $110 ex rights; assume there was no known market value "rights on."

PROBLEMS

Problem 11–1

RL Corporation completed the following transactions relative to their portfolio of stocks held as permanent investments in the order given:

a) Purchased 100 shares of common stock (par value $50) of M Corporation at $70 per share plus a brokerage commission of 4% and transfer costs of $20.

b) Purchased for a lump sum of $58,800 the following stocks of the N Corporation:

Stocks	Number of Shares	Market Price at Date of Purchase
Class A, common, par value $100 200		50
Preferred, par value $50..200		100
Class B, no-par value stock (stated value $125) 200		150

c) Purchased 300 shares of common stock of M Corporation at $80 per share plus a brokerage commission of 4% and transfer costs of $60.

d) Received a stock dividend on the M Corporation stock; for each share held an additional share was received.

e) Sold 400 shares of M Corporation stock at $45 per share (Fifo).

f) Received a two-for-one stock split on the common stock of the N Corporation (the number of shares doubled).

g) Received cash dividends as follows:

M Corporation common stock—$5.00 per share.

N common stock—$3.00 per share.

N preferred—6%.

N no-par value stock—$1.50 per share.

Required:

1. Give entries for RL Corporation for the above transactions. Show calculations and assume Fifo. Use the cost method.

2. Provide an inventory of the permanent investments, including balance sheet valuations, after giving effect to the above transactions.

Problem 11-2

Bower Company owned the following permanent investments:

a) 100 shares of Ajax Corporation common stock acquired in 1949 at $100 per share. No dividends have ever been paid. In recent years the stock has been selling around $6 per share.

b) 600 shares of Preston Mines, Inc., stock acquired in 1950 at $7 per share. In recent years a portion of each dividend has been designated as a liquidating dividend. Dividends have been received as follows:

	Income	Return of Capital	Total
1968...	$3.00	$3.40	$6.40
1969...	2.00	2.35	4.35
1970...	1.60	2.00	3.60
1971...	1.00	.40	1.40

c) 2,000 shares of Brown, Inc., common stock acquired in 1963 at $150 per share; the current market price recently has been $210 per share. The stock regularly pays dividends. A two-for-one stock split has just been announced (the number of shares doubled).

d) 200 shares of common stock (par $50) and 300 shares of preferred stock (par $100) of the Sky Corporation. These shares were purchased as a package in 1970 at a lump-sum cost of $87,000; at the time they were selling at common, $150 and preferred, $200 per share. During 1971 a one-for-one stock dividend was received on the common shares (the number of shares doubled).

Required:

For Bower Company give *all* entries indicated since 1949, including computations with respect to each lot of shares. Explain any assumptions made. Also compute the "book value" and "cost per share" of each lot of shares at the end of 1971. Use the cost method.

Problem 11–3

On March 10, 19A, Bricker Company purchased 10% of the 100,000 outstanding common shares of Core Company at $6 per share. During the years 19A, 19B, and 19C the following additional data were available:

	Bricker Company	Core Company
End 19A:		
Reported profits...$350,000°		$30,000
Cash dividends declared 40,000		15,000
Market value per share...................................... 130		9
End 19B:		
Reported profits...$320,000°		($10,000 loss)
Cash dividends declared 40,000		10,000
Market value per share...................................... 140		7

° Prior to considering the investment in Core Company.

On January 25, 19C, Bricker Company sold 2,000 shares of the Core Company stock at $8 per share.

Required:

1. Give all entries indicated in the accounts of Bricker Company assuming the cost method is utilized.

2. Give all entries indicated assuming that the market value method is utilized and that market changes are considered as "realized."

3. Give all entries indicated assuming that the market value method is utilized and that market changes are considered as "unrealized."

4. Prepare a tabulation to reflect by years, for each of the above requirements, the (*a*) balances in the investment account, (*b*) net income for Bricker Company, and (*c*) balance in any "unrealized" accounts.

Problem 11–4

During January, 19A, Company P purchased 21% of the 30,000 outstanding common shares of Company S at $16 per share. At date of acquisition of the shares the following data in respect to Company S had been assembled by Company P:

	Company S	
	At Book Value	At Estimated Value
Assets not subject to depreciation.............................$250,000		$260,000
Assets subject to depreciation (10-year		
remaining life) 200,000		220,000
	$450,000	

Company S

	At Book Value	At Estimated Value
Liabilities	$ 50,000	$ 50,000
Common stock (par $10)	300,000	
Retained earnings	100,000	
	$450,000	

Selected data available at year-end:

	19A	19B
Reported net income, Company S:		
Ordinary	$ 20,000	($10,000 loss)
Extraordinary	10,000	
Reported net income, Company P (prior to considering the investment in Company S)	120,000	100,000
Cash dividends declared:		
Company S	8,000	5,000
Company P	40,000	30,000
Quoted market price per share, Company S	21	17

At the end of January, 19C, Company P sold enough shares so as to retain exactly a 20% interest in Company S; the sales price was $18 per share.

Required:

1. In parallel columns prepare all entries in respect to the investment in the books of Company P (through January 19C) assuming (*a*) the cost method is utilized, (*b*) the market value method is used (assume market value changes are considered as "realized"), and (*c*) the equity method is utilized. Amortize any goodwill over 20 years.

2. Prepare a tabulation for each assumption in requirement 1 to reflect (*a*) balances in the investment account and (*b*) net income for Company P adjusted for the results of the investment (19A through January 19C).

Problem 11–5

On January 1, 19A, Company P acquired a controlling interest in Company S when the balance sheets reflected the following at book value (summarized):

Book Values at January 1, 19A

	Company P	Company S
Assets not subject to depreciation	$450,000	$140,000
Assets subject to depreciation, net (10-year remaining life)	350,000	100,000
	$800,000	$240,000
Liabilities	$100,000	$ 40,000
Common stock	500,000	150,000°
Retained earnings	200,000	50,000
	$800,000	$240,000

° Par $10 per share.

This problem will focus on four separate conditions (cases) under which Company P acquired the controlling interest in Company S as follows:

Cases	Ownership Percentage	Purchase Price	Consolidation Values to be Recorded for Assets of Company S	
			Nondepreciable Assets	Depreciable Assets
A 100		$200,000	Book value	Book value
B 90		180,000	Book value	Book value
C 80		152,000	$135,000	$ 97,000
D 80		172,000	142,000	104,000

Required:

For each case prepare a consolidation work sheet at acquisition.

Problem 11–6

On January 1, 19A, P Company purchased all of the common stock of S Company (100% interest) at a cost of $197,000 which was equivalent to book value. After one year of operations each company prepared an income statement and balance sheet as follows (summarized):

	Reported at End of Year 19A	
	P Company	S Company
Income Statement:		
Sales..$620,000		$140,000
Interest income... 700		
Total..$620,700		$140,000
Cost of goods sold $370,000		$ 75,000
Depreciation... 40,000		15,000
Other operating expenses... 132,700		36,300
Interest expense... 1,000		700
Total..$543,700		$127,000
Net Income ....$ 77,000		$ 13,000
Balance Sheet:		
Current assets...$273,000		$101,000
Investment in S Company... 197,000		
Fixed assets... 430,000		149,000
Total..$900,000		$250,000
Liabilities...$180,000		$ 40,000
Common stock 600,000		150,000
Retained earnings.. 120,000		60,000
Total..$900,000		$250,000

Intercompany items and adjustments for 19A:

1. S Company sold $17,000 worth of goods (at cost) to P Company during the year.

2. S Company paid P Company $700 interest during the year.
3. At the end of 19A, S Company owed P Company $20,000.

Required:

1. Prepare a work sheet for 19A to develop a consolidated income statement and balance sheet.
2. Prepare another work sheet for the same purpose assuming that P Company acquired an 80% interest (instead of 100%) at book value.

Problem 11-7

On January 1, 19A, Company A purchased in the market 80% of the outstanding common stock of Company B at a cost of $188,000. At date of acquisition, based upon an appraisal, the decision was made for consolidation purposes to increase the fixed assets by $8,000 and to decrease the current assets by $6,000 (the values have already been adjusted to the proportionate ownership).

After one year of operations each company prepared an income statement and balance sheet as follows (summarized):

	Reported at End of Year A	
	Company A	Company B
Income Statement:		
Sales	$630,000	$180,000
Interest income	1,000	
Total	$631,000	$180,000
Cost of goods sold	$370,000	$ 98,000
Depreciation	37,000	16,000
Other operating expenses	140,000	45,000
Interest expense	4,000	1,000
Total	$551,000	$160,000
Net Income	$ 80,000	$ 20,000
Balance Sheet:		
Current assets	$372,000	$110,000
Investment in Company B	188,000	
Fixed assets	360,000	160,000
Total	$920,000	$270,000
Current liabilities	$ 70,000	$ 30,000
Common stock	760,000	200,000
Retained earnings	90,000	40,000
Total	$920,000	$270,000

Data relating to 19A eliminations and adjustments:

1. During the year Company A sold merchandise to Company B for $35,000 (at cost).
2. During 19A Company B paid Company A $1,000 interest on loans.
3. At the end of 19A, Company B owed Company A $20,000.

4. The assets of Company B have an estimated remaining life of 10 years (no residual value, straight-line depreciation).

5. Goodwill is to be amortized over a 20-year period.

Required:

1. Prepare a work sheet to develop a consolidated income statement and balance sheet.

2. Based on the work sheet prepare a consolidated income statement (unclassified) and balance sheet in good form.

Problem 11-8

On January 1, 19A, Corporation Z acquired all of the outstanding stock of Corporation M in order to combine the two businesses. Z issued $100,000 par value of its stock (which had a market value of $300,000) to the stockholders of M in exchange for their stock. Immediately upon the exchange of the stock, Corporation M was dissolved and Z took over the net assets. As of January 1, 19A, Corporation M had $100,000 of stock outstanding; $100,000 of paid-in surplus; and $100,000 of retained earnings.

Required:

1. Give two ways that these transactions may be recorded on the books of Corporation Z.

2. State the circumstances under which each of the two treatments would be appropriate and give the reasoning supporting each treatment.

(AICPA adapted)

Problem 11-9

1. Explain what stock rights are and the accounting for them by recipients as permanent investments. (Disregard income tax considerations.)

2. John Manus holds 100 shares of Harper Company stock, which he purchased in 1967 for $90 a share. On September 10, 1971, Harper Company announces that stock rights will be issued to stockholders of record September 20, the rights to expire on October 10. The rights permit the purchase of one share of stock at $100 for every four shares held. The stock is sold on September 15 "rights on" at $120. The stock has a par value of $25 per share. What is the theoretical value of each right on September 15?

3. If the rights are sold at their theoretical value what gain or loss, if any, would Manus report? Show computations.

(AICPA adapted)

Problem 11-10

Dulan Company had the following transactions in shares of AB Corporation held as a permanent investment:

a) 2,000 shares common, par $25, purchased at $33 on July 1, 1965.

b) 400 shares common received as a stock dividend on July 1, 1969.

c) 800 shares common obtained by exercise of stock rights on July 1, 1971, cash consideration being $20,333. The ex-rights price was $34 per share; rights sold for $2 when received. The 2,400 rights received were exercised.

d) The only credits to the account were for the sale on November 25, 1971, at $40 per share, of all shares received as a dividend and through exercise of rights.

Required:

(Assume the cost method.)

1. Set up the account for the AB investment; make an allocation for rights and keep each block separate.

2. Show gain or loss on sale of stock during 1971.

Problem 11-11

With respect to permanent investments the Jones Company completed the following transactions in stock of the Bay Corporation:

a) January 7, 1964, purchased 200 shares of $100 par-value common stock at $110 per share.

b) The corporation was expanding, and as of March 1, 1965, issued to Jones Company 200 rights, each permitting the purchase of one-fourth share of common stock at par. No entry was made.

The bid price of the stock on March 1, 1965, was 140. There was no quoted price for the rights.

c) Jones Company was advised that they would "lose out on the other stock if they did not pay in the money for the rights." Therefore, they paid for the new shares on April 1, 1965, charging the payment to the Investment account. Since the Jones Company felt that they had been assessed by the company, they credited the dividends (10% in December of each year) to the Investment account until the debit was fully offset.

d) In December 1969 Jones Company received a 50% stock dividend from the company. They made no entry for this dividend because they expected to sell the shares received. They did sell them for $160 per share in January 1970 and credited Income for the proceeds.

e) In December 1970 the stock was split on a two-for-one basis and the new shares were issued as no-par shares. Jones Company found that each new share was worth $5 more than the $110 per share which they paid for the original stock; they debited Investment with the additional shares received at $110 per share and credited Income.

f) In June 1971 Jones Company sold one half of the stock at $92 per share and credited the proceeds to the Investment account.

Required:

(Assume the cost method.)

1. Set up the Investment account as it was kept by Jones Company.

2. Prepare a schedule showing an analysis of the account as the transactions should have been recorded using the "average cost" method for recording stock sold.

3. Prepare the entries that would be necessary to correct the income of each of the years in which Jones Company held the stock.

(AICPA adapted)

chapter 12

Tangible Fixed Assets — Acquisition, Utilization, and Retirement

ACQUISITION OF FIXED ASSETS

Nature of Fixed Assets

Fixed assets, occasionally referred to as capital assets or permanent assets, are those properties and rights which the business retains more or less permanently, not for sale but for utilization in the course of its normal operations in producing goods, distributing goods, and rendering services. For accounting purposes fixed assets are generally classified as follows:

1. Tangible fixed assets—those properties properly classified as fixed assets having bodily substance. They are frequently referred to as plant and equipment, although this term does not encompass all classes of tangible fixed assets. There are three classes of tangible fixed assets, viz:

   a) Those subject to depreciation such as buildings, equipment, tools, and furniture.

   b) Those subject to depletion such as mineral deposits, oil wells, and timber tracts.

   c) Those not subject to depreciation or depletion such as land for plant site, farms, and ranches.

469

2. Intangible fixed assets—those assets properly classified as fixed assets having no bodily substance; the value is represented by grants and business rights which confer some operating, financial, or income-producing advantages on the owner. They are amortized over their useful life in a manner that accords with the expiration of their economic value to the enterprise.

Intangible fixed assets are discussed in detail in Chapter 14; Chapter 12 and 13 consider the problems of accounting for tangible fixed assets.

Idle facilities and land held as a prospective plant site should not be classified as fixed assets unless there is reasonable expectation that they will be put to use for the purpose acquired within a reasonably short period of time. Plants made idle by obsolescence, inadequacy, or permanent overexpansion, even though in good physical condition, should not be classed as fixed assets but as "other" assets.

Capital and Revenue Expenditures

Proper accounting for expenditures and obligations incident to the acquirement of property or of benefits (tangible or intangible) necessitates classification of such outlays as either *capital expenditures* or as *revenue expenditures*. Capital expenditures relate to the acquirement of a benefit that extends over one or more accounting periods beyond the current period, hence they are recorded in appropriate asset accounts. Capital expenditures made for assets having a limited life are subsequently allocated to the periods benefited through depreciation, amortization, or depletion. An expenditure that is debited to an asset account is said to be capitalized. Revenue expenditures relate to the acquirement of property or benefits that do not extend beyond the current accounting period, hence they are recorded in appropriate expense accounts for the current period.

In cases where (a) the expenditure is relatively small, or (b) the future benefit is insignificant, or (c) reasonable measurement of the future benefit is practically impossible, practical reasons suggest classification of the outlay as a revenue expenditure. Many companies have adopted a practical accounting policy in this respect to the effect that, for example, "expenditures under $25 will be classed as revenue expenditures; expenditures above this amount will be classified as capital expenditures only where there is clearly a significant and measurable benefit accruing to a future period."

Valuation Principles Underlying Fixed Asset Accounting

The accounting for fixed assets fundamentally rests upon the *cost and matching principles*. At date of acquisition, assets are recorded in the accounts at cost. The acquisition cost of assets is measured by the cash outlay made to acquire such assets; or, if considerations other than cash are exchanged for the assets, the fair market value of such consideration at the time of the transaction is the proper measure of the cost of the assets so acquired. In the absence of a determinable fair market value for the consideration given, the asset is recorded at its fair market value. An asset is not "acquired" until it has been placed in the position where it is to be used and is ready for productivity in the broad business sense; thus all incidental costs incurred in placing an asset in this status are proper additions to the purchase price of the asset.

Subsequent to acquisition, tangible fixed assets are carried in the accounts and reported at (a) cost (not limited life) or (b) in the case of a limited life, at cost less accumulated depreciation, amortization, or depletion (reflecting continuing application of the matching principle.)

The following is an outline of the principal aspects influencing the accounting for tangible fixed assets:

1. Acquisition cost of tangible fixed assets when acquired:
    a) For cash.
    b) On a deferred payment plan.
    c) For stock or other securities.
    d) Through exchanges.
    e) Through mixed acquisitions at a lump cost.
2. Outlays subsequent to acquisition but before operational use:
    a) Installation costs.
    b) Reinstallation costs.
    c) Repairs and improvements prior to use.
    d) Razing old structures.
    e) Other incidental costs.
3. Assets constructed for own use.
4. Interest during the construction period.
5. Outlays subsequent to the beginning of operational use:
    a) Repairs and maintenance.
    b) Replacements and renewals.
    c) Betterments and improvements.
    d) Additions.
    e) Rearrangements of assets.

Subsequent sections of this chapter develop, in accordance with this outline, the accounting for tangible fixed assets.

At this point we should note that in accounting for tangible fixed assets there are special circumstances where departure from the cost principle has been sanctioned by the accounting profession. These exceptions are discussed subsequently in this chapter.

Assets Acquired for Cash

If a fixed asset is purchased for cash, any outlay that a prudent buyer would make for the asset in an arm's-length transaction, including costs of installation and making ready to use, should be capitalized. The capitalizable costs include the invoice price (less discounts), plus incidental costs such as insurance during transit, freight, duties, drayage, title searching, title registration, installation, and breaking-in costs. All available discounts, *whether taken or not*, should be deducted from the invoice cost. Discounts not taken should be recorded as discounts lost and treated as a current financial expense.

Assets Acquired on Deferred Payment Plan

Assets acquired on a deferred or time payment plan (on credit) should be recorded at the equivalent cash price excluding all interest and carrying charges. Both actual and implied interest and carrying charges should be charged to expense and not to the fixed asset account. If the contract of purchase does not specify interest and carrying charges, such charges, nevertheless, should be taken into account in determining the cost of the asset. If a cash price is determinable, the excess charged under the deferred payment contract should be treated as expense to be apportioned over the period covered by the purchase contract. If no cash price is determinable, a reasonable interest and carrying charge should be recognized in recording the purchase. Although sound in theory these latter distinctions are not always observed in practice, since the amounts involved may be relatively insignificant.

To illustrate the purchase of an asset on a time payment plan, assume a machine was purchased under a contract that required equal payments of $3,741 at the end of each of three years when the going interest rate was 6% per annum. To record the asset purchased at $11,223 (i.e., $3,741 × 3) would include in the asset account the interest cost implicit in the contract. Rather the asset account should be debited for the *present value* of the three payments discounted at 6% as follows:

PV = Annual Payment × P (Table 5–4; page 192)
   = $3,741 × 2.673012 (present value of annuity of 1 at 6% for 3 periods)
   = $10,000 (rounded)

Therefore, the indicated entries are as follows.

At date of purchase:[1]

Asset — Machinery..10,000		
Installments Payable — Machinery Contract......................		10,000

At payment dates (amounts rounded):

	1st Year	2nd Year	3rd Year
Interest Expense°	600	412	211
Installments Payable — Machinery			
Contract 3,141		3,329	3,530
Cash	3,741	3,741	3,741

°Computation of interest:

1st year....... $10,000 × 6%   = $600

2nd year......($10,000 − $3,141) × 6%   = $412

3rd year ......($10,000 − $3,141 − $3,329) × 6% = $212

($211 used due to rounding difference)

Fixed assets frequently are purchased under conditional sales contracts. A conditional sales contract is a purchase of property on an installment plan under which a certain number of payments must be made before title to the property is transferred. Such contracts generally provide that the agreement may be terminated by failure to make regular payments, in which event the vendor, or lessor as he is in some cases, may repossess the property, without legal action, by canceling the unpaid deficit. The accounting question involved is whether an asset account or an expense account should be charged as the periodic payments are made. In the absence of definite intentions to the contrary on the part of the purchaser it should be assumed that payment in full will be made under the contract; therefore the asset, related liability, and interest cost should be recognized. To illustrate, assume a conditional sales contract was entered into whereby five annual payments of $6,000 each were to be paid on a particular machine that normally is sold for $25,274 cash. The contract further stipulated that (a) the vendor may repossess the machinery in case of default in any payment, (b) title passes to the vendee after the fifth payment, and (c) the vendee, at his option, may cease making

---

[1] Alternatively this entry could be made as follows:

Asset — Machinery...10,000		
Deferred Interest Cost 1,223		
Installments Payable — Machinery Contract......................		11,223

The payment entries would be revised accordingly; the net effect would be the same in all respects. The first payment entry would be:

Interest Expense 600		
Installments Payable — Machinery Contract........................... 3,741		
Deferred Interest Cost		600
Cash		3,741

payments and return the machine without further obligation. The accounting entries might be:

1. At date of contract:

Machinery (lease-purchase) 25,274		
Contract Liability on Machinery (lease-purchase).............		25,274

2. At date of first payment:

Interest Expense ($25,274 × 6%)...	1,516	
Contract Liability on Machinery (lease-purchase)...................	4,484	
Cash		6,000

In the above journal entry the implied interest rate of 6% determined as follows:

Data: Present value of the contract payments, $25,274; Contract payments, five at $6,000 each, $30,000.

$PV = $ Annual Payment × Table Value for Present Value of Annuity of 1

$25,274 = $6,000 ×$ Table Value (five periods)

Therefore:

$25,274 ÷ $6,000 = 4.212$, the table value for five periods

Referring to Table 5–4, page 192 we find the value 4.212 indicates an effective interest rate of 6%.[2]

3. Depreciation for first year (10-year life; straight line):

Depreciation Expense...	2,527	
Accumulated Depreciation – Machinery (lease- purchase)...		2,527

4. After completion of contractual payments:

---

[2] A table of debt amortization and interest expense can be readily constructed to indicate the entries over the life of the indebtedness:

Period	Annual Payment (Cash Credit)	Interest Expense (Debit)		Payment on Liability (Credit)	Unpaid Principal
Start............					$25,274
1...................$	6,000	($25,274 × 6%)	$1,516	$ 4,484	20,790
2..................	6,000	($20,790 × 6%)	1,247	4,753	16,037
3..................	6,000	($16,037 × 6%)	962	5,038	10,999
4..................	6,000	($10,999 × 6%)	660	5,340	5,659
5..................	6,000	($ 5,659 × 6%)	341	5,659	–0–
	$30,000		$4,726	$25,274	

Machinery 25,274
Accumulated   Depreciation—Machinery   (lease-purchase)
   $2,527 × 5...12,635
      Machinery (lease-purchase)   25,274
      Accumulated Depreciation—Machinery   12,635

If the contract is defaulted, all balances in the accounts must be removed and a nonrecurring loss recognized.

Assets Acquired in Exchange for Securities

The proper valuation of fixed assets received in exchange for bonds and especially stocks of the company acquiring the assets frequently is difficult to determine for numerous reasons, some of which are:

1. There may be no readily determinable fair market value for the securities or the assets involved.
2. The absence of an arm's-length bargaining with respect to the exchange.
3. The nature of the assets generally involved, such as unexplored or unproven mineral deposits, manufacturing right, patents, chemical formulas, mining claims, and the like, may make value estimates difficult.
4. The tacit assumption on the part of many people that capital stock having a par or stated value issued in exchange for the property imputes a value to the asset rather than that the fair market value of the property constitutes the proper valuation of the capital stock.
5. The current quoted market price of the security may be based upon a market volume far below the volume of shares involved in the exchange.
6. The vagaries of the stock market, involving as it does sometimes, wide fluctuations in price over short periods of time generally casts significant doubt on the relevance of the price per share at a given time.

In general it may be said that the assets received should be valued at an amount equivalent to what would be the cash cost basis. Lacking this figure, valuation of the assets acquired through exchange of securities should be determined as follows:

1. Determine the fair market value of the consideration given, that is, the securities. In the case of a going concern whose capital stock has an established market price, the cost of the asset may be measured by the cash equivalent market value of the securities issued for the asset, assuming there are sound reasons for the presumptions that the current price is indicative that the market would absorb the volume of securities involved at that price.
2. If the fair market value of the securities in the volume exchanged for assets other than cash cannot be determined, the fair market

value of the assets acquired should be estimated. In the absence of an actual cash-basis sale of the assets involved in the immediate past, an independent appraisal of them by a professionally recognized appraiser may be recorded as the "implied cost" of the assets acquired.

3. If a fair market value for either the securities or the assets received cannot be determined objectively, values established by the directors of the corporation may be used. The law generally allows the directors considerable discretion in establishing values in this situation, except in cases where fraudulent intent on the part of the directors can be shown.

When assets are acquired by exchange of securities, any actual or implied discounts or premiums on the securities should be accounted for in the normal manner. Since bonds have a definite and legally enforceable maturity value and interest charge, problems of valuation of assets received in exchange for them may not be as critical as in the case where capital stock is involved. Fixed assets acquired in exchange for bonds payable should be recorded at the cash value of the bonds. If the cash value of the bonds is not ascertainable, the next best basis for valuation of the asset is the independently appraised value of the asset. If neither the cash value of the bonds nor a fair appraised value of the fixed asset is available, the asset should be recorded at the present value of the bonds issued therefor.

Fixed assets acquired for cash *and* securities combined should be capitalized at the sum of the cash and the fair market value of the securities determined in accordance with the standards discussed above. When property is financed through notes, care should be taken so that financing expenses are not charged as a part of the cost of the fixed asset.

In the capacity of an independent auditor the accountant cannot assume responsibility for determining an acceptable fair value of fixed assets acquired through exchange in the absence of objective data; however, he has the responsibility for full disclosure and appropriate qualifications in respect to the financial statements developed in an audit engagement.

Assets Acquired through Exchanges

Many purchases of fixed assets involve the "trading in" of an old asset in part payment for the new asset. Application of the cost principle as applied to fixed assets requires that the new asset be capitalized at the sum of the "fair market value" of the old asset surrendered plus the cash or other consideration (at fair market value) given the seller. Any difference between the book value of the old asset and its fair market value at date of exchange should be recorded as a loss or gain on disposition.

To illustrate the accounting for an exchange, assume that the Brookline Dairy traded in its Truck No. 4, original cost, $2,000, depreciation to date, $1,500 (book value $500), and paid $1,700 cash on the new truck having a firm cash price of $2,500. Thus, in view of the transaction it may be reasonable to assume that the fair market value of the old truck was $800. The exchange should be recorded as follows:

Delivery Equipment—New ($1,700 + $800)..............................2,500		
Accumulated Depreciation—Delivery Equipment—Old..............1,500		
Cash..		1,700
Delivery Equipment—Old...		2,000
Gain on Exchange of Delivery Equipment		300

The gain may be verified as follows:

Exchange value received for old asset:		
Cash price of new $2,500		
Cash paid... 1,700		
Fair market value of old asset............................	$800	
Book value of old asset:		
Cost...$2,000		
Accumulated depreciation.................................... 1,500		
Book value..	500	
Gain on Exchange...	$300	

Alternatively, if the fair market value of the old truck was clearly determined to be $700, the cost of the new truck to be recognized would be $2,400 and a gain of $200 recognized.

This approach capitalized the new asset at its cash equivalent cost and recognized a gain or loss on the old asset on the theory that its book value was not its fair market value. The accumulated depreciation in the past presumably was *incorrect* in terms of market values and as a consequence a loss or gain upon disposition should be recognized just as if it had been sold for the cash equivalent of its fair market value. The Gain (or loss) on Exchange of Delivery Equipment should be accounted for as an extraordinary item. It may be noted that had the exchange taken place during the accounting period, depreciation should have been recognized up to the date of exchange.

The approach illustrated above is not permissible for purposes of calculating federal income taxes since the regulations of the Treasury Department state that "no gain or loss is recognized if a taxpayer exchanges property held for productive use in his trade or business, together with cash for other property of like kind for the same use." The valuation of the new asset for *tax purposes* is the sum of the depreciated value (for tax purposes) of the old asset plus any cash paid (or liability incurred) in respect to the exchange. The exchange illustrated above would be recorded as follows under the "income tax method" assuming "book" and "tax" depreciation to be identical on the old asset:

Delivery Equipment—New ($500 + $1,700)..............................2,200
Accumulated Depreciation—Delivery Equipment.....................1,500
  Cash.. 1,700
  Delivery Equipment—Old.. 2,000

Obviously, under this method no loss or gain on disposition of the old asset will be reported. This method, approved by the Treasury Department to close an obvious tax loophole, is not consistent with sound financial accounting since a continuation of it tends to cause past accumulated depreciation amounts (whether correct or incorrect) to be compounded in the fixed asset accounts. Further, it tends to blend the old and new assets as one cost rather than as distinctly separate assets and costs. Income tax regulations are drawn to assess taxes equitably, to close loopholes, and to encourage certain economic activities by the taxpayer; consequently, they are not always consistent with sound accounting theory. Although accountants feel very strongly that income tax considerations should not influence the application of accounting principles, the tax method is sometimes used as a matter of expediency in those cases where the business is small and it is desirable to maintain the accounts strictly on a tax basis rather than on a sound financial accounting basis. Obviously, this problem would not arise if the old asset were sold separately and the new asset purchased on a cash-equivalent basis.

Departures from Cost in Accounting for Tangible Fixed Assets

Although asset accounting fundamentally is based upon the cost principle, there are special circumstances where departure therefrom may be justified. These exceptions are:

1. Write-up to appraisal value above cost (discussed in next chapter).
2. Write-up due to donation of assets to the company.
3. Write-up due to high and unexpected discovery value.
4. Write-down due to significant and permanent decrease in use value to the company.
5. Write-down due to quasi-reorganization (discussed in Chapter 21).

Items 2, 3, and 4 are discussed in the paragraphs to follow.

Donated Assets and Discovery Value

Assets are sometimes donated to a corporation by stockholders, by municipalities, or local nonprofit organizations as an inducement to locate a plant or other facilities in the area. Frequently, such gifts are conditional upon some particular performance on the part of the corporation such as the employment of a certain number of individuals by a given date.

An exception to the cost principle as applied to fixed assets at acquisition has long been recognized for property acquired by donation.

Strict adherence to the cost principle would involve the recognition of donated fixed assets at only the amount of incidental costs incurred in acceptance of the gift. Accountability for the resources of an enterprise and correct determination of enterprise earning power require that every economic facility employed, regardless of origin, be entered on the books at acquisition at the bargained price or some other equivalent value. In the case of donated assets, an independent and realistic appraisal of the market value of the donated asset should be obtained and recorded, provided the donation is unconditional. Should the donor impose restrictions, however, any "negative values" arising from such conditions should be considered in determination of the valuation to be recorded. To illustrate, assume a large building, including the land is given by a city to the XYZ Corporation as an inducement to establish a plant therein. The related transactions may be recorded as follows:[3]

1. To record the fair market value, per appraisal at date of donation:

Plant Building...8,000
Plant Land...4,000
    Contributed Capital — Donated Plant.............................   12,000°

    ° See page 551 for disposition of accounts of this type.

2. At date of transfer and payment of transfer costs:

Contributed Capital — Donated Plant (basis: the fair market
  value already recognized implicitly includes this cost)..........   900
    Cash   900

3. To record depreciation for first year (10-year life):

Depreciation Expense $\left(\dfrac{\$8,000}{10}\right)$.............................   800
    Accumulated Depreciation — Plant Building.....................   800

    In case the donation is contingent upon the fulfillment in the future of some contractual obligation on the part of the recipient, most accountants agree that the asset should be treated as a contingent asset until such time that the contingent conditions have been met. If the contractual obligation has not been undertaken or if there is some doubt that it will be fulfilled, the donated asset should be shown short or by footnote on the balance sheet. When definite steps are taken to satisfy the obligation or upon conditional transfer of title, the asset should be fully recognized in the accounts. To illustrate, assume the city of Austin donated a plant site having a fair market value of $25,000 to a corporation subject to a provision that title would

---

    [3] Some have argued, somewhat illogically, that assets donated by nonshareholders should give rise to an *extraordinary gain* on the income statement and that donations by shareholders should give rise to a contributed capital account as illustrated. The illustration given appears to be more in harmony with current practice.

transfer one year after the beginning of operations. The transactions may be recorded as follows:

1. At date of agreement:

Contingent Asset — Donated Plant Site 25,000
    Contingent Contributed Capital — Donated Plant Site   25,000

2. At date of transfer of title and incidental costs of $100:

Plant Site.. 25,000
Contingent Contributed Capital — Donated Plant Site 25,000
    Contingent Asset — Donated Plant Site   25,000
    Cash   100
    Contributed Capital — Donated Plant Site   24,900

Depreciable fixed assets received by donation should be depreciated in the normal manner on the basis of the fair market value recorded in the accounts. A contingent asset (as recorded in entry No. 1 above), if depreciable in nature, should be depreciated on the basis of the fair market value from date of initial recognition (or initial use, depending upon the circumstances) as a contingent asset.

Property owned by a company may increase in value substantially as a result of the *discovery* of valuable mineral or other natural resources. In such cases the original cost of the property may not provide a suitable basis for accountability. In the case of discovery value the accounting profession recognizes another exception to the cost principle as applied to fixed assets. The fair market value of the property, in consideration of the valuable natural resource, should be estimated, usually by appraisal, and recorded in the accounts. The resulting credit should be to Unrealized Capital Increment — Discovery Value. Depletion should be recognized on the basis of the increased value. To illustrate, assume a tract of land was purchased in 1954 for $2,000 and that in 1971 a valuable gravel deposit (that would be exploited) was discovered on it. Related entries are:

1. To record purchase in 1954:

Land... 2,000
    Cash   2,000

2. To record discovery value (appraised at $25,000 exclusive of land) in 1971:[4]

Land — Appraisal Increment (gravel deposit) 25,000
    Unrealized Capital Increment (gravel deposit)..................   25,000°

    ° See page 551 for disposition of accounts of this type.

3. To record depletion for first year based on depletion rate of $.25 per ton; 10,000 tons mined during first year:

---

[4] The accounting profession has sanctioned this procedure but has not required it in all cases.

Depletion Expense.. 2,500
    Land — Appraisal Increment (gravel deposit)....................   2,500

Write-Down of Tangible Fixed Assets Based on Decreased Use Value

If a tangible fixed asset loses its operational value it should be written down or written off as the circumstances warrant. Thus, for example, a plant may become idle due to factors such as continuing decline in demand, the obsolescence of its products, or inadquate transportation facilities. Assume further that it has no resale value or convertibility and can only be realized as salvage. In such cases sound accounting would *require* an immediate write-down to approximate realizable value and recognition of the related loss. Normally the write-down should be accomplished through a credit to the accumulated depreciation account (in recognition of obsolescence) and a debit to a nonrecurring loss account.

Outlays Subsequent to Acquisition but Prior to Use

Outlays subsequent to acquisition but prior to operational use of a tangible fixed asset made to improve the asset and to bring it up to operational condition should be capitalized as a part of the cost of the asset. Prior to operational use, a secondhand asset frequently will require considerable outlays for repairs, reconditioning, remodeling, and installation, all of which should be capitalized. Reinstallation and rearrangement costs of machinery, rearrangement of partitions, renovation of buildings, and similar outlays on fixed assets purchased in a used condition should be capitalized as a part of the cost. Overhead items such as insurance, taxes, supervisory salaries, and other incidentals directly related to the asset during a period of renovation also should be capitalized. Depreciation normally should not be recorded until the asset is ready for use.

Acquisitions of Groups of Fixed Assets

It is not unusual for a concern to acquire a group of dissimilar fixed assets for a lump sum. This type of acquisition, frequently referred to as a "basket purchase," creates the problem of apportioning the lump-sum cost to the several assets acquired, some of which may be depreciable and others nondepreciable. The apportionment should be based upon some realistic indicator of the relative values of the several assets involved, such as appraised values, tax assessment values, or discounted value of estimated future earnings (or cost savings). To illustrate, assume that $90,000 was paid for property that included land, a building, and some machinery. Assume further that an independent appraisal showed appraised values of land, $30,000; building, $50,000; and machinery, $20,000. The cost apportionment and entry to record the transaction is shown below.

Fixed Asset	Appraised Value	Multiplier°	Apportioned Cost
Land	$ 30,000	.9	$27,000
Building	50,000	.9	45,000
Machinery	20,000	.9	18,000
Total	$100,000		$90,000

°Multiplier—$90,000 ÷ $100,000 = .9.

Entry to record the purchase:

Land	27,000	
Building	45,000	
Machinery	18,000	
Cash or Payable		90,000

Fixed Assets Constructed for Own Use

Companies may construct buildings, plants, equipment, furniture, and fixtures on occasion for their own use as fixed assets. Fixed assets may be constructed rather than acquired from the outside in order to utilize idle facilities and personnel, to effect an expected cost saving, or to satisfy a need that outsiders cannot meet in the desired time. In the case of assets constructed for a company's own use, several problems arise relative to the amount that should be capitalized as the cost of the asset. Obviously, all material and labor costs directly identifiable with the construction should be capitalized. All overhead costs directly identifiable with the asset being constructed likewise should be capitalized. Capitalizable costs during the construction period also should include charges for licenses, permits and fees, taxes, insurance, and similar charges relating to the assets being constructed. Aside from these directly identifiable costs of construction that should be capitalized, there are two problems that require further consideration, viz:

1. General overhead as a cost of assets constructed for a company's own use.
2. Excess costs on assets constructed for a company's own use.

General Overhead as a Cost of Construction. Assets may be constructed by a company for its own use, under two different operating circumstances.

First, there is the case where for all practical purposes the plant is operating at capacity in producing goods for sale and the management decides to construct some asset to be capitalized rather than sold. Management might make such a decision when the item otherwise is unavailable at the time required. In this case production of regular goods for sale is reduced. Clearly, in this situation the asset should be charged for all additional costs incurred in such construction including (a) additional overhead costs and (b) a share of *general factory overhead* allocated on the same basis as that applied to goods manufactured for sale.

Second, there is the instance where the plant is operating at less than capacity in producing regular goods for sale. In this case the idle plant capacity, or a part of such capacity, is utilized in manufacturing an asset for its own use and production of goods for sale is unaffected. In this case the asset should be charged with all additional costs incurred in such construction including *additional* overhead costs. At this point the question arises as to whether any of the *general factory overhead* also should be allocated to the asset being constructed. On this specific point some accountants take the position that the general factory overhead should be apportioned to the asset on the same basis as it is apportioned to the production for sale; others take the opposite position that none of the general factory overhead should be assigned to the asset being constructed.

When idle plant capacity is used, it is argued in support of assigning a ratable portion of general factory overhead to the asset being constructed that (a) such assets should be accorded the same treatment as regular products; (b) the full cost of the asset should include general factory overhead, otherwise loss from idle capacity is overstated; (c) a future benefit is involved, hence such costs should be deferred; (d) no special favor should be accorded such assets; (e) normal operations should not be penalized by carrying such overhead costs; and (f) that in conformance with the cost principle an allocation is essential if the true cost of both the asset being constructed and the concurrent production for sale is to be assigned.

On the other hand, it is argued in support of not assigning a portion of the general factory overhead to the asset being constructed that (a) such allocation would be reflected as an increase in income due to construction rather than as a result of production and sale of goods; (b) the full cost of the asset should not include overhead that would be incurred even in the absence of such construction; (c) the cost of production for sale should not be influenced by such construction; and (d) management should not consider the general factory overhead in making the decision to construct the fixed asset.

Although there are persuasive arguments for both positions, the authors are of the opinion that in theory it is preferable to capitalize a portion of general factory overhead, when idle plant capacity is used in the construction of assets for a firm's own use. However, allocation should be undertaken only when there is a reasonable basis for such allocation. For this reason, practical considerations frequently overrule theoretical refinements.

Excess Costs of Construction. Ordinarily when management has made a decision to construct assets for its own use, the full cost thereof should be capitalized on the basis that the alternative cost of outside producers is not now available as an alternative. However, when construction costs of such assets are substantially in excess of their business and economic usefulness, the excess cost should be recorded as a period loss, as opposed to a capitalization. Construction costs materially in excess of those of an independent producer may be an indication that the full construction cost is an unwarranted charge to future operations through capitalization.

Interest during Construction Period

Traditionally public utilities have treated interest costs during construction on funds borrowed to finance construction of fixed assets as part of cost of the fixed assets. Governmental regulatory agencies responsible for regulating the rates charged by utilities have allowed interest during construction as a cost of the asset rather than as a current expense. This has the effect of deferring the impact of interest cost on utility rates to the period of usage of the fixed assets. The future impact will be greater because the utility rate base is higher by the amount of interest capitalized. Interest is a cost of borrowing funds rather than a cost of the asset acquired with those funds. Therefore, capitalization of interest during the construction period is not theoretically sound from the accounting point of view and should not be permitted. It has been sanctioned to some extent in the past; however, it seldom is done at present. Obviously, if interest during construction is capitalized, any amortization premium or discount related to the borrowing should be accorded the same treatment.

The concept of capitalizing interest costs during the construction period has been referred to as "the construction-period theory."

COST OUTLAYS SUBSEQUENT TO ACQUISITION

Repairs and Maintenance

After acquisition cost has been properly determined and recorded in the accounts, numerous costs related to *utilization* of the fixed assets must be recognized. The account necessarily must be concerned with the complex problem of determining the correct treatment of outlays related to utilization, such as repairs, maintenance, betterments, and replacements. What outlays should be charged to a fixed asset account, to operating expense, to the accumulated depreciation account, to retained earnings, or to some combination of these accounts? The problem is particularly critical as a result of the difficulty in distinguishing between the several classifications of outlay, such as ordinary repairs as opposed to extraordinary repairs, each of which requires different treatment in the accounts and financial reports.

Maintenance costs are those costs, such as lubrication, cleaning, adjustment, and painting, which are incurred to keep a fixed asset in normal usable condition. Maintenance costs should be accounted for in exactly the same way as *ordinary* repairs, as discussed below. Generally, the two are combined for accounting purposes.

For accounting purposes repairs are classified as (a) ordinary and (b) extraordinary. *Ordinary repairs* are outlays for parts, labor, and other related costs which do not add materially to the use value of the asset, nor prolong its life appreciably, but are necessary to keep the asset in normal operational condition. Ordinary repairs are recurring and normally involve relatively small expenditures. Maintenance and ordinary repair outlays may be accounted for as (a) a revenue expenditure, where an appropriate expense account is debited for the outlay when incurred, or (b) through an "allowance" procedure (in the past referred to as the "reserve for repairs" procedure).

The Allowance Procedure. In the case of a new asset the maintenance and repair costs initially will be low, increasing in amount each year as the asset is utilized. Such costs also will vary on a monthly basis since repair work frequently is deferred, where possible, to the months when operations are low. Rather than charging operating expense as the repairs are incurred, it may be desirable to adopt an allowance procedure to equalize the monthly or annual repair and maintenance expense charge to operations. The allowance procedure requires an estimate of the total cost of ordinary repairs and maintenance during (a) the life of the asset, or (b) during the year, depending on the choice of period over which apportionment is desired. The amount of estimated repairs is allocated to each interim period on the basis of time (an equal amount each month or year as the case may be) or on the basis of production or output. Repair and maintenance expense is debited, and an allowance account is credited. Actual expenditures for maintenance and ordinary repairs are then debited to the allowance account when incurred. To illustrate, assume ordinary repairs and maintenance for the year have been estimated at $1,800 and that this amount is to be apportioned on a time basis (an equal amount each month). Assume that the actual repairs and maintenance costs incurred for the first month amounted to $110. The entries would be:

1. To record the estimated maintenance and ordinary repair cost for the month:

Repairs and Maintenance Expense 150
    Allowance for Maintenance and Repairs.................................   150

2. To record actual outlays for the month for ordinary repairs and maintenance:

Allowance for Maintenance and Repairs 110
    Cash or Payables   110

The income statement would report repairs and maintenance expense of $150 for the month. The $40 credit balance in the allowance account would be reported on the interim balance sheet as a current liability because it reflects a future demand on current assets. In this example, at the end of the year any balance in the allowance account would be closed to the related expense account.

The allowance procedure for maintenance and ordinary repairs has been accorded general acceptability by the accounting profession. The procedure is justifiable for equalizing an expense where there are logical reasons for doing so; it is not acceptable simply as a means of equalizing profits as between several periods. The allowance method is not acceptable for federal income tax purposes.

Extraordinary repairs are major repairs which involve relatively large amounts, are not recurring in nature, and tend to increase the *use value* and perhaps the remaining service life of the fixed asset. If use value (efficiency and utility) is increased, the cost should be charged to the asset account. If the expenditures serve to increase the service life of the related asset, the accumulated depreciation account should be debited, thus increasing the book value of the asset. The depreciation rate must be revised in either case to take into account the new service life, use value, undepreciated cost after the outlay, and the residual value. If the extraordinary repair does not increase the use value or prolong the service life of the asset, it represents cost of neglected repairs and therefore should be expensed as an ordinary repair.

Replacements and Renewals

A replacement involves the removal of an old asset or a part of an asset and the substitution of a new unit of essentially the same type. Replacement may involve specific items or numerous items as would be the case of a major overhaul. Minor replacements are accounted for as an ordinary repair expense, and major replacements are accounted for by removing from the accounts the cost of the parts replaced and the accumulated depreciation thereon and debiting the asset for the cost of the new parts.

Renewals are the same as replacements; although some accountants make a distinction that whereas replacements primarily relate to substitution of new major parts or assemblies for the old, renewals primarily relate to general overhauls where numerous small parts are renewed. Renewals are accorded the same accounting treatment as that indicated above for replacements.

Betterments and Improvements

A betterment or improvement may be defined as a replacement or major renovation of an existing asset or unit of an existing asset by an improved or superior asset or unit, the effect of which is to improve the efficiency of the primary asset. Usually a betterment or improvement results not only in increased efficiency but also lengthens remaining service life. The replacing of an old shingle roof with a tile roof, installing a more powerful motor in a shrimp boat, and the substitution of steel beams for wooden beams in a building are illustrations of betterments and improvements. The accounting treatment for *minor* betterments and improvements is to expense them as indicated above for ordinary repairs. *Major* betterments and replacements necessitate removal from the accounts of the original acquisition cost and accumulated depreciation of the item replaced and recording of the full cost (including installation cost) of the new unit. Normally it will be necessary to recompute the depreciation rate of the primary asset in view of the changed book value, service life, and residual or scrap value.

Additions

Additions are extensions, enlargements, or expansions made to an existing asset. An extra wing or room added to a building and the addition of a production unit to an existing machine are examples of additions. An addition represents a capital expenditure and should be recorded in the fixed asset accounts at the full acquisition cost determined under the principles discussed above for acquisition cost of the original asset. Work done on the existing structure such as the shoring up of the foundation to accommodate the addition or the cutting of an entranceway through an existing wall should be regarded as a part of the cost of the addition and capitalized. The cost of an addition, less any estimated residual value, normally should be depreciated over its own service life or the remaining life of the original asset of which it is a part, whichever period is the shorter.

Rearrangement of Assets

The cost of reinstallation, rerouting, or rearrangement of factory machinery for the purpose of securing greater efficiency in production or reduced production cost should be capitalized if material in amount and if the benefits of the rearrangement definitely will extend beyond the current accounting period. Such costs should be capitalized as a deferred charge and amortized over the ensuing periods benefiting from the rearrangement.

Acquisition Costs of Specific Property

In determining the acquisition cost of any tangible fixed asset, the general principles discussed heretofore are applicable; however, certain items of property give rise to special problems in applying the general principles. These special problems are considered in the immediately succeeding paragraphs.

Land. The acquisition cost of land should be recorded in an account captioned Land or Real Estate. The cost of land includes the price paid the seller plus all incidental costs related to acquisition such as title fees, commissions, legal fees, survey costs, and interest or taxes due at date of acquisition and assumed by the buyer. It is desirable that idle real estate be set up in a separate account, such as Land or Real Estate, and that real estate currently in use be reported in a separate account such as Plant Site or Plant Land. Improvements on land which have a limited life (therefore are depreciable), such as sidewalks, fencing, and water systems, should be recorded in a separate account entitled Land Improvements. Building costs should be recorded in a separate account captioned Buildings.

Costs incurred subsequent to acquisition to *permanently* improve the land for the purpose acquired, such as draining, clearing, landscaping, grading, and subdividing costs, are proper additions to the capitalized cost of the land. Land acquired for a plant site or office building may involve the removal of some existing structures. The costs of removing the existing structures, less any salvage recovery, is a capitalizable cost of the land. Area assessments against the land such as the cost of sewerage and water facilities and streets may be capitalized as a land cost rather than as a land improvement if they are permanent in nature.

Land currently in use should be classified on the balance sheet as a tangible fixed asset. Land held for a future plant site should be classified as Other Assets, and land held for speculation or as an investment should be reported under the caption Funds and Investments. In the case of land held for investment the balance sheet should carry, in addition to cost, a parenthetical notation of its fair market value.

A special problem arises concerning the treatment of taxes and carrying charges in respect to real estate held for investment or for future use. From a conservative point of view such charges should be recorded as current expenses. However, accounting theory tends to hold that in view of the fact that the asset is not producing income against which the charges may be offset, the carrying charges should be capitalized, particularly when the fair market value of the property is increasing. If the real estate is producing income, through rent for example, or is declining in value, there are sound reasons for treating the carrying costs as a current expense. Such charges may be either capitalized or expensed for income tax purposes.

Old Buildings. The capitalizable cost of an old building in addition to the purchase price and related incidentals includes the cost of renovating, repairing, and remodeling necessary to make it suitable for the use for which it was acquired. Building equipment that is an integral part of the building such as lighting equipment and elevators is included in the cost of the building and generally should be depreciated over the life of the building. Removable building equipment may have a shorter life than the building or be subject to removal and improvement, in which case it should be recorded in a separate Building Equipment account and depreciated separately.

Razing costs of a building that has been owned by the firm should be identified with the retirement of the old building and not charged to new construction.

Machinery and Equipment. The terms *machinery* and *equipment* are too general for use in the accounts in the large firms. Normally each major subdivision of equipment or machinery with its related accumulated depreciation should be recorded in separate accounts and reported separately on the balance sheet except in the case of highly condensed statements. Adequate accounting for machinery and equipment normally will involve the use of several *controlling accounts* in the general ledger and a detailed subsidiary ledger account for each unit (except very small items such as hand tools). This detailed accounting is essential to (*a*) safeguard the assets properly, (*b*) depreciate on a sound basis, (*c*) insure proper recording of transfers from one division to another, and (*d*) to account for retirements.

Since machine and hand tools are relatively low in cost per unit, are frequently lost or broken, and thus have a short service life, they normally are not accorded the same treatment as other tangible fixed assets; rather they are accounted for in one of three ways, viz:

1. Capitalized at date of purchase, periodically inventoried, and the asset account adjusted to the inventory value, thereby charging the losses due to breakage, theft, or disappearance to current expense.
2. Capitalized as an asset at a conservative valuation for the ordinary or normal stock; all subsequent tool purchases are then charged to current expense.
3. Expensed as acquired (see Chapter 13).

Patterns and Dies. Patterns and dies are used in the fabrication of many manufactured items such as automobile bodies. Patterns and dies used for regular production over a period of time should be recorded in a fixed asset account, Patterns and Dies, and depreciated over their estimated service life. Patterns and dies that are purchased or constructed for a particular job or order should be charged directly to the cost of that job.

Returnable Containers. Products are frequently sold in containers that have a relatively high value, hence are returnable for reuse. Gas cylinders, oil drums, and steel tanks generally can be returned by the purchaser for value. In some cases the purchaser is charged a deposit for the container and will receive a credit or refund when it is returned. In such cases, until returned, the containers should be carried in the vendor's accounts as a fixed asset and depreciated over their estimated useful life. Containers not returned within a reasonable time are accounted for as retired by sale; the deposit becomes the sales price. In contrast some companies do not bill the customer for the container, although he is expected to hold the container available for pickup. In such cases the vendor may account for the containers as operating supplies rather than as fixed assets and the loss determined by inventory similar to the procedure described for tools.

Leasehold Improvements. Improvements on *leased* property such as buildings, walks, landscaping, and certain types of permanent equipment, unless specifically exempted in the lease agreement, revert to the owner of the property upon termination of the lease. Improvements on leased property of this nature are referred to as *leasehold improvements.* The cost of such improvements should be capitalized by the lessee in a tangible fixed asset account entitled Leasehold Improvements. The cost of the leasehold improvements should be depreciated over the term of the lease or the service life of the improvement, whichever is the shorter. Renewal provisions in the lease agreement normally are disregarded in depreciating leasehold improvements.

RETIREMENT OF TANGIBLE FIXED ASSETS

General

Fixed assets may be retired voluntarily and disposed of by sale, trade, or abandonment—or involuntarily lost as a result of casualty such as fire or storm. Irrespective of the cause of retirement, if the asset is subject to depreciation, it should be depreciated to date of such retirement. Likewise, taxes, insurance premium costs, and similar costs should be accrued up to the date of retirement. At date of retirement the cost of the asset and its related accumulated depreciation should be removed from the accounts; any assets received for the asset retired should be recorded at their fair market value and the resulting loss or gain on retirement of the old asset should be recorded. To illustrate, assume a delivery truck costing $3,200 on February 1, 1967, is sold on July 1, 1971, for $650. Straight line depreciation has been recorded on the basis of an estimated service life of five years and an estimated residual value of $200. The company closes its books on December 31 each year. The entries at date of sale would be as follows:

1. Depreciation of Delivery Equipment 300
      Accumulated Depreciation—Delivery Equipment......   300
      To record 6 months' depreciation for 1971 at $50 per
      month computed as follows:
      Amount to be depreciated ($3,200 – $200) $3,000
      Service life – 5 years or 60 months.
      Monthly depreciation ($3,000/60 months) ......$ 50

2. Cash 650
      Accumulated Depreciation—Delivery Equipment............2,650
      Delivery Equipment...   3,200
      Gain on Sale of Delivery Equipment°   100
      To record retirement of old delivery truck by sale.

°Sales price			$650
Less book value of asset sold:			
Original cost $3,200			
Accumulated depreciation:			
1967 – 11 months $550			
1968 – 12 months 600			
1969 – 12 months 600			
1970 – 12 months 600			
1971 – 6 months 300	2.650		550
Gain on sale...			$100

The gain (or loss) on sale of fixed assets is closed to the Income Summary account as an extraordinary item.

The accounting entries for an exchange were discussed and illustrated earlier in the chapter. In case a fixed asset is abandoned or disposed of because it has no value, the cost and accumulated depreciation amounts should be removed from the accounts and any loss (or gain) on abandonment, including costs of disposal, recognized.

Outlays made to restore and repair uninsured fixed assets damaged through fire, storm, or other casualty should be recorded as extraordinary losses and closed to the Income Summary account. Outlays made where the properties are improved beyond their approximate operating condition prior to the casualty should be apportioned between losses and the fixed asset. Damaged assets not restored should be reduced in book value consistent with the decrease in going-concern utility. Accounting for *insured* casualty losses is discussed in Chapter 14.

Control of Tangible Fixed Assets

Effective control of tangible fixed assets depends upon the establishment of definite management policies relative to acquirement, record keeping, and responsibility for safeguarding.

The acquirement of fixed assets will involve purchase or construction for a company's own use. In either case management should give serious thought and attention to the advisability of committing capital for long periods of time, as is involved in most capital additions. Evaluation of alternatives such as whether to make or buy, the type and size of asset that should be acquired, and the method of financing requires careful planning based upon realistic estimates of *future* results that might be expected. In order to effectively plan and control capital additions, practically all of the better managed companies utilize a *capital additions budget*, which is prepared in detail covering the immediate year ahead, and extended for 3, 5, and sometimes up to 20 years in the future in broader terms. The capital additions budget is established by top management and is revised on at least an annual basis. In developing the capital additions budget the overall future potentials of the company are evaluated and the future needs for fixed assets estimated. Alternatives with respect to capital additions thus are evaluated carefully some time in advance of actual need. Inclusion of specific capital additions in the annual capital additions budget indicates the intent of management to definitely proceed with those particular proposals. Final approval to purchase or construct a fixed asset usually is indicated on an "Authorization for Expenditure (AFE)." Actual expenditures for capital additions throughout the period are compared with the capital additions budget estimates in performance reports to the management.

Detailed record keeping is an important element in the control of tangible fixed assets. Discussions up to this point in this chapter have been concerned primarily with *general ledger* considerations; the basic entries to be made in the control accounts. Subsidiary record accounting for tangible fixed assets frequently involves more detailed record keeping than any other one area. Detailed records generally must be maintained for *each* item which necessitates the adoption of some system for identifying the specific item. For example, assume that among its fixed assets a company has 200 assorted office desks that have been acquired over a period of years at varying costs. Assume further that five of the desks are sold and replaced with new desks. Unless *group depreciation* has been used, the accountant must be able to identify the specific desk with a specific cost and accumulated depreciation for removal from the asset accounts. Specific identification of fixed assets frequently requires a numerical identification system, a number being affixed directly on each item. Most companies charge supervisors with the responsibility for safe-guarding tangible fixed assets assigned to their departments. This policy necessitates the accounting for such assets by location and responsibility; thus when one of the desks, in the example mentioned above, is moved, say, from one office to another, a notification identifying the asset and the new location must be furnished the accounting department so that the detailed records may be changed accordingly. The simple illustration given above will serve to indicate the detail and related problems incident to adequate accounting for tangible fixed assets.

Smaller companies having comparatively few fixed assets generally maintain the detailed asset records by hand. A register form of property record is frequently utilized which lists all the individual assets of a given class on the same sheet, one line being devoted to the data for each unit. Typical headings for this type of register are as shown in Illustration 12–1.

The card form of subsidiary property ledger, one card for each unit of property, is preferred by many smaller companies. The card should carry such information as name and description of the property, item number, location, name of manufacturer, invoice cost, other costs

Illustration 12–1
Property Record

Date Acquired	Vo. No.	Description	Location	Cost	Rate of Deprec.	Deprec. Annual Amount	Depreciation Provided				Trade-in or Scrap	Remarks
							19A	19B	19C	19D		

including installation, estimated service life, residual value, depreciation each period, accumulated depreciation, method of depreciation, and any other significant information. A typical subsidiary property ledger card is shown in Illustration 12–2. Larger companies and other companies having a comparatively large number of fixed assets generally employ machine accounting methods for detailed fixed asset record keeping. One adaptation of punch-card methods to fixed asset accounting is suggested by the card shown in Illustration 12–3.[5] More and more companies are computerizing their property records. The property subsidiary record totals should always tie in with the control accounts. Periodic reconciliation of the detailed records of fixed assets with the related control records should be a part of the routine accounting procedures. Records such as those suggested above are not only important for internal managerial purposes but also for insurance and tax purposes and to assist in settling claims for loss. Detailed data relative to accumulated depreciation for each asset are

---

[5]Courtesy IBM Corporation. This is an illustration of the two-card plan. All information needed for each depreciable asset is contained in the two cards that can be processed at high speed by machine methods.

Illustration 12–2
Equipment Ledger

| ITEM NAME | | | | | | | PLANT | | | |
| ITEM NO. | | | CONTROL ACCOUNT NO. | | | | DEPARTMENT | | | |

MANUFACTURER				SERVICE LIFE		
MANUFACTURER'S NO.				REVISED LIFE		DATE
ACQUIRED FROM				ESTIMATED SCRAP VALUE		

DATE	DESCRIPTION	REF.	TOTAL COST	DEPRECIATION CURRENT YEAR	CHARGES TO ACCUMULATED DEPRECIATION	BALANCE ACCUMULATED DEPRECIATION	BOOK VALUE

essential to assure (*a*) that assets are not over- or underdepreciated, (*b*) proper accounting upon transfer of the property from one division of the company to another, and (*c*) proper accounting upon retirement of the property.

This very brief discussion will serve only to indicate the extreme care which should be exercised in designing and improving a system of record keeping for tangible fixed assets. In this respect the account-

Illustration 12–3
Punched-card Property Record

ant must keep in mind the several objectives mentioned above, some external and some internal in nature, which must be met. Detailed records for fixed assets designed merely to facilitate computation of depreciation, for example, would fall far short of the real planning and control needs of the firm.

QUESTIONS FOR CLASS DISCUSSION

1. Define fixed assets and distinguish between tangible and intangible fixed assets.

2. Distinguish between capital and revenue expenditures. What accounting implications are involved?

3. Relate the *cost principle* to the acquisition of tangible fixed assets. Relate the *matching principle* to fixed asset accounting.

4. How is asset acquisition cost determined when the consideration given is not cash?

5. Define book value with respect to (*a*) assets having no limited service life and (*b*) assets having a limited service life.

6. Explain the relationship between book value and fair market value of a fixed asset.

7. In determining the cost of a tangible fixed asset how should the following items be treated: (*a*) invoice price, (*b*) freight, (*c*) discounts, (*d*) title costs, (*e*) installation costs, (*f*) breaking-in costs, and (*g*) cost of major overhaul before operational use?

8. A machine is purchased on the following terms: cash, $10,000, plus 10 semiannual payments of $3,000 each. How should the acquisition cost of the machine be recorded? Explain.

9. What are the rules for determining acquisition cost of a fixed asset acquired by exchange of the securities of the purchasing company?

10. Distinguish between the "accounting" and "tax" methods of recording tangible fixed assets acquired through exchanges of like items.

11. Explain the procedure for allocating the cost of several assets purchased for a lump sum. Why is apportionment necessary?

12. In case tangible fixed assets are constructed for own use, what costs should be capitalized as a cost of the assets? Explain the considerations relative to (*a*) general company overhead and (*b*) excess construction costs.

13. Should interest during construction be capitalized? Explain.

14. Distinguish between maintenance, ordinary repairs, and extraordinary repairs.

15. Explain the two methods of accounting for ordinary repairs.

16. Explain the accounting for (*a*) extraordinary repairs, (*b*) replacements and renewals, and (*c*) betterments and improvements.

17. The XY Corporation added a new wing at a cost of $50,000, plus $1,000 spent in making passageways through the walls of an old structure to the existing plant. The plant was 10 years old and was being depreciated an equal amount each year over a 30-year life. Discuss the implications in determining the depreciation of the new wing.

18. Explain the three methods of accounting for small tools.

19. What are leasehold improvements? How should they be accounted for?

20. Outline the accounting steps related to the disposition of a tangible fixed asset.

DECISION CASE 12–1

The Bedlam Company issued 5,000 shares of common stock having a par value of $500,000 for an additional plant that was recently appraised at a "conservative" value of $450,000. On the date of the acquisition the stock of the company was selling at $95 per share. The officials of the company desire to record the plant at $500,000.

Later in the year the company purchased some real estate, including three large frame buildings, for the purpose of enlarging the plant. It was expected that the buildings could be moved to adjacent plots owned by the company and used for warehousing purposes. The vendor had offered to remove the buildings and deduct $15,000 from the purchase price of $50,000 for the property. After the deal was closed it was learned that a fire regulation would prevent the removal of the buildings to the other property; consequently, they were torn down and sold as scrap in order to make way for the plant expansion. The scrap recovery amounted to $7,000, and the demolishing costs were $2,000.

The company owned a small manufacturing facility in another part of the city. This particular facility was equipped to manufacture a different item than the usual items manufactured and sold by the company. Although the facility was reasonably efficient under normal conditions, depressed demand for this particular item had caused the management to shut down operations temporarily. Certain costs were being incurred to maintain the facility on a standby basis. The management was concerned with the question as to whether or not it will ever have any future utility as far as the company is concerned.

In respect to one of the original plants the company management had purchased a used gas-steam generator to produce electricity for the plant. The monthly electric bill had averaged $300 per month which was considered to be exorbitant. The net cost of the installed generator was $12,000 ($2,000 purchase price plus $10,000 for moving and installing). With normal usage the generator was expected to last 10 years (straight line basis). It was estimated that the residual value of the generator and the cost of removal would be approximately equal. The generator has been used for two years. Repairs, maintenance, gas, and other operating costs averaged about $120 per month. At the beginning of the current year the company negotiated a contract with the local utility to provide electricity at approximately 50% the original rate. Management has decided to inactivate the generator. Since the generator will not deteriorate appreciably, it is being maintained on a standby basis.

Required:

As the independent CPA employed by the firm to perform the annual audit you have been asked to present tentative recommendations for proper accounting with respect to each situation. Obviously, you are expected to present logical reasons for your recommendations.

EXERCISES

Exercise 12–1

Indicate how each of the following assets would be reported on the balance sheet:

a) Land purchased for future plant site: cost, $4,000.
b) Franchise: cost, $10,000.
c) Building: cost, $100,000; accumulated depreciation thereon, $30,000.
d) Patent: cost, $7,000; amortization to date, $2,000.
e) Plant site in use: cost, $50,000.
f) Office equipment: cost, $15,000; accumulated depreciation, $7,000.
g) Goodwill, $20,000.
h) Plant equipment: cost, $160,000; accumulated depreciation thereon, $60,000.
i) Land purchased for speculative purposes: cost, $25,000.
j) Machine tools, $3,000.

Exercise 12–2

What is the proper cost to use for recording the land in each of the following independent cases? Give reasons in support of your answer.

Case A—Issued 15,000 shares (par value per share $1) par value capital stock with a "market value" of $1.50 per share (based upon a recent sale of 200 shares) for the land. The land was recently appraised at $17,000 by competent appraisers.

Case B—Rejected a prior offer of vendor to sell the land for $7,500 cash—instead issued 1,000 shares of capital stock for the land (market value of the stock based on several recent transactions $7,700; average volume sold 2,000 shares).

Case C—At the middle of the current year gave a check for $5,000 for the land and assumed the liability for unpaid taxes: taxes in arrears last year, $100; assessed for current year, $80.

Case D—Issued 1,000 shares of capital stock for the land. The par value of the stock was $50 per share; the market value (stock sells daily with an average daily volume of 5,000 shares) was $63 per share at time of purchase of land. Vendor offered to sell the land for $62,000 cash. Competent appraisers valued the land at $64,000.

Exercise 12–3

a) Delivery equipment was purchased having a list price of $3,000; terms were 2/10, n/30. Payment was made within the discount period.
b) Delivery equipment was purchased having a list price of $4,000; terms were 2/10, n/30. Payment was made after the discount period.
c) Delivery equipment listed at $10,000 was purchased and invoiced at 2/10, n/30. In order to take advantage of the discount, the company borrowed $8,000 of the purchase price by issuance of a 60-day, 6% note which was repaid with interest at maturity.

Required:

Give entries in each separate situation for costs, borrowing, and any expenses involved.

Exercise 12–4

The Franklin Company purchased a machine, having an estimated 10-year useful life, on a time payment plan. The cash price of the machine was $23,325. Terms were $6,000 cash downpayment plus four equal annual payments to include interest on the unpaid balance at 6% per annum.

Required:

(Round to even dollars).

a) Give entry to reflect the purchase.
b) Give entry for depreciation at the end of one year assuming straight line depreciation.
c) Compute the amount of the annual payments.
d) Prepare a table to reflect the accounting entries for each of the four payments.

Exercise 12–5

The Bacon Company purchased a lot with an office building thereon. Unpaid tax liens on the property amounting to $600 were assumed. The tax rolls showed the property assessed at $15,000, 10% of which pertained to the lot. With the consent of the insurance company a five-year policy (with three years from January 1 of the current year remaining before expiration) costing $500 was transferred from the vendor to the Bacon Company. The purchase agreement was finally executed on July 1 of the current year, and a check for $10,000 and an interest-bearing note for $15,000 (dated July 1) was delivered to the seller. At date of purchase the fair market value of the lot was estimated to be $2,200.

Required:

Give entry to record all aspects of the purchase.

Exercise 12–6

The Cox Manufacturing Company has old machinery carried on its books at $3,800 (original cost, $7,000). This machinery was traded for a new replacement machine with a list price of $11,000; it could be purchased for $10,500 on a cash deal. The dealer "allowed a trade-in value of $4,500"; the balance, $6,500, was paid in cash. Give entries to record the exchange:

a) In accordance with sound accounting practice.
b) In accordance with income tax procedures.

Exercise 12–7

On June 30, Sand Company purchased a new machine, trading in an old machine and paying $23,500 cash; a trade-in allowance of $15,000 was given. The old machine had been depreciated for seven years and originally cost $30,000. Accumulated depreciation at the end of the last year (December 31) was $21,000.

Required:

What entry or entries should be made under each separate assumption to record the exchange —

a) Assuming the list price of the new machine was $34,000 (accounting method).

b) Assuming the fair market value of the old asset was determined to be $4,000 and that there is no established list price for the new machine (accounting method).

c) For each assumption assuming the "income tax method" is used.

Exercise 12–8

The Blue Manufacturing Company purchased a complete factory unit for $176,000. Analysis of tax assessment values of the three elements is set out below. Record the purchase.

Asset	Assessed Value
Land	$ 8,000
Building	40,000
Machinery	32,000

Exercise 12–9

The Spock Company took bids on construction of an addition to its plant. When it developed that the lowest bid was $227,000, the company proceeded to erect the structure with its own force and facilities as follows:

Direct labor to the job	$130,000
Direct materials to the job	74,000
Direct supervision to the job	17,000
Other direct costs to the job	4,000
Executives salaries (estimated they devoted 10% of their time to the job) $70,000 × 10%	7,000
Regular factory overhead (plant continued to operate at normal capacity which was about 15% below potential capacity) $120,000 × 15%	18,000
Total	$250,000

Required:

What entry would you recommend? Justify.

Exercise 12–10

On August 1 Bolt Company paid $12,000 cash for property consisting of land and building valued by the vendor at $9,000 and $3,000, respectively. The property was purchased to secure a building site. Taxes accrued and unpaid at date of purchase amounting to $1,000 were assumed. The company paid $700 for labor necessary to tear down and remove the building. The scrap lumber was sold for $300. The following additional payments were made: (1) fee for examining title to the land purchased, $50; (2) paving assessment, $400; and (3) attorney fee for services in securing zoning change to permit erection of business house on land purchased, $75.

Required:

Give all entries indicated relative to the acquisition of the land.

Exercise 12–11

Indicate for each of the following items the proper account(s) and amount(s) to be debited. Justify your position for doubtful items.

a) Purchased land with usable office building thereon for lump sum, $100,000.
b) Purchased land for future building site at a cost of $30,000 — an old building on this site at date of purchase to be torn down.
c) Net cost of demolishing building mentioned in (b) amounted to $1,000.
d) Cost of excavation for basement of a new building (b) above, $2,000.
e) Attorney fees in connection with purchase of real estate in (b), $400.
f) Taxes paid on land purchased in (b) assessed before completion of building, $100.
g) Rental expense on office during organization of company, $200.
h) Factory superintendent salary for first year, $12,000; spent first six months supervising construction of building, next three months supervising installation of machinery, and last three months supervising operations.
i) Paid $3,600 interest on bonds for first year after organization; bonds issued in partial payment of building; first nine months of bond year coincided with building construction.
j) Cost of grading and paving parking space behind new building, $1,500.

Exercise 12–12

Bowers Corporation made the following expenditures in connection with the erection of an office building for company use: purchase of site, $21,000; fees for clearing title, $100; grading site, $300; building permit, $150; paving assessment, $500; payment to old tenant for canceling lease, $825; razing old structures on site, $800; sale of scrap lumber from old structures on site purchased, $300; excavation for basement, $200; taxes on site during construction, $50; payment to constractor at completion of building, $220,000; damages paid to an individual injured at the construction site, $1,500; there was no insurance coverage (premium on appropriate insurance, $320); and construction of driveways, $550.

Required:

Set up a table and complete for each item as follows:

Expenditures	Land Cost	Building Cost	Other Cost	Assumptions
Purchase of site $15,000				
Etc.				
Total				

Exercise 12–13

A machine originally costing $6,400 on January 1, 1966, was sold for $2,100 on June 30, 1971. The machine had been depreciated over a 10-year life (straight line) and had an estimated residual value of $400.

Required:

1. Assuming the books are closed each December 31, give entry to record the sale. Show computations.

The plant building cost $65,000, residual value $5,000, and was being depreciated over 15 years on a straight line basis. When the building was 10 years old, an additional wing was constructed costing $12,000 (estimated residual value $2,000). The estimated life of the wing when considered separately was 10 years.

   2. *a*) Determine the balances in all related accounts immediately after the additions.

     b) Give entry to record the addition.

     c) Give depreciation entry (entries) one year after the addition.

PROBLEMS

Problem 12–1

In analyzing the fixed asset account of Fumar Company, you find the following items: The company —

a) Issued 200 shares of common stock ($100 par value per share), having a market value of $130 per share at date of transfer, for a tract of land to be used for a factory site. Twelve additional shares of the common stock were given to a lawyer for legal services in getting the corporation charter and clearing title to the land. The lawyer indicated that approximately one fourth of the time was spent on clearing title (charge organization expense for organizing costs.)

b) Purchased a delivery truck having a quoted price of $3,500, paying cash $1,500 and giving a $2,000, one-year, noninterest-bearing note for the balance. Current interest rates at the bank were 5% per annum.

c) Contracted for a building at a flat price of $300,000. The building was paid for by transferring to the contractor $300,000, 20-year, 5% company bonds at which time the bonds were selling at 97.

Required:

Prepare entries to indicate the proper treatment of each item in the accounts of the company at time of initial recording. Where doubtful, justify your position by comment after the entry.

Problem 12–2

Prepare journal entries for Nye Company to record the following transactions relating to the purchase of a new machine. Justify your position on doubtful items.

a) Purchased a new machine having a list price of $20,000. Failed to take a 2% cash discount available upon full payment of the invoice within 10 days. Shipping costs paid by the vendor amounted to $100. Installation costs amounted to $250, including $100 which represented 10% of the monthly salary of the factory superintendent (installation period two days). A wall was torn out and replaced (moved two feet) at a cost of $500 to make room for the machine.

b) Purchased an automatic counter to be attached to the machine purchased in (*a*) above. The counter cost $520. The estimated useful life of the counter was 7 years, whereas the estimated life of the machine was 10 years.

c) During the first month of operations the machine became inoperative due to a defect in manufacture. The vendor repaired the machine at no cost; however, the specially trained operator was idle during the two weeks the machine was inoperative. The operator was paid the regular wages ($300) during the period, although the only work he performed was to observe the repair by the factory representative.

d) A specially designed set of hand tools was purchased at a cost of $175. These tools were necessary for future repair of the machine.

e) After one year of use, exchanged the electric motor on the machine for a heavier motor at an exchange cost of $400. The new motor had a list price of $1,250. The parts list indicated a list price for the original motor of $900.

Problem 12–3

The Fields Company entered into a conditional sales contract to purchase a machine listed at $12,395; payment to be made as follows: $2,000 down and four annual payments of $3,000 each. The vendee could, at his option, stop payments at any time with no obligation, or take full title after last payment. Give entries for the following: (a) at date of contract; (b) at date of first payment including interest recognition; (c) depreciation for first year assuming 10-year life; (d) assuming the contract is canceled after first year; and (e) after completion of all payments. Round to even dollars.

Problem 12–4

The Knox Construction Company entered into a contract for four Master Loaders. The company agreed to make four semiannual payments of $7,500 each. The loaders have a list price of $6,970 each. The machines have an estimated service life of five years. The contract specified that the payments could be discontinued at the option of the Knox Company in which case the machinery would be returned to the lessor. At the end of the 12 months, if all payments were made in accordance with the contract, the machinery would become the property of the Knox Company. Determine the implied interest rate per semiannual period and give appropriate entries on the books of the Knox Construction Company (a) at date of contract, (b) at date of first semiannual payment (assume this is the end of the fiscal year) and develop an amortization table that reflects the effect of the four payments, (c) at date of completion of contractual payments, and (d) after two payments have been made assuming that the machinery is returned to the lessor. Round to even dollars.

Problem 12–5

The following information relates to the purchase of an asset on June 30 of the current year which was paid for by a trade-in of an old asset and the balance in cash:

List price of new asset	$10,000
Cash payment	5,800
Cost of old asset (8-year life, no residual value)	8,000
Depreciation accumulated on old asset (straight line)	4,500
Secondhand market value of old asset	3,600

Required:

Prepare journal entries to show three different ways of recording the transaction. (Assume fiscal period ends December 31 and that depreciation to December 31 of the previous year has been recorded.)

Following each entry give an explanation of the reasoning behind that method of recording and indicate the circumstances in which it might be appropriate.   (AICPA adapted)

Problem 12–6

Eatman Company acquired a new machine with a list price of $12,000 and gave in payment an old machine that originally cost $7,000 (depreciation to date of exchange, $4,000) and paid the difference in cash. Give entries to record the exchange under (1) the financial accounting method and (2) the income tax method assuming:

a) Cash paid was $9,000.
b) Cash paid was $10,000.
c) Cash paid was $8,000.

Problem 12–7

Sussex Company purchased a tract of land on which was located a warehouse and an office building. The cash purchase price was $128,650 plus $350 fees in connection with the purchase. The following data were collected concerning the property:

	Tax Assessment	Vendor's Book Value	Original Cost
Land	$10,000	$10,000	$10,000
Warehouse	20,000	15,000	30,000
Office building	30,000	25,000	60,000

Required:

Journalize the purchase; show computations.

Problem 12–8

The city of Rochelle entered into an agreement with the Watt Manufacturing Company whereby the city would donate to the Watt Company a tract of land near the city on which was located a vacant building suitable for manufacturing operations. The agreement provided that title would transfer to the company at the end of five years (from January 1, 1970) if a plant was put in operation for not less than three years and that the company would employ on the average of 300 or more employees. The Watt Company entered into the agreement on January 1, 1970, and started operations on November 1, 1970, on a reduced scale; by the end of 1971 the plant was in full production and 325 persons were on the payroll.

Just prior to signing the agreement the city had hired a competent appraiser to appraise the property with the following results: plant site, $30,000; and building, $80,000. The appraiser estimated the remaining useful life for the building at 20 years. The Watt Company spent $150 in connection with the title to the site and $16,000 on renovating the building.

Required:

1. Give entries to record the donation, incidental costs, renovating costs, depreciation for 1970 and 1971 (if any), and to record the transfer of title. Disregard residual values.

2. Give entries assuming that the Watt Company did not complete the agreement and abandoned the plant in January 1972.

Problem 12-9

The Chamber of Commerce of Bay City had owned a plot of land for a number of years acquired at a cost of $5,000. During a war period a large building was constructed on the land as a part of the defense effort. The building has been vacant most of the time for the last eight years; consequently, it was in need of considerable repair. Recently the property was conservatively appraised at $40,000 of which $25,000 applied to the building. The Spring Manufacturing Company agreed to locate a small plant at the city on the conditions that the Chamber of Commerce would make the facilities of this property available. As a result an agreement was drawn whereby title to the property would transfer to Spring Company two years after operations began and providing an average of 150 or more persons were employed. During the first year Spring Company spent $35,000 renovating the building and making other improvements prior to the beginning of operations. In addition the Chamber of Commerce repaired and hard-surfaced a short stretch of road from the main highway to the site at a cost of $2,500. The company estimated a 20-year remaining life for the building. Spring Company completed all requirements under the contract and received title to the property. At this time the company expended $300 in checking and clearing the title. In connection with the agreement, give appropriate entries on the books of the company (if none, so state) at each of the following dates:

a) At date of agreement.
b) During the first year of operations.
c) At date of title transfer.

Problem 12-10

The Metz Company utilized its own facilities to construct a small addition to their office building. Construction began on March 1 and was completed on June 30 of the same year. Prior to the decision to construct the asset with its own facilities, the company accepted bids from outside contracts; the lowest bid was $190,000. Detailed costs accumulated during the construction period are summarized below:

Materials used (including $120,000 for normal production).............$180,000
Direct labor (including $200,000 for normal production)................. 300,000
General supplies used on construction... 8,000
Rent paid on construction machinery... 3,000
Insurance premiums on construction... 700
Supervisory salary on construction... 5,000
Total general administrative overhead for the year 115,000
Total factory overhead for the year:
    Fixed ($10,000 due to construction) 100,000
    Variable... 60,000
Direct labor hours (including 100,000 for normal production) 150,000

The company allocates factory overhead to normal production on the basis of direct labor cost.

Required:

Compute the amounts that might be capitalized—

a) Assuming the plant capacity to be 150,000 direct labor hours and that the construction displaced production for sale to the extent indicated.

b) Assuming the plant capacity to be 200,000 direct labor hours and that idle capacity was utilized for the construction.

Hint: Use overhead rates for factory overhead.

Problem 12–11

Prepare journal entries to record the following transactions related to the acquisition of fixed assets. Justify your position on doubtful items.

a) Purchased a tract of land for $20,000, assumed taxes already assessed amounting to $180. Paid title fees, $50, and attorney fees of $300 in connection with the purchase. Payments were in cash.

b) Purchased property which included land and buildings for $78,900 cash. The purchase price included an offset of $300 for unpaid taxes. Purchaser borrowed $30,000 at 7% interest (principal and interest due one year from date) from the bank to help make the cash payment. The property was appraised for taxes as follows: land, $22,000; and building, $44,000.

c) Prior to use of the property purchased in (b) above the following expenditures were made:

Repair and renovation of building...$7,000
Installation of 220-volt electrical wiring....................................... 4,000
Removal of separate shed of no use (sold scrap lumber for $50)..... 300
Construction of a new driveway... 1,000
Repair of existing driveways.. 600
Deposits with utilities for connections... 50
Painting the company name on two sides of the building.............. 400
Installation of wire fence around property.................................. 2,500

d) The land purchased in (a) above was leveled and two retaining walls built to stop erosion that had created two rather large gulleys across the property. Total cash cost of the work was $4,500. The property is being held as a future plant site.

e) Purchased a used machine at a cash cost of $12,500. Subsequent to purchase the following expenditures were made:

General overhaul prior to use	$1,500
Installation of machine	500
Cost of moving the machine	150
Cost of removing two small machines to make way for the larger machine purchased	100
Cost of reinforcing the floor prior to installation	140
Testing costs prior to operation	60
Cost of tool kit (new) essential to adjustment of machine for various types of work	170

Problem 12–12

Utah Manufacturers purchased on March 1 as a site for a factory a certain parcel of land on which some old tenement buildings were standing. The total cost was $85,000. On the seller's books the land was carried at $10,000 and the buildings at $8,000.

Utah paid $3,000 to remove the dwelling houses to make room for the factory and received $300 from the sale of the old building material.

Two months were required to build the factory. Operations started on May 1. Construction work was done under contract for $70,000, one half of which was paid to the contractor at the end of the first month and the balance at the end of the second month. The company was obliged to borrow $12,000 of the second payment to the contractor at 6% for two months.

After the factory had been completed the property was assessed as follows: land, $20,000; and building, $40,000. The company paid taxes from March 1 at the annual rate of $3 per $100.

Insurance for $12,000 on the construction of the building was taken out on March 1. This was increased on April 15 to $42,000. The insurance premium paid was at the rate of $.80 for every $100 of insurance for a period of one year; the policy also covered the completed building after construction.

Legal fees covering search of title to the property amounted to $400 and covering construction contract amounted to $100.

Required:

At what amounts should the land and factory building be recorded? Show computations.

Problem 12–13

The books of the Braley Manufacturing Company had never been audited prior to 1971. In auditing the books for the year ended December 31, 1971, the auditor found the following account for the plant:

Plant and Equipment

1968			1968		
Plant purchased		90,000	Sale of scrap		300
Repairs		5,300	Depreciation (5%)		5,000
Legal		600			
Title fees		50	1969		
Insurance		3,000	Depreciation (5%)		6,700
Taxes		1,200			
			1970		
1969			Cash proceeds from old machine		1,150
Addition to plant		15,000	Depreciation (5%)		6,800
Write-up		20,000			
Interest expense		1,500	1971		
Repairs		500	Depreciation (5%)		7,100
Machinery for new addition		2,000			
1970					
New machine		3,000			
Installation		600			
1971					
Machinery overhaul		1,350			
Replaced roof		900			
Fence		3,400			

(Balance $121,350)

Additional data relating to plant and equipment developed during the audit follow:

a) The plant was purchased during January 1968. At that time the tax assessment listed the plant as follows: plant site at $10,000, the building at $20,000, and the machinery therein at $30,000. The estimated life of the plant and machinery was 20 years.

b) During the first six months of 1968 the company expended the amounts listed in the account for the year in getting the plant ready for operation; operations began July 1. The repairs pertain to both the building and machinery. No breakdown was available. The legal fees were incurred in connection with the plant purchase and applied to all components of it. The $3,000 insurance premium represented a one-year policy on the plant and equipment, dated January 10, 1968 ($1,000 of the premium applied to the machinery). The property tax rate for the year was 2%. The scrap was accumulated during the "repair period."

c) In 1969 a plant addition was completed costing $15,000, at which time the company was paying 10% on some funds borrowed. The addition was under construction for four months. During the year $1,500 was spent for ordinary repairs, of which one third was capitalized. Machine costing $2,000 was purchased. The asset account was written up by $20,000 to bring it in line with the bank's security allowance on loans (Paid-In Surplus credited).

d) During 1970 a new machine was purchased (July 1) for $3,000 plus installation costs of $600; an old machine costing an estimated $2,100 was sold for $1,150. The old machine was acquired when the plant was acquired.

e) During 1971 several items of equipment were completely reconditioned at a cost of $1,350. Minor repairs were charged to expense during the year. The roof was replaced on one wing of the plant. A fence was constructed around the plant to keep unauthorized personnel out; it is estimated that the fence will have the same remaining life as the plant.

Required:

1. Set up a work sheet to compute the correct balances for the following accounts: (suggested top captions) Land, Buildings, Machinery, Land Improvements, and Accumulated Depreciation (assume 5% straight line depreciation on ending balances; disregard residual value and round to even dollars.) Suggested side captions: list each item by year. Justify any assumptions that you make.

2. Give entry to correct the accounts assuming the books are closed for 1971.

Problem 12-14

The Valley Manufacturing Company was incorporated on January 2, 19A, but was unable to begin manufacturing activities until July 1, 19A, because new factory facilities were not completed until that date.

The Land and Building account at December 31, 19A, was as follows:

Date	Item	Amount
Jan. 31, 19A	Land and building	$ 98,000
Feb. 28, 19A	Cost of removal of building	1,500
May 1, 19A	Partial payment of new construction	35,000
May 1, 19A	Legal fees paid	2,000
June 1, 19A	Second payment on new construction	30,000
June 1, 19A	Insurance premium	1,800
June 1, 19A	Special tax assessment	2,500
June 30, 19A	General expenses	12,000
July 1, 19A	Final payment on new construction	35,000
Dec. 31, 19A	Asset write-up	12,500
		$230,300
Dec. 31, 19A	Depreciation—19A at 1%	2,300
	Account balance	$228,000

The following additional information is to be considered:

a) To acquire land and building the company paid $48,000 cash and 500 shares of its 5% cumulative preferred stock, par value $100 per share.

b) Cost of removal of old buildings amounted to $1,500 with the demolition company retaining all materials of the building.

c) Legal fees covered the following:

Cost of organization	$ 500
Examination of title covering purchase of land	1,000
Legal work in connection with construction work	500
	$2,000

d) Insurance premium covered premiums for three-year term beginning May 1, 19A.

e) General expenses covered the following for the period from January 2, 19A, to June 30, 19A:

President's salary	$ 6,000
Plant superintendent covering supervision on new building	5,000
Office salaries	1,000
	$12,000

f) The special tax assessment covered street improvements.

g) Because of a general increase in construction costs after entering into the building contract, the board of directors increased the value of the building $12,500, believing such increase justified to reflect current market at the time the building was completed. Retained Earnings was credited for this amount.

h) Estimated life of building – 50 years.
Write-off for 19A – 1% of asset value (1% of $230,000 = $2,300).

Required:

1. Prepare entries to reflect correct land, and building and depreciation allowance accounts at December 31, 19A.

2. Show the proper presentation of land, building and depreciation allowance on the balance sheet at December 31, 19A.

(AICPA adapted)

	Tangible Fixed Assets —
chapter **13**	Depreciation, Depletion,
	and Restatement

DEPRECIATION

At the outset of the preceding chapter we defined the several classes of fixed assets. Fixed assets are acquired for operational purposes rather than for sale; that is, they are acquired and utilized because of their *future* revenue-generating potentials to the enterprise. Thus, they can be viewed by the enterprise as comprising a store of economic-service values that will expire as they are utilized in the revenue-generating process. Therefore, as these economic-service values are utilized in generating revenue, a portion of their total cost periodically must be matched with (allocated against) the period revenues generated in order to fulfill the economic requirement of income measurement. The process of periodically allocating (matching) a portion of the total cost of a fixed asset against the revenue generated must be applied to most fixed assets. This entails application of allocation procedures to three distinct classes of assets; the accounting terminology commonly utilized in this respect is:

1. Amortization. The accounting process of allocating against periodic revenue the cost expiration of an *intangible* fixed asset represented by *special rights* such as patents, copyrights, and leaseholds. (Discussed in Chapter 14).

2. Depletion. The accounting process of allocating against peri-

odic revenue the cost expiration of an asset represented by a *natural resource* such as mineral deposits, gravel deposits, and timber stands.

3. Depreciation.   The accounting process of allocating against periodic revenue the cost expiration of a *tangible* fixed asset represented by *operational* assets such as machinery, tools, and buildings.

Clearly, the three processes just described are similar conceptually; each focuses on a different class of assets. Conceptually they represent the process of cost allocation as opposed to asset valuation. They constitute an application of the *matching principle* since they focus on allocating a particular kind of period cost to subdivisions of the enterprise, to products, and to services.

In a sense, the cost of a fixed asset may be compared with a prepaid expense; the cost of a fixed asset is prepaid (in advance of utilization of the asset), hence is recorded as an asset; as the economic service life of the asset expires with the passage of time and through use, the cost thereof must be systematically allocated to operations as a current cost. Fixed assets, like goods and services represented by current expenditures for operating costs, make a definite contribution to the operations of the enterprise assets.

In accounting for fixed assets the underlying principles are: (*a*) at acquisition, fixed assets are recorded at cost on the basis of the *cost principle;* (*b*) subsequent to acquisition, those fixed assets that have a determinable limited life are reported at the cost recognized at acquisition less the accumulated allocations of such costs (depreciation amortization and depletion); and (*c*) periodic allocations of acquisition cost, made on a systematic and rational basis, are recognized as current expense in conformance with the *matching principle.*

Nature of Depreciation

Now let's turn our attention specifically to depreciation as defined above. In order to understand fully the nature of depreciation accounting it is necessary to examine its effects as related to (*a*) the income statement; (*b*) retained earnings, and dividends; (*c*) cash flow; and (*d*) balance sheet presentation.

Depreciation is recognized on the income statement as selling, administrative, and manufacturing costs, depending upon the nature and use of the assets involved. The periodic depreciation charge may affect the income statement in two ways. That portion of the depreciation charge properly classified as selling expense and administrative expense directly reduces reported net income by the amount involved. That part of the depreciation charge properly classified as factory cost is reported as a part of the cost of goods manufactured. The goods sold during the current period carry to cost of goods sold a portion of the depreciation charge allocated to manufacturing cost. Such depreciation costs likewise decrease reported net income. On the other hand, that portion of depreciation charge remaining in the valuation of goods on hand at the end of the period is reported as an *asset* (inventory) and deferred until the goods are sold. It follows that net income of a given period is reduced by depreciation initially charged to inventory to the extent that such goods are sold during that period.

Since the depreciation charge reduces reported net income, the amount of retained earnings is likewise reduced. This effect reduces the reported amount of retained earnings available for dividends; consequently, over the life of the tangible fixed asset an amount equivalent to the cost of the tangible fixed asset recognized at acquisition (less any residual value) is "held back" from retained earnings and dividend availability. Thus one of the results of depreciation accounting is to prevent the "impairment of capital" through dividends based upon overstated earnings. Failure to recognize depreciation causes overstatement of income with an attendant possible dissipation of capital through liquidating dividends. Depreciation accounting attempts to measure a cost and to charge it against income. Where revenue is sufficient, depreciation like other expenses is recovered. It should be apparent, however, that the mere booking of depreciation can have no effect upon the amount of assets coming into the business through sales of product. But if a concern can sell its product for enough to cover all operating costs including depreciation, the assets received from customers (cash and receivables) will exceed other expense outlays by at least the amount of the depreciation. Since dividends normally are paid only out of net income, net assets equal to the amount of the depreciation charged off will be retained in the business which operates at a profit or merely at break even.

In view of the above discussion it is important to realize that although the depreciation provision does "hold back" assets from dividends equivalent to the provision, it does not provide or "hold back" cash specifically. The relationship of depreciation and cash flow is simply that although most costs and expenses require cash when incurred, the depreciation charge is a noncash reduction of net income; the cash was disbursed when the fixed asset was acquired. Therefore, the *cash generated by net income is greater* than reported net income by the amount of noncash expenses (less noncash incomes) reported on the income statement.[1] Obviously, the fact that depreciation has been recognized does not mean that cash (or even other assets) necessarily will be available to replace the assets when their service life expires. The assets retained as a result of deducting from gross income a provision for depreciation before making the dividend distribution are not automatically segregated into a fund for replace-

---

[1] See Chapter 25 for an extended discussion of cash flow.

ments. On the contrary, the retained funds will probably find uses in paying off liabilities and in purchase of new and different types of assets and, therefore, seldom are available for actual replacements when old assets reach the end of their service life. Any specific fund for replacement must be the result of planned appropriation of cash or other liquid assets from period to period.

With respect to balance sheet presentation of accumulated depreciation on tangible fixed assets, the acquisition cost of the asset should be reported and the accumulated depreciation provision deducted therefrom, so that the "book or carrying value" of the asset is included in the net asset figure. Significantly, the balance sheet does not present the fair market value of tangible fixed assets but rather the "depreciated-cost value."

The importance of depreciation as a cost may be seen readily upon examination of the operating statements of any concern with a relatively large investment in fixed assets. The importance of depreciation varies with the nature of the business and the degree of mechanization or automation involved. Significantly, the reported net income figure is no more accurate than the estimate of the periodic depreciation figure. Since the periodic depreciation provision as well as certain other expenses are estimates, the reported net income figure reflects such estimates. In view of these considerations any attempt to compute and report the depreciation provision to even pennies, for example, reflects upon the judgment and practicality of the accountant involved. With respect to depreciation provision, rounding of the periodic charge should be consistent with the probable margin of error involved in the estimate. The APB strongly recommended in *Opinion No. 12* (December, 1967) that both the amount of the periodic depreciation charge and the method of depreciation used be reported.

Causes of Depreciation

The causes of depreciation may be classified as follows:

Physical Factors	*Functional Factors*
1. Wear and tear from operation.	1. Inadequacy.
2. Action of time and other elements.	2. Supersession.
3. Deterioration, decay, and disease.	3. Obsolescence.

Significantly it may be noted that a *change in market value* is not recognized as one of the causes of depreciation in the accounting sense. The three physical factors, as they affect the service life of a tangible fixed asset, are self-explanatory. Inadequacy is brought about by expansion of a business, the fixed asset becoming unequal to the increased service required, although still in good condition and quite capable of the service originally expected of it. Supersession results when an asset is superseded by another asset which operates more efficiently. Supersession is brought about when inventions give rise to new assets which may be operated more cheaply in rendering the same or an improved service. In such cases it may be desirable to discard the old asset. Obsolescence may arise from inadequacy, supersession, and other causes. Obsolescence of a tangible fixed asset may arise as a result of the outmoding of the product being produced or the service being rendered.

Depreciation accounting takes into account all predictable factors that tend to limit the economic usefulness of a tangible fixed asset to the enterprise. The periodic apportionment of cost through depreciation must be based upon both the physical and functional causes of depreciation. Generally those factors that operate more or less continuously are given recognition in depreciation accounting, whereas sudden and unexpected factors such as storms, floods, sudden change in demand, and radical outmoding of the asset must be accorded special treatment with respect to the fixed assets involved. One of these special treatments, for example, might result in the immediate removal of an asset from the accounts and the related recording of an extraordinary loss.

While depreciation frequently is referred to as a *fixed* (period) cost, it often varies to a considerable extent with changes in the amount of production. Wear and tear from operation varies almost directly with the volume of output or use of the asset. When depreciation is based on output, it is reflected as a *variable* cost.

The useful life of a tangible fixed asset generally is influenced directly by the repair and maintenance policies of the firm. Low standards of maintenance and repairs may reduce costs temporarily; however, the useful life of the asset will be shortened considerably thereby increasing the periodic depreciation expense. Although some have contended that depreciation should include both amortization of the original cost and current repair costs, accountants have viewed repairs and depreciation (as previously defined) as separate cost elements.

In the case of facilities temporarily idle or being held for possible future use, depreciation should continue since the physical and functional causes, which tend to reduce the ultimate economic usefulness of the asset to the firm, continue. Tangible fixed assets that will not be returned to service should be reduced to their fair market value in anticipation of disposal. Special accounts normally should be established in accounting for idle facilities.

Factors in Determining the Depreciation Charge

The periodic depreciation expense should represent the allocation of the original cost (less the estimated residual value) of the asset to operations in proportion to the economic benefit received from the assets involved. The factors which must be considered in calculating the periodic depreciation charge are:

1. Actual cost (as defined in the preceding chapter).
2. Estimated residual (scrap) value.
3. Estimated service life.

Clearly, determination of depreciation is based on one "actual" and two "estimated" factors. The residual value is the estimated amount which may be recovered through sale, trade-in allowance, or by other means when the asset is finally retired from service. In estimating the residual value, allowance must be made for the costs of dismantling and disposal of the retired asset. For example, assume it is estimated that upon retirement the asset can be sold for $250 and that the costs of dismantling and selling are estimated at $50. In this case the residual value would be $200. In practice, recovery value and dismantling and selling costs are frequently disregarded entirely — a procedure which is acceptable when the recovery and disposal costs may offset, when the amounts involved are immaterial, or when the estimates involve a wide margin of error.

In estimating the service life of an asset for accounting purposes it is important to realize that service life implies (a) use of the asset by the owner, (b) use of the asset for the purpose for which acquired, and (c) a definite repair and maintenance policy over the life of the asset. Allocation of depreciation charges should be representative of the expiration of the "economic-service values" of the asset to the enterprise. Thus, the service life should be measured in terms that are most representative of the expiration of such values. Accordingly, service life may be measured in terms of (a) definite time periods such as months or years, (b) units of output, or (c) hours of operating time. Selection of the appropriate measure of service life should depend upon the nature of the asset involved and the nature of the primary causes of depreciation.

Recording Depreciation

The periodic depreciation amount is recorded as a debit to an expense account or a cost of manufacturing account (factory overhead) and a credit to an asset contra account entitled Accumulated Depreciation. Rather than a direct credit to the related fixed asset account, a special contra account traditionally has been credited in order to maintain a separation of the original cost and the amount of that cost expired through depreciation. The contra account should not be labeled as a "reserve" for depreciation, but as Accumulated Depreciation.

In the subsidiary fixed asset records, the periodic depreciation charges and accumulated depreciation are recorded with respect to each individual asset or group of assets.

When a fixed asset is acquired or retired during a period, a particular problem arises with respect to depreciation for a fractional part of the period. This is a matter on which the management, upon advice of the accountant, should establish a definite and consistent policy. Five alternatives are generally recognized as acceptable, viz:

1. Compute depreciation on the balance in the asset account at the *beginning* of the year.
2. Compute the depreciation on the balance in the asset account at the end of the year.
3. Compute depreciation for a full year on assets *acquired* during the first half of the period and no depreciation on assets acquired during the last half of the period. Compute depreciation for a full year on assets retired during the last half of the period and none if retired during the first half.
4. Compute one-half year depreciation on assets acquired during the year and one-half year depreciation on assets disposed of during the year; compute full year on other assets.
5. When assets are acquired on or before the 15th, depreciate them from the first of the month; when they are disposed of after the 15th, similarly record a whole month's depreciation on them. On the other hand, when acquired or disposed of so that the holding period is for less than one-half month, ignore that month's depreciation. Since depreciation is an estimate, following such a rule does little violence to the concept.

The third method should be assumed in this text (including the assignments) unless there are definite instructions otherwise.

Methods of Depreciation

Basically, there are three categories of depreciation methods, that is (*a*) those related primarily to the passage of time, (*b*) those related primarily to output, and (*c*) those related to a specific depreciation curve peculiar to the asset.

The more important specific methods of depreciation are listed below:

1. Straight line.
2. Service hours.
3. Productive output.
4. Reducing charge.
    a) Sum of years' digits.
    b) Fixed percentage on declining base.
    c) Declining rate on cost.
    d) Double declining-balance.

5. Compound interest methods.[2]
   a) Annuity.
   b) Sinking fund.

In order to illustrate each of these methods the following symbols and simplified amounts are used:

Item	Symbol	Illustrative Figures
Acquisition cost	C	$ 100
Scrap or residual value	S	10
Estimated service life:	n	
Years		3
Service hours		6,000
Productive output in units		9,000
Depreciation rate (per year, per service hour, or per unit of productive output)	r	
Dollar amount of depreciation per period	D	

Straight Line Method. The straight line method has been used widely because of its simplicity. This method relates depreciation directly to the passage of time rather than to specific use. It is called straight line because it results in an equal charge for depreciation in each of the periods of the service life of the asset; thus, when graphed against time, both the accumulated depreciation and the undepreciated asset cost are indicated by straight lines. The use of the formula for computing the periodic depreciation charge (annual in this case) is illustrated below.

$$D = \frac{C - S}{n} \quad \text{or} \quad D = \frac{\$100 - \$10}{3} = \$30 \text{ per period}$$

Depreciation frequently is expressed as a *rate*. For the illustrative figures it should be observed that the periodic (annual) rate (r) may be expressed as either $33\frac{1}{3}\%$ on net depreciable value ($\$90 \times 33\frac{1}{3}\% = \$30$) or 30% on cost ($\$100 \times 30\%$)[3]; the percent on cost generally is used.

Illustration 13–1 summarizes the process of straight line depreciation over the life of the illustrative asset and the accounting entries involved.

Although the straight line method is simple and widely used, it is appropriate as a method of cost allocation only where conditions are such that a logical matching of cost and revenue results from its use. If the level of output is essentially the same from period to period, the straight line method is appropriate. In situations where the eco-

---

[2] These are based on present value concepts discussed in Chapter 5.

[3] Many accountants prefer to express the rate as a percent of depreciable value, viz, $\$30 \div (\$100 - \$10) = 33\frac{1}{3}\%$. In this case, to compute the periodic charge, the "net to be depreciated" is multiplied by the rate.

Illustration 13–1
Depreciation Table and Entries
Straight Line Method (life three years)

Year	Depreciation Expense (Debit)	Accumulated Depreciation (Credit)	Balance Accumulated Depreciation	Undepreciated Asset Balance (Book Value)
0...................				$100
1.................$30	$30	$30	70
2................. 30	30	60	40
3................. 30	30	90	10 (residual
$90	$90		value)

nomic-service potential of the asset decreases primarily as a result of the passage of time, as might be the case where obsolescence is the primary factor, the method is appropriate; however, simplicity can hardly be viewed as a primary criterion of suitability. The method does meet the criterion of "systematic and rational" as specified in *Accounting Terminology Bulletin No. 1* of the AICPA.

The straight line method is theoretically acceptable where the following conditions prevail:

1. The decline in economic-service potential of the asset is approximately the same each period.
2. The decline in economic-service potential of the asset is related to the passage of time rather than to use.
3. Use of the asset is consistent from period to period.

Service-Hours Method. The service-hours method is based upon the assumption that the decrease in service life is conditioned primarily by the actual operational use of the asset rather than by the mere passage of time. Rather than an equal periodic charge for depreciation, this method results in a periodic charge which correlates with the amount of time the asset operated. If a machine were operated twice as much in the current period as in the prior period, the depreciation charge for the current period would be twice as much as that of the last period. In utilizing this method the service life of the asset must be estimated in terms of total probable service or working hours prior to retirement; then a rate per service hour is computed.

Assuming a 6,000-hour service life and 3,000 hours operation during the first year, the formula for computing the depreciation rate would be:

$$r = \frac{C - S}{n} \quad \text{or} \quad r = \frac{\$100 - \$10}{6,000} = \$.015 \text{ per service hour}$$

and for the periodic depreciation charge:

$D = r \times$ Service Hours Current Period   or $D = \$.015 \times 3,000 = \$45$

Illustration 13–2 summarizes the results of the service-hours method over the life of the illustrative asset.

Illustration 13–2
Depreciation Table and Entries
Service-Hours Method (life 6,000 hours)

Year	Service Hours Worked°	Depreciation Expense (Debit)		Accumulated Depreciation (Credit)	Balance Accumulated Depreciation	Undepreciated Asset Balance (Book Value)
0.........						$100
1..........3,000	(3,000 × $.015)	$45	$45		$45	55
2..........2,000	(2,000 × $.015)	30	30		75	25
3..........1,000	(1,000 × $.015)	15	15		90	10 (residual
	6,000		$90	$90		value)

° It is assumed that the asset was actually used in this manner and that the original estimate of useful life was confirmed.

The service-hours method satisfies the criterion of "rational and systematic" and would tend to insure a logical matching of cost and revenue on the assumption that the asset would not be operating unless there was productive output. Consequently, under this method the amount of cost allocated would relate to the productive output of the asset. Where obsolescence is not a primary factor and where the economic-service potentials of the asset to the company are determined primarily by working time, the service-hours method would seem appropriate. Also wide variations in use from period to period would suggest application of the service-hours method. Obviously, relative to many assets, such as buildings, furniture, and typewriters, it would be impracticable, if not impossible, to apply the service-hours method.

Productive-Output Method.   Under this method the service life of the asset is estimated in terms of the number of *units* of output. A proportionate part of the total cost to be depreciated (cost less scrap value) is charged to each unit of output as a cost of production; consequently, depreciation charges fluctuate periodically with changes in the volume of production or output. Each unit of output is charged with a constant amount of depreciation, in contrast to the straight line method where each unit of output will be charged with a different amount of depreciation if output varies from period to period.

In applying the method, the cost to be depreciated over the life of the asset is divided by the service life in units to derive a depreciation rate per unit of output; multiplication of this rate times the output for the period gives the periodic depreciation charge. Thus the computation for the rate (assuming a 9,000-unit service life and 4,000 units of output the first period) would be:

$$r = \frac{C - S}{n} \quad \text{or} \quad r = \frac{\$100 - \$10}{9,000} = \$.01 \text{ per unit of output}$$

and using the same assumption the periodic depreciation charge would be:

$$D = r \times \text{Units of Output Current Period} \quad \text{or} \quad D = \$.01 \times 4,000 = \$40$$

Illustration 13–3 summarizes the results of the productive-output method over the life of the illustrative asset.

Illustration 13–3
Depreciation Table and Entries
Productive-Output Method (life 9,000 units)

Year	Units of Output°	Depreciation Expense (Debit)		Accumulated Depreciation (Credit)	Balance Accumulated Depreciation	Undepreciated Asset Balance (Book Value)
0.........						$100
1.........4,000	(4,000 × $.01)	$40	$40	$40	60
2.........3,000	(3,000 × $.01)	30	30	70	30
3.........2,000	(2,000 × $.01)	20	20	90	10 (residual value)
9,000		$90	$90		

° It is assumed that the asset was actually used in this manner.

The productive-output method and the service-hours method both recognize the fact that some assets, such as trucks and machinery, depreciate more rapidly with higher usage than with lower usage. These methods relate more closely the benefit derived from the use of the asset and the depreciation cost allocated than do other methods. The productive-output method is particularly appropriate where obsolescence is not the primary factor, where actual output can be definitely accounted for, and where the service life in units of output can be reasonably estimated.

The differences between the periodic depreciation in the service-hours method and the productive-output method in the illustrative problem apparently are due to a change in the efficiency of operations – the asset was used more efficiently in some periods than others. This observation would lead to the conclusion that in situations where either method could be applied, the productive-output method generally would be theoretically preferable.

At this point it may be appropriate to note the effect on *total cost of products* and on *unit product cost* of the methods discussed. The straight line method results in depreciation as a cost of being reported as a *fixed cost in total,* but *variable per unit* of output. In contrast, the service-hours method and productive-output method would result in depreciation as a cost being reported as *variable in total,* but *fixed per unit of output.* To illustrate assume an asset costing $600 (no residual value) with an estimated life of five years or 500 units of output. Assume further that output was: Year 1 – 90; Year 2 – 100; Year 3 – 110; Year 4 – 120; and Year 5 – 80. The resultant depreciation charges and unit cost figures for the straight line and output methods are compared below:

Year	Units of Output	Output Depreciation		Straight Line Depreciation	
		Amount	Unit Cost	Amount	Unit Cost
1...................	90	$108	$1.20	$120	$1.33
2...................	100	120	1.20	120	1.20
3...................	110	132	1.20	120	1.09
4...................	120	144	1.20	120	1.00
5...................	80	96	1.20	120	1.50
	500	$600		$600	

These distinctions are particularly important in cost analyses for managerial pricing, control, and decision-making considerations. These relative effects should be considered carefully in selecting a method of depreciation for each tangible fixed asset.

Reducing-Charge Methods. The reducing-charge methods are designed to allocate the cost to be depreciated in such a manner that periodic depreciation expense charges are higher in the early years and lower in the later years of the life of the fixed asset. The reducing-charge methods are based upon the theory that new assets are more efficient than old assets; therefore, the economic-service potentials rendered by the asset are greater during the early life of the asset. If the cost of these greater values being consumed through utilization of the asset is to be matched with the resulting revenue, some form of reducing-charge depreciation (frequently referred to as accelerated depreciation) is theoretically desirable. The reducing-charge methods are also defended on the grounds that the annual depreciation charge should decrease as repair costs on the asset increase, thus resulting in a more equitable charge to the operating periods for the use of the fixed asset.

Numerous procedures have been proposed for computing a reducing depreciation charge from period to period over the life of an asset; however, the principal methods currently being used are:

1. Sum of years' digits.
2. Fixed percentage on declining base.

3. Declining rate on cost.
4. Double declining-balance.

Sum-of-Years'-Digits Method. This method (usually referred to as the SYD method) is based upon the application of a decreasing fraction each succeeding period during the life of the asset to the cost to be depreciated (Illustration 13–4). The fractions are determined by using as the denominator the sum of the years' digits for the life of the asset. The numerator, which changes each period, is the years' digits in inverse order (same as the remaining life including the current period). For example, the asset in the illustration, having an estimated service life of three years, would be depreciated as follows:

Denominator: Sum of the years' digits; $1 + 2 + 3 = 6$.
Numerators: Digits in inverse order; 3, 2, and 1.
Fractions: First period, $\frac{3}{6}$.
               Second period, $\frac{2}{6}$.
               Third period, $\frac{1}{6}$.

Illustration 13–4
Depreciation Table and Entries
Sum-of-Years'-Digits Method (life three years)

Year	Depreciation Expense (Debit)		Accumulated Depreciation (Credit)	Balance Accumulated Depreciation	Undepreciated Asset Balance (Book Value)
0					$100
1 ....($\frac{3}{6}$ × $90)	$45		$45	$45	55
2 ....($\frac{2}{6}$ × $90)	30		30	75	25
3 ....($\frac{1}{6}$ × $90)	15		15	90	10 (residual value)
	$90		$90		

Note that the reducing fraction is multiplied by the cost to be depreciated (cost less residual value) in each period (Illustration 13–4). When the life of the asset is relatively long, the denominator (sum of the digits) can be readily computed by using the following formula:

$$SYD = n\left(\frac{n+1}{2}\right)$$

Illustration for three-year life:

$$SYD = 3\left(\frac{3+1}{2}\right) = 6$$

Illustration for 25-year life:

$$\text{SYD} = 25\left(\frac{25 + 1}{2}\right) = 325$$

Fixed-Percentage-on-Declining-Base Method. In applying this method the book value of the asset (undepreciated asset balance) is multiplied by a constant percentage rate. Since a constant rate is applied to a *declining base,* each subsequent periodic depreciation charge will be less. The rate must be computed taking into account the estimated life, cost, and residual value; consequently, the rate will automatically provide for the residual value at the end of the service life of the asset. The depreciation rate (the fixed percentage) and its application is illustrated below:

$$r = 1 - \sqrt[n]{\frac{S}{C}} \quad \text{or} \quad r = 1 - \sqrt[3]{\frac{\$10}{\$100}} = .536, \text{ or } 53.6\%$$

Calculation of $\sqrt[n]{\frac{S}{C}}$ is readily achieved by use of logarithms.

Observe in Illustration 13–5 that the book value at the end of the service life is precisely the estimated scrap value. It should be pointed

Illustration 13–5
Depreciation Table and Entries
Fixed-Percentage-on-Declining-Base Method

Year	Depreciation Expense (Debit)		Accumulated Depreciation (Credit)	Balance Accumulated Depreciation	Undepreciated Asset Balance (Book Value)
0............					$100.00
1............(53.6% × $100)	$53.60		$53.60	$53.60	46.40
2............(53.6% × $46.40)	24.87		24.87	78.47	21.53
3............(53.6% × $21.53)	11.53		11.53	90.00	10.00 (residual
	$90.00		$90.00		value)

out that where the asset has no scrap value the formula given above for calculation of the depreciation percentage or rate cannot be used unless a nominal scrap value of, say, $1, is assumed. As a matter of practical application it is usually desirable to round the rate to an even percentage, as may have been done in the above example to 54%.

Declining-Rate-on-Cost Method. This method is based on no particular formula; the depreciation rate is different each period, being selected on an arbitrary basis when the depreciation policy is determined with respect to the fixed asset. A series of decreasing percentages are selected to provide the desired reduction in the periodic depreciation charge. The residual or scrap value, as a percent of cost, is provided for by excluding it from the periodic rates. The total of the periodic rates plus the scrap percent must add to 100%. Application of the declining-rate-on-cost method is shown in Illustration 13–6, assuming the declining rates selected are those indicated in the second column.

Illustration 13–6
Depreciation Table and Entries
Declining-Rate-on-Cost Method (estimated life three years)

Year	Declining Rates	Depreciation Expense (Debit)		Allowance for Depreciation (Credit)	Balance Accumulated Depreciation	Undepreciated Asset Balance (Book Value)
0............						$100
1............	55%	(55% × $100)	$55	$55	$55	45
2............	25	(25% × $100)	25	25	80	20
3............	10	(10% × $100)	10	10	90	10 (residual value)
	90%		$90	$90		
Scrap %	10					
	100%					

The primary weakness of the declining-rate method is that the periodic rates, being *arbitrarily* selected, lack objectivity and may not be representative of the actual expiration of service values throughout the life of the asset. On the other hand, in cases where the periodic expiration of the economic-service potentials of the asset can be reasonably estimated, and where they take a form or "curve" not adequately represented by that peculiar to the straight line, SYD, or constant rate on declining-balance methods, the declining-rate method offers a means of approximating an appropriate expiration.

Double Declining-Balance Method. Reducing-charge depreciation is acceptable for federal income tax purposes, except the regulations provide that the amount of depreciation must not be more than double the amount that would result under the straight line method when the residual value is ignored.[4] This provision gave rise to the double declining-balance method. Under this method the fixed percentage used is simply double the straight line rate ignoring

---

[4] For tax purposes, residual value is ignored in computing depreciation. As to assets acquired prior to 1954 the maximum is one and one half of the straight line result.

salvage value. This rate is multiplied each year by the declining book value. Based on the above data the rate would be 67%, i.e., $33\frac{1}{3}\% \times 2$. The depreciation would be:

Year	Book Value	Rate	Depreciation°
1......................................	$100	× 67% =	$ 67
2......................................	33	× 67 =	22
3......................................	11	× 67 =	1
			$ 90
Implicit residual value.....			10
			$100

°At the present time double-declining depreciation may be used for tax purposes only when the life is three years or more and the asset may not be depreciated below its residual value.

Under each of the reducing-charge methods of depreciation, monthly depreciation charges (fractional-period depreciation) are usually computed as one twelfth of the annual charge. To illustrate, assume the annual charge for the current period has been computed to be $4,800 under a reducing-charge method, the monthly charge during the current period would be $400. Obviously, the monthly amount would be less in each succeeding year.

With respect to acceptability of the reducing-charge approach, the Committee on Accounting Procedure of the AICPA stated in *Accounting Research Bulletin No. 44* That:

The declining-balance method is one of those which meets the requirements of being "systematic and rational." In those cases where the expected productivity or revenue-earning power of the asset is relatively greater during the earlier years of its life, or where maintenance charges tend to increase during the later years, the declining-balance method may well provide the most satisfactory allocation of cost. The conclusions of this bulletin also apply to other methods, including the "sum-of-the-years-digits" method, which produce substantially similar results.

Compound Interest Methods

The preceding paragraphs discussed depreciation approaches that provided: (1) a *constant* depreciation charge (expense) per period, (2) a *decreasing* depreciation charge per period, or (3) a *varying* depreciation charge per period (output methods). The *compound interest methods* represent a distinctly different approach since they provide an *increasing periodic* expense effect on net income. The other approaches to depreciation have been criticized because, among other things, they ignore interest, a cost factor in asset ownership. The compound interest methods are based upon the conceptual nature of an investment and the return on that investment (interest). Implicit is the concept that the periodic recovery of an investment over its life is comprised of both principal and interest. Within these generalizations you will observe one conceptual difference between the two compound interest methods; this difference relates to the treatment of the imputed interest.

To illustrate the two methods we will continue the prior example by utilizing the following data:

CV (cost value) $= \$100$
SV (scrap value) $= \$10$
N (years of life) $= 3$
i (interest rate) $= 5\%$
Amount of Annuity $= s_{\overline{n}|i}$ (or $A =$ Table 5–3)
Present Value or Annuity $= a_{\overline{n}|i}$ (or $P =$ Table 5–4)

The Annuity Method of Depreciation. This method is based on the theory that depreciation expense should be comprised of two elements: (1) an allocation of the cost of the asset (the amount allocated *increases* each period) and (2) an imputed interest cost based upon the decreasing asset cost. The imputed interest cost is offset through a credit to interest income. Clearly, the imputed interest income credit will *decrease* in amount from period to period since the unrecovered (undepreciated) asset balance is decreasing. The combined effects of the cost allocation and the imputed interest effect is a *constant* depreciation charge from period to period; however, in view of the decreasing interest income credit the net effect on the income statement is an increasing charge from period to period. These effects, the computations, and the resultant accounting entries are reflected in Illustration 13–7.

Illustration 13–7
Annuity Method of Depreciation

Formula	Illustration
$\dfrac{CV - \dfrac{SV}{(1+i)^n}}{a_{\overline{n}|i}} =$ Periodic Charge	$\dfrac{\$100 - \dfrac{\$10}{(1.05)^3}}{a_{\overline{3}|.05}}$
	$= \dfrac{\$100 - \dfrac{\$10}{1.157625°}}{2.7232480†}$
	$= \underline{\$33.55}$

Illustration 13-7 (continued)
Depreciation Table and Journal Entries — Annuity Method

Year	Depreciation Dr. (a)	Accumulated Depreciation Cr. (b)	Interest Income Cr. (c)	Unamortized Asset Balance (d)
0......................	—	—	—	$100.00
1......................	$ 33.55	$28.55	$ 5.00	71.45
2......................	33.55	29.98	3.57	41.47
3......................	33.55	31.47	2.08	10.00
	$100.65	$90.00	$10.65	

°Table 5-1.
†Table 5-4.
(a) Constant amount from formula.
(b) (a) minus (c).
(c) Previous unamortized asset balance times .05.
(d) Previous balance minus current (b).

The Sinking Fund Method of Depreciation. This method is the same as the annuity method except that the imputed interest is not specifically (separately) recorded and reported. Column (b) in Illustration 13-7 is utilized as the depreciation amounts. Thus, it provides an *increasing* depreciation charge (expense) each period. The "sinking fund" aspect of the designation refers to the historical fact that it assumed also that a fund would be accumulated, on an annuity basis, to replace the asset at the end of its useful life. In this instance the periodic depreciation charge would be the same per period as the increase in the replacement fund. The two compound interest methods are compared in Illustration 13-8.

Illustration 13-8
Compound Interest Methods of Depreciation Compared

	Annuity Method		Sinking Fund Method	
Year 1:				
Depreciation expense......................33.55			28.55	
Accumulated depreciation...........		28.55		28.55
Interest income.........................		5.00		
Year 2:				
Depreciation expense......................33.55			29.98	29.98
Accumulated depreciation...........		29.98		
Interest income.........................		3.57		
Year 3:				
Depreciation expense......................33.55			31.47	
Accumulated depreciation...........		31.47		31.47
Interest income.........................		2.08		

The compound interest methods have been criticized on several counts. Some claim that they are not "rational" since an increasing charge for depreciation over the life of the asset is inconsistent with the fact that ownership costs based on value tend to decrease in later years. Also a part of the depreciation charge under the *annuity method* is for imputed or theoretical interest; the offsetting credit for this element is made to Interest Income and therefore affects the income or loss of the period in which the depreciation is recorded. If the assets being depreciated are used in the production of goods for inventory, the consequence may be that an element of imputed interest will be found in an asset balance rather than in an expense balance at the close of the period.

Compound interest methods of calculating depreciation (annuity and sinking fund methods) occasionally are used by concerns with very large investment in long-lived fixed assets. These two methods view fixed assets as packages of future services, the cost of which reflects the present value of those future services. Thus, the periodic depreciation charge is affected by *imputed interest* at the selected rate. Selection of an appropriate rate for imputation purposes is a critical problem. At the current time it is doubtful that these two methods accord with generally accepted accounting principles.

Special Depreciation Systems

Special problems confronting the firm, due to both internal and external factors, frequently require adaptations of the *depreciation methods* of cost allocation discussed above. The primary adaptations, generally referred to as "systems," are discussed in this section under the captions:

1. Inventory (or appraisal) system.
2. Retirement system.
3. Replacement system.
4. Composite life system.
5. Group system.

Inventory System. Under this system, sometimes referred to as the appraisal system, purchases of depreciable assets are debited to an appropriate asset account in the usual manner and allocations of cost representing depreciation are credited to the same account. The amount to be recorded as depreciation for the period is determined by estimating the "value" of the asset on hand in its present condition; the asset account then is reduced to this amount and depreciation expense is charged. Salvage recovery serves to reduce depreciation expense for the period. The value of the asset on hand is determined by inventory procedures and an estimate of its cost, taking into account present condition.

To illustrate, assume the Hand Tools account showed a balance of $680 and that an inventory of the tools on hand at the end of the period, valued at cost and adjusted for present condition, indicated a value of $560. The entry to record the periodic depreciation is:

```
Depreciation Expense — Hand Tools ............................................120
    Hand Tools ($680 − $560).....................................................        120
```

The inventory system should be used only in situations where the asset account represents numerous asset items of a small unit cost, such as hand tools, machine tools, patterns, and dies. Even in these cases the system should be used only when the usual methods are impractical with respect to the specific asset.

In applying the inventory system care must be exercised to exclude changes in value due to changes in the price level or other market fluctuations, otherwise the depreciation charge will include noncost elements such as unrealized (holding) market gains and losses. A conventional matching of expired cost and periodic revenues requires that the items be valued in terms of original cost adjusted for present condition.

Retirement and Replacement Systems. The retirement and replacement systems of depreciation frequently are used in the public utility field because of the peculiar problems often encountered with respect to certain fixed assets such as poles and other line items. They are also used in accounting for low-cost items such as hand tools. Under both systems, no periodic entry is made for depreciation in the normal manner; instead depreciation is recognized at the time of replacement of the asset. The basic distinction between them is that under the *retirement* system the cost of the *old* asset (less its residual value) is charged to depreciation expense when it is replaced, whereas under the *replacement* system the cost of the *new* asset (less residual value of the *old* asset) is charged to depreciation expense when it replaces the old asset. To illustrate both systems assume the Hi-Power Utility Company replaced 10 utility poles at a cost of $100 each. The old poles replaced originally cost $50 each and have a salvage value of $10 each.

Retirement System

1. To record the retirement of the old poles:

```
Depreciation Expense ............................................................    400
Cash for Salvage (residual value old poles) ..............................    100
    Fixed Asset (cost of old poles)............................................        500
```

2. To record the new asset:

```
Fixed Asset (cost of new poles) ...............................................1,000
    Cash (or inventory) ..........................................................      1,000
```

Replacement System

```
Depreciation Expense..........................................................   900
Cash for Salvage (residual value old poles)..............................   100
    Cash (cost of new poles)...............................................              1,000
```

From this example it should be clear that the retirement system represents a *Fifo* approach whereas the replacement system represents a *Lifo* system in allocating the asset cost to depreciation. The retirement system provides depreciation charges based on older costs and reports the fixed asset at newer costs, whereas the replacement system provides depreciation charges based on newer costs and reports the fixed asset at the older cost. Neither system adequately matches cost with revenue particularly in the early and late life of the business, since depreciation is recognized only when assets are being replaced. Once the company has reached a relatively stable level of growth and replacement, the resulting periodic depreciation charges may approximate cost depreciation. Neither of these systems provides a "systematic and rational" allocation of fixed asset costs. The systems have been used in the utility field because of the practical problems encountered in depreciating large numbers of relatively low-cost items such as poles, cross-members, brackets, and conduits at many locations. In such situations the distinction between ordinary repairs and capitalizable replacements is difficult to establish and apply on a practical basis. Although lacking theoretical justification, the retirement system in particular has practical justification under certain conditions.

Group and Composite-Life Systems. The discussions up to this point have assumed that each item of property will be depreciated as a separate unit. In actual practice, many companies group certain fixed assets for depreciation purposes. For example, all of the one-ton trucks may be grouped, or an entire operating assembly such as a refinery may be depreciated as a single unit. In such cases an *average depreciation* rate is applied to the group or assembly. Where an average rate of depreciation is applied to a number of *homogeneous* assets having similar characteristics and services lives, such as the trucks mentioned above, the procedure is referred to as *group depreciation*. Where an average rate of depreciation is applied to a number of *heterogeneous* assets having dissimilar characteristics and service lives, such as the refinery mentioned above, the procedure is referred to as *composite depreciation*. Many accountants view composite depreciation as a special variation of group depreciation. It is difficult to draw a definite distinction between the two on the basis of characteristics and service lives. From the accounting standpoint there is no difference in mechanical application of the average rate nor in the resulting journal entries as between the two systems.[5]

Under the group system, all of the assets in the group are recorded in one asset account, and one accumulated depreciation account is established for the entire group; consequently, it would be incorrect to consider that any one item in the group has a "book value" — the book value appearing in the account applies to the entire group and not to individual items. Subsequent acquisitions of items belonging to the group are similarly charged to the group asset account at cost. Depreciation is computed by multiplying an *average depreciation rate* times the balance in the group asset account irrespective of the age of the individual assets represented therein. The rate may be computed and applied to cost or cost less salvage value, as desired. The depreciation entry is made by charging Expense and crediting Accumulated Depreciation for the periodic amount of depreciation thus computed. Upon retirement of a unit which is a part of the group, the group asset account is credited for the *original cost* of the item and the Accumulated Depreciation account is debited for the *same amount less any salvage recovery*. The system, therefore, does not recognize "losses or gains" on retirement of group assets.[6]

To illustrate the group system, assume the Derden Wholesale Corporation purchased 10 panel trucks for delivery purposes, each costing $2,400. Each truck has an estimated residual value of $400 at the end of the estimated service life. It is estimated that the average service life is five years. The company desires to depreciate the trucks on a group basis. Assuming depreciation is recognized on the ending balance in the asset account, typical entries under the group system are indicated below:

1. To record the initial purchase of 10 trucks at $2,400 each:

Trucks	24,000	
Cash		24,000

2. To record group depreciation at the end of the first year:

Depreciation Expense ($24,000 × 16⅔%)	4,000	
Accumulated Depreciation		4,000
Cost	$24,000	
Estimated residual value	4,000	
To be depreciated over 5 years	$20,000	
Depreciation per year ($20,000 ÷ 5)	$ 4,000	
Depreciation rate on asset balance ($4,000 ÷ $24,000)	16⅔%	

---

[5] Eugene L. Grant and Paul T. Norton, Jr., *Depreciation* (New York: The Ronald Press Co., 1955), chap. vii.

[6] Ibid.

3. To record retirement of one truck at the end of the second year due to wreck; amount received from insurance, $1,500:

Cash 1,500
Accumulated Depreciation (cost less residual recovery)........... 900
    Trucks.. 2,400

4. To record purchase of two additional trucks at $2,500 each:

Trucks... 5,000
    Cash 5,000

5. To record the retirement of a truck that has been used for $5\frac{1}{2}$ years, and then sold to a salvage yard for $150, original cost, $2,400:

Cash 150
Accumulated Depreciation 2,250
    Trucks.. 2,400

In applying the group system it may be necessary to approximate the "book value" of a specific unit that is a part of the group. For example, when a unit is transferred from one group account to another group account, as might be done when the asset is moved from one organizational division of the company to another, it is desirable that the original acquisition cost and accumulated depreciation to date be transferred in the accounts. In such cases the accumulated depreciation under the group system may be approximated as follows:

$$\frac{\text{Present Age}}{\text{Service Life}} \times (\text{Acquisition Cost} - \text{Residual Value})$$

To illustrate, assume a machine is being transferred from Plant A to Plant B; the machine originally cost $5,300 and has been in operation six years. Its estimated service life is 15 years, and the estimated salvage value, $300. The machine has been depreciated on a group basis, the *average* group rate being used is 8%. The entry to record the transfer might be:

Machinery – Plant B 5,300
Accumulated Depreciation – Machinery – Plant A° 2,000
    Machinery – Plant A 5,300
    Accumulated Depreciation – Machinery – Plant B° 2,000

°Computation: $\frac{6}{15} \times (\$5,300 - \$300) = \underline{\$2,000}$

Under the *composite system* the units making up the operating unit or assembly may have a fairly wide range of service lives. Because of this condition, composite-life depreciation is subject to theoretical objections. In establishing the average rate under composite depreciation, both the *composite life* and *composite rate* may be computed. Composite life is the average life of the various units which go to make up an operating unit or assembly, and the composite rate is

Illustration 13–9
Composite Depreciation — Operating Assembly XY

Component Item	Original Cost	Residual Value	Amount to Be Depreciated	Estimated Service Life	Annual Depreciation
A	$50,000	$5,000	$45,000	15 years	$3,000
B	20,000	4,000	16,000	10 "	1,600
C	7,000	600	6,400	8 "	800
D	3,000	–0–	3,000	3 "	1,000
	$80,000	$9,600	$70,400		$6,400°

° Composite life: $70,400 ÷ $6,400 = 11 years.
Composite depreciation rate:
  $6,400 ÷ $80,000 = 8% on cost.

Depreciation first period:
  Depreciation Expense ($80,000 × 8%).........6,400
    Accumulated Depreciation................... 6,400

Note: Some accountants prefer to compute the rate this way:

$$\frac{\Sigma \text{ Cost} - \text{Residual Value}}{\Sigma \text{ Original Cost} \times \text{Estimated Life}} = \frac{\$70,400}{\$1,015,000} = 7\% \text{ rate.}$$

the ratio of the periodic depreciation to the acquisition cost of all components of the operating unit (Illustration 13–9).

If there are no changes in the asset account the assembly will be depreciated to the residual value (at the end of the 11th year in the above example). However, when replacements of component parts are made, the debit to the asset account for the replacement and the credit to the asset account for the cost of the old component (the compensating entry is a debit to Accumulated Depreciation for this same amount, less any salvage recovery) would tend to spread the total cost of utilizing the asset over the actual service life which would be determined in large part by the repair and replacement policy.

The group and composite-life systems frequently are applied on the grounds of clerical convenience. They should not be applied merely for convenience; rather the characteristics, operating conditions, and groupings should be consistent with the mechanics of the systems so that there is a "rational and systematic" matching of costs and revenue. Many firms find it necessary to revise the average depreciation rate from time to time on the basis of an unrealistic relationship developing between the balance in the asset account (cost) and the balance in the Accumulated Depreciation account. Obviously, such revisions may reflect unfavorably upon objectivity in the accounting function.

Depreciation Policy

Within a company several different methods of depreciation may be employed since there may be wide variations in the nature of the tangible fixed assets employed. In selecting the method of depreciation to use with regard to a specific asset, the nature of the asset and its use are controlling factors. It is fundamental to the process of amortizing the cost of a fixed asset over its service life that there is one depreciation curve that best represents the true depreciation. True depreciation of an asset for a given period on a cost basis is the difference between the present worth of all future services or benefits at the beginning of the period and the end of the period, discounted at the rate of return implicit in the purchase of the asset. These service values cannot be predicted or measured with sufficient accuracy in many cases to permit practical application of this theoretical concept; therefore, accountants are forced to use simplified approximations such as the straight line, sum of the years' digits, and other methods. It is unfortunate that the accountant generally feels the need to employ a very limited range of depreciation curves.

Contrary to traditional thinking there is considerable evidence that some degree of declining-charge depreciation, rather than the commonly used straight line concept, is characteristic of many depreciable assets. Terborgh in analyzing the "Decline of Capital Value with Age," states:

> It is a matter of common observation that the services of capital assets tend to become less and less valuable as time goes on. There is, of course, no mystery about this phenomenon. The majority of such assets require during their service lives a flow of maintenance expenditures, which as a rule rises irregularly with age and use. Most of them suffer a progressive deterioration in the quality or the adequacy of their service. Moreover, in a dynamic technology such as ours they are subject to the competition of improved substitutes, so that the quality of their service declines relative to the available alternatives even when it does not deteriorate absolutely. All of these factors — rising operating costs, impaired service quality or adequacy, and improved alternatives — combine to reduce the value of the service as the assets age. . . .
>
> The main conclusion that emerges from the theoretical and empirical evidence now reviewed may be summed up in two propositions. (1) It seems quite clear that the straight-line writeoff is a gravely retarded method of depreciation for productive equipment. Any realistic allocation procedure should get rid of at least one-half of the initial value over the first third of the service life and at least two-thirds over the first half. (2) The straight-line method is apparently less retarded for buildings and structures than for equipment, how must less it is impossible, on the basis of the available evidence, to say.[7]

Grant and Norton take a somewhat similar position in their treatise on depreciation.[8]

A primary objective of depreciation for financial accounting purposes relates to internal managerial use. Depreciation policy and ac-

---

[7] George Terborgh, *Realistic Depreciation Policy* (Chicago: Machinery and Allied Products Institute, 1954), chaps. iv and v.

[8] Eugene L. Grant and Paul T. Norton, *Depreciation* (New York: The Ronald Press Co., 1955), pp. 368–71.

counting must stand the rigid test of internal usefulness. In evaluating alternative depreciation policies it must be recognized that the resulting data may enter into many important management decisions, such as —

1. Distribution of dividends and utilization of retained earnings.
2. Pricing policy.
3. Establishing wages and salaries.
4. Committing funds to projects, such as capital additions and research.
5. Cost analyses and control.
6. Budgetary considerations.

As previously indicated, numerous methods of depreciation have attained the status of "generally acceptable" accounting procedures. One of the glaring deficiencies in "generally accepted accounting principles" is the fact that any of the "acceptable" methods can be used without regard to the economic realities of the asset in use and its decline in economic service value. To date the profession of accounting has not specifically identified the conditions under which each of the several depreciation methods should be used in order to conform to "generally accepted accounting." Insistence on utilization of an economically defensible method for each set of circumstances would significantly improve accounting results and lend an added measure of economic sophistication to it. The fact that a particular method has general acceptance should not be the criterion for use; rather, within the limits of general acceptance, the characteristics of the asset and the situation in which it is used generally will indicate whether or not a particular depreciation method is appropriate for deriving reported net income.

Depreciation for Income Tax Purposes

The Internal Revenue Code makes provision for deduction of depreciation as an expense in computing taxable net income. Accountants should be careful to make a clear-cut distinction between depreciation for tax purposes and depreciation for accounting purposes. The tax regulations are intended to levy taxes in an equitable manner and in a way that is easy to administer; hence they necessarily must be concerned with closing "tax loopholes" and at the same time not excessively discouraging capital investment. As a result, provisions relating to *exchanges* of similar fixed assets and long-term capital gains, for example, have been incorporated in the tax provisions. A company usually will select the method of depreciation for tax purposes that appears to give the best tax advantage, while at the same time employing the method of depreciation for accounting purposes that best matches cost and revenue. Merely because a particular method is used for tax purposes is no criterion for its use for accounting purposes.

The Revenue Code allows any "reasonable" method but specifically lists the straight line, declining-balance, and the sum-of-years'-digits methods as acceptable (with certain limitations). The code allows depreciation on the basis of either individual units or groups.

Changes and Correction of Depreciation

Since recorded and reported depreciation is based in part on estimates (life and residual value) and several depreciation methods (straight line, SYD, etc.) are generally accepted, accountants frequently encounter situations where a change or correction is advisable. Fundamentally, such changes and corrections can be made *prospectively* (reflected in future accounting values) or *retroactively* (reflected in past accounting values). In respect to depreciation changes and corrections, three distinct categories are involved, viz:

1. Changes in accounting principle—A change from a generally accepted accounting procedure (such as SYD) to another accepted procedure (such as straight line).
2. Changes in estimates—A change in estimated service life or residual value, based on new information or experience (such as a change from a 10- to a 12-year life).
3. Errors—The result of misapplication of the facts due to misunderstanding, oversight, misuse, lack of knowledge of appropriate application, or outright intent.

Each of these three categories will be illustrated and briefly discussed; Chapter 24 incorporates a detailed discussion of these three types of changes.

Change in Principle. The presumption is made that changes in accounting principle are elected only to enhance the value of the resultant financial reports. Thus, an enterprise would change from, say, SYD to straight line only because the latter gives better expression to the continuing decrease in economic-service values of the asset. Once such a change is decided upon, assuming materiality, two questions are posed: (1) How should the change be reflected in the accounts? and (2) How should the change be reported on the periodic financial statements? In response to the two questions, the effect on the net incomes of prior periods between the former method and the new method should be determined and recorded as "Adjustment Due to Accounting Change." This amount should then be reported on the income statement along with extraordinary items.[9]

---

[9] The pro forma effect on prior years' incomes should be reported as a footnote; reference *APB Opinion 20* (July, 1971).

To illustrate, assume XY Corporation has a machine that cost $150,000 (no residual value) and has been depreciated over five years on SYD basis and after the end of year 2 decided to change to straight line depreciation. The results may be compared as follows:

	Prior Method – SYD		New Method –	Difference
Year	SYD	Amount	Straight Line	to Date
1................5/15		$ 50,000	$ 30,000	$20,000
2................4/15		40,000	30,000	10,000
3................3/15		30,000	30,000	
4................2/15		20,000	30,000	
5................1/15		10,000	30,000	
		$150,000	$150,000	$30,000

In year 3 the current depreciation should be based on the new method, and in addition to the usual adjusting entry, the following correcting entry should be made:

Accumulated Depreciation 30,000
    Depreciation Adjustment, Change in Accounting
      Method   30,000

The income statement should reflect the change as follows:

Income before extraordinary items..$60,000
    Extraordinary items (detailed) .... (10,000)
    Adjustment due to accounting change (depreciation)................. 30,000°
Net income $80,000

    ° Appropriate footnote.

This treatment is theoretically sound since it does not permit the adjustment to be reflected as an operating item, documents the item, does not permit it to "bypass" the income statement, and establishes better values for future financial reports.

Changes in Estimates. The presumption is that changes in estimates are made only when new information or experience justifies a change in estimated life or residual value. When such determinations are made the change should be reflected in order to enhance the value of the resultant financial reports. Again, assuming materiality, the dual questions are posed as to the proper way to reflect the effect of the change (*a*) in the accounts and (*b*) on the financial reports. Two positions are widely preferred, viz: (1) prospective treatment, and (2) retroactive treatment.

To illustrate, assume a machine that cost $160,000 (no residual value) is being depreciated over five years ($32,000 per year). Now assume, at the end of the fourth year, on the basis of recent experience it is decided that a more realistic life is eight years ($20,000 per year). What adjustment, if any, should be made in the fourth year to reflect the change in estimate?

Prospective Treatment. The remaining book value (undepreciated balance) would be depreciated over the remaining life and no "adjustment" would be needed. The depreciation entry for the fourth year would be:

Depreciation Expense..12,800
    Accumulated Depreciation ($64,000 ÷ 5)..........................   12,800

This approach is specified in *APB Opinion 9* as follows:

Treatment as prior period adjustments should not be applied to the normal, recurring corrections and adjustments which are the natural result of the use of estimates inherent in the accounting process. For example, changes in the estimated remaining lives of fixed assets affect the computed amounts of depreciation, but these changes should be considered prospective in nature and not prior period adjustments.

Some accountants do not agree with the rationale of this treatment and cite that it establishes a rule "once wrong always wrong" since *both* the past and future periodic depreciation charges will be wrong. Thus, they favor a retroactive adjustment. However, *APB Opinion 20*, "Accounting Changes" (July, 1971) requires prospective treatment.

Retroactive Treatment. The Accumulated Depreciation account would be adjusted to the new balance and prior earnings (retained earnings) corrected as follows:

Accumulated Depreciation 36,000
    Correction Prior Years' Earnings (depreciation)................   36,000
        ($32,000 − $20,000) × 3 years

Depreciation for fourth year:

Depreciation Expense..20,000
    Accumulated Depreciation   20,000

The $36,000 Correction Prior Years' Earnings could be reflected on the income statement as an extraordinary item or on the statement of retained earnings as a prior period adjustment. The authors prefer the former reporting practice on the basis that such items should not by-pass the income statement.

Errors. Outright errors in depreciation should be corrected in the records through a correcting entry and the effect of the correction reflected on the financial statements. To further pinpoint this troublesome area we will cite four examples and illustrate the first one.

Illustration 1. During the third year after acquisition it was discovered that a machine costing $10,000 had been debited directly to an expense account. The asset had an estimated service life of five years and no residual value.

Illustration 2. During the current year (1971) it was discovered that annual depreciation on an asset acquired on January 1, 1967, at a cost of $16,000 (8-year life), through error, was not recorded and reported in 1969.

Illustration 3. Through error or outright intent an asset with a reasonable life of 30 years is being depreciated over 10 years; there has been no change in information.

Illustration 4. At some time during the life of the asset there is a change from an *unacceptable* method of depreciation to a generally accepted method.

In respect to Illustration 1, the following correcting entry is in order during the third year:

Machine	10,000	
Depreciation Adjustment, Due to Error		6,000
Accumulated Depreciation		4,000

Some accountants feel that the correction ($6,000) should be reflected on the income statement as an extraordinary item. Other accountants, including the authors, prefer to reflect it on the statement of retained earnings as a *prior period adjustment.*[10]

In respect to Illustrations 2 through 4 above, the authors prefer that a correcting entry be effected and the amount of the correction reflected as a prior period adjustment in the year of correction.

Depreciation and a Changing Price Level

Significant changes in the general price level (changes in the purchasing power of the dollar) give rise to disturbing effects on depreciation accounting. To illustrate, assume a company purchased a building 20 years ago costing $900,000; the asset is being depreciated on a straight line basis over a 30-year life. At the end of the first year the periodic depreciation charge of $30,000 was *matched* against revenues represented by dollars having essentially the same purchasing power as those represented in the depreciation charge. Now assume that at the end of the 20th year the general price level has doubled so that the value of the dollar is one half what it was when the building was purchased. The current depreciation charge of $30,000 (high-value dollars) is matched against revenues represented by current dollars (low-value dollars), each of which has one half the real value of those represented in the depreciation charge. Current revenue is not being matched with *real cost* as far as the depreciation charge is concerned. Many feel that under these circumstances the depreciation charge should be adjusted for the change in the value of the dollar, in this case to $60,000, to prevent an overstatement of reported net income and consequently of retained earnings.

---

[10] This accords with *APB Opinion 20* (July, 1971).

Many writers have used the term *economic depreciation* to describe the concept of adjusting depreciation charges for changes in the purchasing power of the monetary unit. The position of those advocating economic depreciation may be summarized in the following manner. No one questions the fact that depreciation, which may be correctly defined as *capital consumption,* is a proper cost. In common with revenues and other costs, capital consumption is measured in terms of the accepted monetary unit. To account correctly for capital consumption, there must be periodic amortization of the *original purchasing power* expended (rather than the original dollars expended) to allocate the economic-service values (fixed assets) being consumed. To meet this requirement the periodic amortization is best represented by the number of current monetary units (dollars) required to measure correctly the *original* purchasing power being consumed through exhaustion of fixed assets. The concept of economic depreciation recognizes the fact that the dollar is a changing measure of value. The concept leads to the conclusion that it is incorrect and misleading to match dollars of significantly different real value. The proponents of economic depreciation thus take the position that (assuming inflation) economic depreciation is necessary (*a*) to prevent material overstatement of net income and of retained earnings, (*b*) to prevent "capital deterioration" through excessive dividends, (*c*) to prevent excessive income taxes (a matter of legislation rather than accounting), (*d*) to protect the cash position (overstated profits which may result in excessive dividends and income taxes), (*e*) to provide more realistic cost data for management decisions, and (*f*) to reduce unreasonable union demands for higher wages in view of the overstated earnings.

To date economic depreciation has not been accorded general acceptance by the accounting profession for financial accounting purposes for some very fundamental reasons. Historical cost is useful and necessary; however, economic depreciation data are frequently important for internal management decisions. The best approach under current circumstances is for the accountant to develop such data independently of the financial accounting records. Economic depreciation is an area that needs more research and experimentation particularly in situations where the value of the monetary unit is changing appreciably. Additional discussion of the effect of changes in the general price level on accounting is provided in Chapter 23.

The Investment Credit

From time to time Congress has included in the income tax laws provisions designed to encourage investment in assets, particularly productive facilities. One such provision that created considerable interest and accounting controversy was the *investment credit.* The Revenue Act of 1962 permitted taxpayers to reduce their federal income taxes in the year acquired by an amount equal to 7% of certain depreciable assets subject to specified conditions. The provision was revised in some respects in the Revenue Act of 1964; it was suspended in October 1966 only to be restored by Congress in May 1967. The Tax Reform Act of 1969 again repealed the investment credit; however, special provisions still permit the credit under specific conditions. Unless changed no credit will be allowed under any circumstances on property placed in service after 1975. The investment credit created widespread attention in view of the facts that (a) frequently it resulted in a substantial reduction in income taxes paid and (b) it presented some unusual accounting problems. To illustrate the essential nature of the investment credit, assume data pertaining to X Company for 1968 as follows:

a) Machinery purchased during 1968 that qualified for the investment credit (10-year life, no residual value)............$200,000 (at cost)

b) Annual depreciation on the machinery for 1968 (straight line)... 20,000

c) Net income for 1968 subject to income taxes (after providing for depreciation of $20,000 on the machinery)...... 60,000

d) Income taxes for 1968 prior to the investment credit...... 24,000°

° Assuming a flat 40% rate for illustrative purposes.

The effect of the investment credit would be as follows:

Income taxes for 1968 prior to the investment credit $24,000

Less: Investment credit for 1968 ($200,000 × 7%)......................... 14,000

Amount of Income Taxes for 1968 ....$10,000

In the above example the significant reduction in income taxes, as a result of the investment credit, obviously would be viewed with considerable interest by the taxpayer and surely would influence some of his investment decisions. With respect to proper accounting, the question is posed as to how the $14,000 tax credit should be recorded and reported. Fundamentally, two distinctly different accounting approaches have been vigorously debated by the accounting profession. In these discussions the nature of the investment credit has been viewed as:

a) A reduction in income taxes: The proponents of this view feel that since the investment credit was made available by the Revenue Act, it is in substance a selective reduction in taxes related to the taxable income of the year in which the credit arises. They feel that it is a "tax item"; that to view it as a reduction of the cost of the asset would permit identical items purchased from the same supplier, at the same cost, to be recorded at different costs depending on the respective tax problems of several purchasers and not upon the conditions existing between the buyer and seller of the equipment. They note that various tax consequences as well as the investment credit affect a whole host of managerial decisions. They feel that the investment credit, as an adjustment of income taxes, should affect the net income (after taxes) only in the year in which the tax credit arises. This frequently is referred to as the "flow-through" method.

b) A reduction in the cost of the asset: The proponents of this view (frequently referred to as the asset-reduction method) feel that the investment credit is a direct reduction in the cost of the asset and that its effect should be spread over the life of the asset rather than just the first year. They also note that the original tax provision, although subsequently revised, required that the credit be treated for tax purposes as a reduction of cost. Consistent with these arguments is the position, taken by the proponents of the asset reduction approach, that the investment credit should affect net income over the future life of the asset through the depreciation charge.

The effects of these two diverse positions may be emphasized further by comparing the accounting entries that would result from the illustrative data given above. Entries in 1968 would be as follows:

Investment Credit Treated as a Reduction in Income Taxes	*Investment Credit Treated as a Reduction in Cost of the Assets*

a) To record purchase of the machinery in 1968 for $200,000:

Machinery 200,000		Machinery 200,000	
Cash	200,000	Cash	200,000

b) To record income taxes for 1968:

Income tax expense 10,000		Income tax expense 24,000	
Income taxes		Machinery (investment	
payable	10,000	credit).........................	14,000
		Income taxes payable	10,000

c) Depreciation on machinery for 1968 (10-year life):

Depreciation expense 20,000		Depreciation expense 18,600	
Accumulated de-		Accumulated deprecia-	
preciation	20,000	tion	18,600
Computation:		Computation:	
$200,000 \times 10\% =$		($200,000 − $14,000) ×	
$20,000		10% = $18,600	

The above tabulation of entries clearly reveals that when the investment credit is treated as a reduction in income taxes, its effects, both on the income statement and the balance sheet, are limited to one year, that is, the year in which the tax credit arose. In direct contrast, when the investment credit is treated as a reduction in cost it affects both the income statement (through higher income tax expense the first year and through lower depreciation charges over the life of the asset) and the balance sheet (through a reduction of the recorded asset cost and the accumulated depreciation each period). Clearly, when treated as a reduction in cost the effect of the tax credit is spread over the future life of the asset.

With respect to the investment credit, the Accounting Principles Board of the AICPA issued two opinions, viz:[11]

No. 2 (December 1962) — The board stated a clear preference for the "reduction in cost" approach by saying: "We conclude that the allowable investment credit should be reflected in net income over the productive life of acquired property and not in the year in which it is placed in service."

No. 4 (March 1964) — The board reaffirmed its prior preference for the "reduction in cost" approach, however, it stated: "the alternative method of treating the credit as a reduction of Federal income taxes of the year in which the credit arises is also acceptable."

These two opinions of the board created considerable controversy in view of the facts that (a) they permitted two opposite approaches to be used for the same set of facts, (b) both methods had become widely used prior to the issuance of No. 2, and (c) as one member of the board stated "the effect of *Opinion No. 4* can only be the direct opposite of the Board's ultimate objective of narrowing the areas of difference in practice."

DEPLETION

Nature of Depletion

Depletion in the accounting sense represents allocation against revenue of the cost of a natural resource (wasting asset) that is being exploited. Examples of such resources are ore, oil, coal, timber, and gravel. In accounting for such assets, the original cost is recorded in harmony with the *cost principle* and subsequently amortized over the total production economically available. Allocation between periods, consistent with the *matching principle*, usually is accomplished by dividing the cost of the asset (less any residual value) by the estimated number of units that can be withdrawn economically; the *unit depletion rate* thus computed then is multiplied by the actual units withdrawn during the period to determine the depletion charge for the period. As with other tangible fixed assets, three factors are involved: (1) cost, including all development costs that can be related to the resource; (2) estimated residual value of the property upon exhaustion of the natural resource; and (3) the estimated production over the life of the resource. To illustrate, assume that it is estimated by competent reserve geologists that a particular oil lease has a potential production of 2 million barrels of crude oil, and that the total cost

---

[11] Accounting Principles Board, "Accounting for the 'Investment Credit,'" *Opinion No. 2* (New York: AICPA, December 1962), pp. 5–11; and "Accounting for the 'Investment Credit,'" *Opinion No. 4* (Amending No. 2), March 1964, pp. 21–25.

of the lease, including development costs, is $160,000 with no residual value; the depletion rate per barrel of crude produced and its application would be as follows:

Depletion rate: $160,000 ÷ 2,000,000 = $.08 per barrel
Production for period: 10,000 barrels
Depletion charge for period: 10,000 × $.08 = $800

This method generally is used for financial and cost accounting purposes. For federal income tax purposes, other depletion methods may be employed in accordance with the Revenue Code. For example, the Code permits the taxpayer to elect *statutory depletion* rather than cost depletion illustrated above. Under statutory depletion a stated percentage of gross income may be taken as the depletion deduction on the tax return. The percentage varies from 5% on some minerals to 22% for oil and gas.[12] Under the Code the sum of the statutory depletion charges allowed may exceed the original cost of the resource.

Original acquisition costs, development costs, and tangible property costs associated with a natural resource should be set up in separate accounts. If any of such facilities is likely to have a shorter life than the natural resource, its cost should be amortized over the shorter period. When buildings and similar improvements are constructed in connection with the exploitation of the specific resource, their lives may be limited by the duration of the resource. In such cases costs should be amortized on the same basis as the other costs related to the resource.

In view of the difficulties in estimating underground deposits of minerals, the evaluation of additional information derived through further developmental work and the additional costs incident thereto, the depletion rate must be changed from time to time. The new rate is determined by dividing the unamortized cost plus any additional development costs by the *remaining* estimated reserves. Past depletion charges are not revised.

Dividends frequently are paid by companies exploiting natural resources equivalent to accumulated net income plus the accumulated depletion charge. State laws generally permit such dividends. This practice is common where there are no plans to replace the natural resource in kind and operations are to cease upon exhaustion of the deposit. In such cases, the stockholders should be informed of the portion of each dividend that represents a return of capital (i.e., the depletion charge). To illustrate, assume the Tex Oil Company accounts showed the following (summarized):

---

[12] Changed from 27½% for taxable years beginning after October 9, 1969; certain other depletion rates also were changed.

Assets	$1,000,000
Accumulated depreciation	(200,000)
Allowance for depletion	(100,000)
	$ 700,000
Liabilities..	$ 150,000
Capital stock...	500,000
Retained earnings...	50,000
	$ 700,000

The board of directors could declare a dividend of $150,000 which would be recorded as follows:

Retained Earnings...	50,000	
Return of Capital to Stockholders.....................................	100,000	
Cash		150,000

The Return of Capital to Stockholders would be reported as a deduction in the owners' equity section of the balance sheet.

REVALUATION OF FIXED ASSETS

Throughout the preceding discussions it has been stated that tangible fixed assets should be recorded initially at cost and, subsequently, reported at cost less the accumulated apportionments of such cost (depreciation) to date. The accounting profession consistently has taken the position that, as a general rule, fixed assets should be shown on the books in conformity with the *cost principle.*

Increases or decreases in the market values (current dollar value) of tangible fixed assets may be due to (*a*) a change in the *real worth* of the assets and/or (*b*) a change in the value of the monetary unit itself (inflation or deflation). Present accounting thought holds that, except in certain extreme situations, increases or decreases in the *market values* of tangible fixed assets should not be recognized in the accounts, particularly in view of the cost, continuity, and objectivity principles. This position may be explained as follows:

Tangible fixed assets are acquired for *use,* not for sale; hence current market values have little significance to the going concern (continuity principle) except when such assets actually are being sold or mortgaged as security for debts. Objectivity would similarly call for reflecting historical cost (less amortization) instead of subjective market or appraisal values. Increases or decreases in market values in no way increase or decrease physical productivity of the asset; higher sales values of fixed assets are of little significance to the going concern whose production needs preclude the realization of the higher (or lower) fixed asset values through direct sales in the present or in any foreseeable future market. Sale is not the objective end of the fixed asset; utilization in the business process is the planned objective, usually to the point of total (or near total) consumption.

Accountants consistently have opposed departures from the cost principle in accounting for fixed assets on the basis that "Pandora's box" literally would be opened to many ways for arbitrarily adjusting reported net income. The accounting profession has maintained the position that adherence to the cost principle provides an objective, verifiable, consistent, and understandable approach to tangible fixed asset accounting.

Write-Up of Tangible Fixed Assets Based on Appraisals

In view of frequent increases in the *real worth* of certain fixed assets and of the *devaluation* of the dollar since World War II, there has been considerable discussion and pressure with respect to the write-up of fixed asset values. During this recent period, the primary considerations have related to the income statement, income tax, and asset replacement costs.[13] Currently, strong arguments are being made by many accountants for some form of "fair-value" accounting. Fundamentally, it can take one of two approaches: (*a*) price-level adjusted data or (*b*) revaluation based on appraisals. This section discusses only the latter approach.

The comparative magnitude of inflation since the 1930s has caused many businessmen, economists, and some accountants to seriously question some of the basic concepts of accounting. These individuals have concluded that in recent years the total reported *net income* of American business is grossly overstated, primarily as a result of the effects of inflation and a consequent deficiency in periodic depreciation charges (see Chapter 23). High income tax rates within recent years have caused the businessman to consider more seriously the possibility of any overstatement of net income. As a result, numerous arguments have been developed in support of the idea that depreciation charges should be adjusted for inflation and in general should be sufficient to provide for *replacement in kind* of the assets being depreciated. Otherwise, the argument continues, real capital is being siphoned off through income taxes (being in part on capital rather than entirely on income) and dividends (out of overstated income). In addition it is argued that it enhances comparison of data between companies; provides better data for pricing products; and makes better provision for replacement of assets being depreciated.

In view of the seriousness of the problems of fixed asset valuation, depreciation accounting, income taxes, and asset replacement, the accounting profession has been quite concerned as to what the effect of these problems should be upon accounting theory and practice. The fact that assets have been written up on the basis of appraisals by

---

[13] The discussions to follow do not consider price-level adjustments; see Chapter 23 for a discussion of this particular aspect of accounting for fixed assets.

some companies is serious enough in itself to cause the profession some concern. Accordingly, over the years the accounting profession has taken cognizance of these problems in accounting literature, professional discussions, seminars, committee deliberations, research activities, and in certain pronouncements of the American Institute of Certified Public Accountants and the American Accounting Association.

Appraisals of fixed assets occasionally are made in order to approximate their current fair market value for negotiation purposes relating to such matters as possible sale, merger, credit, and insurance settlement. Of more direct concern to the accountant is the occasional use of appraisal data as a basis for restatement of the fixed assets in the accounts. On this point the accounting profession has continued a rather strong position against such restatement of the accounts particularly when a write-up is involved. The Accounting Principles Board of the AICPA in *Opinion No. 6* dated October 1965, stated:

The Board is of the opinion that property, plant and equipment should not be written up by an entity to reflect appraisal, market or current values which are above cost to the entity. This statement is not intended to change accounting practices followed in connection with quasi-reorganizations or reorganizations. This statement may not apply to foreign operations under unusual conditions such as serious inflation or currency devaluation. However, when the accounts of a company with foreign operations are translated into United States currency for consolidation, such write ups normally are eliminated. Whenever appreciation has been recorded on the books, income should be charged with depreciation computed on the written up amounts.

The primary arguments against revaluation are that (*a*) it is difficult to derive meaningful *values* at each financial statement date; (*b*) highly subjective values are introduced into the financial data; (*c*) the distinction between real-value changes and price-level changes is difficult to apply; (*d*) it opens the door to profit and asset-value manipulation; (*e*) cost and revenue determinations should not be confused with asset replacement problems; and (*f*) both management and investors understand, and are better served, by cost-based accounting.

Appraisals of assets should be done by professional appraisers who are trained adequately, experienced with respect to the type of property involved, and familiar with local and regional conditions that might influence fair market value. Appraisal reports should give a complete description of the fixed assets appraised, together with the date of acquisition, the recorded cost basis, the recorded depreciation to date of appraisal, the reproduction cost (new), an estimate of the future service life, the sound value, and the accumulated depreciation based on the appraisal estimates. Particular terms generally encountered with respect to appraisals are as follows:

1. Reproduction cost (new)—current cost required to replace the fixed asset new.
2. Sound value—the current reproduction cost (new) less the accumulated depreciation to date based upon such value, the appraised residual value, the appraised useful life, and the estimated remaining life. Sound value sometimes is referred to as appraised value in present condition.
3. Condition percent—a percentage expression of the estimated remaining life of the asset per the appraisal; it is the percent of remaining useful life in years to the total useful life per the appraisal. Alternatively, it is the percentage of sound value (less revised residual value) to reproduction cost new (less revised residual value).[14]
4. Appreciation—the net amount of the increase per the appraisal, that is, the sound value minus the book value of the asset after adjustment of the book value for the revised useful life and appraisal residual value.

To illustrate, assume an asset acquired eight years previously was recorded in the accounts at an original cost of $10,000. Based on a 10-year useful life and no residual value, the accumulated depreciation to date (8 years) is $8,000. Now, assume the asset is appraised at $12,000 new, no residual value, and a total useful life of 20 years. Per the appraisal the following values pertain:

1. Reproduction cost (new)..$12,000
2. Sound value, $12,000 − (8/20 × $12,000) 7,200
3. Condition percent, 12/20 or $7,200/$12,000 .... 60%
4. Appreciation, ($12,000 × 12/20) − ($10,000 × 12/20) 1,200

If the appraisal had additionally reported a residual value of $1,000, the following values per the appraisal would pertain:

1. Reproduction cost (new)..$12,000
2. Sound value, $12,000 − (8/20 × $11,000) 7,600
3. Condition percent, 12/20 or $\dfrac{\$\ 7,600 - \$1,000}{\$12,000 - \$1,000}$ 60%
4. Appreciation, $7,600 − [$10,000 − (8/20 × $9,000)] 1,200

Accounting for tangible fixed assets may be affected in one of two ways by appraisal, viz:

1. Revision of depreciation only: In conformance with generally accepted accounting principles most companies give recognition only to the revised useful life and the revised residual value indi-

---

[14]Condition percent is:

$$\frac{\text{Sound Value} - \text{Salvage Value}}{\text{Reproduction Cost} - \text{Salvage Value}} \quad \text{or} \quad \frac{\text{Estimated Remaining Life}}{\text{Estimated Life}}$$

cated by an appraisal. They do not restate the asset valuation from cost, that is, the asset account itself is not disturbed and depreciation is limited to cost less residual value. This procedure is identical to that described under the prior caption "Changes and Correction of Depreciation, Changes in Estimates" (page 537).

2. Restatement of both the asset and the accumulated depreciation accounts: A few companies, despite nonacceptance by the accounting profession, elect to give recognition of the appraisal results in all of the accounts related to the asset. Appropriate accounting procedures for this unusual situation are suggested in the discussions to follow.

Since fixed asset write-ups to appraised values lack general acceptability by the profession, they are made only in rare instances. Since the write-up procedure is followed in some cases, accountants have given attention to the proper approach to follow. Such procedures should be designed so as to disturb as little as possible the flow of *actual cost* data and the determination of *realized* net income. When fixed assets are increased in the accounts to a value greater than that derived through application of the cost principle, both the asset and capital balances are increased. Original cost as recorded in the asset account should not be disturbed; the asset increase based on the appraisal should be recorded in a special asset account appropriately captioned along the following lines: Building—Gross Appreciation; Building—Unrealized Increment per Appraisal; or Building—Appraisal Increase. In a like manner a special accumulated depreciation account should be established to carry the accumulated periodic depreciation relating to the *recorded* appraisal increase. The credit arising from the asset increase should be to a special *unrealized* capital account appropriately captioned such as: Unearned Capital—Appreciation on Building; or Unrealized Capital Increment per Appraisal; or Capital—Appraisal Increase on Building.

In circumstances where the decision has been made to write up a tangible fixed asset to an appraisal value above cost, one of three situations may exist. In the discussions to follow these three situations are illustrated, viz:

Situation 1—No change in either estimated total useful life or estimated residual value.

Situation 2—A change in the estimated total useful life, but not in the estimated residual value.

Situation 3—A change in both estimated total useful life and in the estimated residual value.

Situation 1. No change in estimated useful life or residual value (residual value is zero). Assume the following data relative to a building:

	Data per Books	Data per Appraisal	Appraisal Increase
Original cost..	$200,000		
Reproduction cost new		$300,000	
Difference..			$100,000
Estimated total useful life.....................(20 years)		(20 years)	
Depreciation on cost (end of 15th year) ...	150,000		
Depreciation on reproduction cost (15/20 × $300,000)..........................		225,000°	
Difference..			75,000
Book value..	$ 50,000		
Sound value..		$ 75,000	
Difference — net appreciation.................			$ 25,000

° Condition percent, 5/20 = 25% before and after appraisal.

In view of the fact that the estimated total useful life and residual value were unchanged by the appraisal, no change of depreciation estimates (on cost) is involved. The entry to record the results of the appraisal is as follows:

Building — Unrealized Appraisal Increment...........................100,000		
Accumulated Depreciation on Building — Unrealized Appraisal Increment...		75,000
Unrealized Capital Increment — Appraisal of Building......		25,000

Subsequent to restatement, the periodic depreciation charge should be based upon the *restated* values. The APB, in *Opinion No. 6* which is quoted above, made this point very clear. Accordingly, the annual depreciation charge for the illustrative data, assuming the straight line method, would be recorded as follows:

Depreciation of Building — on Cost 10,000		
Depreciation of Building — on Appreciation.......................... 5,000		
Accumulated Depreciation on Building — on Cost............		10,000
Accumulated Depreciation on Building — Unrealized Appraisal Increment...		5,000

Computation:
On cost: $200,000 ÷ 20 years = $10,000
On appraisal: $100,000 ÷ 20 years = $ 5,000

If the above periodic depreciation entry is made for the remaining life (five years) of the building, the account balances at that time will be as follows:

	Debit	Credit
Building — cost	$200,000	
Accumulated depreciation on building — on cost........		$200,000
Building — unrealized appraisal increment................	100,000	
Accumulated depreciation on building — unrealized appraisal increment		100,000
Unrealized capital increment — appraisal of building...		25,000

Now assume the building is retired with no recovery of cost; the asset and related accumulated depreciation accounts exactly offset leaving the *Unrealized* Capital Increment account (related to the building) with the original $25,000 credit. In view of the fact that the building has been disposed of, the unrealized credit appears to be anomalous. Accordingly, the following proposals have been advanced for disposing of the unrealized credit:

1. Utilize the credit as basis for a stock dividend.
2. Offset the credit against any debits in contributed capital accounts (not Retained Earnings).
3. Each period (during depreciable life) transfer a portion of the unrealized increment to Retained Earnings. The amount to be transferred should exactly *equal* the periodic credit to the account Accumulated Depreciation – Unrealized Appraisal Increment. Consequently, the Unrealized Capital Increment account would have a zero balance at the end of the depreciable life of the asset.

The Committee on Accounting Procedure of the AICPA apparently took no definite position as to what disposition should be made of the *unrealized capital increment* balance. Although theoretically deficient, some accountants appear to have taken the position that the procedure outlined in No. 3 above is preferable.

Situation 2. A change in estimated useful life, but no change in residual value.

To illustrate assume the following data relative to a specific item of equipment:

	Data per Books	Data per Appraisal
Original cost	$100,000	
Reproduction cost new		$150,000
Estimated total useful life	(20 years)	(25 years)
Depreciation on cost (end of 15th year)	75,000	

The above data indicate (*a*) that there should be a revision of depreciation on *cost* and (*b*) that appraised value is above original cost (a basis for possible write-up). Significantly, the management may decide to (1) give recognition only to the new estimated life by means of a revised depreciation schedule on *cost* or (2) recognize the appraisal results in the accounts. We have stated clearly only the first alternative is generally acceptable. In this situation the remaining undepreciated cost would simply be depreciated over the remaining life as indicated by the appraisal; thus the annual depreciation on cost for the next 10 years would be:[15]

Depreciation Expense 2,500
    Accumulated Depreciation—on Cost.............................. 2,500

Computations:
Original cost (less residual value)...................................$100,000
Accumulated depreciation to date (15 years).................... 75,000
    Remaining balance to be depreciated ....$ 25,000
Remaining life per appraisal (25 years − 15 years)............(10 years)
Annual depreciation over remaining life ....$ 2,500

Obviously, under this alternative no write-up entry would be made.

Alternatively, assume the management decides to give the appraisal full recognition in the accounts. In this case the asset appreciation, accumulated depreciation thereon and the unrealized capital would be recorded as follows:[16]

---

[15]This assumes the "change in estimate" (see Chapter 24) is accounted for in conformity with *APB Opinion 20*. Alternatively, some accountants feel that *past* depreciation should be "corrected." Thus, they would record the following *correcting* entry:

Accumulated Depreciation 15,000
    Depreciation Adjustment, Change in Estimate.................. 15,000

Computations:
Depreciation to date (old basis) $100,000 × 15/20.............$75,000
Depreciation to date (new basis) $100,000 × 15/25............ 60,000
    Correction past depreciation......................................$15,000

[16]If the past accumulated depreciation is restated, as noted in the preceding footnote, the entries and computations would be as follows:

	Per Books	Books Adjusted	Per Appraisal	Appraisal Increase
Asset..............................	$100,000	$100,000	$150,000	$50,000
Accumulated depreciation............	75,000	60,000	90,000	30,000
Book value prior to appraisal.............	$ 25,000			
Adjusted book value		$ 40,000		
Sound value.................			$ 60,000	
Appreciation				$20,000

To record restatement:

Equipment—Unrealized Appraisal Increment..........................50,000
    Accumulated Depreciation on Equipment—Unrealized
        Appraisal Increment 30,000
    Unrealized Capital Increment—Appraisal of Equipment 20,000

To record annual depreciation:

Depreciation on Equipment—on Cost................................... 4,000
Depreciation on Equipment—on Appreciation....................... 2,000
    Accumulated Depreciation on Equipment—on Cost.......... 4,000
    Accumulated Depreciation on Equipment—Unrealized
        Appraisal Increment 2,000

Equipment — Unrealized Appraisal Increment.........................50,000
 Accumulated Depreciation on Equipment — Unrealized
  Appraisal Increment ($50,000 × 15/25)......................... 30,000
 Unrealized Capital Increment — Appraisal of Equipment 20,000

Subsequent to the restatement the annual depreciation charges would be recorded as follows:

Depreciation on Equipment — on Cost.................................... 2,500
Depreciation on Equipment — on Appreciation........................ 2,000
 Accumulated Depreciation on Equipment — on Cost.......... 2,500
 Accumulated Depreciation on Equipment — Unrealized
  Appraisal Increment 2,000

Computations:
 ($100,000 − $75,000) ÷ 10 years = $2,500 (cost)
 $ 50,000 ÷ 25 years   = 2,000 (appraisal)

If the asset is sold prior to the end of its useful life, all of the account balances, including those accounts relating to the restatement, are removed and a loss or gain on disposal is recognized. To illustrate, assume that the equipment in the above illustration is sold for $40,000 two years after the restatement. At the date of sale the account balances would be as follows:

	Debit	Credit
Equipment (original cost).....................................	$100,000	
Equipment — unrealized appraisal increment..............	50,000	
Accumulated depreciation on equipment — on cost......		$80,000
Accumulated depreciation on equipment — unrealized appraisal increment...		34,000
Unrealized capital increment — appraisal of equipment...		20,000

The sale would be recorded as follows:

Cash...40,000
Accumulated Depreciation on Equipment — on Cost 80,000
Accumulated Depreciation on Equipment — Unrealized
 Appraisal Increment..34,000
 Extraordinary Gain — Sale of Fixed Asset 4,000
 Equipment (cost) 100,000
 Equipment — Unrealized Appraisal Increment................. 50,000

The $20,000 credit in the Unrealized Capital Increment account should be removed as indicated on page 551.

It may be observed that a *gain* of $20,000 would have been reported had the restatement not been recognized in the accounts, viz:[17]

---

[17] There are two other alternatives that have been advocated for recording the sale, viz:

 a) Under the assumption that the unrealized capital increment is "amortized" each year to Retained Earnings for an amount equal to the depreciation of the appraisal in-

```
Sales price.................................................... $40,000
Original cost ....................................$100,000
    Less: Accumulated depreciation on cost.........  80,000
Book value at date of sale (based on cost)........... $20,000
Gain on Sale ................................................ $20,000
```

In showing fixed assets on the balance sheet after a restatement based on appraisal data, the fact of the appraisal and the related effects must be clearly indicated. Presentation similar to the following is desirable:

ASSETS

```
Equipment—cost......................................................$100,000
    Less: Accumulated depreciation—cost......................  80,000  $20,000
Equipment—unrealized appraisal increment°  ...............$ 50,000
    Less: Accumulated depreciation—unrealized appraisal
       increment......................................................  34,000   16,000  $36,000
```

CAPITAL

```
Unrealized capital increment—appraisal of equipment .....      $20,000
```

° As appraised by the American Appraisal Company, December 19A.

Situation 3. A final illustration is given to show the effect of a change in both the estimated life and the residual value (Situation 3). Assume an asset that cost $215,000 (estimated life 20 years, residual value $5,000) was appraised at the end of 8 years. The appraisal reported a reproduction cost new of $315,000; residual value of $15,000,

---

crease ($2,000 per year) and inclusion of the remaining unrealized capital increment balance in the sale entry:

```
Cash...............................................................................40,000
Accumulated Depreciation on Equipment—on Cost ..............80,000
Accumulated Depreciation on Equipment—Unrealized
    Appraisal Increment .....................................................34,000
Unrealized Capital Increment—Appraisal of Equipment
    ($20,000 − $4,000).......................................................16,000
        Equipment (cost) .....................................................    100,000
        Equipment—Unrealized Appraisal Increment.................     50,000
        Extraordinary Gain—Sale of Fixed Asset .....................     20,000
```

b) Include the unrealized capital increment balance in the sale entry:

```
Cash...............................................................................40,000
Accumulated Depreciation on Equipment—on Cost...............80,000
Accumulated Depreciation on Equipment—Unrealized
    Appraisal Increment .....................................................34,000
Unrealized Capital Increment—Appraisal of Equipment..........20,000
        Equipment (cost) .....................................................    100,000
        Equipment—Unrealized Appraisal Increment.................     50,000
        Extraordinary Gain—Sale of Fixed Asset .....................     24,000
```

Note that the former entry provides the same gain as would have been reported had the appraisal not been recorded in the accounts.

condition percent of 68, and a total useful life of 25 years. These data are arrayed below:

Asset Appreciation:

Value per appraisal..	$315,000	
Cost, per books	215,000	
Increase		$100,000
Accumulated depreciation on appreciation ($100,000 × 8/25)..		32,000
Unrealized Appraisal Increment...		$ 68,000

Analysis of Estimated Life:	*Years*
Present age of asset...	8
Original estimated life..	20
Estimated life per appraisal [8 years ÷ (100% − 68%)].........25	

Annual Depreciation (after appraisal) on cost:

Cost..	$215,000	
Less residual value as revised...	15,000	
Net..	200,000	
Depreciation to date ($210,000 × 8/20).....................................	84,000	
Remaining Balance to be Depreciated...................................	$116,000	
Annual depreciation on cost ($116,000/17 years).........................		$6,820

Annual Depreciation on Appreciation:

($100,000/25 years)...	$4,000

Entry to record appraisal increase:

Building — Unrealized Appraisal Increment...........................100,000		
Accumulated Depreciation Building — Unrealized Appraisal Increment...	32,000	
Unrealized Capital Increment — Appraisal of Building......	68,000	

QUESTIONS FOR CLASS DISCUSSION

1. Distinguish between amortization, depletion, and depreciation.
2. Explain the effects of depreciation on (a) the income statement and (b) the balance sheet.
3. Explain the relationship of depreciation to (a) cash flow and (b) assets.
4. What is the relationship of depreciation to replacement of the assets being depreciated?
5. What are the primary causes of depreciation? What effect do changes in the market value of the asset being depreciated have on the depreciation estimates?
6. List and discuss three factors which must be considered in allocating the cost of a tangible fixed asset.
7. Explain the computation of the straight line method of depreciation. Under what circumstances is the straight line method generally appropriate?
8. Explain the computation of the (a) service-hours method and (b) the

productive-output method. Under what circumstances would these methods generally be appropriate?

9. What is meant by reducing-charge methods of depreciation? Under what circumstances would these methods generally be appropriate?

10. Explain the inventory system of depreciation. When is such a system appropriate?

11. Compare the retirement and replacement depreciation systems.

12. Explain the nature of composite-life depreciation and group depreciation.

13. In accounting for depreciation what are some of the implications of significant changes in the value of the monetary unit?

14. There are three categories in respect to change and correction of depreciation. Briefly explain each and outline the accounting involved.

15. List some important considerations that should be taken into account in selecting a method of depreciation.

16. Define depletion. How is depletion generally computed for financial and cost accounting purposes?

17. What is implied by the statement "a dividend out of depletion reserves"?

18. Define the following relative to fixed assets: (a) reproduction cost new, (b) sound value, (c) condition percent, (d) appreciation, and (e) devaluation.

19. When tangible fixed assets are written up above original cost, what should be the basis for subsequent depreciation charges?

20. What is the nature of the unrealized *credit* that arises when appreciation of tangible fixed assets is recognized in the accounts? What are the alternative treatments that may be subsequently accorded this balance?

DECISION CASE 13–1

Mays, Incorporated, a small manufacturer has just completed its sixth year of life (19X6). Annual financial statements prepared by the company accountant have been distributed to the 150 shareholders who own the 100,000 shares outstanding. The stock is sold over the counter. There has never been an audit. You have been engaged to "perform a complete audit covering the two fiscal years 19X5 and 19X6 and to certify comparative statements for those two years."

To date, except for the three "special items" detailed below, your audit has confirmed the correctness of the following amounts as reflected in the accounts and on the annual financial statements prepared by the company accountant.

	End of Year			
	19X5		19X6	
Machinery and Equipment:				
Machine A—cost (acquired 19X4)............	$ 55,000		$ 55,000	
Accumulated depreciation (SYD)..........	19,000	$36,000	27,000	$28,000
Machine B......................................	$ 75,000		$ 75,000	
Accumulated depreciation (straight line)...	37,500	37,500	45,000	30,000
Machine C......................................	0		0	
Accumulated depreciation (straight line)...	0		0	

Retained Earnings:

Beginning balance	$100,000	$127,000
Net income	27,000	26,400
Ending Balance	$127,000	$153,400

Income Statement:

Depreciation — Machine A	$ 9,000		$ 8,000
" B	7,500		7,500
" C	–0–		–0–
Income before bonus and tax	50,000		60,000
Bonus to executives 10%	5,000		6,000
Subject to tax	$ 45,000		$ 54,000
Income tax (40%)	18,000		21,600
Income before extraordinary items	$ 27,000		$ 32,400
Extraordinary items	0	$(10,000)	
Applicable tax savings	0	4,000	(6,000)
Net Income	$ 27,000		$ 26,400

Earnings per share (100,000 shares outstanding)			
Income before extraordinary item	$ .27		$ .324
Net Income	$ .27		$ .264

Special Items:

1. Machine A cost $55,000 when purchased at the beginning of year 19X4. It is being depreciated on SYD basis over 10 years; no residual value. New information and experience clearly indicates that "more useful financial information" would be provided by straight line amortization; accordingly, this change has been accepted.
2. Machine B cost $75,000 when purchased at the beginning of year 19X1. It is being depreciated on a straight line basis over 10 years; no residual value. New information and experience clearly indicates that "more useful financial information" would be provided by depreciating it over 15 years; accordingly, this change is accepted.
3. Machine C cost $20,000 when purchased at the start of year 19X3. Through error (you have not been able to determine whether intentional or not) the entire purchase price was charged to operating expenses in 19X3 although it had an estimated useful life of five years and no residual value. Accordingly, a change for this item is accepted.

The following assumptions are to be accepted:

a) Income taxes actually paid or payable will not be affected by changes in the three special items.
b) The actual bonus payment will not be affected by changes in the three special items.
c) Financial statements and accounting otherwise will be in conformity with APB Opinions.

Required:

1. Using generally accepted reporting format, including appropriate footnotes, show how you would report machinery and equipment, retained earnings, and the several income statement items on your certified comparative statements. You should conform to *APB Opinions 9* and *20*.

2. Give journal entries for each special item necessary to change the accounts to reflect your recommendations in requirement (1).

3. In what respects do you disagree with the APB requirements as they affected your response to requirements (1) and (2)? Explain the basis for your disagreement.

EXERCISES

Exercise 13–1

Prepare journal entries for each of the following transactions relating to tangible fixed assets:

a) A machine was purchased at a cost of $5,500; installation costs of $200 relating to the machine were paid.

b) At the end of the first year it was decided to utilize straight line depreciation on the machine. The estimated residual value was $700, and the service life, five years.

c) Two years after purchase of the machine an improvement was added to it at a cost of $600; the residual value and service life were unchanged.

d) Three years and eight months after the original purchase the machine was sold for $1,800 cash.

Exercise 13–2

The Dean Company is considering a depreciation policy with respect to the acquisition and disposal of fixed assets during the year. In order to demonstrate how to account under each of the four policies being considered you are to complete the following table. The asset used for illustrative purposes cost $1,200 and has a 10-year life; i.e., $120 per year, or $10 per month, depreciation.

| Alternative Policies under Consideration | Amount of Depreciation to Be Charged for Year— | | | |
| | If Acquired on— | | If Disposed on— | |
	June 1	September 30	May 1	August 31
a) Compute depreciation on balance in asset account at beginning of period.	$_____	$_____	$_____	$_____
b) Compute depreciation on balance in asset account at end of period.	_____	_____	_____	_____
c) Compute depreciation for a full year only on assets acquired during first half and no depreciation if disposed of during first half of the year.	_____	_____	_____	_____
d) Compute one-half year depreciation during year acquired and disposed of and full year otherwise.	_____	_____	_____	_____
e) Depreciate monthly; full month depreciation if on hand more than one-half of the month; if less than one-half month on hand, no depreciation.	_____	_____	_____	_____

Exercise 13-3

In order to demonstrate the mechanical computations involved in several methods of depreciation the following simplified situation is presented:

Acquisition cost......................................$ 3,800
Scrap or residual value..........................$ 200
Estimated service life:
    Years..   4
    Service hours 10,000
    Productive output.............................. 24,000

Required:

Compute the annual depreciation for each year under each of the following situations:

1. Straight line depreciation; compute the depreciation charge and rate for each year.

2. Service-hours method; compute the depreciation rate and charge for the first year assuming 3,000 service hours of actual operation.

3. Productive-output method of depreciation; compute the depreciation rate and charge for the first year assuming 7,000 units of output.

4. Sum-of-years'-digit method; compute the depreciation charge for each year.

Exercise 13-4

Utilizing the data given below compute the depreciation rate and the depreciation charge for each of the three years assuming the fixed-percentage-on-declining-base method is used. The third root of .001 is .10.

Acquisition cost $1,000
Residual value.....................................$1
Estimated service life.........................3 years

Exercise 13-5

An asset that cost $6,400 was being depreciated over a three-year life with an estimated residual value of $400. Prepare a three-year depreciation table (with entries indicated thereon) assuming:

Case A – Straight line depreciation.
Case B – Service-hours depreciation (estimated life 7,500 service hours; actual hours for year 1, 2,000; year 2, 3,000; and year 3, 2,500)

Exercise 13-6

An asset that cost $1,000 was acquired by the Max Company. The estimated life was five years, and the residual value, $10. Prepare a depreciation table (with entries indicated thereon) utilizing the fixed-percentage-on-declining-base method. The fifth root of .01 is .398. Round to nearest dollar.

Exercise 13-7

Equipment costing $100,000 has an estimated five-year life and $20,000 scrap value. Prepare depreciation tables under the annuity method and the sinking fund method covering the entire life of the asset using 5% rates.

Exercise 13–8

Machinery with an estimated life of 10 years and scrap value of 15% of cost is acquired for $10,000. Using a 6% interest rate, what depreciation entries would be made at the end of each of the first two full years (a) under the annuity method and (b) under the sinking fund method (no actual fund maintained)?

Exercise 13–9

Taylor Utility Company purchased 500 poles at $40 per pole; the debit being to the Inventory—Poles P-113 account. Subsequent to the purchase, 100 of the new poles were used to replace an equal number of old poles (Poles M-101) which were carried in the tangible fixed asset account, Poles—Austin Line. The old poles originally cost $30 each and had an estimated salvage value of $10 per pole.

Required:

1. Give all indicated entries (a) assuming the retirement system is employed and (b) assuming the replacement system is used.
2. Compare the effect on the periodic depreciation charge and the asset accounts as between the two systems.

Exercise 13–10

Miton Company owned a power plant which consisted of the following, all acquired on January 1, 1968:

	Cost	Estimated Scrap Value	Estimated Life (Years)
Building......................$450,000		None	15
Machinery, etc. 180,000		$18,000	10
Other equipment............ 100,000		10,000	5

Required:

1. Compute the total straight line depreciation for 1971 on all items combined.
2. Compute the composite depreciation rate on the plant.
3. Determine the composite life of the plant.

Exercise 13–11

Utilizing the following data for a particular operating unit, compute (a) the composite life and (b) the composite depreciation rate.

Compare the periodic depreciation for the first six periods as between the composite system and the straight line method applied to each item separately.

Component Item	Acquisition Cost	Residual Value	Service Life (Years)
A.....................$ 7,500		$ 300	4
B..................... 12,400		2,400	10
C..................... 18,600		600	15

Exercise 13–12

The Marks Company depreciates certain blending machines on a group basis. Transactions relative to the blending machines in Plant A were:

a) Jan. 1, 19A – Purchased six blending machines for $6,600.
b) Dec. 31, 19A – Recorded depreciation on group basis; estimated useful life was five years, residual value for the six machines, $660.
c) Dec. 31, 19B – Recorded depreciation.
d) Jan. 1, 19C – One machine was defective and was sold for $500 cash.
e) Feb. 1, 19C – Two additional blending machines were purchased at the same cost as the original machines ($1,100 each).
f) Dec. 31, 19C – Recorded depreciation (full year on all machines on hand).
g) Jan. 1, 19D – Transferred one of the blending machines to Plant B.

Required:

Give entry for each transaction; show computations.

Exercise 13–13

Downs Company owned 10 warehouses of a similar type except for varying size. The group system is applied to the 10 warehouses, the rate being 8% per year on cost. At the end of the 10th year the asset account Warehouses showed a balance of $530,000 (residual value $30,000), and the Accumulated Depreciation account showed a balance of $240,000. Shortly after the end of the 10th year, Warehouse No. 65, costing $60,000, was retired and demolished. Materials of $5,000 were sold, and $1,500 was spent in demolition.

Required:

Give entries to record (*a*) depreciation for the 10th year, (*b*) retirement of the warehouse, and (*c*) depreciation for the 11th year.

Exercise 13–14

Saxe Company has a plant which originally cost $900,000 10 years ago. The plant has been depreciated as one unit on the basis of a service life of 15 years. Company engineers now estimate that the plant should have been depreciated over a useful life of 20 years.

Prepare entries to record depreciation for the 11th year and to effect any other related adjustments that are acceptable under each of the following assumptions:

a) That adjustment of the profits of past periods is to be effected through revised charges during the remaining service life of the plant.
b) That the Accumulated Depreciation account is to be adjusted for the error in depreciation to date.
c) Under what circumstances should assumption (*a*) and (*b*) be applied?
d) How would the "adjustment account" be reflected on the financial statement?

Exercise 13–15

Box Aggregates, Inc., was engaged in the rock and gravel business. The following transactions relate to the acquisition and development of an extensive gravel pit near a large metropolitan area:

a) 19A—Cost of acquisition and development, $60,000; estimated recoverable tons, 200,000.

b) Dec. 31, 19A—Depletion recorded on the basis of 50,000 tons mined and sold.

c) 19B—Additional development costs, $7,500.

d) Dec. 31, 19B—Depletion recorded on basis of 30,000 tons mined and sold.

e) 19C—Development costs, $28,000; new estimate on remaining recoverable tons, 250,000.

f) Dec. 31, 19C—Depletion recorded on basis of 70,000 tons mined and sold.

Required:

Give the indicated journal entries.

Exercise 13–16

Asset A

```
Cost.......................................................$ 60,000
Residual value ........................................  None
Depreciation to date...............................$ 20,000 (12-year life)
Appraisal results:
    Reproduction cost new..........................$100,000
    Residual value ....................................  None
    Condition percent ..............................  75%
```

Calculate the following using the data above:

> Book value prior to appraisal.
> Reproduction cost new.
> Sound value in dollars.
> Appreciation in dollars.
> Condition percent.
> Remaining years of life per appraisal.

Exercise 13–17

A fixed asset originally costing $100,000, with accumulated depreciation to date of $80,000 at the end of eight years, is appraised at a reproduction cost new of $160,000 and a condition percent of 40. Give entries to recognize the appraisal results and to record depreciation for the next year for each of two separate assumptions: (*a*) Depreciation only is to be affected; (*b*) The fixed asset is to be restated in the accounts. Show computations.

Exercise 13–18

A building, originally costing $200,000 ($20,000 residual value), being depreciated on a straight line basis over 20 years, was appraised at the end of the 10th year. The appraisal showed: reproduction cost new, $280,000; a $30,000 residual value; and a condition percent of 60. Give entries (*a*) to recognize the appraisal results in all respects; and (*b*) depreciation for the first year subsequent to the appraisal.

Exercise 13–19

The XY Corporation recognized in the accounts the results of an appraisal four years previously by making the following entry:

Asset — Unrealized Appraisal Increment (remaining life 10 years) 56,000
    Accumulated Depreciation — Unrealized Appraisal Increment 16,000
    Unrealized Capital Increment 40,000

The account balances to date are as follows:

Asset — cost (acquired eight years ago) $154,000
Asset — unrealized appraisal increment 56,000
Accumulated depreciation — cost 88,000
Accumulated depreciation — unrealized appraisal increment 32,000
Unrealized capital increment (original balance)............ 40,000

Required:

1. Indicate by explanation and related entries alternative treatments that have been suggested for the unrealized capital increment. What alternative is generally preferred?

2. Utilizing the data above illustrate the preferred presentation on the balance sheet and income statement.

PROBLEMS

Problem 13–1

Pressley Company purchased a special machine at a cost of $33,500. It was estimated that the machine would have a net resale value at the end of its useful life for the company of $3,500. Statistics relating to the machine over its service life were as follows:

Estimated service life:
    Years 5
    Service hours 6,000

Actual operations: Year	Service Hours
1	1,400
2	1,300
3	1,000
4	1,100
5	1,200

Required:

Prepare a depreciation table for each assumption below indicating entries for the asset over the useful life under the following methods: (a) straight line, (b) service hours, (c) sum of years' digits, and (d) fixed percentage of 40% on declining base.

Problem 13–2

Welton Company purchased a piece of special factory equipment on January 1, 1968, costing $71,000. In view of pending technological developments it is estimated that the machine will have a resale value upon disposal in four years of $15,500 and that disposal cost will be $4,500.

Data relating to the equipment follows:

Estimated service life:
Years 4
Service hours.........................20,000

Actual operations:

Calendar Year	Service Hours
1968	5,500
1969	5,000
1970	4,800
1971	4,600

Required:

1. Prepare a depreciation table for the service-hours method assuming the books are closed each December 31.

2. Compute depreciation expense for the first and second years assuming: (a) straight line, (b) sum of years' digits, (c) fixed percent on declining base (30% rate), and (d) double declining-balance.

Problem 13–3

Prepare depreciation schedules for equipment costing $1,000 having an estimated life of five years and scrap value of $10 under each of the following depreciation methods:

a) Straight line.
b) Fixed percent on declining base (60.2%).
c) Sum of digits.
d) Annuity (use 5% rate).
e) Sinking fund (use 5% rates and prepare tabulation for a replacement fund as well).

Problem 13–4

White Manufacturing Company utilizes a number of small machine tools in their operations. Although there are numerous variations in the tools, they cost approximately the same and have similar useful lives. The company carries a Machine Tools account in the records; the account showed a balance of $1,200 (200 tools) at the end of 1969. Acquisitions, retirements, and óther data for a period of two years are given below:

	1970	1971
Acquisitions	100 @ $6.20	120 @ $6.30
Retirements:		
Number	150	80
Salvage proceeds	$ 40	$ 20
Inventory	150 @ $5.80	190 @ $5.90

Required:

1. Give entries for each of the two years assuming:

a) The inventory system is used.

b) The retirement system is used.

c) The replacement system is used.

2. Prepare a tabulation covering the two years to present for the annual depreciation charge and the balance in the Machine Tools account under each system.

Problem 13–5

The Slender Company utilizes a large number of identical small tools in operations. On January 1, 1969, the first year of operations, 1,000 of these tools were purchased at a cost of $3 each. On December 31, 1969, 200 of the tools were scrapped, the estimated salvage value being $20 ($.10 each). During the year they had been replaced (200) at a cost of $3.25 each. On December 31, 1970, 300 of the tools were scrapped, having an estimated salvage value of $.10 each and replaced at a cost of $3.40 each. On December 31, 1971, 150 of the tools were scrapped (salvage value $.10 each) each being replaced at a cost of $3.50.

Required:

1. Compute the annual depreciation charge for 1969, 1970, and 1971 and the balance at the end of each year in the Tools account, assuming the company employed the (*a*) retirement system and (*b*) the replacement system.

2. Compare the results.

Problem 13–6

Mays Company utilizes composite depreciation for several operating units, one of which is identified as Unit UT44. The components of Unit UT44 are listed below:

Component	Cost	Estimated Salvage Value	Estimated Life (Years)
A	$14,900	$ 900	10
B	7,000	0	7
C	6,000	1,000	5
D	3,100	100	5
E	19,000	4,000	15

Required:

1. Compute the composite life and composite depreciation rate for Unit UT44.

2. Give the entry to record the depreciation at the end of the first year.

3. During the second year Component B began to give trouble, primarily due to the fact that it was inadequate for the function. As a result Component B was retired and sold for $4,000. A new unit to replace Component B was acquired at a cost of $8,000; the estimated salvage value being $1,300 at the end of its useful life of six years. Give entries to record the retirement and acquisition.

4. Give the entry to record the depreciation at the end of the second year.

Problem 13-7

Brady Petroleum Company utilized the group system of depreciation for automotive equipment. Several groups have been established for the different types of automotive equipment. A new group has been established for "Company Cars" as a result of the recent decision of the management to purchase rather than rent such cars for use at the home office location. The initial purchase and subsequent transactions over a period of three years are given below:

a) January 1, 1969, purchased 10 cars @ $3,000 each.

b) December 31, 1969, recorded annual group depreciation on basis of a four-year average life and a residual value of $600 per car.

c) March 1, 1970, one car was wrecked and was taken over by the insurance company. Insurance received amounted to $2,600.

d) April 1, 1970, purchased two new cars @ $3,100 each; estimated residual value, $650.

e) December 31, 1970, recorded annual group depreciation.

f) The management decided that as of January 1, 1971, three of the cars (purchased in 1969) would be transferred to the three division headquarters. It was decided that two new accounts should be established: "Company Cars – Field" and "Accumulated Depreciation – Company Cars – Field." The three cars to be transferred at their "approximate book value."

g) December 31, 1971, recorded annual depreciation.

Required:

1. Prepare journal entries for each transaction listed above under the group system assuming depreciation is recognized on year-end balances.

2. Reconstruct in account form the tangible fixed asset and related accumulated depreciation accounts.

Problem 13-8

Dwyer Corporation accounts showed the following for three items of equipment as of December 31, end of the fiscal year (straight line depreciation):

	Machine No.		
	1	2	3
Equipment (acquisition cost), 10-year life	$11,950	$25,500	$38,000
Estimated salvage value	950	1,500	2,000

At the beginning of the sixth year the management decided to make the following changes:

a) Machine No. 1 – Change from straight line to sum-of-the-years'-digits depreciation to more nearly reflect expiration of economic-service value.

b) Machine No. 2 – Change estimated life to 15 years; on the basis of experience this appears more realistic.

c) Machine No. 3 – Two years prior (fourth year), through oversight, no depreciation was recorded.

Required:

For each machine give the entries indicated by the change (if any) including the depreciation entry for the sixth year. If alternative approaches are available give entries for them also. Briefly indicate any special effects on the financial statements for the sixth year.

Problem 13–9

The Truck and Accumulated Depreciation accounts of the Miller Department Store are shown below:

Trucks

Debits			*Credits*		
1/1/67	Trucks No. 1 and No. 2 ...	$2,400	1/1/69	Truck No. 1 scrapped.......	$1,200
1/1/69	Truck No. 3	1,260	1/1/70	Truck No. 2 scrapped.......	1,200
1/1/70	Truck No. 4	1,280			
7/1/70	New tires, Truck No. 3.....	200			

Accumulated Depreciation

1/1/69	Truck No. 1 scrapped ($500 received as salvage)....................	$ 800	12/31/67	Depreciation.................	$800
			12/31/68	Depreciation.................	800
			12/31/69	Depreciation.................	820
1/1/70	Truck No. 2 scrapped ($100 received as salvage)....................	1,100	12/31/70	Depreciation.................	820
			12/31/71	Depreciation.................	635

Required:

1. A depreciation schedule showing correct account balances and depreciation by year, assuming the revised lives of Trucks No. 3 and No. 4 were changed from three to four years on January 1, 1971.

2. Journal entries to correct the books as of December 31, 1971, assuming the books were not yet closed for 1971.

Problem 13–10

The Machinery account as of December 31, 1971, on the books of the Michael Company was as follows:

Machinery

1/1/66	Purchase	$50,000	12/31/66	Depreciation..............	$ 5,000
7/1/67	Purchase	10,000	9/ 1/67	Machinery sold	2,000
11/1/68	Purchase	18,000	12/31/68	Depreciation..............	6,000
			12/31/69	Depreciation..............	6,000
			7/ 1/70	Machinery sold	1,000
			12/31/70	Depreciation..............	6,000
			12/31/71	Depreciation..............	7,500
				Balance	44,500
		$78,000			$78,000

Additional data:

Machinery sold September 1, 1967, cost $3,600 on January 1, 1966; machinery sold July 1, 1970, cost $2,500 on January 1, 1966. Machinery costing

$2,000, which was purchased on July 1, 1967, was destroyed on July 1, 1971, and was a total loss.

Required:

1. A depreciation schedule showing correct annual depreciation and account balances. Assume 10-year life on all items, straight line and no residual value.

2. Entries to correct the books on December 31, 1971, assuming the books are not closed for 1971.

Problem 13–11

The Grayson Corporation owned a building acquired 10 years previously at a cost of $200,000. When one-half depreciated, the building was appraised at $300,000 reproduction cost new.

Required:

1. Give entries to recognize:

a) The appraisal results assuming a condition percent of 60.
b) Depreciation for 11th year.
c) Sale at end of 11th year at $178,000.

2. Indicate alternative entries for (*c*).

Problem 13–12

Cleveland Corporation acquired a small outlying plant six years previously. The asset records show the following:

> Land $40,000
> Plant... 90,000
> Accumulated depreciation 36,000

The plant was appraised with the following results:

> Land ....$ 60,000
> Plant—reproduction cost new................... 120,000
>   — sound value 90,000

The management is considering two alternatives: (1) *correcting* the accumulated depreciation only and (2) recognizing in the accounts the *correction* of accumulated depreciation and the appraisal results. In connection with these considerations you are requested to prepare (*a*) entries (supported by appropriate computations) relative to each alternative; (*b*) entries relative to depreciation for the first year subsequent to the appraisal; and (*c*) entries assuming sale of the land and plant for $92,250 three years after the appraisal. You should note especially that *prior* accumulated depreciation is to be adjusted to the new estimates.

chapter **14** | # Intangible Assets; Deferred Charges; Insurance

PART A—INTANGIBLE ASSETS

Nature and Classification of Intangible Assets

The intangible assets of a business are those assets which benefit the enterprise through the special rights and privileges their ownership brings as opposed to the physical characteristics of tangible assets. The evidence of their value is usually some economic advantage derived from ownership. Potential earning power is the fundamental basis of intangible value. Without this potential, there is no basis for assigning a value to "rights and privileges." An enterprise may (a) acquire intangible assets through purchase or (b) develop them internally. Intangible assets may be specifically identifiable such as patents, copyrights, leases, licenses, and franchises, or they may be unidentifiable such as goodwill.

Accounting for intangible assets involves, as with other assets, problems of (a) identification, (b) valuation, and (c) amortization when their future service potentials decline. Intangible assets acquired through purchase should be initially recorded at their "cost" and subsequently amortized by systematic charges to income over the future periods benefited. Internally generated intangibles, unless *specifi-*

569

cally identifiable, should not be capitalized as assets but should be recorded as expenses as the costs are incurred. *APB Opinion 17*, (August 1970) stated:

The Board concludes that a company should record as assets the costs of intangible assets acquired from others, including goodwill acquired in a business combination. A company should record as expenses the costs to develop intangible assets which are not specifically identifiable. The Board also concludes that the cost of each type of intangible asset should be amortized by systematic charges to income over the period estimated to be benefited.

Clearly the significance of the term *specifically identifiable* becomes important in determining when an internally generated intangible should be capitalized. It is subject to interpretation and is likely to become a point of issue in the light of *APB Opinion 17*. It is another of those areas where the accountant must exercise responsible judgment in respect to the circumstances prevailing.

In contrast to *ARB No. 43*, Chapter 5, "Intangible Assets" (which was superseded), *APB Opinion 17* states that:[1]

the value of intangible assets at any one date eventually disappears and . . . the recorded costs of intangible assets should be amortized by systematic charges to income over the periods estimated to be benefited . . . and should not be written off in the year of acquisition . . . the period of amortization should not, however, exceed forty years.

ARB No. 43, Chapter 5, identified two types of intangibles: Type A — those having a limited life and therefore subject to amortization; and Type B — those having an unlimited life and therefore not subject to amortization. Clearly *APB Opinion 17* does not make this distinction, holding instead that all intangibles should be amortized on the basis that none of them have infinite future service potentials. The 40-year maximum is clearly a limit; a concession to practical considerations and the long-range "decision horizons" of the management.

Depending upon their characteristics intangible assets may be classified as current assets, investments, fixed assets, deferred charges or other assets. This chapter discusses intangible assets and some related problems such as insurance.

Accounting Valuation of Intangibles at Acquisition

At acquisition intangibles should be recorded at cost in conformance with the *cost principle*. Where an intangible is acquired for a consideration other than cash, cost is determined either by the fair

---

[1] Accounting Principles Board, AICPA, "Intangible Assets," *Opinion 17* (New York, August 1970), p. 339.

market value of the consideration given or by the fair market value of the right acquired, whichever is the more clearly evident. For example, if a patent is acquired by the issuance of capital stock, the cost of the patent may be determined as the fair market value of the shares of stock issued therefor. However, if the shares issued do not have an established market value, consistent with the volume issued, then evidence of the fair market value of the patent should be sought as the measurement of cost in the transaction. If there is evidence of a definite cash offer to sell the patent, this offering price might be acceptable as a measure of the cost of the intangible asset. Supporting evidence of "fair market value" should be rather conclusive if the "cost" measured thereby is to be accepted as valid.

Classification of the Cost of Intangibles

With intangibles, as in the case of tangible fixed assets, costs must be carefully classified in the accounts to facilitate subsequent accounting. Proper accounting for cost requires that where two or more intangible assets are acquired at a single lump-sum purchase price, an allocation of the joint cost should be made to determine the proper cost basis of each intangible involved. Allocation of the cost of intangibles acquired in a "basket purchase" may be made by using the methods described for tangible assets, such as the relative sales value method.

Amortization of Intangible Costs

The cost of intangibles should be *amortized* by systematic charges to expense over the estimated periods of useful life, just as the cost of tangible fixed assets having a limited period of usefulness is depreciated. Capricious and arbitrary determination of the amount to be charged as expense from period to period distorts income and violates the *matching principle*. Neither is it desirable from the standpoint of correct income determination to accelerate the amortization process and write off the cost of intangibles substantially before the end of their usefulness. In the past, overconservatism frequently resulted in inappropriate accounting in these respects. Intangibles normally are amortized by a direct credit to the asset account and a debit to expense.

In estimating the future useful life of an intangible asset the following factors should be considered:[2]

a) Legal, regulatory, or contractual provisions may limit the maximum useful life.

b) Provisions for renewal or extension may alter a specified limit on useful life.

---

[2] Ibid., p. 340.

c) Effects of obsolescence, demand, competition, and other economic factors may reduce a useful life.

d) A useful life may parallel the service life expectancies of individuals or groups of employees.

e) Expected actions of competitors and others may restrict present competitive advantages.

f) An apparently unlimited useful life may in fact be indefinite and benefits cannot be reasonably projected.

g) An intangible asset may be a composite of many individual factors with varying effective lives.

The method of amortization should be systematic and should reflect over time the decline in economic potential (service value) of the intangible. Thus, straight line, declining period charges, or increasing period charges may be appropriate. Perhaps reflecting precedent rather than economic realities *APB Opinion 17* states that "the straight-line method of amortization — equal annual amounts — should be applied unless a company demonstrates that another systematic method is more appropriate." The Opinion also states that changes in amortization rates should be *prospective*, that is, the remaining unamortized cost should be amortized over the remaining life. Significant adjustments when justified should be reflected, however, in the year of change as an extraordinary item as a correction (see Chapter 24).

Limitation on the Write-Off of Intangibles

Accounting practice in the past has frequently encouraged the arbitrary writing down of intangible costs to a nominal value either by lump-sum charge-off or by amortization over a period much shorter than the period of usefulness on the grounds that such practice was conservative. Contemporary accounting theory does not support such arbitrary write-offs, for improper elimination of costs from the accounts understates the periodic cost of doing business and distorts periodic income. We will now discuss some of the more common specific intangibles.

Patents

A patent is an exclusive grant by the U.S. Patent Office that enables the holder to use, manufacture, sell, and control the patent without interference or infringement by others. In reality the registration of the patent with the Patent Office is no guarantee of protection. Therefore, the patent is not conclusive until it has been successfully defended in court tests. For this reason it is generally held that the cost of *successful* court tests should be capitalized as a part of the cost of the patent.

The cost of a patent acquired by purchase is determined in accordance with the *cost principle,* i.e., cost is the cash or cash-equivalent value of the consideration given. Where the patent is produced in the company's own experimental laboratory, cost includes all developmental expenditures reasonably identifiable with the particular patent. Experimental expenses, cost of working models, drawings, attorney fees, filing fees, and other such expenses comprise the cost of the patent to the inventor.

Patent grants are for a period of 17 years. The useful life of most patents is for a shorter period due to new patents, improved models, substitutes, and general technological progress. Patent costs should be amortized over the period of useful life or legal life, whichever is shorter. In many situations use of a reducing-charge formula of amortization would seem appropriate.

Patent amortizations may be credited directly to the Patent account or to an Accumulated Patent Amortization account; the former is the more common practice. Patents are classified as an intangible fixed asset.

Experimental, Research, and Development Costs

The research department has become a particularly important one in modern industry. Some of the more important functions of this department are: development of new products, improvement of present products, testing of competitors' products, development of new or improved manufacturing methods, development of new and special machines, testing of raw materials, and pure research.

Accounting for the costs of the research department requires careful analysis of the activities of the department. Usually the cost of some of the activities is chargeable as current expense, while others represent expenditures which should be capitalized as an identifiable intangible asset. Costs incurred for such activities as testing of raw materials or finished goods and experiments representing pure research should be expensed currently. Accurate costing may be attained through use of a project cost system. Under this system all direct project costs are charged to specific projects and indirect costs are allocated among the projects on some logical basis. The costs of projects that do not produce useful results should be charged against revenue of the accounting period in which the uselessness is determined. Costs of successful projects should be capitalized and amortized over the future periods benefited.

Some companies operate experimental departments for the sole purpose of developing patented devices. In such cases the problem of accounting for cost of the development work is that of determining the period or periods which should be charged. Three different opinions with respect to the handling of such costs are found:

1. Capitalize the entire cost of operating the department to the successful patents produced.
2. Keep project-cost records and capitalize only the cost specifically assignable to successful patents—the cost of the unsuccessful projects being charged to the current period; frequently impracticable because of an inherent time lag.
3. Charge the entire cost of the department against the revenue of the current period on the theory that this cost is a recurring expense which must be borne period after period if the company is to maintain its competitive position in the industry.

Although there appears to be some justification for each of these methods, the second is theoretically sound. Application in practice may be very difficult since several years of developmental work and field testing may be involved before it is known whether or not the project is successful; therefore, the third method is used widely.

Goodwill

Goodwill represents the potential of a business to earn above "normal" profits. It may be generated internally or purchased; in either case it is not a specifically identifiable asset. Goodwill arises as a result of such factors as customer acceptance, efficiency of operation, reputation for dependability, quality of products, location, internal competences, and financial standing. The "value" of goodwill represents a valuation placed upon the *above-normal earning capacity* of the firm. Conceptually, the goodwill is the *present value* of the expected future excess earnings. Above-normal, or excess earning capacity is the earning power of a firm above what is considered normal for the industry. For example, a firm consistently earning, say, 15% on total assets in an industry averaging a 10% return would have an excess earning capacity of 5%. The basic principle in accounting for goodwill initially is that it should be recorded at cost in conformance with the cost principle since it is not a specifically identifiable asset but a composite. In implementing this principle, goodwill should be recognized only when *actually paid for* in an arm's-length transaction. Consequently, goodwill should be recorded only when a business is purchased (or part of the business is purchased, as in the admission of a new partner) and the price paid exceeds the fair market value of all other identifiable (tangible and specifically identifiable intangible) assets acquired. Goodwill is recognized in the accounts only under these limited conditions so that an objective accounting will result and misrepresentation in financial statements will not occur. In the normal process of building up a business over time an element of goodwill obviously is developed. This is frequently referred to as "internally developed goodwill" and, in contrast to purchased goodwill, is not properly reflected as an asset for two fundamental reasons: (1) directly there has been no disbursement of assets for it as is the case for other assets such as equipment; and (2) to the extent that expenses have been incurred that may have indirectly contributed to it (such as promotion expenditures) they have been reflected in past income statements as expenses and any attempt to separate them out would be quite arbitrary.

Amortization of Goodwill

Goodwill seldom can be purchased or acquired separately therefore it is restricted to situations where the net assets of an enterprise are acquired. The difference between the purchase price in the transaction and the sum of the identifiable assets (tangible and intangible, other than goodwill) represents the cost of purchased goodwill. Thus, if Company A purchases Company B for $1 million and receives tangible assets with a fair value of $750,000 and identifiable intangible assets (such as a patent) with a fair value of $50,000, the purchased goodwill would be $200,000.[3] The question of the correct accounting treatment of purchased goodwill is controversial. One view is that it should not be amortized but should be reported as an intangible fixed asset until there is definite evidence of its demise (such as failure to earn profits). Another view is that it should be deducted in full from capital at date of acquisition. Still another view is that it should be amortized over a realistic period during which the above-normal or superior earnings contemplated in the purchase decision are being realized. Both sides agree that purchased goodwill should be written down when there is clear evidence that it is overstated.

Some argue that there should be no amortization so long as profits are high since it is a permanent asset that has resale value. It is also argued that future profits and earnings per share should not be "penalized" because of a "good deal"; to amortize would penalize the excess profits which justified recording the goodwill in the first instance. The logical extension of this argument would be (a) to write it off directly to capital or (b) to amortize goodwill only when profits fail to materialize.

---

[3] It is sometimes alleged that goodwill can be negative. Cases cited are when the book value of the assets are in excess of the purchase price, or alternatively where the fair market value of the individual assets is in excess of the purchase price. In the opinion of the authors this reasoning flies in the face of both reality and concept. In the first instance book value has no relationship to market value and in the second instance the fair value of a package of assets is the cash consideration given (or its equivalent). It is difficult to perceive, as a practical matter, an informed seller disposing of a group of assets for an amount substantially less than he could derive for them piecemeal. The instances cited usually make an absurd assumption or there is an obvious breakdown in the measurement process. There are situations where a credit may emerge; however, it should be identified for what it is and not carelessly labeled "negative goodwill."

The argument in favor of amortization is that purchased goodwill, like any other fixed asset, was acquired to generate earnings and, like other assets, should be amortized against those earnings. Thus, the conclusion is that goodwill should be amortized when the superior earnings are being realized. The argument continues that the purchase decision contemplated a specific amount of goodwill at the date of purchase which had already been developed. The purchaser envisioned a particularly profitable period in the future for which he would pay a price; that is, the cost of the *original goodwill purchased.* Acquired goodwill should be amortized over the approximate period of excess earnings contemplated in the purchase decision. Obviously, a competent management will continue to build *new* layers of internally generated goodwill the cost of which will flow through the income statements as current operating expenses. Thus, the concept that purchased goodwill represents an established layer; the purchase cost of it should be allocated to the revenues generated by that particular layer. The authors favor the view that purchased goodwill should be allocated to the superior revenues implicit in the investment (purchase) decision. Since investment decisions of this type typically have a long time horizon (10 to 40 years), a similar amortization period should be applied in a systematic and conceptually sound way. Illustration 14–2 presents a theoretically sound approach to amortization.

For income tax purposes amortization of goodwill is not allowed; any tax deduction may be taken only upon sale or liquidation of the business.

Estimating Goodwill

In negotiations relating to the purchase or sale of a business the accountant may be requested to assist in valuing goodwill. However, in such circumstances goodwill value obviously is the result of bargaining between the purchaser and seller. Computations based upon an analysis of asset values and income potentials frequently are useful in such negotiations since goodwill relates to the excess earning capacity of the business. In such analyses it must be emphasized that *future earning potentials* rather than past earnings are significant. Past earnings, properly adjusted, may provide a sound basis for estimating future potentials. In estimating future earnings, the earnings history of the firm should be studied. As a basis for estimating future earnings the following steps may be suggested:

1. Select for study a series of past years' earnings which appears to be most representative of usual operations and indicative of future expectations. A period of five years frequently is used. The period of years should be long enough to reveal the pattern of earnings fluctuations experienced by the company.

2. Adjust these past earnings (*a*) by eliminating all extraneous and nonrecurring gains and losses contained therein; (*b*) for changes in accounting, such as depreciation estimates and methods; (*c*) for changes which are expected to occur in management salaries of the future over those in the past; and (*d*) for any other changes in costs, expenses, and revenue which are expected to occur in the future.
3. Analyze the trend and uniformity of past earnings. Even though earnings in the past have been above normal, any observed downward trend in the immediate past may indicate the disappearance of above-normal earning capacity. Such a downward trend would largely negate any basis for goodwill value.
4. On the basis of the above analysis project the future earnings and assets.

Within the above framework several approaches in *estimating* the value of goodwill are discussed below. To illustrate, assume that on January 1, 1971, it is desired to estimate the goodwill for Company X and that the data in Illustration 14–1 are available.

Illustration 14–1
Estimation of Goodwill

Year	Net Income (Adjusted for Nonrecurring Items)	Total Assets	Liabilities	Owners' Equity
		Book Values		
1966	$18,000	$162,000	$ 82,000	$ 80,000
1967	17,000	172,000	90,000	82,000
1968	19,000	190,000	105,000	85,000
1969	19,000	187,000	90,000	97,000
1970	21,000	200,000	98,000	102,000
Total	$94,000	$911,000	$465,000	$446,000
Five-year average	$18,800	$182,200	$ 93,000	$ 89,200

Assume that after careful analysis of the above data, appraisal of the assets, and other pertinent factors the following estimates are derived:

Average annual earnings expected ....$ 20,000
Estimated average future value of net assets (exclusive of good-
    will) at apprasied values less liabilities to be transferred 100,000

We will illustrate four rather unsophisticated methods followed by a conceptually sound one.

Capitalization of Earnings. The expected earnings may be capitalized at a "normal" rate of return for the industry in order to estimate the total asset value. The difference between this value (total asset value implied) and the average assets expected (exclusive of goodwill) may be considered as an unsophisticated representation of goodwill. To illustrate, assuming a "normal" rate of return of 12%, goodwill for Company X may be computed as follows:

Average annual earnings expected	$20,000	
Normal rate of return for the industry	12%	
Total asset value implied ($20,000 ÷ 12%)		$166,667
Average assets expected (exclusive of goodwill)		100,000
Estimated goodwill		$ 66,667
Total Valuation Including Goodwill ($100,000 + $66,667)		$166,667

Capitalization of Excess Earnings. The preceding method may be deficient in that it does not recognize excess earnings as a special factor. Capitalization of excess earnings requires the selection of a special rate to be applied to such earnings. The special capitalization rate should represent the planned annual rate of recovery of investment in the intangible as a result of excess earnings. The special rate should be higher than the normal rate because of the greater risk of not earning above the "normal" rate. Obviously, the greater the risk the higher the rate should be.

To illustrate the computation for Company X, assume a normal rate on assets of 12% and a capitalization rate for the excess earnings of 20%.

Average annual earnings expected	$20,000	
Return on average assets expected (exclusive of goodwill) at the normal rate ($100,000 × 12%)	12,000	
Excess earnings	$ 8,000	
Goodwill: Excess earnings capitalized at 20% ($8,000 ÷ 20%)		$ 40,000
Total Valuation Including Goodwill ($100,000 + $40,000)		$140,000

Years' Purchase of Average Excess Earnings. The goodwill may be estimated more directly by multiplying the estimated excess earnings by the number of years over which the investor expects to recover his investment in goodwill from the above-normal earnings of the business. To illustrate, assume the expected period of recovery is six years:

Excess earnings (computed above)	$ 8,000
Expected period of recovery	6 years
Estimated goodwill	$ 48,000
Total Valuation Including Goodwill ($100,000 + $48,000)	$148,000

Obviously, there is implicit in this method an amortization period for goodwill of six years.

Other Unsophisticated Methods of Estimating Goodwill Value. Other methods are used in estimating goodwill value. Generally, any method which does not take into account the expectation of above-normal earnings is not recommended. For example, the following method is sometimes used:

Years' Purchase of Average Earnings

Average annual earnings expected	$ 20,000
Four years' purchase (multiply by 4)	× 4
Estimated goodwill	$ 80,000
Total Valuation Including Goodwill ($100,000 +	
$80,000)	$180,000

Under this method some goodwill would be estimated even through below-normal earnings were experienced. For example, if average annual earnings expected were $7,000 an estimated goodwill of $28,000 would result despite the fact that annual earnings were $5,000 *below* normal.

Present Value Estimation of Goodwill

The only conceptually sound approach to estimating (and amortizing) goodwill is to determine the *present value of the future excess earnings purchased.* To illustrate, assume in respect to the above example that the negotiations implied the purchase of future excess earnings for 10 years in addition to the identifiable assets and that the expected earnings rate was 8%.[4] Computation of the implied goodwill would be as follows:

Average annual earnings purchased (estimated for 10 years)	$20,000	
Assets purchased (at fair value)		$100,000
Normal annual earnings expected ($100,000 × 8%)	8,000	
Excess earnings for 10 years.. *EFSE*	$12,000	
Goodwill:		
Present value of future earnings:		
$12,000 × $A_{\overline{n}|i}$ (from Table 5–4)		
$12,000 × 6.7101 = ...		80,521
Total Valuation Including Goodwill		$180,521

The *purchase* at $180,521 would be recorded as follows:

Identifiable Assets (detailed) ....100,000°		
Goodwill.. 80,521		
Cash (or other consideration)		180,521

° At fair value.

---

[4] The short time horizon and relatively low return (8%) was used in this illustration because of the limitations of the table available in Chapter 5.

Conceptually, the goodwill would then be amortized over the 10 years as shown in Illustration 14-2.

Illustration 14-2
Goodwill Amortized on Present Value Basis

Year	Annual Excess Earnings (a)	Return on Goodwill Investment (b)	Goodwill Amortization		Goodwill Investment Carrying Value (e)
			Expense(dr) (c)	Goodwill(cr) (d)	
Start					$80,521
1.........	$12,000	$6,440	$ 5,560	$ 5,560	74,961
2.........	12,000	5,997	6,003	6,003	68,958
3.........	12,000	5,517	6,483	6,483	62,475
4.........	12,000	4,998	7,002	7,002	55,473
5.........	12,000	4,438	7,562	7,562	47,911
6.........	12,000	3,833	8,167	8,167	39,744
7.........	12,000	3,179	8,821	8,821	30,923
8.........	12,000	2,474	9,526	9,526	21,397
9.........	12,000	1,712	10,288	10,288	11,109
10.........	12,000	891°	11,109	11,109	–0–

° Rounding error–$2.
(a) Projected annual excess earnings.
(b) 8% of previous goodwill balance ($80,521 × 8% = $6,440, etc.).
(c) and (d) columns, column (a), minus column (b).
(e) Previous balance minus column (d).

Of course, a crude straight line amortization over the 10-year period could be utilized; however, the present value approach as illustrated above conceptually is in harmony both with the nature of goodwill and the preferred view of its amortization explained on page 575. It may be observed that no "residual" value was recognized in Illustration 14-2 since the *original layer* of purchased goodwill conceptually will have served its purpose of generating excess earnings; new layers of internally generated goodwill normally would have been developed in the meantime.

The recording and reporting of purchased goodwill and its amortization is a central issue in mergers and consolidations; this aspect is discussed in Chapter 11 and 22.

Organization Costs

Expenditures incurred in the original incorporation and promotion of a business enterprise, such as legal fees, state incorporation fees, stock certificate costs, stamp taxes, reasonable underwriting costs, and office expenses incident to organizing, are capitalized as organization costs on the theory that such costs benefit each succeeding year; hence, to charge them off as a cost in the first year of operation would result in an incorrect matching of cost and revenue. Since the life of a corporation generally is indefinite, the length of the period which will receive the benefits of this cost is usually indeterminate. For this reason, and because the recognition of organization costs as a business asset depends entirely upon intangible values presumably attached to the corporate form of organization for the particular business, organization expenses generally are amortized over an arbitrarily selected short period. This practice is encouraged by the tax rules which permit the corporation to amortize most organization costs ratably over such period as the company desires so long as that period is not less than 60 months.

A troublesome problem is posed in respect to stock issue costs; that is, the costs of printing stock certificates, attorney fees related directly to the issue, commissions paid for sale, and accountants fees (such as the cost of filing with the SEC). Three approaches in accounting for these particular costs are found in practice:

1. *Charge such costs to organization costs.*   Although this is a fairly common practice, many accountants feel that it is conceptually deficient.
2. *Offset such costs against the sales price of the stock.*   Under this practice they would be included in the determination of stock discount or premium. In this alternative such costs would not be amortized against revenue. It is conceptually deficient since it may give rise to a recorded discount on stock that does not agree with the amount paid in by the shareholder. This approach appears to be the most widely used primarily because (*a*) frequently the costs are not separable from the issue transaction, and (*b*) such costs benefit the entire life of the corporation.
3. *Charge such costs to an intangible asset and amortize in a manner similar to organization costs.*   This approach is conceptually sound providing such costs are amortized over the useful life of the "asset." As a practical matter they generally are amortized over a short period of time as is done in respect to organization costs.

Leaseholds

The right of a lessee to use real property under the terms of a lease agreement is known as a *leasehold.*[5] A lease agreement calls for periodic rent and may require, in addition, the downpayment of a lump sum. The lump sum is an intangible asset (leasehold) which should be amortized over the life of the lease. Amortization may be (*a*) on a straight line basis or preferably (*b*) on a present value basis. The amortization period is the life of the lease; options to renew the lease

---

[5] These discussions assume operating leases; other types of leases are discussed in Chapter 18.

are usually disregarded in determining the amortization period. Procedurally, the downpayment should be debited to an intangible asset account labeled Leaseholds; the amortization is recorded as a credit to this account and as a debit to rental expense.

To illustrate, assume a property owner is leasing a building for $8,000 per year payable at the start of each year. As a result of bargaining between the lessor (owner) and lessee (tenant), instead of annual rentals, a lump-sum payment at the start of the upcoming year of $40,801.58 would constitute the total rent for six years. This arrangement could be accounted for by each party on a *straight line* amortization basis as follows:

	Lessor			*Lessee*	

1. At date of prepayment.

Lessor	Lessee
Cash..................40,801.58	Prepaid Rent Expense
Prepaid Rent Income 40,801.58	(or leasehold) ..40,801.58
	Cash............ 40,801.58

2. Amortization each year for six years (straight line):

Lessor	Lessee
Prepaid Rent	Rent Expense 6,800.26
Income 6,800.26	Prepaid Rent Expense 6,800.26
Rent Income 6,800.26	
($40,801.58 ÷ 6 years	
$6,800.26)	

The straight line approach does not consider the time value of money, hence the rent income (or expense) is misstated and interest as a factor is not recognized. Theoretically, the leasehold and the amortization (on both sets of books) should be accounted for on a present value basis. The advance payment represents the present value of an annuity of $8,000 for six periods. Since the first payment (rent) is due immediately there is an *annuity* due which may be schematically demonstrated as follows:

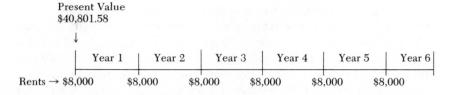

The agreed rate of interest between the parties was 7%; therefore, the advance payment was computed as follows:

Present value of annuity due for six rents at 7%:
  i.e., an annuity due is equivalent to the $(n - 1$ rents$)$ +
    1 value for an ordinary annuity
    Table 5–4, 7%, 5 rents = 4.1001974 + 1 = ... 5.1001974
Multiply by annual rental... × $8,000
Lump-sum payment, if made now $40,801.58

Determination of (1) the periodic amortization using the *scientific* approach and (2) the related accounting entries are best accomplished for either the lessor or lessee by development of an amortization table as shown in Illustration 14–3. Since the annual rent is due at the beginning of each period you should observe that there would be no interest in the sixth year as reflected in the above schematic for the annuity due.

Illustration 14–3
Leasehold Amortization Table (present value basis)
at $8,000 Annual Rental

Rental	Rent	Computation of Interest	Leasehold Amortization	Leasehold Balance
				$40,801.58°
1.............$8,000		($40,801.58 − $8,000)7% = $2,296.11	$5,703.89†	35,097.69‡
2............. 8,000		(35,097.69 − 8,000)7 = 1,896.84	6,103.16	25,994.53
3............. 8,000		(25,994.53 − 8,000)7 = 1,469.62	6,530.38	19,464.15
4............. 8,000		(19,464.15 − 8,000)7 = 1,012.49	6,987.51	15,476.64
5............. 8,000		(15,476.64 − 8,000)7 = 523.36	7,476.64	8,000.00
6............. 8,000			8,000.00	–0–

° Present value of future rents as computed above.
† $8,000.00 − $2,296.11 = $5,703.89.
‡ $40,801.58 − $5,703.89 = $35,097.69.

The interest computations in Illustration 14–3 reflect the characteristics of an annuity due, that is, the *rents* are assumed to be paid at the beginning of each period.

Amortization entries for the lessor and lessee for the first, second, and sixth years are shown in the tabulation below assuming the fiscal and lease years coincide. Entries for the years not shown would be made in accordance with the amortization table shown in Illustration 14–3.

	Lessor			*Lessee*	
Year 1			*Year 1*		
At start of lease:					
Cash...............40,801.58			Leasehold 40,801.58		
Deferred Rent Income		40,801.58	Cash..........		40,801.58

Lessor		*Lessee*	
At end of first year:			
Deferred Rent		Rent Expense.......8,000.00	
Income............5,703.89		Interest	
Interest Expense...2,296.11		Income.......	2,296.11
Rent Income..	8,000.00	Leasehold......	5,703.89
Year 2			
Deferred Rent		Rent Expense.......8,000.00	
Income............6,103.16		Interest	
Interest Expense...1,896.84		Income.......	1,896.84
Rent Income..	8,000.00	Leasehold......	6,103.16
Year 6			
Deferred Rent		Rent Expense 8,000.00	
Income............8,000.00		Interest	
Interest Expense... -0-		Income.......	-0-
Rent Income..	8,000.00	Leasehold......	8,000.00

Clearly the present value (scientific) approach provides more real-istic values for the balance sheet and the income statement than does the straight line approach. The present value approach derives rental and interest values that represent the economic essence of the lease contract. Obviously, the difference between the present value of $40,801.58 and the $48,000.00 that would have been paid is due to the "time value of money" agreed to by the two parties.

Other Intangible Assets

Since the accounting for other intangible assets follows the pro-cedures outlined previously for intangibles, only a brief description of the nature of some of these need be given at this point.

Copyrights. A copyright is an exclusive right granted by the federal government to reproduce, publish, sell, and control a literary product or artistic work. The right is for a term of 28 years with pro-vision for renewal for another 28 years. Obviously, most copyrights have value for a much shorter term, and their costs should be amor-tized over the shorter period. Often these costs are nominal and are written off in the period of expenditure.

Franchises. A common type of franchise is a grant by some govern-mental unit for the use of public properties (or a monopoly to furnish services such as the telephone company) in a manner beneficial to the public. Franchises normally involve rights for a specified period; therefore, the cost of acquiring them should be amortized over that period.

In recent years another type of franchise has become rather com-mon; that is, the granting of a right, by one company to another entity, to utilize a specific designation (such as Colonel Sanders Fried

Chicken) subject to certain obligations agreed to by each party. In these situations appropriate accounting by both parties presents some issues. To date the profession has not taken a specific stand on these particular transactions, hence considerable variation in practice is observed. Clearly, the purchaser of the franchise should capitalize the cost and amortize it over the expected useful life. Of course, the period of amortization is difficult to determine since the franchise may actually gain in value as the operation becomes more successful. On the other hand, the seller of the franchise is inclined to take up the entire sales price as revenue in the year of agreement and at the same time fail to accrue the costs of expected future contractual responsibilities. This practice has been appropriately criticized since it overstates income when the franchises are being sold. Clearly, accrual accounting should be applied in order to realistically reflect both revenue and costs and to match them period by period. At this writing this specific type of franchise is under consideration by the accounting profession with a view to narrowing the alternative (and frequently misleading) accounting treatments.

Trademarks, Trade Names, Brand Names. Trademarks may be registered through the federal patent office in order to aid the user in proving ownership. Proof of prior use of either trademarks, trade names, or brand names is sufficient under the common law to protect the user from infringement. These assets normally involve circumstances such as to warrant amortization.

PART B—DEFERRED CHARGES

Prepaid Expenses and Deferred Charges Distinguished

Prepaid expenses and deferred charges are alike in that they are both destined to be charged to expense in some subsequent period in harmony with the matching principle. They are unlike in that prepaid expenses are of short duration, represent recurring expenses, and are to be allocated to a limited number of future periods; whereas deferred charges are of longer duration, are seldom recurring, and are to be allocated to a number of future periods. The usual prepaid expenses are prepayments of interest, taxes, and rent; unexpired insurance; advanced royalties; and supply inventories. Typical deferred charges are bond issue costs, research and development costs, organization and reorganization costs, and other extraordinary expenses such as national advertising campaigns which logically can be spread over several succeeding fiscal periods. Prepaid expenses are reported on the balance sheet as current assets. Deferred charges are reported on the balance sheet under a special caption, "deferred charges or other assets." Unamortized bond discount, although frequently reported as a deferred charge, preferably should be reported as a contra item to the bond liability.

PART C—INSURANCE

Casualty Insurance

Casualty insurance involves a contract whereby the insurance company in consideration for a premium payment (paid in advance) assumes an obligation under certain circumstances to reimburse the policyholder an amount not exceeding the *fair market value* (at date of loss) of the property lost due to storm, fire, etc., as specified in the policy. The indemnity in no case exceeds the amount stipulated in the contract, that is, the *face* of the policy.

The great diversity in the forms of policies and the legal status of their provisions in the past caused most states to adopt a standard policy. The companies are allowed a certain degree of flexibility in varying the terms of the standard policy by attaching "riders" (standardized paragraphs).

The premium, a charge per $100 of insurance carried, is usually computed on a standard basis, depending upon the nature of the asset insured. For example, in the case of insurance on a building, the premium is adjusted for such things as type of construction, kind of roof, types of flues, occupancy by owner or tenant, space rented, office in building, and location. The fact that a premium discount is given if the term of the policy exceeds one year results in many premiums being paid for periods of three to five years in advance; hence, an *intangible asset* is created (prepaid insurance).

When a policy is canceled at the request of the insurance company, the insured is entitled to a refund of a pro rata portion of the premium, which covers the unexpired time. If the cancellation is requested by the insured, the premium to be returned is computed by reference to a short-rate table which refunds less than the pro rata portion of the premium. For example, one state's schedule provides that the insured who pays $2\frac{1}{2}$ times the annual rate for a three-year policy may recover 60% of the premium if he has the policy canceled at the end of one year.

Coinsurance

In order to encourage adequate insurance coverage many policies carry a *coinsurance clause* which provides that if the property is insured for less than a stated percentage (often 80%) of its fair market value at the time of a loss, the insured is a *coinsurer* with the insurance company. For example, if property having a fair market value of $11,250 is insured for only $7,000 (face of the policy) under a policy that carries a coinsurance clause, the property owner shares the loss with the insurance company. In this case, assuming a loss on the property amounting to $6,300, the insurance company would pay indemnity of $4,900. When there is a coinsurance clause the insurance

company pays as indemnity for a loss the *lowest* of three amounts:
(1) Face of the policy; (2) Fair market value of the loss; (3) Coinsurance indemnity.

To illustrate:

(1) Face of the policy...$7,000
(2) Fair market value of the loss.. 6,300
(3) Indemnity computed by the coinsurance formula...................................... 4,900

Computation:

$$\frac{F}{.80 \times M} \times L = \text{Indemnity} \quad \text{or} \quad \frac{\$7,000}{.80 \times \$11,250} \times \$6,300 = \$4,900$$

F equals the face of the policy; *M* the fair market value of the insured property at the date of the loss; and *L* the fair market value of the loss.

Application of this rule is further illustrated by the cases shown in Illustration 14–4 (assuming in each case that the policy contains an 80% coinsurance clause).

Illustration 14–4
Indemnity under Coinsurance

	Case 1 (When Formula Is Lowest)	Case 2 (When Loss Is Lowest)	Case 3 (When Policy Is Lowest)
Fair market value of property at date of loss	$10,000	$10,000	$10,000
Face of policy carried by insured	7,000	8,800	6,000
Fair market value of loss	5,600	6,000	10,000
Maximum indemnity (formula)	4,900°	6,600†	7,500‡
Actual indemnity payable	4,900	6,000	6,000

$$° \frac{\$7,000}{.80 \times \$10,000} \times \$5,600 = \$4,900.$$

$$† \frac{\$8,800}{.80 \times \$10,000} \times \$6,000 = \$6,600.$$

$$‡ \frac{\$6,000}{.80 \times \$10,000} \times \$10,000 = \$7,500.$$

Blanket Policy

When a company takes out a fire insurance policy covering several items of property (frequently called a blanket policy), the policy usually includes an "average" clause, which provides that the protection shall attach to each item of property in such proportion as each property bears to the entire value (fair market value at time of loss) of the property insured. For example, assume that a blanket policy for $9,000, containing the 80% coinsurance clause, insured two buildings—A having a fair market value at the date of the fire of $10,000 and B of $5,000. The face of the policy would be allocated as $6,000 on A and $3,000 on B. If a fire loss of $2,000 occurred in B, the maximum indemnity would be:

$$\frac{\$3,000}{.80 \times \$5,000} \times \$2,000 = \$1,500$$

Since $1,500 is less than either the loss ($2,000) or the effective policy ($3,000), the actual indemnity would be $1,500, the maximum set by the formula.

Indemnity under Several Policies

Where more than one insurance policy covers the same property and all policies have the same or no coinsurance clause, the total insurance is computed as though all the insurance were issued in a single policy. The indemnity thus computed is then allocated among the different policies in proportion to the face of each policy. To illustrate, assume that property having a fair market value of $100,000 is insured under the policies described below and a fire loss of $60,000 was incurred. If the policies do not contain coinsurance clauses, the actual indemnity would be as shown in Illustration 14–5.

Illustration 14–5
Indemnity under Several Policies with No Coinsurance Clause

Policy	Insurance Carried (Face)	Computation	Indemnity (Amount Collectible)
1	$10,000	10/80 × $60,000	$ 7,500
2	25,000	25/80 × $60,000	18,750
3	40,000	40/80 × $60,000	30,000
4	5,000	5/80 × $60,000	3,750
	$80,000		$60,000

If the policies all contained 90% coinsurance clauses, the actual indemnity would be as shown in Illustration 14–6.

Illustration 14–6
Indemnity under Several Policies with Common Coinsurance Clause

Policy	Coinsurance	(1) Face of Policy	(2) Loss Proration°	(3) Formula†	Indemnity (Lowest)
1	90%	$10,000	$ 7,500	$ 6,667	$ 6,667
2	90	25,000	18,750	16,667	16,667
3	90	40,000	30,000	26,666	26,666
4	90	5,000	3,750	3,333	3,333
		$80,000	$60,000		$53,333

° $10,000/$80,000 × $60,000 = $7,500, etc.
† $\dfrac{\$10,000}{.90\ (\$100,000)} \times \$60,000 = \$6,667$, etc.

If property is insured by several policies having *different* coinsurance clauses, each coinsurance requirement must be taken into account. To illustrate, assume the above example except that the coinsurance clauses are as indicated in Illustration 14–7. Note in particular the last policy; it was the only one on which the coinsurance requirement was not met.

Illustration 14–7
Indemnity under Several Policies with Variable Coinsurance Clauses

Policy	Coinsurance	(1) Face of Policy	(2) Loss Proration°	(3) Formula†	Indemnity (Lowest)
1 ....None		$10,000	$ 7,500	Not applicable	$ 7,500
2 ....75%		25,000	18,750	$20,000	18,750
3 80		40,000	30,000	30,000	30,000
4 90		5,000	3,750	3,333	3,333
		$80,000	$60,000		$59,583

° Computed as in Illustration 14–6.

† $\dfrac{\$25,000}{.75\,(\$100,000)} \times \$60,000 = \$20,000.$

$\dfrac{\$40,000}{.80\,(\$100,000)} \times \$60,000 = \$30,000.$

$\dfrac{\$5,000}{.90\,(\$100,000)} \times \$60,000 = \$ 3,333.$

Accounting for a Casualty Loss

When there is a casualty loss the prepaid expense (Prepaid Insurance) must be adjusted accordingly. To illustrate the nature of the adjustment we will utilize a *fire loss*. When a fire has occurred, an orderly accounting procedure is essential for *separately reporting the loss* and for proper matching of operating cost and revenue. In accounting for a fire loss certain procedures should be followed, viz:

1. Determine to what extent the accounting records have been damaged or destroyed. Take steps to supplement damaged records, or to reconstruct them if they have been destroyed.
2. Adjust the books to the date of the fire for all operating items affected by the fire. Make all necessary adjusting entries for depreciation, amortizations, accrued and prepaid expense, and income items affected by the fire.
3. Determine the *book value* of all assets destroyed by the fire.
4. Open a Fire Loss account in the general ledger and transfer to it the book value of all assets destroyed. Charge the Fire Loss account with any unexpired insurance premium on that portion of the policy which is paid by the insurance company as a result of the casualty, and with any expenses incurred in connection with the fire and the settlement.
5. Determine the amounts recoverable (this determination is made

through negotiations with the adjuster appointed by the insurance company) under the insurance policies in force. Credit the Fire Loss account with these amounts, and with any proceeds from the sale of damaged assets or merchandise whose cost has been charged to Fire Loss.

6. Close the balance of the Fire Loss account as a nonrecurring loss (or gain). It is advisable to close the books as at year-end, when the fire is of major proportions.

In determining the book value of assets destroyed, cognizance must be taken not only of the estimated depreciation recorded for past periods but also of the depreciation to be accrued for the elapsed portion of the present period to date of loss. The portion of the insurance premium to be charged to the Fire Loss account is the unexpired portion at the date of the fire if the full amount of the policy is paid. If only a portion of the policy is paid, then the amount of the payment is endorsed on the policy and the remainder continues in force. In this case, that portion of the unexpired premium which the endorsement bears to the face of the policy is taken out of Prepaid Insurance and charged to Fire Loss. If the policy is continued, the remainder is left in the Prepaid Insurance account; if canceled, this remainder is a cash refund.

If a perpetual inventory system is used, and if the records are not destroyed, the amount of the merchandise on hand at the time of the fire can be determined from the records. In the absence of such records, the amount of the inventory may be estimated by the "gross margin" method as described in Chapter 10.

Illustrative Problem — Fire Loss. The balances of certain accounts on the books of the Fire Alarm Company at January 1 were:

Prepaid insurance	$ 370
Furniture and equipment	2,400
Accumulated depreciation, furniture, and equipment	1,200
Building	30,000
Accumulated depreciation, building	10,000
(Date of fire loss — July 1)	

The prepaid insurance represented two policies, one for $2,400 on the furniture and equipment, dated July 1, of the previous year and running for three years, and the other for $16,800 on the building. The policy on the building was a three-year policy dated the previous January 1 and carried an 80% coinsurance clause. The unexpired premium on the furniture policy was $50 ($50/30 months = $1.67 per month), and that on the building policy, $320 ($320/24 months = $13.33 per month). On July 1, a fire destroyed the furniture and equipment, merchandise estimated by the gross margin method (see Chapter 10) to have cost $3,000, and an estimated two thirds of the building. There was no insurance on the stock of merchandise.

Give the journal entries indicated assuming the fair market values at date of loss were: furniture and fixtures, $1,000; building, $26,250 (loss was $17,500); and inventory at cost.

Solution:

1. Entries to adjust the books to the date of the fire for operating items affected:

Fire Loss (goods destroyed)...	3,000	
Goods Burned (inventory destroyed)...............................		3,000

To set up inventory of unsold merchandise destroyed by fire. (Note: Goods Burned is closed to Income Summary at regular closing. This amount offsets the charges to regular income from the beginning inventory and purchases, part of which was burned).°

° An alternative treatment would be to credit the beginning inventory and purchases to the extent of the loss and to debit the Fire Loss account.

Depreciation on Furniture and Equipment............................	300	
Accumulated Depreciation on Furniture and Equipment...		300

To record depreciation, at a rate of 25% per year, from January 1 to July 1 ($2,400 × 25% × 6/12).

Depreciation on Building..	500	
Accumulated Depreciation on Building............................		500

To record depreciation, 30-year life, from January 1 to July 1 ($30,000 ÷ 30 × 1/2).

Insurance Expense	90	
Prepaid Insurance		90

To record the expired insurance premium from January 1 to July 1, as follows:

Furniture and equipment ($1.67 × 6)	$10
Building ($13.33 × 6)	80

2. Entries to close the book value of assets destroyed to the Fire Loss account:

Fire Loss..	900	
Accumulated Depreciation on Furniture and Equipment.........	1,500	
Furniture and Equipment...		2,400

To close the accumulated depreciation and the asset account into the Fire Loss account.

Fire Loss..	13,000	
Accumulated Depreciation on Building................................	7,000	
Building...		20,000

To close two thirds of the accumulated depreciation and of the asset account into the Fire Loss account.

3. Entry to record the settlement with the insurance company:

Cash	15,000	
Fire Loss...		15,000

To record the payment received from the insurance company, computed as follows: Furniture and equipment, $1,000; Building, per formula ($16,800/.80 × $26,500) × $17,500 = $14,000.

4. To adjust Prepaid Insurance balance:

If policy continued			*If policy not continued*		
Fire Loss 217			Fire Loss 217		
Prepaid Insurance............	217		Cash....................................	63	
			Prepaid Insurance............		280

Analysis of prepaid insurance:

	Furniture and Fixtures	Building	Total
Unexpired January 1...$50		$320	$370
Amortized to July 1 10		80	90
Unexpired July 1...$40		$240	$280
Amount related to indemnity: $1,000/$2,400 × $40 = 17			17
$14,000/$16,800 × $240 =		200	200
Unexpired after fire loss (or cash refund) $23		$ 40	$ 63

The balance in the Fire Loss account is closed to Income Summary.

Life Insurance

General Statement. Life insurance companies sell insurance contracts that call for a stipulated payment (indemnity) in case of death, receiving in return compensation in the form of premiums. In an "ordinary life" policy, the premiums are paid until the death of the insured at which time the stipulated benefit is paid to the beneficiary. During the period the policy is in force it has both a cash surrender value and a loan value. In a "limited payment" policy, the premiums are paid for a stated number of periods or until the death of the insured (if prior to the end of the stipulated period) and the benefit is paid at death or after a stipulated date as an endowment. As with the ordinary life policy there is a cash surrender value and a loan value. In "term" insurance, the premium payments are made for a stated number of periods or until death (if prior to the end of the stipulated period); the benefit is paid only if death occurs within the stated number of periods. In term insurance, there is no cash surrender or loan values and the policy must be renewed at the end of the stipulated period; otherwise it lapses. At renewal, a new premium scale is effective based on the advanced age. As most of the characteristics are involved in "ordinary life" policies, the discussion to follow will be limited to them.

The law and insurance companies have long recognized that a company has an "insurable interest" in certain of its *executives.* Thus, it is not uncommon for a company to insure the life of the company president; the proceeds are payable to the company to compensate for the loss incurred in replacing a deceased executive.

In accounting for a life insurance contract of this type, premiums paid (cash paid less any dividends) and the related asset must be recorded and reported.

Cash Surrender and Loan Value. The cash surrender value of a policy is the sum payable upon the cancellation of the policy at the request of the insured. The loan value of a policy is the sum the insurance company will loan on a policy maintained in force. The cash surrender value is computed as of the end of the year; the loan value is computed as of the beginning of the year. Each policy carries a table that indicates the cash surrender value and the loan value for specific policy years. At any given time the loan value is somewhat less than the cash surrender value.

Premiums paid on insurance carried by a business firm on the life of an officer should be charged to a life insurance expense account. Since the policy could be canceled and a portion of the premiums which have been paid out be returned in the form of the cash surrender value, not all of the premiums paid constitute an expense but only the excess of the total premiums paid over the cash surrender value.[6]

The portion of premiums paid equal to the cash surrender value is an asset and should be shown as such on the balance sheet. Since it is not proposed, however, that the policy be canceled in order to realize the cash surrender value, the asset should be reported under the caption "Funds and Investments."

To illustrate one sequence of entries, assume the following data taken from an insurance policy having an indemnity of $25,000.

Year	Premium (Beginning of Year)	Cash Surrender Value (End of Year)
1	$720	-0-
2	720	-0-
3	720	$1,140
4	720	1,480
5	Etc.	Etc.

Indicated entries:

Year 1:	Life Insurance Expense	720	
	Cash		720
Year 2:	Life Insurance Expense	720	
	Cash		720

---

[6] In mutual companies the "stated" premium is reduced by a dividend credit.

Year 3:   Life Insurance Expense.. 720
         Cash..   720
         At year-end:
         Cash Surrender Value Life Insurance 1,140
            Life Insurance Expense ($\frac{1}{3} \times$ \$1,140).....................   380
            Nonrecurring Adjustment—Prior Year
              ($\frac{2}{3} \times$ \$1,140).....................................   760°

Year 4:   Life Insurance Expense.. 720
         Cash..   720
         At year-end:
         Cash Surrender Value Life Insurance
            (\$1,480 − \$1,140)   340
            Life Insurance Expense.......................................   340

°Another alternative would be to "allocate" the third-year cash surrender value to the first three years on some basis (say, equally) at the time the annual entry for premium is made.

Each year thereafter the Cash Surrender Value of Life Insurance account would be debited for the increase in the cash surrender value as shown by the table in the policy. The above example was simplified by assuming the policy year and the accounting year coincided. If they do not coincide, as is the normal case, an adjusting entry at the end of each accounting period would be required for the prepaid amount of insurance expense.

The following entry would be made when the face of policy is paid at the death of the president, assuming the cash surrender value of the policy at date of death was \$3,500 and that three months' premium is to be refunded in accordance with the insurance contract whereby premiums paid beyond date of death are refunded.

Cash [\$25,000 + ($\frac{3}{12} \times$ \$720)] 25,180
    Life Insurance Expense ($\frac{3}{12} \times$ \$720)...................................   180
    Cash Surrender Value of Life Insurance..........................   3,500
    Gain on settlement of Life Insurance Indemnity...............   21,500

The gain is reported as a nonrecurring gain; therefore it is reported as an extraordinary item on the income statement.

QUESTIONS FOR CLASS DISCUSSION

1. Define intangible assets. How are they reported on the balance sheet?
2. Why is it important in accounting to classify intangibles carefully?
3. What outlays may be considered as a part of the cost of a patent? Should patent costs be amortized over a period of 17 years?
4. Explain the conceptual nature of goodwill and the basis for its amortization.
5. Outline the role of the accountant in "valuation" of goodwill.
6. What items should be charged to organization costs? Should organization costs be amortized? Explain.
7. What is a leasehold?
8. Outline the accounting and reporting for a leasehold.
9. What is the difference between prepaid expenses and deferred charges? List three examples of each.

10. Distinguish between casualty insurance and life insurance.

11. What is the purpose of the coinsurance clause? Does the presence of a coinsurance clause in a policy affect the amount which the insured collects in the case of a total loss by fire of the property which is insured?

12. What is the difference between cash surrender value and loan value on a life insurance policy? Which one affects the accounting entries? How?

13. Why do some companies carry insurance on the lives of their executives?

14. What are the important aspects in accounting for a casualty loss where insurance is involved?

DECISION CASE 14-1

The major processing cost of canned corn, the main product of the Fresho Corporation, has been the cost of cooking. This cost has been large because of the cooking time (52 minutes) required. As a result of this high cost, the Fresho Corporation for the past five years has been engaged in continual research to develop a method to reduce the cooking time. Due to the uncertainty of development of any valuable methods or patents, the Fresho Corporation has followed the practice of writing off research costs currently; however, a very careful record of such costs has been maintained.

Near the end of last year a new process (involving patentable devices and processes) was discovered which reduced cooking time to two minutes per can. This new process was called electronic cooking.

The board of directors of the Fresho Corporation felt that—

a) Write-off of the development costs in the past five years has resulted in material misstatement of incomes and retained earnings and has unduly restricted dividends.

b) Failure to show the cost of the new assets (patents) on the balance sheet will conceal their most valuable economic asset.

c) Failure to amortize the cost of the new patents in future income statements would incorrectly relate costs to incomes.

Consequently, the board proposes to reinstate the cost of the new patents by a debit to the asset account "Patents" and a credit to Retained Earnings.

Required:

Evaluate each proposal.

DECISION CASE 14-2

Company A, a medium-sized manufacturer has been operating for over 50 years; at the present time it has over 10,000 shareholders and is expanding through the acquisition of smaller companies that "fit into our broad long-range goals."

Currently negotiations are underway to purchase, for cash, all of the assets and liabilities of Company B. The single plant owned and operated by Company B for the past 12 years has been quite successful. There are 20 shareholders and they have agreed to the sale pending completion of a price agreement.

Recently published balance sheets reveal the following information:

ASSETS:	Company A	Company B
Cash	$ 630,000	$ 5,000
Accounts receivable (net)	40,000	20,000
Inventory	90,000	10,000
Tangible fixed assets (net)	3,180,000	184,000
Patents	24,000	15,000
Other assets	13,000	6,000
Total Assets	$3,977,000	$240,000
	$ 150,000	$ 10,000
LIABILITIES		
Common Stock		
70,000 shares (par $40)	2,800,000	
5,000 shares (par $10)		50,000
Retained earnings	1,027,000	180,000
Total	$3,977,000	$240,000

The management of Company A has estimated the fair market value of Company B assets, with the professional assistance of the Universal Appraisal Company, with the following results: accounts receivable, $20,000; tangible fixed assets (plant), $450,000; patents, $32,000; and other assets, $8,000. Company A will acquire all of the assets except cash and will assume the liabilities at maturity value ($10,000).

Company A management is preparing for the next round of negotiations in respect to the cash offer to be made. They have decided to offer the fair market value of the identifiable assets, less the liabilities assumed, plus an amount for goodwill "equivalent to the present value of the excess earnings potential of Company B for the next 10 years." The expected earnings rate has been tentatively set at $8\frac{1}{2}\%$, and the projection of average annual earnings expected reflects $62,500.

Required:

1. Compute the estimated goodwill utilizing present value concepts. What would be the total cash offer under the tentative arrangements envisioned by the management of Company A?

2. Assuming the cash offer determined in (1) is made and accepted, give the entry on the books of Company A to record the purchase (assume sufficient cash will be available).

3. Develop an amortization table for Company A based on present value concepts.

4. What other methods of amortization might be considered by Company A? Would you recommend them? Why?

5. Should a residual value be included in the amortization computations for goodwill? Explain.

6. Assume the actual profits on the acquired operations turn out to be better than anticipated. Would you "stretch out" the amortization? What if profits were less than anticipated?

EXERCISES

Exercise 14–1

The following information relates to two completely separate intangible assets:

	Asset X	Asset Y
Cost	$5,250	$4,200
Estimated economic life	Indefinite	14 years

Required:

1. Give entry for amortization, if any, in each case.
2. At end of the eighth year it is determined that Asset Y has only four years of remaining useful life; give any entries indicated.

Exercise 14–2

Pressley Company developed a patent (No. 5) incurring the following costs:

Materials and supplies used	$1,500
Salaries directly related to patent	6,000
Overhead related to patent (based on an allocation procedure recommended by the CPA and approved by the management)	2,200
Miscellaneous costs	1,350

The patent right was effective December 28, 1966. The company believed that the patent would have beneficial value during the entire legal life.

During the latter part of 1969, the company was successful in prosecuting a patent infringement. The cost of the suit was $2,100 and was paid in December 1969.

During February 1968 the company purchased a patent (No. 6) from J. B. Conn paying $9,000 therefor. The patent right had been granted on January 3, 1968. In view of developments in the company laboratory it was expected that the patent will be superseded by other patents within six years of purchase.

Required:

Give entries through 1971 for each patent separately. Explain any assumptions and/or judgments made.

Exercise 14–3

The following projections were developed as a basis for estimating goodwill:

Budgeted average annual earnings expected	$ 8,000
Budgeted average future value of net assets (exclusive of goodwill)	60,000

Required:

Estimate goodwill under each of the following approaches:

a) Goodwill equal to earnings capitalized at 10% (normal rate for industry) over budgeted average assets.

b) Goodwill equal to excess earnings capitalized at 15%; normal earnings rate for industry, 10%.

c) Goodwill equal to seven years of excess earnings; normal earnings rate for industry, 10%.

d) Goodwill based on present value of excess earnings at an 8% expected earnings rate for 5 years. Prove your answer.

Exercise 14–4

The Penn Corporation is negotiating with the Old Company with a view to purchasing the entire assets and liabilities of the latter. You have been asked to help evaluate the "goodwill on the basis of the latest concepts." Accordingly, you decide to utilize the present value approach. The following data have been assembled in respect to Old Company:

	Fair Market Value	Book Value
Total identifiable assets (exclusive of goodwill)	$8,000,000	$5,000,000
Liabilities	3,000,000	3,000,000
Average annual earnings expected (next five years)	420,000	

Required:

(*Round to even dollars.*)

1. Compute goodwill assuming a 7% expected earnings rate.

2. Assume the deal is consummated; Penn's offer, as accepted, was cash equal to the fair market value of the net identifiable assets plus the goodwill computed in (1). Give entry on Penn's books to record the transaction.

3. Prepare an amortization table that is conceptually consistent with your computations in (1).

Exercise 14–5

Miller Company signed a contract on January 1 whereby the company was to pay $4,000 cash plus $400 per month rent for an office building. The contract covered a 10-year period and was renewable at the end of that time for an additional 10 years at a rental not to exceed 10% of that specified for the prior period. The management has no definite ideas as to whether or not the renewal option will be exercised.

Prior to occupancy the Miller Company spent $2,000 in renovation costs. In addition, a large garage was built upon the property costing $9,000. It is estimated that the garage has a 15-year life with no significant residual value. Give all entries indicated for the first year of the lease; assume straight line accounting procedures.

Exercise 14–6

Compute the indemnity under an insurance policy carrying an 80% co-insurance clause under each of the following cases:

	Case A	Case B	Case C
Fair market value of property at date of loss	$20,000	$30,000	$30,000
Insurance carried	24,000	20,000	12,000
Fair market value of the loss by fire	15,000	27,000	15,000

Exercise 14–7

After extended negotiations, a tenant and landlord agree that instead of paying $5,000 annual rental over a five-year term, a lump-sum advance payment of $21,936.06 (including the first rental which is now due) should be paid. Prepare an appropriate leasehold amortization schedule (present value basis) assuming a 7% interest rate. Give journal entries for the first year for lessor and lessee. Show how the advance payment was computed.

Exercise 14–8

Assuming that all policies contain an 80% coinsurance clause, show what each insurance company would pay under each of the following cases:

	Case A	Case B	Case C
Fair market value of property	$25,000	$15,000	$10,000
Amount of loss	24,000	3,000	3,200
Face of policies:			
Written by Company X	10,000	7,500	4,000
Written by Company Y	12,500	5,000	3,500

Exercise 14–9

Determine the liability of each insurance company under policies carrying the coinsurance clauses and the amount carried as indicated. The property had a fair market value at date of fire of $60,000, and the fair market value of the loss was $6,480.

Company	Coinsurance Clause	Face of Policy
A	100%	$15,000
B	70	15,000
C	90	10,000
D	None	5,000

Exercise 14–10

Mason Company sustained a fire loss on February 28. The following data were available (fiscal year ends December 31):

a) Sixty percent of the inventory burned; fair market value of loss, $1,500 (assume periodic inventory procedures).

b) Furniture and fixtures: depreciation $20 per month; fair market value of item burned, $3,900 (original cost, $3,000; accumulated depreciation to January 1, $480).

c) Insurance premium $30 per year paid on last January 1 for one year; payment of the indemnity canceled the policy and the unexpired premium after the fire was refunded in cash.

d) Settled with insurance company; face of policy, $5,000; 90% coinsurance clause; fair market value of property insured, $7,500.

Required:

Give indicated journal entries.

Exercise 14–11

On January 1, a store had $120 unexpired premiums on an 80% coinsurance fire policy, which ran one year, for $15,000 on its merchandise. On January 1, the inventory was $20,000. January purchases were $44,000, and January sales were $60,000. A fire on February 1 destroyed the entire stock on hand. The insurance policy is canceled upon payment of the indemnity and any unexpired premium after the fire was refunded.

Required:

Give journal entries to record the estimated inventory and the fire loss assuming a 30% gross margin rate on sales.

Exercise 14–12

On January 1, the Toms Company purchased a $100,000 ordinary life insurance policy on its president. The following data relate to the first five years:

Year	Annual Advance Premium	Cash Surrender Value (Year-End)	
		Increase	Cumulative
1..........................$2,000		–0–	–0–
2.......................... 2,000		–0–	–0–
3.......................... 2,000		$2,400	$2,400
4.......................... 2,000		900	3,300
5.......................... 2,000		925	4,225
6.......................... Etc.		Etc.	Etc.

Required:

1. Give all entries indicated up to death of the president on July 2 of the fifth year.

2. Give entry to record insurance settlement upon death of the president. The premium unexpired was refunded.

Assume the policy year and accounting year agree; also there are no dividends since the company is not a mutual.

PROBLEMS

Problem 14–1

Carlton Manufacturing Corporation was formed from a partnership. At date of corporate organization 1,000 shares of stock (par $20 per share) were issued to each of five former partners as "payment" for their partnership capital. There were no other stockholders.

Immediately after corporate organization the following data showed on the balance sheet:

Current assets	$ 60,000	Current liabilities	$ 40,000
Fixed assets (net)	111,000	Note payable (five-year)	45,000
Goodwill	30,000	Capital stock	100,000
Organization costs	5,000	Premium on stock	33,000
Franchise	9,000		
Lease cost	3,000		
	$218,000		$218,000

The lease cost represented prepaid rent for one year on office space occupied by the firm. The rental contract provided that the owner be given one-year notice of intent to vacate and that the $3,000 would apply as rent for the last year in case of notice of intent to vacate.

Immediately prior to corporate organization the Goodwill and Franchise accounts were entered on the books, the offsetting credit being to the partner's Capital accounts. The partners had "strong reasons" to believe that the $30,000 goodwill valuation was very conservative. Several years ago several offers were received to sell the business from $15,000 to $30,000 above book value. The company had a 15-year franchise with nine more years before expiration which gave the firm exclusive rights to certain business within the city. The franchise cost $10,000 originally which had been expensed when paid.

The partners felt that their efforts and costs related to corporate organization were worth $5,000 as a minimum. In addition to time, $2,000 had been spent for this purpose.

Shortly after incorporation and incident to plans for borrowing $50,000 from the bank for expansion, a firm of independent CPAs was called in to audit the account.

Required:

You have been requested to indicate the correct treatment of the intangibles in the financial statements being prepared by the independent CPAs. Your response should include a "correct" balance sheet and the basis for any changes.

Problem 14–2

The ABC Corporation was granted a charter authorizing 10,000 shares of $100 par value stock. In connection with organization and sale of the stock the following costs were incurred and paid in cash:

Attorney fees incident to organization	$ 2,000
Attorney fees relating to sale of stock	1,800
Printing costs incident to organization	400
Printing costs relating to sale of stock	200
Charter fee	100
Promoter expenses	4,000
Advertising relating to sale of stock	6,000
Commissions on sale of stock	24,000

The stock was sold as follows:

a) 8,000 shares at $105 per share (cash).
b) 1,000 shares issued for a valuable patent having a 10-year remaining useful life.

Required:

1. Prepare entries to record the above transactions. Justify your treatment on debatable items.
2. Prepare any amortization entries for the first year of operations. Justify your treatment on questionable items.
3. Indicate the correct treatment of each intangible item on year-end financial statements. Justify your position.

Problem 14–3

After considerable analysis the following projections were derived as a basis for estimating the potential value of goodwill in anticipation of negotiations for the sale of the business:

Average annual earnings projected...$ 40,000
Value of net assets purchased.. 350,000
"Normal" rate of return for the industry, $8\frac{1}{2}\%$.
Rate of return expected on excess profits, 10%.
Expected recovery period for excess earnings, five years.
Years purchase of average annual earnings, three.

Estimate the value of goodwill under five different approaches (including a present value determination at $8\frac{1}{2}\%$).

Problem 14–4

Parr Company is negotiating to purchase Slam Company. The latter is a relatively small company which has been moderately successful. It is a family owned company, and the six shareholders are very interested in selling the entire operation (excluding the cash and one building).

Parr has been given access to the records and from them and other sources the following data have been assembled:

a) Average net income reported for the past five years has been $116,000 (unadjusted); this amount is projected to remain stable for the next five years.
b) Administrative salaries for the past five years included $6,000 per year of nonrecurring items.
c) Depreciation was understated for the five-year period by $100,000.
d) Capital additions were understated by $80,000 for the five-year period; this amount was incorrectly charged to expense (depreciation corrected in c).
e) Gains on sales of fixed assets averaged $8,000 per year for the five-year period (two transactions).
f) Fair market value of the assets to be acquired (determined by appraisals):

	Fair Market Value	Book Value
Plant site	$ 18,000	$ 4,000
Plant and equipment (net)	856,000	370,000
Patent (11 years remaining life)	20,000	9,000
Other assets	6,000	8,000

g) Liabilities to be assumed by Parr, $20,000.

Required:

(*Round to even dollars.*):

1. Compute an "average annual net income projection" that would be appropriate for goodwill determination. Also determine the "value of the identifiable net assets" to be purchased.

2. Compute goodwill by capitalization of excess earnings at a 10% rate; assume "normal" industry earnings of 8%.

3. Compute goodwill utilizing the present value approach assuming an expected earnings rate of 8% and a five-year excess earnings period.

4. Assume Parr completed the transaction at the price indicated by your response to (3) and paid cash; give the entry on Parr's books.

5. Prepare a conceptually sound amortization table consistent with your computations in (3).

Problem 14–5

On January 1, 1972, Charmes Company negotiated a five-year lease with the Box Realty Company whereby in lieu of payment of annual rents (at the beginning of the year) of $10,000, the lessor and lessee agreed upon a single lump-sum payment discounted at 8% per annum.

Required:

1. Determine the amount of the lump-sum payment per the agreement.

2. The Box Realty Company (lessor) closes the books on December 31 and intends to utilize present value accounting for the lease. Develop an amortization table and give entries for the first two, and the last, years.

3. The tenant (lessee) also closed the books on December 31 but has adopted straight line accounting procedures for the lease. Give entries for the first two, and the last, years.

4. Which party has adopted the more realistic approach? Explain.

Problem 14–6

On January 1, 1971, the Baker Manufacturing Company rented a building on an eight-year lease, annual rent to be paid in advance. The rent schedule was $8,000 per year for the first four years and $10,000 per year for the last four years. Since Baker had some idle cash to invest, the management decided to approach the owner of the building with a proposition that the entire eight rentals be paid in advance with a discount factor of 8½%. The owner was favorable to the offer; however, he would not accept a discount factor higher than 7%. After some negotiations Baker decided to accept the 7% factor, hence the lump-sum payment was made immediately. Baker wisely decided to utilize present value accounting procedures for the lease.

Required:

1. Compute the amount of the lump-sum payment.
2. Prepare an amortization table for the lease.
3. Give journal entries on Baker's books for the first two, and the last, years assuming the books are closed each December 31.

Problem 14-7

Estimate the amount of insurance collectible on each of the following assets assuming the policies include an 80% coinsurance clause:

Asset	Fair Market Value	Loss Suffered	Insurance Carried
Buildings	$80,000	$40,000	$65,000
Furniture	20,000	18,000	15,000
Delivery equipment	9,000	4,000	5,000
Merchandise	?	60%	10,000

To find the value of the merchandise destroyed, the following facts are submitted from which to select the significant data:

The gross margin averages 30% of sales.
The fair market value of the inventory is the same as its cost.

Purchases for the period	$60,000
Beginning inventory	23,400
Return purchases	2,000
Salesmen's commissions and advertising	8,000
Interest income	200
Postage and stationery	1,000
Sales	84,000
Credit department expense	700
Sales returns	2,000

Problem 14-8

The Knight Mercantile Company operated retail branches in several cities throughout the country. It maintained a warehouse in Kansas City which was a distributing point for five branch stores in Kansas and Missouri. A fire at the warehouse on April 15 resulted in a partial loss.

Branch	Sales to Branches January 1 to April 15
A	$60,000
B	35,000
C	30,000
D	22,000
E	40,000

Sales to branches include a profit of 10% markup on cost.

Purchases by the Kansas City warehouse for the period from January 1 to April 15 totaled $192,000, and purchases returns for the same period were $2,000. Warehouse inventory on January 1 was $52,000.

To arrive at the value of the inventory on April 15 for settlement purposes, it was agreed to deduct for goods shopworn and damaged prior to the fire 3% from the amount on hand, as determined from the above data.

Loss and damage to stock was agreed upon by all parties concerned to have a fair market value of $31,428.

Required:

1. Estimate the amount of merchandise inventory at date of the fire.
2. Determine the amount collectible on a $50,000 insurance policy carrying a 90% coinsurance clause.

Problem 14-9

The records of Company X showed at date of fire (all merchandise destroyed): sales, $240,000; initial inventory, $15,000; purchases, $205,000; insurance (one-year policy for $12,000 with 80% coinsurance clause) premium, $200; salesmen's salaries, $15,000; and general expense, $13,000. The fire occurred six months after the premium was paid; payment of the indemnity canceled the insurance policy, hence any unexpired insurance premium was refunded. It was agreed that the gross margin percentage based on sales was $16\frac{2}{3}\%$.

Required:

1. Compute the indemnity to be received from the insurance company.
2. Give entries relating to the fire loss.
3. Prepare a classified income statement for the period ending on a date immediately following the fire.

Problem 14-10

On July 1, 1971, a fire occurred destroying or damaging the building, equipment, and stock in trade of the Stallings Sales Company. From the books and records which were preserved in a fireproof safe, the following information was available:

Trial Balance, July 1, 1971

Cash	$ 2,100	
Receivables	30,600	
Building and equipment°	180,000	
Accumulated depreciation°		$ 36,000
Land	12,000	
Merchandise inventory, January 1, 1971	10,000	
Office supplies inventory	200	
Unexpired insurance	342	
Accounts payable		38,000
Capital stock		100,000
Retained earnings		47,042
Sales		84,000
Purchases	51,000	
Freight in	1,000	
Selling expenses	11,000	
General and administrative expenses	6,800	
	$305,042	$305,042

° The cost of the building was $150,000. The accumulated depreciation (as of January 1, 1971) was $28,000 related to building, and $8,000 related to the equipment.

The insurance register disclosed the following (all policies carry an 80% coinsurance clause):

	Date of Policy	Term (Years)	Face of Policy	Total Premium Paid
Building	1/1/69	3	$60,000	$450
Merchandise	1/1/71	1	10,000	72
Equipment...............	1/1/71	3	15,000	120

The policy on the building, after endorsement (deduction) for the settlement received from the insurance company, remained in force for the unexpired term of the policy for the face less the indemnity paid; the other policies terminated upon payment of the indemnity. All prepaid premiums after the fire were refunded on the policies terminated.

The adjuster found (a) that the fair market value of the building at the time of the fire was $135,000, (b) that the fair market value of the equipment was $25,000, and (c) that an average rate of markup of 40% on selling price would be recognized in determining value of merchandise destroyed.

The building was only half destroyed. The equipment was almost completely destroyed, only $1,000 being recovered by the insured in a salvage sale. The merchandise was a total loss. It was estimated that office supplies of a value of $150 (not covered by insurance) were destroyed; all supplies were either used or burned.

The annual depreciation rates were: building, 5%; equipment, 10%.

Required:

1. Compute the amount due from insurance companies.

2. Prepare entries to adjust appropriate accounts to date of fire, to record the fire loss, to adjust the books, and to close.

Problem 14–11

The West Company insured the life of its president A. B. West on September 1, 1967, for $50,000. Data concerning the policy are as follows:

Year	Premium	Cash Surrender Value (on Policy Date)
Sept. 1, 1967...............	$3,000	-
Sept. 1, 1968...............	3,000	-
Sept. 1, 1969...............	3,000	$2,700
Sept. 1, 1970...............	3,000	3,900
Sept. 1, 1971...............	3,000	5,460

The policy provides that in case of death the unexpired premium will be refunded up to the end of the month preceding death. The West Company closes its books on December 31. Mr. West died on December 1, 1971.

Required:

1. Give all entries relating to the insurance contract. (Hint: Do not accrue cash surrender value.)

2. Indicate how all amounts relating to the insurance contract would be reported on the financial statement at the end of each year.

chapter 15 | Special Purpose Funds

In preceding chapters current assets, fixed assets (tangible and intangible), investments in stocks, and investments in bonds were discussed in detail. To provide complete coverage of assets in general, this chapter considers *special purpose funds*. Special purpose funds are classified for reporting on the balance sheet in accordance with their particular characteristics; some may be current assets, and others noncurrent; some may be under the direct control of the establishing company, and others may, in accordance with contractual agreements, be under the direct control of a trustee.

The management of a company, at its discretion, may set aside specified assets (usually cash) in a special purpose fund for a particular purpose. A special fund may be simply a segregation of cash (say, in a savings account), or it may consist of investments in securities or other income producing assets. As examples of special purpose funds, a management may set aside funds over a period of time to acquire a new plant site, or to construct a new home office building. Alternatively, the bond sinking fund is typical of one established by contract (the bond indenture). The bond sinking fund typically is accumulated over a period of time and is deposited with a trustee; the funds are to be used to retire the bonds at maturity. Occasionally, special working capital funds are established to meet unusual disbursement requirements such as large current liabilities, special payrolls, cash dividends, and petty cash.

Although the general considerations in this chapter relate to all types of funds, special attention is devoted to those that tend to be significant in amount and to involve long-term arrangements, such as the ones to retire long-term debts, to acquire new or replacement property, and to retire special obligations (such as stock retirement, employee benefit arrangements, and guarantees of performance under long-term contracts). Pension funds are discussed in Chapter 23.

Generally, the accounting for assets constituting special purpose funds should be similar to that for other investments. For example, the same cost and revenue principles apply; the same balance sheet classifications apply; and the same reconciliation and verification procedures should be followed.

Funds Classified

For convenience in discussion the funds and deposits considered in this chapter have been classified as follows:

1. By the use to be made of the assets.
   - *a*) Guarantee of performance of contracts.
   - *b*) Acquisition of noncurrent assets.
   - *c*) Retirement of capital stock.
   - *d*) Payment of noncurrent liabilities.
     - (1) Existing.
     - (2) Prospective.
     - (3) Contingent.
2. By the duration of the fund.
   - *a*) Of temporary nature.
   - *b*) Of an extended nature.
3. By the legal status of the fund.
   - *a*) Voluntarily created.
   - *b*) Legally required.

These classifications overlap; for example, a plant expansion or replacement fund may be classified as follows:

Class	Nature
1(*b*)	When used to acquire new or replacement assets
2(*b*)	When accumulated over a fairly extended period
3(*a*)	When voluntarily created

Similarly, a sinking fund for retirement of bonds payable would be classified as follows:

Class	Nature
1(d)(1)	When accumulated to pay an existing noncurrent liability
2(b)	When accumulated over a fairly extended period
3(b)	When required by a contract

Extent of Fund Accounting

An understanding of the legal status of funds is important to the accountant since he must ascertain whether there has been full compliance with the provisions of the contract when it requires the setting aside of such funds. One principle regarding funds which the accountant should keep in mind is that upon preparing a balance sheet, interest on fund investments should be accrued and added to the fund whereas prospective additions of cash (principal) should not be accrued.

The size, duration, and extent of funds are important because of the effect of such factors upon the records to be maintained. If there are only a few transactions, one account for a fund may suffice since any information desired may be secured readily from an analysis of the account. For example, if it were intended that only cash would be set aside in a sinking fund, the single account, Sinking Fund—Cash, normally would suffice.

On the other hand, if numerous transactions calling for frequent analysis are involved it would seem appropriate to maintain a full set of accounts for the particular fund. For example, the following accounts might be necessary to reflect the sinking fund operations, depending on whether or not the funds are under the control of a designated trustee.

Without Trustee	With Trustee
Sinking fund cash	Sinking fund, X trustee
Sinking fund investments	
Accrued sinking fund income	
Sinking fund income	Sinking fund income
Sinking fund expense	Sinking fund expenses

Essentially, the difference between the two situations above is that where a trustee controls the fund, all fund assets are combined in the single account, "Sinking Fund, X Trustee." Use of the above accounts on the books of the establishing company may be illustrated simply as follows:

Without Trustee   *With Trustee*

1. To record deposit of $5,000 cash in a sinking fund:

Sinking Fund Cash..........5,000		Sinking Fund,	
Cash	5,000	X Trustee 5,000	
		Cash............................	5,000

2. To record purchase of $3,000 of investments:

Sinking Fund Invest-		No entry.
ments..........................3,000		
Sinking Fund		
Cash	3,000	

3. To record $200 accrued interest on the sinking fund investment:

Accrued Sinking Fund In-		No entry.
come...............................200		
Sinking Fund Income...	200	

4. To record $50 expenses on sinking fund:

Sinking Fund Expenses...... 50		No entry.
Sinking Fund Cash	50	

5. To record sinking fund income:

Sinking Fund Income.........200		Sinking Fund, X Trustee.........150		
Sinking Fund		Sinking Fund Income.......		150
Expenses	50			
Income Summary.........	150	Sinking Fund Income.............150		
		Income Summary.............		150

Balance in the sinking			
fund:	$5,150		$5,150

Funds created in accordance with a contract, such as bond sinking fund under a bond indenture or a pension fund for a retirement agreement, generally are administered by a trustee. Where this is the case the specific cash, securities, and other assets of the fund are technically the assets of the trustee. The company's fund asset is actually a claim against the trustee. The company's records should reflect deposits made with the trustee, the fund balance, and a summary of earnings and expenses of the fund based on *periodic reports* from the trustee. The records of the company would not show individual transactions carried on by the trustee such as those relating to the purchase and sale of fund securities and individual security dividend or interest collections and accruals. Of course, it is possible to ignore the separation between company and trustee and to record transactions of the trustee as though the company made them. In order to do this the company obviously would need full and detailed periodic reports from the fund trustee.

Statement Presentation of Funds. Special purpose funds are reported on the balance sheet as current assets or as long-term investments, depending on their nature. Most special purpose funds must be reported as long-term investments. This is true of most special cash funds, as well as for funds in the form of investments in securities. Funds held by trustees are listed as long-term investments even where company withdrawal of the funds is not restricted. Future claims against special purpose funds should be disclosed fully on the balance sheet.

In condensed statements special purpose funds frequently are reported with investments under the general caption "Investments and Funds" immediately after current assets. As an example, recent annual reports of American Motors Corporation and Standard Oil Company (New Jersey) reported them in this manner. When the amount of funds or special deposits is relatively immaterial such assets may be reported with other assets. On the other hand, even when such assets may not be large in relation to other assets it is generally desirable to present them in detail in order to provide adequate disclosure. An interesting example of such reporting is found in Illustration 15–1 which sets out the asset section of the balance sheets of Santa Fe Industries, Inc. Observe that although Special Funds and Investments comprised only about 2.8% of total assets, they are reported in considerable detail and explained by a note.

Illustration 15–1
SANTA FE INDUSTRIES, INC.
Asset Portion of Balance Sheet

ASSETS

	1968	1967
Current Assets:		
Cash ....$	20,649,213	$ 23,875,643
Temporary investments, at cost — approximating market value ...	81,377,689	75,037,263
Accounts receivable...	75,283,277	65,641,409
Inventories, at lower of cost (average or first-in, first-out) or market...	29,953,259	33,243,185
Other current assets..	6,644,976	3,814,755
Total Current Assets ....$	213,908,414	$ 201,612,255
Special Funds and Investments:		
Voluntary bond retirement fund (Note 7) ....$	31,207,735	$ 28,256,203
Other special funds	405,797	371,656
Investments in affiliated companies, at cost...........................	25,213,464	25,351,969
Other investments..	1,175,860	2,082,621
Total Special Funds and Investments...........................$	58,002,856	$ 56,062,449
Properties (See Note below).		
Transportation properties..$2,379,748,629		$2,370,024,852
Other properties.......................................	203,328,736	199,411,494
Total Properties $2,583,077,365		$2,569,436,346
Less — Accumulated depreciation, depletion, and amortization...	815,438,391	843,254,284
Net Properties $1,767,638,974		$1,726,182,062
Other assets and deferred charges.......................................	23,311,183	19,571,566
Total Assets $2,062,861,427		$2,003,428,332

Illustration 15–1 (continued)
Note 7

Long-term debt at December 31, 1968 and 1967 was:

	1968	1967
6¼% subordinated debentures due 1998	$107,529,100	$ —
4% general mortgage bonds due 1995	140,222,000	140,633,000
4% adjustment bonds due 1995	35,782,500	36,343,500
4.3% to 6¾% equipment obligations due 1969 to 1981	134,271,686	127,864,611
5% to 7.9% notes payable due 1969 to 1977	19,354,160	—
Other	1,953,960	1,500,000
Total long-term debt	$439,113,406	$306,341,111
Due within one year	26,990,718	23,570,087
Due after one year	$412,122,688	$282,771,024

The debentures (redeemable after July 31, 1973) are convertible until August 1, 1988, into Industries common stock at $32 per share, subject to adjustment under antidilution provisions.

Approximately 11,990 main track miles, all railroad equipment except equipment subject to prior lien under outstanding equipment trust certificates and purchase contracts and substantially all railroad supporting facilities are subject to lien of the mortgages securing the general mortgage bonds and adjustment bonds.

The contents of the voluntary bond retirement fund at year-end were:

	1968	1967
U.S. government and municipal securities (at cost), accrued interest thereon and cash	$ 31,207,735	$ 28,256,203
General mortgage bonds and adjustment bonds (offset against long-term debt)	23,556,000	21,650,500
	$ 54,763,735	$ 49,906,703

In addition, $5,123,000 of general mortgage bonds and $2,987,000 of adjustment bonds were held in Railway's treasury at December 31, 1968, and such amounts have been deducted from long-term debt.

Planning for Debt Retirement. A bond *sinking fund* is a fund of assets (cash and securities) usually deposited with a trustee, to be used to retire a large bond issue at its maturity. The fund customarily is accumulated over the life of the bond issue by periodic payments made by the corporation to the trustee. The trustee often is authorized to use sinking fund assets to purchase bonds of the funded liability when the market price is favorable. These bonds when purchased by the trustee may be held "alive" in the fund (the corporation continues to pay interest), or they may be canceled. The trustee, in some cases, also serves as the agent of the corporation for the payment of interest on the bonds. In such cases, payments to the trustee must be sufficient to cover sinking fund requirements and also to make the periodic interest payments.

In planning the sinking fund, the amount which will be required to pay the liability as well as the time to maturity are known. It was shown in Chapter 5 how to determine the equal periodic contribution required to accumulate a fixed sum by a given future date on the assumption that a certain earning rate can be realized. It will be recalled that the computation simply involves dividing the principal amount of the bond issue by the *amount of an annuity of 1* for the number of periods at an appropriate interest rate. The computation and related entries are illustrated below.

Illustrative Problem. On January 1, 1971, the XY Corporation issued $200,000 bonds payable, 8% annual interest payable December 31 and June 30, maturity date December 31, 1975. The bond indenture required that a bond sinking fund be established through equal semiannual payments to be made to Trustee X. The payments to the sinking fund were to be made each June 30 and December 31 starting June 30, 1971 and ending on date of maturity; the fund is to earn 4% semiannually and is to be sufficient on maturity date to retire the bond principal. The requirements are: (*a*) to compute the semiannual payments to the sinking fund and (*b*) to prepare a sinking fund table which shows the theoretical fund accumulation.

Solution:

1. To compute the semiannual payments required:

Number of semiannual periods June 30, 1971, to December 31, 1975 = 10.

Periodic payment = $200,000 ÷ amount of annuity of 1 for 10 periods
@4%
= $200,000 ÷ 12.0061071 (Table 5–3)
= $16,658.19

2. A sinking fund table indicating the theoretical fund accumulation is shown in Illustration 15–2.

Illustration 15–2
Sinking Fund Table (theoretical accumulation)

Date	Cash (Cr.)	Sinking Fund Income (Cr.)	Sinking Fund (dr.)	Sinking Fund (Dr.)
6–30–71........$	16,658.19		$ 16,658.19	$ 16,658.19
12–31–71........	16,658.19	$ 666.33°	17,324.52†	33,982.71‡
6–30–72........	16,658.19	1,359.31	18,017.50	52,000.21
12–31–72........	16,658.19	2,080.01	18,738.20	70,738.41
6–30–73........	16,658.19	2,829.54	19,487.73	90,226.14
12–31–73........	16,658.19	3,609.05	20,267.24	110,493.38
6–30–74........	16,658.19	4,419.74	21,077.93	131,571.31
12–31–74........	16,658.19	5,262.85	21,921.04	153,492.35
6–30–75........	16,658.19	6,139.69	22,797.88	176,290.23
12–31–75........	16,658.16	7,051.61	23,709.77	200,000.00
	$166,581.87	$33,418.13	$200,000.00	

° $16,658.19 × .04 = $666.33
† $16,658.19 + $666.33 = $17,324.52
‡ $16,658.19 + $17,324.52 = $33,982.71

Theoretical versus Actual Accumulations

The use of mathematically prepared sinking fund tables, as illustrated above, is predicated on the theory that the fund balance will earn interest at a given rate—which income, in turn, will earn interest at the given rate, hence, the fund theoretically will accumulate and compound to a predetermined accurate balance at a specified future time (theoretical accumulation). Practically, however, the mathematically calculated sinking fund installments will seldom give exactly the correct final balance to the fund because the actual earnings of a fund cannot be forecasted precisely. There are three methods available for resolving this particular problem. The data and computations shown in Illustration 15–2 are continued for illustrative purposes.

1. The semiannual fund installment may be established at an even amount, say, $16,500 in the above example. Any income earned on the fund to be deducted from the next annual installment. For example, if the actual earnings of the fund at 12–31–71 were $650; at 6–30–72, $1,340; and at 12–31–72, $2,120, the payments to the fund would be:

```
12-31-71.................$16,500 - $   650 = $15,850
 6-30-72.................  16,500 -  1,340 =  15,160
12-31-72.................  16,500 -  2,120 =  14,380
```

2. The semiannual sinking fund installment may be set at $16,658.19 plus any amount needed to bring the fund balance to the total shown for the respective date in the table to make up for any shortage of sinking fund income; overages of sinking fund income would have exactly the opposite effect.

For example, assuming the same actual interest earnings as in No. 1 above, the adjusted contributions would be:

Contribution Planned	Interest Shortage or Overage (Add Shortage; Deduct Overage)	Payment Required
$16,658.19..................	$ 666.33 - $ 650.00 = $16.33	$16,674.52
16,658.19..................	1,359.31 - 1,340.00 = 19.31	16,677.50
16,658.19..................	2,080.01 - 2,120.00 = (39.99)	16,618.20

3. The basic semiannual sinking fund installment may be set at a figure approximating the sum computed by using the annuity tables, usually by rounding to the next highest figure, and the firm may guarantee that the fund will earn the designated rate of interest. Shortages or overages of periodic sinking fund income would then be eliminated by adjusting the next semiannual installment so that the actual sinking fund balance will be the predetermined balance. Any small varia-

tion due to rounding off the semiannual sinking fund installment would be adjusted during the last period.

Example:

Assume the periodic payments are to be $16,600, plus or minus income supplements (or decrements) to equal the theoretical balance.

Dates	Desired Balance	−	Previous Balance	+	Actual Income	=	Period's Payment
12–31–71............$33,982.71		−	($16,600.00°)	+	$ 650.00)	=	$16,732.71
6–30–71............ 52,000.21		−	(33,982.71)	+	1,340.00)	=	16,677.50
12–31–72............ 70,738.41		−	(52,000.21)	+	2,120.00)	=	16,618.20

° Payment first period.

Methods 2 and 3 usually are preferred over Method 1, since for a bond issue with a long maturity, they should give approximately uniform periodic payments.

Sinking Funds to Pay Bond Interest and Retire Bond Principal

Governmental units quite frequently levy a constant tax to establish a sinking fund to provide for *both* the interest and principal of an issue of municipal bonds. Industrial firms may also use such a fund, making payments to a trustee to retire principal and make the periodic interest payments to bondholders. The entries for a sinking fund to retire both the principal and the periodic interest coupons are similar to the entries for an ordinary sinking fund as shown in Illustration 15–2.

To illustrate the situation where the trustee is to make the periodic interest payments and also retire the bonds at maturity, we can again utilize the data presented above for Illustration 15–2. The data are repeated for convenience. The XY Corporation issued $200,000 bonds payable, dated January 1, 1971, maturity December 31, 1975, interest 9% per annum payable on June 30 and December 31. A sinking fund is to be created by equal semiannual payments made to Trustee X starting June 30, 1971, of sufficient amount to (a) pay the semiannual interest to the bondholders of $9,000 (i.e., $200,000 × 4½%) and (b) to accumulate a $200,000 fund by maturity date to retire the bonds. It is assumed that the fund will earn 4% each semiannual period. The semiannual payment to the trustee would be computed as follows:

Sinking fund requirement (as computed on page 614)
$200,000 ÷ 12.0061071...............................$16,658.19
Semiannual interest requirement $200,000 ×
4½% 9,000.00
Total Semiannual Contribution................$25,658.19

Illustration 15–3

Tabulation of Entries for Bond Sinking Fund to Pay Interest and Principal

		Cash, Cr.°	Sinking Fund Income Dr., Cr.°	Accrued Sinking Fund Income Dr., Cr.°	Bond Sinking Fund Dr., Cr.°	Bond Interest Expense Dr., Cr.°	Accrued Bond Interest Payable Dr., Cr.°	Income Summary Dr.
6-30-71	Payment to fund	$25,658.19°			$25,658.19			
6-30-71	Payment of bond interest†				9,000.00°	$ 9,000.00		
8-31-71	Adjusting entry		$ 222.11°	$ 222.11		3,000.00	$3,000.00°	
8-31-71	Closing entry		222.11			12,000.00		$11,777.89
9-1-71	Reversing entry		222.11	222.11°		3,000.00°	3,000.00	
12-31-71	Payment to fund	25,658.19°	666.33°		26,324.52			
12-31-71	Payment of bond interest				9,000.00°	9,000.00		
6-30-72	Payment to fund	25,658.19°	1,359.31°		27,017.50			
6-30-72	Payment of bond interest				9,000.00°	9,000.00		
8-31-72	Adjusting entry		693.37°	693.37		3,000.00	3,000.00°	
8-31-72	Closing entry		2,496.90			18,000.00°		15,503.10
9-1-72	Reversing entry		693.37	693.37°		3,000.00°	3,000.00	
12-3-72	Payment to fund	25,658.19°	2,080.01°		27,738.20			
12-31-72	Payment of bond interest				9,000.00°	9,000.00		
6-30-73	Payment to fund	25,658.19°	2,829.54°		28,487.73			
6-30-73	Payment of bond interest				9,000.00°	9,000.00		
8-31-73	Adjusting entry		1,203.02°	1,203.02		3,000.00	3,000.00°	
8-31-73	Closing entry		5,419.20			18,000.00°		12,580.80
9-1-73	Reversing entry		1,203.02	1,203.02°		3,000.00°	3,000.00	

† ($25,658.19 − $9,000.00) × .04 × 2/12 = $222.11

A tabulation of all of the related entries including adjusting, closing, and reversing entries is presented in Illustration 15–3. The tabulation assumes that interest earnings were exactly as anticipated in the theoretical accumulation; to the extent this assumption might not be borne out in actual experience, procedures discussed in the preceding section can be applied. It is also assumed in Illustration 15–3 that the fiscal year of XY Corporation ends on August 31. The tabulation is carried through September of the third year of the sinking fund —a sufficient period to illustrate the pertinent entries.

Alternatives to Present Value Calculation Bases

Earlier illustrations in this chapter have been based on traditional sinking fund procedures. Modern corporate financial practice may differ in several respects because there is a growing recognition that ultimate security to bondholder rests more on the corporation's ability to earn profits and to generate cash than on regular contributions of uniform amounts to a sinking fund. Some alternatives to following a rigid actuarial schedule of sinking fund contribution include basing the contribution on some variables which cannot be predicted precisely. This recognition that the amount of cash available for fund deposits may vary sharply with operating and business conditions is manifest in basing the periodic fund contributions on variables such as:

1. *Output.* Where, for example, bonds are secured by a mortgage on wasting property, it is logical to increase fund contributions as the security decreases in value through removal and as revenue fluctuates more or less in proportion to output.

2. *Earnings.* This plan is particularly appropriate to stock redemption funds in that the amount of stock to be retired in a given year frequently is based upon the amount of net income of the preceding year.

3. *Scheduled variables.* For example, if bond issue proceeds are used for plant construction, the effect of the improvement on company earnings is delayed until completion and then may show only a gradual rise in revenue. Accordingly, arrangements may be made to postpone contributions for a number of years, then to adopt a schedule of fixed or increasing contributions.

Appropriation of Retained Earnings

The same contract or plan calling for accumulation of a fund frequently requires a related restriction on dividend payments. By making a portion of retained earnings unavailable for dividends, disbursements which might otherwise be made to stockholders may be reduced or eliminated. The result sought by such a restriction is continued ability of the company to make fund contributions as they come due by restricting the demand for funds during the interim period.

Traditional sinking fund practice was to maintain a balance in Retained Earnings Appropriated for Bond Sinking Fund (sometimes called Reserve for Bond Sinking Fund) parallel in amount to the sinking fund balance. For example, the company creating the fund shown in Illustration 15–2 would have made the following additional entries:

	6/30/71	12/31/71	6/30/72
Retained Earnings	16,658.19	17,324.52	18,017.50
Retained Earnings Appropriated for Bond Sinking Fund.................	16,658.19	17,324.52	18,017.50

	12/31/72	6/30/73
Retained Earnings	18,738.20	19,487.73
Retained Earnings Appropriated for Bond Sinking Fund.................	18,738.20	19,487.73

In such a case the sinking fund is said to be provided "out of income." Actually the money set aside could come from a variety of sources and would have to be contributed, regardless of profits, to prevent the bonds from becoming defaulted. Of course, if the company continuously failed to realize net income, ability to continue to make fund contributions would be jeopardized and default might occur. The appropriation is provided "out of income," but the income may be past rather than current income.

Sound financial practice frequently indicates the need for a restriction on dividend payments so long as long-term debt is outstanding, but the determination of the amount of the restriction is likely to be somewhat different from that which has just been illustrated. We have seen that the increase in the sinking fund appropriation did not necessarily come from most recent income. Indeed, so long as any balance remained in unappropriated Retained Earnings, the appropriation balance could be augmented. Since this is true it would follow also that dividends could be paid so long as any balance remained in unappropriated Retained Earnings. Thus, a gradual buildup of a Reserve for Sinking Fund out of Retained Earnings (currently accumulated or otherwise) does not necessarily provide the protection sought by the reserve requirement. For this reason modern bond indentures may provide for the "freezing" of all or part of the Retained Earnings balance as of date of issuance, the restriction to remain effective until the bonds are retired. This would mean that no dividends could be paid from the restricted portion. Other restrictions to safeguard bondholders are employed, sometimes in conjunction with surplus freezing. Examples of these include limitations on added borrowing, limitation on redemption of stock, maintenance of working capital above a certain minimum figure, and maintenance of the specified financial statement ratios in excess of a certain minimum. Disclosure of these restrictions should be made in notes accompanying the balance sheet.

A growing number of the 600 companies included in the survey *Accounting Trends and Techniques* report the existence of restrictions on retained earnings as a result of bond or note indentures or other credit agreements. In 1969, 420 companies reported such restrictions; there has been a modest increase since 1960 when 392 of the 600 companies reported such restrictions.[1]

Purchase of Own Bonds with Sinking Fund Assets

It is a common practice to use sinking fund assets to acquire bonds of the issue for which the fund was created to retire. Acquisition of the bonds for which the fund was created usually is done because it may effect a net saving of interest. A net saving would be effected when the bonds pay a higher rate of interest than the sinking fund is scheduled to earn (after deduction of trustee expenses and investment costs).

When bonds of an issue are purchased before maturity with assets of the sinking fund dedicated to the redemption or retirement of that issue, the accounting treatment is dependent on whether the bonds are formally canceled or kept "alive" in the sinking fund. If the repurchased bonds are kept "alive" by the trustee as a part of the sinking fund assets, he should account for them like any other sinking fund investment. He would receive regular interest payments on them from the issuer and would report such interest as a part of sinking fund income. In some instances he may decide to resell the bonds being held, should he deem the market price favorable at a later date. If the bonds of the issuer acquired by the trustee are to be canceled, an entry for retirement should be made. If the sinking fund is under the direct control of the issuing corporation, reacquired bonds should either be canceled or recorded as treasury bonds. To illustrate these situations, assume that $100,000 bonds payable, out of a $1 million issue that is funded, are purchased at 100.5 from sinking fund assets dedicated to their retirement. Assume further that the unamortized bond discount on the books of the issuer with respect to the $100,000 bonds reacquired was $800 on the date of purchase, which was an interest date. The indicated entries on the books of the issuing corporation under several assumptions are indicated below:

Situation A: Sinking fund under direct control of trustee; reacquired bonds to be kept alive in the sinking fund.

---

[1] *Accounting Trends and Techniques*, 1970 ed., p. 150.

No entry on books of issuing corporation except to reflect any sinking fund income subsequently reported by trustee. Issuing corporation pays interest on the reacquired bonds (to trustee).

Situation B: Sinking fund under direct control of trustee; reacquired bonds to be canceled.

Bonds Payable	100,000	
Loss on Redemption of Bonds Payable	1,300	
Unamortized Discount on Bonds Payable		800
Sinking Fund, Trustee		100,500

Situation C: Sinking fund under direct control of issuing corporation (no trustee); reacquired bonds to be formally retired.

Bonds Payable	100,000	
Loss on Redemption of Bonds Payable	1,300	
Unamortized Discount on Bonds Payable		800
Sinking Fund Cash		100,500

Situation D: Sinking fund under direct control of issuing corporation (no trustee); reacquired bonds not to be retired.

Treasury Bonds (payable)	100,000	
Loss on Acquisition of Treasury Bonds	1,300	
Unamortized Discount on Bonds Payable		800
Sinking Fund Cash		100,500

In this case interest payments would not be made or recognized on the books of the corporation for the bonds held in the treasury. The treasury bonds should be deducted from bonds payable on the balance sheet. Loss on bond redemption would ordinarily be reported on the income statement as extraordinary items (net of tax effect).

It should be pointed out that there is some difference of opinion among the authorities as to whether the "repurchased bonds held alive" by the trustee should be considered a fund asset and any interest paid on them be treated as both interest expense and fund income, or as to whether the bonds should be considered as a reduction of liabilities and, therefore, any interest paid on them treated as merely an additional contribution to the fund. In the latter event, bond interest expense and fund interest income are reduced by the amount of the cash transfer to the sinking fund trustee which is treated as an added sinking fund contribution rather than as interest. If the trustee bought the bonds at a price different from their carrying value on the issuer's books the two parties would have different amounts of amortization to reflect in adjusting bond values toward par as maturity approached (unless, of course, they were carried at par).

Regulation S-X of the SEC provides:

Reacquired evidences of indebtedness shall be shown separately as a deduction, under the appropriate liability caption. However, reacquired evidences of indebtedness held for pension and other special funds not related to the particular issues may be shown as assets of such funds, provided that there be stated parenthetically the amount of such evidences of indebtedness, the cost thereof, and the amount at which carried.

Sinking Funds for Serial Bonds

One of the advantages claimed for serial bond issues is that they eliminate the need for sinking funds. This is particularly the case where uniform maturities occur at regular intervals, payments of bonds as they mature would impose cash requirements similar to those attending accumulation of a sinking fund. To illustrate, assume a $200,000 serial bond issue dated January 1, 1971, had the following maturity schedule:

Date Due	Amount
1/1/72	$ 40,000
1/1/73	40,000
1/1/74	40,000
1/1/75	40,000
1/1/76	40,000
	$200,000

Instead of making five annual payments of approximately $40,000 to a bond sinking fund, the debtor directly retires $40,000 of debt annually. Alternatively, serial bond issues that call for *irregular* payments to retire the bond issue create a potential need for a bond sinking fund. To illustrate this latter situation, assume $60,000 is borrowed on January 1, 1971, with maturities scheduled as below:

Date Due	Amount
1/1/72	$10,000
7/1/72	20,000
1/1/73	30,000
	$60,000

Note that irregular amounts are to be repaid at irregular intervals (no payment is due until 12 months elapse). Installments for a sinking fund calling for regular payments at the end of four six-month intervals may be calculated as follows:

Step 1: Ascertain the sum of the compound amounts (amount of 1) of the different maturity payments from the due date of the first payment to the last maturity date.

Step 2: Divide this sum by the amount of an ordinary annuity of 1 for the number of periods of the bonds with the last maturity date. On the assumption the sinking fund can earn 2% each semiannual interest period, the calculation would show:

$$\$10,000 \times (1.02)^2 = \$10,404$$
$$20,000 \times (1.02) = 20,400$$
$$30,000 = \underline{30,000}$$
$$\underline{\underline{\$60,804}}$$

Periodic payment
to sinking fund = $60,804 ÷ Amount of annuity of 1, 4 periods @ 2%
= $60,804 ÷ 4.121608 (Table 5–3)
= $\underline{\$14,752.49}$

The correctness of this answer and the related entries are indicated in Illustration 15–4.

Illustration 15–4
Bond Sinking Fund Table—for Serial Bonds

End of—	Cash Cr.	Income Cr.†	Sinking Fund Dr., Cr.°	Bonds Payable Dr.	Sinking Fund Balance
6 months	$14,752.49	–	$14,752.49	–	$14,752.49
12 months	14,752.49	$295.05	15,047.54	–	29,800.03
12 months	–	–	10,000.00°	$10,000.00	19,800.03
18 months	14,752.49	396.00	15,148.49	–	34,948.52
18 months	–	–	20,000.00°	20,000.00	14,948.52
24 months	14,752.51	298.97	15,051.48	–	30,000.00
24 months	–	–	30,000.00°	30,000.00	–

† 2% of previous fund balance.

Funds for Other Purposes

While the discussion in this chapter has centered on funds for bond retirement, funds also are provided for other long-range purposes. The classification under item 1 on page 609 indicates the nature of some of these. Generally speaking, the same accounting procedures apply to these other funds; viz., they may or may not call for payments to maintain their rate of growth on an actuarial basis, they may or may not be paralleled by an appropriation of retained earnings, they may or may not be managed by an independent trustee, etc. The chapter is now concluded with a brief discussion of some funds for other purposes.

Deposits to Secure Guarantee of Performance. Bidders on long-term construction contracts and potential suppliers of materials under contracts which cannot be fulfilled promptly under a single delivery are often required to deposit a proportion of the consideration of the contract or other material lump-sum amount as a guarantee of performance. The amount put up by the successful bidder remains on deposit with the purchaser until fulfillment of the contract at which time it is refunded, possibly with interest added. While such guarantees of performance are often secured under an insurance contract called a performance bond contract, some bidders may prefer to put up cash or other liquid assets in order (1) to save premiums which would otherwise have to be paid to the bondsman or (2) to possibly earn interest during the deposit period. If cash or securities owned are thus placed in escrow or turned over to the other party to the long-term contract, it is necessary to reflect this fact in the financial statements. A journal entry would be required crediting the assets transferred and debiting an account such as Cash (or Securities) on Deposit to Secure Contract Performance. The balance in such an account normally should be reported as a fund rather than as a current asset.

Plant Expansion Funds. Funds established for this purpose should be accounted for in essentially the same manner as bond sinking funds. Plant expansion funds, unlike bond sinking funds, are purely discretionary. Such funds can be diverted by management for other purposes. A plant expansion fund should be reported under the investments and funds caption and not under plant and equipment. The latter treatment would be unsound because the fund is not used as a plant asset. Plant expansion funds might be created in view of such considerations as an expected change in construction costs or present unavailability of materials (as in wartime or other emergency periods), or simply as an orderly means of accumulating the assets needed for a particular purpose.

Stock Retirement Funds. Companies which have issued *redeemable* preferred stock sometimes accumulate funds for redemption of the callable shares. Provision of a fund for this purpose may be required under terms of the stock issue contract. The assets of a stock retirement fund should be accounted for in essentially the same manner as other funds discussed earlier in this chapter and would be reported under the investments and funds caption of the balance sheet.

QUESTIONS FOR CLASS DISCUSSION

1. Define special purpose funds.
2. Basically, funds may be classified on three bases; indicate the nature of each classification.
3. What is the distinction between (a) a fund under the direct control of a trustee and (b) a fund under the direct control of the establishing company?
4. Basically, how does the distinction made in Question 3 affect the accounting for funds?
5. How should special purpose funds be reported on the balance sheet?
6. What is a bond sinking fund?

7. Distinguish between theoretical accumulation and actual accumulation of a bond sinking fund.

8. How may a bond sinking fund be related to the appropriation of retained earnings?

9. Under what conditions might it be desirable to use sinking fund assets to purchase bonds of the issue for which the fund was created?

10. Under what conditions might it be desirable to hold "alive" bonds purchased before maturity with funds from a sinking fund accumulated to retire those bonds at maturity?

11. Outline the accounting for bonds purchased before maturity out of sinking fund assets accumulated to retire those bonds at maturity.

DECISION CASE 15–1

The Hassett Company, Inc., issued $1 million of 20-year, 8% bonds dated May 1, 1972, interest payable May 1 and November 1. The company used the proceeds for plant expansion. The indenture requires the establishment of a sinking fund by annual payments of $50,000 to a trustee, starting March 31, 1973. The indenture also requires an annual appropriation of $50,000 "to be set aside out of earnings."

The 1973 payment was made on March 31, and on April 1, 1973, the trustee purchased $50,000 face amount of the company's bonds on the open market. In view of this "reacquisition of bonds," the annual appropriation of retained earnings was omitted.

A financial analyst criticized the company's statement of net income for the fiscal year ended April 30, 1973, on the basis that "it overstates earnings by $50,000, since it shows no charge for the annual payment to the trustee and leads investors to believe there are earnings available for dividends which the company is in no position to pay."

Required:

1. Explain whether or not the omission of the appropriation was justified and evaluate the analyst's criticism.

2. What advantages might attend the purchase of the company's own bonds instead of securities issued by other corporations?

(AICPA adapted)

DECISION CASE 15–2

The STU Company issued bonds of a par value of $500,000 to finance plant expansion. Pursuant to the terms of bond indenture, a sinking fund was created for the eventual retirement of the bonds, and also a sinking fund reserve was established. At the maturity date of the bonds, the sinking fund was utilized to retire the bonds.

Required:

1. What purposes were served by having both a sinking fund and a sinking fund reserve?

2. Discuss fully the disposition of the sinking fund reserve after the bonds have been retired, including consideration of various alternatives.

(AICPA adapted)

EXERCISES

Exercise 15–1

The AB Corporation issued $1 million, 6% bonds payable; they were issued at par and mature December 31, 1972.

On December 29, 1972, the sinking fund balances were: Cash, $172,000; investments, $900,000 (at cost).

The AB Corporation has apporpriated retained earnings for the bond sinking fund amounted to $965,000.

The sinking fund earned $5,000.

On December 30, 1972, the sinking fund securities were sold for $927,000.

On December 31, 1972, the last semiannual interest payment on the bonds was paid and the bonds were retired in full; both payments were made out of the bond sinking fund.

Required:

1. Assume the fund was under the direct control of the AB Corporation. Give all entries indicated on books of AB Corporation (use totals when detail is not available) relative to the fund.

2. Assume the fund was under the direct control of Trustee Y. Give all entries indicated on the books of AB Corporation (use totals when detail not available) relative to the fund.

Exercise 15–2

Ace Corporation will need a special fund of $200,000 by January 1, 1973. Beginning January 1, 1969, the treasurer of the company feels the company can afford to set aside as much as $36,000 each January 1 to accumulate the required sum. Jim Mathwhiz is an employee of the company; he calculates that periodic contributions to a fund in the amount of $35,479.28 will result in accumulation of the required amount if the funds invested earn 6% per annum, and the earnings are allowed to remain in the fund to earn additional interest. Set up a table to show that Mathwhiz is right or wrong.

Exercise 15–3

Prepare a sinking fund table to show the theoretical accumulation of a $400,000 sinking fund under an arrangement whereby an equal amount is contributed each year on September 30, beginning September 30, 1968. The desired amount is to be accumulated by September 30, 1973, date of the last payment. The fund earns 6% compounded annually.

Exercise 15–4

A $90,000 plant expansion fund is desired; semiannual deposits of $21,407.98 have been decided upon, starting March 1, 1972. The fund will earn 2% interest each semiannual period and the fund is needed one period after the last deposit. You are to (a) compute the number of deposits and (b) construct a fund accumulation table.

Exercise 15–5

Company X has need of a $200,000 sinking fund by June 30, 1974, date of the last payment, to retire a bond issue. Semiannual contributions are to be made each six months beginning December 31, 1969. Compute the required contribution on the assumption 4% can be earned each six months. If on June 30, 1973, the sinking fund balance was $153,492.35, give Company X's entries at December 31, 1973, and June 30, 1974. Assume a sinking fund reserve is being maintained parallel with the fund.

Exercise 15-6

On January 1, 1971, Cox Corporation authorized and sold an issue of 10-year, $500,000, 5% bonds at 90. The issue of bonds of $500 and $1,000 denominations provided for annual interest payments. The trust deed provided that "there shall be established a fund to be called the Bond Sinking Fund, to the account of which there shall on the 31st day of December of each year be carried a sum equal to 7% of the total par value of the bonds issued, and that, out of the monies so carried to the account of said fund, the company shall pay the interest on the bonds as it becomes due, and the balance of said monies shall be expended each year in purchasing the bonds of the company in the open market."

In January 1972 the company purchased $10,000 of its bonds at 97 and retired and canceled them. In January 1973 the market price of the bonds was 98.

Required:

1. How many bonds can be purchased from the bond sinking fund in January 1973?

2. Make journal entries for all the transactions from the date of the sale of the bonds to and including the purchase for the sinking fund in January 1973.

3. Show trial balance of the accounts involved after posting the above entries.

Exercise 15-7

The Baker Corporation issued $100,000, 5% bonds payable at 95. The bonds mature in 10 years, and the interest is payable on an annual basis. A sinking fund has been established; payments were started at the beginning of the fifth year of the life of the bonds. The sinking fund is to increase one fifth each year.

At the end of the eighth year $50,000 of the outstanding bonds were purchased exinterest at 90 with sinking fund assets; the purchase was on the eighth interest date.

Give entry, or entries, on the issuer's books for the acquisition under each of the following separate assumptions. If no entry is required indicate the reason therefor.

a) The sinking fund is under the direct control of a trustee and the reacquired bonds are to be kept alive in the sinking fund.

b) The sinking fund is under the direct control of a trustee and the reacquired bonds are to be canceled.

c) The sinking fund is under the direct control of the issuing corporation (no trustee); the reacquired bonds are to be kept alive.

d) The sinking fund is under the direct control of the issuing corporation (no trustee); the reacquired bonds are to be canceled.

PROBLEMS

Problem 15–1

Part A. In order to manufacture and sell its products a company must invest in inventories, plant and equipment, and other operating assets. In addition, a manufacturing company often finds it desirable or necessary to invest a portion of its available resources, either directly or through the operation of special funds, in stocks, bonds, and other securities.

Required:

1. List the reasons why a manufacturing company might invest funds in stocks, bonds and other securities.
2. What are the criteria for classifying investments as current or noncurrent assets?

Part B. Because of favorable market prices the trustee of Walker Company's bond sinking fund invested the current year's contribution to the fund in the company's own bonds. The bonds are being held in the fund without cancellation. The fund also includes cash and securities of other companies.

Required:

Describe three methods of classifying the bond sinking fund on the balance sheet of Walker Company. Include a discussion of the propriety of each method.

(AICPA adapted)

Problem 15–2

Give journal entries for the transactions listed below relating to the bond sinking fund; include year-end entries at December 31. The MO Company maintains a balance in Retained Earnings Appropriated for Sinking Fund equal to the sinking fund. Compute interest on a 360-day basis. There is no trustee.

12/31/69 Transferred $10,000 cash to sinking fund.
1/5/70 Sinking fund cash used to purchase $10,000 face value of 5% bonds of X Company at 98 plus accrued interest from January 1; amortize discount over 20 years.
7/1/70 Coupons on above bonds collected (semiannual).
12/31/70 Another $10,000 transferred to sinking fund.
1/1/71 Coupons collected.
1/2/71 Sinking fund cash used to purchase $11,000 face value of 5% bonds of Y Company at 95 plus accrued interest from January 1; amortize discount over 10 years; semiannual interest.
7/1/71 Coupons collected.
12/31/71 Sinking fund expenses of $125 paid.
12/31/71 Another $10,000 transferred to sinking fund.
1/1/72 Coupons collected.
1/10/72 Sinking fund cash used to purchase $10,000 face value of 5% bonds of Z Company at 101 plus accrued interest from January 1.

(AICPA adapted)

Problem 15–3

Lemmon Corporation issued $50,000 of bonds payable on January 1, 1971, at par. The bonds mature December 31, 1975; the 6% per annum interest is payable each June 30 and December 31. Arrangements are made to make all interest payments through a sinking fund trustee, the Zenon Trust Company. It is calculated that semiannual payments of $6,033.33 to the trustee will handle interest requirements and will provide a $50,000 sinking fund at the maturity date of the bonds provided the sinking fund trustee invests the amounts in excess of interest expense requirements to earn 2% each semi-annual interest period on a compound interest basis. Lemmon Corporation adjusts and closes its books annually each August 31.

Required:

Prepare a tabulation of all entries related to the sinking fund and interest, including adjusting, closing, and reversing entries through September 1, 1973, for Lemmon Corporation.

Problem 15-4

Under terms of a bond indenture contract, XYZ Company was required to maintain a sinking fund administered by an independent trustee. Accordingly XYZ entered into a contract with the National Trust Company which provided for payments of $10,000 into a fund to be administered by the trust company. These payments were to be made each January 1, and the trust company agreed to invest the money in Grade Aa (or better) bonds and Grade Aa (or better) preferred stocks. The contract provided that for the next five years the yield on all money in the fund was to be a minimum of 3%. In the event the fund failed to earn 3% (before trustee's commission) in any year the trust company was to receive no compensation for administering the fund. Otherwise it would earn 7% of the income of the fund as a commission.

The trust company further agreed to pay a flat 1% on the minimum balance of uninvested cash in the fund during each year. The 7% commission would not be computed on this 1% penalty interest but would be figured on the basis of all other income earned by the fund.

On January 1, 1972, $10,000 was deposited with the trust company as a first installment. On March 1, 1972, $8,216 was invested in $8,000 par value bonds of ABC Company. Interest is at the rate of 5% per annum and is paid semi-annually each February 28 and August 31. The bonds mature August 31, 1976 (use straight line amortization). On April 1, $1,000 was invested in $800 par value 6% cumulative preferred stock of Arco Company. This stock has regularly paid dividends each January 31, and no dividends are in arrears.

Interest credited by the trustee and commission paid to trustee both affect sinking fund cash and are to be paid each December 31.

Required:

1. Journalize all transactions by the trustee during 1972 including year-end adjustments and payments.

2. Give entries on the XYZ Company's books to reflect the sinking fund transactions with the trustee.

Problem 15-5

Richardson Corporation will need a $100,000 sinking fund at the end of 1980. It contracts with Milton Trust Company to make equal annual deposits commencing December 31, 1971; the last deposit to occur December 31,

1980. The trust company agrees to pay 6% per annum compound interest on the deposits.

Required:

1. Calculate the proper amount of each annual deposit under terms of the proposed contract.

2. Prepare a tabulation showing the theoretical accumulation of 6% is in fact earned and credited by the trust company.

3. Assuming that Richardson also maintains a sinking fund reserve parallel to the fund, give entries for the reserve as of December 31, 1971, 1972, and 1973.

Problem 15-6

XYZ Corporation issued serial bonds on March 1, 1972, in the amount of $500,000 maturing as follows:

Serial A—March 1, 1973 ....$100,000
Serial B—March 1, 1975 200,000
Serial C—March 1, 1976 200,000

Required:

Assuming the sinking fund earns 4% compounded annually and four equal contributions are to be made—

a) Compute the annual sinking fund installment for retirement of the serial bonds.

b) Prepare a table of entries covering the entire life of the fund; assume that the first contribution to the sinking fund is made on March 1, 1973.

Problem 15-7

The directors of the SMT Corporation authorized the establishment of an Employees' Purchases Fund to be under the direction of an officer of the company as trustee and ordered the treasurer of the company to transfer from general cash to the trustee of the Employees' Purchases Fund the sum of $100,000 for his use in carrying out the purpose for which the fund was created.

In its authorizing resolution the directors stipulated that—

a) The fund was established for the purpose of purchasing automobiles, refrigerators, stoves, furniture and the like, to be resold to SMT Corporation employees at cost plus 5%.

b) Merchandise would be sold for cash or in accordance with a deferred payment plan which provided for interest at the rate of one half of 1% per month on any unpaid balance.

c) No trade-ins would be accepted as part payment.

d) Any merchandise recovered by the trustee as the result of nonpayment of installments was to be transferred to the corporation, for its use or disposal, at the value allowed by the trustee as a basis of recovery.

e) The trustee was to deposit in a separate bank account the sum received from the corporation for the initial capital of the fund and to handle through such account all subsequent transactions, including operating expenses, incident to the purchase of merchandise and its sale to employees.

f) The amount appropriated was to be a revolving fund, to be considered an investment of the corporation.

g) An adequate system of accounts was to be set up to reflect the current transactions, to provide a general ledger control of inventories and a basis for adequate financial statements relative to its condition and operating results.

Required:

Submit a classification of the trustee's general ledger accounts with descriptions of typical entries for each and their resulting balances.

(AICPA adapted)

<table>
<tr><td>chapter 16</td><td>Current and
Contingent Liabilities</td></tr>
</table>

Current and Contingent Liabilities

In general, liabilities are obligations that result from past transactions to pay assets or render services in the future which are definite in amount (or subject to reasonable estimation) as stated or implied in oral or written contracts. Consequently, the problems of their identification and measurement are not as serious as those encountered with respect to assets. From the going-concern viewpoint, all liabilities are payable at some point in time. Broadly, liabilities may be classified as (*a*) current, (*b*) long term, and (*c*) contingent.[1] In accounting for liabilities, the primary problem is one of making certain that no liabilities are omitted from the records and reports. The presence of an asset generally can be determined, whereas the existence of certain liabilities may be hard to ascertain. Accountants frequently are in situations where it is to the advantage of certain parties to overstate assets and understate liabilities. In particular, the accountant on occasion may find it almost impossible to learn of all liabilities, such as those owed obscure parties in other states or regions. Once all liabilities are identified, there remains an important problem of *measurement* or *valuation*. Conceptually, a liability when incurred is the *present value* of the future outlays required. Current accounting practice, however, generally reflects

---

[1] Long-term liabilities are discussed in Chapter 17, Part B.

current liabilities at their face value (maturity value) since the difference between the two values usually is not large.

Measurement or valuation of liabilities must be in accordance with the *cost principle*, for that principle applies to the determination of costs, assets, liabilities, and proprietary equities. Although many liabilities are definite as to amount, occasions frequently arise where a liability is known to exist but the amount is not specifically determinable at the time. As a consequence, liabilities are comprised of (*a*) known obligations of a definite amount and (*b*) known obligations of an estimated amount.

PART A—CURRENT LIABILITIES

Accounting for current liabilities involves the identification of certain types of items, such as short-term debts; accrued liabilities; deposits and advances received from customers, clients, and others; deferred credits; and implied contractual obligations. A particular problem of measurement arises because some of these liabilities are seldom shown on the books in full before some adjustment. For example, liabilities, such as wages payable, requiring periodic payments for services rendered continuously are seldom fully recorded in the accounts prior to end-of-the-period adjustments. Such liabilities frequently are not recorded in full except after an analysis has been made of certain financial facts preliminary to adjustments and other procedures have been performed preliminary to preparation of the financial statements. The identification, measurement, and reporting of these more or less fugitive liabilities are of some considerable significance. The primary objective of accounting for liabilities then is to identify and measure them so that reporting will be in conformity with the full-disclosure *principle*. The amount and all other pertinent facts relative to liabilities must be identified and reported so that a company's financial condition may be evaluated.

Current Liabilities Defined

Current liabilities for many years were defined as those obligations due within one year of balance sheet date. This definition was related to the older definition of current assets (liquidation within one year). It was recognized that these definitions were unrealistic for many concerns. As a consequence the Committee on Accounting Procedure of the AICPA defined current liabilities as follows:

The term *current liabilities* is used principally to designate obligations whose liquidation is reasonably expected to require the use of existing resources properly classifiable as current assets, or the creation of other current liabilities.

The committee further elaborated as follows:

As a balance-sheet category, the classification is intended to include obligations for items which have entered into the operating cycle, such as payables incurred in the acquisition of materials and supplies to be used in the production of goods or in providing services to be offered for sale; collections received in advance of the delivery of goods or performance of services; and debts which arise from operations directly related to the operating cycle, such as accruals for wages, salaries, commissions, rentals, royalties, and income and other taxes. Other liabilities whose regular and ordinary liquidation is expected to occur within a relatively short period of time, usually 12 months, are also intended for inclusion, such as short-term debts arising from the acquisition of capital assets, serial maturities of long-term obligations, amounts required to be expended within one year under sinking fund provisions, and agency obligations arising from the collection or acceptance of cash or other assets for the account of third persons.

This concept of current liabilities would include estimated or accrued amounts which are expected to be required to cover expenditures within the year for known obligations (a) the amount of which can be determined only approximately (as in the case of provisions for accruing bonus payments) or (b) where the specific person or persons to whom payment will be made cannot as yet be designated (as in the case of estimated costs to be incurred in connection with guaranteed servicing or repair of products already sold).[2]

This definition has gained wide acceptance particularly since it recognizes operating cycles of varying lengths in different industries.

The principal types of current liabilities are:

Known liabilities of a definite amount:

1. Accounts payable.
2. Short-term notes payable.
3. Cash dividends payable.
4. Advances and funds held as returnable deposits.
5. Accrued liabilities.
6. Deferred revenues.

Known liabilities, amount dependent on operations:

7. Taxes (income, sales, and social security).
8. Bonus obligations.

Known liabilities of an estimated amount:

9. Guarantee and warranty obligations.
10. Premium obligations.

Special accounting problems related to these types of current liabilities are discussed in the following sections.

---

[2]Committee on Accounting Procedure, AICPA, "Restatement and Revision of Accounting Research Bulletins," *Accounting Research Bulletin No. 43* (New York, 1961), pp. 21–22.

Accounts and Notes Payable.   Accounts payable and notes payable generally constitute the largest portion of current liabilities. Accounts payable as a designation is usually reserved for the normally recurring trade obligations of the business; other payables are separately designated and reported. Both notes payable and "open" payables should be reported separately as (*a*) trade obligations, (*b*) bank borrowings, (*c*) loans from officers, or (*d*) other obligations. This division in recording and reporting indicates the *source* of short-term funds and the *nature* of the obligation.

In determining the amount of accounts payable for goods purchased near the end of a specific period, careful attention should be given to goods that might be in transit. The purchase and liability should be recorded when *title passes.* In view of the fact that it is frequently difficult to determine precisely what goods are in transit, it is customary, for practical reasons, to record the liability for purchases when the goods are received. Frequently, goods are received during the last few days of the period; hence, there is a delay in checking the merchandise and the invoice may not be entered in the records. If the purchase is not recorded, liabilities are understated. Similarly, the inventory will be understated if the goods are not included in the count; thus, both the current assets and current liabilities are understated.

Short-term notes payable may be secured by collateral (pledged or mortgaged assets) or may be unsecured. Secured notes should be accounted for separately, and the nature of the collateral should be reported both with respect to the notes and to the specific assets involved. One method would be to report pledged assets by a footnote which refers both to the assets involved and the specific obligation. Perhaps a preferable method would be to report pledged assets parenthetically under both the asset and liability captions. To illustrate:

Investment: Current Liabilities:
Stock in X Corp., at cost (pledged   Notes payable (secured by stock
   for $1,000 note to "Y" Bank)...$5,000   in X Corp.)............................$1,000

Dividends Payable.   Cash (or property) dividends payable should be reported as a current liability if there is an intention to pay them in the near future. Stock dividends payable are not reported as a current liability but as an element of the capital section as explained in Chapter 21. Cash dividends payable are reported as a liability between date of declaration and date of payment on the legal basis that such a declaration is an enforceable contract, whereas stock dividends declared are revocable by the board of directors at any time prior to issuance. Liabilities are not recognized for undeclared dividends in arrears on preferred stock nor for any other dividends not yet declared formally by the board of directors. Script dividends payable (liability dividends) are properly reported as a current liability unless there is no intention to make payment within the near future.

Advances and Returnable Deposits. A special type of liability arises when a firm receives deposits from customers and employees. Deposits may be received from customers as guaranties to cover payment of obligations that may arise in the future or to guarantee performance of a contract or service. For example, when an order is taken, a firm may require an advance payment to cover losses that would be incurred should the order be canceled. Such advances are liabilities of the firm receiving the order until the underlying transaction is completed. Deposits are frequently received from customers as guaranties for possible damage to property left with the customer. For example, deposits taken from customers by gas, water, light, and other public utilities are liabilities of such companies to their customers. Employees may make deposits for the return of keys and other company property, for locker privileges, and for club memberships. Some of the deposits are fairly permanent; others are current. Deposits should be reported as current or noncurrent liabilities depending upon the time involved between date of deposit and expected termination of the relationships. In cases where the advances or deposits are interest bearing, accrual of such interest costs is required.

Accrued Liabilities. Accrued liabilities arise through accounting recognition of costs and expenses that have "materialized" but have not been paid. For example, property taxes usually are assessed near the end of the calendar year and are payable in the following year. The *matching principle* requires that such expenses and the related liabilities be estimated in advance and then recognized in the accounts and reported on the interim financial statements on an accrual basis. Determination of expense accruals may be made from an examination of the historical expense accounts and other supplementary records. In recording such liabilities it is especially important that appropriate account titles be used such as Wages Payable, Estimated Property Taxes Payable, and Interest Payable.

In respect to the accrual of property taxes the Committee on Accounting Procedure of the AICPA stated:

Generally, the most acceptable basis of providing for property taxes is monthly accrual on the taxpayer's books during the fiscal period of the taxing authority for which the taxes are levied. The books will then show, at any closing date, the appropriate accrual or prepayment.[3]

For some liabilities established on an accrual basis such as Property Taxes Payable, the amount actually paid and the amount accrued sometimes will differ. Such differences should be accounted for as an adjustment of the related annual expense.

---

[3] Ibid., pp. 83–84.

Deferred Revenues. Frequently a caption "deferred credits" or "deferred revenues" positioned after liabilities and before owners' equity may be observed on published balance sheets. Usually one finds under this caption four types of items, viz:

1. Revenues collected in advance such as prepaid interest income, prepaid rental income, and advances received for services to be rendered. These items require that obligations, benefits, or services be rendered in the future before the income is realized. Expenses may or may not be incurred in meeting the future obligations.
2. Credits arising through certain external transactions, such credits being difficult to classify otherwise. Examples of this type of item are: premium on bonds payable, unearned deposit on royalties, discount on reacquired securities, and deferred income on installment sales.
3. Credits arising through certain internal transactions. Examples of such credits are: deferred repairs, allowance for rearrangement costs, and equities of minority interests (on consolidated statements).
4. Credits arising from income tax allocation procedures (income taxes payable in future years).

The wide variation in usage of this caption suggested by these four types of items indicates some of the problems involved. Most of the items listed above as examples are difficult to classify and report on the balance sheet in such a manner that a clear understanding on the part of the reader is assured. These reasons underlie the fairly wide usage of this somewhat vague balance sheet classification.

It should be observed that the classification, reported as it is below liabilities and above owners' equity, is not consistent with the basic accounting equation Assets = Liabilities+ Owners' Equity. This treatment fails to identify clearly the true nature of the various items reported thereunder. Certain of these items are clearly in the nature of liabilities; others represent offsets or additions to related items. It is for these reasons that modern accounting theory and practice consider the "deferred" classification on the balance sheet to be objectionable. The authors of this text have chosen to indicate a preference throughout on this point, that is, to avoid this caption to the fullest extent possible (see Chapter 3). A sound basis for classification of the various items (listed above) appears to be as follows:

1. Classify as *current liabilities* (a) those items that represent a claim against current assets whether or not there is an obligation to a specific individual or entity and (b), those items that will represent revenues when the current obligations for goods, benefits, or services are met.

2. Classify as *other liabilities* all items that are consistent with (1) above, except that they are not *current*, that is, extended periods of time are involved.
3. Classify all other items according to their characteristics as asset offsets, owners' equity, or additions to regular liabilities.

On the above basis the following classifications are suggested:

Item	*Classification*
Prepaid interest income	Current liability
Prepaid rental income	Current liability
Advances received for services to be rendered	Current liability
Unearned deposit on royalties	Current liability
Magazine subscriptions collected in advance	Current liability
Deferred repairs	Current liability (represents a "claim" against current assets—may be long-term liability if related to several future periods)
Allowance for rearrangement costs	Current liability
Premium on bonds payable	Long-term liability (add to related bonds payable)
Equities of minority interests	Owners' equity (special caption separate from controlling interest)
Long-term refundable deposits	Long-term liability
Leasehold advances (leaseholds)	Current or long-term liability
Income taxes payable in future years	Current or long-term liability depending upon the element of time involved.

Strictly defined deferred revenues are items of prepaid income, that is, amounts received in advance of being "earned" hence they are current liabilities. Such items are properly reported as liabilities until the services are furnished or there is a transfer of title to goods, as the case may be. For example, subscriptions collected in advance on magazines represent deferred revenues (there is a liability to deliver a certain number of issues) until such issues are provided the subscriber. As the issues are delivered the liability Prepaid Subscriptions is canceled by a transfer to an income account such as Subscription Income.

Funds Collected for Third Parties. Within recent decades numerous state and federal laws have been passed which require the individual business enterprise to collect taxes from customers and employees for remission to certain governmental agencies. Taxes collected but not yet remitted represent current liabilities. To illustrate, assume there is a 2% sales tax and that sales for the period were $200,000. The indicated entries are:

```
Cash or Accounts Receivable..............................................204,000
    Sales..........                                                                      200,000
    Sales Taxes Payable .................................................           4,000

Sales Taxes Payable ......................................................    4,000
    Cash........                                                                           4,000
```

Federal income tax laws require the employer to withhold from the pay of each employee an amount representing anticipated income taxes payable by the employee. The amount withheld depends upon the number of dependents and the level of income of each employee. Employers compute the amounts withheld according to a government-prescribed formula or take them directly from withholding tax tables provided by the government. While income taxes withheld must be remitted to the Treasury through local depositaries (banks), such amounts are current liabilities of the employer until the time of remittance.

Social security legislation also requires that the employer deduct a tax from the pay of each employee under specified conditions. In addition the employer must match the contribution of the employee and remit the sum of both taxes to the Treasury along with income taxes withheld. Currently (1971–72) the tax amounts to 10.4%, one half of which is paid by the employee (5.2%) and one half by the employer.[4] The tax applies to the first $7,800 in 1971 and $9,000 in 1972 paid to each employee during the calendar year. Such taxes are referred to as F.I.C.A. taxes since the enabling act is the Federal Insurance Contributions Act. This tax is to provide retirement pay to the contributor at a specified retirement age and survivor benefits.

Another social security tax levied by the federal government is to provide for *unemployment* insurance. This tax is required by the Federal Unemployment Tax Act and is generally referred to as F.U.T.A. taxes. This tax is paid wholly by the employer (of four or more persons) and amounts to 3.1% on the first $3,000 in wages paid each employee. The law provides that 2.7% is payable to the state and .4% is payable to the federal Treasury.

Accounting for withholding taxes, F.I.C.A. taxes, and F.U.T.A. taxes may be illustrated simply. Assume salaries of $5,000 for the month of January and income tax withholdings of $600.

1. To record salaries and employee payroll taxes:

Salaries	5,000	
Withholding Taxes Payable		600
F.I.C.A. Taxes Payable – Employees ($5,000 × 5.2%)		260
Cash		4,140

2. To record employer payroll taxes:

Expense – Payroll Taxes	415	
F.I.C.A. Taxes Payable – Employer ($5,000 × 5.2%)		260
F.U.T.A. Taxes Payable – Federal ($5,000 × .4%)		20
F.U.T.A. Taxes Payable – State ($5,000 × 2.7%)		135

When the taxes are remitted, cash is credited and the current liability accounts established in the preceding entries are debited.

---

[4] The rate scheduled for 1973–75 is 5.65%. These rates are changed by Congress from time to time.

Tax and Bonus Problems. It is not unusual to find employment contracts providing for the payment of a *bonus* to an officer, branch manager, or other employees of a corporation. A bonus should be treated as an operating expense and set up as a current liability when accrued and pending payment. Bonus payments generally are deductible in computing corporate taxable income under federal tax laws. Bonus contracts relating to income earned are usually one of two classes, viz:

1. The bonus is computed on the net income after deducting income taxes but before deducting the bonus.
2. The bonus is computed after deducting both the bonus and the income tax.

Since the tax is not determinable before the bonus is computed or vice versa, a special problem of computation arises which requires the use of simultaneous equations. To illustrate a typical situation, assume the Bryan Company reported an income of $100,000 before deducting income taxes and before the bonus to the general manager. Assume the tax rate, or T, is 52% and the bonus rate or B, is 10%. Two situations are illustrated:

Situation 1. The bonus of 10% is based on income after deducting income taxes but before deducting the bonus.

$$B = .10(\$100,000 - T) \qquad (1)$$
$$T = .52(\$100,000 - B) \qquad (2)$$

Substitute value of T in (2) for T in (1):

$$B = .10[\$100,000 - .52(\$100,000 - B)] \qquad (3)$$
$$B = .10[\$100,000 - \$52,000 + .52B]$$
$$B = \$10,000 - \$52,000 + .052B$$
$$B - .052B = \$4,800$$
$$.948B = \$4,800$$
$$B = \underline{\underline{\$5,063}}$$

Substitute value of B in (2):

$$T = .52(\$100,000 - \$5,063)$$
$$T = \$52,000 - \$2,633$$
$$T = \underline{\underline{\$49,367}}$$

Situation 2. The bonus of 10% is based on net income after deducting both income taxes and the bonus.

$$B = .10(\$100,000 - B - T) \qquad (1)$$
$$T = .52(\$100,000 - B) \qquad (2)$$

Substitute value of T in (2) for T in (1):

$$B = .10[\$100.000 - B - .52(\$100,000 - B)]$$
$$B = .10[\$100,000 - B \; \$52,000 + .52B] \qquad (3)$$
$$B = \$10,000 - .10B - \$5,200 + .052B$$
$$B + .10B - .052B = \$4,800$$
$$1.048B = \$4,800$$
$$B = \underline{\underline{\$4,580}} \qquad (4)$$

Substitute value of B in (2):

$$T = .52(\$100,000 - \$4,580) \qquad (5)$$
$$T = \underline{\underline{\$49,618}}$$

Proof of Computations

	Situation 1	Situation 2
Computation of taxes:		
Income before tax and bonus	$100,000	$100,000
Deduct bonus (as computed)	5,063	4,580
Taxable income	$ 94,937	$ 95,420
Multiply by tax rate	.52	.52
Tax	$ 49,367	$ 49,618
Computation of bonus:		
Income before taxes and bonus	$100,000	$100,000
Taxes	49,367	49,618
	$ 50,633	$ 50,382
Bonus (as computed)		4,580
Income subject to bonus	$ 50,633	$ 45,802
Multiply by bonus rate	.10	.10
Bonus	$ 5,063	$ 4,580

The entries to record the bonus and income taxes in Situation 2 would be as follows:

1. To record bonus:

Expense—Manager's Bonus	4,580	
Bonus Payable		4,580

2. To record income taxes:

Expense—Income Taxes	49,618	
Income Taxes Payable		49,618

3. To record payment of bonus:

Bonus Payable	4,580	
Cash		4,580

Estimated Liabilities. Estimated liabilities are *known* liabilities which are uncertain in amount at the time the financial statements are prepared. Estimated liabilities should be reported as an integral part of the balance sheet (usually as a current liability) rather than by footnote. The amount of each should be estimated realistically on the basis of all information available. The account title should indicate clearly that the amount is estimated. For example, it was suggested in preceding paragraphs that appropriate account titles such as Estimated Property Taxes Payable, Estimated Income Taxes Payable, Estimated Liability under Guarantee, and Estimated Premium Claims Outstanding be used. The term *reserve* definitely should not be used in account titles for liabilities.

There are numerous situations where known liabilities must be estimated as to amount. In the following paragraphs several situations involving special problems are discussed.

Premiums and Price Offers to Customers. As a promotional device many concerns offer premiums to customers in return for wrappers, coupons, labels, box tops, and other parts of the containers in which the products are packed. At the end of the accounting period many coupons, wrappers, etc., will be outstanding and a portion of these will have to be redeemed in subsequent periods as they are presented. The claim for premiums outstanding represents a current liability, and the cost of such premiums is a proper charge to expense in the period in which the sales were made. The following example illustrates accounting for premiums:

The Baker Coffee Company offered to customers a silver coffee spoon costing 75 cents each on the return of 20 coupons, one coupon being placed in each can of coffee when packed. The company estimated, on the basis of past experience, that only 70% of the coupons would ever be redeemed. The following additional data for two years are available:

	First Year	Second Year
Number of coffee spoons purchased @ $.75	6,000	4,000
Number of coupons redeemed	40,000	120,000
Number of cans of coffee sold	100,000	200,000

The indicated entries are as follows:

1. To record purchases of spoons:

	First Year		Second Year	
Premiums — Silverware	4,500		3,000	
Cash		4,500		3,000

2. To record estimated liability and premium expense on sales:

	First Year		Second Year	
Premium Expense°	2,625		5,250	
Estimated Premium Claims Outstanding		2,625		5,250

°Computations:
Year 1: $100,000 × .75/20 × .70 = $2,625
Year 2: $200,000 × .75/20 × .70 = $5,250

First Year   *Second Year*

3. To record redemption of coupons:

Estimated Premium Claims Outstanding° 1,500   4,500
    Premiums — Silverware.............................. 1,500   4,500

  °Computations:

    First year: $\dfrac{40,000}{20} \times \$.75 = \underline{\$1,500}$

    Second year: $\dfrac{120,000}{20} \times \$.75 = \underline{\$4,500}$

4. To close:

Income Summary 2,625   5,250
    Premium Expense 2,625   5,250

Balances (ending) for financial statements:

Balance Sheet:
Premiums — silverware (inventory)
  ($4,500 − $1,500)..$3,000
  ($3,000 + $3,000 − $4,500) $1,500
Estimated premium claims outstanding (liability)
  ($2,625 − $1,500)... 1,125
  ($1,125 + $5,250 − $4,500)   1,875

Income Statement:
Premium expense (distribution expenses)............................... 2,625   5,250

The Premiums — Silverware account balance should be reported as a current asset. The balance in the Estimated Premium Claims Outstanding should be reported as a current liability.

Liability from Guarantees. Merchandise frequently is sold under a guarantee or warranty ranging from a few days to one or more years. Under such circumstances correct accounting would require that the guarantee costs be recognized during the period of the sale so that cost and revenue are matched properly. Since the guarantee will involve future expenditures, a liability exists. When guarantee costs are apt to be immaterial in amount, the exception principle overrides the theoretical matching principle; no attempt is made to match them with the related sales. However, when the costs are material, an estimate of such costs should be made. The estimate is recorded in the accounts through a debit to operating expense and a credit to a current liability account. When actual costs are incurred in the future in fulfilling the terms of the guarantee, Cash (or some other appropriate asset) is credited and the liability account debited. Similar procedures are appropriate when service contracts are undertaken in connection with the sale of merchandise.[5]

Goods frequently are sold in returnable containers; the seller requiring a deposit subject to return. In these situations the accounts must be organized to reflect the container inventory, container de-

[5] See Chapter 18 for discussion of liabilities under pension plans.

posits (a current liability), and sale of containers not to be returned, i.e., purchased by customers.

Reporting Current Liabilities

When there is a legal debt which has the criterial attributes of a current liability, then a current liability must be reported whether the amount is known precisely or is estimated. The *detail* that is to be reported concerning current liabilities should be sufficient to meet adequately the requirement for full disclosure. Appropriate account titles such as Wages Payable are preferable over Accrued Wages; footnotes should be utilized to clarify the reporting with respect to special problems. Within the current liability section the items sometimes are listed in *order* of maturity, although this concept frequently is hard to apply from a practical point of view. Secured liabilities should be identified clearly, and the related assets pledged as collateral (or security) indicated. Current maturities of long-term obligations should be reported as current liabilities. Current liabilities, such as bank overdrafts, should not be offset against assets. An exception is permitted where a company has two accounts in the same bank; these may be offset.

PART B—CONTINGENT LIABILITIES

Definition

Contingent liabilities are potential claims that may materialize as legal debts provided certain reasonably probable contingencies occur in the future. They are potential liabilities arising from acts, events, or circumstances occurring before the date of the balance sheet or from conditions existing as of that date, but for which any legal indebtedness is contingent upon some *future* event or circumstance. Contingent liabilities should be accorded special accounting treatment and should not be regarded as liabilities. Contingent liabilities may involve potential indebtedness of known or unknown amounts; the distinction between liabilities and contingent liabilities hinges on the point of certainty or uncertainty as to the existence of a legal debt, not on the point of whether the amount is known precisely. Contingent liabilities also may involve contingent *losses*. Conversely, all contingent losses do not involve contingent liabilities. For example, there is always a possibility that some catastrophe may destroy assets in which case there would be a loss but no liability.

Some of the more common forms of contingent liabilities are:

1. *Notes receivable discounted.* When a note receivable is discounted, a contingent liability is created since there is a possibility that the endorser will have to make payment should the maker default. The method of accounting for, and reporting, this type of contingent liability was discussed in Chapter 11.

2. *Accounts receivable assigned.* This contingent liability is very similar to that of discounted notes as was discussed in Chapter 11.

3. *Accommodation endorsements.* Individuals may cosign a note for a friend, promising to make payment should the primary maker default. Many accountants prefer to give formal recognition in the accounts to accommodation endorsements that bind the entity by debiting a receivable from the party accommodated and crediting a contingent liability account such as "Contingent Liability from Endorsements." On the balance sheet these two accounts should be reported under contingent liabilities as offsets so that their net effect on the totals is nil.

4. *Guarantees.* When merchandise is sold under guarantees as to quality or performance, an estimated liability normally should be recognized. However, in some cases the probability of any future claim is so remote that recognition of a contingent liability rather than an actual obligation (current or long-term liability) is justified as discussed in a preceding paragraph.

5. *Purchase commitments.* When goods are ordered for future delivery a contingent liability is created. The amount of the contingent liability is the full purchase price, but since there is also a contingent asset equal to the value of the merchandise at the time of delivery, the purchase commitment is usually ignored, unless due to falling prices the amount of the contingent liability is substantially in excess of the contingent asset. Where there is a falling market, the amount of the contingent loss is the excess of the commitment price over the market price at date of delivery.

6. *Lawsuits pending.* Where unsettled lawsuits give rise to the probability that damages or judgments may have to be paid, a contingent liability should be recognized and reported.

7. *General.* There are numerous other contingent liabilities in addition to those listed above. Some of those most frequently encountered are:

a) Guarantees to customers against price declines.

b) Contingent liability under leases and other agreements.

c) Guaranteed bonds and other liabilities of subsidiary companies.

Reporting Contingent Liabilities

Contingent liabilities should be reported on the financial statements so that there is full disclosure of all pertinent aspects of the potential claim. Contingent liabilities may be reported on the balance sheet (*a*) as a footnote, (*b*) parenthetically in the body of the balance sheet between liabilities and capital, (*c*) as an appropriation of retained earnings coupled with a footnote, or (*d*) in the body of the balance sheet between liabilities and capital as a special caption "contingent liabilities." The first method generally is preferred since the requirements of full disclosure are best satisfied. The last method requires that the contingent liabilities be listed but shown "short," that is, not included in the balance sheet totals.

In situations where there is a particularly strong possibility that a contingent liability may materialize, the management may direct that retained earnings be *appropriated* in an amount equivalent to the potential claim. In this case Retained Earnings is debited and an appropriation account (appropriately captioned) is credited.[6] In reporting the contingent liability on the balance sheet, in this situation, the appropriation of retained earnings would be shown in the usual manner and a footnote added to provide sufficient explanation for full disclosure. When the contingency finally is determined the appropriation is returned to retained earnings. If the claim does not materialize, no further accounting is involved; if the claim does materialize, the legal liability and any resultant loss should be recognized in the normal manner without reference to the prior appropriation of retained earnings. Ordinarily contingent liabilities are not recorded formally in the accounts; however, the following manners of recognition in the accounts (in addition to reporting on the balance sheet) are used:

1. Appropriation of retained earnings.
2. A memorandum type entry whereby two offsetting accounts are established such as described above under the caption "accommodation endorsements."

QUESTIONS FOR CLASS DISCUSSION

1. In evaluating a balance sheet for their purposes, bankers consistently report that the liability section is the most important part. What is the primary reason for their position on this point?
2. How is the "cost principle" involved in accounting for current liabilities?
3. Define current liabilities.
4. Distinguish between the two types of current liabilities: those that are known as to amount and those that represent estimates. Explain why both are classified as true liabilities.
5. Differentiate between secured and unsecured liabilities. Explain proper reporting procedures for each.
6. What is the proper balance sheet classification for cash dividends payable? Stock dividends payable? What is the basis for such classification?
7. What are deferred revenues? What is the basis for classifying them as current liabilities?
8. Define contingent liabilities. Give several examples.
9. How may contingent liabilities be recognized formally in the accounts?

---

[6] Refer to Chapter 22.

10. How are contingent liabilities reported on the balance sheet?

11. Under what circumstances would you consider appropriation of retained earnings with respect to a contingent liability?

12. How would each of the following items be reported on the balance sheet?

a) Cash dividends payable.
b) Bonds payable.
c) Accommodation endorsement.
d) Reserve for lawsuit pending.
e) Stock dividend payable.
f) Notes receivable discounted.
g) Estimated taxes payable.
h) Prepaid rent income.
i) Deferred interest income.
j) Customer deposits on containers.
k) Current payment on bonds payable.
l) Accounts payable.
m) Reserve for bond sinking fund.
n) Loans from officers.
o) Accrued wages.
p) Deferred repairs.

13. Distinguish between each of the following by indicating how they would be reported on the balance sheet.

a) Short-term obligations — known amount.
b) Potential obligations — known amount.
c) Short-term obligations — estimated amount.
d) Potential obligations — estimated amount.

DECISION CASE 16–1

The firm of Allen and Cross, independent certified public accountants, was completing the annual audit of the Keeler Company. Assume you are a member of the staff of the CPA firm and have been asked by the managing partner to "write appropriate footnotes for the financial statements for each of the following which relate to the audit of the Keeler Company." Also be prepared to justify your written comments and to point out alternative treatments and related problems. Note any additional information that you should have.

a) The company tax returns for the past five years have recently been checked by the Internal Revenue Service. Items involving additional taxes of approximately $6,000 have been questioned. It appears that the company will have to appear before the tax court since most of the items are "borderline."

b) The Keeler Company owns 80% of the stock in another (and smaller) company. Notes payable owed by the other company to two different banks amounting to $40,000 have been cosigned by the Keeler Company. These notes are unsecured and are due in 18 months. The subsidiary is particularly short of cash.

c) The Keeler Company has notes receivable recorded on the books of $60,000 of which $20,000 have been discounted at the National Bank.

d) The company sells one line of items on which there is a two-year warranty. It has been conservatively estimated that costs of fulfilling the warranties outstanding at year-end will be $8,000. No recognition of this amount has been made in the accounts.

e) Dividends in arrears on cumulative preferred stock amounts to $10,000. No dividends were paid during the year just ended or the prior year.

EXERCISES

Exercise 16–1

The books and related records of the Watson Corporation provided the following information at December 31, 19A:

a) Notes payable, short term (including a $4,000 note on the purchase of equipment that cost $20,000; the assets were mortgaged in connection with the purchase) $14,000

b) Bonds payable ($10,000 due each April 1) 60,000

c) Open accounts owed (including $6,000 due the president of the company) 43,000

d) Accrued taxes (property) payable 1,000

e) Stock dividends payable, September 1, 19A (at par value) 8,000

f) Scrip dividends payable (declared January 1 of current year; to be paid 24 months later) 8,000

g) Cash dividends payable, September 1, 19A 3,000

Required:

Assuming the fiscal year ends December 31, show how each of the above items should be reported on the financial statements at December 31, 19A.

Exercise 16–2

During the month of September, the first month in which the first general sales tax (2%) was effective, the Corner Grocery had cash sales of $155,040 and credit sales of $18,360 including the sales tax collections (all sales were subject to tax). The tax was remitted to the state collection agency. Illustrate with entries a suitable method of accounting for the sales taxes.

Exercise 16–3

Le Ferve Company paid salaries for the month amounting to $50,000. Of this amount $10,000 was received by employees who had already been paid $7,800. In addition to the $50,000 another $5,000 was paid to employees who had already been paid $3,000. Withholding taxes amounted to $4,300, and $1,000 was withheld for investment in company stock per an agreement with certain employees. Use the following rates: F.I.C.A., 10.4%; F.U.T.A.— state, 2.7%; F.U.T.A.—federal, 4%.

Required:

Give entries to record (a) the salary payment including the deductions, (b) the employer payroll costs, and (c) remittance of the taxes (assume it is at the end of the first quarter).

Exercise 16–4

Lanning Company gives the general manager a bonus equal to 20% of net income after tax. The bonus is deductible for tax purposes. For simplicity assume a tax rate of 40%. Net income prior to taxes and bonus was $80,000.

Required:

1. Compute the tax and the bonus.

2. Prove your computations.

3. Give entries to record the tax and the bonus.

Exercise 16–5

Blue Company has an agreement with its president to pay him a bonus of 10% of net income, after deducting federal income taxes and after deducting an amount equal to 6% on the invested capital. Invested capital amounted to $300,000. The income before deductions for bonus and income taxes was $50,000. The bonus is deductible for tax purposes; assume the company is in the 25% bracket.

Required:

Compute the bonus, tax, and net income after deducting both bonus and tax. Prove the computations.

Exercise 16–6

Ryans Grocery has just initiated a promotion program whereby customers are given coupons redeemable in U.S. savings bonds. One coupon is issued for each dollar of sales. On the surrender of 750 coupons, one $25 savings bond (cost $18.75) is given. It is estimated that 20% of the coupons issued will never be presented for redemption. Sales for the first period were $400,000, and the coupons redeemed totaled 225,000. Sales for the second period were $440,000, and the coupons redeemed totaled 405,000.

Required:

Prepare journal entries relative to the premium cost for the two periods including closing entries. Show ending balances and computations.

Exercise 16–7

XYZ Corporation sells a line of products that carry a three-year guarantee. Based on past experience the estimated guarantee costs based on dollar sales are: first year after sale – 1% of sales; second year after sale – 3% of sales; and third year after sale – 5%. Sales and actual guarantee expenditures for a three-year period were:

	Sales	Actual Guaranty Expenditures
19A	$100,000	$ 960
19B	120,000	4,400
19C	110,000	9,600

Required:

1. Give entries for the three years related to sales and the guarantee provisions.

2. Determine the balance in the liability account at the end of each year.

Exercise 16–8

For each of the following indicate the balance sheet classifications and preferred title:

a) Accounts payable.
b) Deposits received from customers — trade.
c) Deferred interest income.
d) Accrued wages.
e) Endorsements for subsidiary.
f) Reserve for rearrangement
   costs.
g) Customer advances — orders.
h) Sales taxes collected.
i) Bonds payable.
j) Advance on rent (five years).

k) Stock dividend declared.
l) Notes receivable discounted.
m) Premium on bonds payable.
n) Accrued property taxes.
o) Reserve for bond sinking
   fund.
p) Scrip dividends declared.
q) Reserve for lawsuit in process.
r) I.O.U. to company president.
s) Reserve for repairs.
t) Bonds payable (portion due
   next year).

Exercise 16–9

Scott Company sells its products in 50-gallon metal containers that are to be returned. The customer is required to make a deposit of $5 on each container which is refunded when it is returned. The following data relate to operations for a two-month period:

a) Purchased 100 new containers at $4 each.
b) Sold merchandise in 60 containers for $12,000 plus container deposits.
c) Twenty containers were returned.
d) At customers' requests six containers are to be kept permanently by them.
e) Two containers were damaged beyond repair; no salvage value.
f) Assume remaining containers outstanding will be returned in good condition (ignore depreciation).

Required:

1. Give all entries indicated.
2. Compute the value of the container inventory and the related current liability.

PROBLEMS

Problem 16–1

For each of the situations to follow indicate (1) the correct balance sheet classification and (2) the amount to be reported and (3) factors affecting the balance sheet reporting. (Suggestion: Set up three columns for your response.)

a) Accounts payable (including $1,000 owed to the company presi-
   dent)...$15,000
b) Notes payable (including $3,000 for equipment)............................   9,000
c) Notes receivable (including $10,000 discounted)............................ 30,000
d) Long-term note payable (secured by stock in X Company)..............   5,000
e) Dividends payable 10,000
f) Deposits from customers..   3,000
g) Prepaid rent income   6,000
h) Premium on bonds payable   4,800

  i) Bonds payable (annual payment $10,000)..................................... 40,000
  j) Deferred repairs... 1,000
  k) Leasehold advance received (five years) 7,500
  l) Estimated taxes payable... 4,000
  m) Reserve for lawsuit pending 7,000
  n) Estimated future costs of guarantee.. 6,000
  o) Accommodation endorsement 2,000

Problem 16–2

During an audit of the books of Thomas Company the following data were developed:

a) The corporation discounted a $1,000 note at the bank that had been received from a customer. The note is due 120 days hence (disregard interest).

b) The corporation has been sued for $10,000 damages arising out of an accident involving one of the company trucks. The attorneys believe that the suit will be settled for $6,000 cash.

c) The company has signed a firm contract for 100 special tools that are sold to customers along with the primary product. These tools are essential to adequate maintenance. The special tools are sold to the customers at the "market price," that is, about what competitors are asking. It now appears that there will be a 15 to 25% drop in the price prior to delivery, yet the corporation will have to pay the contract price of $62 per tool.

d) T. H. Thomas the owner of the company recently cosigned a $5,000 note for a business associate as an accommodation.

Required:

Give two alternatives indicating how each item may be accounted for and reported on the financial statements. Indicate the preferred alternative.

Problem 16–3

The following transactions occurred during the year just ended for Rollins Corporation. You are requested (1) to provide appropriate journal entries for each item and (2) to indicate the current liabilities, long-term liabilities, and contingent liabilities on December 31 after giving effect to these transactions:

a) Bonds payable dated January 1 with a maturity value of $80,000 were sold at par plus accrued interest on April 1. The bonds mature in 10 years and bear 6% interest per annum payable on January 1.

b) Merchandise sold on account amounted to $400,000. Collections were $340,000; accounts carried over from the preceding year were $30,000.

c) Cosigned a $5,000 note payable for wholly owned subsidiary.

d) Notes totaling $12,000 were received from customers on accounts receivable.

e) A $10,000 note receivable from a customer was discounted at the bank; proceeds, $9,300.

f) Payroll records showed the following (assume amounts given are correct):

	Employee			Employer		
Gross Wages	With-holding	F.I.C.A.	Union Dues	F.I.C.A.	F.U.T.A.-State	F.U.T.A.-Federal
$17,000.........$1,500		$450	$130	$450	$400	$45
19,000......... 1,700		500	140	500	444	51

Remittances were: union, $250; withholding taxes, $3,000; F.I.C.A., $1,800; and F.U.T.A.-state, $640.

g) The company had been sued for $25,000 damages. It appears now that a judgment against the company of about $10,000 can be expected.

h) At the beginning of the year, the company estimated machinery rearrangement costs expected to be incurred during August of $1,800, which were accrued on a monthly basis; actual expenditures amounted to $2,050.

i) The company accrued $250 per month for "special repairs." At the end of the year only $2,000 had been spent for this purpose. It was decided to put off certain repairs until January, although they were definitely scheduled for December. The basic reason was that certain parts, although purchased, had not arrived by year-end.

j) Dividends in arrears (not declared) on cumulative preferred stock amounted to $6,000.

k) Dividends declared but not paid: cash, $5,000; stock, $2,000.

l) On December 31 accrued interest on the bonds.

Problem 16-4

Barry Corporation was formed for the purpose of constructing buildings. The first contract involved the construction of an office building. Since the corporation was short of ready cash, an agreement was made with the supervising engineer whereby his compensation would be a share of the profits. The agreement provided that the supervising engineer would receive 20% of the profits on the contract after providing for federal income tax.

Upon completion of the construction the records of the corporation showed the following:

Income before tax and before payment to the supervising
    engineer (assume a 30% tax rate)...............................$300,000
Costs already deducted from the net income, not allowable
    as deductions in computing income taxes but allowed as
    a deduction before computing the profit to be paid the
    supervising engineer.. 20,000

Assume the compensation to the supervising engineer is deductible for income tax purposes.

Required:

1. Compute the compensation and the income taxes assuming the compensation is not an expense in determining the basis for the compensation. Show proof of computations.

2. Compute the amount of the compensation to the supervising engineer and the income taxes assuming the compensation is an expense in determining the basis for the compensation. Show proof of computations.

Problem 16–5

Standard Products Company has an executive bonus plan whereby the management receives one fifth of the annual net income after deducting state and federal income taxes but before deducting the bonus.

On the state return, the federal tax and the bonus are deductions. On the federal return, the state tax and the bonus are deductions. Net income for the year before bonus, state tax, and federal income taxes was $50,000.

No minimum income exemptions are allowable in computing the state tax. The state tax rates are: 1% on the first $1,000, 2% on the next $1,000, 3% on the next $1,000, 4% on the next $1,000, 5% on the next $1,000, and 6% on net income in excess of $5,000. Assume a federal tax rate of 25%.

Required:

1. Compute the state tax, federal tax, and bonus.
2. Present proof of computations.

Problem 16–6

For the purpose of stimulating sales, Black Coffee Company places a coupon in each can of coffee sold, the coupons being redeemable in chinaware. Each premium costs the company 60 cents. Ten coupons must be presented by the customers to receive one premium. The following data are available:

Month	Cans of Coffee Sold	Premiums Purchased	Coupons Redeemed
January	650,000	50,000	220,000
February	500,000	30,000	410,000
March	700,000	70,000	310,000

It is estimated that only 70% of the coupons will be presented for redemption.

Required:

Compute the amount of the premium inventory, liability for premiums outstanding, and premium expense at the end of each month and give the related entries.

Problem 16–7

Crunchy Cereal Company gives a premium costing $.30 each for five box tops received plus "$.10 for mailing costs." Actual mailing costs average $.05 per premium. Data covering three periods are as follows:

	Period		
	First	Second	Third
Premiums purchased	20,000	20,000	25,000
Tops redeemed for premiums	50,000	110,000	150,000
Boxes of cereal sold at $.70 per box	200,000	300,000	310,000

It is estimated that 60% of the tops distributed will never be returned.

Required:

1. Give entries for each period to record the sales, premium purchases, redemptions, adjustments, and closing entries. Hint: Set up parallel columns for the three periods.

2. Indicate how premiums and any related liabilities would be reported on the balance sheet at the end of each period.

Problem 16–8

Green Appliance Company provides a warranty on two lines of items sold. Line A carried a two-year warranty for all labor and service (but not parts). The company contracts with a local service establishment to provide the requirements of the warranty. The local service establishment charges a flat fee of $40 per unit payable at date of sale. It is estimated by Green Appliance that the warranty requirements are greater in the second year than in the first year by 60%.

Line B carried a three-year warranty for labor and parts on service due to "defects not due to ordinary use." Green Appliance purchases the parts needed under the warranty and has service personnel who perform the work. On the basis of past experience it is estimated that the three-year warranty costs are 3% of dollar sales for parts and 7% for labor and overhead. It is further estimated that warranty requirements are greater in the second than in the first year by 100% and the same in the third year as in the second. Additional data available are:

	Period		
	1	*2*	*3*
Sales in units, Line A..........................	700	1,000	
Sales price per unit, Line A...............$	550	$ 600	
Sales in units, Line B..........................	600	800	
Sales price per unit, Line B...............$	700	$ 740	
Actual warranty costs:			
Parts	$2,500	$ 9,100	$11,000
Labor and overhead......................	$6,200	$20,000	$28,000

Required:

1. Give entries for sales and warranties in periods 1, 2, and 3. Hint: Set up parallel columns for the three periods.

2. Indicate income statement and balance sheet figures related to the warranties at the end of each period.

Problem 16–9

Illustrate how each of the following items preferably should be reported on the balance sheet. Indicate any assumptions that you make.

a) Accounts receivable: balance in accounts receivable, $150,000, including $30,000 that has been "discounted with recourse."

b) Dividends declared but not yet "paid."

Cash	$10,000
Scrip...	20,000
Stock...	30,000

c) Bonds payable outstanding, $90,000; annual payments, $10,000. Premium on bonds payable unamortized, $4,000.

d) The following items labeled as "reserves" on the books:

Reserve for bond sinking fund $40,000
Reserve for lawsuit pending 7,000
Reserve for repairs 1,000
Reserve for income taxes... 9,000
Reserve for rearrangement costs.. 3,000

e) Accruals and deferrals:

Prepaid rent income 900
Deferred interest income 400
Estimated property taxes accrued... 800
Accrued interest expense 700

f) Accommodation endorsement for partially owned company......... 10,000
g) Customer deposits held... 1,000
h) Premiums outstanding 2,000
i) Future guarantee costs on sales to date.................................... 5,000
j) Amount of contract signed to purchase 100 subassemblies during next three months at $500 each ($10,000 down payment made; there is a possibility now that the price may drop) 40,000

Accounting for Bonds

chapter **17**

A bond is a formal (written) promise to pay a specified principal at a designated date in the future and, in addition, periodic interest at a specified rate on the principal. Bonds are almost exclusively long-term obligations of business units, governmental units, and certain nonprofit units. With respect to a bond there are two parties, the investor who holds the document evidencing a future claim, and the borrower (issuer) who owes the obligation; thus, there is a reciprocal relationship between them. As a consequence, essentially the same accounting concepts and procedures are applicable to accounting for bonds by the investor and the borrower. To illustrate, note the similarities in the following example:

Borrower's Books — X Corporation	*Investor's Books — Y Company*

1. X Corporation sold $10,000, 10-year bonds, 6% annual interest, to Y Company for $10,200:

Borrower's Books		Investor's Books	
Cash 10,200		Investment in Bonds	
Bonds Payable	10,000	Payable..................10,000	
Premium on Bonds		Premium on Bond	
Payable	200	Investment..............	200
		Cash....................	10,200

2. Payment of annual interest and amortization of bond premium:

Interest Expense	580			Cash	600	
Premium on Bonds				Premium on Bond		
Payable	20			Investment		20
Cash		600		Interest Income ...		580

In view of these apparent similarities, accounting for bond *investments* and bond *liabilities* is discussed in this chapter. Specifically, similarities relate to valuation of bonds for accounting purposes, interest payments, amortization of premium and discount on bonds, and reporting.[1] The first part of the chapter deals with bond investments and the second part with bond liabilities.

Since bonds characteristically are long-term obligations under normal circumstances, they are classified as long-term liabilities by the borrower and as long-term or permanent investments by the investor. With respect to liabilities, it will be recalled that the current and long-term classifications were defined and considered in detail in Chapter 3. With respect to investments, it will be recalled that temporary investments were considered in detail in Chapter 6. In that chapter two distinguishing characteristics of temporary investments were noted: (*a*) ready marketability and (*b*) a clear management intention to convert them to working capital in the near future. All investments not meeting both of these tests are classified as permanent (long term) for accounting purposes. Permanent investments in stocks, as opposed to bonds, were considered in Chapter 11. Thus, in this chapter we are considering only one type of permanent investment (bonds) and also only one type of long-term liability (bonds).

PART A—PERMANENT INVESTMENTS IN BONDS

Nature of Permanent Investments in Bonds

Bonds intended to be held for relatively long periods should be classed under a balance sheet caption such as "investments and funds." Such a caption commonly is found immediately following current assets.

A typical bond issue is divided into a number of units (individual bonds) of $1,000 maturity amount (face value) although some issues offer other denominations such as $25, $50, $100, and $10,000. Interest payments usually are made semiannually, but despite this fairly common practice, interest rates generally are expressed on an annual basis.

---

[1] For no reason, other than precedent, the investor frequently "nets" the premium (or discount) against the maturity amount in one account Investment in Bonds Payable $10,200. The periodic amortization then is to this account so that at maturity its balance corresponds to the maturity amount of the bond. Obviously, the results are the same.

Because bonds have fixed maturity values, definite maturity dates, and specified interest payments, they tend to fluctuate in price less than do stocks. As a class of securities, bond value fluctuates in market price inversely with changes in the market rates of interest. When the market rate of interest rises, the market price of outstanding bonds falls; when the market rate of interest falls, the market price of bonds rises. These market fluctuations are the means by which the fixed-dollar interest return specified on the bonds is adjusted to the prevailing *yield rate* in the particular market. The price of individual bond issues tends to move with the interest market; however, the price also is influenced by changes in the issuer's financial standing and the approach of maturity (when the market value and redemption amount normally will coincide).

Valuation of Permanent Investments in Bonds

Permanent investments in bonds should be recorded at *cost* on the date of acquisition. The price paid for a bond (its market value) is the result of a rather delicate appraisal of the risk involved in the investment commitment together with an effective valuation of the *nominal* interest rate (as specified on the bond) in comparison with the market rate of interest (yield rate) for that type of security. If a bond has an adequate margin of security and there is confidence that it will be paid at maturity in full, the price paid will depend in the main upon the rate of interest in the current money market. Once the bond has been recorded in the accounts, changes in market or realizable values which occur because of changes in the interest rates have no effect upon the accounting for interest earned on the investment. Permanent investments in bonds should be reported on the balance sheet at cost with the aggregate market value, where available, reported parenthetically or otherwise. "Cost" as applied to permanent investments in bonds after acquisition means original cost adjusted for appropriate amortization of premium or discount. Where a *substantial* decline in market prices has taken place and if the decline appears to be a long-term adjustment in market values, the amount of such decline should be set up in a valuation allowance similar to that used for temporary investments.[2]

To the extent to which premiums or discounts enter into the cost of the bonds, adjustments of the cost are made to reflect an amortization of the premium or discount over the remaining life of the bond. Actually this amortization has the effect of gradually bringing the book value into agreement with the maturity amount and also adjusts the interest earned each period to the effective yield.

---

[2] In practice there appears to be a trend toward classification of long-term investments as marketable and nonmarketable. The trend also is to value marketable securities at market price on the date the financial statements are prepared and to value nonmarketable securities at "fair value."

Investment houses quote bonds on a yield basis. A 5% bond quoted on a 4-20 basis signifies that the bond can be bought at a price that will yield the purchaser an income of 4.20% each year on his investment to its maturity. Thus, a $1,000 bond with a nominal interest rate of 5%, payable semiannually, if purchased on a 4.20% basis (yield rate) five years before maturity, would cost $1,035.74. The $35.74 premium paid is an adjustment of interest from the 5% nominal rate to a 4.2% yield rate and must be amortized over the remaining life of the bond. Amortization is necessary because the investor's proceeds at maturity (usually par) are less than the price paid for a bond bought at a premium. Amortization is against interest because the excess of the investor's total receipts over his disbursement is regarded as his return or interest income. During each of the ensuing years the interest actually earned will be the $50 collected from the bond less the amortized premium of $7.15 (straight line; $35.74 ÷ 5) thus giving an actual yield of $42.85 on the investment (4.2%). The investment account (cost less amortized premium) at the end of the first year will stand at $1,035.74 − $7.15, or $1,028.59.

Yield and Nominal Rates

Some elaboration on bond interest rates is in order. The rate called for by the terms of a bond is known as the *nominal, contract,* or *stated* rate. Thus, the nominal interest on the $1,000 bond described above is $25 each six months, $50 a year; and the nominal interest rate is 5%. The *yield* rate is the true rate of interest earned (or paid) after taking into account the premium or discount. For bonds purchased at par, the *yield, effective,* or *market* rate corresponds to the *nominal* rate. In the case of bonds purchased at a discount, the *yield* rate is higher than nominal rate. Conversely, bonds purchased at a premium have a higher *nominal* rate than yield rate. In the foregoing example of a bond bought at a $35.74 premium the yield rate is 4.2% while the nominal rate is 5%. Throughout this text the terms *nominal* rate and *yield* rate will be preferred. To summarize, the nominal rate is the interest rate a bond says it will pay (and is the actual rate if bought at par), while yield rate is the rate of interest actually earned in a year. If the yield rate is the lower of the two the bond will be bought at a premium; the longer its life, the greater the premium because of the longer period over which the premium will be amortized. If, on the other hand, the yield rate exceeds the nominal rate the bond will be bought at a discount, and the longer its life, the greater the amount of discount.

Mathematical Valuation of Bonds

A bond is essentially a contractual obligation to pay (1) a principal amount plus (2) periodic interest. The market value of a bond theoretically is the sum of the *present values* of these two payments.

Since the principal of a bond is payable at some specified date in the future, the present value of the principal amount is obtained by discounting that amount at the yield rate of interest for the time between the present and its maturity; this is accomplished by multiplying the principal by the present value of 1. The stated (nominal) interest is payable periodically, that is, annually, semiannually, or at some other periodic date. The present value of the interest is the discounted value of those periodic payments. The present value of such a series of periodic payments is the present worth of an annuity. By multiplying the present value of an ordinary annuity of 1 by the number of dollars constituting the periodic interest payment, the present value of the interest to be paid over the life of the bond is obtained. The present value of 1 multiplied by the principal of the bond gives the present value of that amount. By adding these two present values together, that of the interest and that of the principal, the present value of the bond is obtained.

Thus, all bonds maturing at a fixed date may be valued by the following formula:

$$V = \left[M \times \frac{1}{(1+i)^n} \right] + \left[I \times a_{\overline{n}|i} \right]$$

where M is the maturity or redemption value of the bonds, I the periodic nominal interest payment, i the yield rate to the investor per interest period, n the number of interest payments over the bond life, $1/(1+i)^n$ the present value of 1 at the yield rate, and $a_{\overline{n}|i}$ the present value of an annuity of 1 for n periods at the yield rate. Thus, for accounting purposes, the value of a bond is the present value of its maturity amount plus the present value of its interest payments, both discounted at the yield rate of interest.

To illustrate simply, assume $10,000 of 5% bonds, interest payable semiannually, maturing in five years, were purchased on a 6% yield basis. What was the purchase price? Refer to Table 5–2, for the present value of 1 and Table 5–4 for the present value of an annuity of 1. The computation follows:

$$V = \$10,000 \times \frac{1}{(1.03)^{10}} \quad + \$250 \times a_{\overline{10}|.03}$$

$$= \$10,000 \times .74409391 + \$250 \times 8.53020284$$
$$= \$7,440.94 \qquad\qquad + \$2,132.55$$
$$= \$9,573.49$$

purchase price of the bond may be verified in the bond table shown in Illustration 17–1.

Illustration 17–1
Bond Table
(values to the nearest cent of a bond for $1,000,000 at 5%
interest, payable semiannually)

Yield or Net Income	3 Years	3½ Years	4 Years	4½ Years	5 Years
4.00.........	1,028,007.65	1,032,359.96	1,036,627.41	1,040,811.19	1,044,912.93
4.85.........	1,004,141.48	1,004,775.67	1,005,394.84	1,005,999.36	1,006,589.56
4.90.........	1,002,758.67	1,003,180.75	1,003,592.72	1,003,994.85	1,004,387.36
4.95.........	1,001,378.18	1,001,588.86	1,001,794.45	1,001,995.07	1,002,190.85
5.00.........	1,000,000.00	1,000,000.00	1,000,000.00	1,000,000.00	1,000,000.00
5.25.........	993,143.53	992,100.89	991,084.91	990,094.92	989,130.25
5.50.........	986,344.08	984,276.48	982,264.21	980,305.80	978,399.81
5.75.........	979,601.10	976,525.98	973,536.79	970,631.15	967,806.71
6.00.........	972,914.05	968,848.59	964,901.54	961,069.45	957,348.98

Use of Bond Tables to Determine Bond Prices and Yield Rates

In the preceding illustration the price (value) of a specified bond was computed by using values from two compound interest tables (present value of 1 and present value of annuity of 1). Bond tables are available which in effect combine these two values, so as to facilitate computation of both bond prices and bond yields. For a bond redeemable at par, five elements are considered in a bond table: (1) nominal rate, (2) number of periods to maturity, (3) maturity value, (4) bond price, and (5) yield rate. If the first three and either of the latter are known, the missing or unknown element can readily be determined from the bond table. The tabulation in Illustration 17–1, excerpted from a complete set of bond tables, serves to illustrate how such tables can be used.

To illustrate, assume a three-year, $10,000 bond, interest at 5%, payable semiannually, is purchased at a price to yield the investor 4.90%, the price of the bond can be read directly from the table in Illustration 17–1 as $10,027.59 (column for three years and line for 4.90 yield). If the bond is purchased at a yield rate not shown in the table, for example 4.925%, the approximate price may be obtained by interpolation as shown below:

To restate the problem:

Yield   Valuation
.04900 = $10,027.59
.04925 = To be determined by interpolation between the two values
.04950 = $10,013.78

Interpolation:

Valuation at .04925

$$= \$10{,}013.78 + \left[\left(\frac{.04950 - .04925}{.04950 - .04900} \right) \times (\$10{,}027.59 - \$10{,}013.78) \right]$$

$$= \$10{,}013.78 + \left[\left(\frac{.00025}{.00050} \right) \times \$13.81 \right]$$

$$= \$10{,}013.78 + \$6.90$$

$$= \underline{\$10{,}020.68} \text{ (the approximate price of the bond)}$$

In some cases the price (valuation) of a bond is known but the yield rate is not known, in which case the latter must be determined. The bond itself will provide data relative to the maturity value, the nominal interest rate, and the remaining life of the bond. With these four factors known, the unknown factor, the yield rate, can be determined by reference to a bond table. To illustrate, assume a bond is purchased for $9,921 and that it has a maturity value of $10,000, a nominal interest rate of 5% payable semiannually, and has a remaining life of $3\frac{1}{2}$ years. What is the implied yield rate? Reference to a bond table (Illustration 17–1) for a 5% bond, semiannual interest payments, under the $3\frac{1}{2}$-year column will show the price ($9,921) to be on the 5.25 line, thus the yield rate is 5.25% per annum. Frequently, the price (valuation) of the bond may not be precisely the amount shown in the bond table (as was the case in the above example). In such cases the yield rate can be closely approximated by interpolation from the valuations given in the table. To illustrate, assume that a three-year $10,000 bond, interest 5%, payable semiannually, is purchased for $10,020.68. What is the yield rate? by interpolation of the bond table values the yield rate may be determined as follows:

To restate the problem:

Valuation

$10,027.59 = .04900

10,020.68 = To be determined by interpolation between the two values

10,013.78 = .04950

Interpolation:

Valuation at $10,020.68

$$= .04900 + \left[\left(\frac{\$10{,}027.59 - \$10{,}020.68}{\$10{,}027.59 - \$10{,}013.78} \right) \times (.04950 - .04900) \right]$$

$$= .04900 + \left[\frac{\$6.91}{\$13.81} \times .00050 \right]$$

$$= \underline{.04925} \text{ (approximate yield of the bond)}$$

Amortization of Bond Premium and Bond Discount

As previously noted, bond premium and bond discount are considered as adjustments to interest over the number of periods the bonds are to be held. In the process of determining interest income from bond investments, part of the discount is added to the interest collected or accrued while part of any premium is deducted (whichever the case may be). The process of making these adjustments involving premium or discount is called *amortization*.

There are two widely used methods of amortizing bond premium and bond discount; both are utilized by borrowers as well as by investors. They are:

1. Straight line amortization.   The total discount or premium is prorated in equal dollar amounts to interim periods between the date of purchase and the maturity date of the bond. This method results in a uniform amount (dollars) of amortization per period; hence, there is a stable amount of interest on the bonds recognized in the accounts each interim period. Straight line amortization is easy to understand, simple to apply, and is considered sufficiently accurate in most cases. Thus, on these *practical* grounds it is widely utilized; however, it is conceptually deficient.

2. Present value amortization.   This method also is referred to as the compound interest or scientific approach; the total discount or premium is prorated to interim periods on the basis of a constant *rate* (as opposed to a constant dollar amount), so that a uniform rate of interest income on the bonds is recognized in the accounts. The uniform rate corresponds with the yield rate of the bonds. This method is sound theoretically, in contrast with the straight line approach. However, it is somewhat more complex and more difficult to apply than is the straight line method.

Each of the two methods of amortizing bond discount and premium on long-term investments will be illustrated in concluding this section of the chapter.

Straight Line Amortization Illustrated

Bonds Purchased at a Premium.   Assume that, on April 1, 1971, an investor purchased bonds with a maturity value of $10,000 for $10,280.07. The bonds mature on April 1, 1974, and pay interest at an annual rate of 5% semiannually on April 1 and October 1. The table in Illustration 17–2 gives the investor's entries (tabulated) during the holding period except for purchase of the bonds, their redemption, and closing entries (which, of course, would vary depending on the fiscal period; any necessary adjustments would similarly vary depending on this factor).

Under the straight line method the amount of the premium amortization is obtained by dividing the total to be amortized by the num-

Illustration 17–2
Premium Amortized by Straight Line Method

Date	Cash Dr. (a)	Interest Income Cr. (b)	Premium on Bond Investment Cr. (c)	Investment Carrying Value (d)
4/1/71..................	–	–	–	$10,280.07
10/1/71...................$250.00		$203.32	$ 46.68	10,233.39
4/1/72................... 250.00		203.32	46.68	10,186.71
10/1/72................... 250.00		203.32	46.68	10,140.03
4/1/73................... 250.00		203.32	46.68	10,093.35
10/1/73................... 250.00		203.32	46.68	10,046.67
4/1/74................... 250.00		203.33	46.67	10,000.00
			$280.07	

(a) $10,000 × 5% × 6/12 = $250.00.
(b) Cash interest $250.00 − $46.68 = $203.32.
(c) Total premium $280.07 ÷ 6 periods = $46.68.
(d) Preceding carrying value minus the amortization of premium ($10,280.07 − $46.68 = $10,233.39).

ber of interest periods from date of purchase to maturity (i.e., $280.07 ÷ 6 = $46.68). It should be noted that the amortization on 4/1/74 was adjusted so as to write off the remaining premium exactly.

Bonds Purchased at a Discount. To illustrate bonds purchased at a discount, assume that the $10,000, 5% bonds in the preceding illustration instead cost $9,729.14. The discount on bond investment amounts to $270.86. The amortization and related entries are tabulated in Illustration 17–3.

Illustration 17–3
Discount Amortized by Straight-Line Method

Date	Cash Dr. (a)	Interest Income Cr. (b)	Discount on Bond Investment Dr. (c)	Investment Carrying Value (d)
4/1/71..................	–	–	–	$ 9,729.14
10/1/71...................$250.00		$295.14	$ 45.14	9,774.28
4/1/72................... 250.00		295.14	45.14	9,819.42
10/1/72................... 250.00		295.14	45.14	9,864.56
4/1/73................... 250.00		295.14	45.14	9,909.70
10/1/73................... 250.00		295.14	45.14	9,954.84
4/1/74................... 250.00		295.16	45.16	10,000.00
			$270.86	

(a) $10,000 × 5% × 6/12 = $250.00
(b) $250.00 + $45.14 = $295.14
(c) $\frac{\$10,000 - \$9,729.14}{6} = \$45.14$
(d) Preceding carrying value plus (c).

Under the straight line method the amount of the periodic discount amortization is obtained by dividing the total to be amortized by the number of interest periods (i.e., $270.86 ÷ 6 = $45.14). It should be noted that it was necessary to adjust the last period's amortization so as to write off the discount exactly. Commonly the investment is reflected in a single account at its actual cost, but for illustrative purposes separate premium and discount accounts have been shown.

Investor's Entries When Interest and Fiscal Closing Dates Do Not Coincide

If the interest payment dates on a bond investment do not coincide with the date on which the investor closes his books, it is necessary to adjust the Interest Income account for the interest accrued since the date of the last interest receipt. It is also necessary to adjust for any premium or discount which should be amortized over the time since the last interest receipt. Using the example of straight line premium amortization shown in Illustration 17–2, if the investor uses only one investment account and adjusts and closes his books annually on December 31, his entries on December 31, 1971, to adjust for the period from October 1, date of the last interest receipt, to year-end would be as follows:

December 31, 1971

Bond Interest Receivable ($\frac{3}{6}$ of $250) 125.00		
Bond Investment ($\frac{3}{6}$ of $46.68)		23.34
Interest Income ($\frac{3}{6}$ of $203.32)		101.66

To record accrued interest and premium amortization for the last three months of 1971 (assumes amortization at each interest date).

Interest Income 304.98	
Income Summary	304.98

To close interest earned on bond investment from April 1 to December 31, 1971, $203.32 + $101.66 = $304.98.

The adjustment would be reversed on January 1, 1972.

Some accountants prefer to record premium or discount amortization only at the close of the fiscal period rather than at each interest date. Under this procedure entries during 1971 subsequent to purchase of the bonds would be as follows:

October 1, 1971

Cash 250.00	
Interest Income	250.00

To record collection of interest on bonds for six months ($10,000 × 5% × 6/12 = $250).

December 31, 1971

Bond Interest Receivable 125.00	
Interest Income	125.00

To accrue three months' interest on bond investment ($250 × $\frac{3}{6}$ = $125).

The preceding entry would be reversed on January 1, 1972, but the one which follows would not:

Interest Income ($46.68 + ⅜ of $46.68) 70.02
  Bond Investment..   70.02
To amortize nine months' premium (April 1 to December
31).

(Note: In subsequent years this entry would be for 12 months' amortization.)

Interest Income ($250.00 + $125.00 − $70.02)........................304.98
  Income Summary 304.98
To close nine months' interest earned.

(Note: In subsequent years this entry would be for 12 months' interest.)

Bonds Bought between Interest Dates

When bonds are purchased between interest dates, part of the
total consideration paid must be allocated to accrued interest; the
remainder, of course, is allocable to the cost of the bonds. For example, if an investor purchased bonds with a maturity value of $10,000
on July 1, 1971, for a total consideration of $10,381.73, and the bonds
pay 5% interest per annum on April 1 and October 1, the first $125
represents payment for three months' accrued interest (April 1 to
July 1) while the remainder is the cost of the bond investment. This
purchase would be recorded as follows:

Bond Investment...10,256.73
Interest Income ($10,000 × 5% × 3/12).......................... 125.00
  Cash 10,381.73

(Premium = $381.73 − $125.00 = $256.73.)

If these bonds matured on April 1, 1974, remaining entries throughout 1971 would be similar to those illustrated for bond investments in
the example in Illustration 17–2, as can be seen below (December 31
closing assumed):

October 1, 1971

Cash (full six months' interest)...250.00
  Bond Investment°..   23.34
  Interest Income...   226.66
To record collection of six months' interest on first interest
date (three months after purchase) and amortization of pre-
mium.

° Remaining months to maturity (July 1, 1971, to April 1, 1974) = 33. Amortization
for three months (July 1 to Oct. 1) = 3/33 × $256.73 = $23.34

December 31, 1971

Bond Interest Receivable (3/6 of $250)..................................125.00
  Bond Investment (3/33 of $256.73) 23.34
  Interest Income...   101.66
To adjust for three months' accrued interest and three
months' amortization of premium.

Interest Income ($226.66 + $101.66 − $125.00) 203.32
  Income Summary 203.32
To close interest earned since purchase.

Bonds Sold between Interest Dates

The sale of all or a portion of bonds held as a permanent investment between their interest dates calls for removal of the carrying value of the bonds sold as of the date of sale. The carrying value must be adjusted to the date of sale (unless, of course, the bonds had been purchased at par), interest should be accrued, and the difference between the proceeds and the adjusted carrying value plus accrued interest should be recorded as gain or loss on the sale. Thereafter, if a portion of the bonds is still held, a new amortization table should be prepared, or at each interest date the fraction of the bonds still held should be multiplied times the original table values to arrive at the new proper amounts.

To illustrate, refer to the bonds (maturity value, $10,000) purchased on April 1, 1971, for $9,729.14, for which an amortization table was given in Illustration 17–3; the interest dates are April 1 and October 1. Now assume that the investor sold 40% of them ($4,000 maturity value) on July 1, 1972, for $3,930, including accrued interest. The sequence of related entries during 1972 relative to the 40% sold and the 60% retained, assuming the books are closed each December 31, would be as follows:

January 1, 1972

Interest Income...	147.57	
Bond Investment (3/6 × $45.14)		22.57
Bond Interest Receivable (3/6 × $250)		125.00

To reverse the adjusting entry made on December 31, 1971, for three months' accrued interest and discount amortization.

April 1, 1972

Cash (six months' interest).................................	250.00	
Bond Investment (six months' amortization of discount)........	45.14	
Interest Income......................................		295.14

To record collection of semiannual interest and amortization on entire bond portfolio; refer to Illustration 17–3 for computations.

July 1, 1972

Bond Interest Receivable $\left(40\% \times \dfrac{\$250}{2}\right)$	50.00	
Bond Investment $\left(40\% \times \dfrac{\$45.14}{2}\right)$	9.03	
Interest Income...		59.03

To accrue interest for three months on 40% of bonds sold and to amortize three months' discount to adjust the accounts up to date of sale.

Cash 3,930.00
Loss on Sale of Bond Investment 56.80
    Bond Interest Receivable 50.00
    Bond Investment [(40% × $9,819.42) + $9.03]............. 3,936.80
    To record sale of 40% of the bonds by removal of the bond interest receivable account and 40% of the bond investment balance.

October 1, 1972

Cash (60% × $250) 150.00
Bond Investment (60% × $45.14 − amortization)................. 27.08
    Interest Income... 177.08
    Collection of semiannual interest and six months' amortization on 60% of the bonds not sold.

December 31, 1972

Bond Interest Receivable 60% × $\left(\dfrac{\$250}{2}\right)$ 75.00

Bond Investment 60% × $\left(\dfrac{\$45.14}{2}\right)$ 13.54

    Interest Income... 88.54
    To record accrued interest and discount amortization for last three months of 1972 on portion (60%) of bonds still held.

Interest Income.. 472.22
    Loss on Sale of Bond Investment 56.80
    Income Summary 415.42
    To close nominal accounts for the year.

Separate amortization tables for the sold and unsold portions of the bonds could be prepared dated from the last interest date on which the entire portfolio was held. If this were done, the tables would show the information given in Illustration 17–4. Use of these tables would facilitate recording the 40% and 60% allocations shown in the preceding entries.

Illustration 17–4
Amortization Table

Date	Cash Dr.	Interest Income Cr.	Discount on Bond Investment Dr.	Investment Carrying Value
For 40% Sold 4/1/72	$100.00	$118.06	$18.06	$3,927.77
10/1/72	100.00	118.06	18.06	3,945.83
For 60% Not Sold 4/1/72	150.00	177.08	27.08	5,891.65
10/1/72	150.00	177.08	27.08	5,918.73
4/1/73	150.00	177.08	27.08	5,945.81
10/1/73	150.00	177.08	27.08	5,972.89
4/1/74	150.00	177.11	27.11	6,000.00

Bonds Callable before Maturity

Often the bond contract provides that the issuer may elect to call the bonds for payment before maturity. The call for payment may be on or after a date specified in the bond and usually is at a price in excess of maturity (par) value. Where such a call provision is included, the investor must adjust his amortization to provide for the possibility of the prepayment of the bond investment. Thus, where a bond is purchased at 109½ and is callable in 10 years at 102, although the maturity date is 20 years from date of purchase, the premium to be amortized on such a bond of a par value of $10,000 would be as follows:

> Cost of $10,000 par-value bond purchased at 109½...............$10,950
> Call price in 10 years from date of purchase....................... 10,200
>   Premium to Be Amortized over 10-Year Period...........$ 750

If the bond is not called by the issuer at the time it has been amortized to $10,200 (end of 10 years), the investor should amortize the remaining $200 over the second 10-year period.

If a bond is purchased at a discount and is callable at a premium, it is not considered desirable practice, because of conservatism, to amortize more than the discount from the par value of the bond, unless there is definite assurance that the bond will be called on the call date. For example, if the above bond were purchased for $9,800 and were callable at 102 in 10 years, the $200 discount ($10,000 par value less $9,800 cost) should be amortized over the full 20 years from date of purchase to date of maturity. Then if the bond is called at the end of 10 years, the excess of the call price over the amortized value of the bond investment should be taken up as a gain in the year of the call.

Present Value Amortization Illustrated

The present value (compound interest) method of amortizing views the premium or discount as the amount of an annuity, and the amount to be written off in any given period is determined by the present value of the annuity at that time. Since bonds are purchased to yield a given rate of interest, the amount of the premium or discount written off (amortized) each period is obtained by taking the difference between the effective interest on the carrying value and the nominal interest on the par value for the period. In the illustrations which follow the bond purchase prices, dates, and rates correspond, for comparative purposes, with those shown in the straight line amortization examples in Illustrations 17-2 and 17-3; for convenience, however, the illustrative data are restated below.

Bonds Purchased at a Premium. To illustrate present value amortization of bond premium, assume an investor purchased bonds on April

Illustration 17–5
Premium Amortized by Present Value Method

Date	Cash Dr. (a)	Interest Income Cr. (b)	Premium on Bond Investment Cr. (c)	Investment Carrying Value (d)
4/1/71	—	—	—	$10,280.07
10/1/71	$ 250.00	$ 205.60	$ 44.40	10,235.67
4/1/72	250.00	204.71	45.29	10,190.38
10/1/72	250.00	203.81	46.19	10,144.19
4/1/73	250.00	202.88	47.12	10,097.07
10/1/73	250.00	201.94	48.06	10,049.01
4/1/74	250.00	200.99	49.01	10,000.00
	$1,500.00	$1,219.93	$280.07	

(a) $10,000 × 5% × 6/12 = $250.00.
(b) $10,280.07 × 4% × 6/12 = $205.60.
(c) $250.00 − $205.60 = $44.40.
(d) $10,280.07 − $44.40 = $10,235.67.

1, 1971, with a maturity value of $10,000. The bonds mature on April 1, 1974, and annual interest of 5% is paid the holder every six months beginning with October 1, 1971. The investor paid $10,280.07 for the bonds, which price will yield the investor 4% annual interest (paid semiannually) on the amount of the investment. A table which shows the amortization of the premium and the related entries using the present value method is shown in Illustration 17–5.

You should compare the results in Illustration 17–5 with those in Illustration 17–2. Note that when straight line amortization is used the *amount* of interest income is constant each period (Illustration 17–2). In contrast, when present value amortization is used the amount of interest income is less each period. That is because a constant rate (the yield rate) is applied to a decreasing investment carrying value. This comparison clearly demonstrates the conceptual superiority of the present value method of amortization.

Bonds Purchased at a Discount

To illustrate present value amortization of bond discount, assume an investor purchased bonds having a par value of $10,000 on April 1, 1971. The bonds mature on April 1, 1974, and annual interest of 5% is paid the holder every six months beginning with October 1, 1971. The investor paid $9,729.14 for the bonds, a price which will yield the investor 6% annual interest (paid semiannually) on the amount of the investment. The table in Illustration 17–6 shows the amortization of the discount and the related entries using the scientific (present value) method.

Illustration 17–6
Discount Amortized by the Present Value Method

Date	Cash Dr. (a)	Interest Income Cr. (b)	Discount on Bond Investment Dr. (c)	Investment Carrying Value (d)
4/1/71	–	–	–	$ 9,729.14
10/1/71 .... $	250.00	$ 291.87	$ 41.87	9,771.01
4/1/72	250.00	293.13	43.13	9,814.14
10/1/72	250.00	294.42	44.42	9,858.56
4/1/73	250.00	295.76	45.76	9,904.32
10/1/73	250.00	297.13	47.13	9,951.45
4/1/74	250.00	298.55	48.55	10,000.00
	$1,500.00	$1,770.86	$270.86	

(a)$10,000 × 5% × 6/12 = $250.00.
(b)$9,729.14 × 6% × 6/12 = $291.87.
(c)$291.87 − $250.00 = $41.87.
(d)$9,729.14 + $41.87 = $9,771.01.

Entries under Present Value Method When Interest and Closing Dates Do Not Coincide

Using the present value amortization example involving a premium (Illustration 17–5), if the investor adjusts and closes his books each December 31, the following entries would be made on December 31, 1971. It is assumed the premium was debited to the Bond Investment account.

December 31, 1971

Bond Interest Receivable (3/6 of $250)...................................125.00
    Interest Income (3/6 of $204.71)..................................... 102.35
    Bond Investment (3/6 of $45.29 premium)....................... 22.65
    To record accrued interest and premium amortization for the
    last three months of 1971.

Interest Income...307.95
    Income Summary 307.95
    To close.

The adjusting entry shown above could be reversed on January 1, 1972.

Bonds Bought between Interest Dates

When bonds are purchased between interest dates *on a specified yield basis*, the total payment must include the value of the bonds on the agreed yield basis plus the nominal (cash) interest accrued since the last interest date. For example, if the bonds shown in Illustration 17–5 had been purchased on July 1, 1971, which is three months past the issue date, and at the same annual yield basis of 4% paid semiannually, the total price of the bond investment would be computed as follows:

Valuation (price) on April 1, 1971 (per Illustration 17–5)..............$10,280.07
Premium amortization, 4/1/71 to 7/1/71, 3/6 × $44.40................... −22.20
Valuation (price) of the bond investment on 7/1/71 on 4%
    annual yield basis..$10,257.87
Cash interest accrued for three months (April 1 to July 1)............ +125.00
Total Cash Outlay for the Bond Investment on 7/1/71 ....$10,382.87

Since $44.40 represents the change in carrying value (due to amortization of premium) for the six-month period and the bonds were purchased at the midpoint of the six months, one half of $44.40 or $22.20 must be subtracted from the April 1 value to secure the July 1 value on the 2% yield basis (semiannual). To this amount must be added the nominal interest of $125 for the three months since the entire $250, representing six months' interest, will be paid to the holder at the next interest date regardless of what fraction of the six months he actually owned the bond.

The entry to record the purchase would be:

July 1, 1971

Bond Investment (par)...10,000.00
Premium on Bond Investment...................................... 257.87
Bond Interest Income (accrued interest purchased – three
    months).. 125.00
    Cash...   10,382.87

Assuming present value amortization, the entry to record the receipt of the first interest payment (for six months) would be:

October 1, 1971

Cash ($10,000 × 5% × 6/12)...250.00
Premium on Bond Investment ($10,257.87 less
    $10,235.67°)..   22.20
    Bond Interest Income 227.80

° $10,235.67 is taken from Illustration 17–5.

The table for present value amortization after October 1, 1971, would be the same as that shown for the bond when purchased on an interest date, such as April 1, 1971 (Illustration 17–5).

If the bond investment (purchased at a discount on a 6% annual yield basis, interest paid semiannually) shown in Illustration 17–6 had instead been purchased between interest dates, for example, on July 1, 1971, the amount paid for it would have been computed in a manner similar to that illustrated above for the situation where a premium was involved. However, the discount amortization for the three months between the preceding interest date and the date of sale would be added to the preceding carrying value instead of being subtracted; the accrued interest would be treated as previously illustrated. Assuming purchase of the discounted bonds (Illustration 17–6) on July 1, 1971, the computations would be:

Valuation on April 1, 1971 (per Illustration 17–6)............................$9,729.14
Add discount amortization, 4/1/71 to 7/1/71, 3/6 × $41.87 ....   +20.93
Valuation (price) of the bond investment on 7/1/71 on a 6%
    annual yield basis $9,750.07
Cash interest accrued for three months, 4/1/71 to 7/1/71..................   +125.00
Total Cash Outlay for the Bond Investment $9,875.07

Indicated entry for purchase on July 1, 1971:

Bond Investment (par)..10,000.00
Bond Interest Income (accrued interest purchased, three
    months) 125.00
    Discount on Bond Investment..............................   249.93
    Cash...   9,875.07

Sale of Part of Permanent Bond Investment between Interest Dates

When part of a permanent investment in bonds is sold between interest dates, the procedures and entries are the same when present value amortization of premium or discount is used as those with respect to straight line amortization, except for calculation of the respective amounts for the entries. As with straight line amortization, the accrued interest and amortization of premium or discount relative to the portion of the bond investment sold should be brought up to the date of the sale. Next the entry for the sale can be made to remove the carrying value of the sold bonds as of the date of the sale.

To illustrate a sale between interest dates when present value amortization is being used, assume an investor purchased $5,000 bonds, dated and purchased on January 1, 1971, due in 5 years, 5% annual interest, payable semiannually on January 1 and July 1, at a cost of $5,141.39 which will yield an annual return of 4%. In addition, the bonds have a provision that they can be redeemed at 101 on January 1, 1973. The investor closes his books each March 1. Subsequently, on May 1, 1972, the investor sold one fifth ($1,000 par value) of the bonds for $1,015 plus any accrued interest; assume that later it was decided to redeem them. Assume the solution required all entries with respect to the bond investment.

As a first step in the solution it would be desirable to prepare an amortization table for the total investment as shown in Illustration 17–7.

The next logical step would be to develop the entries for the total investment through the year-end entries at March 1, 1972, that is, immediately preceding the sale. These entries are separately identified in the tabulation given in Illustration 17–8.

Next, an entry should be made to bring the accrued interest and premium amortization up to the date of the sale. In view of the re-

Illustration 17–7
Premium Amortization, Present Value Method

Date	Cash Dr. (a)	Interest Income Cr. (b)	Premium on Bond Investment Cr. (c)	Investment Carrying Value (d)
1/1/71				$5,141.39
7/1/71	$125.00	$102.83	$22.17	5,119.22
1/1/72	125.00	102.38	22.62	5,096.60
7/1/72	125.00	101.93	23.07	5,073.53
1/1/73	125.00	101.47	23.53	5,050.00

(a) $5,000 × 5% × 6/12 = $125.00.

(b) $5,141.39 × 4% × 6/12 = $102.83.

(c) $125.00 − $102.83 = $22.17.

(d) $5,141.39 − $22.17 = $5,119.22.

versing entry after March 1, the accrual and premium amortization entry must be for the period January 1 (last interest date) through May 1, 1972 (date of sale), that is, for four months on those bonds sold (one fifth of the total). This entry would be as follows, assuming no separate account for premium:

May 1, 1972

Bond Interest Receivable ($1,000 × 5% × 4/12) 16.67
    Bond Investment (premium amortization for
      four months)° 3.08
    Bond Interest Income... 13.59

°Computation of amortization:

Amortization indicated in the above table for
  six months...$23.07

Amortization applicable to bonds sold
  ($23.07 × 1/5) ....$ 4.61

Amortization for four months ($4.61 × 4/6)................................ $3.08

Having brought the accrued interest and amortization up to date, the sale entry can now be made as follows:

May 1, 1972

Cash ($1,015.00 + $16.67, four months interest per
  above) 1,031.67
Loss on Sale of Permanent Investments........................... 1.24
    Bond Interest Receivable (per above) 16.67
    Bond Investment (unamortized balance)° 1,016.24

°Computation of the credit to bond investment:

Unamortized balance indicated in above table
  for the investment on 1/1/72 ....$5,096.60

Unamortized balance on 1/1/72 on bonds sold
  ($5,096.60 × 1/5)..$1,019.32
Deduct amortization for period 1/1/72 to
  5/1/72 (date of sale) on bonds sold
  (per above).. 3.08

    Difference — Unamortized Balance on
    5/1/72..$1,016.24

Illustration 17-8
Entries for Bond Investment

Date	Explanation	Cash Dr., Cr.*	Bond Interest Income Dr., Cr.*	Premium on Bond Investment Dr., Cr.*	Bond Investment Dr., Cr.*	Bond Interest Receivable Dr., Cr.*	Income Summary Dr., Cr.*
	Entries prior to partial sale:						
1/1/71	For purchase of bond investment	$5,141.39*	—	$141.39	$5,000.00		—
3/1/71	Adjusting entry—2 months	—	$ 34.28*	7.39*	—	$41.67	—
3/1/71	Closing entry	—	34.28		—		$ 34.28*
3/2/71	Reversing entry	—	34.28	7.39	—	41.67*	—
7/1/71	Collection of interest for 6 months	125.00	102.83*	22.17*	—	—	—
1/1/72	Collection of interest for 6 months	125.00	102.38*	22.62*	—	—	—
3/1/72	Adjusting entry—2 months	—	33.98*	7.69*	—	41.67	—
3/1/72	Closing entry	—	204.91		—		204.91*
3/2/72	Reversing entry	—	33.98	7.69	—	41.67*	—
	Entries for sale of one fifth of the bond investment:						
5/1/72	To accrue interest and premium to date of sale	—	13.59*	3.08*	—	16.67	—
5/1/72	To record sale of one fifth of the investment	1,031.67	—	16.24*	1,000.00*	16.67*	1.24
	Entries for remainder (four fifths) of the bond investment:						
7/1/72	Collection of interest for 6 months	100.00	81.54*	18.46*	—	—	—
1/1/73	Collection of interest for 6 months	100.00	81.18*	18.82*	—	—	—
1/1/73	Collection on bond investment (redemption)	4,040.00	—	40.00*	4,000.00*	—	—
3/1/73	Closing entry		142.33	—		—	142.33*
		$ 380.28					$380.28*

The two entries given above are shown on the tabulation of entries given in Illustration 17–8. Entries for the remaining investment (four fifths) are also included. To repeat an earlier statement, a careful study of Illustration 17–8 will reveal that the entries were precisely the same as if straight line amortization were used—the only difference being in the dollar amount of premium amortization computed for the several entries.

Treatment of Extreme Fluctuations of Bond Values

If a bond on which interest or principal or both have been defaulted is held or purchased, special treatment is warranted. Clearly, there must be an adjustment of carrying value if default occurs while the bond is held as an investment. Valuation of bonds in default is not easy. There may or may not be a market value for them. The fact that there is no bid price at a particular time does not prove the bond to be worthless. Even when bid quotations are available, they should not be used without first checking to determine probable proceeds of liquidation of the underlying bond security, the mortgaged property. Transfer from the regular investment account to an appropriately titled special account at fair value with recognition of the loss is necessary, especially since defaulted bonds are frequently turned over to a trustee pending settlement. Interest on bonds in default should not be accrued.

When defaulted bonds are purchased *flat*, i.e., a single price is paid for the bond and accrued interest, the cost should be recorded in a single account. Subsequent receipts, regardless of how designated by the payer, should be accounted for under the "cost recovery or sunk cost method." That is, receipts should be treated as a recovery of investment cost, unless, of course, they ultimately exceed cost because of full recovery. A favorable change in the financial fortunes of the issuer may warrant reclassification of the defaulted bond investment and resumption of accrual of interest. However, until indications of the ultimate solvency of the issuer are very clear, the conservative treatment described above should be followed.

PART B—LONG-TERM LIABILITIES (BONDS)

Nature and Purpose of Long-Term Liabilities

The long-term debts of a business entity are also known as fixed liabilities. Long term is understood to mean liabilities not maturing within the ensuing year or the operating cycle of the entity, in case the cycle extends beyond the year. Bonds maturing within one year or the next operating cycle may still properly be classed as long-term or fixed if they are expected to be refunded (replaced with other bonds of longer maturity and lower interest rate) or to be liquidated by funds reflected in noncurrent asset classifications (such as where adequate sinking funds exist).[3]

Fixed liabilities generally are incurred for the purpose of securing a part of the more permanent capital of the concern, such as for the acquisition of fixed assets.

The term *mortgages payable* is misleading. The fixed liability is the long-term note, and the mortgage is a related lien on specified assets (a conditional transfer of title) which serves as security for the amount borrowed.

Classes of Bonds Payable

Bonds may be classified on the following bases:

1. Character of issuing corporation. The borrower may be a private corporation issuing *industrial* bonds or a public corporation issuing *municipal* or *government* bonds.

2. Character of security. Secured bonds are supported by a lien on specific assets, whereas unsecured bonds have no such support. Unsecured bonds are frequently called *debenture bonds*. *Guaranty security bonds* are those which, in case of default, will be paid as to principal and interest by the guarantor. For example, a parent corporation may guarantee payment of the bonds issued by its subsidiary companies. *Lien security bonds* may be secured by a lien on personalty consisting of securities (collateral trust bonds), rolling stock (car trust and equipment bonds), and funds (sinking fund bonds), or by a lien on realty.

3. Purpose of issue. *Funding bonds* are issued to retire current or other long-term debt. *Purchase money bonds* are issued in full or part payment for property. *Refunding bonds* are issued to retire maturing obligations and usually have the same security as the redeemed bonds. *Consolidated bonds* replace several prior issues and unite the securities for the retired issues.

4. Payment of interest. *Income bonds* differ from ordinary bonds in that the payment of interest on income bonds depends on the earning of net income. *Participating bonds* have a specified minimum rate of interest plus a participation in profits; they may have a specific maximum (in limited participation) or an unlimited maximum (in unlimited participation). Most bonds carry a specified rate of interest payable semiannually; if this interest is remitted by individual checks made payable to the "holder of record," the bonds are called *registered bonds* (i.e., by name); if the interest checks (coupons) are attached to the bonds to be detached by whoever has possession of the bond and cashed when due, the bonds are called *coupon bonds*.

---

[3]Committee on Accounting Procedure, AICPA, "Restatement and Revision of Accounting Research Bulletins," *Accounting Research Bulletin No. 43* (New York, 1961), pp. 21–23.

5. Maturity of principal. Bonds maturing at a fixed date are either *straight* (ordinary) *bonds,* i.e., maturing all at one time, or *serial,* i.e., maturing in stated installments. *Callable* or *redeemable bonds* give the issuing company the right to retire them at a stated price before the obligatory maturity date. *Convertible bonds* are, at the payee's option, convertible into other specified securities of the issuer.

Contents of Bond Indenture

Accounting for a bond issue must be consistent with the provisions of the bond indenture, mortgage, or other loan agreement. The accountant must have full knowledge of these provisions in order to make "full disclosure" on the financial statements.

The bond indenture contains information on the following points of special concern to accounting and financial supervisors in complying with the requirements of the loan.

1. Deposits to cover bond interest.
2. Deposits to the sinking fund.
3. Provisions affecting mortgaged property—taxes, insurance payments, proceeds collected on destroyed mortgaged property, collections of interest and dividends on pledged securities, release of part of mortgaged property from the lien of the mortgage, etc.
4. Trustee's access to corporate books and records.
5. Prescribed ratios of bonds outstanding to (a) net tangible assets and (b) net current assets.
6. Certification of bonds by trustee.
7. Period of grace allowed to issuing corporation.
8. Maturity of issue and provisions for repayment.
9. Other descriptive characteristics of the bonds, such as interest provisions, call provisions, and conversion privileges.

Amortization of Premium or Discount on Bonds Payable

The section on bond investments sets out amortization procedures under both the straight line and present value methods for the investor. The same principles and procedures apply to amortization of premium or discount on bond liabilities for the issuer. One minor difference is worthy of mention. In the case of bond investments it was noted that two accounts could be set up to reflect the permanent bond investment—one for the principal, the other for the premium or discount. However, the more common practice for bond investments is to maintain a single account for each bond investment, the balance of which is the amount of the principal plus any premium or minus any discount. In contrast, in the case of bond liabilities it is customary to maintain separate accounts—one for the principal or face amount of the debt, the other for discount or premium. There also may be a separate account for bond issue costs.

Since the relative amounts of a bond issue are likely to be material as compared to other statement items on the issuer's books, present value amortization of premium or discount ordinarily is preferable since it results in a theoretically correct accounting for both interest expense and the carrying value of the debt.

It goes almost without saying that valuation of bonds payable, determination of effective interest rates, and usage of bond tables and formulas for bonds payable follow the same principles as for permanent investments in bonds. Accordingly there is no repetitive discussion of these topics here; however, an illustration is presented.

Present Value Amortization Illustrated on Bonds Payable

To illustrate the entries for a bond issue, assume a $10,000 bond issue was dated and sold April 1, 1971, for $10,190.39. The nominal annual interest rate was 5%; the yield rate at this price for an issue maturing in two years is 4% per annum; interest is payable semi-annually.

An amortization table using the present value method is shown in Illustration 17–9.

Illustration 17–9
Present Value Amortization Table—Premium on Bonds Payable

Date	Cash Cr. (a)	Bond Interest Expense Dr. (b)	Bond Premium Dr. (c)	Liability Carrying Value (d)
4/1/71	—	—	—	$10,190.39
10/1/71 ....$ 250.00		$203.81	$ 46.19	10,144.20
4/1/72	250.00	202.88	47.12	10,097.08
10/1/72	250.00	201.94	48.06	10,049.02
4/1/73	250.00	200.98	49.02	10,000.00
	$1,000.00	$809.61	$190.39	

(a) $10,000 × 5% × 6/12 = $250.00.
(b) $10,190.39 × 4% × 6/12 = $203.81.
(c) Column (a) minus column (b).
(d) $10,190.39 − $46.19 = $10,144.20.

If the issuer's fiscal year ends December 31, he would make the entries tabulated in Illustration 17–10 relative to the bonds in 1971, 1972, and 1973.

Some accountants prefer to amortize premiums or discounts only at year-end. This procedure, of course, can be followed for bond investments and for bond liabilities. The end results and the effect on statements are the same. Year-end amortization is reflected in Illustration 17–11 using the same data as in Illustration 17–10.

Illustration 17–10

Bonds Payable – Amortization on Interest Dates

Date	Explanation	Cash Dr., Cr.°	Bonds Payable Dr., Cr.°	Bond Interest Expense Dr., Cr.°	Accrued Bond Interest Dr., Cr.°	Income Summary Dr., Cr.°	Bond Premium Dr., Cr.°
4/1/71	Sale of bonds	$10,190.39	$10,000.00°				$190.39°
10/1/71	Interest payment and amortization	250.00°		$203.81			46.19
12/31/71	Adjusting entry			101.44	$125.00°		23.56
12/31/71	Closing entry			305.25°		$305.25	
12/31/71	Reversing entry			101.44°	125.00		23.56°
4/1/72	Interest payment and amortization	250.00°		202.88			47.12
10/1/72	Interest payment and amortization	250.00°		201.94			48.06
12/31/72	Adjusting entry			100.49	125.00°		24.51
12/31/72	Closing entry			403.87°		403.87	
12/31/72	Reversing entry and amortization			100.49°	125.00		24.51°
4/1/73	Interest payment and amortization	250.00°		200.98			49.02
4/1/73	Payment of bonds	10,000.00°	10,000.00				
12/31/73	Closing entry			100.49°		100.49	
		$ 809.61°	nil	nil	nil	$809.61	nil

Illustration 17-11

Bonds Payable—Amortization at Year-End Only

Date	Explanation	Cash Dr., Cr.°	Bonds Payable Dr., Cr.°	Bond Interest Expense Dr., Cr.°	Accrued Bond Interest Dr., Cr.°	Income Summary Dr., Cr.°	Bond Premium Dr., Cr.°
4/1/71	Sale of bonds	$10,190.39	$10,000.00°				$190.39°
10/1/71	Interest payment	250.00°		$250.00			
12/31/71	Adjusting entry			125.00	$125.00°		
12/31/71	Premium amortization			69.75°			69.75
12/31/71	Closing entry			305.25°		$305.25	
12/31/71	Reversing of accrued interest			125.00°	125.00		
4/1/72	Interest payment	250.00°		250.00			
10/1/72	Interest payment	250.00°		250.00			
12/31/72	Adjusting entry			125.00	125.00°		
12/31/72	Premium amortization			96.13°†			96.13
12/31/72	Closing entry			403.87°		403.87	
12/31/72	Reversing of accrued interest			125.00°	125.00		
4/1/73	Payment of interest	250.00°		250.00			
4/1/73	Payment of bonds	10,000.00°	10,000.00				
12/31/73	Premium amortization			24.51°			24.51
12/31/73	Closing entry			100.49°		100.49	
		$ 809.61°	nil	nil	nil	$809.61	nil

†First three months of 1972 ($47.12 ÷ 2)..................$23.56
April 1–October 1, 1972..................48.06
Last three months of 1972 ($49.02 ÷ 2)..................24.51
Total Amortization for 1972..................$96.13

Use of Unissued Bonds Account

Illustrations in this chapter have shown issues of bonds being credited to Bonds Payable and redemptions debited to this account. An alternate procedure using accounts for Unissued Bonds Payable and Authorized Bonds Payable is illustrated below:

```
Unissued Bonds Payable...........................................1,000,000
    Authorized Bonds Payable ....................................        1,000,000
    To record authorization of $1,000,000 face value of 4%,
    first-mortgage bonds maturing 10 years from date.
```

Immediate sale of four fifths of this issue at 102 would be recorded as below:

```
Cash........................................................................ 816,000
    Unissued Bonds Payable.......................................        800,000
    Premium on Bonds Payable...................................         16,000
    To record sale of $800,000 face value of bonds at 102.
```

A balance sheet prepared at this stage would show:

```
Fixed Liabilities:
Bonds payable, 4%, secured by first mortgage on
    land and buildings, maturing July 1, 19—:
    Authorized...................................................$1,000,000
    Less: Unissued.............................................    200,000
    Outstanding ................................................$  800,000
    Premium on bonds payable............................     16,000  $816,000
```

There is no legal necessity to distinguish between unissued bonds and reacquired bonds which have not been canceled since both can be issued at a discount without imposing a liability on the buyer.

Balance Sheet Presentation of Related Bond Accounts

Balance sheet presentation of bonds payable has been discussed in the preceding paragraphs of this section and illustrated immediately above. Several special accounts related to bonds payable have been illustrated; some additional discussion of the theoretical implications is desirable.

Bond Discount and Bond Premium on Balance Sheet. Discount on bonds payable is sometimes reported on the balance sheet under the deferred charges caption. Bond premium similarly is set out under deferred credits. An inconsistency in accounting treatment is suggested. Conceptually, these items should be shown as adjustments of the bond liability under the long-term debt caption. This latter treatment of bond premium was illustrated in the preceding section. A discount would be shown in the same place and subtracted. To illustrate the point, if a single investor had purchased the $800,000 face value of bonds for $816,000, he would report an $816,000 asset. His asset is the issuer's liability. By maturity the issuer will amortize the premium to zero so that the liability becomes $800,000; the owner of the bonds will similarly adjust his asset value to $800,000 by that time. Showing bond discount as an asset on the issuer's books also is objectionable because the amount really represents money the issuer did not receive when the bonds were marketed as a consequence of their nominal rate being lower than their market interest rate. Some have contended the bond discount balance represents prepaid interest because amortization of the balance increases the periodic interest expense. Rather than a prepaid balance, the discount represents an unpaid sum—a sum the issuer could not borrow because of a disparity between the nominal and market interest rates. There is less controversy concerning the reporting of premium on bonds payable as an adjustment of the bond liability on the balance sheet. The account naturally appears on the equities side because of its credit balance. Since many accountants are opposed to the use of a deferred credits caption (because it does not fit into the basic concept: Assets = Liabilities + Capital), its elimination leaves no caption but liabilities under which to report bond premium. For this reason, and for those cited favoring presentation of bond discount as a liability adjustment, reporting of bond premium as a liability adjustment has gained fairly widespread acceptance.

Treasury Bonds. Par value of bonds reacquired but not canceled should be debited to Treasury Bonds. The balance in this account should be subtracted from Bonds Payable when a balance sheet is prepared.

Bond Issue Costs. Costs such as legal expenses of preparing the bond indenture, printing, registration and filing fees, commissions to bond sellers, etc., should be amortized over the life of the bond issue. These costs are frequently either added to Bond Discount or netted against Bond Premium. Theoretically, it may be argued that this is an objectionable practice. These costs, unlike discount, are a true deferred charge. While expediency calls for lumping the two and disposing of them through a single amortization process, sound theory calls for maintaining them in separate accounts and displaying them in different sections of the balance sheet. Bond issue costs should be presented under deferred charges. In cases where an underwriter handles the planning, issue, and sale of bonds, it may be difficult to distinguish issue costs from discount as an element affecting net proceeds of the bond issue. *APB Opinion 21* (August, 1971) requires that they be accounted for separately. If recorded separately, bond issue costs should be amortized on the same basis (time and method) as is used for amortization of the premium or discount.

Sale of Bonds after Day on Which Bonds Were Dated

A bond bears interest after the date specified on the bond itself. Bonds frequently are sold after the date the bond interest starts at a price plus accrued interest. The interest normally will be accrued, to the date of sale, for the exact number of days elapsed from the date of the bond or from the last interest date based upon a 360-day year. For example, if a 10-year $10,000 bond bearing 6% interest payable semi-annually from June 1, 1971, is sold for $10,500 plus accrued interest on July 18, 1971, the following entries would be made for the sale and the first interest payment:

1. To record sale of bonds, July 18, 1971:

```
Cash ($10,500 + $80, accrued interest)..........................10,580.00
    Bonds Payable...................................................        10,000.00
    Premium on Bonds Payable ...............................        500.00
    Bond Interest Expense°........................................        80.00
```

° Computation of accrued interest:
  $10,000 × 6% = $600 per year
  June 1 to July 18 = 48 days
  48/360 × $600 = $80 (accrued interest on date of sale)

2. To record payment of semiannual interest on December 1, 1971:

```
Bond Interest Expense ..............................................    281.42
Premium on Bond Payable (straight line amortization)°...    18.58
    Cash ($10,000 × 6% × 6/12) ...............................        300.00
```

° Amortization of premium:
    From date of sale (July 18, 1971) to maturity is 118.4 months
    Monthly amortization, $500 ÷ 118.4 = $4.22+
    Amortization from date of sale (July 18, 1971) to first interest
        date (December 1, 1971):
        $4.22 × 4⅖ or 4.4 months = $18.58

Bonds Redeemed before Maturity

Bonds payable, when provided for in the indenture, frequently are redeemed (paid) prior to the maturity date. Any unamortized premium or discount and bond issue costs pertaining to bonds redeemed before maturity date should be removed from the accounts, i.e., the balance in the Bond Premium or Bond Discount account and Bond Issue Costs should be reduced so that the balance remaining is that part which applies to bonds still outstanding. The difference between the "book value" of the bonds retired and the redemption price should be recorded as a "gain or loss on bond redemption." For practical reasons, bonds are usually redeemed on an interest date; therefore, there normally will be no accrued interest to contend with, but premium or discount must be amortized through the interest date, that is, up to date of redemption. To illustrate, assume $1,000 par of the bonds shown in Illustration 17–9 were purchased (redeemed) and retired on April 1, 1971, for $1,010, the amortization for the years affected would be as shown in Illustration 17–12.

Refunding Bonds Payable

A corporation having outstanding bonds payable with an optional redemption provision is faced with the decision as to whether or not redemption is advantageous at a particular time. The issuing corpora-

Illustration 17–12
Bonds Payable—Partial Redemption

Date	Explanation	Cash Cr.	Bond Interest Expense Dr.	Bond Premium Dr.	Bonds Payable Dr.	Loss on Retirement Dr.	Liability Carrying Value
4/1/71	Bonds outstanding	—	—	—	—	—	$10,097.08
4/1/71	Bonds repurchased, $1,000 (10%)	$1,010.00	—	$ 9.71°	$1,000.00°	$.29	9,087.37
10/1/71	Payment of interest on 90% outstanding	225.00	$181.75	43.25	—	—	9,044.12
4/1/72	Payment of interest on 90% outstanding	225.00	180.88	44.12	—	—	9,000.00
4/1/72	Payment of balance of bonds	9,000.00	—	—	9,000.00	—	—

° 10% of carrying value $10,097.08 .... $ 1,009.71
Par value .... −1,000.00
Premium Retired .... $ 9.71

tion's decision as to whether or not to exercise the option to call its outstanding bonds involves primarily the question of future costs. Issue prices, yields to investors, etc., are past history. The decision rests primarily on the questions: can future costs be reduced by refunding? Use of the following formula is helpful in answering this question. Let S denote the saving by refinancing, V the present value of the bonds outstanding for the unexpired term at the current (new) interest rate, and R the call redemption price of the bonds. Then:

$$S = V - R$$

Using the bond valuation formula (page 660), to substitute for V, the equation becomes:

$$S = \left[M \times \frac{1}{(1 + i)^n} \right] + \left[I \times a_{\overline{n}|i} \right] - R$$

To illustrate, should a corporation which can borrow money at 4% per annum, compounded semiannually, redeem 5% semiannual bonds, par $100, due in five years, callable immediately at 101? Application of the formula indicates a saving through refunding, viz:

$$S = \left[\$100 \times \frac{1}{(1.02)^{10}} \right] + \left[\$2.50 \times a_{\overline{10}|.02} \right] - \$101$$
$$= [\$100 \times .820348] + [\$2.50 \times 8.982585] - \$101$$
$$= [\$82.03 + \$22.46] - \$101$$
$$= \$104.49 - \$101.00$$
$$= \$3.49, \text{ the savings on each bond by calling at 101}$$

Thus, the present value of the outstanding obligation at the new interest rate is $104.49. Since it will cost $101.00 to call them now there is a net saving of $3.49 for each $1,000 bond. Clearly, it sometimes becomes advantageous for a corporation to retire a bond issue before maturity. If the bonds are callable or if they can be purchased in the market at an advantageous price, the corporation may reacquire the bonds and cancel them as discussed in the preceeding paragraph. Alternatively, it may be necessary, however, for the corporation to borrow the money to retire the old issue. This may be done by issuing new bonds with a lower interest rate either in exchange for the old bonds or to secure the cash to pay off the old bonds. This new issue of bonds is called a refunding bond issue.

When bonds are refunded, an accounting problem arises as to the proper disposition of any unamortized discount and issue costs on the old issue and of any call premium that must be paid to reacquire the old bonds. For example, assume that a $10 million bond issue was sold at a discount of $400,000, the bonds maturing in 20 years and bearing interest at 8%. Assume also that issue costs in connection with the bonds amounted to $100,000. After the bonds have been outstanding for 10 years they are called at 105 (the price provided in the bond contract if the bonds were called before maturity). A new 20-year 6% bond issue is sold and the proceeds used to retire the old issue. The following charges applicable to the old bond issue must be accounted for (assuming straight line amortization):

Unamortized discount and issue costs on the old issue........$250,000
Call premium paid on the old issue 500,000
             Total $750,000

Three methods of accounting for unamortized discount, issue costs, and redemption premium have been used in accounting practice. These were listed by the former Committee on Accounting Procedure of the AICPA as follows:[4]

1. Direct write-off of the $750,000 to income as a nonrecurring item.
2. Amortize the $750,000 over the remainder of the original life of the issue retired (10 years) as a financing cost.
3. Amortize the $750,000 over the life of the new refunding issue (20 years) as a financing cost.

This committee expressed a preference for Method 2; agreed that Method 1 was acceptable; and rejected Method 3. However, the Accounting Principles Board later reconsidered Method 3 and stated that "The third method, amortization over the life of the new issue, is appropriate under circumstances where the refunding takes place because of currently lower interest rates or anticipation of higher rates in the future. In such circumstances, the expected benefits justify spreading the costs over the life of the new issue, and this method is, therefore, acceptable."[5] The original committee stated that any write-off under Method 1 should be limited to the excess of the unamortized discount over the reduction of current taxes to which the refunding gives rise. The amount written off under Method 1 should be accounted for as an extraordinary item on the income statement.[6]

The Committees of the American Accounting Association have consistently supported Method 1. Generally, there has been considerable disagreement among accountants as to which of the methods proposed for handling unamortized discount, issue costs, and redemption premium on bonds refunded should be used. A brief summary of the pros and cons for each method follows.

Theoretical support for Method 1 rests on the view that the unamortized discount and redemption premium represent the cost of terminating a borrowing contract which has become disadvantageous and, therefore, a loss or expense should be recognized not later than the time when the series of transactions giving rise to it is ended.

---

[4] Ibid., p. 130.

[5] Accounting Principles Board, AICPA, *Opinion No. 6*, October 1965, p. 43.

[6] For income tax purposes Method 1 must be followed.

Method 2 results in reflection of the refinancing expense as a direct charge under an appropriate classification in a series of income statements related to the term of the original borrowing contract. Costs whose benefits are to be realized over a future period should be charged to that period. Here the unamortized discount and redemption premium represent a cost of making a more advantageous agreement for the remaining term of the old issue. Following this line of reasoning, the cost of borrowing over the entire term of the original issue is affected by that original contract. If the cost of accelerating maturity is incurred because it has become advantageous to do so, the saving over the unexpired term of the old issue should exceed the unamortized discount and the redemption premium. Such costs then should be spread over that unexpired term as a cost of borrowing.

Method 3, which has been rather widely used by companies subject to jurisdiction of regulatory bodies, finds some support in this line of reasoning: funds of a given amount are obtained for the time both the old and new issues are outstanding. While it is true there has been a break—a point when one uniform charge ceases and another begins, essentially there is merely an extension of the original borrowing period. All costs of borrowing should be charged as ratably as possible to the entire period of indebtedness. That which has been written off is gone but that which remains applies to the extended debt term. Therefore, to such extent as they have not already been systematically charged off, costs incident to the refunded issue should be spread over the term of the replacement issue. One rather unlikely possibility we have not mentioned is the fact that the life of the refunding issue could be shorter than the remaining life of the retired issue. In this event, of course, either use of the first method or the life of the refunding issue as the basis of amortization would be proper. In case debt is discharged other than by refunding before the original maturity date, any balance of discount and other issue cost then remaining on the books and any redemption premium should be treated as a direct charge to income in the period the debt is settled.

Clearly, early retirement of a debt (bond issue) may be accomplished by disbursing cash, by issuing other debt, or by exchange of stock for the debt. Many accountants feel that irrespective of the mode of retirement the accounting treatment of unamortized discount (or premium) should be identical. For cash and stock modes of retirement, Method 1 is followed; they ask, why should it be different for a refunding situation? They also argue that to carry forward such items is just as illogical for a refunding situation as it would be for spreading the gains and losses on "early" retirements of fixed assets. In the opinion of the authors when the new issue clearly is a continuation of the old, with a revised interest rate, Method 3 appears most appropriate; in all other instances the weight of logic is favorable to Method 1.

Issuance of Convertible Bonds

During the 1960s the issuance of bonds (convertible debt securities or debentures) that could be, at the option of the investor, converted to common stock of the issuer became quite popular. Typically, the indenture also provided for a call or cash redemption price, exercisable at the option of the issuer. In the rising market for common stocks such securities seemed to offer advantages to both the issuer and the investors. A *conversion ratio* specified the number of shares of common stock the holder of the convertible security would receive if and when he surrendered his bond for conversion. The *conversion price* is the relationship between the par or maturity value of the bond and the number of shares of common stock received in exchange for it. To illustrate assume X Corporation issued 100 $1,000 convertible bonds on January 1, 1971. Investor Y purchased one of the bonds which could be converted or exchanged for 20 shares of the common stock of X Corporation prior to January 1, 1978. Any time prior to that date X Corporation had the option of calling the bonds at 104. The conversion *ratio* in this situation was 20 (shares of stock) to 1 ($1,000 par-value bond); the conversion *price* was $50 (that is, $1,000 ÷ 20 shares).

The conversion price and conversion ratio are established when the convertible bond is sold. While these are usually fixed for the life of the bond, a changing conversion ratio is sometimes used. For example, Litton Industries convertible debentures are convertible into 12.5 shares until 1972, into 11.76 shares from 1972 until 1982, and into 11.11 shares from 1982 until maturity in 1987. Thus the conversion price begins at $80, rises to $85, then to $90. In other words, the $1,000 bond respectively divided by 12.5, 11.76, and 11.11 shares will yield conversion prices of $80, $85, and $90.

Since most convertible securities are callable for cash at the option of the issuer, conversion can be forced for all practical purposes, because if the security is called and the redemption price is below the market value of the common stocks for which the convertible security can be exchanged, only a foolish investor would take cash in lieu of stock. Even if he does not want to hold the stock, he can dispose of it for cash and be better off than if he took cash directly from the issuer in exchange for his bond.

Convertible debt securities offer certain advantages to both the issuer and the investors. From the issuer's standpoint, interest rates were usually lower and the securities could often be viewed as essentially means of raising equity capital. If common stock prices rose, the issuer could force conversion of bonds into common stock by calling the debt for redemption. In the event the market values of stocks into which bonds were convertible did not rise, issuers still had the benefit of borrowing at relatively low cash interest costs. From the investor's standpoint there was, at a minimum, assurance of receiving back the amount lent, and the chance of receiving instead at his option common stock with considerably appreciated value.

An accounting question arose as to whether convertible debt securities should be treated solely as *debt* or whether the conversion option should receive *separate* accounting recognition at time of issuance. The essence of the problem can be pinpointed by way of illustration. Assume that AB Corporation issued 6% bonds payable with a maturity value of $100,000. The bonds sold for $96,000; therefore the transaction would be recorded as follows:

```
Cash.................................................................96,000
Discount on Bonds Payable .............................  4,000
    Bonds Payable.....................................                100,000
```

Now let's assume, hypothetically, that AB Corporation instead sold $100,000 bonds that include a feature that permitted each holder of a $1,000 bond to convert it to 10 shares of common stock of AB Corporation. As a consequence of this feature the bonds could be sold with a 4% interest rate (as opposed to the prior 6% rate). How should the sale be recorded assuming receipt of $106,000 cash for them? Clearly, two alternatives should be considered:

1) Consider the transaction as involving debt only:

```
Cash.................................................................106,000
    Premium on Bonds Payable.........................                 6,000
    Bonds Payable.....................................                100,000
```

2) Account for the debt and conversion option separately:

```
Cash.................................................................106,000
Discount on Bonds Payable .............................  4,000
    Bonds Payable.....................................                100,000
    Contributed Capital-Conversion Option on Bonds .........          10,000
```

In *Opinion 9* (1966) the APB recommended the second alternative; in *Opinion 12* (1967) it suspended this recommendation pending further study. Finally, in *Opinion 14* (1969) the board stated that: "no portion of the proceeds from the issuance of the types of convertible debt securities described in paragraph 3 should be accounted for as attributable to the conversion feature." Thus the board opted for the first alternative. The principal arguments for the last position centered on the inseparability of the debt and the conversion option. Another reason for preferring the first alternative was that valuation of the conversion option, or the debt security without the conversion option, presents difficult practical problems. In the absence of separate transferability, values cannot be established in the market, hence must be somewhat subjective. Further, there are uncertainties as to the future values of the stock to be obtained upon conversion and, in some cases, uncertainties as to how long the conversion option might remain effective. The board stated that in reaching its last Opinion (in favor of the first alternative) that it "placed greater weight on the inseparability of the debt and the conversion feature than on the practical difficulties." Presumably this was an argument for conceptual justification of the Opinion.

In contrast it may be noted that the APB in *Opinion 14* stated that the debt and the conversion option should be accounted for separately (the second alternative above) when the conversion feature is represented by *detachable stock warrants* (rights). The basis for this position was that the debt and the conversion option (represented by the warrants) are separable elements; that the warrants trade separately; and that an allocation on the basis of fair market value is generally possible. The Opinion stated: "the portion of the proceeds of debt securities issued with detachable stock purchase warrants which is allocable to the warrants should be accounted for as paid-in capital."

Bond Conversion

The first step is to adjust to a current status all balances relating to the bonds being converted. Thus, any premium or discount amortization or interest accrual to date of conversion should be recorded. Conversion is usually at an interest date; when at other dates interest would ordinarily be paid down to the date of conversion. The second step is less simple because it involves a choice from among alternatives:

1. The conversion can be recorded on a "book value" basis, i.e., the book or amortized value of the bonds determines the book value assigned to the stock issued. If the stock has par or stated value and these amounts do not agree with the amortized bond value at date of conversion, the resultant difference is recorded as a premium or discount on stock.

2. The conversion can be recorded on a "market value" basis whereby either the market value of the bonds or the market value of the stock, whichever is the more clearly determinable at the time of conversion is used as the measure of consideration. Ordinarily there should not be much disparity between the market values of convertible bonds and the shares which can be received in exchange for them.

For purposes of illustration, assume that a corporation has outstanding a $10 million convertible bond issue. On a date when all accrued interest has been paid and on which the currently adjusted balance (up to date of conversion) of unamortized Bond Premium is $300,000, holders of 100 bonds of $1,000 denomination ($100,000 maturity value) exercise their option to turn in their bonds and receive in exchange 2,000 of the $40 par value common shares ($80,000 par value) of the corporation. On this date the stock was selling for $54 per share (total market value $108,000) and the bonds at 108 (total market value $108,000).

Under Method 1 the market values would be ignored and the exchange would be recorded as follows:

```
Bonds Payable (100 bonds @  $1,000) .................................100,000
Bond Premium (100 × $30) ...............................................  3,000
    Common Stock (2,000 shares × par $40) .........................          80,000
    Premium on Common Stock.........................................          23,000
    To record exchange of 100 bonds of $1,000 denomination for
    2,000 shares of common stock, par $40, in accordance with
    bond conversion privilege.
```

Under Method 2 the exchange would be recorded as below:

```
Bonds Payable (100 bonds @  $1,000) .................................100,000
Bond Premium (100 × $30) ...............................................  3,000
Loss on Bond Conversion 100 ($80 − $30) ............................  5,000
    Common Stock (par value) .........................................          80,000
    Premium on Common Stock 2,000 ($54 − $40) ................          28,000
    To record exchange of 100 bonds of $1,000 denomination for
    2,000 shares of common stock, par $40, in accordance with
    bond conversion privilege when bonds have market value
    of $1,080 and stock of $54 per share.
```

Of course, the market values of the bonds and stocks may not coincide as assumed, but they should be fairly close. On this point the American Accounting Association's Committee on Concepts and Standards in expressing a preference for Method 2 stated:

Any difference between the amortized amount of a liability as reflected in the accounts and the amount of assets released or equities created should be recognized as a gain or loss in the period of liquidation. When a liability is discharged by conversion to a stock equity, the market value of the liability is ideally the measure of the new equity created. However, if a reliable market price for the liability is not available, the market value of the stock issued may be used.[7]

Assuming the bonds were quoted at 107.5 (total market value $107,500), when the foregoing transaction was consummated and the stock price was either unknown or was $54 as before (total market value $108,000) recording would be as follows:

```
Bonds Payable .................................................................100,000
Bond Premium...............................................................  3,000
Loss on Bond Conversion .................................................  4,500
    Common Stock.........................................................          80,000
    Premium on Common Stock (based on market value of the
        liability)...........................................................          27,500
```

On the other hand, if the stock price was $55 (total market value

---

[7] AAA, *Accounting and Reporting Standards for Corporate Financial Statements and Supplements* (Columbus, Ohio, 1957), p. 7.

$110,000) per share and the bond price was either unknown or was *unreliably* reported at 108, the recording would be as follows:

Bonds Payable	100,000	
Bond Premium	3,000	
Loss on Bond Conversion	7,000	
Common Stock		80,000
Premium on Common Stock (based on market value of the stock)		30,000

The first method can be supported on the grounds that when the corporation issued the convertible bonds it reckoned that the bond sales price could, to a large extent, represent consideration received for stock. When conversion occurs the book value of the obligation is simply transferred to the stock exchanged for it.

The second method can be supported by reasoning that the exchange of stock for bonds completes the transaction cycle for the bonds and begins a new cycle for stock. The consideration of value used in this new transaction cycle is the amount which would be received if the bonds were sold anew or if the stock were sold rather than exchanged. Since this method recognizes changes in property values which have been occurring and subordinates a consideration determined years or decades ago when the bonds were issued, it is theoretically preferable.

Serial Bonds

An issue of bonds with provision for repayment in a series of installments is called a serial bond issue. One of the principal advantages of a serial bond issue is the avoidance of need for a sinking fund. Serial bonds are particularly well adapted for use by school districts and other taxing authorities which borrow money upon agreement that a special tax will be levied to pay off the obligation. As the taxes are collected, the money so raised can best be utilized by paying off a part of the indebtedness. This may be done by having a part of the bond issue mature each year. Of course, some of the same advantages can be secured by the industrial firm, for by using funds which otherwise would have to be invested in a sinking fund (the earnings of which would likely be less than the interest on the bonds payable) and by retiring a part of the indebtedness, a saving can be effected.

The selling price of serial bonds may be obtained by valuing each series separately in the same way that a straight bond issue is valued and then totaling the valuations of the several series. For example, assume that serial bonds carrying 7% interest payable semiannually are sold to yield 5% semiannually with the following maturity dates: $10,000 at end of 12 months, $20,000 at end of 18 months, and $30,000 at end of 24 months. The selling price of each of the three series as well as that of the whole issue may be computed as follows by using the bond valuation formula given earlier in the chapter:

Series No. 1 (Due in 12 Months):

$$V = \left[\$10,000 \times \frac{1}{(1.025)^2} \right] + \left[\$350 \times a_{\overline{2}|.025} \right]$$

$$= [\$10,000 \times 0.9518144] + [\$350 \times 1.9274242]$$
$$= \$9,518.14 + \$674.60 \qquad\qquad\qquad = \$10,192.74$$

Series No. 2 (Due in 18 Months):

$$V = \left[\$20,000 \times \frac{1}{(1.025)^3} \right] + \left[\$700 \times a_{\overline{3}|.025} \right]$$

$$= [\$20,000 \times 0.9285994] + [\$700 \times 2.8560236]$$
$$= \$18,571.99 + \$1,999.21 \qquad\qquad = 20,571.20$$

Series No. 3 (Due in 24 Months):

$$V = \left[\$30,000 \times \frac{1}{(1.025)^4} \right] + \left[\$1,050 \times a_{\overline{4}|.025} \right]$$

$$= [\$30,000 \times 0.9059506] + [\$1,050 \times 3.7619742]$$
$$= \$27,178.52 + \$3,950.07 \qquad\qquad = \underline{31,128.59}$$

Total Price..$61,892.53

Amortization of Premium and Discount on Serial Bonds. Premium and discount on serial bonds may be based on either the straight line method or the present value method. As with ordinary or straight bonds, the only difference between the two methods is computation of the dollar amount to be amortized each period. The straight line method will be considered first. Either of two approaches may be used with respect to the straight line method; both give the same results. One approach is based on the assumption that the premium or discount is known for each *separate series*. To illustrate, in the above example the selling price, and hence the premium on each series, was known as summarized in columns (*d*) and (*e*) in Illustration 17–13. The premium on each series then is allocated equally to each time period as shown in columns (*f*) through (*i*). The last line shows the totals to be amortized each period.

The second approach under the straight line method is based on the assumption that *only* the *total* premium or discount on the several series combined is known. For example, in the above illustration only the single premium amount $1,892.53 is presumed to be known. In this situation the *dollar-periods* approach may be used. The computation is based on an allocation of the premium or discount to the several series and time periods in relationship to the dollars of par outstanding for each series. The computations are shown in Illustration 17–14. Note that the fractions, based on dollar periods, are used only to allocate the premium or discount to each serial, then the

Illustration 17-13

Amortization of Premium on Serial Bonds—Straight Line Method

Serial No. (a)	Months Outstanding (b)	Par Value (c)	Sales Price (d)	Premium to Be Amortized (e)	Amortization of Premium—Straight Line				
					At End of 6 Months (f)	At End of 12 Months (g)	At End of 18 Months (h)	At End of 24 Months (i)	Total Premium (j)
1	12	$10,000	$10,192.74	$ 192.74	$ 96.37	$ 96.37			$ 192.74
2	18	20,000	20,571.20	571.20	190.40	190.40	$190.40		571.20
3	24	30,000	31,128.59	1,128.59	282.15	282.15	282.15	$282.14	1,128.59
Total Amortization per Period					$568.92	$568.92	$472.55	$282.14	$1,892.53

Illustration 17–14
Amortization of Premium on Serial Bonds—
Straight Line (dollar-periods method)

Serials	Par	Periods Outstanding (6 Months)	Dollar Periods	Fraction	Total Amortization by Serials
No. 1 ....$10,000		2	20,000	20/200	$ 189.25
No. 2 20,000		3	60,000	60/200	567.76
No. 3 30,000		4	120,000	120/200	1,135.52
			200,000	200/200	$1,892.53

| Amortization Dates | Amortization by Serials | | | Total Amortization by Time Periods |
	No. 1	No. 2	No. 3	
End of 6 months..............$ 94.63		$189.25	$ 283.88	$ 567.76
End of 12 months............ 94.62		189.26	283.88	567.76
End of 18 months............ –		189.25	283.88	473.13
End of 24 months............ –		–	283.88	283.88
	$189.25	$567.76	$1,135.52	$1,892.53

amount so allocated to each serial is spread equally to each period over the life of each serial.

It should be observed that under both methods illustrated above (Illustrations 17–13 and 17–14) the amortization was developed both by *time period* and *by serial*. In many situations (and problems) the issuer needs to know the premium or discount with respect to each serial as well as by time period. If any of the serials, or part of a serial, is retired or purchased before its maturity date, both the serial and time-period amortizations are essential. On the other hand, if only the periodic amortization in total is needed a direct computation may be made as follows:

Date	Par Outstanding	Fraction	Amortization
End of 6 months.......................$ 60,000		60/200	$ 567.76
End of 12 months.................... 60,000		60/200	567.76
End of 18 months.................... 50,000		50/200	473.13
End of 24 months.................... 30,000		30/200	283.88
	$200,000	200/200	$1,892.53

This short-cut approach frequently is referred to as the "bonds outstanding" computation. Before using it, one should ascertain whether or not amortization data by serial are needed.

The entries with respect to the foregoing example, are given below, with the added assumption that $5,000 par of the Serial No. 3 bonds, which were to mature at the end of 24 months, were purchased and retired at the end of 12 months.

1. To record sale of the bonds:

Cash	61,892.53	
Premium on Bonds Payable		1,892.53
Bonds Payable		60,000.00

2. To record payment of interest and amortization of premium at the end of six months:

Bond Interest Expense	1,532.24	
Premium on Bonds Payable	567.76	
Cash		2,100.00

3. To record payment of interest and amortization of premium at end of 12 months:

Bond Interest Expense	1,532.24	
Premium on Bonds Payable	567.76	
Cash		2,100.00

4. To record payment of Serial No. 1 bonds:

Bonds Payable (Serial No. 1)	10,000.00	
Cash		10,000.00

5. To record retirement of $5,000 of Serial No. 3 bonds at end of 12 months:

Bonds Payable	5,000.00	
Bond Premium	94.62°	
Loss on Bonds Retired	5.38	
Cash		5,100.00

　　° ($5,000/$30,000) × ($283.88 × 2) = $94.62

6. To pay interest, amortize premium, and pay off Serial No. 2 bonds at end of 18 months:

Bond Interest	1,149.18	
Bond Premium [$189.25 + ($\frac{5}{6}$ × $283.88)]	425.82	
Cash		1,575.00

Bonds Payable	20,000.00	
Cash		20,000.00

7. To pay interest, amortize premium, and pay off Serial No. 3 bonds at end of 24 months:

Bond Interest	638.43	
Bond Premium ($\frac{5}{6}$ × $283.88)	236.57	
Cash		875.00

Bonds Payable	25,000.00	
Cash		25,000.00

It should be noted that the premium amortized in these entries, $94.62, $425.82, and $236.57, totals the same as the amortizations, $473.13 and $283.88, orginally tabulated for the end of 18 months and end of 24 months.

In order to apply the present value method of amortization, the yield rate of interest must be known as well as the selling price. When serial bonds are involved, an amortization table should be prepared in the same manner as the amortization table for ordinary (nonserial) bonds except that the maturity values of each installment must be deducted from the "carrying value" figures when the installments are paid. An amortization table showing present value amortization of the premium and the payment of the three serial installments on the serial bond issue illustrated in the preceding section is given in Illustration 17–15. In that example, it will be recalled that the sales price

Illustration 17–15
Amortization of Premium on Serial Bonds – Present Value Amortization

Date	Cash Cr.	Bond Interest Expense Dr.	Bond Premium Dr.	Bonds Payable Dr.	Carrying Value
At issue......................	–	–	–	–	$61,892.53
End 6 months............$	2,100.00	$1,547.31°	$ 552.69	–	61,339.84
End 12 months..........	2,100.00	1,533.50	566.50	–	60,773.34
End 12 months..........	10,000.00	–	–	$10,000.00	50,773.34
End 18 months..........	1,750.00	1,269.33	480.67	–	50,292.67
End 18 months..........	20,000.00	–	–	20,000.00	30,292.67
End 24 months..........	1,050.00	757.33	292.67	–	30,000.00
End 24 months..........	30,000.00	–	–	30,000.00	–
	$67,000.00	$5,107.47	$1,892.53	$60,000.00	

° $61,892.53 × .025 = $1,547.31.

was $61,892.53 and the yield rate was $2\frac{1}{2}\%$ semiannually. In the amortization table (Illustration 17–15) it may be observed that the computations are identical with that illustrated for nonserial bonds except for the payment on principal as each serial matures.

If some of the serial bonds, where premium is amortized under the present value method are retired before maturity, the carrying value as of date of redemption must be reduced by the value of the retired bonds as computed by using the given nominal and yield interest rates and a life corresponding to the periods between the redemption date and the normal maturity of the specific bonds (serial) retired. To illustrate, if $5,000 par of the bonds in the foregoing illustration, which were to mature at the end of 24 months (Serial No. 3), were repurchased for $5,100 and retired at the end of 12 months, the reduction of the carrying value of the portion being redeemed before maturity would be:

$$V = \left[\$5,000 \times \frac{1}{(1.025)^2} \right] + [\$175 \times a_{\overline{2}|.025}]$$
$$= [\$5,000 \times .951814] + [\$175 \times 1.927424] = \$5,096.37$$

Illustration 17–16
Serial Bond Entires Tabulated—Present Value Amortization

Date	Cash Cr.	Bond Interest Expense Dr.	Bond Premium Dr.	Bonds Payable Dr.	Loss on Retirement Dr.	Carrying Value
Balance end 12 months...........	—	—	—	—	—	$50,773.34°
End 12 months..........$	5,100.00	—	$ 96.37	$ 5,000.00	$3.63	45,676.97
End 18 months..........	1,575.00	$1,141.92	433.08	—	—	45,243.89
End 18 months..........	20,000.00	—	—	20,000.00	—	25,243.89
End 24 months..........	875.00	631.11	243.89	—	—	25,000.00
End 24 months..........	25,000.00	—	—	25,000.00	—	—

° From Illustration 17–15, line 4.

QUESTIONS FOR CLASS DISCUSSION

Part A

1. Distinguish between a temporary and a permanent investment.
2. What are the primary characteristics of a permanent investment in bonds?
3. What is the relationship between a bond and a mortgage?
4. How should permanent investments in bonds be valued at acquisition? Subsequent to acquisition?
5. Distinguish between the nominal rate of interest and the yield rate of interest.
6. What is the market value of a bond? Explain.
7. Distinguish between straight line amortization and present value amortization of bond premium and discount.
8. Why must accrued interest be paid for from the last interest date to date of purchase of a bond investment?
9. Over what period should premium and discount on a bond investment be amortized? Explain.
10. Outline the accounting steps necessary with respect to sale of a part of a bond investment.

Part B

11. Distinguish between a current liability and a long-term liability.
12. Define each of the following classes of bonds payable: (a) industrial bonds, (b) governmental bonds, (c) secured bonds, (d) unsecured bonds,

(e) income bonds, (f) serial bonds, (g) callable bonds, and (h) convertible bonds.

13. What is a bond indenture?

14. What are the two methods of amortzing premium and discount on bonds payable? Explain each.

15. Relate the problems and approaches in amortization of premium and discount on bonds from the investor's and the issuer's respective viewpoints.

16. How are bonds payable valued at issue date? Subsequent to issuance?

17. How should the following items related to bonds payable be reported on the balance sheet: (a) par of bonds payable, (b) unissued bonds payable, (c) premium on bonds payable, (d) discount on bonds payable, and (e) treasury bonds.

18. Outline the accounting steps necessary with respect to the redemption of bonds payable prior to maturity.

19. What is meant by "refunding bonds payable"? Explain the essential accounting procedures.

20. What are convertible bonds? How did the Accounting Principles Board decide they should be accounted for at the time of issuance and for what reasons?

21. Bonds are sometimes sold with detachable warrants to purchase stock. Initially the two are often issued as a "package." How should such a sale be accounted for?

22. What is meant by "bond conversion"? Explain the essential accounting procedures.

23. What are serial bonds? Outline the basic accounting procedures including amortization of premium and discount.

DECISION CASE 17-1

The Capital Budget Committee of the Walton Corporation was established to appraise and screen departmental requests for plant expansions and improvements at a time when these requests totaled $10 million. The committee thereupon sought your professional advice and help in establishing minimum performance standards which it should demand of these projects in the way of anticipated rates of return before interest and taxes.

The Walton Corporation is a closely held family corporation in which the stockholders exert an active and unified influence on the management. At this date, the company has no long-term debt and has 1 million shares of common capital stock outstanding. It is currently earning $5 million (net income before interest and taxes) per year. The applicable tax rate is 50%.

Should the projects under consideration be approved, management is confident the $10 million of required funds can be obtained either:

a) By borrowing—via the medium of an issue of $10 million, 4%, 20-year bonds.

b) By equity financing—via the medium of an issue of 500,000 shares of common stock to the general public. It is expected and anticipated that the ownership of these 500,000 shares would be widely dispersed and scattered.

The company has been earning $12\frac{1}{2}\%$ return after taxes. The management and the dominant stockholders consider this rate of earnings to be a fair capitalization rate (eight times earnings) as long as the company remains free of long-term debt. An increase to 15% or six and two-thirds times earnings would constitute an adequate adjustment to compensate for the risk of carrying $10 million of long-term debt. They believe that this reflects, and is consistent with, current market appraisals.

Required:

1. Prepare a schedule comparing minimum returns, considering interest, taxes, and earnings ratio, which should be produced by each alternative to maintain the present capitalized value per share.

2. What minimum rate of return on new investment is necessary for each alternative to maintain the present capitalized value per share? Explain.

(AICPA adapted)

EXERCISES

Part A (1 through 9)

Exercise 17–1

X Corporation sold to Y Corporation bonds payable having a maturity value of $120,000. The bonds were due in 10 years and carried a nominal interest rate of 5% per year payable each March 1 and September 1. The Y Corporation purchased the bonds on March 1 for $129,000.

Required:

Assuming straight line amortization, give in parallel columns entries on the borrower's books and the investor's books for the first complete year following the transaction. Assume both parties close their books on December 31.

Exercise 17–2

An investor purchased $50,000 par bonds dated January 1, 1972, interest January 1 and July 1, to yield 2% half-yearly. If the bonds are due at par on January 1, 1974, and pay $2\frac{1}{2}\%$ half-yearly, what was their cost?

Exercise 17–3

Determine the price investors would be willing to pay for each of the following:

a) A 10-year $1,000 par value bond; annual interest at 5% (payable semi-annually) purchased to yield 4% effective interest.

b) An eight-year $5,000 par value bond; annual interest at 6% (payable annually) purchased to yield 5% effective interest.

c) A 12-year $1,000 par value bond; annual interest at 4% (payable semi-annually) purchased to yield 5% effective interest.

Exercise 17–4

1. Using the bond table given in the chapter, what price must an investor pay for a $10,000 bond, 5% annual interest, payable semiannually, maturing in five years if the yield rate is 5.25%? If 4.92%?

2. What is the yield rate on a $10,000, 5% bond (interest payable semiannually), maturing in five years if purchased for $9,800?

Exercise 17–5

John M. Rockwell purchased $50,000 maturity value bonds on January 1, 1972, for $50,929.25. The bonds carried a nominal interest rate of 7% per annum, payable semiannually on January 1 and July 1, and were to mature on January 1, 1974.

Required:

1. Prepare an amortization table for Mr. Rockwell showing a tabulation of interest, amortization, and carrying value. Assume the books are closed on the interest date purchased. Use straight line amortization.

2. Prepare an amortization table assuming the bonds were acquired for $49,668.61.

Exercise 17–6

WXY Corporation adjusts and closes its books each April 30. On February 1, 1971, it purchased as a permanent investment $200,000 par-value bonds of BCD Company. Purchase price, including accrued interest, was $201,380. The bonds mature June 30, 1975, and pay 3% interest each June 30. On September 30, 1971, $50,000 par value of the bonds were sold at a gain of $500. Give entries for all transactions concerning these bonds, including adjusting, closing, and reversing entries, through May 1, 1972. Use straight line amortization.

Exercise 17–7

Prepare an amortization table for a $50,000 bond investment; the nominal interest rate is 6% per annum, effective interest rate is 7%. The bonds were purchased for 48,306.39 on January 1, 1971, and mature four years later. Interest is payable each January 1. Use present value amortization.

Exercise 17–8

An investor purchased $50,000 maturity-value bonds on January 1, 1973, for $50,940.49. The bonds carried a nominal interest rate of 6% per annum, payable semiannually on January 1 and July 1, and were to mature on January 1, 1975. The price paid resulted in a yield rate of 5% per annum.

Required:

1. Prepare an amortization table for the investor showing a tabulation of interest, amortization, and carrying value. Assume the books are closed on the interest date purchased. Use present value amortization.

2. Prepare an amortization table assuming the bonds were acquired for $49,059.50 to give a yield rate of 5% per annum. Assume further that the nominal rate was 4% per annum paid semiannually on January 1 and July 1 and were to mature as above.

Exercise 17–9

1. Refer to the bond table in the chapter to determine the price of a $100,000, 5% bond, interest payable March 1 and September 1, purchased March 1, 1967, maturing March 1, 1970, purchased to yield $5\frac{1}{2}$%.

2. Verify your results by using an appropriate formula.

3. Prepare an amortization table for the bond using the present value method.

4. Record all transactions incident to the bonds on the books of its owner for the calendar year 1968 including adjusting, closing, and reversing entries.

Part B (10 through 21)

Exercise 17–10

The K Corporation issued $100,000 bonds payable with a 5% nominal interest rate, payable semiannually. The bonds mature in five years and were sold at a yield rate of 6%. The bonds were dated and sold on the same date.

Required:

1. Using the formula approach determine the sales price of the bonds.

2. Determine the sales price of the bonds by reference to the bond table given in the chapter.

3. What would be the amount of discount to be amortized for the first full year after sale, assuming straight line amortization?

4. What would be the amount of discount to be amortized for the first full year after sale, assuming present value amortization?

Exercise 17–11

At a time when the no-par-value common stock of the Baker Company was selling on the open market for $40 per share (stated value $50 per share), the company authorized issuance of $200,000 in 4% coupon bonds. Three months later an investment syndicate agreed to purchase the entire issue of bonds "at par, provided however that 100 shares of stock will be included as a bonus and further provided no charge will be made for the interest accrued." Because no better offer to buy the bonds had been received, the syndicate's offer was accepted. Assuming the market price of the stock has not changed, give the entry to record the sale of the bonds to the syndicate.

Exercise 17–12

The Kawasak Corporation issued $30,000 bonds payable with a nominal interest rate of 6% payable annually. The bonds were dated March 1 and matured in five years. They were sold at a yield rate of 7% per annum on the date of the bond issue.

Required:

1. Compute the sales price of the bonds.

2. Prepare an amortization table for the life of the bonds assuming straight line amortization.

3. Prepare an amortization table for the life of the bonds assuming present value amortization.

Exercise 17–13

The Korn Corporation prepared a bond indenture for the issuance of $60,000 bonds payable to be dated March 1, 1971. The bonds carried a nominal interest rate of 5%, payable semiannually on March 1 and September 1, and were due in 10 years from March 1, 1971. The bonds sold at $62,360 plus accrued interest on May 1, 1971. The corporation closes its books on December 31.

Required:

Give all entries indicated through January 1, 1972, assuming straight line amortization.

Exercise 17–14

Zakin Co. recently issued $1 million face value, 5%, 30-year sub-ordinated debentures at 97. The debentures are redeemable at 103 upon demand by the issuer at any date upon 30 days notice 10 years after the issue. The debentures are convertible into $10 par-value common stock of the company at the conversion price of $12.50 per share for each $500 or multiple thereof of the principal amount of the debentures.

Required:

1. Explain how the conversion feature of convertible debt has a value to the (a) issuer and (b) purchaser.

2. Management of Zakin Co. has suggested that in recording the issuance of the debentures a portion of the proceeds should be assigned to the conversion feature.

a) What are the arguments for according separate accounting recognition to the conversion feature of the debentures?

b) What are the arguments supporting accounting for the convertible debentures as a single element?

3. Assume that no value is assigned to the conversion feature upon issue of the debentures. Assume further that five years after issue, debentures with a face value of $100,000 and book value of $97,500 are tendered for conversion on an interest payment date when the market price of the debentures is 104 and the common stock is selling at $14 per share and that the company records the conversion as follows:

Bonds Payable	100,000	
Bond Discount		2,500
Common Stock		80,000
Premium on Common Stock		17,500

Discuss the propriety of the above accounting treatment.

(AICPA adapted)

Exercise 17–15

Indicate the gain or loss from redemption of bonds payable prior to maturity in each of the following cases. Use straight line amortization.

Case	Issue Date	Maturity Date	Redemption Date	Face Amount	Issue Price	Redemption Price
A........	1/1/66	1/1/76	1/1/73	$100,000	105	102
B........	7/1/69	7/1/79	1/1/77	200,000	110	103
C........	1/1/61	1/1/81	1/1/74	250,000	100	101
D........	3/1/61	3/1/81	3/1/75	100,000	96	100
E........	8/1/65	8/1/75	2/1/71	300,000	95	97

Exercise 17–16

The Tom Corporation issued $30,000 bonds payable carrying 6% annual interest, payable semiannually on January 1 and July 1. The bonds matured in five years from their date of January 1, 1971. The bonds were sold on January 1, 1971, for $29,640. The books are closed on August 31. On January 1, 1972, the corporation recalled (by purchase) $5,000 (par) of the bonds at 105.

Required:

Give all entries indicated through July 1, 1972; assume straight line amortization.

Exercise 17–17

Should a corporation which can borrow on a new issue at 6% per annum, compounded semiannually, redeem 7% bonds, par $1,000, due in six years, callable immediately at 104? Indicate any advantage in dollars per bond.

Exercise 17–18

The Comfort Corporation has outstanding two different bond issues as follows:

Maturity Value	Life Years	Nominal Interest Rate	Interest Payment	Privileges	Present Carrying Value	Remaining Life-Years
$90,000	20	6%	Payable annually	Redeemable	$84,000	12
30,000	10	4%	Payable semiannually	Convertible	31,680	6

The redeemable bonds can be recalled (purchased) at any time after the fifth year at 102. The convertible bonds, at the option of the investor, can be converted to common stock on a "par-for-par" basis at any time after the fourth year.

Required:

1. A new issue of 3.90% (annual interest) bonds of $100,000 (par) have just been sold for $101,000; the proceeds are to be used to refund the redeemable bonds immediately. Give entries for (a) sale of the new bonds, (b) redemption of the 6% bonds, and (c) the first interest payment on the new bonds; assume 10 years to maturity, annual interest, and straight line amortization.

2. An investor holding $10,000 of the 4% bonds has delivered them for immediate conversion to common stock. The common stock currently is selling at $110 per share. Give entry for the conversion under two different methods.

Exercise 17–19

Compute the selling price of a 3% half-yearly (yield basis) serial bond issue, 2½% nominal interest half-yearly, sold on January 1, 1972, due at par as follows: $10,000, January 1, 1973; $15,000, July 1, 1974; and $25,000, January 1, 1975.

Exercise 17–20

On May 1, 1971, Star Corporation sold an $800,000 serial bond issue for $872,000. These bonds which pay 5% interest each May 1 mature in $100,000 annual installments, the first maturity being May 1, 1972, Star Corporation adjusts and closes books each October 31. Give all entries pertaining to these bonds through November 1, 1972.

Exercise 17–21

The Stone Corporation sold a small bond issue that carried a 4% annual interest rate, payable annually, with a total maturity value of $6,000. The bonds were sold for $5,400 on the date of the indenture. The bonds were to be paid as follows:

Serial	At End of Year	Maturity Value
A	2	$1,000
B	3	2,000
C	4	3,000

Required:

1. Set up an amortization table utilizing straight line amortization so as to show the amortization by serial, by year. Assume the discount is known for each serial, that is: A, $60; B, $180; and C, $360.

2. Set up an amortization table utilizing straight line amortization so as to show the amortization by serial, by year. Assume the discount for each serial is unknown.

3. Set up an amortization table that shows the straight line amortization by year only.

4. Give entry to pay off one third of Serial C, at par, assuming it is paid one year before maturity, that is, at the end of the third year.

PROBLEMS

Part A (1 through 6)

Problem 17–1

Arrow Company purchased as an investment, to be held until maturity (December 1, 1979), 10 of the 7% debenture bonds issued by Bow Corporation at $1,010 each plus accrued interest. Interest dates are June 1 and December 1. Date of purchase is March 1, 1976.

Required:

Give all entries on Arrow Company's books pertaining to the bond investment during 1976 if the entry for amortization of the premium is made only at the close of the fiscal year, December 31, 1976. Give also any reversing entry needed at January 1, 1977.

Problem 17–2

Argo Company purchased as a permanent investment, for a total consideration of $10,250, bonds of Fulatot Corporation having a maturity value of $10,000. The bonds were purchased on March 1, 1972, and bear interest at 6% per annum, payable each June 1 and December 1. The bonds mature on December 1, 1975. A separate account is set up for the premium, and a portion of the balance of this account is amortized (straight line) each interest collection date. The investor's books are adjusted and closed each December 31.

Required:

Give all entries pertaining to the bonds through December 31, 1975, including adjusting, closing, and reversing entries. For purpose of compliance with this requirement, use a table with the following headings:

Date	Bond Investment Dr., Cr.	Premium on Bond Investment Dr., Cr.	Bond Interest Income Dr., Cr.	Accrued Bond Interest Income Dr., Cr.	Cash Dr., Cr.	Income Summary Dr.

Problem 17–3

The Ray Company completed the following transactions during 1971.

Feb. 1   Purchased as a permanent investment $100,000 (par value) of American Corporation, 5% bonds, maturing October 1, 1980, interest payable April 1 and October 1, at 96 plus brokerage fee of $200 and accrued interest.

Mar. 20   Purchased 200 shares of Grace Utilities common stock, par $100, at $120 (permanent investment).

Apr. 1   Deposited the semiannual interest coupons on the American Corporation bonds.

May 15   Purchased for temporary investment $10,000 par value, Amtex Company, 4% bonds for $9,860, including interest accrued since March 1.

July 2   Purchased 1,000 shares of A & B no-par common stock for $9,800 as a temporary investment.

Aug. 1   Received a 25% stock dividend on the Grace Utilities common.

Sept. 1   Cashed semiannual interest coupons on the Amtex bonds.

Sept. 3   Received a quarterly dividend of $.25 per share on the A & B common.

Oct. 1   Collected coupons on American Corporation bonds.

Oct. 1   Received stock rights to subscribe for one new share of Grace Utilities common for each five shares held at a special subscription price of $100 per share. The market price of the stock, ex rights, was $108 on October 1.

Oct. 15   Exercised 100 of the Grace Utilities stock rights, and sold the rest at $1.50.

Nov.   4   Sold the Grace Utilities stock obtained on the exercise of stock rights
at $106 per share; also sold 100 shares of the old shares at the same price.

Dec. 10   Sold $2,000 Amtex bonds at 99 and accrued interest.

Dec. 15   Received notice that a quarterly dividend of $.25 per share had been
declared on A & B common, payable to stockholders of record on December 30.

Required:

1. Give entries for each transaction appropriately identifying both the
temporary and permanent investments.

2. Maintain ledger accounts for the investments; set up premium and
discount on permanent investments in separate accounts.

3. Present any adjusting and closing entries at the end of the fiscal year,
December 31. Use the straight line method and amortize at year-end.

4. Present any reversing entries.

5. Show how the investments should be reported on the balance sheet at
December 31 (assume cost method).

Problem 17-4

On April 1, 1972, Merritt, Inc., purchased as a permanent investment
bonds of the Shane Corporation having a maturity value of $100,000. The
bonds were purchased to yield 8% annual interest. The bonds mature on
April 1, 1982, and carry a nominal interest rate of 6% per annum, payable
semiannually on April 1 and October 1.

Required:

1. Compute the purchase price of the bond investment.

2. Prepare an amortization table assuming the straight line method
through April 1, 1976.

3. Prepare an amortization table assuming the present value method
through April 1, 1976.

4. Give the adjusting, closing, and related reversing entries in parallel
columns for both methods of amortization for December 31, 1972.

5. On December 31, 1975, Merritt sold $30,000 (par) of the bond invest-
ment at 95 plus accrued interest. Give all related entries in parallel columns
for both methods of amortization.

6. Give the adjusting and closing and related reversing entries in parallel
columns for both methods of amortization for December 31, 1975.

Problem 17-5

On April 1, 1973, the Pierce Company purchased $1 million of the par
value of 5% bonds of Eastern Utilities Company for $926,399.14. Interest
is payable annually on April 1. (The annual effective rate of interest was
6%.)

Required:

1. Give entry for purchase.

2. If these bonds matured in 10 years, prepare adjusting and closing
entries on December 31, 1973, using straight line amortization.

3. Prepare an amortization table using the present value method of
amortization.

4. Prepare adjusting and closing entries as of December 31, 1973, and as of December 31, 1968, using the table in 3.

5. If $100,000 of the par value of these bonds are sold on September 1, 1977, at 97½ plus accrued interest, prepare entry to record sale. (Compute book value from table prepared in 3.)

6. After the bonds are sold in 5, prepare adjusting and closing entries at end of calendar and fiscal year, 1977.

Problem 17–6

Compute the sales price of the following bond payable issues:

a) $100,000 issue of 6% bonds, interest payable quarterly, sold to yield 8% effective interest, maturing in five years.

b) Serial bond issue totaling $90,000 maturing $15,000 at the end of two years, $30,000 at the end of four years, and $45,000 at the end of six years. Stated interest rate is 7% payable annually; effective rate is 5%.

c) Issue of $100,000 bonds paying a stated interest rate of 5% annually sold to yield 7%, bonds mature in 10 years.

d) Same as in (c) except the bonds are not sold until 12 months after authorized.

Part B (7 through 19)

Problem 17–7

On March 31, 1974, a corporation sold a $100,000 issue of 6% bonds maturing four years from that date. The bonds were sold for $105,000 and pay interest each September 30 and March 31. The corporation's fiscal year ends on December 31. Premium is amortized on each interest payment date using the straight line method. Reflect all entries pertaining to the bonds (including adjusting, closing, and reversing entries) in a table with the following headings:

Date	Cash Dr., Cr.	Premium Bonds Payable Dr., Cr.	Bond Interest Expense Dr., Cr.	Accrued Bond Interest Expense Dr., Cr.	Income Summary Dr.	Bonds Payable Dr., Cr.

Problem 17–8

On July 1, 1970, Deep Mine Company authorized a $50,000, 6% bond issue (including a first mortgage) maturing four years from date. Interest is payable each January 1 and July 1. The bonds were sold September 1, 1970, at 103.59 plus accrued interest.

The bond indenture provided (1) that 25 cents per ton mined would be deposited each June 30 to provide a sinking fund for bond retirement and (2) that retained earnings would be appropriated on a straight line basis.

The production of coal was as follows:

Year Ended June 30	Tons
1971	42,000
1972	56,000
1973	50,000
1974	58,000

Required:

The sinking fund earned 4% the first year and 5% thereafter. Submit all journal entries necessary to express all of these particulars on the company's books. Amortize bond premium by the straight line method. Hint: To save time the bond interest and sinking fund entries may be tabulated. Omit adjusting and closing entries.

(AICPA adapted)

Problem 17-9

The BK Corporation issued $100,000 in bonds payable on January 1, 1968. To simplify this problem assume they matured on July 1, 1971. They carried a 5% annual interest rate (nominal) payable January 1 and July 1. You are to prepare amortization tables under each of the following assumptions:

1. The bonds sold for $98,427.65 (excluding accrued interest) so as to yield 5½% per annum.
   a) Assuming straight line amortization.
   b) Assuming present value amortization.
2. The bonds sold for $100,318.08 (excluding any accrued interest) so as to yield 4.9% per annum.
   a) Assuming straight line amortization.
   b) Assuming present value amortization.

Problem 17-10

A $1 million bond issue dated May 1, 1973, due in five years, paying 6% interest annually was authorized by directors of Mayo Corporation.

Required:

1. Give the entry for sale of the bonds on May 1, 1973, if priced to yield 4%.
2. Prepare an amortization table using the present value method.
3. Give adjusting and closing entries at December 31, 1974.
4. On July 1, 1975, one fourth of the issue was purchased on the market by Mayo Corporation for $267,000 plus accrued interest. Record the purchase and cancellation of these bonds.
5. Refer to transaction (1). Assume instead that the bonds had not been sold until January 1, 1974, at which time, they were sold to yield 4%. Give entry for the sale.

Problem 17-11

Bearing Corporation sold a $100,000 par-value bond issue on April 1, 1972, for $93,267.26. At this price the effective interest rate is 8% per annum on the bonds which pay 6% per annum on interest dates of April 1 and October 1. Record sale of the bonds and all entries pertaining to them through January 1, 1974. The corporation's fiscal year ends December 31.

The corporation decided that it could retire half of the issue on January 1, 1974, for $48,500 including accrued interest. Give entry or entries for this transaction and the reversing entry on January 1, 1974. Check figure: At the end of four periods carrying value of the bonds is $96,370.12 using present value amortization.

Problem 17-12

Nixon Company sold a $1 million bond issue on December 31, 1966. Interest is payable annually on December 31 at $3\frac{3}{4}\%$, and the bonds are purchased by an investment syndicate to yield 4%. The bonds mature December 31, 1976.

Required:

1. Prepare an amortization table (present value method) for Nixon Company.
2. Give entry for sale of the bonds.
3. Give adjusting, closing, and reversing entries with respect to the bonds on September 30, 1970, using table prepared in 1. Fiscal period of Nixon Company ends September 30.
4. On June 30, 1973, the company redeems 20% of the bonds outstanding at 99 plus accrued interest. Give entry for the redemption.
5. Give the adjusting and closing entries on September 30, 1973.

Problem 17-13

1. Starnes Corporation can redeem its Series A bonds payable now outstanding at 103 and substitute a new issue with interest at 5% per annum payable semiannually. The current bonds have eight years to run and bear 6% per annum, payable semiannually. Indicate the saving per $1,000 bond.
2. In addition to the foregoing $200,000 issue, Starnes Corporation has outstanding another $200,000 issue (Series B) which matures in 12 years, pays 7% per annum, payable semiannually, and is callable at 106. Show which series should be called.

Problem 17-14

On January 1, 1971, Cohen Company had outstanding $1 million in 4% convertible bonds, interest payable January 1 and July 1. After the interest payment of January 1, 1971, unamortized Bond Discount amounted to $20,800. Straight line amortization is used; the bonds mature July 1, 1973. Give all entries necessary at July 1, 1971, if on that date holders of $200,000 of the bonds turn them in for common stock, under each of the following independent cases:

1. Each $1,000 bond can be exchanged for 200 shares of no-par stock, and
   a) The market value of the stock is $5.50 per share; market value of the bonds is less certain.
   b) Market value of the bonds is at 108; market value of the stock is less certain.
   c) The book value method is to be used.
2. Each $1,000 bond can be exchanged for 18 shares of the $50 par-value stock of the company, and
   a) The market value of the stock is $61; market value of the bonds is less certain.
   b) Market value of the bonds is at 106; market value of the stock is less certain.
   c) The book value method is to be used.

Problem 17-15

A serial issue of $700,000 of bonds dated April 1, 1971, was sold on that date for $707,600. The interest rate is 4% per annum payable semiannually on April 1 and October 1. Scheduled maturities are as follows:

Serial	Due Date	Amount
1	April 1, 1972	$100,000
2	April 1, 1973	200,000
3	April 1, 1974	200,000
4	April 1, 1975	200,000

Required:

The $200,000 group due April 1974 was retired October 1, 1973, at 101. Give all entries relating to the bonds including closing entries through January 1, 1973. The company adjusts and closes its books each December 31. Use straight line amortization (dollar periods).

Problem 17-16

Supreme Corporation, in need of some additional funds covering a short period of time, decided to float a serial bond issue totaling $75,000. These bonds were all taken by one investment house and the corporation received $69,500 therefor. The bonds were all dated January 1, 1967, and were to be redeemed in the following manner: January 1, 1968, $5,000; January 1, 1969, $10,000; January 1, 1970, $15,000; January 1, 1971, $20,000; January 1, 1972, $25,000. Total, $75,000.

Required:

1. Prepare a schedule of amortization of bond discount showing the following:

a) Amount of discount applicable to each serial.
b) Amount of discount to be charged against each year's operation with due regard to the amount of money in use each year.

2. Assume that on January 1, 1970, the corporation realized $25,000 on some life insurance policies and with the proceeds redeemed the serial issue of $25,000 regularly due on January 1, 1972. Prepare a table to show what changes, if any, in the annual amortization would result from this prepayment.

Problem 17-17

The ABC Corporation sold serial bonds due as follows: $10,000, January 1, 1971; $15,000, July 1, 1971; and $25,000, January 1, 1972. The bonds carried a 2½% coupon (nominal) interest per semiannual period (5% per annum) and were sold to yield 2% interest per semiannual period (4% per annum). Prepare a table of amortization for the life of the bond issue assuming: (*a*) straight line amortization and (*b*) present value amortization. To yield 2% interest per semiannual period the bond issue sold for $50,789.33 on January 1, 1970.

Problem 17–18

On April 1, 1948, Company X issued at par $100,000 bonds, $2\frac{1}{2}\%$ coupons half-yearly, due at par, April 1, 1973. On April 1, 1971, the sinking fund had a balance of $87,882.59. Contributions to the fund are made semiannually.

Required:

For each case indicated below:

a) Compute the semiannual contribution to the sinking fund.

b) Assuming the sinking fund earns 2% half-yearly, prepare a sinking fund table for the last two years of the life of the bonds.

c) Assuming Company X closes its books on December 31, tabulate Company X's journal entries with the bond interest, the sinking fund, and the appropriation of Retained Earnings during 1972 and 1973. The fund and appropriation of Retained Earnings are kept in agreement. The amount of an annuity of 1 at 2% is 84.5794014 for 50 periods.

Case A – the bond interest is not paid out of the sinking fund.

Case B – the bond interest is paid out of sinking fund.

Problem 17–19

Rich Corporation authorized and had certified by the trustee $800,000 of $4\frac{1}{2}\%$ first-mortgage, sinking fund bonds, dated April 1, 1972, due 20 years from date, interest payable April 1 and October 1. The trust indenture states that the company shall make contributions as of January 1 of each year "out of profits" to a sinking fund of one fifteenth of the outstanding bonds on that date.

On April 1, 1972, $200,000 of the bonds were sold by the company at par on the open market. On July 1, 1972, another $200,000 block was sold by the company at a premium of $2,370 plus accrued interest.

On August 1, 1972, a syndicate took the remaining bonds at 97.935 and accrued interest with the proviso that any unsold bonds on October 1, 1972, might be returned to the company at $97\frac{1}{2}$. Under this provision $100,000 was returned (ex interest) on October 1, 1972.

Required:

1. Journalize all transactions in connection with the bonds, interest, and fund through January 1, 1973, including adjusting, closing, and reversing entries at December 31, 1972.

2. Prepare a partial balance sheet at January 1, 1973 (based on the accounts used with respect to the above transactions).

	Pensions and
chapter **18**	Leaves

PART A—ACCOUNTING FOR PENSION PLANS

A pension plan is an arrangement whereby a company establishes a plan to provide its employees with retirement benefits that can be estimated or determined in advance from the provisions of an agreement (document) or from the company's practices. Ordinarily, such benefits are in the form of monthly pension payments, but they may also include death and disability payments. Pension plans may be either written or implied from a well-defined company policy. However, a policy of paying random benefits to selected employees on a case-to-case basis cannot classify as a viable pension plan.[1]

Since the cost of a pension plan falls upon the employer over a period of time, the central accounting issues are (*a*) *timing* of the employer's charges to expense and (*b*) *presentation* of the effects of the plan on the income statement and balance sheet over time. Accounting for pension plans is frequently complex since it involves actuarial determinations (estimates) and present value applications. The purpose of this section is to present the broad aspects of accounting for

---

[1] This definition is essentially the same as provided in the most recent AICPA documents on pension plans: Ernest L. Hicks, "Accounting for the Cost of Pension Plans," *Accounting Research Study No. 8* (New York: AICPA, 1965), and "Accounting for the Cost of Pension Plans," *APB Opinion 8* (New York: AICPA, November 1966).

pension plans. Detailed study should include the two relatively recent AICPA documents cited in footnote 1.

The growth of pension plans is a relatively recent phenomenon. In 1969 there were approximately 33,000 private pension plans covering an estimated 30 million employees. According to statistics compiled by the Securities and Exchange Commission, financial assets of company pension funds have risen from $52 billion in 1960 to $126 billion in 1966.[2]

The first AICPA pronouncement on accounting for pension plans was an *Accounting Research Bulletin* in 1948, which was timely enough, because prior to that time the number of plans and the relative magnitude of the problem probably did not warrant much attention. That bulletin was reaffirmed in 1953 and was augmented in 1956 in *Accounting Research Bulletin No. 47*, "Accounting for Costs of Pension Plans." In response to the growing magnitude of the problem the Accounting Principles Board published *Research Study No. 8* in 1965 and followed the next year with *APB Opinion 8* (see footnote 1). The discussions to follow are in accord with the latter Opinion.

Pension Plan Fundamentals

Most pension plans are formally established through a "retirement plan" that qualifies under the Internal Revenue Code so that:

a) The employer's contributions are deductible for tax purposes.

b) Interest on "pension funds" is not subject to income tax.

c) Retirement benefits are not taxable to the recipient.

The company may, at its choice, establish a pension plan that is either *funded* or *nonfunded*. Under a nonfunded plan, pension payments to retired employees are made directly by the company as they become due. Under a funded plan the employer makes payments (1) to a funding agency such as a trustee (an independent third party) who, in turn, makes payments to the recipient as they become due, or (2) to an insurance company who assumes all obligations for payments of benefits as they become due. A company may set up its own special internal fund for pension plans; however, if the funds are under the control of the employer the plan would be classified as nonfunded.

A pension plan may be contributory, where the employees bear part of the cost, or noncontributory, where the employer bears the entire cost. An employee's right to receive a present or future pension benefit is said to *vest* when his right to eventually receive the benefit is no longer contingent upon his remaining an employee of the company. Vesting occurs when the employee retires, but may occur prior

---

[2] *U.S. News and World Report*, January 11, 1971, p. 58.

to that date. For example, a benefit may vest after a specified number of years of service or at a specified age.

Actuarial determinations and estimates are an integral part of pension plans since *pension costs* are related to a number of significant uncertainties concerning future events, such as: retirement age, mortality (the average life expectancy of employees both before and after retirement), employee turnover, interest rates, gains and losses of fund investments, administrative requirements, future salary levels, pension benefits, and vesting provisions.

A pension plan may be initiated under one of two quite different circumstances which would have significant effects on pension costs, funding requirements, and accounting, viz:

1. A pension plan may be initiated when the company is organized, in which case persons upon initial employment would qualify for the pension plan. Subsequent to inception of the plan only *normal pension costs* would be incurred (each year) by the company.

2. A pension plan may be initiated some years after the company was organized. In this case *present* employees, as well as new employees subsequently hired, would qualify for the plan. *Normal* pension costs would be incurred (each year) by the company for both groups of employees. However, in this case an additional pension cost also would be incurred at date of inception of the pension plan. All employees working for the enterprise at date of the inception of the pension plan generally are given past service credits under the plan for prior years' employment with the company. Thus, the company must bear a one-time pension cost (in addition to the normal pension cost incurred on a year-to-year basis) to provide for the "catch-up" for prior employees; this cost generally is referred to as *past service pension cost.*

Accounting for Pension Plans

Accounting for pension plans should be on an accrual basis and maintain a distinction between pension costs (normal cost and past service cost) and pension funding. Funding is an important aspect of accounting for a pension plan since the common pattern is to establish a "pension fund," either internally or externally, into which cash is paid currently as the employees earn "service credits" from year to year. The pension benefits are payable many years later when the employee retires. Obviously, the total cash paid in for service credits is apt to be significantly different than the total disbursements subsequently made for pension benefits (whether on an individual or group basis) due to earnings (interest) on the funds between dates of deposit and dates of disbursement as benefits, mortality experience, and other future uncertainties.

In accounting for pension plans all costs, including fund gains and losses, must be identified, recorded, and reported in a manner consistent with the long-term characteristics of a pension plan; on this point *APB Opinion* 8 states:

In the absence of convincing evidence that the company will reduce or discontinue the benefits called for in a pension plan, the cost of the plan should be accounted for on the assumption that the company will continue to provide such benefits. This assumption implies a long-term undertaking, the cost of which should be recognized annually whether or not funded. . . . The entire cost of benefit payments ultimately to be made should be charged against income subsequent to the adoption or amendment of a plan and that no portion of such cost should be charged directly against retained earnings.

In accounting for pension plans it is essential that a careful distinction be made between *pension costs* and *pension funding.* In the discussions and illustrations to follow, however, you will observe that they are intimately related. We have already identified the two basic types of pension costs; they may be more precisely defined as follows:

1. Normal pension costs—the amount of cost, on an accrual basis, that should be assigned annually to the pension plan for current services of the employees during the year, exclusive of any element representing a portion of past service cost or interest thereon. More directly, it is the cost assigned, for purposes of actuarial calculations, for the service credits earned by the employees during the specific period (year).

2. Past service cost—the cost assigned to service credits for employees for years prior to the inception of the pension plan. Past service cost arises (*a*) when an established company institutes a pension plan which recognizes past services and (*b*) when a pension plan is amended.

Although these two basic types of pension costs may be reported on a combined basis, their determination (as to amount) and accounting requirements are quite different. These differences will be emphasized in the paragraphs to follow.

In respect to *funding* a pension plan, assuming a funded plan, the company must disburse funds for each of the two types of pension costs, viz:

1. For normal pension costs, the company disburses cash (to the fund or funding agency) each period in an amount sufficient to satisfy the *normal* pension credits being earned currently by the employees.

2. For past service pension cost (a one-time cost), the company may elect to disburse cash at date of inception of the plan sufficient to satisfy this obligation, or, as is the usual case, to spread the payments over a selected number of periods in the future (say 10) from date of inception of the plan. The latter choice, obviously, is tantamount to

paying a currently due debt on an installment basis which would give rise to an interest charge.

Past service pension costs represent a "catch-up" obligation and the question as to when it should be reflected in the accounts and the manner of reflecting it has been the concern of the accounting pronouncements mentioned above. Obviously, since it is a one-time, and generally significant, amount that relates to past service of the employees, this has caused it to be somewhat controversial. All accountants agree that it must be given recognition at date of inception of the plan; however, there is a difference of opinion as to whether past service cost should be reflected as (1) an adjustment to prior period earnings (retained earnings), (2) an extraordinary item on the income statement in the year of inception of the plan, or (3) spread over a selected number of years (as a current cost) in the future (after inception of the plan). The quotation on page 717 from *APB Opinion 8* clearly requires the latter. The details of the Opinion state, in effect, that past service cost must be amortized after date of inception of the plan as a part of total pension cost each year; the period of amortization is variable, being subject to the particular circumstances. The following quotation from *APB Opinion 8* applies:

To be acceptable for determining cost for accounting purposes, an actuarial cost method should be rational and systematic and should be consistently applied so that it results in a reasonable measure of pension cost from year to year. Therefore, in applying an actuarial cost method that separately assigns a portion of cost as prior service cost, any amortization of such portion should be based on a rational and systematic plan and generally should result in reasonable stable annual amounts.

For analytical and problem-solving purposes it is sometimes helpful to diagram a pension plan along the following lines:

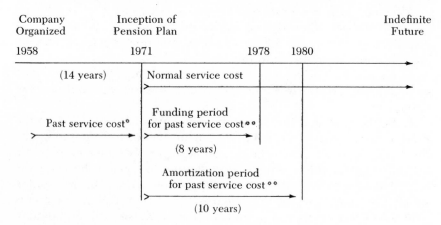

Company Organized	Inception of Pension Plan		Indefinite Future
1958	1971	1978 1980	

(14 years)   Normal service cost

Past service cost°   Funding period for past service cost°°

(8 years)

Amortization period for past service cost°°

(10 years)

° $70,000 (present value)
°° Must be on present value basis; see Case B page 724

The accounting entries themselves are not involved; rather computation of the amounts of (a) the normal pension cost for the period, (b) the past service cost and its amortization, and (c) the amount of funding can be rather complex. To illustrate the essence of the accounting entries, rather than the complexity of the computations, we will present five highly simplified cases with "straight line" relationships. Present value determinations and actuarial estimates, as required by *APB Opinion 8* (straight line is unacceptable), will be incorporated in subsequent illustrations. Both funding and amortization of past service costs will be illustrated.[3]

Case A. A new company; a nonfunded pension plan is initiated the first year, hence there are no past service costs.

To record normal pension costs appropriately determined:

	Year 1	Year 2
Pension Cost...10,000		12,000
Liability under Pension Plan	10,000	12,000

To record payment (in later years) to a retired employee:

| Liability under Pension Plan .... | xxx | |
| Cash... | | xxx |

Case B. Same as Case A except the plan is funded.

| Pension Cost...10,000 | | 12,000 |
| Cash (paid to trustee).............................. | 10,000 | 12,000 |

No entry would be required for payments to retired employee; payment would be made by the funding agency (trustee).

Case C. An old company; a new plan is initiated (funded); past service costs appropriately determined to total $70,000.

To record pension costs and funding (assuming a 10-year amortization period and a 10-year funding period):

| Pension Costs°...17,000 | | 19,000 |
| Cash (paid to trustee).............................. | 17,000 | 19,000 |

°Computation:	Year 1	Year 2
Normal pension cost.........................$10,000		$12,000
Past pension cost $70,000 allocated over the next 10 years on straight line basis; for this illustration only.)..... 7,000		7,000
Total Pension Cost $17,000		$19,000

Case D. Same as Case C except funding is $3,000 *less* than the period pension costs.

Pension Costs...17,000		19,000
Liability—Pension Costs in Excess of Payments...	3,000	3,000
Cash...	14,000	16,000

[3] The 1970 issue of *Accounting Trends and Techniques,* p. 177, reported that of 597 companies, 381 amortize past service costs.

Case E. Same as Case C except funding is $3,000 *more* than the period pension costs.

Pension Cost	17,000		19,000
Deferred Charge—Payments in Excess of			
Pension Costs	3,000		3,000
Cash		20,000	22,000

Determination of Pension Cost. The preceding illustrations and discussions emphasized that the critical aspects of accounting for pension plans are determination (estimation) of (*a*) the periodic pension cost for accounting purposes and (*b*) the funding required each period (in the case of funded plans). Accountants generally agree that pension costs should be accounted for on an accrual basis; however, there is not general agreement as to the precise nature of periodic pension costs in relationship to the future (prospective) benefits that will have to be paid. Clearly, interest earned on funds set aside many years before disbursement as benefits will significantly affect certain accounting values to be recorded. *Opinion 8*, as quoted above, clearly specifies that both "normal" and "past service" costs should be included in the periodic charge (pension cost). The board also stated in *Opinion 8* that the annual provision for pension cost should be based on an *accounting method* that uses an acceptable *"actuarial cost method"* (as defined below) and results in a provision between the *minimum* and *maximum* stated below:[4]

Minimum. The provision for pension cost should not be less than the *total* of:
1. Normal cost.
2. An amount equivalent to interest on any unfunded past service cost.
3. If indicated—a provision for vested benefits.

Maximum. The annual provision for pension cost should not be greater than the *total* of:
1. Normal cost.
2. Ten percent of the past service cost (until fully amortized).
3. Ten percent of the amounts of any increases or decreases in past service costs arising on amendments of the plan (until fully amortized); in effect, a 10-year minimum period.
4. Interest equivalents on the difference between provisions (pension costs) and amounts funded.

The *actuarial cost methods* mentioned immediately above are approaches that have been developed primarily as funding techniques

---

[4]Adapted. Also note that the minimum amortization period is 10 years; to minimize computations shorter periods are utilized in the chapter and in the exercises and problems. This simplification for instructional purposes does no violence to the concepts involved.

in that they provide the specific amounts for periodic payments to be made to the funding agency (funded plans) such as insurance companies or trustees (trust agreements). Since determination of the funding requirements explicitly requires estimation of the underlying pension costs for several of the actuarial cost methods they are also useful in determining pension costs for accounting purposes. Although these methods are alike in that they utilize present value concepts and rest on actuarial assumptions, they differ significantly in their approach and can produce quite different results for the same situation.

We noted above that, in accordance with *APB Opinion 8*, the *accounting method* utilized in accounting for pension plans must use an acceptable *actuarial cost method*. The Opinion states:

(1) Accrued Benefit Cost Method (Unit Credit Method) — under the unit credit method, future service benefits are funded as they accrue — that is, each employee works out the service period involved. The past service cost is the present value at the plan's inception date of the units of future benefit credited to employees for service prior to inception of the plan. Thus, the annual contribution (and cost) comprises primarily (*a*) the normal cost and (*b*) the past service cost.

(2) Projected Benefit Cost Methods — There are four methods in this group; entry age normal, individual level premium, aggregate, and attained age normal methods. The amount assigned (for funding) to the current year usually represents a level or constant amount that will provide for the estimated projected retirement benefits over the service lives of either the individual employees or the employee group, depending on the method selected. Pension cost projected under these methods tends to be stable or decline year by year, depending on the method selected.

Although the APB, in *Opinion 8*, listed these methods as acceptable it recognized that other methods may be acceptable if they conform to the guidelines established in the Opinion.

Recording Pension Costs Illustrated. Now that we have reviewed the basic approaches utilized by actuaries in determining funding requirements, normal pension costs, and past service costs, the essential steps leading to development of the periodic accounting entries may be listed as follows:

1. Determination of *past service cost* by the actuary. This involves a complicated actuarial estimate derived by applying an acceptable actuarial method taking into account factors such as those listed on page 716. The actuary develops the present obligation (present value) of the cost of credits for services prior to the inception of the pension plan.

2. Determination of normal pension cost for the period by the actuary. This involves a complicated determination based upon service credits for the current year. There must be a separate determination for each year as it occurs. Obviously, the number of employees,

salaries, and terms of the plan must underlie this actuarial determination for each period.

3. Verify that the total pension cost as computed in No. 1 and 2 comes within the maximum and minimum limits; if not, utilize the closest limit.

4. When there are past service costs, develop a present value amortization schedule for the period of amortization (at an appropriate interest rate). If the past service costs are to be funded, as is the usual case, develop a funding schedule for the funding period (at an appropriate interest rate). The two schedules may be combined in one table as shown in Illustration 18–1.

5. Based upon (a) the normal pension cost for the period, (b) the amortization schedule, and (c) the funding schedule, develop the accounting entries for the period.

To illustrate, assume the AB Corporation, having been in operation for 14 years, decided in 1971 to adopt a funded pension plan for its employees. A trust agreement has been entered into with a bank (trustee) whereby the required payments to the fund will be made each year. The pension plan provides for vesting after 20 years of service by each eligible employee; it is noncontributory. An actuary was engaged on a consultation basis to develop the normal and past service costs and fund contributions each period. The management decided to utilize the "unit credit method." After an extended analysis, and based upon certain actuarial assumptions, the actuary developed the following:

1. Normal pension cost for 1971, $10,000 (within the maximum and and minimum limits). .

2. Present value of the past service cost at date of inception of the pension plan (January 1, 1971), $70,000.

The management, upon recommendation of the actuary, decided to assume a 4% interest rate and to amortize the past service costs over a 10-year period.

Three cases will be illustrated in respect to *funding* of the past service costs (funding payments to be made at the end of each year):

Case A. Past service costs to be funded over a 10-year period (same as the amortization period).

Case B. Past service costs to be funded over an 8-year period (two years less than the amortization period; see page 718).

Case C. Past service costs to be funded over a 12-year period (two years more than the amortization period).

Case A. The next step is to compute the periodic *amortization* and *funding* for the *past service costs.* In this case the amortization and funding periods are identical; therefore, the two schedules (periodic amounts) are the same; that is, we have two questions and they have identical responses:

1. Assuming a present obligation of $70,000 to be paid in equal installments over 10 years, at 4%, what is the periodic payment?
2. Assuming a $70,000 value (cost) to be amortized over 10 equal periods (years) on a present value basis, at 4%, what is the periodic amortization?

Computation:

Periodic payment
(or amortization) = $70,000 ÷ Present value of annuity of 1 for
                                10 rents at 4% (Table 5–4)
              = $70,000 ÷ 8.1108958
              = $ 8,630.37

Indicated entries for the pension costs and funding at year-end:

1971

Pension Cost (normal)...10,000.00
Pension Cost (amortization of past service cost)° 8,630.37
    Cash (paid to trustee)...   18,630.37

1972 (assuming normal pension cost of $12,000):

Pension Cost (normal)...12,000.00
Pension Cost (amortization of past service cost)° 8,630.37
    Cash (paid to trustee)...   20,630.37
    ° Observe that these amounts implicitly include an interest factor that decreases each period.

Clearly, after the 10th year the past service costs, and the related funding, would drop out and only the normal costs and normal funding would be recognized thereafter.

Case B. This case introduces another complexity; that is, the amortization period is 10 years whereas the funding period is 8 years. Clearly, in this situation we must compute the amortization schedule on one basis and the funding schedule on another basis. Since funds will be disbursed at a greater rate than the cost accrual we also must adjust the *amortization* schedule for the interest differential. A special table is essential to this determination (Illustration 18–1).

In respect to the distinctive features of Illustration 18–1 you should observe the following:

1. This table relates only to past service costs (not normal pension costs).
2. The periodic amortization of past service costs (column *a*) is *reduced* by the interest on the funding paid in *excess* of the periodic amortization; this causes a decreasing periodic amortization (column *c*).

Illustration 18–1

Schedule of Past Service Pension Costs and Related Funding†
(amortization period 10 years; funding period 8 years)

Year	Amortization of Past Service Cost – 10 Years			Funding – 8 Years	Balance Sheet – Deferred Charge	
	10-Year Accrual Factor (a)	Reduction for Interest (b)	Past Pension Cost (Debit) (c)	Cash (Credit) (d)	Debit/ Credit° (e)	Account Balance (f)
1971	$8,630.37‡		$ 8,630.37	$10,396.95§	$1,766.58	$ 1,766.58
1972	8,630.37	$ 70.66	8,559.71	10,396.95	1,837.24	3,603.82
1973	8,630.37	144.15	8,486.22	10,396.95	1,910.73	5,514.55
1974	8,630.37	220.58	8,409.79	10,396.95	1,987.16	7,501.71
1975	8,630.37	300.07	8,330.30	10,396.95	2,066.65	9,568.36
1976	8,630.37	382.73	8,247.64	10,396.95	2,149.31	11,717.67
1977	8,630.37	468.71	8,161.66	10,396.95	2,235.29	13,952.96
1978	8,630.37	558.12	8,072.25	10,396.95	2,324.70	16,277.66
1979	8,630.37	651.11	7,979.26	–0–	7,979.26°	8,298.40
1980	8,630.37	331.97	8,298.40	–0–	8,298.40°	–0–
			$83,175.60	$83,175.60		

† It may be observed that this table assumes (1) amortization at end of the period (year), (2) that the present value of the past service cost is at the beginning of the period, and (3) that the funding payments are made at the end of each period. Other viable assumptions are possible.

‡ Amortization: (10 periods, @ 4%):
  Periodic amortization = $70,000 ÷ 8.110895 (Table 5–4)
  = $ 8,630.37 to column (a)

§ Funding: (8 periods, @ 4%):
  Periodic payment = $70,000 ÷ 6.7327449 (Table 5–4)
  = $10,396.95 to column (d)

(a) Independently computed above.
(b) 4% of the preceding balance of column (f).
(c) Column (a) less column (b).
(d) Independently computed above.
(e) Column (d) minus column (c).
(f) Preceding balance plus (or minus) column (e).

3. The periodic funding payments cease at the end of year 8 (1978).

4. Payments to the fund are constant each year.

5. The amortization of past service costs terminates at the end of the 10th year (1980).

6. Total pension costs (column c) and total fund payments (column d) are equal ($83,175.60) although their timing is different.

7. The deferred charge (column f) to be reported on the balance sheet is due to the fact that funding payments exceed amortization; however, at the end of the amortization period the deferred charge balance is zero.

8. Funding payments are comprised of two elements; principal, $70,000, and interest, $13,175.60.

9. Accounting entries are indicated by the table but do not include normal pension costs.

Entries for pension costs and funding at year-end:

1971:

Pension Cost (normal)...	10,000.00	
Pension Cost (amortization of past service cost)..............	8,630.37	
Deferred Charge-Payments in Excess of Pension Costs ...	1,766.58	
Cash (paid to trustee)...		20,396.95

1972:

Pension Cost (normal)...	12,000.00	
Pension Cost (amortization of past service cost)..............	8,559.71	
Deferred Charge-Payments in Excess of Pension Costs ...	1,837.24	
Cash (paid to trustee)...		22,396.95

Case C. This is the same as Case B except that the amortization period for past service costs is two years less than the funding period. As a consequence, the Schedule of Past Pension Costs and Related Funding (as shown in Illustration 18–1) obviously must be changed in two respects: (1) in the amortization portion the interest differential must be added (rather than deducted) and (2) in the balance sheet column a *liability* (rather than a deferred charge) must be reflected. Illustration 18–2 reflects these differences.

Illustration 18–2
Schedule of Past Service Pension Costs and Related Funding
(amortization period 10 years; funding period 12 years)

	Amortization of Past Service Cost – 10 Years			Funding – 12 Years	Balance Sheet – Liability	
Year	10-Year Accrual Factor (a)	Addition for Interest (b)	Past Pension Cost (Debit) (c)	Cash (Credit) (d)	Credit Debit° (e)	Account Balance (f)
1971 ......$8,630.37†			$ 8,630.37	$ 7,458.65‡	$1,171.72	$ 1,171.72
1972 ...... 8,630.37	$ 46.87	8,677.24	7,458.65	1,218.59	2,390.31
1973 ...... 8,630.37	95.61	8,725.98	7,458.65	1,267.33	3,657.64
1974 ...... 8,630.37	146.31	8,776.68	7,458.65	1,318.03	4,975.67
1975 ...... 8,630.37	199.03	8,829.40	7,458.65	1,370.75	6,346.42
1976 ...... 8,630.37	253.86	8,884.23	7,458.65	1,425.58	7,772.00
1977 ...... 8,630.37	310.88	8,941.25	7,458.65	1,482.60	9,254.60
1978 ...... 8,630.37	370.18	9,000.55	7,458.65	1,541.90	10,796.50
1979 ...... 8,630.37	431.86	9,062.23	7,458.65	1,603.58	12,400.08
1980 ...... 8,630.37	496.00	9,126.37	7,458.65	1,667.72	14,067.80
1981 ...... –0–	562.71	562.71	7,458.65	6,895.94°	7,171.86
1982 ...... –0–	286.79	286.79	7,458.65	7,171.86°	–0–
			$89,503.80	$89,503.80		

†Periodic amortization = $70,000 ÷ 8.1108958 (Table 5–4)
                 = $ 8,630.37 To column (a)

‡Periodic funding = $70,000 ÷ 9.3850738 (Table 5–4)
               = $ 7,458.65 To column (d)

(a) Independently computed above.
(b) 4% of the preceding balance of column (f).
(c) Column (a) plus column (b).
(d) Independently computed above.
(e) Column (c) less column (d).
(f) Preceding balance plus (or minus) column (e).

The entries indicated in Illustration 18–2 are:

1971:

Pension Cost (normal)..10,000.00		
Pension Cost (amortization of past service cost)............. 8,630.37		
Liability – Pension Cost in Excess of Payments		1,171.72
Cash (paid to trustee)...		17,458.65

1972:

Pension Cost (normal)..12,000.00		
Pension Cost (amortization of past service cost)............. 8,677.24		
Liability – Pension Cost in Excess of Payments		1,218.59
Cash (paid to trustee)...		19,458.65

Actuarial Gains and Losses

You will recall that the entries presented in respect to Cases A, B, and C presumed that the interest rate (4%) materialized on the fund and that the determinations of past service costs would not change over time. Obviously, actuaries must deal with several uncertainties in making these estimates. Regardless of the degree of competence, it is likely that some of these determinations will subsequently have to be revised. The effects on actuarially calculated pension costs of (a) changes in the underlying assumptions and (b) deviations between planned and actual results are called actuarial gains and losses. Adjustments for actuarial gains and losses may be needed annually to reflect actual experience or from time to time to reflect a revision in the underlying assumptions. There are two related accounting questions: (a) determination of the actuarial loss or gain and (b) the timing of their recognition in the accounts. In practice three methods are to be found: immediate recognition, spreading on a prospective basis, and averaging. On this point *Opinion 8* states:

Actuarial gains and losses, including realized investment gains and losses, should be given effect in the provision for pension cost in a consistent manner that reflects the long-range nature of pension cost. . . . Accordingly, (with certain exceptions) actuarial gains and losses should be spread over the current year and future years or recognized on the basis of an average.

Disclosure

According to *APB Opinion No. 8*, the following disclosures should be made in financial statements or their notes:

1. A statement that such plans exist, identifying or describing the employee groups covered.
2. A statement of the company's accounting and funding policies.
3. The provision for pension cost for the period.
4. The excess, if any, of the actuarially computed value of vested benefits

over the total of the pension fund and any balance-sheet pension accruals, less any pension repayments or deferred charges.

5. Nature and effect of significant matters affecting comparability for all periods presented, such as changes in accounting methods (actuarial cost method, amortization of past and prior service cost, treatment of actuarial gains and losses, etc.), changes in circumstances (actuarial assumptions, etc.), or adoption or amendment of a plan.[5]

The consolidated income statement, balance sheet, and related footnotes for Bethlehem Steel are presented in Illustration 18–3 as an excellent example of the reporting of pension costs and pension liability; footnote C is especially noteworthy. In addition, the statement for the Pension Trust Fund and the accountants' opinion are presented. Note that the fund is separate and apart from the financial statements of the company; the fund is controlled and operated by the trustees.

Illustration 18–3
BETHLEHEM STEEL
Consolidated Statement of Income
and Income Invested in the Business

(Dollars in Thousands)

	1969	1968
Revenues:		
Net sales	$2,927,657	$2,862,734
Interest, dividends, and other income	28,595	33,521
	$2,956,252	$2,896,255
Costs and Expenses:		
Cost of sales	$2,250,050	$2,180,394
Depreciation (Note B)	213,112	211,641
Pensions (Note C)	40,516	36,143
Taxes, other than taxes on income	103,043	94,080
Selling, administrative, and general expense	137,463	125,527
Interest and other debt charges	22,536	18,942
Provision for taxes on income (Note D):		
Current	(32,900)	20,800
Deferred	65,900	48,200
	$2,799,720	$2,735,727
Net Income	$ 156,532	$ 160,528
Net income per share°	3.56	3.55
Income Invested in the Business, January 1	1,369,412	1,281,230
	$1,525,944	$1,441,758
Dividends	76,966	72,346
Dividends per share	1.75	1.60
Income Invested in the Business, December 31	$1,448,978	$1,369,412

° Based on average number of shares outstanding.

---

[5] The 1970 issue of *Accounting Trends and Techniques*, p. 177, reported that of 597 companies, 536 disclosed the basis for determining pension costs.

Illustration 18–3 (continued)

Consolidated Balance Sheet

ASSETS

(Dollars in Thousands)

Current Assets:	1969	1968
Cash	$ 60,168	$ 47,314
U.S. government and other marketable securities, at cost (approximately market)	208,439	235,945
Receivables—less allowance for doubtful receivables	313,056	269,963
Inventories	462,094	437,696
Total Current Assets	$1,043,757	$ 990,918
Investments and Long-term Receivables:		
Investments in 50% or less owned enterprises, at cost	205,734	201,260
Miscellaneous investments, at cost, and receivables	40,820	99,782
Property, plant, and equipment, net	1,924,394	1,753,314
Deferred charges	9,539	15,080
Total	$3,224,244	$3,060,354

LIABILITIES AND STOCKHOLDERS' EQUITY

Current Liabilities:		
Accounts payable (Note E)	$ 254,312	$ 348,926†
Notes payable	11,310	32,000
Accrued taxes (Note D)	99,127	100,985
Accrued employment costs	182,261	139,965
2¾% bonds, Series I, due July 15, 1970	45,714	—
Other	82,310	66,815
Total Current Liabilities	$ 675,034	$ 688,691
Accrued liabilities payable after one year (Note E)	101,700	99,840†
Deferred income taxes (Note D)	64,100	19,700
Long-term debt	418,963	368,294
Stockholders' Equity (Notes F and G):		
Preferred stock—$1 par value—		
authorized 20,000,000 shares	—	—
Common stock—$8 par value—		
authorized 80,000,000 shares; issued 45,987,118 shares	$ 575,992	$ 575,992
Income invested in the business	1,448,978	1,369,412
	$2,024,970	$1,945,404
Less—1,964,894 and 2,000,066 shares of common stock held in treasury, at cost	60,523	61,575
Total Stockholders' Equity	$1,964,447	$1,883,829
Total	$3,224,244	$3,060,354

† Restated for purposes of comparison.

Notes to Consolidated Financial Statements

A. *Principles of Consolidation*

The consolidated financial statements include the accounts of the Corporation and its majority owned subsidiaries. During 1969, the Corporation acquired several related companies. The accounts of the companies for the period since acquisition have been included in the consolidated financial statements.

Illustration 18–3 (continued)

B. *Depreciation*

Substantially all the annual additions to property, plant, and equipment made between 1953 and 1968 are being depreciated under the sum-of-the-years'-digits method. Substantially all additions since January 1, 1968, are being depreciated under the straight line method for financial accounting purposes, while the sum-of-the-years'-digits method has been retained for federal income tax purposes.

C. *Pensions*

The amounts charged against income for pensions were mainly in respect of pensions under the Pension Plan, which provides retirement benefits for substantially all employees. Effective August 1, 1969, the amounts so charged reflect an increase in cost resulting from additional benefits then effective and a decrease in cost resulting from certain revisions in the actuarial assumptions. Such revisions did not have a material effect on consolidated net income for 1969.

The Pension Plan is noncontributory and covers approximately 24,000 participants now receiving pensions and approximately 135,000 participants who may become entitled to pensions in the future. Normal retirement age is 65 and benefits are related to compensation and years of continuous service.

The assets, at cost, of the Pension Trust Fund at December 31, 1969, amounted to $536,567,000 and are sufficient to fully fund pensions already granted and to provide substantial additional amounts for pensions which may be subsequently granted. In the opinion of the Corporation and its independent actuary, such additional amounts constituted, in the light of the circumstances prevailing at December 31, 1969, a reasonable provision for the estimated actuarial liability at that date in respect of nonretired employees. The aggregate market value of the assets of the Pension Trust Fund is substantially more than the cost thereof. The Pension Trust Fund is not the property of the Corporation or its subsidiaries and therefore is not included in the consolidated financial statements.

D. *Provision for Taxes on Income*

Net income for 1969 and 1968 reflects reductions in the provision for current federal income taxes equal to the estimated investment tax credits for such years of approximately $32,000,000 and $19,900,000, respectively.

The tax effects of material timing differences in the recognition of income and expense for financial accounting purposes and for the calculation of income taxes payable are included in the financial statements in accordance with *Opinion 11* of the Accounting Principles Board of the American Institute of Certified Public Accountants.

E. *Raw Materials Transactions*

In December of 1967, 1968, and 1969, several of the Corporation's wholly owned subsidiaries sold mineral production payments aggregating $296,000,000, $18,800,000, and $57,700,000, respectively, in primary sums. The purchasers are entitled, until the primary sums and certain additional amounts have been paid, to the proceeds from the sales of raw materials mined after December 31 of the year of sale from properties of such subsidiaries. The transactions are taken into income as the minerals are produced. The unpaid balance of the primary sums at December 31, 1969, was $97,839,000 and was reflected in accounts payable and in accrued liabilities payable after one year in the ratio of the amounts that were expected to be repaid out of production in the following 12 months and thereafter.

Based on its proportionate stock interest in certain 50% or less owned raw material enterprises, the Corporation is entitled to receive its share of the raw materials produced by such enterprises and is committed to pay its share of their costs, including amortization of their long-term indebtedness. The Corporation's share of such amortization averages approximately $8,000,000 annually through 1983. In addition, the Corporation has guaranteed indebtedness of various enterprises, including that of certain 50% or less owned raw material enterprises, with maturities which average approximately $7,000,000 annually through 1973.

Illustration 18–3 (continued)

F. *Capital Stock*

During 1969, the Corporation reacquired 61,603 shares of its common stock and used 96,775 shares of treasury stock to acquire the companies mentioned in Note A.

At December 31, 1969, 457,700 shares of common stock were reserved for the exercise of options granted under the Stock Option Plan prior to 1963. The option prices range from $41 to $45 per share and the options expire on various dates prior to May 1972. During 1969, no options were exercised and options covering 156,200 shares terminated. No additional options may be granted under the plan.

G. *Kusan Acquisition*

Under date of December 15, 1969, Bethlehem and Kusan, Incorporated, entered into a Reorganization Agreement and Plan providing for the sale of all the assets, properties, and business of Kusan to a wholly owned subsidiary of Bethlehem in exchange for shares of common stock of Bethlehem at the rate of 93/100ths of a share of Bethlehem for each share of Kusan and the assumption of substantially all the liabilities of Kusan. It is contemplated that the acquisition will be accounted for on the basis of a pooling of interests and that Bethlehem will use a maximum of 679,455 shares of treasury stock to effect the exchange. The acquisition is subject to various conditions, including approval by Kusan stockholders.

Pension Trust Fund

STATEMENT OF ASSETS

(Dollars in Thousands)
December 31,

	1969	1968
Cash and accrued interest receivable	$ 2,267	$ 2,480
Contributions receivable from employing companies	38,171	8,291
Investments, at cost:		
Short-term obligations	22,107	37,018
Other bonds, notes, and obligations	112,117	121,190
Preferred stocks	16,125	11,001
Common stocks	345,780	329,557
Total°	$536,567	$509,537

STATEMENT OF CHANGES IN FUND

	1969	1968
Balance in Fund, January 1	$509,537	$471,908
Additions:		
Contributions from employing companies	40,440	36,069
Income from investments	22,750	23,132
Net gain on disposition of investments	10,776	18,453
	$583,503	$549,562
Deduction: Pension payments	46,936	40,025
Balance in Fund, December 31	$536,567	$509,537
Pensioners at year-end	24,573	23,053

° The Pension Trust Fund is not the property of the Corporation or its subsidiaries and therefore is not included in the consolidated financial statements. The aggregate market value of the total assets of the fund is substantially more than the cost thereof.

Opinion of Independent Accountants

To the Trustees of the Pension Trust of Bethlehem Steel Corporation and Subsidiary Companies:

In our opinion, the accompanying statement of assets and statement of changes in the Fund present fairly the assets of the Pension Fund under the Pension Trust of Bethlehem Steel Corporation and Subsidiary Companies at December 31, 1969 and the changes in the Fund during the year, in conformity with generally accepted accounting principles applied on a basis consistent with that of the preceding year. Our examina-

Illustration 18-3 (continued)

tion of these statements was made in accordance with generally accepted auditing standards and accordingly included such tests of the accounting records and such other auditing procedures as we considered necessary in the circumstances, including confirmation by the custodian of investments owned at December 31, 1969.

Price Waterhouse Co.
New York, N.Y.
January 26, 1970

PART B—ACCOUNTING FOR LEASES

Operating Leases

Up to this point in your study only simple operating-type leases have been encountered. Part B of this chapter discusses leases of varying complexity, the basic distinctions that influence accounting for them, and the accounting concepts and procedures essential to recording and reporting their economic essence by both parties—the lessor and the lessee.

A lease is a contract whereby real or personal property is furnished by one party (lessor, or owner) to another party (lessee) for a specified period of time in return for a compensation in one form or another (rent). A lease may vary from a very long period covering the entire useful life of the asset (such as a 50-year lease on a building) to a very few hours or days (such as the rental of an automobile). In discussing appropriate accounting for lease agreements the lessor and lessee must be carefully distinguished.

Leases may be broadly classified as *operating* leases and *financing* leases. The essential characteristics of an operating lease are: (*a*) the owner (lessor) retains the usual risks and rewards of ownership, (*b*) rental revenue is computed to cover, in addition to profit, the usual ownership costs such as depreciation, taxes, insurance, maintenance, and so forth, (*c*) no special property rights or lease-purchase agreements are transferred, (*d*) the lease agreement is readily cancellable, and (*e*) the arrangement is not designed as a major financing method for the lessee. Thus, operating leases comprise what most of us consider to be the ordinary leasing situations. First we will discuss operating leases.

The two broad classifications of leases mentioned in the preceding paragraph (operating leases and financing leases) have influenced the development of accounting concepts and procedures in accounting for lease agreements. In the discussions to follow and in Illustrations 18-4 and 18-5 operating leases will be accounted for under the following accounting methods:[6]

---

[6] John H. Myers, "Reporting Leases in Financial Statements," *Accounting Research Study No. 4* (New York: AICPA, 1962). "Reporting Leases in Financial Statements of Lessee," *Opinion of the Accounting Principles Board No. 5* (New York: AICPA, 1964). "Accounting for Leases in Financial Statements of Lessors," *Opinion of the Accounting Principles Board No. 7* (New York: AICPA, 1966).

Lessor—rental (or operating) method
Lessee—noncapitalization (or expense) method

These methods are consistent in that both sides of the lease agreement as represented by the lessor and the lessee recognize revenue, expense, and amortization on the same conceptual basis. Both methods focus on determination of net income by recognizing revenues and expenses on an accrual basis; they ignore *future* rights, obligations, and commitments (because such rights normally do not exist in an operating lease situation).

An example of the simplest operating lease situation is presented in Illustration 18–4. The situation assumed is that A owns a small office building, part of which he rents to B for an annual rental of $1,200 payable in advance each January 1. It is assumed that the fiscal period of each party ends October 31. This is an operating lease since the lessor retains all the normal risks of ownership and the lessee gains no special property or purchase rights, but only temporary and cancellable occupancy rights.

Illustration 18–4
Simple Operating Lease Situation—Accounting by Lessor and Lessee
(typical entries only)

Lessor A (Rental Method)		Lessee B (Noncapitalization Method)	

January 1, 19A:
To record annual rental payments:

Cash	1,200	Rent Expense	1,200
Rent Income	1,200	Cash	1,200

October 10, 19A:
To record payment of property taxes:

Expense	60	No Entry	
Cash	60		

October 13, 19A:
To report payment of monthly telephone bill:

No Entry		Expense	15
		Cash	15

October 31, 19A:
To record adjusting entry (2 months' rent unexpired):

Rent Income	200	Prepaid Rent Expense	200
Unearned Rent Income	200	Rent Expense	200

An operating lease becomes slightly more complex when, in addition to the annual rental, there is an additional payment made in advance (a downpayment). In this situation the additional payment must be allocated (amortized) over the life of the lease on a realistic basis. Two amortization methods are commonly used, viz:

1. Straight line method—a constant dollar amount of the prepayment is allocated to each period covered by the lease.
2. Present value (or interest) method—a constant rate of allocation

is utilized as determined by application of the annuity concept to the prepayment. This method necessitates utilization of the present value of an annuity (Table 5–4).

This type of situation, including both methods of amortization of the prepayment, is presented in Illustration 18–5. This illustration

Illustration 18–5
Operating Lease with Amortization—Accounting by Lessor and Lessee
(typical entries only)

Lessor A	*Lessee B*
(Rental Method)	*(Noncapitalization Method)*

January 1, 19A:

To record prepayment of rent:

Cash..............................3,000	Leasehold (prepaid rent
Prepaid Rent	expense) 3,000
Income................ 3,000	Cash................................. 3,000

To record annual rental:

| Cash..............................1,200 | Rent Expense...........................1,200 |
| Rent Income ....   1,200 | Cash.................................   1,200 |

December 31, 19A:

To record amortization of advance rental payment (for 12 months):

Case A—Straight line method:

Prepaid Rent	Rent Expense...........................1,000
Income° 1,000	Leasehold........................... 1,000
Rent Income 1,000	
° Computation:	
3,000 × 12/36 = $1,000	

Case B—Present value method (see computations below):

Prepaid Rent Income...... 942.33	Rent Expense...........................1,122.33
Interest Expense............ 180.00	Interest Income 180.00
Rent Income 1,122.33	Leasehold........................... 942.33

December 31, 19A:

Closing entry (Case B):

Rent Income 2,322.33	Income Summary......................2,142.33
Interest Expense...... 180.00	Interest Income 180.00
Income Summary 2,142.33	Rent Expense.................... 2,322.33

Computations:

Schedule of Amortization (see note)

Period	Periodic Rent	Interest (6%)	Amortization of Prepayment	Unamortized Balance
1–1–19A				$3,000.00
12–31–19A.........$1,122.33°	$180.00†	$ 942.33‡	2,057.67§
12–31–19B......... 1,122.33	123.46	998.87	1,058.80
12–31–19C......... 1,122.33	63.53	1,058.80	–0–

° Implied periodic rent = $3,000 ÷ Present value of ordinary annuity (3 rents, 6%)
                     = $3,000 ÷ 2.6730120 (Table 5–4)
                     = $1,122.33

† $3,000 × 6% = $180.00

‡ $1,122.33 − $180.00 = $942.33

§ $3,000.00 − $942.33 = $2,057.67

Note: An ordinary annuity is assumed; that is, that the advance payment represents the present value of three equal year-end amounts of $1,122.33 each. Alternatively, an annuity due could have been assumed; that is, that the three payments would be at the *beginning* of each period. In this case the Table 5–4 value would be $(n − 1) + 1$. An annuity due for advance rentals was illustrated in Chapter 14, page 583; also see page 746.

734 INTERMEDIATE ACCOUNTING [Ch. 18

is identical with the preceding one (18–4) with the additional provision that (a) there is a three-year lease agreement, (b) there is an advance payment of $3,000 (in addition to the $1,200 annual rental), and (c) the fiscal year for both parties ends on December 31. A 6% annual interest rate is assumed.

Clearly, the present value method of amortization is theoretically preferable to the straight line method since it expresses the economic essence of the prepayment of a series of periodic rents and the time value of money. In applying the present value method some accountants prefer, for practical reasons as opposed to conceptual reasons, to offset the rent and inputed interest and thereby report one amount on the income statement ($942.33 in 19A). The straight line method is used solely on the basis of simplicity and materiality.

In summary, we may observe that the lessor, under the rental (or operating) method, did not recognize any transfers of rights or property, or any "purchase" agreements. Alternatively, he did recognize the prepayment as a deferred credit (or liability) and then amortized it to derive a periodic credit to income. The lessee, under the non-capitalization (or expense) method, did not capitalize any property rights or recognize any "purchase" agreements. The prepayment was capitalized as a deferred charge (or intangible fixed asset) and then amortized to derive a periodic charge to expense.

Financing Leases

The discussions to follow will relate to much more complex lease arrangements than to operating leases. Financing leases have become rather common in recent years and they represent a fairly wide range of contractual specifications. They are commonly referred to as financing leases in view of their dominant characteristic as a form of major financing; the lessor primarily is in the business of providing financing and the lessee is using the lease as a major source of financing. Financing leases are generally longer term contracts than are operating leases. Fundamentally, there are two types of financing leases to be considered:

1. Leases that give rise to *special property rights* and related obligations (discussed on pages 735 to 743 inclusive).
2. Leases which are in fact *purchases;* they are generally referred to as lease-purchase contracts (see page 744).

These two types of financing leases, although quite similar, will be separately discussed for both the lessor and the lessee.

The relationship between the accounting methods for leases may be outlined as follows:

Operating Leases

Lessor   Lessee

(1) Rental (operating) method ⟵ $\dfrac{\text{Conceptually}}{\text{comparable}}$ ⟶ (1) Noncapitalization (expense) method

Financing Leases

(2) Financing method ⟵ $\dfrac{\text{Conceptually}}{\text{comparable}}$ ⟶ (2) Capitalization method

The discussions to follow will focus on financing leases and accounting for them by both the lessor and the lessee.

Leases That Give Rise to Special Property Rights and Obligations

Frequently, the primary business activities of the lessor-owner are providing financing by lending money and by leasing assets such as equipment and buildings. Basically, the lessor-owner has money to invest for a return and may choose to invest it in property acquired for rental purposes and thus gain a return on his investments through rents. In these circumstances the lessor-owner may offer lease contracts that give rise to *special* property rights for the lessee. On the other side, by renting under these conditions, the lessee basically is using this approach as one means of major financing of his business. The lessor provides the capital through the assets leased and the lessee makes "installment" payments in the form of rent. These payments include both principal and interest; generally they are fully deductible for tax purposes by the lessee. Thus, in accounting for leases of this type the underlying concept is that the *special* property rights and related liabilities (and receivables) should be measured, accounted for, and reported in the financial statements of the two parties to the transaction. Special property rights may be evidenced by a lease-purchase agreement (discussed later), or by a lease agreement having the following characteristics:

1. Length of lease—the lease covers substantially the full useful life of the property (thus, the residual value at the termination of the lease is relatively small).
2. Cancellation—the lease is noncancellable for all practical purposes.
3. Periodic rent—the periodic rent over the term of the lease is essentially equivalent to the owner's investment in the property (its fair value) plus a "fair" return on that investment.
4. Costs of ownership—maintenance, insurance, renovation, taxes, and other costs of ownership are assumed (paid directly rather than as rent) by the lessee.

5. Risks—the risks and rewards of ownership essentially are transferred to the lessee.
6. In contrast to a lease-purchase, the property leased is returned to the lessor at the termination of the lease.

The underlying accounting concept for *financing leases* as they relate to the lessor-owner and the lessee may be summarized as follows:

Party	Accounting Method	Characteristics
Lessor	Financing Method	Underlying concept—in essence the lessor is providing financing for the lessee by purchasing assets, which are conveyed to the lessee, and the latter assumes the risks of ownership without a formal transfer of title.
		Accounting—recognizes (*a*) a receivable from the lessee for the life of the lease; (*b*) a "sale" of the leased asset; and (*c*) an unearned lease revenue. The receivable and unearned revenue, recognized at inception of the lease, should be amortized over the life of the lease on a present value (interest) basis as the periodic rentals are collected.
Lessee	Capitalization Method	Underlying concept—in essence the lessee is obtaining major financing by contracting for *special* property rights on a noncancellable basis. As a consequence, over the life of the property rented, the rental payments to the lessor constitute a payment of principal plus interest. The ordinary costs of ownership will be paid by the lessee, hence they must be recognized as current expenses as paid (or accrued) by him.
		Accounting—recognizes (*a*) a fixed asset "lease-rights" for the life of the lease; (*b*) a payable "lease obligation" to the lessor extending over the life of the lease; (*c*) rental payments as reductions of the payable to the lessor; (*d*) the interest should be amortized over the life of the lease on a present value (interest) basis; and (*e*) depreciation of the fixed asset over the life of the lease (or if acquired finally, over its useful life).

Accounting by the lessor under the financing method and by the lessee under the capitalization method will now be illustrated separately with a common situation.

Illustration of Financing Method (Lessor). To illustrate accounting for financing leases by the *lessor* assume that the Lessor Company is primarily engaged in leasing out heavy construction equipment. Among the equipment that the company has available for leasing is a newly acquired package of machines that cost $200,000 with an estimated useful life of five years and no residual value. Lessor Company has been negotiating with Lessee Company in respect to the capital needs of the latter. As a result of these negotiations a lease agreement was signed on January 1, 19A, by the two parties with the essential provisions that: (*a*) Lessor Company would provide a package of new machines on a five-year contract; (b) Lessee Company would pay an equal annual rent at the *end* of each year amounting to $47,479.28; (c) the contract is noncancellable; (d) Lessee Company would assume (pay directly in addition to the rent) all of the normal ownership costs such as taxes, maintenance, and insurance; and (e) at the termination of the lease the equipment reverts to the lessor. On January 1, 19A, the effective date of the agreement, the equipment was turned over to Lessee Company. Using these data we will illustrate accounting by the lessor; the next section will consider accounting by the lessee.

Lessor Company established the annual rental amount quoted to Lessee Company (and incorporated in the lease agreement) on the basis that it had an investment with a present value of $200,000 and expected a 6% return on that investment. The resultant computations were:

Annual rent = $200,000   ÷   Present value of an ordinary annuity
                              (5 periods @ 6%) (Table 5–4)
           = $200,000   ÷   4.2123638
           = $ 47,479.28

The following amortization schedule for the life of the lease (investment) was then developed as a basis for the accounting entries for the lessor:

Lessor—Schedule of Lease Amortization and Related Accounting Entries
(financing method)

Date	Annual Rental (a)	Interest on Unrecovered Investment (b)	Investment Recovery (c)	Unrecovered Investment (d)
Jan. 1, 19A				$200,000.00
Dec. 31, 19A	$ 47,479.28	$12,000.00	$ 35,479.28	164,520.72
Dec. 31, 19B	47,479.28	9,871.24	37,608.04	126,912.68
Dec. 31, 19C	47,479.28	7,614.76	39,864.52	87,048.16
Dec. 31, 19D	47,479.28	5,222.89	42,256.39	44,791.77
Dec. 31, 19E	47,479.28	2,687.51	44,791.77	–0–
	$237,396.40	$37,396.40	$200,000.00	–0–

(a) computed directly per above.
(b) preceding balance in columns (d) times 6%.
(c) column (a) minus column (b).
(d) preceding balance minus column (c).

Based on the amortization schedule, the lessor would make the following accounting entries under the financing method:

Jan. 1, 19A:

To record the inception of the lease by recognizing the receivables, the "constructive" sale of the asset, and the unearned lease revenue:

Receivables under Contracts for Equipment
Rentals ....$237,396.40°
    Equipment.. 200,000.00
    Unearned Lease Revenue............................ 37,396.40°

° Obviously, these two amounts could be recorded "net" in the receivables account, thus the balance in the receivables account would accord with column (d) in the above tabulation from period to period.

Dec. 31, 19A:

To record first rental collection and to recognize the revenue earned (per above schedule):

Cash...... .... 47,479.28
    Receivables under Contracts for Equipment
    Rentals.., ... 47,479.28

Unearned Lease Revenue.................................. 12,000.00
    Lease Revenue Earned................................ 12,000.00

Dec. 31, 19B:

To record second rental and to recognize revenue earned:

Cash.. 47,479.28
    Receivables under Contracts for Equipment
    Rentals 47,479.28

Unearned Lease Revenue.................................. 9,871.24
    Lease Revenue Earned................................ 9,871.24

Entries for the remaining periods of the lease would follow the pattern established above. Obviously, after the December 31, 19E, entries, each account established in the initial entry on January 1, 19A, would have a zero balance and the cash account of the lessor would have been increased by the investment ($200,000) plus the interest earned ($37,396.40) and the lessor would reclaim the worn-out equipment which has little value. Alternatively, should the lessor sell the worn-out equipment, say as scrap, at an amount in excess of the cost of disposal, a "gain on sale of scrap" would be recorded. You should note that the lessor recorded no depreciation on the machinery; the recovery of his principal was included in the rental payments which served to reduce the receivable from the lessor.

In respect to reporting and disclosure on the periodic financial statements, during the life of the lease the lease revenue earned would be reported as an operating income by the Lessor Company. On the balance sheet the debit balance in the receivables account would be reduced by the credit balance in the Unearned Lease Revenue account. The current portion would be reported as a current asset and the remainder under the "other" asset caption. To illustrate, the Lessor Company would report at December 31, 19B, as follows (refer to the above amortization schedule for source of amounts):

Income Statement:
    Lease revenue ....$ 9,871.24
Balance Sheet:
    Current Assets:
        Receivables under contracts for equipment rentals........... 47,479.28
        Less: Unearned lease revenue 7,614.76 $39,864.52
    Other Assets:
        Receivables under contracts for equipment rentals........... 94,958.56
        Less: Unearned lease revenue 7,910.40   87,048.16

Appropriate footnote.

In respect to disclosure by the lessor *APB Opinion 7* states:

In addition to an appropriate description in the balance sheet of the investment in property held for or under lease, the principal accounting methods used in accounting for leasing activities should be disclosed. Further, where leasing is a substantial portion of a nonfinancing institution's operations, the Board believes that financial statements should disclose sufficient information to enable readers to assess the significance of leasing activities to the company. Leases and leased property are also subject to the conventional disclosure requirements affecting financial statements as, for example, disclosure of pledges of leased property and leases as security for loans.

Illustration of Capitalization Method (Lessee). For this purpose we will utilize the preceding example with no changes thus enabling you to compare the two methods. You should observe that they are internally consistent conceptually. Upon signing the five-year lease, which called for five equal rentals of $47,479.28, payment annually at *year-end*, Lessee Company should debit an asset account for the *present value* of the special property rights accruing under the lease agreement and credit a liability to Lessor Company for the total amount of the obligation – the difference is an interest discount factor. To determine the capitalizable value of the special rights the Lessor Company would make the following computation:

Present value of the special
property rights   = $ 47,479.28 × Present value of an
                                           ordinary annuity (5
                                           periods @ 6%)
                                           (Table 5–4)
                                   = $ 47,479.28 × 4.2123638
                                   = $200,000

The Lessee Company would then develop the following schedule of amortization and related entries for the period covered by the lease:

Lessee — Schedule of Lease Amortization and Related Accounting Entries
(capitalization method)

Date	Annual Rental (a)	Interest on Unpaid Liability (b)	Payment on Principal (c)	Unpaid Principal (d)
Jan. 1, 19A......				$200,000.00
Dec. 31, 19A......$	47,479.28	$12,000.00	$ 35,479.28	164,520.72
Dec. 31, 19B......	47,479.28	9,871.24	37,608.04	126,912.68
Dec. 31, 19C......	47,479.28	7,614.76	39,864.52	87,048.16
Dec. 31, 19D......	47,479.28	5,222.89	42,256.39	44,791.77
Dec. 31, 19E......	47,479.28	2,687.51	44,791.77	–0–
	$237,396.40	$37,396.40	$200,000.00	–0–

(a) computed directly per above.
(b) preceding balance in column (d) times 6%.
(c) column (a) minus column (b).
(d) preceding balance minus column (c).

Based on the amortization schedule, the lessee would make the following accounting entries under the capitalization method:

Jan. 1, 19A:

To record the inception of the lease by capitalizing the present value of the special property rights; to recognize the liability and the interest:

Asset — Leasehold Rights (equipment)....................200,000.00
Discount on Lease Obligations .... 37,396.40°
  Liability — Obligations under Lease
  Agreements ....   237,396.40°

° Obviously these two amounts could be recorded "net" in the liability account, thus the balance therein from period to period would accord with column (d) of the above tabulation.

Dec. 31, 19A:

To record payment of the first rental (per above schedule):

Liability — Obligation under Lease Agreements......... 47,479.28
  Cash 47,479.28

To record interest expense (per above schedule):

Interest Expense (or lease expense)....................... 12,000.00
  Discount on Lease Obligations 12,000.00

To record amortization of asset — leasehold rights (straight line):

Expense — Amortization of Property Rights
  (equipment)... 40,000.00
  Asset — Leasehold Rights (equipment)..............   40,000.00

Note: Frequently the interest expense and amortization expense is reported on the income statement as one expense item; also these three entries generally are combined.

Oct. 15, 19B:

To pay a cost of ownership such as repairs:

Repair Expense 600.00
    Cash 600.00

Dec. 31, 19B:

To record payment of the second rental:

Liability—Obligation under Lease Agreements 47,479.28
    Cash 47,479.28

To record interest expense (per above schedule);

Interest Expense 9,871.24
    Discount on Lease Obligations 9,871.24

To record amortization of asset—leasehold rights (straight line):

Expense—Amortization of Property Rights
    (equipment) 40,000.00
    Asset—Leasehold Rights (equipment)................   40,000.00

Observe in the above tabulation that two distinctly separate series of entries are involved, viz:

1. Recording the annual (equal) payments on the liability; each rental constitutes in part a payment on the principal and in part a payment of interest for the period. Since the principal is reduced each period by a progressively greater amount, the interest is less each period. This reflects the economic essence of installment payments on debt.[7]

2. Recording periodic amortization (or depreciation) of the asset, leasehold rights. The lessee should depreciate the asset following conventional approaches: straight line, decreasing charge, etc. Alternatively, a strong conceptual argument can be made for amortizing leasehold rights on a present value basis in view of the "financing" characteristics of the leasing arrangement. In this instance the periodic amortization would accord with column (c) in the above schedule; this approach would be comparable to depreciation by the sinking fund method discussed in a prior chapter. Obviously, the lessee has no residual value to consider.

Entries for the remaining periods would follow the pattern established above. Obviously, after the December 31, 19E entries, the balances in the asset, liability, and discount accounts, established at the inception of the lease, would be zero. The worn-out equipment would be returned to the lessor and no further entries would be needed. Note that the lessee, by virtue of the lease agreement, re-

---

[7]Although conceptually unsound in every respect a few have argued for "straight line" recognition of the interest expense.

ceived $200,000 financing which he repaid over a five-year period plus 6% interest (total interest expense, $37,396.40).

In respect to reporting and disclosure on the periodic financial statements, during the life of the lease, the expense (amortization and interest) would be reflected as an operating item by the Lessee Company. On the balance sheet the asset "leasehold rights" would be reported as an intangible fixed asset and the payable, less the unamortized discount, under liabilities appropriately classified as to current and noncurrent. To illustrate, the balance sheet for Lessor Company on December 31, 19B, should reflect the following (refer to above amortization schedule for source of amounts):

```
Intangible Fixed Assets:
  Leasehold rights capitalized..........................................$120,000.00
Current Liabilities:
  Obligations under lease agreements..............................   47,479.28
    Less: Unamortized discount° ....................................    7,614.76   $39,864.52
Long-Term Liabilities:
  Obligations under lease agreements..............................   94,958.56
    Less: Unamortized discount° ....................................    7,910.40    87,048.16
```

°A less desirable alternative would be to report this as a deferred charge.

In respect to disclosure by the lessee *APB Opinion 5* states: "The property and the obligation should be stated in the balance sheet at an appropriate discounted amount of future payments under the lease agreement. A note or schedule may be required to disclose significant provisions of the transaction."

Salvage Value of Leased Assets – Financing Leases

In respect to accounting for financing leases, salvage values of leased property must be recognized in the computations and entries by the lessor (financing method). To illustrate, we will continue the example of the Lessor and Lessee companies with the following changes:

1. The property cost Lessor Company $210,000.
2. The estimated residual value at the end of five years is $10,000.

In order to attain the 6% desired return on the *total* investment the annual rent would have to be increased by the required amount of interest on the residual value ($10,000 × 6% = $600 per year). Thus, additional interest amounting to $3,000 over the life of the lease must be incorporated in the accounting procedures. Note that the lessor gets back the asset at the end of the fifth year which then has a value of $10,000. Several approaches for incorporating the residual value have been developed: a straightforward, and yet conceptually sound, approach is illustrated.

Jan. 1, 19A:

At inception of the lease the following entry would be made by the Lessor Company:

Receivables under Contracts for Equipment Rentals
($237,396.40 + $3,000.00)...240,396.40
    Equipment ($210,000 − $10,000) 200,000.00
    Unearned Lease Revenue
      ($37,396.40 + $3,000.00) 40,396.40

Refer to the amortization schedule on page 737 for the source of the amounts; to them are added the interest on the residual value. The effect of this entry is to leave the residual value in the asset account and to record a receivable that incorporates the principal ($200,000) plus interest on that principal and interest on the residual value. This compensates the lessor, in interest, for the total outlay of $210,000. The residual value is reported as an asset on the balance sheet of the lessor at a constant amount over the life of the rental agreement. It would be included on the balance sheet along with other equipment held for rental purposes.

Dec. 31, 19A:

To record receipt of first rental and to amortize:

Cash ($47,479.28 + $600.00) 48,079.28
    Receivables under Contracts for Equipment
      Rentals..   48,079.28

Unearned Lease Revenue ($12,000 + $600.00)................12,600.00
    Lease Revenue Earned...   12,600.00

This approach is sound theoretically since the residual value is viewed in the same manner as a cash loan to the lessee which is payable, as to principal, at the termination of the lease. Each year the lessor collects interest on the salvage value (as a part of the periodic rental) at the established rate of interest. Thus, the lessor has the inflow of cash (interest) for reinvestment each period. His principal (the salvage value) comes back, not periodically, but as a lump sum at the termination date (as would be the case in a loan repayment). Clearly the economic essence of the salvage value aspect of the lease agreement is captured by this treatment, thus there is no reason to "present value" the salvage value.[8] In respect to the lessee, he would

---

[8] Another alternative would not increase the receivable and the Unearned Lease Revenue by the amount of interest on the residual value ($3,000 in this instance); each rental collection would reflect the periodic interest income on the residual value ($600 in this instance) as a direct credit to income.

Still another alternative would involve computation of the present value of the residual value along with the specified rental payments. In this approach the residual value would appear in the accounts of the lessor at its present value at date of initiation of the lease ($7,472.58 in this instance). In each subsequent period this value would be increased on a present value basis through the amortization entry so that at the termination of the lease the lessor's accounts would reflect the original residual value ($10,000 in this instance). Obviously, this approach would be conceptually sound but more complex in application than the one illustrated above.

capitalize the "special rights" on the basis of the total periodic rental payments. Thus, the lessee would not recognize the salvage value in a direct manner.

Lease-Purchase Contracts

Property contracts sometimes are drawn in such a way that, what is called a lease, in substance is a purchase-sale agreement. *APB Opinion 5* states the criteria for a purchase (lease-purchase) essentially as follows:

The presence, in a noncancellable lease or in a lease cancellable only upon the occurrence of some remote contingency, of one or more of the following *usually* will establish that a lease should be considered in substance a sale (by the lessor) and a purchase (by the lessee):

1. The initial term is materially less than the useful life of the property, and the lessee has the option to renew the lease for the remaining useful life of the property at substantially less than the fair rental value; or
2. The lessee has the right, during or at the expiration of the lease, to acquire the property at a price which at the inception of the lease appears to be substantially less than the probable fair value of the property at the time or times of permitted acquisition by the lessee.
3. The property was acquired by the lessor to meet the special needs of the lessee and will probably be usable only for that purpose and only by the lessee.
4. The term of the lease corresponds substantially to the estimated useful life of the property, and the lessee is obligated to pay costs such as taxes, insurance, and maintenance, which are usually considered incidental to ownership.
5. The lessee has guaranteed the obligations of the lessor with respect to the property leased.
6. The lessee has treated the lease as a purchase for tax purposes.

The distinction between a lease transferring "special property rights" only and a "lease-purchase" is simply one of degree; both are financing types of leases and both should be accounted for in the same manner except for minor changes in account titles. The special property rights type of lease, in its pure form, does not result in a consummated purchase-sale; the property reverts to the lessor at the termination of the lease. Alternatively, in a lease-purchase situation the presumption is that the leased property will accrue to the lessee either during or at the termination of the lease agreement. Many accountants do not make a distinction between the two situations particularly since most financing lease agreements, by their specific terms, are somewhere between these two situations.

Accounting for a lease-purchase situation should follow the financing method (by the lessor) and the capitalization method (by the lessee) as illustrated above. Fundamentally, the lessor should record a sale of the property leased, and the lessee should record a purchase of a fixed asset. Periodic rents represent installment payments on the obligation. Typically, some of the account titles will be revised, and the lessee will account for depreciation in the usual manner since he will record and report the specific asset rather than special property rights.

To illustrate, assume Company X leased a new machine, that cost $20,000, to Company Y with the following basic terms:

1. Five annual rentals of $4,479.18 each payment at the *beginning* of each year, starting January 1, 19A.
2. At any time after January 1, 19A, Company Y can purchase the machine for $22,395.90, total consideration, provided that all rents paid to date will be applied as reduction in the remaining cash to be paid.
3. A noninterest-bearing note with a face amount of $22,395.90 was attached to the lease agreement.

Assume further that the machine has a five-year life and no residual value and that Company X expects a 6% return on its investment.

Since the rents are due at the *beginning* of each year the present value of an annuity due must be utilized in the computations. Typical computations and entries for both the lessor (vendor) and the lessee (buyer) are presented below.

Computations of the annual rent by the vendor (Company X):

$$
\begin{aligned}
\text{Periodic rent} &= \$20,000 \div \text{Present value of annuity due (5 rents @ 6\%)} \\
&= \$20,000 \div (n-1 \text{ rents}) + 1 \text{ (from Table 5--4)} \\
&= \$20,000 \div 3.4651056 + 1 \ (= 4.4651056) \\
&= \underline{\$\ 4,479.18}
\end{aligned}
$$

Alternatively, the lessee (Company Y) knowing only the periodic rent (and assuming a 6% rate) would compute as follows:

$$
\begin{aligned}
\text{Present value of machine} &= \$\ 4,479.18 \times 4.4651056 \\
&= \underline{\$20,000}
\end{aligned}
$$

An amortization schedule, appropriate for both the lessor and lessee, can now be developed on an *annuity due* basis as follows:

Lease-Purchase—Amortization Schedule (annuity due basis)

Date	Rental Amount	Interest (6%) on Balance	Reduction in Unamortized Balance	Unamortized Balance
Jan. 1, 19A start............				$20,000.00
Jan. 1, 19A payment ......$ 4,479.18			$ 4,479.18	15,520.82
Dec. 31, 19A accrual........		($15,520.82 × 6%) = $ 931.25	(931.25)	16,452.07
Jan. 1, 19B payment	4,479.18		4,479.18	11,972.89
Dec. 31, 19B accrual........		($11,972.89 × 6%) = 718.37	(718.37)	12,691.26
Jan. 1, 19C payment	4,479.18		4,479.18	8,212.08
Dec. 31, 19C accrual........		($ 8,212.08 × 6%) = 492.72	(492.72)	8,704.80
Jan. 1, 19D payment	4,479.18		4,479.18	4,225.62
Dec. 31, 19D accrual........		($ 4,225.62 × 6%) = 253.56	(253.56)	4,479.18
Jan. 1, 19E payment	4,479.18		4,479.18	–0–
	$22,395.90	$2,395.90	$20,000.00	

Entries for the first two years of the life of the lease for the lessor and lessee would be (account titles abbreviated):

Lessor—Company X	Lessee—Company Y
(Financing Method)	(Capitalization Method)

January 1, 19A:
To record lease-purchase:

Notes Receivable-Leases ....22,395.90°		Machinery (lease-purchase) 20,000.00	
Machinery	20,000.00	Deferred Interest Expense......................... 2,395.90°	
Unearned Revenue (or deferred interest income).........	2,395.90°	Liability (lease-purchase)	22,395.90°

January 1, 19A:
To record first rental payment:

| Cash...................... 4,479.18 | | Liability (lease-purchase) .... 4,479.18 | |
| Notes Receivable-Leases ... | 4,479.18 | Cash .... | 4,479.18 |

December 31, 19A:
To record interest earned:

| Unearned Revenue.............. 931.25 | | Interest Expense................ 931.25 | |
| Earned Revenue (or interest income)......... | 931.25 | Deferred Interest Expense................... | 931.25 |

° Alternatively these could be recorded "net" in which case the account balance would accord with the last column in the above amortization schedule.

This pattern of entries would continue throughout the life of the lease by both parties. The lessee would record annual depreciation in the normal manner as well as other ownership costs since he owns (as assumed by the concept) the machine.[9] Reporting and disclosure

[9] In respect to special property rights we stated that a sound conceptual argument could be made for present value amortization of the leasehold amount by the lessee (p. 741). It would appear that this position has less validity in respect to lease-purchase situations.

requirements would follow those discussed for financing leases generally. Preferably deferred interest should be deducted from the related obligation.

Sale and Leaseback

Not infrequently there are agreements whereby one party, desiring not to have large amounts of resources tied up in long-lived assets (such as buildings), will sell such an asset to another party. Coupled with the contract will be a long-term agreement to lease back the asset for an annual rent (either fixed in amount each period or related to a factor such as sales volume). Thus, the original owner converts a fixed asset to immediate cash and substitutes in its place a long-term obligation to make periodic rental payments for its continued use. The substitution of one periodic amount to be paid for all of the individual costs of ownership such as insurance, taxes, casualty losses, obsolescence, and depreciation has certain other advantages such as full and immediate deductibility of the rental payment for income tax purposes. On the other side, the lessor (buyer) has made a long-term investment which is further enhanced by a long-term lease agreement. Clearly, the sale and leaseback aspects are interrelated. *APB Opinion 5* states:

The principal details of any material sale-and-leaseback arrangement should be disclosed in the year in which the transaction originates. The Board is of the opinion that the sale and leaseback usually cannot be accounted for as independent transactions. Neither the sale price nor the annual rental can be objectively evaluated independently of the other. Consequently, material gains or losses resulting from the sale of properties which are the subject of sale-and-leaseback transactions, together with the related tax effect, should be amortized over the life of the lease as an adjustment of the rental cost (or, if the leased property is capitalized, as an adjustment of depreciation).

APB Opinions on Leases

The APB has issued two Opinions on leases—*Opinion 5* relates to the lessee and *Opinion 7* to the lessor. These Opinions outline accounting approaches and disclosure provisions for the several types of leases discussed in this chapter. *Opinion 7* is in agreement with the preceding discussions; that is, the *lessor* must, under the Opinion, utilize the:

a) Rental (operating) method for all leases that have characteristics that would identify them as *operating leases* (as defined in this chapter);

b) Financing method for all leases that have characteristics that would identify them as *financing leases* (as defined in this chapter).

In contrast, a *lessee* following the provisions of *Opinion 5* would not be consistent with the preceding discussions (nor with *Opinion 7*). *Opinion 5* specifies that the *lessee* must utilize the:

a) Noncapitalization (expense) method for all operating leases *and also for all financing leases except those that are of the lease-purchase type;*

b) Capitalization method only for lease-purchase contracts or agreements that have similar provisions.

Many accountants feel that both parties to the same lease should utilize conceptually consistent accounting methods. They feel that the conceptual error is in *Opinion 5* (as regards the lessee); that is, they believe that the lessee should utilize the noncapitalization (expense) method for operating leases only and that the capitalization method should be used for both types of financing leases (i.e., property rights and lease-purchase agreements.)[10]

At this writing the APB is developing an Opinion that is expected to remove the inconsistency and also provide some sharper distinctions in application of the concepts.

The 1969 financial statement for Kellwood Company as shown in Illustration 18–6 represents one presentation of capitalized leases. You should note the appropriate footnotes as well as the basic statements.

Illustration 18–6
KELLWOOD COMPANY AND SUBSIDIARIES
Consolidated Balance Sheet

ASSETS

October 31,

	1969	1968
Current Assets:		
Cash	$ 7,650,886	$ 6,197,994
Receivables:		
Sears, Roebuck and Co.	22,088,940	16,653,589
Other	11,389,685	6,344,344
	$ 33,478,625	$ 22,997,933
Inventories—at lower of cost (first-in, first-out method) or market:		
Finished goods	$ 54,527,573	$ 45,158,593
Work in process	10,585,840	10,053,428
Raw materials	30,283,980	25,571,494
	$ 95,397,393	$ 80,783,515
Prepaid expenses	606,832	472,076
Total Current Assets	$137,133,736	$110,451,518
Property, Plant, and Equipment, at cost (Notes C and D):		
Land	$ 406,381	$ 98,939
Buildings	2,396,268	1,366,926
Leasehold improvements	3,751,458	2,792,880
Machinery and equipment	31,751,714	25,098,159
	$ 38,305,821	$ 29,356,904
Less accumulated depreciation and amortization	18,804,046	15,328,397
	$ 19,501,775	$ 14,028,507

[10] *APB Opinion 7* recognized this point as follows: "The Board takes notice of a question that has been raised as to whether certain conclusions herein are inconsistent with conclusions in *Opinion No. 5*, 'Reporting of Leases in Financial Statements of Lessee'—specifically, the question is whether leases accounted for on the financing method by lessors should be capitalized by lessees."

Illustration 18–6 (continued)

	1969	1968
Carried forward from page 748	$ 19,501,775	$ 14,028,507
Capitalized facility leases, less accumulated amortization of $854,638 – 1969 and $446,899 – 1968	10,078,360	6,718,017
	$ 29,580,135	$ 20,746,524
Other Assets (Note B)	3,792,932	2,206,680
	$170,506,803	$133,404,722

LIABILITIES AND SHAREOWNERS' EQUITY

Current Liabilities:

	1969	1968
Short-term notes payable	$ 74,819,750	$ 43,823,303
Accounts payable:		
Sears, Roebuck and Co.	14,941,922	10,227,280
Other	13,025,318	12,814,875
	$ 27,967,240	$ 23,042,155
Accrued employees' compensation and other expenses	9,319,527	8,391,147
Federal and state income taxes	647,732	2,811,755
Dividends payable	566,678	559,747
Current portion of long-term debt	486,250	926,906
Current portion of capitalized lease obligations	925,679	532,433
Total Current Liabilities	$114,732,856	$ 80,087,446

Deferred Items:

	1969	1968
Federal income taxes	$ 1,493,106	$ 798,890
Investment tax credit	884,816	674,761
Incentive stock credits (Note E)	165,875	–
	$ 2,543,797	$ 1,473,651

Long-Term Debt, less portion due within one year (Note D):

	1969	1968
Term loan from banks	–	$ 5,600,000
Capitalized lease obligations	$ 14,025,015	10,061,721
Other	918,158	212,914
	$ 14,943,173	$ 15,874,635

Shareowners' Equity (Note E):

	1969	1968
Preferred stock – without par value; authorized 200,000 shares	–	–
Common stock – without par value; authorized 6,000,000 shares; issued and outstanding shares, 1969 – 3,135,337, 1968 – 3,084,356 stated at	$ 4,866,826	$ 4,213,281
Retained earnings	33,420,151	31,755,709
	$ 38,286,977	$ 35,968,990
	$170,506,803	$133,404,722

Statement of Consolidated Earnings

EARNINGS

Net Sales:

	1969	1968
Sears, Roebuck and Co.	$198,909,994	$179,657,756
Other	44,308,500	40,485,669
	$243,218,494	$220,143,425

Costs and Expenses:

	1969	1968
Cost of products sold	$212,680,429	$190,918,121
Selling, general, and administrative expenses	14,232,623	12,458,851
Interest expense	6,073,167	3,679,051
Operating loss – Aladdin (Note A)	664,557	–
	$233,650,776	$207,056,023

Illustration 18–6 (continued)

	1969	1968
Earnings before Income Taxes and Extraordinary Charge	$ 9,567,718	$ 13,087,402
Federal and State Income Taxes	4,923,869	6,737,224
Earnings before Extraordinary Charge	$ 4,643,849	$ 6,350,178
Extraordinary Charge—Aladdin, net of applicable income taxes (Note A)	720,000	—
Net Earnings	$ 3,923,849	$ 6,350,178
Weighted Average Shares Outstanding	$ 3,110,612	$ 3,060,520
Per Average Share Outstanding:		
Earnings before extraordinary charge	$1.49	$2.07
Extraordinary charge—Aladdin	.23	—
Net Earnings	$1.26	$2.07

SHAREOWNERS' EQUITY

Year Ended October 31, 1969

	Common Stock		Retained Earnings
	Number of Shares	Amount	
Balance, November 1, 1968 (common stock balances exclusive of $202,293 cost of 52,728 shares in treasury)	1,542,178	$4,213,281	$31,755,709
Adjustment for two-for-one stock split on February 25, 1969 (Note E)	1,542,178		
Stock options exercised	50,981	653,545	
Net earnings			3,923,849
Cash dividends declared of $.72 per share			(2,259,407)
Balance, October 31, 1969	3,135,337	$4,866,826	$33,420,151

Statement of Consolidated Source and Application of Funds

Year Ended October 31,

	1969	1968
Beginning Working Capital	$30,364,072	$28,804,813
Funds Provided:		
Earnings	$ 3,923,849	$ 6,350,178
Depreciation and amortization expense..	3,878,080	2,789,683
Book value of fixed assets sold	324,054	169,491
Stock options exercised	653,545	492,580
Increase in deferred items	1,070,146	1,069,997
Increase in other long-term debt	705,244	(5,633)
Increase in lease obligations	3,963,294	4,625,750
Total Funds Provided	$14,518,212	$15,492,046
Funds Used:		
Payment of term loan	$ 5,600,000	$ 800,000
Purchases of fixed assets	9,267,663	7,330,104
Dividends declared	2,259,407	1,886,403
Increase in facility leases	3,768,082	2,828,443
Increase in other assets	1,586,252	1,087,837
Total Funds Used	$22,481,404	$13,932,787
Net Increase (decrease)	(7,963,192)	1,559,259
Ending Working Capital	$22,400,880	$30,364,072

Illustration 18–6 (continued)

Notes to Consolidated Financial Statements
Year Ended October 31, 1969

A. *Principles of Consolidation*

The financial statements include the accounts of the company and each of its subsidiaries.

During the year the company purchased, for cash, all of the outstanding stock of Allsheer Hosiery Mills, Inc., and its subsidiary. This transaction has been accounted for as a purchase and results of operations are included in the statement of consolidated earnings from August 15, 1969, the date of purchase.

On March 1, 1969, the company purchased, for cash and notes, all of the outstanding stock of Aladdin Knit Mills, Inc., and its subsidiary companies. The loss from operations of Aladdin from date of purchase to October 31, 1969, has been separately reflected in the statement of consolidated earnings. Management has made the decision to dispose of the Aladdin operation either in whole or in part. A number of alternatives are under consideration. There has been additionally provided an extraordinary charge in an amount estimated to be sufficient to meet the anticipated loss on eventual disposition of this operation.

B. *Other Assets*

Other assets include $3,042,295 of start-up costs at new or expanded facilities and deferred engineering costs which are recoverable in future years under merchandise contracts with the company's major customer. Although a portion of these costs will be recovered in the next fiscal year, the amount is indeterminable at this time and the entire balance has been considered noncurrent.

C. *Depreciation and Amortization Policy*

Depreciation and amortization is computed principally on the double declining-balance method for buildings and machinery and equipment; and on the straight line method for leasehold improvements, using asset lives as follows:

Asset	*Years*
Buildings	45
Machinery and equipment	3–14
Leasehold improvements	Life of lease or asset, whichever is shorter
Capitalized facility leases	Life of asset

D. *Long-Term Debt*

Capitalized machinery and equipment leases aggregating $3,322,704 are payable, including interest factors ranging from 5% to 9%, in amounts of approximately $680,000 through 1972, $647,000 – 1973, $617,000 – 1974 with declining payments thereafter to 1979. Machinery and equipment having a depreciated cost of approximately $3,200,000 at October 31, 1969, is subject to the related obligations.

Capitalized facility leases aggregating $10,702,311 relate principally to land, buildings, and improvements leased from various governmental agencies. The initial term of such leases is generally 20 years with annual rental payments, including interest factors ranging from 4% to 6¾%, approximately $994,000 through 1974, $985,000 through 1979, $880,000 through 1985 with declining payments thereafter to 1993.

Other debt consists of 6% – 11% unsecured notes in the amount of $501,959 due ratably to 1973 and $416,199 of 4% – 7¾% mortgage notes with various maturities to 1980. Property with a net book value of $497,928 is subject to the lien of the mortgages.

E. *Shareowners' Equity*

On February 25, 1969, the shareowners approved an amendment to the company's Certificate of Incorporation to increase the authorized number of common shares of stock of the company from 2,500,000 to 6,000,000 shares without par value, and at

Illustration 18–6 (continued)

the same time approved a two-for-one split of the company's outstanding common stock. All the share data have been adjusted to give effect to the stock split.

The company's stock option plans provide that options for a maximum of 350,000 shares may be granted to key employees of the company at an option price of 100% of the fair market value on the date of grant. Each option granted prior to January 1, 1964, expires 10 years from the date of grant, and each option granted subsequent to December 31, 1963, expires 5 years from the date of grant. The options are exercisable cumulatively in installments over the aforementioned periods at prices ranging from $10.25 to $41.75 per share.

Changes during the 1969 fiscal year under the plans were as follows:

	Shares		
	Reserved	Granted	Available
Balance, November 1, 1968............................ 279,842		174,172	105,670
Granted...		36,400	(36,400)
Exercised at an aggregate price of $653,530.......(50,981)		(50,981)	
Canceled..		(9,050)	9,050
Balance, October 31, 1969 228,861		150,541	78,320
Exercisable at October 31, 1969		75,791	

The company's Restricted Stock Compensation Plan of 1969, approved by shareowners on February 25, 1969, provides for the issuance of a maximum of 100,000 shares to key employees of the company.

Shares granted to qualified employees under the "high performance bonus" portion of the plan are limited to an aggregate of 20,000 shares for any plan year, are granted on January 1 following the plan year, may not be transferred, sold, pledged, or otherwise disposed of prior to the lapse of restrictions, and are released from restrictions ratably over five years.

Qualified employees under the "deferred compensation" portion of the plan may elect prior to the beginning of a plan year to have a part or all of any bonus awarded to him for the plan year paid in restricted stock in an amount up to 30% of his annual compensation. Such shares may not be transferred, sold, pledged, or otherwise disposed of prior to the lapse of restrictions, unless first offered to the company in accordance with the plan, and are released from restrictions ratably over a 5- or 10-year elected period from the date of death, retirement, or age 65 if no longer an employee.

No shares were granted in respect of the "deferred compensation" portion of the plan for the current year. On January 1, 1970, grants totaling 6,635 shares were made under the "high performance bonus" portion of the plan and $165,875 has been charged to earnings for the year ended October 31, 1969, with respect thereto.

F. Pension Plan

The company and its subsidiaries have two pension plans covering substantially all of their employees. The total pension expense for the year was approximately $1,289,000 ($1,130,000 – 1968) which includes the normal cost of the plans and interest on unfunded past service cost and, for one of the plans, amortization of prior service cost over a period of 30 years. The company's policy is to fund pension cost accrued. As of November 1, 1968, the latest date for which actuarial computations are available, the assets of the plans plus balance sheet accruals exceeded the actuarially computed value of vested benefits.

G. Long-Term Leases

Rental expense under noncapitalized leases during the year ended October 31, 1969, amounted to $1,105,000 ($1,111,000 – 1968). In addition, with respect to most

Illustration 18–6 (*continued*)

of these leases, the company and its subsidiaries pay taxes, insurance, and maintenance costs. Most of the leases are for terms ranging from 5 to 20 years and generally include options to renew for additional periods. Minimum fixed annual rentals for the next five years required under leases in effect as of October 31, 1969, ratably decline from $1,068,000 in 1970 to $761,000 in 1974.

Accountants' Report

January 7, 1970

Board of Directors and Shareowners,
Kellwood Company,
St. Louis, Missouri.

We have examined the accompanying consolidated balance sheet of Kellwood Company and subsidiaries as of October 31, 1969, the related statements of consolidated earnings and shareowners' equity, and the statement of consolidated source and application of funds for the year then ended. Our examination was made in accordance with generally accepted auditing standards, and accordingly included such tests of the accounting records and such other auditing procedures as we considered necessary in the circumstances; however, it was not practicable to confirm the accounts receivable from Sears, Roebuck and Co., as to which we have satisfied ourselves by means of other auditing procedures.

In our opinion, the financial statements referred to above present fairly the consolidated financial position of Kellwood Company and subsidiaries at October 31, 1969, and the consolidated results of their operations, and the sources and applications of funds, for the year then ended, in conformity with generally accepted accounting principles applied on a basis consistent with that of the preceding year.

Touche Ross & Co.
St. Louis, Missouri

QUESTIONS FOR CLASS DISCUSSION

1. In connection with pension plans, explain the meaning of (*a*) normal service cost and (*b*) past service cost.

2. Over what period are past service costs usually amortized? Why?

3. Under *APB Opinion 8* guidelines for pension plan accounting, what *minimum* and *maximum* annual provisions should be made?

4. In respect to pension plans, what are actuarial gains and losses?

5. Under *APB Opinion 8* guidelines for pension plan accounting, what disclosures should be made in financial statements or their related notes?

6. If accounting charges for past service costs exceed funding payments, what kind of account arises and how should it be reported in financial statements? Suppose the reverse is true, i.e., payments exceed charges, what then?

7. When an established company adopts a pension plan, the costs related to past services of employees should be charged to which of these?
   a) Operations of current and future periods.
   b) Operations of prior periods.
   c) Operations of the current period.
   d) Retained earnings.

(AICPA adapted)

8. Distinguish between operating leases and financing leases.

9. What are the generally accepted methods of accounting for (a) operating leases and (b) financing leases?

10. Outline appropriate accounting procedures for operating leases (a) by lessor and (b) by lessee.

11. Outline appropriate accounting procedures for financing leases (a) by lessor and (b) by lessee.

12. Sometimes a part of the total rent is paid in advance (as a downpayment covering several future periods); outline the accounting procedures in respect to the advance payment.

13. Why are present value concepts fundamental in accounting for financing leases?

14. Distinguish between (a) leases that give rise to "special property rights" and (b) those that are lease-purchase agreements.

15. Complete the following to indicate what would appear on the financial statement:

Type of Lease and Accounting Method	Financial Statement Items	
	Income Statement	Balance Sheet
Operating Lease:		
Lessor—rental method		
Lessee—noncapitaliza-tion method		
Financing Lease:		
Lessor—financing method		
Lessee—capitalization method		

DECISION CASE 18–1

XYZ Corporation has decided to establish a pension plan for its employees. Excerpts from the proposed scale of benefits appear below:

Average Annual Salary	Annual Pension Based on Years of Service			
	10 Years	20 Years	30 Years	40 Years
$ 5,000	$ 700	$ 1,400	$ 2,100	$ 2,800
10,000	1,800	3,500	5,300	7,000
20,000	3,800	7,700	11,500	15,300
30,000	5,900	11,800	17,700	23,600

Suppose at the time of adoption the eligible employees are as follows:

Salary	Number	Years of Service											
		1	2	3	4	5	6	7	8	9	10	11	12
$ 5,000	7	3	0	1	1	0	0	2	0	0	0	0	0
10,000	8	1	1	2	0	2	0	0	1	1	0	0	0
20,000	4	0	0	0	0	0	1	0	0	1	1	0	1
30,000	1	0	0	0	0	0	0	0	0	0	0	0	1

Required:

1. What additional *facts* would be required as a starting point to calculation of the liability for past service costs?

2. What *assumptions* would have to be made before calculation of the liability for past service costs could be undertaken?

3. As to the present work force only, what factors might cause *current cost* for 19E (four years hence) to increase over *current cost* for 19A? (Do not assume any change in the scale of proposed benefits.)

4. As to the present work force only, what factors might cause *current cost* for 19E to be less than *current cost* for 19A?

DECISION CASE 18–2

The increasing amount of fringe benefits has focused the attention of accountants on these costs. One of the principal costs is that of pension plans.

Required:

1. Distinguish between pay-as-you-go (unfunded) and funded pension plans.

2. The total cost of contributions that must be paid ultimately to provide pensions for the present participants in a plan cannot be determined precisely in advance; however, reasonably accurate estimates can be made by the use of actuarial techniques. List the factors entering into the determination of the ultimate cost of a funded pension plan.

3. When a funded pension plan is adopted its total cost to the employer for the first year may be apportioned to past service and current-service (normal) cost.

a) Distinguish between these two costs.

b) How should these costs be charged as between accounting periods?

c) What should be the balance sheet treatment of these costs if the employer must (by contract) accumulate in a trusteed fund enough to guarantee the employees their benefits upon retirement?

(AICPA adapted)

EXERCISES

Exercise 18–1

The TP Company decided to initiate a funded pension plan and to give employees credit for prior employment. The plan is noncontributory, and the benefits vest at age 60. The actuary estimated the past service cost at date of inception of the plan to be $50,000. To keep the problem short assume the past service cost is to be amortized over three years and that the interest rate is 5%.

Required:

1. Compute the periodic amortization *factor* and the periodic funding payment assuming:

Case A—Funding is over a three-year period.
Case B—Funding is over a four-year period.
Case C—Funding is over a two-year period.

2. Prepare an amortization and funding schedule for the past service cost for Case C.

3. Give entries for the four years for Case C assuming the actuarially determined normal pension costs to be: Year 1, $15,000; Year 2, $18,000; Year 3, $20,000; and Year 4, $24,000.

4. Indicate the amounts that would be reflected on the income statement and the balance sheet under Case C for the four years.

Exercise 18–2

Several years after formation, AA Corporation decided to initiate a pension plan on a funded, noncontributory basis. The actuary determined that the past service cost at date of inception of the plan to be $362,989.52.

Required:

1. Using a 4% interest rate prepare a schedule that reflects the amortization of the past service cost over a four-year period and a funding over a three-year period.

2. Assuming the actuary determined the normal pension cost to be: Year 1, $40,000, and year 2, $44,000, give the entries in respect to the pension plan for both years.

3. What items would be reported on the income statement and balance sheet for each of the two years?

Exercise 18–3

Several years after formation, Brown Company decided to adopt a funded, noncontributory pension plan. The actuary determined that the past service cost at date of inception of the plan to be $367,307.92.

Required:

1. Using a 3½% rate prepare a schedule that reflects the amortization of the past service cost over a four-year period and a funding over a six-year period.

2. Assuming the actuary determined the normal pension cost to be: Year 1, $140,000, and Year 2, $160,000, give entries in respect to the pension plan for both years.

3. What items would be reported on the income statement and balance sheet for each of the two years?

Exercise 18–4

This is a library assignment which calls for you to consult the AICPA publication *Accounting Trends and Techniques*. You are to research and prepare a report on your findings as to *pensions*.

Required:

Write a report covering the following matters:

1. Number of the 600 companies which indicate existence of pension plans.
2. As to the companies having plans, indicate:
   a) Extent to which they are funded.

b) Where the charge to income is set forth.

c) Number of plans newly adopted during the year.

d) Number of plans amended during the year.

3. Quote two of the more interesting excerpts reproduced from reports of companies having plans and state why you selected those particular excerpts.

4. Comment on any aspect of the coverage of pensions in *Trends* which particularly impressed you.

Exercise 18–5

On August 1, 1971, Y Company leased some unused space in its office building to Z Company for an annual rental of $4,800 payable August 1 each year. It was agreed that Z Company would occupy the space at least two years and that three months advance would be given prior to moving; likewise Y Company agreed to give six months notice if it needed the space. The fiscal year for each company ends on December 31.

Required:

1. What type of lease is involved? Explain. What accounting method should each party use?

2. Give all entries for the lessor and lessee for 1971 and 1972 in parallel columns.

Exercise 18–6

On January 1, 1971, Dell Company leased a small building to Mason Company on a three-year contract that required an annual rental of $9,000, payable each January 1, plus an advance payment of $6,000. There was no specific renewal agreement and Dell Company was to pay all normal ownership costs. Each company closes its books on December 31.

Required:

1. What type of lease is this? Explain. What accounting approach should be used by each party; indicate any alternatives.

2. Develop an amortization table that would be suitable for either party. Assume 7% interest and present value amortization.

3. What would be the amount of amortization each period assuming straight line?

4. Give all entries for 1971 and 1972 for the lessor and lessee in parallel columns. Use present value (interest) amortization.

5. What would be reported on the income statement and balance sheet by each party at the end of 1971 and 1972?

Exercise 18–7

On January 1, 1971, Crown Leasing Company entered into a leasing contract whereby it would provide a new special truck to Dawn Contractors on a four-year basis. The truck cost Crown $22,000 (estimated useful life, four years, no residual value) and the annual rental, payable each year-end, was $6,642.26. Dawn agreed to pay all of the normal ownership costs including maintenance, taxes, and insurance. On January 1, 1971, the truck was delivered to Dawn Contractors. Crown expects an 8% rate of return. Assume a financing lease, but not a lease-purchase.

Required:

1. How might Crown compute the periodic rental?
2. How would Dawn compute the present value of the special property rights?
3. Develop an amortization schedule that would be suitable for either party.
4. For both the lessor and lessee give entries for (a) inception of the lease and (b) the first and second rental collections and the related amortization. Present the entries in parallel columns; you may use abbreviated account titles. Assume the present value approach to asset amortization.
5. What values would be reported on the income statement and balance sheet at the end of 1971?

Exercise 18–8

M Leasing Company leased a new machine that cost $24,000 to Company N on a three-year noncancellable contract. N Company agreed to assume all risks of normal ownership including such costs as insurance, taxes, and maintenance. The machine has a three-year useful life and no residual value. The lease was signed on January 1, 19A; M Company expected an 8% return. The annual rentals were payable on each December 31. The fiscal period of each party ends on December 31. Assume a financing lease, but not a lease-purchase.

Required:

1. How should the lessor compute the periodic rental?
2. How should the lessee compute the present value of the special property rights under the contract?
3. Develop an amortization table that would be suitable for both the lessor and lessee.
4. Give entry for lessor and lessee, in parallel columns, at date of inception of the lease. You may utilize abbreviated account titles.
5. Give entry for lessor and lessee, in parallel columns, for first rental (present value amortization).
6. Give entry for lessor and lessee, in parallel columns, for adjustment of the lease accounts at December 31, 19A.
7. Show how each party would report the lease amounts on the financial statements at the end of 19A.

Exercise 18–9

Cooper Company leased an item of equipment to Brown Contractors at the start of period 1. Under the lease agreement equal rentals are payable at the end of the first six months and semiannually thereafter for six periods (three years). The contract contained all of the characteristics of a financing type of lease. At termination of the lease the equipment reverts to the lessor. The equipment had no net salvage value; as a consequence the following amortization schedule was developed:

Period	Periodic Rental (a)	3½% of (d) Interest (b)	(a)−(b) Investment Recovery (c)	Unrecovered Investment (d)
Initial				$300,000.00
1 ....$56,300.46		$10,500.00	$45,800.46	254,199.54
2 .... 56,300.46		8,896.98	47,403.48	206,796.06
3 .... 56,300.46		7,237.86	49,062.60	157,733.46
4 .... 56,300.46		5,520.67	50,779.79	106,953.67
5 .... 56,300.46		3,743.38	52,557.08	54,396.59
6 .... 56,300.46		1,903.87°	54,396.59	—

° Rounded.

Required:

1. What was the annual rate of return expected by the lessor?
2. How did the lessor compute the periodic rent?
3. How did the lessee compute the present value of the property rights?
4. Give entry, or entries, for lessor and lessee at inception of the lease; you may abbreviate account titles.
5. Give entry, or entries, for lessor and lessee for first rental (present value amortization).
6. Assume the equipment cost $330,000 and had a residual value of $30,000 at the termination of the lease. (a) Give entry for lessor at inception of the lease and (b) Give entry for lessor for first rental.

PROBLEMS

Problem 18-1

The Simpson Company was organized in 1964. The decision was made to initiate a funded, noncontributory pension plan starting January 1, 1971. The First Security Bank will be the funding agency. The actuary determined the past service cost at date of inception of the plan (as of January 1, 1971) to be $30,000 and the normal pension cost for the year 1971 to be $10,000. Since the company had an excess of ready cash, it was decided to completely fund the past pension cost at the end of 1971. Past pension cost will be amortized over four years; a 6% rate of interest will be assumed.

Required:

1. Prepare a schedule of funding and amortization of past service costs.
2. Give all entries indicated for 1971.
3. Give entries for 1972–76 assuming the following normal pension costs: 1972, $11,000; 1973, $12,000; 1974, $13,000; 1975, $14,000; and 1976, $15,000.
4. Assume a long-time employee retired during 1976 and was paid his first monthly pension benefit of $300. Give any entries indicated. Explain.
5. What would be reported on the income statement and balance sheet for each period 1971–76 inclusive?

Problem 18–2

Rake Corporation has been in business for approximately 25 years. Recently the management made a decision to institute a funded, noncontributory pension plan. A trustee has been selected to receive and disburse the pension funds in accordance with the plan. To shorten this problem the amounts are relatively small and the number of periods limited. Assume that the program started on January 1, 1971, and that estimates through 1975 made by the actuary were:

1. Past service costs at the beginning of 1971, $60,000.
2. Normal service costs: 1971, $8,000; 1972, $8,400; 1973, $9,000; 1974, $9,500; and 1975, $10,200.
3. Interest rate, 5%.

In respect to amortization of past service costs and their funding there are four separate cases:

	Periods	
Case	*Amortization*	*Funding*
A	4	4
B	3	4
C	4	3
D	4	1

Required:

For each case, show computations.

1. Schedule of amortization and funding (assume funding at year-end).
2. Journal entries for years 1971, 1974, and 1975.
3. Balances to be reported on financial statements for 1971, 1974, and 1975.

Problem 18–3

The Maron Company has been operating for a number of years. Recently a decision was made (year 1) to initiate a pension plan on a funded, noncontributory basis. The actuary determined the past service cost (at the start of year 1) to be $1 million. A decision has been made by the management to amortize it over a 10-year period at an assumed interest rate of 4%. The normal service cost at the end of year 1 was determined to be $90,000. The Capitol Bank will act as the funding agency.

Required:

1. Construct a schedule of amortization and funding for past service cost assuming the funding of past service cost will be over an eight-year period.
2. Give entries for year 1 in respect to the pension plan.
3. Give entries for years 2, 3, 10, 11, and 12 assuming the following normal (current) service costs: year 2, $92,000; year 3, $93,000; year 10, $110,000; year 11, $115,000; and year 12, $118,000.
4. Give entry (if any) assuming long-time employee Jones retired in year 10 and received his first pension benefit, a check for $375. Explain.
5. What values would be reflected on the income statement and balance sheet for years 1, 2, 3, 10, 11, and 12?

Problem 18-4

Knox Manufacturing Company has been operating for a number of years. Recently a decision was made (assume year 1) to initiate a pension plan on a noncontributory funded basis. The actuary determined that the past service cost (at the start of year 1) to be $1 million. A decision was made to amortize past service costs over a 10-year period and to fund them over a 12-year period. The Irvin Trust Company will act as trustee; a 6% interest rate has been assumed.

Required:

1. Construct a schedule of amortization and funding for past service cost.

2. Give entries for years 1, 2, 3, 10, 11, and 12 assuming the following normal pension costs: year 1, $110,000; year 2, $116,000; year 3, $122,000; year 10, $130,000; year 11, $140,000; and year 12, $150,000.

3. Give entry (if any) assuming long-time employee Smith retired in year 9 and received his first pension benefit, a check for $410. Explain.

4. What values would be reflected on the income statement and balance sheet for the years 2, 10, and 12?

Problem 18-5

On January 1, 19A, Company A rented an office to Company B for an annual rental of $1,200 payable each January 1. In addition, an advance payment of $3,000 was required. The lease was for three-year period. The advance payment represented three annual rentals that would have been payable each January 1; the $3,000 was somewhat less than the sum of the three annual payments that would have been made in addition to the normal rent of $1,200.

(Note: This situation is identical with Illustration 18-4 in the chapter except that the downpayment is viewed as advance annual rentals rather than year-end annual rentals. It is particularly useful for comparing the two alternative assumptions.)

Required:

1. Give all entries, including closing entries, for both the lessor and lessee assuming (*a*) both parties' fiscal year ends December 31 and (*b*) a 6% interest rate for amortization purposes. Utilize present value amortization and present the two sets of entries in parallel columns. Show all computations. Also assume that this is an operating lease.

2. Show amounts that would be reported on the income statement and balance sheet for each year for both the lessor and lessee.

Problem 18-6

Lessor Company and Lessee Company entered into a financing type of lease on January 1, 19A. The lease was for new construction equipment which cost the Lessor Company $200,000 (useful life five years, no residual value). Lessor Company expects 6% return over the five-year period of the lease. The lease calls for five annual rentals payable each January 1, i.e., at the *beginning* of each year starting on January 1, 19A. Lessee Company is to assume all the risks and normal costs of ownership and the machines revert to the lessor at the termination of the lease.

(Note: This situation is identical with the example in the chapter for the same two companies, page 736, except that the rentals are payable at the *beginning* rather than at the end of each period. It is particularly useful for comparing the two alternative assumptions.)

Required:

1. Show how the Lessor Company would compute the annual rental amount. How would the Lessee Company compute the present value of the lease rights?

2. Prepare an amortization table that would be suitable for each party (straight line amortization).

3. Give the entries for both the lessor and lessee, in parallel columns, for the years 19A and 19B. You may use abbreviated account titles.

4. Show the items and amounts that would be reported on the income statement and balance sheet at the end of 19B for both the lessor and lessee.

Problem 18–7

Stokes Corporation is a newly formed subsidiary of a financial institution. Stokes will be engaged in leasing a basic machine that costs $50,000 each and has a six-year life and no residual value at the end of its useful life. Stokes started operations with 10 of the machines; its equities consist of a $150,000 note due in three years which bears 5% interest payable each December 31 and $350,000 capital stock. The fiscal year ends on December 31. The machines will be rented under six-year contracts whereby annual rentals are paid on at year-end; 6% return on the investment is expected. The lessee assumes all risks and costs of normal ownership, and the lease is noncancellable. The machines revert to the lessor at the termination of the lease.

Required:

1. Show how the lessor would compute the annual rental on a machine.

2. Show how the lessee would compute the present value of the special property rights.

3. Prepare an amortization table that would be suitable for either the lessor or lessee.

4. Give journal entries for the lessor for the following transactions; you may use abbreviated account titles.

Jan. 1, 19A—Concluded leases on all 10 machines with various lessors.
Dec. 31, 19A—Collected lease rentals due; paid salaries and other expenses, $20,000; paid interest due on the note.
Dec. 31, 19A—Adjust the lease accounts and accrue income taxes at 20%; closing entries not required.

5. Prepare a classified balance sheet for the lessor as of December 31, 19A.

6. Give journal entries for a lessee who leased one of the machines on Jan. 1, 19A, for the following: (*a*) to record the lease and (*b*) to record payment of first rental and adjustment of lease accounts (present value amortization of the asset).

Problem 18–8

RST Company leases all types of machinery and is offering leases of the financing type; its budgeted rate of return on all leased property is 6% per annum. A new machine which cost $120,000 (estimated useful life of five years, zero residual value) is leased to SA Company for an annual rental of $28,487.57 payable at the end of each of the five years of the lease agreement. SA Company is to assume all costs of ownership such as maintenance, taxes, and insurance. The lease is to be effective January 1, 1971 (designated as year 1 for convenience). The machine reverts to the lessor at termination of the lease.

Required:

1. Show how the lessor (RST Company) computed the annual rental amount.

2. Show how SA Company would compute the present value of the special property rights under the lease agreement.

3. Prepare a schedule of amortization that could be utilized for either the lessor or lessee.

4. Give journal entries for the lessor and lessee, side by side, for years 1 and 2. You may use abbreviated account titles (assume a property-rights type of lease and present value amortization of the asset).

5. Show amounts that would be reported on the financial statements for both the lessor and lessee for year 1.

Problem 18–9

On January 1, 19A, Virginia Leasing Company entered into a noncancellable agreement with James Company whereby the latter would be provided a new machine on a four-year rental basis. Annual rentals are to be paid each December 31 (at year-end) and James Company assumed all normal ownership risks and costs. At the end of the fourth year the machine will revert to the lessor.

Virginia Company paid $72,000 for the machine which had an estimated life of four years and a residual value of $12,000. The Virginia Company expects an 8% return on its investment. The fiscal year for each company ends on December 31.

Required:

1. Compute the annual rental to be quoted by Virginia Company.

2. How would James Company compute the present value of the special property rights under the lease assuming the quoted rental is incorporated in the lease agreement?

3. Prepare separate amortization tables for the lessor and the lessee.

4. Give the following entries for the lessor and lessee (you may utilize abbreviated account titles): (a) at date of inception of lease, (b) collection of first rental, and (c) adjustment of lease accounts on December 31, 19A (assume straight line amortization).

5. How would the lease amounts be reflected on the financial statements of the lessor and lessee on December 31, 19A?

Problem 18–10

James Leasing Company rented a new machine to Conway Contractors that cost $18,000; having a four-year life and no residual value at that time. The lease was signed on January 1, 19A, and the lessee was to assume all normal risks and costs of ownership; the lease was noncancellable. The James Company computed the rent on the basis of a 7% return and the lessee utilized this same rate for accounting for the lease. The property will revert to the lessor at termination of the lease.

Required:

1. Assuming the annual rentals are payable at the end of each year complete the following: (*a*) lessor computation of periodic rental payments; (*b*) lessee computation of the present value of the special property rights under the lease; and (*c*) an amortization table that would be suitable for both the lessor and lessee.

2. Assuming the annual rentals are payable at the start of each year complete the same three items required in (1).

3. Give the entries for the lessor and lessee, in parallel columns, for requirement (2) throughout 19A. You may utilize abbreviated account titles (straight line amortization).

4. Indicate the asset and liability amounts that would be reported on the balance sheets at December 31, 19A, by the lessor and lessee.

Problem 18–11

The practice of obtaining the right to use property by noncancellable leases is becoming more prevalent.

Required:

1. Assets acquired under noncancellable leases that are in substance installment purchases should be capitalized in the accounts of the lessee in order to show the facts properly. List the defects in the lessee's balance sheet and income statement that would result from *not* recording assets acquired under such contracts.

2. Other noncancellable leases that give the lessee essentially all the rights and obligations of ownership are not installment purchases in substance.

a) Discuss the case *against* recording assets acquired by such leases.

b) The case for recording assets acquired by such leases rests primarily on the belief that the opportunity to exercise the right of use creates an asset that should be recognized in the accounts with its related liability. Discuss the arguments that *support* this belief.

(AICPA adapted)

chapter **19**

Corporations —
Contributed Capital
at Formation

The Concept of Corporate Capital

The corporate form of business organization has become a dominant one in the United States. This particular form of business organization gained widespread use primarily as a result of the legal foundations upon which it is built. A corporation is, in the eyes of the law, an entity separate and apart from the owners. Limited liability of corporate owners, provision for succession of ownership, facility for capital accumulation, separation of management from ownership, and the legal right to act in the same capacity as an individual in the transaction of authorized business are four important factors contributing to the growth of the corporate form of business. In view of the unique features of the corporate form and its extensive use, accountants have shown considerable concern with respect to the special accounting problems encountered. This chapter and the three following consider these special accounting problems.

Unique problems are encountered in accounting for a corporation in respect to the *proprietary equities*. In other respects the accounting treatment of transactions is largely unaffected by the form of business organization. At the outset it is well for the student to realize that there is not complete agreement in the accounting profession on a number of the issues related to accounting for corporate capital. In a sole proprietorship, owner's equity usually is represented by a single owner's equity account and in a partnership by separate equity accounts for each partner. In contrast, accounting for a corporation generally requires a number of owners' equity accounts.

In accounting for corporate proprietary equities, accountants adhere to a concept of *source of capital resources*. In order to apply this concept, corporate capital accounts are established in such manner that the *sources* of the capital used in the enterprise are clearly segregated. In accounting by *source*, aside from the funds supplied by creditors (liabilities), the primary sources of corporate capital are (*a*) contributions by the owners and (*b*) earnings retained in the business.

The term *capital* standing alone has different meanings to various individuals. The accountant should be familiar with the four following classes of capital:

1. *Total equity (enterprise capital)*. Total equity represents the total interests of all lenders and owners of a particular corporation in the properties of that business; it is the sum of the creditors' equity and the owners' equity.
2. *Proprietary equity (owners' equity)*. Proprietary equity represents the total equity at a given time of the legal owners of the enterprise; it is the total of contributed capital and all subsequent accretions thereto in the form of additional contributions and retained earnings.
3. *Contributed capital*. Contributed capital is the investment made by the owners; in a corporation it is the total amount paid in by all parties other than creditors.
4. *Legal or stated capital*. Legal capital is that portion of corporate capital that is required by statute to be retained in the business for the protection of creditors.

Classifications of Corporations

The laws of the several states provide for the formation and operation of corporations. Although state laws relating to corporations vary in many respects, there is much similarity in basic provisions. The statutes of all states provide for the existence of a separate entity and for the basic capital structure (capital stock). Corporations are brought into legal existence by submitting an application (articles of incorporation) for a charter to the secretary of state; if approved, a charter is then issued which specifies the detailed conditions under which the corporation may operate such as what business activities are permitted, types of capital stock to be issued, and the method of electing officers. The charter is supplemented with bylaws which are adopted by the stockholders.

Corporations may be classified as follows:

1. Public corporations, when they relate to governmental units or business operations owned by governmental units.
2. Private corporations, when they are privately owned. Such corporations may be nonstock (nonprofit organizations such as colleges and churches) or stock (usually organized for profit making).
3. Domestic corporations, when operating in the state in which incorporated.
4. Foreign corporations, when operating in states other than the one in which incorporated.
5. Open corporations, when the stock is available for purchase. The stock is usually widely held.
6. Close corporations, when the stock is not available for purchase and is generally held by a few shareholders.

Nature of Capital Stock

Shares of capital stock, represented by stock certificates, evidence ownership in a corporation. Shares may be transferred freely by shareholders unless there is an enforceable agreement not to do so. Ownership of shares entitles the holder to certain basic rights. These rights are:

1. The right to participate in the *management* of the corporation through participating and voting in stockholder meetings.
2. The right to participate in the *profits* of the corporation through dividends declared by the board of directors.
3. The right to share in the distribution of *assets* of the corporation at liquidation or through "capital" dividends.
4. The right to purchase shares of stock on a *pro rata basis* in the corporation when such shares represent additional capital stock issues. This right is designed to protect the proportional interests of each shareholder in the ownership.

These rights are shared equitably and proportionately by all stockholders unless the charter or bylaws (and stock certificates) specifically provide otherwise. In the case of one class of stock, all holders enjoy equal rights; in the case of two or more classes of stock, the holders of one class of stock may have rights that have been withheld from the others.

In order to comprehend clearly the nature of capital stock, and to account for it correctly, the accountant must understand the following terms:

1. Authorized capital stock — the number of shares of stock that can be issued legally as specified in the charter.

2. Issued capital stock—the number of shares of authorized stock that have been issued to date.
3. Unissued capital stock—the number of shares of authorized capital stock that have *never* been issued.
4. Outstanding capital stock—the number of shares of stock that have been issued and are being held by shareholders at a given date.
5. Treasury stock—those shares once issued and later reacquired by the corporation, i.e., the difference between issued shares and outstanding shares.
6. Subscribed stock—unissued shares of stock set aside to meet subscription contracts. Subscribed stock will be issued upon full payment of the subscription price.

In accounting for corporate capital, definite categories have been evolved by the accounting profession. Although in practice there is some variation in such categories and in terminology, the following appears to represent current trends:[1]

1. Contributed capital (sometimes referred to as paid-in capital):
   a) Capital stock.
      (1) Preferred stock.
      (2) Common stock.
   b) Other contributed capital (in past years frequently referred to as capital surplus):
      (1) From owners:
         Premium on stock (and amounts paid in excess of par or stated value on stock).
      (2) From outsiders:
         Donations of assets.
2. Retained earnings (in past years referred to as earned surplus):
   a) Appropriated (frequently referred to as reserves).
   b) Unappropriated.
3. Unrealized increment arising through revaluation (upward) of assets.

Item (1) is considered in Chapters 19 and 20, items (2) and (3) in Chapters 13, 21, and 22. Throughout these chapters the categories and terminology listed above will be followed.

The above classifications of corporate capital are observable in a properly prepared balance sheet. To illustrate, the corporate capital section of a balance sheet might be reported as shown in Illustration 19–1.

---

[1] On page 30 of AICPA *Accounting Terminology Bulletin No. 1*, "Review and Résumé," the Committee on Terminology recommended: "The use of the term *surplus* (whether standing alone or in such combination as *capital surplus, paid-in surplus, earned surplus, appraisal surplus*, etc.) be discontinued."

Illustration 19–1
Capital Section of a Corporation Balance Sheet

Contributed Capital:
Capital stock:

Preferred stock, 6%, par $10, cumulative and nonparticipating, 20,000 shares authorized, 15,000 issued	$150,000	
Preferred stock subscribed, 100 shares	1,000	
Total	$151,000	
Common stock, no-par value, authorized 10,000 shares, issued and outstanding 8,000 shares at stated value, $5	40,000	$191,000

Other contributed capital:
By owners:

Premium on preferred stock	$ 12,000	
From sale of common stock in excess of stated value	3,000	15,000

By outsiders:

From donation of plant site		5,000
Total Contributed Capital		$211,000

Retained Earnings:
Appropriated:

Reserve for bond sinking fund	$40,000	
Reserve for possible loss on suit pending	10,000	$ 50,000
Unappropriated		70,000
Total Retained Earnings		120,000
Unrealized increment from write-up of fixed assets		50,000
Total Capital		$381,000

Although in practice one frequently observes different terms and arrangements of the various subclassifications of corporate capital shown in Illustration 19–1, the emphasis should be on *source, clarity of presentation,* and *avoidance of needless technical terminology.*

Classes of Capital Stock

Modern corporate structure utilizes different classes of capital stock, the ownership of which gives rise to varying privileges, restrictions, and responsibilities among the respective classes. Some of these restrictions may result from provisions of the state statutes, the charter, or the bylaws of the corporation and are made operative by contract between the corporation and the shareholders. The two primary classifications of capital stock are (*a*) par-value and no-par-value stock and (*b*) common and preferred stock.

Par-Value Stock. The laws of the several states provide for the issuance of par-value stock, that is, shares of stock with a designated dollar "value" per share as provided for in the articles of incorporation and as printed on the face of the stock certificates. Par-value stock may be either common or preferred. In the early history of corporations in the United States, only par-value stock was authorized. Since the owners of a corporation were not liable to creditors (beyond the assets of the corporation), statutes provided for a "par value" to afford some measure of protection to creditors. In this respect the courts tended to hold that shareholders who had paid *less* than par value for their stock could be assessed for the discount to satisfy creditors' claims. Par-value stock sold initially at less than par is said to have been issued at a discount, whereas par-value stock sold above par is said to have been issued at a premium. Today the issuance of stock at a discount is illegal in most states. Subsequent to issue, par value has no necessary relationship to market value.

No-Par-Value Stock. True no-par-value stock does not carry a designated or assigned value per share — nor is such provided for in the articles of incorporation. Many states also authorize the issuance of no-par-value stock with a *stated* or *assigned* value. The stated or assigned value is established by the corporate directors or the bylaws of the corporation. No-par-value stock with a stated or assigned value is encountered more frequently than is true no-par stock. The use of assigned or stated-value stock serves to place the no-par stock on practically the same basis as par-value stock for accounting purposes. Both common and preferred stock may be represented by no-par shares. No-par-value stock was first permitted by statute in New York in 1912; since that date the authorization of stock without par value has become so generally accepted that today practically all states permit its issuance. During the past 30 years many new corporations (and old corporations reorganized) have issued no-par-value stock. The chief advantages claimed for this type of stock are as follows:

1. It avoids stock discount and hence eliminates a contingent liability of stockholders to creditors for purchase of stock below par.
2. It places the investor on guard to determine the true value of the stock rather than blindly to assume it to be worth the par value.
3. It facilitates the accounting for capital in that the total amount paid in generally is credited to the capital stock account.
4. It does away with the dubious expediency, frequently encountered in par-value stock, of overvaluing assets received for stock in order to report such stock fully paid. The use of no-par-value stock is particularly advantageous in connection with issuance for property such as patents, leaseholds, manufacturing rights, goodwill, and other intangibles, the true worth of which has not been proved.

The disadvantages of no-par stock result from excessive franchise and other taxes levied by some jurisdictions and the opportunity to manipulate part of the proceeds of the issue so as to give the appearance of excessive paid-in capital or even retained earnings upon organization. Conversely, in some jurisdictions there is less tax on no-par shares.

Common Stock. Common stock represents the basic issue of

shares and normally carries all of the basic rights listed on page 767. When there is only one class of stock all of the shares are common stock.

Preferred stock is a type which entitles the owners to some preference or priority over the common stock shareholders. The preference or priority usually relates to dividends and asset distributions upon liquidation and may be "positive" or "negative" when compared with the common stock. For example, nonvoting preferred stock represents a preference that is negative.

Legal Capital. The total proprietary equity in a corporation is represented by capital contributed by owners, capital contributed by outsiders, retained earnings, and unrealized increment arising from appraisal increases on fixed assets. *Legal capital,* sometimes referred to as *stated capital,* is defined by statute. It will be recalled that the stockholders in a corporation have limited liability; that is, they cannot be held legally liable for the debts of the corporation. In order to afford some measure of protection to creditors, the statutes of the several states designate some minimum investment in the corporation to be identified specifically as legal capital. This legal capital cannot be returned to the owners through dividends or by purchase of shares held by them, unless creditor claims are first satisfied.

When par-value stock is issued, most states require that the par value of all outstanding shares shall represent the legal capital. In the case of no-par stock the legal capital generally is regarded as the stated or assigned value per share. In the case of true no-par stock most states require that the full proceeds from the sale of no-par stock must be treated as legal capital. In case the legal capital is impaired through dividend payments or purchase of the corporation's own shares (treasury stock), the courts generally have held that creditors may obtain payment from the shareholders for claims to the extent of such impairment.

The concept of legal capital is particularly important in correctly accounting for corporate ownership equities. The capital accounts should be maintained so that sources are reported, thereby providing appropriate data for determination of legal capital in conformance with the statutes of the particular state in which incorporated. Since state statutes define legal capital and there is considerable variation as between states, careful accounting for corporate capital is essential.

The amount of legal capital should be entered in the capital stock account, and investments in excess of legal capital should be recorded in other appropriately designated capital accounts.

Preferred Stock. Preferred stock is so designated because it has some preference or priority over the common stock. The preference or priority may relate to —

1. Dividends:
   a) Cumulative or noncumulative.
   b) Fully participating, partially participating, or nonparticipating.
2. Assets.
3. Redemption.
4. Convertibility.

Since the right to vote is a basic right, preferred shareholders have full voting rights unless specifically prohibited in the stock agreement relating to the original issue. Likewise, all the other basic rights listed in a preceding paragraph apply to preferred stock unless specifically stated otherwise in the stock agreement (charter).

Preferred stock is usually par-value stock, in which case the dividend preference is expressed as a percentage. For example, 6% preferred stock would carry a dividend preference of 6% of the *par value* of each share. In the case of no-par preferred stock a dividend preference is expressed as a specific dollar *amount* per share. Occasionally a corporation may issue two or more classes of preferred stock each having different preferences.

In order to identify correctly the preferences relating to preferred stock, corporations must indicate on the stock certificate the exact nature of the preferences; that is, whether the stock is cumulative, participating, callable, or convertible.[2]

Cumulative Preferences on Preferred Stock. Noncumulative preferred stock provides that dividends not declared (passed) for any year or series of years are lost permanently as far as the preferred shareholder is concerned. As a result the noncumulative restriction generally is viewed as an undersirable feature by potential investors.

Cumulative preferred stock provides that dividends passed (dividends in arrears) for any year or series of years accumulate and must be paid to the preferred shareholders when dividends are declared before the common stockholders may receive a dividend. If only a part of the preference is met for any one year, then the balance of the preference is in arrears. Cumulative preferred stock does not carry the right, in liquidation of the corporation, to dividends in arrears if there are no retained earnings. However, express provisions may be made in the charter and stock contract concerning dividends in arrears in such situations. At common law, where the charter is silent as to the cumulative feature, preferred stock is considered to be cumulative.

Participating Preferences on Preferred Stock. Preferred stock is *fully* participating when the preferred shareholders are entitled to extra dividends on a pro rata basis (based on par or stated value) with

---

[2] In some cases the distinction between common and preferred stock represents restrictions or negative features. For example, noncumulative, nonparticipating, and nonvoting are definite negative features.

the holders of common stock. In this case the preference relates to a prior claim to dividends up to a stated percent of par (the preferential rate), after which both classes of stock share ratably (including the preference).

Preferred stock is nonparticipating when the dividends on such stock for any one year are limited in the charter, stock contract, and on the stock certificate to a specified preferential rate.

In the case of *partially* participating preferred stock, the shareholders thereof participate above the preferential rate with the common stockholders but only up to an additional rate which is specified in the charter and on the stock certificate. For example, a corporation may issue 6% preferred stock, with participation up to a total of 8%, in which case participation privileges with the common shareholders would be limited to an additional 2%.

In the absence of an expressed stipulation most courts have taken the view that preferred stock has no right to participate with the common stock, unless this preference is stated expressly in the preferred stock contract (charter).

Since accountants frequently are called upon to advise management with respect to dividend declarations, it is important that computations with respect thereto be clearly understood. In order to illustrate dividend computations assume the following:

Preferred stock, 5% ($100 par value per share – 1,000 shares).........$100,000
Common stock ($100 par value per share – 2,000 shares)............... 200,000

	Preferred	Common
Illustration No. 1: Preferred stock is cumulative, nonparticipating; dividends two years in arrears; dividends declared, $28,000.		
Step 1 – Preferred in arrears	$10,000	
Step 2 – Preferred, current (at 5%)	5,000	
Step 3 – Common (balance)		$13,000
	$15,000	$13,000
Illustration No. 2: Preferred stock is cumulative, fully participating; dividends two years in arrears; dividends declared, $28,000.		
Step 1 – Preferred in arrears	$10,000	
Step 2 – Preferred, current (at 5%)	5,000	
Step 3 – Common, current (to match preferred at 5%)		$10,000
Step 4 – Balance (ratably with par)	1,000	2,000
	$16,000	$12,000
Illustration No. 3: Preferred stock is noncumulative, partially participating up to 7%; dividends declared, $28,000.		
Step 1 – Preferred, current (at 5%)	$ 5,000	
Step 2 – Common, current (to match preferred at 5%)		$10,000
Step 3 – Preferred, partial participation, additional 2%	2,000	
Step 4 – Common (balance)		11,000
	$ 7,000	$21,000

	Preferred	Common
Illustration No. 4: Preferred stock is noncumulative; partially participating up to 7%; dividends declared, $16,000.		
Step 1—Preferred, current at 5%	$ 5,000	
Step 2—Common, current (to match preferred at 5%)		$10,000
Step 3— {Preferred, partial participation	333	
{Common		667
	$ 5,333	$10,667

Preferred stock that is preferred as to *assets* provides that the holders thereof upon corporate dissolution will have a priority up to par value or other stated amount per share over common shareholders. Once the priority for the preferred is satisfied, the remainder of the assets are distributed to the common shareholders.

Preferred stock having *redemption* privileges (redeemable stock), provides that the shareholder, at his option, may, under the conditions specified, turn in his shares to the corporation at a specified price per share.

Preferred stock may carry a provision of *convertibility* (convertible stock), at the option of the holder, for other securities such as common stock. Conversion privileges frequently turn out to be particularly valuable and, hence, are favored by investors.

Preferred stock may be *callable,* that is, the corporation may, at its option, call the stock (purchase it) for cancellation under specified conditions of time and price. *APB Opinion 10* states that "the liquidation preference of the stock (preferred) be disclosed in the equity section of the balance sheet in the aggregate, either parenthetically or 'in short' rather than on a per share basis or by disclosure in notes."

Accounting for Issuance of Par-Value Stock

In accounting for corporate capital it will be recalled that *source* is particularly important; accordingly, if a corporation has more than one class of stock, separate accounts must be maintained for each class. In case there is only one class of stock, an account "Capital Stock" is usually employed. In cases where there are two or more classes of stock, titles such as "Common Stock," "Capital Stock, 5% Preferred," and "Common Stock, No Par" are appropriate. The sequence of transactions related to issuance of stock is (*a*) authorization of shares, (*b*) subscriptions, (*c*) collections on subscriptions, and (*d*) issuance of the shares.

Authorization. The authorization in the charter to issue a specified number of shares may be recorded (*a*) by notation or (*b*) by a formal journal entry. To illustrate, under the first method the notation for the journal and the ledger account heading may be as follows:

Capital Stock, Common—Par Value $100 per Share
(authorized 5,000 shares)

In case of formal journal entry is made it would be as follows:

```
Unissued Capital Stock, Common ......................................500,000
    Capital Stock, Common, Authorized ...........................        500,000
    To record authorization of 5,000 shares of common stock,
    par value $100 per share.
```

It should be noted that these are offsetting accounts.

Subscriptions. Prospective stockholders frequently sign a contract to purchase a specified number of shares — payment to be made at one or more stated dates in the future. Such a contract is known as a *stock subscription.* Since a legal contract is involved, accounting recognition must be given to this transaction. The purchase price is debited to Stock Subscriptions Receivable. Since the subscriber is given full status as a stockholder at this time (unless specifically withheld by the agreement), a capital account, Capital Stock Subscribed, is credited for the par value — any difference being debited to a stock discount account or credited to a stock premium account, as the case may be. To illustrate, assume 1,000 of the shares in the preceding illustration are subscribed for at $102; the entry would be:

```
Stock Subscriptions Receivable — Common Stock .................102,000
    Common Stock Subscribed........................................        100,000
    Premium on Common Stock ......................................         2,000
```

The Common Stock Subscribed account recognizes the corporation's obligation to issue the 1,000 shares upon fulfillment of the terms of the agreement by the subscribers. This account is reported on the balance sheet in a manner similar to the related capital stock account. Subscriptions receivable is classified as a current asset if the corporation expects current collection. If there are no plans for collection, subscriptions receivable cannot be considered a realizable asset and therefore should be offset against capital stock subscribed in the capital section of the balance sheet. In some cases subscription contracts call for installment payments. In such cases separate "call" accounts may be set up for each installment. In all cases a *subscribers' ledger* is maintained as a subsidiary record to the subscriptions receivable account in a manner similar to that maintained for regular accounts receivable.

Collections on Subscriptions. Collections on stock subscriptions may be in cash, property, or services. The appropriate account is debited, and subscriptions receivable is credited. If a service or property is received, the *amount* recorded would result from an agreement between the individual and the corporate officials as to the value to be placed on the property or services. To illustrate, assume five of the shares subscribed are to be issued in payment for legal services that otherwise would have required a $510 cash payment. The payment of the subscription would be recorded as follows:

```
Legal Costs (or organization costs) ....................................  510
    Stock Subscriptions Receivable — Common Stock ..........          510
```

Issuance of Shares. Stock certificates frequently are not issued to the subscriber until the subscription price is paid in full. The entry upon issuance depends upon the manner in which the authorized shares were recorded. To illustrate, suppose the 1,000 shares subscribed for above are paid in full. Assuming no prior entry was made for the authorization, the entry would be:

```
Common Stock Subscribed.............................................100,000
    Capital Stock, Common.............................................          100,000
```

On the other hand, assuming a prior entry was made to record the authorization, the issue would be recorded as follows:

```
Common Stock Subscribed.............................................100,000
    Unissued Capital Stock, Common .............................          100,000
```

In order to issue the stock, a *stock certificate* is prepared for each shareholder specifying the number of shares represented. An entry for each shareholder would be made in the *stockholder ledger* which is a subsidiary ledger to the capital stock account.

In case stock is sold directly for cash in full, entries for subscriptions and collections thereon, obviously, are not made. Instead the cash account would be debited, capital stock credited, and the premium or discount recorded.

Accounting for No-Par Capital Stock

In view of the fact that present-day statutes in many states give rise to two types of no-par-value stock—true no-par stock and stated no-par-value stock—some variation in accounting is observed. No-par-value stock with a stated value may be accounted for as discussed above for par-value stock, since the stated value places the no-par stock on practically the same basis as par-value stock. Amounts received in excess of stated value should be credited to an account with a descriptive title such as "Contributed Capital on No-Par Common Stock—Excess of Sales Price over Stated Value."

In the case of *true* no-par stock, no entry can be made for the authorization; instead of notation may be made in the journal and in the ledger account heading such as:

Capital Stock, Common—No-Par Value
(authorized 10,000 shares)

With respect to no-par-value stock most states require that the total number of shares authorized, as well as the number of shares represented by the individual stock certificate, be shown on the face of each such certificate. It is important to note that entries concerning true no-par-value stock should indicate the *number of shares* involved as well as the dollar amounts. In the case of true no-par-value stock the accounting treatment should follow the applicable legal require-

Illustration 19–2
Entries for No-Par Value Stock

Stated Value Method
(No-Par Value with $5 Stated Value per Share)

---

1. To record authorization of 10,000 shares of no-par stock:

Unissued Common Stock, No Par (stated value $5 per share) 50,000
    No-Par Common Stock Authorized (stated value $5)..........   50,000

(Note: This entry could also take the form of a notation as explained for par-value stock.)

2. To record sale of 5,000 shares at $6 per share:

Cash 30,000
    Unissued Common Stock, No Par....................................   25,000
    Contributed Capital, No-Par Common Stock—Excess Re-
    ceived over Stated Value...   5,000

3. To record sale of 5,000 shares at $6, with 20% paid in cash:

Cash 6,000
Subscriptions Receivable—No-Par Common Stock 24,000
    Contributed Capital, No-Par Common Stock—Excess Re-
    ceived over Stated Value...   5,000
    No-Par Common Stock Subscribed   25,000

4. To record final collection and issuance of shares:

Cash 24,000
    Subscriptions Receivable—No-Par Common Stock   24,000

No-Par Common Stock Subscribed 25,000
    Unissued Common Stock, No Par..................................   25,000

No Stated Value Method
(True No-Par Stock)

---

1. To record authorization of 10,000 shares of no-par stock:

Notation: To record authorization of 10,000 shares of no-par-
value common stock.

2. To record sale of 5,000 shares at $6 per share:

Cash 30,000
    No-Par Common Stock (5,000 shares).............................   30,000

3. To record sale of 5,000 shares at $6, with 20% paid in cash:

Cash 6,000
Subscriptions Receivable—No-Par Common Stock 24,000
    No-Par Common Stock Subscribed (5,000 shares).............   30,000

4. To record final collection and issuance of shares:

Cash 24,000
    Subscriptions Receivable—No-Par Common Stock   24,000

No-Par Common Stock Subscribed 30,000
    No-Par Common Stock (5,000 shares).............................   30,000

ments. If the statutes provide that all proceeds represent legal capital, then the capital stock account should be credited for the full amount received, so that no excess or shortage from a certain amount need be recorded separately. If the statutes establish a minimum amount per share, then at least this amount should be credited to the capital stock account. In the absence of legal requirements the total amount received normally should be credited to the capital stock account.

The entries in Illustration 19–2 (page 777) show the accounting for no-par-value stock, assuming that the corporation is authorized to issue 10,000 shares of no-par-value common stock.

Defaults on Installment Subscription

When a subscriber defaults after fulfilling a part of the subscription contract, certain complexities arise. In case of default the corporation simply may decide to (1) return to the subscriber all payments made or (2) issue shares equivalent to the number paid for in full, rather than the total number contracted. These two options obviously involve no disadvantage to the subscriber, although the corporation may incur a resultant loss. The laws of most states cover the contingency where the corporation does not elect either of these alternatives. Such laws vary considerably; two contrasting provisions follow—

a) That the stock is *forfeited* and all payments made by the defaulting subscriber are lost to him, hence they become a source of contributed capital to the corporation. Further, the corporation is free to sell the shares again. Obviously provisions of this type favor the corporation.

b) That the stock is forfeited and the corporation must resell the stock under a *lien*, whereby the original subscriber must be reimbursed for the amount that the total receipts for the stock (his payments plus the later sale proceeds), less the costs incurred by the corporation in making the second sale, exceed the original subscription price. The reimbursement to the defaulting subscriber cannot exceed the amount paid by him to date of default.

To illustrate the various possibilities, assume an original subscription price of $10,500 for $10,000 par-value stock; payments by the subscriber of $4,200 prior to default; second sale at $11,000; and cost of subsequent sale, $600. Computation of the refund would be as follows:

Collection from original subscriber	$ 4,200	
Collection from second sale	11,000	$15,200
Less: Costs incident to second sale		600
		$14,600
Original subscription price		10,500
Amount to Be Refunded to First Subscriber		$ 4,100°

° Not in excess of $4,200.

Each of the four situations may be illustrated using the above data:

1. The corporation decides to return all payments to the subscriber:

Refund to subscriber:
Capital Stock Subscribed..10,000
Premium on Capital Stock.. 500
   Stock Subscriptions Receivable ($10,500 − $4,200).........   6,300
   Cash   4,200

Second sale:
Cash 11,000
   Capital Stock..   10,000
   Premium on Capital Stock   1,000

Payment of costs incident to resale:
Premium on Capital Stock.. 600
   Cash   600

2. The corporation decides to issue shares equivalent to the amount paid:

Issuance of 40% of shares subscribed: ($4,200 ÷ $10,500 = 40%):
Capital Stock Subscribed..10,000
Premium on Capital Stock ($500 × 60%)............................ 300
   Stock Subscriptions Receivable ($10,500 − $4,200).........   6,300
   Capital Stock ($10,000 × 40%)   4,000

Subsequent sale of remaining shares for $6,600:
Cash 6,600
   Capital Stock..   6,000
   Premium on Capital Stock   600

Payment of $360 ($600 × 60%) costs incident to subsequent sale:
Premium on Capital Stock.. 360
   Cash   360

3. The corporation prefers to follow the statute (assumed to provide for forfeiture):

Forfeiture recorded:
Capital Stock Subscribed..10,000
Premium on Capital Stock.. 500
   Stock Subscriptions Receivable.....................................   6,300
   Contributed Capital, Forfeited Subscriptions.................   4,200

Subsequent sale for $11,000:
Cash 11,000
   Capital Stock..   10,000
   Premium on Capital Stock   1,000

Costs incident to resale:
Premium on Capital Stock.. 600
   Cash   600

4. The corporation prefers to follow the statute (assumed to provide for lien on resale):

Forfeiture recorded:

Capital Stock Subscribed	10,000	
Premium on Capital Stock	500	
Stock Subscriptions Receivable		6,300
Payable to Subscriber (pending resale)		4,200

Subsequent sale for $11,000:

Cash	11,000	
Capital Stock		10,000
Premium on Capital Stock (original amount)		500
Payable to Subscriber		500

Costs incident to resale:

Payable to Subscriber (cost of resale)	600	
Cash		600

Refund to subscriber:

Payable to Subscriber (refund computed above)	4,100	
Cash		4,100

Accounting for Stock Premium and Discount

In the preceding discussions and illustrations, amounts received in excess of par value were credited to a stock premium account. Similarly, amounts received less than par were debited to a stock discount account. Premium constitutes an increase in total corporate capital, whereas stock discount serves to reduce total corporate capital. In view of the advent of no-par-value stock and the passage of laws in many states forbidding the sale of stock at a discount, accountants seldom encounter the problem of stock discount.

Premium on stock is properly classified as contributed or paid-in capital and should be retained in the accounts until retirement of the stock. Upon retirement of the stock the related premium should be removed from the accounts. Some states allow such contributed capital to be used for stock dividends; a few allow charges to such accounts for cash dividends as well. When state laws allow such charges, the shareholders receiving such dividends should be informed that they represent a return of original investment (liquidating dividend) rather than a distribution of earnings.

Separate premium (and discount) accounts should be established for each class of stock. Premium and discount should not be offset one against the other. Discount can be disposed of by additional collections (stock assessments) from shareholders or through retirement of the related stock. On the balance sheet, stock premium and discount are reported as a part of corporate capital. Discount is reported on the balance sheet (a) preferably as a negative item directly under the particular class of stock to which it relates or (b) secondarily as a negative item under the "other contributed" capital section. See Chapter 14 for a discussion of stock issue costs.

Special Sales of Stock

A corporation may sell each class of stock separately as assumed in the preceding discussions or it may sell two or more classes of securities for one lump sum. Further, a corporation may sell stock for services or property rather than for cash. Each of these situations presents special accounting problems.

In the situation where two or more classes of securities are sold for a single lump sum, the proceeds must be allocated between the several classes of securities on some logical basis. Two methods available for such situations are (a) the proportional method where the lump sum received is allocated between the classes of stock on a proportional basis such as the relative fair market value of each security related to the units involved and (b) the incremental method where the market value of one security is used as a basis for that security and the remainder of the lump sum is allocated to the other class of security. Selection of an appropriate method should depend upon the information available. In order to illustrate several situations, assume 100 shares of common stock (par value $100 per share) and 50 shares of preferred stock (par value $80 per share) are sold for a lump sum of $15,000.

Assumption 1. The common stock is selling at 104, and the preferred stock at 101 — apportionment on basis of relative fair market values.

Cash	15,000	
Premium on Common Stock°		100
Premium on Preferred Stock†		900
Capital Stock, Common...		10,000
Capital Stock, Preferred		4,000

Computations (rounded):

$$° \text{Common:} \frac{\$10,400}{\$15,450} \times \$15,000 = \$10,100 \qquad \$10,100 - \$10,000 = \$100$$

$$† \text{Preferred:} \frac{\$5,050}{\$15,450} \times \$15,000 = \frac{4,900}{\$15,000} \qquad \$\ 4,900 - \$\ 4,000 = \$900$$

Assumption 2. The common stock is selling at 104; no market has been established for the preferred stock — apportionment on basis of fair market value of one class of shares.

Cash	15,000	
Premium on Common Stock ($4 per share)......................		400
Premium on Preferred Stock...		600
Capital Stock, Common..		10,000
Capital Stock, Preferred		4,000

Assumption 3. No current market value is determinable for either class of stock. In this case an arbitrary allocation is the only alternative. In the absence of any other logical basis the allocation may be made on the basis of relative par values. Should a market value be

established for one of the securities in the relatively near future, a correcting entry based on such value would be appropriate. The entry to record the arbitrary allocation would be:

```
Cash ...................................................................................15,000
    Premium on Common Stock° .........................................        714
    Premium on Preferred Stock† .......................................        286
    Capital Stock, Common................................................     10,000
    Capital Stock, Preferred .............................................      4,000
```

Computations:

$$°\frac{\$10,000}{\$14,000} \times \$15,000 = \$10,714 \qquad \$10,714 - \$10,000 = \$714$$

$$†\frac{\$4,000}{\$14,000} \times \$15,000 = \$ \ 4,286 \qquad \$ \ 4,286 - \$ \ 4,000 = \$286$$

Stock Warrants Issued with Debt. Debt, usually in the form of bonds payable, may be issued with warrants to purchase stock under specified conditions. Detachable warrants often trade separately from the debt instrument. Usually the sale of debt instruments with warrants results in a lower cash interest cost than otherwise. The terms of the warrants generally are such that whether or not they will ultimately be exercised depends upon the market price of the stock to which they relate. The central problem is to give appropriate accounting recognition to both the debt and the stock warrant aspects of the transaction when the bonds and warrants are issued. Accounting theory would require that a portion of the proceeds be assigned to the debt and the balance to the stock warrants (that is, contributed capital). To illustrate, assume X Company issues $100,000, 4% bonds, 10-year maturity, and that each $1,000 bond carries two stock warrants. Each stock warrant provides an option to purchase one share of common stock of X Company (par $100) at $120 per share. Current market value of the stock is $110, and immediately after issue, the warrants sold for $10 each. Cash proceeds were $97,000. One sequence of entries would be:

1. To record issuance of debt and warrants:

```
Cash.................................................................................97,000
Discount on Bonds Payable ............................................. 5,000
    Stock Warrants Outstanding (200 × $10) ........................        2,000
    Bonds Payable........................................................      100,000
```

2. To record amortization of discount (five years, straight line):

```
Bond Interest Expense..................................................... 2,500
    Discount on Bonds Payable .......................................        2,500
```

3. To record exercise of 90% of the warrants when stock is selling at $125 per share:

```
Cash.................................................................................21,600
Stock Warrants Payable ................................................... 1,800
    Capital Stock.........................................................       18,000
    Premium on Capital Stock .........................................       5,400
```

4. To record lapse of remainder of warrants:

Stock Warrants Outstanding	200	
Contributed Capital-Lapse Stock Warrants		200

In some situations convertible debt does not include detachable warrants but are convertible directly into common stock of the issuer at a specified rate, and the sales price of the debt cannot be realistically allocated between debt and contributed capital, in which case there should be no allocation to contributed capital. The increasing use of convertible debt generated *APB Opinion 14*, "Accounting for Convertible Debt and Debt Issued with Stock Purchase Warrants." The Opinion stated:

the portion of the proceeds of debt securities issued with detachable stock purchase warrants which is allocable to the warrants should be accounted for as paid-in capital. The allocation should be based on the relative fair values of the two securities at time of issuance. . . . However, when stock purchase warrants are not detachable from the debt and the debt security must be surrendered in order to exercise the warrant, the two securities taken together are substantially equivalent to convertible debt . . . no portion of the proceeds . . . should be accounted for as attributable to the conversion feature.

Noncash Sale of Stock. When a corporation issues stock as payment for services, the question of stock valuation for accounting purposes arises. The values to apply in this situation, in determination of the proceeds, are as follows, in order of preference:

1. Fair value of the services rendered.
2. Current market value of the stock issued. (Presumably this would be the same as (1), if known, since it would be strong evidence of the value of the services.)
3. Book value of the stock.
4. Par value of the stock.

The valuation should be as of the date of the contract for services rather than the date of issuance of the shares. Income tax regulations prescribe the date of issuance; however, the contract is viewed in the accounting sense as a subscription; therefore, the contract date is more appropriate.

When assets other than cash are received in payment for capital stock, the question of asset and stock valuations for accounting purposes must be resolved. In such situations accountants generally have followed these preferences, in the following order:

1. Current market value of the assets received.
2. Current market value of the stock issued.
3. Appraised value of the assets received.
4. Valuation of the assets as established by the board of directors.
5. Par or stated value of the stock issued.

The exchange of noncash assets for stock has given rise to many cases of abuse over the years through improper valuation of the assets received. Over-valued assets create an overstatement of the corporate capital—a condition frequently referred to as *watered stock*. On the other hand, undervaluation of assets creates an understatement of corporate capital giving rise to what is frequently referred to as *secret reserves*. Secret reserves also may be created by depreciating or amortizing assets over a period substantially less than their useful life.

Assessments on Shareholders

Some states permit the issuance of *assessable stock*, providing the charter includes such a provision. A stock assessment involves the collection of cash from the stockholders in proportion to the shares held without the issuance of additional stock. Stock assessments seldom are used; generally only when the corporation is in dire need of cash or when the stock originally was issued at a discount. If the stock was issued originally at a discount, the assessment (up to the amount of the discount) may be credited to the discount account. If there is no stock discount carried in the accounts, the credit is to a contributed capital account with an appropriate title such as Contributed Capital, Stock Assessments.

Incorporation of a Going Business

The owner, or owners, of a going business may decide to incorporate, or a corporation may acquire another business in exchange for shares of stock. Certain accounting problems arise in such situations, particularly with respect to (a) the values to be placed on the assets received for shares of stock and (b) proper entries to record the exchange.

In accounting for assets in the situation where the unincorporated business is selling its assets, the basic principle is to record them at their fair market value as of the date of the exchange. If this is not determinable, then the fair market value of the stock issued for the assets should be used. In many situations neither of these values can be determined; in such cases the responsible parties involved must be relied upon to establish appropriate values. It is not unusual in the case of a going business for the parties to agree to an exchange value in excess of the fair market value of the tangible assets acquired because of the recognition of goodwill. In cases where goodwill is paid for, it should be recorded as an intangible asset at the purchased price.[3]

In situations where the only change is in the form of organization;

---

[3] See Chapter 11 in respect to business combinations.

that is, the ownership and management is continuous, as where a partnership is simply incorporated, a strong case can be made for carrying forward the book values and no recognition of goodwill.

The entries to record the exchange of a going business for shares of stock will depend upon whether the original books of the acquired business will be continued or whether new books will be opened for the corporation, and any adjustments to fair market values.

If the *original books* are retained, two basic steps are required in the accounting, viz:

1. Entries must be made to revalue the assets (and any other items agreed upon) in accordance with the restated values for the new business.
2. Entries must be made to close out the old proprietary accounts and to replace them with corporate capital accounts.

If *new books* are to be opened, the old books must be closed and new books for the corporation opened. The procedure in this situation may be outlined as follows: Entries should be made on the *old books* to –

1. Revalue the assets (and any other items agreed upon) in accordance with the restated values for the new business.
2. Record the transfer of the assets.
3. Record receipt of the stock and the distribution thereof.

Entries must be made on the *new books* to –

1. Record the stock authorization.
2. Record the receipt of the assets.
3. Record issuance of the stock.

To illustrate each situation, assume the books for the AB Partnership showed the following:

Cash	$ 2,000	Accounts payable	$ 5,000
Accounts receivable	10,000	Notes payable	2,000
Allowance for doubtful accounts	(1,000)	A, capital	30,000
Inventory	21,000	B, capital	20,000
Fixed assets	40,000		
Accumulated depreciation	(15,000)		
	$ 57,000		$57,000

The XYZ Corporation is formed with 20,000 shares of capital stock authorized (par value $5 per share); 12,000 of the shares are issued in exchange for the assets, except the cash; the liabilities are assumed by the corporation. It was agreed that the inventory should be written down to $16,000 and that the accumulated depreciation should be $14,000. The book value of the remaining assets essen-

Illustration 19-3

Entries, Corporation Acquires a Partnership

Entries on New Books

Entries on Old Books

Notation: Capital stock authorized, 20,000 shares, $5.00 par value per share.

1. To record authorization of capital stock:

2. To record adjustments agreed upon:

Accumulated Depreciation	1,000	
Adjustment Account	4,000	
Inventory		5,000

3. To record goodwill (as computed in Assumption 1):

Goodwill	17,200	
Adjustment Account		17,200

4. To close Adjustment account to capital accounts:

Adjustment Account	13,200	
A, Capital		6,600
B, Capital		6,600

5. To record transfer of assets and liabilities as adjusted:

Allowance for Doubtful Accounts	1,000	
Accumulated Depreciation	14,000	
Accounts Payable	5,000	
Notes Payable	2,000	
Receivable from XY Corporation	61,200	
Accounts Receivable		10,000
Inventory		16,000
Fixed Assets		40,000
Goodwill		17,200

Accounts Receivable	10,000	
Inventory	16,000	
Fixed Assets	40,000	
Goodwill	17,200	
Allowance for Doubtful Accounts		1,000
Accumulated Depreciation		14,000
Accounts Payable		5,000
Notes Payable		2,000
Payable to AB Partnership		61,200

6. To record transfer of stock:

Payable to AB Partnership 61,200
    Capital Stock 60,000
    Premium on Capital Stock.................1,200
Stock in XY Corporation 61,200
    Receivable from XY Corporation.................61,200

7. Distribution of stock and cash:

A, Capital.................36,600
B, Capital.................26,600
    Stock in XY Corporation 61,200
    Cash.................2,000

8. To record sale of 8,000 shares at $5.10 per share:

Cash.................40,800
    Premium on Capital Stock.................800
    Capital Stock.................40,000

tially represented fair market value at the time of transfer to XYZ Corporation. The 12,000 shares and the $2,000 cash are to be divided between A and B according to their capital balances after the above adjustments. The partners had divided profits and losses equally. The remaining 8,000 shares were sold to the public at $5.10 per share.

Assumption 1. The old books are to be retained.

1. To record the adjustments:

Accumulated Depreciation	1,000	
Adjustment Account	4,000	
Inventory		5,000

2. To record goodwill:[4]

Goodwill°	17,200	
Adjustment Account		17,200

° Computation:

Value of shares exchanged (12,000 at $5.10)		$61,200
Value of net assets (after adjustment and excluding cash)		44,000
Goodwill		$17,200

3. To close Adjustment account to partners' capital accounts:

Adjustment Account	13,200	
A, Capital		6,600
B, Capital		6,600

4. Notation: Capital stock authorized, 20,000 shares, par $5 per share.

5. To record distribution of $2,000 cash and issuance of 12,000 shares of stock to the partners for the other assets (net):

A, Capital	36,600	
B, Capital	26,600	
Cash		2,000
Capital Stock		60,000
Premium on Capital Stock (12,000 shares @ $.10)		1,200

6. To record sale of 8,000 shares at $5.10 per share:

Cash	40,800	
Premium on Capital Stock		800
Capital Stock		40,000

Assumption 2. New books are opened and the old books closed (see Illustration 19–3, pages 786–87).

For tax purposes, if control is continued by the original owners (at least 80% of the voting stock), no loss or gain is recognized and the valuation basis for tax purposes remains unchanged.

---

[4] See Chapter 14 for discussion of amortization of goodwill.

QUESTIONS FOR CLASS DISCUSSION

1. Discuss the unique features of the corporate form of business noting those that have been particularly important in the rapid growth of the number of corporations in this country.

2. Explain the meaning of each of the following: total equity, contributed capital, proprietary equity, and legal capital.

3. Distinguish between public, private, domestic, foreign, open, and closed corporations.

4. What are the four basic rights of shareholders? How may one or more of these rights be withheld from the shareholder?

5. Explain each of the following: authorized capital stock, issued capital stock, unissued capital stock, outstanding capital stock, subscribed stock, and treasury stock.

6. In accounting for corporate capital why is *source* particularly important?

7. Distinguish between par and no-par stock.

8. Distinguish between common and preferred stock.

9. Explain the difference between cumulative and noncumulative stock.

10. Explain the difference between nonparticipating, partially participating, and fully participating stock.

11. Under what circumstances should stock subscriptions receivable be reported (a) as a current asset, (b) as a noncurrent asset, and (c) as a deduction in the corporate capital section of the balance sheet?

12. Explain and illustrate "secret reserves" and "watered stock."

13. How are premium on capital stock and discount on capital stock accounted for and reported?

14. Indicate the priorties for stock valuation when assets other than cash are received in payment therefor.

15. Explain stock assessments.

16. When should fair market values for assets and liabilities be used with respect to the formation of a new corporation to take over another company?

DECISION CASE 19–1

Clyde Banfield, an engineer, developed a special device to be installed in backyard swimming pools that would set off an alarm should anything fall into the water. Banfield spent his spare time over a two-year period developing and testing the device. After receiving a patent thereon, three of his friends, including a lawyer, considered plans to market the device. Accordingly, a charter was obtained which authorized 25,000 shares of $10 par value stock. Each of the four organizers contributed $1,000, and each received in return 100 shares of stock. They agreed to distribute another 500 shares to each. The remaining shares were to be held as unissued stock. Each organizer made a proposal as to how he would pay for the additional 500 shares. These individual proposals were made independently; then the group considered them as a package. The four proposals were:

BANFIELD: The patent would be turned over to the corporation as payment for the 500 shares.

LAWYER: One hundred shares to be received for legal fees already rendered during organization, 100 shares to be received as advance payment for legal retainer fees for the next three years, and the balance to be paid for in cash at par.

FRIEND NO. 3:   A small building, suitable for operations, would be turned over to the corporation in payment for 400 shares; the remainder would be paid for in cash at $7.50 per share. It was estimated that $750 would be needed for renovation. The owner estimates that the fair value of the property is "$25,000 and there is a $18,000 loan on it to be assumed by the corporation."

FRIEND NO. 4:   To pay $1,000 cash on the stock and to give a noninterest-bearing note for $4,000 "to be paid out of dividends over the next five years."

Required:

You have been engaged as an independent CPA to advise the group. Specifically, you have been asked the following questions:

1. How would the above proposals be recorded in the accounts? Indicate the basis therefor.

2. What are your recommendations for an agreement that would be equitable to each organizer, including the basis for such recommendations?

EXERCISES

Exercise 19–1

May Corporation received a charter authorizing 30,000 shares of stock, par value $10 per share. During the course of the first year 20,000 shares were sold at $12 per share. One hundred additional shares were issued in payment for legal fees. At the end of the first year, reported net income was $12,000. Dividends of $2,000 were paid as of the last day of the year. Liabilities at the year-end amounted to $9,800.

Required:

Complete the following tabulation (show calculations):

Item	Amount	Assumptions
a) Total equity	$	
b) Owners' equity	$	
c) Contributed capital	$	
d) Legal capital	$	
e) Issued capital stock	$	
f) Outstanding capital stock	$	
g) Unissued capital stock	$	
h) Treasury stock	$	

Exercise 19–2

Cade Corporation has the following stock outstanding:

Common, $50 par value. — 6,000 shares
Preferred, 6%, $100 par value. — 1,000 shares

Required:

Compute the amount of dividends payable in total and per share on the common and preferred for each separate case:

Case A: Preferred is noncumulative and nonparticipating; dividends declared, $18,000.

Case B: Preferred is cumulative and nonparticipating; three years in arrears; dividends declared, $33,000.

Case C: Preferred is noncumulative and fully participating; dividends declared, $18,000.

Case D: Preferred is noncumulative and fully participating; dividends declared, $32,000.

Case E: Preferred is cumulative and participating up to an additional 3%; three years in arrears; dividends declared, $50,000.

Case F: Preferred is cumulative and fully participating; three years in arrears; dividends declared, $41,000.

Exercise 19–3

Standard Corporation reported net earnings during four successive years as follows: $1,000; $2,000; $3,000; and $10,000.

The capital stock consisted of $60,000 common (par $20 per share) and $40,000 of 5% preferred (par $10 per share).

Required:

If net earnings in full were declared as dividends each year, determine the amount to be paid on each class of stock for each of the three years assuming:

Case A: Preferred is noncumulative and nonparticipating.
Case B: Preferred is cumulative and nonparticipating.
Case C: Preferred is noncumulative and fully participating.
Case D: Preferred is cumulative and fully participating.

Exercise 19–4

Tavis Corporation received a charter authorizing the issuance of 50,000 shares of common stock with a par value of $4 per share. Give the journal entries for the following transactions assuming (1) an unissued stock account is used and (2) the authorization is not recorded in a special account. Set up two columns so that the entries required in (1) are to the left and those for (2) to the right.

a) Authorization recorded.
b) Received subscriptions for 10,000 shares at $4.20 per share; collected 60% of the subscription price.
c) Sold 20,000 shares at $4.10; collected in full and issued shares.
d) Issued 100 shares to attorney in payment for legal fees; agreed price was $4.10 per share.
e) Issued 8,000 shares and paid cash $20,000 in payment for a building; the agreed price for the stock was $4.25 per share.
f) Collected balance on subscriptions receivable in (b).

Exercise 19–5

Roger Manufacturing Company charter authorized the issuance of 20,000 shares of no-par common stock. Give journal entries for the following transactions assuming (1) the stated value method of recording is used (the board of directors set a stated value of $6 per share) and (2) the stock is true no par (has no stated or assigned value). Set up two columns so that requirement (1) is to the left and (2) to the right.

a) Authorization recognized.
b) Received subscriptions for 5,000 shares at $7.00 per share; collected 40% of the subscription price.
c) Sold 2,000 shares at $6.80 and collected in full; shares were issued.
d) Issued 100 shares for legal services; the agreed price being $7.00 per share.
e) Issued 1,500 shares and paid $4,500 cash for some used machinery; the agreed price of the shares being $7.00.
f) Collected balance of subscriptions in (*b*).

Exercise 19–6

Anson Corporation charter authorized 2,000 shares of $50 par-value stock. A. B. Cook subscribed to 400 shares at $60 per share, paying $3,000 down, the balance to be paid $1,000 per month. After paying for three months he defaulted. Subsequently the corporation sold the stock for $55 per share. Costs incidental to the second sale amounted to 3% of the par value.

Required:

1. Give entries prior to default relative to the Cook sale.
2. Give all entries related to the default under each separate case listed below. Use Capital Stock Subscribed account.

Case A: The corporation decided to return all payments to the subscriber.
Case B: The corporation decided to issue shares equal to the amount paid.
Case C: The corporation followed the statute which provided for forfeiture.
Case D: The corporation followed the statute which provided for a lien upon resale and refund to the original subscriber.

Exercise 19–7

York Manufacturing Company has authorized 25,000 shares of common stock ($100 par value) and 10,000 shares of preferred stock ($50 par value). The company issued 1,000 shares of common and 500 of preferred for some used machinery.

Required:

For each separate situation give the entry to record the purchase of the machinery assuming (*a*) the common stock currently is selling at $110 and the preferred at $55; (*b*) there is no current market price for either class of stock; and (*c*) there is no current market price for either class of stock and the machinery has been appraised at $150,000.

Exercise 19–8

The XYZ Corporation charter authorized 1,000 shares of $100 par-value common stock and 1,000 shares of $50 preferred stock. The following "special" transactions were completed. Assume each is completely independent.

a) Sold 10 shares of common and 10 shares of preferred for a lump-sum amounting to $1,870. The common had been selling at 110 and the preferred at 60.

b) Sold a $1,000, 6% bond payable at 102 and gave as a bonus one share of preferred stock which had been selling at 60.

c) Issued 10 shares of common stock for equipment. The equipment had been appraised at $1,200; the book value shown by the seller was $1,000. No market had been established for the stock.

d) A 10% assessment was voted on both the common and preferred when 600 shares of common and 400 shares of preferred were outstanding. The assessment was paid in full.

Required:

Give the indicated journal entries.

Exercise 19–9

Nevada Corporation charter authorized 20,000 shares of common stock, no-par value, and 5,000 shares of 5%, cumulative and nonparticipating preferred stock, par value $50 per share. Stock issued to date: 10,000 shares of common sold at $130,000 and 4,000 shares of preferred stock sold at $55 per share. Subscriptions for 1,000 shares of preferred have been taken, and 30% of the purchase price of $55 has been collected. Accumulated earnings amount to $50,000 of which $20,000 has been set aside as a reserve for bond sinking fund.

Required:

Prepare the corporate capital section of the balance sheet in good form.

Exercise 19–10

Prepare in good form the corporate capital section of the balance sheet for the Olds Manufacturing Company.

Retained earnings—unappropriated	$ 30,000
Premium on common stock	10,000
Preferred stock subscribed (1,000 shares)	10,000
Preferred stock, 6%, par $10, authorized 15,000 shares	140,000 (issued)
Common stock, par $20, authorized 10,000 shares	160,000 (issued)
Stock subscriptions receivable, preferred	10,000
Reserve for contingencies	10,000
Donation of plant site	5,000
Unrealized capital increment per appraisal fixed assets	30,000
Payable to subscriber to common stock	1,000

Exercise 19–11

Model Corporation was incorporated with 250 shares of capital stock, par $100; 210 of the shares were issued for the equity in the Brown and Black partnership. The remaining 40 shares were sold at par. The balance in the accounts for the partnership were as follows:

Cash	$ 1,000	Accounts payable	$10,000
Notes receivable	3,000	Allowance for doubtful	
Accounts receivable	7,000	accounts	1,000
Inventory	6,000	Accumulated depreciation	2,000
Fixed assets	15,000	Brown, capital	10,000
		Black, capital	9,000
	$32,000		$32,000

The following adjustments were to be made prior to the exchange: decrease inventory to $4,000 and increase accumulated depreciation to $3,000. The partners shared profits equally.

Required:

1. Give entries assuming the old books are to be continued (compute goodwill assuming the fair market value of the stock issued was $100 per share).

2. Give entries assuming new books are being opened (compute goodwill assuming the fair market value of the stock issued was $100 per share).

PROBLEMS

Problem 19–1

Gary Corporation was organized under a charter authorizing 5,000 shares of 5% preferred stock, par value $10 per share, and 10,000 shares of common stock, no-par value. No stated or assigned value was identified with the common stock. During the first year the following transactions occurred:

a) Subscriptions were received for 4,000 shares of preferred stock at $11.50 per share; 40% was received as a down payment, and the balance in two equal installments.

b) 6,000 shares of common stock were sold for cash at $5 per share.

c) 1,000 shares of common stock were issued as reimbursement to promoters and 30 shares of preferred stock for legal costs of incorporation.

d) The first installment on the preferred subscriptions was collected.

e) 1,500 shares of common stock, 500 shares of preferred stock, and $25,000 cash were given as payment for a small plant that the company needed. This plant originally cost $40,000 and was depreciated on the books of the selling company to $28,000.

f) 100 shares of preferred stock sold for cash at $11.50.

g) Dividends of 5% on the preferred and $.20 per share on the common were declared and paid. No dividends are paid on subscribed stock.

Required:

1. Give journal entries to record the above transactions assuming an Unissued Preferred Stock account is not used.

2. Prepare the capital section of the balance sheet at year-end. Retained earnings, before the dividends, amounted to $13,370.

Problem 19–2

Hartford Company received a charter to conduct a manufacturing business. The authorized capital was common stock, $500,000, par value per share, $80; and 5% preferred stock, $300,000, cumulative and nonparticipating, par value per share $60. Six incorporators subscribed to 500 shares each of the common and 100 shares each of the preferred, both at par. One half of the subscription price was paid, and one half of the subscribed shares issued. Another individual purchased 1,500 shares of common and 1,500 shares of preferred stock paying $218,400 therefor. One of the incorporators purchased a going plant for $105,800 and immediately transferred it to the Hartford Company for 200 shares of common stock, 200 shares of preferred stock, and a five-year interest-bearing note for $75,000. Subsequently, an investor purchased 1,000 shares of common stock at $82 paying cash therefor. It is not anticipated that the subscriptions due from the incorporators will be called in the next year but will be in the year following. Retained earnings to date are $100,000.

Required:

1. Give all entries indicated for the Hartford Company.
2. Prepare a classified balance sheet.

Problem 19–3

The capital section of the balance sheet for the Cutter Metals Company at the end of the first fiscal year was reported as follows:

Contributed Capital:
Capital stock:
Preferred 6% cumulative, $100 par value, redeemable at $125 per share, authorized 5,000 shares,
issued 4,500 shares ....$ 450,000
Preferred stock subscribed, 150 shares ....   15,000 $ 465,000

Common stock, stated value $8 per share, authorized 1,500,000 shares, issued 1,050,000 shares
at stated value $8,400,000
Common stock subscribed, 10,000 shares   80,000   8,480,000
Other contributed capital:
Premium on preferred stock ....$ 15,000
Excess received over stated value of common
stock   21,200   36,200
Retained earnings   110,000
Total Capital $9,091,200

Required:

Prepare journal entries indicated by the above report. Assume unissued stock accounts are used and that all stock was purchased through subscriptions under terms of 60% down and 40% six months later.

Problem 19–4

Tampa Corporation received a charter authorizing capital stock consisting of (1) 5,000 shares of 6% preferred, noncumulative, par $50, and (2) 10,000 shares of no-par common stock. No stated value was assigned to the common stock. During the first year the following transactions occurred:

a) Subscriptions were received for 1,500 shares of preferred stock at $51 per share; 20% of the subscription price was collected, the balance to be paid in two equal installments.

b) 1,000 shares of no-par common stock were sold at $15 per share; the shares were issued.

c) Subscriptions were received for 600 shares of no-par common stock at $16 per share; 20% of the subscription price was collected, the balance to be paid in two equal installments.

d) The first call on the preferred stock was collected.

e) 300 shares of preferred and 100 shares of common were issued for used machines.

f) The first call on the common stock was collected.

g) 50 shares of the common stock were issued to the promoters as payment for their services, and 30 shares of preferred stock to an attorney for legal fees.

h) The second call on the preferred stock was collected, and the stock was issued.

i) The second call on the common stock was collected except for the amount due on 50 shares. The shares fully paid were issued.

j) The defaulting subscriber stated that he could not make payment in the near future. Consequently, the shares were sold at the current quoted market of $15; selling costs paid were $40. The state laws required that the corporation sell the stock under a lien.

k) Received subscriptions to 100 shares of preferred stock at $52; one half of the price was collected in cash.

Required:

1. Give entries for the above transactions (use an unissued account for the preferred stock).

2. Prepare the capital section of the balance sheet at year-end, assuming retained earnings of $15,000.

Problem 19–5

Western Corporation reported net earnings during five successive years as follows: $20,000; $30,000; $9,000; $5,000; and $50,000. The capital stock consisted of $300,000 par-value common and $200,000 par value of 5% preferred.

Required:

For each separate case prepare a table showing the amount each class of stock would receive in dividends (a) if the entire earnings were distributed each year and (b) if three fifths of the earnings were distributed each year.

Case A: Preferred stock is noncumulative and nonparticipating.
Case B: Preferred stock is cumulative and nonparticipating.
Case C: Preferred stock is cumulative and participating.

Problem 19–6

"X" Company charter authorized 5,000 shares of 6% preferred stock with a par value of $20 per share and 8,000 shares of common stock with a par value of $50 per share, all of which have been issued. In a five-year period, total dividends declared were $4,000; $40,000; $32,000; $5,000; and $40,000.

Required:

Compute the amount of dividends payable to each class of stock for each year under the following separate cases:

Case A: Preferred stock is noncumulative and nonparticipating.
Case B: Preferred stock is cumulative and nonparticipating.
Case C: Preferred stock is noncumulative and fully participating.
Case D: Preferred stock is cumulative and fully participating.
Case E: Preferred stock is cumulative and partially participating up to an additional 2%.

Problem 19–7

Folsom Company was incorporated January 1, 19A, with authorized capital of $200,000. One share of stock (par $100) was issued to each of the three incorporators, A, B, and C, in order to compensate them for promotional efforts (organization expense); five shares were given to a lawyer, D, as compensation for legal services performed in organizing the corporation.

A broker agreed to sell the remainder of the stock to investors less 100 shares of stock, which he was to receive as compensation for his services. Payments for the stock were to be made in four equal installments on the first day of March, June, September, and December.

a) On March 1 the broker reported that all the stock was subscribed for at par and the first installment paid. One hundred shares of stock were issued to the broker for his services.
b) On June 1 the second installment was paid.
c) On September 1 the third installment was paid by all subscribers except F, who had subscribed for 10 shares.
d) On December 1 the fourth and last installment was paid. F again defaulted on the payment of his installment.
e) On January 2, 19B, the treasurer of the X Company offered F's shares for sale at public auction. The shares sold to G for $800. The expenses of the sale amounted to $30. A stock certificate for the 10 shares was issued to G. After deducting expenses and interest on unpaid installments at 8%, the balance was remitted to F (lien method).

Required:

1. Give entries for the above transactions.
2. Assume that instead of offering F's shares for sale at auction, the directors elected to bring action at law against him for the amount due from him, together with interest thereon. The action was entered on February 1, 19B, for $560 covering expenses, unpaid subscriptions, and other charges. Judgment was obtained on March 1. At the end of 30 days, since the judgment remained unpaid, the directors declared all amounts previously paid by F forfeited to the corporation. Make necessary entries.

Problem 19–8

The Washington Corporation charter authorized 10,000 shares of preferred stock, par value $50, and 20,000 shares of common stock; par value $100. Subscriptions were taken from 20 individuals for a total of 9,000 shares of preferred stock at an average price of $53 per share and for 12,000 shares of common stock at par. All of the subscriptions were paid and the stock issued except the following:

A. B. Moot: 100 shares preferred, defaulted on subscription after paying 60% of the purchase price.

C. V. Word: 100 shares common, defaulted on subscription after paying 40% of the purchase price.

B. R. Ray: 500 shares of preferred, one-half paid, hence not issued (not in default.

A. K. Sams: 700 shares of common, one-half paid, hence not issued (not in default).

The stock in default was resold as follows:

a) Preferred sold at 52 with cost of sale $40.
b) Common sold at par with cost of sale $50.

Required:

1. Give all entries indicated. Assume stock in default is sold under lien.
2. Prepare the capital section of the balance sheet. Assume accumulated earnings of $12,000.

Problem 19–9

Using appropriate data from the information given below, prepare in good form the corporate capital section of a balance sheet for the Raleigh Corporation.

Stock subscriptions receivable, preferred stock...................$ 8,000	Common stock, no par, 5,000 shares authorized and outstanding............................$250,000
Reserve for bond sinking fund... 60,000	Donation of plant site............... 6,000
Unrealized capital increment per appraisal of fixed assets 45,000	Premium on preferred stock...... 12,000
Authorized 6% preferred stock, par $100 per share, cumulative and participating............... 100,000	Preferred stock subscribed........ 10,000
	Unissued preferred stock.......... 40,000
Bonds payable........................ 125,000	Payable to subscriber............... 2,000
	Discount on bonds payable....... 1,000
	Retained earnings (free) 50,000

Problem 19–10

The Topeka Corporation charter authorized the issuance of 20,000 shares of 5% cumulative, nonparticipating preferred stock, par $10 per share, and 5,000 shares of common stock, par value $20 per share. The promoters sold 9,000 shares of the preferred stock at par, and the stock was issued. In addition, subscriptions were received for an additional 1,000 shares at $10.20 per share; 10% was collected, the balance to be paid in three equal installments. Each of the three promoters took 1,000 shares of common stock (only the common stock carried voting privileges) at par paying one half in cash, and the remainder was considered to be reimbursement for promotional activities; these shares were issued at par. The remaining common stock was sold for $61,000 including one share of preferred given as a bonus for each share of common stock. Cash was collected in full on these sales, and the shares were issued. A 5% dividend on all outstanding shares was declared and subsequently paid.

Required:

1. Prepare journal entries to record the foregoing transactions.
2. Prepare the capital section of the balance sheet assuming retained earnings (after dividends) of $38,800.

Problem 19–11

Town Corporation was formed with 750 shares of capital stock authorized. The shares were to be issued as follows:

a) 200 shares for $20,400 cash.
b) 400 shares for the equity in the RT Partnership which reported the following balance sheet at "fair value."

Cash	$10,000	Notes payable	$ 6,000
Accounts receivable	13,000	R, capital	20,000
Inventory	22,000	T, capital	19,000
	$45,000		$45,000

Required:

Give entries for the acquisition of the partnership on the partnership books and on the corporation books (new books are opened) in each separate case below, assuming profits are divided equally:

Case A: The capital stock has a par value of $100, and the implied goodwill is recognized.

Case B: The capital stock is no-par value with a stated value of $80 per share. Goodwill of $1,000 is to be recognized.

Case C: The capital stock is no-par value and is to be recorded on a consideration-received basis. No goodwill is to be allowed.

Hint: Set up six columns across the top; that is, a debit and credit column for each case. List entries down the left side. Do not use unissued and subscription accounts.

Problem 19–12

Madison Corporation was formed to take over the partnership of Brown and Smith. Authorized capital stock, with a par value of $100 per share, was 10,000 shares. The balance sheet as of June 30 for Brown and Smith was as follows:

ASSETS		LIABILITIES AND PROPRIETORSHIP	
Cash	$ 10,000	Accounts payable	$ 29,000
Accounts receivable	13,000	Accrued expenses	4,000
Allowance for doubtful accounts	(1,000)	Brown, proprietorship	60,000
Prepaid expenses	1,000	Smith, proprietorship	40,000
Buildings	90,000		
Accumulated depreciation	(20,000)		
Equipment	60,000		
Accumulated depreciation	(30,000)		
Land	10,000		
	$133,000		$133,000

The partnership profits and losses were being divided 70% to Brown and 30% to Smith. Incorporators were Brown, Smith, Franks, Box, and Cane. The latter three purchased 2,000 shares each at $102. Fifteen hundred shares were to be issued to Brown and Smith, based upon their capital balances, in payment for the business (including the liabilities), except for cash $10,000 which was to be distributed pro rata (related to profit ratios) to the two partners prior to adjustments to "fair value."

The following adjustments prior to the exchange were also agreed upon:

a) Allowance for doubtful accounts to be increased to $3,000.

b) Accumulated depreciation, buildings to be decreased to $7,000.

c) Land to be revalued to $20,000.

d) Goodwill recognition based on the "adjusted values."

Required:

1. Prepare entries relative to the above data assuming the old books are to be retained.

2. Prepare entries relative to the above data assuming new books are to be opened.

chapter 20 | # Corporations — Retained Earnings

The Concept of Retained Earnings

In the prior chapter the three major categories of corporate capital were noted: contributed capital, retained earnings, and unrealized increment from revaluation of assets. Contributed capital was discussed in Chapter 19, and unrealized increment (appraisal write-ups) in Chapter 14. This chapter and the following one consider retained earnings.

Retained earnings represent the accumulated gains and losses of a corporation to date reduced by any dividend distributions to shareholders and any amounts transferred to permanent capital accounts. *Earnings* and *losses* may come from regular operations, nonrecurring transactions (such as gains on the sale of fixed assets), and corrections of prior accountings. If the accumulated losses and distributions of retained earnings exceed the accumulated gains, a deficit in retained earnings will be reported.

Retained earnings may be reduced by the following:

1. Cash and property dividends.
2. Stock dividends.
3. Treasury stock requirements (Chapter 22).
4. Recapitalizations (Chapter 21).
5. Absorption of losses.
6. Prior period adjustments.

In accounting for *total* retained earnings a number of accounts may be involved. Total retained earnings at a given date may be represented in two categories of accounts: various *appropriated* retained earnings accounts (see Chapter 21) and the *Unappropriated* Retained Earnings account. The Unappropriated Retained Earnings account usually is simply labeled *retained earnings*. Net income (or net loss) for the period is transferred to this account directly from the Income Summary account. In practice, numerous appropriated retained earnings accounts are used, most of which are discussed in the next chapter. Appropriated retained earnings accounts are created by credits; the offsetting debits are to the Unappropriated Retained Earnings account. It is important to note again that *total* retained earnings at a given date is the sum of the balances of all the retained earnings accounts, both appropriated and unappropriated.

Some variation in terminology with respect to retained earnings may be noted in practice. In prior years the term *earned surplus* was commonly used to denote what has been defined above as retained earnings. The modern terminology is much preferred since the basic concept involved is strongly implied, whereas the older term is quite inappropriate in that no "surplus" is involved. On this point the AICPA Committee on Terminology recommended:

> The use of the term *surplus* (whether standing alone or in such combinations as *capital surplus, paid-in surplus, earned surplus, appraisal surplus,* etc.) be discontinued. . . .
> The term *earned surplus* be replaced by terms which will indicate source, such as *retained income, retained earnings, accumulated earnings* or *earnings retained for use in the business.*[1]

In accounting for corporate capital a very careful distinction must be maintained between contributed capital (comprised of the capital stock and "other" contributed capital accounts) and retained earnings (see page 768). Not infrequently one observes improper accounting whereby contributed capital accounts are utilized to absorb items that should be reflected in retained earnings and vice versa. The following list represents some "other" or "additional" contributed capital items:

1. Premium and discount on capital stock.
2. Excess over stated value of no-par stock.
3. Gains on treasury stock transactions.
4. Gains and losses on conversion of the corporation's own stock.
5. Assessments on stockholders.
6. Reductions in par or stated value of the corporation's own stock.

---

[1] Committee on Terminology, AICPA, "Review and Résumé," *Accounting Terminology Bulletin No. 1* (New York, 1961), pp. 30–31.

7. Donations received by the corporation.
8. Forfeiture of stock subscriptions.
9. Certain quasi-reorganization adjustments.

It is reemphasized that in accounting for retained earnings, as with respect to other elements of corporate capital, reporting in terms of *source* is of fundamental importance.

Dividends

Dividends consist of distributions to the stockholders of a corporation in proportion to the number of shares of each class of stock held. In most cases such distributions take place at regular intervals; however, on occasion, extraordinary or interim dividends may be distributed. The term *dividends* used alone usually refers to cash dividends. Whenever dividends in any form other than cash are distributed, they should be labeled according to the form of disbursement. The following types of dividends are encountered with some frequency by accountants:

1. Cash dividends.
2. Property dividends.
3. Liability or scrip dividends.
4. Liquidating dividends.
5. Stock dividends.

Distributions to stockholders may involve:

1. The distribution of corporate assets and a decrease in *total* corporate capital as in the case of cash, property, or liquidating dividends.
2. The creation of a liability and a decrease in *total* corporate capital as in the case of liability dividends or a cash dividend declared but not yet paid.
3. No change in assets, liabilities, or *total* corporate capital, but only a change in the internal categories of corporate capital as in the case of a stock dividend.

The question always arises as to the "use" of retained earnings for dividends. Obviously, dividends are not *paid* out of retained earnings but are paid out of cash or some other asset (except in the case of a stock dividend). More appropriately, dividends generally reduce both retained earnings and assets. Cash or property dividends cannot be paid without this dual effect. As noted above, assets other than cash and even liabilities may be involved in dividend distributions. In a similar manner other elements of corporate capital may be affected rather than retained earnings. The laws of all states allow retained earnings to be used as a basis for dividends, although some states place restrictions even here, such as a provision that dividends to a particular class of shareholders in any one year may not exceed the earnings for the preceding year. Some states permit debits to certain contributed capital accounts such as stock premium as a basis for cash dividends, providing creditor interests are not jeopardized.[2] Generally statutes are much more liberal with respect to stock dividends. The statutes of the particular state are controlling; however, in the absence of any statement or information to the contrary one should assume a debit to Retained Earnings when dividend distributions are recorded.

In accounting for dividends three dates are important: (1) the date of declaration, (2) the date of record, and (3) the date of payment. Dividends must be formally *declared* by the board of directors of the corporation. Stockholders normally cannot force a dividend declaration; the courts have consistently held that dividend declaration is a matter of prudent management to be decided upon by the duly elected board of directors. Of course, the board must meet all statutory, charter, and bylaw requirements, act in good faith, and protect the interests of all parties involved. In deciding whether or not to declare a dividend (and of what type), the board of directors should consider the financial impact on the company including the adequacy of cash and retained earnings, and financial expectations for the future including corporate growth and expansion needs.

On the *date of declaration* the board formally announces the dividend declaration. In the case of a *nonrevocable* declaration, the declaration is recorded on this date by debiting Retained Earnings (or other appropriate account) and crediting Dividends Payable. In the absence of fraud or illegality,[3] the courts have held that formal announcement of the declaration of a cash, property, or liability dividend constitutes an enforceable contract (nonrevocable declaration) between the corporation and the shareholders. In view of the irrevocable aspects of this action, the liability is recorded on declaration date as noted above. In the case of stock dividends, no assets are involved, directly or indirectly, as far as the corporation is concerned; therefore, the courts generally have held that the stock dividend declaration is revocable. Consequently, no formal entry need be made on declaration date in the case of a stock dividend.[4]

The *date of record* is selected by the board and is stated in the announcement of the declaration. The date of record is the date on which the list of stockholders of record is prepared. Individuals holding stock at this date receive the dividend, irrespective of sales or

---

[2] A liquidating dividend may be involved; see subsequent section on liquidating dividends.

[3] Questions of legality should be referred to an attorney.

[4] Many accountants prefer to make a formal entry at this date. See subsequent section on stock dividends.

purchases of stock after this date. No formal dividend entry is made in the records on this date.

The *date of payment* is also determined by the board and generally is stated in the announcement of the declaration. At date of payment, in the case of cash or property dividends, the liability recorded at date of declaration is debited, and the appropriate asset account is credited. In the case of a stock dividend the distribution is recorded on this date as illustrated in a subsequent section.

Dividends on par-value stock may be stated as a certain percent of the par value, but dividends on no-par-value stock must be stated as a definite amount per share.

Cash Dividends. The usual form of distributions to stockholders involves cash dividends. The declaration must meet the preferences of the preferred stockholders and then may extend to the common stockholders. In declaring a cash dividend the board of directors should be careful that the cash position for the coming months is not jeopardized and the retained earnings balance is sufficient. The cash problem may be met, in part, by careful selection of the *payment* date. To illustrate a cash dividend, assume the following announcement is made: The board of directors of the Bass Company, at their meeting on January 20, 19A, declared a dividend of $.50 per share, payable March 20, 19A, to shareholders of record as of March 1, 19A. Assume further that 10,000 shares of stock having a par value of $10 per share are outstanding.

At date of declaration (January 20, 19A):

Retained Earnings	5,000	
Cash Dividends Payable		5,000

At date of record (March 1, 19A):

No entry. (Stockholders' record is "closed" and list of dividend recipients is prepared.)

At date of payment (March 20, 19A):

Cash Dividends Payable	5,000	
Cash		5,000

Cash Dividends Payable is reported on the balance sheet as a current liability.

Property Dividends. Corporations occasionally pay dividends in a form of assets other than cash. Such dividends are known as property dividends. The property may be in the form of securities of other companies held by the corporation, real estate, merchandise, or any other asset designated by the board of directors. Property received by the stockholder as a dividend is subject to income tax at its fair market value. Accounting practice has tended toward recording the dividend paid as a debit to retained earnings at the *book value* of the assets distributed on the basis that there has been no "two-way or arm's-length" transaction. Alternatively, there are strong theoretical arguments, buttressed by the opinions of many accountants, that the property first should be written up to fair value and then the dividend should be recorded at that value. This would provide the same result should the assets be sold for their fair value and the proceeds immediately distributed as a cash dividend. The fair value approach also resolves the critical problem of dividend preferences when preferred stock is involved. As a matter of practice, property dividends are usually in securities of *other* companies (or subsidiaries) held as an investment because of problems of divisibility of units and delivery to the stockholders when other assets are utilized.

To illustrate one sequence of entries, assume a $10,000 balance in the account "Investment in X Company Stock (at cost)" and a fair market value of $15,000. Assume further that a $15,000 property dividend is declared and that this stock is to be used for payment. The transactions may be recorded as follows:

(1) Investment in X Company Stock 5,000
    Gain on Disposal of Stock Investment   5,000

(2) Retained Earnings 15,000
    Dividends Payable (stock of X Company)   15,000

(3) Dividends Payable (stock of X Company) 15,000
    Investment in X Company Stock   15,000

Liability Dividends. Strictly speaking, any dividend involving the distribution of assets is a liability dividend between the declaration date and the date of payment. Nevertheless, liability or *scrip* dividends refer to instances where the board of directors declares a dividend and issues promissory notes, bonds, or scrip to the stockholders. In most cases scrip dividends are declared where the corporation has sufficient retained earnings to serve as a basis for dividends but is short of cash. The stockholder may hold the scrip until due date and collect the dividend or possibly may discount it to obtain immediate cash. When bonds or notes are involved, the due date and rate of interest are specified. Scrip may or may not be interest bearing and is usually payable at a specified date; however, in some cases the maturity date is indefinite, being left to the option of the issuing corporation. The immediate effect of a scrip or liability dividend is a charge to Retained Earnings and a credit to a liability account such as Scrip Dividends Payable or Notes Payable to Stockholders. Upon payment, Cash is credited and the liability account debited. A liability dividend is in effect a cash dividend with a considerable time lapsing between declaration date and payment date. Since interest on a liability dividend is not a part of the dividend itself, such payments should be charged to interest expense.

Liquidating Dividends. Distributions that constitute a *return of capital* rather than of earnings are known as liquidating dividends.

Liquidating dividends may be either intentional or unintentional. Intentional liquidating dividends occur when the board of directors knowingly declares dividends which will, in effect, represent a return of investment to the shareholders as in the case when a corporation is discontinuing operations or when there is excessive capitalization.

In mining operations companies frequently pay dividends on the basis of earnings prior to a deduction for depletion. In such cases there is an intentional liquidating dividend equal to the depletion not deducted. Stockholders should be informed of the portion of any dividend that represents a return of capital. Such dividends are not taxable to the shareholder as income but serve to reduce the cost basis of his stock.

In accounting for liquidating dividends, contributed capital rather than retained earnings should be charged since a portion of stockholder investment is being returned. Rather than debiting the capital stock accounts, as would be done if shares were being retired, other contributed capital accounts such as premium accounts may be charged. In some cases it may be desirable to set up a special account, Capital Repayment, which would be treated as a deduction in the corporate capital section of the balance sheet.

Unintentional liquidating dividends may occur when net income, and hence retained earnings, is overstated through error or omission. The omission or understatement of depreciation charges, amortizations, and depletion charges would cause retained earnings to be overstated. In such cases if reported retained earnings (prior to correction) were used in full as a basis for dividends, part of the resulting dividend would represent a return of contributed capital.

Stock Dividends. A stock dividend is a distribution of additional shares, without cost, to the shareholders in proportion to their holdings. A stock dividend may be in the form of treasury stock or unissued stock; common or preferred shares may be involved. When the stock dividend is of the same class as that held by the recipients, there is an *ordinary* stock dividend; on the other hand, when a different class of stock is involved it is a *special* stock dividend. It was noted in a preceding section that state laws are quite varied as to the availability of various classes of corporate capital for stock dividends. Some states permit the use of certain *contributed* capital, such as stock premium, and unrealized capital increment from revaluation of assets to be used as a basis for a stock dividend. All states permit retained earnings to be used as a basis for stock dividends. In the absence of information to the contrary it should be assumed that the charge is to Retained Earnings.

There are a number of circumstances and reasons that might make a stock dividend advisable. The principal reasons are:

1. To permanently retain profits in the business by *capitalizing* a

portion of the retained earnings. The effect of a stock dividend, through a charge to Retained Earnings and an offsetting credit to permanent capital, is to raise the contributed (and legal) capital.

2. To continue dividends without distributing assets needed for expansion and working capital. This action may be motivated by a desire to pacify stockholders, since many shareholders are willing to accept a stock dividend representing accumulated profits almost as readily as a cash dividend. Ordinary stock dividends are not subject to income tax; however, they do serve to reduce the cost per share to the holder.

3. To increase the number of shares outstanding, thus reducing the market price per share. An indirect effect of a stock dividend may cause increased trading of the shares in the market.

It is especially important that the exact nature of a stock dividend be understood and that it be clearly differentiated from a *stock split*. A stock dividend does not require the distribution of assets or the creation of a liability. It does not change *total* corporate capital. Rather, a stock dividend is no more than an interequity transaction. Normally, the only effect on the issuing corporation s balance sheet is a transfer of part of the retained earnings to contributed capital and an increase in the number of shares outstanding. A stock dividend does not affect the par value per share. Thus, a stock dividend does not affect the assets, liabilities, or total capital, but only the internal content of corporate capital. In contrast, a *stock split* increases the number of shares and at the same time it involves a pro rata reduction in the par value per share. A stock split is accomplished by replacing the old shares with a greater number of new shares with a smaller par value per share; total par value outstanding remains the same after a stock split. A stock split does not cause a transfer of retained earnings to contributed capital; neither is changed. In the case of stock split only the content (number of shares, but not the amount) of contributed capital is changed, whereas in a stock dividend the amount of contributed capital is changed. To illustrate, assume X Corporation has 40,000 shares of common stock, par $100, authorized, of which 10,000 shares were sold at par, and $1,600,000 in retained earnings. The effects of a stock dividend versus a stock split may be summarized:

	Prior to Change	After Stock Dividend	After Stock Split
Stock outstanding:			
10,000 shares, par $100 ......$1,000,000			
20,000 shares, par $100		$2,000,000	
20,000 shares, par $50			$1,000,000
Retained earnings.............. 1,600,000		600,000	1,600,000
Total Capital...............$2,600,000		$2,600,000	$2,600,000

Since a stock dividend involves the capitalization of retained earnings, the question arises as to the amount of retained earnings that should be capitalized (transferred to contributed capital) for the additional shares issued. The *statutory minimum* in most states is the par value.[5] In the case of preferred stock it may be the liquidating value. However, the amount transferred from retained earnings to contributed capital should not necessarily be limited to the statutory minimum. The Committee on Accounting Procedure of the American Institute of Certified Public Accountants has stated a definite position on this matter. The committee recognized two distinct situations and indicated a different accounting procedure for each, viz:

Situation 1 — A Small Stock Dividend. The proportion of additional shares is *small* in relation to the total shares previously outstanding. In this situation the *fair market value* of the additional shares should be capitalized as the committee stated:

many recipients of stock dividends look upon them as distributions of corporate earnings and usually in an amount equivalent to the fair value of the additional shares received. Furthermore, it is to be presumed that such views of recipients are materially strengthened in those instances, which are by far the most numerous, where the issuances are so small in comparison with the shares previously outstanding that they do not have any apparent effect upon the share market price and, consequently, the market value of the shares previously held remains substantially unchanged. The committee therefore believes that where these circumstances exist the corporation should in the public interest account for the transaction by transferring from earned surplus (retained earnings) to the category of permanent capitalization . . . an amount equal to the fair value of the additional shares issued.[6]

Situation 2 — A Large Stock Dividend. The proportion of additional shares is *large* in relation to the total shares previously outstanding. In this situation the legal minimum (generally par value) should be capitalized, as the committee stated:

Where the number of additional shares issued as a stock dividend is so great that it has, or may reasonably be expected to have, the effect of materially reducing the share market value, the committee believes that the implications and possible constructions discussed in the preceding paragraph are not likely to exist. . . . Consequently, the committee considers that under such circumstances there is no need to capitalize earned surplus (retained earnings), other than to the extent occasioned by legal requirements.[7]

---

[5] Most of the states specify as the legal minimum either the par value, stated value, or average price per share originally paid in.

[6] Committee on Accounting Procedure, AICPA, "Restatement and Revision of Accounting Research Bulletins," *Accounting Research Bulletin No. 43* (New York, 1961), p. 51. (Words in parentheses supplied.)

[7] Ibid., p. 52. (Words in parentheses supplied.)

The dividing line between the two situations described above (a small versus a large stock dividend) is rather difficult to draw. The significant distinction is the effect of the additional shares on the market price rather than the exact proportion between the new and old shares. The market price per share will depend upon a number of factors such as the economic characteristics of the company itself, the vagaries of the market, the general condition of the economy, and the number of additional shares issued. In considering this problem the committee further stated: "It would appear that there would be few instances involving the issuance of additional shares of less than, say, 20% or 25% of the number previously outstanding where the effect would not be such as to call for the procedure" for a small stock dividend outlined above as Situation 1.

From the above discussion it can be seen that there is a minimum amount per share (the legal amount required) that should be capitalized in some situations and a preferred higher amount per share (fair market value) that should be capitalized in other situations. In the past many corporate managements have elected to capitalize an amount between these two extremes, frequently using the *average* contributed capital per share on the old shares. It may be noted further that the above discussions are particularly applicable to *ordinary* stock dividends. In the case of special stock dividends, such as a stock dividend in preferred stock issued to common shareholders, theoretical considerations would suggest that fair market value be capitalized.

In order to illustrate several situations involving stock dividends assume the following:

```
Preferred stock, par value $20, 10,000 shares author-
    ized, 5,000 shares outstanding..........................$100,000
Common stock, par value $10, 20,000 shares author-
    ized, 10,000 shares outstanding........................  100,000
Premium on preferred stock ...................................   10,000
Premium on common stock...................................   15,000
Retained earnings...............................................  150,000
        Total Capital.............................................              $375,000

Market price per share prior to stock dividend:
    Preferred.......................................................      25
    Common .......................................................      11
```

Illustration 1. A 10% common stock dividend is declared on the common stock. The market price per share does not change perceptibly — a small stock dividend.

1. At date of declaration:

```
Retained Earnings (1,000 shares at market of $11)...................11,000
    Common Stock Dividends Payable (1,000 shares at par).....          10,000
    Premium on Common Stock (1,000 shares at $1) ...............           1,000
```

2. At date of payment (issuance):

```
Common Stock Dividends Payable...................................10,000
    Common Stock (1,000 shares).........................................      10,000
```

Illustration 2. A 50% common stock dividend is declared on the common stock. The market value per share reduces to $7.50 — a large stock dividend.

1. At date of declaration:

```
Retained Earnings (5,000 shares at par $10)............................50,000
    Common Stock Dividends Payable................................      50,000
```

2. At date of payment (issuance):

```
Common Stock Dividends Payable...................................50,000
    Common Stock (5,000 shares).........................................      50,000
```

Illustration 3. A 50% common stock dividend is declared on the common stock. The market value per share reduces to $7.50, the management decides to capitalize on the basis of the "average contributed."

1. At date of declaration:

```
Retained Earnings (5,000 shares at $11.50) ............................57,500
    Common Stock Dividends Payable (5,000 shares at par).....      50,000
    Premium on Common Stock .........................................      7,500
       ($100,000 + $15,000 ÷ 10,000 = $11.50)
```

2. At date of payment (issuance):

```
Common Stock Dividends Payable...................................50,000
    Common Stock (5,000 shares).........................................      50,000
```

Illustration 4. A common stock dividend (20% of the shares outstanding) is declared on both common and preferred stock. The market price per share does not change materially — a small stock dividend.

1. At date of declaration:

```
Retained Earnings (3,000 shares at market of $11)...................33,000
    Premium on Common Stock (3,000 shares at $1) ..............      3,000
    Common Stock Dividends Payable (3,000 shares at par).....      30,000
       (10,000 + 5,000 × 20% = 3,000 shares)
```

2. At date of payment (issuance):

```
Common Stock Dividends Payable...................................30,000
    Common Stock (3,000 shares).........................................      30,000
```

Illustration 5. A common stock dividend is declared whereby each common stock shareholder shall receive one share of common stock for each five shares held. The market price per share does not change significantly — a small stock dividend. Assume further that in view of the ratio of new shares to old shares it is necessary that 1,350 *fractional share warrants* (see Chapter 22, stock rights) be issued to various shareholders calling for 270 shares (1,350 ÷ 5). Each fractional share warrant is for one fifth of a share of stock. In order to obtain a share, five such warrants have to be presented; fractional share warrants are commonly bought and sold.

1. At date of declaration:

Retained Earnings (2,000 shares at market of $11)...................22,000
    Common Stock Dividends Payable (1,730 shares at par)....... 17,300
    Fractional Share Warrants Outstanding, Common (1,350
      warrants requiring 270 shares at par) 2,700
    Premium on Common Stock (2,000 shares at $1) 2,000

2. At date of payment (issuance):

Common Stock Dividends Payable.......................................17,300
    Common Stock (1,730 shares)....................................... 17,300

Assuming all warrants are turned in:

Fractional Share Warrants Outstanding, Common.................. 2,700
    Common Stock (270 shares)... 2,700

Assuming 90% of the warrants are turned in and the remainder lapse:

Fractional Share Warrants Outstanding, Common.................. 2,700
    Common Stock (243 shares at par)................................. 2,430
    Contributed Capital, from Lapse of Stock Warrants (27
      shares)[*] 270

[*] An alternative would be to reverse the $270.

If a balance sheet is prepared between the date of declaration and date of issuance of a stock dividend, the stock dividends payable and the warrants outstanding would be reported in the corporate capital section of the balance sheet as follows:

CAPITAL

Contributed Capital:		
Capital stock:		
Preferred stock, $20 par value, 10,000 shares authorized, 5,000 shares outstanding........................		$100,000
Common stock, $10 par value, 20,000 shares authorized, 10,000 shares outstanding........................	$100,000	
Stock dividend to be issued, 2,000 shares on (date) including fractional share warrants for 270 shares	20,000	120,000
Total Capital Stock......................................		$220,000
Other contributed capital:		
Premium on preferred stock ....$	10,000	
Premium on Common stock....................................	17,000	27,000
Total Contributed Capital..............................		$247,000
Retained Earnings:		
Unappropriated...		128,000
Total Capital..		$375,000

It will be observed that stock dividends payable are reported as an element of capital, whereas cash or property dividends payable are reported as current liabilities. There are three reasons for reporting stock dividends payable (and warrants payable) as an element of corporate capital. First, there is no obligation on the part of the corporation to distribute assets. Second, a stock dividend declaration is revocable up to date of issuance of the stock. Third, there is a formally announced intent to issue capital stock of a specific number of shares and shares must be reserved for this purpose.

If *treasury stock* is used for stock dividends, the procedures for regular stock dividends apply. In the case of a "small" dividend the amount capitalized should be the maximum (current fair market value). In the case of a "large" stock dividend at least the legal minimum (par) should be capitalized.

To illustrate a stock dividend involving treasury stock, assume a corporation issued 6,000 shares of $20 par-value common stock at $22 per share of which 5,000 shares are currently outstanding and 1,000 shares are held as treasury stock acquired (and recorded) at $21 per share. The board of directors declared a stock dividend whereby one share of treasury stock shall be transferred for each five shares of stock held. The current market value per share remained essentially unchanged at $23 per share. The indicated entry assuming a small stock dividend is:[8]

```
Retained Earnings (1,000 shares at market of $23)..................23,000
    Treasury Stock (1,000 shares at cost of $21) .....................     21,000
    Contributed Capital, from Treasury Stock Dividend..........      2,000
```

Accumulated Dividends on Preferred Stock

Dividends in arrears on cumulative preferred stock, prior to formal declaration of such dividends, do not constitute a liability to the corporation. However, full disclosure requires that cumulative dividends in arrears be reported on the balance sheet. The preferable method of reporting is to include a footnote on the balance sheet indicating the years and amounts relative to arrearages. An alternative method is to report the dividends in arrears separately from the unappropriated retained earnings figure. For example, retained earnings may be reported as follows:[9]

```
Retained earnings:
    Amount equal to preferred stock dividends in arrears ............$10,000
    Unappropriated balance ...................................................  20,000   $30,000
```

---

[8] Any related restriction on retained earnings should be reversed.

[9] *APB Opinion 10* recommends that "the liquidation preference of the stock be disclosed in the equity section of the balance sheet in the aggregate, either parenthetically or 'in short' rather than on a per share basis or by disclosure in notes" and that amounts in arrearages in cumulative preferred also should be disclosed.

Legality of Dividends

The availability of retained earnings and certain elements of contributed capital as a basis for dividends was mentioned in the first section of this chapter. To attempt to define or comprehend just what elements of corporate capital are available as a basis for cash, property, and stock dividends would require a minute and detailed study of the laws of each of the states. Manifestly, such a study is far beyond the scope of this text; further, a question of law rather than accounting is involved. There are at least two limitations which appear uniform, namely, that dividends may not be paid from *legal capital* (usually represented by the capital stock accounts; see Chapter 19), and that unappropriated retained earnings are available for dividends.[10] Between these two limits there are numerous variations, depending upon the respective state statutes, some of which are:

1. All contributed capital, other than legal capital, is available for dividends.
2. Specified items of contributed capital, other than legal capital, are available for dividends.
3. Contributed capital, other than legal capital, is available for dividends on preferred stock but not on common stock.
4. Unrealized capital increment from revaluation of assets is not available for dividends.
5. Unrealized capital increment from revaluation of assets is available for stock dividends only.
6. Capital losses and deficits must be restored before payment of any dividends.
7. Dividends from retained earnings must not reduce such balance below the cost of treasury stock held.

The accountant has a definite responsibility in circumstances where the propriety and legality of dividends is at issue to (a) insure that such matters are passed upon by an attorney and (b) ascertain that the financial statements fully disclose all known and material facts concerning such dividends.

Unrealized Capital Increment from Revaluation of Assets

The revaluation of fixed assets and the resulting unrealized capital increment (appraisal increase) were discussed in Chapter 13. Since the unrealized increment is essentially different from other elements of corporate capital, it must be treated as a separate and fundamentally different item. Unrealized increment from revaluation of assets is

---

[10] Some states permit the payment of dividends from current earnings even though the corporation has an accumulated deficit in retained earnings.

not derived from any transaction or contractual obligation since it represents the difference between the appraised value and the book value of the particular assets involved. This increase in value may be due to qualitative or quantitative causes. *Qualitative* appreciation usually is referred to as "unrealized increment" and results from causes extraneous to the efforts of the business unit, such as economic and social changes. For example, the construction of a power dam may enhance significantly the value of a nearby plant site; or a decrease in the purchasing power of money in periods of rising prices may cause the present replacement value of the plant and equipment to be valued at a dollar figure in excess of its book value. (See Chapter 23 for a discussion of the basic problems of price-level changes.)

Quantitative appreciation results from the discovery of resources unknown at time of purchase. A "wildcat" oil well drilled at a cost of $100,000 may result in the discovery of a new oil field on the property having a potential oil recovery value of $5 million. Both qualitative and quantitative appreciation if placed on the books and shown on the balance sheet should be reflected under an appropriate caption in the capital section such as "unrealized appreciation from revaluation of (asset)." Whatever the title, it is important that if reported, a caption separate and apart from contributed capital and retained earnings be set up in the capital section of the balance sheet. In addition, other information pertinent to full disclosure should be included as a footnote to the balance sheet.

One type of adjustment which should not be reflected under this caption results from past errors in distinguishing between capital and revenue expenditures. Asset restatements resulting from excessive depreciation charges and the charging of capital items to operations during past periods should be accounted for as adjustments of prior accounting and not as unrealized increments. The difficulty, of course, is in determining what portion of an asset revaluation is due to past errors in accounting and what part is due to qualitative and/or quantitative appreciation.

Unrealized capital increment accounts should never be charged with items other than those which relate directly to the identical property which was the original source of the unearned appreciation. Any subsequent write-down of the same property may be made against the related unrealized capital increment account; but the writing down of other assets against nonrelated unrealized increment accounts is obviously improper. Unrealized capital increment balances are not available for absorbing losses since they represent wholly unrealized amounts and can be realized only through recovery from future income through depreciation charges on the full appraised value or through sale. Cash or stock dividends, then, should not be based upon unrealized capital increment balances unless the statutes specifically permit such action, in which case the accountant has a responsibility for full disclosure.

QUESTIONS FOR CLASS DISCUSSION

1. It has been said that retained earnings is the meeting place of the income statement and the balance sheet. Explain what is implied.

2. What are the principal sources and dispositions of retained earnings?

3. Differentiate between total retained earnings and the balance of the Retained Earnings account.

4. What is the position of the accounting profession relative to use of the word *surplus?* What is the basis for this position?

5. What are the three important dates relative to accounting for dividends? Explain the importance of each.

6. Distinguish between cash dividends, property dividends, and liability dividends.

7. What is a liquidating dividend? What are the responsibilities of the accountant with respect to such dividends?

8. Explain the difference between intentional and unintentional liquidating dividends.

9. Basically what is the difference between a dividend involving the distribution of assets and a stock dividend?

10. Distinguish between a stock dividend and a stock split.

11. Explain the two distinct situations that determine the method of accounting for stock dividends.

12. Explain how cash dividends payable and stock dividends payable should be reported on the balance sheet. Why are they reported in a different manner?

13. What is the proper method of reporting dividends in arrears on cumulative preferred stock?

14. What elements of capital are available for dividends?

15. What is meant by "unrealized capital increment"? What are the primary reporting problems?

DECISION CASE 20-1

Bland Plastics, Incorporated, was formed in 1964 to manufacture a fairly wide range of plastic products from three basic components. The company was originally owned by 23 shareholders; however, five years after formation the capital structure was expanded considerably at which time preferred stock was issued for the first time. At the present time there are over 250 holders of preferred and common stock. The preferred stock is nonvoting, cumulative 6% stock. The company had experienced a very substantial growth in business over the years. This growth was due to two principal factors: (*a*) the dynamic management and (*b*) geographical location. The firm served a rapidly expanding area with relatively few regionally situated competitors.

The last audited balance sheet showed the following (summarized):

Balance Sheet, December 31, 1971

Cash	$ 11,000
Other current assets	76,000
Investment in K Company stock (at cost)	30,000
Plant and equipment (net)	310,000
Intangible assets	15,000
Other assets	8,000
	$450,000
Current liabilities	$ 38,000
Long-term loans	60,000
Preferred stock, par value $100°	50,000
Common stock, no-par value (10,000 shares)°	157,000
Premium on preferred stock	2,000
Retained earnings	18,000
Profits invested in plant	125,000
	$450,000

°Authorized shares — preferred, 2,000; common, 20,000.

The board of directors had not declared a dividend since organization; instead, the profits were used "to expand the company." This decision was based on the facts that the original capital was small and that there was the desire to limit the number of shareholders. At the present time the common stock is held by slightly fewer than 50 individuals. Each of these individuals also owns preferred shares; the total of their holdings approximate 46% of the outstanding preferred. The preferred was issued at the time of the expansion of capital.

The board of directors had been planning to declare a dividend during the early part of 1972, payable June 30. However, the cash position as shown by the balance sheet had raised serious doubts as to the advisability of a dividend in 1972. The president had explained that "most of the cash was temporarily tied up in inventory and plant."

The company had a chief accountant but no controller. The board had relied on an outside CPA for advice concerning financial management. The CPA was asked to advise with respect to the contemplated dividend declaration. Four of the seven members of the board felt very strongly that "some kind of a dividend must be declared so that all shareholders will get something."

Required:

You have been asked to analyze the situation and make whatever dividend proposals that appear to be worthy of consideration by the board. Present figures to support your recommendations in a form suitable for consideration by the board in reaching a decision. Provide the basis for your proposals and indicate any preferences that you may have.

EXERCISES

Exercise 20-1

Starnes Corporation's books on January 1 showed the following balances (summarized):

Cash	$ 25,000	Current liabilities	$ 20,000
Other current assets	25,000	Long-term liabilities	60,000
Fixed assets (net)	250,000	Capital stock, 2,000 shares	200,000
Other assets	50,000	Premium	10,000
		Retained earnings	60,000
	$350,000		$350,000

The board of directors is considering a cash dividend, and you have been requested to provide certain assistance as the independent CPA. The following matters have been referred to you:
1. What is the maximum amount of dividends that can be paid? Explain.
2. What amount of dividends would you recommend based upon the data from the accounts? Explain.
3. What entries would be made assuming a $15,000 dividend is declared with the following dates: (*a*) January 20, declaration date; (*b*) February 15, date of record; and (*c*) March 15, date of payment.
4. Assuming a balance sheet is prepared between declaration date and payment date, how would the dividend declaration be reported?

Exercise 20–2

Summers Manufacturing Corporation had outstanding 11,500 shares of capital stock having a par value of $10 per share. The shares were held by 10 stockholders, each having an equal number of shares. The Retained Earnings account showed a balance of $40,000, although the company was short of cash. The company owned 1,000 shares of stock in the Green Company that had been purchased at $8,000; the current market value was $11 per share. The board of directors of the Summers Corporation declared a dividend of $2 per share "to be paid with Green stock within 30 days after declaration date and scrip to be issued for the difference. The scrip will be payable at the end of 12 months from issue date and will earn 4% interest per annum."

Required:
1. Give all entries indicated through date of payment of the scrip.
2. What items related to the dividend declaration would be reported on the interim balance sheets prior to payment of the scrip?

Exercise 20–3

The board of directors of the Fast Mining Company declared a dividend. There were 50 stockholders, each holding 300 shares of stock having a par value of $50 per share. The laws of the state provide that "dividends may be paid equal to accumulated profits prior to depletion charges." Earnings account showed a balance of $12,000; accumulated depletion charges amounted to $10,000. The dividend was $2 per share payable within 60 days of declaration date.

Required:
1. What entries are indicated?
2. What special notification, if any, should be given the shareholders?
3. What items related to the dividend declaration would be reported on the balance sheet between declaration date and payment date?

Exercise 20-4

The records of the Davidson Corporation showed the following balances:

Capital stock authorized, par $100 ....$300,000
Capital stock unissued.. 120,000
Premium on stock.. 10,800
Retained earnings.. 60,000

On June 1 the board of directors declared a stock dividend (from the un-issued stock) of one additional share for each five shares outstanding; issue date September 1. The market value of the stock prior to the declaration was $110 per share.

Required:

1. Give entries in parallel columns for the stock dividend assuming (*a*) the fair market value is capitalized, (*b*) the par value is capitalized, and (*c*) average paid in is capitalized.
2. Explain when each should be utilized.

Exercise 20-5

Assume the Starnes Corporation, whose data are given in Exercise 20-1, declared a 15% stock dividend instead of the cash dividend (same dates prevailing); currently the stock is selling at $108.

Required:

1. Compute three alternative amounts that might be capitalized.
2. What entries would be made in the accounts? Give basis for the amount capitalized.
3. Assuming a balance sheet is prepared between declaration date and payment date, how would the dividend declaration be reported?

Exercise 20-6

The books of Fast Sales Corporation showed the following:

Preferred stock, 6% cumulative, nonparticipating, $20 par.........$240,000
Common stock, no-par value, 60,000 shares issued 360,000
Premium on preferred stock.................................... 25,000
Treasury stock (common 2,000 shares at cost)......................... 16,000
Retained earnings.. 100,000

The preferred stock has dividends in arrears for the past year. The board of directors has just passed the following resolution: "The current year dividend shall be 6% on the preferred and $.40 per share on the common; the dividends in arrears shall be paid by issuing one share of treasury stock for each 10 shares of preferred stock held."

Required:

Give all entries indicated.

Exercise 20-7

Orleans Corporation has been in operation for over 40 years. The corporation has 20,000 shares of $100 par-value capital stock authorized of which

12,000 shares are outstanding. There are 105 shareholders. Most of the growth of the corporation has been "out of earnings." In view of a large balance in retained earnings the board of directors declared a 20% stock dividend, to be capitalized at "the average paid in per share." The accounts showed the following balances prior to the dividend:

Capital stock outstanding $1,200,000	
Paid-in capital in excess of par......................... 90,000	
Retained earnings.. 700,000	

The shares were to be distributed within six months of declaration date. Upon issuance, fractional share warrants were issued for 600 shares. Subsequently, 90% of the warrants were exercised and 10% lapsed.

Required:

Give all entries indicated.

PROBLEMS

Problem 20-1

The balance sheet for the Northern Manufacturing Company is shown below in summary:

Cash ....$ 18,000		Current liabilities.................$ 26,000
Receivables 36,000		Bonds payable 50,000
Inventory 110,000		Preferred stock.................... 100,000
Investments – 7,000 shares		Common stock (3,000
of Taylor stock at cost...... 56,000		shares) 330,000
Fixed assets (net) 280,000		Premium on preferred 5,000
Other assets....................... 86,000		Retained earnings 75,000
$586,000		$586,000

The preferred stock is 5%, $100 par value, and cumulative. Dividends have not been paid for the past three years. The common stock is no-par value. The board of directors has just passed a dividend declaration to the effect that "two months after declaration date the dividends in arrears shall be paid in the form of a property dividend by transferring within 60 days one share of Taylor stock for each share of preferred stock. The current year's dividend on the preferred shall be paid in cash. A dividend of $13 per share on the common is hereby declared. This dividend shall be paid as follows: $5 per share in cash within 60 days and the balance in scrip due in nine months. The scrip shall earn 6% interest per annum from the declaration date."

Stock warrants were issued for 10 shares of Taylor stock. Warrants for two shares lapsed; the balance was exercised.

Required:

1. Give all entries required by the dividend provisions.
2. Prepare the capital section of the balance sheet prior to the dividend payment date (one month after declaration date). Assume a reported net income of $17,000 (including interest on scrip).

3. What items related to the dividend declaration will be reported on the balance sheet referred to in (2) other than those in the capital section?

Problem 20–2

Dayton Corporation's board of directors declared a stock dividend whereby "each holder of common stock shall receive one share of common for each five shares held, and each holder of preferred stock shall receive one share of common for each five shares held. The average originally paid in per share of common shall be capitalized." At this date the records of the corporation showed:

> Preferred stock, 5%, $10 par value, authorized.............$150,000
> Preferred stock, 5%, $10 par value, unissued............... 30,000
> Common stock, no par, authorized 200,000 shares
> Common stock, no par, issued 120,000 shares 360,000
> Premium on preferred stock.....................................   5,000
> Contributed capital — excess paid in on common
>   stock over stated value   24,000
> Retained earnings 160,000

Upon issuance stock warrants were distributed for 500 shares of stock; subsequently 450 of the warrants were exercised. The remaining warrants are outstanding to date.

Required:

1. Give entries to record the dividend declaration and payment.

2. Prepare the capital section of the balance sheet after giving effect to the entries in (1) above.

Problem 20–3

The accounts for the Cherokee Corporation showed the following balances:

> Assets..$600,000
> Liabilities 90,000
> Capital:
> Preferred stock, 5%, par value $20, 10,000 shares
>   authorized... 180,000
> Common stock, no-par value, assigned value $10,
>   authorized 20,000 shares, issued 15,000 shares...... 150,000
> Premium on preferred   10,000
> Excess of paid-in over assigned value on common
>   stock...   30,000
> Retained earnings 140,000

During the subsequent year the following sequential transactions were recorded relating to the capital accounts:

a) A stock dividend was declared whereby each holder of 10 preferred shares would receive one share of common stock, and each holder of 6 shares of common stock would receive one share of common. The board directed that the "average originally paid in per share of common" be capitalized.

b) In issuing the stock dividend, warrants were issued for 150 shares.

c) All of the warrants were redeemed except those for 10 shares which remained outstanding.

d) A 5% cash dividend on the preferred shares and $.50 per share on the common shares were declared and paid.

e) Reported net income was $30,000.

Required:

1. Prepare journal entries for the above transactions.
2. Prepare the capital section of the balance sheet.

Problem 20–4

The capital accounts for the Reno Corporation showed the following balances at year-end:

Current assets ....$	185,000	Current liabilities ....$	80,000
Fixed assets	980,000	Long-term liabilities..........	100,000
Other assets	260,000	Preferred stock	300,000
Investment in X		Common stock..................	800,000
Corporation stock		Premium on preferred.......	9,000
(5,000 shares at cost) ...	5,000	Retained earnings.............	141,000
	$1,430,000		$1,430,000

The preferred stock is 5%, $100 par value, cumulative. One million shares of no-par-value common stock were authorized. The average selling price was $1 per share. No dividends have been declared for the preceding year.

During the subsequent two years the following transactions affected capital:

19A:

a) Declared and immediately issued one share of X Corporation stock to each shareholder of preferred stock as a dividend. The current market value of $1.30 per share to be recognized in the dividend. In addition, $3.70 per share cash dividend was paid the preferred.

b) Declared and immediately issued scrip dividends amounting to 5% on the preferred and $.10 per share on the common stock.

c) Reported net income $110,000 including gain or loss on X Corporation stock.

19B:

d) Paid the scrip dividends including 5% per annum interest thereon.

e) Declared a stock dividend, payable in common stock to holders of both preferred and common stock. The preferred holders to receive "value" equivalent to 5%, and the common holders to receive one share for each five shares held. The value and the amount capitalized per share shall be the fair market value. The current price per share on the common stock is $1.25.

f) Issued the stock dividend except for 800 shares for which stock warrants were issued; of these, 100 warrants related to the preferred.

g) Warrants for 600 shares were honored; of these, 90 warrants related to preferred. The remaining warrants are outstanding.

h) Reported net income $187,000.

Required:

1. Prepare journal entries for each of the foregoing transactions (round to even dollars).

2. Prepare the capital section of the balance sheet after giving recognition to the foregoing transactions.

Problem 20-5

The Carter Manufacturing Company was organized with an authorization for 50,000 shares of $10 par-value stock. During the first five years of operations the following transactions affected corporate capital:

19A:

a) Received subscriptions for 20,000 shares of stock at $11 per share; 50% was collected as a downpayment.

b) Balance was collected on all shares except 1,500.

c) Reported net income was $3,800.

19B:

d) Balance was collected on 1,400 shares. Subscriptions for the other 100 shares were defaulted. The subscriber was refunded the amount paid in less 20% of the purchase price per agreement.

e) One original subscriber to 200 shares was badly in need of cash; the corporation refunded the full amount and received the stock. (Record treasury stock at cost.)

f) Reported net income, $6,300.

19C:

g) Declared cash dividend amounting to 3% on shares outstanding.

h) Reported net income, $14,300.

19D:

i) Sold 5,000 shares of stock at $10; collected cash and issued stock.

j) Reported net income, $18,800.

19E:

k) Declared a 10% stock dividend. The board of directors directed that the "average paid in to date per share" be capitalized.

l) Issued the stock dividend and stock warrants for 260 of the shares issued.

m) Reported net income, $12,700.

n) Stock warrants for 120 shares received and stock issued; balance lapsed.

o) Declared a 4% dividend — one half payable in cash, balance in scrip payable in six months with interest at 5% per annum.

Required:

1. Prepare entries for the foregoing transactions.

2. Prepare the capital section of the balance sheet after giving effect to the foregoing entries.

Problem 20-6

The Roz Corporation, a client, is considering the authorization of a 5% common stock dividend to common stockholders. The financial vice president of the corporation wishes to discuss the accounting implications of such an authorization with you before the next meeting of the board of directors.

Required:

1. The first topic he wishes to discuss is the nature of the stock dividend to the recipient.

a) Discuss the case *for* considering the stock dividend as income to the recipient.

b) Discuss the case *against* considering the stock dividend as income to the recipient.

2. The other topic for discussion is the propriety of issuing the stock dividend to all "stockholders of record" or to "stockholders of record exclusive of shares held in the name of the corporation as treasury stock."

a) Discuss the case *for* issuing stock dividends on treasury shares.

b) Discuss the case *against* issuing stock dividends on treasury shares.

3. These topics raise several issues about the nature of the accounting entity and the equities for which it is accountable. Of the theories which explain accounting equities, describe the

a) Proprietary theory.
b) Entity theory.
c) Residual equity theory.
d) Fund theory.

(*Hint:* Refer to Chapter 1.)

(AICPA adapted).

chapter **21**

Corporations — Appropriations of Retained Earnings, Reporting Retained Earnings; Quasi-Reorganization

PART A—APPROPRIATIONS OF RETAINED EARNINGS

Retained Earnings and Reserves

In view of certain terminology used in past years (and continuing to some extent at the present time), consideration of retained earnings necessitates a discussion of the term *reserves*. No other term appears to have been accorded greater variation of meaning and use in accounting. Reserves have been set up in so many different ways and handled so differently in accounting practice that the profession deemed it essential to take a definite position with respect to the proper use of the term (No. 5 below). The term *reserves* has been used in accounting in the five manners set forth below:

1. *Valuation or asset reduction reserves.* Asset valuation accounts

825

entitled Reserve for Depreciation, Reserve for Bad Debts, and Reserve to Reduce Inventory to Lower of Cost or Market were in common usage even in the 1940s. These accounts were deducted on the balance sheet from the related asset accounts. In recent years accountants generally have ceased using such terminology; instead more descriptive titles are employed, such as Accumulated Depreciation, Allowance for Doubtful Accounts, and Allowance to Reduce Inventory to Lower of Cost or Market.

2. *Liability reserves.* Where the amount of a liability was not definitely ascertainable at the statement date, the estimated amount thereof often was set up as a credit to a reserve account, such as the account, Reserve for Income Taxes. The account was then reported as a liability. In recent years accountants have used more appropriate account titles for liabilities of this type, such as Estimated Income Taxes Payable.

3. *Contingent liability reserves.* A reserve account was used to give recognition in the accounts to an obligation which it was thought would probably arise as a result of certain events which had already occurred; although final determination of whether or not a liability existed had not yet been made. Since the amount of the possible loss from the contingency could seldom be estimated at the statement date with reasonable accuracy, the offsetting charge in setting up this reserve was to Retained Earnings. For example, account titles such as Reserve for Contingencies were credited for this purpose. Thoughtful accountants have come to recognize the necessity for more descriptive account titles for recognizing such contingent liabilities in the accounts.

4. *Equalization or budgetary reserves.* Certain costs and expenses which clearly are applicable to the production (or revenue) of a specific period may not be determined precisely as to amount nor paid until a subsequent period. Accounting practice recognizes the validity and soundness of recording such expenses based on estimates by a charge to expense or cost and a credit to an account which is subsequently debited when the payment is made. For example, a plant whose production is seasonal may defer all but the most necessary repairs to the slack season. Without a procedure for accruing repair costs, months of high production would be charged with low repair expense, while months of low production would be charged with the high repair costs actually incurred during those months when the operational and related events transpired which created the need for repairs. To avoid a possible inequitable and inaccurate distribution of repair costs, the total repair expense for the year may be estimated in advance, then each month's revenue is charged with an equitable proportion of this total, the offsetting credit being to a temporary account such as Deferred Repairs. When repair costs are actually

paid or incurred, they are debited to the Deferred Repairs. Where such expense is estimated for a period of one year and apportioned on a realistic basis (i.e., related to causative factors) to each month, any balance in the account at the end of the year (such as Deferred Repairs) is closed to the Income Summary account as an adjustment to the annual repair cost, or may be carried forward for any repairs scheduled but not completed before the end of the year. Deferred Repairs and similar accounts are properly reported on the balance sheet under the current liability caption. In past years the practice was to use an account entitled Reserve for Repairs rather than Deferred Repairs. Thoughtful accountants have discontinued use of the "reserve" terminology.[1] These procedures are acceptable when there is a sound accrual basis for allocating the item over time; the use of these procedures for "income-leveling" purposes definitely is unacceptable.

5. *Surplus reserves.* During the period when retained earnings was labeled "earned surplus," appropriations of such earnings were credited to reserve accounts such as Reserve for Bond Sinking Fund, Reserve for Contingencies, and Reserve for Plant Expansion. The latter terminology has been continued in use; however, modern terminology prefers "Retained Earnings" over "Earned Surplus" and "Appropriation of Retained Earnings for . . ." over "Reserve for . . .".

Significantly, the Committee on Terminology of the AICPA took the definite position that usage of the term *reserve* if used in accounting should be restricted to the *fifth* concept discussed above.[2] This chapter focuses on this aspect of reserves; other chapters discuss the other four concepts outlined above.

Where a so-called reserve is set up by a charge against revenue (debit to expense or cost account), subsequently it should be debited with the actual expenses and losses provided for in the estimate. Any balance remaining in such account after their purpose is served should be closed out to the current income summary account. A so-called reserve set up by charges against retained earnings should *never* be used to relieve the income statement of charges which should be made therein. In other words, losses and expenses should never be charged against such a reserve but should be reported in the year of their determination in the current income statement. Balances in appropriated reserves after their purposes have been served should be returned intact to retained earnings. The fundamental

---

[1] Equalization reserves were sometimes distinguished from budgetary reserves in that the former extend over several years.

[2] Committee on Terminology, AICPA, "Review and Résumé," *Accounting Terminology Bulletin No. 1* (New York, 1961), p. 27.

reason for these guidelines in respect to charges and credits to "appropriation" accounts is to conform to the revenue, cost, and matching principles. It is not uncommon to observe instances where the appropriation device is utilized to circumvent the income statement in respect to charges and credits that should be reflected thereon. To illustrate, assume a Reserve for Inventory Losses is created as an appropriation of retained earnings in year A; then in year B the actual inventory losses (from whatever cause) are debited to that account rather than being reflected, as they should be, as an operational item (on the income statement) for the year in which sustained. Any objective survey of a number of published financial reports will reveal widespread, and obviously intentional, misuse of reserves of various types.

Basis for Appropriations of Retained Earnings

Incomes and losses from operations and extraordinary losses and gains are transferred to the Retained Earnings account. This account is also charged for dividends in the manner explained previously. From time to time *appropriations* of retained earnings may be made on the books of the corporation and so reported in the financial statements. Appropriations of retained earnings constitute a *restriction* on a specified portion of accumulated earnings for specific purposes. It must be remembered that such specifically designated accounts nevertheless represent a part of *total* retained earnings. Thus, retained earnings collectively is comprised of two subcategories of accounts: (1) appropriated retained earnings and (2) unappropriated retained earnings; each may be represented by one or more separate accounts. A statement of retained earnings is presented in Illustration 21–2 (page 840).

When the need for an appropriation ceases to exist, the special appropriation account is debited and the regular Retained Earnings account is credited. In accounting for appropriated retained earnings, accountants follow a basic principle that the special appropriation account is *never* debited for a loss or for any reason other than to return the balance to the original source, that is, to the Retained Earnings account. Even in the case of a stock dividend or when a new appropriation is being established as the consequence of closing another such account, balances of any appropriated retained earnings accounts involved should be returned first to the *Unappropriated Retained Earnings* account, and the new transaction should be recorded in the normal manner.

Although retained earnings fundamentally are appropriated to indicate that such amounts are not available as a basis for dividends, thereby protecting the working capital position of the corporation, such restrictions arise from a number of situations, the primary reasons being:

a) To fulfill a *legal requirement* as in the case of a restriction on retained earnings equivalent to the cost of treasury stock held as
required by the law of the specific state. This situation will be
discussed and illustrated in Chapter 22.

b) To fulfill a *contractual agreement* as in the case of a bond issue
where the bond indenture requires a sinking fund and carries a
stipulation providing for a restriction on retained earnings. Such
agreements have been used much less in recent years than formerly.

c) To record formally a discretionary action by the board of directors
to restrict a portion of retained earnings as a matter of *financial
planning*.

d) To record formally a discretionary action by the board of directors
to restrict a portion of retained earnings in anticipation of *possible
future losses*.

Since item (a) above will be discussed in Chapter 22, the remaining
items will be discussed below. Preliminary to the discussions to
follow, we should note that the appropriation of retained earnings
fundamentally has absolutely no effect upon the composition of assets
unless actions are taken in addition to the "clerical" identification of
specific portions of retained earnings. This point should be particularly noted in the discussions to follow.

Appropriation Related to a Bond Sinking Fund

In order to offer more security to purchasers of a bond issue the
bond indenture (contract) may include various provisions favorable
to the bondholders (also see Chapter 17). One such provision, generally referred to as a bond sinking or redemption fund, might call
for the periodic deposit of a specified amount of cash in a fund, held
by a trustee, to be used to pay the bonds at maturity. A second provision might also call for the periodic *appropriation* of a specific
amount of retained earnings. The amount to be appropriated may or
may not be the same as the cash contributed to the fund. Or in some
cases there may be an appropriation agreement without a fund provision. This situation is frequently true in the case of serial bonds.
The appropriation of retained earnings related to a bond sinking fund
has two avowed purposes: (1) to inform readers of statements of the
use (or planned use) of assets derived from earnings in the retirement of the fixed liability; and (2) to assure creditors (bondholders)
that new assets received from revenue are being "retained" to offset
the drain occasioned by the bond liability requirement.

To illustrate, assume a $1 million bond issue, sold at par with the
provisions that (a) $100,000 per year, for 10 years, shall be deposited
in a special fund and (b) that an equal amount shall be set aside as an
appropriation of retained earnings. The indicated entries would be:

1. At date of sale of bonds:

Cash 1,000,000
　　Bonds Payable .... 　　　　　1,000,000

2. At end of each of the 10 years:

Bond Redemption Fund (or bond sinking fund)............ 100,000[3]
　　Cash .... 　　　　　100,000

Retained Earnings....................................... 100,000
　　Retained Earnings Appropriated for Bond Redemp-
　　tion Fund (or reserve for bond sinking fund)........ 　　　　　100,000

3. At date of maturity:

Bonds Payable...1,000,000
　　Bond Redemption Fund....................................... 　　　　　1,000,000

Retained Earnings Appropriated for Bond Redemption
　　Fund 1,000,000
　　Retained Earnings... 　　　　　1,000,000

Since the original proceeds of the bond issue may have been used to acquire fixed assets, upon payment of the bonds the management may desire to reappropriate the $1,000,000 or to "capitalize" it through a stock dividend. To illustrate each situation:

1. The board of directors directed that $1,000,000 be reappropriated formally in view of investment in plant:

Retained Earnings...1,000,000
　　Retained Earnings Appropriated for Investment in
　　Plant .... 　　　　　1,000,000

2. The board of directors declared and issued a $1,000,000 stock dividend (to be capitalized at par value):

Retained Earnings...1,000,000
　　Capital Stock .... 　　　　　1,000,000

Similar contractual appropriations may relate to agreements such as the purchase of specific assets, capital stock for retirement, and payment of various obligations.

Appropriations as a Matter of Financial Planning

Many corporations began with a small capital investment and have grown large "through earnings," that is, a good portion of the earnings have been retained in the business in order to expand, purchase fixed assets, and increase working capital. In such circumstances a portion of accumulated earnings may be permanently "capitalized" through

---

[3] Interest income on the fund balance is disregarded in this example. Interest normally is recorded as a credit to interest income and a debit to the sinking fund. This procedure would serve to reduce the amount of cash transferred to the sinking fund each year (see Chapter 17).

stock dividends (or increases in par values); or instead, the management, at least temporarily, may set aside a portion of accumulated earnings in one or more appropriation accounts such as the following:

Retained Earnings Appropriated for Future Investment in Plant
Retained Earnings Appropriated for Working Capital
Retained Earnings Invested in Fixed Assets

These appropriated accounts are established through a debit to the regular Retained Earnings account (unappropriated) and are returned to this account when the purpose has been served. Obviously, they represent only a restriction on retained earnings and do not relate to *specific* earnings or assets since accounting does not identify assets with specific items of corporate capital or vice versa. In many cases upon return of the appropriation to the regular Retained Earnings account (unappropriated), a stock dividend for the same amount is declared and issued as was illustrated above for the bond transactions.

Appropriation for Possible Future Losses

In anticipation of possible future losses it is not uncommon for the board of directors to direct that a portion of accumulated earnings be restricted or set aside and specifically identified in accounts such as the following:

Retained Earnings Appropriated for Contingencies
Retained Earnings Appropriated for Possible Storm Damage
Retained Earnings Appropriated for Possible Future Inventory
   Cost Declines
Retained Earnings Appropriated for Possible Loss in Lawsuit
   Pending
Retained Earnings Appropriated for Self-insurance

Such accounts are established through a debit to the Unappropriated Retained Earnings account and are subsequently returned to this same account. As stated earlier, even though the anticipated contingency does materialize, any actual loss arising therefrom should be charged to operations or to the regular Retained Earnings account as would be done when there is no related appropriation account; such losses are not properly charged to the appropriation account. If the balance of an appropriation account needs adjustment, such changes should directly involve the Unappropriated Retained Earnings account.

With respect to the appropriation for possible future inventory cost decline, attention should be called to the fact that this is not the same account discussed in Chapter 8 which related to the valuation of inventory under the lower of cost or market rule (Allowance to Reduce Inventory to Lower of Cost or Market). That account was related to a cost decline that had *already* materialized, whereas the appropriation account relates to a possible cost decline in the future, that is, one that has not materialized and may not materialize but the possibility does exist.

Retained Earnings Appropriated for Self-insurance. Most companies insure against casualty losses to the fullest extent practicable. Casualty losses arising from fire, storm, hurricane, frost, hail, explosion, and accidents involving either property or individuals normally are covered at least in part by insurance policies. Nevertheless, a management may decide that a saving can be effected by "self-insurance," that is, by carrying no insurance, or insufficient insurance, on a particular risk. In addition, there are situations where insurance may not be available or the rates are prohibitive.

When a company carries no insurance, the management may direct that some recognition of risk be given in the accounts and reported on the financial statements. In this situation, there are two possible alternative accounting treatments:

1. *Appropriation Method.* Retained earnings may be appropriated so as to aggregate the maximum expected loss at any one time. In some cases the appropriation from period to period may approximate the premium cost of adequate insurance covering the risk. The appropriation balance logically should not exceed the maximum expected loss at any one time. Under this alternative, actual losses are *never* charged to the appropriation account, rather losses are recorded in the same manner as if the appropriation was not existent.

2. *Accrual Method.* Current expense may be debited and a *liability* account credited from period to period so as to approximate the amount of the loss chargeable to the current period on an *accrual basis*. Under this alternative, actual losses are charged to the liability account.

The appropriation method (alternate 1 above) may be used in any situation involving self-insurance since there is no allocation or accrual of the expected losses. In establishing the appropriation, the Retained Earnings account is charged and the appropriation account is credited. The appropriation account is not charged for actual losses; rather the losses are recognized only as they occur by means of a charge to a loss account for the actual amount of the loss. The effect of this procedure is a varying charge to current expense for losses, rather than a stable charge, such as would result from premium payments on an insurance contract.

To illustrate the appropriation method as applied to self-insurance, assume the board of directors decided to carry no hurricane-loss insurance. It has been estimated by the company as a result of a study covering the past 15 years that the maximum expected loss at any one time is $45,000 and that the total losses probably will be considerably less than the accumulated premiums on adequate insurance. Assume further that the board of directors has requested that some accounting recognition be accorded the self-insurance plan. Under these circumstances it appears that the only acceptable alternative accounting-wise is the appropriation method since the losses cannot be estimated with sufficient confidence and accuracy (for a single company with limited operations) to justify *accrual accounting* of such losses. Therefore, the indicated entries are:

1. To record the annual appropriation, assuming further that it is decided to accumulate the desired amount in the appropriation account over a three-year period:

Retained Earnings..15,000
    Retained Earnings Appropriated for Self-Insurance (or re-
    serve for self-insurance)   15,000

2. To record actual hurricane damage involving assets having a cost of $17,000 and accumulated depreciation of $5,000 to date of loss:

Hurricane Loss..12,000
Accumulated Depreciation 5,000
    Assets Involved...   17,000

The accrual method (alternate 2 above) involves a periodic charge to current expense and an offsetting credit to a liability account, Estimated Claims (self-insurance). The amount of the charge is based upon a sound estimate of the expected future losses. This procedure apportions the estimated losses to current periods as a stable charge (similar in effect to insurance premium cost), and actual losses are charged to the liability account. *This approach should be used only when there is a sound objective basis for accrual accounting with respect to such losses.* Accrual accounting is acceptable for such situations where the loss can be estimated with reasonable accuracy. Consistency of losses from period to period and other evidence on which to base reliable estimates must be considered carefully.

To illustrate the application of the accrual method to self-insurance, assume a company has 50 salesmen who are employed on a commission basis, and that the company agrees to be responsible for the medical costs of certain specific illnesses of the salesmen. For the past 15 years the company has covered these illnesses with an insurance policy. The company had been paying an average annual premium of $1,000. A careful record of claims had been maintained. As a result of a careful study of the claims, the management estimated that future claims would average $800 per year and that there would be relatively little variation from year to year since the claims for the past years had been very consistent as to amount. In view of the indicated savings possible, the board of directors did not renew the policy and directed that *accrual accounting* recognition be accorded to the self-insurance program. The indicated entries would be:

1. To recognize (accrue) estimated losses each year:

Expense—Salesmen Illness Claims..800
    Estimated Claims—Self-Insurance (liability)............................   800

2. To recognize claim by a salesman:

Estimated Claims—Self-Insurance..100
    Cash..   100

The expense account (operating) would be closed to the Income Summary account and reported in the normal manner; the estimated claims account would be reported on the balance sheet as a current liability.

In each of the above illustrations the company management may well have also decided to *fund* the self-insurance program. To illustrate, assume in the latter case the board of directors also decided that a special fund would be established for the self-insurance. The indicated entries for both the accrual and the fund would be:

1. To recognize (accrue) estimated losses each year and to establish the fund:

Expense—Salesmen Illness Claims..800
    Estimated Claims—Self-Insurance......................................   800

Self-Insurance Fund..800
    Cash..   800

2. To recognize payment of a claim:

Estimated Claims—Self-Insurance..100
    Self-Insurance Fund...   100

The primary precaution which the accountant should observe with respect to accounting for self-insurance is that it must not be used as a device for arbitrarily equalizing earnings from period to period. There must be a sound basis for accrual accounting with respect to recognition of expense on the basis of estimates and to apportionment of expense to the various periods; otherwise, the appropriation basis is the only acceptable alternative.

Positions of the Committees of AICPA and the AAA on Appropriations

Appropriations of retained earnings occasionally are discussed under the caption of *reserves*. In a preceding section of this chapter the position of the accounting profession with respect to terminology was outlined. In that discussion pronouncements from the Committee on Terminology of the AICPA were noted. Both AICPA and AAA committees have published statements relating to appropriations of retained earnings (at that time referred to as *surplus reserves*). The statement of the Committee on Accounting Procedure of the AICPA relative to reserves is quoted in part below:

The committee is therefore of the opinion that reserves such as those created:

a) for general undetermined contingencies, or
b) for any indefinite possible future losses, such as, for example, losses on inventories not on hand or contracted for, or
c) for the purpose of reducing inventories other than to a basis which is in accordance with generally accepted accounting principles, or
d) without regard to any specific loss reasonably related to the operations of the current period, or
e) in amounts not determined on the basis of any reasonable estimates of costs or losses

are of such a nature that charges or credits relating to such reserves should not enter into the determination of net income.

Accordingly, it is the opinion of the committee that if a reserve of the type described in paragraph 7 (the above paragraph) is set up:

a) it should be created by a segregation or appropriation of earned surplus,
b) no costs or losses should be charged to it and no part of it should be transferred to income or in any way used to affect the determination of net income for any year,
c) it should be restored to earned surplus directly when such a reserve or any part thereof is no longer considered necessary, and
d) it should preferably be classified in the balance sheet as a part of shareholders' equity.[4]

The statement of the Committee on Concepts and Standards Underlying Corporate Financial Statements of the AAA is quoted below:

1. The term "reserve" should not be employed in published financial statements of business corporations.
2. The "reserve section" in corporate balance sheets should be eliminated and its elements exhibited as deduction-from-asset, or liability, or retained income amounts.
3. Appropriations of retained income should not be made or displayed in such a manner as to create misleading inferences.
    (a) Appropriations of retained income which purport to reflect managerial policies relative to earnings retention are ineffective, and frequently misleading, unless all retained income which has in fact been committed to operating capital is earmarked. Partial appropriation fosters the implication that retained earnings not earmarked are available for distribution as dividends.

---

[4]Committee on Accounting Procedure, AICPA, "Restatement and Revision of Accounting Research Bulletins," *Accounting Research Bulletin No. 43* (New York, 1961), pp. 42–43.

(b) Appropriations of retained income required by law or contract preferably should be disclosed by footnote. If required to be displayed as
balance sheet amounts, such appropriations should be included in the
proprietary section.

(c) Appropriations of retained income reflecting anticipated future losses,
or conjectural past or present losses (when it is not established by
reasonably objective evidence that any loss has been incurred) preferably should be disclosed by footnote. If displayed as balance sheet
amounts, such appropriations should be included in the proprietary
section.

(d) In any event, whenever appropriations are exhibited in a balance
sheet, the retained income (excluding amounts formally capitalized)
should be summarized in one total.

4. The determination of periodic earnings is not affected by the appropriation of retained income or the restoration of such appropriated amounts to
unappropriated retained income.[5]

Thus, committees of both organizations question the use of the term
reserves, although the AICPA accepts its usage with respect to appropriations of retained earnings. The AICPA accepts the concept of
appropriation of retained earnings for specific purposes, whereas the
AAA looks upon the procedure with disfavor, preferring footnote
treatment instead. If appropriations are made, both appear in agreement as to the appropriate accounting treatment. Accountants generally view appropriations which are based upon vague, indefinite, and
general purposes as undesirable. For example, entitling an appropriation account "Reserve for Contingencies" would not be considered
good accounting procedure. More fundamentally, many thoughtful
accountants question the usefulness of the device of "appropriating"
retained earnings. Admittedly, it is done under the guise of a *reporting device;* many feel that much more informative and understandable
approaches to the reporting problem can, and should, be devised.
Despite the questioning, appropriation of retained earnings continues
to be a very pervasive practice as reflected in published financial
reports. Even more serious is the not uncommon use of the appropriation device to circumvent the income statement for appropriate credits
and charges that should be reported thereon.

Reporting Retained Earnings

Within recent years there has been considerable diversity of views
as to how net income and retained earnings should be reported. Two
conflicting views attracted considerable support. One view commonly
referred to as the *current operating performance concept* placed primary emphasis on reporting in the income statement *only* current

---

[5] AAA, *Accounting and Reporting Standards for Corporate Financial Statements
and Preceding Statements and Supplements* (Columbus, Ohio, 1957), p. 19.

operating data. As a consequence extraordinary nonrecurring items of loss and gain and adjustments of prior period results (when material) were viewed as proper items to report on the statement of retained earnings rather than on the income statement. The opposite view, commonly referred to as the *all-inclusive concept,* placed primary emphasis on reporting *all* nonrecurring items of loss and gain and adjustments of prior period results on the income statement. As a consequence, there would be relatively few items reported on a statement of retained earnings. Although there were many variations of these two opposite viewpoints, recommendations of the committees of the AICPA tended toward the current operating performance concept, whereas those of the committees of the AAA tended toward the all-inclusive concept. The net result was that both views, including reasonable adaptations of them, became "generally accepted" through use (also see Chapter 4).

Upon publication by the AICPA of *APB Opinion No. 9,* "Reporting the Results of Operations," dated December 1966 the diversity of views perhaps has largely been resolved.[6] In this opinion the APB essentially adopted the *all-inclusive concept.* As a consequence of the more general agreement now, it is reasonable to suppose that this view will represent "generally accepted" accounting procedures in the future. Four pertinent excerpts from *Opinion No. 9* are:

(1) On the basic position:
    The Board has considered various methods of reporting the effects of extraordinary events and transactions and of prior period adjustments which are recorded in the accounts during a particular accounting period. The Board has concluded that net income should reflect all items of profit and loss recognized during the period with the sole exception of the prior period adjustments described below. *Extraordinary* items should, however, be segregated from the results of ordinary operations and shown separately in the income statement, with disclosure of the nature and amounts thereof. . . .

(2) On financial statement presentation:
    Under this approach, the income statement should disclose the following elements:

    Income before extraordinary items
    Extraordinary items
    (less applicable income tax)
    Net income

(3) On defining prior period adjustments:
    Adjustments related to prior periods – and thus excluded in the determination of net income for the current period – are limited to those

---

[6] Accounting Principles Board, AICPA, *Opinion No. 9* (New York, 1967), various pages.

material adjustments which (a) can be specifically identified with and directly related to the business activities of particular prior periods, and (b) are not attributable to economic events occurring subsequent to the date of the financial statements for the prior period, and (c) depend primarily on determinations by persons other than management and (d) were not susceptible of reasonable estimation prior to such determination. Such adjustments are rare in modern financial accounting. . . .

Treatment as a prior period adjustment should not be applied to the normal, recurring corrections and adjustments which are the natural result of the use of estimates inherent in the accounting process. For example, changes in the estimated remaining lives of fixed assets affect the computed amounts of depreciation, but these changes should be considered as prospective in nature and not prior period adjustments.

(4) On defining extraordinary items related to current period:
Such events and transactions are identified primarily by the nature of the underlying occurrence. They will be of a character significantly different from the typical or customary business activities of the entity. Accordingly, they will be events and transactions of material effect which would not be expected to recur frequently and which would not be considered as recurring factors in any evaluation of the ordinary process of the business. Examples of extraordinary items . . . include material gains or losses (or provisions for losses) from (a) the sale or abandonment of a plant or a significant segment of the business, (b) the sale of an investment not acquired for resale, (c) the write-off of goodwill due to unusual events or developments within the period, (d) the condemnation or expropriation of properties and (e) a major devaluation of a foreign currency. . . .

Certain gains or losses (or provisions for losses), regardless of size, do not constitute extraordinary items (or prior period adjustments) because they are of a character typical of the customary business activities of the entity. Examples include (a) write-downs of receivables, inventories and research and development costs, (b) adjustments of accrued contract prices and (c) gains or losses from fluctuations of foreign exchange. These effects of items of this nature should be reflected in the determination of income before extraordinary items.

Significant in the Opinion is the very careful definition of what is to be included and what is not to be included in (*a*) prior period adjustments (a very narrow range of items) and (*b*) extraordinary items. Also of significance is the manner of reporting net income and consequently retained earnings. The only items to be reported on the statement of retained earnings are:

1. Beginning balance.
2. Adjustments for prior periods (as narrowly defined above).
3. Net income or loss for the current period.
4. Dividends.
5. Appropriations of retained earnings.
6. Adjustments made pursuant to a quasi-reorganization.
7. Adjustments, charges, or credits, resulting from transactions in the company's own capital stock (e.g., treasury stock and stock conversion).
8. Ending balance.

With respect to prior period adjustments on the statement of retained earnings *Opinion No. 9* states:

When financial statements for a single period only are presented, this disclosure should indicate the effects of such restatement on the balance of retained earnings at the beginning of the period. When financial statements for more than one period are presented, which is ordinarily the preferable procedure, the disclosure should include the effects for each of the periods included in the statements. Such disclosures should include the amounts of income tax applicable to the prior period adjustments.

In order to illustrate the reporting of retained earnings the following summarized data at the end of 1971 are presented for the Model Stores, Incorporated:

Sales		$520,000
Cost of goods sold		300,000
Expenses		120,000
Income taxes on ordinary income		52,000
Gain on sale of Albany plant		25,000
Income taxes related to sale of Albany plant		6,000
Loss on sale of permanent investments		15,000
Balance in retained earnings January 1, 1971:		
Unappropriated	$120,000	
Bond sinking fund	40,000	
Appropriation for plant expansion	60,000	220,000
Refund from renegotiation of 1969 income taxes		27,000
Damages from 1970 lawsuit (paid this year)	15,000	
Less: Related income tax adjustment	7,000	8,000
Dividends for current year		30,000
Appropriation of retained earnings for bond sinking		
fund for current year		10,000

The resultant income statement and statement of retained earnings are shown in Illustrations 21–1 and 21–2. Obviously, in instances where there have been only one or two changes in retained earnings, full disclosure is possible on the balance sheet and the statement of retained earnings need not be prepared.

Illustration 21–1
MODEL STORES, INCORPORATED
Income Statement
For the Year Ended December 31, 1971

Sales..		$520,000
Less: Cost of goods sold..		300,000
Gross margin on sales..		$220,000
Less: Expenses	$120,000	
Income taxes	52,000	172,000
Income before extraordinary items		$ 48,000
Extraordinary items:		
Gain on sale of Albany plant....................................	$ 25,000	
Loss on sale of permanent investments......................	(15,000)	
	$ 10,000	
Less: Applicable income tax	6,000	
Total extraordinary items...............................		4,000
Net Income		$ 52,000

Note: see Chapter 26 in respect to earnings per share data.

Illustration 21–2
MODEL STORES, INCORPORATED
Statement of Retained Earnings
For the year Ended December 31, 1971

Unappropriated Retained Earnings:			
Unappropriated balance, January 1, 1971		$120,000	
Adjustments applicable to prior periods:			
Refund from renegotiation of 1969 income taxes	$27,000		
Damages from lawsuit (1970) $15,000			
Less: Tax adjustment 7,000	8,000	19,000	
Corrected balance...		$139,000	
Add: Net income for current year.........................		52,000	
		$191,000	
Deductions and appropriations:			
Dividends...	$30,000		
Appropriation to reserve for bond sinking fund......	10,000	40,000	
Unappropriated balance, December 31, 1971			$151,000
Appropriated Retained Earnings:			
Reserve for bond sinking fund, balance January 1, 1971...	$40,000		
Addition for current year.....................................	10,000		
Reserve for bond sinking fund, balance December 31, 1971.....................................		$ 50,000	
Appropriation for plant expansion.........................		60,000	
Appropriated balance, December 31, 1971			110,000
Total Appropriated and Unappropriated, Balance December 31, 1971..................			$261,000

Note: Since the publication of *APB Opinion No. 9* some difficulty has been experienced in distinguishing between "extraordinary" items and "prior period adjustments." Primarily the difficulties have related to three categories of items: (*a*) accounting changes, (*b*) changes in accounting estimates, and (*c*) correction of accounting errors. These aspects of financial reporting are discussed and illustrated in Chapters 4, 13, and 24.

PART B – QUASI-REORGANIZATIONS

The subject of quasi-reorganizations was mentioned in Chapter 13 in respect to fixed assets since a departure from the cost principle in accounting for fixed assets is involved in such a reorganization. When a corporation has sustained heavy losses over a period of time so that there is a significant deficit in the Retained Earnings account and a related *overstatement* of the carrying value of certain assets, a quasi-reorganization may be both desirable from the prudent management point of view and from the accounting point of view.

A quasi-reorganization refers to a procedure whereby a corporation may, without formal court proceedings of dissolution of the corporation, establish a new basis for accounting for assets and corporate capital. In effect, a quasi-reorganization is an accounting reorganization in which a "fresh start" is effected in the accounts with respect to certain assets, legal capital, and retained earnings.

The Committee on Accounting Procedure of the AICPA recognized the procedure provided it is properly safeguarded.[7] The Securities and Exchange Commission listed certain safeguards or conditions with respect to a quasi-reorganization. These conditions are summarized below:

1. Retained earnings after the quasi-reorganization must be zero.
2. Upon completion of the quasi-reorganization no deficit shall remain in any corporate capital account.
3. The effects of the whole procedure shall be made known to all stockholders entitled to vote and appropriate approval in advance obtained from them.
4. A fair and conservative balance sheet shall be presented as of the date of the reorganization and the readjustment of values should be reasonably complete, in order to obviate as far as possible future readjustments of like nature.[8]

Characteristics of a quasi-reorganization are: (a) the recorded values relating to appropriately selected assets are restated downward; (b) the capital accounts are restated, and the Retained Earnings account has a zero balance after the reorganization; (c) the Retained Earnings account is "dated" for a period of time (5 to 10 years) following the reorganization; (d) full disclosure of the procedure and the effects thereof are reported on the financial statements; and (e) the corporate entity is unchanged.[9]

---

[7] *Accounting Research Bulletin No. 43*, pp. 45–47.

[8] Securities and Exchange Commission, *Accounting Series Release No. 25.*

[9] For a detailed treatment of quasi-reorganization see: James S. Schindler, *Quasi-Reorganization* (Michigan Business Studies, vol. XIII, no. 5) (Ann Arbor: Bureau of Business Research, University of Michigan, 1958).

To illustrate the accounting for a quasi-reorganization assume the following simplified balance sheet at January 1, 19A:

Current assets.................\$ 200,000		Capital stock \$1,500,000
		Premium on stock............ 100,000
Fixed assets 1,000,000		Retained earnings............ (400,000)
\$1,200,000		\$1,200,000

Assume further that it is clearly determined that the inventories are overvalued by \$50,000 and that fixed asset carrying value should be reduced by \$250,000 if a realistic accounting is to be made in the future.

Under these conditions the company might consider two alternatives. First, the corporation may be dissolved and a new corporation formed. The new corporation would receive the assets, record them at \$900,000, and report the same amount as corporate capital. Second, the corporation may effect a quasi-reorganization (without dissolution) which would be less cumbersome and less expensive than legal reorganization. By complying with the conditions set forth above, including stockholder approval, the quasi-reorganization may be effected through the following entries assuming capital stock is to be reduced to \$900,000:

1. To write down assets:

Clearance – Quasi-Reorganization......................................300,000	
Current Assets (inventories)	50,000
Fixed Assets..	250,000

2. To eliminate the deficit in retained earnings:

Clearance – Quasi-Reorganization......................................400,000	
Retained Earnings...	400,000

3. To write off premium:

Premium on Stock...100,000	
Clearance – Quasi-Reorganization..............................	100,000

4. To reduce legal capital from \$1,500,000 to \$900,000:

Capital Stock 600,000	
Clearance – Quasi-Reorganization..............................	600,000

The balance sheet after the quasi-reorganization would be:

Current assets.....................\$150,000		Capital stock.......................\$900,000
Fixed assets....................... 750,000		Retained earnings (Note 1) ... –
\$900,000		\$900,000

Note 1. Retained earnings accumulated since January 1, 19A at which time a \$4,000 deficit was eliminated as the result of a quasi-reorganization.

In general, a quasi-reorganization is justified when (a) a large deficit from operations exists, (b) it is approved by the stockholders and creditors, (c) the cost basis of accounting for fixed assets becomes unrealistic in terms of going-concern values, (d) a break in continuity of the historical cost basis is clearly needed so that realistic financial reporting is possible, (e) the retained earnings balances are totally inadequate to absorb an obvious decrease in going-concern asset values, and (f) a "fresh start" in the accounting sense appears to be desirable or advantageous to all parties properly concerned with the corporation.

QUESTIONS FOR CLASS DISCUSSION

1. What is the relationship between retained earnings and reserves?

2. What is the position of the accounting profession generally with respect to the term *reserves*?

3. What is the nature of the account sometimes referred to as "Reserve for Repairs"?

4. What are the basic reasons for appropriation of retained earnings?

5. Explain the distinction between (a) a bond sinking fund and (b) an appropriation of retained earnings for bond sinking fund. What is the purpose of each?

6. What is a "funded" appropriation?

7. What is a "general contingency" appropriation? What is the position of the accounting profession generally with respect to such appropriations?

8. What debits may be made to an appropriations account? Explain.

9. Explain what is meant by self-insurance. What are the two alternative accounting treatments available? Indicate the conditions under which each may be properly applied.

10. Outline the respective positions of the committees of the AICPA and the AAA with respect to appropriations.

11. How should retained earnings be reported on the balance sheet? Under what conditions should a statement of retained earnings be prepared?

12. What items are properly reported on the statement of retained earnings?

13. Is the following statement correct? "Retained earnings was reduced by $10,000 appropriated for plant expansion." Explain.

14. What is a quasi-reorganization? Under what conditions is it acceptable?

15. What is meant by "dated" retained earnings?

16. In what way may a quasi-reorganization affect the accounting for tangible fixed assets?

DECISION CASE 21–1

The following were excerpted from published financial statements (source: G. E. Phillips and R. M. Copeland, *Financial Statements, Problems from Current Practice*, Englewood Cliffs, N.J.: Prentice-Hall, Inc., 1970):[10]

---

[10] This is an excellent source for reviewing current practice.

a) Duffy-Mott Company, Inc., under current assets:
Accounts receivable (less reserves for returns and
allowances) $2,792,022

b) Studebaker Corporation, under current liabilities:
Reserve for product warranty 1,787,600

c) Bendix Corporation, under noncurrent assets:
Real estate not used in the business — at depreciated
cost (less reserve, $75,000)................................... 720,130

d) Union Oil Company of California, above stockholders'
equity:
Reserves:

Self-insurance..	$3,757,006	
Contingent management compensation	391,388	
Other..	383,059	4,531,453

e) Amerada Petroleum Corporation, above stockholders'
equity:

Reserves:	Dec. 31, 1966	Dec. 31, 1965
Insurance...	$689,432	$ 691,333
Contingencies°	—	6,238,606
Total Reserves...	$689,432	$6,929,939

° Financial review: The reserve for contingencies shown on the 1965 balance sheet was eliminated in 1966 by transfers of $1,800,000 to reserve for investment in and advances to Esperanza Petroleum Corporation, $2,500,000 to reserve for income taxes for prior years, and the remainder to extraordinary income.

Required:

For each separate situation (*a*) explain the nature of the event(s) being reported on and (*b*) assess conformity with sound accounting.

EXERCISES

Exercise 21-1

The records of the Bastle Sales Company showed the following:

a) Reserve for bond sinking fund.
b) Earned surplus.
c) Reserve for depreciation
d) Reserve for lawsuit pending.
e) Reserve to reduce inventory
to lower of cost or market.

f) Reserve for vacation wages.
g) Reserve for bad debts.
h) Reserve for contingencies.
i) Reserve for repairs.
j) Reserve for income taxes.

Required:

For each account give (1) type of account, (2) a preferable title, and (3) balance sheet classification.

Exercise 21-2

Staten Manufacturing Company books carried an account entitled "Reserve for Profits Invested in Fixed Assets, $150,000" and another account entitled "Reserve for General Contingencies, $80,000." The retained earnings balance was $75,000 and capital stock outstanding, par value $100, amounted to $700,000.

The board of directors voted a 30% stock dividend and directed that the fair market value of the stock. $110 per share, be capitalized using as a basis therefor "the general reserves."

The company also had bonds outstanding of $100,000. In respect to the bond issue the following accounts were carried also: Bond Sinking Fund, $90,000; Bond Sinking Fund Reserve, $80,000.

Required:

Give entries for the following:

a) To establish the fixed asset and general contingency "reserves."
b) To record the stock dividend.
c) To establish the bond sinking fund.
d) To establish the sinking fund reserve.
e) To record payment of the bonds.

Exercise 21–3

The ending inventory records of Silber Company showed the following:

| | | Per Unit | |
Item	Units	Cost	Market
A	200	$ 9	$10
B	50	10	10
C	100	15	12
D	20	8	8
E	300	21	20

The company utilized periodic (physical) inventory procedures and is in the process of adjusting and closing the books for the year. The lower of cost or market rule is applied to inventories. The management also expects a future drop in market prices amounting to $1,050 prior to disposal of the inventory.

During the first few months of the succeeding year the market price of the items in inventory dropped by $600 prior to disposal. By the end of April all of the goods carried in inventory had been sold.

Required:

Give all entries indicated that are directly related to the inventory including recognition of management's expectation.

Exercise 21–4

Canning Sales Company has decided to discontinue two insurance policies because it is thought that "the premiums are excessive in view of the losses sustained over the years." The two policies were as follows:

Coverage	Face of Policy	Annual Premium	Average Annual Loss Over Last 10 Years
Fire loss on old plant	$50,000	$2,800	$1,360°
Workmen's compensation		2,000	1,200°°

° High loss, $4,000 based on 4 experiences.
°° Relatively stable each year.

In considering the matter the board of directors decided that "appropriate provision in the accounts should be made for each risk. A fund of $3,000 shall be maintained for the workmen's compensation risk and an annual recognition of $1,200 cost recorded." The board was of the opinion that the average fire loss on the plant would not increase. During the following year the plant sustained a fire loss of $4,700; workmen's compensation payments totaled $1,100. Indicate appropriate accounting (including entries) for each risk and the subsequent losses. Justify your position.

Exercise 21–5

Using the simplified data below construct (1) an income statement and (2) a statement of retained earnings in good form. Assume all amounts are material and omit per share data.

a)	Sales	$320,000
b)	Cost of sales	111,000
c)	Operating expenses	98,000
d)	Financial expenses	6,000
e)	Gain on sale of fixed asset	1,000
f)	Loss on sale of permanent investment	16,000
g)	Appropriation to bond sinking fund	10,000

Balances – beginning of period:

h)	Retained earnings	$130,000
i)	Reserve for bond sinking fund	50,000
j)	Damages arising from lawsuit (instituted in prior year)	1,200
k)	Dividends	44,000

Income taxes:

l)	On income before extraordinary items	40,000
m)	On sale of fixed asset	100
n)	On sale of permanent investments (tax saving)	(2,900)
o)	On damages from lawsuit	500

Exercise 21–6

Using the simplified data below construct comparative statements of (1) income and (2) retained earnings for 19A and 19B. Assume all amounts are material and omit per share data.

		19A	19B
a)	Sales	$ 80,000	$90,000
b)	Cost of sales	45,000	50,000
c)	Expenses	24,000	27,000

Income taxes: [(d) through (g)]

		19A	19B
d)	On income before extraordinary items	4,000	5,000
e)	On sale of fixed assets	700	
f)	On sale of permanent investments (tax saving)		(300)
g)	On damages from lawsuit (see m below)		1,100
h)	Gain on sale of fixed assets	3,000	
i)	Loss on sale of permanent investments		1,800
j)	Dividends	12,000	10,000
k)	Appropriation for profits invested in fixed assets	40,000	

l) Beginning balances:
    Unappropriated retained earnings.....................................$110,000   ?
    Appropriation for profits invested in fixed assets ....   –0–   ?
m) In 19A the corporation was sued for $10,000 damages; the suit
    was settled in 19B requiring the payment of $4,000 damages;
    this caused a reduction in income taxes of $1,100 (*g* above).

Exercise 21–7

Fast Company had experienced a net loss for a number of years. Recently
a new management had been installed. The board of directors had agreed to
a quasi-reorganization and to "restate" certain items in the accounts as outlined by the new management, subject to stockholder approval. Prior to the
restatement the balance sheet reported the following (summarized at July 1,
19A):

Cash and receivables...........$ 21,000	Current liabilities................$ 50,000
Inventories......................... 210,000	Fixed liabilities.................... 85,000
Fixed assets (net) 560,000	Capital stock (8,000
Other assets....................... 44,000	shares) 800,000
	Premium on stock 40,000
	Retained earnings .... (150,000)
	Reserve for contingencies 10,000
$835,000	$835,000

The stockholders approved the quasi-reorganization which carried the
following provisions:

a) The inventories to be reduced to a lower of cost or market value of $145,000.
b) Receivables of $5,000 to be written off as worthless.
c) The fixed assets to be reduced to a net carrying value of $400,000.
d) The capital structure to be adjusted so that the deficit will be eliminated
    and the paid-in capital reduced by the net adjustment made to assets.

Required:

1. Give entries to record the restatement as approved by the stockholders.
2. Prepare a balance sheet after giving effect to the restatement.

PROBLEMS

Problem 21–1

The following account titles (with credit balances) appeared on the books
of the Baker Company. You are asked to set up a tabulation with the following headings: (1) title per books, (2) appropriate title, (3) balance sheet classification, (4) offsetting debit to create the account, and (5) offsetting credit to
decrease or dispose of the account.

a) Reserve for federal income taxes.
b) Reserve for future bond redemption.
c) Reserve for pensions.
d) Reserve for inventory fluctuations.
e) Reserve for appraisal of fixed assets.
f) Reserve for undeclared dividends.

g) Reserve for uncollectible notes
    and accounts.
h) Reserve for depletion.
i) Reserve for discount on sales.
j) Reserve for self-insurance,
    fire and liability.

k) Reserve for social security taxes.

l) Reserve for plant expansion.

m) Reserve for depreciation.

n) Reserve for repairs.

o) Reserve for treasury stock purchased.

p) Reserve for contingencies.

q) Reserve for bond sinking fund.

r) Reserve for vacation wages.

Problem 21-2

Mason Manufacturing Company adopted the following policies prior to the beginning of 19A:

a) Inventories shall be reported at the lower of cost or market.

b) Provision shall be made in the accounts for expected future decline in inventory prices.

c) The company shall carry self-insurance on (1) storm damage to warehouses in the Western Division and (2) collision losses (but not liability) on the 10 company autos. The records relating to these two risks showed the following:

| | Annual Premium | | Actual Losses | |
Past Years	Storm Damage	Auto Collision	Storm Damage	Auto Collision
1	$1,400	$650	$ 300	$480
2	1,400	680	2,200	300
3	1,800	680	100	330
4	1,800	680	1,200	290
5	1,900	700	300	350

During the three-year period following the adoption of the above policies the records revealed the following:

| Future Years | Actual Losses | | Inventory | | Inventory Future Price Decline | |
	Storm	Collision	Cost	Market	Expectation	Actual
19A	$ 500	$480	$190,000	$180,000	$12,000	$10,000
19B	200	270	205,000	203,000	9,000	none
19C	1,600	200	200,000	185,000	5,000	11,000

Required:

1. What accounting entries should have been made for each of the three years 19A-19C in implementation of the policies? Observe the fact that certain data given would not have been known at the time the entry had to be made. Explain the basis for your decision on entries that might be questioned.

2. Indicate how balances in the accounts should be reported at the end of 19C in the financial statements.

Problem 21–3

The following data were taken from the records of Brooklyn Corporation at the end of the current year (assume all amounts material, that items in parenthesis are credit balances, and omit per share data.)

a)	Sales	($340,000)
b)	Cost of sales	211,000
c)	Operating expenses	83,500
d)	Financial income	(5,000)
e)	Loss on sale of fixed assets	16,000
f)	Gain on sale of permanent investments	(4,500)
g)	An expense incorrectly charged to a nondepreciable asset in a prior year	3,000
h)	Stock dividend	20,000
i)	Cash dividend	8,000
j)	Income tax renegotiation (recovery of prior year taxes)	(11,000)
k)	Damages paid on lawsuit (pending for past 3 years)	9,000

Income taxes:

l)	On income prior to extraordinary items	19,000
m)	On sale of fixed assets (tax saving)	(4,000)
n)	On sale of permanent investments	1,000
o)	On damages from lawsuit (tax reduction)	(3,200)

Beginning balance in retained earnings:

p)	Unappropriated	(80,000)
q)	Bond sinking fund	(50,000)
r)	Appropriation for plant expansion	(60,000)
s)	Current appropriation to bond sinking fund	10,000
t)	Current appropriation for plant expansion	30,000

Required:

Based on the above data prepare in good form (1) an income statement and (2) a statement of retained earnings.

Problem 21–4

Detroit Corporation records provided the following data for the years 19A and 19B. Based on these data comparative statements of (1) income and (2) retained earnings are to be prepared. Assume all amounts to be material and omit per share data.

		19A	19B
a)	Sales	$240,000	$260,000
b)	Cost of sales	134,000	143,000
c)	Expenses	71,000	77,000
d)	Income from sale of temporary investments		4,000
e)	Loss from sale of permanent investments	7,000	1,000
f)	Gain on sale of fixed assets	3,000	5,000
g)	Stock dividend		15,000
h)	Appropriation to bond sinking fund (current)	10,000	10,000

Adjustments in accounts due to a change in the application of accounting principles that gave rise to corrections that reduced net income (income tax not affected):

	19A	19B
i) Prior to 19A (debit)	9,000	
j) Prior to 19A (credit)	1,000	
k) Correction of error in depreciation prior to 19A (debit)	2,000	2,000

Beginning balances in retained earnings:

l) Unappropriated	140,000	?
m) Appropriated for bond sinking fund	50,000	
n) Appropriated for plant expansion	100,000	

Income taxes:

o) On income before extraordinary items	12,000	16,000
p) On sale of temporary investments (reduction)		(2,000)
q) On sale of fixed assets	1,000	2,000
r) On sale of permanent investments (reduction)	(2,000)	(400)

Problem 21–5

Holstrom Corporation records provided the following unclassified data. Select appropriate data and prepare (1) a summary income statement, (2) a statement of retained earnings, and (3) a listing of contributed capital excluding legal capital for the year ended December 31. Omit per share data.

a) Additional appropriation of retained earnings for sinking fund, $10,000; the prior balance was $50,000.
b) Deficit in Retained Earnings account per books at end of prior year, $90,000.
c) Dividends declared on preferred stock December 31 of the year just ended, payable the following January 15 amounting to $10,000.
d) Balance at end of prior year in account entitled "Excess Paid-in over Stated Value of Capital Stock," $60,000.
e) Cash collected July 1 of the year just ended, less cash surrender value of life insurance from Model Insurance Company on insurance policy on life of the company president, $75,000.
f) Declared stock dividend on common stock July 1 of year just ended; issue date October 1 of same year, $12,000.
g) Premium on sale of preferred stock during year just ended, $2,000.
h) Income statement data for current year: sales, $330,000; cost of sales, $150,000; operating expenses, $82,000; and financial income, $1,500.
i) Treasury stock donated to the company November 1 of prior year; credited to Retained Earnings at par value, $12,500.
j) Additional assessment during year just ended by Internal Revenue Service for prior years' income taxes, $4,000.
k) Damages paid on prior year lawsuit, $8,000.
l) Income taxes:

On income prior to extraordinary items	$32,500
On extraordinary items	15,000
On corrections to retained earnings balance (tax reduction)	(3,000)

Problem 21–6

The books of Pacific Corporation are being audited. The books show an account entitled "Surplus" which is reproduced below covering a five-year period, January 1, 1967, to December 31, 1971.

Credits

1967–70	Net income carried to surplus	$980,000
1967	By debit to goodwill — authorized by board	40,000
1/1/67	Patents granted to stockholder January 1, 1964; donated to company; valued by board	23,800
12/31/68	Premium on capital stock sold	6,000
1/1/69	Donation to company 10 shares of treasury stock (entered at par)	1,000
11/1/69	Discount (on purchase) of 1,000 shares of capital stock acquired and retired	2,000
12/31/69	Gain on sale of fixed assets	9,000
7/1/70	Reduction in capital stock from par value $100 to par value $50 with no change in the number of shares outstanding (10,000); approved by shareholders	500,000
12/31/71	Net income 1971	75,000

Debits

1967–71	Cash dividends paid	750,000
1/1/67	To reserve for bond sinking fund (annually)	10,000
12/31/68	To establish reserve for general contingencies	100,000
12/31/69	Bond sinking fund reserve	10,000
12/31/70	Bond sinking fund reserve	10,000
9/1/71	Fifty percent stock dividend	250,000

The following additional information has been developed: The Patent account was being amortized on the basis of a 17-year life from 1/1/67.

Required:

1. Prepare a work sheet suitable for analyzing the above account and related data so that appropriate correcting entries may be made. It is suggested that the work sheet carry the following headings (five columns): (a) surplus account per books, (b) corrected net income 1971, (c) corrected retained earnings, and (d) other accounts (columns for amount and specific account).

2. Give the appropriate correcting entry or entries.

Problem 21–7

The Bosley Company, a medium-sized manufacturer, has been experiencing losses for the five years that it has been doing business. Although the operations for the year ended resulted in a loss, several important changes resulted in a profitable fourth quarter and the future operations of the company are expected to be profitable.

The treasurer suggests that there be a quasi-reorganization to (a) eliminate the accumulated deficit of $423,620, (b) write up the $493,100 cost of operating land and buildings to their fair value, and (c) set up an asset of $203,337 representing the estimated future tax benefit of the losses accumulated to date.

Required:

1. What are the characteristics of a quasi-reorganization? That is, of what does it consist?

2. List the conditions under which a quasi-reorganization generally would be justified.

3. Discuss the propriety of the treasurer's proposals to:
a) Eliminate the deficit of $423,620.
b) Write up the value of the operating land and buildings of $493,100 to their fair value.
c) Set up an asset of $203,337 representing the future tax benefit of the losses accumulated to date.

(AICPA adapted)

	Corporations –
	Contributed
chapter **22**	Capital Changes
	after Formation

Changes in Capital after Formation

Once the corporate charter is granted and the bylaws are approved, provisions for corporate capital are established; however, this does not mean that such provisions may not be changed. Initial sales of capital stock may involve all or only part of the authorized shares. Numerous changes in contributed capital after formation (other than those due to sales of unissued stock) are possible. The corporation may, in effect, reduce contributed capital by purchasing and then canceling some of its own outstanding stock. Or it may purchase some of its own stock and hold it without cancellation. Shares of one class may be called in and redeemed, or shares of one class may be called in and exchanged for another class. The corporation may undergo a corporate reorganization involving a significant change in the entire capital structure; or it may combine with other entities. These changes are controlled in various manners: by state laws, by charter and bylaw provisions, or by the shareholders themselves. Obviously, upon approval of the shareholders the bylaws may be changed and even a new or amended charter obtained. As a result, there is a good possibility that the accountant can expect to encounter one or more such changes from time to time.

In accounting for such changes four basic principles have general applicability, viz:

1. Accounting must be such that *sources* of all capital are recorded clearly and reported accurately.
2. Accounting must provide the necessary information for full disclosure and reporting in accordance with the prevailing legal requirements.
3. Since a corporation cannot realize income on capital transactions between itself and its owners, accounting recognition of increases and decreases resulting from transactions relating to the corporation's own stock involve contributed capital rather than retained earnings (except as noted in [4] below.)
4. Certain payments by a corporation to its shareholders for their shares above the original contributions may be considered to be a form of cash dividends (affecting retained earnings).

Treasury Stock

Changes in contributed capital after formation frequently arise as a result of treasury stock transactions. The statutes of most states permit a corporation to purchase its own stock subject to certain limitations. *Treasury stock* is a corporation's own stock (preferred or common) that (*a*) has been issued; (*b*) subsequently reacquired by the issuing corporation; and (*c*) not resold or canceled. Treasury stock may be held as treasury stock, resold, or canceled. When resold it is again classified as outstanding stock. It may be noted, however, that the courts generally have held that a discount liability does not apply to treasury stock resold (Chapter 19), assuming the second purchaser did not have knowledge of a prior discount liability. The purchase of a corporation's own stock serves to contract both assets and corporate capital, whereas a resale of treasury stock serves to expand both assets and corporate capital. Treasury shares may be obtained by purchase, by settlement of an obligation, or through donation. Obviously, treasury stock does not carry voting, dividend, and liquidation privileges. In contrast to treasury stock, a corporation may have issued redeemable stock callable at a specified price in the future and at the option of the issuer. Redemption of stock entails acquisition and immediate cancellation of shares.

Recording Treasury Stock Transactions

There are a number of prevailing views as to the exact approaches that should be used in accounting for treasury stock. These views may be grouped broadly under two approaches: (1) the "one-transaction" concept, i.e., the purchase and subsequent sale of treasury stock are viewed, in effect as *one continuous capital transaction* (generally referred to as the cost method); (2) the "dual-transaction" concept, i.e., the purchase and subsequent sale of treasury stock constitute *two separate and distinct transactions* (generally referred to as the par-value method). Under this latter concept then the acquisition of treasury shares has essentially the same effect on contributed capital as does the purchase and cancellation of capital stock. The resale is viewed simply as a sale of capital stock, and it is treated in the same manner as the sale of unissued capital stock. Both concepts are utilized extensively, often with numerous variations. Rather than attempting to discuss and illustrate all the variations of each approach, the authors have decided to present one representative application of each approach.

The One-Transaction Concept (Cost Method). Under this approach, upon the purchase of treasury stock, a *treasury stock account* is debited for the *cost* of the shares acquired and upon resale is credited for the cost in a manner similar to an inventory account. As a consequence, it is frequently referred to as the "cost method." In the case of several purchases at different costs per share, the acquisition price, upon resale, should be identified with the specific shares if practicable, and if not, Fifo or average cost may be used. Since the "one-transaction" approach rests upon the concept that the purchase and subsequent resale are viewed as one continuous transaction, the purchase is the initial step, involving the use of assets to effect a temporary contraction of total cápital. The final step in the transaction is the resale of the treasury shares and a consequent expansion of assets and total capital. Under this particular approach the balance in the Treasury Stock account is viewed as an *unallocated reduction of total capital.* The following illustration indicates the accounting treatment under the *one-transaction concept* (cost method):

1. To record the initial sale of 10,000 shares of capital stock, par $25, at $26 per share:

Cash	260,000	
Premium on Capital Stock ($1 per share)		10,000
Capital Stock (10,000 shares, par $25)		250,000

2. To record a purchase of 1,000 shares of treasury stock at cost ($28):

Treasury Stock (by type of stock)	28,000	
Cash		28,000

3a. To record a sale of 500 of the shares of treasury stock at $28 per share (same as the purchase price):

Cash	14,000	
Treasury Stock (500 shares @ $28)		14,000

b. Now assume instead a sale of the 500 shares at $30 per share (i.e., $2 per share above the purchase price):

```
Cash ($500 shares @ $30).................................................  15,000
    Contributed Capital, from Sale of Treasury Stock in
        Excess of Cost (500 shares @ $2) ...........................          1,000
    Treasury Stock (500 shares @ $28)...............................         14,000
```

c. Now assume again a sale of the 500 shares but at $22 per share (i.e., $6 per share below the purchase price; also below par):

```
Cash ...............................................................................  11,000
Contributed Capital (see discussion below)........................   3,000
    Treasury Stock (500 shares  @ $28) ............................         14,000
```

There seems to be general agreement where the one-transaction concept is being followed that when treasury stock is sold at a price in excess of its cost, the excess should be recorded as contributed capital (in a special contributed capital account similar to that employed in 3*b*). But where the shares are sold at less than their cost, there is no uniformity in practice as to the account to be charged for the loss of capital on the resale. Where the laws of the state of incorporation require that amounts paid in for capital stock be retained as a credit to legal or stated capital, the capital lost on the sale of treasury shares at less than cost should be charged to Retained Earnings. But since most state laws do not have this requirement, and generally are not specific as to the treatment of this "lost capital," the following treatments are the more common ones suggested by accountants and used by industry:

1. Charge the difference (lost capital) to any existing contributed or paid-in capital above legal requirements and related to the same class of stock in the following order:
   a) First to capital arising from prior treasury stock transactions.
   b) Second to any capital related to the same class of stock.
   c) After utilizing balances in (*a*) and (*b*) charge remainder to Retained Earnings.
2. Charge contributed capital with a pro rata amount per share of any premium (or discount) that was recorded on *original sale* of the stock, and charge any remaining loss to Retained Earnings. For example, the latter situation 3(*c*) illustrated above would be recorded as follows under this procedure:

```
Cash ...............................................................................11,000
Premium on Capital Stock (500 shares at original premium of $1
    per share) ...............................................................    500
Retained Earnings...........................................................  2,500
    Treasury Stock .........................................................        14,000
```

3. Charge the entire difference (lost capital) to Retained Earnings.

The second alternative is preferred from a theoretical point of view since it recognizes a return of the original investment ($26 per share) and a form of dividend distribution ($2 per share) to the *prior* owner. The third alternative is used primarily because of its simplicity and conservatism, or because of the lack of appropriate contributed capital accounts to absorb the charge.

The one-transaction approach, as illustrated above for the several assumptions, is frequently used because of its simplicity. It may avoid the necessity of developing specific data concerning the original premiums, discounts, etc., relating to the specific stock involved. It can be defended largely on practical grounds; theoretical justification is difficult even if no gain or loss is involved. The primary objection from the point of view of theory is that the *sources* of the various components of capital are not maintained. Under this procedure the actual capital contributed (after the treasury stock transactions are recorded) for the outstanding stock is not specifically identified in the accounts. As illustrated in a later section of this chapter, the balance in the Treasury Stock account (at cost) is deducted on the balance sheet from total capital (after retained earnings) as an *unallocated* deduction.

The Dual-Transaction Concept (Par-Value Method). The accounting objectives to be accomplished under this concept are:

1. To make a final accounting with the retiring stockholder (from whom the treasury shares were acquired).
2. To record precisely the capital contributed by the new stockholder (the purchaser of the treasury shares).

The final accounting with the retiring stockholder (at date of purchase of the treasury shares) involves comparing the amount withdrawn (price paid for the treasury shares) with the amount originally invested by the stockholder (computed on an average basis for all shares issued). If the amount withdrawn exceeds the original investment, the excess is charged to Retained Earnings. If the original investment exceeds the amount withdrawn, the difference is credited to Contributed Capital (from retiring stockholders).

When the treasury shares are sold, the entire proceeds of the sale are treated as capital invested by the new shareholders. The amount of this contributed capital is credited to the Capital Stock and, where above par, to the Premium on Capital Stock accounts. If the shares are sold at less than par or stated value, the debit should be charged to Retained Earnings since no discount liability attaches to Treasury Stock sold at less than par.

This concept usually is accomplished by recording treasury stock purchases at *par value*. As a consequence, it is frequently referred to as the "par-value method." This approach is based upon the theory that when treasury shares are purchased, the contributed capital is reduced; all original capital balances identifiable with the shares should be removed. Since resale is considered as a completely separate transaction giving rise to an expansion of contributed capital, new capital balances are created.

The following entries illustrate the accounting under the dual-transaction concept where treasury stock is recorded at *par value:*

1. To record sale of 10,000 shares of capital stock, par $25, at $26 per share:

Cash..260,000		
Premium on Capital Stock ($1 per share)......................		10,000
Capital Stock (10,000 shares, par $25)..........................		250,000

2. To record a purchase of 1,000 shares of treasury stock at $28 per share:

Treasury Stock (1,000 shares at par).....................................	25,000	
Premium on Capital Stock (1,000 shares at $1)....................	1,000	
Retained Earnings...	2,000	
Cash..		28,000

3a. To record a sale of 500 shares of treasury stock at $28 per share (same as the purchase price; $3 above par):

Cash.. 14,000		
Treasury Stock (500 shares at par)...............................		12,500
Premium on Capital Stock ($3 per share)		1,500

b. Now assume instead a sale of the 500 shares of treasury stock at $30 per share ($5 per share above par):

Cash (500 shares @ $30).. 15,000		
Treasury Stock (500 shares at par)...............................		12,500
Premium on Capital Stock (or contributed capital from sale of treasury stock in excess of par) ($30 − $25) × 500 shares...		2,500

c. Now assume again a sale of the 500 shares but at $22 per share ($3 per share below par):

Cash (500 shares @ $22).. 11,000		
Retained Earnings ($25 − $22) × 500 shares...................... 1,500°		
Treasury Stock (500 shares at par, $25)		12,500

°Discount on stock is not debited since a discount liability is not created.

The dual-transaction concept, as illustrated above, theoretically is sound in that the *sources* of capital are maintained intact. An exact record of capital received on all outstanding stock is maintained. The principal disadvantage is the necessity of identifying the various components of contributed capital with the specific shares involved.[1]

---

[1] The dual-transaction approach may be adapted whereby treasury stock is recorded at cost. This variant approach is not illustrated here since it is seldom used.

With respect to accounting for treasury stock, two of the major accounting associations have made reasonably definite statements. The following statements by these two associations indicate that they strongly favor the dual-transaction concept as illustrated above.

Preferably, the outlay by a corporation for its own shares is reflected as a reduction of the aggregate of contributed capital, and any excess of outlay over the pro-rata portion of contributed capital as a distribution of retained earnings. The issuance of reacquired shares should be accounted for in the same way as the issuance of previously unissued shares, that is, the entire proceeds should be credited to contributed capital.[2]

Apparently there is general agreement that the difference between the purchase price and the stated value of a corporation's common stock purchased and retired should be reflected in capital surplus. Your committee believes that while the net asset value of the shares of common stock outstanding in the hands of the public may be increased or decreased by such purchase and retirement, such transactions relate to the capital of the corporation and do not give rise to corporate profits and losses. Your committee can see no essential difference between (a) the purchase and retirement of a corporation's own common stock and the subsequent issue of common shares, and (b) the purchase and resale of its own common stock.[3]

Accounting for No-Par Treasury Stock

If no-par stock having a *stated* or *assigned* value per share is purchased, it may be accounted for in exactly the same manner as illustrated above for par-value treasury stock under either of the two approaches. The stated or assigned value per share is treated as if it were a par value in all of the entries. However, if *true* no-par stock is purchased as treasury stock (no stated or assigned value per share), the transactions would be recorded as in the following examples.

Assume that a total of 10,000 shares of no-par stock has been issued by the company for a total of $120,000. It then reacquired 1,000 shares by purchase at $15 per share and subsequently sold 500 of these treasury shares at $18 per share. The accounting for these transactions under the two concepts would be as follows:

One-transaction concept (record treasury stock at cost):

To record purchase at $15:

No-par Treasury Stock (1,000 shares, @ $15) 15,000
    Cash   15,000

---

[2] AAA, *Accounting and Reporting Standards for Corporate Financial Statements and Preceding Statements and Supplements* (Columbus, Ohio, 1957), p. 7.

[3] Committee on Accounting Procedure, AICPA, "Restatement and Revision of Accounting Research Bulletins," *Accounting Research Bulletin No. 43* (New York, 1961), p. 14.

To record sale at $18:

```
Cash (500 × $18) ...............................................................  9,000
    No-Par Treasury Stock (500 shares  @  $15).....................      7,500
    Contributed Capital — on Treasury Stock Transactions (500
        shares  @  $3).......................................................      1,500
```

Dual-transaction concept (record treasury stock at original sales price):

To record purchase at $15:

```
No-Par Treasury Stock (1,000 shares  @  $12)..........................12,000
Retained Earnings ................................................................  3,000
    Cash (1,000 shares  @  $15)...........................................     15,000
```

To record sale at $18:

```
Cash (500 shares  @  $18)..................................................  9,000
    No-Par Treasury Stock (500 shares  @  $12).....................      6,000
    No-Par Capital Stock (the only contributed capital account
        in the true no-par stock method)................................      3,000
```

It should be noted that the same basic procedures are followed for no-par treasury stock as for par-value treasury stock. The resale of no-par treasury shares at "cost" and at a price below cost are not illustrated since no different problems are posed.

Restriction of Retained Earnings for Treasury Stock

In a preceding chapter legal capital was discussed and the point was made that the laws frequently attempt to protect creditor interests through the maintenance of legal capital requirements and restriction of dividends. When treasury stock is purchased, assets of the corporation are disbursed to the owners of the shares purchased. Should a corporation have a completely free hand in this matter, it is not difficult to perceive how creditor interests (or even the interests of a particular class of shareholders) may be jeopardized through the distribution of corporate assets via treasury stock purchases, even though legal capital may be "reported intact." To prevent this situation most states have laws limiting the amount of treasury stock that may be held at any one time to some amount such as the total retained earnings.[4] This provision has the effect (*a*) of requiring that retained earnings equivalent to the cost of treasury stock be restricted (appropriated) and (*b*) of reducing the amount of retained earnings that may be used for dividends until the treasury shares are resold. To illustrate, assume a corporation reports the following capital structure:

---

[4] In most states the restriction applies to retained earnings; on the other hand, some states permit the purchase of treasury stock equivalent in cost to other capital items such as premium. Throughout these discussions we will assume the restriction extends only to retained earnings.

Capital stock, par value $25, 10,000 shares..........................$250,000
Premium on capital stock.. 10,000
Retained earnings 30,000

Assuming the statutory limitation extends only to retained earnings, in this case the corporation may purchase treasury stock costing up to $30,000, and if it did so, no dividends could be declared. Should the corporation purchase treasury stock costing $26,000, dividends up to $4,000 could be declared. The restriction of retained earnings could be removed (a) by sale of the treasury shares or (b) by their cancellation. In case of cancellation, statutory requirements would have to be complied with relating to reduction of legal capital.

The restriction on retained earnings may be reported on the balance sheet (a) as a separate item of retained earnings, (b) as a parenthetical note to retained earnings, or (c) as a footnote. The authors prefer (a) or (b) over (c) on the basis that such presentation is clear, concise, and less apt to be overlooked by readers. Each of these methods of reporting the restriction on retained earnings is illustrated in the next section.

Many accountants (and some state laws) take the position that the restriction on retained earnings should be given *formal* recognition in the accounts. For example, the entry to record the restriction in the above illustration would be as follows:

Retained Earnings..26,000
    Retained Earnings Appropriated for Cost of Treasury Stock
    Held 26,000

When the treasury stock is sold, the above entry would be reversed; if only part of the treasury stock is sold, a proportionate amount equal to the cost of the treasury shares sold would be reversed.[5] In states where such restrictions are not required, the management, as a matter of prudence, frequently directs that similar procedures be followed.

Treasury Stock on the Balance Sheet. A corporation having treasury shares cannot exercise the basic rights that attach to stock ownership such as the right to vote, receive dividends, share in assets upon liquidation, or the right to purchase pro rata shares in new issues. Treasury stock cannot be considered as an asset in the same manner as investments in other stocks. Treasury stock is instead a *reduction* in the capital section of the balance sheet. Although treasury stock may have been purchased as part of a special fund, such as a sinking fund, it should not be reported as a part of the fund assets.

---

[5] There is some basis for the opinion that the amount of the reversal be the same as the *cash received* upon resale rather than a proportionate part of the original cost. In case state law requires an appropriation, the wording of the statute may clearly indicate which procedure is required. Further, it may be argued that the restriction should be equal to the par value rather than the cost.

Methods of presenting treasury stock on the balance sheet under several assumptions are illustrated below.

Assumption No. 1. Treasury stock accounted for at *par value* (dual-transaction concept), and the restrictions on retained earnings reported as a separate item:

CAPITAL

Contributed Capital:		
Capital stock, par value $25, 10,000 shares authorized and issued...		$250,000
⊗——▶Less: Treasury stock, 500 shares at par $25......................		12,500
Total Capital Stock Outstanding, 9,500 Shares............		$237,500
Other contributed capital:		
Premium on capital stock..		9,500
Total Contributed Capital......................................		$247,000
Retained Earnings:		
⊗——▶Appropriated for cost of treasury stock held.......................$14,000		
Unappropriated... 15,000		29,000
Total Capital...		$276,000

Note: An alternate approach would report appropriated retained earnings at $13,000 since $1,000 was charged to Retained Earnings when the treasury stock was acquired.

Assumption No. 2. Treasury Stock accounted for at *cost*, (one-transaction concept), earnings restriction reported as separate item:

CAPITAL

Contributed Capital:		
Capital stock, par value $25, 10,000 shares authorized and issued of which 500 shares are held as treasury stock........		$250,000
Other contributed capital:		
Premium on capital stock...		10,000
Total Contributed Capital.......................................		$260,000
Retained Earnings:		
⊗——▶Appropriated equal to cost of treasury stock.......................$14,000		
Unappropriated.. 16,000		30,000
Total..		$290,000
⊗▶Less: Cost of treasury stock (500 shares)..............................		14,000
Total Capital..		$276,000

Assumption No. 3. This is the same as assumption no. 2 except the retained earnings restriction is reported parenthetically.

Total Contributed Capital (reported as above)..........................$260,000	
⊗▶Retained Earnings (including a restriction of $14,000, equivalent to the cost of 500 shares of treasury stock held).....................................	30,000
Total..$290,000	
⊗▶Less: Cost of treasury stock (500 shares)...	14,000
Total Capital...$276,000	

Assumption No. 4. This is the same as assumption no. 2 except the retained earnings restriction is reported as a footnote.

Total Contributed Capital (reported as above)......................$260,000
ⓧ→Retained Earnings (see note).. 30,000
Total $290,000
ⓧ→Less: Cost of treasury stock (500 shares)............................... 14,000
Total Capital $276,000

ⓧ——→ Note: Retained earnings are restricted in the amount of $14,000, the cost of 500 shares of treasury stock held. Dividends are limited to the excess of the balance of retained earnings above this amount.

Treasury Stock Received through Donations

Shareholders may donate shares of stock back to the corporation. Such donations may (*a*) be to raise needed working capital, through resale of the donated stock; (*b*) represent a gift to the corporation; or (*c*) represent the return of the stock in recognition of an overvaluation of assets originally given in exchange for the stock.[6] Stock received by donation is classified as treasury stock. Neither total assets nor *total* equity is changed by the donation of treasury stock. Three methods have been employed in recording the receipt of donated treasury stock, viz:

1. Since no outlay is involved in a receipt of donated stock, a memorandum entry is made in the accounts. The memorandum entry should indicate the class of stock, number of shares, donor, and identifying stock certificate numbers. Upon resale the entire proceeds are credited to appropriate contributed capital accounts.
2. The Treasury Stock account may be debited for the fair market value of the shares when received; a Contributed Capital account is credited for the same amount.
3. The Treasury Stock account may be debited for the par or stated value, any original premium (or discount) pertaining to the shares removed from the accounts, and an appropriate contributed capital account is credited. Subsequent to this entry the Treasury Stock account is carried at par or stated value.

Although all of the approaches are sound in various respects, the first approach generally is utilized in view of the cost principle; however, the third approach is theoretically preferable.

Retirement of Treasury Shares

Corporations, upon occasion, decide to retire treasury stock held and thereby give it the status of unissued shares. This action may be taken assuming the corporation meets all legal requirements with

---

[6] In some cases donated stock may involve a "treasury stock subterfuge." This situation involves a collusive agreement to issue an excess number of shares for properties (when valued at fair market value) followed by a donation back to the corporation of a part of such shares. In some jurisdictions the donated shares have then been sold at a discount with no discount liability since such liability attaches only to the *first* issuance.

respect thereto. The entries to be made will depend upon whether the treasury stock was recorded at cost or at par value and whether or not retained earnings equal to the cost thereof have been appropriated. To illustrate, assume 1,000 shares of treasury stock are being retired, that the par value per share is $10, and that they originally sold at $12 per share. Assume further that the shares were purchased as treasury stock at $12.50 per share. Entries for retirement would be as follows:

1. Assuming the Treasury Stock account was debited for cost ($12,500) at acquisition:

```
Capital Stock (at par)...................................................10,000
Premium on Capital Stock ...............................  2,000
Retained Earnings ...........................................    500
     Treasury Stock (at cost) ...............................          12,500
```

2. Assuming the Treasury Stock account was debited for par value ($10,000) at acquisition:

```
Capital Stock (at par)...................................................10,000
     Treasury Stock (at par) ...............................          10,000
```

Assuming retained earnings were appropriated for the cost of treasury stock, the following entry also would be necessary under either method:

```
Retained Earnings Appropriated for Cost of Treasury
     Stock Held.........,............................................................12,500
     Retained Earnings ......................................          12,500
```

Assuming the treasury stock was purchased at $9 per share, the entries for retirement would be:

1. Assuming the Treasury Stock account was debited for cost ($9,000) at acquisition:

```
Capital Stock (at par)...................................................10,000
Premium on Capital Stock ...............................  2,000
     Contributed Capital from Retirement of Capital Stock .......    3,000
     Treasury Stock (at cost) ...............................    9,000
```

2. Assuming the Treasury Stock account was debited for par value ($10,000) at acquisition:

```
Capital Stock (at par)...................................................10,000
     Treasury Stock (at par) ...............................          10,000
```

Assuming retained earnings had been appropriated for the cost of treasury stock, the following entry also would be necessary under either method:

```
Retained Earnings Appropriated for Cost of Treasury
     Stock Held.......................................................... 9,000
     Retained Earnings ......................................          9,000
```

Purchase of Stock for Retirement

Corporations frequently issue callable preferred stock, that is, stock that may be called in, at the option of the corporation, after a specified date. The stock contract usually will specify the call price per share which usually is at some amount above par value. Most purchases of stock for immediate retirement are related to call privileges.[7]

When stock is purchased and immediately retired, all capital items relating to the specific shares are removed from the accounts, any "loss" is charged to Retained Earnings as a form of dividends and any "gain" is recorded in a contributed capital account appropriately designated. If the stock is cumulative preferred and there are dividends in arrears, such dividends are paid and charged to Retained Earnings in the normal manner. To illustrate several possibilities, assume a corporation had 2,500 shares of preferred stock (par value $100) outstanding, $250,000; premium on preferred stock, $10,000; contributed capital from other sources, $5,000; and retained earnings, $45,000. Now assume the corporation purchased and retired 1,000 shares of the preferred stock. Four different assumptions as to cost of retirement are illustrated below:

Assumption 1. Preferred stock is purchased at the original issue price of $104 per share.

Preferred Stock (1,000 shares at par)	100,000	
Premium on Preferred Stock ($4 per share)	4,000	
Cash		104,000

Assumption 2. The preferred stock is purchased at $110 per share — a price above the original issue price of $104.

Preferred Stock (1,000 shares at par)	100,000	
Premium on Preferred Stock ($4 per share)	4,000	
Retained Earnings	6,000	
Cash		110,000

Assumption 3. The preferred stock is purchased at $98 per share — a price below both the original issue price and par value.

Preferred Stock (1,000 shares at par)	100,000	
Premium on Preferred Stock ($4 per share)	4,000	
Contributed Capital from Retirement of Preferred Stock		6,000
Cash		98,000

Assumption 4. The preferred stock is 5% cumulative; three years' dividends are in arrears. The stock is purchased at 101 plus the dividends in arrears.

---

[7]*APB Opinion No. 10* recommends that "the liquidation preference of the stock be disclosed in the equity section of the balance sheet in the aggregate, either parenthetically or 'in short' rather than on a per share basis or by disclosure in notes." Amounts of arrearages in cumulative preferred dividends also should be disclosed.

Retained Earnings ($100,000 × 5% × 3 years)	15,000	
Cash		15,000

Note: The remaining preferred shares are not considered in this entry; presumably cumulative dividends on them also would be paid and recorded at this time.

Preferred Stock (1,000 shares at par)	100,000	
Premium on Preferred Stock ($4 per share)	4,000	
Contributed Capital from Retirement of Preferred		
Stock		3,000
Cash		101,000

If true no-par stock is being retired, the average price per share originally credited to the stock account is removed and the "loss" or "gain" accounted for as illustrated above. If no-par stock with a stated or assigned value is being retired, the procedures illustrated above for par-value stock are appropriate.

Conversion of Stock

Corporations frequently issue *convertible* stock which permits the shareholder, at his own option within specified time periods, to exchange shares currently held for other classes of capital stock (or bonds) at a specified rate. Conversion privileges require the issuing corporation to set aside a sufficient number of shares to fulfill the conversion rights until they are exercised or expired. The entries to record conversion depend upon the par values of the respective shares and the original issue price of the shares being converted. To illustrate three possible situations assume the following data:

Preferred stock, 100,000 shares outstanding, par $2 per	
share	$200,000
Premium on preferred stock	20,000
Common stock, par $1 per share, 500,000 shares authorized;	
100,000 shares outstanding	100,000
Premium on common stock	5,000
Retained earnings	50,000

Assumption 1. 10,000 shares of preferred stock are turned in for conversion; an equal number of common shares are issued to replace them:

Preferred Stock (10,000 shares at par)	20,000	
Premium on Preferred Stock ($.20 per share)	2,000	
Common Stock (10,000 shares at par)		10,000
Contributed Capital from Conversion of Preferred		
Stock		12,000

Assumption 2. 10,000 shares of preferred stock are turned in for conversion; 20,000 shares of common stock are issued to replace them:

Preferred Stock (10,000 shares at par)	20,000	
Premium on Preferred Stock ($.20 per share)	2,000	
Common Stock (20,000 shares at par)		20,000
Contributed Capital from Conversion of Preferred		
Stock		2,000

Assumption 3. 10,000 shares of preferred stock are turned in for conversion; 30,000 shares of common stock are issued to replace them:

```
Preferred Stock (10,000 shares at par) ....................................20,000
Premium on Preferred Stock ($.20 per share)......................... 2,000
Retained Earnings............................................................... 8,000
    Common Stock (30,000 shares at par).............................          30,000
```

Conversion of bonds into stocks was discussed in Chapter 17.

Changing Par Value

By proper corporate action to conform with the state laws, charter, and corporate bylaws, the par value of one or more classes of stock may be changed. Par-value stock may be called in and replaced with no-par-value stock; or conversely, no-par-value stock may be replaced with par-value stock. Entries to record such changes in the capitalization depend upon the new capital structure authorized.[8] To illustrate several different situations usually encountered, assume the following data:

```
Capital stock, 50,000 shares outstanding, par value
    per share $2 ...........................................................$100,000
Premium on capital stock............................................. 20,000
Retained earnings....................................................... 30,000
```

Assumption 1. The shares are changed from par value to an equal number of true no-par-value shares.

```
Capital Stock, Par Value (50,000 shares).............................100,000
Premium on Capital Stock............................................... 20,000
    Capital Stock, No-Par Value (50,000 shares) ..................          120,000
```

Note: The board of directors may direct that a lesser amount be credited to the new capital stock account, in which case the difference should be credited to an appropriately designated contributed capital account.

Assumption 2. The shares are changed from par value to an equal number of no-par shares with a stated value of $1 per share.

```
Capital Stock, Par Value (50,000 shares).............................100,000
Premium on Capital Stock............................................... 20,000
    Capital Stock, No Par, Stated Value $1 (50,000 shares) ...          50,000
    Contributed Capital from Change to No-Par-Value
        Stock ...............................................................          70,000
```

Assumption 3. The shares are changed from par value to an equal number of no-par shares with a stated value of $2.50 per share.

```
Capital Stock, Par Value (50,000 shares).............................100,000
Premium on Capital Stock............................................... 20,000
Retained Earnings......................................................... 5,000
    Capital Stock, No Par, Stated Value $2.50 (50,000
        shares) ..............................................................          125,000
```

Assumption 4. The original shares were true no-par value, and

---

[8] Stock splits are considered in Chapter 21.

the capital account was credited for $120,000. The no-par shares are changed to an equal number of shares having a par value of $2.

```
Capital Stock, No Par (50,000 shares).................................120,000
    Capital Stock, Par Value $2 (50,000 shares)...................        100,000
    Contributed Capital from Conversion to Par-Value
       Shares.........................................................................        20,000
```

Stock Rights

A corporation may extend *rights* to certain individuals to acquire shares of a particular class of stock in the corporation subject to certain conditions that the individual must meet. These stock rights are evidenced by certificates known as *stock warrants*.[9] The warrants specify the conditions that must be met in order to acquire each share of stock. In the absence of a restriction, stock rights may be bought and sold on the market similar to shares of stock. The market value of a right will approximate the difference between the current market value of the stock involved (ex rights) and the option price specified on the stock warrant divided by the number of rights needed to purchase one share of stock. Situations where stock warrants frequently are issued are as follows:

1. Evidence of the basic right of a current stockholder to purchase pro rata shares in new stock issues by the corporation.
2. Evidence of a contractual right to acquire certain securities based upon the purchase of another type of security such as convertible debt.
3. Evidence of rights to acquire stock by virtue of employee stock options established by the corporation.
4. Evidence of rights by current stockholders to acquire stock by virtue of a stock dividend.

Each of these situations presents somewhat different accounting problems. The first situation requires a memorandum entry only. The second was discussed in Chapter 19 and the third is discussed below; the last one was discussed in Chapter 20. A warrant specifies (*a*) the option price for the specified security, (*b*) the number of rights required to obtain each share of the specified security, (*c*) the expiration date of the right, and (*d*) instructions for exercise of the right.

Stock Options Issued to Officers and Employees

Corporations frequently grant stock options to officers and other employees which entitle them to purchase stock in the future at a stated price per share. The objective of stock options to employees is to provide for additional compensation both for services rendered and to be rendered. In addition, there is the objective of letting the em-

---

[9] See Chapter 11 for discussion of stock rights from the investor's point of view.

ployees share in the benefits of their own efficiencies as reflected in increased earnings. Definite tax advantages accrue to the recipient in many cases. The typical stock option to officers specifies that a number of shares may be purchased at a stated price per share within a stated period of time. Increase in market price per share above the option price provides the additional compensation. The advantage to the employee is particularly favorable since the opportunity for gain is great and the chance of loss is zero. In addition, current tax laws recognize income to the employee only when the stock is sold by him, and if he has held the shares a minimum of three years from date of exercising the option, a long-term capital gain is recognized.

Stock warrants are issued to those entitled to purchase stock under an option plan. Generally there is a restriction that such rights cannot be sold. Current tax laws require under a "qualified" plan that the options must be exercised within five years from the date the option is granted.

Accounting recognition must be given to the issuance of such rights (stock options) as well as to the *exercise* of such rights. In accounting for the issuance of stock rights under employee option plans, two basic problems arise: (1) At what date should the issuance of the rights be given accounting recognition? (2) What value should be used in the accounting? Provisions of the tax laws have tended to preclude theoretically sound accounting treatment of stock options. Under current tax laws a "qualified" stock option plan requires that (a) the option price be not less than the current market price of the stock at the date the option is granted and (b) no compensation expense is deductible by the company for tax purposes. As a consequence most stock option agreements specify an option price identical with the current market price of the shares.

Theoretically, at the date the option is granted, accounting recognition should be accorded the "value" of the services for which the stock option is granted. From an economic point of view the company is compensating certain employees by conveying (a) cash and (b) a stock option. The total bargained value of the compensation should be recorded and matched with the revenue of the enterprise. The accounting profession has not yet developed a satisfactory approach for measuring the compensation represented by stock options. Since the option price and the current market price of the stock, as noted above, usually are the same, any valuation approach necessarily must look to the future period when the option can be exercised.

Several years back the AICPA's Committee on Accounting Procedure dealt with both the *date* and the valuation; however, those positions are not as relevant as they were when issued in view of (a) changes in the tax laws and (b) changes in the typical option contract. The committee listed six possible dates:

a) The date of adoption of the option plan.

b) The date on which an option is granted to a specific individual.

c) The date on which the grantee has performed any conditions precedent to exercise of the option.

d) The date on which the grantee may first exercise the option.

e) The date on which the option is exercised by the grantee.

f) The date on which the grantee disposes of the stock acquired.[10]

The committee "concludes that in most cases, including situations where the right to exercise is conditional upon continued employment, valuation of the option should be made as of the date of the grant." This preference for the date of the grant, (*b*) above, was based upon the theory that "the date of the grant also represents the date on which the corporation foregoes the principal alternative use of the shares which it places subject to option, i.e., the sale of such shares at the then prevailing market price."[11]

With respect to *valuation* of the rights (amount of compensation), the committee held that it should be the difference between the market value of the shares "at the date on which an option is granted to a specific individual," (*b*) above, and the agreed option price. This position is based upon the theory that "when compensation is paid in a form other than cash the *amount* of compensation is ordinarily determined by the fair value of the property which was agreed to be given in exchange for the services to be rendered."[12]

In granting employees stock options the presumption is that they are in payment for services (*a*) already rendered, (*b*) currently being rendered, and/or (*c*) to be rendered in the future. The valuation placed on the rights must be charged to an appropriate account, or accounts, depending upon the the services involved. Theoretically, for services already rendered the charge should be to Retained Earnings (very seldom the case); for services currently being performed to current expense; and for future services to a deferred expense account. As a matter of actuality, a close distinction on this score may be impossible; consequently, the accountant should follow the intentions of the board of directors if ascertainable or look to other evidence as a basis for charging the appropriate account or accounts.

To illustrate stock options to employees, assume a corporation authorizes stock options to each of three officers of 5,000 shares of common stock, par value $10 per share. The option may be exercised at any date beginning three years after the date of the option agreement, but must be exercised within five years. The option price of a

---

[10] *Accounting Research Bulletin No. 43*, p. 121.

[11] Ibid., p. 122.

[12] Ibid., p. 122. The accounting approach envisioned by the committee was theoretically sound; the questionable aspect of it is the manner in which the amount of the compensation is *measured*.

share is $15, and the current market price (on date of the option) is $20 per share. The valuation of the rights, or amount of the compensation, is:

```
Market value at date of option, 15,000 shares at $20.................$300,000
Option price, 15,000 shares at $15 ......................................... 225,000
       Valuation of Rights (amount of compensation).................$ 75,000
```

The entry at date of the option to record the issuance of the warrants would be:

```
Retained Earnings, or Current Expense, and/or Deferred
   Expense ....................................................................75,000
       Common Stock Warrants Outstanding (15,000 @ $5)..........          75,000
```

The entry to record the exercise of 5,000 rights would be:

```
Cash (5,000 shares at $15)....................................................75,000
Common Stock Warrants Outstanding (5,000 @ $5) .................25,000
       Common Stock (5,000 shares at par)................................          50,000
       Premium on Common Stock .........................................          50,000
```

Assuming the rights are never exercised (market value below option price), the entry at expiration date would be:

```
Common Stock Warrants Outstanding (15,000 @ $5)................75,000
       Contributed Capital from Lapsed Stock Options ...............          75,000
```

Should the market value of the stock be the same or less than the option price at the date of recognition, date (b) above, a memorandum entry only would be made relative to the rights outstanding. During the time stock options are outstanding a careful record must be kept of the number not exercised and stock must be reserved to meet the requirements of the options. Full disclosure on the balance sheet is required concerning stock options. Information should be given relative to the terms of the option, the number of options outstanding, and the number of shares reserved. In order to "qualify" for tax purposes the option price generally is set at or above, the market price at date option is granted.

The warrants outstanding account should be reported in the capital section of the balance sheet as an item of contributed capital immediately below the capital stock to which it relates. Relative to reporting, *Bulletin 43* states:

In connection with financial statements, disclosure should be made as to the status of the option or plan at the end of the period of report, including the number of shares under option, the option price, and the number of shares as to which options were exercisable. As to options exercised during the period, disclosure should be made of the number of shares involved and the option price thereof.[13]

---

[13] Ibid., p. 124.

The accounting profession, including the APB, continues to be concerned with developing appropriate approaches for measuring the compensation in stock option plans. Hopefully, a theoretically viable approach will be forthcoming from these efforts.

The capital structure of a corporation also is affected through (a) stock splits and (b) quasi-reorganizations. These topics were discussed in Chapter 21.

QUESTIONS FOR CLASS DISCUSSION

1. Define treasury stock.

2. Explain the basic difference in theory between the one-transaction concept and the dual-transaction concept in accounting for treasury stock.

3. In comparing the recording of treasury stock at cost with recording at par "total capital is unaffected, however subdivisions thereof are affected." Explain this statement.

4. Why have many states limited purchases of treasury stock to the amount reported as retained earnings? How may the restriction on retained earnings be removed?

5. In recording treasury stock transactions why are "gains" recorded in a contributed capital account, whereas "losses" are debited to Retained Earnings?

6. How is treasury stock reported on the balance sheet (a) under the cost method and (b) under the par-value method?

7. How is the restriction on retained earnings, equal to the cost of treasury stock held, reported on the balance sheet?

8. How is stock donated back to the corporation recorded? Indicate any preference.

9. What are stock rights? In what situations are stock warrants frequently issued?

10. How is the compensation valued when stock rights are given to employees? What date is pertinent in this respect?

11. How is "stock warrants outstanding" reported on the balance sheet?

DECISION CASE 22-1

Smiley, Incorporated, has issued 5,000 shares of 6% cumulative preferred stock, par value $20 per share, and 10,000° shares of common stock, par value $25 per share. The preferred stock is nonvoting and is callable at a liquidating value of $30 per share plus any cumulative dividends. The current market value of the preferred stock is $23 per share, although the three largest shareholders of preferred (representing 76% of the shares) will not sell their shares, as they say, "at any price." For the past three years the corporation has been averaging 5% earnings on the par value of the shares outstanding. Retained earnings currently total $152,000; cash on hand amounts to $29,000; and the working capital position is approximately 3:1.

° Currently includes 1,000 shares of treasury stock purchased at $26; current market, $27.

In view of the rate of earnings during the past five years and the privileges of the preferred stock, no dividends have been declared for the past three years prior to the current year. The common stockholders are "pressuring" the board of directors to "do something about dividends." The board feels that something must be done and consequently has considered three alternatives, viz: (1) declare dividends of approximately $30,000, (2) call in the preferred shares, or (3) pass dividends again.

Required:

As the independent CPA for the company you have been asked to consult with the board on the problems posed by the pressure from the common stockholders. Specifically, the board requests you to (1) analyze the present situation, (2) analyze all reasonable alternatives, and (3) specifically recommend an alternative. Feel free to comment on any related matters.

DECISION CASE 22-2

The Unknown Corporation purchased $144,000 of equipment in 1970 for $90,000 cash and a promise to deliver an indeterminate number of treasury shares of its $5 par common stock, with a market value of $15,000 on January 1 of each year for the next four years. Hence $60,000 in "market value" of treasury shares will be required to discharge the $54,000 balance due on the equipment.

The corporation then acquired 5,000 shares of its own stock in the expectation that the market value of the stock would increase substantially before the delivery dates.

Required:

1. Discuss the propriety of recording the equipment at—

a) $90,000 (the cash payment).
b) $144,000 (the cash price of the equipment).
c) $150,000 (the $90,000 cash payment + the $60,000 market value of treasury stock that must be transferred to the vendor in order to settle the obligation according to the terms of the agreement).

2. Discuss the arguments *for* treating the balance due as—

a) A liability.
b) Treasury stock subscribed.

3. Assuming that legal requirements do not affect the decision, discuss the arguments *for* treating the corporation's treasury shares as—

a) An asset awaiting ultimate disposition.
b) A capital element awaiting ultimate disposition.

(AICPA adapted)

EXERCISES

Exercise 22-1

Tyler Company had 1,000 shares of $100 par-value stock outstanding, originally sold at 103. On January 15, Tyler purchased 18 shares of its own stock at 105. On March 1, 10 of the treasury shares were sold at 106. Retained earnings balance was $10,000.

Required:

Give all entries indicated in parallel columns, assuming (*a*) the one-transaction concept (cost) and (*b*) the dual-transaction concept (par value). Disregard appropriation of retained earnings. Indicate resulting balances in the capital accounts.

Exercise 22–2

Iowa Corporation had the following stock outstanding:

1,000 shares, par value $100, sold initially at $104...............$104,000
1,000 shares, true no par, sold initially at $26 26,000

The following treasury stock transactions occurred:

a) Purchased 15 shares of the par-value stock at $105.
b) Purchased 10 shares of the no-par-value stock at $27.
c) Sold 10 shares of the par-value stock at $103.
d) Sold 5 shares of the no-par-value stock at $30.

Required:

1. Give all indicated entries; assume dual-transaction (par-value basis) concept; and disregard appropriation of retained earnings.
2. Give resulting balances in the capital accounts; assume starting balance in retained earnings of $8,500.

Exercise 22–3

Topeka Corporation had outstanding 6,000 shares of preferred stock, par value $10, and 5,000 shares of common stock, par value $20. Premium on preferred stock amounted to $2,000, premium on common stock amounted to $7,500, and retained earnings, $28,000. The company purchased 300 shares of preferred at $11 per share and 150 shares of common stock at $20 per share.

Required:

1. Give the entries to record the acquisition of the treasury stock assuming the one-transaction concept (cost basis) is used and retained earnings are appropriated.
2. Prepare the capital section of the balance sheet.

Exercise 22–4

The year-end reports for the Watson Corporation showed the following:

Capital stock, $100 par value, 6,000 shares issued....................$600,000
Premium on capital stock.. 18,000
Retained earnings 175,000

The state law requires that retained earnings be appropriated equal to the cost of treasury stock.

During the year the following transactions affecting corporate capital were recorded:

a) Purchased 700 shares of treasury stock at $102 per share.
b) Purchased 200 shares of treasury stock at $105 per share.
c) Sold 100 shares of treasury stock at $106.

Required:

1. Give all entries indicated in parallel columns, for (*a*) the one-transaction concept (cost basis) and (*b*) the dual-transaction concept (par-value basis).
2. Give resultant balances in the capital accounts.

Exercise 22–5

Johnson Corporation balance sheet reported the following data:

Capital stock, par $100. issued and outstanding
    1,000 shares $100.000
Premium on stock.. 4.000
Retained earnings... 43.000

State laws require restriction of retained earnings for cost of treasury stock. During the current year the following transactions affecting corporate capital were recorded:

a) Purchased 100 shares of treasury stock at $106 per share.
b) Purchased 200 shares of treasury stock at $103 per share.
c) Sold 110 shares of treasury stock at $107 per share.

Required:

1. Give entries in parallel columns for the above transactions (*a*) assuming the one-transaction concept (cost basis) is used and (*b*) assuming the dual-transaction concept (par-value basis) is used.
2. Prepare the capital section of the balance sheet, using parallel columns, for each assumption.

Exercise 22–6

The Denison Manufacturing Corporation balance sheet at December 31 showed the following:

Assets..$90,000
Liabilities... 10,000
Capital:
    Capital stock, 5,000 shares, par $10................................ 50,000
    Treasury stock, 1,000 shares (at cost)............................. 11,000
    Premium on capital stock 2,500
    Retained earnings... 38,500

Required:

1. Prepare a balance sheet for the corporation with special emphasis on the capital section assuming an amount equal to the cost of treasury stock is to be restricted in retained earnings. The one-transaction concept (cost basis) of accounting for treasury stock is used.

2. Prepare the capital section of the balance sheet assuming the dual-transaction concept (par-value basis) of accounting is used and retained earnings is restricted.

3. Illustrate each of the three methods of reporting the restriction on retained earnings.

Exercise 22–7

Karmin Corporation had 30,000 shares of $10 par-value stock authorized of which 20,000 shares were issued three years ago having been sold at $12 per share. During the current year the corporation received 500 shares of stock as a bequest from a deceased shareholder; in addition, 1,000 shares were purchased at $11 per share. State law requires a restriction of retained earnings equal to the cost of treasury stock. At the end of the year a dividend of $.50 per share was paid; prior to the dividend, retained earnings amounted to $35,000.

Required:

1. Prepare entries relative to the above transactions assuming the one-transaction concept (cost basis) for treasury stock is used.

2. Prepare the capital section of the balance sheet at year-end. Assume the donated stock is recorded at fair market value.

Exercise 22–8

Manhattan Manufacturing Company balance sheet at the end of the annual fiscal period reported the following corporate capital:

a) Preferred stock, par $50, issued 2,000 shares.
b) Preferred treasury stock, 200 shares (cost $54 per share).
c) Premium on preferred stock at original issue was $1 per share.
d) Common stock, par $100, issued 3,000 shares.
e) Common treasury stock, 300 shares (cost $98 per share).
f) Premium on common stock at original issue was $2 per share.
g) Retained earnings $110,000 including a restriction equal to cost of the treasury shares.

The shareholders voted to retire all of the treasury stock forthwith and another 400 shares of common stock that could be purchased immediately at $101 per share.

Required:

Give entries, in parallel columns, for purchase and retirement of the 400 shares and the retirement of the 500 shares already in the treasury assuming (a) the one-transaction concept (cost basis) was used in recording treasury stock and (b) the dual-transaction concept (par-value basis) was used.

Exercise 22–9

The balance sheet for the Babson Corporation reported the following:

Preferred stock, 1,000 shares issued, par $100 .... $100,000
Common stock, 1,000 shares issued, par $50 50,000
Premium on preferred stock 5,000
Premium on common stock 2,000
Retained earnings 50,000

The preferred stock is convertible into common stock. Give entry, or entries, required in each of the following cases:

Case A: The preferred shares are converted to common stock on a par-for-par basis; that is, two shares of common are issued for each share of preferred.

Case B: The preferred shares are converted to common share for share.

Case C: The preferred shares are converted to common stock on a one-for-three basis; that is, three shares of common are issued for each share of preferred.

Case D: The preferred shares are converted for a new class of stock known as Common Class B, no-par share for share.

Exercise 22–10

The balance sheet for Gary Corporation at the beginning of the year reported the following:

Common stock, $50 par value, authorized 50,000 shares,
    issued 10,000 .... $500,000
Premium on common stock 3,000
Retained earnings 47,000

During the current year the following transactions were recorded:

a) The company sold at par 20 $10,000 bonds payable giving a stock warrant with each bond which provided for the purchase of two shares of common stock at $58 per share; the current market value of the common stock was $60 per share. The options were to lapse six months from date of issuance.

b) By year-end 60% of the warrants had been exercised, 10% had lapsed, and the remainder were outstanding and in good standing.

c) The stockholders approved a stock option plan for five top executives whereby each received rights to purchase up to 1,000 shares of common stock at $52 per share. When the option was granted to each executive, the shares were selling for $58. The options were nontransferable, and the executive had to remain in the employ of the company to exercise the option; they were to expire at year-end.

d) By year-end four of the executives had exercised their options.

Required:

1. Give entries to record the above transactions.

2. Prepare the capital section of the balance sheet. Assume retained earnings at year-end of $57,528.

PROBLEMS

Problem 22–1

Sprague, Incorporated, reported the following data on the balance sheet at December 31:

Assets	$633,000	Capital:	
Less: Liabilities	100,000	Preferred stock, $10 par	$300,000
		Common stock, $25 par	
		value, 6,000 shares	150,000
		Premium on preferred	15,000
		Retained earnings	68,000
	$533,000		$533,000

The state law requires restriction of retained earnings equal to the cost of treasury stock held.

Subsequent to December 31, the following transactions affecting corporate capital were recorded:

a) Purchased treasury stock (preferred), 300 shares at $13.
b) Purchased treasury stock (common), 500 shares at $24.
c) Sold treasury stock (preferred), 100 shares at $14.50.
d) Sold treasury stock (common), 300 shares at $23.

Required:

1. Give entries in parallel columns for the above transactions (*a*) assuming the one-transaction concept (cost basis) and (*b*) assuming the dual-transaction concept (par-value basis) is used.

2. Indicate the balances in the capital accounts for each assumption.

Problem 22–2

Memphis Corporation reported the following data on the balance sheet at the end of the year:

Common stock, $20 par value, 40,000 shares issued	$800,000
5% preferred stock, $10 par value, 10,000 shares	
authorized, 8,000 issued	80,000
Premium on common stock	24,000
Premium on preferred stock	6,400
Retained earnings	200,000

Subsequent to this date the following transactions affecting corporate capital were recorded:

a) 2,000 shares of treasury stock (common) were purchased at $21 per share.
b) 1,000 shares of treasury stock (preferred) were purchased at $10.50 per share.
c) 1,000 shares of the treasury stock (common) were sold for $21.40 per share.
d) 10 shares of treasury stock (preferred) were transferred to M. R. Battle as payment for services rendered the corporation.

Required:

1. Assuming the state law requires restriction of retained earnings, using parallel columns, record the above transactions (*a*) under the one-transaction concept (cost basis) and (*b*) under the dual-transaction concept (par-value basis). Reflect the restriction on retained earnings in the accounts.

2. Prepare the capital section of the balance sheet for each assumption.

Problem 22–3

Catlett Corporation balance sheet showed the following:

Capital stock, $30 par value, 15,000 shares issued and
  outstanding $450,000
Premium on capital stock.. 30,000
Retained earnings 60,000

Transactions relating to corporate capital were recorded during the year:

a) 300 shares of treasury stock were purchased at $33 per share.
b) 100 shares of Catlett stock were received as a donation.
c) 200 shares of treasury stock were purchased at $31 per share.
d) 100 shares of treasury stock were sold at $28. (Use Fifo.)
e) 300 shares of treasury stock were sold at $32.
f) Dividends of $.50 per share were paid at year-end.
g) Net income amounted to $10,000 for the year.

Required:

1. State law requires restriction of retained earnings for cost of treasury stock. Give entries for the above transactions, assuming the dual-transaction concept (par-value basis) is used in recording treasury stock. Assume Fifo flow on treasury stock sales and that the restriction on retained earnings is reflected in the accounts.

2. Prepare capital section of the balance sheet.

Problem 22–4

The Pure Corporation had authorized and outstanding 5,000 shares of common stock, par value $50 per share. The stockholders approved the recall of the old stock and the exchange for each share of old stock two shares of new common stock. The new authorization was for 15,000 shares of new stock.

Required:

Prepare entries to record the change under each of the following separate cases (assume a sufficient balance in retained earnings):

Case A: The old stock originally was sold at a premium of $2 per share and the new stock was $25 par-value common stock.

Case B: The old stock was sold at a premium of $3 per share and the new stock was no-par-value stock with no stated or assigned value.

Case C: The old stock was sold at a premium of $1 per share and the new stock was no-par-value stock with no stated or assigned value.

Case D: The old stock was sold at par and the new stock was no-par-value stock with no stated or assigned value.

Case E: The old stock was sold at a premium of $2 per share and the new stock was no-par-value stock with a stated value of $20 per share.

Case F: The old stock was sold at a premium of $5 per share and the new stock was no-par-value stock with a stated value of $30 per share.

Case G: The old stock was sold at par and the new stock was no-par-value stock with a stated value of $27.50 per share.

Problem 22-5

The following account balances were shown on the books of Wonder Corporation at December 31:

```
Cumulative preferred stock, par $100, 6% 1,000 shares ............$100,000
Common stock, par $50, 4,000 shares ..................................... 200,000
Retained earnings (deficit) ................................................... (45,000)
```

At a stockholders' meeting (including holders of preferred shares) the following plan was decided on:

a) That an amendment to the charter be obtained authorizing a total issue of 2,000 shares of noncumulative 8% preferred, par $100 per share, and 20,000 shares of no-par common stock.

b) That all outstanding stock be returned in exchange for new stock as follows:

1) For each share of old preferred, one share of new preferred. Purchased for cash at par 20 shares of old preferred stock from a dissatisfied stockholder.

2) For each share of old common, two shares of new common, with the understanding that $50,000 of the amount originally paid in for this stock be transferred to a paid-in capital account.

c) That the past operating deficit be written off against the credit created by the stock conversion.

During the ensuing year the following transactions were effected:

d) One hundred shares of the new preferred stock were sold at 101, payable 10% down and 10% per month until fully paid. Stock to be issued after last monthly payment.

e) The downpayment and the first two monthly installments were collected on the stock sold in (d).

f) All of the third monthly payment on the stock sold in (d) was collected except that due from one subscriber to 10 shares. His subscription was declared forfeited; state law does not require the corporation to account to the subscriber.

g) The company issued 1,200 shares of no-par common in payment for a patent tentatively valued by the seller at $20,000. (The market value of a share was $15.)

h) The company sold 50 shares of no-par common at 15, receiving cash, and at the same time issued 100 $1,000 bonds at 102, giving one share of common stock as a bonus with each bond.

i) At the end of the year the board of directors met and was informed that the net income before deductions for bonuses to officers was $100,000. The directors took the following actions:
  1) Ordered that 500 shares of no-par common stock (from authorized but unissued shares) be issued to officers as a bonus. The market price of a no-par common share on this date was $16.
  2) Declared dividends (for one year) on the preferred stock outstanding.

Required:

  1. Prepare journal entries to record the above capital transactions.
  2. Prepare capital section of the balance sheet.

Problem 22–6

On January 1, the books of the AB Corporation provided the following trial balance (condensed):

Assets	$450,000	
Liabilities		$ 46,000
Preferred stock, par $100 (authorized 2,000 shares)		100,000
Common stock, par $20 (15,000 shares authorized)		200,000
Premium on preferred stock		10,000
Premium on common stock		2,000
Donated capital (plant site)		15,000
Common stock subscribed (at par)		20,000
Treasury stock, preferred (200 shares at cost)°	23,000	
Retained earnings		80,000
	$473,000	$473,000

°One-transaction concept (cost basis).

During the ensuing period the following transactions occurred:

a) Collected the $5,000 balance due on the subscribed stock; issued the shares.

b) Purchased 100 shares of treasury stock, common at $23 per share (use cost basis).

c) Sold 50 shares of preferred treasury stock at $108 per share.

d) Paid $20,000 on liabilities.

e) Purchased machinery costing $40,000, paid 60% down, balance due in one year.

f) Received subscriptions to 500 shares of common stock at $24, collected 20% down.

g) Transferred 100 shares of preferred treasury stock for a patent; at the time preferred shares were selling at $112.

h) Issued 1,000 common stock rights to each of three executives. The option provided that the rights could be exercised at any time at a price of $21. Common stock was selling at $25. Debit retained earnings.

i) One executive exercised the rights received in (*h*).

j) Net income for the year amounted to $21,050.

k) Declared and paid dividends on all outstanding stock as follows: preferred, 8%; common, $1.50 per share.

Required:

1. Set up a four-column interim worksheet with headings for beginning balances, entries debit, entries credit, and ending balances. Enter the above transactions, keying the entries. Use one account for all assets, one account for all liabilities, and detailed accounts for capital.

2. Prepare a balance sheet with particular attention to the capital section.

Problem 22-7

The following condensed trial balance was taken from the books of the Flint Corporation at December 31:

Assets	$584,000	
Liabilities		$ 60,000
Common stock, $10 par value (100,000 shares authorized; 40,000 shares issued)		400,000
Premium on common stock		4,000
Retained earnings		120,000
	$584,000	$584,000

During the year the following transactions were recorded:

a) Subscriptions were received for 10,000 shares of common stock at $11 per share; 40% of the subscription price was collected.

b) A patent was acquired in exchange for 5,000 shares of common stock. The owner valued the patent at $60,000. Common stock was selling at $11.

c) An original stockholder desired to get his money back from the corporation for 1,000 shares he had purchased at $10.10 per share. The corporation purchased the shares paying $10.50 per share. The dual-transaction concept (par-value method) is used for treasury stock.

d) The balance on subscriptions (a) was collected; the stock was issued.

e) Machinery costing $34,000 was purchased; 50% was paid down, the balance due in one year.

f) The charter was amended authorizing 200,000 shares of no-par common stock, (to replace the par-value common stock) and 5,000 shares of preferred stock, par $100.

g) The old common stock (54,000 shares outstanding) was exchanged for the new no-par stock; two shares of the new stock were issued for each share of old stock. The 1,000 shares of treasury stock were canceled.

h) 1,000 shares of the preferred stock were sold at $105.

i) Officers were given stock options to purchase 4,000 shares of preferred stock at $101 when the stock was selling at $105. Debit Retained Earnings.

j) 2,000 shares of preferred stock were issued under the stock option agreement.

k) 200 shares of common were reacquired as treasury stock at $12; and 100 shares of preferred at $105.

l) Net income for the period was $34,364.

m) A 3% dividend was declared on the preferred, and $.50 per share was declared on the common stock.

Required:

1. Set up an interim worksheet with debit and credit columns for beginning balances, interim entries, and ending balances (six columns). Enter the beginning balances and the transactions. Key the entries. Do not detail the assets and liabilities; use one account "Assets" and one account "Liabilities."

2. Prepare a balance sheet with particular emphasis on the capital section.

Problem 22-8

You have just commenced your audit of Shaky Company for the year ended December 31, 19B. The president advises you that the company is insolvent and must declare bankruptcy unless a large loan can be obtained immediately. A lender who is willing to advance $450,000 to the company has been located, but he will only make the loan subject to the following conditions:

1. A $600,000, 6% mortgage payable on the company's land and buildings held by a major stockholder will be canceled along with four months' accrued interest. The mortgage will be replaced by 5,000 shares of $100 par-value, 6%, cumulative if earned, nonparticipating preferred stock.

2. A $450,000, 8% mortgage payable over 15 years on the land and buildings will be given as security on the new loan (cash received $450,000).

3. On May 1, 19A, the company's trade creditors had accepted $360,000 in notes payable on demand at 6% interest in settlement of all past-due accounts. No payment has been made to date on the notes. The company will offer to settle these liabilities at $.75 per $1.00 owed or to replace the notes payable on demand with new notes payable for full indebtedness over five years at 6% interest. It is estimated that $200,000 of the demand notes will be exchanged for the longer term notes and that the balance will accept the offer of a reduced cash settlement.

4. A new issue of 500 shares of $100 par-value, 5%, noncumulative, nonparticipating preferred stock will replace 500 outstanding shares of $100 par-value, 7%, cumulative, participating preferred stock. Preferred stockholders will repudiate all claims to $21,000 of dividends in arrears. The company has never formally declared the dividends.

5. A new issue of 600 shares of $50 par-value, class A common stock will replace 600 outstanding shares of $100 par-value, class A common stock.

6. A new issue of 650 shares of $40 par-value, class B common stock will replace 650 outstanding shares of $100 par-value, class B common stock.

The president of the Shaky Company requests that you determine the effect of the foregoing on the company and furnishes the following condensed account balances, which you believe are fairly presented:

Bank overdraft	$ 15,000
Other current assets	410,000
Fixed assets	840,000
Trade accounts payable	235,000
Other current liabilities	85,000
Contributed capital in excess of par value	125,000
Retained earnings deficit	345,000

Required:

1. Prepare pro forma journal entries that you would suggest to give effect to the foregoing as of January 1, 19C. Entries should be keyed to numbered information in order.

2. Prepare a pro forma balance sheet for the Shaky Company at January 1, 19C, as if the recapitalization had been consummated.

(AICPA adapted)

chapter **23**

Some Special
Problems of
Income Determination

PART A – INCOME TAX ALLOCATION

There are two distinct aspects of income tax allocation, viz:

1. Intraperiod (interstatement) allocation of income tax expense. The total income tax expense[1] for the period is first determined; the total then must be allocated to appropriate classifications on the period financial statement. Thus, the total income tax expense for the period is allocated to (a) ordinary income, (b) extraordinary items, (c) retained earnings, and (d) other owners' equity accounts, to the extent that each of these classifications reports items that affected the total income tax expense for the period. The concept of intraperiod tax allocation is that the tax consequences must follow the item on the financial statement. Illustration 23–1 presents a hypothetical situation that demonstrates (a) *intraperiod* (or interstatement) tax allocation affecting three primary financial statements and (b) the basic reason why intraperiod tax allocation is essential. *Intraperiod* income tax allocation was discussed in Chapter 4 (pages 142 to 143); it is strongly

---

[1] Income tax expense for the period is the algebraic sum of income taxes payable for the period (per the income tax return) and the effects of timing differences for the period; see subsequent paragraphs in this part.

recommended that you return to that discussion preliminary to studying Part A of this chapter.[2]

Illustration 23-1
Interstatement (Intraperiod) Tax Allocation — Hypothetical

1. Assumed income tax rate for illustrative purposes, average rate of 40% on all items.
2. Items subject to income taxes:
   a) Pretax operating income, $100,000
   b) Extraordinary loss, $5,000
   c) Prior period adjustment (decrease in retained earnings), $20,000
   d) Decrease in owners' equity, $10,000
3. Income tax expense, $26,000

	Without Intraperiod Tax Allocation (Incorrect)	With Intraperiod Tax Allocation (Correct)	
Income statement:			
Pretax operating income	$100,000		$100,000
Less: Income tax expense	26,000		40,000
Income before extraordinary item	$ 74,000		$ 60,000
Extraordinary loss	(5,000)	$ 5,000	
Less: Applicable tax saving		2,000	(3,000)
Net income	$ 69,000		$ 57,000
Statement of retained earnings:			
Prior period adjustment (decrease)	$ 20,000	$20,000	
Less: Applicable tax saving		8,000	$ 12,000
Balance sheet:			
Owners' equity (decrease)	$ 10,000	$10,000	
Less: Applicable tax saving		4,000	$ 6,000

2. **Interperiod allocation of income tax expense.** The allocation of income tax expense between accounting periods is occasioned by the fact that some transactions (or items) affect the determination of net income for financial reporting purposes in one reporting period and the computation of income taxes payable in a different reporting period. Part A of this chapter focuses on *interperiod* income tax allocation.

Need for Interperiod Allocation of Income Tax Expenses

Federal income taxes are, by far, the most significant tax levied on the corporation both in respect to complexity and to the impact on decisions of the management and on the resultant financial reports. In the early days income taxes were levied primarily on a cash basis; since 1918 this approach has been modified to more generally conform to accrual accounting as reflected on the periodic financial reports. Despite this trend there are today many divergencies be-

---

[2] Both timing differences and permanent differences affect intraperiod (interstatement) tax allocation; see page 890.

tween *accounting* net income and *taxable* net income for any given period. Clearly, the objectives of income taxation, in addition to that of raising revenues (presumably according to ability to pay), encompass such aims as: to control the economy, to promote full employment, to stimulate capital expenditures, and to attain certain social ends (i.e., tax deductibility of contributions to certain types of institutions). Thus, there are many differences between accounting net income and taxable net income.

For many years following the passage of the first federal income tax law, considerable difference of opinion as to the essential nature of the income tax payment existed among both accounting theorists and practitioners. Some held that income taxes were in reality a partial *distribution of earnings* (somewhat analogous to a dividend payment) and should be so reflected on the financial reports of the corporation. In contrast, as tax rates increased many became convinced that income taxes should be considered an *expense* or cost of doing business and should be so reflected on the periodic financial statements. This latter view has tended to prevail and provides the basis for the allocation of income taxes (both intraperiod and interperiod). Since income tax is viewed as an expense, accrual accounting concepts should be applied to it. The following statement of the Committee on Accounting Procedure of the AICPA has received general acceptance: "Income taxes are an expense that should be allocated, when necessary and practicable, to income and other accounts, as other expenses are allocated. What the income statement should reflect under this head, as under any other head, is the expense properly allocable to the income included in the income statement for the year."[3]

The numerous differences between accounting income and taxable income give rise to *tax differences,* some of which must be given recognition in the accounts and in the resultant financial statements. The central question is the extent to which accounting recognition should be given to these income tax differences. Accounting recognition of the tax differences is contingent upon the *type* of difference; there are two distinct types: (1) timing differences and (2) permanent differences.

1. *Timing Differences.* Differences between the periods in which transactions or items affect accounting income and the periods in which they affect taxable income give rise to a tax difference between the periods; these are known as timing differences. Timing differences originate in one period and reverse or turn around in one or more subsequent periods. Some timing differences reduce income taxes that would otherwise be payable in the current period while other differences increase income taxes that would otherwise be paya-

---

[3] Committee on Accounting Procedure, AICPA, "Restatement and Revision of Accounting Research Bulletins," *Accounting Research Bulletin No. 43* (New York, June, 1961), p. 88.

ble in the current period. "Interperiod tax allocation is an integral part of the determination of income tax expense, and income tax expense (as reported on the financial statements) should include the tax effects of revenue and expense transactions included in the determination of pretax accounting income."[4] Four types of transactions give rise to timing differences, viz.:

a) Revenues or gains are included in taxable income one or more periods after they are included in accounting income; for example, gross profit on installment sales.

b) Expenses or losses are deducted in determining taxable income one or more periods after they are deducted in determining accounting income; for example, estimated (accrued) warranty costs.

c) Revenues or gains are included in taxable income before they are included in accounting income; for example, rent collected in advance.

d) Expenses or losses are deducted in determining taxable income before they are deducted in determining accounting income; for example, depreciation on an accelerated basis for tax purposes, but on a straight line basis for accounting income purposes.

2. *Permanent Differences.* Items that are reflected on the income statement but are *never* permitted on the income tax return; and alternatively, items that are *never* reflected on the income statement but must be reflected on the income tax return are known as permanent differences. Illustrations are:

Expense on income statement but not permitted on the tax return — allocable portion of premiums paid on officers' life insurance.

Income on income statement but not permitted on tax return — interest income received on municipal bonds.

Expense deduction on tax return but not on income statement — statutory depletion on natural resources (in excess of cost depletion).

Thus, permanent differences in income tax, as defined above, never balance out over time as between accounting income and taxable income. "*Since permanent differences do not affect other periods, interperiod tax allocation is not appropriate to account for such differences.*"[5]

The essential characteristics of *interperiod* tax allocation and the related accounting recognition can be simply illustrated. Assume

---

[4] AICPA, "Accounting for Income Taxes," *APB Opinion No. 11* (New York, 1967) (parentheses added), p. 158.

[5] AICPA, "Accounting for Income Taxes," *APB Opinion No. 11* (New York, 1967), p. 169.

that XY Corporation reported pretax operating income of $18,000 in year A and also in year B. Assume further that the income tax rate was 40% and that in year A a $12,000 expense item was deducted on the income statement but was not allowable as a deduction on the tax return until year B; thus there is a timing difference. The results would be as follows:

	Year A		Year B
Without tax allocation:			
Pretax operating income................................	$18,000		$18,000
Less applicable income tax expense (per tax return) ($18,000 + $12,000) × .40...........	12,000	($18,000 − $12,000) × .40	2,400
Net income..	$ 6,000		$15,600
With interperiod tax allocation:			
Pretax income...	$18,000		$18,000
Less applicable income tax expense (allocation basis) $18,000 × .40......................	7,200		7,200
Net income..	$10,800		$10,800

Observe that *total* income for the two years, with and without allocation, is identical ($21,600) although the detail reported is quite different for each year. The same is true in respect to the income tax expense. The results are dissimilar due to the effect of a *timing difference* of $4,800 in income tax expense between the two years. Note that the timing difference in year A reverses in year B. The illustration has been drawn to pinpoint the fundamental basis for interperiod tax allocation, that is, to reflect the income tax expense on the income statement on an accrual basis. Note that, although pretax operating income is identical in both years, without interperiod tax allocation materially different net income amounts are reported as between year A and year B. In contrast, under allocation procedures, the reported net income amounts are identical. The interperiod income tax allocations reflected on the above income statements would be *recorded in the accounts* at each year-end as follows:

Year A

Income Tax Expense..	.7,200	
Deferred Income Taxes	.4,800	
Income Taxes Payable		12,000

Year B

Income Tax Expense..	.7,200	
Deferred Income Taxes		4,800
Income Taxes Payable		2,400

The balance in the deferred income tax account would be reported on the *balance sheet* at the end of year A as explained in a subsequent paragraph. A more comprehensive example, involving both intraperiod (interstatement) and interperiod tax allocations, is shown in Illustration 23–2.

Illustration 23-2
Interperiod Tax Allocation — Installment Sales

Assumptions:
(1) Income tax rates: First $25,000, 22%; above $25,000, 48%; capital gains, 25%.
(2) Income on installment sales is included in the income tax return in period of collection rather than in period of sale. Collections on installment sales assumed to be in year following sale.
(3) Data per accounts:

	19A	19B
Income on regular sales	$100,000	$140,000
Income on installment sales	40,000	-0-
Extraordinary gain on sale of fixed assets	9,600	9,600

Computations on income tax return:

	19A	19B
On regular sales:	$25,000 × 22% = $ 5,500	$ 25,000 × 22% = $ 5,500
	75,000 × 48% = 36,000	115,000 × 48% = 55,200
On installment sales:°		40,000 × 48% = 19,200
On extraordinary gain:	9,600 × 25% = 2,400	9,600 × 25% = 2,400
	$43,900	$82,300

°Other assumptions are acceptable in respect of "order" of regular and installment sales.

Partial Income Statement — with Intraperiod and Interperiod Tax Allocation

		19A		19B
Income on regular sales		$100,000		$140,000
Income on installment sales		40,000		
Total income before tax and extraordinary items		$140,000		$140,000
Less: Applicable income taxes†		60,700		60,700
Income before extraordinary items		$ 79,300		$ 79,300
Extraordinary items:				
Gain on sale of fixed assets	$9,600		$9,600	
Less: Applicable income tax†	2,400	7,200	2,400	7,200
Net Income		$ 86,500		$ 86,500

†Computation of income tax expense (accrual or allocation basis)
Same for each year
$ 25,000 × 22% = $ 5,500
115,000 × 48% = 55,200 $60,700
9,600 × 25% =   2,400
Total tax expense $63,100

Entries in the accounts to reflect the tax allocation:

19A

Income Tax Expense	63,100	
Deferred Income Taxes		19,200
Income Taxes Payable		43,900

19B

Income Tax Expense	63,100	
Deferred Income Taxes	19,200	
Income Taxes Payable		82,300

Note: For comparative purposes observe that, without income tax allocation, reported net income for 19A would have been $105,700 and for 19B, $67,300; each amount is materially different than that reported under allocation procedures.

Nature of Deferred Income Taxes

When the Deferred Income Taxes account has a debit balance inferentially at least the account could be construed as a deferred charge. When this account has a credit balance, as in Illustration 23-2, a deferred credit might be inferred. In Chapter 3 and elsewhere, the authors have indicated a preference for classifying *real* accounts with credit balances as either contra asset accounts, liabilities, or part of capital. Accounting practice, unfortunately, seems to show little hesitancy in reporting some such accounts, including those arising from tax allocation, under a deferred credits caption.

Suppose, for the moment, the word *expense* is added to "deferred income tax" when the account has a debit balance and the word *liability* is added when it has a credit balance. Even so titled, neither account accords very well with the standard definition of assets and liabilities. "Deferred income tax expense" arises when the current tax liability actually exceeds the tax applicable to income reported on the income statement. However, the government would not view any tax as having been prepaid. The account is a result of an attempt at better matching of expense with revenue. Essentially parallel reasoning can be applied to "deferred income tax liability." This account arises out of matching because the current tax liability is less than the amount charged on the income statement as tax expense. The credit amount reported in the account is not currently owed to the government (and may never be).

Some accountants view a *real* account arising from tax allocation as a deferred credit; others view it as a liability. While debit balances in such accounts are somewhat less common, it seems reasonable to infer that adherents to the deferred credit concept would view such debit balances as deferred charges. There does not seem to be a single, easy answer to the question of classification or of terminology. One matter is fairly certain: when the account has a credit balance it is not to be reported as part of *capital*. Attempts to do this by several public utilities a number of years ago evoked specific rejections from both an AICPA committee and the SEC. On this point *APB Opinion 11* on tax allocation reads:

Deferred charges and deferred credits relating to timing differences represent the cumulative recognition given to their tax effects and as such do not represent receivables or payables in the usual sense. They should be classified in two categories — one for the net current amount and the other for the net noncurrent amount. This presentation is consistent with the customary distinction between current and noncurrent categories and also recognizes the close relationship among the various deferred tax accounts, all of which bear on the determination of income tax expense. The current portions of such deferred charges and credits should be those amounts which relate to assets and liabilities classified as current. Thus, if installment receivables are a current asset, the deferred credits representing the tax effects of uncollected installment sales should be a current item; if an estimated provision for warranties is a current liability, the deferred charge representing the tax effect of such provision should be a current item.[6]

Some terminology which has been suggested when a *debit balance* is developed includes "deferred income tax expense," "prepaid income tax expense," and "deferred charges to income tax expense." The authors favor deferred income tax expense because it is comparatively short and does not connote that it is a working capital item. Terms suggested when there is a *credit balance* include "deferred income tax liability," "income taxes payable in future years," "deferred income tax credit," "deferred credit to income tax expense," and "deferred federal taxes on income." It should be noted that the brief title used in the illustrations — "deferred income taxes" — is used by some accountants (and in the illustrations in this chapter for simplicity) and is unlikely to be misunderstood so long as there is but a single type of balance (debit or credit) arising from tax allocation and is properly classified on the balance sheet.[7]

Disclosure of Tax Allocation

Disclosure of the components of income tax expense (including deferred income taxes) can be complex. In respect to the income statement *APB Opinion 11* states that "the components of income tax expense should be disclosed," that is, in addition to *intraperiod* allocation, taxes estimated to be payable and the tax effects of timing differences should be reported. The Opinion states that these amounts "may be presented as separate items in the income statement or, alternatively, as combined amounts with disclosure of the components parenthetically or in a note to the financial statements." An example of the footnote approach is shown in Illustration 23–3.

Balance sheet disclosure requires (*a*) that income taxes payable be set out separately from deferred tax amounts and (*b*) that deferred tax balances be reported in two amounts — a net *current* amount and a net *noncurrent* amount. The classification of the deferred amounts as current or noncurrent is on the basis of the related assets and liabili-

---

[6] "Accounting for Income Taxes," *APB Opinion No. 11* (New York: AICPA. December 1967), p. 178.

[7] It can be demonstrated that so long as a business continues to replace property which is depreciated more rapidly for tax than for book purposes, the "deferred income tax liability" will not mature. Indeed, if the replacement cost of such property rises or the total investment in depreciable property rises, the liability account will grow and grow and if one ignores "turnover" will never be paid. It is also true that if a business becomes less profitable in the future or if its income for that reason or for another reason is taxed at lower rates, the full amount will not be paid. It is also true that if a business fails to generate taxable income in the future, the amount will never be owed; a prediction this will occur is probably a departure from the continuity or going-concern assumption.

Illustration 23–3
Disclosure of Income Tax Allocation – Income Statement
B CORPORATION
Income Statement (partial)
For the Year Ended December 31, 19B

Income from operations		$120,000
Less: Income tax expense (Note A)		48,000°
Income before extraordinary items		$ 72,000
Extraordinary items:		
Loss on sale of fixed asset	$30,000	
Less: Applicable income tax	12,000	18,000
Net income		$ 54,000

Note to Financial Statement

A. Income tax payable was computed as follows:

Income tax expense on current operations	$48,000
Add decrease in current deferred tax credit	2,000
Deduct increase in noncurrent deferred tax credit	(3,000)
Income taxes payable on current operations	$47,000
Deduct tax saving on sale of fixed asset	12,000
Income taxes currently payable	$35,000

°An average tax rate of 40% is assumed on all items for illustrative purposes.

ties. For example, if a deferred tax credit arises as a result of installment receivables that are classified as current assets, then the tax
credit would be classified as current. Reporting in this manner is
reflected in Illustration 23–4.

Disclosure of income taxes and the related tax allocations in an

Illustration 23–4
Disclosure of Deferred Taxes – Balance Sheet
B CORPORATION
Balance Sheet (partial)
December 31, 19B

Current liabilities:	
Income taxes payable (Note A)	$35,000
Deferred income taxes (Note B)	11,000
Long-term liabilities:	
Deferred income taxes (Note B)	19,000

Notes to Financial Statement

A. Shown in Illustration 23–3.

B. The current portion of deferred income taxes is for gross
profit on installment sales not yet taxed; the net decrease
for the current year was $2,000. The noncurrent portion
was for the excess tax credit for accelerated depreciation
on the tax return over straight line depreciation reflected
on the income statement; the net increase for the year was
$3,000.

actual situation may be observed in Illustrations 18–3 and 18–6 (pages 727 and 728).

Methods of Interperiod Income Tax Allocation

There are three methods (or concepts) in respect to how the income tax effects of timing differences should be accounted for. The three methods briefly are:

1. *Deferred Method.* This method is utilized throughout this book; in *Opinion 11* the APB stated: "the deferred method of tax allocation should be followed since it provides the most useful and practical approach to interperiod tax allocation and the presentation of income taxes in financial statements."

Under this method the timing differences are recognized in the period in which they originate and are not adjusted subsequently for changes in tax rates or to reflect the imposition of new taxes. The tax effects of transactions which reduce taxes currently payable are reflected as deferred tax charges. The future effect on income tax expense is reflected when the timing differences reverse.

2. *Liability Method.* This method recognizes changes in tax rates and the imposition of new taxes. The difference between the income tax expense for the current period and the taxes currently payable (or prepaid) is recorded as a liability for taxes (or as a receivable), computed by using the tax rates *expected* to be in effect in the future when the timing differences reverse. Under the liability method the initial computations (and entries) are considered to be tentative and subject to future adjustment to reflect changes in tax rates. The liability method has considerable merit theoretically; however, it is not currently used much in view of the APB preference.

3. *Net of Tax Method.* Under this method the tax effects of timing differences (determined by either the deferred or liability methods) are factors in the valuation of assets and liabilities and the related revenues and expenses. The tax effects are applied to reduce specific assets or liabilities on the basis that taxability are relevant factors in their valuation. Thus, many assets, liabilities, revenues, and expenses under this method would be reflected at their "net of tax" amount. This method has gained very little practical support.

Comprehensive versus Partial Tax Allocation

There are continuing disagreements in respect to interperiod tax allocation; there appears to be little disagreement in respect to inter-statement allocation. It appears that practically all accountants favor interperiod tax allocation; however, there is disagreement as to how far it should be extended. The proponents of *comprehensive* allocation feel that the effects of *all* timing differences should be reflected in the accounts and financial statements. They believe that only by giving timely recognition to the tax effects of all timing differences is it possible to obtain a consistent and thorough application of the matching principle, one of the basic processes of income determination. On the other hand, those who favor *partial* tax allocation feel that there is only a narrow range of situations that justify tax allocation. They start with the general presumption that the income tax *expense* reported for the period should be the computed income taxes *payable* for that period. They then argue that this general presumption should be changed only when there are specific, nonrecurring differences between accounting income and taxable income that if not recognized as to their tax effects would lead to material misstatement of income tax expense and net income. Thus, they would not apply allocation procedures to (*a*) recurring timing differences, (*b*) differences that result in indefinite postponement of income tax liability, (*c*) differences that reflect remote contingencies, and (*d*) accruals that do not reflect actual tax liabilities (or receivables). The APB in *Opinion 11* took a firm position in favor of comprehensive tax allocation; for this reason, and for those cited in preceding paragraphs, the discussions in this chapter assumed comprehensive tax allocation.

Operating Losses and Tax Allocation

Federal tax laws allow corporations which sustain losses to carry back and carry forward such losses (which are subject to various adjustments before they become carrybacks or carryforwards). The effect can be that a corporation may secure refunds of income taxes paid in three prior years, and if the loss is so large that after adjustment it is not absorbed fully when offset against the profitable years to which it is carried back, it can be carried forward for as many as five years during which it may serve to reduce taxes that would otherwise be owed on income of those years.

Loss Carryback. In a period where an operating loss follows a period of net income sufficient to offset the loss, the resultant tax carryback will give rise to a refund of income taxes paid in the prior period. Since the refund is virtually certain, the effect should be recorded in the accounts and reflected in the financial statement for the loss period. *APB Opinion 11* states the following:

The tax effects of any realizable loss carry*backs* should be recognized in the determination of net income (loss) of the loss periods. The tax loss gives rise to a refund (or claim for refund) of past taxes, which is both measurable and currently realizable; therefore the tax effect of the loss is properly recognizable in the determination of net income (loss) for the loss period. Appropriate adjustments of existing net deferred tax credits may also be necessary in the loss period.

To illustrate, assume AB Corporation reported net income before taxes of $80,000 in 19A, its first year of operations. Since the average tax rate was 40% (for illustrative purposes) and book and taxable income coincided, the corporation paid $32,000 in income tax. In 19B, due to a recession, the books showed a net loss. This loss was subject to certain technical adjustments which reduced it to a carryback of $20,000, entitling the company to a refund of $8,000 taxes paid in 19A. The books would reflect the following entry:

19B:

```
Receivable for Refund of 19A Income Taxes..............................8,000
    Refund of Income Taxes Due to Loss.................................        8,000
```

The bottom portion of the 19B income statement would show:

```
Net loss before recognition of tax effect.................$25,000
Deduct estimated refund of prior year income tax due
    to loss carryback...........................................    8,000
Net Loss...............................................................$17,000
```

Loss Carryforward. In the situation where a company has experienced a net operating loss, which cannot be offset through a carryback, it may be realized as a carryforward up to five years in the future. Where the years preceding a loss year have been profitable there can be little doubt that a carry*back* equal to or less than the profits of the years to which it can be applied will be fully realized. On the other hand, uncertainty must necessarily attend the realizability of a carry*forward* since future profits are uncertain. On this point the APB in *Opinion 11* stated:

The tax effects of loss carry*forwards* also relate to the determination of net income (loss) of the loss periods. However, a significant question generally exists as to realization of the tax effects of the carry*forwards*, since realization is dependent upon future taxable income. Accordingly, the Board has concluded that the tax benefits of loss carry*forwards* should not be recognized until they are actually realized, except in unusual circumstances when realization is *assured beyond any reasonable doubt* at the time the loss carry*forwards* arise. When the tax benefits of loss carry*forwards* are not recognized until realized in full or in part in subsequent periods, the tax benefits should be reported in the results of those periods as extraordinary items.

To illustrate the carry-forward case assume that Z Corporation sustained a $50,000 net operating loss during the first year of operations. Assuming, for illustrative purposes, a 40% corporate average tax rate a potential loss carryforward of $20,000 arises. Whether or not Z Corporation will be able to avail itself of this as a *future* tax saving depends upon whether or not future income is earned. In view of the uncertainty of future income, appropriate accounting for the potential carryforward in the year of the loss is somewhat troublesome. Fundamentally, three accounting approaches are available:

1. Recognize the tax carryforward as an asset (receivable for tax refund) and reduce the current operating loss by the amount of the tax carryforward; to illustrate:

Year of loss:

```
Receivable for Tax Refund (carryforward)..............................20,000
    Income Summary (income tax expense)..........................          20,000
```

```
Income Statement:
    Pretax operating loss...............................................$50,000
        Less: Tax carryforward ($50,000 × 40%)..................  20,000
    Net Loss...........................................................$30,000
```

Succeeding year; assuming a pretax net operating profit of $80,000:

```
Income Tax Expense ........................................................32,000
    Receivable for Tax Refund (carryforward).........................          20,000
    Income Taxes Payable ................................................          12,000
```

```
Income Statement:
    Pretax operating income...........................................$80,000
        Less: Income tax expense....................................  32,000
    Net Income ......................................................$48,000
```

2. Do not recognize the tax carryforward in the period of the loss; report the tax saving in the future period(s) when realized as an extraordinary item (correction of prior period loss); to illustrate:

Year of loss: No entry.

```
Income Statement:
    Pretax operating loss ....................................$50,000
    Income tax expense (carryforward).................   -0-
    Net Loss.................................................$50,000
```

Succeeding year; assuming a pretax net operating profit of $80,000:

```
Income Tax Expense ........................................................32,000
    Extraordinary Item (correction) ......................................          20,000
    Income Taxes Payable ................................................          12,000
```

```
Income Statement:
    Pretax operating income ..............................$80,000
        Less: Income tax expense..........................  32,000
    Income before extraordinary items.................$48,000
    Extraordinary item:
        Tax carryforward......................................  20,000
    Net Income................................................$68,000
```

3. Do not recognize the tax carryforward in the period of the loss; report the tax saving in the future period(s) when realized as an offset to the current income tax expense; to illustrate:

Year of loss: No entry.

Income Statement:

Pretax operating loss	$50,000
Income tax expense (carryforward)	–0–
Net Loss	$50,000

Succeeding year; assuming pretax net operating profit of $80,000:

Income Tax Expense	12,000	
Income Taxes Payable		12,000

Income Statement:

Pretax operating income		$80,000
Less: Income tax expense	$32,000	
Less: Tax carryforward	20,000	12,000
Net Income		$68,000

Selection of the appropriate alternative depends upon the circumstances. Clearly, in the absence of *uncertainty* alternative 1 is preferable. Since the tax saving in the succeeding year was due solely to the loss in year 1, the benefit should be reflected in the loss period. Seldom is the degree of certainty sufficient to justify alternative 1. On this point the APB in *Opinion 11* stated that alternative 1 was appropriate only when realization is assured. The Opinion stated that:

Realization of the tax benefit of a loss carry*forward* would appear to be assured beyond any reasonable doubt when both of the following conditions exist: (a) the loss results from an identifiable, isolated and nonrecurring cause and the company either has been continuously profitable over a long period or has suffered occasional losses which were more than offset by taxable income in subsequent years, and (b) future taxable income is virtually certain to be large enough to offset the loss carry*forward* and will occur soon enough to provide realization during the carry*forward* period.

Since alternative 1 is appropriate *only* when realization of the tax benefit of the loss carry*forward* is assured beyond reasonable doubt; alternative 2 or 3 must be utilized for all other circumstances. *APB Opinion 11* clearly stated a preference for alternative 2 (see quotation from the Opinion on page 896).

In selecting between alternatives 2 and 3 observe that if the potential tax saving *materializes* (i.e., after the decision was made in the year of loss not to recognize it) alternative 2 is preferable. In this case net loss in year 1 is misstated; in year 2 income before extraordinary items is correctly stated, yet net income is misstated. On the other hand, under method 3 all of these amounts would be misstated. Alternatively, if the potential tax saving does *not* materialize method 3 would give the correct amounts; so too would method 2. Thus, on balance it appears that method 2 is preferable when there is a material degree of uncertainty.

Some Problems in Tax Allocation

There are special problems in tax allocation that we have not discussed up to this point; they will be considered briefly in this section.

Tax Rates. The deferred method, approved by *APB Opinion 11*, utilizes the tax rates in effect when the timing difference originates and ignores future changes in such rates, thus resolving the problem of changing rates, at least temporarily. Another rate problem affecting tax allocation is due to the fact that in any given period the taxable income may be subject to normal, surtax, and capital gains rates. As noted earlier in the text, some accountants prefer to utilize an "average" rate; *APB Opinion 11* requires application of the differential rates, with the "first cut" being applied to operating income. Another problem is posed when taxable income fluctuates above and below the $25,000 amount subject to the normal rate; in such cases sound judgment would suggest the use of an average rate.

Discounting of Deferred Taxes. In view of the fact that a significant amount in the deferred tax account may not "reverse" in the short run, strong arguments have been made that discounting (present value computations) should be applied to such amounts in order properly to measure the income tax expense and deferred credit (or charge) for postponed income taxes. On this point *APB Opinion 11* stated that "deferred taxes should not be accounted for on a discounted basis." Currently the Board and other interested parties are giving further study to this proposal.

Special Problems in Intraperiod Tax Allocation

In the last few years primary attention has been devoted to interperiod tax allocation as opposed to intraperiod tax allocation. As a consequence, numerous instances have been observed of misstatement and misleading inferences on financial statements resulting from failure to apply appropriate *intraperiod* tax allocation. Intraperiod tax allocation requires that the income tax consequences follow the related items as they are reflected in income before extraordinary items, extraordinary items, prior period adjustments (retained earnings), and owners' equity accounts. To illustrate, assume AB Corporation with an average 40% tax rate on all items and $12,000 income taxes payable for the period reported the following:

Partial Income Statement

Operating income		$ 60,000
Less: Applicable income tax expense		4,000
Income before extraordinary items		$ 56,000
Extraordinary item:		
Extraordinary gain	$20,000	
Less: Applicable income tax expense	8,000	12,000
Net Income		$ 68,000

Partial Statement of Retained Earnings

Balance, beginning of year	$110,000
Less: Prior period adjustment (loss)	50,000
Adjusted balance	$ 60,000
Add: Net income for year	68,000
Balance, End of Year	$128,000

Clearly, there was an overstatement of reported net income due to failure to apply intraperiod tax allocation; the prior period adjustment (loss) of $50,000 reduced income taxes by $20,000 (i.e., $50,000 × 40%) which was offset against income tax expense on the income statement. In this case the $50,000 loss was "used" to increase *reported* net income. Correct reporting would require appropriate intraperiod tax allocation as follows:

Partial Income Statement

Operating income		$ 60,000
Less: Applicable income tax expense		24,000
Income before extraordinary items		$ 36,000
Extraordinary items:		
Extraordinary gain	$20,000	
Less: Applicable income tax expense	8,000	12,000
Net Income		$ 48,000

Partial Statement of Retained Earnings

Balance, beginning of year		$110,000
Less: Prior period adjustment (loss)	$50,000	
Reduced by tax saving	20,000	30,000
Adjusted balance		$ 80,000
Add: Net income for the year		48,000
Balance, End of Year		$128,000

The above example would have been even more dramatic had we selected, instead of a prior period adjustment, a tax item that directly affected owners' equity as is the case frequently in respect to some of the "phantom" and "tandem" bonus and stock option plans currently in vogue.

The application of both interperiod and intraperiod tax allocation to all types of situations is reflected in Illustration 23–5. Note that intraperiod allocation is required for all categories except the last one.

Illustration 23–5
Interperiod and Intraperiod Income Tax Allocation

Item Category (of Revenue or Expense)	Type of Difference	Tax Allocation	
		Interperiod	Intraperiod
1. Item on tax return and financial statement same period	No difference	No	Yes
2. Item on tax return prior to financial statement	Timing difference	Yes	Yes
3. Item on financial statement prior to tax return	Timing difference	Yes	Yes
4. Item on tax return; never will be on financial statement	Permanent difference	No	Yes
5. Item on financial statement; never will be on tax return°	No tax to be recognized at any time either on financial statement or tax return	No	No

°*APB Opinion 11* does not explicitly recognize this category; however it needs careful attention. Instances have been observed where items of this type are incorrectly included in income tax expense on the financial statement and consequently are included in deferred taxes.

Evaluation of Tax Allocation

Intraperiod (interstatement) tax allocation is not particularly controversial and is widely accepted. *Interperiod* allocation has gained less acceptance, and it cannot be said to be noncontroversial.

The authors favor both types of tax allocation and believe the examples cited amply justify their use wherever there is a material difference between the actual tax liability and the tax expense based on the reported income. In the interests of objectivity it is appropriate that the principal theoretical objections to tax allocation be presented. These objections and some counterarguments to them follow:

1. Future income tax rates and rules concerning determination of taxable income may change materially making the amount of any tax allocation excessive or deficient or even unnecessary. In answer to this objection it has been pointed out that the assumptions involving a tax allocation are often no less certain than those involved in other allocation or estimation procedures regarded as routine. Examples of routine procedures involving future uncertainties include asset amor-

tization and depreciation, estimation of liabilities for products sold under warranties, and valuations of securities or inventories under cost or market. Furthermore, an attempt to relate the tax expense to the amount of income reported on the income statement which, on hindsight, proves to be erroneous in amount nevertheless gave better results in reporting than had there been no allocation.

2. Income tax allocation is a form of income normalizing or smoothing. One answer given to this objection is that tax allocation merely attempts to correct some artificial and temporary conditions which arise as a result of tax incentives granted by Congress or as a result of vagaries of the tax law based on administrative convenience instead of logic.

3. The validity and reality of deferred charges or credits arising from interperiod tax allocation depend on continued earning of income by the entity in future periods. In answer to this objection it has been pointed out that while no entity is necessarily expected to produce net income each and every fiscal year, the very essence of the continuity assumption is that the entity will be profitable. If this is so, there will be future income and the possibility thereby of absorbing the balances objected to. Some accountants feel that to argue against tax allocation on these grounds is to abandon the continuity concept.

4. Classification of credit balance (deferred income taxes) arising when the tax expense under allocation exceeds the tax expense derived from the tax return is not uniform and is difficult. Earlier in the chapter it was noted that both the AICPA Committee on Accounting Procedure and the SEC had disapproved classifying the item as owners' equity. These rejections came about as a result of a concerted effort by representatives of a basic industry to do just that. While specifically rejecting owners' equity as a proper caption, both left considerable leeway for classifying the credit elsewhere on the equities' side of the balance sheet.

5. Tax allocation is complex and not readily comprehensible to users of financial statements. In answering this objection some accountants express the opinion that failure to apply tax allocation is a disservice to more sophisticated users of statements. They have pointed out that those same persons who would have difficulty understanding tax allocation would also fail to understand other accounting practices which affect statements.

6. It is difficult to fit the deferred income tax accounts into the accepted definitions of assets and liabilities since they neither represent things of value owned nor legal obligations. In rebuttal it has been noted that certain other accepted items which appear on the balance sheet similarly do not represent things of value owned or debts. Consider for example many of the items commonly found under the de-

ferred charge and deferred credit captions such as unamortized bond discount or premium, unrealized gross margin on installment sales, and accrued loss on purchase commitments, etc.

Two additional objections to tax allocation which are particularly difficult to counter will now be cited. The first concerns a business which adopts accelerated depreciation of assets for tax purposes while straight line depreciation is used on the books. It is a fact that if such a business expands or remains a constant size and consistently replaces worn-out assets with new ones as soon as they are (for the entity's purposes) fully depreciated, a more or less permanent tax deferment will theoretically result; hence the deferred liability for future taxes will never have to be paid. It has been pointed out, however, that not even the most ardent supporter of tax allocation would expect sustained ability to predict future tax rates with such precision that the amount of taxes deferred would never vary. There would be opportunities to adjust the account at least annually. Further, the balance is actually turning over on a "Fifo basis"; i.e., tax liabilities of specific years are being paid continuously while new liabilities in equal or greater amounts are being created simultaneously, and the total liability therefore remains constant or even increases. Somewhat closely akin to the "permanent" balance arising from differences of depreciation is the balance that arises from tax allocation necessitated when a company reports income on installment sales on a regular sales basis for financial accounting purposes while using the installment method for tax purposes. Again, from a "continuity assumption" (going-concern) standpoint, the balance arising from tax allocation will remain fairly constant and appear more or less permanently on the books and statements unless there is a marked change in the volume of installment business, gross profit, or tax rates.

The second of these more compelling objections rests on one's concept of the nature of taxes. If income taxes are viewed as distributions of income rather than as expenses, and hence income is viewed as enterprise income rather than that which becomes available to stockholders as potential dividends, it is more difficult to justify tax allocation. In this case taxes become an expense only in periods in which there is taxable income, that is, where revenue (per tax return) exceeds period costs (per tax return). Perhaps the strongest counter to this argument is that taxes are an expense and, unlike dividends, do not represent distributions that are both voluntary and controlled. In the final analysis, all expenses, as distinguished from losses, are voluntarily incurred. There is very little that is voluntary about any tax, particularly income taxes that frequently take away more than half of the income remaining after all other expenses. Almost any objective study of the tax laws and regulations and of hearings which precede legislative action on tax proposals will reveal that controlling factors get pretty far from the pale of acceptability within the framework of generally accepted accounting principles.

Some of the organizations which have done most to shape current accounting theory and practice have not wholly agreed as to the desirability of using tax allocation procedures. The Committee on Accounting Procedure of the AICPA took the lead in supporting tax allocation. While no single statement of the committee can accurately summarize its entire thinking, this brief one perhaps comes close to doing so.

Financial statements are based on allocations of receipts, payments, accruals, and various other items. Many of the allocations are necessarily based on assumptions, but no one suggests that allocations based on imperfect criteria should be abandoned in respect of expenses other than income taxes, or even that the method of allocation should always be indicated. Income taxes are an expense that should be allocated, when necessary and practicable, to income and other accounts, as other expenses are allocated. What the income statement should reflect under this head, as under any other head, is the expense properly allocable to the income included in the income statement for the year.[8]

The APB, successor to the Committee on Accounting Procedure, has consistently favored tax allocation and has essentially reaffirmed its predecessor's pronouncements on the subject. On the other hand, the AAA's Committee on Concepts and Standards Underlying Corporation Financial Statements in its latest pronouncement supports disclosure by other means and commented on tax allocation procedures as follows.

Disclosure is sometimes accomplished by recording the differences as prepayments (given an expectation of future tax savings) or accruals (given the opposing prospect). However, these items do not present the usual characteristics of assets or liabilities; the possible future offsets are often subject to unusual uncertainties; and treatment on an accrual basis is in many cases unduly complicated. Consequently, disclosure by accrual may be more confusing than enlightening and is therefore undesirable.[9]

The first reaction on the subject of tax allocation by the SEC was in opposition to it.[10] Later Accounting Series Releases reversed the original stand and approved tax allocation.[11]

It should be noted again that in its latest comprehensive Opinion

---

[8] *Accounting Research Bulletin No. 43*, p. 88.

[9] AAA, *Accounting and Reporting Standards for Corporate Financial Statements* (Columbus, Ohio, 1957), p. 6.

[10] *Accounting Series Release No. 53*, November 1945.

[11] *Accounting Series Release Nos. 85, 86, and 102* dated, respectively, February 1960; April 1960; and December 1965.

dealing with the matter, the Accounting Principles Board has expressed a distinct preference for the deferred method.

PART B—CHANGING PRICES AND FINANCIAL STATEMENTS

Instability of Money

One of the basic tenets of accounting held for many years was that the monetary unit could be assumed to be stable. While such an assumption regarding the U.S. dollar has never been altogether true, it has, unfortunately, been far from true since 1940. This stability assumption was discussed in Chapter 1. This section of the present chapter takes cognizance of actual price-level changes which have occurred, points out their impact on financial statements, and describes briefly some solutions which have been advanced to deal with the problem.

The extent of price changes in the United States as measured by the U.S. Department of Commerce's gross national product Implicit Price Deflator is revealed by Illustration 23–6.

Illustration 23–6
Prices in the United States

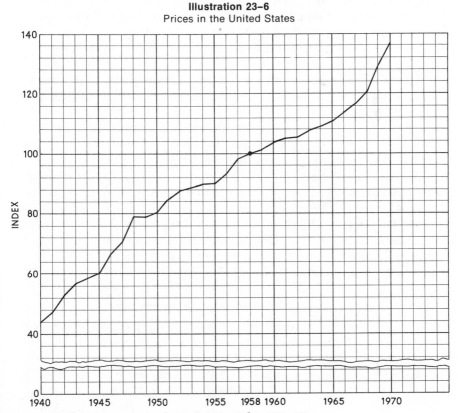

As measured by the gross national product Implicit Price Deflator 1958 = 100
Source: Office of Business Economics, U.S. Department of Commerce.

Simple Illustration of Price-Level Change Impact

Two simple examples of the effects of inflation will be given to point up the problem. An investor who purchased a 20-year corporate bond in 1940 for $100,000 at par and held it until maturity in 1960 would be repaid as many dollars as given up and would have received interest over the 20-year term. However, in 1940 the Implicit Price Deflator averaged 43.9 for the year. (The index for 1958 was 100.) In 1960 the index average level was over 103. This means (aside from interest) the bondholder received dollars worth about 43% of the purchasing power parted with. In other words, in 1940 he could have bought well over twice as much of the things consumers buy as he could in 1960 with the same $100,000. Yet from a financial accounting standpoint his financial statements would have shown no gain or loss (aside from interest) for the 20-year period from the buying and redemption of the bond.

Suppose another investor had bought land in 1940 costing $100,000. If he sold the land in 1960 for $280,000, a book gain before taxes of $180,000 would be reported. Deduction of taxes on this gain at the long-term capital gain rate of 25% ($45,000) would leave him $235,000 in cash, and his financial accounting records would show an increase in his capital after taxes of $135,000 (i.e., $180,000 − $45,000). His purchasing power, after taxes, measured by the Implicit Price Deflator is almost exactly the same as it was when he had $100,000 20 years earlier thus indicating no *real* gain for the period. In order to achieve this break-even position the value of his land had to rise faster than prices measured by the index because of the income tax factor. This second illustration ignores the facts that his money earned no interest during the 20 years and that he would doubtless have had to pay some property taxes throughout the period.

In an economic sense the bondholder lost money, but conventional accounting revealed he broke even as to the buying and selling of the bond. He would, of course, have earned considerable interest which would have been subject to income tax if the bond had been issued by a business corporation. In an economic sense the landowner broke even, but conventional accounting reported that he made a 135% profit *after* income taxes.

Illustration of Price-Level Impact on Financial Statements

A more extended illustration will serve to show effects of inflation on a business. Suppose a corporation erected a warehouse on land it owned and immediately leased the property on January 1, 1940, for 20 years at an annual rent of $18,000. Assume the balance sheet at the date the warehouse was completed was as follows:

Balance Sheet, January 1, 1940

Cash	$ 10,000	Capital stock	$125,000
Warehouse	100,000		
Land	15,000		
	$125,000		$125,000

If the cash expenses (other than income taxes at 40%) were $3,000 and the warehouse was depreciated over a 20-year life (straight line basis), statements at the end of 1940 would appear as follows:

1940 Income Statement

Revenue from lease		$18,000
Deduct expenses:		
Paid in cash (property tax, etc.)	$3,000	
Depreciation	5,000	8,000
Net income before taxes		$10,000
Income taxes (at 40%)		4,000
Net Income		$ 6,000

Balance Sheet, December 31, 1940

Cash		$ 25,000	Income tax payable	$ 4,000
Warehouse	$100,000		Capital stock	125,000
Less: Depr	5,000	95,000	Retained earnings	6,000
Land		15,000		
		$135,000		$135,000

At December 31, 1941, assuming no dividends were paid, the balance sheet would appear as below, and the 1941 income statement would be identical to the one for 1940:

Balance Sheet, December 31, 1941

Cash		$ 36,000	Income tax payable	$ 4,000
Warehouse	$100,000		Capital stock	125,000
Less: Depr	10,000	90,000	Retained earnings	12,000
Land		15,000		
		$141,000		$141,000

While it is unrealistic to assume no dividends would be paid throughout the 20-year lease term and that cash would be allowed to accumulate idly, nevertheless consider what the balance sheet would look like after 18 more years or at December 31, 1959, under such circumstances:

Balance Sheet, December 31, 1959

Cash..................	$234,000	Income tax payable ....$	4,000
Warehouse $100,000		Capital stock......................	125,000
Less: Depr....... 100,000	–0–	Retained earnings	120,000
Land	15,000		
	$249,000		$249,000

Or if it is assumed all profits had been paid out as dividends as earned, the last balance sheet would have shown:

Balance Sheet, December 31, 1959

Cash..................	$114,000	Income tax payable ....$	4,000
Warehouse $100,000		Capital stock......................	125,000
Less: Depr....... 100,000	–0–		
Land	15,000		
	$129,000		$129,000

In this latter event the corporation would have the $100,000 to replace its warehouse after saving a $10,000 operating cash balance and after paying its $4,000 debt. If construction prices have risen as much as consumer prices, the company has actually lost money because it could now afford to erect a warehouse less than half as large. The Implicit Price Deflator index was at 43.9 in 1940 and at 103.3 in 1960 on the basis that 1958 prices averaged 100. Therefore, a new warehouse identical to the original one would cost $235,300:

$$(\$100,000 \times \frac{103.3}{43.9} = \$235,300)$$

Or if no dividends had ever been paid, the owners would have received no return on their $125,000 investment over the years and the corporation could, by spending all of its cash, erect about the same kind of warehouse as it had in 1940. Meanwhile, of course, it has paid income taxes of $80,000 based on book income. Clearly, there has been an erosion of real capital due to overstated profits; the real capital eroded was expended for income taxes and dividends since both were based on overstated income.

Various Statement Items Affected Differently

In a period of rapid price changes not all financial statements are affected uniformly or even in the same direction. Because prices have been rising since the 1930s, let us base our discussion on a background of price increases. However, it is well to bear in mind that at times in our history prices have dropped sharply, in which case the effects tend to be opposite of those accompanying a price rise.

If a business merely maintains a constant cash balance during a period of rising prices, it loses purchasing power. The same thing can be said of investments in bonds. Receivables tend to turn over rapidly, are a product of revenue which is presumably geared to current prices, and hence ordinarily reflect current price levels.[12]

It is less easy to generalize about effect of price changes on inventories. Physically inventories experience turnover; hence one might assume they stay current, i.e., move with prices. Whether they do or not depends largely on the pricing flow method used. If Lifo is employed, cost of goods sold or issued tends to reflect current prices, but the residual of inventories shown on the balance sheet may consist of prices which are quite out of date. On the other hand, with Fifo the balance sheet values tend to be current, but the extent to which cost of goods sold figures are current depends on the rate of inventory turnover. Generally speaking, the average methods tend to give results between those provided by Lifo and Fifo.

It is in the area of noncurrent assets and long-term liabilities that the problem of inflation becomes most serious. Plant items, intangibles, and possibly also sinking fund assets tend to turn over very slowly. The account balances are likely to include a substantial proportion of such assets acquired in the relatively distant past. As a consequence, carrying values and periodic amortization of these assets are likely to reflect values completely out of line with current prices. In the warehouse enterprise example given earlier in the chapter it was noted that replacement of the asset with funds held back equivalent to depreciation charges based on 1940 costs would have been impossible in terms of the 1960 price level. Most tangible and intangible assets have relatively long lives and, with the exception of land, affect the income statement through depreciation and amortization.

If a business remains in debt during a period of inflation, it tends to gain because the dollars borrowed have greater purchasing power than those repaid.[13] What is true of long-term debt tends to be applicable also to redeemable preferred stock. As to other elements of owner's equity, common stock and retained earnings, these are residuals and are the net resultant of other balance sheet changes.

---

[12] A business which maintained a $100,000 constant but revolving balance of receivables would sustain a loss over a period in which prices changed materially. The loss is realized gradually as collections occur and the unrealized loss on the current receivables would be relatively small. See discussion on pages 915–19.

[13] If a company remained in debt $100,000 on a bond issue and maintained a constant but revolving balance of $100,000 in accounts payable over a period which saw prices double, purchasing power gain on both would be the same. The gain on the bonds would be unrealized until they are paid, while that relating to the accounts payable would be realized gradually and the unrealized gain at any given time would be small. See page 915.

The reader is reminded again of what happened to this group of equity interests in the warehouse enterprise example given earlier in the chapter.

Pros and Cons of Price-Level Accounting

Clearly, accountancy is faced with a most serious challenge because one of its basic assumptions—that the money unit is stable—has been demonstrably untrue. Should conventional accounting procedures, founded as they are on objectively determined historical cost, be supplemented or abandoned for some new procedures or should these procedures which worked well for many decades be adhered to? The controversy over this point has raged for over two decades and has probably accounted for more pages in accounting periodicals during that period than any other single topic with the possible exception of income taxes.[14]

A summary of leading arguments for and against supplementation or abandonment of the traditional historical cost basis of recording and statement presentation follows.

Critics of conventional accounting procedures cite these arguments in favor of the adoption of alternative procedures and reporting techniques:

1. Reported income determined under present methods contains a mixture of dollars of different purchasing power. The greater the investment in fixed assets the more serious this effect becomes. Pre-World War II dollars and current dollars are essentially noncomparable unless adjusted in some way to express both in terms of equivalent purchasing power. Revenue is usually expressed in current dollars. To determine income by subtracting expenses based on a mixture of past dollars (e.g., depreciation) and of current dollars (e.g., wages) is to violate a fundamental principle of mathematics, as well as economics, because the items are not alike. Income tends to be overstated when prices are rising and to be understated when they are falling. This gives rise to added pressures for increases in wage and dividend payments during periods of inflation.

2. The use of depreciation based on historical costs for income tax purposes does not allow tax-free recovery of sufficient purchasing power to enable the assets to be replaced. The income tax thereby becomes to some extent a tax on capital. Unless the inadequacy of the depreciation charge is explained to stockholders, many of them are unable to understand why amounts in excess of the depreciation

---

[14] Here it should be noted that most articles dealing with taxation are expository and designed to keep readers abreast of constant changes rather than being argumentative.

deduction must be retained to enable the entity to maintain its present productive capacity.

3. Balance sheets fail to reflect current values of almost all items outside the current classifications.

4. Financial statement readers can better appraise management's effectiveness in the preservation of the current dollar equivalent of the capital invested in the business, and can make a more useful analysis of the entity's earning power in terms of current economic conditions.

5. Computation of the gain or loss on monetary items provides information that measures effectiveness of monetary management and the impact of inflation on net quick assets and long-term debt.[15]

6. Both public officials and the public generally would be better informed regarding the effects of price changes on the general economy and on corporate prices and profits. In developing policies as to taxation, pricing, and regulation, information which reflects the effects of price-level changes is essential if those policies are to be sound. This is particularly true for regulated industries such as public utilities which tend to have relatively heavy capital investments and cannot determine their own charges for services or products.

7. Financial statements that reflect current values would be particularly useful to investors.

On the other hand, those who defend traditional accounting recording and reporting procedures and the presentation of financial statements based solely on unadjusted historical cost cite these arguments:

1. Traditional methods are uniform, objective, based on verifiable evidence, and widely understood. Any limitations they may have are known and recognized. Advocates of changing to other procedures have been unable to agree on what techniques or combinations of techniques should be used or on which measures (index numbers or other means of determination current cost) ought to be used. Changing to other systems would seriously impair whatever comparability of statements has been achieved by present uniform methods.

2. Actual depreciation is measured by costs which have been incurred, not by some future cost estimate arrived at by resort to appraisals, index numbers, or other means. The Lifo inventory method which is cited as a precedent to charge current costs against revenue does not use costs yet to be incurred.

3. Solutions proposed by those advocating change are often piecemeal. These and comprehensive solutions almost invariably become unsatisfactory or tedious to explain in the case of statements of

---

[15] An explanation of monetary items is given on pp. 915–16 of this chapter.

several periods over which prices have continued to fluctuate. There is also the possibility of statement manipulations and other malpractices if price indexes or other measures of current cost could be applied on a subjective basis.

4. The use of unadjusted historical cost is deeply imbedded in law and in income tax matters. Income tax relief is not dependent on financial accounting technique employed. There are numerous differences between what is reported on tax returns and on published statements of the same enterprise. If no tax relief is realized, additional dollars for replacement of assets will not be generated by revision of accounting procedures or reporting.

5. The importance of the price-level problem may have been exaggerated. In view of changing technology, a substantial part of the assets of manufacturing companies and others have been recently acquired and are, therefore, valued at fairly current prices. Inventory turnover results in cost of goods sold being stated on a current basis without reference to the flow method adopted and only in the case of Lifo is balance sheet valuation of inventory markedly out of line with current prices.

6. Investors might become confused with attendant severe market fluctuations following if on the basis of alternate or substitute statements, a less favorable financial picture is presented.

7. No real need exists for placing of statement items on a common price-level basis. Mixtures and averages have traditionally been employed by accountants with satisfactory results.

Thinking on the price-level problem and what to do about it covers a very broad spectrum. At one end are those who feel price changes are not much of a problem because the United States has comparatively experienced a "creeping inflation." Persons who hold this viewpoint contend most of our prices have changed slowly enough that conventionally prepared statements present operating results and financial position reasonably fairly. Others, near this first group in the spectrum, acknowledge that conventional statements are deficient in the face of changing price levels but can point out that statements have other deficiencies as well, and they lack confidence in some of the proposed remedies or the public's reaction to them. Among practitioners at least this end of the spectrum seems to have the largest number of adherents. Near the middle is a group which views the problem as more serious. Many here think statements based on historical cost should be supplemented by statements which reflect price-level changes.[16] There seems to be a large number of

---

[16] It seems reasonable to speculate that some members of this middle segment of the spectrum expect that in time the supplementary statements would be so well received that they would become primary statements and might supplant statements based on historical cost.

academicians in this middle group. The other end of the spectrum is represented by persons who would, on a broad scale, substitute data based on appraisals, market quotations, and index numbers for historical cost data in the basic accounting records. They would, of course, report in statements what had been recorded in the basic records. It does not appear that this end of the spectrum is heavily populated; most of its residents appear to be academicians.

AICPA and the Price-Level Problem

The history of the AICPA in respect to the price-level problem is interesting. In 1947, its Committee on Accounting Procedure (a forerunner to today's APB) specifically considered the problem of "Depreciation and High Costs" and concluded:

1. At that time it would not be satisfactory to increase depreciation charges against current income to reflect higher replacement costs of plant or to recognize such costs by recording appraisals.
2. In considering depreciation in connection with product costs, prices, and business policies, management must take into consideration the likelihood that replacement costs of plant assets then in use would greatly exceed their historical costs.
3. Periodic appropriation of net income or retained earnings in contemplation of replacement of plant at higher costs was a proper managerial action.

This basic position was reaffirmed by the same committee the next year in a letter addressed to the AICPA membership.

In 1953 the same committee again considered the problem and reaffirmed its earlier position. The vote was 14 to 6, whereas in 1947 it had been 20 for, none against, with one member not voting and another voting favorably but with qualification.

The Committee on Accounting Procedure was replaced in 1959 by the Accounting Principles Board—a like-sized and somewhat similar group. Initially the APB commissioned research studies on six problem areas; one dealt with price-level accounting. *Accounting Research Study No. 6*, "Reporting the Effects of Price-Level Changes," was published in 1963. After considering reactions to this study the APB set about the development of *Statement No. 3*, "Financial Statements Restated for General Price-Level Changes," which was published in 1969. In the process of developing the statement, the techniques recommended in it were experimentally applied over a two-year period to the financial records of 18 cooperating businesses. Results of this application were reported in an article in the *Journal of Accountancy* (June 1969).

Timing of the issuance of *Statement No. 3* was fortunate in one sense, unfortunate in another. The statement was timely in that it appeared when prices were again rising sharply. Concurrently though, business profits began to fall off in 1969 and continued to decline in 1970. As a consequence, business managements were loath to adopt the recommended procedures of *Statement No. 3* in such an economic climate. *Statement No. 3* recommends preparation of a set of supplemental statements to accompany the regularly prepared balance sheet, income statement, and retained earnings statement. The supplemental statements would reflect the application of a price index reflective of price changes broadly to specific statement items and amounts. Given the long inflation which preceded 1969 and the sharp acceleration of prices in that year and in 1970, given also the drop in profits as as compared with 1968 and earlier, one can understand the reluctance of the typical company management to adopt on a voluntary basis an accounting procedure which would result generally in a less favorable showing while conventional statements were already tending to make managerial performance look worse. Application of the procedures recommended in *Statement No. 3* would have had such effects for most companies in 1969 and 1970 because depreciation and cost of goods sold tended to be higher while most other income-determining items remained about the same (at least as to net effect). At the same time, for most companies the capital (investment base) would be higher. The overall effect was to report less profit on a higher investment base; this was simply unacceptable to management of the typical company. To date the authors have been unable to learn of a single instance in which a major U.S. company implemented the provisions of *Statement No. 3* insofar as published statements are concerned. It is true that Indiana Telephone Corporation has continued to prepare both conventional and price-level adjusted statements (as has been its practice for many years), but the procedures used do not wholly accord to the recommendations of *Statement No. 3*.

Summarized Description of Stabilized Accounting

As in previous editions of this book, by way of illustrating a set of procedures which permit the reflection of price-level changes in financial statements, we have chosen to present a description of "stabilized accounting." This is an older, proven technique. Its application will yield results quite similar to those obtained from application of procedures recommended in *Statement No. 3*. In addition, statements prepared by the stabilized accounting technique will yield more relevant information than will the techniques of *Statement No. 3*. Neither procedure seems to have any advantage insofar as ease and simplicity are concerned. It should be noted that other well-developed systems for reflecting the effects of price-level changes in financial statements have existed for some time.

Stabilized accounting represents the earliest comprehensive approach to overcoming the inadequacies of financial statements prepared according to the concept that the money unit is stable when in fact it has been quite unstable. A complete description of this system is beyond the scope of a portion of a single chapter, but certain highlights will be presented. Readers interested in details are referred to a series of articles by Henry W. Sweeney which appeared in the *Accounting Review* in the early 1930s and to his book *Stabilized Accounting*.[17] To paraphrase Sweeney's words, his purpose in writing *Stabilized Accounting* was to show how accounting figures become wrong because of the fluctuating dollar and how the attendant errors can largely be eliminated.

Sweeney actually developed two techniques for stabilizing accounting data. He referred to these as "stabilization of each entry" and "balance sheet stabilization." While the latter is easier to apply, it is less satisfactory for use as an illustration to impart some of the rudiments of the stabilized accounting system; it also results in a less satisfactory form of income statement unless some supplementary procedures are applied. Accordingly, the illustration which follows uses the stabilization-of-each-entry technique.

Assets and liabilities are divided into two main groups according to the way they are affected by changes in the value of money. The first kind, called *money-value assets and liabilities,* consists of those items whose amounts are set at specified dollar figures which cannot change as the value of money changes. Cash, receivables, marketable securities, and payables are examples of money-value items. If a money-value asset is held while the value of the dollar is decreasing (price index is rising), an *unrealized loss* results; conversely, if such assets are held while the value of the dollar is increasing, an *unrealized gain* occurs. On the other hand, a business which remains in debt during a period of price rises has an *unrealized gain* while it would have an *unrealized loss* if prices fell during the period of indebtedness. A principal objective of stabilized accounting is to present financial results in terms of purchasing power measured by index numbers. Since money-value assets and liabilities reflect receivables and payables in a fixed amount of money (their maturity amount) they cannot be restated for balance sheet purposes. Significantly, however the resultant unrealized (purchasing power) loss or gain must be measured and accounted for in stabilized accounting.

Unrealized losses resulting from the holding of cash during rising prices become *realized* when that cash is disbursed, while unrealized gains on debt held during a period of rising prices become *realized* when the debt is paid.

---

[17] The book was first published in 1936 by Harper & Bros., New York. It subsequently went out of print, but it became such a "classic" it was republished by Holt, Rinehart & Winston, Inc., essentially unchanged in 1964. Articles by Sweeney concerning his technique appeared in the following issues of the *Accounting Review:* September 1931; June 1932; September 1933; December 1934; June 1935.

Other assets and equities are known as *real-value items*. These consist of those assets and equities which are not payable in a fixed amount of money and whose prices change as the price level fluctuates. Examples of real-value items are inventory, equipment, land, and capital (other than preferred stock). Real-value items are restated on a balance sheet which reflects stabilized values if there has been a change in the level of the index number between the time the real-value item was initially recorded and the date of the stabilized balance sheet. Although adjusted for balance sheet purposes, real-value assets, prior to their disposal, do not give rise to unrealized (purchasing power) losses or gains in stabilized accounting.

Illustrative Problem.   Assume that a general price index has changed very rapidly as evidenced in the following tabulation:

Date	Index	Date	Index
January 1	100	April 1	130
February 1	110	June 1	140
March 1	120	July 1	150

The following trial balance was taken at January 1, and all balances can be assumed to have developed when the price index stood at 100:

Cash	$8,100	
Liability		$3,000
Capital stock		4,000
Retained earnings		1,100

Transactions during the ensuing six months were as follows:

a) February 1: Cash receipts representing revenue for services amounted to $4,620.

b) March 1: Equipment having an estimated four-year life and no scrap value was purchased for $6,000 cash.

c) April 1: A payment of $2,860 was made to apply on the liability balance.

d) June 1: A payment of $2,100 for general expenses was made.

e) July 1: Depreciation on the equipment was recorded for the four months ended July 1.

These transactions as they would be reflected in the regular ledger accounts, at cost, are shown in Illustration 23–7.

To apply stabilization to the money-value items (cash and liability in the foregoing ledger), it is necessary separately to (*a*) stabilize the beginning balances, (*b*) calculate unrealized gain or loss inherent in the ending balances, and (*c*) stabilize increases by *dates of origin* and decreases by *dates of occurrence*. These steps are necessary to provide data essential to measure the purchasing power (unrealized)

Illustration 23-7
Work Sheet and Ledger for the Period January 1 to July 1

	January 1 Balances		Transactions				July 1 Balances	
Cash	8,100		(a) 4,620	(b) 6,000		1,760		
				(c) 2,860				
				(d) 2,100				
Equipment			(b) 6,000			6,000		
Accumulated deprecia-								
tion				(e) 500			500	
Liability		3,000	(c) 2,860				140	
Capital stock		4,000					4,000	
Retained earnings		1,100					1,100	
Revenue				(a) 4,620			4,620	
General expenses			(d) 2,100			2,100		
Depreciation			(e) 500			500		
Total	8,100	8,100	16,080	16,080		10,360	10,360	

Cash					Retained Earnings		
Bal. (100)°	8,100	(b) (120)	6,000			Bal. (100)	1,100
(a) (110)	4,620	(c) (130)	2,860				
		(d) (140)	2,100				

Equipment				Revenue		
(b) (120)	6,000				(a) (110)	4,620

Accumulated Depreciation				General Expenses		
		(e) (150)	500	(d) (140)	2,100	

Liability				Depreciation		
(c) (130)	2,860	Bal. (100)	3,000	(e) (150)	500	

Capital Stock		
	Bal. (100)	4,000

° Figures in parentheses are index number values prevailing when the balance or transactions were originally recorded.

losses and gains due to price-level changes. Two terms used above call for some explanation or elaboration. Sweeney used "date of origin" to relate to transactions which resulted in increases in balances of asset or equity accounts and "date of occurrence" to relate to decreases. It seems likely that he chose to use "date of origin" for *increase* items because at origin they were recorded at historical cost (the prime source of difficulty if prices changed). For clarity and convenience, some alternate terminology was needed when an *original* cost balance was reduced or fully removed from an account; here, he chose to use "date of occurrence." His terminology is retained here because it is descriptive and to enable readers who may wish to engage in more extended study of his technique to do so without having to learn

Illustration 23–8
Steps in Stabilizing Money-Value Items
Schedule (*a*)
Stabilization of Beginning Balances (money-value items)

Account	Type Balance	Ledger Amount (A)	Index Ratio (B)	Stabilized Amount (A) × (B)
Cash...................	Debit	$8,100	150/100	$12,150
Liability................	Credit	3,000	150/100	4,500

Schedule (*b*)
Calculation of Unrealized Gain or Loss in Ending Balances (money-value items)

Account	Type Balance	Ledger Amount (A)	Index Ratio (B)	Stabilized Amount (C)= (A) × (B)	Unrealized Gain or Loss° (C) − (A)
Cash°	Debit	$1,760	150/110	$2,400	$640°
Liability..........	Credit	140	150/100	210	70
Net Unrealized Loss in Ending Balances					...$570°

° Denominator of 110 used to convert ending cash balance because of *Fifo* flow assumption (i.e., the $1,760 ending balance is assumed to be from the $4,620 receipt; the cash balance with a value of "100" was completely used up).

Schedule (*c*)
Stabilization of Increases by Dates of Origin and Decreases by Dates of Occurrence (money-value items)

Debits			Account	Credits		
Unstabilized	Index Ratio	Stabilized		Unstabilized	Index Ratio	Stabilized
(*a*) $4,620	150/110	$6,300	CASH	(*b*) $ 6,000	150/120	$ 7,500
				(*c*) 2,860	150/130	3,300
				(*d*) 2,100	150/140	2,250
$4,620		$6,300		$10,960		$13,050
			LIABILITY			
(*c*) $2,860	150/130	$3,300				

new terminology. The three stabilization steps are shown in Schedules (a), (b), and (c) in Illustration 23–8. They are necessary as a basis for calculation of *net realized gains or losses in money-value items;* this latter step is shown in Schedule (d) (see Illustration 23–9). Cash is assumed to have been disbursed on a *Fifo* basis.

Illustration 23–9
Schedule (d)
Computation of Net Realized Gain/Loss on Money-Value Items

Explanation	Cash	Liability
Beginning balances stabilized—Schedule (a)................	$12,150	$4,500
Add: Increases stabilized by dates of origin—		
Schedule (c)	6,300	0
Total..	$18,450	$4,500
Less: Ending balances stabilized—Schedule (b)	2,400	210
Total Decreases Stabilized by Dates of		
Origin...	$16,050	$4,290
Less: Decreases stabilized by dates of occur-		
rence—Schedule (c)...	13,050	3,300
Realized Gain or (Loss)...($	3,000)	$ 990
Net Realized Loss from Stabilization on		
Money-Value Items		$2,010

It is appropriate to emphasize that stabilization is being effected as of July 1 at which time the price index value is 150. Thus, 150 is the numerator value of each index ratio (IR) applied, while the denominator value is the value of the index when the transaction originated or occurred. Amounts derived in the foregoing calculations are now used to compute *realized* gain or loss on money-value items. You should observe that in Schedule (b) an *unrealized* loss or gain is determined, whereas in Schedule (d) a *realized* loss or gain is determined.

Illustration 23–10
Income Statements, Six Months Ended July 1

	Unstabilized	Index Ratio	Stabilized
Revenue $4,620		150/110	$6,300
General expenses $2,100		150/140	$2,250
Depreciation 500		150/120°	625
Total Expenses...............$2,600			$2,875
Operating income $2,020			$3,425
Deduct stabilized losses:			
Deduct realized stabilized loss—			
Schedule (d)......................			2,010
Change in stabilized retained			
earnings...........................			$1,415
Unrealized stabilized loss—			
Schedule (b)......................			$ 570

° The denominator used for depreciation, accumulated depreciation, and for the equipment itself is 120, the index value prevailing when the equipment was bought.

Illustration 23–10 (continued)

Balance Sheets, July 1

	Unstabilized	Index Ratio	Stabilized
Cash	$1,760		$1,760
Equipment	$6,000	150/120	$7,500
Less: Accumulated depreciation	500	150/120	625
Net value	5,500		6,875
Total Assets	$7,260		$8,635
Liability	$ 140		$ 140
Capital stock	4,000	150/100	6,000
Retained earnings, January 1	1,100	150/100	1,650
Add: Increase – per income statement	2,020		1,415
Deduct: Unrealized loss – Schedule (b)	–		(570)
Total Equities	$7,260		$8,635

Financial statements reflecting both unstabilized and stabilized amounts are shown in Illustration 23–10. The point at issue is the extent to which usefulness to users is enhanced.

AAA and the Price-Level Problem

Committees of the American Accounting Association have also considered the problems caused by changing price levels from time to time. In August 1951 its Committee on Concepts and Standards Underlying Corporate Financial Statements issued a supplementary statement entitled "Price Level Changes and Financial Statements" from which the following excerpt is quoted:

Management may properly include in periodic reports to stockholders comprehensive supplementary statements which present the effects of the fluctuation in the value of the dollar upon net income and upon financial position.

(a) Such supplementary statements should be internally consistent; the income statement and the balance sheet should both be adjusted by the same procedures, so that the figures in such complementary statements are co-ordinate and have the same relative significance.

(b) Such supplementary statements should be reconciled in detail with the primary statements reflecting unadjusted original dollar costs, and should be regarded as an extension or elaboration of the primary statements rather than as a departure therefrom.

(c) Such supplementary statements should be accompanied by comments and explanations clearly setting forth the implications, uses, and limitations of the adjusted data.[18]

While this particular committee did not prescribe the structure or techniques to be used, another AAA sponsored research project culminated in the publication in 1955 and 1956 of three books – two

---

[18]Published in the October 1951 issue of the *Accounting Review*.

authored by Professor Ralph C. Jones which aggregated almost 400 pages and a shorter work by Professor Perry Mason. One of the studies by Jones is particularly interesting in that it contains case study presentations of the effects of price-level changes on four companies and applies uniform statement-adjusting techniques to their financial data for 11 years.[19] A comparison of the effects of fluctuating prices on reported net income of Armstrong Cork Company, one of the four, is shown in Illustration 23–11.

Illustration 23–11

In 1957 the association's Committee on Accounting Concepts and Standards issued the fourth of a series of overall statements briefly setting out the entire framework of financial accounting principles. The principal provisions dealing with the price-level problem are quoted:

Because money has meaning only with respect to a given level and structure of prices, substantial changes in prices affect the comparability of money amounts. Under such conditions, any unadjusted money measurement should be interpreted in the light of the price situation extant at the time of the transaction in which it originated . . . .

---

[19] Ralph C. Jones, *Price Level Changes and Financial Statements, Case Studies of Four Companies* (Columbus, Ohio: American Accounting Association, 1955). Other studies in this series are: Ralph C. Jones, *Effects of Price Level Change on Business Income, Capital and Taxes;* and Perry Mason, *Price Level Changes and Financial Statements, Basic Concepts and Methods.*

Adjustments for price level change . . . can be made meaningful only when the underlying asset amount is objectively stated . . . .

Until reasonably uniform principles of adjustment for price changes are commonly accepted, investors should be furnished such supplementary data as would be helpful in evaluating the significance of price fluctuations in the interpretation of financial reports of the particular enterprise. Supplementary data may be reported to reflect the effect of price changes in the specific assets held by the enterprise during the period, to show the effect upon the enterprise of movements in the general price level, or to achieve both purposes. Adjustment for individual price changes may be effected by determinations of replacement cost or by the use of specific price indexes; adjustment for changes in the general purchasing power of money requires the use of general rather than specific price indexes.[20]

In 1964, the AAA Executive Committee decided that perhaps the association's pattern of efforts to enunciate accounting principles should change.[21] A new Committee to Prepare a Statement of Basic Accounting Theory was established and told that it "should not feel bound in any way by the format or content of previous statements issued by this or other organizations." The committee was charged "to develop an integrated statement of basic accounting theory . . . [to] serve as a guide to educators, practitioners, and others interested in accounting."[22] Within two years the committee completed a 100-page statement with which eight of its nine members substantially agreed. One of the major recommendations of *A Statement of Basic Accounting Theory* was that financial statements prepared for external users should reflect both historical cost and current cost information. One of the two appendixes deals with means of obtaining current cost information; the other sets out illustrative multivalued statements with detailed explanations of the handling of current cost information.

Concluding Note

Price-level accounting procedures have not been given the trial and usage they deserve. However, unless inflation (which has been a worldwide way of life for three decades) is halted, it seems inevitable that sooner or later more widespread experimentation with price-level accounting will occur. If this should happen, usefulness of statements reflecting price changes should make them a regular part of the accounting scene until an era of price stability is reached. Then, and only then, validity of the stability of the unit-of-measure assumption would be reestablished and the need for price-level accounting would disappear.

---

[20] AAA, *Accounting and Reporting Standards for Corporate Financial Statements* (Columbus, Ohio, 1957).

[21] The pattern dated back to 1936 when the first of a series of four statements was published; revisions were published in 1941, 1948, and 1957.

[22] *A Statement of Basic Accounting Theory* (Evanston, Ill.: AAA, 1966), p. v.

QUESTIONS FOR CLASS DISCUSSION

1. In fairly general terms, under what circumstances may income tax allocation be appropriate?

2. Give specific examples of *timing* differences which would call for income
tax allocation.

3. In illustrating various situations involving tax allocation, regardless of
whether a debit balance or credit balance was created, an account titled
"deferred income taxes" was used in the chapter. (*a*) Give some appropriate synonyms where debit balances are involved. (*b*) Give some appropriate synonyms where credit balances are involved.

4. Cite four different objections which have been raised against tax allocation.

5. What are the respective positions of the following organizations in respect to income tax allocation: (*a*) SEC? (*b*) Accounting Principles Board?
(*c*) AAA Committee on Concepts and Standards?

6. Taxwise, what happens in case a corporation which has operated profita-
bly for several consecutive years sustains a large loss?

7. As between *carrybacks* and *carryforwards*, which can be accounted for
with greatest certainty at the time they arise? Why?

8. Interperiod income tax procedures are not appropriate when (check best
answer):
   a) An extraordinary loss will cause the amount of income tax expense to
   be less than the tax on ordinary net income.
   b) An extraordinary gain will cause the amount of income tax expense to
   be greater than the tax on ordinary net income.
   c) Differences between net income for tax purposes and financial reporting occur because tax laws and financial accounting principles do
   not concur on the items to be recognized as revenue and expense.
   d) Differences between net income for tax purposes and financial reporting occur because, even though financial accounting principles
   and tax laws concur on the items to be recognized as revenues and
   expenses, they do not concur on the timing of the recognition.
   (AICPA adapted)

9. An investor bought a 20-year, 5% corporate bond at par for $100,000. He
collected interest annually throughout the period and realized the face
amount of the bond at maturity. How did he fare economically if (*a*)
prices steadily rose throughout the 20 years and were twice as high as
at the start of the period? (*b*) prices fell steadily and were half as high
as at the start of the period?

10. If prices are rising steadily, from a standpoint of balance sheet adequacy,
which of the following would be most realistically valued: (*a*) buildings,
(*b*) inventories, or (*c*) receivables?

11. Classify each of the following as money-value or as real-value items:
   a) Equipment.   *d*) Inventories (Lifo basis used).
   b) Unamortized discount on   *e*) Accumulated depreciation —
   bonds payable.   buildings.
   c) Retained earnings.   *f*) Account payable (incurred for
                                         item *d*).

12. During an era of rising prices, would the following items give rise to (1) unrealized gains, (2) realized gains, (3) unrealized losses, (4) realized losses, or (5) none of these?

 a) Holding cash in a plant expansion fund.

 b) Using the fund in (*a*) after a large enough amount had been accumulated.

 c) Giving a note payable when an account payable became due.

 d) Selling capital stock at a premium.

 e) Owing money for five years after having sold bonds at par.

13. It is generally correct to say the AICPA has been cognizant of the price-level problem for more than two decades. Cite specific evidence this is a true statement.

14. Would you say publications of the AAA have tended to (*a*) encourage implementation of price-level accounting procedures, (*b*) discourage them, or (*c*) take a neutral position in respect to them? Support your answer.

DECISION CASE 23–1

The following quotations and other data are from pages 239–40 of the May 15, 1969, issue of *Fortune*.

"The accounting that appears in annual reports sometimes serves a cosmetic purpose—it is there not so much to inform stockholders as to help management keep them happy, or at least quiet, by touching up blemishes and brightening beauty spots. When a company is not doing well, and at the same time is trying to fend off an unwanted merger, the cosmeticians of accountancy can sometimes perform wonders—even when they are limited to shades of red. Quite a number of companies in this year's directory [*Fortune's* directory of 500 large companies featured annually in one of its issues] used bookkeeping devices of various kinds to brighten their results. But Allis-Chalmers Manufacturing outdid them all at the rouge pot.

"As 1968 ended, long-suffering Allis-Chalmers, No. 130 among the 500, found itself with some conflicting needs and desires. It presumably wanted to put the best possible face on 1968 results in order to maintain stockholder support in a bitter battle against a take-over by White Consolidated Industries, No. 143. But the new president of Allis-Chalmers, David C. Scott, who took office September 1 wanted to write off at once the tremendous charges associated with past mistakes and thereby turn the company around. To do that, he had to slap stockholders with some very bad news just when White Consolidated's onslaught was hotting up.

"Allis-Chalmers resolved this conflict with some intricate accounting that let it accept Scott's write-off while minimizing the bad news that had to be reported to stockholders. The published results were still pretty dismal: on sales of $767,313,100, the company reported a loss of $54,589,720. That was, however, a whole lot better than the $121,588,931 that the company *actually* lost last year.

"To understand how an actual loss of $122 million can become a reported loss of $55 million requires some comprehension of tax accounting. It is well known, of course, that a corporate dollar earned is roughly 50 cents lost to the tax collector. The converse is also true, i.e., *a dollar lost is 50 cents earned.*"

Required:

1. In terms of data given to this point, does the general tenor of the article seem overcritical? What is Allis-Chalmers apparently doing?

(Additional data for Requirement 2.)

The article went on to add:

"The tax carry-forward created by a loss can be used only in years succeeding the one in which the loss occurred. For this reason alone, then, Allis-Chalmers' tax return for 1968 can bear only a passing resemblance to its stockholder report. In addition, not all of that $122 million represented operating losses. The figure included $69 million that Scott charged off in 1968 in the form of special reserves for costs that he expected to incur later; i.e., the company provided for losses that had not yet occurred and that can't be claimed on the tax return until they do occur.

. . . .

"To be sure, not all the $60-odd million of tax credits that Allis-Chalmers used were anticipatory. Some $14 million represented a carryback against losses that were paid on earnings for 1965, 1966, and 1967. No problem there . . . but included in the total tax credits used to cut down the 1968 loss that the company reported was around $43 million in 'estimated future income tax benefits.' In fact, Allis-Chalmers will not get the benefit of any such amount until it comes up with some $86 million in pre-tax profits."

2. In the light of the added data, would you agree with the tone of the article? Comment on the practice in respect to reserves for future losses.

DECISION CASE 23–2

1. What is the common objective of depreciation based on replacement cost and the last-in, first-out method of pricing inventories?
2. Outline some conditions necessary for the last-in, first-out method to accomplish the results expected of it.
3. A basic monetary concept underlying accounting and financial statements conventionally prepared is primarily responsible for the development of these methods of accounting. Identify and discuss this monetary concept as it is related to these methods of accounting.

(AICPA adapted)

EXERCISES

Exercise 23–1

This is a hypothetical situation to illustrate both interperiod and intraperiod (interstatement) income tax allocation. For illustrative purposes use a flat 40% income tax rate. Items in parentheses are losses, and items indicated with an asterisk represent permanent differences.

	19A		19B	
	On Income Tax Return	On Financial Statement	On Income Tax Return	On Financial Statement
Pretax operating income	$100,000	$120,000	$140,000	$120,000
Extraordinary item	(10,000)°	(10,000)°		
Prior period adjustment	(10,000)°	(10,000)°		

Required:

1. Reflect the application of interperiod tax allocation procedures for each year as follows:

a) Compute income taxes payable for each year.
b) Compute income tax expense for each year.
c) Give entry for each year to reflect income tax allocations.

2. Reflect the application of intraperiod (interstatement) income tax allocation procedures for each year as they would be reported on the financial statements.

3. Did permanent tax differences enter into your determinations of either (1) or (2)? Explain.

Exercise 23–2

Income tax returns of Albirt Corporation reflected the following:

	Years Ended Dec. 31		
	19A	19B	19C
Royalties	$150,000	$170,000	$140,000
Interest	80,000	50,000	60,000
Rent	240,000	–	–
Total revenues	$470,000	$220,000	$200,000
Deductible expenses	220,000	180,000	170,000
Taxable income	$250,000	$ 40,000	$ 30,000

Assume the average income tax rate for each year was 35%.

The only differences between the tax returns and the income recognized on the books of the corporation relate to rent. On the tax return, $240,000 of rent collected October 1, 19A, relating to the 24-month period ending September 30, 19C, was included in 19A taxable income. For book purpose, this rent revenue was recognized ratably over the period it covered.

Required:

1. Prepare income statements for each year reflecting tax allocation.

2. Give journal entries such as would appear at the end of each year to reflect income tax accrual and allocation.

Exercise 23–3

Irma Retailers, Inc., would have had identical net income before taxes results on both its income tax returns and income statements for the years 19A through 19D were it not for the fact that for tax purposes fixed assets which cost $120,000 were depreciated by the sum-of-the-digits' method, whereas for book purposes the straight line method was used. These fixed assets have a four-year estimated life and zero scrap value. Excess of revenue over expenses other than depreciation and income taxes for the years concerned were as follows:

	19A	19B	19C	19D
Excess revenue over other expenses.......	$90,000	$100,000	$75,000	$75,000

Assume the average income tax rate for each year was 40%.

Required:

1. Prepare income statements for each year as completely as possible to reflect tax allocation under the deferred credit concept.
2. Give journal entries such as would appear at the end of each year to reflect income tax accrual and allocation.

Exercise 23–4

The actual tax liability of XYZ Corporation for each of three years was as follows: 19A, $76,000; 19B, $39,400; and 19C, $29,800.

Due to differences in timing of reporting of income for book purposes and tax purposes, the following variations existed in these three years:

19A – Book income exceeded income per tax return, $11,000.
19B – Income per tax return exceeded book income, $7,000.
19C – Book income exceeded income per tax return, $16,200.

Required:

Assuming these differences will ultimately cancel out, prepare journal entries to record the tax accrual and to reflect tax allocation procedures. Assume an average tax rate of 40%.

Exercise 23–5

Botts Corporation reported an operating profit (pretax) in 19A amounting to $60,000, the first year of operations. In 19B the corporation experienced a $50,000 operating loss (pretax). Assume a flat 40% income tax rate for problem purposes.

Required:

1. Compute the income tax consequences for each year.
2. Show how the tax consequences for each year would be reflected in the income statement.
3. Give appropriate entries to reflect income tax allocation in the accounts.

Exercise 23–6

Davis Corporation experienced a $100,000 net operating loss (pretax) for 19A, the first year of operations. Assume a flat 40% tax rate for problem purposes.

Required:

1. Assume the loss resulted from an identifiable, isolated nonrecurring cause and that future taxable income over the next five years is virtually certain to be sufficient to offset the loss carryforward.

a) Give entry and a partial income statement for 19A to reflect appropriate tax allocation consequences.
b) Assume it is now the end of 19B and that a net operating profit (pretax) in 19B is reported amounting to $150,000. Give entry and a partial income statement for 19B to reflect appropriate tax allocation consequences.

2. Assume that at the time of the loss there did not exist an assurance "beyond reasonable doubt" that profits in the next five years would be sufficient to absorb the loss carryforward.

a) Give entry and a partial income statement for 19A to reflect appropriate tax allocation consequences.
b) Assume operating incomes (pretax), following the year of loss, as follows: 19B, breakeven; 19C, $40,000; and 19D, $90,000. Give entry and a partial income statement for each of these three years to reflect appropriate tax allocation consequences.

Exercise 23-7

The following data were taken from income statements of Zee Corporation:

	19A	19B	19C	19D	19E
Net income (loss) before income taxes	$5,000	$15,000	$10,000	($20,000)	$15,000

For purpose of computing any carrybacks or carryforwards, the loss in 19D is subjected to a reduction of $5,000 under income tax regulations. Assume the average income tax rates were 40% for 19A and 19B and 30% for all other years.

Required:

1. Give journal entries in respect to the carrybacks such as would be appropriate at year-end, 19D.
2. Assume instead that the net loss per books before considering income taxes had been $10,000 greater. Calculate the amount of tax refund claim the loss would generate (journal entries not required).
3. Without reference to requirement 2, how large would the book loss have to be before the amount of tax for 19E would amount to only $2,400? Show your calculations.

Exercise 23-8

Machinery purchased for $10,000 on January 1, 19A, when the price index used was at 120 is being depreciated over a 10-year life with no scrap value assumed. Prices rose so that at December 31, 19A, the index was at 132 and a year later was at 150.

Required:

1. What is the adjusted depreciation expense charge on the income statement for the years ended December 31, 19A, and 19B?

2. If the price index remains at 150 until the asset is fully depreciated and the income tax rate to which the owner is subject is uniformly 52%, how much will have to be taken in to enable replacement of the asset?

Exercise 23-9

Excerpts from the trial balance of ABC Company as of July 1 include:

Cash	$ 480	
Accounts receivable	3,000	
Accounts payable		$1,800

The transactions affecting these accounts for the following several months were as follows:

Date	Index	Date
July 1	125	Sold $1,000 of merchandise on account.
Aug. 1	125	Secured a loan for $1,500 from an affiliate by issuance of a six-month note.
Sept. 1	130	Collected $2,600 of the receivables from June.
Sept. 15	150	Paid the entire balance of the account payable.
Oct. 1	145	Collected the remainder of the initial balance of receivables plus $325 of receivables created on July 1.

Required:

Applying Sweeney's stabilized accounting technique, calculate the realized and unrealized gains (to the nearest dollar) as to cash, receivables, and payables. Assume that the opening balances were acquired when the index used stood at 120 and that the value at date of conversion was 160. Fifo flow of cash is to be assumed.

Exercise 23-10

A speculator purchased land for $50,000 on January 1, 19A, when an index measuring general purchasing power of the dollar stood at 80. Assuming any gain on sale of the land is taxable at the capital gains rate of 25%, at what price would the land have to be sold on each of the following dates in order for the investor to have the same purchasing power after taxes? In each case the index number on the date of sale is as given below:

Date of Sale	Index
a) July 1, 19B	90
b) January 1, 19C	107
c) March 1, 19D	110
d) August 1, 19E	104
e) October 15, 19F	113

Round answers to the nearest dollar.

Exercise 23–11

The following trial balance was acquired when the price index stood at 105.

Cash	$57,235	
Land	79,500	
Liability		$ 2,570
Capital stock		100,000
Retained earnings		34,165

The following transactions took place during the first quarter of the current fiscal year.

Date	Index	Data
Oct. 1	110	Purchased machinery costing $8,500 on account.
Oct. 15	120	Paid for machinery purchased on Oct. 1.
Oct. 31	135	Billed customers for services rendered, $7,500.
Nov. 15	140	Paid $1,230 of the initial liability balance.
Nov. 30	145	Collected half of the billed revenue.
Dec. 10	150	Paid general expense of $5,700.
Dec. 31	160	Accrued three months' depreciation on machinery which has a five-year life with no scrap value.

Required:

Record the above balances and entries in T-accounts. Applying Sweeney's stabilized accounting technique, prepare conventional statements as well as stabilized statements for the quarter. Support these statements with the type of schedules shown in the chapter. Assume Fifo flow of cash and round all items to the nearest dollar.

Exercise 23–12

A common objective of accountants is to prepare meaningful financial statements. To attain this objective many accountants maintain that the financial statements must be adjusted for changes in price level. Other accountants believe that financial statements should continue to be prepared on the basis of unadjusted historical cost.

Required:

1. List arguments for adjusting financial statements for changes in price level.

2. List the arguments for preparing financial statements on only the basis of unadjusted historical cost.

3. In their discussions about accounting for changes in price levels and the methods of measuring them, uninformed individuals have frequently failed to distinguish between adjustments for changes in the price levels of specific goods and services and adjustments for changes in the general purchasing power of the dollar. What is the distinction? Which are "price-level adjustments"? Discuss.

(AICPA adapted)

PROBLEMS

Problem 23-1

Markwell Construction Company has contracts for construction of three major bridges. The percentage-of-completion method of accounting is used on the books while the completed contract method is used in filing income tax returns. Data pertaining to these contracts are as follows:

Project	Year Begun	Year Completed	Profit
C	1971	1973	$30,000
E	1972	1973	75,000
F	1972	1974	81,000

Degree of completion during each year:

	1971	1972	1973	1974
C	40%	50%	10%	
E		20	80	
F		10	70	20%

Required:

Assume the average tax rate is 40% and prepare journal entries to accrue income tax expense and to reflect tax allocation procedures for each year according to the deferred credit method illustrated in the chapter. Assume that the other income (aside from the three contracts) is $35,000 in 1971, $20,000 in 1972, and $50,000 in 1973.

Problem 23-2

Kozmetsky Corporation would have had the same amounts of income on its books and tax returns before depreciation and taxes for the years 19A through 19E were it not for the fact that fixtures acquired at the start of 19A were depreciated differently for the two purposes.

The fixtures in question cost $315,000 and have a six-year estimated life with a probable zero scrap value at the end of that period. For tax purposes, they are depreciated by the sum-of-the-digits' method, while on the books, straight line depreciation is used. In 19A and 19B the tax rate was 40%; in 19C it rose to 45% and remained at that level.

Excess of revenue over expenses other than depreciation and income taxes for 19A through 19E inclusive were as follows:

	19A	19B	19C	19D	19E
Excess of revenue over expenses other than depreciation and income taxes	$110,000	$90,000	$95,000	$50,000	$70,000

Required:

1. Prepare journal entries at the end of 19A through 19E inclusive to reflect income tax accrual and tax allocation under the deferred credit method.
2. Prepare (partial) income statements for each year 19A through 19E.

Problem 23-3

This is a hypothetical problem involving both intraperiod and interperiod income tax allocations reflected in (a) ordinary income, (b) extraordinary items, and (c) prior period adjustments. To simplify assume a flat 40% tax rate on all items properly included on the tax return. Assume all timing differences reverse in 19B and that all items are "gains." The following data relate to accounting income and taxable income as specified:

	19A	19B
Operating income:		
Item A—On financial statement and tax return same period	$100,000	$115,000
B—On financial statement in 19A and tax return in 19B	10,000	
C—On financial statement only, in 19A (never will be on tax return)	6,000°	
D—On tax return only, in 19A (never will be on financial statement)	4,000°	
Extraordinary items:		
Item E—On financial statement and tax return same period	30,000	20,000
F—On tax return in 19A and financial statement in 19B	9,000	
G—On financial statement only, in 19A (never will be on tax return)	5,000°	
H—On tax return only, in 19A (never will be on financial statement)	2,000°	
Prior period adjustments:		
Item I—On financial statement and tax return same period	50,000	40,000
J—On financial statement in 19A and tax return in 19B	7,000	
K—On financial statement only, in 19A (never will be on tax return)	8,000°	
L—On tax return only, in 19A (never will be on financial statement)	12,000°	

° Permanent differences.

Required:

1. For each year compute income taxes payable by statement component.
2. For each year compute income tax expense by statement component.
3. Give entries for each year to record income taxes and allocation consequences.
4. Reconcile the timing differences with the amount of deferred taxes recorded in (3).
5. For each year prepare financial statements to reflect both interperiod and interstatement (intraperiod) tax allocation consequences.

Problem 23-4

Income statements of Apex Corporation for the years 19A through 19F reflect the following:

	19A	19B	19C	19D	19E	19F
Net income (loss) before income tax	$20,000	$20,000	$15,000	$20,000	($45,000)	$22,000
Tax rates	28%	28%	30%	26%	30%	30%

Prevailing income tax rates for the years involved are shown above. The 19E loss per books must be reduced by $7,000 under income tax regulations for purpose of computing any carrybacks or carryforwards.

Required:

1. Based on information given in the chapter concerning tax carrybacks and carryforwards, journalize their recognition on the books of Apex Corporation at year-end 19E.

2. Calculate the amount of claim for income tax refund which would arise if the net loss had been $10,000 greater and if tax rates for each year had been 2% lower (i.e., 28% in 19A, 28% in 19C etc.).

3. Without reference to requirement 2, how large would the book loss have to be to cause the amount of income tax to be owing for 19F to amount to only $1,500? Show calculations.

Problem 23-5

On January 1, 19A, XYZ Company bought for $150,000 cash machinery which, for income tax purposes is to be depreciated by the straight line method over a five-year life. For financial accounting purposes a 15-year life is to be used; for both purposes the scrap value is assumed to be zero. Current and expected income tax rates are 45%. XYZ Company has annual net income of $200,000 before considering depreciation of the machinery in question or income taxes.

Required:

1. Give journal entries at December 31, 19A, and at December 31, 19F, to accrue XYZ's income tax liability and to reflect tax allocation.

2. Now assume that it is January 1, 19F, and that the five-year life has been used both for book and tax purposes in writing off the machinery. Directors of XYZ Company decide that the total economic life of the machinery is actually 15 years and that a portion of its value should be restored to the books. Give entries to reflect the restoration if:

a) It is to be reflected at "net of taxes" value.
b) It is instead to be reflected at gross value.

3. List some of the theoretical objections to interperiod income tax allocation.

Problem 23-6

The financial statements of the Shinn Corporation recognize profits on installment sales in the period during which the merchandise is shipped. The profits on such sales, however, are reported in the corporate income tax returns on the installment basis.

Under this tax reporting method the corporation will defer for tax purposes $10,000 of profits on $50,000 of accounts receivable at year-end. All related expenses will be reported in the financial statements and in the federal income tax return. The corporation plans to carry $4,800 as a liability for federal income taxes to be paid in future years.

Required:

Interperiod tax allocation is necessary because there are differences in the timing of revenues and expenses between financial statements and federal income tax returns. List the categories of circumstances that result in such timing differences and give examples of them.

(AICPA adapted)

Problem 23–7

Apply Sweeney's stabilized accounting technique to the following situation. The price index stood at 120 when these trial balance items were acquired:

Cash	$5,800	
Equipment	3,000	
Accumulated depreciation		$ 600
Liability		900
Capital stock		5,000
Retained earnings		2,300

Transactions during the first quarter of the current fiscal year were as follows. Index values prevailing at the time are indicated parenthetically.

Jan. 15   A payment of $480 on the liability balance is made (125).
Jan. 31   Revenue for services is billed to customers, $1,300 (130).
Feb. 15   Half of the revenue billed is collected (140).
Mar. 10   Land is purchased for $5,200 cash (130).
Mar. 20   General expenses are paid, $700 (140).
Mar. 31   Accrued three months' depreciation on the equipment which has a six-year life and no scrap value (150).

The index at March 31 was 150.

Required:

Record in appropriate T-accounts. Convert all items to the nearest dollar and prepare conventional statements as well as stabilized statements supported by the type of schedules illustrated in the chapter. Fifo flow of cash is to be assumed.

Problem 23–8

The following trial balance was acquired when the price index stood at 115.

Cash	$ 7,245	
Land	12,075	
Liabilities		$ 3,220
Capital stock		11,500
Retained earnings		4,600

The following transactions took place during the first quarter of the current fiscal year:

Date	Index	Data
Oct. 1	120	Purchased machinery costing $6,000 on account.
Oct. 15	125	Paid for machinery purchased on Oct. 1.
Oct. 31	130	Billed customers for services rendered, $4,680.
Nov. 15	135	Collected half of the billed revenue.
Dec. 1	140	Paid $700 of the initial liability balance.
Dec. 10	145	Paid general expenses of $2,610.
Dec. 31	150	Accrued three months' depreciation on machinery which has a 10-year life with no scrap value.

Required:

Record the above balances and entries in T-accounts. Applying Sweeney's stabilized accounting technique, prepare conventional statements as well as stabilized statements for the quarter. Support these statements with the type of schedules illustrated in the chapter. Assume Fifo flow of cash and round all items to the nearest dollar.

Problem 23-9

1. In considering the merits of using price indexes for the purpose of converting the accounting data as reflected in the conventional historical accounts, some people have suggested that *these price-level adjustments should be confined to the fixed assets and related depreciation.*

What can be said in favor of such a proposal? Against it?

2. The price index rose from 125 to 175 during the previous year and from 175 to 225 during the current year. The dollar sales during the previous year were $240,000 and during the current year were $300,000.

a) For comparative income statement purposes you are to convert the sales figures for both years to the price level existing at the end of the current year. You are to assume that sales were made uniformly throughout both years, and that the change in price level was also uniform.

b) What additional information is revealed by a comparison of the converted figures? How do you interpret them?

(AICPA adapted)

Problem 23-10

It has been said that "income determination is now based on a questionable concept which, for companies with a large investment in plant and equipment, distorts reported income unfavorably when prices are rising and favorably when prices are falling."

Required:

1. Explain fully the principal arguments used by those expressing the foregoing view.

2. What specific changes in presently accepted methods of determining income have been recommended by supporters of this view? Explain fully, including illustrations if appropriate.

3. What are the arguments used by those opposing the foregoing view?

(AICPA adapted)

Problem 23–11

Apply Sweeney's stabilized accounting technique to the following situation. The price index stood at 150 when these trial balance items were acquired:

Cash	$ 7,500	
Equipment	10,000	
Accumulated depreciation		$2,000
Liability		1,900
Capital stock		8,000
Retained earnings		5,600

Transactions during the first half of current fiscal year were as follows. Index values prevailing at the time are indicated parenthetically.

Jan. 10   A payment of $800 on the liability balance is made (160).
Feb. 15   Revenue for services is billed to customers, $2,500 (175).
Mar.   1   Four fifths of the revenue billed is collected (180).
Apr. 20   Land is purchased for $8,000 cash (190).
May   5   General expenses are paid, $500 (185).
June 30   Accrued six month's depreciation on the equipment which has a 10-year life and no scrap value (200).

The index at June 30 was 200.

Required:

Record in appropriate T-accounts. Convert all items to the nearest dollar and prepare conventional statements as well as stabilized statements supported by the type of schedules illustrated in the chapter. Fifo flow of cash is to be assumed.

	Changes in Accounting
chapter **24**	Methods and Estimates, Errors and Incomplete Records

Whether in public practice or in industrial accounting, situations are frequently encountered where changes in accounting methods, estimates and error corrections must be made. Similarly, situations are encountered, particularly in very small businesses, where the records maintained are incomplete in many respects. In recognition of these two distinctly different problems, this chapter is divided into two parts: Part A is concerned with changes in accounting; Part B is concerned with the preparation of financial statements from single-entry and other incomplete records.

In view of the nature of the two problems considered in this chapter there are no new accounting principles and concepts introduced; rather, the chapter deals exclusively with guidelines and techniques designed for orderly resolution of the two specific types of problems. The techniques presented herein have been developed and tested over many years and have been found to be efficient for problem-solving purposes whether for the student, the independent CPA, or the accountant in government or private industry.

PART A—CHANGES IN ACCOUNTING METHODS, ESTIMATES AND ERROR CORRECTIONS

Current practices and procedures for accommodating accounting changes and errors have evolved gradually and no authoritative body such as the APB or the AAA dealt with them comprehensively prior to *APB Opinion 20* (August, 1971). As a consequence there has existed a diverse range of accounting approaches for recording and reporting their effects. These approaches have been conceptually inconsistent and lacking in forthright disclosure in some cases. The recent pronouncements of the APB (as reflected in *Opinion 9* in particular) tended to focus attention on this problem area. It is not unusual that changes in accounting, depending on how they are recorded and reported, may result in (*a*) a particular amount (revenue or expense) over time "passing through" the income statement twice (or even three times), or (*b*) a particular amount (revenue or expense) over time completely missing the income statement. This is an area where diversity and alternatives should be narrowed since certain accounting values may be significantly affected. The discussions in this part of the chapter reflect distinctions and approaches currently being sharpened to resolve the problem. Those familiar with earlier practices and procedures, and their evolution, will be quite aware of the importance of these new directions. Attention is being focused on (1) reporting problems on comparative financial statements and (2) accounting recognition in the accounts. The changes discussed in this part may be outlined as follows:

A. Accounting Changes
   1. Change in accounting principle. When the enterprise adopts a different generally accepted accounting principle or procedure from the one previously used. An example would be: A change from straight line depreciation to double-declining depreciation.
   2. Change in accounting estimate. As more current and improved data are obtained in respect to accounting determinations based on estimates, the prior estimate may be changed. An example would be: Based on new information it is decided to depreciate Asset X over 12 years rather than on the 10-year life currently being utilized.
   3. Change in reporting entity. Because of changes in the reporting entity, such as including or excluding financial statements of subsidiaries in consolidated statements, accounting applications may be affected. Accommodating such changes constitutes one class of accounting changes.
B. Error Correction
   4. Change due to discovery of an error. An error is defined as

misapplication of facts existing at the time of the exchange; the misapplication may have been through oversight or intentional. An example would be: expensing an item of equipment in a prior period that should have been capitalized.

In considering the appropriate accounting approach for the four types of changes defined above, the impact on the financial statements must be focused upon. This particular facet of the problem increases in complexity when *comparative* financial statements are presented as is the usual case. In the view of many accountants, comparability is of such importance that the statements for *all* periods currently presented should be retroactively restated on the "new" basis. Other accountants are of the opinion that retroactive restatement in this manner would destroy confidence of the users in all amounts reported on the financial statements. Thus, a problem is posed that, fundamentally, has three alternative solutions. That is, in respect to presentation of comparative financial statements, how should changes be reflected thereon; the *reporting alternatives* are:

1. Current application. Utilize an adjustment on the financial statement for the *current period only* (an extraordinary item on the income statement or a prior period adjustment on the statement of retained earnings) for the amount necessary to "catch up or change over" to the new status.
2. Retroactive application. Restate financial statements for all prior periods presented currently with a catch-up adjustment when needed to the beginning balance of retained earnings (as a prior period adjustment) for the *first period* for which the comparative statements are presented.
3. Prospective application. Reflect no catch-up or change-over adjustment and do not restate any prior periods; rather spread the effect of the change over the *current and future periods*.

Because of the differing characteristics of each accounting change the preferable alternative relates to the type of change (listed on page 938). The major objectives, in respect to accounting changes, are (*a*) to narrow the areas of differences so that like changes are treated in a similar manner across industries and (*b*) to attain consistency in the accounting treatment accorded changes having similar characteristics. In view of the wide diversity of situations in each change category, these objectives are difficult to attain.

A related accounting problem is the entry (or entries) to be recorded in the accounts to reflect the change. In the case of alternatives 1 (current application) and 3 (prospective application) the entry obviously can, and should, parallel the effects to be reflected on the comparative financial statements presented for the period. On the other hand, alternative 2 (retroactive application) would not permit this internal consistency since the catch-up adjustment for the *first period presented* usually could not be recorded directly in the accounts as presented on the comparative financial statements. Obviously, a current adjusting entry involving different amounts generally would, of necessity, have to be made. This situation will be illustrated in the paragraphs to follow.

Fundamental to all changes is the presumption that an entity initially should adopt accounting principles which, on the basis of the circumstances then existing, provide results most useful to statement users. An accounting principle once selected should not be changed unless the change clearly and significantly will enhance the usefulness of the financial statements of the users.

We will now discuss and illustrate each of the four types of changes and indicate the appropriate reporting and accounting alternatives. Prior to those discussions we should note an essential feature of *APB Opinion 9* (December 1966) to the effect that charges and credits to *retained earnings* should be limited to certain capital transactions, including dividends and *prior period adjustments*. The latter were very narrowly defined as those material adjustments which:

a) can be specifically identified with and directly related to the business activities of particular prior periods, and
b) are not attributable to economic events occurring subsequent to the date of the financial statements for the prior period, and
c) depend primarily on determinations by persons other than the management, and
d) were not susceptible of reasonable estimation prior to such determination.

The Opinion also stated that "Such adjustments are rare in modern financial accounting." We have noted in several prior chapters that the thrust of that Opinion was to the "all-inclusive" income statement which was facilitated through specification of a section thereon captioned *extraordinary items*. As a consequence, adjustments such as those arising from accounting changes and error corrections generally have been reported as extraordinary items. However, it must be realized that *Opinion 9* did not deal directly with the problem of presentation of the effects of these changes on comparative financial statements. *APB Opinion 20* deals directly with these problems.

Change in Accounting Principle

A change in accounting principle occurs when a company adopts a generally accepted accounting principle or procedure different from a previously used one that *also* was generally accepted at the time adopted.[1] *APB Opinion 20* states: "A characteristic of a change in accounting principle is that it concerns a choice." It excludes the adoption of a principle occasioned by events occurring for the first time or that were previously immaterial in their effect. Examples of a change in accounting principle are:

1. A change from straight line to some other acceptable method of depreciation.
2. A change in inventory cost flow such as from Lifo to Fifo.
3. A change in accounting for long-term construction contracts from completed contract basis to percentage of completion.
4. A change from expensing research and development costs to capitalization and amortization.

There is some disagreement among accountants in respect to the preferable accounting approach to recording and reporting the effects of a change in accounting principle. *APB Opinion 20* states that the effect of most changes in accounting principle should be recorded in the period of change and that any resultant adjustment should be reported similar to an "extraordinary" item and reported on the current income statement.[2] The catch-up adjustment, if material in amount, should be clearly identified on the face of the income statement and elaborated on by way of footnote that clearly *justifies* the reason for the change. The current income statement should reflect the operational effect on the new basis. On comparative statements, data for previous periods should not be retroactively restated to the new basis; however, full disclosure and comparability require that net income and earnings per share data be provided on a pro forma basis assuming retroactive application.[3] This position is in harmony with current practice (alternative 1 above) and is consistent with *APB Opinions 9, 15,* and *20.*

To illustrate *a change in accounting principle,* assume Company M has been depreciating an asset, which cost $200,000, on a straight line basis over 10 years and no residual value. Starting in the third year the decision was made to adopt double-declining depreciation.[4]

---

[1] See page 946 for a discussion of a change from a nonacceptable accounting approach to a generally accepted one. Also you should note that *accounting principle* as used here is much broader than the definition provided in Chapter 1 of this book; as used in the present chapter it includes not only accounting principles and practices but also methods of applying them.

[2] *APB Opinion 20,* "Changes in Accounting," August, 1971, Appendix A.

[3] *Pro forma* is defined in *Webster's Dictionary* as "for the sake of or as a matter of form." Pro forma statements are "as if" statements; the as if assumptions should be clearly stated.

[4] This illustration disregards tax effects; depending upon the circumstances deferred taxes should be taken into account (i.e., net of tax effects).

1. The effect of the change in accounting principle would be:

Double-declining depreciation to date:
Year 1 – $200,000 × 20% $40,000
Year 2 – $160,000 × 20% 32,000 $72,000
Straight line depreciation recorded:
Years 1 and 2 – ($200,000 ÷ 10) × 2   40,000
Effect of the change in accounting principle
   (catch-up adjustment) $32,000

2. Entry to record the effect of the change in accounting principle (catch-up adjustment) in year 3:

   Adjustment Due to Accounting Change (depreciation) 32,000
      Accumulated Depreciation   32,000

3. Income statement presentation (comparative) at the end of year 3:

	Year 2	Year 3
Depreciation expense	$ 20,000	
($200,000 – $40,000 – $32,000) × 20% = $25,600		$ 25,600
Income before extraordinary items	$100,000	$110,000
Extraordinary items, specified°	(6,000)	10,000
Accounting change effect°		(32,000)
Net income	$ 94,000	$ 88,000
Pro forma net income, assuming retroactive application of accounting change‡	$ 82,000	$120,000
Earnings per share (100,000 shares outstanding):		
Income before extraordinary items and changes	$1.00	$1.10
Extraordinary items	(.06)	.10
Accounting change	–	(.32)
Net income	$ .94	$ .88
Pro forma assuming retroactive application of accounting change:‡		
Income before extraordinary items‡	.88	1.10
Net income‡	.82	1.20

°Appropriate footnote.

‡The pro forma share amounts represent what "would have been" had the new method been used from the beginning. *APB Opinion 15* recommends, but noes not require, earnings per share amounts for the extraordinary items.

‡Computations:	Year 2	Year 3
As reported	$100,000	$110,000
Add back straight line depreciation	20,000	
Deduct double-declining depreciation	(32,000)	Already deducted
Income before extraordinary items	$ 88,000	$110,000
Extraordinary item	(6,000)	10,000
Net income	$ 82,000	$120,000

On page 941 we stated that "most changes in accounting principle should be recorded in the period of change and any resultant adjustment should be reported similar to an extraordinary item." A few changes in accounting principle are particularly unique and require different treatment. On this point *APB Opinion 20* states:

Certain changes in accounting principle are such that the advantages of retro-active treatment outweigh the disadvantages. Accordingly, for those few changes, the Board concludes that the financial statements of all prior periods presented should be restated (retroactive restatement). The changes that should be accorded this treatment are: (a) a change from the Lifo method of inventory pricing to another method, (b) a change in the method of accounting for long-term construction type contracts, and (c) a change to or from the "full cost" method of accounting which is used in the extractive industries.

Change in Accounting Estimate

Accounting necessarily requires the use of estimates because future developments and events cannot be perceived with certainty. For example, the periodic depreciation charge is the result of one known (cost) and two estimates (residual value and useful life). Estimates result from judgments which are based on specific assumptions and projections concerning future events. As the anticipated event, or events, approach reality in time it is generally possible to improve on the accuracy of the estimates. As a consequence, the accountant is frequently faced with the problem of what to do about improved estimates.[5] For example, during the first few years' life of a firm the estimated loss rate due to uncollectible accounts neces-sarily may have a relatively wide range of error due to the lack of historical experience on collections; as time progresses the rate is refined, and used, as a result of additional information. Thus, changes in accounting estimates are a *natural consequence* of the accounting process. A change in an accounting estimate is quite different in cause than is a change in accounting principle or an accounting error. Examples of a change in accounting estimates are:

1. Change in the residual value or estimated useful life of an asset subject to depreciation, amortization, or depletion.
2. Change in the estimated loss rate on receivables.
3. Change in the expected recovery of a deferred charge.
4. Change in the expected realization of a deferred revenue.
5. Change in the expected warranty cost on goods sold under guar-antee.

When a change in an estimate has been decided upon the accountant is faced with the dual problem of (a) how to reflect the change on the comparative financial statements and (b) how to record the effect of the change of estimate in the accounts. The accountant presumes

---

[5] This definition of a change in estimates assumes that the original estimate and the new estimate both represent realistic and good faith determinations based upon the information available at the time the respective estimates were made. Changes in esti-mates not meeting these criteria must be classified as an "accounting error" as defined and discussed in the next section of this chapter.

that a change in an accounting estimate will be made only when there are sound reasons for doing so as opposed to intent to manipulate reported net income; changes for the latter purpose are unacceptable.

Generally accepted accounting principles tend to recognize that changes in estimates are occasioned primarily by uncertainties that are influenced by external conditions. As a consequence, changes in accounting estimates generally are not accorded current catch-up or retroactive treatments but rather are accounted for *prospectively*. On this point *APB Opinion 20* states:

The Board concludes that the effect of a change in accounting estimate should be recognized in (a) the period of change if the change affects that period only or (b) the period of change and future periods if the change affects both.

Thus, a change in accounting estimate normally will be reflected prospectively in the current and future financial statements. To illustrate, assume a company is utilizing an estimated loss rate on receivables of one half of 1% of credit sales and on the basis of more recent experience has decided to reduce the rate to one fourth of 1%. In this instance, normally there would be no catch-up adjustment; rather the current and future "loss from doubtful accounts" amounts reported on the income statement would be based on the new rate. Similarly, changes in the estimated future useful life of a natural resource would be effected simply by recomputing the depletion rate so as to spread the remaining cost over the remaining life. The same approach would follow for changes in depreciation estimates. However, one must recognize that prior to *APB Opinions 9* and *20* general practice, in respect to depreciation, appeared to be to adjust the accumulated depreciation account to the new basis assuming the latter had been applied from the beginning. In the absence of apparent attempts to manipulate reported net income through unrealistic estimates or numerous changes from one method to another the *prospective approach* appears to be preferable. Thus, a change in an estimate should not result in restatement of previously reported balances on the financial statements.[6]

To illustrate a *change* in an *estimate* assume an asset that cost $120,000 (no residual value) is being depreciated over a 10-year life, and on the basis of new information after 5 years' use, a 15-year life appears to be more realistic. The change in the depreciation estimate, starting in the sixth year, would be recognized as follows:

---

[6] Unrealistic estimates, resulting from misapplication of known information, give rise to an "accounting error" when corrected and should be accounted for as explained in the next section of this chapter.

	Per Year	After Five Years
Depreciation recognized to date (10-year life)	$12,000	$60,000
Depreciation on revised basis (15-year life)	8,000	40,000
Difference	$ 4,000	$20,000

Depreciation for sixth year:

Depreciation Expense [($120,000 − $60,000) ÷ 10 years]	6,000	
Accumulated Depreciation		6,000

Entry to record effect of the change: None required.

The nature of the change and its effect on net income should be clearly disclosed.

In some situations a change in accounting principle and a change in estimate may be concurrent and hence indistinguishable. In such cases it is generally preferable to account for it as a *change in estimate*.

Change in Reporting Entity

Changes in the reporting entity are to be effected and reported through retroactive restatement; that is, "they should be reported by restating the financial statements of all prior periods presented in order to show financial information for the new reporting entity for all periods." *APB Opinion 20* also defines this type of accounting change as follows:

One type of accounting change results in financial statements which, in effect, are those of a different reporting entity. This type is limited mainly to (a) presenting consolidated or combined statements in place of statements of individual companies, (b) changing specific subsidiaries comprising the group of companies for which consolidated statements are presented and (c) changing the companies included in combined financial statements. A different group of companies comprise the reporting entity after each change.

This type of change is discussed in detail in another book in this series.[7]

Change Due to Discovery of an Error

The independent CPA frequently must deal with accounting errors made by the client. Obviously, such errors must be corrected prior to issuance of the financial statements to which the CPA certifies. Seldom is an error discovered in statements on which the independent CPA has expressed an opinion. Accounting errors usually are inadvertent and reflect a lack of sophistication; at the same time, the

---

[7] C. H. Griffin, T. H. William, and K. L. Larson, *Advanced Accounting* (Homewood, Ill.: Richard D. Irwin, Inc., 1971).

auditor must be alert for intentional errors designed to manipulate income or financial position or to conceal fraud.

An accounting error is specifically defined as the *misapplication* of facts existing at the time the exchange is recorded or when some other related effects are recorded, or reported. The following are examples of accounting errors as distinguished from changes in accounting principle or changes in estimates:

a) Use of an inappropriate or unacceptable accounting principle. Thus a change from an unacceptable accounting principle to a generally accepted one would require the correction of an error (not a change in accounting principle).

b) Use of an unrealistic accounting estimate, that is, the misapplication of known information at the date of the decision in respect to the estimate. Thus, the adoption of a clearly unrealistic depreciation rate would require the correction of an error when the change is effected (not a change in accounting estimate).

c) Misstatement of an accounting value, such as inventory, deferred charge or credit, liabilities, owners' equity.

d) Failure to recognize accruals and deferrals.

e) Incorrect classification of an expenditure as between a revenue charge and an asset charge.

f) Incorrect or unrealistic allocations of accounting values.

As with the other types of changes a dual problem is posed: (a) how should the effects of the error correction be reflected on the financial statements and (b) the entry, or entries, essential to appropriate correction of the accounts.

There is general agreement that accounting errors, when discovered, should be corrected in the accounts forthwith. The incorrect account balances should be adjusted to their correct balances and the net adjustment, if any, should be recorded as "Adjustment — Correction of Error." This item as specified in *APB Opinion 20,* should be closed to retained earnings and reported as a *prior period adjustment* although many accountants feel that it should be reported on the income statement as an extraordinary item. Consideration of the reporting requirements will reveal the essential nature of the adjustment.

In respect to the comparative financial statements, accountants generally agree that incorrect financial data for each period reported should be corrected for all subsequently discovered errors. Thus, in the case of comparative financial statements, the data for each year being presented (including the current period) should be restated to the correct basis (that is retroactive restatement) and any catch-up adjustment should be shown as a *prior period adjustment to retained earnings* for the first period being reported. On this point *APB Opinion 20* states:

Disclosure. The nature of an error in previously issued financial statements and the effect of its correction on income before extraordinary items, net income, and the related per share amounts should be disclosed in the period in which the error was discovered and corrected. Financial statements of subsequent periods need not repeat the disclosures.

To illustrate the correction of an accounting error, assume a $6,000 expenditure for an asset, having a six-year estimated life (no residual value), was recorded in January, 19A, as an expense. Assume it is now 19C, and in the process of preparing the 19C year-end financial statement, the error was discovered. Net income originally reported in 19A was $14,000 and in 19B, $19,000. Accounting and reporting recognition of the error at the end of 19C, assuming straight line depreciation, would be as follows:

1. Entry to correct the accounts:

Asset (specified)	6,000	
Depreciation Expense (19C)	1,000	
Accumulated Depreciation		3,000
Adjustment—Correction of Error (retained earnings)		4,000

2. Closing entries:

Income Summary	1,000	
Depreciation Expense		1,000
Adjustment—Correction of Error (retained earnings)	4,000	
Retained Earnings		4,000

3. Financial statements at end of 19C (comparative):

	19B	19C
Balance Sheet:		
Asset	$ 6,000	$ 6,000
Less: Allowance for depreciation	2,000	3,000
	$ 4,000	$ 3,000
Income Statement:		
Depreciation expense	$ 1,000	$ 1,000
Net income (Note 1)	18,000	21,000
Statement of Retained Earnings:		
Beginning balance	$70,000	$ 93,000
Prior period adjustment—depreciation correction	5,000	
Adjusted balance	$75,000	$ 93,000
Net income	18,000	21,000
Ending Balance	$93,000	$114,000

Note 1. Appropriate explanation.

Observe that the $19,000 net income reported in the prior financial statement for year 19B has been restated to the correct amount,

Illustration 24-1
Accounting Changes and Error Correction Summarized

Type of Change	Reporting of Effect on Comparative Financial Statements	Recording of Effect in Accounts in Year of Changes (Accounting Entries)	Rationale
Change in principle°	Current application and pro forma reporting. Report current results on new basis; report the change-over adjustment as an *extraordinary item* on the current income statement. Do not restate previously reported statements. Present pro forma data on net income and EPS for all prior periods being presented.	Use change-over entry to restate all affected accounts; as of the *beginning* of the current period. The change-over adjustment should be recorded as an *extraordinary item.*	On balance, preferable when comparability and user confidence is considered. Comparability is sacrificed since user confidence would be destroyed by continual retroactive restatement of financial statements. Pro forma reporting satisfies principle of comparability.
Change in estimate	Prospective and current reporting. Report current and future financial statements on new basis. No restatement or "adjustments" to current or past financial statements. (Note: A major change in an estimate tends to suggest a change due to *error.*)	No change-over entry required since remaining accounting value is allocated over remaining future periods.	Estimates are a necessary consequence of the accounting process. Estimates are made on the basis of information available at the time. As new information becomes available a judgmental change in the prior estimate may be imperative. Past accounting results should not be restated as a result of the necessary improvement of estimates derived on a sound basis.

Change due to error	Retroactive application. All prior financial statements presented must be corrected for errors. When effects extend prior to statements for first period presented, the beginning balance of retained earnings for that period should be restated through a prior period adjustment.	Use a change-over entry to correct all current account balances. The correction adjustment, if any, should be recorded as a prior period adjustment to retained earnings.	There is absolutely no reason for reporting financial data known to be in error, notwithstanding prior reporting of the data. Thus, all financial statements being presented must be restated to remove the effects of error.
Change due to both principle and estimate	Report as a *change in estimate*.	Account as a *change in estimate*.	In those instances where a change in principle and estimate are inseparable, this must be accounted for as a change in estimate because the retroactive effect cannot be separately identified.

---

* Several exceptions are specified in *APB Opinion 20*.

$18,000, and that the catch-up adjustment reported on the statement of retained earnings was up to the *beginning* of year 19B. This amount is different by one year from the adjustment recorded in the accounts.

In overall perspective, we can observe that the four types of *changes* discussed are diverse in situation, characteristics, and accounting treatment. This is another area where the judgment and professional responsibility of the independent accountant is paramount. The distinctions discussed and illustrated in the preceding paragraphs focus on one central issue, that is, the distinction between changes occasioned by change in circumstances (change in principle, change in estimate, and change in entity) that provide a good faith and logical basis for change and those occasioned either by lack of good faith or unsophistication (accounting errors). The accounting treatments that appear most appropriate are related to these circumstances and are designed to best serve the statement user through accuracy, full disclosure, and the absence of misleading inferences. These issues are not fully agreed upon since judgment is a dominant aspect of accounting. In summary we may also reemphasize the mechanical differences posed in (a) correcting or restating the accounts by means of one or more entries at a specific point in time and (b) appropriate reporting of the effect of the change in a set of financial statements that normally extend backward one or more periods from the current period. These distinctions are summarized for your convenience in Illustration 24–1 (pages 948–49).

Analytical Procedures for Accounting Changes

Both the independent accountant and the internal accountant must utilize efficient analytical procedures for dealing with accounting changes whether they are due to principles, estimates, or errors. Change or correction entries must be determined and previously prepared financial statements frequently must be revised. This section presents some analytical techniques that are useful for these purposes as well as for problem-solving purposes for students, CPA candidates, and others.

Changes may be classified according to which financial statements are affected. Some may affect only the balance sheet. For example, a debit to the Temporary Investment account instead of the Permanent Investment account would affect only the balance sheet. Correction of this error would involve a transfer from one balance sheet account to another real account. In this case, balance sheets for future periods would be in error until correction of the respective account balances. Other changes affect only the income statement. For example, a credit to the Sales account instead of Interest Income would affect only the income statement. Correction of this error would involve a transfer from one nominal account to another nominal account. In this case financial reports of future periods would be unaffected whether or not the error is corrected.

A third type of change affects both the balance sheet and the income statement. This type may be further classified on the basis of its effect on future statements as follows:

1. *Counterbalancing errors.* These errors result from failure to allocate properly a cost or revenue item between two consecutive accounting periods. They produce no discernible effect upon the balance sheet at the end of the second period, since the total income and expense to that date is correct, leaving no error in retained earnings or other balance sheet accounts. Examples of counterbalancing errors are:

a) Errors in adjusting for prepaid expenses, accrued expenses, prepaid incomes, or accrued incomes. Such errors cause an incorrect statement of income in the period in which the incorrect adjustment was made or omitted, with an equal misstatement in the opposite direction on the income statement for the following period. To illustrate, assume accrued wages were not recognized in 1970. The effect of this error is as follows:

1970 income statement — Wage expense understated
— Net income overstated
1970 balance sheet   — Current liabilities understated
— Retained earnings overstated
1971 income statement — Wage expense overstated
— Net income understated
1971 balance sheet   — No misstatements

b) Errors in the merchandise inventory. Errors of this type are counterbalancing because the final inventory of the first period is the beginning inventory of the next period and the beginning and ending inventories have an opposite effect on net income. To illustrate, assume the final inventory for 1970 is understated. The effect of this error is as follows:

1970 income statement — Ending inventory understated
— Cost of goods sold overstated
— Net income understated
1970 balance sheet   — Assets (inventory) understated
— Retained earnings understated
1971 income statement — Beginning inventory understated
— Cost of goods sold understated
— Net income overstated
1971 balance sheet   — No misstatements

2. *Noncounterbalancing.* These errors continue to affect account balances until corrected; hence, one or more balance sheet accounts

continue to be reported inaccurately. Examples of noncounterbalancing errors are:

a) Over- or understatement of the depreciation charge; the accumulated depreciation and retained earnings balances are in error until corrected or the asset is disposed of. The income statements are inaccurate only for the periods in which the incorrect charges were recorded.

b) Recognition of a capital expenditure as an expense, or vice versa, results in incorrect asset balances, depreciation charges, and retained earnings.

Recording Changes

In analyzing the effect of errors in the accounts the analyst must know whether or not the books have been closed. The following illustrations involving both counterbalancing and noncounterbalancing *errors* demonstrate *correcting entries* for the accounts and some of the aspects of the status of the accounts at date of correction. Observe that when correcting an error the "adjustment" account is closed to retained earnings as a prior period adjustment.

1. Error in merchandise inventory. Assume that the final inventory in 1970 was understated by $1,000.

Case A. The error was found at the end of 1971; books not closed for 1971. Correcting entry:

```
Beginning Inventory ................................................................1,000
    Adjustment – Inventory Correction.....................................        1,000
```

Case B. The error was found after books were closed for 1971:

Counterbalanced in 1971 – no correcting entry required: restate financial statements.

2. Error in purchases and inventory. Assume that a $2,000 purchase in 1970 was not recorded until 1971. The goods were not included in the 1970 ending inventory.

Case A. The error was found in 1971; books not closed for 1971. Correcting entry:

```
Beginning Inventory ..............................................................2,000
    Purchases...................................................................        2,000
```

Note: Since the item was omitted from both purchases and inventory, 1970 reported net income was correct. However, on the balance sheet for 1970, inventory and payables each were understated by $2,000.

Case B. Same facts except that the books were closed for 1971:

Counterbalanced in 1971 – no correcting entry required; restate financial statements.

3. Error in purchases only. Assume that a $2,000 purchase in 1970 was not recorded until 1971. The goods were included in the 1970 ending inventory.

Case A. The error was found in 1971; books not closed for 1971. Correcting entry:

Adjustment—Purchases Correction 2,000
    Purchases...   2,000

Case B. The error was found after books were closed for 1971:

Counterbalanced in 1971—no correcting entry required; restate financial statements.

4. Error in prepaid expense. Assume that a five-year fire insurance policy was acquired on January 1, 1970; the premium of $500 was charged to expense in 1970.

Case A. The error was found at the end of 1971; books not closed for 1971. Correcting entry:

Prepaid Insurance.. 300
Insurance Expense (1971)...................................... 100
    Adjustment—Insurance Correction.....................................   400

Case B. The error was found after books were closed for 1971:

Prepaid Insurance.. 300
    Adjustment—Insurance Correction.....................................   300

5. Error in accrued expenses. Assume accrued taxes of $100 for 1970 were not recorded at year-end.

Case A. The error was found at the end of 1971; books not closed for 1971. The taxes were paid in 1971. Correcting entry:

Adjustment—Tax Expense Correction 100
    Tax Expense   100

Case B. The error was found after books were closed for 1971:

Counterbalanced in 1971—no correcting entry required; restate financial statements.

6. Error in accrued income. Assume accrued interest income of $75 for 1970 was not recorded at year-end.

Case A. The error was found at the end of 1971; books not closed for 1971. Correcting entry:

Interest Income 75
    Adjustment—Interest Income Correction...........................   75

Case B. The error was found after books were closed for 1971:

Counterbalanced in 1971—no correcting entry required; restate financial statements.

7. Expense capitalized. Assume that $500 was expended for ordinary repairs January 1, 1970; the $500 was debited to the related fixed asset account which was being depreciated 10% per year.

Case A. The error was found at the end of 1971; books were adjusted but not closed for 1971. Correcting entry:

Accumulated Depreciation (1970–71)	100	
Adjustment — Depreciation Correction	450	
Depreciation Expense (1971)		50
Fixed Assets		500

Case B.   The error was found after books were closed for 1971:

Accumulated Depreciation	100	
Adjustment — Depreciation Correction	400	
Fixed Assets		500

8. Error in doubtful accounts. Assume there has been no provision for doubtful accounts; losses have been recognized when the account was written off. The following data are available:

Accounts	Bad Accounts Written Off 1969	1970	1971	Additional Losses Expected
1969	100	200	300	150
1970		400	500	250
1971			600	350

Case A.   Error to be corrected at end of 1971; books not closed for 1971. Correcting entry:

Adjustment — Bad Debt Correction	1,200	
Bad Debt Expense°		450
Allowance for Doubtful Accounts		750

°Computations:
Allowance — establish $750 balance to cover future expected losses
($150 + $250 + $350).
Bad debt expense:

Charged in 1971 ($300 + $500 + $600)	$1,400
Correct charge for 1971 ($600 + $350)	950
Overcharge in 1971	$ 450

Case B.   Error to be corrected after 1971 books closed. Correcting entry:

Adjustment — Bad Debt Correction	750	
Allowance for Doubtful Accounts		750

Work Sheet Techniques for Analyzing Changes

Generally, changes can be analyzed and appropriate accounting developed without a work sheet; however, when changes are numerous and complicated, utilization of the work sheet technique is desirable. An efficient work sheet can be designed for any of a number of types of changes and related requirements. For example, the requirement for correction of a series of income statements would suggest a different work sheet than the requirement for correction of a series of balance sheets. Of necessity, accountants must develop skill in designing efficient work sheets for specific problems as they arise. In the remainder of this Part work sheet techniques are presented for some of the more common types of changes and the requirements with respect to their resolution.

Work Sheet to Correct Net Income and Provide Correcting Entries.
A type of error frequently encountered is where adjusting entries have
not been made for a series of periods. The related requirement usually
is (a) to determine the correct net income for each period and (b) to
provide the entries necessary to correct the accounts. To illustrate,
assume the following simplified data are available:

	1969	1970	1971
Reported net income	$5,000	$7,000	$6,000
Errors made in the records:			
a) Prepaid expenses not recognized	100	200	400
b) Prepaid incomes not recognized	300	500	100
c) Accrued expenses not recognized	600	800	500
d) Accrued incomes not recognized	500	400	600
e) Depreciation understated	200	200	200

Required:

1. Determine the correct income for each year.

2. Give correcting entries required at the end of 1971 assuming the
books have not been closed.

3. Give correcting entries required at the end of 1971 assuming the
books have been adjusted and closed.

Solution:

Req. 1: Work Sheet to correct net income and provide correcting
entries.

Particulars	1969	1970	1971	Corrections	
				Amount	Account
Reported net income (loss)	5,000	7,000	6,000	18,000°	Balancing
Corrections:					
a) Prepaid expenses −1969	100	100°			
(not recognized) 1970		200	200°		
1971			400	400°	Prepaid expenses
b) Prepaid incomes −1969	300°	300			
(not recognized) 1970		500°	500		
1971			100°	100	Prepaid incomes
c) Accrued expenses −1969	600°	600			
(not recognized) 1970		800°	800		
1971			500°	500	Accrued expenses
d) Accrued incomes −1969	500	500°			
(not recognized) −1970		400	400°		
1971			600	600°	Accrued incomes
e) Depreciation −1969	200°				
(understated) 1970		200°		600	Accumulated
1971			200°		depreciation
Correct net income (loss)	4,500	6,400	6,900	17,800°	Balancing

° Denotes debit.

Note: As an arithmetic check note that the last line and last column sum to the same total.

Req. 2: Correcting entries at the end of 1971 assuming the books have not been closed.

a) Prepaid Expenses...400
    Expenses–1971 ($400 – $200)..   200
    Adjustment–Prepaid Expense Correction   200
b) Adjustment–Prepaid Incomes Correction 500
    Incomes–1971 ($500 – $100)..   400
    Prepaid Incomes   100
c) Adjustment–Accrued Expenses Correction 800
    Expenses–1971 ($800 – $500)..   300
    Accrued Expenses   500
d) Accrued Incomes...600
    Incomes–1971 ($600 – $400)..   200
    Adjustment–Accrued Incomes Correction...........................   400
e) Depreciation expense–1971...200
    Adjustment–Depreciation Correction....................................400
    Accumulated Depreciation   600

Req. 3: Correcting entries at the end of 1971 assuming the books have been adjusted and closed.

a) Prepaid Expenses (or expenses)..400
    Adjustment – Expense Correction.......................................   400

b) Adjustment – Income Correction 100
    Prepaid Incomes (or incomes)   100

c) Adjustment – Expense Correction...500
    Accrued Expenses (or expenses)   500

d) Accrued Incomes (or incomes)...600
    Adjustment – Income Correction   600

e) Adjustment – Depreciation Correction 600
    Accumulated Depreciation   600

Work Sheets to Recast Financial Statements. Another group of problems commonly require that the income statement, balance sheet, and statement of retained earnings be recast in detail as corrected.

In order to demonstrate adaptation of the interim work sheet to problems where an uncorrected trial balance is available and the requirement is to provide correct statements of income, retained earnings, and assets and equities, the following illustrative problem is presented. The data given below are analyzed and recorded on the work sheet in Illustration 24–2. The resulting financial statements and correcting entries will not be presented since they may be taken directly from the work sheet. The reader should trace each transaction to the work sheet; the entries are keyed to facilitate study.

Illustrative Problem. Based upon the uncorrected and unadjusted trial balance provided (as listed on the work sheet shown in Illustration 24–2) and the following additional data, prepare a work sheet

Illustration 24-2. Work Sheet Starting with Uncorrected Trial Balance (January 1, 1971, to December 31, 1971)

	Trial Balance Debit	Trial Balance Credit	Correcting Entries Debit	Correcting Entries Credit	Income Summary Debit	Income Summary Credit	Retained Earnings Debit	Retained Earnings Credit	Balance Sheet Debit	Balance Sheet Credit
Cash	9,000								8,000	
Receivables	20,000								20,000	
Allowance for doubtful accounts				(i) 1,000						4,000
Initial inventory	30,000			(f) 4,000; (a) 4,000	26,000					
Equipment	60,000			(g) 20,000					60,000	
Accumulated depreciation		5,000								20,000
Accounts payable										5,000
Capital stock, par $10, 7,500 shares outstanding		76,000	(j) 1,000							75,000
Retained earnings		25,000		(h) 8,000				33,000		
Nonrecurring items:										
Inventory correction			(a) 4,000		4,000					
Salaries correction			(d) 1,000		1,000					
Bad debt correction			(f) 1,000		1,000					
Depreciation correction			(g) 15,000		15,000					
Sales		130,000				130,000				
Purchases	90,000				90,000					
Selling expenses	17,000			(b) 2,000; (d) 1,000	14,000					
General expenses	10,000		(e) 1,000; (f) 3,000; (g) 5,000; (i) 1,000	(c) 2,000	18,000					
	236,000	236,000								
Prepaid advertising			(b) 2,000						2,000	
Prepaid insurance			(c) 2,000						2,000	
Accrued rent				(e) 1,000						1,000
Dividends paid 1971			(h) 8,000				8,000			
Final inventory						32,000			32,000	
Premium on capital stock				(j) 1,000						1,000
Net loss after extraordinary items						7,000	7,000			
Retained earnings balance							18,000			18,000
			44,000	44,000	169,000	169,000	33,000	33,000	124,000	124,000

that presents detailed data for preparation of an income statement, statement of retained earnings, and balance sheet.

a) Merchandise inventory December 31, 1970, overstated $4,000.

b) Prepaid advertising of $2,000 at December 31, 1971, not recorded.

c) Prepaid insurance of $2,000 at December 31, 1971, not recorded; the entire premium paid on June 1, 1971, was debited to general expense.

d) Accrued sales salaries of $1,000 at December 31, 1970, not recorded.

e) Accrued rent expense of $1,000 at December 31, 1971, not recorded; treat as general expense.

f) No provision was made for doubtful accounts. The following estimates have been made: 1970, $1,000; 1971, $3,000. Treated as general expense.

g) No provision was made for depreciation. The following amounts have been computed: prior to 1971, $15,000; 1971, $5,000. Treated as general expense.

h) Dividends paid and properly recorded in 1971, $8,000. (Note: Transactions occurring during the current year and affecting retained earnings may be entered on the work sheet so that the work sheet will provide detail concerning all changes in retained earnings.)

i) Cash shortage, $1,000.

j) Correct for implied premium on capital stock (par value-7,500 shares @ $10).

k) The final inventory was $32,000.

PART B—STATEMENTS FROM SINGLE-ENTRY AND OTHER INCOMPLETE RECORDS

Most businesses maintain a reasonably complete record of all transactions directly affecting the firm. Usually complete records are best accomplished through an accounting model based on (a) the double-entry concept and (b) the accounting equation. However, some small entities, especially if a sole proprietorship, may not maintain a record of any more than what is considered at the time as the "bare essentials." The proprietor may maintain his own records and may not be familiar with standard record-keeping procedures nor appreciate the importance of good records to sound management.

Actually, single-entry record keeping includes all those records, whether kept systematically or not, deemed necessary by the proprietor but which do not attempt to record the *dual effect* of each transaction on both assets and equities as expressed in the accounting equation. In some cases only records of cash, accounts receivable, accounts payable, and taxes paid may be maintained. No record may be kept, except perhaps in memorandum form, of fixed assets, inventories, expenses, revenues, and other elements considered essential to adequate accounting. Yet, in spite of incomplete data provided by the single-entry method, it is generally feasible to prepare a balance sheet, an income statement, and an income tax return.

Preparation of the Balance Sheet from Single-Entry Records

Since single-entry records usually provide no information about assets other than cash and accounts receivable; preparation of the balance sheet involves inventorying, counting, and verification procedures to determine the nature and amount of most of the assets and liabilities. The cost of the fixed assets must be determined from such data as are available. Canceled checks, receipts, bills of sale, deeds, papers transferring title to real estate, and other similar records provide much of the needed data. Once the cost of the fixed assets is determined, depreciation can be computed. The amount of merchandise, supplies on hand, and other inventories are obtained by actual count. The original cost of these items is determined in order to place a value on the inventory. If original cost cannot be obtained, merchandise and supplies are priced at current replacement cost.

Similarly, notes payable and other liabilities (except accounts payable for which there is generally a record) must be obtained from memoranda, correspondence, and even by consultation with creditors. Usually in this manner a fairly reliable statement of assets and equities can be developed.

To illustrate, assume that a balance sheet is being prepared for Mr. A. A. Brown who maintains single-entry records. The bank statement balance plus cash on hand amounted to $2,345. An inventory of merchandise, priced at replacement cost, amounted to $1,550. Inspection of miscellaneous records revealed that he had acquired store and office equipment on January 1 costing $500. A reasonable rate of depreciation of this asset was estimated to be 5% per annum. An interest-bearing note, dated December 31, 19A, for $50 signed by a customer was on hand. In addition the "charge" book showed that four customers owed bills amounting to $90. From the cashbook it was determined that Mr. Brown had purchased supplies costing $15 during the period. Since no supplies were on hand, it must be assumed that they were used during the period. There were no liabilities except for two accounts payable (from an "accounts payable" file amounting to $240).

The balance sheet in Illustration 24–3 was prepared from these data. Note that proprietorship was determined by subtracting total liabilities from total assets.

Computation of Net Income. The computation of net income where single-entry records are kept may be based on an analysis of the changes in the owner's equity for the period. For example, if it is determined that the only change in Mr. Brown's proprietorship resulted from a gain or loss from operations, the summary income state-

Illustration 24–3
A. A. BROWN
Balance Sheet, December 31, 19A

ASSETS

Current Assets:

Cash		$2,345	
Notes receivable		50	
Accounts receivable:			
A. B. Cottle	$25		
R. S. Thomas	30		
N. O. Page	10		
B. C. Davis	25	90	
Merchandise inventory		1,550	
Total Current Assets			$4,035
Fixed Assets:			
Office and store fixtures (depreciated cost)			475
Total Assets			$4,510

CURRENT LIABILITIES

Accounts Payable:

Lee and Jackson	$ 90	
Mason Company	150	
Total Current Liabilities		240

PROPRIETORSHIP (DIFFERENCE)

A. A. Brown, proprietorship	$4,270

ment in Illustration 24–4 may be prepared (proprietorship, January 1, 19A, taken from balance sheet for prior period).

If there had been additional investments or withdrawals during the period, these must be considered in the computation of net income or net loss. The following equation indicates the procedure when there have been investments or withdrawals during the period:

$$\text{Net Income} = \text{Present Proprietorship} - \text{Past Proprietorship} + \text{Withdrawals} - \text{Additional Investments}$$

The two examples of the single-entry income statement computations shown in Illustration 24–5 indicate the procedure when there have been investments or withdrawals during the period.

Illustration 24–4
A. A. BROWN
Computation of Net Loss
For the Year Ended, December 31, 19A

Proprietorship, January 1, 19A	$4,500
Proprietorship, December 31, 19A	4,270
Net Loss for Period	$ 230

Illustration 24–5
Income Determination – Single Entry

	Computation Where There Has Been –	
	A Net Income	A Net Loss
Present proprietorship (end of period)	$8,000	$5,500
Prior proprietorship (beginning of period)	7,100	6,300
Change (increase)	$ 900	
(decrease)		$ (800)
Add: Withdrawals during period	1,200	1,000
	$2,100	$ 200
Deduct: Additional investments during period	500	400
Income for Period	$1,600	
Loss for Period		$ (200)

Preparation of a Detailed Income Statement from Incomplete Data

Computation of the amount of net income or loss can be accomplished as shown in the preceding section. However, knowing only the amount of net income or loss certainly does not meet the internal needs of management for information about operations nor does it meet the needs of other interested parties. Banks and other credit grantors usually request a statement setting out the details of operations. The Internal Revenue Service requires a detailed statement of revenues and expenses for income tax purposes.

An itemized income statement in the conventional form may be prepared from single-entry records and supplemental data without converting the records to double-entry form. By analyzing the cash receipts and disbursements, much of the needed detail may be obtained. The preparation of an income statement from single-entry data may be simply illustrated as follows:

The following information was obtained from the single-entry records of John Mercer. Balance sheets as of January 1 and December 31 and an income statement for the year are to be prepared:

	19A	
	January 1	December 31
Accounts and trade notes receivable (no doubtful accounts)	$35,000	$48,000
Inventory (per physical count)	6,900	8,700
Building and equipment (appraised at estimated cost less depreciation)	17,000	17,400
Prepaid expenses (per memoranda)	100	110
Accounts payable (per files)	8,100	9,200
Notes payable (for equipment per files)		500
Cash on hand (register)	60	110
Accrued expenses (per memoranda)	120	150

An analysis of the bank statements indicated deposits and disbursements as follows:

Bank overdraft, January 1, 19A.....................................$ 2,800
Deposits during year:
    Collections on account.. 42,000
    Additional capital contributions................................ 10,000
Checks drawn during year:
    Purchases 26,000
    Expenses.. 6,000
    Salaries of employees... 7,000
    Withdrawals by owner 3,000
    Purchase of equipment.. 340

Balance Sheet Preparation. In preparing the balance sheets the cash in the bank on December 31, 19A, must be computed; there was an overdraft on January 1, 19A. Total deposits of $52,000 less the January 1 overdraft of $2,800 and total checks drawn of $42,340 indicates a December 31, 19A, balance of $6,860. The balance sheets would be as shown in Illustration 24–6.

Illustration 24–6
JOHN MERCER
Balance Sheets

	19A	
	January 1	December 31
ASSETS		
Cash in bank..$		$ 6,860
Cash in register	60	110
Accounts and notes receivable	35,000	48,000
Inventory...	6,900	8,700
Prepaid expenses...	100	110
Buildings and equipment	17,000	17,400
	$59,060	$81,180
LIABILITIES		
Notes payable ....$	—	$ 500
Bank overdraft...	2,800	—
Accounts payable...	8,100	9,200
Accrued expenses payable	120	150
	$11,020	$ 9,850
PROPRIETORSHIP (DIFFERENCE)		
John Mercer..$48,040		$71,330

Computation of Net Income. Using the single-entry method, net income may be computed by analysis of the change in proprietorship as follows:

Proprietorship on December 31, 19A $71,330
Proprietorship on January 1, 19A.................................. 48,040
Increase in proprietorship $23,290
Add withdrawals during year 3,000
$26,290
Deduct additional investments during year 10,000
Net Income, 19A $16,290

Analysis of Revenue and Expenses. In order to prepare a detailed income statement, each item of revenue and expense to be included thereon must be determined. Such a determination may be made by summarizing all the transactions in debit and credit form, which in effect would involve conversion to double-entry procedures. This approach is subsequently illustrated (in work sheet form) in this chapter. Alternatively, the desired figures may be derived directly by analyzing the respective items as illustrated below.

Computation of Sales. Cash and credit sales combined may be determined by analyzing cash receipts and changes in accounts receivable and trade notes receivable as follows:

SCHEDULE 1

Accounts and trade notes receivable, December 31, 19A ...$48,000
Cash collected from customers and deposited................ 42,000
Increase in cash on hand... 50
$90,050
Less: Accounts and trade notes receivable,
    January 1, 19A.. 35,000
Sales for the Period, 19A $55,050

Alternatively, to determine the sales for the period, the student may prefer simply to reconstruct the T-accounts for the *accounts receivable* and *sales* accounts as follows:

Accounts Receivable			Sales	
Beg. bal.		Cash col-		
(Jan. 1)	35,000	lections		
		(depos-		
		ited)	42,000	
(A) Sales		Cash col-	(A)	55,050
(amount		lections		
necessary		(on hand)	50	
to com-				
plete ac-		End balance		
count)	55,050	(Dec. 31)	48,000	
	90,050		90,050	
Balance				
carried				
forward	48,000			

Many students find the T-account approach preferable to the schedule in that the problem of whether to add or subtract a given amount is easily resolved by making the "normal" entries; also there is a built-in self-check. The items are simply entered in the account in the normal manner and the missing amount (sales in the above case) is the "squeeze" figure. Note that the *ending* balance is always entered on the "opposite side" for balancing purposes in reconstructing the account as is done in the normal year-end closing of accounts with balances to be carried forward.

Note that the increase of cash on hand is assumed to represent collections from customers. If there had been data relative to cash discounts on sales, returned sales, or accounts charged off as uncollectible, both the sales discounts and the bad debts written off should be added to the total in Schedule 1. In such cases if the T-account analysis is being used, it would appear advisable to reconstruct the following accounts: Accounts Receivable, Allowance for Doubtful Accounts, Loss from Doubtful Accounts, Sales Discounts, Sales Returns, and Sales.

Computation of Purchases. The amount of purchases may be determined by the analysis of cash disbursements and changes in both accounts payable and trade notes payable.

SCHEDULE 2

Accounts and trade notes payable, December 31, 19A	$ 9,200
Payments to creditors	26,000
	$35,200
Less: Accounts and trade notes payable, January 1, 19A	8,100
Purchases for the Period, 19A	$27,100

It should be noted that cash discounts may have been taken. If this is the case, such discounts should be added in the schedule (or included in the T-account analysis) to derive gross purchases.

Computation of Depreciation. The building and equipment were valued at appraised cost less depreciation. The decrease in the net book value of the asset, taking into account additions and dispositions of equipment during the period, is the amount of depreciation for the period as computed below:

SCHEDULE 3

Net balance of buildings and equipment, January 1, 19A	$17,000
Purchases of equipment during 19A:	
By issue of note payable	500
By cash payment	340
Balance before depreciation	$17,840
Less: Net balance on December 31, 19A (after current depreciation)	17,400
Depreciation for the Period, 19A	$ 440

Computation of Expenses. The expenses paid in cash, determined from an analysis of cash disbursements, must be adjusted for prepaid and accrued items at the beginning and at the end of the period as follows:

SCHEDULE 4

Expenses paid in cash during 19A........................	$6,000
Add: Expenses accrued on December 31, 19A.......	150
Prepaid expenses on January 1, 19A	100
	$6,250
Deduct: Accrued expenses, January 1, 19A............$120	
Prepaid expenses, December 31, 19A....... 110	230
Expenses for the Period, 19A.............................	$6,020

Students generally find it much easier to analyze the more involved situations, such as this one, by reconstructing the related accounts in the following manner:

Prepaid Expenses			Accrued Expenses	
Beginning bal- ance (Jan. 1) 100	(A) Transfer to expense 100		(B) Transfer to expense 120	Beginning Bal- ance (Jan. 1) 120
(C) To record final balance (Dec. 31) 110				(D) To record final balance (Dec. 31) 150

Expenses		
Paid in cash during 19A	6,000	(B) Transfer from accrued 120
(A) Transfer from prepaid	100	(C) Final balance prepaid 110
(D) Final balance accrued	150	

(Expenses for 19A – account balance, $6,020.)

Note again that the beginning balances are entered, then the "normal" accounting entries are made in the accounts.

The information does not reveal an adjustment to salaries paid in cash. The amount of that expense is $7,000.

Preparation of the Income Statement. All information needed to prepare the income statement has now been determined. That statement would appear as shown in Illustration 24–7.

Illustration 24-7
JOHN MERCER
Income Statement
For Year Ended December 31, 19A

Sales (Schedule 1)		$55,050
Cost of goods sold:		
Inventory, January 1, 19A ....$ 6,900		
Purchases (Schedule 2)...................................... 27,100		
Goods available for sale................................$34,000		
Less: Inventory, December 31, 19A................ 8,700		
Cost of goods sold.....................................		25,300
Gross margin on sales		$29,750
Less: Expenses:		
Depreciation (Schedule 3) ....$ 440		
Expenses (Schedule 4) 6,020		
Salaries.. 7,000		13,460
Net Income...		$16,290

Work Sheets for Problems from Single-Entry and Other Incomplete Records

The preceding example, although simplified, demonstrates the need for a work sheet approach to reduce clerical work and the possibility of errors and omissions. In problem-solving situations, whether in study or in practice, the *interim* work sheet described in Chapter 2 is particularly useful. The interim work sheet provides for several internal checks on accuracy and recognizes each group of transactions in their debit and credit effects. In order to provide a "track record" such work sheets should be accompanied by explanations and computations of the analyses involved.

The following illustrative problem is presented to demonstrate adaptation and use of the interim work sheet in solving problems involving incomplete data:

J. C. Main had been in business two years and had not maintained double-entry records. A financial statement was prepared by an accountant at the end of last year, 19A. This balance sheet (dated January 1, 19B) and one developed at the end of the current year (dated December 31, 19B) are presented in Illustration 24–8. They were developed by "inventorying" all assets and liabilities.

The following additional information for 19B was developed:

(A) Mr. Main kept no record of cash receipts and disbursements, but an analysis of canceled checks showed the following payments: accounts payable, $71,000; expenses, $20,700; and for purchase of equipment, $3,700. No checks appeared to be outstanding.

(B) Mr. Main stated that he withdrew regularly $100 cash each week from the cash register for personal use. No record was made of these personal withdrawals.

Illustration 24-8
J. C. MAIN
Balance Sheets

	January 1	December 31
Cash	$ 10,000	$ 22,000
Notes receivable	5,000	3,000
Accounts receivable	61,000	68,000
Inventories	25,000	27,000
Prepaid expenses	500	200
Furniture and equipment (net)	10,600	12,400
	$112,100	$132,600
Bank loan	$ —	$ 5,000
Accounts payable	30,000	36,000
Accrued expenses	800	650
J. C. Main, capital	81,300	90,950
	$112,100	$132,600

(C) The bank loan was for one year, the note was discounted by the bank at 6% on July 1, 19B.

(D) Mr. Main stated that he sold equipment listed in the January 1 balance sheet at $900 for $620 cash.

(E) The bank reported that it had credited Mr. Main with $4,000 during the year for customers' notes left for collection.

(F) One $400 note on hand December 31, 19B, was past due and appeared to be worthless. Therefore, this note was not included in the $3,000 notes receivable listed in the December 31 balance sheet. Assume no allowance for doubtful accounts; bad debts are written off directly to expense.

Mr. Main needs a detailed income statement for the current year, 19B.

Solution. An eight-column or five-column interim work sheet may be adapted for this problem. A five-column work sheet is shown in Illustration 24–9. Note that a five-column work sheet is achieved by placing "debits over credits." Columns are set up for beginning balances, interim entries (debit and credit), income statement, and ending balances.

The beginning and ending balances, taken from the two balance sheets, are entered directly on the work sheet as illustrated with sufficient line spacing for the anticipated entries. Next the interim entries for all transactions are reconstructed (as explained below) to account for all changes in each account during the period. Last, all items not listed in the column "ending balances" are carried as debits or credits to the column headed "Income Statement." At this point in the solution the *net income* (or loss) is the difference between

Illustration 24–9

J. C. MAIN

Work Sheet for Year Ended December 31, 19B

	Beginning Balances January 1, 19B	Interim Entries Debit	Interim Entries Credit	Income Statement	Ending Balances December 31, 19B
Debit accounts:					
Cash	10,000	(C) 4,700 (D) 620 (E) 4,000 (H) 103,280	(A) 95,400 (B) 5,200		22,000
Notes receivable	5,000	(G) 2,400	(E) 4,000 (F) 400		3,000
Accounts receivable	61,000	(I) 112,680	(G) 2,400 (H) 103,280		68,000
Inventories	25,000	(J) 27,000	(J) 25,000		27,000
Prepaid expenses	500	(C) 150 (K) 50	(K) 500		200
Furniture and equipment (net)	10,600	(A) 3,700	(D) 900 (L) 1,000		12,400
Expenses		(A) 20,700 (K) 500 (N) 650	(K) 50 (N) 800	21,000	
Interest expense		(C) 150		150	
Loss on sale of equipment		(D) 280		280	
Loss on worthless note		(F) 400		400	
Depreciation		(L) 1,000		1,000	
Purchases		(M) 77,000		77,000	
Net income to capital		(O) 14,850		14,850	
	112,100			114,680	132,600
Credit accounts:					
Bank loan			(C) 5,000		5,000
Accounts payable	30,000	(A) 71,000	(M) 77,000		36,000
Accrued expenses	800	(N) 800	(N) 650		650
J. C. Main, capital	81,300	(B) 5,200	(O) 14,850		90,950
Sales		(I) 112,680	(I) 112,680	112,680	
Income summary (inventory change)		(J) 25,000	(J) 27,000	2,000	
	112,100	476,110	476,110	114,680	132,600

the debits and credits in the latter column. Particular attention should be called to the fact that considerable data needed for reconstruction of the entries are missing; therefore, care must be exercised as to sequence of developing the entries. Note that all of the data available are used first (entries A through F) then subsequent entries are developed by computing the "missing data" as illustrated in entry G and following. Problems such as this one are frequently referred to as missing data problems.

Explanation of Entries on the Work Sheet:

(A) To record payments shown by analysis of canceled checks.
(B) To record Main's cash withdrawals of $100 per week for 52 weeks.
(C) To record bank loan of $5,000 less $300 interest of which $150 was prepaid as of December 31, 19B.
(D) To record sale of equipment, cost less depreciation, $900, for $620 cash.
(E) To record $4,000 notes receivable collected by bank.
(F) To record charge-off of bad note, $400. (Reported as a loss since there is no provision for doubtful accounts.)
(G) To record notes from customers, computed as follows (data taken directly from work sheet):

Notes collected	$4,000
Note written off	400
Notes on hand December 31, 19B	3,000
	$7,400
Less: Notes on hand January 1, 19B	5,000
New Notes Receivable	$2,400

(H) Cash collected from customers (observe that it does not matter whether the collection was at time of sale or on account) is computed as follows from data shown in the Cash account on the work sheet:

Cash paid out ($95,400 + $5,200)	$100,600
Cash balance, December 31, 19B	22,000
	$122,600
Cash collected from all sources other than from customers:	
($4,700 + $620 + $4,000)	9,320
	$113,280
Less: Cash balance, January 1, 19B	10,000
Cash Collected from Customers	$103,280

(I) Sales are computed by finding the only entry missing on the work sheet in accounts receivable, which entry is for sales on account. (Balance in notes receivable has been already reconciled on the work sheet.)

Notes received on account		$ 2,400
Cash collected from customers		103,280
Final balance of accounts receivable		68,000
Total credits and balance		$173,680
Less: January 1 balance		61,000
Total Debits for the Year (Sales)		$112,680

(J) To close the January 1 inventory and to record the December 31 inventory (to income summary).

(K) To close the January 1 balance of prepaid expenses and to increase the prepaid expense balance as of December 31 to $200 as given.

(L) To set up the depreciation allowance for the period. All entries have been made in the Furniture and Equipment accounts on the work sheet except the depreciation credit. Depreciation is computed as follows:

Furniture and equipment, January 1, 19B		$10,600
Equipment purchased		3,700
		$14,300
Less: Equipment sold		900
		$13,400
Less: Balance of furniture and equipment, December 31, 19B		12,400
Depreciation for the Period		$ 1,000

(M) Purchases are computed by finding the missing entry in accounts payable on the work sheet as follows:

Payments on accounts payable		$ 71,000
Balance of accounts payable, December 31, 19B		36,000
		$107,000
Less: Accounts payable, January 1, 19B		30,000
Purchases for the Period		$ 77,000

(N) To close the January 1 balance of accrued expenses and to record accrued expenses as of December 31.

(O) To close net income to capital. The net income may be computed by analyzing the changes in capital from January 1 to December 31, 19B, as illustrated previously or by extending nominal accounts balances to the column "Income Statement" and then computing the difference between the debits and credits. Obviously, one computation would serve as a check on the other.

The resulting income statement taken directly from the work sheet is shown in Illustration 24–10.

Illustration 24–10

J. C. MAIN

Income Statement

For Year Ended December 31, 19B

Revenues:

Sales		$112,680
Costs and expenses:		
Cost of goods sold.		
Beginning inventory, January 1, 19B	$ 25,000	
Purchases	77,000	
Total Goods Available for Sale	$102,000	
Less: Final inventory, December 31, 19B	27,000	75,000
Gross margin on sales		$ 37,680
Less: Expenses:		
Expenses	$ 21,000	
Depreciation	1,000	
Loss on worthless note	400	22,400
Operating income		$ 15,280
Less: Other costs and losses:		
Interest expense	$ 150	
Loss on sale of equipment	280	430
Net Income		$ 14,850

Analysis of the Use of Single-Entry Bookkeeping

Single-entry record keeping is employed by a large number of particularly small businesses, by nonprofit organizations, by persons acting in a fiduciary capacity as administrators or executors of estates, and by many individuals relative to their personal affairs. Even some regular systems of record keeping recommended for retail outlets by trade associations and by manufacturers are based on single entry. For example, one such system is used by a large number of small retail druggists. Single-entry systems are used in the interest of simplicity and generally are less expensive to maintain than double-entry records since they do not require the services of a trained person. In fact, more often than not, single-entry records are maintained by the proprietor or someone closely associated with the activities being recorded.

Single-entry record keeping is generally inadequate except where operations are especially simple and the volume of activity is small. Some of the more important disadvantages of single-entry systems are:

1. Data are not available to the management for effectively planning and controlling the business.
2. Lack of systematic and precise record keeping may lead to inefficiency in administration and control over the affairs of the business.
3. They do not provide a check against clerical errors, as does a

double-entry system. This is one of the most serious of the defects of single entry.

4. They seldom make provision for recording all transactions. Many internal transactions (i.e., those normally reflected through adjusting entries) in particular are not recorded.

5. Since no accounts are provided for many of the items appearing in both the balance sheet and income statement, omission of important data is always a possibility.

6. In the absence of detailed records of all assets, lax administration of those assets is quite likely.

7. Theft and other losses are less likely to be known.

QUESTIONS FOR CLASS DISCUSSION

1. Identify and briefly describe the four distinctly different types of changes.

2. What are the two central accounting issues in dealing with accounting and error changes?

3. What are the three basic alternatives for reflecting the effects of accounting and error changes on financial statements and in the accounts?

4. Basically how should changes in accounting principles, estimates, and error changes be reflected (a) in the accounting entries and (b) on the comparative financial statements?

5. What is a counterbalancing error? Explain why certain errors are counterbalancing.

6. Why is it that some errors are not counterbalancing? Give some examples and briefly state what must be done to correct them.

7. Give two examples of errors that affect only the balance sheet and also two examples of errors that affect only the income statement.

8. Give examples of three errors that affect both the balance sheet and the income statement. Are they counterbalancing?

9. Distinguish between single-entry and double-entry records.

10. What are the usual elements of a single-entry system?

11. What are the chief shortcomings of the single-entry method?

DECISION CASE 24-1

A special committee of accountants has been analyzing the "whole problem of accounting changes with a view to developing an operational yet conceptually sound position" in respect to them. One particularly difficult facet of the committee's efforts centered on appropriate accounting when an accounting "principle" is changed. Typical situations would be where the company changes the method of depreciation (say, from double declining to straight line), a change from Fifo to Lifo inventory procedures, and a change from capitalizing and amortizing research and development costs to expensing them as incurred. In these types of changes it is assumed that the change is from one generally accepted procedure to another generally accepted procedure.

Illustrative data (hypothetical) has been developed to clearly delineate the results of several suggested accounting procedures for reflecting the effects of the change in the comparative financial statements. A change from capitalizing and amortizing research and developments costs to expensing them as incurred has been selected for the hypothetical illustration. The hypothetical data in thousands follow:

	1969	1970	1971°	1972	1973
Revenues	$1,000	$1,000	$1,000	$1,000	$1,000
Cost of goods sold	$ 540	$ 540	$ 540	$ 540	$ 540
Research and development costs†	60	60	80	80	80
Other costs and expenses	200	200	200	200	200
Income before extraordinary items	$ 200	$ 200	$ 180	$ 180	$ 180
Extraordinary items	0	0	0	0	0
Net income	$ 200	$ 200	$ 180	$ 180	$ 180

°Current year.
†Amortized amount determined as follows:

Deferred Research and Development	1965	1966	1967	1968	1969	1970	1971°	1972	1973
Beginning balance	$ 0	$ 60	$105	$135	$150	$150	$150	$170	$185
Incurred (end of period)	60	60	60	60	60	60	80	80	80
Total	$ 60	$120	$165	$195	$210	$210	$230	$250	$265
Amortized (4 years)	0	15	30	45	60	60	60	65	70
Ending balance	$ 60	$105	$135	$150	$150	$150	$170	$185	$195

To simplify the illustration and in order to bring out the differences created by the issue (change) the effect of income taxes has been ignored.

In 1971 a change from capitalization of research and development costs and their amortization over four years to expensing them as incurred will be implemented. This case focuses specifically on how the change should be implemented (a) in the accounts and (b) on the comparative income statement (use 1970 and 1971 for this purpose). You are to develop the approach that in your judgment best serves the needs of the statement user, notwithstanding current practice or pronouncements by the APB or other groups. Your response should include as a minimum the following:

a) Your recommendation and your arguments to support it (including any assumptions).
b) The entry, or entries, required in the current period (1971) to implement your recommendation.
c) A comparative income statement for 1971 which includes 1970 results for comparative purposes.
d) A list of other alternative recommendations that you considered and the reasons for your rejection of them.

EXERCISES

Exercise 24–1

Witt Corporation has been depreciating Machine A over a 10-year life on a straight line basis. The machine cost $130,000 and has an estimated residual value of $20,000. On the basis of an engineering study of its economic potential to the company completed during the fifth year (19B), the management decided to change to sum-of-the-years' depreciation with no change in the estimated useful life or the residual value. The annual financial statements are prepared on a comparative basis (two years presented). Net incomes (no extraordinary items) prior to giving effect to this change (i.e., on the old basis) were: 19A, $40,000; 19B, $46,000. Assume the income tax rate is 50% and that the change in method is acceptable for tax purposes. Shares of stock outstanding, 100,000.

Required:

1. Identify the type of accounting change involved and analyze the effects of the change.

2. Prepare the entry, or entries, to appropriately reflect the change in the accounts in 19B (fifth year), the year of the change.

3. Illustrate how the change should be reflected on the 19B financial statement which includes 19A results for comparative purposes.

Exercise 24–2

Witt Corporation has been depreciating Machine B over a 10-year life on a straight line basis. The machine cost $96,000 and has an estimated residual value of $6,000. On the basis of experience since acquisition (four years prior to 19B) the management has decided to depreciate it over a total life of 13 years instead of 10, and no change in the estimated residual value. The annual financial statements are prepared on a comparative basis (two years presented). Net incomes (no extraordinary items) on the old basis were: 19A, $40,000; 19B, $46,000. Shares of stock outstanding, 100,000. Assume the income tax rate is 50% and that the change is acceptable for tax purposes.

Required:

1. Identify the type of accounting change involved and analyze the effects of the change.

2. Prepare entry, or entries, to appropriately reflect the change in the accounts for 19B (fifth year), the year of the change.

3. Illustrate how the change should be reflected on the 19B financial statement which includes 19A results for comparative purposes.

Exercise 24–3

Jackson Corporation has never had an audit prior to 19D, the current year. Prior to the arrival of the auditor the company accountant had prepared a comparative financial statement with 19C and 19D shown thereon for comparative purposes. The books for 19D have not been closed. During the audit it was discovered that an invoice dated January 19A for $10,000 (paid in cash at that time) was debited to operating expenses although it was for the purchase of Machine X. Machine X has an estimated useful life of ten years and no residual value.

Reported net income reflected on the comparative financial statement prepared by the company auditor (prior to discovery of the error) was: 19C, $44,000; 19D, $46,000. Shares of stock outstanding, 100,000. Disregard tax considerations.

Required:

1. Identify the type of accounting change involved and analyze the effects of the change.

2. Prepare entry, or entries, to appropriately reflect the change in the accounts for 19D, the year of the change.

3. Illustrate how the change should be reflected on the 19D financial statement which includes 19C results for comparative purposes.

Exercise 24-4

Give journal entries to correct the accounts for each of the errors listed below assuming (*a*) the corrections were made on December 31, 1971, before the books were closed and (*b*) the corrections were made on January 12, 1972, after the books were closed on December 31, 1971. Also assume that each item is material.

a) Merchandise costing $7,000 was received on December 28, 1970, and was included in the final inventory of 1970, but the purchase was not recorded in the purchases journal until January 3, 1971.

b) An entry was made on December 30, 1971, for write-off of organization expense as follows (assume only one half of the amortization was justified):

General Expense	20,000	
Deferred Organization Expense		20,000

c) Discount of $6,600 on a permanent bond investment purchased on May 1, 1970, was written off to retained earnings on that date. These bonds mature on July 1, 1979.

d) Machinery costing $600 was purchased and charged to repairs expense on June 30, 1970. The depreciation rate on machinery is 10% per year.

Exercise 24-5

You are in the process of auditing the accounts of the Walker Corporation for the year ended December 31, 1971. You discover that the adjustments made on the previous audit for the year 1970 were not entered in the accounts; therefore, the accounts are not in agreement with the audited amounts as of December 31, 1970. The following adjustments were included in the 1970 audit report:

a) Invoices for merchandise purchased in December 1970, not entered on the books until January 1971 and not included in the December 31, 1970, inventory, $8,500.

b) Invoices for merchandise received in December 1970 were not recorded in the accounts; the goods were included in the 1970 ending inventory, $12,000.

c) Provision for doubtful accounts for 1970 understated by $2,000.

d) Factory expense bills for 1970 not entered in the accounts until January 1971, $2,500.

e) Accrued payroll at December 31, 1970, not recorded at that date, $5,000.

f) Insurance premiums relating to unexpired insurance at December 31, 1970, $300.

g) Taxes for year ended December 31, 1970, not entered in the accounts until January 1971, $3,000.

h) Depreciation not taken up in the accounts prior to January 1970, $5,000; for year ended December 31, 1970, $2,000.

i) To write off unlocated difference in the Accounts Receivable control account at December 31, 1970, $150. The difference was subsequently located in the subsidiary ledger and corrected during 1971.

Required:

Assume the books have not been adjusted or closed at December 31, 1971, and that you have at hand a trial balance from the books. Give the journal entries related to the above items, incident to the 1971 audit. Assume that each item is material.

Exercise 24–6

O'Dell Company failed to recognize accruals and prepayments since organization three years previously. The net income, accruals, and prepayments at year-end are given below:

	19A	19B	19C
Reported net income	$4,000	$2,000°	$5,000
Items not recognized at year-end:			
a) Prepaid expenses	200	300	100
b) Accrued expenses	250	200	240
c) Prepaid incomes	325	350	290
d) Accrued incomes	275	200	190

    ° Net loss.

Required:

1. Compute the correct net income for each year.

2. Give entries to correct the accounts at year-end 19C assuming books were not closed.

3. Give entries to correct the accounts at year-end 19C assuming the books were closed.

Exercise 24–7

Spence Company, organized three years ago, has never made provision for doubtful accounts. Losses have been recognized when the account was written off as bad. Data relative to net income, sales, and bad debts were as follows:

	19A	19B	19C
Reported net income	$3,000	$ 2,000°	$ 5,000
Credit sales	9,000	14,000	16,000
Accounts written off:			
19A	100	130	140
19B		70	150
19C			210

° Net loss.

After analyzing the losses to date and accounts on the books, the management estimated that bad debt losses will approximate 4% of credit sales.

Required:

1. Compute correct net income for each period.
2. Give entry to correct the accounts at year-end 19C assuming books have not been closed.
3. Give entry to correct accounts at year-end 19C assuming books have been closed.

Exercise 24-8

During the year ended December 31, 1971, Mark Lane, a retail merchant who had started business January 2, 1971, paid trade creditors $49,062 in cash, and final inventory per count (Fifo basis) was $9,563. Ledger account preclosing balances available on December 31, 1971, were the following: accounts payable, $16,125; expenses, $2,450; capital (representing total investment in cash January 2, 1971), $45,000; accounts receivable, $13,188; and sales, $50,000. There were no withdrawals. All sales and purchases were on credit.

Required:

From the above data prepare the following:

1. A work sheet for development of income statement and balance sheet amounts for the year.
2. Statement of cash receipts and payments for the year ended December 31, 1971.

Exercise 24-9

From the following data taken from single-entry records compute the net income or loss:

	Jan. 1, 19A	Dec. 31, 19A
Total assets	$83,000	$95,000
Total liabilities	20,000	25,000

Case 1: The proprietor's withdrawals were $6,000, and his additional investments during the year, $2,000.

Case 2: The proprietor's withdrawals were $1,000, and his additional investments, $10,000.

Exercise 24–10

On January 1 Frank Blue invested $5,000 cash in a television repair shop. Memoranda revealed that he withdrew $50 per week for living expenses. He invested his personal automobile, having a fair market value of $2,500 at that time, in the business for use as a service car. The shop then paid $500 for body changes on the car to make it suitable for its needs; this amount was capitalized. On January 10 Paul Grey was taken in as a partner. He invested equipment valued at $3,000 and $1,000 cash. It was agreed that the partners would share profits equally after July 1. Grey withdrew $800 cash during the last half of the year.

On December 31 the following assets and liabilities were determined from memoranda and incomplete records: cash, $4,810; equipment (less depreciation), $4,600; receivables, $1,200; call truck (less depreciation), $2,250; notes payable, $1,000.

Required:

Prepare a balance sheet showing capital balances for each partner and a schedule to compute the gain or loss for the year.

Exercise 24–11

Make the computations needed for the income statement from the following data (each item is independent):

a) Wages: amount paid, $15,000; accrued on January 1, $1,000; accrued on December 31, $2,000.

b) Rent income: amount collected, $8,000; prepaid $500 on January 1 and $300 on December 31; accrued rental, $200 on January 1 and $600 on December 31.

c) Sales:

Cash: balance, January 1, $26,000; balance, December 31, $33,000; total disbursements for the year, $39,000. Cash receipts were from customers. Accounts receivable: balance, January 1, $40,160, balance, December 31, $59,000; accounts written off during the period as uncollectible, $960.

d) Purchases (before discounts): accounts payable balance on January 1, $28,320, and on December 31, $33,000; payments made on accounts during the year, $46,000; cash discounts taken, $820.

Exercise 24–12

Give the journal entry to account for the missing amount in each of the following situations:

a) Unexpired Insurance: starting balance, $1,400; final balance, $1,900; amount expired, $1,200.

b) Allowance for Doubtful Accounts: starting balance, $5,000; final balance, $6,000; bad debts written off, $2,700.

c) Sinking Fund: starting balance, $90,000; final balance, $102,000; current payment to sinking fund, $20,000.

d) Premium on Bonds Payable: starting balance, $6,000; final balance, $4,500.

e) Capital Stock: starting balance, $200,000; final balance, $250,000; stock sold at par during the year, $30,000.

f) Retained Earnings: starting balance, $34,000 (credit); appropriation to reserve for bond sinking fund, $10,000; charge for stock dividend, $20,000; net income, $42,000; final balance, $36,000 (credit).

g) Accounts Receivable: starting balance, $25,000; collections on accounts, $27,000; bad accounts written off, $1,200; sales returns on account, $900; notes received on accounts, $3,000; final balance, $25,900.

h) Accounts Payable: starting balance, $17,300; cash paid on accounts, $30,200; cash discounts taken, $600; final balance, $15,500.

Exercise 24–13

For each account indicate the amount that should be reported on the income statement. Show computations.

	Beginning of Period	End of Period
a) Deferred interest income	$ 50	$ 75
Uncollected interest income	65	20
Interest collected during period, $200.		
Interest income should be reported as $_____.		
b) Accrued wages	$ 1,000	$ 1,800
Prepaid wages	400	200
Wages paid during period, $12,000.		
Wages should be reported as $_____.		
c) Accounts receivable	$10,000	$14,000
Notes receivable	2,000	1,000
Cash sales	$120,000	
Collections on accounts	40,000	
Return sales (on account)	2,000	
Collection on trade notes	5,000	
Accounts written off as bad	500	
Discounts given (on account)	600	
Gross sales should be reported as $_____.		
d) Accounts payable	$ 5,000	$ 7,000
Notes payable (trade)	10,000	6,000
Payments on accounts	$ 40,000	
Cash purchases	100,000	
Discounts taken on credit purchases	1,000	
Purchase returns (on account)	1,500	
Payments on trade notes	8,000	
Gross purchases should be reported as $_____.		

Exercise 24–14

The following data were obtained from single-entry records. Prepare a detailed income statement for 1971 together with schedules showing computations. As proof of the income statement, compute net income by analyzing the changes in capital.

	December 31			December 31	
	1970	1971		1970	1971
Accounts receivable	$6,000	$7.600	Accounts payable	$2,400	$3,000
Inventories	3,200	4,300	Accrued expenses	900	870
Prepaid expenses	480	550			
Equipment (net)	4,100	3,800			

A summary of the cashbook was as follows:

Balance, January 1, 1971		$ 1,100
Receipts:		
From customers	$8,400	
Additional capital invested	1,000	9,400
		$10,500
Disbursements:		
For expenses	$3,680	
Proprietor's withdrawals..............................	1,800	
Payments on accounts payable......................	5,100	10,580
Overdraft at Bank		$ 80

Exercise 24–15

Mrs. Fay Sharp operated a hat shop but had not kept careful records of her business. The following data were secured from various memoranda and records:

An analysis of canceled checks revealed the following cash expenditures: expenses, $4,800; accounts payable, $9,200. Mrs. Sharp stated that she had withdrawn money from time to time from the cash register for personal living expenses. These withdrawals were estimated to total $3,600. All other receipts were deposited in the bank.

A list of assets and liabilities that was developed follows:

	Jan. 1, 19A	Dec. 31, 19A
Cash...	$ 1,200	$ 900
Account receivable..........................	1,000	1,500
Inventories.....................................	3,900	4,600
Prepaid expenses	100	60
Equipment (net)..............................	4,200	3,800
	$10,400	$10,860
Accounts payable	1,100	1,300
Proprietorship.................................	$ 9,300	$ 9,560

Required:

Prepare a work sheet to develop the revenues, costs, expenses, and net income.

PROBLEMS

Problem 24–1

The accounting department of the Virginia Corporation had completed the comparative financial reports for the period ending 19C prior to the initiation of the independent audit by the outside certified public accountant. This problem relates specifically to three changes recommended by the CPA after the statements were prepared by the company. You are to (a) analyze the nature of the changes to be made, (b) determine their effects on the financial statements, (c) develop appropriate entries to effect them, and (d) revise the comparative financial statements in accordance with generally accepted accounting principles. State any assumptions that you make and justify any debatable items or recommendations made by you.

The statements have been summarized for problem purposes; details are provided only in respect to the recommended changes; the statements were:

	19A	19B	19C
Balance Sheet:			
Assets:			
Machinery	$ 300,000	$ 300,000	$ 300,000
Accumulated depreciation	(80,000)	(100,000)	(120,000)
Remaining assets	2,280,000	2,290,000	2,420,000
Total	$2,500,000	$2,490,000	$2,600,000
Liabilities	$ 373,000	$ 349,000	$ 410,000
Capital stock (200,000 shares)	2,000,000	2,000,000	2,000,000
Retained earnings	127,000	141,000	190,000
Total	$2,500,000	$2,490,000	$2,600,000
Income Statement:			
Sales (all on credit)	$1,000,000	$1,100,000	$1,200,000
Cost of goods sold	600,000	650,000	700,000
Gross margin	$ 400,000	$ 450,000	$ 500,000
Operating expenses	$ 300,000	$ 330,000	$ 360,000
Income taxes (assume 50%)	50,000	60,000	70,000
Income before extraordinary items	$ 50,000	$ 60,000	$ 70,000
Extraordinary items	10,000	(20,000)	14,000
Less income tax effect	(3,000)	4,000	(5,000)
Net income	$ 57,000	$ 44,000	$ 79,000
Earnings per share data:			
Income before extraordinary items	.250	.300	.350
Net income	.285	.220	.395
Statement of Retained Earnings:			
Beginning balance	$ 100,000	$ 127,000	$ 141,000
Net income	57,000	44,000	79,000
Dividends	(30,000)	(30,000)	(30,000)
Ending balance	$ 127,000	$ 141,000	$ 190,000

The three changes recommended by the CPA and approved by the president, to be effective for 19C, were:

1. Change the loss experience rate on credit sales from one half of 1% to one fourth of 1%. This change was dictated by collection experience and losses during the past two years. These analyses indicate a drop in expected losses due to bad debts. The company has initiated a tight control on credit granting and stepped up collection efforts.

2. Six years previously a machine costing $20,000 (10-year life, no residual value) was inadvertently debited to operating expense at that time. The error was discovered by the CPA at the end of 19C; the machine has four more years of useful life (after 19C).

3. The Internal Revenue Service has approved a change from expensing research and development (R&D) costs as incurred to capitalization and amortization over 10 years; the management has decided to reflect the change in the accounting system. The accounting records provided the following data relevant to the change:

	Prior Year	Prior Year	19A	19B	19C
Old accounting policy:					
R&D costs expensed by year $1,000		$2,000	$3,000	$4,000	$5,000

New accounting policy:
 (1) Capitalize R&D costs for 19C plus the four preceding years.
 (2) Amortize R&D costs capitalized over 10 years (straight line).
 (3) Disregard tax allocation of prior years (before 19A).

You are to assume that each of these changes are consistent with the treatment of them on the income tax return.

Problem 24–2

Cooper Hat Shop maintained incomplete records. After investigation you found the following assets and liabilities:

ASSETS

	Jan. 1, 19A	Dec. 31, 19A
Cash on hand...................................	$ 90	$ 160
Cash in bank	1,250	870
Accounts receivable..........................	6,700	6,830
Inventory	3,100	3,800
Equipment (net of depreciation)	5,200	5,600
Prepaid insurance	120	60
	$16,460	$17,320

LIABILITIES

Accounts payable ....$ 1,000		$ 2,200
Bank loan.......................................		3,000
Accrued expenses payable................	90	50
	$ 1,090	$ 5,250
Proprietorship...............................$15,370		$12,070

An analysis of bank deposits and disbursements showed:

Deposits:
    Collections from customers $8,900
    Proceeds of bank loan.. 3,000
    Additional investment by proprietor........................... 1,200
Checks and charges:
    Payments to creditors 6,100
    Expenses... 4,500
    Refunds on sales (allowances).................................... 350
    Proprietor's withdrawals 1,500
    Interest on bank loan.. 30
    Purchase of equipment 1,000

Required:

1. Compute the net income or loss by analyzing the changes in proprietorship.

2. Prepare a detailed income schedule including computation schedules.

Problem 24–3

Mayes Company was organized on January 1, 19A, with a capital stock of $50,000 paid for in cash at par value. The promoters, who were also chief stockholders and officers of the company, failed to provide for an adequate system of records, and when called on to present statements as of April 1, 19A, were unable to do so. An accountant was called in, and his investigation revealed the following:

a) Total cash receipts (including capital investment) from January 1 to April 1, 19A, $109,850. Included in receipts were the proceeds from notes payable, face value $2,000, dated February 15, payable in six months and discounted at 6%.

b) An analysis of the canceled checks and other bank debits showed the following:

Payments for land and building	$35,000
Payment for furniture and fixtures	8,150
Salaries	2,850
Other expenses	825
Accounts payable	51,165

c) On April 1 accounts payable totaled $2,160, and total accounts receivable, $5,680. From a study of the invoices and from conversations with the president of the company, it was learned that goods costing $500 were purchased and paid for that were for one of the officers who had not reimbursed the company. Accounts receivable marked off as uncollectible during the three months totaled $350. Past uncertainties have made the specific charge-off basis of accounting preferable.

d) The cost of the land was $6,000. The building should be depreciated at a rate of 6%, and the furniture and fixtures at 16% per annum. All of these assets may be assumed to have been purchased on January 1.

e) The inventory of merchandise on April 1 was $8,925, and the prepaid expenses other than interest were $180. Accrued expenses amounted to $210.

Prepare a balance sheet as of April 1, 19A, and a detailed income statement. Show computations.

Problem 24–4

Harper Company has maintained incomplete records. In applying for a loan that was very important to the company, a financial statement was needed. An analysis of the records provided the following data:

Cash receipts:	
Cash sales	$130,000
Collections on credit sales	43,000
Collections on trade notes	1,000
Purchase allowances	1,500
Miscellaneous	250
Cash payments:	
Cash purchases	84,500
Payments to trade creditors	34,100

Payment on mortgage plus annual interest............................	4,020
Sales commissions	7,200
Rent..	2,400
General expenses...	14,590
Other operating expenses	29,800
Sales returns ($3,000 of which $1,000 was cash)	1,000
Insurance (renewal three-year premium, April 1)..................	468
Fixed assets purchased...	1,500

	Balances	
	Jan. 1, 19A	Dec. 31, 19A
Cash..	$14,100	$10,172
Accounts receivable.....................................	13,000	18,000
Trade notes receivable...............................	2,000	1,500
Inventory	10,000	18,400
Unexpired insurance	39	?
Prepaid interest expense.............................	600	510
Trade accounts payable...............................	26,500	23,800
Income taxes payable		1,984
Accrued operating expenses	600	400
Fixed assets (net)	35,400	33,290
Other assets..	11,861	11,861
Capital stock...	40,000	40,000
Mortgage payable (6% dated July 1)..............	20,000	?

No fixed assets were sold during the year.

Required:

Prepare a work sheet that will provide data for a detailed income statement for the year and a balance sheet for 19A. Show computations.

Problem 24–5

The following data were taken from the incomplete records of Baker's Sporting Goods Store:

	Balances	
	Jan. 1, 19A	Dec. 31, 19A
Accounts receivable......................................	$2,300	$ 3,900
Notes receivable (trade)...............................	1,500	2,000
Accrued interest on notes receivable..............	90	70
Prepaid interest on notes payable	75	60
Inventory	9,255	10,400
Prepaid expenses (operating)........................	100	130
Store equipment (net).................................	8,500	8,600
Other assets...	—	500
Accounts payable	1,700	1,900
Notes payable (trade).................................	11,000	11,500
Notes payable (equipment)...........................	—	500
Accrued interest payable.............................	40	30
Accrued expenses (operating)	170	210
Prepaid interest income	30	40

An analysis of the checkbook, canceled checks, deposit slips, and bank statements provided the following summary for the year:

Balance, Jan. 1, 19A..		$4,200
Cash receipts:		
Cash sales	$23,000	
On accounts receivable	7,600	
On notes receivable..	1,000	
Interest income..	160	
Cash disbursements:		
Cash purchases	11,800	
On accounts payable...	2,400	
On notes payable (trade)	500	
Interest expense...	560	
Operating expenses	14,130	
Miscellaneous nonoperating expenses	970	
Other assets purchased	500	
Withdrawals by Mr. Baker..	2,400	
Balance, Dec. 31, 19A..		$2,700

Required:

1. Compute the net income by analyzing the changes in the capital account.

2. Prepare a detailed income statement with supporting schedules to show computations.

Problem 24–6

The books of Rox Company, with outstanding capital stock of $25,000, have been maintained by single entry. On December 31, 1971, an inventory of the assets and liabilities revealed the following:

Cash on hand............................	$ 1,584	Merchandise inventory	$21,737
Cash in bank A.........................	10,824	Prepaid expenses	5,081
Accounts receivable..................	29,521	Overdraft, bank B......................	5,003
Investments	1,000	Accounts payable	19,747
Plant and equipment.................	65,006	Mortgage payable......................	25,000
Notes payable	20,000		

a) Depreciation of plant and equipment in the amount of $11,392 had been deducted from the inventory valuation of this asset for the year 1971.

b) The balance sheet at the beginning of the year showed retained earnings of $35,703.

c) From an analysis of canceled checks and accounts payable it was found that total purchases of merchandise amounted to $661,910 and expenses for salaries, wages, repairs, etc., amounted to $120,115. The purchases, however, included $450 paid out for some special items for personal use by John Smith, an employee; he had not reimbursed the company. The total expense payments included $250 advanced to a buyer as a working fund.

d) The merchandise inventory at the beginning of the year was $18,125, and prepaid expenses were $2,653.

e) Customers' accounts written off as uncollectible (as a direct charge) during the year amounted to $3,206. Interest payments were $1,061 on notes payable and $1,500 on mortgage.

f) A 10% cash dividend had been declared but not paid.

Required:

1. Prepare a balance sheet at December 31, 1971. (Hint: Determine net income as a "squeeze" figure.)

2. Prepare a detailed income statement.

Problem 24-7

White Department Store was destroyed by fire on March 20, 1971, and relatively few items were salvaged. From the general ledger, the one book of account saved, the following figures were abstracted as of February 28, 1971:

Fixtures	$ 10,543	
Accumulated depreciation		$ 8,673
Accounts receivable	53,484	
Petty cash	250	
Cash in bank	5,285	
Bank loan		10,000
White, capital (after drawings)		130,253
Merchandise (purchases)	106,838	
Sales		59,977
Expenses	32,503	
	$208,903	$208,903

The last fiscal closing was October 31, 1970.

Correspondence with creditors revealed unrecorded obligations to wholesale houses at March 20 amounting to $17,100. An inspection of checks returned from the bank at the end of March showed $22,924, and indicated cash purchases of merchandise from March 1–20 of $15,267, the balance representing cash withdrawals by Mr. White. Merchandise in transit at March 20 was recovered by suppliers and not billed. Bank deposits during that period, as shown by the bank statement, amounted to $20,930; and with the exception of a refund of $200 on March 2 from a merchandise creditor, which Mr. White recalls that he deposited shortly thereafter, these may be assumed to be payments on account by customers. Indebtedness acknowledged by customers totaled $52,876; it is estimated that an additional $10,000 due from them will never be acknowledged or recovered. Of the acknowledged indebtedness, $1,000 will probably be uncollectible. Returns to suppliers, not yet accounted for by them, amounted to $1,252.

The estimated inventory valuation at March 20, 1971, was $90,000. The merchandise stock was insured for $50,000; the insurance company agreed to pay this amount.

Salvaged items were:

a) Fixtures, to be sold to a secondhand dealer, with the approval of the insurer, at an estimated price of $200; the fixtures were insured for $700 of which $500 will be collected in full from the insurance company. Additions to the fixtures account during the current fiscal year have been $300. Depreciation rates are 10% per year on the old items and 5% per year (4⅔ months) on the additions.

b) Petty cash box containing cash and stamps amounting to $103.

c) Damaged merchandise, sold to dealer in salvage stocks, $5,264; sold at auction, $12,821.

d) The balance in the proprietor's account at October 31, 1970, was $140,718.

Required:

A work sheet showing the general ledger balances at February 28, 1971, adjusting journal entries, the adjusted asset and liability balances as at March 20, 1971; proprietor's equity; and the income statement figures for the 4⅔ months ended on that date. Provide explanations for all entries on the work sheet and related computations. (Solution hint: Set up debit and credit columns for each of the following: Balances, February 28, 1971; Transactions, March 1–20; Income Summary, November 1, 1970, to March 20, 1971; White Capital; and Balance Sheet.)

Problem 24–8

Landon Company failed to recognize accruals and deferrals in the accounts. In addition, numerous other errors were made in computing net income. The net incomes for the past three years are given below along with a list of the items that were not recognized in the record keeping.

You are to set up a work sheet to correct net income for each year. Set up columns for the following: particulars, 19A, 19B, 19C, and accounts to be corrected. Key and briefly identify the errors under the "particulars" column and enter amounts under the respective years as plus or minus so that the last line will report corrected net income. Maintain equality of balances in the work sheet. Assume that all items are material.

	19A	19B	19C
a) Reported net income	$4,000	$(3,500)	$10,000
Items not properly recognized at each year-end:			
b) Accrued expenses	400	250	300
c) Prepaid incomes	100		200
d) Prepaid expenses	320	410	120
e) Accrued incomes	170	140	
f) Annual depreciation overstated (not cumulative)		1,000	1,200
g) Annual provision for doubtful accounts understated	170	200	190
h) Goods purchased on December 31, included in ending inventory; not recorded until following year	460	210	150
i) Sales on December 31 not recorded until following year; not included in final inventory	290	770	390
j) Ending inventory overstated	130	240	290
k) Checks written and mailed on December 31 as payment on accounts payable; not recorded until next year	1,100	1,500	1,400
l) Bad debts not written off to allowance for doubtful accounts by year-end	800	950	1,170

Problem 24–9

Russell Waters established a retail business in 1969. Early in 1972, he entered into negotiations with John Jones with a view to forming a partnership. You have been asked by the two men to check Waters' books for the past three years, and to compute correct net income for each year.

The profits per clients' statements were as follows:

Year Ending 12/31

	1969	1970	1971
Net Income	$9,000	$10,109	$8,840

During the audit, you found the following:

Year Ending 12/31

		1969	1970	1971
	Omissions from the books:			
Item				
A	Accrued expenses at end of year	$2,160	$2,094	$4,624
B	Accrued income at end of year	200	–	–
C	Prepaid expenses at end of year	902	1,210	1,406
D	Deferred income at end of year	–	610	–
	Goods in transit at end of year omitted from inventory:			
E	For which purchase entry had been made	–	2,610	–
F	For which purchase entry had not been made	–	–	1,710
	Other points requiring consideration:			
G	Depreciation of equipment had been recorded monthly by a charge to expense and a credit to an allowance for depreciation account at a blanket rate of 1% of end-of-month balances of equipment accounts. However, the sale during December 1970 of certain equipment was entered as a debit to Cash and a credit to the asset account for the sale price of	–	5,000	–
	(This equipment was purchased in July 1969 at a cost of $6,000.)			
H	No allowance had been set up for uncollectible accounts. It is decided to set up one for the estimated probable losses as of December 31, 1971, for:			
	1970 accounts	–	–	700
	1971 accounts	–	–	1,500
	and to correct the charge against each year so that it will show the losses (actual and estimated) relating to that year's sales.			
	Accounts had been written off to expense as follows:			
	1969 accounts	1,000	1,200	–
	1970 accounts	–	400	2,000
	1971 accounts	–	–	1,600

(AICPA adapted)

Problem 24–10

Kelley-Thomas Company is a partnership that has not maintained adequate accounting records because it has been unable to employ a competent bookkeeper. The company sells hardware items to the retail trade and also wholesales to builders and contractors. As the company's CPA, you have been asked to prepare the company's financial statements as of June 30, 19B.

Your work papers provide the following postclosing trial balance at December 31, 19A:

KELLEY-THOMAS COMPANY
Postclosing Trial Balance
December 31, 19A

	Debit	Credit
Cash	$10,000	
Accounts receivable	8,000	
Allowance for bad debts		$ 600
Merchandise inventory	35,000	
Prepaid insurance	150	
Automobiles	7,800	
Allowance for depreciation – automobiles		4,250
Furniture and fixtures	2,200	
Allowance for depreciation – furniture and fixtures		650
Accounts payable		13,800
Bank loan payable		8,000
Accrued expenses		200
Kelley, capital		17,500
Thomas, capital		18,150
Total	$63,150	$63,150

You are able to collect the following information at June 30, 19B:

a) Your analysis of cash transactions, derived from the company's bank statements and checkbook stubs, is as follows:

Deposits:
Cash receipts from customers	$65,000

($40,000 of this amount represents collections on receivables
including redeposited protested checks totaling $600)

Bank loan, 1/2/19B (due 5/1/19B, 5%, face $8,000)	7,867
Bank loan, 5/1/19B (due 9/1/19B, 5%, face $9,000)	8,850
Sale of old automobile	20
Total Deposits	$81,737

Disbursements:
Payments to merchandise creditors	$45,000
Payment to Internal Revenue Service on Thomas' 19B declaration of estimated income taxes	3,000
General expenses	7,000
Bank loan, 1/2/19B	8,000
Bank loan, 5/2/19B	8,000
Payment for new automobile	2,400
Protested checks	900
Kelley withdrawals	5,000
Thomas withdrawals	2,500
Total Disbursements	$81,800

b) The protested checks include customers' checks totaling $600 that were redeposited and a $300 check from an employee that is still on hand.

c) Accounts receivable from customers for merchandise sales amounts to $18,000 on June 30, 19B, and includes accounts totaling $800 that have been placed with an attorney for collection. Correspondence with the client's attorney reveals that one of the accounts for $175 is uncollectible. Experience indicates that 1% of credit sales will prove uncollectible.

d) On April 1 a new automobile was purchased. The list price of the automobile was $2,700, and $300 was allowed for the trade-in of an old automobile, even though the dealer stated that its condition was so poor that he did not want it. The client sold the old automobile, which cost $1,800 and was fully depreciated at December 31, to an auto wrecker for $20. The old automobile was in use up to the date of its sale.

e) Depreciation is recorded by the straight line method and is computed on acquisitions to the nearest full month. The estimated life for furniture and fixtures is 10 years and for automobiles is 3 years. [Salvage value is to be ignored in computing depreciation. No asset other than the car in item *(d)* was fully depreciated prior to June 30, 19B.]

f) Other data as of June 30, 19B, include the following:

Merchandise inventory	$37,500
Prepaid insurance	80
Accrued expenses	166

g) Accounts payable to merchandise vendors total $18,750 on June 30, 19B. There is on hand a $750 credit memorandum from a merchandise vendor for returned merchandise; the company will apply the credit to July merchandise purchases. Neither the credit memorandum nor the return of the merchandise had been recorded on the books.

h) Profits and losses are divided equally between the partners.

Required:

Prepare a work sheet that provides, on the accrual basis, information regarding transactions for the six months ended June 30, 19B, the results of the partnership operations for the period, and the financial position of the partnership at June 30, 19B. (No need to prepare formal financial statements or formal journal entries.)

(AICPA adapted)

| chapter 25 | Statement of Changes in Financial Position – Working Capital and Cash |

Significance of Analysis of Changes in Financial Position

Throughout the preceding chapters the primary focus has been on the income statement, the statement of retained earnings, and the balance sheet. This chapter focuses on another statement which is included in the overall *financial report* of a business enterprise; that is, the statement of changes in financial position. This statement is a direct descendant of what was formerly called a "statement of sources and applications of funds" which was variously developed on the basis of an analysis of *either* (a) working capital flows or (b) cash flows. For many years accountants, at their option, included (or excluded) such a statement in the overall financial report. In 1963 the APB issued *Opinion 3* ("The Statement of Source and Application of Funds") which provided some guidelines for preparation and presentation of such statements. Significantly, *Opinion 3* did not specify it as a requirement, i.e., "The Board believes that a statement of source and application of funds should be presented as supplementary information in financial reports. The inclusion of such information is not mandatory, and it is operational as to whether it should be covered in the report of the independent accountant." The AAA and other accounting groups have tended to

991

favor the presentation of such information. In March 1971 the APB issued *Opinion 19*, entitled "Reporting Changes in Financial Position," which made it *mandatory* in the following terms:[1]

The Board concludes that information concerning the financing and investing activities of a business enterprise and the changes in its financial position for a period is essential for financial statement users, particularly owners and creditors, in making economic decisions. When financial statements purporting to present both financial position (balance sheet) and results of operations (statement of income and retained earnings) are issued, a statement summarizing changes in financial position should also be presented as a basic financial statement for each period for which an income statement is presented. These conclusions apply to all profit-oriented business entities, whether or not the reporting entity normally classifies its assets and liabilities as current and noncurrent.

The Opinion also states that, "The Board therefore recommends that the title be Statement of Changes in Financial Position." This title likely will become generally used; therefore it is used throughout this chapter. *Opinion 19* is noteworthy in that, in addition to making the statement mandatory, it requires application of an "all resources" concept in contrast to simply a working capital or cash concept. This broad concept of the statement is elaborated in the paragraphs to follow.

Historically, "funds" statements have experienced a wide diversity in terminology and content. They have been concerned with the inflow and outflow of *funds;* a term that has been accorded several diverse and frequently vague definitions. Some people and groups have viewed funds as cash items only; others have viewed them as cash *plus* temporary investments; still others have viewed them as working capital (current assets and current liabilities). Then there is an entirely different meaning of funds, that is, assets set aside for a particular purpose such as a bond sinking fund; further, in governmental accounting the term has a unique meaning. In order to establish a basis for clear-cut delineation, the discussions in this chapter are categorized as follows:

Part A. Changes in Financial Position (Working Capital Basis)
Part B. Changes in Financial Position (Cash Basis)

The significance of the new statement of changes in financial position rests primarily upon the need of statement users for *comprehensive* information concerning all of the financing and investing activities of the enterprise. These activities encompass a broad problem area of major import to both managers, shareholders, and others. It encompasses cash flows, working capital flows, and all of the non-cash financing and investing activities (such as the retirement of debt

---

[1] AICPA, *Opinions of the Accounting Principles Board, No. 19,* (New York, March 1971), p. 373.

through the issuance of capital stock). These items are intimately related to *profit* since this is generally the primary source that meets the continuing needs for cash and working capital. In addition, the new statement is deemed essential to "fair" reporting of the *causes* of the changes in financial position (balance sheet) from one period to the next. The income statement reports changes as a *result of operations*, and the statement of retained earnings reports only *certain* changes in owners' equity. Both of them do not, in large measure, reflect all of the changes in financial position between two consecutive balance sheets. The broad all-resources concept of the statement of changes in financial position expressed in *APB Opinion 19*, as opposed to the earlier working capital and cash concepts of "funds statements," aims to provide the missing link in reporting on *all changes in financial position* between two consecutive balance sheets. The Opinion states that "The Board also concludes that the statement summarizing changes in financial position should be based on a broad concept embracing all changes in financial position — The Statement of each reporting entity should disclose all important aspects of its financing and investing activities regardless of whether cash or other elements of working capital are directly affected." Thus, the concept clearly is much broader than the former concepts of reporting on working capital or cash.

The all-resources concept has not been accorded much attention in literature to date.[2] Perry Mason, in the *Accounting Research Study 2*, recognized the concept as follows:[3]

All Financial Resources. A different and somewhat broader approach is sometimes taken to the problem of interpreting the term "funds." It is conceived as purchasing or spending power, or as all financial resources, arising, as several writers have pointed out, from external rather than internal transactions of the business enterprise. In other words, it extends the concept to include assets or financial resources which do not affect or flow through the working capital accounts.

This conception of what is meant by "funds" seems to us to be the most useful meaning of the term. The narrower definitions, such as cash or working capital, have often led to the omission from the statement of the effect of transactions which do not directly affect cash or working capital, but which nevertheless are important items in the financial administration of the business. Examples are the purchase of property in exchange for shares of stock or bonds, gifts or subsidies, exchanges of property, and the like. The inclusion of such transactions is sometimes justified by assuming intermediate steps,

---

[2] "The Funds Statement Reconsidered," by Louis Goldberg, *Accounting Review*, October 1951, pp. 485–91; "Reporting on the Flow of Funds," by Maurice Moonitz, *Accounting Review*, July 1956, pp. 375–85; and "The Sources and Applications of Funds Statement: Suggested Improvements," By Donald A. Corbin, *Proceedings of the Thirty-Fifth Annual Conference of the Western Association* (1960), pp. 29–33.

[3] Mason, Perry, "Cash Flow Analysis and the Funds Statement," *Accounting Research Study 2* (New York: AICPA, 1961), pp. 54–55.

e.g., the issue of bonds for cash and the purchase of the property with cash. This introduction of hypothetical transactions would usually be unnecessary under the "all financial resources" concept since the changes in such items would naturally fall into the scope and purpose of the funds statement.

It may be proper and useful for some purposes, such as cash budgeting, to prepare a statement which is literally limited to changes in cash or in working capital, but for general use and reporting to stockholders, the broader approach provides a more complete and informative presentation. There would still be a need for a funds statement even though there were no change in cash or working capital.

The narrower concepts also tend to restrict the form in which the statement is prepared and to introduce too high a degree of uniformity in the arrangement of the items. The funds statement should be a flexible device, designed to disclose and emphasize all significant changes and transactions, whether they are within or without the current asset and liability groups. Too often a single figure of increase or decrease in working capital is shown, when one of the most significant changes may have been an increase or decrease in inventories, receivables, or some other current item.

On the basis of the provisions of the Opinion and the all-resources concept explained above, the objectives of the new statement of changes in financial position are: (*a*) to report on all of the financing and investing activities of the enterprise, (*b*) to report on the generation and application (use) of funds (either on a working capital or cash basis), and (*c*) to complete the reporting of the causes of all of the changes in financial position during the period.

Since a statement of changes in financial position may be prepared *in part* on either a working capital basis or a cash basis, we will consider each separately. First we will discuss the working capital basis.

PART A. STATEMENT OF CHANGES IN FINANCIAL POSITION – WORKING CAPITAL BASIS

In preparing an all-resources statement of changes in financial position (working capital basis), fundamentally two categories of items must be identified and analyzed for the period: (1) working capital generated (inflows) and working capital applied (outflows) and (2) all financing and investing activities that did not affect (flow through) working capital during the period.

Working capital for this purpose comprises all current assets and all current liabilities (net working capital is the difference between current assets and current liabilities). Thus, working capital is composed of positive current items (cash, temporary investments, short-term receivables, inventories, prepaid expenses, etc.) and a series of negative current items (accounts payable, short-term notes payable, accrued liabilities, etc.); the difference represents a "liquid pool" of net working resources. In a transaction where there is a net increase in working capital it is said that working capital has been "generated," and where there is a net decrease in working capital it is said that working capital has been applied (used). Thus, transactions such as the payment of a current liability, the collection of a current receivable, or the purchase of inventory for cash will not either generate or apply working capital; they merely rearrange the internal *content* of working capital. In contrast, certain other transactions, such as the purchase of a fixed asset for cash or the payment of a long-term debt, will cause both the *content* and the *amount* of net working capital to change. Thus, in the *analysis of working capital* we must be concerned with (a) changes in the internal content of working capital and (b) causes of changes in the amount of net working capital. Maintaining this distinction in the discussions to follow is important to adequate understanding.

Working Capital Generation and Application. Working capital is generated primarily from the following sources: (a) sale of capital stock for cash or for current receivables; (b) sale of a fixed asset for cash or for current receivables; (c) increase in long-term debt for cash or current receivables; and (d) net income for the period (represented by cash and/or current receivables). In order to explain the concepts of working capital generation, particularly for analytical purposes, each of these types of transactions is illustrated below. Both the working capital and cash effects are presented in order to contrast their differences. The four examples with comments follow.

Transaction	Cash Generated	Working Capital Generated
(a) Sold 1,000 shares of common stock during the period resulting in the following entry:		
Cash... 3,000	3,000	3,000
Special Receivable (current) 4,000		4,000
Special Receivable (noncurrent) 5,000		
Common Stock (par $10).......... 10,000		
Premium on Common Stock..... 2,000	____	____
Total generated	3,000	7,000

Observe that working capital for the period was generated by the amount of current assets received and not by the selling price, the par value of the stock, or the noncurrent receivable.

(b) Sold a fixed asset during the period resulting in the following entry:		
Cash... 4,000	4,000	4,000
Notes Receivable, Short-Term........ 5,000		5,000
Mortgage Receivable, Long-Term ...14,000		
Accumulated Depreciation.............10,000		
Fixed Asset........................... 31,000		
Gain on Sale of Fixed Asset..... 2,000	____	____
Total Generated	4,000	9,000

Observe that working capital generated for the period was the sum of cash and current receivables recognized and not the amount of the sales price, the gain recognized on the sale, or the noncurrent receivable.

(c) Borrowed from the bank resulting in the following entry:

Cash.................................30,000		30,000	⎫ 10,000	
Notes Payable, Short-Term	20,000		⎭	
Notes Payable, Long-Term	10,000			
Total Generated		30,000		10,000

Observe that, although there was an inflow of cash of $30,000, working capital increased by only $10,000. This was because the increase in current liabilities for the short-term debt "offset" $20,000 of the inflow. Thus, working capital was increased by the amount of the increase in long-term debt.

(d) Net income for the period was as follows:

Sales: Cash 40,000		+40,000	+40,000
On account........................10,000	50,000		+10,000
Cost of goods sold:			
Goods purchased for cash 18,000		−18,000	−18,000
Goods purchased on account....... 7,000			− 7,000
Goods from inventory................. 3,000	28,000		− 3,000
Gross margin.........................	22,000		
Expenses:			
Paid in cash 10,000		−10,000	−10,000
Accrued (liability)...................... 2,000			− 2,000
Depreciation 4,000	16,000		
Income before extraordinary items...	6,000		
Extraordinary item–gain on sale of			
fixed asset, (b) above.	2,000		
Net Income.....................	8,000		
Total Generated from			
Operations°		+12,000	+10,000
Total Generated from All			
Transactions.........................		49,000	36,000

° The results of this analysis are: (a) Net income on accrual basis of $8,000 converted to "net income on a working capital basis" is $10,000 and (b) Net income on accrual basis of $8,000 converted to "net income on a cash basis" is $12,000.

Observe that more cash than working capital was generated in the four transactions. In respect to the net income analysis (d), note that sales, whether cash or short-term credit, generated working capital. Thus, a change in the balance of accounts receivable does not affect working capital although it does affect cash flow. Expenses whether paid in cash or recorded as a current liability apply (use) working capital. In direct contrast, depreciation expense did not affect working capital for the period, since a working capital account was not affected by the credit to accumulated depreciation. The working capital effect of depreciation occurs when the asset was acquired and paid for, not when the depreciation estimate is recorded. Also you should note that the gain on sale of fixed assets ($2,000) did not generate working capital for the reasons noted in the analysis of transaction (b) above which gave rise to it; rather it was the amount of cash and current receivables recognized in the period of sale that generated working capital. In view of these concepts it should be clear that working capital generated by net income can be computed directly thus:

Net income as reported ....$ 8,000
Add back nonworking capital expenses that were deducted
 from net income:
 Depreciation 4,000
Total $12,000
Deduct gain on sale of fixed assets 2,000
Working capital generated for the period by net income $10,000

This short-cut approach to computing working capital generated from net income is widely used. It is important to observe that (a) depreciation is added back to net income, not because it generated working capital, but because it had been deducted from net income although it did not require working capital; (b) the gain (or loss, as the case may be) is deducted from net income because this amount does not represent a working capital increase or decrease although it had been added to net income. The working capital flow from the transaction that gave rise to the gain is identified by another analysis as in (b) above.

In summarizing we can say that the general effect of revenue transactions is to increase working capital and the effect of expense transactions generally is to decrease working capital. There are significant exceptions to this general rule in respect to depreciation, amortizations, and depletion.

Working capital normally is applied (used) to (a) acquire noncurrent (fixed) assets, (b) pay ordinary dividends, (c) pay noncurrent (long-term) debts, and (d) retire or repurchase capital stock. The concepts of working capital application, particularly for analytical purposes, are illustrated below for each of these types of transactions. The cash effects are included in order to contrast their differences. The examples to follow should be viewed as a continuation of the examples immediately above.

Transaction		Cash Applied	Working Capital Applied
(a) Purchased a fixed asset during the period resulting in the following entry:			
Fixed Asset 30,000			
Cash	3,000	3,000	3,000
Note Payable, Short-Term	7,000		7,000
Mortgage Payable, Long-Term	20,000		
Total Applied		3,000	10,000

Observe that working capital applied for the period was the sum of the cash paid plus the current liability recognized, not the purchase price or the long-term debt incurred.

(b) Ordinary dividends declared, or paid, resulted in the following entry:			
Retained Earnings 12,000			
Cash	8,000	8,000	8,000
Dividends Payable (current)	4,000		4,000
Total Applied		8,000	12,000

Transaction	Cash	Applied	Working Capital Applied

(c) Payments on debts during the period resulted in the following entry:

		Cash Applied	Working Capital Applied
Accounts Payable 15,000			
Notes Payable, Long-Term...................25,000			
Cash	40,000	40,000	25,000
Total Applied		40,000	25,000

Observe that although $40,000 cash (and working capital) was disbursed, the decrease in net working capital was only $25,000. This was because the $15,000 paid on a working capital debt constituted an "offset." Thus the working capital applied was equivalent to the decrease in long-term debt only.

(d) Treasury stock purchased during the period resulted in the following entry:

		Cash Applied	Working Capital Applied
Treasury Stock (at cost)........................ 8,000			
Cash	5,000	5,000	5,000
Special Payable, Short-Term...........	3,000		3,000
Total Applied		5,000	8,000
Total Applied for the Period (all transactions).............................		56,000	55,000

In summarizing the results of the eight transactions for a given period as analyzed above, we observe a significant difference between cash flow and working capital results. Additionally, by reviewing the analysis we can readily pinpoint the *causes* of the changes in both cash and working capital for the period, viz:

	Cash Basis	Working Capital Basis
Financial resources generated:		
Sale of common stock...............................$ 3,000	$ 3,000	$ 7,000
Sale of fixed assets	4,000	9,000
Borrowing...	30,000	10,000
From operations......................................	12,000	10,000
Noncash and/or nonworking capital/ resources.....................................	–	–
Total Financial Resources Generated..............................	$49,000	$36,000
Financial resources applied:		
Purchase of fixed assets ....$ 3,000	$ 3,000	$10,000
Ordinary dividends	8,000	12,000
Retire debt..	40,000	25,000
Acquire treasury stock	5,000	8,000
Noncash and/or nonworking capital resources applied.............................	–	–
Total Financial Resources Generated..............................	$56,000	$55,000
Net decrease for the period: Cash..............	$ 7,000	
Working capital		$19,000

This final summary clearly demonstrates the fundamental difference between the cash and working capital analyses of funds flow.

With these concepts in mind we can move to a slightly more complex illustration that includes the *noncash and nonworking capital* types of financing and investing activities.

Determining Changes in the Content of Working Capital. Changes in the content of working capital involve merely the preparation of a comparative listing of the beginning and ending balances in the current asset and current liability accounts. To illustrate, assume the data presented in Illustration 25–1.

Illustration 25–1
ADAMSON COMPANY
Summarized Data for the Year Ended December 31, 1971

	Dec. 31, 1971	Dec. 31, 1970
(1) Balance Sheet:		
Cash	$ 45,000	$ 30,000
Accounts receivable (net)	38,000	40,000
Inventory	67,000	60,000
Permanent investments	162,000	200,000
Land	128,000	100,000
Building (net)	98,000	
Total	$538,000	$430,000
Accounts payable	$ 36,000	$ 40,000
Notes payable, short term (nontrade)	24,000	30,000
Bonds payable	35,000	50,000
Mortgage payable	100,000	
Common stock	295,000	270,000
Retained earnings	48,000	40,000
Total	$538,000	$430,000
(2) Income Statement:		
Sales	$100,000	
Cost of goods sold	$ 51,000	
Expenses (including interest and taxes)	16,000	
Total	$ 67,000	
Net Income	$ 33,000	

(3) Summary of transactions for 1971:
  (a) Net income, $33,000.
  (b) Purchases, $58,000, on account.
  (c) Increase in inventory, $7,000.
  (d) Sales, $100,000, on account.
  (e) Expenses, $14,000, cash.
  (f) Collection on accounts receivable, $102,000.
  (g) Paid on accounts payable, $62,000.
  (h) Sold bonds payable, $10,000, for cash at par value.
  (i) Purchased land, $28,000 cash.
  (j) Paid cash dividend, $25,000.
  (k) Paid short-term notes payable, $6,000 (nontrade).
  (l) Sold permanent investment for cash, $38,000 (sold at book value).
  (m) Retired $25,000 bonds payable by issuing common stock.
  (n) A new building was completed on the land in January 1971 at a cost of $100,000; gave an interest-bearing mortgage for the full amount. The building had an estimated life of 50 years and no residual value (straight line).
  (o) Depreciation expense, $2,000.

Changes in the internal *content* of working capital from the beginning to the end of the year can be taken directly from the above data as reflected in Illustration 25–2. You should note in particular that this illustration merely reflects what specific working capital accounts changed and the amount that each changed; thus it reflects only changes in content. Significantly, it does not reflect (1) the *causes* of the changes in working capital, (2) the amount of working capital generated (sources), and (3) the uses (applications) of working capital. Additionally we must identify (4) all of the *nonworking capital* investing and financing activities for the period. In order to develop these four items, which are necessary to prepare a statement of changes in financial position (working capital basis), we must turn to a somewhat complex analysis of the changes in the balances of the *nonworking capital accounts* during the period.

Illustration 25–2
ADAMSON COMPANY
Changes in the Content of Working Capital Accounts

| | Balances, Dec. 31 | | Working Capital |
	1971	1970	Increase (Decrease)
Current Assets:			
Cash	$ 45,000	$ 30,000	$15,000
Accounts receivable (net)	38,000	40,000	(2,000)
Inventory	67,000	60,000	7,000
Total Current Assets	$150,000	$130,000	
Current Liabilities:			
Accounts payable	$ 36,000	$ 40,000	4,000
Notes payable – short term (nontrade)	24,000	30,000	6,000
Total Current Liabilities	$ 60,000	$ 70,000	
Working Capital	$ 90,000	$ 60,000	$30,000

Developing a Statement of Changes in Financial Position. The statement to be developed for the Adamson Company is reflected in Illustration 25–3. You should observe that the four primary captions in the statement parallel the requirements listed immediately above. There are four major captions: (1) working capital generated (inflows of working capital), (2) working capital applied (outflows of working capital), (3) financing and investing activities that did not affect (flow through) working capital, and (4) a detailed report of changes in the internal content of working capital. This illustration was designed to meet the *minimum* criteria specified in *APB Opinion 19*.

Illustration 25-3
ADAMSON COMPANY
Statement of Changes in Financial Position—Working Capital Basis
(for the year ended December 31, 1971)

1) Working Capital Generated:

From operations:
Net income before extraordinary items $33,000
Add expenses not requiring working capital in
the current period:
Depreciation   2,000

Total working capital generated by operations (exclusive
of extraordinary items).. $ 35,000
Extraordinary items generating working capital:
Permanent investments sold...   38,000
Other sources of working capital:
Bonds payable issued...   10,000
Total Working Capital Generated.................................... $ 83,000

2) Working Capital Applied:
Land purchased...$28,000
Cash dividend paid... 25,000
Total working capital applied...   53,000
Net Increase in Working Capital during the Period........... $ 30,000

3) Financing and Investing Activities Not Affecting Working Capital:
Bonds retired by issuing common stock..................................... $ 25,000
Building acquired in exchange for long-term mortgage payable......   100,000
Total... $125,000

4) Changes in Working Capital Accounts:

	Balances December 31		Working Capital Increase (Decrease)
	1971	1970	
Current assets:			
Cash..	$ 45,000	$ 30,000	$15,000
Accounts receivable (net)....................	38,000	40,000	(2,000)
Inventory...	67,000	60,000	7,000
Total current assets......................	$150,000	$130,000	
Current liabilities:			
Accounts payable...............................	$ 36,000	$ 40,000	4,000
Notes payable—short term (nontrade) ...	24,000	30,000	6,000
Total current liabilities..................	$ 60,000	$ 70,000	
Working Capital	$ 90,000	$ 60,000	$30,000

The Work Sheet Approach. In the unrealistically simple situations, such as the hypothetical Adamson Company, it would be possible to develop the statement of changes in financial position haphazardly by "inspection" of the data or in a more rational way by using the elementary T-account approach. However, for more complex and typical situations one would find the use of a work sheet more convenient if not absolutely essential. A work sheet practically is necessary to handle the large quantities of data and the complex transactions found in extensive problems frequently encountered by students and in real-life situations. Illustration 25–4 presents an efficient work sheet that has been designed for analysis of the nonworking capital accounts and to sort out the data needed for each major classification on the statement of changes in financial position. In contrast to some work sheets (which involve complex reversing and reclassifying entries) this one simply requires summary restatement of the former entries without change of format or direction. The interim entries are keyed to the list of transactions on page 999.

Illustration 25–4
ADAMSON COMPANY
Work Sheet to Develop Statement of Changes in Financial Position—Working Capital Basis
(for the year ended December 31, 1971)

Debits	Beginning Balance Dec. 31, 1970	Analysis of Interim Entries Debit		Credit		Ending Balance Dec. 31, 1971
1) Working Capital	$ 60,000	(p)	$ 30,000			$ 90,000
2) Nonworking Capital Accounts:						
Permanent investments	200,000			(l)	$ 38,000	162,000
Land	100,000	(i)	28,000			128,000
Building (net)		(n – 1)	100,000	(o)	2,000	98,000
	$360,000					$478,000
Credits						
Bonds payable	$ 50,000	(m – 1)	25,000	(h)	10,000	$ 35,000
Mortgage payable				(n – 2)	100,000	100,000
Common stock	270,000			(m – 2)	25,000	295,000
Retained earnings	40,000	(j)	25,000	(a)	33,000	48,000
	$360,000		$208,000		$208,000	$478,000

3) Working Capital Generated:					
From operations:					
Net income before extraordinary items		(a)	$ 33,000		
Adjustments for nonworking capital items:					
Depreciation		(o)	2,000		
Extraordinary items generating working capital:					
Permanent investments sold		(l)	38,000		
Other sources of working capital:					
Bonds payable issued		(h)	10,000		
4) Working Capital Applied:					
Land purchased				(i)	$ 28,000
Cash dividends paid				(j)	25,000
5) Financing and Investing Activities Not Affecting Working Capital:					
Bonds retired by issuing common stock		(m – 2)	25,000	(m – 1)	25,000
Building purchased; gave long-term mortgage		(n – 2)	100,000	(n – 1)	100,000
Increase in net working capital for the period				(p)	30,000
			$208,000		$208,000

It is significant to observe that this work sheet is built around the fact that the *causes* of the changes in working capital and nonworking capital financing and investing activities can be found only in an analysis of the *nonworking capital accounts*. In contrast, an analysis of *only* the working capital accounts will divulge only changes in the *content* of working capital; observe that the work sheet does not deal with the content of working capital.

The work sheet is set up with four amount columns and five major side captions. The first column (beginning balance) and last column (ending balance) are taken from the two consecutive balance sheets; the two interim columns (debit and credit) are provided for "reconciling through analysis" the beginning and ending balances for each account listed. The five side captions may be explained as follows.

Basic Data:

1. Working Capital. This is the net working capital at the beginning and ending dates; it is entered on the work sheet only for "balancing" purposes since the work sheet does not deal with an analysis of the content of working capital accounts themselves.

2. Nonworking Capital Accounts. These are the accounts to be analyzed in detail; they are grouped by "debits" and "credits" only for convenience. The amounts are taken directly from the two consecutive balance sheets; sufficient space should be provided between accounts that may have had high activity during the period.

Data to be Elicited and Grouped from the Analysis:

3. Working Capital Generated. This section, paralleling the statement to be developed, provides for listing the various sources of working capital inflow. The amounts under this section normally will be reflected on the work sheet as debits.

4. Working Capital Applied. This section parallels the statement to be developed and the amounts normally will be reflected as credits.

5. Financing and Investing Activities Not Affecting Working Capital. This section parallels the statement being developed and will reflect each item as both a debit and credit. This effect is due to the fact that the type of transactions to be identified in the analysis (nonworking capital effects) represent simultaneous financing and investing activities.

Completion of the work sheet involves an analysis of each transaction that affected a nonworking capital account (transactions that affect working capital *only* are not entered on the work sheet) and entering them on the work sheet in the debit-credit format used when they were originally recorded in the accounts; all debits and credits to working capital accounts (such accounts are not on the work sheet) are reflected under the third and fourth captions on the work sheet. Transactions that did not affect (flow through) working capital result in debits and credits under the fifth caption (financing and investing activities not affecting working capital). The following is a step-by-step approach to be used in completing the work sheet (Illustration

25-4) for the Adamson Company (original data given on page 999).

Step 1: Set up the four amount columns and the five major side captions.

Step 2: Enter the original data from the balance sheets for beginning and ending balances for (*a*) net working capital and (*b*) each nonworking capital account.

Step 3: Analyze each transaction; enter on the work sheet under "analysis of interim entries" only those that affected one or more nonworking capital accounts so that all differences between the beginning and ending balances are finally accounted for. The analysis may be explained as follows (the entries are keyed to the transactions listed on page 999):

	Original Entry	*Worksheet Entry*
(a) Net income for the period:		
Income Summary.....................................33,000		
Working Capital Generated,		
Net Income...		33,000
Retained Earnings	33,000	33,000

Analysis: Net income for the period (*a*) generated working capital and (*b*) affected a noncurrent account (Retained Earnings). The work sheet entry repeats the original entry except for the debit; on the work sheet this reflects the generation of working capital.

The following transactions are not entered on the work sheet since each one did not affect a noncurrent account: (*b*) purchase on accounts; (*c*) inventory increase; (*d*) sales on account; (*e*) expenses paid in cash; (*f*) collection on accounts receivable; and (*g*) paid on accounts payable.

(h) Sold bonds payable for cash:		
Cash..10,000		
Working Capital Generated,		
Other Sources		10,000
Bonds Payable................................	10,000	10,000

Analysis: This transaction used working capital; a noncurrent account, Land, was affected. This work sheet entry corresponds to the original entry except that the original debit to a working capital account (cash) is reflected in the lower part of the work sheet as a debit to Working Capital Generated, Other Sources. The original debit to cash (a working capital account) cannot be entered as such on the work sheet since no working capital accounts are listed; this is a built-in safety feature.

(i) Purchased land for cash:		
Land 28,000		28,000
Cash...	28,000	
Working Capital Applied..................		28,000

Analysis: This transaction used working capital; a nonworking capital account, Land, was affected. This work sheet entry corresponds to the original entry except for the original credit to working capital (cash); on the work sheet this is reflected as a credit under Working Capital Applied.

(j) Paid cash dividend:

Retained Earnings 25,000		25,000
Cash...	25,000	
Working Capital Applied..................		25,000

Analysis: This transaction used working capital; a noncurrent account, Retained Earnings, was affected. The work sheet entry reflects the original credit to cash as a credit under Working Capital Applied.

(k) Paid short-term notes payable: Not entered on the work sheet since noncurrent accounts were not affected.

(l) Sold permanent investment for cash:

Cash...38,000		
Working Capital Generated,		
Other Sources		38,000
Permanent Investments.....................	38,000	38,000

Analysis: This transaction generated working capital; a noncurrent account, Permanent Investments, was affected. The work sheet entry reflects the original debit (to cash) under working capital generated as a debit.

(m) Retired bonds payable by issuing common stock:

Bonds Payable..................................... 25,000		25,000[1]
Common Stock...............................	25,000	25,000[2]
Financing and Investing		
Activities Not Affecting		
Working Capital...............................		25,000[2] 25,000[1]

Analysis: This transaction (1) did not affect working capital and (2) affected only noncurrent accounts; yet it constituted a "financing and investing" activity. It must reflect on the statement of changes in financial position; therefore, it must be entered on the work sheet under the caption Financing and Investing Activities Not Affecting Working Capital. Obviously, if one were to simply repeat the original entry on the work sheet this aspect would be omitted. As a consequence, it is desirable to reflect on the work sheet two interrelated and concurrent entries as shown above. The view is that entry (1) reflects payment of a debt (the debit) and an outflow for that purpose (the credit) and entry (2) reflects the issuance of common stock (the credit) and an inflow from that source. This is what is commonly called an "in and out" item of financing and investing. At this point you should follow this entry through the work sheet and back to the statement (Illustration 25–3).

(n) Purchased new building; gave long-term mortgage note for purchase price:

Building...................................100,000		100,000[1]	
Mortgage Payable.....................	100,000		100,000[2]
Financing and Investing Activities Not Affecting Working Capital.........................		100,000[2]	100,000[1]

Analysis: This transaction is of the same type as analyzed in (m) above. This transaction (1) did not affect working capital and (2) affected only noncurrent accounts; yet it constituted a "financing and investing" activity. It is reflected on the work sheet as an "in and out" item as explained immediately above.

(o) Depreciation expense for the period:

Expenses, Depreciation..................	2,000		
Working Capital Generated, Net Income (adjustment).....................		2,000	
Accumulated Depreciation........	2,000		2,000

Analysis: This transaction did not generate working capital, yet it affected a noncurrent account—accumulated depreciation. Since depreciation is an expense it was deducted from net income; however, it did not require the use of working capital in the period of recognition in contrast to other expenses that are either paid in the period or recognized as a current liability (accrual). Significantly, then we see an item that reduced net income but did not require working capital; as a consequence, to determine the amount of working capital generated from operations, depreciation must be added back. The work sheet entry (a debit to working capital generated) reflects this effect. At this point you should follow this item through the work sheet and back to the statement.

(p) Entry (p) does not represent a transaction; it is an optional entry that may be made simply to "balance" the work sheet. After this entry is made, two internal checks for accuracy and completeness can be made, viz:

(1) Check each line on the work sheet horizontally to be sure that the interim entries "clear out" all differences between the beginning and ending balances.
(2) Total the debit and credit columns under "Analysis of Interim Entries" at two levels on the work sheet as illustrated; the work sheet debits and credits in these columns will balance at these two levels.

One of the special features of this work sheet is that the formal statement of changes in financial position (Illustration 25–3) can be copied directly from the lower portion of the work sheet, adding thereto the last section wherein the *content* of the working capital accounts is presented. For examinations and problem-solving purposes by students, the work sheet generally will suffice without the added burden of preparing a formal statement.

Some Special Problems. In developing the work sheet, several special situations may require careful attention; they are:

1. Transactions that affect only owners' equity accounts. Generally, changes, such as a common stock dividend on common stock, are not reported on the statement of changes in financial position. However, *APB Opinion 19* specifies that the statement should disclose: "Conversion of long-term debt or preferred to common stock." This is interpreted to mean that basic changes in owners' equity should be reported. The exchange of preferred stock for common stock then would be reflected on the work sheet and on the statement as an "in and out" item similar to that previously illustrated for the exchange of debt for stock.

2. Amortization of long-term items. Long-term (noncurrent) amortizations (either debits or credits) reduce, or increase, reported net income although they do not require or provide working capital during the current period. Examples of this type of item are discount and premium on bonds payable. To illustrate, assume $1,000 discount on bonds payable is being amortized over a 10-year period on a straight-line basis. The annual amortization of $100 would appear on the income statement as an increase in bond interest expense although it would not require the application of working capital during the current period. Therefore, the work sheet entry would be a debit to "Net Income — Adjustment" similar to depreciation and a credit to Discount on Bonds Payable.

3. Reclassification of a long-term liability. When a long-term liability becomes payable within the upcoming year it is usually reclassified as a current liability. The reclassification has the effect of decreasing working capital; therefore, there should be recognition on the work sheet and in the statement of a working capital application. The entry on the work sheet would be a debit to long-term liabilities and a credit to working capital applied.

Criteria for the Statement of Changes in Financial Position

In view of the wide diversity observed in the past in respect to the funds statements, the APB in *Opinion 19* specified certain criteria that should be satisfied in presenting a statement of changes in financial position; these criteria may be summarized as follows:

1. The statement should be presented as a basic financial statement for each period in which an income statement is prepared.
2. The statement applies to all profit-oriented business entities whether or not there is a classification of assets and liabilities between current and noncurrent.
3. The statement should be based on a broad concept embracing all

changes in financial position (not limited to working capital or cash). The statement should disclose all important changes in financial position for the period.

4. The statement should begin with the income or loss before extraordinary items, if any, and add back (or deduct) items recognized in determining income (or loss) which did not use (or provide) working capital or cash during the period.[4]

5. The items to be added back (or deducted) in 4 above should be clearly presented to avoid the interpretation that they provided funds (e.g., "Add – Expenses not requiring outlay of working capital in the current period").

6. The effects of extraordinary items (see *APB Opinion 9*) should be reported separately from the effects of normal operating items.

7. The effects of all financing and investing activities, as well as working capital or cash, should be *individually* disclosed.

8. If the format shows the flow of working capital and two-year comparative balance sheets are presented, the detailed changes in working capital accounts nevertheless must be presented.

9. Working capital or cash provided from (or used) should be appropriately described (e.g., Working capital provided from (used in) operations for the period, exclusive of extraordinary items).

10. If the format shows the flow of cash, detailed changes in other working capital accounts should be disclosed in the body of the statement.

11. Terms referring to Cash should not be used unless all noncash items have been appropriately adjusted.

12. There should be flexibility in form, content, and terminology in the statement; flexibility should be used to develop the presentation that is most informative in the circumstances.

13. It was strongly recommended that isolated statistics of working capital and cash, especially per-share amounts, not be presented.

Comprehensive Illustration

The comprehensive illustration that follows for F. P. Corporation presents a situation where the data are more complex and the analysis more involved than those shown in the previous example. The illustration includes the following:

Illustration 25–5 Basic Data for Illustration

---

[4] An acceptable alternative procedure, which gives the same result, starts with revenues that generated working capital or cash during the period and deducts therefrom operating expenses that required the outflow of working capital or cash. This approach has the advantage of not suggesting that "adjustments" to net income, such as depreciation, generated working capital or cash.

The work sheet (Illustration 25-6) has been adapted to provide more information than the one shown in Illustration 25-4. This adaptation is to provide data for *maximum reporting* under the concepts espoused in *APB Opinion 19*. Observe that the side captions have been designated differently; that is, (1) financial resources generated and (2) financial resources applied. This is consistent with the concept of reporting separately all of the investing and financing activities of the enterprise. Under each of these major captions observe the subcaptions for (a) working capital and (b) other resources generated (or applied) that did not affect working capital. This revised classification on the work sheet readily provides reporting data for either minimum or maximum reporting of information. As with all work sheets the analyst should adapt it to meet his particular needs and preferences.

Illustration 25-5
F. P. CORPORATION
Basic Data for Illustration

	Amounts Reported on	
	12/31/19A	*12/31/19B*
Cash	$ 30,000	$ 96,000
Marketable securities	10,000	8,000
Accounts receivable (net)	50,000	80,000
Inventory	20,000	30,000
Prepaid expenses		2,000
Land	60,000	60,000
Machinery	80,000	65,000
Accumulated depreciation	(20,000)	(24,900)
Other assets	29,000	39,000
Discount on bonds payable	1,000	900
Total	$260,000	$356,000
Accounts payable	$ 40,000	$ 55,000
Dividends payable		15,000
Bonds payable	70,000	80,000
Common stock	100,000	111,000
Preferred stock	20,000	49,000
Retained earnings	30,000	46,000
Total	$260,000	$356,000

Illustration 25–5 (continued)

	12/31/19A	12/31/19B
Sales		$180,000
Cost of goods sold		90,000
Distribution expenses		35,000
Administrative expenses (including interest and taxes)		20,000
Depreciation		7,900
Amortization of discount on bonds payable		100
Total Costs		$153,000
Income before extraordinary items		$ 27,000
Extraordinary items:		
Gain on sale of land		8,000
Gain on sale of machinery		10,000
Net Income		$ 45,000

Additional data; summary of transactions for the year:

(a) Sales (on account), $180,000.
(b) Purchases (on account), $100,000.
(c) Inventory increase, $10,000.
(d) Administrative expenses, $20,000 (cash); to simplify tax allocation is disregarded.
(e) Depreciation, $8,000.
(f) Distribution expenses paid, $37,000, of which $2,000 is prepaid.
(g) Ordinary dividend declared, $15,000.
(h) Common stock dividend issued; retained earnings debited for $10,000.
(i) Purchased land costing $25,000 paid for by issuing bonds payable at par.
(j) Issued bonds payable for cash, $5,000.
(k) Sold land for $45,000 cash; book value, $35,000.
(l) Purchased land for $10,000 cash.
(m) Purchased marketable securities, $2,000 cash.
(n) Paid dividend on preferred stock with marketable securities, $4,000.
(o) Retired $20,000 bonds payable by issuing preferred stock.
(p) Sold machinery for $20,000 cash: cost, $15,000; accumulated depreciation, $3,000.
(q) Collected cash on accounts receivables, $150,000.
(r) Paid cash on accounts payable, $85,000.
(s) Acquired other assets for $10,000 by issuing preferred stock.
(t) Amortization of discount on bonds payable, $100.

Illustration 25–6
F. P. CORPORATION
Work Sheet to Develop Statement of Changes in Financial Position – Working Capital Basis
(for the year ended December 31, 19B)

Debits	Balance Dec. 31, 19A	Analysis of Interim Entries Debit	Analysis of Interim Entries Credit	Balance Dec. 31, 19B
Working Capital	$ 70,000	(u) $ 76,000		$146,000
Nonworking Capital Accounts:				
Land	60,000	(i) 25,000	(k) $ 35,000	60,000
		(l – 1) 10,000		
Machinery	80,000		(p) 15,000	65,000
Other assets	29,000	(s – 1) 10,000		39,000
Discount on bonds payable	1,000		(t) 100	900
Total	$240,000			$310,900

Illustration 25–6 (continued)

Credits

Accumulated depreciation	$ 20,000	(p)	3,000	(e)	7,900	$ 24,900
Bonds payable	70,000	(o – 1)	20,000	(i – 2)	25,000	80,000
				(j)	5,000	
Common stock	100,000			(h)	10,000	110,000
Preferred stock	20,000			(o – 2)	20,000	50,000
				(s – 2)	10,000	
Retained earnings	30,000	(g)	15,000	(e)	45,000	46,000
		(h)	10,000			
		(n)	4,000			
Total	$240,000		$173,000		$173,000	$310,900

Financial Resources Generated:
Working Capital Generated:

Net income	(a)	$ 45,000	(k)	$ 10,000
			(p)	8,000
Adjustments:				
Depreciation expense	(e)	7,900		
Amortization of bond				
discount	(t)	100		
Extraordinary items:				
Land sold	(k)	45,000		
Machinery sold	(p)	20,000		
Other sources of working				
capital:				
Bonds payable sold	(j)	5,000		
Nonworking capital resources				
generated:				
Bonds issued to acquire				
land	(i – 2)	25,000		
Preferred stock issued to				
retire bonds	(o – 2)	20,000		
Preferred stock issued for				
other assets	(s – 2)	10,000		
Financial Resources Applied:				
Working capital applied:				
Dividends declared			(g)	15,000
Land purchased			(l)	10,000
Dividends on preferred				
stock, paid with				
marketable securities			(n)	4,000
Nonworking capital resources				
applied:				
Land acquired by issuing				
bonds payable			(i – 1)	25,000
Bonds payable retired by				
issuing preferred stock			(o – 1)	20,000
Other assets acquired by				
issuing preferred stock			(s – 1)	10,000
Increase in net working				
capital for the period			(u)	76,000
		$178,000		$178,000

The analysis of transactions and the related entries on the work sheet are explained below; the discussions and entries are keyed to the basic data given in Illustration 25–5. Only those transactions that represent situations different from those explained above for Adamson Company are discussed.

	Original Entry	Worksheet Entry

(h) Common stock dividend issued:

Retained Earnings............................10,000		10,000	
Common Stock	10,000		10,000

Analysis: This transaction (a) did not affect working capital and (b) does not represent a "financing and investing" activity although two noncurrent accounts were affected. It merely represents a transfer of one equity account to another and is generally considered not to be encompassed in the provisions of APB Opinion 19. The work sheet entry, identical to the original entry, must be made for "clearing" purposes.

(k) Sold land for cash at a profit:

Cash...45,000			
Working Capital Generated,		45,000	
Extraordinary Items........................			
Land..	35,000		35,000
Gain on Sale of Land (extraor-			
dinary item).............................	10,000		
Working Capital Generated, Net			
Income (adjustment).................			10,000

Analysis: This transaction generated working capital by the amount of cash received ($45,000) rather than the gain ($10,000). Since net income included the $10,000 gain, it must be removed from the net income amount through an adjustment (credit on the work sheet). This has the effect of restoring net income to the amount desired "income before extraordinary items," and reflects the working capital generated rather than the gain. This transaction should be traced through the work sheet and then to the statement of changes in financial position.

(n) Paid dividends with marketable securities:

Retained Earnings............................. 4,000		4,000	
Marketable Securities....................	4,000		
Working Capital Applied			4,000

Analysis: This transaction utilized working capital (marketable securities) and affected a nonworking capital account.

(o) Retired bonds payable by issuing preferred stock:

Bonds Payable..................................20,000		20,000[1]	
Preferred Stock............................	20,000		20,000[2]
Financing and Investing Activities			
Not Affecting Working Capital.....		20,000[2]	20,000[1]

Analysis: This transaction affected two nonworking capital accounts but did not affect working capital; it is an "in and out" item that must be reported (see page 1005 for further explanation).

(p) Sold machinery for cash at a profit:

Cash...20,000
Working Capital Generated, Other
   Sources...   20,000
Accumulated Depreciation.................. 3,000   3,000
   Machinery....................................   15,000   15,000
   Gain on Sale of Machinery............   8,000
   Working Capital Generated, Net
      Income (adjustment)..................   8,000

Analysis: This transaction generated working capital by the amount of cash received and also affected two nonworking capital accounts (machinery and accumulated depreciation). The gain must be "cleared" from net income as explained in transaction (k) above.

(s) Acquired other assets by issuing preferred stock:

Other assets.....................................10,000   10,000[1]
   Preferred Stock............................   10,000   10,000[2]
   Financing and Investing Activities
     Not Affecting Working Capital.....   10,000[2]   10,000[1]

Analysis: This transaction did not affect working capital; it affected two nonworking capital accounts. It is an "in and out" item that represents a financing and investing activity; hence it must be recognized on the worksheet (see page 1005 for further explanation).

(t) Amortization of discount on bonds payable:

Expenses, Amortization of Bond
   Discount....................................... 100
Working Capital Generated, Net
   Income (adjustment)......................   100
   Discount on Bonds Payable...........   100   100

Analysis: This transaction did not affect working capital; it affected a nonworking capital account — Discount on Bonds Payable — and reported net income. Since it was deducted from net income, but did not affect working capital, it must be added back to net income as a nonworking capital charge. This item is similar in effect to depreciation expense for the period previously discussed.

The following transactions were not entered on the work sheet since they affected only working capital accounts: (a), (b), (c), (d), (f), (m), (q), and (r). Entry (u), you will recall, is merely an optional balancing entry on the work sheet.

Statement Format

APB Opinion 19 stated that "Provided that these guides are met, the statement may take whatever form gives the most useful portrayal of the financing and investing activities and the changes in financial position of the reporting entity." In the light of this statement there is apt to be a wide range of variation in the forms developed by industry. Clearly, numerous variations of form could meet the criteria provided in the *Opinion* (see list of criteria above). In order to illustrate both extremes of the scale of reporting, we have prepared Illustration 25–7 as an example of what we consider to represent *minimum* reporting within the criteria of the *Opinion*. Alternatively, we

Illustration 25–7
F. P. CORPORATION
Statement of Changes in Financial Position—Working Capital Basis—
Minimum Reporting
(for the year ended December 31, 19B)

Working Capital Generated:

From operations:
Income before extraordinary items $27,000
Add expenses not requiring working capital in the
current period:
Depreciation and amortization 8,000

Working capital provided by operations exclusive of
extraordinary items .... $ 35,000
Working capital from extraordinary items:
Land sold $45,000
Machinery sold 20,000
Working capital provided by extraordinary items 65,000
Other sources of working capital:
Bonds payable issued 5,000
Total Working Capital Generated $105,000

Working Capital:
Cash dividends declared $15,000
Land purchased 10,000
Dividends on preferred stock paid in marketable securities 4,000
Total working capital 29,000
Net Increase in Working Capital during the Period .... $ 76,000

Financing and Investing Activities Not Affecting
Working Capital:
Bonds payable issued for land acquired .... $ 25,000
Preferred stock issued to retire bonds 20,000
Preferred stock issued for other assets acquired 10,000
Total .... $ 55,000

	Account Balances		Working Capital Increase (Decrease)
Changes in Working Capital Accounts:	12/31/19B	12/31/19A	
Current assets:			
Cash	$ 96,000	$ 30,000	$66,000
Marketable securities	8,000	10,000	(2,000)
Accounts receivable (net)	80,000	50,000	30,000
Inventory	30,000	20,000	10,000
Prepaid expenses	2,000		2,000
Total current assets	$216,000	$110,000	
Current liabilities:			
Accounts payable	$ 55,000	$ 40,000	($15,000)
Dividends payable	15,000		(15,000)
Total current liabilities	$ 70,000	$ 40,000	
Working Capital	$146,000	$ 70,000	$ 76,000

have presented Illustration 25–8 as an example of what we consider maximum reporting within the criteria of the *Opinion*. Note in particular that the "in and out" items; that is, the investing and financing activities not affecting working capital are reported in Illustration 25–7 as one-line items in a nonintegrated manner. In contrast, in Illustration 25–8 these items are reported as an integral part of the statement; therefore, they are reflected both as an inflow and outflow of resources. The authors prefer the latter disclosure in general and, at this point in time, anticipate that practice will vary between these two extremes with a tendency toward the minimum.

Illustration 25–8
F. P. CORPORATION
Statement of Changes in Financial Position — Working Capital Basis —
Maximum Reporting
(for the year ended December 31, 19B)

Financial Resources Generated:

Working capital generated:

Income before extraordinary items	$27,000	
Add: Expenses not requiring working capital in the current period:		
Depreciation expense	7,900	
Amortization bond discount	100	
Working capital generated by operations exclusive of extraordinary items		$ 35,000
Extraordinary items:		
Land sold	$45,000	
Machinery sold	20,000	
Working capital generated by extraordinary items		65,000
Other sources of working capital:		
Bonds payable sold		5,000
Total working capital generated		$105,000
Financial resources generated not affecting working capital:		
Bonds issued for land acquired	$25,000	
Preferred stock issued to retire bonds payable	20,000	
Preferred stock issued to acquire other assets	10,000	
Total		55,000
Total Financial Resources Generated		$160,000

Financial Resources Applied:

Working capital applied:

Cash dividend payable	$15,000	
Land purchased	10,000	
Dividends paid on preferred stock in marketable securities	4,000	
Total working capital applied		$ 29,000
Financial resources applied not affecting working capital:		
Land acquired by issuing bonds payable	$25,000	
Bonds payable retired by issuing preferred stock	20,000	
Other assets acquired by issuing preferred stock	10,000	
Total		55,000
Increase in net working capital during the period		76,000
Total Financial Resources Applied		$160,000

Changes in Working Capital Accounts:
Same as reflected in Illustration 25–7

PART B.   STATEMENT OF CHANGES IN FINANCIAL POSITION—
CASH BASIS

The critical problems of cash planning and cash control create a serious need by internal management for meaningful statements of cash inflows and outflows coupled with the other financing and investing activities. Similarly, in decision making the external investor has a critical need for relevant information on the ability of the enterprise to generate cash inflows, the cash requirements, and the related noncash financing and investing activities. Although a statement of changes in financial position prepared on a "working capital" basis as discussed in the first part of this chapter serves useful purposes, similar statements prepared on a "cash flow" basis generally are considerably more relevant both for internal management and the investor. Clearly, cash, as opposed to the concept of working capital, is more commonly understood by management and the investor alike. Also, all working capital problems "come to rest" in the cash position. A statement of financial position prepared on the cash basis would preclude the need for a similar statement on the working capital basis although the opposite is not the case. In direct contrast to a "cash flow" statement, a working capital statement submerges the critical problems of cash position, receivables out of control, inventory position, and accounts payable. In view of the obvious superiority of cash-flow-based statements, one may ask the question as to why working-capital-based statements have tended to dominate in published financial statements (although not in internal managerial accounting reports). The answer probably lies in the facts that working-capital-based statements (a) tended to be developed first historically, (b) are easier to prepare, (c) divulge less about the critical financing strengths and weakness of the enterprise, (d) have been given more attention in textbooks on financial accounting, and (e) represent precedent (which is difficult to change). In *Opinion 19* the APB was very careful to specify that the statement of changes in financial position could be presented either on a working capital or cash basis. Unfortunately the board did not specifically recognize the obviously greater relevance of the cash flow approach. However, a major concession to the cash flow approach is evidenced by the requirement, under the working capital approach, that: "Whether or not working capital flow is presented in the Statement, net changes in each element of working capital (as customarily defined) should be appropriately disclosed for at least the current period, either in the Statement or in a related tabulation." In contrast, in respect to the cash flow approach the *Opinion* states: "If the format shows the flow of cash, changes in other elements of working capital (e.g., in receivables, inventories, and payables) constitute sources and uses of cash and should accordingly be disclosed in appropriate detail in the *body* of the Statement" (italics supplied). This difference in reporting can be clearly observed by comparing the illustrations in Part A with Part B (identical data are assumed in both parts) of this chapter.

Cash flow analyses may be prepared from two distinctly different points of view:

1. A summary of the debits and credits (including changes) to the cash account.

2. A statement of the sources that generated cash inflow (such as net income, sale of fixed assets, increase in a liability, or sale of capital stock) and the applications (uses) of cash (such as the purchase of fixed assets, payment of a liability, payment of a dividend, or the purchase of treasury stock).

A summary of the cash account, (1) above, is generally considered to be a superficial presentation; in contrast the concept of sources and applications of cash is particularly relevant. This latter concept is explicit throughout the discussions in this chapter; it has much more relevance for decision making both by the management and the investor.

On pages 995 through 998 a series of transactions were analyzed to demonstrate their effects upon both cash and working capital. At this point in your study it would be desirable to review that illustration paying particular attention to the cash flow effects. Observe in those simple transactions that it was easy to identify the cash generated and applied in each instance and also the cash generated by net income (operations) of $12,000. Alternatively, this amount could have been derived by the short-cut method of starting with reported net income and by adding (and deducting) thereto the noncash items included on the income statement. This would convert net income computed on an accrual basis to net income on a cash basis. Using the data given on page 996 the short-cut computation would be:

Net income reported (accrual basis) ....$ 8,000
Add (deduct) noncash items affecting the income statement:
   Trade receivables increase .... (10,000)
   Trade payables increase 5,000
   Inventory decrease 3,000
   Depreciation expense 4,000
   Accrued expense increase.. 2,000
   Gain on sale of fixed asset .... (2,000)
Cash generated by operations (net income adjusted
   to a cash basis) $10,000

The summary presented on page 998 reflects the *cash generated and applied* by the eight illustrative transactions. In that summary you can observe the fundamental distinction between a statement of changes in financial position prepared on a cash basis versus a working capital basis. With these concepts in mind we can proceed directly to the development of the statement on a cash basis in more complex situations.

Work Sheet to Develop Statement of Changes in Financial Position—Cash Basis

Development of a statement of changes in financial position on the cash basis, except in the simplest of situations, requires an organized approach to analyzing the transactions for the period. For complex situations and those involving a large number of transactions the work sheet approach is practically necessary. Since the general format of the statement of changes in financial position is the same under either the working capital or cash approaches, we can utilize the same work sheet approach for each. In order to simplify the illustrations in this part of the chapter we have decided to parallel the work sheet format shown in Illustration 25-6 with a few changes in terminology (essentially from the words *working capital* to *cash*). For the first and simplified example, we will utilize the data for Adamson Company given on page 999. The cash basis work sheet for these data is shown in Illustration 25-9. In preparing the work sheet the summarized transactions are analyzed and entered in debit-credit format under the pair of columns headed "Analysis of Interim Entries." Observe that, as under the working capital basis, the original entries are repeated with adaptation and entry at the bottom of the work sheet for the original debits and credits to cash. Fundamentally the work sheet reflects the following major side captions:

Cash—Entered on the work sheet simply as a "balancing" feature.

Noncash Accounts—All of the noncash accounts from the beginning and ending balance sheets are entered on the worksheet for analysis and reconciliation. It is in the analysis of the noncash accounts that we find the sources and applications of cash; or, to state it another way, to identify the *causes* of the changes in cash during the period. As with the working capital approach, we are also able to identify and "pull out" the effects of the "in and out" items. You will recall that these are noncash investing and financing activities that did not affect (flow through) cash.

Financial Resources Generated—This major caption is subdivided for net income, extraordinary items, other sources of cash, and finally for the noncash financing activities.

Financial Resources Applied—This major caption is subdivided for cash applied for nonoperating items and for noncash resources applied.

Net Increase (Decrease) in Cash for the Period

In developing the work sheet (and the related statement) on a working capital basis, *net income* is converted from an accrual basis amount

Illustration 25–9
ADAMSON COMPANY
Work Sheet to Develop Statement of Changes in Financial Position — Cash Basis
(for the year ended December 31, 1971)

Debits	Balance Dec. 31, 1970	Analysis of Interim Entries Debit		Analysis of Interim Entries Credit		Balance Dec. 31, 1971
Cash	$ 30,000	(p)	$ 15,000			$ 45,000
Noncash Accounts:						
Accounts receivable (net)	40,000			(d & f)	$ 2,000	38,000
Inventory	60,000	(c)	7,000			67,000
Permanent investments	200,000			(l)	38,000	162,000
Land	100,000	(i)	28,000			128,000
Building (net)		(n − 1)	100,000	(o)	2,000	98,000
Total	$430,000					$538,000

Credits						
Accounts payable	$ 40,000	(b & g)	4,000			$ 36,000
Notes payable, short term (nontrade)	30,000	(k)	6,000			24,000
Bonds payable	50,000	(m − 1)	25,000	(h)	10,000	35,000
Mortgage payable				(n − 2)	100,000	100,000
Common stock	270,000			(m − 2)	25,000	295,000
Retained earnings	40,000	(j)	25,000	(a)	33,000	48,000
Total	$430,000		$210,000		$210,000	$538,000

Financial Resources Generated:					
Cash generated:					
Net income	(a)	$ 33,000			
Adjustments for noncash items:					
Inventory increase			(c)	$ 7,000	
Accounts payable decrease			(b & g)	4,000	
Accounts receivable decrease	(d & f)	2,000			
Depreciation expense	(o)	2,000			
Extraordinary items generating cash:					
Permanent investment sold	(l)	38,000			
Cash from other sources:					
Bonds payable sold	(h)	10,000			
Noncash Financing Activities:					
Common stock issued to retire bonds payable	(m − 2)	25,000			
Mortgage payable issued for building	(n − 2)	100,000			
Financial Resources Applied:					
Cash applied for nonoperating items:					
Land purchased			(i)	28,000	
Dividends paid			(j)	25,000	
Notes paid, short term (nontrade)			(k)	6,000	
Noncash resources applied:					
Bonds payable retired by issuing common stock			(m − 1)	25,000	
Building acquired, gave long-term mortgage			(n − 1)	100,000	
Net increase in cash for the period			(p)	15,000	
		$210,000		$210,000	

to a working capital basis (i.e., working capital generated by operations exclusive of extraordinary items). This identical concept is carried over to the cash basis work sheet (and the related statement); that is, net income on an accrual basis is converted to a *cash basis* (i.e., cash generated by operations exclusive of extraordinary items). Therefore, in Illustration 25–9 (work sheet, cash basis) and Illustration 25–10 (statement, cash basis) you will observe that the "adjustments" to net income are for all *noncash charges and credits* reported on the income statement.[5]

In studying Illustration 25–9 (Adamson Company) you are urged to compare it with the comparable work sheet under the working capital basis shown in Illustration 25–4. The interim entries reflected in Illustration 25–9 (cash basis) are identical with those entered in Illustration 25–4 (working capital basis) except for the following:

	Original Entry	Worksheet Entry
(c) Inventory increase of $7,000:		
Inventory..7,000		7,000
Cost of Goods Sold	7,000	
Cash Generated, Net Income (adjustment)...............................		7,000

Analysis: This change in a noncash account must be reconciled. Cash generated is credited as an adjustment to net income since this item represents a noncash credit to cost of goods sold through the inventory increase.

(b & g) Decrease in accounts payable, $4,000:		
Accounts payable..4,000		4,000
Cash..	4,000	
Cash Generated, Net Income (adjustment).....................................		4,000

Analysis: This is the net effect of two entries: (b) purchases of goods on account, $58,000, and (g) payment on accounts, $62,000. They

---

[5] General practice is to start with net income and add (or deduct) the noncash items to derive the cash or working capital generated from operations. Alternatively, many accountants prefer instead to start with "cash (or working capital) revenues" and then deduct therefrom the "cash (or working capital) expenses." This approach gives precisely the same cash or working capital generated by operations. Both approaches were demonstrated in respect to the data given on pages 996–97. On this point *APB Opinion 19* states: "An acceptable alternative procedure, which gives the same result, is to begin with total revenue that provided working capital or cash during the period and deduct operating costs and expenses that required the outlay of working capital or cash during the period. In either case the resulting amount of working capital or cash should be appropriately described, e.g., 'Working capital provided from [used in] operations for the period, exclusive of extraordinary items.' This total should be immediately followed by working capital or cash provided or used by income or loss from extraordinary items, if any; extraordinary income or loss should be similarly adjusted for items recognized that did not provide or use working capital or cash during the period."

could be represented on the work sheet as two entries; however, it is convenient to combine them for the net effect. The decrease in accounts payable affects one noncash account that must be reconciled. Cash generated is credited as an adjustment to net income since this item represents a noncash credit through cost of goods sold.

(d & f) Decrease in accounts receivable $2,000:

Cash..2,000			
Cash Generated, Net Income (adjustment).......		2,000	
Accounts Receivable.............................		2,000	2,000

Analysis: This is the net effect of two entries: (d) sales on account of $100,000, and (f) collections on receivables, $102,000. They could be represented on the work sheet as two entries; however, it is convenient to combine them for the net effect. Cash generated is debited as an adjustment to net income since this item represents a noncash debit to income (sales).

(k) Paid short-term notes payable (nontrade) $6,000:

Notes Payable – Short Term (nontrade)............6,000		6,000	
Cash..	6,000		
Cash Applied for Nonoperating Items.......			6,000

Analysis: This item affected a noncash account and represented the use of cash for an item not related to the income statement. Note – It did not appear on the working capital analysis since the transaction did not affect a nonworking capital account.

Since the work sheet involves an analysis of all noncash accounts, it is obvious that all transactions as summarized (except the rare cash to cash transaction) would be reflected on the work sheet. Entry (p) is an optional "balancing" entry. Observe, the arithmetical checks at two horizontal levels on the work sheet.

Preparing the Statement of Changes in Financial Position (Cash Basis)

The completed work sheet (Illustration 25–9) provides all of the details needed to prepare the statement of changes in financial position (cash basis) in conformity with the criteria of *APB Opinion 19*. Observe on the cash basis statement, in contrast to the working-capital-basis statement, that it is not necessary to include a section comparable to "Changes in Working Capital Accounts." As was discussed in respect to the working capital basis, the statement on a cash basis may be prepared under flexible guidelines. Accordingly, we offer two alternative presentations that tend to be on the extreme ends of the scale between minimum reporting (Illustration 25–10) and maximum reporting (Illustration 25–11). As practice develops under the guidance of *APB Opinion 19*, some middle ground between these two alternatives is likely to dominate.

Illustration 25-10
ADAMSON COMPANY
Statement of Changes in Financial Position—Cash Basis—
Minimum Reporting
(for the year ended December 31, 1971)

Cash Generated:
Income before extraordinary items $33,000
  Add (deduct) items not requiring, or generating,
  cash during the current period:
    Inventory increase .... (7,000)
    Trade payables decrease... (4,000)
    Trade receivables decrease 2,000
    Depreciation expense 2,000
  Total cash generated by operations exclusive of
    extraordinary items... $ 26,000
Extraordinary items generating cash:
  Permanent investments sold... 38,000
Other sources of cash:
  Bonds payable sold 10,000
    Total cash generated .... $ 74,000
Cash Applied:
  Land purchased.. $28,000
  Dividends paid.. 25,000
  Notes—short term (nontrade) paid...................................... 6,000
    Total cash applied.. 59,000
    Increase in Cash for the Period .... $ 15,000

Financing and Investing Activities Not Affecting Cash:
  Bonds payable retired by issuing common stock...................... $ 25,000
  Building acquired, gave long-term mortgage payable 100,000
    Total... $125,000

Illustration 25-11
ADAMSON COMPANY
Statement of Changes in Financial Position—Cash Basis—
Maximum Reporting
(for the year ended December 31, 1971)

Financial Resources Generated:
Cash generated:
Income before extraordinary items .... $ 33,000
  Add (deduct) items not requiring, or generating,
  cash during the current period:
    Inventory increase.. (7,000)
    Trade payables decrease .... (4,000)
    Trade receivables decrease.. 2,000
    Depreciation expense.. 2,000
  Total cash generated by operations exclusive of
    extraordinary items.. $ 26,000
Extraordinary items generating cash:
  Permanent investments sold 38,000
Other sources of cash:
  Bonds payable sold... 10,000
    Total cash generated... $ 74,000
Financial resources generated not affecting cash:
  Common stock issued to retire bonds payable .... $ 25,000
  Mortgage payable issued for building acquired...................... 100,000
    Total... 125,000
    Total Financial Resources Generated $199,000

Illustration 25–11 (*continued*)

Financial Resources Applied:		
Cash applied for nonoperating items:		
Land purchased	$ 28,000	
Dividends paid	25,000	
Notes – short term (nontrade) paid	6,000	
Total cash applied for nonoperating items		$ 59,000
Financial resources applied not affecting cash:		
Bonds payable retired by issuing common stock	$ 25,000	
Building acquired, gave long-term mortgage	100,000	
Total		125,000
Increase in cash during the period		15,000
Total Financial Resources Applied		$199,000

Comprehensive Illustration

The data for F. P. Corporation provided in Illustration 25–5 are also used to illustrate some of the complexities omitted from the previous illustration. The cash basis work sheet is reflected in Illustration 25–12 and the resultant statement of changes in financial position (cash basis) is shown in Illustration 25–13. You are urged to

Illustration 25–12

F. P. CORPORATION

Work Sheet to Develop a Statement of Changes in Financial Position – Cash Basis
(for the year ended December 31, 19B)

Debits	*Balance Dec. 31, 19A*	*Analysis of Interim Entries* *Debit*		*Credit*		*Balance Dec. 31, 19B*
Cash	$ 30,000	(u)	$ 66,000			$ 96,000
Noncash Accounts:						
Marketable securities	10,000	(m)	2,000	(n – 2)	$ 4,000	8,000
Accounts receivable (net)	50,000	(a & q)	30,000			80,000
Inventory	20,000	(c)	10,000			30,000
Prepaid expenses		(f)	2,000			2,000
Land	60,000	(i – 1)	25,000	(k)	35,000	60,000
		(l)	10,000			
Machinery	80,000			(p)	15,000	65,000
Other assets	29,000	(s – 1)	10,000			39,000
Discount on bonds payable	1,000			(t)	100	900
Total	$280,000					$380,900
Credits						
Accumulated depreciation	$ 20,000	(p)	3,000	(e)	7,900	$ 24,900
Accounts payable	40,000			(b & r)	15,000	55,000
Dividends payable				(g – 2)	15,000	15,000
Bonds payable	70,000	(o – 1)	20,000	(i – 2)	25,000	80,000
				(j)	5,000	
Common stock	100,000			(h)	10,000	110,000
Preferred stock	20,000			(o – 2)	20,000	50,000
				(s – 2)	10,000	
Retained earnings	30,000	(g)	15,000	(a)	45,000	46,000
		(h)	10,000			
		(n – 1)	4,000			
	$280,000		$207,000		$207,000	$380,900

Illustration 25–12 (*continued*)

Analysis of Interim Entries

	Debit	Credit
Financial Resources Generated:		
Cash generated:		
Net income............................	(a) $ 45,000	(k) $ 10,000
		(p) 8,000
Adjustments for noncash items:		
Depreciation expense	(e) 7,900	
Amortization of bond discount	(t) 100	
Inventory increase..............		(c) 10,000
Prepaid expenses increase.......................		(f) 2,000
Accounts receivable increase....................		(a & q) 30,000
Accounts payable increase...	(b & r) 15,000	
Extraordinary items generating cash:		
Land sold.......................	(k) 45,000	
Machinery sold	(p) 20,000	
Cash from other sources:		
Bonds payable sold..........	(j) 5,000	
Noncash financing activities:		
Liability for dividends declared........................	(g – 2) 15,000	
Bonds payable issued for land acquired..................	(i – 2) 25,000	
Preferred stock issued to retire bonds....................	(o – 2) 20,000	
Marketable securities used to pay dividends on preferred stock..............................	(n – 2) 4,000	
Preferred stock issued for other assets.....................	(s – 2) 10,000	
Financial Resources Applied:		
Cash applied for nonoperating items:		
Land purchased		(l) 10,000
Marketable securities purchased......................		(m) 2,000
Noncash resources applied:		
Dividends declared but not paid..............................		(g – 1) 15,000
Land acquired by issuing bonds payable................		(i – 1) 25,000
Bonds retired by issuing preferred stock...............		(o – 1) 20,000
Dividends on preferred stock paid with marketable securities........................		(n – 1) 4,000
Other assets acquired by issuing preferred stock.....		(s – 1) 10,000
Net increase in cash during the period		(u) 66,000
	$212,000	$212,000

follow each transaction through the work sheet, remembering the principles and concepts previously discussed. In this respect it should be helpful to compare this work sheet and statement with those for the F. P. Corporation on a working capital basis as reflected in Illustrations 25–6, 25–7 and 25–8.

Illustration 25–13
F. P. CORPORATION
Statement of Changes in Financial Position—Cash Basis—Maximum Reporting
(for the year ended December 31, 19B)

Financial Resources Generated:

Cash generated:

Net income before extraordinary items	$27,000	
Add (deduct) items not requiring, or generating, cash during the current period:		
Depreciation expense	7,900	
Amortization of discount on bonds payable	100	
Inventory increase	(10,000)	
Prepaid expenses increase	(2,000)	
Trade accounts receivable increase	(30,000)	
Trade accounts payable increase	15,000	
Total cash generated by operations exclusive of extraordinary items		$ 8,000
Extraordinary items generating cash:		
Land sold	$45,000	
Machinery sold	20,000	
Total cash generated by extraordinary items		65,000
Other sources of cash:		
Bonds issued		5,000
Total cash generated		$ 78,000
Financial resources generated not affecting cash:		
Liability for dividends declared but not paid	$15,000	
Bonds payable issued for land acquired	25,000	
Preferred stock issued to retire bonds payable	20,000	
Marketable securities used to pay dividends on preferred stock	4,000	
Preferred stock issued for other assets	10,000	
Total		74,000
Total Financial Resources Generated		$152,000

Financial Resources Applied:

Cash applied for nonoperating items:

Land purchased	$10,000	
Marketable securities purchased	2,000	
Total cash applied for nonoperating items		$ 12,000
Financial resources applied not affecting cash:		
Dividends declared but not paid	$15,000	
Land acquired by issuing bonds payable	25,000	
Bonds payable retired by issuing preferred stock	20,000	
Dividends on preferred stock paid with marketable securities	4,000	
Other assets acquired by issuing preferred stock	10,000	
Total		74,000
Increase in cash during the period		66,000
Total Financial Resources Applied		$152,000

Concluding Note

The statements of changes in financial position, and the related work sheets, are being presented approximately three months after the issuance of *APB Opinion 19*. This *Opinion* is noteworthy in that it (*a*) for the first time, requires that a statement reporting all of the financing and investing activities be included in the annual financial report (and subject to the auditor's opinion), (b) narrows reporting alternatives by establishing specific criteria that the report must satisfy, and (c) leaves the development of the format to be developed by "practice." Over the next few years it will be particularly interesting to see how "practice" handles this new assignment and the extent to which the decisional needs of investors generally are met. The authors hope that generally these needs will be met by a trend toward what we suggest as "maximum" reporting. In any event one should appreciate that both problem-solving approaches (the work sheet and the statement format) involve a wide range of alternatives and judgments.

QUESTIONS FOR CLASS DISCUSSION

1. Briefly explain the objectives and significance of the statement of changes in financial position.

2. Define the "working capital" concept of funds and explain why a statement reflecting the changes in working capital does not explain all financing and investing activities.

3. Explain the difference between (a) changes in the content of working capital and (b) causes of the changes in working capital.

4. Why is it necessary that the changes in the noncurrent accounts rather than the changes in the current accounts be analyzed in developing the statement of changes in financial position?

5. Why is it that the net change in a nonworking capital account balance frequently will not provide a full explanation of the effect on working capital? Give an example to illustrate this point.

6. The income statement for X Company reported a net income of $10,000. The statement also showed a deduction for depreciation of $5,000. Give the working capital generated by operations and explain why it is different from the net income.

7. The income statement for Y Company reported a net loss of $7,000. The statement also showed a deduction for depreciation of $6,000 and amortization of patents of $3,000. In addition the statement showed amortization of premium on bonds payable of $1,000. Compute the working capital generated by operations and explain why it is different from net profit or loss.

8. Give an example of working capital generated involving (a) noncurrent assets, (b) noncurrent liabilities, (c) capital stock, and (d) retained earnings.

9. Give an example of working capital applied involving (a) noncurrent assets, (b) noncurrent liabilities, (c) capital stock, and (d) retained earnings.

10. Assume the sale of a fixed asset costing $10,000, one-half depreciated, for $6,000. Give the working capital generated by this transaction. Ex-

plain why an adjustment to the net income for the loss or gain in this transaction may be necessary to determine the amount of working capital generated.

11. Explain why net income is adjusted for the depreciation amount but not for the estimated bad debt amount in determining working capital generated.

12. In general, what is the effect on working capital of a net loss from operations? Explain how working capital may be generated from operations although there is a net loss.

13. What is the essential difference between a statement of changes in financial position prepared on a cash basis compared with one prepared on a working capital basis?

14. Why is the cash basis generally more relevant than the working capital basis for evaluating the financing and investing activities of an enterprise?

15. Distinguish between (a) a summary of the debits and credits to the cash account and (b) a report on the sources and applications of cash.

DECISION CASE 25–1

The following statement was prepared by the controller of the Clovis Company. The controller indicated that this statement was prepared under the "all financial resources" concept of funds, which is the broadest concept of funds and includes "all financing and investing activities."

CLOVIS COMPANY
Statement of Source and Application of Funds
(December 31, 19B)

Funds were provided by:

Contribution of plant site by the city of Camden (Note 1)	$115,000
Net income after extraordinary items per income statement (Note 2)	75,000
Issuance of note payable—due 19F	60,000
Depreciation and amortization	50,000
Deferred income taxes relating to accelerated depreciation	10,000
Sale of equipment—book value (Note 3)	5,000
Total Funds Provided	$315,000

Funds were applied to:

Acquisition of future plant site (Note 1)	$250,000
Increase in working capital	30,000
Cash dividends declared but not paid	20,000
Acquisition of equipment	15,000
Total Funds Applied	$315,000

Notes to Financial Statement

1. The city of Camden donated a plant site to Clovis Company valued by the board of directors at $115,000. The company purchased adjoining property for $135,000.
2. Research and development expenditures of $25,000 incurred in 19B were expensed. These expenses were considered abnormal.
3. Equipment with a book value of $5,000 was sold for $8,000. The gain was included as an extraordinary item on the income statement.

Required:

1. Why is it considered desirable to present a statement similar to the above in the financial reports?

2. Define and discuss the relative merits of the following three concepts used in funds flow analysis in terms of their measurement accuracy and freedom from manipulation (window dressing) in one accounting period:

a) Cash concept of funds.

b) Net monetary assets (quick assets) concept of funds.

c) Working capital concept of funds.

3. In view of *APB Opinion 19*, identify and discuss the weaknesses in presentation and disclosure in the above statement for Clovis Company. Your discussion should explain why you consider them to be weaknesses and what you consider the proper treatment of the items to be. Do not prepare a revised statement.

(AICPA adapted)

EXERCISES

Exercise 25–1

The balance sheets for Heinen Company showed the following information.

	December 31	
	19A	*19B*
Cash	$ 4,000	$ 5,000
Accounts receivable (net)	5,000	9,000
Inventory	10,000	12,000
Permanent investments	2,000	
Fixed assets	30,000	47,000
	$51,000	$73,000
Accumulated depreciation on fixed assets	$ 5,000	$ 7,000
Accounts payable	3,000	5,000
Notes payable, short term (nontrade)	4,000	3,000
Long-term notes payable	10,000	18,000
Common stock	25,000	29,000
Retained earnings	4,000	11,000
	$51,000	$73,000

Additional data concerning changes in the noncurrent accounts:

a) Net income for the year 19B, $14,000.

b) Depreciation on fixed assets for the year, $2,000.

c) Sold the permanent investments at cost.

d) Paid dividends of $7,000.

e) Purchased fixed assets costing $5,000; paid cash.

f) Purchased fixed assets and gave a $12,000 long-term note payable.

g) Paid a $4,000 long-term note payable by issuing common stock.

Required:

1. Determine the increase or decrease in working capital.

2. Prepare a statement of changes in financial position (working capital basis) without the use of a work sheet. Use the format of Illustration 25–3 as a guide.

Exercise 25–2

The records of Bland Company reflected the following data.

Balance Sheet Data

	December 31	
	19A	*19B*
Cash	$ 34,000	$ 34,500
Accounts receivable (net)	12,000	17,000
Inventory	16,000	14,000
Permanent investments	6,000	
Fixed assets	80,000	93,000
Treasury stock		11,500
	$148,000	$170,000
Accumulated depreciation	$ 48,000	$ 39,000
Accounts payable	19,000	12,000
Bonds payable	10,000	30,000
Common stock	50,000	61,000
Retained earnings	21,000	28,000
	$148,000	$170,000

Additional data for the period January 1, 19B, through December 31, 19B:

a) Sales on account, $70,000.
b) Purchases on account, $40,000.
c) Depreciation, $5,000.
d) Expenses paid in cash, $18,000.
e) Decrease in inventory, $2,000.
f) Sold fixed assets for $6,000 cash; cost $21,000 and two-thirds depreciated (loss or gain is an extraordinary item).
g) Purchased fixed assets for cash, $4,000.
h) Purchased fixed assets, exchanging therefor bonds payable of $30,000.
i) Sold the permanent investments for $9,000 cash (extraordinary item).
j) Purchased treasury stock for cash, $11,500.
k) Retired bonds payable by issuing common stock, $10,000.
l) Collections on accounts receivable, $65,000.
m) Payments on accounts payable, $47,000.
n) Sold unissued common stock for cash, $1,000.

Required:

1. Prepare a work sheet to develop a statement of changes in financial position (working capital basis). Use Illustration 25–4 as a guide.

2. Prepare a statement of changes in financial position (working capital basis). Use Illustration 25–3 as a guide.

Exercise 25-3

The records of Stelec Company showed the following information relating to the balance sheet accounts.

Balance Sheet Data

	December 31	
Debits	*19A*	*19B*
Cash	$ 10,000	$ 11,000
Accounts receivable (net)	19,000	24,000
Inventory	52,000	50,000
Prepaid expenses	3,000	4,000
Permanent investments	10,000	
Buildings	90,000	120,000
Machinery	40,000	62,000
Patents	5,000	4,000
	$229,000	$275,000
Credits		
Accounts payable	$ 12,000	$ 8,000
Notes payable—short term (nontrade)	9,000	13,000
Accrued wages	3,000	2,000
Accumulated depreciation	40,000	39,000
Notes payable—long term	30,000	35,000
Common stock	120,000	150,000
Retained earnings	15,000	28,000
	$229,000	$275,000

Additional data relating to the noncurrent accounts:

a) Net income for the year was $24,000.

b) Depreciation recorded on fixed assets was $8,000.

c) Amortization of patents amounted to $1,000.

d) Purchased machinery costing $15,000; paid one third in cash and gave a five-year interest-bearing note for the balance.

e) Purchased machinery costing $25,000 which was paid for by issuing common stock.

f) Sold old machinery for $7,000 that originally cost $18,000 (one-half depreciated); loss (or gain) reported on income statement.

g) Made addition to building costing $30,000; paid cash.

h) Paid a $5,000 long-term note by issuing common stock.

i) Sold permanent investments for $12,000 cash.

j) Paid cash dividends.

k) Sales of $120,000 on account.

l) Collections on accounts receivable, $115,000.

Required:

1. Prepare a work sheet to determine changes in financial position (working capital basis). Use Illustration 25-6 as a guide.

2. Prepare a statement of changes in financial position; follow the format of Illustration 25-7.

Exercise 25-4

Utilize the data given in Exercise 25-1 to:

1. Prepare a statement of changes in financial position (cash basis) without

the use of a work sheet. Use the format of Illustration 25–10 as a guide unless directed otherwise by your instructor.

2. If Exercise 25–1 has been solved, reconcile the difference in results between your statement (cash basis) and one prepared as required in Exercise 25–1 (working capital basis).

Exercise 25–5

Utilize the data given in Exercise 25–2 to:

1. Prepare a work sheet to develop a statement of changes in financial position (cash basis). Use Illustration 25–9 as a guide unless directed otherwise by your instructor.

2. Prepare a statement of changes in financial position (cash basis). Use Illustration 25–10 as a guide unless directed otherwise by your instructor.

3. If Exercise 25–2 has been solved, reconcile the differences between your results in requirement 2 above (cash basis) with the statement developed in Exercise 25–2 (working capital basis).

Exercise 25–6

Utilize the data given in Exercise 25–3 to:

1. Prepare a work sheet to develop a statement of changes in financial position (cash basis). Use Illustration 25–12 as a guide.

2. Prepare a statement of changes in financial position (cash basis). Use Illustration 25–13 as a guide unless directed otherwise by your instructor.

3. If Exercise 25–3 has been solved, reconcile the differences between your results in requirement 2 above (cash basis) with the statement developed in Exercise 25–3 (working capital basis).

PROBLEMS

Problem 25–1

The balance sheets of Fisher Company provided the information shown below.

	December 31	
	19A	19B
Cash	$ 4,000	$ 7,000
Accounts receivable (net)	9,000	12,000
Inventory	8,000	5,000
Permanent investments	2,000	
Plant	30,000	30,000
Equipment	20,000	22,000
Land	10,000	40,000
Patents	8,000	7,000
	$91,000	$123,000
Accumulated depreciation – plant	$ 7,000	$ 10,000
Accumulated depreciation – equipment	10,000	8,000
Accounts payable	8,000	2,000
Accrued wages	1,000	
Long-term notes payable	10,000	19,000
Common stock	50,000	75,000
Retained earnings	5,000	9,000
	$91,000	$123,000

Additional data:

a) Net income for the year, $8,000.
b) Depreciation on plant for the year, $3,000.
c) Depreciation on equipment for the year, $2,000.
d) Amortization of patents for the year, $1,000.
e) Sales on account, $67,000.
f) Purchases on account, $35,000.
g) Expenses paid in cash (including accrued wages), $15,000.
h) At the end of the year sold equipment costing $8,000 (50% depreciated) for $3,000 cash; the gain or loss was recorded in the income summary account.
i) Purchased land costing $10,000; paid $2,000 cash, gave long-term note for the balance.
j) Paid $4,000 on long-term notes.
k) Sold $10,000 capital stock at par.
l) Purchased equipment costing $10,000; paid one-half cash, balance due in three years (interest-bearing note).
m) Issued $15,000 common stock for land; cost $20,000, balance in cash.
n) Collections on accounts receivable, $64,000.
o) Payment on accounts payable, $41,000.
p) Sold permanent investments at book value.
q) Paid dividends, $4,000.

Required:

1. Prepare a work sheet to develop a statement of changes in financial position (working capital basis) for 19B. Key your entries.
2. Prepare a statement of changes in financial position (use Illustration 25–8 as a guide).

Problem 25–2

The records of Supreme Trading Company provided the following summaries and incomplete data:

1. Income statement for the month of April 19XX:

Sales		$ 80,000
Less: Purchases	$ 40,000	
Increase in inventory	5,000	35,000
		$ 45,000
Expenses:		
Depreciation	$ 5,000	
Allowance for doubtful accounts	1,000	
Insurance	1,000	
Interest expense	2,000	
Salaries and wages	12,000	
Other expenses	16,000	37,000
Net income before extraordinary items		$ 8,000
Extraordinary items:		
Loss on sale of fixed assets		2,000
Net Income		$ 6,000

2. Balance sheets (unclassified):

	March 31, 19XX	April 30, 19XX
Cash	$ 15,000	$ 31,000
Accounts receivable	30,000	28,500
Allowance for doubtful accounts	1,500°	2,000°
Inventory	10,000	15,000
Prepaid insurance	2,400	1,400
Fixed assets	80,000	81,000
Accumulated depreciation	20,000°	16,000°
Land	40,100	81,100
Total	$156,000	$220,000
Accounts payable	$ 10,000	$ 11,000
Wages payable	2,000	1,000
Accrued interest expense		1,000
Long-term notes payable	20,000	46,000
Common stock	100,000	136,000
Retained earnings	24,000	25,000
Total	$156,000	$220,000

°Deductions

3. Cash account:

Debits			*Credits*	
Balance	$15,000	Purchases		$10,000
Sales	20,000	Salaries and wages		5,000
Fixed assets	4,000	Accounts payable		4,000
Sales	15,000	Salaries and wages		2,000
Notes payable	20,000	Purchases		5,000
Sales	15,000	Expenses		6,000
Accounts receivable	31,000	Dividends		5,000
Common stock	5,000	Purchases		5,000
		Expenses		10,000
		Accounts payable		6,000
		Land		20,000
		Accounts payable		9,000
		Wages		6,000
		Interest		1,000

4. Retained Earnings account showed a debit for dividends, $5,000.

5. Wrote off $500 accounts receivable as uncollectible.

6. Acquired land for common stock issued at par.

7. Acquired fixed assets costing $16,000; gave three-year, interest-bearing note.

8. Paid a $10,000 long-term note by issuing the creditor common stock at par.

Required:

1. Prepare a work sheet to develop a statement of changes in financial position (working capital basis) using Illustration 25–6 as a guide.

2. Prepare the statement of changes in financial position.

Problem 25-3

The comparative balance sheets for Reno Corporation reflected a significant increase in current assets, a relatively minor increase in current liabilities, and a low profit. The executive committee of the corporation has requested a report that shows the detailed financing and investing activities for the year 19B. You have been provided the incomplete data below and requested to prepare:

1. A work sheet that will provide data for the report (working capital basis); assume all amounts are material.

2. The formal report for the executive committee.

Balance Sheet Data

	December 31	
	19A	19B
Cash	$ 2,000	$ 11,510
U.S. bonds		2,000
Accounts receivable	7,000	8,300
Inventory	39,000	43,500
Prepaid insurance	250	225
Office supplies inventory	75	80
Sinking fund		300
Delivery equipment	5,000	16,500
Office equipment	2,000	1,900
Organization expense	600	400
Discount on 6% bonds	100	
Patents	1,000	800
Cash surrender value of life insurance policies	1,000	1,100
Land		20,000
	$58,025	$106,615
Notes payable, short term (nontrade)	$ 300	$ 250
Accounts payable	2,000	2,590
Dividends payable		1,500
Allowance for repairs	25	75
Six percent bonds payable	2,000 ·	
Seven percent bonds payable		25,000
Premium on 7% bonds		700
Allowance for doubtful accounts	700	900
Accumulated depreciation – delivery equipment	2,500	3,050
Accumulated depreciation – office equipment	400	520
Preferred stock	3,500	
Common stock	40,000	60,000
Retained earnings	6,600	11,480
Other contributed capital		250
Reserve for bond sinking fund		300
	$58,025	$106,615

Selected additional data:

a) Net income for 19B was $6,990 after extraordinary items.

b) Preferred stock, par value $500, purchased at 110 and canceled. Premium charged to Retained Earnings.

c) Common stock par value $5,000, sold at $105 per share.

d) Typewriter costing $100, recorded depreciation $80, was sold for $15. Loss reported on income statement as an extraordinary item.

e) Truck costing $500, recorded depreciation $450, sold for $30. Loss reported as extraordinary item.

f) Depreciation for the year: delivery equipment, $1,000; office equipment, $200.

g) Discount on the 6% bonds was written off as follows: July 1 amortized $25 to interest expense; July 2 by recording the retirement of the issue before maturity by payment of $1,775 cash.

h) Amortized $200 organization expense to income.

i) Paid $100 legal costs in defense of the patent rights. Amortized $300 patent costs.

j) Paid dividends on preferred stock, $260.

k) Declared $1,500 dividends on common stock, payable January 15 next year.

l) Sold $5,000 of the 7% bonds at 115 on July 1 and amortized $50 of the premium to expense.

m) Paid premium on life insurance on certain executives, $500; cash value increased $100.

n) Bad debts written off during the period totaled $1,000; the bad debt allowance for the period was $1,200.

o) During the year Repair Expense was debited for $300 and Allowance for Repairs credited; also Allowance for Repairs was debited and Cash credited for $250. Allowance for Repairs is a working capital account.

p) Office supplies of $250 were purchased during the year.

q) The U.S. bonds were purchased on August 1 as temporary investments.

r) Property insurance premiums paid totaled $150; expired premiums totaled $175.

s) Retired the preferred stock by issuing common stock.

t) Issued 7% bonds at par value for land, $20,000.

u) Acquired delivery equipment costing $12,000 by issuing common stock at par value.

Problem 25-4

Utilize the data for the Fisher Company given in Problem 25-1 to:

1. Prepare a work sheet to develop a statement of financial position (cash basis). Use Illustration 25-12 as a guide.

2. Prepare a statement of changes in financial position (cash basis). Use Illustration 25-10 as a guide unless directed otherwise by your instructor.

3. If directed to do so by your instructor, prepare a reconciliation between your results in requirement 2 above (cash basis) and the results under the working capital basis (as required in Problem 25-1).

Problem 25-5

Utilize the data for the Supreme Trading Company given in Problem 25-2 to:

1. Prepare a work sheet to develop a statement of financial position (cash basis). Use Illustration 25-12 as a guide.

2. Prepare a statement of changes in financial position (cash basis). Use Illustration 25–13 as a guide.

3. If directed to do so by your instructor, prepare a reconciliation between your results in requirement 2 above (cash basis) and the results under the working capital basis (as required in Problem 25–2).

Problem 25–6

Utilize the data for Reno Corporation given in Problem 25–3 to:

1. Prepare a work sheet to develop a statement of financial position (cash basis). Use Illustration 25–12 as a guide.

2. Prepare a statement of changes in financial position (cash basis). Use Illustration 25–13 as a guide.

3. If directed to do so by your instructor, prepare a reconciliation between your results in requirement 2 above (cash basis) and the results under the working capital basis (as required in Problem 25–3).

chapter 26	# Comparative Statements and Ratio Analyses

The purpose of this and the next chapter is to explain certain techniques by means of which accounting data may be used in the analytical and interpretive processes. The principal reason for discussing these techniques is to present to the reader the primary essentials needed for developing information whereby management, creditors, investors, and the general public may be assisted in passing financial judgment on operations and guided in estimating the probable future and operating results. These chapters do not attempt to cover the whole range of possible financial statement analyses and interpretations, but rather are limited to certain techniques having general application. Although the emphasis throughout this book has been on external reporting, most of the techniques discussed in this and the following chapter are also useful for internal purposes.

In prior chapters, principles underlying the classification, valuation, and reporting of items represented by accounting data have been described and wherever practicable illustrated. It is axiomatic that accounting principles must be followed and appropriate form observed if financial statements are to serve their full potential. Carefully prepared statements generally become more useful to the management, owner, investor, creditor, and general public when analyzed and interpreted in the light of both internal and external factors as related to the interests of the particular reader. Significantly, each group of readers has essentially different interests and needs with reference to financial statements; consequently, one of the responsibilities of the accountant is to identify these differing needs and to present analyses and interpretations consistent with them. Clearly, no one "approach" to the analysis, interpretation, and presentation of accounting data can adequately meet these diverse interests and needs.

COMPARATIVE STATEMENTS

Need for Comparative Statements

The annual financial statements relate to one period in the financial history of the entity. Trends in the financial development of a firm have particular significance to all readers. Trends in financial data may be presented in comparative statements wherein current data are shown and compared with those of one or more past periods. In addition, the comparison of current results with those of one or more prior periods provides the reader with a sense of orientation in evaluating the reasonableness of the current data; that is, the prior results provide some basis for evaluation of progress, improvement, or deterioration. In recognition of the desirability of presenting comparative financial data, the AICPA Committee on Accounting Procedure, in *Bulletin 43*, Chapter 2, stated:

1. The presentation of comparative financial statements in annual and other reports enhances the usefulness of such reports and brings out more clearly the nature and trends of current changes affecting the enterprise. Such presentation emphasizes the fact that statements for a series of periods are far more significant than those for a single period and that the accounts for one period are but an instalment of what is essentially a continuous history.

2. In any one year it is ordinarily desirable that the balance sheet, the income statement, and the surplus statement be given for one or more preceding years as well as for the current year. Footnotes, explanations, and accountants' qualifications which appeared on the statements for the preceding years should be repeated, or at least referred to, in the comparative statements to the extent that they continue to be of significance. If, because of reclassifications or for other reasons, changes have occurred in the manner of or basis for presenting corresponding items for two or more periods, information should be furnished which will explain the change. This procedure is in conformity with the well recognized principle that any change in practice which affects comparability should be disclosed.

Your attention is directed particularly to the effect of accounting changes on comparative statements; see Chapter 24.

Techniques of Comparative Statements

Some companies present comparative financial data in their published financial statements for each year covering periods of five or more years, whereas other companies present the results for the current year and prior year with an increase and decrease column. A common variation of the latter type of comparative statement is shown in part in Illustration 26–1.

Illustration 26–1
STANDARD MANUFACTURING COMPANY
Comparative Balance Sheets (incomplete)
December 31, 1970 and 1971

	December 31		Increase Decrease°
	1971	1970	1971 over 1970
ASSETS			
Current Assets:			
Cash	$ 9,000	$ 8,000	$1,000
Notes receivable	$ 1,000	$ 2,000	$1,000°
Accounts receivable	12,500	12,000	500
Total Receivables	$13,500	$14,000	$ 500°
Less: Allowance for doubtful accounts	500	480	20
Net receivables	$13,000	$13,520	$ 520°
Inventory	$22,000	$20,000	$2,000
Prepaid insurance	200	300	100°
Total Current Assets	$44,200	$41,820	$2,380

In addition to form, Illustration 26–1 points up two technical aspects of comparative statements. In the preparation of a balance sheet for one date only, use is made of two, three, or possibly four money columns. This arrangement permits the use of a single line (underscore) to indicate addition or subtraction. The placing of balance sheets for two or more periods in juxtaposition on the same report suggests that only one money column be used for each period. The subtotaling of group accounts requires, therefore, a third use of the single ruling, to denote a subtotal. Also, it may be noted that in the case of allowance for doubtful accounts, in the increase-decrease column, the increase in the allowance *adds* to the amount of the *decrease* in net receivables.

Similar techniques may be applied to the income statement, statement of retained earnings, manufacturing statement, and other accounting statements.

Percentage Analysis of Financial Statements

Financial data expressed in absolute amounts are necessary for practically all purposes; nevertheless a weakness is involved in that proportionate relationships are not clearly revealed. Thus, the expression of relationships in terms of percentages or ratios frequently adds significantly to the interpretation of financial data. There are two common forms of percentage analyses — vertical and horizontal.

Vertical analysis involves the expression of each item on a particular financial statement as a percent or ratio of one specific item which is referred to as the base. For example, the component items on the income statement generally are expressed as a percent of net sales as shown in Illustration 26–2. Note that the base (net sales) representing 100% is divided into each component item to derive the component percentages, and that the percentages may be summed. Alternatively, the relationships may be expressed as ratios, in which case net sales would represent 1.00 (rather than 100%) and the components likewise would be expressed in terms of this base.

Illustration 26–2
AUSTIN DRY GOODS STORE
Comparative Income Statements (condensed)
For the Years Ended December 31, 1970 and 1971
(vertical analysis)

	1971		1970	
	Amount	Percent of Net Sales	Amount	Percent of Net Sales
Gross sales	$151,500	101.0	$141,540	101.1
Less: Returns and allowances ...	1,500	1.0	1,540	1.1
Net sales	$150,000	100.0	$140,000	100.0
Cost of goods sold	105,000	70.0	99,400	71.0
Gross margin	$ 45,000	30.0	$ 40,600	29.0
Expenses:				
Selling expenses	$ 7,500	5.0	$ 7,560	5.4
General expenses	4,500	3.0	4,500	3.2
Financial expenses – net	750	.5	560	.4
Total Expenses	$ 12,750	8.5	$ 12,620	9.0
Net Income for Year	$ 32,250	21.5	$ 27,980	20.0

In applying vertical analysis to balance sheet data, the base (representing 100% or 1.00) generally used is the balance sheet total as shown in Illustration 26–3.

In applying vertical analysis to the statement of retained earnings, the beginning balance is commonly used as the base; in the manufacturing statement the total cost of manufacturing usually is appropriate as the base, and the analysis should not extend to the in-process inventories. Statements expressed in terms of percentages only are often referred to as *common-size* statements.

Horizontal analysis refers to the development of percentages or ratios indicating the proportionate change in the same item over *time*. The conversion of absolute amounts of change to percentages or ratios facilitates interpretation with particular reference to trends. For example, horizontal percentages shown on the partial balance

Illustration 26–3
AKRON CORPORATION
Comparative Balance Sheets (condensed)
December 31, 1970 and 1971
(vertical analysis)

	1971		1970	
	Amount	Percent	Amount	Percent
ASSETS				
Current assets	$300,000	60	$283,900	59
Long-term investments	30,000	6	38,400	8
Plant and equipment	$200,000	40	$182,400	38
Less: Accumulated depreciation	40,000	8	36,500	7
Net	$160,000	32	$145,900	31
Intangible assets	10,000	2	11,800	2
Total Assets	$500,000	100	$480,000	100
LIABILITIES				
Current liabilities	$ 75,000	15	$ 42,800	9
Long-term liabilities	125,000	25	150,000	31
Total Liabilities	$200,000	40	$192,800	40
CAPITAL				
Common stock	$200,000	40	$200,000	42
Premium on common stock	20,000	4	20,000	4
Retained earnings	80,000	16	67,200	14
Total Capital	$300,000	60	$287,200	60
Total Liabilities and Capital	$500,000	100	$480,000	100

sheets and income statements in Illustration 26–4 serve to emphasize the trend of each component.[1]

It should be noted in the examples relating to horizontal analysis that in computing the percent as well as the amounts of increase or decrease, the base year usually is the earlier period. The percents may not be added or subtracted as between lines since each separate component percentage has a different base. In this respect, attention should be called to the incorrectness of percentages of increase and decrease which are computed from negative or zero base-year amounts. For example, assume a net loss in 19A of $5,000 and a net gain in 19B of $5,000. With an actual increase of $10,000 the ratio of increase appears to be a minus 200% (+10,000 ÷ −$5,000), a computation which is positively misleading as well as mathematically incorrect. Manifestly, percentage figures should not be computed for accounts which for the base year had no balance or a negative balance. The table in Illustration 26–5 points out the proper procedure to be

---

[1] In percentage and ratio analysis it is generally desirable to round to whole percents.

Illustration 26–4
(Horizontal Analysis)
(a) Partial Balance Sheets

	December 31		Increase or Decrease° 1971 over 1970	
	1971	1970	Amount	Percent
Current Assets:				
Cash	$ 18,000	$ 15,000	$ 3,000	20
Accounts receivable	$ 44,000	$ 40,000	$ 4,000	10
Less: Estimated bad debts	1,800	2,000	200°	10°
Net receivables	$ 42,200	$ 38,000	$ 4,200	11
Inventory	$ 51,000	$ 60,000	$ 9,000°	15°
Prepaid expenses	525	500	25	5
Total Current Assets	$111,725	$113,500	$ 1,775°	2°

(b) Partial Income Statements

Gross sales	$126,000	$105,000	$21,000	20
Less: Returns and allowances	7,000	5,000	2,000	40
Net sales	$119,000	$100,000	$19,000	19
Cost of goods sold:				
Beginning inventory	$ 30,000	$ 20,000	$10,000	50
Purchases	79,000	80,000	1,000°	1°
Total	$109,000	$100,000	$ 9,000	9
Final inventory	25,000	30,000	5,000°	17°
Cost of goods sold	$ 84,000	$ 70,000	$14,000	20
Gross Margin	$ 35,000	$ 30,000	$ 5,000	17

Illustration 26–5
Computing Differences

	December 31		Increase-Decrease°	
	19B	19A	Amount	Percent
Positive amounts in the base year (19A):				
Item No. 1	$ 200°	$800	$1,000°	125°
2	—	800	800°	100°
3	200	800	600°	75°
4	1,200	800	400	50
Negative amounts in the base year (19A):				
Item No. 5	1,000°	800°	200°	—
6	200	800°	1,000	—
7	—	800°	800	—
No amounts in the base year (19A):				
Item No. 8	200	—	200	—
9	200°	—	200°	—

followed in the computation of percentages resulting from horizontal increases and decreases.

In considering percentage increases or decreases the analyst also should be aware of misleading inferences when the amounts are small. For example, assume a particular expense in 19A was $10 and in 19B, $30. The percentage increase is 200% which appears significant despite the fact that there was only a $20 increase.

When the statements for more than two years are to be compared, the columns may be shown as in Illustration 26–6. Note that the base for 19B changes is 19A, while the base for 19C changes is 19B.

Illustration 26–6
Determination of Base Period

	December 31			Increase–Decrease°		Percent of Increase–Decrease°	
	19C	19B	19A	During 19C	During 19B	During 19C	During 19B
Item No. 1..........	$200	$400	$300	$200°	$100	50.0°	33.3
2..........	400	300	200	100	100	33.3	50.0
3..........	400	300	400	100	100°	33.3	25.0°

Use and Interpretation of Comparative Statements

Practically all serious readers of financial statements will benefit significantly from comparative data and percentage analyses. In this respect a word of caution is in order; the accountant, whether industrial or public, must be discriminating in the selection of data to be presented to the several groups of readers; for example, an income statement prepared for internal use may well be quite different from one prepared for external use. Frequently, the quantitative data presented are so voluminous that the reader is confused rather than enlightened, or perhaps completely discouraged, thereby precluding serious consideration of the data. It should be realized that large volumes of complex tabulations dismay the average person. Discrimination must be exercised in selecting (a) data relevant to the normal problems of the intended reader and (b) appropriate analyses of data that will shed light on the situations generally confronting the reader. These comments reemphasize that no one set of statements is appropriate for all readers — reports, and the data therein, must be consistent with the needs of the primary user.

In developing and presenting financial data, the accountant should keep in mind a fundamental principle of management — the *exception principle*. This principle holds that management should devote detailed attention chiefly to the exceptions, the out-of-line items, rather than the routine items, thereby having sufficient time for overall policy and planning considerations. As applied to accounting data and reports, the exception principle would require the emphasis of differences or *variations* which reveal for the reader the unusual or exceptional items. This principle has particular application for internal financial reports designed to aid management in planning and controlling operations.

It was mentioned previously that comparative statements are significant in that *trends* are indicated; however, it must be realized that they have somewhat limited application for internal control purposes. In comparing actual current data with actual data from a prior period for control purposes, the prior period data are given the status of a *standard*. In this connection it is important to realize that actual data for a prior period generally represent a very unreliable standard against which current performance may be measured since:

1. General and/or specific economic conditions may have changed during the current period.
2. Internal operations (products, methods of manufacture, organization, etc.) may be different from those of the prior period.
3. Accounting procedures and classifications may have been changed.
4. Volume of business (goods sold, manufactured, inventoried, etc.) may be more or less than in the prior period.
5. General price-level changes (change in value of the dollar) may have occurred.
6. Prior period's figures may represent the results of gross inefficiencies.

Comparison of actual data with *budgeted* data and *standards* is a significantly more meaningful comparison for management planning and control purposes.

In interpreting comparative data and the related percentage analyses, the accountant, and reader as well, should recognize unusual or nonrecurring items that are reflected in the data for each of the periods. Where possible, nonrecurring items should be removed from the data prior to analysis. Changes in the general price level (value of the dollar) may have a significant monetary effect on financial data covering a long period of time. In such cases it may be desirable to express data for all periods in terms of dollars of current (or common) purchasing power (see Chapter 23).

RATIO ANALYSES

Nature of Ratio Analyses

A ratio is an expression of a relationship between two amounts. Such a relationship may be expressed as a fraction, a percent, or a decimal. The application of ratio analyses to financial data involves the selection of two separate amounts (balances of accounts or groups of accounts) and the dividing of one by the other. For example, assume a direct labor cost of $10,000 and sales of $200,000, the relationship between these two factors ($10,000/$200,000) could be expressed as $\frac{1}{20}$, 5%, or .05. Obviously, the horizontal and vertical percentage analyses discussed in the preceding section are specific examples of ratio analyses.

Ratio analyses are significant only when the relationship between the selected factors sheds additional light on the interpretation of the individual absolute amounts. Ratio analyses may compare (a) two items from the same statement or (b) items from two different financial statements such as the balance sheet and the income statement. In view of the large number of ratios that could be computed it is important that the accountant select for presentation only those ratios that appear to have the greatest significance. In determining "significance," consideration must be given to the purposes for which the ratios are to be used. Investors, managers, and creditors have essentially different interests and problems; consequently, they would have somewhat different needs with respect to ratio analyses. Since a complete study of ratio analyses is outside the scope of this text, only representative ratios having general application are discussed. The selected ratios will be explained under the following general headings:

1. Ratios indicating current position.
2. Ratios indicating equity position.
3. Ratios indicating income position and operating results.

Ratios Indicating Current Position

The current position of a firm refers to the relationship of current assets to current liabilities. Analyses designed to provide a basis for evaluating the current position are of particular interest to practically all interested groups — management, investors, and creditors. The principal ratios that are generally useful in analyses of working capital (defined as current assets less current liabilities) are shown in Illustration 26–7.

It will be observed that the analysis of current position involves (a) tests of overall solvency and (b) evaluations of the movement of current assets (turnovers).[2]

Current Ratio. The current or working capital ratio has long been recognized as an index of solvency, or the ability of the firm to meet the currently maturing creditor claims and operating costs. The amount of working capital and the related ratio have a direct bearing

---

[2] The reader should be cautioned that there is no single "generally accepted" method of computing specific ratios or of determining the values to be substituted in the formulas. Generally the precise computation should be determined by (1) the data available and (2) the use and interpretation expected in the particular situation. The formulas given herein are indicative of the general approach.

on the amount of short-term credit that should be granted. Traditionally, a working capital ratio of 2 to 1 has been considered to be adequate; however, the recent trend has been away from the use of such rule-of-thumb standards.

Illustration 26-7
Ratios Indicating Current Position

Ratio	Formula for Computation	Significance
Tests of overall solvency:		
1. Current ratio or working capital ratio	$\dfrac{\text{Current Assets (Net)}}{\text{Current Liabilities}}$	Primary test of solvency— indicates ability to meet current obligations from current assets as a going concern. Measure of adequacy of working capital.
2. Acid-test ratio or quick ratio.	$\dfrac{\text{Quick Assets (Net)}}{\text{Current Liabilities}}$	A more severe test of immediate solvency than the current ratio. Tests ability to meet sudden demands upon current assets.
3. Working capital to total assets.	$\dfrac{\text{Working Capital}}{\text{Total Assets (Net)}}$	Indicates relative liquidity of total assets and distribution of resources employed.
Ratios indicating movement of current assets (turnover):		
4. *a)* Receivable turnover.	$\dfrac{\text{Net Credit Sales}}{\text{Average Receivables (Net)}}$	Velocity of collection of trade accounts and notes. Test of efficiency of collection.
b) Age of receivables.	$\dfrac{365 \text{ (Days)}}{\text{Receivable Turnover}}$ (Computed per [*a*] Above)	Average number of days to collect receivables.
5. Inventory turnover. *a)* Merchandise turnover (retail firm).	$\dfrac{\text{Cost of Goods Sold}}{\text{Average Merchandise Inventory}}$	Indicates liquidity of inventory. Number of times inventory "turned over" or was sold on the average during the period. Will exhibit tendency to over- or understock.
b) Finished goods turnover (manufacturing firm).	$\dfrac{\text{Cost of Goods Sold}}{\text{Average Finished Goods Inventory}}$	Same as 5(*a*)
c) Raw material turnover.	$\dfrac{\text{Cost of Raw Materials Used}}{\text{Average Raw Materials Inventory}}$	Number of times raw material inventory was "used" on the average during the period.
d) Days' supply in inventory.	$\dfrac{365 \text{ (Days)}}{\text{Inventory Turnover}}$ (Computed per [*a*], [*b*], or [*c*] Above)	Average number of days' supply in the ending inventory. Indicates general condition of over- or understocking as the case may be.
6. Working capital turnover.	$\dfrac{\text{Net Sales}}{\text{Average Working Capital}}$	Indicates adequacy and activity of working capital.
7. Percent of each current asset to total current assets.	$\dfrac{\text{Each Current Asset}}{\text{Total Current Assets}}$	Indicates relative investment in each current asset.

It must be realized that the peculiarities of the industry in which the firm operates and other factors, such as methods of operations and seasonal influences, should be taken into account in evaluating the current ratio. In computing the ratio, *restricted* assets should be excluded and all current liabilities should be included. (Such as the so-called liability reserves owed externally.)

It should be realized that the working capital ratio is only one measure or index of solvency and ability to meet short-term obligations. A high working capital ratio may be the result of overstocking of inventory; a firm may have a high current ratio while at the same time it may have a cash deficit. In addition an extremely high working capital ratio may indicate excess funds which should be invested or otherwise put to use. As with all ratios there is a delicate balance between a ratio that is too high and one that is too low. The determination of the most desirable ratio varies from firm to firm, and the determination of the optimum ratio for a particular firm is a complex problem.

Acid-Test Ratio. Cash, accounts receivable, short-term notes receivable, and temporary investments in marketable securities generally represent funds which may be made readily available for paying current obligations, hence are referred to as *quick assets*. Inventories, on the other hand, must be sold and collection made before cash is available for paying obligations. In many cases, particularly where there are raw materials and work in process inventories, the time element as well as marketability involve considerable uncertainty. In view of these considerations the acid-test or quick ratio (quick assets divided by current liabilities) has come into general usage as a significant test of immediate solvency. An acid-test ratio of 1 to 1 traditionally, by the rule-of-thumb standard, has been considered to be desirable. As with the current ratio, the acid-test ratio for a particular company must be evaluated in the light of industry characteristics and other factors discussed throughout this chapter.

Working Capital to Total Assets. The ratio of working capital to total assets generally is considered to be an important ratio in that it is a generalized expression of the distribution and liquidity of the assets employed after current liabilities have been deducted from the current assets. An excessively high ratio might indicate excess cash and/or overstocking of inventory, whereas a low ratio would indicate a definite weakness in the current position.

A related analysis involves a *vertical* percentage analysis of current assets employing *total current assets* as the base (100%). This analysis has particular significance in that (*a*) the relative composition of the current asset structure is revealed and (*b*) when compared with similar data from prior periods, important trends may be revealed.

Evaluation of Movement of Current Assets. The usual trading cycle is from cash to inventory to receivables and back to cash. The analysis of the movement of inventory and receivables is significant in that efficiency with respect to these individual items of current assets has a direct bearing on the current position and the overall efficiency with which operations are conducted. Receivable turnover (collections) and inventory turnover (investment) are especially important control points from the management point of view.

Receivable Turnover. In some lines of business cash sales predominate, whereas in others credit sales predominate. In either case the amount of trade receivables on the average should bear some relationship to the sales for the period and the terms of credit. The application of the receivable turnover in these respects may be illustrated by assuming net credit sales of $1,300,000 and average net receivables of $100,000:

$$\frac{\$1,300,000}{\$100,000} = 13 \text{ receivable turnover per period}$$

$$\frac{365}{13} = 28 \text{ average number of days to collect}$$

If we assume the terms of sale are 1/10, n/20, it appears that collections are lagging terms by eight days or more on the average—a reflection of lack of care and inefficiencies with which credit is granted and collection made.

The above simplified illustration also points up several technical aspects of the computation, viz:

1. Should the total of cash and credit sales, or credit sales only, be used in the computation? A more stable and meaningful ratio will result if credit sales only are used; otherwise a shift in the proportion of cash to credit sales will affect the ratio although collection experience is unchanged. For internal use credit sales should be used (since the figure is available or may be reconstructed readily); however, for comparison with other firms the total of cash and credit sales generally must be used since published data seldom provide the credit sales figures for the other firms.
2. Should the ending balance of receivables or average receivables be used? The average *monthly* receivables balance generally should be used in order to smooth out seasonal influences. The average should be determined by adding the 13 monthly balances (January 1, January 31, and through December 31) of trade accounts and notes receivable, then dividing by 13. In the absence of monthly balances the average of the annual beginning and ending balance or only the ending balance may be used. For comparison with other firms the ending balance may, by necessity, have to be used.
3. Receivables should be net of the estimated bad debts.

4. Trade notes receivable should be included in averaging receivables.

Whether to express the receivable movement as a "turnover" or as "number of days to collect" is principally a matter of personal preference. It is appropriate to note that if the company uses a "natural" business year, the receivables reported on the balance sheet normally will be quite low which would cause the turnover to look better than is actually the case on the average.

Merchandise Turnover. The merchandise turnover is the ratio between the cost of goods sold (or used) and the average inventory balance. The procedures for determining the average inventory balance are similar to those discussed above for average receivables. For comparisons with other firms the analyst may have to use *sales* rather than cost of goods sold. Obviously, such a ratio would at best represent an approximation since the markup in the sales amount (but not in the inventory amount) would distort the ratio. This error may be avoided by restating inventory at retail.

The merchandise inventory turnover may be expressed as a "turnover" or as "days' supply"; the latter appears to predominate in current usage.[3] The turnover or days' supply figure has significance in that the amount of inventory on hand normally should bear a close relationship to the sales (cost of sales). The relationship necessarily will vary from industry to industry—a grocery store normally would have a high inventory turnover, whereas an antique dealer would have a comparatively low turnover. Also, it must be remembered that the ratio represents an average—a generalization that does not reflect how fast a particular item is moving but rather how fast all items on the average are moving. For example, a grocer may have a turnover of 15, yet have items on the shelves that have not turned over at all during the entire year.

Inventory turnover is directly related to profitability. To illustrate, assume that the inventory turnover is 12 (cost of sales, $1,200,000 average inventory, $100,000) and that the entrepreneur realizes a profit of $1,000 each time the $100,000 investment in inventory turns over. A $12,000 profit is indicated. Now assume another firm identical in every respect except that the inventory turnover is 6 indicating a $6,000 profit on a similar $100,000 investment.

Work in process inventory turnover is computed by dividing cost of goods manufactured by the average work in process inventory. With respect to all inventories, turnover computations based on appropriate units, when practicable, will provide more reliable results than when based on dollar amounts.

---

[3] Some analysts prefer to use 300 days; that is, the approximate number of business days in the year.

Ratios Indicating Equity Position

The right (credit) side of the balance sheet presents the two basic sources of funds, that is, (a) the creditors' equity (total liabilities) and (b) the owners' equity (total net worth) for the firm. Identification of the interrelationships between these two distinct equities and the

Illustration 26–8
Ratios Indicating Equity Position

Ratio	Formula for Computation	Significance
Equity ratios:		
1. Owners' equity to total assets.	$\dfrac{\text{Owners' Equity (Total Net Worth)}}{\text{Total Assets (Net of Depreciation)}}$	Proportion of assets provided by owners. Reflects financial strength and cushion for creditors.
2. Creditors' equity to total assets.	$\dfrac{\text{Total Liabilities}}{\text{Total Assets (Net of Depreciation)}}$	Proportion of assets provided by creditors. Extent of "trading on the equity."
3. Owners' equity to total liabilities. (Sometimes computed as total liabilities to owners' equity.)	$\dfrac{\text{Owners' Equity}}{\text{Total Liabilities}}$	Relative amounts of resources provided by owners and creditors. Reflects strengths and weaknesses in basic financing of operations.
Equities related to profits and sales:		
4. Net income to owners' equity.	$\dfrac{\text{Net Income}}{\text{Owners' Equity}}$	Return on the resources provided by the owners.
5. Sales to owners' equity.	$\dfrac{\text{Sales (Net)}}{\text{Owners' Equity}}$	Number of times net worth is "turned over" in sales. Indicative of the utilization of owner capital; may suggest overcapitalization in relation to volume of business done.
Miscellaneous ratios related to equities:		
6. Fixed assets to fixed liabilities.	$\dfrac{\text{Fixed Assets (Net)}}{\text{Fixed Liabilities}}$	Reflects extent of resources from long-term debt. May suggest potential borrowing power. If the fixed assets are pledged—degree of security.
7. Fixed assets to owners' equity.	$\dfrac{\text{Fixed Assets (Net)}}{\text{Owners' Equity}}$	May suggest over- or under-investment by owners; also weakness or strength in "trading on the equity."
8. Fixed assets to total equity.	$\dfrac{\text{Fixed Assets (Net)}}{\text{Total Liabilities and Owners' Equity}}$	May suggest overexpansion of plant and equipment.
9. Sales to fixed assets (plant turnover).	$\dfrac{\text{Sales (Net)}}{\text{Fixed Assets (Net)}}$	Turnover index which tests roughly the efficiency of management in keeping plant properties employed.
10. Book value per share of common stock.	$\dfrac{\text{Common Stock Equity}}{\text{Number of Outstanding Shares}}$	Number of dollars of equity (at book value) per share of common stock.

assets and earnings are important aspects of financial statement analysis. Ratios of this type are particularly appropriate in evaluating the long-term solvency and soundness of the enterprise. The principal ratios in this category are listed in Illustration 26–8.

Equity Ratios

The three equity ratios should be interpreted together in evaluating the financial condition of a firm. Significantly, what is desirable from the stockholders' point of view may not necessarily be desirable from the creditors' point of view. For example, a low ratio of total liabilities to total assets is desirable from the creditors' point of view, but from the stockholders' viewpoint a higher ratio might be favorable since "trading on the equity" might be advantageous. Trading on the equity is a common term referring to the advantage to be gained by a firm which borrows funds at, for example, 6%, when the earnings on stockholder investment is, for example, 20%; in such case there is a distinct leverage factor in favor of the owners resulting from borrowing.

In computing the equity ratios where owners' equity (total net worth) is employed, it is important that all components of capital, such as the "reserves" and revaluation capital increment, be included. In this respect it may be noted that some analysts prefer to subtract the carrying value of intangible assets thereby using *tangible* net worth for owners' equity. The authors see no basic reason for this approach since we assume the intangibles are accounted for properly.

Book Value per Share of Common Stock

Book value per share generally has limited significance in that a good portion of the asset book values may have little relationship to current market values notwithstanding the fact that generally accepted accounting principles and procedures have been followed. Nevertheless, book value per share does have some use in measuring owners' equity in the enterprise. When there is only one class of stock, book value per share is computed by simply dividing the number of shares outstanding into total net worth. However, in computing book value per share of common stock, special problems arise when the firm also has preferred stock outstanding. In this case total net worth (including retained earnings) must be allocated to the respective common and preferred equities. The allocation will depend upon the *preferential rights* of the preferred stock. Liquidation, cumulative, and participating preferences of the preferred stock must be satisfied; the balance of the net worth then becomes the common stock equity. To illustrate the allocation, assume the Stone Manufacturing Company's net worth to be as follows:

Preferred stock, 6%, cumulative, nonparticipating, par value $100 per
   share, 1,000 shares outstanding...$100,000
Common stock, $100 par value (2,000 shares issued)................................ 200,000
Premium on preferred stock.. 10,000
Premium on common stock 15,000
Retained earnings 75,000
Treasury stock — common (100 shares at cost) .... (17,000)
     Total Net Worth (owners' equity)..$383,000

Preferred preferences — liquidation value $105 per share — two years'
   dividends in arrears.
Book value per share:
   Total net worth $383,000
   Allocation to preferred stock:
     Liquidation value — 1,000 shares @ $105...........................$105,000
     Cumulative dividends — $100,000 × 6% × 2 (two years in
     arrears at 6% including current year just ended)............... 12,000   117,000
   Allocation to common stock (1,900 shares outstanding) $266,000

Book value per share of preferred:

$$\frac{\$117,000}{1,000} = \$117$$

Book value per share of common:

$$\frac{\$266,000}{1,900} = \$140$$

    Book value per share has been accorded much more attention in
recent years in view of the widespread trend toward business combinations. It will be recalled (Chapter 11) that book value and fair
market value were important factors in the purchase versus pooling
methods of accounting for business combinations. Obviously, adjustments and corrections for improper accounting should be accomplished prior to computing book value per share. Not infrequently
special provisions of contracts between the parties in a combination
require adjustments prior to such computations. In many situations
it may be desirable to compute *pro forma* book value per share
amounts under certain assumed (as if) conditions such as fully diluted
for convertible securities, stock warrants, and options.

Ratios Indicating Income Position and Operating Results

    Within recent years increasing attention has been given to the
ability of a concern to earn a satisfactory income, rather than to the
"value of the assets." Although ratios relating to income are perhaps
of more interest to investors than to creditors, the latter are giving
increasing attention to profitability. A creditor may be unwilling to
make loans or grant merchandise credit if an unhealthy profit picture
exists in the prospective borrower's business, even though adequate
collateral is available. Management is particularly concerned with

Illustration 26-9
Ratios Indicating Income Position and Operating Results

Ratio	Formula for Computation	Significance
1. Net income to net sales (profit margin).	$$\frac{\text{Net Income}}{\text{Net Sales}}$$	Indicates net productivity of each dollar of sales.
2. Net income to owners' equity.	$$\frac{\text{Net Income}}{\text{Average Owners' Equity}}$$	Earnings rate on resources provided by owners (also see [4] on page 1050).
3. Investment turnover.	$$\frac{\text{Net Sales}}{\text{Total Investment}}$$	Number of times total investment (total assets) turns. Indicative of efficiency with which total resources are utilized.
4. Net income earned per share of common stock.	$$\frac{\text{Net Income Minus Preferred Dividend Requirements}}{\text{Average Number of Shares of Common Stock Outstanding}}$$	Profit earned on each share of common stock. Indicative of ability to pay dividends.
5. Earnings rate on market value per share.	$$\frac{\text{Net Income per Share}}{\text{Market Price per Share}}$$	Earnings rate based on cost of share of stock on the market. Indicates profitableness of firm related to market value of stockholders' equity.
6. Price-earnings ratio.	$$\frac{\text{Market Price per Share}}{\text{Net Income per Share}}$$	Another way to express the relationship in 5 above.
7. Return on investment (return on assets employed).	$$\frac{\text{Net Income Plus Interest Expense}^{\circ}}{\text{Total Investment (Total Assets)}}$$	Represents rate earned by management on all resources committed to the firm. Indicates ability of management to conduct profitable operations.

°Adjusted for "tax savings."

evidences of the income position. The principal ratios indicative of the income position are summarized in Illustration 26-9.

Net Income to Net Sales

The ratio of net income to net sales, generally referred to as the *profit margin*, is widely used as an index of profitability; however, it must be realized that one significant factor related to profitableness—investment—is given no consideration in the ratio. To illustrate, assume the accounts of the Conway Company showed the following statistics: net income, $10,000; net sales, $2,000,000; and total assets, $100,000. In this case the profit margin is only one half of 1%, whereas the return on total investment of 10% appears to be satisfactory. Thus, the profit margin appears inadequate as a measure of profitability. The profit margin has value primarily for evaluation of trend and for comparison with industry and competitor statistics.

Net Income to Owners' Equity

The ability of management to earn a favorable rate on owner's equity (net worth) is an important factor in evaluating operating results and income position. Some analysts prefer to deduct the intangible assets thereby basing the ratio on *tangible* net worth. The deduction of intangibles may be consistent with the viewpoint of the creditors since in many situations such assets would have little or no value in case of forced liquidation. On the other hand, since intangibles normally have real value and represent funds that were invested they should not be deducted.

Earnings per Share on Common Stock

The two ratios, net income per share (4 in the tabulation above), and earnings rate per share (5 and 6 in the tabulation above) have particular significance to the investor. When there is only one class of stock outstanding net income per share is computed simply by dividing the shares outstanding into the reported net income. However, when there are both common and preferred shares outstanding net income must be allocated between them.

To illustrate computation of these ratios assume the following:

Seven percent preferred, nonparticipating, cumulative (2 years in arrears), par $100 per share, 1,000 shares outstanding $100,000
Common stock, par $50 per share, 4,000 shares outstanding
  (average during year)... 200,000
Retained earnings (excluding current year net income) 45,000
Net income 34,000
Market value per share common stock.................................... 70

Net annual income earned per share of common stock:[4]

$$\frac{\text{Net Income Minus Preferred Dividends}}{\text{Average Shares Common Stock Outstanding}} = \frac{\$34,000 - \$7,000}{4,000}$$

$$= \$6.75$$

Earnings rate on market value per share:

$$\frac{\text{Net Income per Share}}{\text{Market Value per Share}} = \frac{\$6.75}{\$70.00} = 9.6\%$$

Price-earnings ratio:

$$\frac{\$70.00}{\$6.75} = 10.4 \text{ times}$$

Due to the increasing importance ascribed to earnings per share figures, particularly by security analysts, and the resultant over-

---

[4] Note that since the preferred stock is nonparticipating, its allocation is limited to the preferential amount for one year; the dividends in arrears are viewed as a claim against retained earnings.

statement of such figures by certain corporations through manipulation of financial data (and complex securities) the APB included in *Opinion 9* (December 1966) specific computational and reporting guidelines. After approximately three years, in the light of new trends, the APB reexamined the issue particularly in respect to convertible debt and stock purchase warrants. As a consequence the board issued *Opinion 15* in May 1969. This Opinion superseded the portion of *Opinion 9* dealing with earnings per share (EPS). *Opinion 15* provided detailed guidelines for complex situations and dealt comprehensively with the effect of convertible securities and stock warrants on EPS computations.[5] The Opinion states that "earnings per share amounts should be presented (on the face of the income statement) for (*a*) income before extraordinary items and (*b*) net income. It may also be desirable to present earnings per share amounts for extraordinary items, if any." The Opinion distinguishes between two situations, viz.:

1. Corporations having only common shares (that is, no convertible securities). In this situation the EPS amounts should be computed as illustrated above and captioned "Earnings per common share."
2. Corporations with complex capital structures (that is, having convertible securities). In this situation two types of EPS data must be presented, viz.:
    a) Primary earnings per share. Based on the outstanding common shares and those securities that are in substance equivalent to common shares and have a dilutive effect. An example would be bonds payable convertible to common stock.
    b) Fully diluted earnings per share. A pro forma (as if) presentation which "reflects the dilution of earnings per share that would have occurred if *all* contingent issuances of common stock that would individually reduce earnings per share had taken place."

The Opinion further stated that "Earnings per share data should be presented for all periods covered by the statement of income or summary of earnings."

Detailed discussion and illustration of this subject is deferred to another volume in this series.[6]

Return on Investment

Return on investment is derived by dividing income by total investment (total assets). Return on investment is referred to variously

---

[5] Recently the AICPA issued a 189-page book focusing on technical interpretations of the Opinion: J. T. Ball, *Computations of Earnings per Share* (New York: AICPA, 1970).

[6] C. H. Griffin, T. H. Williams, and K. D. Larson, *Advanced Accounting* (Homewood, Ill.: Richard D. Irwin, Inc., 1971). Also see Chapter 4.

as capital yield, return on assets employed, return on capital, or simply rate of return. Return on investment has two important applications in business situations:

1. Evaluating proposed capital additions (not discussed herein).[7]
2. Measuring the relative success of a company and subdivisions thereof (discussed below).

Although return on investment may be derived directly as indicated above:

$$\left(\frac{\text{Net Income Plus Interest Expense}}{\text{Total Assets}}\right)$$

the significance of the concept is clearer when it is realized that it is the direct result of two other ratios—the profit margin (No. 1 on page 1053) and investment turnover (No. 3 on page 1053). To illustrate, assume: sales, $200,000; income, $20,000; and investment, $100,000: The ratios are:

1. $\dfrac{\text{Income}}{\text{Sales}} = \dfrac{\$20,000}{\$200,000} = 10\%$ (profit margin)

2. $\dfrac{\text{Sales}}{\text{Investment}} = \dfrac{\$200,000}{\$100,000} = 2$ (investment turnover)

3. 10% (profit margin) × 2 (investment turnover) = 20% return on investment

or

$$\frac{\text{Income}}{\text{Investment}} = \frac{\$20,000}{\$100,000} = 20\% \text{ return on total investment}$$
$$\text{(total assets employed)}$$

In the above computation interest expense was added to net income since it was deducted on the income statement as an expense although it is part of the "return" when total assets are utilized as the base. Extraordinary items are usually excluded from the computation since they are nonrepresentative. The return may be computed both before and after tax.

Return on investment has gained wide acceptance in the last few years as an important tool of managerial control.[8] The measure has the distinct advantage of directing management attention clearly and forcefully to a combination of the three principal factors affecting profit—sales, costs, and total assets employed.[9]

---

[7] For an excellent discussion see Harold Bierman, Jr., and Seymour Smidt, *The Capital Budgeting Decision* (New York: The Macmillan Co., 1960).

[8] Charles T. Horngren, *Cost Accounting* (2d ed; Englewood Cliffs, N.J.: Prentice Hall, Inc.,), ch. XI.

[9] A related but distinctly different ratio frequently is derived by dividing net income by net worth. See No. 2 on page 1053.

Use, Application, and Presentation of Ratio Analyses

In evaluating the financial position of a firm the relationships as indicated by both the absolute amounts and the ratios, it is especially important that the limitations of the data be realized. Significantly, ratios represent average conditions; therefore, they must be interpreted rather broadly. In addition, changes in the accounting system and classification of data may significantly affect a ratio. One writer has suggested that the idea of their use may be conveyed by a comparison with the interpretation of a thermometer reading by a doctor—beyond a certain range the fever reading indicates *something* is wrong with the patient, but not exactly what it is. An unfavorable ratio can be thought of as a red flag—the matter should be investigated. Additionally, one ratio or even several ratios standing alone, whatever their values, may be insignificant. Consequently, a primary problem confronting both the analyst and the reader relates to the evaluation of a specific ratio. For example, is it good or bad that the inventory turnover for a company is 12? In determining what constitutes an unfavorable, or favorable, ratio for a particular firm the following comparisons are suggested:

1. Comparison of ratios for the current year with those of preceding years for the company. The trend of certain ratios may be highly significant.
2. Comparison of the company's ratios with those of leading competitors (when available from published financial statements).
3. Comparison with ratios of the industry within which the company operates. Industry statistics may be obtained from the following sources:
   a) Industry trade associations—practically all industries support one or more trade associations which generally collect and publish financial statistics relating to the industry. The National Retail Dry Goods Association is a good example.
   b) Bureaus of business research of universities—the Universities of Harvard and Michigan compile and publish comparative data for department stores; the University of Texas prepares comparative data on approximately 100 Texas retail stores, etc.
   c) U.S. Department of Commerce, Washington, D.C.
   d) Publications of Robert Morris Associates.
   e) Dun & Bradstreet, Inc., in the magazine *Modern Industry* and separate booklets.
4. Comparison with budgeted or standard ratios developed for the company.

Because differences in product lines, methods of operation, size, geography, accounting methods, and variations in the method of computing the ratios may significantly influence the statistics, caution should be exercised in comparing ratios with those from other sources.

When comparing ratios over a period of several years, the price-level problem,[10] in addition to those mentioned above, assumes considerable significance.

Despite the shortcomings mentioned above, ratio analysis is a very useful tool in interpreting financial statements and in evaluating the financial strength of a firm. The accountant, both public and industrial, should employ this useful tool to the extent consistent with the situation and the needs of the reader.

The presentation of ratio analyses is an important aspect of financial reporting. The accountant should report the results of the analyses in a manner that is consistent with the problem at hand. A special report involving a tabulation of specific data generally is required for creditor purposes. External reporting in the annual financial statement usually involves a limited number of ratios, although it is fairly common to include some graphical representation based on ratios such as a pie chart indicating the "disposition" of the sales dollar.

The presentation of ratio analyses to management for internal use should involve (a) special reports related to specific nonrecurring problems and (b) repetitive reports having a bearing on general management planning and control problems. The former reports should take a form consistent with the problem and the needs of a particular executive or executives. The latter type of report should involve, at least annually, an "analytical report" for top management developed along the following lines:

1. As a separate report.
2. Initially the report should include a minimum number of pertinent ratios — new ones being added as executives become familiar with those presented to date.
3. There should be adequate narrative-type explanations and comments.
4. Presentation should include graphs, illustrations, and nontechnical interpretations to bring out clearly and forcefully trends, comparisons, and exceptional developments. When graphs and diagrams are used the related data also should be reported.

QUESTIONS FOR CLASS DISCUSSION

1. In what ways do management, investors, creditors, and the public generally have different interests and needs with respect to financial statement analyses?
2. What is the position of the accounting profession with reference to the presentation of comparative financial data?

---

[10] See Chapter 23.

3. In what ways may the expression of relationships in terms of percentages or ratios add to the interpretation of financial data?

4. Distinguish between horizontal and vertical percentage analyses.

5. In applying vertical analysis one amount is selected as the base; with respect to each of the statements listed below indicate an appropriate base:

   a) Income statement.
   b) Balance sheet.
   c) Statement of retained earnings.
   d) Manufacturing statement.

6. In what respects should the accountant be discriminating in the selection of financial data to be presented for particular users?

7. What is meant by the management by exception principle? How is the principle related to financial reporting?

8. For control purposes what weaknesses are involved when current results are compared with the results of a prior period?

9. What are the three primary tests of overall solvency?

10. Distinguish between the current ratio and the acid-test ratio.

11. Current assets and current liabilities for two companies having the same amount of working capital are summarized below; evaluate their relative solvency.

	X Company	*Y Company*
Current assets	$200,000	$900,000
Current liabilities	100,000	800,000
Working capital	$100,000	$100,000

12. Explain the interpretation of receivable turnover and age of receivables.

13. Explain the interpretation of inventory turnover and days' supply in inventory.

14. Explain and illustrate trading on the equity.

15. Compute and explain the meaning of the book value per share of common stock of the Pride Manufacturing Company assuming the following data are available:

   Preferred stock, 5%, cumulative, nonparticipating, 200
   shares outstanding .... $ 20,000
   Common stock, par value $100, 1,000 shares
   outstanding 100,000
   Retained earnings 7,000
   (Three years dividends in arrears on preferred stock
   including current year.)

16. Discuss the usefulness of the profit margin as an index of profitability.

17. Explain the return on investment concept, noting in particular why it has been recognized as a particularly useful concept.

18. What are the principal limitations that should be kept in mind in evaluating ratios?

19. Discuss the importance of appropriate presentations of the results of analytical procedures.

DECISION CASE 26-1

The condensed balance sheet for the Crandon Corporation is shown below. The board of directors is contemplating raising $150,000 additional funds to finance a proposed $100,000 fixed asset expansion and to replenish working capital. Two proposals for raising the $150,000 are under consideration, viz:

Proposal A: Issue a 4½% bond issue (10 year).

Proposal B: Issue additional stock at par to present stockholders.

It is estimated that the fixed asset expansion will increase profits by approximately $18,750 per year, excluding any additional interest costs and any additional income taxes. For several years the company has paid a 6% annual dividend. It is estimated that the average income tax rate on the additional income will be 25% under Proposal A and 27% under Proposal B.

CRANDON CORPORATION
Balance Sheet, December 31, 1971

Current assets	$ 33,000	Current liabilities	$ 30,000
Fixed assets (net)	267,000	Fixed liabilities (notes)	100,000
Other assets	1,700	Common stock ($100 per	
Deferred charges	8,300	share)	150,000
		Retained earnings (1971 earnings $17,250; dividends	
		paid $9,000	30,000
	$310,000		$310,000

Average ratios for the industry that are available:

Current ratio	2.36
Fixed assets to owners' equity	1.48
Net income to owners' equity	8.14
Inventory turnover	11.62
Total liabilities to owners' equity	.80
Return on investment (total assets)	6.1
Total assets to total liabilities	3.5

Required:

Evaluate the proposals in the light of the above data. Assume "other" assets and deferred charges will not change. (Obviously other factors not included herein also would influence the final decision.)

DECISION CASE 26-2

Sudan Corporation needs additional funds for plant expansion. The board of directors is considering obtaining the funds by issuing additional short-term notes, long-term bonds, preferred stock, or common stock.

Required:

1. What primary factors should the board of directors consider in selecting the best method of financing plant expansion?

2. One member of the board of directors suggests that the corporation should maximize trading on equity, that is, using stockholders' equity as a basis for borrowing additional funds at a lower rate of interest than the expected earnings from the use of the borrowed funds.

a) Explain how trading on equity affects earnings per share of common stock.

b) Explain how a change in income tax rates affects trading on equity.

c) Under what circumstances should a corporation seek to trade on equity to a substantial degree?

3. Two specific proposals under consideration by the board of directors are the issue of 7% subordinated income bonds or 7% cumulative, non-participating, nonvoting preferred stock, callable at par. In discussing the impact of the two alternatives on the debt to stockholders' equity ratio, one member of the board of directors stated that he felt the resulting debt-equity ratio would be the same under either alternative because the income bonds and preferred stock should be reported in the same balance sheet classification. What are the arguments (*a*) for and (*b*) against using the same balance sheet classification in reporting the income bonds and preferred stock?

(AICPA adapted)

EXERCISES

Exercise 26–1

The Victoria Trading Company income statements (condensed) for two monthly periods are shown below. Prepare a comparative statement including amount of change and a vertical percentage analysis. (Round to even per-cents.)

	March, 19A	March, 19B
Gross sales	$202,000	$212,200
Returns and allowances	2,000	2,200
Net sales	$200,000	$210,000
Cost of goods sold	102,000	111,000
Gross margin	$ 98,000	$ 99,000
Expenses:		
Selling expenses	$ 61,000	$ 59,800
Administrative expenses	31,000	30,200
Financial expenses (net of financial incomes)	2,000	3,100
Total expenses	$ 94,000	$ 93,100
Net income before extraordinary items	$ 4,000	$ 5,900
Extraordinary items, net of tax	2,000	(1,800)
Net Income	$ 6,000	$ 4,100

Exercise 26–2

Prepare a horizontal percentage analysis for both years for the Victoria Trading Company utilizing the data given in Exercise 26–1. (Round to even percents.)

Exercise 26–3

What are the "increase–decrease" amounts and percents for the following items (parentheses indicate negative balance)? Where it is inappropriate to express a percent, say "invalid."

Items	This Year	Last Year	Items	This Year	Last Year
No. 1......................	$320	$200	No. 6....................	$350	—
No. 2......................	350	500	No. 7....................	(250)	—
No. 3......................	—	500	No. 8....................	(300)	$(200)
No. 4......................	(200)	400	No. 9....................	200	(100)
No. 5......................	400	200	No. 10....................	—	(600)

Exercise 26–4

The condensed financial data given below were taken from the annual financial statements of Hunt Corporation:

	19A	19B	19C
Current assets (including inventory)..............$	220,000	$ 255,000	$ 264,000
Current liabilities......................................	160,000	170,000	120,000
Cash sales	700,000	740,000	800,000
Credit sales	250,000	279,000	260,000
Cost of goods sold	540,000	590,000	600,000
Inventory	116,000	120,000	80,000
Quick assets..	70,000	85,000	72,000
Accounts receivable (net)	60,000	64,000	66,000
Total assets (net)	1,000,000	1,000,000	1,640,000

Required:

1. Based on the above data, calculate the following for 19B and 19C (carry computations one place):

a) Current ratio.

b) Acid-test ratio.

c) Working capital to total assets.

d) Receivable turnover.

e) Age of receivables.

f) Merchandise turnover.

g) Days' supply in inventory.

h) Working capital turnover.

2. Evaluate the results of each computation including trends. Use 360 days for computation purposes.

Exercise 26–5

The following data were taken from the financial statements of the Stuchell Company. Based on these data compute (a) the working capital, (b) the current ratio, and (c) the acid-test ratio (carry percents to one place). Evaluate each change.

	19A	19B
Cash ....$	15,000	$ 37,000
Temporary investments.......................................	25,000	20,000
Trade accounts receivable (net)...........................	48,000	52,000
Notes receivable	5,000	7,000
Inventory	140,000	60,000
Prepaid expenses	7,000	4,000
Total Current Assets................................$	240,000	$180,000
Current liabilities..$	80,000	$100,000

Exercise 26–6

The following data were taken from the financial statements of the Smith Company:

	19A	19B	19C
Sales – cash	$190,000	$200,000	$220,000
Sales – credit	100,000	120,000	130,000
Average receivables	25,000	34,000	50,000
Average inventory	60,000	70,000	80,000
Cost of goods sold	180,000	190,000	200,000

Required:

What conclusions may be made relative to (a) inventories and (b) receivables? (Use 300 business days in year; credit terms are 90 calendar days.)

Exercise 26-7

The Corn Manufacturing Corporation balance sheet showed the following as of December 31, 19A:

Preferred stock, 7%, par value, $50 per share.....................$150,000
Common stock, no-par value, 20,000 shares outstanding...... 300,000
Premium on preferred stock... 20,000
Retained earnings... 40,000

Required:

Compute the book value per share of preferred and common assuming:

a) None of the preferred shares have been issued.
b) Preferred is noncumulative and nonparticipating.
c) Preferred is cumulative and nonparticipating (three years' dividends in arrears including current year).
d) Preferred has a liquidation value of $60 per share and is noncumulative and nonparticipating.
e) Preferred has a liquidation value of $60 per share and is noncumulative and nonparticipating, and the Retained Earnings account shows a *deficit* of $40,000.

Exercise 26-8

The Brown Corporation financial statement for 19C reported complete comparative statements. The following data were taken therefrom:

	19A	19B	19C
Net sales	$11,000,000	$12,000,000	$14,000,000
Net income	100,000	132,000	112,000
Owners' equity	1,310,000	1,330,000	1,470,000
Shares of common stock outstanding	22,000	22,000	25,000
Total assets	3,000,000	3,000,000	3,500,000
Market value per share	$ 65.00	$ 75.00	$ 70.00

Required:

1. Based on the above financial data compute the following ratios for 19B and 19C: (a) profit margin, (b) net income to owners' equity, (c) earnings per share of stock, (d) earnings rate on market value per share, (e) price-earnings

ratio, (f) investment turnover, and (g) return on investment. (Carry computations to one decimal place.)

2. Note any significant trends that appear to be developing.

Exercise 26–9

The following data relate to the Economy Printing Company:

	19A	19B	19C	19D	19E
Net income	$ 10,000	$ 14,300	$ 21,600	$ 33,600	$ 39,000
Sales	100,000	130,000	180,000	240,000	260,000
Total assets	50,000	71,500	108,000	168,000	195,000

Required:

Evaluate the company in terms of the (a) profit margin, (b) investment turnover, and (c) return on investment.

PROBLEMS

Problem 26–1

The following income statements (condensed) of the Garner Corporation were presented to you with instructions to prepare (a) a comparative statement, (b) a vertical analysis, and (c) pertinent comments relative to the results. (Round to even percents.)

GARNER CORPORATION

For Year Ended December 31

	19A	19B
Sales	$285,600	$301,800
Return sales	5,600	1,800
	$280,000	$300,000
Cost of goods sold	$131,600	$142,000
Selling expenses	84,000	77,000
Administrative expenses	61,600	64,000
Other expenses	16,800	15,000
Income taxes		1,000
Subtotal	$294,000	$299,000
Net Income (Loss)	$ (14,000)	$ 1,000

Problem 26–2

The following condensed data (rounded to even $1,000) relative to the Mid-States Manufacturing Company financial position are being analyzed. Assume you are the chief accountant and have been requested to prepare the analysis; accordingly, you decide to prepare (among other analyses which are not required in this problem) a statement showing both vertical and horizontal analyses along with comments that appear appropriate. (Round to even percents.)

ASSETS

	19A	19B
Cash	$ 470,000	$ 380,000
Trade receivables	182,000	222,000
Allowance for doubtful accounts	(6,000)	(7,000)
Inventories	800,000	610,000
Prepaid expenses	21,000	23,000
Bond sinking fund	400,000	100,000
Land	1,600,000	2,000,000
Plant and equipment	6,100,000	6,470,000
Accumulated depreciation	(750,000)	(1,070,000)
Goodwill	100,000	
Deferred charges	83,000	72,000
Total	$9,000,000	$8,800,000

LIABILITIES AND CAPITAL

Accounts payable	$ 325,000	$ 360,000
Income taxes payable	51,000	44,000
Accrued wages	39,000	43,000
Bonds payable	1,200,000	1,000,000
Capital stock	7,000,000	7,000,000
Retained earnings	385,000	353,000
Total	$9,000,000	$8,800,000

Problem 26–3

The following data were taken from the annual financial statements of the Vance Corporation:

	19A	19B	19C
Current Assets:			
Cash	$ 100,000	$ 75,000	$ 80,000
Trade receivables	90,000	110,000	130,000
Less: Allowance for doubtful accounts	(5,000)	(6,000)	(8,000)
Notes receivable (nontrade)	110,000	125,000	134,000
Marketable securities	45,000	30,000	20,000
Inventories	298,000	345,000	341,000
Prepaid expenses	12,000	11,000	13,000
Total	$ 650,000	$ 690,000	$ 710,000
Current Liabilities:			
Trade payables	$ 70,000	$ 158,000	$ 158,000
Notes payable	90,000	72,000	98,000
Accrued wages payable	72,000	46,000	52,000
Income taxes payable	19,000	23,000	24,000
Deferred rent income	2,000	2,000	2,000
Accrued liabilities	17,000	19,000	16,000
Total	$ 270,000	$ 320,000	$ 350,000
Additional Data:			
Cash sales	$3,300,000	$3,500,000	$3,200,000
Credit sales	1,500,000	1,700,000	1,800,000
Cost of goods sold	2,500,000	2,900,000	2,800,000
Total assets (net)	6,600,000	7,200,000	7,200,000

Required:

(Carry computations to one place.)

1. Compute ratios which highlight the overall solvency of the Vance Corporation.

2. Compute ratios which highlight the movement of current assets of the Vance Corporation.

Problem 26–4

The financial statements of the Green Manufacturing Company for a three-year period showed the following:

	19A	19B	19C
Total assets (net)	$2,000,000	$2,040,000	$1,940,000
Total current liabilities	230,000	150,000	150,000
Fixed assets (net)	1,248,000	1,257,600	1,260,000
Total fixed liabilities	860,000	960,000	750,000
Common stock (par value $100 per share)	600,000	600,000	700,000
Retained earnings	310,000	330,000	340,000
Sales (net)	6,600,000	7,000,000	7,100,000
Net income	50,000	70,000	40,000

Required:

1. Based on the above data calculate the following ratios for each year (round to even numbers):

a) Owners' equity to total assets.

b) Owners' equity to total liabilities.

c) Total liabilities to total assets.

d) Net income to owners' equity.

e) Sales to owners' equity.

f) Fixed assets to fixed liabilities.

g) Fixed assets to owners' equity.

h) Fixed assets to total equity.

i) Sales to fixed assets.

j) Book value per share of stock.

k) Earnings per share.

2. Note any favorable or unfavorable trends that appear to be developing.

Problem 26–5

Utilizing the year-end data presented below for the Clayton Trading Company evaluate the profitability of the firm:

	1967	1968	1969	1970	1971
Sales	$400,000	$420,000	$450,000	$440,000	$490,000
Net income	12,000	10,600	11,500	11,500	12,500
Total assets	200,000	212,000	220,000	225,000	230,000
Owners' equity	100,000	106,000	109,000	107,000	102,000
Shares outstanding	4,000	4,000	4,000	3,900	3,800
Market value per share	50	48	45	48	52

Problem 26-6

The following summarized data were taken from the published statements of two companies that are being compared.

	(In Thousands)	
	Company A	Company B
Sales	$3,000	$9,000
Cost of goods sold	1,900	6,942
Operating expenses	400	1,600
Depreciation expense included	100	400
Interest expense	8	108
Extraordinary items (gain)	22	(550)
Income taxes	240	300
Current assets	1,000	4,000
Tangible fixed assets	5,000	19,000
Accumulated depreciation	2,000	7,000
Investments; long term	400	100
Other assets	600	7,900
Current liabilities	900	2,000
Longterm liabilities	100	1,800
Capital stock ($100 par value)	3,000	18,000
Retained earnings	1,000	2,200
Current market value per share	$ 165.00	$ 11.20

Compute the one ratio that would best respond to each of the following questions (show computations). Justify your choice.

a) Which company has the best current position?
b) Which company has the best working capital turnover?
c) Which company is earning the best rate on resources available to the management?
d) Which company has the advantage in "trading on the equity"?
e) Which company has the best profit margin?
f) Which company has the highest book value per share?
g) Which stock is the best buy?

Problem 26-7

Derr Sales Corporation's management is concerned over the corporation's current financial position and return on investment. They request your assistance in analyzing their financial statements and furnish the following statements:

DERR SALES CORPORATION
Statement of Working Capital Deficit
(December 31, 1968

Current liabilities		$223,050
Less current assets:		
Cash	$ 5,973	
Accounts receivable, net	70,952	
Inventory	113,125	190,050
Working capital deficit		$ 33,000

DERR SALES CORPORATION
Income Statement
For the Year Ended December 31, 1968

Sales (90,500 units)	$760,200
Cost of goods sold	452,500
Gross profit	$307,700
Selling and general expenses, including $22,980 depreciation	155,660
Income before taxes	$152,040
Income taxes	76,020
Net income	$ 76,020

Additional data:

Assets other than current assets consist of land, building, and equipment with a book value of $352,950 on December 31, 1968.

Required:

1. Assuming Derr Sales Corporation operates 300 days per year compute the following (show your computations):

a) Number of days' sales uncollected.
b) Inventory turnover.
c) Number of days' operations to cover the working capital deficit.
d) Return on total assets as a product of asset turnover and the net income ratio (sometimes called profit margin).

2. Sales of 100,000 units are forecasted for 1969. Within this relevant range of activity costs are estimated as follows (excluding income taxes):

	Fixed Costs	Variable Costs per Unit
Cost of goods sold		$4.90
Selling and general expenses, including $15,450 depreciation	$129,720	1.10
Totals	$129,720	$6.00

The income tax rate is expected to be 50%. Past experience indicates that current assets vary in direct proportion to sales. Management feels that in 1969 the market will support a sales price of $8.30 at a sales volume of 100,000 units. Compute the rate of return on book value of total assets after income taxes assuming management's expectations are realized.

(AICPA adapted)

Problem 26-8

In the course of your audit of Mystic Company, you were requested to prepare comparative data from the company's inception to the present. Toward this end you determined the following:

1. Mystic Company's charter became effective on January 2, 1962, when 1,000 shares of no-par common and 1,000 shares of 6% cumulative, non-participating, preferred stock were issued. The no-par common stock was

sold at its stated value of $150 per share, and the preferred stock was sold at its par value of $100 per share.

2. Mystic was unable to pay preferred dividends at the end of its first year. The owners of the preferred stock agreed to accept one share of common stock for every 20 shares of preferred stock owned in discharge of the preferred dividends due on December 31, 1962. The shares were issued on January 2, 1963, which was also the declaration date. The fair market value was $120 per share for common on the date of issue.

3. On April 30, 1964, Mystic paid a 10% stock dividend in preferred stock (1 share for every 10 shares held) to all common stockholders. The fair market value of preferred stock was $85 per share on that date.

4. Mystic Company acquired all of the outstanding stock of Homes Corporation on May 1, 1964, in exchange for 600 shares of Mystic common stock. The transaction was recorded as a purchase. Homes reported a net income of $12,000 for its fiscal year ended April 30, 1964, and had reported a net income of $15,000 per year in each of its two prior years.

5. Mystic split its common stock three for two on January 1, 1965, and two for one on January 1, 1966.

6. Mystic tendered an offer to convert 20% of the preferred stock to common stock on the basis of two shares of common for one share of preferred. The offer was fully accepted, and the conversion was made on July 1, 1966.

7. The company reported the following in income statements for the years indicated:

Year	Operating Income (Loss)	Other Income	Income Tax Expense	Net Income (Loss)
1962	$(9,600)			$(9,600)
1963	23,421		$ 4,146°	19,275
1964	47,920†		16,960	30,960
1965	60,221†	$13,200‡	25,706§	47,715
1966	57,365†		23,615¶	33,750

° After net operating loss deduction; tax rate = 30%.

† Includes net income of combined companies.

‡ Gain from sale of land.

§ Includes $3,300 tax on gain from sale of land.

¶ Includes $2,580 tax applicable to 1964.

8. No cash dividends were paid on common stock until December 31, 1964. Cash dividends per share of common stock were paid as follows:

	June 30	December 31
1964		$3.19
1965	$1.75	2.75
1966	1.25	1.25

Required:

1. Prepare schedules which show the computation of:

a) The number of shares of each class of stock outstanding on the last day of each year.

b) The number of shares of common stock outstanding each year expressed as a weighted average of the current equivalent shares. (A current equivalent share is a share adjusted for stock splits.)

c) Cash dividends paid on common stock.

2. Prepare a five-year summary of financial statistics by years of "net income," "earnings per share," and "dividends per share" for common stock and "earnings coverage" for preferred stock. The summary is to be included in the Mystic Company's annual report and should be properly footnoted. Supporting computations should be in good form. (Earnings coverage indicates the number of times preferred dividends were earned).

(AICPA adapted)

	Analysis of Variations
chapter **27**	in Income, Gross
	Margins, and Cost

VARIATION IN INCOME AND GROSS MARGINS

The preceding chapter indicated methods of reporting that emphasize variations between the results of one period and those of another period. While the emphasis of those variations may point up areas of concern, mere reporting of such differences does not reveal the probable causes of variations generally. This chapter is concerned with analyses directed toward identification of the *causes* of variations. In addition the effect of changes in volume of business upon costs and profits (break-even analysis) is considered.

Obviously, the analyses discussed in this chapter are particularly appropriate for internal managerial use as opposed to external use. The significance of analyses of variations depends upon (*a*) the data available upon which to base the analyses, (*b*) the materiality of the variations being analyzed, and (*c*) the usefulness of the results. The analyses discussed in this chapter have considerable usefulness only when properly interpreted and wisely used. It is important to realize that such analyses are based upon certain assumptions and that the results are no more reliable than the underlying assumptions.

Causes of Variations in Net Income

The variation in *net income* as between two different periods may be due to (*a*) changes in gross margin, (*b*) changes in operating expenses, (*c*) changes in financial incomes and expenses, and (*d*) changes in extraordinary gains and losses.

Changes in *gross margin* may be due to —[1]

1. Variation in sales revenue resulting from —
   a) Changes in the sales price (per unit) of the goods sold.
   b) Changes in the volume (quantity) of goods sold.
2. Variation in the cost of goods sold resulting from —
   a) Changes in the cost (per unit) of the goods sold.
   b) Changes in the volume (quantity) of goods sold.

Analysis of changes in gross margin is discussed in the next section.

Variations in net income due to changes in operating expenses, items of financial income and expense, and the extraordinary gains and losses generally are not subject to the type of analysis explained in this chapter. Control of expenses is achieved primarily through the use of budgets, standard costs, responsibility accounting, and performance reporting. Variations in expenses between two different periods may result from numerous causes, among which the chief reasons are (*a*) inefficiencies, (*b*) changes in the physical volume of business, (*c*) changes in managerial policy and efficiency, (*d*) changes in methods of operation, (*e*) external influences, and (*f*) managerial discretionary decisions which increase or decrease such expense-creating items as salaries, plant investment, inventory, advertising, and research. Obviously, determination of the specific causes of variations in expenses involves detailed analysis relative to each expense or group of related expenses.

Illustrative Problem

In order to illustrate the mathematical premises and procedures involved in the analysis of variations in gross margin, the simplified data in Illustration 27–1 are provided.

In this illustration note that net income decreased $65 as the net result of a decrease in expenses of $2 and a decrease in gross margin of $67. We are interested in determining the *causes* of the $67 decrease in gross margin. What are the underlying factors that gave rise to this decrease? The comparative statement indicates that the $67 decrease in gross margin resulted from a $320 increase in *sales* which was more than offset by a $387 increase in cost of goods sold. Thus, we are faced with the problem of determining the *causes* of the variations in these two factors — sales and cost of goods sold.

---

[1] In the case of more than one product, gross margin may be affected by a change in sales mix, that is, a change in the relative proportion of the various products sold.

Illustration 27–1
THE XYZ COMPANY
Comparative Income Statement (condensed)

	This Year	Last Year	Increase–Decrease° This Year over Last Year
Sales:			
Units.................................	1,100	1,000	100
Unit sales price..................	$ 1.20	$ 1.00	$ .20
Amount............................	$1,320	$1,000	$320
Cost of goods sold:			
Units.................................	1,100	1,000	100
Unit cost	$ 1.17	$ .90	$ .27
Amount.............................	$1,287	$ 900	$387
Gross margin	$ 33	$ 100	$ 67°
Expenses.............................	13	15	2°
Net Income	$ 20	$ 85	$ 65°

Analysis of Gross Margin Variations

Determination of the causes of the variation in gross margin (profit) as between two periods necessitates an analysis of the causes of variations in sales and cost of sales. It was noted above that a variation in sales may be due to the effect of two factors – price and quantity.

Sales price variation represents the effect on sales revenue of a change in sales price per unit, or in the case of groupings of products, average sales price, as between two periods. In computing sales price variation, *volume* (physical quantity) is held *constant* and price is treated as a variable. Utilizing the data in Illustration 27–1, the sales price variation may be computed as follows:

Constant – physical volume (units) sold this year...................... 1,100
Variable – increase in unit sales price during year
    ($1.20 – $1.00) ....$ .20
Sales price variation, 1,100 × ($.20) $220

Alternate computation:

1. Quantity sold this year at *this* year's sale price
    (1,100 units @ $1.20) $1,320
2. Quantity sold this year at *last* year's sale price
    (1,100 units @ $1).. 1,100
    Sales price variation... $220

By finding what this year's sales figure would have been had selling prices remained the same (item 2) and comparing it with the actual sales this year (item 1), the amount by which sales increased due to the effect of the price factor alone is indicated. In the illustration $220 of the increase in sales is due solely to the effect of a 20% increase in unit sales price.

Sales volume variation represents the effect on sales revenue of a change in physical sales volume (units) as between two periods. In computing sales volume variation, *sales price* is held *constant* and physical volume is treated as a variable. Utilizing the data in Illustration 27–1, the sales volume variation may be computed as follows:

```
Constant—unit sales price last year..........................................$1.00
Variable—increase in physical units during year
    (1,100 − 1,000)...........................................................................  100
    Sales volume variation, $1 × (100)........................................            $100
```

Alternate computation:

```
1. Quantity sold this year at last year's price (1,100 @ $1) ........$1,100
2. Quantity sold last year at last year's price (1,000 @ $1).........  1,000
       Sales volume variation ................................................            $100
```

By finding what sales would have been this year with no change in price (item 1) and comparing it with the physical volume last year at the price last year (item 2), the amount by which sales increased due solely to the effect of the quantity factor is indicated.

Up to this point the causes of the $320 increase in sales revenue have been determined to be as follows:

```
Sales price variation (increase in sales due to increase in
    sales price)..........................................................................$220
Sales volume variation (increase in sales due to increase in
    physical volume) .................................................................  100
Variation in Sales (increase)...........................................................$320
```

The next step in analyzing the variation in gross margin involves determination of the causes of the $387 *increase* in cost of goods sold. Cost of goods sold also is influenced by two factors—cost per unit and physical volume of goods sold.

Cost price variation represents the effect on cost of goods sold of a change in the cost per unit, or in the case of groupings of products, average cost, as between two periods. In computing cost price variation, *volume* (physical quantity) is held *constant* and unit cost is treated as a variable. Utilizing the data in Illustration 27–1, the cost price variation may be computed as follows:

```
Constant—physical volume (units) sold this year...................... 1,100
Variable—increase in unit cost during year ($1.17 − $.90).........$  .27
    Cost price variation, 1,100 × ($.27) ......................................        $297
```

Alternate computation:

```
1. Quantity sold this year at this year's cost (1,100 @ $1.17).....$1,287
2. Quantity sold this year at last year's cost (1,100 @ $.90) .......   990
       Cost price variation.......................................................        $297
```

In the illustration, cost of goods sold increased by $297 as a result of the 30% increase in unit cost for the year.

Cost volume variation represents the effect on cost of goods sold of a change in physical volume (units) of goods sold as between two periods. In computing cost volume variation, *unit cost* is held *constant* and physical volume is treated as a variable. Utilizing the data in Illustration 27-1, the cost volume variation may be computed as follows:

Constant — unit cost last year ....$ .90
Variable — increase in physical units during year (1,100 − 1,000) 100
    Cost volume variation, $.90 × 100 .... $90

Alternate computation:

1. Quantity sold *this* year at last year's cost (1,100 @ $.90) $990
2. Quantity sold *last* year at last year's cost (1,000 @ $.90) 900
    Cost volume variation $90

By holding last year's cost per unit constant and varying physical quantity, the effect of the volume change is determined.

The causes of the $387 increase in cost of goods sold have been determined to be as follows:

Cost price variation (increase in cost of goods sold due to
    increase in unit cost) $297
Cost volume variation (increase in cost of goods sold due
    to increase in physical volume)   90
Variation in Cost of Goods Sold (increase) $387

The results of the analysis to determine the causes of the $67 variation (decrease) in gross margin may be reported to management as shown in Illustration 27-2.

In considering analyses, such as illustrated above for gross margin variations, it is important that the accountant make a careful distinction between computational formats and presentations of the results for managerial use. The accountant must remember that most management users of accounting data are not accountants; therefore, methods of presentation should be selected which clearly tell the story in nontechnical terms. Frequently, narrative and graphic presentations of the results of analyses are preferable to tabulations of quantitative results.

Gross margin analysis, along the lines illustrated above, though useful, should be interpreted with care. Computation of the effect of the several factors — price, cost, and volume — is based upon the unrealistic premise that each factor operates independently. This premise is not wholly accurate since there is a dependent interrela-

Illustration 27–2

THE XYZ COMPANY

Analysis of the Variation in Gross Margin

For the Period (Last Year) to (This Year)

The $67 decrease in gross margin resulted from the following factors:

		Effect on Gross Margin *(Increase – Decrease°)*
Increase of $320 in sales due to –		
1. Sales price variation – increase in sales revenue resulting from management decision to increase unit sales price by 20% for the year......................$220		
2. Sales volume variation – increase in sales revenue resulting from 10% increase in physical volume of goods sold† 100		$320
Increase of $387 in cost of goods sold due to –		
3. Cost price variation – increase in cost of goods sold due to a 30% higher unit cost for the year..$297°		
4. Cost volume variation – increase in cost of goods sold due to 10% increase in physical volume of goods sold.. 90°		387°
Decrease in Gross Margin		$ 67°

† Some analysts prefer to combine sales volume variation and cost volume variation into one amount – volume variation.

tionship between sales, cost, and volume as they affect gross margin. The analysis does not purport to show the effect of a change in price on sales volume (quantity of goods sold).

Alternate Analysis of Gross Margin Variation

In the above analyses each variation in sales and cost of goods sold was identified with two factors – price and volume. This approach is frequently referred to as a *two-way analysis* of the sales and cost variations. Some analysts prefer what may be referred to as a *three-way analysis*. The additional variation is generally referred to as the *quantity-price variation* with respect to sales and the *quantity-cost variation* with respect to cost of goods sold. This approach may be illustrated as follows (based on data given in Illustration 27–1):

A. Causes of the $320 increase in sales:
  1. Sales price variation, $1,000 \times (\$1.20 - \$1.00)$............................$200
  2. Sales volume variation, $\$1 \times (1,100 - 1,000)$............................ 100
  3. Quantity-price variation:
      Variation in units $(100) \times$ variation in price $(\$.20)$.................. 20
      Variation in sales.. $320
B. Causes of the $387 increase in cost of goods sold:
  4. Cost price variation, $1,000 \times (\$1.17 - \$.90)$............................$270°
  5. Cost volume variation, $\$.90 \times (1,100 - 1,000)$ .... 90°
  6. Quantity-cost variation:
      Variation in units $(100) \times$ variation in cost $(\$.27)$ .... 27°
      Variation in cost of goods sold .... 387°
Variation in Gross Margin .... $ 67°

° Decrease.

Comparison of the results of the three-way analysis with the results of the two-way analysis in the above illustration for sales shows
an amount of $20 (quantity-price variation) as a separate variation in
the three-way analysis, whereas in the two-way analysis this amount
was included in the sales price variation. The two-way computation
could have been made in such a way that the $20 in question would
be reflected in the sales volume variation rather than in the sales
price variation. There seems to be no particularly logical basis to
support favoring one approach over the other. Some accountants
prefer to adjust the computation so that this "difference" is identified with the larger of the price or volume variation; others prefer a
three-way analysis as explained above.

The two-way and three-way analyses may be conveniently compared graphically as shown in Illustration 27–3.

Illustration 27–3
Variation Analysis Graphed

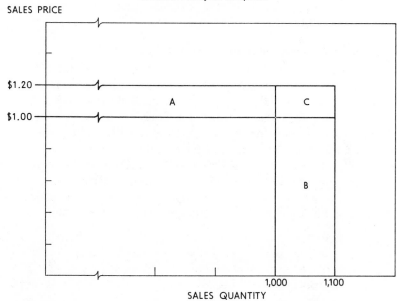

Variation	Computation	Amount	Graphic Identification
Two-way analysis:			
Sales price variation ....($1.20 − $1.00)1,100		$220	A + C
Sales quantity variation......(1,100 − 1,000)$1.00		100	B
Total Sales Variation		$320	(A + C) + B
Three-way analysis:			
Sales price variation ....($1.20 − $1.00)1,000		$200	A
Sales quantity variation......(1,100 − 1,000)$1.00		100	B
Quantity-price variation......(1,100 − 1,000)($1.20 − $1.00)		20	C
Total Sales Variation		$320	A + B + C

A three-way analysis may be developed in the same manner with respect to the variation in cost of goods sold. The resultant *quantity-cost variation* would be $27, computed immediately above. ($1.17 − $.90) (1,100 − 1,000).

The "third" variance in each analysis may be explained as follows:

1. Quantity-price variation—additional increase in sales revenue due to the simultaneous effect of increased sales price and increased physical volume.
2. Quantity-cost variation—additional increase in cost of goods sold due to the simultaneous effect of increased unit cost and increased physical volume.

The three-way analysis appears to be preferable from a theoretical point of view; nevertheless, the two-way analysis appears to be used more in actual practice because of the difficulty of explaining the meaning and significance of the quantity-price and quantity-cost factors in simple terms for reporting purposes.

Gross Margin Analysis Using Percents of Change

The preceding illustration and discussions have assumed that detailed statistics are available relative to units sold, unit sales price, and unit cost price. Obviously, this assumption would limit the analysis to situations where there are detailed statistics by product or where there is only one product. Frequently, it is impractical to attempt an analysis for each product separately. In many such cases the accountant can develop an analysis for groups of products or for the entire company by resorting to percentages based on averages. If the analyst can obtain a reasonably accurate estimate of any *one* of the following percentages, the analysis can be performed.

A. Sales price percentage—the average percent of increase or decrease in selling prices. This estimate may be developed by the sales executives or from data from the accounting records.
B. Cost price percentage—the average percent of increase or decrease in cost prices. This estimate may be developed by the manufacturing executives (or buyers) or from accounting data.
C. Quantity percentage—the average percent of increase or decrease in physical volume of goods sold. This estimate may be developed by the sales executives or from accounting data.

Computations based on percentages (rather than on unit data) under several different assumptions as to data available are illustrated below in two separate cases.

Case A—Sales Price Percent Known. This situation can be posed by adapting the data given in Illustration 27-1. Assume that these data represent not one but several products; that physical quantities, unit prices, and unit costs are not known; and that it has been estimated by the sales executives that there was an *average increase of 20% in selling prices* for the year. In order to determine the several variations reflecting the cause of the variation in gross margin, percentage of change must be derived for (*a*) price (given as 20% increase in this case), (*b*) cost, and (*c*) volume. The computation mechanically may be facilitated by setting up a tabulation similar to Illustration 27–4. Data for columns (1) and (5) will be available from the account-

Illustration 27–4
Variation Analysis Based on Sales Percentage

	(1)	(2)	(3)	(4)	(5)	(6)
			Quantity This Year			
	This Year Actual	*Price and Cost Percents*	*at Last Year's Price and Cost*	*Quantity Percents*	*Last Year Actual*	*Varia- tions*
Sales $1,320	120% (*a*)	$1,100 (*b*)	110% (*c*)	$1,000	$320
Cost of goods sold..... 1,287	130% (*e*)	990 (*d*)	110% (*c*)	900	387°
Gross Margin..........$ 33				$ 100	$ 67°

° Decrease.

ing records (see Illustration 27–1). It is assumed that item (*a*) under column (2) has been *estimated* (20%) with reasonable accuracy. The remaining amounts and percentages under columns (2), (3), and (4), are computed *in order* as follows:

a) Given.
b) $1,320 ÷ 120% = $1,100 (This year's sales divided by the average price percentage gives this year's sales volume at last year's prices.)
c) $1,100 ÷ $1,000 = 110% (This year's sales volume at last year's prices divided by last year's sales gives the volume or quantity percent for sales due to change in volume only.)
The 110% quantity percent applies to both sales volume and cost volume, hence it is carried down to the cost line in column (4).
d) $900 × 110% = $990 (Last year's cost of sales multiplied by the quantity percent gives this year's sales volume at last year's cost.)
e) $1,287 ÷ $990 = $130% (This year's sales divided by this year's sales volume at last year's cost gives the average cost percent.)

The variations may be readily computed by utilizing the derived percentages as follows:

Effect on Gross Profit
(*Increase − Decrease°*)

Two-Way Analysis:
1. Sales price variation, $1,100 × 20% $220
2. Sales volume variation, $1,000 × 10%................................... 100

    Variation in sales (increase)... $320
3. Cost price variation, $990 × 30% ....$297°
4. Cost volume variation, $900 × 10%.....................................   90°

    Variation in cost of goods sold (increase).........................   387°

    Variation in Gross Margin (decrease)............................... $ 67°

Three-Way Analysis:
1. Sales price variation, $1,000 × 20% $200
2. Sales volume variation, $1,000 × 10%.................................. 100
3. Quantity-price variation, $1,000 × 20% × 10%......................   20

    Variation in sales (increase)... $320
4. Cost price variation, $900 × 30% ....$270°
5. Cost volume variation, $900 × 10% ....   90°
6. Quantity-cost variation, $900 × 30% × 10%.......................   27°

    Variation in cost of goods sold (increase).........................   387°

    Variation in Gross Margin (decrease)............................... $ 67°

Case B — Cost Price Percentage Known. Assume that data given in the tabulation in columns (1), (5), and (6) are available and that it has been *estimated* that there was an *average increase of 20% in cost price* (as opposed to volume) for the year (see Illustration 27–5). In this case 120% is entered on the last line in column (2). Next the $162,000 in column (3) was derived ($194,400 ÷ 120%); then the quantity percents in column (4) ($162,000 ÷ $180,000) = 90%. In turn, the $180,000 in column (3) ($200,000 × 90%) and finally the 105% ($189,000 ÷ $180,000) in column (2) were computed.

In deciding whether a particular variation as computed represents an *increase* or *decrease* as it affects gross margin, it is well to remember that —

1. An increase in unit sales *price,* or a price percent above 100%, indicates an increase in gross margin, whereas a decrease in unit price or a price percent below 100%, indicates the opposite effect.
2. An increase in unit *cost,* or a cost percent above 100%, indicates a decrease in gross margin, whereas a decrease in unit cost, or a cost percent below 100%, indicates the opposite effect.
3. An increase in physical *volume,* or a quantity percent above 100%, indicates an increase in gross margin through *sales,* but indicates a decrease in gross profit through *cost of goods sold.* A decrease in physical volume, or a quantity percent below 100%, would indicate the opposite effects.
4. In computing the quantity-price and quantity-cost variations, the increases (plus) and decreases (minus) must be observed in the mathematical computations.

Illustration 27–5
Variation Analysis Based on Cost Percentage

	(1) This Year Actual	(2) Price and Cost Percents	(3) Quantity This Year at Last Year's Price and Cost	(4) Quantity Per-cents	(5) Last Year Actual	(6) Variations (Increase − Decrease°)
Sales	$189,000	105%	$180,000	90%	$200,000	$11,000°
Cost of goods sold ...	194,400	120	162,000	90	180,000	14,400
Gross Margin...........	$ (5,400)				$ 20,000	$25,400°

Computation of Variations

Effect on Gross Margin
(Increase − Decrease°)

Two-Way Analysis:
1. Sales price variation, $180,000 × 5%................................$ 9,000
2. Sales volume variation, $200,000 × 10%............................ 20,000°
3. Cost price variation, $162,000 × 20% .... 32,400°
4. Cost volume variation, $180,000 × 10%............................. 18,000

    Variation in Gross Margin... $25,400°

Three-Way Analysis:
1. Sales price variation, $200,000 × 5%...............................$10,000
2. Sales volume variation, $200,000 × 10%............................ 20,000°
3. Quantity-price variation, $200,000 ×
    5% × 10%.. 1,000°
4. Cost price variation, $180,000 × 20% .... 36,000°
5. Cost volume variation, $180,000 × 10%............................. 18,000
6. Quantity-cost variation, $180,000 ×
    20% × 10%... 3,600

    Variation in Gross Margin... $25,400°

The procedures discussed above may be applied in a similar manner to analyze gross margin variations between *budget allowances*
and actual results for a specific period of time. Many accountants
and other executives believe that this application is much more useful
than when applied only to historical data.

BREAK-EVEN ANALYSIS

Break-even analysis, more descriptively referred to as cost-volume-
profit analysis, relates to analytical procedures used to determine and
express the interrelationships of different volumes of activity (sales),
costs, sales prices, and sales mix[2] to *profits*. Specifically, the analysis
is concerned with what will be the effect on profits of changes in sales

---

[2] Sales mix refers to the relative proportions of the several products sold. For example if 5,000 units of Product A and 10,000 units of Product B are sold in January
and 6,000 of A and 9,000 of B in February, there has been a change in sales mix.

volume, sales prices, sales mix, and costs. These relationships are not easy to determine even with reasonable approximation. Break-even analysis may relate to either historical data or to future estimates (budget data); obviously, the more significant application relates to future estimates.

The *break-even point*, defined as that volume at which revenue exactly equals cost, is somewhat incidental to cost-volume-profit analysis. The analysis of cost-volume-profit relationships, when reasonably accurate, can provide management with data which give an insight into certain *economic characteristics* of the firm having considerable significance in many areas of managerial decisions.

Break-even analysis fundamentally rests upon the important concept of *cost variability*. This concept requires that *all* manufacturing, distribution, and administrative costs be identified as to their *fixed* and *variable* components. *Fixed* costs are defined as those costs that remain constant over short time periods, for all practical purposes, irrespective of changes in physical volume of business (sales volume). In direct contrast, *variable* costs are defined as those costs that, for all practical purposes, vary *proportionately* (in direct ratio to) changes in physical volume of business (sales volume). Both definitions are subject to a *relevant range* of volume changes.

In addition, an understanding of break-even analysis requires an appreciation of the mathematical process involved. To illustrate these concepts assume the following simplified data are available:

Sales (10,000 units @ $100)			$1,000,000
Costs:	*Fixed*	*Variable*	
Direct material		$100,000	
Direct labor		200,000	
Factory overhead	$ 80,000	300,000	
Administrative expenses	90,000	40,000	
Distribution expenses	100,000	60,000	
Total Costs	$270,000	$700,000	970,000
Net Income			$ 30,000

Note: Maximum capacity of plant is 12,000 units.

The break-even point may be determined, once the requisite data are available, by means of simple mathematical procedures, or may be approximated by plotting the data on a graph. There are a number of computational formulas that may be used; the three usually employed are as follows:

1. Based on the accounting equation:

$$\text{Sales} = \text{Fixed Costs} + \text{Variable Costs} + \text{Profit}$$

Adapted:

$$\text{Break-Even Point in Sales} = \text{Fixed Costs} + \frac{\text{Variable Costs at}}{\text{Break-Even Sales}}$$

$$+ \frac{\text{Profit at}}{\text{Zero}}$$

Therefore:

$$\text{BES} = \text{FC} + \frac{\text{VC}}{\text{S}}(\text{BES}) + 0$$

Substituting the illustrative data:

$$\text{BES} = \$270,000 + \frac{\$700,000}{\$1,000,000}(\text{BES}) + 0$$
$$\text{BES} = \quad 270,000 + .70\ \text{BES}$$
$$.30\ \text{BES} = \quad 270,000$$
$$\text{BES} = \$900,000$$

2. Based on the contribution equation:

$$\text{BES} = \frac{\text{Fixed Costs} + \text{Profit}}{1 - \dfrac{\text{Variable Costs}}{\text{Corresponding Sales}}}$$

Substituting the illustrative data we have —

$$\text{BES} = \frac{\$270,000 + \$0}{1 - \dfrac{\$700,000}{\$1,000,000}} = \frac{\$270,000}{1 - .70}$$

$$= \frac{\$270,000}{.30}$$

$$= \$900,000 \text{ (or } \$900,000 \div \$100 = 9,000 \text{ units at break even)}$$

This formula may be explained as follows: Dividing variable costs by the corresponding sales revenue figure gives the part (.70) of each sales dollar that is required to cover variable costs; this value generally is referred to as the *variable-cost ratio* or percentage. Subtraction of this value from unity (1) gives the contribution of each sales dollar to cover *fixed costs* and *profit*. The contribution of each sales dollar to cover fixed costs and profit, .30 in the illustration, frequently is referred to as the P/V (profit/volume) ratio. Profit is zero at break even; therefore, division of the total fixed costs by the P/V ratio gives the dollar amount of sales revenue that is required to exactly cover all fixed costs, that is, the break-even point.

This equation also may be explained by rearranging the income statement in a "direct costing" format, viz:

Sales	$1,000,000	100%
Variable costs	700,000	70 (variable cost ratio)
Contribution margin	$ 300,000	30% (P/V ratio)
Fixed costs	270,000	
Net Income	$ 30,000	

$$\text{BES} = \frac{FC}{P/V \text{ Ratio}} = \frac{\$270,000}{30\%} = \$900,000$$

3. Based on unit price and unit cost:

Unit sales price ($1,000,000 ÷ 10,000 units) $100
Unit variable cost ($700,000 ÷ 10,000 units) 70
Difference—contribution of each unit sold to cover fixed
  costs and profit .... $ 30

Fixed costs to be recovered ($270,000) divided by unit contribution ($30) gives the break-even volume in *units* (9,000).

Obviously, unit cost computations can be used only in the case of the single product or in application of the analysis to each product separately.

Proof of computations (for all approaches):

	Fixed	*Variable*	*Total*
Sales at break even as computed (9,000 units × $100)			$900,000
Cost at break even:			
Direct material (9,000 units × $10)		$ 90,000	
Direct labor (9,000 units × $20)		180,000	
Factory overhead—fixed	$ 80,000		
Variable (9,000 units × $30)		270,000	
Administrative expense—fixed	90,000		
Variable (9,000 units × $4)		36,000	
Distribution expense—fixed	100,000		
Variable (9,000 units × $6)		54,000	
Total Costs	$270,000	$630,000	900,000
Net Income at Break Even			nil

The illustrative data analyzed above are plotted in Illustration 27–6 in such manner that the break-even point and the effect of various sales volumes on costs and profits are indicated. It may be observed that costs and dollar revenue are plotted on the vertical scale against volume (units sold) on the horizontal scale. Note that each scale is from zero to capacity. In case more than one product

Illustration 27–6
Break-Even Chart

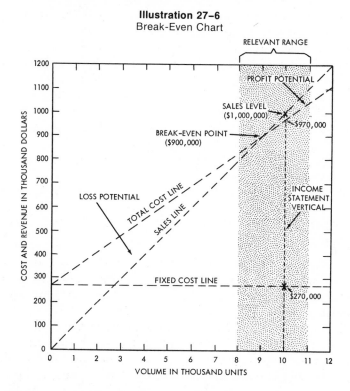

is involved, the horizontal scale must be expressed in terms of *dollars* of volume.

The chart is easily constructed by first plotting the "income statement vertical," marking thereon three key values — fixed costs ($270,000), total costs ($970,000), and sales ($1,000,000). The fixed cost line is then plotted horizontally through the fixed cost point; the sales line is plotted from the sales level point to the zero intersection at the left; and the total cost line is plotted from the total cost point to the point of intersection of the fixed cost line with the left vertical scale. Charts of the type shown in Illustration 27–6 are excellent devices for presenting the concepts and interpretations in nontechnical terms for managerial use.

The illustrations above clearly bring out the basic short-run assumptions and concepts which underlie break-even analysis. These assumptions and concepts may be briefly outlined as follows:

1. That the concept of cost variability is valid; therefore, costs can be classified realistically as *fixed* and *variable*. Fixed costs are those items of cost which do not vary with changes in sales volume or productive activity within a relevant range of operations. They

accrue with the passage of time and remain relatively constant in the short run. Variable costs vary in direct proportion to sales or productive activity within a relevant range of operations.

2. That selling price does not change as physical volume of sales changes.
3. That there is only one product, or in case of multiple products, that sales mix remains constant.
4. That productivity per worker remains essentially unchanged in the short run.
5. That the general price level remains essentially stable in the short run.
6. That there is synchronization between sales and production; that is, inventory remains constant, or is zero.
7. That there is a relevent range of validity for all of the other underlying assumptions and concepts.

The assumption that all costs may be classified as fixed or variable places a serious burden upon break-even analysis since the results are no more reliable than the classification of costs. In most situations many costs such as salaries, taxes, depreciation, and insurance can be identified readily as fixed for all practical purposes. Similarly, many costs such as direct labor and direct material may be identified readily as variable. Generally, there will remain a number of costs that are neither fixed nor variable but are semivariable in nature. These semivariable costs must be resolved into their fixed and variable components if break-even analysis is to be applied. Numerous approaches have been developed for resolving semivariable costs into fixed and variable components.[3] In many situations, such procedures are appropriate, whereas in other situations they may be impractical, if not impossible. In applying and interpreting break-even analysis results, the margin of error in expense classification must be kept in mind.

The concept of *relevant range* is particularly important with respect to interpretation of break-even analysis results. Although the break-even chart extends from zero to capacity, it has significance only within the narrow band of relevance indicated by the shaded area. The relevant range is indicative of the fact that the data upon which the analysis is developed relate to a narrow range of operations. Outside the relevant range a revised break-even analysis would be in order. In other words, the linear relationships assumed do not prevail from zero volume to capacity, but only in a segment of that range which is called the "relevant range."

In situations where break-even analysis on a reasonably valid basis can be developed, numerous applications are possible in the areas of

---

[3] See Glenn A. Welsch, *Budgeting: Profit Planning and Control* (Englewood Cliffs, N.J.: Prentice-Hall, Inc., 1970), chap. ix.

managerial planning, control, and decision making. The following illustrations (based on the illustrative data) are indicative of some applications:

1. What is the margin of safety?

The margin of safety (M/S) is the relationship of sales to the break-even point. It is important that management realize how close to the break-even point the concern is operating. The margin of safety may be expressed in one of several ways; the simplest expression results from dividing sales by break even. To illustrate, the margin of safety may be computed as follows, utilizing the data above:

$$\frac{\text{Sales}}{\text{Break Even}} = \frac{\$1,000,000}{\$900,000} = 111\%$$

Interpretation: The concern is operating 11% above the break-even point.

Alternative computation:

$$\frac{\$1,000,000 - \$900,000}{\$900,000} = 11\%$$

2. What sales volume is required to generate a net profit of $40,000?

Computation:

$$S \text{ (Sales)} = \frac{\text{Fixed Costs} + \$40,000}{1 - \dfrac{\text{Variable Costs}}{\text{Corresponding Sales}}}$$

$$= \frac{\$270,000 + \$40,000}{1 - \dfrac{\$700,000}{\$1,000,000}}$$

$$= \frac{\$310,000}{.30}$$

$$= \$1,033,333 \text{ (or 10,333 units)}$$

3. What is the break-even point if management makes a decision which increases fixed costs by $9,000?

Computation:

$$\text{BEP} = \frac{\$279,000}{.30}$$

$$= \$930,000 \text{ (or 9,300 units)}$$

4. What is the break-even point if management makes a decision which increases variable costs by 10%?

Computation:

$$BEP = \frac{\$270,000}{1 - \dfrac{\$700,000 \times 110\%}{\$1,000,000}}$$

$$= \frac{\$270,000}{.23}$$

$$= \$1,173,913 \text{ (or } 11,739 \text{ units)}$$

5. What is the break-even point if management decides to increase selling price by 10%?

Computation:

$$BEP = \frac{\$270,000}{1 - \dfrac{\$700,000}{\$1,000,000 \times 110\%}}$$

$$= \frac{\$270,000}{1 - .6364} = \frac{\$270,000}{.3636}$$

$$= \$742,574 \text{ (or } \$742,574 \div \$110 = 6,751 \text{ units)}$$

6. What sales volume is required to generate a $30,000 net profit assuming management decides to increase selling price by 10%?

Computation:

$$Sales = \frac{\$270,000 + \$30,000}{.3636}$$

$$= \$825,083 \text{ (or } 7,501 \text{ units)}$$

ANALYSIS AND REPORTING OF INCOME AND COST IN TERMS OF RESPONSIBILITIES

One of the more significant developments in recent years has been the concern of accountants with the internal application of accounting data to the planning and control needs of management. This development in accounting reflects the well-established principle of management that sound organizational structure and careful delineation and assignment of individual managerial responsibilities in terms of organizational structure are essential to efficient operations. A result of this concern on the part of both management and accountants has been the wide acceptance of the concepts of *profit-center* accounting, *responsibility-center* accounting, and *performance* reporting.

A basic principle of these concepts, with respect to internal use, is that the collection, classification, and reporting of accounting data should be oriented primarily to *organizational responsibilities* and secondarily in terms of cost of products. This idea reflects the fact that planning and control in the business situation are attained through *people*. Acceptance of the concepts of profit-center and responsibility-center accounting requires that the chart of accounts and internal accounting reports be designed to correspond with the organizational responsibilities of each individual having managerial status.

Although certain allocations are desirable for specific purposes such as determining the full cost of each product, a basic principle is that financial data for planning and control purposes should not be cluttered up with arbitrary allocations over which the individual executive has no control.

Although income statements by departments, for example, are not new, the concepts of responsibility accounting and performance reporting along with the decentralization of operations in many firms into numerous "profit or responsibility centers" have caused renewed interest in the collection and reporting of accounting data in terms of responsibilities. Preparation of income statements by profit centers poses a problem relative to presentation of certain allocations of overhead costs. One procedure for reporting by profit centers (departments in this case) is shown in Illustration 27–7. Note that (*a*) direct departmental profit is clearly shown and (*b*) allocations over which the departmental manager has no control are clearly set out.

Illustration 27–7
FRIENDLY DEPARTMENT STORE
Income Statement
For the Month Ending January 31, 1971

	Department		
	1	*2*	*Total*
Sales	$80,000	$140,000	$220,000
Cost of goods sold	62,000	110,000	172,000
Gross margin	$18,000	$ 30,000	$ 48,000
Direct departmental costs	6,000	11,000	17,000
Direct departmental income (loss)	$12,000	$ 19,000	$ 31,000
Allocation of indirect overhead	5,000	6,000	11,000
Net Departmental Income (before tax)	$ 7,000	$ 13,000	$ 20,000

A third principle of responsibility accounting and performance reporting is that actual results should be compared with some realistic standard. Thus, actual results accumulated through the accounts should be compared with (*a*) budget standards or (*b*) standard costs. The comparison of the actual results of one period with the actual results of a prior period for this purpose suffers from several serious weaknesses, principally due to the noncomparable conditions as between two different periods.

Illustration 27–8
Articulation of Performance Reports by Responsibility
A. REPORT FOR TOP MANAGEMENT
Division Cost Summary—February 1971

	Actual		(Over) Under Budget	
	This Month	Year to Date	This Month	Year to Date
Controllable Costs:				
Sales Division ....$	45,000	$ 88,000	($1,880)	($2,700)
Finance Division	5,500	10,500	(150)	150
Production Division	62,000	123,000	(1,520)	(2,720)
Administrative Division..........	18,200	36,500	970	1,600
Others	9,300	18,000	80	(30)
Total all divisions ....$	140,000	$276,000	($2,500)	($3,700)

$2,720, etc.

B. REPORT FOR MIDDLE MANAGEMENT
Factory Cost Summary—February 1971

	Actual		(Over) Under Budget	
	This Month	Year to Date	This Month	Year to Date
Controllable Costs:				
Power Department....................$	9,400	$ 17,000	($380)	($790)
Purchasing Department............	3,200	6,000	110	160
Production Department............	31,000	60,000	(360)	(460)
Maintenance Department	15,500	34,200	(980)	(1,740)
Others	2,900	5,800	90	110
Total all departments ....$	62,000	$123,000	($1,520)	($2,720)

$460, etc.

C. REPORT FOR LOWER MANAGEMENT
Production Department Report—February 1971

	Actual		(Over) Under Budget	
	This Month	Year to Date	This Month	Year to Date
Controllable Costs:				
Direct labor.............................	$17,500	$34,000	($340)	($560)
Direct material used................	9,600	18,700	90	120
Indirect labor	1,400	2,700	(70)	(180)
Set up costs............................	400	900	(20)	(50)
Repairs	1,200	1,900	(80)	110
Supplies.................................	600	1,300	40	90
Others	300	500	20	10
Totals	$31,000	$60,000	($360)	($460)

A simplified example of performance reporting (by responsibility) for internal control purposes with respect to costs is presented in Illustration 27–8. Note in particular (a) the "tie-in" between the separate reports following organizational structure, (b) the comparison with budget standards, (c) the simplification of the report, and (d) the exclusion of noncontrollable items of cost. Also of note is the fact the higher the level of management the greater the summarization.

QUESTIONS FOR CLASS DISCUSSION

1. What are the primary causes of the variation in gross margin as between two different periods?

2. What are the two factors that give rise to variation in sales as between two different periods?

3. What are the two factors that give rise to variation in cost of goods sold as between two different periods?

4. Explain the computation and interpretation of sales price variation. Use the following simplified data from the records of the XY Company for illustrative purposes:

	Last Year	This Year
Units sold	1,000	900
Unit selling price	$1.00	$1.20

5. Explain the computation and interpretation of sales volume variation. Use the data given in 4 above for illustrative purposes.

6. Explain the differences in computation and interpretation of the variation in sales as between the two-way and three-way analyses. Use the data given in 4 above for illustrative purposes.

7. Explain the computation and interpretation of cost price variation. Use the following simplified data from the records of XY Company for illustrative purposes:

	Last Year	This Year
Units sold	1,000	900
Unit cost price	$.60	$.69

8. Explain the computation and interpretation of cost volume variation. Use the data given in 7 above for illustrative purposes.

9. Explain the differences in computation and interpretation of the variation in cost of goods sold as between the two-way and three-way analyses. Use the data given in 7 above for illustrative purposes.

10. What approach must the analyst employ in analysis of the gross margin variation when quantity data are not available?

11. What is meant by break-even analysis? Define the break-even point.

12. Explain the computation of the break-even point (a) based on the accounting equation, (b) based on the contribution equation, and (c) based on unit sales price and cost. Use the following simplified data of the RT Company for illustrative purposes:

Sales (5,000 units)..................		$50,000
Costs:		
Fixed $24,000		
Variable........................... 20,000	44,000	
Income...............................		$ 6,000

13. What is meant by the P/V ratio? What is the P/V ratio for the RT Company (12 above)?

14. Utilizing the data for the RT Company (12 above) compute and interpret the effect of each of the following contemplated changes. Consider each change separately.

a) An increase of $3,000 in fixed costs.

b) An increase of $3,000 in variable costs.

15. Explain the meaning and significance of the concept of relevant range as related to break-even analysis.

16. What are the basic assumptions and concepts which underlie break-even analysis? Why is an appreciation and understanding of them essential to proper interpretation of the results of break-even analysis?

17. Explain the concept of responsibility accounting. Why is it important from the management control point of view?

18. Why is the problem of cost allocation critical with respect to the problem of cost control?

DECISION CASE 27–1

Watt Company has been operating for over 40 years; it is a publicly held corporation and its common stock is listed on the stock exchanges. The company manufactures seven lines of products; four in Plant No. 1 and three in Plant No. 2. The company sells to wholesale outlets throughout the United States. The country is divided into four sales regions. Plant No. 1 has six producing departments and Plant No. 2 has four such departments; each has three service departments (administration, maintenance, and production planning and scheduling). Both plants utilize a "normal" absorption cost system that collects and reports costs by lines of products. All sales activities in the company are conducted under the supervision of the central sales function. Production levels are geared to sales projections which are revised monthly based upon actual sales to date, economic analyses, estimates provided by the four regional sales managers, and executive judgment. Quarterly, financial statements for internal management use are prepared by the controller's department. The company has not utilized a comprehensive budget program. The quarterly financial statements compare the current quarter (just ended) with the preceding quarter for sales, costs, and income. In respect to each plant the quarterly report provides data on plant output for the quarter, inventory levels, number of employees, and actual expenses.

Recently executive management decided to implement a "comprehensive profit planning and control program" which would entail the development of a three-year, long-range plan and an annual profit plan. The annual profit plan will be detailed by month and revised each quarter. An important facet of the new program will be restructuring of the internal performance reporting system.

Required:

List and briefly explain the primary concepts (and changes) that you think should be incorporated into the new reporting system. Concentrate your attention primarily on internal reporting problems.

EXERCISES

Exercise 27–1

The sales records of the Sexton Company reflected the following:

	Sales	
Year	Units	Amount
19A..........................	2,000	$200,000
19B..........................	2,200	228,800

Required:

1. Prepare a two-way analysis to reflect the effect of price and volume changes.
2. Prepare a three-way analysis.
3. Develop a graphic analysis to reflect the analyses; identify each variance.

Exercise 27–2

The records of the Home Company provided the following information relative to the main product:

	Year Ended December 31	
	19A	19B
Sales...	$400,000	$409,500
Cost of sales	260,000	256,200
Gross margin	$140,000	$153,300
Operating expenses..........................	110,000	109,300
Net Income	$ 30,000	$ 44,000

Units sold: 19A.........20,000
19B.........21,000

Required:

Analyze the causes of the $13,300 increase in gross margin using a two-way analysis of the sales and cost of sales variations.

Exercise 27–3

Based on the data given in Exercise 27–2 and the solution to it, prepare a suitable report to management.

Exercise 27–4

Utilizing the data given in Exercise 27–2 for the Home Company, analyze the $13,300 increase in gross margin using a three-way analysis of the sales and cost of sales variations.

Exercise 27–5

Based on the data given in Exercise 27–2 and the solution to Exercise 27–4, prepare a suitable report to management.

Exercise 27–6

The records of the Conrad Company showed the following statistics relative to the one product distributed by the company:

	Year Ended June 30	
	19A	19B
Sales	$1,200,000	$1,176,000
Cost of sales	840,000	812,000
Gross margin	$ 360,000	$ 364,000
Operating expenses	270,000	264,000
Net Income	$ 90,000	$ 100,000

Average sales prices: 19A, $40; 19B, $42.

Required:

Analyze the causes of the $10,000 increase in net income assuming a two-way analysis of the sales and cost of sales variations.

Exercise 27–7

Utilizing the data given in Exercise 27–6 for the Conrad Company (a) analyze the $10,000 increase in net income assuming a three-way analysis of the sales and cost of sales variations and (b) show how the results might be presented to management.

Exercise 27–8

In 1971 the Almo Cement Company sold 10% more in volume than in 1970, yet the net income declined substantially. Condensed income statements for the two years were as follows:

	1971	1972
Sales	$1,372,800	$1,300,000
Cost of cement sold	920,200	845,000
Gross margin	$ 452,600	$ 455,000
Operating expenses	360,000	280,000
Net Income	$ 92,600	$ 175,000

Required:

Analyze the causes of the variation in net income assuming (a) a two-way analysis of the sales and cost of sales variations and (b) a three-way analysis. Round to even $100.

Exercise 27–9

The Cox Wholesale Company handles 15 different products. Statistics relating to quantities sold by product are not maintained. The company has experienced a drop in gross margin. The management is interested in an evaluation of the factors causing the decrease in gross margin. Since no detailed statistics are available, upon request the executive in charge of sales estimated that sales prices were increased on the average of 6% for the year. The income statement provided the following data:

	19A	19B
Sales	$850,000	$855,950
Cost of sales	540,000	554,040

Required:

Analyze the causes of the variation in gross margin using (a) a two-way analysis of the sales and cost of sales variations and (b) a three-way analysis.

Exercise 27-10

The Linden Corporation executives prepared a budgeted income statement for the coming year which showed the following data (summarized):

Sales ($20 per unit)		$2,400,000
Costs:		
Fixed	$1,200,000	
Variable	960,000	2,160,000
Net Income		$ 240,000

Required:

1. Compute the break-even point using the formula based on the accounting equation.
2. Compute the break-even point using the formula based on the contribution equation.
3. Compute the break-even point employing unit price and cost data.
4. Prove your computations of the break-even point.
5. Compute the margin of safety.
6. Compute the P/V ratio.

Exercise 27-11

The Smart Distributing Company income statement for the past year showed the following data (condensed):

Sales		$900,000
Cost of sales		600,000
Gross margin		$300,000
Selling and general costs:		
Fixed	$106,000	
Variable	120,000	226,000
Net Income		$ 74,000

Required:

1. Compute the break-even point for the past year.
2. What sales revenue would have been necessary assuming no increase in sales prices, to earn 10% on sales?

3. Compute the break-even point assuming an increase of $45,000 in variable costs at the same physical volume.

4. Compute the break-even point assuming an increase of $45,000 in fixed costs at the same physical volume. Disregard requirement 3.

Exercise 27–12

The Lanier Manufacturing Company is in the process of developing a budget for the coming year. The management is concerned about the probable profit; therefore, several alternatives are under consideration which might improve the profit picture and the break-even situation. The tentative budget indicates the following:

Sales...		$8,000,000
Cost of sales:		
Fixed...$3,000,000		
Variable 1,800,000		4,800,000
Gross margin		$3,200,000
Selling and general expenses:		
Fixed...$1,500,000		
Variable 1,400,000		2,900,000
Net Income		$ 300,000

Required:

1. Compute the break-even point.

2. Management is considering increasing sales prices by 5%. Evaluate the effect on profits and the break-even point assuming physical volume of sales is unaffected.

3. Management is considering actions that would reduce fixed costs by 5%. Evaluate the effect on profits and the break-even point. Disregard requirement 2 above.

4. Management is considering actions that would reduce variable costs by 5%. Evaluate the effect on profits and the break-even point. Disregard requirements 2 and 3 above.

5. Evaluate the effect on profits and the break-even point assuming requirements 2, 3, and 4 are accepted.

Exercise 27–13

The Towncraft Company manufactures and sells one product. The budget for the coming year showed the following unit data:

Unit selling price..$12.00
Unit costs:
Fixed manufacturing cost.. 3.00
Variable manufacturing cost 3.30
Fixed selling cost.. 1.35
Variable selling cost .... .60
Fixed general cost.. 1.68
Variable general cost .... .06

Net income budgeted for the year, $201,000.

Required:

1. Compute the break-even point.

2. Prepare a break-even chart. Scale volume in units and assume relevant range 70,000 to 120,000 units.

3. How many units must be sold, assuming no change in unit sales price, to earn 15% on sales?

4. Plot the effect of a 10% increase in sales price on the chart prepared in requirement 2. Recompute the break-even point.

PROBLEMS

Problem 27–1

The financial report for the Birch Manufacturing Company provided the following statistics:

	19B			19A		
Product	Units Sold	Net Sales	Cost of Sales	Units Sold	Net Sales	Cost of Sales
X................................	900	$54,000	$36,000	1,000	$53,000	$42,000
Y................................	1,750	63,000	49,000	1,500	48,000	33,000

Required:

1. Prepare a comparative statement (19A and 19B) by product for the components of gross margin.

2. Prepare an analysis of the causes of the variations in gross margins, using a two-way analysis of the sales and cost of sales variations.

3. Compute the variations assuming a three-way analysis.

Problem 27–2

The Black Manufacturing Company income statement showed the following data:

	This Year	Last Year
Sales	$126,000	$112,000
Cost of goods sold..........................	102,000	84,000

Average sales price per unit this year, $42.
Average cost price per unit last year, $30.

Required:

1. Analyze the variation in gross margin assuming a two-way analysis of the sales and cost of sales variations. Prepare a report suitable for presentation to management.

2. Analyze the variation in gross margin assuming a three-way analysis and prepare a report for presentation to management.

3. Account for the differences resulting from the two solutions required above.

Problem 27–3

Ransom Sales Company distributes two products. Quantity records are maintained for each product. The president of the company in examining the summary of operations presented below noted that gross margin increased "around 14% whereas sales increased only 7%." He suggested the "possibility of an error" in the data. An examination of the records revealed no errors.

Required:

You are requested to prepare a statement indicating the causes of the differences noted by the president. Show (*a*) your computations and (*b*) the report for the president. Assume a two-way analysis of the sales and cost of sales variations:

	Product A		Product B		Total	
	Last Year	This Year	Last Year	This Year	Last Year	This Year
Sales............................	$40,000	$45,600	$100,000	$104,500	$140,000	$150,100
Cost of sales.................	30,000	32,400	80,000	83,600	110,000	116,000
Gross margin.................	$10,000	$13,200	$ 20,000	$ 20,900	$ 30,000	$ 34,100
Operating expenses.......					16,000	18,100
Net Income...................					$ 14,000	$ 16,000
Units sold	10,000	12,000	20,000	19,000		

Problem 27–4

Benson Specialties Company manufactures and distributes two groups of products, each consisting of numerous individual products. Statistics are not accumulated relative to units sold by individual product. You are called upon to prepare a statement for management showing the causes of the variation in gross margin for each group of products (two-way analysis). You have obtained the following statistics:

Product Group A: Average increase in cost during 19B was 4%.
Product Group B: Average decrease in physical volume sold during 19B was 6%.

	For Year Ended December 31			
	19A		19B	
	Group A	Group B	Group A	Group B
Sales	$200,000	$300,000	$208,000	$279,180
Cost of sales	150,000	180,000	160,680	165,816
Gross margin	$ 50,000	$120,000	$ 47,320	$113,364

Problem 27–5

The operating results of the Walker Manufacturing Company for the last two years in summary were as follows:

	Last Year	This Year
Net sales	$480,000	$690,000
Cost of sales	428,000	503,000
Gross margin	$ 52,000	$187,000
Distribution and administrative expenses	76,000	89,500
Operating income	$ (24,000)	$ 97,500

At the start of this year management decided that an increase in selling prices was necessary if further losses were to be avoided. Accordingly, a general increase of 15% was made in all prices for the year. At the same time a new plant manager was appointed who gave considerable attention to reducing plant costs during the year.

At the end of the year a dispute arose between the new plant manager and the executive in charge of sales. Both recognized that the increase in operating income was influenced significantly by the increase in selling prices; however, the plant manager insists that savings in factory costs were greater in amount than the increase in gross profits due to the increased volume of sales. The sales manager is equally insistent that the opposite is the case.

Required:

Present an analysis which will indicate who is correct. (Prepare a two-way and a three-way analysis.)

Problem 27-6

The income statement of Wimberley Manufacturing Corporation, whose operations are confined to production of one mechanical device, showed the following results:

	Year Ended December 31	
	19A	19B
Quantity sold	18,000	21,600
Net sales	$144,000	$190,080
Manufacturing cost	81,000	118,800
Gross margin	$ 63,000	$ 71,280
Selling and administrative expenses	27,000	37,280
Net Income	$ 36,000	$ 34,000

In view of the larger volume in 19B, the management is disappointed with the results and requested an analysis of the reasons for the decline in income.

Required:

You are to prepare the following:

a) A two-way analysis.
b) A three-way analysis.
c) A report to management based on the three-way analysis.

Problem 27-7

Certain budget data from the budgeted income statement of the Metropolitan Department Store are summarized below:

Sales...		$30,000,000
Costs:		
Fixed...	$13,050,000	
Variable......................................	16,500,000	29,550,000
Net Income		$ 450,000

Required:

(Round to even $1,000.)

1. Compute the break-even point.
2. Compute the break-even point assuming fixed costs are increased by 10%.
3. Compute the break-even point assuming variable costs only are increased by 10%.
4. Compute the break-even point assuming sales prices are increased by 10%. Disregard requirements 2 and 3.
5. Compute the break-even point assuming physical sales volume is increased by 10%. Disregard requirements 2, 3, and 4.
6. Prepare a break-even chart comparing the results of requirement 1 with the results of 2, 3, and 4 combined. Verify the indicated break-even points with computations. The relevant relationships are expected to remain stable over a volume range above and below the planned sales volume.

Problem 27-8

The Bingham Company income statement for the past year showed the following results:

Sales		$2,000,000
Cost of goods manufactured and sold:		
Fixed..	$400,000	
Variable.....................................	800,000	1,200,000
Gross margin.................................		$ 800,000
Selling and general expenses:		
Fixed..	$230,000	
Variable.....................................	300,000	530,000
Net Income...................................		$ 270,000

In planning for next year it is estimated that sales volume can be increased to $2,800,000, but that to do so would require an expensive addition to the plant. The addition would add $150,000 to fixed factory overhead and would save $30,000 of present variable factory overhead. Selling and administrative costs would not be affected by the addition; however, $30,000 would be added to fixed interest cost.

Required:

1. Prepare an estimated income statement for next year assuming the addition is made.
2. Compare the break-even points before and after the addition.
3. Compute profits after the addition at the past year's sales volume.
4. Compute the volume of sales needed, after the addition, to yield $250,000 profit assuming no change in sales prices.

Problem 27-9

The Western Manufacturing Company income statement for 19A provided the following summarized data:

Sales		$700,000
Cost:		
Fixed	$487,500	
Variable	175,000	662,500
Net Income		$ 37,500

Executive management is in the process of developing plans and policies for the budget for the coming year. Since the plant operated at practical capacity during 19A, and a continuing increase in demand for the products is expected (expectations: a 10% increase for 19B), consideration is being given to plant expansion. Two alternatives in particular have been given considerable study. Certain estimates developed with respect to them are as follows:

	Estimated Effect on—		
Plan	*Fixed Costs*	*Variable Costs*	*Plant Capacity*
A......Increase by $35,000	Increase the variable cost to sales ratio by 10%		Increase by 10%
B......Increase by $73,000	Increase the variable cost to sales ratio by 5%		Increase by 40%

Required:

1. Compute the break-even point for 19A.
2. Assuming Plan A is accepted compute (a) the break-even point and (b) the probable income for 19B. Assume no change in sales prices.
3. Assuming Plan B is accepted compute (a) the break-even point and (b) the probable income for 19B. Assume no change in sales prices.
4. Which plan would you recommend? Why?

Problem 27-10

The income statement of the Hill Company for the past year showed the following statistics:

Sales		$5,000,000
Cost of sales:		
Fixed	$1,600,000	
Variable	1,750,000	3,350,000
Gross margin		$1,650,000
Selling and general expenses:		
Fixed	$ 556,000	
Variable	800,000	1,356,000
Net Income		$ 294,000

In developing plans and policies for the coming year the executive in charge of sales estimated a potential sales volume of $7,500,000. The executive in charge of manufacturing realized that this volume of sales would necessitate major additions to fixed plant. The controller and other executives estimated that the expansion required would have the following effects:

Increase in depreciation, taxes, and insurance on factory	$220,000
Increase in superintendence salaries	20,000
Increase in miscellaneous fixed factory overhead	60,000
Increase in monthly sales salaries	200,000
Increase in annual advertising appropriation	100,000
Increase in interest cost	50,000

Required:

1. Prepare an estimated income statement for the contemplated plan.
2. Compare the break-even points before and after the expansion.
3. Compare profits before and after the expansion at present sales levels.
4. Compute the sales needed after the expansion to yield $1 million profit assuming (a) no change in selling prices and (b) the additional sales revenue is derived by means of a price increase.

chapter **28** | # Accounting for Consignments

Nature of Consignments

A consignment is a conveyance of the custody of goods from the owner, designated the *consignor,* to one who acts as his agent, designated the *consignee.* The agent, who is often locationally more accessible to available markets than is the consignor, undertakes to sell the consigned merchandise for the owner under a commission arrangement. Viewed legally, the transfer of the custody of goods is a bailment; accordingly, the laws of agency control in respect to determining the rights and responsibilities of each party (the consignor as principal, the consignee as agent). In respect to the consignor, the transaction for the transfer of goods is described as a *consignment out;* to the consignee, the receipt of these goods is termed a *consignment in.*

The basic distinction between a sale and a consignment relates to the time of legal title passage. In a transaction of sale, legal title vests in the buyer concurrently with the delivery of goods – either to the buyer or to a common carrier depending upon the terms of the sale. In both sale and consignment transactions there is a change in the *custody* of goods; however, in a consignment transaction legal title continues to identify with the consignor until the goods are sold by the consignee to a *third party.* Legal title thus passes directly from the consignor to the ultimate transferee, the buyer, when the sale is completed.

1103

In recognition of the unique characteristics of consignment transactions, the following fundamental criteria are appropriate guidelines for accounting procedures:

1. Since title to consigned goods continues to vest in the consignor, such goods should be reported in the inventory of the consignor and excluded from the inventory of the consignee.
2. Goods on consignment do not create revenue, or satisfy the revenue for either the consignor or consignee until they are sold to a third party.
3. The consignor is accountable as owner for all costs incurred which directly relate to the goods from date of shipment to the date of sale by the consignee, except as may otherwise be provided by specific contractual agreement between the parties.
4. The consignee, in his capacity as an agent, is charged with the exercise of due care of the goods held on consignment; accordingly, it is appropriate to maintain a memorandum record of consigned goods awaiting sale.

Several reasons why a consignment arrangement may be advantageous to both the consignor and the consignee are: *First*, it may be an appropriate means of enlarging channels of distribution for new products, particularly where the demand for these products is uncertain. Additionally, if the goods are high unit-cost items and if the risks of obsolescence and price change are great, retailers may hesitate to purchase such goods; yet, they may be willing to display and to sell them on the condition that the consignor carry the burden of inventory investment and risk. *Second,* there is an obvious investment advantage to the consignee, since he is not compelled to make a commitment of funds in advance of ultimate sale. *Third,* the retention of legal title may serve to reduce the credit risk of the consignor. In the event of the legal dissolution of the consignee enterprise, creditors of the consignee may not attach these goods as would be possible if the goods were *sold* to the consignee on credit. *Fourth,* the consignor establishes and continues to retain control over the selling price of consigned merchandise; the exercise of this authority seldom is possible when the goods are sold to the retailer. Notwithstanding these apparent advantages to the consignor and consignee, there has been a noticeable decrease in the use of consignments in recent years, primarily due, no doubt, to improvements in the distribution function generally and to more liberal return privileges on sales contracts.

Rights and Responsibilities Relating to Consignments

Consignment provisions should be outlined clearly in a legally executed written contract between the consignor and the consignee, dealing with such matters as commissions, terms of sale, responsibility for the collection of accounts receivable and losses from uncollectible accounts, expenses of the consignee incident to the receipt, maintenance, and sale of consigned merchandise, remittances to the consignor, care and protection of the consigned goods, and the nature and time schedule for reports to be rendered by the consignee. In respect to matters not specifically referred to in the consignment agreement, the laws of bailment and agency establish the rights and responsibilities of the parties. Since these rights and responsibilities are reciprocally related, i.e., a right of the consignee translates as a responsibility of the consignor, the primary provisions relating to the consignee only are enumerated below:

1. *Rights of the consignee:*
   a) The right to compensation for selling the consigned goods and reimbursement for necessary expenses connected therewith. The commission (or other form of reimbursement) to be allowed the consignee normally is a percentage of sales. Reimbursement for necessary expenses often covers such expenditures as freight, insurance, storage, and the usual warranty costs.
   b) The right to make the usual, but not extraordinary, warranties in respect to the quality of merchandise; the consignor is then bound by such warranties.
   c) The right to extend credit for the sale of consigned merchandise in terms consistent with those which are conventional in business enterprises selling similar goods; the consignor may limit this right by express agreement. The receivables from the sale of consigned merchandise (and any related bad debt losses) are those of the consignor. If the consignee, by contractual agreement, assumes responsibility for the collection of these receivables, he is called a *del credere agent*, and normally is allowed extra compensation for the additional risk assumed.
2. *Responsibilities of the consignee:*
   a) To care for and protect the goods held on consignment in a prudent and responsible manner.
   b) To exert reasonable efforts to sell the goods in compliance with the terms of the consignment contract. In granting credit (if this is not denied by the contract), the consignee must exercise a degree of prudence consonant with the credit standards of similar types of business enterprises. The goods should be sold at prices specified by the consignor and, in the absence of specification, at a price that appears to represent the best interests of the consignor. Similarly, the consignee must exercise reasonable diligence in the collection of receivables if he has collection responsibility.
   c) To keep the consignor's goods separate and apart from other

goods in order to assure their easy identification. This requirement normally presumes physical separation; however, in the
event this proves to be impractical, the consignee must maintain accounting records in sufficient detail to permit identification of consigned goods. A collateral obligation, although related
to the separation of consigned merchandise, is the responsibility to preserve the separateness of consignment transactions
in the accounting records; sales, reimbursable expenses, inventory, and accounts receivable from consignments all must be
clearly designated in order that the interests of the consignor
may be distinguished and protected.

  d) To render periodic reports and to make liquidating settlements
for consignment transactions (goods received, sold, and on
hand) as specified in the consignment contract. The contract
may require monthly, weekly, or even daily reports to the consignor. The periodic report typically is referred to as an *account*

Illustration 28–1

ACCOUNT SALES
Matthewson Retailers
Houston, Texas
(Consignee)

No. J-4

March 31, 1970

Date

Sold for Account and Risk of (consignor):

Jackson Manufacturing Company

231 Makin Street

Moline, Illinois

Account sales of:

Color Television Sets (Model AK-320)

Date	Explanation	Quantity		Amount
March 1	Balance on hand (carried forward)	–0–		$ –0–
March 1–31	Received	15		
	TOTAL	15		$ –0–
March 1–31	Sales:			
	TV Sets (AK-320) @ $400 each	10		4,000
	GROSS			$4,000
	Charges:			
	Warranty adjustments (on sets sold)		$ 20	
	Local freight (on 15 sets)		15	
	Commissions (20%)		800	835
	NET			$3,165
March 31	Remittance enclosed			$3,165
March 31	Balances	5		$ –0–

---

sales. It should specify the goods received on consignment, those sold, related expenses, the amount due the consignor, and the amount remitted. A representative form of an account sales is shown in Illustration 28–1.

ACCOUNTING BY THE CONSIGNEE

Since legal title to consigned goods does not vest in the consignee, formal inclusion of these units in the inventory of the consignee is unwarranted and incorrect. However, as previously noted, the consignee usually will find it desirable to use various memoranda to record merchandise held on consignment, detailing both the kind and quantity of the consigned units.

In respect to transactions involving the sale of consigned merchandise and related expenses, it is customary for the consignee to record the relevant data in a special summary Consignment In account. This account is credited with the proceeds from the sale of consigned merchandise and is debited for reimbursable expenses incurred in connection therewith and for commissions earned by the consignee. Consequently, the Consignment In account is essentially a reflection of a debtor-creditor relationship. If the account shows a residual credit balance, it indicates that the consignee is indebted to the consignor; alternatively, should a debit balance exist, it indicates a receivable due from the consignor.

The Consignment In account may be supported by subsidiary records, depending upon the need for additional account detail. The data usually contained in the summary account and the related subsidiary records are the basic source information for the *account sales*, which is fundamentally a classified enumeration of all transactions between the consignor and the consignee, concluding with the calculation of their reciprocal balance status. Where transactions are executed with several consignors, a separate account sales must be submitted to each; accordingly, it also is necessary to establish a separate Consignment In account for each consignor. In the event the number of consignors is unusually large, a Consignment In Control account supported by the various detailed accounts with each consignor may be desirable.

Illustrative Entries

Following are the entries made by a consignee (Matthewson Retailers) for certain typical consignment transactions (the data used are the March transactions reported in the account sales in Illustration 28–1):

1. To record the receipt of 15 color TV sets on consignment from the Jackson Manufacturing Company:

Make a memorandum entry indicating receipt of the consigned goods, the name of the consignor, the quantity of units ordered and received, sales price, and the storage or display location.

2. To record local freight paid on the 15 TV sets received from the Jackson Manufacturing Company:

Consignment In – Jackson Manufacturing Company................... 15
    Cash... 15

3. To record sale of 10 of the TV sets held on consignment @ $400 each:

Cash (or accounts receivable – consignment sales) 4,000
    Consignment In – Jackson Manufacturing Company............. 4,000

4. To record the payments for warranty adjustments on the TV sets sold during March:

Consignment In – Jackson Manufacturing Company................... 20
    Cash... 20

5. To record the 20% commission earned on the March sales of TV sets held on consignment:

Consignment In – Jackson Manufacturing Company................... 800
    Commissions Earned – Consignment Sales 800

6. To record the remittance to accompany the March 31 account sales forwarded to the consignor:

Consignment In – Jackson Manufacturing Company....................3,165
    Cash... 3,165

After the above entries are posted, the Consignment In account will appear as follows:

Consignment In – Jackson Manufacturing Company

March 1–31	Local freight	15	March 1–31	10 TV sets sold	4,000
	Warranty				
	adjustments	20			
	Commissions	800			
March 31	Cash remitted	3,165			
		4,000			4,000

Modifications of Entries and Account Structure

On some occasions the consignee may remit cash to the consignor in advance of the sale of any of the consigned goods; such an advance should be debited to the Consignment In account (or a special receivable account) and serves to reduce subsequent remittances to the consignor. Additionally, if the consignor assumes the responsibility for credit sales (i.e., the consignee is not a *del credere* agent), the remittance accompanying the account sales may consist of both cash and transferred open accounts. Of course, if the ultimate purchasers of consigned goods remit directly to the consignor, it is probable that the account sales will reflect an amount due to the consignee.

Should there be only one monthly consignment transaction or several transactions involving the same type of merchandise, there is little need for subsidiary account detail. Procedural variations may be required, however, to accommodate special or unique consignment arrangements. For example, if a second shipment of consigned merchandise of a different type is received from the Jackson Company, e.g., 20 black and white TV sets (Model SS-100), a more formal set of unit inventory records may be required. Additionally, the accumulation of cost and revenue data may be reflected in more detailed records as follows:

Controlling account: Consignment In Control—Jackson Manufacturing Company

Subsidiary accounts: Consignment In—Jackson Manufacturing Company (Model AK-320)

Consignment In—Jackson Manufacturing Company (Model SS-100)

This type of account structure would facilitate the preparation of a *control account sales,* expressed in dollars only, supported by *subsidiary account sales* for each type of merchandise expressed in both units and dollar amounts.

Financial Statement Presentation

In the income statement of the consignee, the *commissions earned* should be reported as an item of operating income. A balance in the Consignment In account represents either a debt to or from the consignor, and should be reported in the balance sheet as a current asset if a debit balance and as a current liability if a credit balance. Consignment In account balances which relate to different consignors should not, however, be offset; rather, the sum of the debit balances should be reported as an asset, and the sum of the credit balances should be reported separately as a liability.

ACCOUNTING BY THE CONSIGNOR

The specific accounting procedures for the consignor depend upon the following two circumstances: (1) whether he elects to record the consignment transactions in separate accounts, or to record them in the regular account classifications slightly altered to accommodate both consignment and nonconsignment transactions, and (2) whether the perpetual inventory method or the periodic inventory method is being used in the existing accounting system of the consignor. Whatever the basic format and inventory method elected by the consignor, he must maintain records reflecting consigned units shipped, sales of consigned goods and related expenses, and the status of his accountability with each consignee.

Consignment Out Account

In the event consignment transactions are entered in the regular accounts, no unique accounting problems are presented. If it is desired to record separately the regular and consignment sales, a special account, *Consignment Out,* is created in which are summarized the basic data concerning consignment transactions. The normal inclusions in the account are as follows:

Consignment Out – (Name of Consignee)

Cost of goods shipped on consignment
Expenses related to consignment, incurred by consignor
Expenses related to consignment, incurred and reported by the consignee on the account sales
Commissions earned on consigned goods sold by the consignee and reported on the account sales
Debit (credit) adjustment to yield the correct end-of-period account balance – the cost of the inventory of goods held on consignment, and other deferred costs which relate thereto

Sales of consigned goods as reported by consignee on account sales

During the accounting period, the Consignment Out account serves as a summary account in respect to all consignment transactions. At the end of the period, however, it is adjusted so that the residual balance represents the sum of the *cost* of unsold consigned goods and the related deferred expenses. The deferred expenses – including those of both the consignor and the consignee – may then be reallocated and separately identified as Deferred Consignment Costs in the accounts and/or balance sheet of the consignor. These capitalizable outlays include all expenditures incurred to place the goods in position for sale, e.g., freight charges, drayage costs, and shipping insurance; they do not include expenditures for direct selling costs such as advertising, and commissions.

Illustrative Entries – Perpetual Inventory

Illustration 28–2 presents in tabular form the entries made by the consignor (Jackson Manufacturing Company) for the transactions relative to the consignment arrangement reflected in the account sales in Illustration 28-1; additionally, the necessary end-of-period adjustments are illustrated. Entries are given under two assumptions: (1) a separate set of accounts is used for consignment sales and regular sales, and (2) one set of accounts is used for *both* regular and consignment sales. Under each assumption, a perpetual inventory system is used.

At the end of the period (the month of March), the Consignment Out account would appear as follows:

Consignment Out — Matthewson Retailers

Shipped 15 TV sets (Model AK-320) @ $150		2,250	Sale of 10 TV sets @ $400 (Model AK-320)		4,000
Consignor's expenditures:					
Crating costs	45				
Freight-out	60	105			
Consignee's expenditures:					
Warranty adjustments	20				
Local freight	15				
Commissions	800	835			
End-of-period adjustment (consignment profit)		1,600	Balance carried forward		790
		4,790			4,790
April 1 inventory — 5 TV sets (Model AK-320) @ $158		790			

The assignment of costs for purposes of inventory valuation and the determination of profit on consignment sales is analyzed in detail in Illustration 28-3.

Inventoriable and Noninventoriable Costs

In respect to the tabular calculation in Illustration 28-3, it is important to note the fundamental distinction between inventoriable costs and noninventoriable costs. The inventoriable costs include the original merchandise costs and subsequent cost increments; to the extent that these costs attach to unsold units, they are properly deferred to future periods to be matched against related revenues when the goods are sold. Packing, freight, and drayage paid by the consignee are illustrative of expenditures usually regarded as increasing the value of the consigned units; they add locational utility to the inventory in that these costs are necessary to place the goods in position for sale.

Illustration 28–2

Entries by Consignor (perpetual inventory method)

Separate Accounts Used for Consignment Transactions		*Regular Accounts Used for Consignment Transactions*	
(1) To record cost of 15 TV sets shipped on consignment, at $150 per set:			
Consignment Out—Matthewson Retailers 2,250		Merchandise on Consignment 2,250	
Inventory	2,250	Inventory	2,250
(2) To record crating costs, $45, incurred by the consignor on the above shipment:			
Consignment Out—Matthewson Retailers 45		Deferred Consignment Costs 45	
Cash	45	Cash	45
(3) To record $60 freight paid by the consignor on the shipment in (1):			
Consignment Out—Matthewson Retailers 60		Deferred Consignment Costs 60	
Cash	60	Cash	60
(4) To record transaction details reported in the account sales (Illustration 28–1):			
Cash 3,165		Cash 3,165	
Consignment Out—Matthewson Retailers (costs)° 835		Warranty Expense 20	
Consignment Out—Matthewson Retailers (sales)	4,000	Deferred Consignment Costs 15	
		Commissions 800	
		Sales	4,000

°Warranty adjustments (on sets sold) ...... $ 20
Local freight on 15 sets 15
Commissions on sets sold 800
$835

(5) To adjust the balance in the Consignment Out account to the end-of-the-period capitalizable costs for the unsold goods, and to recognize profit on consignment sales:

Consignment Out—Matthewson Retailers° 1,600
    Consignment Profit.................................... 1,600

°Inventoriable costs related to 15 sets:
Inventory value when shipped................$2,250
Packing expense.................................... 45
Freight out.. 60
Local freight—consignee...................... 15
    Total..$2,370

Unit cost ($2,370 ÷ 15).......................... $ 158

Inventory valuation ($158 × 5)............... $ 790
Preadjustment *credit* balance in Consign-
    ment Out account.............................. 810
    Debit adjustment required $1,600

(6) To close:

Consignment Profit.............................1,600
    Income Summary 1,600

To adjust inventory account (Merchandise on Consignment) for the end-of-the period cost of goods held by the consignee:

Cost of Goods Sold° 1,580
    Merchandise on Consignment† 1,500
    Deferred Consignment Costs‡ 80

°The expired portion of deferred consignment costs, $80, may be identified as a separate expense in this entry.
†Computation:
  Total deferred consignment costs ($45 +
  $60 + $15)...................................... $ 120
  Amount related to unsold goods:
    $120 × 5/15...................................... 40
  Amount to charge as a cost.............. $ 80
†Inventory Credit $2,250 × 10/15 = ... $1,500

Sales...4,000
    Cost of Goods Sold............................... 1,580
    Warrant Expense.................................... 20
    Commissions 800
    Income Summary 1,600

Illustration 28–3
Analysis of Consignments

	Total Consigned Merchandise			Sets Remaining in Inventory		Sets Sold		
	Units	Total Cost	Unit Cost	Units	Valuation	Units	Costs	Amounts
Sales (10 units @ $400)...............								$4,000
Inventoriable costs:								
Incurred by consignor:								
Merchandise cost when shipped........	15	$2,250	$150	5	$750	10	$1,500	
Packing expense.................	15	45	3	5	15	10	30	
Freight out....................	15	60	4	5	20	10	40	
Incurred by consignee:								
Local freight...................	15	15	1	5	5	10	10	1,580
								$2,420
Selling expenses incurred by consignee:								
Warranty adjustments...........							$ 20	
Commissions.................							800	820
Profit on consignment sales......								$1,600
Inventory valuation............			$158	5	$790			

Contrariwise, the noninventoriable costs are those expenditures that fail to add place utility value to the unsold consigned units, and they are accordingly charged to expense in the period of outlay. In addition to the normal selling expenses of the consignee, there are frequently other, sometimes unusual, expenditures which generally are regarded as noninventoriable costs. In respect to transshipments of consigned goods, the ultimate valuation of the inventory should reflect costs of transportation which are not in excess of those normally incurred by direct shipment from the consignor; any additional transportation cost should be regarded as a current expense. Similarly, in the event that a portion of unsold consigned goods are returned to the consignor, they should be restored to the inventory account at their original acquisition cost, and the additional expenditures, to the extent they are not recoverable from the consignee, should be reported as current expenses. Expenditures for repairs and other charges incident to the care and safety of consigned goods usually are accounted for as period costs, and accordingly are charged to expense in the period in which incurred.

Deferred Consignment Costs

Fundamentally, there are two alternative methods of recording and reporting the additional inventoriable costs incurred in shipping goods on consignment. The entries under both assumptions shown in Illustration 28–2 are consistent with the concepts of asset valuation at cost and the matching of revenues and expenses.

In Illustration 28–2 the additional costs were entered in the inventory account. In contrast, the consignor may elect to identify separately the additional inventoriable costs in a separate deferred cost account. These amounts are easily calculated by using the transaction details such as are depicted in Illustration 28–3. In the event that a Deferred Consignment Costs account is to be used in conjunction with a Consignment Out account, entry 5 in Illustration 28–2 would be modified as follows:

```
Deferred Consignment Costs (5 units @ $8) ............................    40
Consignment Out—Matthewson Retailers................................1,560
     Consignment Profit .............................................................    1,600
```

The total capitalized value of consignment costs, as before, would consist of—

```
Inventory of goods on consignment:
    Consignment out—Matthewson Retailers
        (5 units @ $150) .................................................$750
    Deferred consignment costs...........................................  40
        Total .......................................................................$790
```

The balance in the Deferred Consignment Costs account would remain $40 until the end of the succeeding accounting period, at which time it would require additional adjustment. Alternatively, the Deferred Consignment Costs account may be debited for each additional cost when incurred, as in the procedure where "regular" accounts are used for both consignment and nonconsignment transactions.

In those circumstances where separate accounts are not maintained, the entries in Illustration 28–2 may also be modified. In particular, the packing and freight expenditures may be charged directly to their standard expense classifications. If this practice were followed, the individual expense accounts would have to be adjusted at the end of the period to give effect to the $40 cost deferment in respect to unsold goods. In the opinion of the authors, the previously illustrated technique is preferable. Also it is simpler in that less analysis is required to separate items applicable to consignments for adjustments and for reporting purposes.

Entries for Periodic Inventory Method

The entries in Illustration 28–2 assumed that a perpetual inventory was maintained by the consignor. In the event that the periodic inventory method was followed, only minor modifications of the entries are required.

When consignment transactions are recorded separately, entry 1 takes the following form:

Consignment Out—Matthewson Retailers................................2,250
    Consigned Shipments... 2,250

The Consigned Shipments account is essentially a suspense credit to Purchases, and is created primarily to effect dollar control of current shipments. No other changes are required except to close this account to Purchases at the end of the accounting period.

If the "regular" accounts are used to record consignment transactions, the changes are equally minor. Only a memorandum record is made of a consignment shipment (entry 1). Subsequent transactions are recorded as before. In the closing sequence, a Merchandise on Consignment account is created with a balance of $750, and the Deferred Consignment Costs account is adjusted to yield a residual balance of $40.

Financial Statement Presentation by the Consignor

In some cases the consignee may remit more or less than the amount due the consignor as reported on the account sales. If more is remitted than is due (or an advance is made), the consignor should credit the excess to a separate account, Payable to Consignee, rather than to the Consignment Out account. The balance in this account is reported as a current liability in the balance sheet of the consignor, as in most instances, it will be abated, or eliminated by offset, as amounts due are reported on subsequent account sales. If an advance is for an extended period, it should, of course, be reported as a long-term liability.

Where the consignee remits less than the reported amount due, the deficiency should be debited by the consignor to an asset account, Due from Consignee, and reported as a receivable under the current asset caption in the balance sheet. For example, if Matthewson Retailers (Illustration 28–2) had remitted only $2,165 with the account sales, the consignor's entry to record the receipt would be as follows:

```
Cash................................................................................2,165
Due from Consignee — Matthewson Retailers ............................1,000
Consignment Out — Matthewson Retailers ...................... 835
    Consignment Out — Matthewson Retailers ...........................        4,000
```

If, however, the $1,000 differential consists of trade accounts receivable transferred to the consignor by the consignee, the above entry should be modified to reflect this circumstance.

The balance in the Consignment Out account, after adjustment at the end of the accounting period, should be reported on the balance sheet of the consignor as follows:

```
Current Assets:
  Inventories:
    Merchandise on hand ...........................$12,500
    Consigned merchandise.........................    790   $13,290
```

In the event a Deferred Consignment Costs account is used, it should be classified as a current asset — either in the inventory or prepaid expense category.

With respect to the income statement, the operating data for consignment transactions often are merged with other reported revenues and costs. However, a more prominent form of disclosure, and one that is especially appropriate if consignment sales are significant in respect to total revenues, is shown in Illustration 28–4.

A word of caution should be sounded in respect to the above type of presentation. The reported profit on consignment sales may be overstated, perhaps significantly, in view of the fact that the administrative costs are totally charged against the regular sales. Even if management desires to analyze the consignment transactions on a direct cost, or contribution margin, basis, this reporting implicitly assumes that *all* administrative costs are unrelated to the consignment activity. For some purposes it may be useful to allocate such costs.

Illustration 28-4

THE BISHOP WHOLESALE CORPORATION
Income Statement
For Year Ended December 31, 1970

	Consignment Sales	Regular Sales	Total
Sales	$40,000	$100,000	$140,000
Cost of goods sold	24,000	58,000	82,000
Gross margin on sales	$16,000	$ 42,000	$ 58,000
Operating expenses:			
Selling expenses	$ 8,000	$ 14,000	$ 22,000
Administrative expenses		25,000	25,000
Total operating expenses	$ 8,000	$ 39,000	$ 47,000
Net income	$ 8,000	$ 3,000	$ 11,000

QUESTIONS FOR CLASS DISCUSSION

1. What is a consignment? Identify the consignor and consignee. Distinguish between a consignment in and a consignment out.
2. In respect to consignment sales, when does title pass? What are the accounting implications in this regard?
3. Indicate the primary advantages of a consignment arrangement.
4. What are the primary rights and responsibilities of a consignee?
5. What is a *del credere agent?*
6. What is an account sales?
7. What is the nature and purpose of the Consignment In account?
8. What is the nature and purpose of the Consignment Out account?
9. What are deferred consignment costs? Explain the accounting treatment of them.
10. Explain why the inventory method used by the consignor affects his accounting for consignments.
11. In respect to consignments what is the difference between inventoriable and noninventoriable costs?
12. How should goods on consignment be reported on the financial statements (a) by the consignor, (b) the consignee?

EXERCISES

Exercise 28-1

The transactions listed below took place between a consignor and a consignee during the year:

a) Consignor shipped 10 units; unit cost $80; to sell for $150 each.
b) Consignor paid packing and shipping costs on the shipment of $20.
c) Consignee paid local transportation costs on the shipment of $10, which is reimbursable by the consignor.
d) Consignee paid advertising costs on the items amounting to $60; one half is reimbursable by the consignor.

e) Consignee sold 6 of the units at the regular sales price; cash collected in full.

f) Consignee rendered an account sales deducting therein a 20% commission.

Required:

1. In parallel columns give all entries on (*a*) the books of the consignor, assuming perpetual inventory procedures and that the regular accounts are used for consignments, and (*b*) the books of the consignee.

2. Prepare the account sales rendered by the consignee.

3. List the balances in each account relating to consignments that would be reported on the financial statements of each party.

Exercise 28–2

1. Prepare all entries relating to the following transactions for the Smith Office Supply Company, consignor.

a) A consignment of 100 secretarial desks was sent to the Jones Company. The cost of each desk was $62, and each was marked to sell for $100.

b) $150 freight on the above shipment was paid by the consignor.

c) The following account sales was received by the Smith Office Supply Company at the end of the fiscal year:

```
Desks received.........................100
Unsold desks........................... 25
Desks sold .............................. 75  @ $100        $7,500
Less:
    Commission ........................        $750
    Advertising ........................         100         850
    Amount remitted.....................                   $6,650
```

Assume perpetual inventory procedures and that consignment sales are recorded separately.

2. Prepare all entries for the Jones Company, consignee.

Exercise 28–3

The AB Corporation signed a consignment contract with the XY Company to sell a particular item designated ARKAY. The consignee can bill AB Corporation for shipping and transportation costs and one half of any advertising related to goods held on consignment. Both companies use perpetual inventory procedures and close their books on December 31. XY Company, by the terms of the contract, is a *del credere agent*. The following transactions took place during 1970.

a) Shipped 10 units of ARKAY to XY Company; cost $150 each; to sell for $250 each.

b) AB Corporation paid freight on the consignment amounting to $30.

c) XY Company received the 10 units and paid local hauling costs of $10.

d) XY Company spent $80 for advertising the product.

e) XY Company sold seven of the units and collected 60% of the selling price in cash; the balance is due February 1, 1971.

f) XY Company rendered an account sales; deducting therefrom their 20% commission on total sales and reimbursable expenses. Cash was remitted in respect to collections.

Required:

1. Prepare the account sales submitted by the consignee.

2. In parallel columns give all entries for 1970 on the books of the consignor assuming (a) separate accounts are used for consignment transactions and (b) regular accounts are used for the consignment transactions.

Exercise 28-4

The Stans Corporation ships goods on consignment to Law Distributors, a consignee. The consignment contract provides that the consignor shall bear all expenses incurred by the consignee which relate to the consignments; an agency commission of 30% of all consignment sales shall be paid to the consignee. The consignee is required to render an account sales at each year-end and to remit all cash due plus a $5,000 advance because of the existence of a considerable quantity of unsold merchandise. The accounts of the Stans Corporation showed the following balances at December 31, 1970 (end of the accounting period):

Cash	$ 60,000	
Accounts receivable (net)	180,000	
Plant and equipment (net)	250,000	
Accounts payable		$ 80,000
Advance from consignee		5,000
Merchandise inventory (regular)	140,000	
Consignment out (valuation of goods on consignment at December 31, 1970, exclusive of deferred shipping costs)	30,000	
Deferred shipping costs—goods on consignment (paid by consignor)	2,000	
Commission on consignment sales	30,000	
Deferred shipping costs—goods on consignment (paid by consignee)	1,000	
Advertising costs (paid by consignee)	13,000	
Sales, regular		800,000
Sales, consignment		100,000
Cost of goods sold, regular	320,000	
Cost of goods sold, consignment	40,000	
Selling expenses	190,000	
Administrative expenses	150,000	
Capital stock		400,000
Retained earnings (January 1, 1970)		21,000
	$1,406,000	$1,406,000

Assume an income tax rate of 52% and that 20% of the tax liability is paid at the year's end; income taxes are not reflected by the above balances.

Required:

Based upon the above data prepare an income statement for 1970, reporting consignment transactions separately, and a balance sheet as of December 31, 1970.

PROBLEMS

Problem 28–1

Sommerfeld, Inc., shipped 200 Super-X appliances to Jones Bros., retail distributors, for sale on a 15% *del credere* commission basis. The cost of each appliance was $83, with an additional payment of $2.20 per unit to crate and ship to the consignee. It was agreed that Sommerfeld would draw a sight draft on the consignee for 60% of the cost of the appliances, the advance to be recovered periodically by monthly deductions (in proportion to units sold) from the remittances which accompany the account sales. All expenses of the consignee are to be deducted monthly as incurred.

The following account sales was rendered by the consignee at the conclusion of the first month's operations:

Sales of Super-X appliances (60 units @ $100)............		$6,000
Deductions for:		
Expenses paid by the consignee..............................$310		
Advance .... ?		
Commission... 900		?
Remittance to consignor..		$?

Required:

1. Give all entries on the books of the consignee.
2. Give entries tor the month's transactions in the consignor's books assuming the use of a perpetual inventory and with the further assumptions that:

a) Consignment transactions are commingled with regular transactions.
b) Consignment transactions are recorded separately.

Problem 28–2

The Columbian Manufacturing Company and Marks Retailers entered into a consignment agreement whereby the latter would sell sets of Columbian silverware on a consignment basis. The terms of the agreement provided that Marks would receive a commission of 25% on sales price and bill Columbian for all expenses except 10% of advertising expenditures. Both firms close their books on December 31. Marks agreed to render an account sales at each year's end and remit all cash then due. Columbian utilizes perpetual inventory procedures; both firms keep consignments separate from other merchandise transactions. Transactions were:

a) November 15, 19A. Columbian shipped goods on consignment, 100 sets to sell at $30, cost $12 per set. Packing and freight costs, $200, were paid by the consignor.
b) December 31, 19A. An account sales was rendered by the consignee, reporting no sales but expenditures of $100 for local freight and $50 for advertising. No cash was transferred.
c) January–April, 19B. Consignee sold 90 sets at the agreed sales price.
d) April 30, 19B. Columbian shipped goods on consignment, 200 sets to sell at $31, cost $13 per set. Packaging and freight costs, $400, were paid by the consignor.

e) April 30, 19B. Consignee paid $200 for local freight on the above shipment.

f) May, 19B. Consignee paid $300 for advertising, all of which related to consigned merchandise.

g) May–December, 19B. Consignee sold 110 sets at the agreed sales prices, which include the remainder of the sets from the first shipment.

h) December 31, 19B. An account sales was prepared; the required remittance was made.

Required:

1. Give all entries on the books of the consignee for 19A and 19B. Prepare an account sales for each year.

2. Give all entries on the books of the consignor for 19A and 19B.

Problem 28–3

Transactions are to be executed between Consignor X and Consignee Y under provisions of a contract stipulating that (*a*) the consignor will reimburse the consignee for all costs related to piano consignments except advertising costs, which are to be borne 60% by the consignor and 40% by the consignee, (*b*) the consignee's commission will be 20% of sales, and (*c*) receivables arising from consignment sales are to be carried on the books of the consignor.

Inventoriable expenditures incurred in addition to merchandise cost at shipment date are carried in a deferred cost account by the consignor. Both parties close their books at calendar year-end.

The transactions during the first accounting period were:

a) The consignor shipped 10 pianos to the consignee, cost $300 each, to sell at $700.

b) The consignor paid $150 for crating, freight, and insurance on the 10 pianos shipped on consignment.

c) The consignee paid $50 drayage upon receiving the above shipment of 10 pianos.

d) The consignee sold three pianos for $500 cash downpayment (per piano), the balance to be paid at the end of 12 months.

e) The consignee paid $300 advertising costs relating to the pianos.

f) The consignee sold five pianos for cash at the agreed price.

g) The consignee submitted an account sales and remitted the cash due on the eight pianos sold. No collections had been made on the receivables.

h) The books were adjusted and closed.

Required:

1. Prepare in parallel columns all entries for the period (including any memorandum entries) on the books of both the consignor and the consignee as indicated by the above information. Assume that both parties utilize perpetual inventory procedures and that consignment transactions are recorded separately.

2. Prepare the account sales.

Problem 28–4

You are examining the December 31, 19B, financial statements of the Conol Sales Company, a new client. The company was established on January 1, 19A, and is a distributor of air-conditioning units. The company's income statements for 19A and 19B were as follows:

THE CONOL SALES COMPANY
Statements of Income and Expense
For Years Ended December 31, 19A and 19B

	19B	19A
Sales	$1,287,500	$1,075,000
Cost of goods sold	669,500	559,000
Gross margin	$ 618,000	$ 516,000
Selling and administrative expenses	403,500	330,000
Net income before income taxes	$ 214,500	$ 186,000
Provision for income taxes @ 50%	107,250	93,000
Net income	$ 107,250	$ 93,000

Your examination disclosed the following:

a) Some sales were made on open account; other sales were made through dealers to whom units were shipped on a consignment basis. Both sales methods were in effect in 19A and 19B. In both years, however, the company treated all shipments as outright sales.

b) The sales price and cost of the units were the same in 19A and 19B. Each unit had a cost of $130 and was uniformly invoiced at $250 to open account customers and to consignees.

c) During 19B the amount of cash received from consignees in payment for units sold by them was $706,500. Consignees remit for the units as soon as they are sold. Confirmations received from consignees showed that they had a total of 23 unsold units on hand at December 31, 19B. Consignees were unable to confirm the unsold units on hand at December 31, 19A.

d) The cost of sales for 19B was determined by the client as follows:

		Units
Inventory on hand in warehouse, December 31, 19A		1,510
Purchases		4,454
Available for sale		5,964
Inventory on hand in warehouse, December 31, 19B		814
Shipments to: Open account customers	3,008	
Consignee customers	2,142	5,150

Required:

1. Compute the total amount of the Conol Sales Company's inventory at—
a) December 31, 19B.
b) December 31, 19A.

2. Prepare the auditor's working-sheet journal entries to correct the financial statements for the year ended December 31, 19A.

3. Prepare the formal adjusting journal entries to correct the accounts at December 31, 19B. (The books have not been closed.)

(AICPA adapted)

Problem 28–5

The Stone Manufacturing Company closes its books annually on December 31. In making an investigation of the accounts of the company in respect to 1971, you discover the following facts:

a) During November and December, the company shipped stoves to two dealers, A and B, on a consignment basis. The consignment agreements provided that the stoves were to be sold by the consignee at a list price of $180 each. The consignee was to be allowed a 25% commission on each sale and was to be reimbursed for all expenses paid in connection with the stoves. Sales on account are at the risk of the consignee.

b) At the time of shipment, the consignor debited Trade Accounts Receivable and credited Sales $120 for each stove, this being the usual sale price received by the consignor on the basis of which a gross profit of 20% on cost is realized.

c) All cash received from these two consignees was credited to Trade Accounts Receivable. No other entries have been made in respect to these accounts.

d) Information as to all of the transactions with the consignees is given following:

    1) Stoves shipped out: to A — 100, to B — 40.

    2) Stoves unsold by consignees as of 12/31/71: A—35, B—25.

    3) Crating and shipping cost to consignor—$84.

    4) Freight paid by consignees: A—$130, B—$100.

    5) Cash advanced by A at date of receipt of the first 100 stoves—$4,000. Cash subsequently remitted by A—$5,395.

    6) Cash remitted by B—$575.

Required:

1. Show, by entries in T-accounts, transactions completed and adjustments required by the Stone Company.

2. Prepare a trial balance of the accounts affected by these transactions and adjustments.

(AICPA adapted)

	Installment
chapter **29**	**Sales**

Nature of Installment Sales

The installment sales contract is a special type of credit arrangement which provides for a schedule of predetermined, periodic collections from the sale of real estate, merchandise, or other personal property. In the usual credit sale, the collection interval is comparatively short and title passes unconditionally to the buyer concurrently with the completion of the sale. In contrast, installment sales contracts are characterized by (1) a cash downpayment at the date of sale followed by periodic (frequently equal) payments over a relatively long period of time and (2) a transfer of title which remains conditional until the debt is fully discharged.

In view of the typically long collection period and the concomitant increase in risk, a variety of contractual arrangements are used to provide some additional measure of protection to the seller. Most of these agreements involve some form of title retention by the seller; among these are the following:

1. Conditional sales contracts, whereby the seller retains legal title of transferred property until the installment collections are completed.
2. Hire-purchase contracts, whereby the vendor, in effect, leases the property to the buyer until the final installment (rental) payment is made, at which time title is conveyed to the buyer for some nominal consideration.

3. Custodial arrangements, wherein legal title to property is vested in a third party (a trustee) until payment is completed, at which time title transfers to the purchaser; this arrangement is primarily applicable to sales of realty.

In other types of agreements, title passes to the purchaser under a mortgage or lien arrangement. Such contracts enable the vendor to reclaim possession of transferred property in those instances where the purchaser is in default.

Despite these safeguards, losses from installment sales tend to be significantly larger than those from short-term credit sales. This may be attributed, in part, to such factors as the extended collection period, the relatively small value of many items of repossessed merchandise (whether due to physical deterioration, obsolescence, or depreciation), increased collection expenses, and necessary costs of repossession.

In view of the unique aspects of installment sales the accounting profession has been quite concerned with the accounting problems posed; basically these problems relate to the timing of the recognition of gross profit. For many years an approach to this problem, usually identified as the *installment sales method,* has been recognized as generally acceptable by the accounting profession. In addition it has been, and continues to be recognized, for income tax purposes and by the Securities and Exchange Commission. Significantly, the Accounting Principles Board, in *Opinion No. 10,* dated December 1966 restricted somewhat the usage of the method. In *Opinion 10* the board stated:

Chapter 1A of *ARB No. 43,* paragraph 1, states that "Profit is deemed to be realized when a sale in the ordinary course of business is effected, unless the circumstances are such that the collection of the sale price is not reasonably assured." The Board reaffirms this statement; it believes that revenues should ordinarily be accounted for at the time a transaction is completed, with appropriate provision for uncollectible accounts. Accordingly, it concludes that, in the absence of the circumstances referred to above, the installment method of recognizing revenue is not acceptable.[1]

However, the board stated in a related footnote that "there are exceptional cases where receivables are collectible over an extended period of time, and, because of the terms of the transactions or other conditions, there is no reasonable basis for estimating the degree of collectibility. Where such circumstances exist, and as long as they exist, either the installment method or the cost recovery method of accounting may be used." In view of the position taken by the board,

---

[1] AICPA, *Accounting Principles Board Opinion No. 10* (New York, December 1966), p. 149.

one may conjecture that the installment method will be used much less in the future than at present. However, in view of the income tax provision,[2] SEC regulations, and the footnote quoted above, it is reasonable to assume that the installment method will continue to be used by various companies. For this reason a fairly brief discussion of the topic is presented in this chapter.

Criteria for Gross Margin (Profit) Recognition

The accounting process of measuring net income from installment sales theoretically should follow the treatment accorded ordinary credit sales; that is, as the APB Opinion quoted above states, "revenues should ordinarily be accounted for at the time the transaction is completed." In this approach provision necessarily must be made for the accrual of certain costs expected to be incurred in the future (e.g., those associated with collection) and for estimated losses due to uncollectible receivables. However, because of the prolonged collection period, the frequent high losses due to bad debts, and the difficulty of estimating other future costs (related expenses) the treatment accorded ordinary credit sales frequently is thought to be inadequate.

For these and other reasons, special methods of accounting for installment sales which accent cash collections have been developed. Among the various proposed income determination concepts, each of which focuses primarily on the recognition of gross profit, are the following:

1. *Cost Recovery Method.* Gross margin (sales less cost of goods sold) is not given accounting recognition until collections are equivalent in amount to the cost of the transferred property; all subsequent receipts then are recorded as realized gross margin. This deferral of gross margin until cost is totally recovered appeals to accounting conservatism. Perhaps a circumstance involving a one-time installment sale with an extremely high degree of risk may justify the application of this method; however, it appears to be an overly cautious criterion for income recognition when applied to a business regularly engaged in installment sales transactions. Accordingly, this method seldom is used.

2. *Installment Sales Method.* Each collection is regarded as a

---

[2] Internal Revenue Code, Section 453 (a) states: "A person who regularly sells or otherwise disposes of personal property on the installment plan may report as income therefrom in any taxable year that proportion of the installment payments actually received in that year which the gross profit, realized or to be realized when payment is completed, bears to the total contract price." (Section 453 [b] also extends the treatment to the sale of realty.) Use of the installment basis for tax purposes and of the sale basis for accounting purposes necessitates resort to tax allocation procedures if material amounts are involved.

partial recovery of cost and a partial realization of gross profit (margin), in the same proportion that these two elements are present in the original selling price. This method is discussed in the paragraphs to follow.

The Installment Sales Method

With respect to regular sales, revenue is realized upon completion of the sale transaction; accordingly, it is recognized in the accounting period when title transfers to the buyer. This identification of revenue with the period of sale appears reasonable in view of the fact that there is either an immediate recovery of the total sales price, or collection is made within a relatively short period of time. However, in the case of installment sales, the collection period is frequently an extended interval and the probability of loss because of uncollectible receivables is significantly greater than for regular sales; for this reason, attention is diverted from the date of sale to the _dates of collection_. Under the installment sales method, revenue, or more precisely gross profit, is considered realized in the period of collection rather than in the period of sale. The amount of gross profit (margin) recognized in a given period depends upon the relevant gross profit rate and the amount of installment receivables collected.

To illustrate, assume an installment sale of property, the cost of which was $3,000, was made on December 31, 1968, for $5,000, with a cash downpayment of $1,000 and 40 monthly payments of $100 plus interest scheduled thereafter. The total gross margin to the seller was $2,000,

$$\frac{\$5,000 - \$3,000}{\$5,000} = 40\% \text{ of the selling price}$$

Under the installment sales method, annual realized gross margin would be recognized according to the following table:

Year	Cash Collected	Gross Margin Recognized Computations	Amount
1968	$1,000	$1,000/$5,000 × $2,000	$ 400
1969	1,200	1,200/ 5,000 × 2,000	480
1970	1,200	1,200/ 5,000 × 2,000	480
1971	1,200	1,200/ 5,000 × 2,000	480
1972	400	400/ 5,000 × 2,000	160
Total	$5,000		$2,000

The deferral of gross profit (margin) recognition, which is the essence of the installment sales method, compels the accountant to examine the consistency of the treatment of related expenses. It is evident that the deferral of gross profit, in effect, constitutes a delayed recognition of both sales revenue *and* cost of goods sold. Significantly, however, other operating expenses—some of which relate directly to installment selling, such as distribution costs, collection expenses, and other administrative overhead—are accounted for as period costs in the usual way. Accordingly, the matching of revenue from installment sales relates only to those product costs incident to, and directly associated with, the acquisition or manufacture of merchandise (i.e., cost of goods sold); the matching process in this application does not extend to other operating expenses. At best, this inconsistency can be explained in terms of materiality and conservatism.

The treatment of bad debt losses poses a special problem. The installment sales method is predicated upon somewhat more uncertain collection prospects, and accordingly defers the recognition of gross margin. Additionally, it is frequently assumed that the repossession privilege affords the vendor an opportunity to recover the amount of uncollectible installment receivables, at least to the extent of the unrecovered costs of the reclaimed merchandise which are implicit in these balances. Under these circumstances, it would appear that provision for estimated bad debt losses is not required. However, when it becomes evident that the value of repossessed merchandise fails to compensate for corresponding losses of uncollectible accounts (viz, unrecovered cost and previously recognized gross profit), estimates of these losses should be made in the same manner as for other credit sales. Since the cost of the merchandise transferred at date of sale is often the principal component of the ultimate loss, the provision for bad debts is reported properly in the period of sale.

Interest on Unpaid Installment Receivable Balances

Because the collection period for installment sales is prolonged and may involve unliquidated receivable balances of unusual magnitude, interest often is charged on these unpaid balances. Where this condition prevails, each installment collection consists of (1) a reduction of the principal (receivable) and (2) interest income. The installment contract may expressly provide for an allocation of the scheduled payments, detailing that portion of each collection which shall relate to the debt principal and interest.

The interest requirement may follow one of several common patterns. These include the following:

1. Cash payments of equal amount are made each period. Each successive installment collection includes an *increased* reduction of principal and a corresponding *decrease* in interest. This is the conventional method of payment on installment sales contracts and will be illustrated subsequently.
2. Interest is charged on the receivable balance unpaid at the begin-

ning of each period. Normally, where this approach is followed, there is a constant reduction of principal in each successive period. Also, the amount of cash received decreases with each collection as a consequence of a decreasing amount of interest.

The first approach is illustrated using the following data:

Installment sale made on January 1, 1970 ....$2,500.00
Cash downpayment 500.00
Annual installment collection for four consecutive years (in-
 cluding 5% interest) .... 564.02°

°Computation of equal periodic payment:
 Periodic payment = Original unpaid receivable balance
  ÷ Present value of an annuity of $1 for 4 periods at 5%
  = $2,000 ÷ 3.5459505
  = $564.02.
Note: See Chapter 5 for a discussion of compound interest fundamentals and related tables.

Table of Entries for Periodic Collections

Date	Cash (Debit)	Interest Earned (Credit)	Installment Accounts Receivable (Credit)	Unpaid Balance
1/1/70				$2,500.00
1/1/70	$500.00		$500.00	2,000.00
1/1/71	564.02	$100.00†	464.02	1,535.98
1/1/72	564.02	76.80‡	487.22	1,048.76
1/1/73	564.02	52.44§	511.58	537.18
1/1/74	564.04°	26.86‖	537.18	–0–

°Adjusted to reflect the requirements of the terminal payment.
†$2,000.00 × 5% = $100.00.
‡$1,535.98 × 5% = $ 76.80.
§$1,048.76 × 5% = $ 52.44.
‖$ 537.18 × 5% = $ 26.86.

Although no further detailed illustrations are offered at this time, the second interest pattern described is illustrated subsequently with a journal entry sequence for the sale of realty on an installment basis.

Accounting Procedures for the Installment Sales Method

Various accounting procedures may be used to record transactions using the installment sales method. The sequence of entries described and illustrated in the following pages is essentially a distillate of current accounting practice.

Although there are no substantive differences in the several applications of this income concept, it is convenient to consider separately two basic types of property transfers, with their attendant procedural details:

1. Installment sales of items other than regular merchandise — realty and casual sales of personal property (see Illustration 29–1).
2. Installment sales of conventional merchandise (see Illustration 29–3).
   a) Perpetual inventory basis.
   b) Periodic inventory basis.

Entries for Installment Sale of Realty (and Other Casual Sales).
The following installment sale transaction is assumed to have occurred on January 31, 1970:

Sales of realty (Plot 9)	$100,000
Cost of the realty	70,000
Gross margin on sale (30% of the sales price)	$ 30,000
Expenses of sale	$ 2,000
Collection schedule:	
Cash downpayment at date of sale	20,000
Note secured by a mortgage lien on the realty. Liquidation is to be made by eight annual payments of $10,000. Six percent interest is payable each January 31 on the unpaid balance at the beginning of the year	80,000

Illustration 29–1

	Accrual (Conventional) Method (Gross Margin Recognized in Period of Sale)		Installment Sales Method (Gross Margin Recognized with the Progress of Collection)	
(1) January 31, 1970. Sale of Plot 9, cost $70,000, for $100,000, and collection of cash down payment of $20,000 (gross margin rate = 30%).				
Cash	20,000		20,000	
Note Receivable	80,000		80,000	
Real Estate (Plot 9)		70,000		70,000
Gain on Sale of Realty		30,000		
Deferred Gross Margin on Sale of Realty				30,000
(2) January 31, 1970. Payment of expenses related to sale.				
Expenses of Realty Sales	2,000		2,000	
Cash		2,000		2,000
(3) December 31, 1970. Realized gross margin on installment basis: $20,000 × 30% = $6,000.				
Deferred Gross Margin on Sale of Realty			6,000	
Realized Gross Profit on Sale of Realty				6,000

Illustration 29–1 (continued)

	Accrual (Conventional) Method (Gross Margin Recognized in Period of Sale)		Installment Sales Method (Gross Margin Recognized with the Progress of Collection)	

(4) December 31, 1970. Accrued interest income on note receivable for 11 months: $80,000 × 6% × 11/12 = $4,400.

Interest Receivable 4,400			4,400	
Interest Earned		4,400		4,400

(5) December 31, 1970. Year-end closing.

Gain on Sale of Realty....................................30,000				
Realized Gross Margin on Sale of Realty			6,000	
Interest Earned 4,400			4,400	
Expenses of Realty Sales		2,000		2,000
Income Summary....................................		32,400		8,400

(6) January 1, 1971. Reversal of entry (4).

Interest Earned 4,400			4,400	
Interest Receivable		4,400		4,400

(7) January 31, 1971. Receipt of first installment on note receivable and interest of $4,800 ($80,000 × 6%).

Cash..14,800			14,800	
Note Receivable		10,000		10,000
Interest Earned		4,800		4,800

(8) December 31, 1971. Gross Margin on installment basis: $10,000 × 30% = $3,000.

Deferred Gross Margin on Sale of Reality........			3,000	
Realized Gross Profit on Sale of Realty.......				3,000

(9) December 31, 1971. Accrued interest income on note receivable for 11 months: $70,000 × 6% × 11/12 = $3,850.

Interest Receivable 3,850			3,850	
Interest Earned		3,850		3,850

(10) December 31, 1971. Year-end closing.

Realized Gross Margin on Sale of Realty			3,000	
Interest Earned 4,250			4,250	
Income Summary....................................		4,250		7,250

In order to emphasize the special effect of the installment sales method on revenue recognition from the sale of realty, entries which indicate the recognition of gross margin under the installment method (i.e., ratably over the periods in which collections are made) are juxtaposed against entries determining net income by the conventional accrual method (i.e., in the period of sale) for a two-year period in Illustration 29–1. A comparative analysis of the annual amounts of recognized gross profit over the total time interval is given in Illustration 29–2.

Illustration 29–2
Accrual and Installment Methods Compared

Year	Collections	Uncollected Balance at Year-End	Recognized (Realized) Gross Margin on Sale of Realty		Deferred Gross Margin at Year-End	
			Accrual Method	Installment Method	Accrual Method	Installment Method
1970	$ 20,000	$80,000	$30,000	$ 6,000	-0-	$24,000
1971	10,000	70,000	-0-	3,000	-0-	21,000
1972	10,000	60,000	-0-	3,000	-0-	18,000
1973	10,000	50,000	-0-	3,000	-0-	15,000
1974	10,000	40,000	-0-	3,000	-0-	12,000
1975	10,000	30,000	-0-	3,000	-0-	9,000
1976	10,000	20,000	-0-	3,000	-0-	6,000
1977	10,000	10,000	-0-	3,000	-0-	3,000
1978	10,000	-0-	-0-	3,000	-0-	-0-
Total	$100,000		$30,000	$30,000		

Note: Interest earned and period costs are accorded equivalent treatment under both methods, and thus are excluded from this analysis.

Entries for Installment Sale of Merchandise.   In application of the installment sales method to a merchandising operation, it is important that the accounting system be modified sufficiently to accommodate the necessary account detail and additional procedures. This involves several considerations, among which are the following:

1. Sales, accounts receivable, and cost of goods sold should be given separate account designations identifying them as either "regular" or "installment."
2. Installment receivables should be identified by year of sale.
3. Gross margin should be recognized each period in proportion to the current collections of installment accounts receivable; this recognition becomes an essential part of the sequence of adjusting entries.

Recording procedures also are influenced by the method of inventory accounting used; accordingly, entries are presented in Illustration 29–3 based upon two assumptions: (1) that perpetual inventory records are maintained and (2) that periodic inventory procedures are followed.

Assume the following data relate to the XY Corporation:

	1970	1971
Sales:		
Regular	$200,000	$220,000
Installment	100,000	110,000
Merchandise inventory, January 1	10,000	20,000
Merchandise inventory, December 31	20,000	15,000
Purchases	185,000	189,900
Cost of goods sold:		
Regular	115,000	130,000
Installment	60,000	64,900
Selling expenses	50,000	65,000
Provision for doubtful accounts (regular sales)	1,000	1,100
Collections on account:		
Installment accounts receivable — 1970	30,000	40,000
Installment accounts receivable — 1971		50,000
Accounts receivable (regular)	180,000	230,000

Illustration 29–3

	Installment Sales Method			
	Perpetual Inventory		Periodic Inventory	
(1) January–December 1970. Regular and installment sales in 1970.				
Accounts Receivable (regular)	200,000		200,000	
Installment Accounts Receivable — 1970	100,000		100,000	
Sales (regular)		200,000		200,000
Installment Sales		100,000		100,000
(2) January–December 1970. Purchases of merchandise in 1970.				
Merchandise Inventory	185,000			
Purchases			185,000	
Accounts Payable (cash)		185,000		185,000
(3) January–December 1970. Selling expenses and provision for doubtful accounts during 1970.				
Selling Expenses	50,000		50,000	
Estimated Loss on Doubtful Accounts	1,000		1,000	
Accounts Payable (cash)		50,000		50,000
Allowance for Doubtful Accounts		1,000		1,000
(4) January–December 1970. Collection of receivables during 1970.				
Cash	210,000		210,000	
Accounts Receivable (regular)		180,000		180,000
Installment Accounts Receivable — 1970		30,000		30,000

Illustration 29–3 (continued)

Installment Sales Method

	Perpetual Inventory	*Periodic Inventory*

(5) Determination of cost of sales for 1970:

  (*a*) January–December 1970.

    Cost of Goods Sold (regular).....115,000

    Cost of Goods Sold on

      Installment.......................... 60,000

        Merchandise Inventory...... 175,000

  (*b*) December 31, 1970.

    Cost of Goods Sold (regular)° ...　　　115,000

    Cost of Goods Sold on

      Installment° ....　　　60,000

      Merchandise Inventory............　　　10,000

        Purchases.......................　　　　　　　　185,000

(6) December 31, 1970. Determination of 1970 deferred gross profit on installment sales. Gross profit rate $= \dfrac{\$100,000 - \$60,000}{\$100,000} = 40\%.$

Installment Sales..........................100,000　　　100,000

  Cost of Goods Sold on

    Installment.......................　　　60,000　　　　　　60,000

  Deferred Gross Profit on

    Installment Sales – 1967.......　　　40,000　　　　　　40,000

(7) December 31, 1970. Realized gross profit in 1970 on installment sales.

Year of Sale	Gross Profit Rate	Collec- tions	Realized Gross Profit
1970	40%	$30,000	$12,000

Deferred Gross Profit on

  Installment Sales – 1970............. 12,000　　　12,000

    Realized Gross Profit on

      Installment Sales.................　　　12,000　　　　　　12,000

(8) December 31, 1970. Year-end closing for realized gross profit.

Realized Gross Profit on

  Installment Sales...................... 12,000　　　12,000

    Income Summary...................　　　12,000　　　　　　12,000

° In view of the paucity of inventory detail under the periodic method, this cost allocation may be necessarily based on some estimating process in actual practice, frequently in the same ratio as sales.

Illustration 29–3 (continued)

Installment Sales Method

	Perpetual Inventory		Periodic Inventory	
(9) December 31, 1970. Year-end closing for other nominal accounts.				
Sales (regular)............................200,000			200,000	
Cost of Goods Sold (regular).....		115,000		115,000
Estimated Loss on Doubtful Accounts		1,000		1,000
Selling Expenses...................		50,000		50,000
Income Summary		34,000		34,000
Income Summary 46,000			46,000	
Retained Earnings.................		46,000		46,000
(10) January–December 1971. Regular and installment sales in 1971.				
Accounts Receivable (regular)........220,000			220,000	
Installment Accounts Receivable— 1971 110,000			110,000	
Sales (regular).......................		220,000		220,000
Installment Sales...................		110,000		110,000
(11) January–December 1971. Purchases of merchandise in 1971.				
Merchandise Inventory.................189,900				
Purchases.................................			189,900	
Accounts Payable (cash).........		189,900		189,900
(12) January–December 1971. Selling expenses and provision for doubtful accounts during 1971.				
Selling Expenses......................... 65,000			65,000	
Estimated Loss on Doubtful Accounts 1,100			1,100	
Accounts Payable (cash).........		65,000		65,000
Allowance for Doubtful Accounts		1,100		1,100
(13) January–December 1971. Collection of receivables during 1971.				
Cash 320,000			320,000	
Accounts Receivable (regular)...		230,000		230,000
Installment Accounts Receivable—1970...............		40,000		40,000
Installment Accounts Receivable—1971...............		50,000		50,000

Illustration 29–3 (continued)

Installment Sales Method

	Perpetual Inventory	*Periodic Inventory*

(14) Determination of cost of sales for 1971:

(a) January–December 1971.

Cost of Goods Sold (regular) 130,000		
Cost of Goods Sold on		
Installment......................... 64,900		
Merchandise Inventory......	194,900	

(b) December 31, 1971.

Cost of Goods Sold (regular)		130,000
Cost of Goods Sold on		
Installment.........................		64,900
Merchandise Inventory......		5,000
Purchases.........................		189,900

(15) December 31, 1971. Determination of 1971 deferred gross profit on installment sales. Gross profit rate = $45,100 ÷ $110,000 = 41%.

Installment Sales.........................110,000		110,000
Cost of Goods Sold on		
Installment.........................	64,900	64,900
Deferred Gross Profit on		
Installment Sales – 1971.......	45,100	45,100

(16) December 31, 1971. Realized gross profit in 1971 on installment sales.

Year of Sale	Gross Profit Rate	Collec- tions	Realized Gross Profit
1970	40%	$40,000	$16,000
1971	41	50,000	20,500

Deferred Gross Profit on		
Installment Sales – 1970............. 16,000		16,000
Deferred Gross Profit on		
Installment Sales – 1971............. 20,500		20,500
Realized Gross Profit on		
Installment Sales.................	36,500	36,500

(17) December 31, 1971. Year-end closing for realized gross profit.

Realized Gross Profit on		
Installment Sales...................... 36,500		36,500
Income Summary..................	36,500	36,500

Illustration 29–3 (*continued*)

Installment Sales Method

	Perpetual Inventory	Periodic Inventory
(18) December 31, 1971. Year-end closing for other nominal accounts.		
Sales (regular).............................220,000		220,000
Cost of Goods Sold (regular).....	130,000	130,000
Estimated Loss on Doubtful Accounts	1,100	1,100
Selling Expenses...................	65,000	65,000
Income Summary	23,900	23,900
Income Summary 60,400		60,400
Retained Earnings.................	60,400	60,400

Although the comparative interperiod effect of electing the installment sales method is not again calculated, it remains essentially consistent with the results derived in Illustration 29–2. Since sales of merchandise on the installment basis often extend over many periods of business operations, however, net income under the conventional accrual method and the installment sales method eventually will tend to be approximately equal.

Financial Statement Presentation

Transactions involving installment sales introduce several problems in respect to informative reporting. As with other special types of transactions, adequacy of disclosure is a compelling consideration. Significantly, however, informative reporting may be accomplished in a number of ways, depending upon the characteristics of each particular situation. For this reason, various alternative approaches are illustrated in the following pages using the data contained in Illustration 29–3.

Income Statement. With respect to the income statement, the degree of detail to be reported frequently will vary, depending upon the magnitude of installment sales revenues in relation to total sales. For example, if installment sales are relatively insignificant in amount, the type of presentation in Illustration 29–4 may be preferable.

Illustration 29–4
THE XY CORPORATION
Income Statement
For Year Ended December 31, 1971
(installment sales are not significant in amount)

Sales $220,000
Cost of goods sold... 130,000
Gross margin...$ 90,000
Realized gross margin on installment sales............ 36,500
Total gross profit..$126,500
Expenses 66,100
Net income ....$ 60,400

Alternatively, should installment sales represent a material amount of the total revenues of a business enterprise, additional detail may be required for a full and informative disclosure. Illustration 29–5 shows one way to present the appropriate details. Manifestly, many other variants on these illustrative statement forms are possible.

Illustration 29–5
THE XY CORPORATION
Income Statement
For Year Ended December 31, 1971
(installment sales are significant in amount)

			Sales	
		Total	Regular	Installment
Sales		$330,000	$220,000	$110,000
Cost of goods sold:				
Merchandise inventory, January 1	$ 20,000			
Purchases	189,900			
	$209,900			
Merchandise inventory, December 31	15,000			
Total		194,900	130,000	64,900
Accrual-basis gross margin on 1971 sales		$135,100	$ 90,000	$ 45,100
Less: Gross margin to be deferred on 1971 installment sales		24,600		24,600
		$110,500		$ 20,500
Add: Realized gross margin in 1971 on installment sales of prior year – 1970		16,000		16,000
Total gross margin realized in 1971 on installment sales°				$ 36,500
Total realized gross margin		$126,500		
Expenses (detailed)		66,100		
Net income		$ 60,400		

° Approximately one third of the sales of the XY Corporation are represented by installment sales for which the average collection period is three years. Gross margin on these sales is deferred until realized (or confirmed) through collection of receivable balances. This procedure is used for both financial accounting and income tax purposes.

Balance Sheet. With respect to balance sheet presentation, installment accounts receivable from the sale of merchandise usually are classified as current assets and reported as follows:

ASSETS

Current Assets:		
Notes receivable	$25,000	
Accounts receivable	60,000	
	$85,000	
Less: Allowance for doubtful accounts	5,000	$ 80,000
Installment accounts receivable:		
From 1970 sales	$50,000	
From 1971 sales	90,000	140,000

This treatment accords with the accepted definition of current assets as consisting of "cash and other assets or resources commonly identified as those which are reasonably expected to be realized in cash or sold or consumed during the normal operating cycle of the business."[3] Installment transactions generate an operating cycle, at least for one segment of the enterprise's operations, which by definition includes the *collection* of these accounts. On the other hand, it would be difficult to justify this classification for an installment contract, or contracts, resulting from a transaction which is unrelated to normal operations (e.g., the infrequent sale of land held for expansion); consequently, receivable balances which derive from such a source should be reported in the "other assets" section of the balance sheet.

The balance of Deferred Gross Margin on Installment Sales at the end of an accounting period frequently is classified as a current liability and reported as follows:

LIABILITIES

Current Liabilities:
  Deferred revenues:
    Deferred gross margin on installment sales —
      1970..$28,000
    Deferred gross margin on installment sales —
      1971.. 42,000 $70,000

Differences of opinion exist, however, concerning the most desirable balance sheet classification of this account. At least six different viewpoints can be identified:

1. Deferred gross profit on installment sales should be reported as a current liability, although identified separately as a deferred revenue, as illustrated above. This approach has been accorded the widest acceptance because of its simplicity and because it prudently compromises other views with respect to the several issues involved.

2. The balance of deferred gross profit should be reported in the enumeration of other current liability items without separate subclassification. A common argument often made against this classification is that there is no commitment, now or in the future, for the use of the firm's resources.

3. Such balances should be identified in a separate classification between liabilities and stockholders' equity. This position has gained some measure of approval, although it patently begs the question of a precise classification within the enumeration of conventional equity interests.

4. Deferred gross margin is a valuation adjustment of the related

---

[3] AICPA, *Accounting Research and Terminology Bulletins, Final Edition* (New York, 1961), p. 20.

Installment Accounts Receivable. Although this produces a conservative valuation of the receivable, the amount of deferred gross profit has no inherent relationship with the estimated collectible value of the accounts receivable.

5. Deferred gross profit should be reported as a separate designation in the stockholders' equity section of the balance sheet. The strength of this position is to be found in the argument that installment sales have actually given rise to profits in the same manner as have regular sales; realization of profits in both cases is contingent upon the receivables collection. The varying time periods involved in the collection process are recognized in the form of different classes of "accumulated" earnings. Notwithstanding these arguments, this method of classification has gained very little following to date.

6. Such balances consist essentially of three basic elements which should be classified as follows:

a) That portion of the deferred gross margin that is equivalent to the estimated income tax liability to be eventually paid when the sales are reported as realized revenue should be reported as an estimated current liability.

b) That portion of the deferred gross margin estimated as being necessary to offset collection expenses and possible bad debt and repossession losses should be reported on the balance sheet as a deduction from installment accounts receivable.

c) The residual balance of deferred gross margin represents net income associated with installment sales and should be reported as net income from installment sales, restricted as to dividend availability, in the retained earnings statement.

As collections progress, these elements must be appropriately reclassified. Although this proposal synthesizes the best features of (2), (4), and (5) above, it essentially represents a commitment to a new concept of income determination, controverting the notion of profit deferral. Additionally, it generates little practical support because of the difficult problem of allocating deferred gross profit between the three basic elements.

Defaults and Repossessions

If one who has purchased goods on an installment contract defaults in any of the scheduled payments, the vendor may repossess or reclaim the units sold to satisfy the remaining indebtedness. Normally, the goods repossessed are subsequently resold, either in their reclaimed condition or after costs have been incurred to restore them to a more marketable state. Default and repossession require that the vendor (1) record the repossessed item in an appropriate inventory account as its market value at date of repossession, (2) remove the uncollected receivable balance of the defaulted account, (3) write off the amount of deferred gross profit related to the above receivable balance, and (4) record the resulting gain or loss on repossession.

To illustrate, assume the following data in respect to a default and concurrent repossession on April 15, 1971, of goods sold in 1969:

Installment accounts receivable – 1969 .... $1,000
Deferred gross profit on installment sales – 1969
(gross profit rate 30% of selling price)   300
Estimated market value of item repossessed in its
reclaimed condition...   600

The entry for repossession on April 15, 1971, would be as follows:

Inventory of Repossessed Merchandise.......................................600
Deferred Gross Profit on Installment Sales – 1969.........................300
Loss on Defaults (repossessions)..100
    Installment Accounts Receivable – 1969..............................   1,000

Costs of restoration which relate to repossessed merchandise should be accounted for as a cost increment to the Inventory of Repossessed Merchandise account; resale of repossessed merchandise should be accounted for in the conventional manner for regular or installment sales transactions.

With respect to the valuation of repossessed merchandise (or other property), the above entry assumes that *fair market value in present condition* at date of repossession is appropriate. This value is the estimated cash purchase price of the repossessed units as established in the local used-goods, or wholesale, market. Arguments are also made for several other valuation bases:

1. The value of repossessed property should be the *book value* of the unliquidated indebtedness, i.e., the uncollected balance of the relevant installment account receivable reduced by the amount of deferred gross profit which relates thereto. Clearly, the actual value of repossessed goods may have little relationship to the book value of the indebtedness. The seller is compelled to reclaim the merchandise to minimize a potential loss; the magnitude of that loss should be determined preferably by a comparison of the used-goods replacement cost of the item repossessed and the book value of the indebtedness. Accordingly, the residual net book value of uncollected receivables has gained comparatively little support as a valuation basis for repossessed merchandise.
2. No value should be assigned to the repossessed asset; rather, a loss at date of repossession should be recognized in the amount of the book value of the indebtedness (i.e., the amount due less the deferred gross profit). Upon resale of the repossessed item, the total sales price is regarded as revenue. This treatment, which fails to ascribe *any* value to repossessed property, can be justified

only on the grounds of conservatism; consequently, it is seldom used in accounting practice.

3. The value of repossessed property should be that amount which will allow the recognition of a "normal profit" on its resale. This approach is deficient in several important respects. Primarily, it violates the cost principle in respect to asset valuation and accordingly incorrectly measures the loss on repossession; it effectively capitalizes profits (at an arbitrary rate) which are yet to be realized; and it invokes the practical problem of estimating future costs to repair, to resell, and, conceivably, to repossess again.

As a consequence of the above considerations, the use of the fair market value as an inventory valuation basis for repossessed goods generally is subscribed to by most accountants.

The balance in the Repossessed Merchandise Inventory account usually is reported on the balance sheet as a current asset; gain or loss on repossessions is reported variously in the income statement either as an adjustment to realized gross profit on installment sales, as a separately identified item of gain or loss, or as an addition to, or deduction from, the loss on doubtful accounts. Alternatively, if a provision has been previously made for losses on doubtful accounts which included an allowance for installment sales, the loss on repossessions should be charged to Allowance for Doubtful Accounts (regular and installment sales).

QUESTIONS FOR CLASS DISCUSSION

1. Define installment sales. How do they differ from ordinary credit sales?
2. What is the installment sales method?
3. In respect to the installment sales method what is the position of: (a) the Accounting Principles Board of the AICPA, (b) the Securities and Exchange Commission, and (c) the Internal Revenue Code?
4. Distinguish briefly between (a) the cost recovery method and (b) the installment sales method.
5. Why is interest an important consideration with respect to installment sales?
6. How should the results of installment sales be reported on the income statement?
7. How should the accounts "Installment Accounts Receivable" and Deferred Gross Margin on Installment Sales" be reported on the balance sheet?
8. How should repossessed merchandise be valued prior to resale?

DECISION CASE 29-1

The Jones Company sells furniture on the installment plan. For its federal income tax returns, it reports its profit from sales on the "installment basis." For its financial reports, it considers the entire profit to be earned in the year of sale.

Required:

1. Discuss the relative merits of the two methods of reporting income.
2. Explain the installment basis as used for income tax purposes.
3. Discuss the effects of the use of these two bases by the Jones Company on the significance of its reported annual net income.

(AICPA adapted)

EXERCISES

Exercise 29–1

The Swazey Company sold a parcel of real estate on January 1, 1971, which cost $7,000. The terms of the sale were: $5,000 downpayment, plus five equal payments of $1,000 payable on January 1 each year.

Required:

1. Prepare a table which shows the collections, status of the receivable balance, and the gross profit to be recognized each year assuming the installment sales method is used. (Disregard interest considerations.)
2. Give entries for the sale, collections, and gross profit recognition through 1973.
3. Indicate the relevant amounts that would be reported on the balance sheet and income statement through 1976.

Exercise 29–2

On January 2, 1971, the ABC Company purchased display equipment under the following terms: $2,000 downpayment to be paid upon installation, plus five annual payments of $1,000, the first installment payment to be made on December 31, 1971. Title to the display equipment was retained by the seller until the final payment was made. It is estimated that the display equipment will be used for 10 years with no residual value.

This same display equipment was available at a cash price of $6,600.

Ignore income tax aspects of the transaction.

Required:

Prepare all accounting entries for ABC Company relating to the display equipment as of January 2 and December 31, 1971, and as of December 31, 1972. For each entry, give your supporting reasons.

(AICPA adapted)

Exercise 29–3

The following is the preclosing trial balance of the Gamma Company on December 31, 1971:

Cash	$100,000	
Installment accounts receivable – 1970	40,000	
Installment accounts receivable – 1971	60,000	
Installment sales		$100,000
Cost of installment sales	70,000	
Deferred gross profit – 1970		30,000
Capital stock		80,000
Retained earnings		60,000
	$270,000	$270,000

Required:

1. Prepare entries on December 31, 1971, to record the gross profit realized in 1971 and complete the closing of the accounts. The rate of gross profit on sales in 1970 was 25%.

2. On February 10, 1972, a customer defaulted on his payments and the merchandise was repossessed. Prepare the journal entry for the repossession given the following information:

> Original sale...$500
> Date of sale...July 1970
> Collections to date $300
> Estimated market value of repossessed goods $100

Exercise 29–4

On October 1, 1970, the Television Company sold a set costing $400 to Jones for $600. Jones made a downpayment of $150 and agreed to pay $25 the first of each month for 18 months thereafter.

The first two installments due on November 1 and December 1, 1970, were paid. In 1971, five payments were made by Jones, who then defaulted on the balance of his payments. The set was repossessed on November 1, 1971. The company closes its books on December 31.

Required:

1. Give three different amounts that might be shown as realized gross profit for 1970 and indicate the circumstances under which each of these amounts would be acceptable.

2. Assuming that the repossessed television set has a wholesale value of $50 and a retail value of $75, prepare a journal entry to record the repossession under the "installment method" of accounting. Explain fully the reasoning applicable to your entry.

(AICPA adapted)

Exercise 29–5

On April 1, 1971, the Kiley Department Store sold an item of furniture which cost $160, for $280. A downpayment of $30 was made with the provision that additional payments of $25 be made monthly thereafter. Interest was to be charged the customer at a monthly rate of 1% on the unpaid contract balance; the monthly remittance was to apply first to the accrued interest and the balance to the principal.

After completing four monthly payments, the customer defaulted and the furniture was reclaimed; the replacement value of the furniture (used) was estimated to be $75.

The Kiley Department Store maintains a perpetual inventory with respect to major appliances and furniture.

Required:

Make all journal entries for the installment sale, from April 1, 1971, through September 1, 1971.

PROBLEMS

Problem 29-1

The Cox Realty Company sold a plot of real estate for $80,000 designated as the Baker Addition. The property originally cost $25,000, and $35,000 was subsequently spent for grading, drainage, and other similar costs. Expenses incident to sale were $6,000. The terms of the sale were: 20% downpayment and a note specifying five annual payments (at year-end) including a constant reduction in principal *and* 6% interest per annum on the unpaid balance at the start of each year.

Required:

1. Prepare a schedule of payments.

2. Prepare journal entries through the second installment assuming the installment sales method is used.

3. Indicate how the amounts relating to the second period should be reported on the income statement and balance sheet.

4. Prepare a schedule of payments assuming five equal payments at year-end (6%). Also give entries for (*a*) collection of the first installment and (*b*) recognition of realized gross profit at end of year one.

Problem 29-2

The AB Company completed the following transactions:

	1971	1972
Sales (all on account):		
Regular	$100,000	$112,000
Installment	60,000	50,000
Selling expenses	23,000	24,000
Collections on accounts:		
Regular	83,000	96,000
Installment—1971	42,000	12,000
Installment—1972		30,000
Cost of goods sold:		
Regular	42,000	47,300
Installment	24,600	21,000

Required:

1. Set up in parallel columns all entries for the two years in respect to the above transactions under two assumptions for installment sales: (1) the installment sales method and (2) the "regular" sales method. Assume perpetual inventory procedures.

2. Prepare a tabulation showing the balances on the financial statements for the following: (1) receivables; (2) deferred gross profit, (3) realized gross profit on installment sales, and (4) net income. Classify as to the balance sheet and income statement.

Problem 29-3

The Oyster Bay Sales Company balance sheet on January 1, 1971, reported the following:

Cash	$ 20,000	Accounts payable....................	$ 30,000
Merchandise inventory	120,000	Deferred gross profit on install-	
Accounts receivable (regular)...	11,000	ment sales – 1969...............	12,000
Allowance for doubtful		Deferred gross profit on install-	
accounts	[1,000]	ment sales – 1970...............	29,400
Installment accounts receiv-		Capital stock	203,000
able – 1969......................	30,000	Retained earnings...................	75,600
Installment accounts receiv-			
able – 1970......................	70,000		
Various assets	100,000		
	$350,000		$350,000

Transactions during 1971 were (summarized):

Sales:
Regular (on credit)....................................$300,000
Installment 100,000
Purchases of merchandise (cash) 238,000
Ending inventory (periodic basis)...................... 130,000
Cost of installment sales.................................. 57,000
Selling expenses... 105,000
Allowance for doubtful accounts........................¼ of 1% of
                                                    regular sales

Collections on installment receivables:
1969 accounts...$ 20,000
1970 accounts... 40,000
1971 accounts... 55,000
Regular accounts 280,000

Required:

1. Compute gross profit rates for 1969, 1970, and 1971.
2. Prepare journal entries for 1971, including adjusting and closing entries at December 31.
3. Prepare an income statement for 1971.
4. Prepare a balance sheet as of December 31, 1971.

Problem 29–4

Pitts-Marvel Sales Corporation sells goods and accounts for such sales on the installment basis. At the end of each year it takes up gross profit on the basis of the year(s) of collection rather than the year of sale; accordingly, each collection consists of cost and gross profit elements.

The balances of the control accounts for Installment Accounts Receivable at the beginning and end of 1971 were:

	Jan. 1, 1971	Dec. 31, 1971
Installment Accounts Receivable 1969.................	$ 24,020	–0–
1970.................	344,460	$ 67,440
1971.................		410,090

As collections are made, the company debits Cash and credits Installment Accounts Receivable. During 1971, upon default in payment by customers, the company repossessed merchandise having an estimated wholesale value of $1,400. The sales had been made in 1970 for $5,400, and $3,200 had been collected prior to default. The company recorded the default and repossession by a debit to Inventory of Repossessed Merchandise and a credit to Installment Accounts Receivable—1970 for the uncollected receivable balance.

The company's sales and cost of sales for the three years involved are summarized below:

	1969	1970	1971
Net sales	$380,000	$432,000	$602,000
Cost of sales	247,000	285,120	379,260

Required:

1. Prepare journal entries to record at December 31, 1971, the recognition of profits and any other adjustments arising from the above data. Give complete explanations in support of your entries.

2. Give one acceptable alternate method of handling the repossession and discuss the relative merits of it as compared to the method you used in (1).

(AICPA adapted)

Problem 29–5

A specialty appliance distributor selling on the installment basis was organized as a retail sales outlet on January 1, 1968. Reorganization was begun, however, after three and one-half years operations, on July 1, 1971. Operating data for this interim period are summarized following:

Year	Sales	Cost of Sales	Expenses°
1968	$ 60,000	$36,000	$15,000
1969	100,000	61,000	16,000
1970	120,000	75,600	17,500
1971	70,000	32,900	14,000

° Excludes gains or losses from defaulted accounts.

	Collections				Accounts Defaulted		
Year of Sale	1968	1969	1970	1971	1969	1970	1971
1968	$40,000	$19,000			$1,000		
1969		80,000	$ 18,000			$2,000	
1970			100,000	$15,000			$5,000
1971				68,000			2,000

Repossessed merchandise is assumed to have no resale value.

Required:

Prepare an analysis of net income for each year (or fractional year) contrasting the differences when—

a) Net income is computed using the installment method of accounting for sales revenue.

b) Net income is computed on the assumption that revenue is recognized at the time of sale, and bad debts are charged to expense as they occur.

Problem 29–6

The Jones Appliance Store started business on January 1, 1970. Separate accounts were set up for installment and cash sales, but no perpetual inventory record was maintained. On the installment sales, a downpayment of one third was required, with the balance payable in 18 equal monthly installments. A Deferred Gross Profit account was created at each year-end in respect to the current year's installment sales. When contracts were defaulted, the unpaid balances were charged to Bad Debt Expense, and sales of repossessed merchandise were credit to this account. The expense account was adjusted at the year-end to reflect the actual loss.

A summary of the transactions of the Jones Appliance Store for 1970 and 1971 follows:

	1970	1971
Sales:		
New merchandise for cash	$ 21,348	$ 29,180
New merchandise on installment (including one-third cash downpayment)	188,652	265,320
Sales of repossessed merchandise	600	700
Purchases	154,000	173,585
Physical inventories at December 31:		
New merchandise at cost	36,400	48,010
Repossessions at realizable (market) value	150	160
Unpaid balances of installment contracts defaulted:		
1970 sales	2,865	3,725
1971 sales		3,010
Cash collections on installments contracts, exclusive of downpayments:		
1970 sales	42,943	61,385
1971 sales		55,960

Required:

1. Compute the gross profit rates for the years 1970 and 1971.

2. In T-account form, reproduce the ledger accounts for installment accounts receivable.

3. Calculate the net loss on defaulted accounts for the year 1970; it is assumed that realizable value is an appropriate value basis for repossessed merchandise.

4. Prepare a schedule showing the realized gross profit for the year 1971 that would be reported on the income statement.

(AICPA adapted)

Index

1151

This book has been set in 10 and 9 point Caledonia, leaded 2 points. Chapter numbers are in 12 point Caledonia and chapter titles are in 18 point Helvetica Regular. The size of the type page is 27 by 46^1/$_2$ picas.